2017
Guidebook to
NEW YORK
TAXES

Mark S. Klein

Contributing Editor

 Wolters Kluwer

Wolters Kluwer Editorial Staff Publication

Editor .... Fred Conklin

Production Coordinator .... Govardhan L

Production .... T Chandrasekhar

This publication is designed to provide accurate and authoritative information in regard to the subject matter covered. It is sold with the understanding that the publisher is not engaged in rendering legal, accounting, or other professional service and that the author is not offering such advice in this publication. If legal advice or other expert assistance is required, the services of a competent professional person should be sought.

ISBN 978-0-8080-4468-0

Printed in the United States of America

PREFACE

This *Guidebook* gives a general picture of the taxes imposed by the state of New York and the general property tax levied by the local governments. All 2016 legislative amendments received as of press time are reflected, and references to New York and federal laws are to the laws as of the date of publication of this book.

The emphasis is on the law applicable to the filing of income tax returns in 2017 for the 2016 tax year. However, if legislation has made changes effective after 2016, we have tried to note this also, with an indication of the effective date to avoid confusion.

The taxes of major interest—income and sales and use—are discussed in detail. Other New York taxes, including the bank franchise tax and estate or inheritance taxes, are summarized, with particular emphasis on application, exemptions, returns, and payment.

Throughout the *Guidebook*, tax tips are highlighted to help practitioners avoid pitfalls and use the tax laws to their best advantage.

The *Guidebook* is designed as a quick reference work, describing the general provisions of the various tax laws, regulations, and administrative practices. It is useful to tax practitioners, businesspersons, and others who prepare or file New York returns or who are required to deal with New York taxes.

The *Guidebook* is not designed to eliminate the necessity of referring to the law and regulations for answers to complicated problems, nor is it intended to take the place of detailed reference works such as the CCH NEW YORK TAX REPORTS. With this in mind, specific references to the publisher's New York and federal tax products are inserted in most paragraphs. By assuming some knowledge of federal taxes, the *Guidebook* is able to provide a concise, readable treatment of New York taxes that will supply a complete answer to most questions and will serve as a time-saving aid where it does not provide the complete answer.

SCOPE OF THE BOOK

This *Guidebook* is designed to do three things:

1. Give a general picture of the impact and pattern of all taxes levied by the state of New York and the general property tax levied by local governmental units.

2. Provide a readable quick-reference work for the personal income tax and the tax on corporate income. As such, it explains briefly what the New York law provides and indicates whether the New York provision is the same as federal law.

3. Analyze and explain the differences, in most cases, between New York and federal law.

HIGHLIGHTS OF 2016 NEW YORK TAX CHANGES

The most important 2016 New York tax changes received by press time are noted in the "Highlights of 2016 New York Tax Changes" section of the *Guidebook*, beginning on page 13. This useful reference gives the practitioner up-to-the-minute information on changes in tax legislation.

LOCAL TAXES

The *Guidebook* also features a chapter on New York City taxes. Included in this chapter are the principal features of the New York City personal income tax on residents. Persons subject to tax, computation, basis of tax, and rate of tax are covered. Also discussed are taxes on estates, and partners and partnerships.

FINDERS

The practitioner may find the information wanted by consulting the general Table of Contents at the beginning of the *Guidebook*, the Table of Contents at the beginning of each chapter, the Topical Index, or the Law and Regulation Locator.

The Topical Index is a useful tool. Specific taxes and information on rates, allocation, credits, exemptions, returns, payments, collection, penalties, and remedies are thoroughly indexed and cross-referenced to paragraph numbers in the *Guidebook*.

The Law and Regulation Locator is an equally useful finders tool. Beginning on page 745, this finding list shows where sections of New York statutory law and administrative regulations referred to in the *Guidebook* are discussed.

November 2016

About the Editor

Mark S. Klein, J.D., is a partner of the New York law firm of Hodgson Russ LLP. Mr. Klein concentrates in New York State and New York City tax matters. He also has extensive federal, multistate, and local tax experience. He teaches courses on state taxation and tax practice and procedure at the State University of New York (SUNY) at Buffalo, School of Management Tax Certificate Program, and has lectured extensively throughout the United States and Canada. He has written and edited numerous books, articles, and treatises on New York, multistate, and e-commerce taxation. Mr. Klein earned his law degree at SUNY at Buffalo.

CONTENTS

HIGHLIGHTS OF 2016 NEW YORK TAX CHANGES

The most important late 2015 and 2016 tax changes received by press time are noted below.

Multiple Taxes
(See also specific tax headings below)

• *New York's 2016-17 budget affects personal income and franchise taxes*

New York's 2016-17 budget includes a variety of corporate franchise and personal income changes, as detailed below (Ch. 60 (S.B. 6409), Laws 2016, effective April 13, 2016). Separate stories cover sales tax, property tax, and miscellaneous tax changes contained in the legislation.

Middle class tax cut: The personal income tax rate for affected taxpayers will drop beginning in 2018. Taxpayers eligible for a tax rate reduction to 5.5%, when fully implemented, include single filers with taxable income up to $75,000, head of household filers with taxable income up to $100,000, and married joint filers with taxable income up to $150,000. Taxpayers eligible for a tax rate reduction to 6%, when fully implemented, include single filers with taxable income between $75,000 and $200,000, head of household filers with taxable income between $100,000 and $250,000, and married joint filers with taxable income between $150,000 and $300,000. (¶106)

Conformity to new federal filing dates: The legislation aligns various state and New York City tax filing deadlines with new deadlines at the federal level (*i.e.*, generally changing the due date from March 15 to April 15 for corporations and from April 15 to March 15 for partnerships, for taxable years beginning on or after January 1, 2016). (¶601, ¶859, ¶1401, ¶2813, ¶3207)

Farm workforce retention credit: For taxable years beginning on or after January 1, 2017, and before January 1, 2022, the legislation creates a new farm workforce retention credit available against the corporate franchise and personal income taxes. The credit amount is determined by multiplying the total number of eligible farm employees by a dollar amount, which increases from $250 in 2017 to $600 in 2021. (¶163, ¶961)

STAR credit: The legislation provides for transitioning the school tax relief (STAR) property tax exemption into a personal income tax credit. (¶162)

New York City school tax reduction credit: The school tax relief credit for New York City taxpayers is converted from a city personal income tax credit into a state personal income tax credit. The change applies to taxable years beginning on or after January 1, 2016. (¶3009)

Electronic filing mandate: Electronic filing mandate provisions are extended for three years, until December 31, 2019.

Low-income housing credit: Over a five-year period, the legislation increases the aggregate dollar amount of credits available for the low-income housing credit from $64 million to $104 million. (¶138, ¶941)

Hire-a-veteran credit: The hire-a-veteran credit is extended for two years, through taxable years beginning before January 1, 2019. As extended, the credit is available for the hiring of qualified veterans who commence employment before January 1, 2018. (¶158, ¶957)

Empire state commercial production credit: The empire state commercial production credit is extended for two years, through taxable years beginning before January 1, 2019. (¶147, ¶949)

Credit for transporting disabled individuals: The credit for companies that provide transportation to individuals with disabilities is extended for six years, through 2022. (¶134, ¶947)

Enhanced EITC for noncustodial parents: The legislation makes the enhanced earned income tax credit (EITC) for noncustodial parents permanent. Previously, the credit was scheduled to expire after 2016. (¶126)

Tax shelter reporting: The expiration date of tax shelter reporting provisions is delayed from July 1, 2015, until July 1, 2019. (¶3703)

Clean heating fuel credit: The clean heating fuel credit is extended so that it applies to purchases before January 1, 2020 (previously, 2017). In addition, the legislation provides that, beginning January 1, 2017, the credit does not apply to bioheat that is less than 6% biodiesel per gallon of bioheat. (¶150, ¶950)

Excelsior jobs program: The legislation provides that 100% of the unawarded amounts remaining at the end of 2024 can be allocated in subsequent years. However, no tax credits are allowed for taxable years beginning on or after January 1, 2027. In addition, the maximum aggregate credit components are reduced from $200 million to $183 million for 2016 through 2021, from $150 million to $133 million for 2022, from $100 million to $83 million for 2023, and from $50 million to $36 million for 2024. (¶135, ¶940)

New York City biotechnology credit: The New York City biotechnology credit against the general corporation and unincorporated business taxes is extended for three years, through taxable years beginning before January 1, 2019. (¶2806, ¶3206)

Alcoholic beverage production credit: For taxable years beginning on or after January 1, 2016, the beer production credit is renamed the alcoholic beverage production credit, and the credit is expanded to include cider, wine, and liquor. (¶149, ¶955)

Real property tax credit for manufacturers: Provisions regarding the real property income tax credit for manufacturers are amended to specify that for corporation franchise tax purposes, in the case of a taxpayer principally engaged in the production of goods by farming, agriculture, horticulture, floriculture, viticulture, or commercial fishing, the taxpayer is eligible if the taxpayer (1) satisfies the required conditions and (2) leases the real property from a related or unrelated party. (¶958)

Urban youth jobs program credit: The legislation enhances the urban youth jobs program tax credit by increasing the amount of money allocated to programs four and five from $20 million to $50 million each. (¶137, ¶953)

• *New York's 2015-16 budget affects personal income and franchise taxes*

New York's 2015-2016 budget makes changes to numerous tax provisions. Sales and use tax, property tax, and miscellaneous tax changes are discussed separately below. Personal income and corporate franchise (income) tax changes are as follows (Ch. 59 (A.B. 3009), Laws 2015):

New York City personal income tax: The budget law eliminates the New York City STAR personal income tax rate reduction benefit for taxpayers having income above $500,000, applicable to taxable years beginning after 2014. (¶23, ¶3005)

Charitable contributions: The budget law extends for two years (through 2017) the provision reducing the amount of charitable contributions allowed as a New York itemized deduction from 50% to 25% for taxpayers with New York adjusted gross income above $10 million. (¶304)

Enhanced real property tax circuit breaker credit: With respect to the enhanced real property tax circuit breaker credit, the budget clarifies that a taxpayer's residence must be in New York City in order to qualify for the credit. (¶122)

MCTMT: The budget law clarifies that all self-employed taxpayers subject to the metropolitan commuter transportation mobility tax (MCTMT), and not just New York state residents, may be required to report their MCTMT liabilities on their personal income tax returns. (¶106, ¶601)

Manufacturers' real property tax credit: Personal income tax provisions regarding the manufacturers' real property tax credit are amended to clarify that the credit is limited to real property taxes that are not deducted from the taxpayer's New York adjusted gross income. In addition, an erroneous reference to combined groups has been eliminated. The law also adds language making the credit available to certain farming businesses that lease real property from related or unrelated parties. (¶122)

START-UP NY telecommunication services excise tax credit: Personal income tax provisions regarding the START-UP NY telecommunication services excise tax credit are amended to clarify that the credit is limited to taxes that are not deducted from the taxpayer's New York adjusted gross income. (¶114)

Excelsior Jobs Program: The law expands eligibility under the Excelsior Jobs Program to include certain business entities operating in music production or as an entertainment company. An "entertainment company" is defined to include entities principally engaged in the production or post-production of motion pictures, instructional videos, televised commercial advertisements, animated films or cartoons, music videos, television programs, or programs primarily intended for radio broadcast. Certain types of companies are specifically excluded (*e.g.*, those principally engaged in the live performance of events). "Music production" means the process of creating sound recordings of at least eight minutes, recorded in professional sound studios, and intended for commercial release; the term does not include live concert recordings, recordings that are primarily spoken word or wildlife or nature sounds, or recordings produced for instructional use or advertising or promotional purposes.

The definition of "net new jobs" is expanded to include jobs obtained by an entertainment company in New York (1) as a result of the termination of a licensing agreement with another entertainment company, (2) that are at risk of leaving the state as a direct result of the termination, (3) that are either full-time wage-paying jobs or equivalent to full-time wage-paying jobs requiring at least 35 hours per week, and (4) that are filled for more than six months.

New provisions are added specifying that a business entity operating predominately in music production must create at least five net new jobs, and a business entity operating predominantly as an entertainment company must create or obtain at least 100 net new jobs. The definition of a "regionally significant project" is expanded to include an entertainment company creating or obtaining at least 200 net new jobs in New York and making a significant capital investment in the state. (¶135, ¶940)

Employee training credit: A new tax credit is available for employers that procure certain training for employees. The credit equals 50% of a taxpayer's eligible training costs, up to a credit of $10,000 per employee completing eligible training, and 50% of the stipend paid to an intern, up to a credit of $3,000 per intern completing eligible training. The credit applies to taxable years beginning on or after January 1, 2015, and to eligible training costs incurred on or after April 13, 2015. (¶161, ¶960)

Corporate tax reform technical changes: The amount of investment income that may be deducted is capped at 8% of the taxpayer's entire net income in cases where the taxpayer's investment income is determined without regard to the interest deductions allowed. This and other technical changes to the corporate tax reform statute are retroactive to tax years beginning after 2014. (¶1001)

The law clarifies that net operating losses (NOLs) are required to be carried back to the earliest of the three years. Additionally, taxpayers are entitled to make an irrevocable election to relinquish the entire carryback period. (¶1001)

The law adds apportionment rules for marked-to-market gains (¶1301), as well as for receipts from the operation of vessels (¶1303).

Alternative fuel vehicle refueling and electric vehicle recharging credit: Technical changes relating to the treatment of grants are made to the tax credit for alternative fuels and electric vehicle recharging property. The credit is available against the corporate and personal income tax. (¶148, ¶935)

Biennial information statement: The law combines the N.Y. Department of State biennial information statement and tax return filings and repeals the $9 Department of State filing fee. (¶4001, ¶4002)

Libraries exemption (MCTDMT): The law is amended in relation to the exemption of libraries from the metropolitan commuter transportation mobility tax. This change applies to taxable periods on or after January 1, 2016. (¶106, ¶905)

• *STAR income tax credit clarified*

Enacted New York legislation makes technical and clarifying personal income tax modifications to the school tax relief (STAR) credit that was created by the 2016 budget legislation (discussed above), applicable to tax years beginning on or after January 1, 2016. Among other changes, the legislation generally allows a full credit to owners of cooperative apartments and provides for a minimum credit amount in the case of mobile homes (*i.e.,* no less than the credit that would be allowed for property with a $20,000 assessed value).

The legislation also provides that, if property is sold, the seller will remain eligible to claim the credit if the property was his or her primary residence during the taxable year and he or she paid qualifying taxes on the property while still an owner. In addition, the credit application process is clarified.

The law also clarifies eligibility for the STAR property tax exemption, in addition to clarifying that a STAR exemption may be continued on a marital residence that had been solely owned by one spouse and has since passed to the other spouse through inheritance. (Ch. 73 (S.B. 8159), Laws 2016) (¶162)

• *Combative sports events now subject to gross receipts tax; event admissions exempted from sales tax*

On and after September 1, 2016, a gross receipts tax is imposed on authorized "combative sports" (*i.e.,* kick boxing, single discipline martial arts, or mixed martial arts events) held in New York, other than any professional or amateur boxing, sparring or wrestling exhibition or match, at a rate of 8.5% of gross receipts from ticket sales, and 3% of the sum of gross receipts from broadcasting rights and gross receipts from digital streaming over the Internet. The tax is limited to $50,000 for any match or exhibition.

Charges for admission to taxable combative sports events in New York are exempt from sales tax. (Ch. 32 (S.B. 5949), Laws 2016) (¶2723, ¶2010)

• *Film production credit enhancement applies in additional counties*

Legislation effective November 4, 2016, expands the number of upstate counties outside the metropolitan commuter region in which services can be performed to qualify for the additional empire state film production income tax credit. The new counties are Columbia, Dutchess, Greene, Orange, Putnam, Rensselaer, Saratoga, Suffolk, Sullivan, Ulster, Warren, and Washington County. (Ch. 420 (S.B. 6987), Laws 2016) (¶127, ¶944)

• *Enrolled agents may represent taxpayers before the DOTF*

"Enrolled agent" has been added to the list of taxpayer representatives recognized by the Department of Taxation and Finance, and a taxpayer is permitted to suspend an interview with the department in order to request representation from an enrolled agent. (Ch. 345 (A.B. 8674), Laws 2016, effective September 29, 2016) (¶3802)

Personal Income Tax
(See also "Multiple Taxes," above)

• *Extension of collection period for military members does not extend to hospitalization*

The personal income tax provision that extends various time limits for certain individuals serving in the U.S. armed forces has been amended to provide that the collection period after an assessment will not be extended due to a hospitalization. Specifically, the legislation states that, with respect to any period of continuous hospitalization described in Sec. 696(a), Tax Law, and the next 180 days thereafter, the provision will not apply to the collection of personal income tax liabilities. The amendment applies to any assessed taxes for which there is an outstanding tax liability. (Ch. 411 (A.B. 9191), Laws 2016) (¶605)

Sales and Use Taxes
(See also "Multiple Taxes," above)

• *New York's 2016-17 budget includes new and amended sales and use tax exemptions*

New York's 2016-17 budget package includes a variety of sales and use tax provisions, including those detailed below (Ch. 60 (S.B. 6409), Laws 2016, effective April 13, 2016, except as noted).

Purchases of hotel room occupancies by room remarketers: Applicable to rent paid for hotel occupancies on or after June 1, 2016, an exemption is provided for the purchase of hotel room occupancies by room remarketers when those purchases are made from hotels for later resale and an exemption certificate is provided to the hotel operator by the room remarketer. Previously, there was no an exemption for room remarketers' purchases of hotel room occupancies they supplied to their customers. Instead, room remarketers had to seek a credit or refund for the tax they paid to the hotel operators if the room remarketers satisfied certain conditions. (¶2009)

Fuel used in commercial and general aviation aircraft: Sales of fuel for use in commercial and general aviation aircraft are exempt from local sales taxes and from the prepayment of sales tax on motor fuels, effective December 1, 2017. (¶2106; ¶2203)

Commercial fuel cell electricity generating systems equipment: An exemption is provided for commercial fuel cell electricity generating systems equipment and the service of installing and maintaining such systems, effective June 1, 2016. For purposes of the exemption, "fuel cell electricity generating systems equipment" means an electric generating arrangement or combination of components installed upon nonresidential premises that utilize solid oxide, molten carbonate, proton exchange membrane or phosphoric acid fuel cell, or linear generator.

Also effective June 1, 2016, an exemption is provided for the sale of hydrogen gas or electricity by a person primarily engaged in the sale of fuel cell electricity generating system equipment and/or electricity generated by such equipment pursuant to written agreement under which the electricity is generated by commercial fuel cell electricity generating system equipment that is: (a) owned by a person other than the purchaser of such electricity; (b) installed on the non-residential premises of the purchaser of such electricity; (c) placed in service; and (d) used to provide heating, cooling, hot water or electricity to such premises. (¶2102)

Alternative fuels: The sunset date for the exemption for alternative fuels, including E85, Compressed Natural Gas (CNG), hydrogen, and B20, is extended from September 1, 2016 to September 1, 2021. (¶2106)

• *New York's 2015-16 budget includes new and amended sales and use tax exemptions*

New York's 2015-2016 budget makes the following sales and use tax changes, applicable as noted (Ch. 59 (A.B. 3009), Laws 2015):

General aviation aircraft: An exemption is provided for sales or uses of general aviation aircraft, and machinery or equipment to be installed on such aircraft, effective September 1, 2015. For purposes of the exemption, "general aviation aircraft" means an aircraft that is used in civil aviation and that is not a commercial aircraft, military aircraft, unmanned aerial vehicle or drone. (¶2102)

Also effective September 1, 2015, leases of noncommercial aircraft having a seating capacity of less than 20 passengers and a maximum payload capacity of less than 6,000 pounds are not subject to accelerated sales or use tax provisions. (¶2021)

Beverage tasting: Effective June 1, 2015, the sales and use tax exemption for wine tasting is extended to other alcoholic beverages (*i.e.*, liquor, beer, or cider) and items used to package such beverages (*i.e.*, bottles, corks, caps, and labels). Also, the law makes technical corrections to clarify that the exemption applies to tastings held off the premises of an alcoholic beverage producer. In addition, charges for admission to tour the facilities of an alcoholic beverage producer are not taxable. (¶2102)

Vessels: An exemption is provided for sales, leases or uses of vessels in excess of $230,000, effective June 1, 2015. In addition, a use tax exemption is provided for the use of a vessel within New York until (1) the boat is registered, or is first required to be registered, under New York's vehicle and traffic laws, or (2) the boat is used in New York for more than 90 days. (¶2102)

Prepaid mobile calling services: The budget law clarifies that sales tax applies to prepaid mobile calling services under the same rules that apply to prepaid telephone calling services (tax generally imposed based on retail location). "Prepaid mobile calling service" means the right to use a commercial mobile radio service, whether or not sold with other property or services, that must be paid for in advance and is sold for use over a specified period of time or in predetermined units or dollars that decline with use in a known amount, whether or not that right is represented by or includes the transfer to the purchaser of an item of tangible personal property. (¶2007)

Solar energy system equipment: The existing sales tax exemptions for solar energy system equipment are expanded to include electricity generated by such equipment that is sold under a power purchase agreement, effective December 1, 2015. Specifically, the law expands the existing exemptions from state and local sales tax for residential and commercial solar equipment to include electricity purchased from a person primarily engaged in the sale of solar energy systems equipment and/or electricity generated by such equipment if the electricity is sold under a written agreement and generated by equipment that is: (1) owned by a person other than the purchaser of the electricity; (2) installed at the purchaser's residence or nonresidential premises; and (3) used to provide heating, cooling, hot water or electricity. The existing local option provisions are amended to include the expanded exemptions. (¶2106)

Sales to certain related persons: An exemption is provided for certain related persons' tangible personal property or service transactions related to requirements of the federal Dodd-Frank Wall Street Reform and Consumer Protection Act, effective September 1, 2015. The exemption sunsets on June 30, 2019. (¶2103)

• *Feminine hygiene products exempted*

Effective September 1, 2016, there is a New York state and local sales and use tax exemption for feminine hygiene products, including but not limited to, sanitary napkins, tampons and panty liners. (Ch. 99 (A.B. 7555), Laws 2016) (¶2102)

• *Taxes on adult entertainment clubs upheld against Constitutional attack*

The New York Supreme Court, Appellate Division, held that the "amusement tax" and the "cabaret tax" were constitutional on their face and as applied to the taxpayers. Specifically, the taxpayers, who operated an adult entertainment club, challenged the sales taxes imposed on their "Beaver Bucks" or "scrip," which was the club's in-house currency used by patrons to tip topless dancers, floor hosts, and to gain admission to private rooms to view entertainers and for lap dances. The taxpayers asserted that the tax laws infringed on their right to free speech under the United States and New York Constitutions by imposing a differential tax on protected expression based on content, thereby penalizing disfavored expression without furthering any important governmental interest. The taxpayers also claimed that the tax laws violated the Equal Protection Clauses of the United States and New York Constitutions by discriminating against protected expression based on its content, and allowing for different treatment of New York businesses engaging in constitutionally protected activities.

The court rejected all of the taxpayers' constitutional arguments, concluding that the tax laws were of general application and do not enforce any differential treatment based on the content of ideas or viewpoints expressed in the entertainment provided at the club. By enacting the exemptions for certain types of entertainment (*i.e.*, live theatre, musical performances, and choreographed dancing), the legislature simply exercised its authority to pick and choose among the forms of expression it decides to subsidize through a tax exemption. (*CMSG Restaurant Group, LLC, v. The State of New York*, Appellate Division of the Supreme Court of New York, First Department, No. 153539/14 1214, November 3, 2016, CCH New York Tax Reports, ¶ 408-896) (¶ 2010)

Property Tax
(See also "Multiple Taxes," above)

• *STAR property tax exemption closed and transition to a personal income tax credit begins*

New York's 2016-17 budget package includes statutory changes to convert the existing School Tax Relief (STAR) exemption program to a personal income tax credit. (Ch. 60 (S.B. 6409), Laws 2016)

Transitional provisions: Beginning with the 2016-2017 school district assessment rolls, the STAR exemption is closed to new applicants and a new refundable personal income tax credit is available instead. Current recipients of STAR exemptions are permitted to keep the exemptions as long as they continue to own their homes, but upon transfer of the property to a new owner, the new owner would only be eligible for the income tax credit program. Current STAR exemption recipients have the option of giving up their STAR exemptions in favor of the personal income tax credit, though it is not required. Details of the personal income tax credit are discussed above and at ¶ 162.

Applications: Applications for renewal of enhanced STAR) and senior citizen property tax exemptions may be filed after the taxable status date in certain cases. No later than the last day for paying taxes without incurring cost or penalty, owners may submit a written request to the assessor requesting a filing extension. The assessor may extend the deadline and grant the exemption if good cause existed for failure to timely file the renewal application and if the applicant is otherwise entitled to the exemption. (¶ 2504)

Recoupment: Additionally, the STAR recoupment program is amended to clarify that improperly granted exemptions for the current school year or one or more of the three preceding school years may be recouped. In order for the recoupment procedure to be considered timely, the required notice must be mailed no later than three years after the conclusion of the school year for which the exemption in question was granted, or in the case of an exemption granted for the 2012-2013 school year, no later than September 30, 2016. (¶ 2504)

• *All property tax assessing units must offer enhanced STAR exemption*

Effective November 21, 2015, all New York property tax assessing units are required to participate in the enhanced school tax relief (STAR) exemption. (Ch. 451 (A.B. 7375), Laws 2015) (¶ 2507)

• *STAR exemption extended to farm dwellings owned by an LLC*

Legislation effective January 1, 2016, extends the school tax relief (STAR exemption) program to farm dwellings owned by a limited liability company (LLC) if the property serves as the primary residence of one or more of the owners. The same provisions continue to apply to farm dwellings owned by S corporations and partnerships. (Ch. 564 (A.B. 1421), Laws 2015) (¶ 2507)

• *School districts may provide exemptions for Cold War veterans*

Legislation effective August 19, 2016, authorizes school districts to provide, by resolution, a property tax exemption from school taxes for eligible Cold War veterans. (Ch. 253 (A.B. 3379), Laws 2016) (¶ 2504)

• *Exemptions for certain veterans may be prorated*

Municipalities are authorized to prorate a veteran's property tax exemption if such veteran moves within the same county, or in the case of a city having a population of 1 million or more persons, within the same city. Previously, the proration was authorized for veterans relocating within the same city, town, or village. (Ch. 538 (S.B. 2938), Laws 2015, effective January 2, 2016, and applicable to assessment rolls prepared on the basis of taxable status dates occurring on and after that date) (¶ 2504)

• *SCRIE and DRIE exemptions may be transferred to surviving household members*

Surviving members of a household may to apply for a transfer of the former head of household's property tax benefit under the Senior Citizens Rent Increase Exemption (SCRIE) and Disability Rent Increase Exemption (DRIE) programs. The option to transfer either benefit is available for six months after the head of household dies or permanently leaves the household or for 90 days after the date of notice from the supervising agency informing the household that the rent increase exemption benefit has expired, whichever is later. (Ch. 580 (S.B. 5826), Laws 2015; Ch. 31 (S.B. 6427), Laws 2016) (¶ 2504)

• *Persons excluded from SCRIE and DRIE exemptions may reappply the next year*

Individuals who are dropped from the Senior Citizen Rent Increase Exemption (SCRIE) and the Disability Rent Increase Exemption (DRIE) programs due to a nonrecurring item of income may reapply the following year and be accepted at the previously frozen rent amount. (Ch. 343 (A.B. 8228), Laws 2016) (¶ 2504)

• *Subsurface rights included in property tax foreclosure sales*

New York legislation effective January 1, 2016, provides that oil, gas, and mineral rights are to be sold along with any property sold pursuant to a property tax foreclosure sale. (Ch. 500 (S.B. 5288), Laws 2015) (¶ 2507)

Miscellaneous Taxes; Administration

• *2016-2017 budget extends alternative fuel tax exemptions and more*

New York's 2016-17 budget package makes the following changes affecting motor fuel and petroleum businesses (Ch. 60 (S.B. 6409), Laws 2016):

Alternative fuels: The repeal date for the full motor fuel tax and petroleum business tax exemption for sales of E85 (85% ethanol), CNG (methane), or hydrogen fuel, and the partial 20% tax exemption for B20 (20% biodiesel) fuel, is extended from September 1, 2016, to September 1, 2021. (¶ 2709, ¶ 2716)

Motor fuel wholesalers: Effective December 1, 2016, wholesalers of motor fuel are required to register with the Department and file motor fuel tax returns. "Wholesaler of motor fuel" is defined as a person, firm, association or corporation who (1) is not a distributor of motor fuel; (2) makes a sale of motor fuel in New York other than a retail sale not in bulk; and (3) makes any purchases of motor fuel for resale within specified regions. Bond or security may be required to register. Wholesalers are required to file returns on or before the 20th day of each month. Grounds and procedures for cancellation or suspension of registration are provided by the law. Unregistered wholesalers are prohibited from making sales of motor fuel in New York other than a retail sale not in bulk. Any person not registered as a motor fuel wholesaler who makes a sale in New York other than a retail sale not in bulk may be guilty of a class E felony. (¶2709)

Highway use tax: The $15 application fee and $4 decal or special decal fees for highway use tax registration decals are repealed and replaced with a single application fee of $1.50. A fee of $1.50 is also imposed for replacement due to loss, mutilation, or destruction of decals; however, no additional fee is charged for issuance of a corrected certificate of registration. (¶2705)

• *Tax on interactive fantasy sports contests enacted*

A new privilege tax has been enacted on interactive fantasy sports contests in New York, effective August 3, 2016. Registrants are required to pay a tax equivalent to 15% of their interactive fantasy sports gross revenue generated within New York; in addition, registrants must pay a tax equal to 0.5%, but not to exceed $50,000 annually.

"Interactive fantasy sports contest" or "contest" means a game of skill wherein one or more contestants compete against each other by using their knowledge and understanding of athletic events and athletes to select and manage rosters of simulated players whose performance directly corresponds with the actual performance of human competitors on sports teams and in sports events. Operators of interactive fantasy sports contests must register with the N.Y. State Gaming Commission. (Ch. 237 (A.B. 10736), Laws 2016) (¶2723)

New York City Taxes
(See also "Multiple Taxes," and "Property Taxes," above)

• *Corporate tax reform enacted for New York City*

New York legislation significantly revises the New York City corporate income tax system, generally applicable to taxable years beginning on or after January 1, 2015. However, S corporations remain subject to the existing New York City general corporation tax or banking corporation tax. (Ch. 60 (S.B. 4610), Laws 2015)

For affected corporations (*i.e.*, corporations and banks that are not S corporations), the new provisions make numerous changes, similar to those enacted last year for New York State' corporation franchise (income) tax, including the following:

— merging the banking and general corporation taxes; (¶2803)

— in place of the general 8.85% tax rate, allowing a reduced rate for certain small businesses and qualified manufacturing corporations; (¶2805)

— applying a 9% tax rate to certain financial corporations having more than $100 billion in assets; (¶2805)

— adopting combined reporting for unitary corporations that meet a more-than-50% stock ownership test; (¶2813)

— replacing the entire net income tax base with a business income tax base; (¶2805, ¶2807)

— adopting the phase-in of a single receipts factor, as previously contained in the general corporation tax; (¶2811)

— applying customer-based sourcing rules; (¶2811)

— eliminating the separate treatment of subsidiary capital and income; (¶2811)

— modifying the definitions of "investment capital" and "investment income" and exempting both from tax; (¶2805)

— for pre-2015 net operating losses (NOLs), providing for a prior NOL conversion subtraction; (¶2808)

— allowing a three-year carryback for NOLs incurred in tax years beginning after 2014; (¶2808)

— repealing the alternative minimum tax base for income plus compensation; (¶2805)

— eliminating the tax on assets for banks (¶2805, ¶2903); and

— increasing the maximum capital base tax to $10 million, but allowing a $10,000 reduction for all capital base tax calculations. (¶2805)

• *Beer production credit enacted for New York City*

New York legislation has created a beer production credit available against the New York City unincorporated business, general corporation, and business corporation taxes, applicable to taxable years beginning on or after January 1, 2017. The legislation provides taxpayers with a credit of 12 cents per gallon for the first 500,000 gallons produced in New York City and 3.86 cents per gallon for the next 15 million gallons produced in New York City in the taxable year. To be eligible for the credit, a taxpayer must be registered as a distributor under Tax Law Article 18 and must produce 60 million or fewer gallons of beer in the state during the taxable year. (Ch. 333 (A.B. 1719), Laws 2016) (¶2806, ¶3206)

TAX CALENDAR

The following table lists significant dates of interest to New York taxpayers and tax practitioners.

January

1st—Real property generally valued as of this date.

5th—New York City property tax—taxable status date.

15th—Declaration and payment of estimated New York City unincorporated business tax due from businesses, $2/3$ of whose estimated taxable income is from farming, or which have an estimated tax of $40 or less. For others, installment of estimated tax and declaration or amendment of previous declaration due, if required.

31st—Highway use tax returns due from carriers (annual filers).

February

15th—Business corporations on a calendar-year basis filing reports by this date and paying the balance of the full tax shown to be due on such reports are not required to make declarations or amended declarations otherwise due on or before December 15.

Banks and financial corporations who file report by this date and pay the balance of the full tax shown to be due on the report are not required to file declarations or amended declarations otherwise due to New York State on or before December 15.

Utilities filing reports by this date and paying the balance of the full tax shown to be due on the reports are not required to file declarations or amended declarations otherwise due on or before December 15.

Insurance corporations filing reports by this date and paying the balance of the full tax shown to be due on the reports are not required to file declarations or amended declarations otherwise due on or before December 15.

New York State and City of New York withholding statement due to employees by this date.

Calendar-year corporations who file the New York City general corporation tax return by this date, and pay the balance of tax due, are not required to file an estimated tax declaration or amended declaration otherwise due by December 15.

Return and payment of New York City unincorporated business tax may be made in lieu of December 15 declaration or amended declaration and payment of estimated tax.

Information returns, with respect to payments of $600 or more to taxpayers subject to New York State and City of New York personal income tax, due.

March

1st—Real property taxable status date for cities and towns.

Real property applications for exemption or special assessment generally due.

15th—Foreign corporations subject to Article 9-A or under Section 183 or 185 increasing assets employed in New York must file a report and pay the tax.

S corporation tax returns due.

Partnership and limited liability company tax returns and filing fees due.

Cooperative agricultural corporations must file franchise tax report and pay tax.

Utilities tax returns and payment of tax due (returns for tax surcharge on transportation and transmission companies are due one year after the due date for the return covering the tax).

Utilities filing return for preceding calendar year on which tax exceeds $1,000 must pay percentage of preceding year's tax at time of filing return to apply against estimated tax and further installment payments thereafter.

Insurance corporation franchise tax returns and payment due for calendar-year corporations.

Insurance corporations filing return for preceding calendar year on which tax exceeds $1,000 must pay percentage of preceding year's tax at time of filing return to apply against estimated tax and further installment payments thereafter.

New York City general corporation tax annual return and payment due for calendar-year corporation. Activities report of a foreign corporation disclaiming liability for tax due.

Taxpayers whose tax liability for New York City general corporation tax for the preceding year is over $1,000 pay installment of estimated tax for current year.

20th—Annual sales and use tax return and remittance for persons filing on an annual basis; election as to filing on annual basis due for succeeding year.

April

15th—Last day for calendar-year taxpayers to file return and pay New York State personal and corporation franchise (income) taxes and New York City personal and general corporation income taxes for preceding year.

Declaration and first installment of estimated New York State and New York City personal income taxes due for current year.

Last day for making calendar-year return and paying New York City unincorporated business tax for the preceding year.

Declaration and first installment of estimated New York City unincorporated business tax due for current year.

June

20th—Returns and payment of New York City motor vehicle tax due.

25th—New York City tax on retail licensees of alcoholic beverages due.

August

20th—New York City coin-operated amusement devices tax and annual return due.

Quarterly Recurring Dates

Within 60 days from end of calendar quarter—Persons subject to premiums tax on commercial insurance contracts directly placed with insurers not authorized to do business in New York within the preceding calendar quarter must file returns and pay tax by this date.

1st—July, October, January and April—Real property taxes due for New York City.

15th—January, April, June, September—Installments of estimated New York State and New York City personal income tax due. New declaration or amendment of previous declaration due, if required.

Installments of estimated New York City unincorporated business tax due. Declaration or amendment of previous declaration due, if required.

15th—June, September, December—Installments of New York State estimated business corporation franchise tax due for calendar-year corporations. New declaration due, if required.

Installments of New York State estimated utilities tax due for calendar-year corporations.

Installments of New York State estimated insurance corporation franchise tax due for calendar-year corporations.

Installments of New York City estimated general corporation tax due for calendar-year corporations. New declaration due, if required.

20th—March, June, September, December—Lubricating oil tax returns and payment of tax due.

           Sales and use tax returns and payment due for quarterly taxpayers.

           Report and payment of New York City commercial rent or occupancy tax due.

           Report and payment of New York City hotel room occupancy tax due.

Monthly Recurring Dates

15th—Monthly reports of cigarette tax agents due for New York State.

           Monthly reports of cigarette tax agents due for New York City.

20th—Petroleum business tax returns and payment of tax due.

           Alcoholic beverage distributors return and tax due for New York State.

           Diesel motor fuel tax returns and payment due.

           Motor fuel tax returns and payment due.

           Alcoholic beverage distributors return and tax due for New York City.

           Sales and use tax returns and payment due from monthly taxpayers.

25th—Public utility excise return and tax in New York City due.

Last day—Highway use tax returns and payment of tax due from carriers whose total highway use tax liability for the preceding calendar year exceeded $4,000.

           Highway supplemental use tax returns and tax due (unless Commissioner had authorized quarterly filing).

Semimonthly Recurring Dates

Within 15 days after the date of transfer—Persons liable for the payment of real estate transfer gains tax must pay the tax due to the Commissioner by this date. A statement of tentative assessment and return must accompany the payment. If the tax due exceeds $10,000 and is greater than 50% of the cash portion of the consideration received on or before the date of transfer, installment payments of tax may be made.

PART I

TABLES

TAX RATES

¶1 Corporation Franchise (Income)—Tax Rates

The minimum taxable income base (alternative minimum tax) is eliminated for tax years beginning on or after January 1, 2015, as is the additional tax on subsidiary capital (Sec. 210, Tax Law). Accordingly, the tax is generally the highest of the amounts under the entire net income (ENI)/business income base, the capital base, or the fixed dollar minimum. However, the capital base tax is phased out over six years, beginning in 2016.

ENI/Business income base.—The applicable rates are as follows (Sec. 210, Tax Law):

— qualified New York manufacturers: 0%

— qualified emerging technology companies (QETCs): 5.7% (2015), 5.5% (2016 and 2017), 4.875% (2018 and thereafter).

— small businesses: for 2015, the same graduated rates applicable in 2014 continue to apply (see ¶905); for 2016 and thereafter, a flat rate of 6.5% applies.

— other taxpayers: 7.1% (2015), 6.5% (2016 and thereafter).

Capital base.—The applicable rates are as follows (Sec. 210, Tax Law):

— For qualified New York manufacturers and QETCs, the rates are: 0.132% (2015), 0.106% (2016), 0.085% (2017), 0.056% (2018), 0.038% (2019), 0.019% (2020), and 0% (2021 and thereafter).

— For cooperative housing corporations, the rates are: 0.04% (through 2019), 0.025% (2020), and 0% (2021 and thereafter).

— For other taxpayers, the rates are: 0.15% (2015), 0.125% (2016), 0.1% (2017), 0.075% (2018), 0.05% (2019), 0.025% (2020), and 0% (2021 and thereafter).

For tax years beginning on or after January 1, 2015, the tax is capped at $350,000 for qualified New York manufacturers and QETCs, and at $5 million for all other taxpayers.

Fixed dollar minimum.—For taxable years beginning after 2014, the fixed dollar minimum varies according to the taxpayer's New York receipts, as follows (Sec. 210(1)(d), Tax Law):

New York receipts	Fixed dollar minimum
Not more than $100,000	$25
$100,001 to $250,000	$75
$250,001 to $500,000	$175
$500,001 to $1,000,000	$500
$1,000,001 to $5,000,000	$1,500
$5,000,001 to $25,000,000	$3,500
$25,000,001 to $50,000,000	$5,000
$50,000,001 to $100,000,000	$10,000
$100,000,001 to $250,000,000	$20,000
$250,000,001 to $500,000,000	$50,000
$500,000,001 to $1 billion	$100,000
Over $1 billion	$200,000

Innovation Hot Spots: A qualified entity that is located within an innovation hot spot will only be subject to the fixed dollar minimum tax (Sec. 209(11), Tax Law; *TSB-M-13(6)C*, CCH NEW YORK TAX REPORTS, ¶ 407-897; *TSB-M-14(1)C*, CCH NEW YORK TAX REPORTS, ¶ 408-039).

Qualified New York manufacturer C corporations and QETCs: The amounts range from $22 to $4,385 (depending on New York receipts) for tax year 2015; from $21 to $4,230 for tax years 2016 and 2017; and from $19 to $3,750 for tax year 2018 and thereafter.

For tax year 2016 and 2017, the fixed dollar minimum (FDM) tax for qualified New York manufacturers and QETCs that are not S corporations is as follows:

New York receipts	Fixed dollar minimum
Not more than $100,000	$21
$100,001 to $250,000	$63
$250,001 to $500,000	$148
$500,001 to $1,000,000	$423
$1,000,001 to $5,000,000	$1,269
$5,000,001 to $25,000,000	$2,961
Over $25,000,000	$4,230

• *Metropolitan Commuter Transportation District taxes*

Surcharge: A surcharge is imposed on that portion of the corporation franchise tax attributable to business activity carried on within the Metropolitan Commuter Transportation District, which consists of the City of New York and the counties of Dutchess, Nassau, Orange, Putnam, Rockland, Suffolk, and Westchester. The surcharge rate is increased from 17% to 25.6% for taxable years beginning after 2014 and before 2016 (Sec. 209-B(1), Tax Law). See ¶ 905 for the calculation method. See ¶ 1317 for a discussion of the apportionment of tax within and without the District.

S corporations: New York S corporations are not subject to the temporary metropolitan commuter transportation business tax surcharge.

MCTD mobility (payroll) tax: For employers (including professional employer organizations), the MCTDMT is imposed at the following rates (see ¶905).

— 0.11% for employers with payroll expense over $312,500 but no greater than $375,000 in any calendar quarter;

— 0.23% for employers with payroll expense no greater than $437,500 in any calendar quarter;

— 0.34% for employers with payroll expense exceeding $437,500 in any calendar quarter.

Employers accepted into the START-UP NY program (see ¶923) are exempt from the MCTDMT (Sec. 803(b), Tax Law).

¶2 Banks—Tax Rates

NOTE: For taxable years beginning after 2014, the Article 32 bank franchise tax is repealed, and banks are merged into the Article 9-A corporate franchise tax. For 2014 tax rates, see ¶1605, and for the pre-2015 explanation of the bank franchise tax, see Part IV, Chapters 16-18, beginning at ¶1601.

¶5 Personal Income Tax—Tax Rates

Tax is imposed at a graduated rate determined on the basis of income and filing status (¶106—107). For the New York State tax rate schedules, see ¶6.

¶6 Personal Income Tax—New York State Tax Rate Schedules

Reproduced below are the New York State tax rate schedules in effect for taxable year 2016, as published in Form IT-2105-I (2016).

CAUTION—A supplemental tax may change the calculation of tax for taxable incomes over $100,000. See ¶106 for a complete explanation, and consult the worksheets found in the official instructions.

See ¶23 for the schedules applicable to New York City.

• *Tax rates for taxable year 2016*
Resident married taxpayers filing joint returns and resident surviving spouses

Taxable year 2016

If the New York taxable income is:	The tax is:
Not over $17,050	4% of the New York taxable income
Over $17,050 but not over $23,450	$682 plus 4.5% of excess over $17,050
Over $23,450 but not over $27,750	$970 plus 5.25% of excess over $23,450
Over $27,750 but not over $42,750	$1,196 plus 5.9% of excess over $27,750
Over $42,750 but not over $160,500	$2,081 plus 6.45% of excess over $42,750
Over $160,500 but not over $321,050	$9,676 plus 6.65% of excess over $160,500
Over $321,050 but not over $2,140,900	$20,352 plus 6.85% of excess over $321,050
Over $2,140,900	$145,012 plus 8.82% of excess over $2,140,900

Resident heads of household

Taxable year 2016

If the New York taxable income is:	The tax is:
Not over $12,750	4% of the New York taxable income
Over $12,750 but not over $17,550	$510 plus 4.5% of excess over $12,750
Over $17,550 but not over $20,800	$726 plus 5.25% of excess over $17,550
Over $20,800 but not over $32,000	$897 plus 5.9% of excess over $20,800
Over $32,000 but not over $106,950	$1,557 plus 6.45% of excess over $32,000
Over $106,950 but not over $267,500	$6,392 plus 6.65% of excess over $106,950
Over $267,600 but not over $1,605,650	$17,068 plus 6.85% of excess over $267,500
Over $1,605,650	$108,732 plus 8.82% of excess over $1,605,650

Resident unmarried taxpayers, resident married filing separately, and residents estates and trusts

Taxable year 2016

If the New York taxable income is:	The tax is:
Not over $8,450	4% of the New York taxable income
Over $8,450 but not over $11,650	$338 plus 4.5% of excess over $8,450
Over $11,650 but not over $13,850	$482 plus 5.25% of excess over $11,650
Over $13,850 but not over $21,300	$598 plus 5.9% of excess over $13,850
Over $21,300 but not over $80,150	$1,037 plus 6.45% of excess over $21,300
Over $80,150 but not over $214,000	$4,833 plus 6.65% of excess over $80,150
Over $214,000 but not over $1,070,350	$13,734 plus 6.85% of excess over $214,000
Over $1,070,350	$72,394 plus 8.82% of excess over $1,070,350

Supplemental tax: For tax years beginning after 2011 and before 2018, Sec. 601(d-1), Tax Law, imposes a temporary supplemental tax that is in addition to the tax imposed under Sec. 601(a), Sec. 601(b), and Sec. 601(c). This supplemental tax is intended to recapture the tax benefit that a taxpayer receives in calculating taxes from the tax table rates that are below the highest applicable rate. The supplemental tax applies to taxpayers whose adjusted gross income exceeds $100,000. For complete details, see ¶106

¶10 Sales and Use Taxes—Statewide Tax Rate

In general, the New York State sales and use tax is imposed at the rate of 4% (Sec. 1105, Tax Law; Sec. 1110, Tax Law).

The tax is imposed on (1) retail sales of tangible personal property, (2) sales of enumerated services, (3) use of tangible personal property and enumerated services, (4) sales of certain utility services, (5) hotel occupancies, (6) restaurant meals (including alcoholic beverages), (7) certain admission charges, and (8) social and athletic club dues (¶2001).

An additional $3/8$ of 1% state tax is imposed within the Metropolitan Commuter Transportation District (¶2022).

Special taxes are also imposed on passenger car rentals (¶2014) and entertainment and information services that are provided exclusively aurally (¶2007).

¶11 Sales and Use Taxes—Local Tax Rates

In addition to the statewide sales and use tax, some cities and counties impose sales and use taxes on all the items subject to the statewide tax. Other local jurisdictions impose an additional tax only on consumer utilities or on restaurant meals (including alcoholic beverages), hotel occupancies, or admissions, club dues and cabaret charges. The following table lists the combined state and local rates.

The combined rates include the additional $3/8$ of 1% state tax within the Metropolitan Commuter Transportation District (MCTD) where applicable. The MCTD consists of New York City and the Counties of Dutchess, Nassau, Orange, Putnam, Rockland, Suffolk and Westchester.

Combined State and Local Sales Tax Rates

Albany County	8%	Delaware County	8%
Allegany County	8$1/2$%	Dutchess County	8$1/8$%
Auburn (Cayuga Co.)	8%	Erie County	8$3/4$%
Bronx—see New York City		Essex County	8%
Brooklyn—see New York City		Franklin County	8%
Broome County	8%	Fulton County	8%
Cattaraugus County	8%	Genesee County	8%
Cayuga County	8%	Glen's Falls (Warren County)	8%
Chautauqua County	8%	Gloversville (Fulton County)	8%
Chemung County	8%	Greene County	8%
Chenango County	8%	Hamilton County	8%
Clinton County	8%	Herkimer County	8$1/4$%
Columbia County	8%	Hornell (Steuben County)	8%
Corning (Steuben Co.)	8%	Ithaca (Tompkins County)	8%
Cortland County	8%	Jefferson County	7$3/4$%

Johnstown (Fulton County) 8%
Kings (Brooklyn)—see New York City
Lewis County 8%
Livingston County 8%
Madison County 8%
Manhattan—see New York City
Monroe County 8%
Montgomery County 8%
Mount Vernon (Westchester Co.) . . . . $8^3/8$%
Nassau County . . . . $8^5/8$%
New Rochelle (Westchester Co.) . . . . . . $8^3/8$%
New York City . . . . $8^7/8$%
Niagara County 8%
Norwich (Chenango County) 8%
Olean (Cattaraugus County) 8%
Oneida County . . . . $8^3/4$%
Oneida (Madison County) 8%
Onondaga County 8%
Ontario County . . . . $7^1/2$%
Orange County . . . . $8^1/8$%
Orleans County 8%
Oswego County 8%
Oswego (city) (Oswego County) 8%
Otsego County 8%
Putnam County . . . . $8^3/8$%
Queens—see New York City
Rensselaer County 8%

Richmond (Staten Island)—see New York City
Rockland County . . . . $8^3/8$%
Rome (Oneida County) . . . . $8^3/4$%
St. Lawrence County 8%
Salamanca (Cattaraugus County) 8%
Saratoga County 7%
Saratoga Springs (Saratoga County) 7%
Schenectady County 8%
Schoharie County 8%
Schuyler County 8%
Seneca County 8%
Staten Island—see New York City
Steuben County 8%
Suffolk County . . . . $8^5/8$%
Sullivan County 8%
Tioga County 8%
Tompkins County 8%
Ulster County 8%
Utica (Oneida County) . . . . $8^3/4$%
Warren County 7%
Washington County 7%
Wayne County 8%
Westchester County . . . . $7^3/8$%
White Plains (Westchester County) . . . . $8^3/8$%
Wyoming County 8%
Yates County 8%
Yonkers (Westchester County) . . . . $8^7/8$%

The following localities impose a local tax on hotel room occupancy only:

Niagara Falls City 8%
Niagara County (outside cities of Niagara Falls and Lockport) 8%
Lockport City 8%

The following localities impose a local tax on food and drink only:

Lockport City 8%
Niagara County (outside cities of Niagara Falls and Lockport) 8%
Niagara Falls City 8%

The following localities impose a tax on hotel room occupancy and/or food and drink:

Long Beach (city only) . . . . $8^5/8$%   Nassau County (outside city of Long Beach) . . . . $8^5/8$%

The following localities impose a local tax on admissions, club dues, and cabaret charges:

Lockport City 8%
Niagara County (outside cities of Lockport and Niagara Falls) 8%
Niagara Falls City 8%

Consumer utility rates: See Publication 718-U at ¶ 65-909 in CCH NEW YORK TAX REPORTS.

¶15 Estate and Gift Taxes—Tax Rates

Estate tax: If the decedent's New York taxable estate is less than or equal to the basic exclusion amount ($2,062,500 from April 1, 2014, through March 31, 2015; $3,125,000 from April 1, 2015, through March 31, 2016; $4,187,500 from April 1, 2016, through March 31, 2017; $5,250,000 from April 1, 2017, through December 31, 2018; and $5 million plus an annual cost-of living adjustment beginning January 1, 2019), the estate will receive a credit equal to the amount of tax due. No credit will be allowed to the estate of any decedent whose New York taxable estate exceeds 105% of the basis exclusion amount.

For decedents dying on and after April 1, 2014, the New York state estate tax rates range from 3.06% to 16.0% of the taxable estate after exclusion (see ¶ 2602).

Gift tax: The gift tax law, Art. 26-A, was repealed by Ch. 389, Laws 1997, effective January 1, 2000, applicable to gifts made on or after January 1, 2000.

¶20 New York City General Corporation Tax—Tax Rates

For taxable years beginning after 2014 and before 2018, corporations subject to the New York City general corporation tax must determine their tax under three (previously, four) alternative methods and pay whichever of the three produces the greatest liability.

For taxable years beginning after 2014 and before 2018, the alternatives are as follows (Sec. 11-604, NYC Adm. Code):

(1) a tax at the rate of 8.85% on allocated business income (9% for certain financial corporations having more than $100 billion in assets); or

(2) a tax at the rate of 0.15 on each dollar of allocated business capital (0.04 per dollar in the case of cooperative housing corporations), not to exceed $10 million (a $10,000 reduction applies to all capital tax calculations); or

(3) a fixed dollar minimum tax of that varies according to the taxpayer's New York City receipts, as follows (Sec. 11-604(1)(E), NYC Adm. Code):

The rate for qualified manufacturing corporations ranges from 4.425% to 8.85%, depending on the amount of business income.

The rate for small businesses ranges from 6.5% to 8.85%, depending on the amount of business income.

The portion of total business capital directly attributable to stock in a subsidiary that is taxable as a utility within the meaning of the New York City Utility Tax or would have been taxable as an insurance corporation under the former New York City Insurance Corporation Tax is taxed at the rate of 0.75%.

S corporations and qualified subchapter S subsidiaries remain subject to the existing, pre-reform general corporation tax provisions. (Sec. 11-602.1, NYC Adm. Code)

New York receipts	Fixed dollar minimum
Not more than $100,000	$25
$100,001 to $250,000	$75
$250,001 to $500,000	$175
$500,001 to $1,000,000	$500
$1,000,001 to $5,000,000	$1,500
$5,000,001 to $25,000,000	$3,500
$25,000,001 to $50,000,000	$5,000
$50,000,001 to $100,000,000	$10,000
$100,000,001 to $250,000,000	$20,000
$250,000,001 to $500,000,000	$50,000
$500,000,001 to $1 billion	$100,000
Over $1 billion	$200,000

For taxable years beginning after 2014, the alternative minimum tax base for income plus compensation is repealed. This was a tax at the rate of 8.85% of an amount that is 30% (subject to reduction; see below) of the taxpayer's entire net income plus salaries and other compensation paid to 5%-plus stockholders and less the sum of $40,000 (prorated for fractional years)

¶21 New York City Banking Corporation Tax—Tax Rates

Beginning in 2015, the New York City tax on financial corporations is merged with the New York City general corporation tax; see ¶20.

¶22 New York City Personal Income Tax on Residents— Tax Rates

New York City imposes its base personal income tax on residents at a graduated rate determined on the basis of income and filing status (¶2805). City residents, estates, and trusts are subject to an additional tax surcharge for taxable years beginning before 2015. The surcharge is imposed at the rate of 14% of the city personal income tax (¶3007).

Minimum tax: In addition to other taxes, a minimum income tax is imposed at the rate of 2.85% of city minimum taxable income.

¶23 New York City Personal Income Tax on Residents—New York City Tax Rate Schedules

The following tax rate schedules, which incorporate the base rate and the additional surcharge rate, may be used by City residents for computing New York City tax.

Married filing joint returns and qualifying widow(er)s

For taxable years beginning after 2009

If the New York City taxable income is:	The tax is:
Not over $21,600	2.907% of the NYC taxable income
Over $21,600 but not over $45,000	$628 plus 3.534% of excess over $21,600
Over $45,000 but not over $90,000	$1,455 plus 3.591% of excess over $45,000
Over $90,000 but not over $500,000	$3,071 plus 3.648% of excess over $90,000
Over $500,000	$19,155* ($18,028, before 2015) plus 3.876% of excess over $500,000

Heads of households

For taxable years beginning after 2009

If the New York City taxable income is:	The tax is:
Not over $14,400	2.907% of the NYC taxable income
Over $14,400 but not over $30,000	$419 plus 3.534% of excess over $14,400
Over $30,000 but not over $60,000	$970 plus 3.591% of excess over $30,000
Over $60,000 but not over $500,000	$2,047 plus 3.648% of excess over $60,000
Over $500,000	$19,230* ($18,098, before 2015) plus 3.876% of excess over $500,000

Single and married filing separately

For taxable years beginning after 2009

If the New York City taxable income is:	The tax is:
Not over $12,000	2.907% of the NYC taxable income
Over $12,000 but not over $25,000	$349 plus 3.534% of excess over $12,000
Over $25,000 but not over $50,000	$808 plus 3.591% of excess over $25,000
Over $50,000 but not over $500,000	$1,706 plus 3.648% of excess over $50,000
Over $500,000	$19,255* ($18,122, before 2015) plus 3.876% of excess over $500,000

* These amounts include an additional amount to recapture the School Tax Reduction (STAR) Program rate reduction benefit for tax rates on taxable income below $500,000 (Form IT-2150-I (5/15)).

¶25 New York City Unincorporated Business—Tax Rate

Tax is imposed at a rate of 4% on unincorporated business taxable income.

¶26 New York City Sales and Use Taxes—Tax Rate

The New York City sales and use tax is imposed at the rate of 4%. Thus, the combined state and local tax rate imposed in New York City is 8³/₈%. This includes the 4% state tax, the ³/₈% Metropolitan Commuter Transportation District tax, and the 4% city tax. The tax also applies to restaurant meals, admissions, and hotel occupancies.

¶30 Mortgage Recording Tax Rates

• *County tax rates*

The following chart lists mortgage recording taxes by county. Rates are for each $100 and remaining major fraction thereof of principal debt that is secured by a mortgage.

Albany $1.25
Allegany 1.00
Broome 1.00
Cattaraugus 1.25
Cayuga 1.00
Chautauqua 1.25
Chemung 0.75
Chenango 0.75
Clinton 1.00
Columbia 1.25
Cortland 1.00
Delaware 1.00
Dutchess 1.05*
Erie 1.00
Essex 1.25
Franklin 1.00
Fulton 1.00
Genesee 1.25
Greene 1.25
Hamilton 1.00
Herkimer 1.00
Jefferson 0.75
Lewis 1.00
Livingston 1.00
Madison 0.75
Monroe 1.00
Montgomery 0.75
Nassau 1.05*
Niagara 1.00
Oneida 1.00
Onondaga 1.00
Ontario 1.00
Orange 1.05*
Orleans 1.00
Oswego 1.00

¶30

Otsego 0.75

Putnam 1.05*

Rensselaer.. 1.25

Rockland..1.30*

Saratoga 1.00

Schenectady 1.25

Schoharie 1.00

Schuyler 1.00

Seneca.. 1.00

St. Lawrence 0.75

Steuben... 1.25

Suffolk 1.05*

Sullivan.. 1.00

Tioga.. 0.75

Tompkins 0.75

Ulster 0.75

Warren 1.25

Washington... 1.00

Wayne... 1.25

Westchester 1.30*

Wyoming 1.25

Yates 1.00

Yonkers (Westchester County) 1.80*

*Includes MCTD tax.

Additional information.—Additional information concerning the tax rate imposed in a particular county may be obtained by:

(1) calling (518) 457-8637; or

(2) calling the recording officer of the county where the real property subject to the mortgage is located.

New York City: The tax in NYC is imposed at the following rates

(1) $1 for each $100 or major fraction thereof with respect to real property securing a principal debt or obligation of less than $500,000;

(2) $1.125 for each $100 or major fraction thereof with respect to one-, two-, or three-family houses, and individual residential condominium units securing a principal debt or obligation of $500,000 or more; and

(3) $1.75 for each $100 or major fraction thereof with respect to all other property.

¶35 Administrative Agencies

The general revenue laws of the state of New York are administered by the Department of Taxation and Finance. For information on the Department and other agencies that administer taxes, see ¶3601. For contact information for the various agencies, including the New York City Department of Finance, see Chapter 39.

FEDERAL/STATE COMPARISON OF KEY FEATURES

¶40 Personal Income Tax Comparison

The following is a comparison of key features of the New York personal income tax law and federal income tax law. New York taxable income is based on federal adjusted gross income (AGI) (see ¶202). State modifications to federal adjusted gross income required by law differences are discussed beginning at ¶203.

Nonresidents and part-year residents: Nonresidents and part-year residents are subject to New York income tax only on income derived from New York sources (see ¶206).

Alternative minimum tax (IRC Sec. 55—IRC Sec. 59).—New York imposes a minimum income tax on certain tax preference items. The tax preference items are based on federal tax preference items with certain modifications (see ¶502, 504).

Asset expense election (IRC Sec. 179 and IRC Sec. 1400N).—Generally, the same as federal because the starting point for New York taxable income is federal adjusted gross income (see ¶202). However, an addition is required with respect to the expensing of certain sport utility vehicles (see ¶203).

Bad debts (IRC Sec. 166).—The same as federal because the starting point for New York taxable income is federal adjusted gross income (see ¶202).

Capital gains and capital losses (IRC Sec. 1(h), IRC Sec. 1211, IRC Sec. 1212, and IRC Sec. 1221).—New York does not have a special tax rate for capital gains. Capital gains and losses are determined in the same manner as under federal law because the starting point for New York taxable income is federal adjusted gross income (see ¶202).

Charitable contributions (IRC Sec. 170 and IRC Sec. 1400S).—New York follows the federal treatment of charitable contributions.

Child care credit (IRC Sec. 45F).—New York has no equivalent to the federal child care credit. However, New York does provide a credit for child and dependent care expenses (see ¶121).

Civil rights deductions (IRC Sec. 62).—The same as federal because the starting point for New York taxable income is federal adjusted gross income (see ¶202).

Dependents (IRC Sec. 152).—The same as federal because the New York exemption for dependents is based on the dependent exemptions to which the taxpayer is entitled under the IRC (see ¶105).

Depreciation (IRC Sec. 167, IRC Sec. 168 and IRC Sec. 1400N).—Generally, the same as federal because the starting point for New York taxable income is federal adjusted gross income (see ¶202). However, except with respect to certain property, New York is decoupled from bonus depreciation under IRC Sec. 168(k); accordingly, amounts claimed as bonus depreciation on the federal return must be added back (see ¶203). Other modifications are required with respect to safe harbor leases and certain property placed in service before 1994.

Earned income credit (IRC Sec. 32).—New York has an earned income credit that is a percentage of the federal credit, and an enhanced EIC is also available for noncustodial parents (see ¶126).

Educational benefits and deductions (IRC Sec. 62(a)(2)(D), IRC Sec. 127, IRC Sec. 221, IRC Sec. 222, IRC Sec. 529).—The same as federal because the starting point for New York taxable income is federal adjusted gross income (see ¶202). In addition, New York provides a college tuition credit (see ¶140) or deduction (see ¶303).

Foreign earned income (IRC Sec. 911 and IRC Sec. 912).—The same as federal because the starting point for New York taxable income is federal adjusted gross income (see ¶202).

Health insurance and health savings accounts (HSAs) (IRC Sec. 105(b), IRC Sec. 106(e), IRC Sec. 139C, IRC Sec. 139D, IRC Sec. 162(l), IRC Sec. 223).—The same as federal because the starting point for New York taxable income is federal adjusted gross income (see ¶202).

Indebtedness (IRC Sec. 108 and IRC Sec. 163).—Generally, the same as federal because the starting point for New York taxable income is federal adjusted gross income (see ¶202). However, under New York's expense disallowance provisions, an addition may be required for certain interest payments made to a related member (see ¶203). An addback is also required for interest on loans to buy tax-exempt securities.

Interest on federal obligations (IRC Sec. 61).—Interest income on obligations of the U.S. and its possessions may be subtracted from federal AGI in computing New York adjusted gross income (see ¶203).

Interest on state and local obligations (IRC Sec. 103).—New York requires an addback for interest income on state and local bonds and obligations, but not those of New York State or its local governments (see ¶203).

Losses not otherwise compensated (IRC Sec. 165 and IRC Sec. 1400S).—New York follows the federal treatment.

Net operating loss (IRC Sec. 172 and IRC Sec. 1400N).—New York follows the federal treatment of net operating losses (see ¶202).

Personal residence (IRC Sec. 121, IRC Sec. 132(n), IRC Sec. 163(h)(3), and IRC Sec. 1033).—The same as federal because the starting point for New York taxable income is federal adjusted gross income (see ¶202).

Retirement plans (IRC Sec. 401—IRC Sec. 424 and IRC Sec. 1400Q).—New York generally conforms to federal provisions regarding retirement plans. However, an addition to federal adjusted gross income is required for certain public employee retirement contributions, and employees are allowed subtractions for certain pension and annuity income, government pensions, railroad retirement income, and social security benefits (see ¶203).

Start-up expenses (IRC Sec. 195).—The same as federal because the starting point for New York taxable income is federal adjusted gross income (see ¶202).

Taxes paid (IRC Sec. 63(c)(1) and IRC Sec. 164).—State, local, and foreign income taxes deducted federally must be added back for New York purposes (see ¶203). The addback requirement does not apply with respect to state and local general sales tax that a taxpayer may opt to claim (instead of income tax) in federal itemized deductions. New York allows a subtraction for state and local income tax refunds included in federal adjusted gross income (¶203), and a credit is provided for income taxes paid to other states (see ¶117). Because New York has its own standard deduction amounts (see ¶306), New York does not follow the federal provision allowing nonitemizers an additional standard deduction for (1) property taxes for the 2008 and 2009 tax years or (2) state sales and excise taxes on new motor vehicles purchased after February 17, 2009, and prior to 2010.

Unemployment compensation (IRC Sec. 85).—The same as federal because the starting point for New York taxable income is federal adjusted gross income (see ¶202).

¶45 Corporate Income Tax Comparison

The following is a comparison of key features of the New York corporation franchise tax law and federal law. The starting point for computing New York entire net income is federal taxable income (see ¶1001). State modifications to taxable income required by law differences are discussed at ¶1002 and 1003.

IRC Sec. 27 foreign tax credit.—New York does not allow a deduction for foreign taxes on, or measured by income or profits; such amounts must be added back to federal taxable income (see ¶1002). If the foreign tax credit is claimed in lieu of a deduction, then no adjustment is required.

IRC Sec. 40 alcohol fuels credit.—New York has no direct equivalent to the federal alcohol fuels credit. However, New York does provide a biofuel production credit (see ¶952).

IRC Sec. 41 incremental research expenditures credit.—New York has no equivalent to the federal incremental research expenditures credit. However, New York allows a subtraction from federal taxable income for the portion of wages and salaries not allowed as a business expense deduction for federal purposes under IRC Sec. 280C because a federal credit was taken (see ¶1003). In addition, New York does provide a credit for investment in research and development property (¶924) and an Excelsior Jobs Program credit that includes a research and development component (¶940).

IRC Sec. 42 low-income housing credit.—New York provides a low-income housing credit that coordinates with the federal low-income housing credit under IRC Sec. 42 (¶941).

IRC Sec. 44 disabled access credit.—New York has no equivalent to the federal disabled access credit.

IRC Sec. 45A Indian employment credit.—New York has no equivalent to the federal Indian employment credit. However, New York allows a subtraction from federal taxable income for the portion of wages and salaries not allowed as a business expense deduction for federal purposes under IRC Sec. 280C because the Indian employment credit was taken (see ¶1003).

IRC Sec. 45B employer social security credit.—New York has no equivalent to the federal employer social security credit.

IRC Sec. 45C orphan drug credit.—New York has no equivalent to the federal orphan drug credit. However, New York allows a subtraction from federal taxable income for the portion of wages and salaries not allowed as a business expense deduction for federal purposes under IRC Sec. 280C because a federal credit was taken (see ¶1003).

IRC Sec. 45D new markets credit.—New York has no equivalent to the federal new markets credit. However, New York provides a credit for contributions to certain community development projects (¶929).

IRC Sec. 45E small business pension start-up costs credit.—New York has no equivalent to the federal small business pension start-up costs credit.

IRC Sec. 45F employer-provided child care credit.—New York has no equivalent to the federal employer-provided child care credit.

IRC Sec. 45K fuel from nonconventional source credit.—New York has no equivalent to the federal fuel from nonconventional source credit.

IRC Sec. 45L new energy efficient homes credit.—New York has no equivalent to the federal new energy efficient homes credit.

IRC Sec. 45M energy efficient appliance credit.—New York has no equivalent to the federal energy efficient appliance credit.

IRC Sec. 46—IRC Sec. 49 investment credit (former law).—With respect to the former federal investment credit (repealed effective for property placed in service after 1985), New York allows a comparable investment credit (see ¶924). New York does not have an equivalent to the current federal investment credits (IRC Sec. 47, IRC Sec. 48, IRC Sec. 48A, IRC Sec. 48B, and IRC Sec. 48C). In addition, New York allows a credit for renovation of historic barns, which uses IRC Sec. 47 definitions (see ¶933), a biofuel production credit (see ¶952), a green building credit for costs related to meeting environmental and energy efficiency standards (see ¶942), and an Excelsior Jobs Program credit that includes jobs tax credit and investment tax credit components (see ¶940). A credit for historic property rehabilitation is also available (see ¶948).

IRC Sec. 51—IRC Sec. 52 (and IRC Sec. 1396) wage credits.—Although New York has no direct equivalent to the federal work opportunity credit (IRC Sec. 51—IRC Sec. 52) or the empowerment zone employment credit (IRC Sec. 1396), New York allows a subtraction from federal taxable income for the portion of wages and salaries not allowed as a business expense deduction for federal purposes under IRC Sec. 280C because a federal credit was taken (see ¶1003). New York provides credits for employing disabled persons (¶928) and for employment in an emerging technology company (¶936). In addition, the Excelsior Jobs Program includes a jobs tax credit (see ¶940).

IRC Sec. 55—IRC Sec. 59 alternative minimum tax.—New York has no equivalent to the federal alternative minimum tax on tax preference items. However, New York imposes an alternative minimum tax on the state "minimum taxable income" base that resembles, but is not based directly on, the federal definition of "alternative minimum taxable income" (see ¶1105).

IRC Sec. 78 deemed dividends.—All amounts of foreign dividend gross-up under IRC Sec. 78 are subtracted from federal taxable income for New York purposes (see ¶1003).

Interest on federal obligations.—Any interest received on federal obligations that was exempt from federal taxation is added back for New York corporation franchise tax purposes (see ¶1002).

IRC Sec. 103 interest on state obligations.—Interest income received on state or local obligations, including those of New York and its political subdivisions, must be added back to federal taxable income (see ¶1002, ¶1005).

IRC Sec. 108 discharge of indebtedness.—The same as federal because the starting point for New York entire net income is federal taxable income before the net operating loss and special deductions (see ¶1001, ¶1005).

IRC Sec. 163 interest on indebtedness.—Generally, the same as federal because the starting point for New York entire net income is federal taxable income (see ¶1001). However, interest deducted in computing federal taxable income for interest on indebtedness paid to a corporate stockholder owning more than 50% of issued stock is added back to taxable income (see ¶1002).

IRC Sec. 164 income and franchise tax deductions.—Income taxes paid to states (including New York), local governments, or foreign governments that were deducted from federal taxable income are added back for New York purposes (see ¶1002).

IRC Sec. 165 losses.—Generally, the same as federal because the starting point for computing New York entire net income is federal taxable income (see ¶1001); however, losses from subsidiary capital must be added back (see ¶1002).

IRC Sec. 166 bad debts.—The same as federal because the starting point for computing New York entire net income is federal taxable income (see ¶1001).

IRC Sec. 167 and IRC Sec. 168 (and IRC Sec. 1400N) depreciation.—Generally the same as federal because the starting point for computing New York entire net income is federal taxable income (see ¶1001). However, for taxable years beginning after 2002, and applicable to property placed in service on or after June 1, 2003, New York is decoupled from federal bonus depreciation provisions under IRC Sec. 168(k), except with respect to qualified Resurgence Zone property and qualified New York Liberty Zone property. In addition, adjustments may be required for property placed in service in taxable years beginning before 1994 (see ¶1002).

IRC Sec. 168(f) safe harbor leasing (pre-1984 leases).—New York does not follow federal treatment of safe harbor leases under former IRC Sec. 168(f)(8); adjustments to federal taxable income are required (see ¶1002 and ¶1003).

IRC Sec. 169 pollution control facilities amortization.—The same as federal because the starting point for computing New York entire net income is federal taxable income (see ¶1001).

IRC Sec. 170 (and IRC Sec. 1400S) charitable contributions.—The same as federal because the starting point for computing New York entire net income is federal taxable income (see ¶1001).

IRC Sec. 171 amortizable bond premium.—The same as federal because the starting point for computing New York entire net income is federal taxable income (see ¶1001).

IRC Sec. 172 (and IRC Sec. 1400N) net operating loss.—New York allows a modified and apportioned net operating loss, which is generally the same as the federal NOL, except that the carryback is limited to the first $10,000 of loss in any taxable year (see ¶1008).

IRC Sec. 174 research and experimental expenditures.—The same as federal because the starting point for computing New York entire net income is federal taxable income (see ¶1001).

IRC Sec. 179 asset expense election.—Generally the same as federal because the starting point for computing New York entire net income is federal taxable income (see ¶1001). An addition is required, however, with respect to the expensing of certain sport utility vehicles (see ¶1002).

IRC Sec. 179D energy efficient commercial buildings deduction.—The same as federal because the starting point for computing New York entire net income is federal taxable income (see ¶1002).

IRC Sec. 190 deduction for barriers removal.—The same as federal because the starting point for computing New York entire net income is federal taxable income (see ¶1001).

IRC Sec. 195 start-up expenditures.—The same as federal because the starting point for computing New York entire net income is federal taxable income (see ¶1001).

IRC Sec. 197 amortization of intangibles.—The same as federal because the starting point for computing New York entire net income is federal taxable income (see ¶1001).

IRC Sec. 199 domestic production activities.—New York requires an addition modification for amounts deducted under IRC Sec. 199 (see ¶1001).

IRC Sec. 243—IRC Sec. 245 dividends received deduction.—The federal deduction for dividends received is not allowed for New York corporation franchise tax purposes. However, New York allows a 100% deduction of dividends from more than 50% owned subsidiaries, and a 50% deduction of all dividends received from other corporations, except for a few special types (see ¶1003, ¶1005).

IRC Sec. 248 organizational expenditures.—The same as federal because the starting point for New York entire net income is federal taxable income (see ¶1001).

IRC Sec. 301—IRC Sec. 385 corporate distributions and adjustments.—The same as federal because the starting point for computing New York entire net income is federal taxable income (see ¶1001).

IRC Sec. 441—IRC Sec. 483 accounting periods and methods.—Generally, the same as federal. New York has a provision similar to IRC Sec. 482 that authorizes the Tax Commissioner to allocate income and deductions to clearly reflect income (see ¶1313). In addition, case law indicates that New York will accept income allocations made on the basis of IRC Sec. 482 (see ¶1404).

IRC Sec. 501—IRC Sec. 530 exempt organizations.—An organization that is exempt from federal income taxation pursuant to IRC Sec. 501(a), will be presumed to be exempt from the New York corporation franchise tax (¶903). Exempt organizations are subject to the unrelated business income tax, which conforms to federal law (¶2713).

IRC Sec. 531—IRC Sec. 547 corporations used to avoid shareholder taxation.—New York has no provisions regarding corporations used to avoid shareholder taxation. New York does not impose a tax on accumulated earnings or an additional tax on the undistributed income of personal holding companies (IRC Sec. 541).

IRC Sec. 581—IRC Sec. 597 banking institutions.—New York has no provisions comparable to the federal provisions regarding banking institutions. Banks and other financial institutions are exempt from the corporation franchise tax, but are subject to the franchise tax on banking corporations (see ¶1602).

IRC Sec. 611—IRC Sec. 638 natural resources.—The same as federal because the starting point for computing New York entire net income is federal taxable income (see ¶1001).

IRC Sec. 801—IRC Sec. 848 insurance companies.—There is no equivalent to the federal provisions relating to insurance companies. Insurance companies are exempt from the corporation franchise tax, but are subject to the franchise tax on insurance companies (see ¶2702).

IRC Sec. 851—IRC Sec. 860L RICs, REITs, REMICs, and FASITs.—RICs are subject to tax to the same extent as under federal law (see ¶911). REITs are also subject to the corporation franchise tax (see ¶918). REMICs are exempt (see ¶918). See also ¶854. New York has no provisions regarding former FASITs (see ¶854). Special combined reporting provisions apply to captive RICs (see ¶911) and captive REITs (see ¶918).

IRC Sec. 861—IRC Sec. 865 foreign source income.—New York does not follow the federal foreign sourcing rules. Multistate and international businesses that conduct business both inside and outside New York use the state's allocation rules (see ¶1302) for determining whether income is attributable to state sources. Income from sources outside the U.S., less allowable deductions, which was not included in federal taxable income is added back for New York purposes if the taxpayer is a corporation organized outside the U.S. (see ¶1002).

IRC Sec. 901—IRC Sec. 908 foreign tax credit.—New York has no provisions comparable to the federal foreign tax credit.

IRC Sec. 1001—IRC Sec. 1092 gain or loss on disposition of property.—Generally, the same as federal, but the amount of the special additional mortgage recording tax that was paid and that is reflected in the computation of the basis of the property must be added back to federal taxable income (see ¶1002).

IRC Sec. 1201 alternative capital gains tax.—New York does not provide for an alternative tax rate on capital gains.

IRC Sec. 1211 and IRC Sec. 1212 capital losses.—Generally, the same as federal, except that federal taxable income and entire net income must be recomputed to determine the amount to be carried back or forward, adding back any loss from subsidiary capital (see ¶1009).

IRC Sec. 1221—IRC Sec. 1260 determining capital gains and losses.—The same as federal because the starting point for computing New York entire net income is federal taxable income (see ¶1001).

IRC Sec. 1361—IRC Sec. 1379 S corporations.—New York S corporations are subject to a corporate-level franchise tax (*i.e.*, fixed dollar minimum tax amounts, based on the level of New York receipts). In addition to the corporate level tax, New York S corporation shareholders are liable for personal income tax on their shares of pass-through S corporation income and losses (see ¶914).

IRC Sec. 1391—IRC Sec. 1397F and IRC Sec. 1400E—IRC Sec. 1400J empowerment zones and renewal communities.—The same as federal because the starting point for computing New York entire net income is federal taxable income. Taxpayers may deduct expenses for which a federal empowerment zone employment credit was claimed (see ¶1003).

IRC Sec. 1501—IRC Sec. 1504 consolidated returns.—New York does not allow the filing of a consolidated return except by all corporate stockholders in a tax-exempt DISC (see ¶919). New York generally requires combined reporting for related corporations with substantial intercorporate transactions (see ¶1404).

BUSINESS INCENTIVES AND CREDITS

¶50 Introduction

New York has created a number of tax incentives designed to attract business to the state, stimulate expansion, and/or encourage certain economic activity. These incentives are listed below, by tax, with a brief description and a cross-reference to the paragraph at which they are discussed in greater detail. Exemptions and deductions, which are too numerous to be fully included below, are discussed under the taxes to which they apply (see the Table of Contents or the Topical Index).

Business tax credit deferral: For tax years 2010, 2011, and 2012, taxpayers with more than $2 million in aggregated business tax credits were required to defer the amounts above $2 million until 2013. The total amount of credits deferred will be paid back to taxpayers over tax years 2013, 2014, and 2015. (¶923—952)

¶55 Corporation Franchise (Income) Tax

• *Investment tax credit (ITC)*

An investment tax credit is allowed for tax years during which qualified production facilities are placed in service within New York. The credit is a percentage of the basis of qualified tangible property, less the amount of certain financing. The percentage used to compute the credit depends on the period during which the property was acquired. (Secs. 208, 210, Tax Law) (¶924)

• *Employment incentive credit (EIC)*

Corporate taxpayers that qualify for an investment tax credit (discussed above) may be entitled to receive an additional employment incentive credit (EIC) for each of the two years following the year in which the ITC is allowed. The credit is a percentage of the original investment credit base on which the ITC was computed. (Sec. 210(12-D), Tax Law) (¶925)

• *Excelsior jobs program credits*

The Excelsior Jobs Program, which replaced the expiring Empire Zones program to provide job creation and investment incentives to firms in targeted industries, includes the following corporate franchise, bank franchise, insurance franchise, and personal income tax credits (Sec. 31, Tax Law; Sec. 210(41), Tax Law) (¶ 940):

— a jobs tax credit equal to 6.85% of gross wages per new job;

— an investment tax credit, equal to 2% of qualified investments;

— a research and development credit, equal to 50% of the federal credit, capped at 3% of R&D expenditures in New York; and

— a real property tax credit.

• *Economic Transformation and Facility Redevelopment Program credits*

The Economic Transformation and Facility Redevelopment Program provides a fully refundable credit available to personal income taxpayers, agricultural cooperatives, general business corporations, banks, and insurance companies and consisting of four components (Sec. 35, Tax Law) ¶938:

— *Jobs tax credit component:* 6.85% of the gross wages of each net new job created;

— *Investment tax credit (ITC) component:* 10% of the cost of investments at a closed facility, with a facility-based cap of $8 million; 6% of the cost of investments elsewhere in an ETA, with a cap of $4 million per entity (if the participant is a partnership, a limited liability company, or an S corporation, the $4 million limitation is applied at the entity level);

— *Job training credit component:* 50% of training expenses for employees displaced by a facility closure, up to $4,000 per employee per year (the employees for whom the expenditures are made must be employed in a full-time, full-year position primarily located at the site in the economic transformation area during the training, and for 180 days after its completion); and

— *Real property tax credit component:* 50% of real property taxes for projects located entirely within the grounds of a closed facility, declining by 10% a year; 25% of real property taxes for projects elsewhere in an ETA, declining by 5% a year.

• *Credit for historic property rehabilitation*

A credit is available for 100% of the federal credit for the rehabilitation of historic properties (Sec. 210(40), Tax Law). (¶ 948)

• *Historic barn renovation credit*

A 25% credit is allowed for qualified rehabilitation expenditures to renovate or rehabilitate qualified historic barns in New York. (Sec. 210(12(I)), Tax Law) (¶ 933)

• *Agricultural property tax credit*

Taxpayers whose federal gross income from farming is at least $2/3$ of their total federal gross income in excess of $30,000 may take a credit for school district property taxes paid on qualified agricultural property. (Sec. 210(22), Tax Law) (¶ 934)

• *Credits for employing qualified disabled persons*

Employers that hire qualified disabled persons for at least 180 days or 400 hours a year may take a credit for 35% of the qualified employee's first $6,000 in wages. (Sec. 210(23), Tax Law; TSB-M-98(2)C, TSB-M-98(3)C, and TSB-M-98(1)I) From 2015 through 2019, an additional credit may be claimed for hiring workers with developmental disabilities (Sec. 210-B(48), Tax Law). (¶ 928)

• *Credit for disabled-accessible taxis*

Until December 31, 2022, a company providing taxicab or livery service may claim a credit for the incremental cost, up to $10,000, of upgrading a vehicle so that it is "accessible by individuals with disabilities," as defined in federal law (Sec. 210 [40], Tax Law). (¶947)

• *Emerging technology credits*

A taxpayer may take a 10% or 20% capital credit for qualified investments in a qualified emerging technology company (QETC), up to $150,000 or $300,000, and a QETC may take an employment credit equal to $1,000 per employee in excess of its base year employment. (Sec. 210(12-E), (12-F), Tax Law) (¶936)

• *Automated external defibrillator credit*

A credit is available for the purchase of automated external defibrillators. The credit is equal to the cost of each defibrillator or $500, whichever is less. (Sec. 210(25), Tax Law) (¶937)

• *Green building*

A credit is allowed for a portion of the costs incurred in performing qualified construction or rehabilitation to enhance the supply of environmentally sound buildings in New York. (Sec. 210(31), Tax Law) (¶942)

• *Low-income housing*

A credit is provided for the construction or rehabilitation of rent-restricted housing that, with some differences, qualifies for the federal low-income housing credit. (Sec. 210(30), Tax Law) (¶941)

• *Long-term care insurance*

A credit is allowed for 20% of the premium paid during the taxable year for long-term care insurance premiums. (Sec. 210(25-a), Tax Law) (¶939)

• *Brownfield remediation*

Three refundable brownfield credits are available to taxpayers that own or develop a qualified site for which a certificate of completion has been issued to the taxpayer by the Commissioner of Environmental Conservation. (Secs. 21-23, 210(33-35), Tax Law) These credits are designated the brownfield redevelopment tax credit, credit for remediated brownfields, and environmental remediation insurance credit (¶943).

• *Real property tax credit for qualified manufacturers*

Effective for tax years beginning on or after January 1, 2014, a credit is available for property taxes paid by qualified New York manufacturers. (Sec. 210(48), Tax Law) (¶958)

• *Film production credit*

A credit is available through 2019 to qualified film production companies, or sole proprietors of qualified film production companies. The amount of the credit is generally 30% of the qualified production costs of a qualified film and may be increased for post-production costs (Secs. 24, 210(36), Tax Law). In addition, New York City has adopted a 5% film production credit against general corporation and unincorporated business taxes. (¶944, ¶2806)

• *Commercial production credit*

A credit is available to qualified commercial production companies, or sole proprietors of qualified film production companies for a percentage of its qualified production costs, applicable to tax years beginning after 2006, and before 2019 (Sec. 28, Tax Law). (¶949)

¶55

• *Musical and theatrical production credit*

For tax years 2015 through 2019, a credit is available 25% of the qualified production expenditures and transportation costs incurred by eligible production companies to produce a live, dramatic stage presentation in a qualified production facility on a tour that consists of eight or more shows in three or more localities (Sec. 24-a(B), Tax Law). (¶959)

• *Credit for security training*

Qualified building owners may claim a refundable credit for a portion of the cost of training security officers. (Sec. 210(37), Tax Law) (¶946)

• *Biofuel production credit*

A biofuel production credit is available for taxable years beginning after 2005 and before 2020. The credit equals 15¢ for each gallon of biofuel produced at a biofuel plant, after the production of the first 40,000 gallons per year presented to market. (Sec. 28, Tax Law) (¶952)

• *Credit for conservation easement property taxes*

A credit is available in the amount of 25% of the school district, county, and city real property taxes paid on land that is under a conservation easement. The credit amount claimed by a taxpayer may not exceed $5,000 in any given year. (Sec. 210(38), Tax Law) (¶951)

• *Youth Works credit*

The New York Youth Works Tax Credit Program provides tax credits of up to $1,000 for a six-month period to qualified businesses employing at-risk youths in full-time and part-time positions in 2012 through 2018. The program is administered by the Department of Labor. (Sec. 210[44], Tax Law) (¶953)

• *Empire State Jobs Retention Program*

The Empire State Jobs Retention Program creates tax credits equal to 6.85% of the gross wages paid for impacted jobs in order to retain strategic businesses and jobs that are at risk of leaving the state due to the impact on business operations of an event (such as a natural disaster) leading to an emergency declaration by the governor. (Sec. 36, Tax Law; Sec. 210[44], Tax Law) (¶954)

• *Alcoholic beverage production credit*

For taxable years beginning on or after January 1, 2016, the beer production credit is renamed the alcoholic beverage production credit, and the credit is expanded to include cider, wine, and liquor. (Sec. 210(45), Tax Law) (¶955)

• *Alternative fuel vehicle refueling and electric vehicle recharging property credit*

A credit of up to $5,000 is available for investment in alternative fuel vehicle refueling property and/or electric vehicle recharging property for tax years beginning on or after January 1, 2013, but before January 1, 2018. (Sec. 210(24), Tax Law) (¶935)

• *Minimum wage reimbursement credit*

A credit in varying amounts is available for taxable years 2014 through 2019 for employers that hire eligible employees at the minimum wage rate. (Sec. 38, Tax Law; Sec. 210(46), Tax Law) (¶956)

• *Hire a veteran credit*

For taxable years beginning on or after January 1, 2015 and before January 1, 2019, a 10% credit is available for employers that hire a qualified veteran. The credit is 15% for employers that hire a disabled veteran. (Sec. 210(23-a)(a), Tax Law) (¶957)

• *Employee training incentive credit*

For taxable years beginning on or after January 1, 2015, a refundable tax credit is available against corporation franchise and personal income tax for eligible training costs incurred on or after April 13, 2015, by employers that procure certain training for their employees. (Sec. 606(ddd), Tax Law). (¶960)

• *START-UP NY program*

The SUNY Tax-Free Areas to Revitalize and Transform Upstate (START-UP) New York program provides several personal and corporate income tax, sales and use tax, property tax, and transfer tax incentives to promote business and job creation by transforming public higher education through designated tax-free communities in upstate New York and other strategically-designated locations. A tax-free NY area tax elimination credit against corporation franchise tax is provided. (Sec. 40(b), Tax Law) (¶923)

• *Business Incubator and Innovation Hot Spot incentives*

The New York State Business Incubator and Innovation Hot Spot Support Act supports the growth of companies in the early stages of development. The Empire State Development Corporation (ESD) may designate five "New York State Innovation Hot Spots" in SFY 2013-14 and an additional five in SFY 2014-15. Entities designated as Innovation Hot Spots must demonstrate an affiliation with and the support of at least one college, university, or independent research institution, and offer programs consistent with regional economic development strategies. Qualified entities in Innovation Hot Spots are eligible for various tax benefits for five taxable years, beginning with the year the entity becomes a tenant in or part of an Innovation Hot Spot. Qualified entities are subject only to the fixed dollar minimum tax under Article 9-A. Also, qualified entities are allowed a deduction for the amount of income or gain attributable to operations in the hot spot. (Part C, Ch. 59 (S.B. 2609, Laws 2013)) (¶923)

¶60 Sales and Use Taxes

• *Manufacturing (Secs. 1105, 1115, and 1118, Tax Law; Reg. Sec. 528.13)*

Machinery and equipment are exempt when they are used or consumed directly and predominantly for various purposes, including:

— production for sale of tangible personal property, gas, electricity, refrigeration, or steam by manufacturing, processing, generating, assembling, or refining; and

— mining and extracting operations (¶2105).

A use tax exemption may also apply for property that is converted into or becomes a component part of the product produced for sale by the purchaser (¶2104).

The exemption for machinery and equipment used in manufacturing or processing is applicable for purposes of the New York City sales and use taxes.

¶60

Services performed on exempt property are also exempt. These services include producing, fabricating, processing, printing, and imprinting performed on tangible personal property furnished by the customer, and installing, maintaining, servicing, or repairing tangible personal property not held for sale in the regular course of business (¶2102).

Parts with a useful life of more than one year that are used directly and predominantly in production are exempt from sales and use taxes. There is also an exemption for parts with a useful life of one year or less and for tools and supplies used in connection with production machinery and equipment (¶2105).

Fuel, utilities and utility services used or consumed directly and exclusively in the production for sale of tangible personal property, gas, electricity, refrigeration or steam by manufacturing, processing, assembling, generating or refining are not taxable (¶2106).

• *Research and development*

Tangible personal property used or consumed directly and predominantly in research and development in the experimental or laboratory sense is exempt, as is gas, electricity, refrigeration, steam and gas, electric, refrigeration and steam service used or consumed directly and exclusively in research and development in the experimental or laboratory sense (Secs. 1115(a)(10), 1115(40)(b)(ii), Tax Law). The exemption does not extend to installation and repair services for property used or consumed directly and predominantly in research and development (Reg. Sec. 528.11(a)(2)). (¶2108)

• *Economic transformation areas*

Under the Economic Transformation and Facility Redevelopment Program (Article 18, Secs. 400- 404), incentives are provided to attract new businesses and jobs in communities affected by the closing of certain correctional and youth facilities. In addition to other incentives available, a participant may also be eligible for a refund of New York state sales or use tax paid for certain purchases of tangible personal property. The tangible personal property must be used in construction, expansion, or rehabilitation of industrial or commercial real property and must become an integral part of the property that is located within an economic transformation area. (¶2112)

• *Computer hardware and software*

Computer system hardware used or consumed directly and predominantly in designing and developing computer software or websites is exempt. Software designed and developed to the specifications of a specific purchaser is exempt. Software that is otherwise taxable may be exempt if provided as part of an Internet access service. (Secs. 1101(b)(14), 1115(a)(35), Tax Law) (¶2102)

• *Advertising*

Certain advertising and promotional materials and services are exempt, including:

— fees for the services of advertising agencies;

— charges for running advertisements on the Internet, provided the taxpayer does not sell tangible personal property in conjunction with the services;

— advertising supplements, when distributed as inserts in a newspaper, periodical or shopping paper;

— certain promotional materials and services. (Secs. 1105(c)(1), 1105(v)(1), and 1115(n), Tax Law; Reg. Secs. 527.3(b)(5) and 528.6(e)(1)) (¶2102)

¶60

• *Packaging*

Cartons, containers, wrapping and packaging materials, as well as supplies and components purchased, for use and consumption by a vendor in performing a taxable service or in packaging or packing tangible personal property for sale are tax-exempt when transferred by the vendor to the purchaser (Sec. 1115(19), Tax Law; Reg. Sec. 528.20(a)(1)). Returnable containers (such as drums, barrels, or acid carboys), when purchased at retail by a person who does not transfer ownership of the container, are subject to tax (Reg. Sec. 528.20(c)(1)). (¶2102)

• *Agriculture*

Tangible personal property and services used or consumed directly and predominantly in farm production are exempt. Also, fuel and utility services used in farming are exempt. (Secs. 1115(a)(6), 1115(c), Tax Law) (¶2102)

• *Motion picture production*

Items such as cameras, projectors and sound recorders constitute exempt machinery used in production when purchased for use in movie, video or sound productions. Projectors and sound recorders purchased for use in movie, video or sound productions qualify for exemption as equipment used in production. Wardrobes, backdrops, art work, settings and props used in movie, video or sound productions constitute nontaxable supplies. (Sec. 1105-B(a), Tax Law) In addition, exemptions are available for (1) tangible personal property used or consumed directly and predominantly in the production, including editing, dubbing, and mixing, of a film for sale, regardless of the medium used to convey the film to a purchaser (Sec. 1115(a)(39)); (2) the services of producing, fabricating, processing, printing, imprinting, installing, maintaining, servicing, or repairing such property (Sec. 1115(bb)(1)); and (3) fuel, gas, electricity, refrigeration, or steam, as well as gas, electric, refrigeration, or steam service, used or consumed directly and exclusively in the production of a film for sale. (Sec. 1115(bb)(2)) (¶2102)

• *Pollution control and cleanup equipment*

The manufacturing exemption applies to machinery and equipment used to dispose of industrial waste in the prevention of water or air pollution, and a specific exemption applies to machinery or equipment used in the control, prevention, or abatement of pollution or contaminants from manufacturing or industrial facilities. (Sec. 1115(a)(12) and (40); Reg. Sec. 528.13(d)(1)) (¶2105)

• *Waste removal*

Removal of waste material from a facility regulated as a transfer station or construction and demolition debris processing facility by the New York Department of Environmental Conservation exempt from New York sales and use tax, provided that the waste material to be removed was not generated by the facility. (¶2103)

• *Solar energy systems*

Receipts from the retail sale and installation of residential solar energy systems equipment are exempt from tax. All municipalities, including New York City, are authorized to grant the same exemption. (¶2106)

Effective January 1, 2013, the sale and the installation of commercial solar energy systems equipment are exempt from state sales and use tax. (¶2106)

• *Internet data centers*

An exemption applies to machinery, equipment, and other tangible personal property for use in providing website services in an Internet data center located in New York. (Secs. 1115(a)(37), 1115(y), Tax Law) (¶2102)

¶60

• *Broadcasting equipment*

Machinery, equipment, or other tangible personal property (including parts, tools, and supplies) used by a broadcaster directly and predominantly in the production and post-production of live or recorded programs for the purpose of broadcast over-the-air, cable television transmissions, or direct broadcast satellite system transmissions are exempt. In addition, services such as editing, dubbing, and mixing are exempt. (Sec. 1115(aa), Tax Law) (¶2102)

• *Telecommunications equipment*

Exemptions apply to tangible personal property used or consumed in providing telecommunications services for sale or Internet access services for sale. Also, machinery, equipment, or apparatus to upgrade cable television systems to digital, and related parts with a useful life of one year or less and tools or supplies are exempt. (Sec. 1115(a)(12-a), Tax Law) (¶2102)

• *Alcoholic beverage tasting*

Wine or wine products furnished by the official agent of a farm winery, winery, wholesaler, or importer at a wine tasting to a customer or prospective customer who consumes the wine at the tasting is not subject to sales and use taxation (Sec. 1115(a)(33), Tax Law).

Effective June 1, 2015, the wine tasting exemption is extended to include other alcoholic beverages (*i.e.*, liquor, beer or cider) and items used to package such beverages (*i.e.*, bottles, corks, caps, and labels). (Sec. 1118(13), Tax Law) (¶2102)

• *START-UP NY program*

The SUNY Tax-Free Areas to Revitalize and Transform Upstate (START-UP) New York program provides several tax incentives to promote business and job creation by transforming public higher education through designated tax-free communities in upstate New York and other strategically-designated locations. A business in such a tax-free community is eligible for a credit or refund of sales and use taxes imposed on the retail sale of tangible personal property or services and similar taxes. The credit or refund is allowed for 120 consecutive months beginning with the month during which the business locates in the tax-free NY area. (Ch. 68 (A.B. 8113), Laws 2013) (¶2112)

• *Business Incubator and Innovation Hot Spot incentives*

The New York State Business Incubator and Innovation Hot Spot Support Act supports the growth of companies in the early stages of development. The Empire State Development Corporation (ESD) may designate five "New York State Innovation Hot Spots" in SFY 2013-14 and an additional five in SFY 2014-15. Entities designated as Innovation Hot Spots must demonstrate an affiliation with and the support of at least one college, university, or independent research institution, and offer programs consistent with regional economic development strategies. Among other incentives, qualified entities are also eligible for a credit or refund of sales and use tax imposed on the retail sale of tangible personal property or services. (Part C, Ch. 59 (S.B. 2609, Laws 2013)) (¶2109)

¶65 Property Tax

• *Agriculture*

Land used in agricultural production may be assessed at its agricultural value if (1) the land is located within an agricultural district, or (2) the owner commits the land exclusively to agricultural uses for a period of eight years. A limited property tax exemption is allowed for certain land used for crop expansion or replanting in connection with an orchard or vineyard. Also, permanent agricultural structures with specified uses are exempt from taxation, special ad valorem levies and special assessments. (Secs. 481, 483a, Real Property Tax Law) (¶2504)

• *Business investment*

A 10-year partial exemption from tax and special levies is allowed for the cost of construction, alteration, installation or improvement of business property (such exemption does not include fire district taxes and does not apply in New York City). Certain real property used in manufacturing steel is exempt if owned by a corporation subject to the franchise tax. (Sec. 485-b, Real Property Tax Law) (¶2504)

• *Capital improvements*

Municipalities other than New York City may authorize limited exemptions for increases in the assessed value of residential buildings that have been reconstructed, altered or improved. (Sec. 421-f, Real Property Tax Law) (¶2504)

• *Energy conservation improvements*

Real property that contains a solar or wind energy system approved by the New York State Energy Research and Development Authority is exempt from taxation for a period of 15 years to the extent of any increase in assessed value due to the system. (Secs. 487, 489, Real Property Tax Law) There is also an exemption for nuclear powered electric generating facilities. (¶2504)

• *"Green" building improvements*

A property tax exemption is authorized for the construction of improvements to real property initiated on or after January 1, 2013, that meet Leadership in Energy and Environmental Design (LEED) certification standards for green buildings, the green building initiative's green globes rating system, the American National Standards Institute, or substantially equivalent standards for certification. The exemption amount ranges from 100% in the first year for certified/silver, gold, or platinum LEED exemption to 20% in the 10th year for platinum LEED exemption. (¶2505)

• *Alteration of property for disabled access*

Municipalities and villages may provide a limited 10-year tax exemption for real property altered, installed, or improved for the purpose of removing architectural barriers for the disabled. (Sec. 459-a, Real Property Tax Law) (¶2504)

• *Historic property*

If authorized by local law, real property that is altered or rehabilitated for historic preservation is eligible for an exemption from taxation and special levies. Cities and towns to which the multiple dwelling law applies may provide a 14-year exemption for the value of alterations or improvements to the exterior walls of buildings or structures completed within 36 months of the starting date, in order to comply with building codes in an area designated a historic or landmark area or that are designated as historic or landmark buildings or structures. Also, local governments may provide for 10-year partial property tax exemptions for increases in assessed values that would otherwise result from the reconstruction or rehabilitation of historic barns. (Secs. 483-b, 444-a, and 489(1)(a)(4), (6), Real Property Tax Law) (¶2504)

• *Pollution control facilities*

Industrial waste treatment facilities and air pollution control facilities that are constructed or reconstructed to comply with environmental conservation law and codes are exempt to the extent of any increase in value by reason of such construction or reconstruction. (Secs. 477, 477a, Real Property Tax Law) (¶2504)

¶65

• *START-UP NY program*

The SUNY Tax-Free Areas to Revitalize and Transform Upstate (START-UP) New York program provides several tax incentives to promote business and job creation by transforming public higher education through designated tax-free communities in upstate New York and other strategically-designated locations. Private universities and colleges will maintain tax-exempt status on property that is currently tax exempt and that they subsequently lease to businesses participating in the START-UP NY program. Only the portion of the property that is used for purposes of the START-UP NY program will be exempt. (Ch. 68 (A.B. 8113), Laws 2013) (¶2504)

PART II

PERSONAL INCOME TAX

CHAPTER 1
IMPOSITION OF TAX, EXEMPTIONS, RATES, CREDITS

¶101 Overview of Personal Income Tax

The New York personal income tax was first enacted in 1919. The present law is codified as Article 22 of the Tax Law and generally adopts for New York purposes the provisions of the federal Internal Revenue Code relating to items of income, deduction, gain and loss, and uses federal adjusted gross income and deductions, with certain modifications, as the basis of tax.

The tax is imposed at rates listed at ¶106 on the taxable income of resident individuals, estates, and trusts. Nonresident individuals, estates, and trusts are taxed only upon their taxable income from New York sources. The tax is imposed at graduated rates. A separate tax computation is applicable to nonresidents and part-year residents.

Imposition of the tax, issues of residence, tax rates, exemptions, credits, and accounting methods are discussed in Chapter 1.

The starting point for the computation of New York taxable income is federal adjusted gross income, with certain adjustments and modifications, as discussed in Chapter 2.

Standard and itemized deductions for New York purposes are discussed in Chapter 3, while the apportionment of business income and the allocation of salaries and wages earned partly within and outside New York are the subjects of Chapter 4.

Prior to repeal (see ¶501), a minimum tax was imposed on items of tax preference.

Estimated taxes, withholding, returns, and payment of tax are explained in Chapter 6, and the application of tax to estates, trusts, and partnerships is discussed in Chapter 7.

Taxpayer remedies are treated in Chapter 8, along with information on penalties and interest.

¶102 Who is a Resident?

Law: Sec. 605, Tax Law; Reg. Secs. 105.20, 105.23 (CCH New York Tax Reports, ¶15-105—15-130, 15-205).

New York taxes its residents on all income from all sources, regardless of whether the income is attributable to New York activities or property. In certain cases, income taxes imposed by other states (generally on income "sourced" to those states) may be available as a credit to a New York taxpayer (¶117). Income taxes imposed by other states on intangible income (*e.g.,* interest, dividends, capital gains, etc.) may be subjected to double tax. According to New York's courts, this potential for double taxation does not offend the U.S. Constitution. See *Tamagni v. Tax Appeals Tribunal,* 91 NY2d 530, *Cert denied,* 119 Supreme Court 340 (1998), CCH New York Tax Reports, ¶403-055; *Zelinsky v. Tax Appeals Tribunal,* New York Court of Appeals, No. 129, 2003 N.Y. LEXIS 3968, November 24, 2003, CCH New York Tax Reports, ¶404-683.

Nonresidents pay tax to New York only on income that is "derived or connected with New York sources." This includes wages and salaries (including stock option income and deferred compensation) as well as rents and gains associated with the lease or sale of assets located within New York's borders. Income from a New York business, trade, profession or occupation is also sourced to New York. This includes a nonresident's share of New York income from any flow-through entity (*e.g.,* partnerships, S corporations, LLCs, etc.) doing business in the State.

A "resident individual" is defined as (Sec. 605(b)(1), Tax Law; Reg. Sec. 105.20):

— any person domiciled in New York (unless such person does not maintain a permanent place of abode in New York, maintains a permanent place of abode elsewhere and spends in the aggregate not more than 30 days of the taxable year in New York), or

— any person not domiciled in New York who maintains a permanent place of abode in New York and spends in the aggregate more than 183 days of the taxable year in New York. This is generally known as "statutory residence." A place of abode will not be deemed to be permanent if it is maintained only during a temporary stay for the accomplishment of a particular purpose. However, an apartment suitable for permanent dwelling is a permanent place of abode even if used only as a temporary or second lodging for shopping trips, visits, or related purposes. See *Barker,* New York Division of Tax Appeals, Tax Appeals Tribunal, DTA No. 822324, January 13, 2011, CCH New York Tax Reports, ¶407-100.

For discussion of what constitutes a "permanent place of abode," see *TB-IT-690,* New York Department of Taxation and Finance, December 15, 2011, CCH New York Tax Reports, ¶407-439.

Temporary lodgings: For taxable years ending on or after December 31, 2008, New York no longer recognizes a temporary stay exception in determining whether a taxpayer maintains a permanent place of abode inside or outside New York (see *TSB-M-09(2)I,* January 16, 2009, CCH New York Tax Reports, ¶406-297).

Presence within New York for any part of a calendar day is deemed to be a day spent within the state. However, such presence within New York State may be disregarded if it is solely for the purpose of boarding a plane, ship, train or bus for travel to a destination outside New York State, or while traveling by motor, plane or train through New York State to a destination outside New York State.

CCH Advisory: Undergraduate Students

Reg. Sec. 105.20(e)(1) excludes dwelling places maintained by qualified undergraduate students from the definition of "permanent place of abode" for purposes of considering whether a taxpayer is a resident or nonresident for personal income tax purposes. This applies to New York State, New York City, and Yonkers personal income taxes for tax years 2009 and after.

A "permanent place of abode" is defined as a dwelling place of a permanent nature maintained by the taxpayer, whether or not owned by the taxpayer, and will generally include a dwelling place owned or leased by the taxpayer's spouse. However, a dwelling place maintained by a full-time student enrolled at an institution of higher education, as defined in Sec. 606(t)(3), Tax Law, in an undergraduate degree program leading to a baccalaureate degree, and occupied by the student while attending the institution is not a permanent place of abode with respect to that student. For purposes of this rule, a full-time student means an individual who is carrying a minimum courseload in a baccalaureate program of 12 hours per semester for at least two semesters, or the equivalent, during the tax year. Accordingly, there is no exception for graduate students pursuing a post-baccalaureate degree. (TSB-M-09(15)I, New York Department of Taxation and Finance, December 16, 2009, CCH NEW YORK TAX REPORTS, ¶406-626)

Presence in foreign countries: For taxable years beginning on or after January 1, 2009, a domiciliary is not a New York resident for tax purposes if (Sec. 605(b)(1), Tax Law):

(1) the taxpayer is present in one or more foreign countries for at least 450 of 548 consecutive days; and

(2) during the period of 548 consecutive days, the taxpayer, the taxpayer's spouse (unless legally separated), and the taxpayer's minor children are not present in New York for more than 90 days.

Practitioner Comment: Medical Days

New York's Tax Department has also recognized that a day spent in a New York hospital or nursing home is involuntary and will not be treated as a New York "day." Schmitz, TSB-A-00(3)I; CCH NEW YORK TAX REPORTS, ¶403-701; Stranahan, 416 NYS2d 836 (1979), CCH NEW YORK TAX REPORTS, ¶98-049. Presence in New York for outpatient treatment, however, is considered time in New York. And time spent visiting or tending to a hospitalized spouse is considered "purposeful and voluntary" under New York's day-count rules. (Brush, ALJ 4/12/01)

Mark S. Klein, Esq., Hodgson Russ LLP

The term "resident individual" does not include a person domiciled in New York who, within any 548-day period, is present in a foreign country or countries for at least 450 days, is not present in New York for more than 90 days, and does not maintain a permanent place of abode in New York at which his or her spouse (unless legally separated) or minor children are present for more than 90 days. (In the case of a short taxable year because of a change of residence status, the 90-day period is prorated.) In addition, domiciliaries excluded from the definition of "resident" include those who, during the nonresident portion of the taxable year within which the 548-day period begins and the nonresident portion of the taxable year within which such period ends, are not present in New York for a number of days that exceeds the amount that bears the same ratio to 90 as the number of days contained in such portion of the taxable year bears to 548. (Sec. 605(b)(1), Tax Law; Reg. Sec. 105.20)

¶102

Minor children: A child will be considered a minor for purposes of the rule until he or she is 18 years of age. Therefore, in determining whether the taxpayer's children are present in New York for more than 90 days during the applicable 548-day period, each day that the children are present in New York and under the age of 18 during the 548-day time period will be counted. (*TSB-A-12(5)I*, New York Commissioner of Taxation and Finance, September 27, 2012, CCH New York Tax Reports, ¶ 407-658)

Practitioner Comment: Proof of Whereabouts

Auditors will review credit card statements, automated teller machine withdrawal locations, E-ZPass charges, cellular and other telephone bills and cancelled checks in an effort to determine a taxpayer's whereabouts on any particular day. In recent years, auditors have been issuing subpoenas to wireless cell phone carriers to determine a taxpayer's location (by latitude and longitude) each time a call is made or received. The burden of proof rests with the taxpayer, however, and auditors will generally assume that an undocumented day is a day spent in New York.

Mark S. Klein, Esq., Hodgson Russ LLP

The New York State Department of Taxation and Finance devotes substantial resources to its residency audit program. Lifelong residents of New York State who decide to move to another jurisdiction can expect their first nonresident return (or their failure to file a return after departure) to be closely scrutinized by New York's auditors. If the taxpayers change their residence but continue to maintain a home (or any permanent place of abode) in New York, auditors will expect to see detailed records confirming that the taxpayers did not set foot in any part of the State for more than 183 days during the calendar year. Trips to New York for gasoline, shopping, dinner or the theater are all considered "days" spent in New York.

Even if the taxpayers are able to satisfy their burden of proof and demonstrate that they did not spend too many days in New York, auditors will then scrutinize the purported change of domicile, to see if the taxpayers made a significant change in their lifestyle that reflects a permanent move to a new location.

For a discussion of domicile, see ¶ 103.

A "nonresident individual" is defined as an individual who is not a resident or a part-year resident. (Sec. 605(b)(2), Tax Law)

A "part-year resident individual" is an individual who is not a resident or nonresident for the entire taxable year. (Sec. 605(b)(5), Tax Law)

Practitioner Comment: Change of Residence

Practitioners should appreciate the interplay of the domicile and statutory residence rules. Taxpayers who decide to change their domicile from New York to another state during the second half of the year who also retain a home (or any permanent place of abode) in New York for the remainder of the year, must carefully review their New York day count. For example, assume that taxpayer S, a lifelong New York domiciliary, decides to retire and move to Florida on September 1, 2017. S retains his modest New York home or apartment either as an investment or as a place to visit during the summer months. Although S may have changed his domicile to Florida, he may still be taxed as a New York resident for all of 2017 if, during the 2017 calendar year, he spent more than 183 days in New York. According to the New York taxing authorities, it does not matter that the "New York days" occurred before S changed his domicile. This interpretation of the law has recently been successfully challenged. See *Sobotka* (ALJ Order, 8/20/15). New York's Tax Department does not agree with this decision.

Mark S. Klein, Esq., Hodgson Russ LLP

• *Estates and trusts*

A "resident estate or trust" is defined as (Reg. Sec. 105.23):

— the estate of a decedent who at the time of death was domiciled in New York;

— a trust, or a portion of a trust, consisting of property transferred by will of a decedent who at the time of death was domiciled in New York; or

— a trust, or portion of a trust, consisting of the property of (a) a person domiciled in New York at the time such property was transferred to the trust, if such trust or portion of a trust was then irrevocable, or if it was then revocable and has not subsequently become irrevocable, or (b) a person domiciled in New York at the time such trust, or portion of a trust, became irrevocable, if it was revocable when such property was transferred to the trust but has subsequently become irrevocable.

CCH Advisory: Future Interests

The transfer of future interests to nonresident trusts by a resident trust did not make them resident trusts until the event that vested the principal occurred. (*The Amauris Trust*, New York Division of Tax Appeals, Administrative Law Judge Unit, DTA Nos. 821369 and 821497, July 24, 2008, CCH NEW YORK TAX REPORTS, ¶ 406-118)

A trust is deemed revocable if subject to a power to revest title in the person whose property constitutes such trust or portion of a trust. A trust becomes irrevocable when the possibility that such power may be exercised has been terminated.

A "nonresident estate" is defined as an estate that is not a resident, while a "nonresident trust" is defined as a trust that is not a resident or part-year resident.

A "part-year resident trust" is a trust that is not a resident or nonresident for the entire taxable year.

CCH Advisory: Nontaxable Resident Trusts

A resident trust is not taxable if (1) all the trustees are domiciled outside New York State; (2) the entire corpus of the trust, including real and tangible property, is located outside New York; and (3) all income and gains of the trust are from or connected with sources outside the state and are determined as if the trust were a nonresident trust (Reg. Sec. 105.23(c)).

Intangible property is considered to be located in New York if at least one of the trustees is domiciled in the state (Sec. 605(b)(3)(D)(ii), Tax Law).

A banking corporation located outside New York continues to be a nonresident corporate trustee even if it later becomes an office or branch of a corporate trustee domiciled in New York (Sec. 605(b)(3), Tax Law).

Resident trusts must file a New York state fiduciary income tax return if the trust (TSB-M-10(5)I, July 23, 2010, CCH NEW YORK TAX REPORTS, ¶ 406-891):

— is required to file a federal income tax return for the tax year;

— had any New York taxable income for the year;

— had tax preference items for minimum income tax purposes in excess of the specific deduction; or

— is subject to a separate tax on lump-sum distributions.

For treatment of members of the armed forces, see ¶ 111.

For additional information on resident and nonresident trusts and estates, see Chapter 7, beginning at ¶ 701.

¶103 Domicile

Law: Sec. 605, Tax Law; Reg. Sec. 105.20 (CCH NEW YORK TAX REPORTS, ¶ 15-110, 15-255, 15-305).

Generally, a person's domicile is the place that the person intends to be his or her permanent home; that is, the place to which the person intends to return whenever absent.

Domicile is not dependent on citizenship; for example, an immigrant who has permanently established his or her home in New York is domiciled in New York regardless of whether the immigrant has become a U.S. citizen or has applied for citizenship. However, a U.S. citizen will not ordinarily be deemed to have changed domicile by going to a foreign country unless it is clearly shown that the citizen intends to remain there permanently. (Reg. Sec. 105.20)

Husband and wife: The domicile of a husband and wife is usually the same. However, if they are separated in fact they may each, under some circumstances, acquire their own separate domiciles, even though there is no judgment or decree of separation. (Reg. Sec. 105.20)

Children: A child's domicile ordinarily follows that of the child's parents, until the child reaches the age of self-support and actually establishes his or her own separate domicile. (Reg. Sec. 105.20) When the mother and father have separate domiciles, the domicile of the child is generally the domicile of the parent with whom the child lives for the major portion of the year. The domicile of a child for whom a guardian has been appointed is not necessarily determined by the domicile of the guardian.

Military personnel: Federal law provides that, for purposes of taxation, military and naval personnel are not deemed to have lost their residence or domicile in any state solely by reason of being absent from the state in compliance with military or naval orders. Thus, federal law insures that personnel who are domiciled in New York will not be deemed domiciliaries for income tax purposes in other states in which they are stationed. On the other hand, an individual who is domiciled in another state and stationed in New York will not be deemed a domiciliary, for tax purposes, of New York. The rule is, generally, that the domicile of a person is in no way affected by service in the armed forces of his or her country. A change of domicile has to be shown by facts that objectively manifest a voluntary intention to make the new location a domicile. Although it is possible for a military or naval person to change domicile, the requisite intent is difficult to prove. (Reg. Sec. 105.20)

See also the discussion of military personnel at ¶111. For a discussion of allocation of military pay received by non-New York domiciliaries, see ¶403.

• *Change in domicile*

A domicile, once established, continues until the person moves to a new location with a bona fide intention of making the new location his or her fixed and permanent home. (Reg. Sec. 105.20) *Intention* is the decisive factor in determining whether a particular residence occupied by a person qualifies as the person's domicile; no change of domicile results from a removal to a new location if the intention is to remain there only for a limited time.

There is a legal presumption against a change in domicile from one location to another. (Reg. Sec. 105.20) Accordingly, the burden is on the taxpayer to establish, by clear and convincing evidence, both a change in residence and the intention to effect a change in domicile.

Practitioner Comment: The "Leave and Land" Rule

Before they will respect a change of domicile, New York auditors insist that taxpayers must both leave New York and land in their new home. In *Knight*, TAT 11/9/06, the Tax Appeals Tribunal provided a succinct illustration:

"If a domiciliary of New York terminated his residency in New York with the intention of never returning and spent the following several years traveling among the capitals of Europe, residing for a few months in each, and finally returned to the United States to make a home in Florida, he would remain a domiciliary of New York until his new home in Florida was established."

¶103

In spite of the fact that the taxpayer abandoned New York, tax would be imposed on his worldwide income until he "landed," in Florida by establishing a residence in the new location.

Mark S. Klein, Esq., Hodgson Russ LLP

Audit guidelines: The Department of Taxation and Finance has revised its District Office Audit Manual to simplify the factors considered by auditors in determining whether a taxpayer successfully establishes both a change in residence and an intention to change domicile. The guidelines list six "primary" and eight "other" factors. The "primary" factors are fundamental and first in line toward developing a case for New York domicile. Information concerning the "other" factors are only requested when a basis for New York domicile, using the primary factors, is found to exist or when primary factors are at least equal in weight for New York and another location.

Primary factors: The primary factors evidencing a change in domicile include the following:

— The individual's use and maintenance of a New York "residence," compared to the nature and use patterns of a non-New York residence;

— The individual's pattern of employment, as it relates to compensation derived by the taxpayer in the particular year being reviewed, including active participation in a New York trade, business occupation or profession and/or substantial investment in, and management of, any New York closely held business;

— An analysis of where the individual spends time during the year;

— The location of items that the individual holds "near and dear" to his or her heart, or those items that have significant sentimental value, such as family heirlooms; works of art; collections of books; stamps and coins; and those personal items that enhance the quality of lifestyle; and

— An analysis of the taxpayer's family connections both within and without New York.

Practitioner Comment: Impact of Primary Domicile Factors

In 2014, New York's Department of Taxation and Finance revised its nonresident audit guidelines and identified the five primary factors that must be examined in a residency audit. According to the guidelines, the primary factors include a review of a taxpayer's home, active business involvement, time spent in New York, the location of near and dear items and family connections. The guidelines state, "in virtually all cases, the review of the primary factors will result in a decision on domicile." (*Nonresident Audit Guidelines,* Department of Taxation and Finance. V.A.) Unfortunately, in practice, this is almost never the case.

Mark S. Klein, Esq., Hodgson Russ LLP

Secondary factors: When the primary factors indicate a New York domicile, "other" (secondary and tertiary) factors will be reviewed. These "other" factors are not considered to carry the weight and significance of the primary factors. The guidelines note that, in situations where it remains unclear as to the strength of a domicile determination by an analysis of the primary factors, an analysis of these "other" factors is warranted and takes on a greater significance. The "other" factors are as follows:

— The address at which bank statements, bills, financial data and correspondence concerning other family business is primarily received;

— The physical location of the safe deposit boxes used for family records and valuables;

¶103

— Location of auto, boat, and airplane registrations as well as the individual's personal driver's or operator's license;

— Indication as to where the taxpayer is registered to vote and an analysis of the exercise of said privilege;

— The frequency and nature of business conducted within New York State for legal, medical and other professional services in relationship to the services performed at other locations;

— Possession of a New York City parking tax exemption;

— An analysis of telephone services at each residence, including the nature of the listing, the type of service features, and the activity at the location.

Practitioner Comment: Consequences of Changing Domicile

Auditors strictly scrutinize a taxpayer's purported move from New York to another state or country and expect consistency in a nonresident's lifestyle. Ex-New Yorkers must remember that, when they return to New York for visits, they no longer qualify for resident recreational privileges, New York's real property "STAR" credit or resident hunting/fishing licenses. Similarly, when a nonresident ultimately sells a New York State home, the sale may not qualify for the generous federal exclusion of gain applicable to a taxpayer's "principal residence" under IRC Sec. 121.

Mark S. Klein, Esq., Hodgson Russ LLP

Tertiary factors: Tertiary factors, which are below secondary and far below primary in importance, include: the place of interment; the location where the taxpayer's will is probated; passive interest in partnerships or small corporations; the mere location of bank accounts; contributions made to political candidates, or causes; the location where the taxpayer's individual income tax returns are prepared and filed; and religious organization membership.

¶104 Same-Sex Marriages

Law: New York Marriage Equality Act (CCH NEW YORK TAX REPORTS, ¶15-125, 15-520, 16-615).

Comparable Federal: Sec. 151 (U.S. MASTER TAX GUIDE ¶133—149).

Equal treatment has been given to individuals legally married to different-sex spouses and same-sex spouses since the enactment of the state's Marriage Equality Act, which took effect on July 24, 2011 (see *TSB-M-11(8)I*, July 29, 2011, CCH NEW YORK TAX REPORTS, ¶407-326). Based on the U.S. Supreme Court's *Windsor* decision and IRS Revenue Ruling 2013-17, this equal treatment now also applies for earlier periods. For tax years 2013 and after, same-sex married couples must file using the general married filing status rules. (*TSB-M-13(5)I*, Sept. 13, 2013, CCH NEW YORK TAX REPORTS, ¶407-911)

Withholding: Employers and same-sex married employees should follow the general withholding tax rules for married employees; see ¶608 *et seq.*, (*Notice*, New York Department of Taxation and Finance, September 2013).

Prior law: For tax years 2011 and 2012, same-sex married couples had to file their New York personal income tax returns using a married filing status even if they used a filing status of single or head of household on their federal income tax returns.

For tax years before 2011, individuals who were legally married to a same-sex spouse and who filed their New York personal income tax returns using a filing status of single or head of household could (but were not required to) file an amended New York return to use a married filing status (*e.g.*, married filing jointly, married filing separate). A New York amended personal income tax return can be filed for any tax year where the statute of limitations for filing an amended return remains open. Generally, an amended return must be filed within three years from the date the return was filed or two years from the date the tax was paid, whichever is later. To complete a New York amended income tax return, taxpayers must report and/or compute any federal information required to be shown on the New York amended return by applying the federal rules in effect for married taxpayers for the same tax year (regardless of whether an amended federal return is filed).

¶105 Deductions for New York Exemptions

Law: Secs. 616, Tax Law (CCH New York Tax Reports, ¶15-535).

Comparable Federal: Sec. 151 (U.S. Master Tax Guide, ¶133—149).

A resident or nonresident individual is entitled to a New York exemption of $1,000 for each dependent claimed on the taxpayer's federal income tax return (Sec. 616(a), Tax Law). The personal exemption is not allowed for the taxpayer and spouse. If a husband and wife file a joint federal return but file separate New York returns, each is separately entitled to the number of exemptions to which he or she would have been separately entitled if separate federal returns had been filed (Sec. 616(b), Tax Law).

CCH Advisory: Exemptions

Unlike federal law, New York allows exemptions for dependents, but not for the taxpayer or the taxpayer's spouse.

¶106 Tax Rates

Law: Secs. 601, 602, 699, 800—804, Tax Law (CCH New York Tax Reports, ¶15-355—15-365).

Forms: IT-201, Resident Income Tax Return; IT-203, Nonresident and Part-Year Resident Income Tax Return.

Comparable Federal: Sec. 1 (U.S. Master Tax Guide, ¶25, 1401—1480).

The personal income tax is imposed at a graduated rate determined on the basis of income and filing status.

For taxable years beginning after 2012 and before 2018, a cost of living adjustment will be applied to the brackets and the standard deduction; however, after 2017 the standard deduction will be fixed at the 2017 amount.

Nonresidents: See ¶206.

• *Tax rates for taxable year 2016*
Resident married taxpayers filing joint returns and resident surviving spouses

Taxable year 2016

If the New York taxable income is:	The tax is:
Not over $17,050	4% of the New York taxable income
Over $17,050 but not over $23,450	$682 plus 4.5% of excess over $17,050
Over $23,450 but not over $27,750	$970 plus 5.25% of excess over $23,450
Over $27,750 but not over $42,750	$1,196 plus 5.9% of excess over $27,750
Over $42,750 but not over $160,500	$2,081 plus 6.45% of excess over $42,750
Over $160,500 but not over $321,050	$9,676 plus 6.65% of excess over $160,500
Over $321,050 but not over $2,140,900	$20,352 plus 6.85% of excess over $321,050
Over $2,140,900	$145,012 plus 8.82% of excess over $2,140,900

Resident heads of household

Taxable year 2016

If the New York taxable income is:	The tax is:
Not over $12,750	4% of the New York taxable income
Over $12,750 but not over $17,550	$510 plus 4.5% of excess over $12,750
Over $17,550 but not over $20,800	$726 plus 5.25% of excess over $17,550
Over $20,800 but not over $32,000	$897 plus 5.9% of excess over $20,800

Taxable year 2016

If the New York taxable income is:	The tax is:
Over $32,000 but not over $106,950	$1,557 plus 6.45% of excess over $32,000
Over $106,950 but not over $267,500	$6,392 plus 6.65% of excess over $106,950
Over $267,600 but not over $1,605,650	$17,068 plus 6.85% of excess over $267,500
Over $1,605,650	$108,732 plus 8.82% of excess over $1,605,650

Resident unmarried taxpayers, resident married filing separately, and residents estates and trusts

Taxable year 2016

If the New York taxable income is:	The tax is:
Not over $8,450	4% of the New York taxable income
Over $8,450 but not over $11,650	$338 plus 4.5% of excess over $8,450
Over $11,650 but not over $13,850	$482 plus 5.25% of excess over $11,650
Over $13,850 but not over $21,300	$598 plus 5.9% of excess over $13,850
Over $21,300 but not over $80,150	$1,037 plus 6.45% of excess over $21,300
Over $80,150 but not over $214,000	$4,833 plus 6.65% of excess over $80,150
Over $214,000 but not over $1,070,350	$13,734 plus 6.85% of excess over $214,000
Over $1,070,350	$72,394 plus 8.82% of excess over $1,070,350

Taxable years after 2012: For tax years 2013 through 2017, the tax rates shown in the 2016 tax tables above are the same. However, the dollar amounts in the tax tables will be indexed by a cost of living percentage adjustment, if applicable. (Sec. 601, Tax Law; Sec. 601-a, Tax Law; *TSB-M-12(3)I*, CCH NEW YORK TAX REPORTS, ¶407-472)

Supplemental tax: For tax years beginning after 2011 and before 2018, Sec. 601(d-1), Tax Law, imposes a temporary supplemental tax that is in addition to the tax imposed under Sec. 601(a), Sec. 601(b), and Sec. 601(c). This supplemental tax is intended to recapture the tax benefit that a taxpayer receives in calculating taxes from the tax table rates that are below the highest applicable rate. The supplemental tax applies to taxpayers whose adjusted gross income exceeds $100,000.

Generally, the supplemental tax, is calculated by multiplying the "tax table benefit" by a fraction, the numerator of which is the lesser of $50,000 or the excess of the taxpayer's New York adjusted gross income for the taxable year over $100,000, and the denominator of which is $50,000.

The "tax table benefit" is the difference between (1) the amount of taxable income specified in a taxpayer's tax table that is not subject to the highest rate of tax for the taxable year, multiplied by such rate, and (2) the dollar denominated tax for such amount of taxable income set forth in the tax table applicable to the taxable year.

For tax years 2013 through 2017, the computation of the supplemental tax will be indexed by a cost of living percentage adjustment, if applicable, computed under Sec. 601-a, Tax Law.

Practitioner Comment: Impact of Supplemental Tax Phase-In

The supplemental tax is a mechanism to eliminate the graduated tax benefit for incomes that are taxed below the highest possible rate. Since the phase-out occurs within $50,000 of additional income, the supplemental tax can create a marginal tax rate in excess of 70%.

Mark S. Klein, Esq., Hodgson Russ LLP

Minimum income tax rate (repealed): See ¶502.

• *Tax rates for taxable years after 2017*

For tax years beginning after 2017, the tax rates will be as shown below. However, the dollar amounts in the tax tables will be indexed by the cost of living percentage adjustments. (Sec. 601, Tax Law; Sec. 601-a, Tax Law)

The personal income tax rate for affected taxpayers will drop beginning in 2018 (Sec. 601, Tax Law). Taxpayers eligible for a tax rate reduction to 5.5%, when fully implemented, include:

— single filers with taxable income up to $75,000,

— head of household filers with taxable income up to $100,000, and

— married joint filers with taxable income up to $150,000.

Taxpayers eligible for a tax rate reduction to 6%, when fully implemented, include:

— single filers with taxable income between $75,000 and $200,000,

— head of household filers with taxable income between $100,000 and $250,000, and

— married joint filers with taxable income between $150,000 and $300,000.

Tax rate schedules for recent years are below:

- **Tax rates for taxable year 2015**

Resident married taxpayers filing joint returns and resident surviving spouses

Taxable year 2015

If the New York taxable income is:	The tax is:
Not over $16,950	4% of the New York taxable income
Over $16,950 but not over $23,300	$678 plus 4.5% of excess over $16,950
Over $23,300 but not over $27,550	$964 plus 5.25% of excess over $23,300
Over $27,550 but not over $42,450	$1,187 plus 5.9% of excess over $27,550
Over $42,450 but not over $159,350	$2,066 plus 6.45% of excess over $42,450
Over $159,350 but not over $318,750	$9,606 plus 6.65% of excess over $159,350
Over $318,750 but not over $2,125,450	$20,206 plus 6.85% of excess over $318,750
Over $2,125,450	$143,965 plus 8.82% of excess over $2,125,450

Resident heads of household

Taxable year 2015

If the New York taxable income is:	The tax is:
Not over $12,700	4% of the New York taxable income
Over $12,700 but not over $17,450	$508 plus 4.5% of excess over $12,700
Over $17,450 but not over $20,650	$722 plus 5.25% of excess over $17,450
Over $20,650 but not over $31,800	$890 plus 5.9% of excess over $20,650
Over $31,800 but not over $106,200	$1,548 plus 6.45% of excess over $31,800
Over $106,200 but not over $265,600	$6,346 plus 6.65% of excess over $106,200
Over $265,600 but not over $1,594,050	$16,947 plus 6.85% of excess over $265,600
Over $1,594,050	$107,945 plus 8.82% of excess over $1,594,050

Resident unmarried taxpayers, resident married filing separately, and residents estates and trusts

Taxable year 2015

If the New York taxable income is:	The tax is:
Not over $8,400	4% of the New York taxable income
Over $8,400 but not over $11,600	$336 plus 4.5% of excess over $8,400
Over $11,600 but not over $13,750	$480 plus 5.25% of excess over $11,600
Over $13,750 but not over $21,150	$593 plus 5.9% of excess over $13,750
Over $21,150 but not over $79,600	$1,029 plus 6.45% of excess over $21,150
Over $79,600 but not over $212,500	$4,800 plus 6.65% of excess over $79,600
Over $212,500 but not over $1,062,650	$13,637 plus 6.85% of excess over $212,500
Over $1,062,650	$71,873 plus 8.82% of excess over $1,062,650

- **Tax rates for taxable year 2014**

Resident married taxpayers filing joint returns and resident surviving spouses

Taxable year 2014

If the New York taxable income is:	The tax is:
Not over $16,700	4% of the New York taxable income
Over $16,700 but not over $22,950	$668 plus 4.5% of excess over $16,700
Over $22,950 but not over $27,150	$949 plus 5.25% of excess over $22,950
Over $27,150 but not over $41,800	$1,170 plus 5.9% of excess over $27,150
Over $41,800 but not over $156,900	$2,034 plus 6.45% of excess over $41,800
Over $156,900 but not over $313,850	$9,458 plus 6.65% of excess over $156,900
Over $313,850 but not over $2,092,800	$19,895 plus 7.45% of excess over $313,850
Over $2,092,800	$141,753 plus 8.82% of excess over $2,092,800

¶106

Resident heads of household

Taxable year 2014

If the New York taxable income is:	The tax is:
Not over $12,550	4% of the New York taxable income
Over $12,550 but not over $17,200	$502 plus 4.5% of excess over $12,550
Over $17,200 but not over $20,350	$711 plus 5.25% of excess over $17,200
Over $20,350 but not over $31,350	$877 plus 5.9% of excess over $20,350
Over $31,350 but not over $104,600	$1,526 plus 6.45% of excess over $31,350
Over $104,600 but not over $261,550	$6,250 plus 6.65% of excess over $104,600
Over $261,550 but not over $1,569,550	$16,687 plus 6.85% of excess over $261,550
Over $1,569,550	$106,285 plus 8.82% of excess over $1,569,550

Resident unmarried taxpayers, resident married filing separately, and residents estates and trusts

Taxable year 2014

If the New York taxable income is:	The tax is:
Not over $8,300	4% of the New York taxable income
Over $8,300 but not over $11,450	$332 plus 4.5% of excess over $8,300
Over $11,450 but not over $13,550	$474 plus 5.25% of excess over $11,450
Over $13,550 but not over $20,850	$584 plus 5.9% of excess over $13,550
Over $20,850 but not over $78,400	$1,015 plus 6.45% of excess over $20,850
Over $78,400 but not over $209,250	$4,727 plus 6.65% of excess over $78,400
Over $209,250 but not over $1,046,350	$13,428 plus 6.85% of excess over $209,250
Over $1,046,350	$70,770 plus 8.82% of excess over $1,046,350

- **Tax rates for taxable year 2013**

Resident married taxpayers filing joint returns and resident surviving spouses

Taxable year 2013

If the New York taxable income is:	The tax is:
Not over $16,450	4% of the New York taxable income
Over $16,450 but not over $22,600	$658 plus 4.5% of excess over $16,450
Over $22,600 but not over $26,750	$935 plus 5.25% of excess over $22,600
Over $26,750 but not over $41,150	$1,153 plus 5.9% of excess over $26,750
Over $41,150 but not over $154,350	$2,002 plus 6.45% of excess over $41,150
Over $154,350 but not over $308,750	$9,304 plus 6.65% of excess over $154,350
Over $308,750 but not over $2,058,550	$19,571 plus 7.45% of excess over $308,750
Over $2,058,550	$139,433 plus 8.82% of excess over $2,058,550

Resident heads of household

Taxable year 2013

If the New York taxable income is:	The tax is:
Not over $12,350	4% of the New York taxable income
Over $12,350 but not over $16,950	$494 plus 4.5% of excess over $12,350
Over $16,950 but not over $20,050	$701 plus 5.25% of excess over $16,950
Over $20,050 but not over $30,850	$864 plus 5.9% of excess over $20,050
Over $30,850 but not over $102,900	$1,501 plus 6.45% of excess over $30,850
Over $102,900 but not over $257,300	$6,148 plus 6.65% of excess over $102,900
Over $257,300 but not over $1,543,900	$16,416 plus 6.85% of excess over $257,300
Over $1,543,900	$104,548 plus 8.82% of excess over $1,543,900

Resident unmarried taxpayers, resident married filing separately, and residents estates and trusts

Taxable year 2013

If the New York taxable income is:	The tax is:
Not over $8,200	4% of the New York taxable income
Over $8,200 but not over $11,300	$328 plus 4.5% of excess over $8,200
Over $11,300 but not over $13,350	$468 plus 5.25% of excess over $11,300
Over $13,350 but not over $20,550	$575 plus 5.9% of excess over $13,350
Over $20,550 but not over $77,150	$1,000 plus 6.45% of excess over $20,550
Over $77,150 but not over $205,850	$4,651 plus 6.65% of excess over $77,150
Over $205,850 but not over $1,029,250	$13,209 plus 6.85% of excess over $205,850
Over $1,029,250	$69,612 plus 8.82% of excess over $1,029,250

- **Tax rates for taxable year 2012**

Resident married taxpayers filing joint returns and resident surviving spouses

Taxable year 2012

If the New York taxable income is:	The tax is:
Not over $16,000	4% of the New York taxable income
Over $16,000 but not over $22,000	$640 plus 4.5% of excess over $16,000
Over $22,000 but not over $26,000	$910 plus 5.25% of excess over $22,600
Over $26,000 but not over $40,000	$1,120 plus 5.9% of excess over $26,000

Taxable year 2012

If the New York taxable income is:	The tax is:
Over $40,000 but not over $150,000	$1,946 plus 6.45% of excess over $40,000
Over $150,000 but not over $300,000	$9,041 plus 6.65% of excess over $150,000
Over $300,000 but not over $2,000,000	$19,016 plus 6.85% of excess over $300,000
Over $2,000,000	$135,466 plus 8.82% of excess over $2,000,000

- *Resident heads of household*

Taxable year 2012

If the New York taxable income is:	The tax is:
Not over $12,000	4% of the New York taxable income
Over $12,000 but not over $16,500	$480 plus 4.5% of excess over $12,000
Over $16,500 but not over $19,500	$683 plus 5.25% of excess over $16,500
Over $19,500 but not over $30,000	$840 plus 5.9% of excess over $19,500
Over $30,000 but not over $100,000	$1,460 plus 6.45% of excess over $30,000
Over $100,000 but not over $250,000	$5,975 plus 6.65% of excess over $100,000
Over $250,000 but not over $1,500,000	$15,950 plus 6.85% of excess over $250,000
Over $1,500,000	$101,575 plus 8.82% of excess over $1,500,000

Resident unmarried taxpayers, resident married filing separately, and residents estates and trusts

Taxable year 2012

If the New York taxable income is:	The tax is:
Not over $8,000	4% of the New York taxable income
Over $8,000 but not over $11,000	$320 plus 4.5% of excess over $8,000
Over $11,000 but not over $13,000	$455 plus 5.25% of excess over $11,000
Over $13,000 but not over $20,000	$560 plus 5.9% of excess over $13,000
Over $20,000 but not over $75,000	$973 plus 6.45% of excess over $20,000
Over $75,000 but not over $200,000	$4,521 plus 6.65% of excess over $75,000
Over $200,000 but not over $1,000,000	$12,833 plus 6.85% of excess over $200,000
Over $1,000,000	$67,633 plus 8.82% of excess over $1,000,000

- *MCTD payroll tax*

The Metropolitan Commuter Transportation District Mobility Tax (MCTDMT) is imposed on certain employers and self-employed individuals engaging in business within the Metropolitan Commuter Transportation District. Specifically, the tax applies to (Sec. 800, Tax Law; Sec. 801, Tax Law; *TSB-M-09(1)MCTMT*, June 1, 2009, CCH NEW YORK TAX REPORTS, ¶ 406-407):

> (1) employers required to withhold New York state income tax from employee wages and whose payroll expense exceeds $312,500 in any calendar quarter; and

> (2) individuals with net earnings from self-employment allocated to the MCTD that exceed $10,000 for the tax year. (according to the Department of Taxation and Finance, this includes partners in partnerships and members of a limited liability company (LLC) treated as a partnership).

An advisory opinion discusses the taxability of nonqualified deferred compensation earnings (*TSB-A-14(2)MCTMT*, New York Commissioner of Taxation and Finance, July 2, 2014, CCH NEW YORK TAX REPORTS, ¶ 408-150).

Exemptions: The tax does not apply to the United Nations, federal agencies, interstate agencies or public corporations, or certain educational institutions, including public or free association libraries (Sec. 800, Tax Law). Wages paid to federal work-study students are not subject to the MCTMT; see *TSB-A-16(6)I*, New York Commissioner of Taxation and Finance, August 29, 2016, CCH NEW YORK TAX REPORTS, ¶ 408-874.

Practitioner Comment: The Use of Independent Professionals Does Not Implicate the MCTMT

The MCTDMT applies to self-employed individuals engaged in a trade or business within the metropolitan commuter transportation district (MCTD). The use of independent professionals (a business manager or accountant) located in the MCTD does not, by itself, constitute engaging in a trade or business within the district. (*TSB-A-14(1) MCTMT*)

Mark S. Klein, Esq., Hodgson Russ LLP

Rate of tax: For self-employed individuals, tax at the rate of 0.34% applies if earnings attributable to the Metropolitan Commuter Transportation District exceed $50,000 for the tax year. For employers (including professional employer organizations), the MCTMT is imposed at the following rates (Sec. 801, Tax Law):

— 0.11% for employers with payroll expense no greater than $375,000 in any calendar quarter;

— 0.23% for employers with payroll expense no greater than $437,500 in any calendar quarter;

— 0.34% for employers with payroll expense exceeding $437,500 in any calendar quarter.

For quarters before the quarter beginning April 1, 2012, the tax rate was 0.34% of total payroll expense for employees employed within the MCTD.

An employer cannot deduct from an employee's wages or compensation any amount representing all or a portion of the tax imposed on the employer (Sec. 802, Tax Law).

Any exemption from tax specified in any other New York state law does not apply to the MCTDMT, except that the net earnings from self-employment of an individual from a business that is accepted into the START-UP NY program are exempt from the tax. (Sec. 803, Tax Law)

Payment of tax: Beginning in 2015, the MCTMT final return due date is changed from April 30 to April 15, to conform to the personal income tax return due date. (Sec. 804, Tax Law). Procedures to obtain approval to file on a group basis and related topics are discussed in *TSB-M-09(2)MCTMT*, August 5, 2009, CCH NEW YORK TAX REPORTS, ¶406-476.

Beginning with tax year 2015, self-employed individuals (including partners) paying MCTDMT must do so on their personal income tax returns. See ¶601 and **http://www.tax.ny.gov/bus/mctmt/mctmt_changes_self_employed.htm**.

Also beginning in 2015, quarterly estimated MCTMT payments instead are due on the same date as quarterly estimated personal income tax payments (April 15, June 15, September 15, and January 15). Previously, the tax had to be paid quarterly, at the same time as the statewide wage reporting system report is required. For additional information, see *TSB-M-14(1)MCTMT*, August 25, 2014, CCH NEW YORK TAX REPORTS, ¶408-206.

The Department of Taxation and Finance has a website dedicated to the MCTDMT tax at **http://.tax.ny.gov/sbc/mta.htm**.

The New York Department of Taxation and Finance has issued an advisory opinion discussing the metropolitan commuter transportation mobility tax (MCTMT) treatment of compensation paid by a temporary staffing services company to certain of its employees. The company presented two different factual situations involving employees assigned to both New York projects and out-of-state projects during the year. In the case of temporary staffing assignments, when billable employees perform distinct, consecutive job assignments for the same employer, the determination of whether the employee is a covered employee whose wages are included in the employer's payroll expense when calculating MCTMT liability should be made separately for each of the employee's assignments. Accordingly, the employees are considered covered employees under the MCTMT for the duration of their assignments within the Metropolitan Commuter Transportation District (MCTD) because their services will be performed entirely within the MCTD during this period. However, the employees should not be considered covered employees under the MCTMT for their assignments outside the MCTD because they will not perform any services in the MCTD during this period. (*TSB-A-11(1)MCTMT*, New York Commissioner of Taxation and Finance, July 21, 2011, CCH NEW YORK TAX REPORTS, ¶407-331)

A New York appellate court has reversed a lower court's ruling that the metropolitan commuter transportation mobility tax (MCTMT) was unconstitutionally passed by the Legislature without a home rule message. The lower court found that the tax was a special law that did not serve a substantial state interest (*Mangano v. Silver*, Supreme Court, 10th Judicial District (New York), No. 14444/10, August 22, 2012, CCH NEW YORK TAX REPORTS, ¶407-628).

However, the appellate court concluded that the law, which provides a funding source for the preservation, operation, and improvement of essential transit and transportation services in the Metropolitan Commuter Transportation District, does serve a substantial state concern. Therefore, the law was not unconstitutionally passed without a home rule message. (*Mangano v. Silver*, Appellate Division of the Supreme Court of New York, Second Department, Nos. 2012-09463 and 2012-09991, June 26, 2013, CCH NEW YORK TAX REPORTS, ¶407-866; motion for leave to appeal denied, New York Court of Appeals, January 14, 2014)

¶107 Separate Tax on Lump-Sum Distributions

Law: Secs. 603, 620-A, 624, 637, Tax Law (CCH NEW YORK TAX REPORTS, ¶15-355).

Comparable Federal: Sec. 402 (U.S. MASTER TAX GUIDE ¶2153).

A separate tax is imposed on the ordinary income portion of a lump-sum distribution to a resident or nonresident individual, estate, or trust that has made an election of lump-sum treatment under IRC Sec. 402. (Sec. 603, Tax Law) This tax is in addition to any other tax imposed under Article 22 of the Tax Law.

For computation information, see CCH NEW YORK TAX REPORTS, ¶15-800.

The special five-year averaging of lump-sum distributions (former IRC Sec. 402(e)) is generally unavailable for tax years beginning after 1999.

Ten-year averaging or a flat 20% federal tax remains available, but only in the case of a qualifying lump-sum distribution to an employee born before 1936. In that case, the separate New York tax is imposed on the 10-year basis, but using tax rates in effect as of 1986.

For computation information, see CCH NEW YORK TAX REPORTS, ¶15-800.

¶108 Accounting Periods and Methods

Law: Sec. 605, Tax Law; Reg. Sec. 105.3 (CCH NEW YORK TAX REPORTS, ¶15-455).

Comparable Federal: Secs. 441, 446, 481 (U.S. MASTER TAX GUIDE, ¶1501—1577).

New York adopts the accounting periods and the methods of accounting used by the taxpayer in determining federal income tax for the taxable year. (Sec. 605(a), Tax Law)

¶109 Changes in Accounting Periods and Methods

Law: Sec. 605, Tax Law; Reg. Sec. 105.3 (CCH NEW YORK TAX REPORTS, ¶15-455—15-460).

Comparable Federal: Secs. 442, 443, 446, 481 (U.S. MASTER TAX GUIDE, ¶1501—1577).

New York adopts the accounting periods and methods used by the taxpayer in determining federal taxable income tax liability for the taxable year. (Sec. 605(a), Tax Law) New York also adopts any changes in accounting periods or accounting methods that are made for federal purposes.

Change in accounting period: If changes in the accounting period result in a taxable year of less than 12 months, New York requires the proration of the New York exemptions (¶105) and the New York standard deduction (¶306).

¶110 Income and Deductions in Respect of Decedents

Law: Sec. 651, Tax Law (CCH NEW YORK TAX REPORTS, ¶15-355).

Comparable Federal: Sec. 691 (U.S. MASTER TAX GUIDE ¶182).

The return for any deceased individual must be filed by the executor, administrator, or other person charged with the individual's property. If a final return of a decedent is for a fractional part of a year, the due date of the return is the 15th day of the fourth month following the close of the 12-month period that began with the first day of the fractional part of the year. (Sec. 651, Tax Law)

¶111 Members of Armed Forces

Law: Secs. 605, 696, Tax Law; Reg. Sec. 132.11; Publication 361 (CCH NEW YORK TAX REPORTS, ¶15-180).

Comparable Federal: Secs. 112, 121(9), 132(n), 134, 692 (U.S. MASTER TAX GUIDE ¶889—896, 1078, 2609, 2533).

New York's taxation of pay and benefits received by members of the U.S. Armed Forces is generally the same as federal because the starting point for New York adjusted gross income is federal adjusted gross income (¶201). Military pay received by a nonresident member of the Armed Forces does not constitute income derived from New York sources. For taxable years beginning after 2003, income received by a member of the New York state organized militia as compensation for performing active duty service, other than training, of the state or federal government within New York may be subtracted from federal adjusted gross income.

The following income of military personnel is subject to both federal and New York income taxes:

— active duty and reserve training pay;

— enlistment and reenlistment bonuses;

— incentive pay;

— lump-sum payments for accrued leave;

— severance, separation, or release pay;

— readjustment pay;

— travel and per diem allowances;

— payments received from a former employer, even if paid directly to dependents;

— personal allowances for high-ranking officers;

— military retirement pay based on age or length of service;

— scholarships and student loan repayments.

• *Residency and domicile*

Under the provisions of the Soldiers' and Sailors' Civil Relief Act of 1940, a member of the Armed Forces retains, while in service, the same domicile as when entering military service. Members of the armed forces who were domiciled in New York (¶103) at the time of entrance into military service continue to be New York domiciliaries, regardless of where they may be assigned to duty or how long. Consequently, such individuals will continue to be taxed as New York residents unless during the taxable year *all* of the following three conditions in either Group A or Group B were satisfied:

Group A:

— The individual maintained no permanent place of abode in New York during the taxable year;

— The individual did maintain a permanent place of abode outside New York during the entire taxable year; and

— The individual did not spend more than 30 days in New York during the taxable year.

Group B:

— The individual was present in a foreign country or countries for at least 450 days within any period of 548 consecutive days;

— The individual was not present in New York more than 90 days and did not maintain a permanent place of abode in New York at which his spouse (unless legally separated) or minor children were present for more than 90 days within this 548 consecutive day period; and

— During any period of less than one year within the 548 day period, which would be treated as a separate taxable period if the individual changed his or her resident status during the year, the individual was present in New York for no more than the number of days bearing the same ratio to 90 as the number of days in the less than one year period bears to 548.

Members of the armed forces who were not domiciled in New York at the time of entrance into the armed forces will not be considered New York residents during their period of service even though they may be assigned to duty in New York for more than 183 days in the taxable year and even though they established a permanent place of abode in New York.

Military personnel temporarily assigned and living in New York are not subject to tax on their income or compensation for military service unless they have changed their domicile with intent to establish a New York residence (50 U.S.C. § 574). However, income from nonmilitary New York sources is subject to New York income tax and must be reported on a nonresident return.

Family members: Civilian spouses and dependents of military personnel who are living in New York temporarily because of assignment of the military spouse are subject to tax as nonresidents. Taxpayers who are nonresidents of New York who marry military personnel who live outside New York and are New York residents are not subject to New York income tax merely because the military spouse is a resident.

Federal legislation: Applicable to state or local income tax returns for tax years beginning after 2008, the Military Residency Relief Act of 2009 (P.L. 111-97) prohibits a service member's spouse from either losing or acquiring a residence or domicile for purposes of taxation because he or she is absent or present in any U.S. tax jurisdiction solely to be with the service member in compliance with the service member's military orders, if the residence or domicile is the same for the service member and the spouse.

P.L. 111-97 also prohibits a spouse's income from being considered income earned in a tax jurisdiction if the spouse is not a resident or domiciliary of such jurisdiction when the spouse is in that jurisdiction solely to be with a service member serving under military orders.

CCH Advisory: NY Implementation of Military Residency Relief Act

For purposes of New York State, New York City, and Yonkers personal income taxes, a military spouse will not be treated as a resident of New York State for tax purposes (that is, the spouse will be treated as a nonresident) if the following conditions are met:

— the military spouse is located in New York State solely to be with the servicemember and the servicemember is located in New York State in compliance with his or her military orders; and

— the servicemember and his or her spouse were residents or domiciliaries in a state other than New York State before being located in New York.

Additionally, a military spouse's income that is earned in New York State will not be treated as New York source income and will therefore be exempt from any personal income tax if:

— the military spouse is a nonresident of New York State; and

— the military spouse is in New York State solely to be with the servicemember and the servicemember is in New York State in compliance with his or her military orders.

A military spouse who is a domiciliary or resident of New York State should be aware that the federal law could affect the amount of New York tax he or she has to pay if he or she:

— is required to file a New York State resident personal income tax return;

— is in another state solely to be with the servicemember when the servicemember is in that state in compliance with his or her military orders; and

— is employed or operates a business in that state.

Under the federal Military Spouses Residency Relief Act, a military spouse's net earnings from self-employment attributable to a trade or business carried on in the Metropolitan Commuter Transportation District (MCTD) are exempt from the MCTMT if: (1) the military spouse is a nonresident of New York State; and (2) the military spouse is located in New York State solely to be with the servicemember and the servicemember is located in New York State in compliance with his or her military orders. (*TSB-M-10(1)I*, *TSB-M-10(1)MCTMT*, Office of Tax Policy Analysis, New York Department of Taxation and Finance, January 11, 2010, CCH NEW YORK TAX REPORTS, ¶ 406-652; *Publication 361*, New York State Income Tax Information for Military Personnel and Veterans)

• *Service in combat zone*

Armed forces members are entitled to an exemption from New York personal income tax for military pay received while serving in a combat zone, applicable to taxable years commencing after 2007 (Sec. 612(c)(8-c), Tax Law). Previously, they were exempt to the same extent that military pay is exempt from federal income tax. The federal exclusion for a commissioned officer is limited to the highest rate of enlisted pay for each month.

Service members directly supporting operations in Iraq from other locations, who are receiving imminent danger pay or hostile fire pay, are deemed to be serving in a combat zone (*Important Notice N-03-07*, April 2003, CCH NEW YORK TAX REPORTS, ¶ 320-113).

Hospitalization: The monthly exclusion also applies if the service member is hospitalized anywhere as the result of wounds, disease, or injury sustained while serving in a combat zone, but is limited to two years after the termination of combatant activities in the combat zone. Payments for leave accrued during service in a combat zone are also excluded.

• *Tax forgiveness for decedents*

Income tax is forgiven for members of the Armed Forces who die as the result of wounds, disease, or injury incurred in a combat zone or as a result of wounds or injuries sustained in terroristic or military action. Forgiveness includes the entire taxable year in which the death occurs, not just the shortened tax year, and extends to any earlier year ending on or after the first day of service in a combat zone. Taxes for those years are abated, credited, or refunded. However, refunds are subject to the statute of limitations.

CCH Advisory: Spouse of Deceased Member

The tax forgiveness applies only to the deceased person, not to the spouse.

The forgiveness provisions also include astronauts who die in the line of duty.

• *Combat zones and hazardous duty areas*

There are three designated (by Executive Order of the President) combat zones, which include the airspace above, as follows:

— **Arabian Peninsula.** Beginning January 17, 1991: Bahrain, Iraq, Kuwait, Oman, Qatar, Saudi Arabia, the United Arab Emirates, Gulf of Aden, Gulf of Oman, Persian Gulf, Red Sea, and part of the Arabian Sea. Beginning January 1, 2003: Israel and Turkey. Beginning April 11, 2003: part of the Mediterranean Sea.

— **Kosovo.** Beginning March 24, 1999: Yugoslavia (Serbia and Montenegro), Albania, the Adriatic Sea, and the northern Ionian Sea. Additional areas have been designated in support of Operation Enduring Freedom, including Pakistan, Tajikistan, and Jordan (beginning September 19, 2001); Incirlik Air Base, Turkey (beginning September 21, 2001); Kyrgyzstan and Uzbekistan (beginning October 1, 2001); Phillipines (beginning January 9, 2002); Yemen (beginning April 10, 2002); and Djibouti (beginning July 1, 2002).

— **Afghanistan.** Beginning September 19, 2001. Separately, the Department of Defense (DOD) has certified that military personnel in Uzbekistan, Kyrgystan, Pakistan, Tajikistan, and Jordan are eligible for all combat zone related tax benefits due to their service in direct support of military operations in the Afghanistan combat zone.

A "qualified hazardous duty area" is treated as if it were a combat zone. Bosnia, Herzegovina, Croatia, and Macedonia have been designated as hazardous duty areas.

Additional information on combat zone area designations is available at **http://www.irs.gov/uac/Combat-Zones**.

• *Other nontaxable items*

Miscellaneous items of income received by service members are nontaxable, as follows:

— living allowances, including Basic Allowance for Quarters (BAQ), Basic Allowance for Subsistence (BAS), Variable housing Allowance (VHA), and housing and cost-of-living allowances abroad;

— family allowances, including those for emergencies, evacuation, separation, and certain educational expenses for dependents;

— death allowances, including those for burial services, travel of dependents, and the death gratuity payment to eligible survivors;

— moving allowances for dislocation, moving household and personal items, moving trailers or mobile homes, storage, and temporary lodging;

— other benefits, including dependent care, disability, medical benefits, group-term life insurance, professional education, defense counseling, ROTC allowances, survivor and retirement protection plan premiums, uniform allowances for offices, and uniforms furnished to enlisted personnel.

• *Sale of residence*

Two important benefits are available to members of the military who sell their homes.

¶111

Homeowner's Assistance Program (HAP): The HAP reimburses military homeowners for losses incurred on the private sale of their homes after a base closure or reduction in operations. The HAP payment is the difference between 95% of the home's fair market value before the closure or reduction announcement and the greater of the home's fair market value at the time of sale or the actual sale price.

HAP payments made after November 11, 2003, are excludable from gross income. Payments made before that date are taxable as compensation.

Capital gains: All homeowners may exclude up to $250,000 ($500,000 on a joint return) of gain on the sale of a home if they have owned and used the home as their personal residence for two of the five years preceding the date of sale. Because members of the military, Public Health Service officers, and Foreign Service officers may be required to move frequently, the Military Family Tax Relief Act of 2003 provided for these personnel by suspending the five-year testing period for up to 10 years. The suspension applies whenever the person is on qualified official extended duty for more than 90 days and is stationed at least 50 miles from the person's residence or is under orders to reside in government quarters.

• *Moving expenses*

Armed forces members, their spouses and dependents may deduct moving expenses without regard to the distance and time requirements that otherwise would apply. The move must be pursuant to a military order that results in a permanent change of station.

• *Filing requirements*

Certain extensions of time for filing returns, payment of tax, etc., are provided for members of the armed forces serving in combat zones (including personnel serving outside the United States in a contingency operation) or hospitalized as a result of such service (¶605).

For a discussion of allocation of military pay received by non-New York domiciliaries, see ¶403.

Additional information may be found in Publication 361, *New York State Income Tax Information for Military Personnel and Veterans.*

¶112 Shareholders of S Corporations

Law: Sec. 660, Tax Law (CCH NEW YORK TAX REPORTS, ¶15-190).

Comparable Federal: Sec. 1366 (U.S. MASTER TAX GUIDE ¶309—333).

Forms: CT-6, Election by a Federal S Corporation to be Treated as a New York S Corporation.

If an S corporation is subject to the New York tax on business corporations, the shareholders of the S corporation may elect to take into account the S corporation items of income, loss, deduction, and reductions for taxes (described in IRC Sec. 1306(f)(2) and (3)) that are taken into account for federal income tax purposes for the taxable year. All of the shareholders must consent. (Sec. 660, Tax Law)

Generally, for such an election to be valid for a taxable year, it must have been made during the previous taxable year or on or before March 15 of the tax year to which the election will apply. The election will be effective until terminated.

For additional information, see ¶856.

Practitioner Comment: S Election Rules Strictly Enforced

New York's Department of Taxation and Finance requires strict compliance with the S corporation election rules. According to an ALJ, "the legislature left no room for the exercise of discretion where the failure to make [an S election] was due to error" (*Unger*, ALJ 1/2/03, CCH NEW YORK TAX REPORTS, ¶404-422). However, in *Dohan*, ALJ 1/6/05,

CCH NEW YORK TAX REPORTS, ¶405-006, a judge recognized that the "reliance on the advice of a professional . . . provides a reasonable basis for the late filing of the New York State election for S corporation treatment."

Mark S. Klein, Esq., Hodgson Russ LLP

¶113 Limited Liability Company Members

Law: Secs. 601(f), 658(c), Tax Law; Sec. 507, Banking Law (CCH NEW YORK TAX REPORTS, ¶15-190).

Comparable Federal: Secs. 704, 721, 731(b) (U.S. MASTER TAX GUIDE ¶402B).

New York authorizes the formation of domestic and foreign limited liability companies (LLCs), professional service limited liability companies, and limited liability partnerships. Domestic LLCs may be formed for any lawful business purpose or purposes other than engaging in activities for which another statute specifically requires some other business entity or natural person to be formed or used. Unlike domestic partnerships, which require at least two persons or entities, LLCs, at the time of formation, may consist of one member.

LLCs classified as partnerships for federal purposes are not subject to New York income tax. (Sec. 601(f), Tax Law)

Annual filing fees: For purposes of New York personal income tax, New York LLCs and foreign LLCs doing business in New York are treated as partnerships, unless classified as corporations for federal tax purposes. Domestic and foreign LLCs with New York source income are subject to an annual filing fee (see ¶851).

• *Limited liability investment and trust companies*

Certain investment companies that are established and regulated under Article 12, Banking Law, may organize themselves as limited liability investment companies (LLICs). (Sec. 507, Banking Law) Generally, the LLIC option is available only to Article 12 investment companies that serve as holding companies for foreign banking operations. Limited liability trust companies (LLTCs) are also authorized under the New York Banking Law.

An LLIC or LLTC that is treated as a partnership for federal tax purposes will be treated as a partnership for New York State income tax purposes. Accordingly, members of LLICs or LLTCs that are classified as partnerships for federal purposes will be taxed as partners in a partnership, and will be liable for personal income tax in their separate or individual capacities.

LLICs or LLTCs that are treated as partnerships for federal tax purposes are subject to the same annual filing fees that apply to limited liability companies (see discussion above).

¶114 Credits Against Tax and Other Tax Incentives—In General

Law: Sec. 38, 208(9)(a)(18), 209(11), 210(49), 606, 612(c)(39), Tax Law (CCH NEW YORK TAX REPORTS, ¶16-805).

The New York personal income tax law provides numerous credits against the tax, as discussed in the following paragraphs.

• *Carryovers; recapture*

Most credits may not reduce a taxpayer's tax liability below zero, although some "refundable" credits may generate a refund to the taxpayer even if there is no tax liability. With some exceptions, credits not used in one year may be carried forward indefinitely. Recapture of credits may be required if property does not remain in qualified use.

• *Effect of certain criminal convictions on credits*

If a taxpayer stands convicted (or is a shareholder of an S corporation or a partner in a partnership that is convicted) of certain penal law offenses concerning corruption, bribery, and misconduct, then the taxpayer will not be eligible for any tax credit allowed under the corporate franchise tax or any business tax credit allowed under the personal income tax. The provision applies to acts committed on or after April 30, 2014. (Sec. 41, Tax Law)

• *Order of credits*

Credits that cannot be carried forward and that are not refundable must be deducted first. Credits that can be carried over to subsequent years, and carryovers of such credits, must be deducted next; among such credits, those whose carryover is of limited duration must be deducted before those whose carryover is of unlimited duration. Credits that are refundable must be deducted last.

• *Refunds of credits*

The New York Department of Taxation and Finance has issued a corporate and personal income tax memorandum explaining how refunds of certain state business tax credits are treated.

At the federal level, the Internal Revenue Service (IRS) previously determined that the amount of the Qualified Empire Zone Enterprise (QEZE) credit for real property taxes that is refunded, or credited as an overpayment to estimated tax, is considered income to the taxpayer. The IRS recently determined that amounts of the Empire Zone (EZ) investment tax credit and the EZ wage tax credit that are refunded or credited as an overpayment to estimated tax are also considered income to the taxpayer and must be included in the taxpayer's federal taxable income or federal adjusted gross income.

At the state level, under existing New York law, the amount of the refund of these credits included in a taxpayer's federal taxable income or federal adjusted gross income is not taxable. Therefore, New York taxpayers are allowed a subtraction modification for that refund amount.

For information on how to apply the subtraction modification for tax years 2015 and after, taxpayers should refer to Forms CT-225, CT-225-A, and IT-225. The memorandum discusses the amended return requirements for both corporate franchise and personal income taxes.

If the IRS determines that other New York business tax credits refunded, or credited as an overpayment to estimated tax, are considered income to the taxpayer, then the memorandum notes that those credits will also be allowed a subtraction modification on New York returns. (*TSB-M-10(9.1)C, (15.1)I*, New York Department of Taxation and Finance, April 7, 2016, CCH NEW YORK TAX REPORTS, ¶408-713)

• *Business tax credits deferred*

For tax years 2010, 2011, and 2012, taxpayers with more than $2 million in aggregated business tax credits were required to defer the amounts above $2 million until 2013. The total amount of credits deferred were paid back to taxpayers over tax years 2013, 2014, and 2015. (Secs. 33, 34, Tax Law; TSB-M-10(11)I, New York Department of Taxation and Finance, September 13, 2010, CCH NEW YORK TAX REPORTS, ¶406-976)

Beginning with tax year 2010, Form IT-500, *Income Tax Deferral Credit*, provides taxpayers with detailed instructions and schedules regarding the temporary deferral of tax credits.

• *Obsolete credits*

The following credits are no longer available, but unused credits may be carried forward until exhausted:

Special additional mortgage recording taxes: For taxable years beginning before 1988, a credit against personal income tax was allowed for special additional mortgage recording taxes paid on mortgages recorded on or after January 1, 1979. (Sec. 606(f), Tax Law) The credit was revived for taxable years beginning after 2003 (see ¶ 145).

Alternative fuel vehicle property: Applicable to property placed in service after 1997 (after 1999 for qualified hybrid vehicles) and before 2005, a credit was available for a percentage of expenditures on electric vehicles, clean-fuel vehicles, and qualified hybrid vehicles (Sec. 606(p), Tax Law). A credit for alternative fuel vehicle refueling property and electric vehicle recharging property is in effect for tax years beginning on or after January 1, 2013, but before January 1, 2018 (see ¶ 148).

• *Business Incubator and Innovation Hot Spot incentives*

The New York State Business Incubator and Innovation Hot Spot Support Act (Part C, Ch. 59, Laws 2013) was enacted to support the growth of companies in the early stages of development. The Act authorizes the Empire State Development Corporation (ESDC) to designate five "New York State innovation hot spots" in SFY 2013-14 and an additional five in SFY 2014-15.

ESD is authorized to issue an annual request for proposals for grants and assistance based on available appropriations and to designate qualified applicants as New York State incubators. In addition, in each of state fiscal years 2013 and 2014, ESD was authorized to designate five qualified New York State incubators as New York State Innovation Hot Spots. These New York State Innovation Hot Spots can certify certain clients as a qualified entities eligible for tax benefits under Sec. 38, Tax Law.

Entities designated as innovation hot spots must demonstrate an affiliation with and the support of at least one college, university, or independent research institution, and offer programs consistent with regional economic development strategies. Qualified entities in innovation hot spots are eligible for the tax benefits listed below for five taxable years, beginning with the year the entity becomes a tenant in or part of an innovation hot spot:

— A qualified entity that is located within an Innovation Hot Spot is subject only to the fixed dollar minimum tax under Article 9-A (¶ 905).

— Qualified entities located within and without the Hot Spot and corporate partners of qualified entities are allowed a deduction for the amount of income or gain attributable to operations in the Hot Spot (¶ 1003).

— Individuals who are sole proprietors of a qualified entity, or are partners/members/shareholders of a partnership, limited liability company, or New York S corporation, respectively, that is a qualified entity are allowed a deduction for the amount of income or gain attributable to operations at the Hot Spot. This benefit is also available under the New York City personal income tax on residents. (¶ 303; ¶ 3010)

— Qualified entities are also eligible for a credit or refund of sales and use tax imposed on the retail sale of tangible personal property or services (¶ 2109).

Taxpayers claiming the above tax benefits are not eligible for any other New York State exemptions, deductions, credits, or refunds to the extent the exemption, deduction, credit, or refund is attributable to the business operations in the Innovation Hot Spot.

(Secs. 38, 208.9(a)(18), 209(11), 612(c)(39), and 1119(d)(1); Sec. 1(16-v), Urban Development Corporation Act; Sec. 11-1712(c)(35); NYC Admin. Code; *TSB-M-14(1)C, (1)I, (2)S*, March 7, 2014, CCH NEW YORK TAX REPORTS, ¶ 408-039)

• *START-UP NY Program*

The SUNY Tax-Free Areas to Revitalize and Transform Upstate (START-UP) New York program (Ch. 68 (A.B. 8113), Laws 2013; Sec. 39, Tax Law, Sec. 40, Tax Law, Sec.

606(ww), Tax Law) provides several personal and corporate income tax, sales and use tax, property tax, and transfer tax incentives to promote business and job creation by transforming public higher education through designated tax-free communities in upstate New York and other strategically-designated locations. For ten years, through applicable credits and refunds, participating businesses will pay no corporate franchise or personal income taxes on business income and no sales and use taxes on tangible personal property and services related to the area.

Applicability: The tax benefits apply to taxable years beginning on or after January 1, 2014, to calendar quarters beginning on or after January 1, 2014, to sales tax quarters beginning on or after March 1, 2014, or to transactions occurring on or after January 1, 2014, whichever is applicable. (Sec. 23, Part A, Ch. 68 (A.B. 8113), Laws 2013; Sec. 39, Tax Law; Sec. 40, Tax Law)

Qualifications: Among other requirements for eligibility, a business must be a new start-up company, an out-of-state company relocating to New York, or an expansion of an existing New York company. The business must also create and maintain net new jobs. Businesses will not be eligible if they compete with existing businesses that are not within the tax-free area, and certain types of businesses are specifically excluded (*e.g.,* restaurants, real estate management companies, and retail, wholesale, or personal service businesses). (Sec. 433, Econ. Dev. Law)

Corporate income tax provisions: A tax-free NY area tax elimination credit is provided. The amount allowed is the product of two factors (Sec. 40(b), Tax Law):

(1) the tax-free area allocation factor, which is the percentage representing the business's economic presence in the tax-free NY area in which the business was approved to locate, and

(2) the tax factor, which is the largest of the amounts of tax determined for the taxable year under Sec. 210(1)(a)—(d), Tax Law, after the deduction of any other corporate income tax credits allowable.

The legislation also enhances the Excelsior Jobs Program by reducing the applicable job creation requirements (*e.g.,* a participant is required to create 10 manufacturing jobs, rather than 25 (Sec. 353(4), Econ. Dev. Law)). In addition, a taxpayer that creates at least 75% of the estimated jobs will be allowed a proportionally reduced credit. See also ¶135.

In addition, an exemption from the metropolitan commuter transportation mobility tax (MCTMT) is created (¶106).

Applicable to taxable years beginning on and after January 1, 2014, a refundable credit is available for the excise tax on telecommunication services paid by a START-UP NY business (Sec. 210(49), Tax Law). The credit is equal to the 2.5% of the excise tax paid on purchased telecommunication services under Article 9, Section 186-e, Tax Law.

Personal income tax provisions: Employees working at such businesses will be authorized to claim a personal income tax deduction equal to the wages earned from the business in the tax-free area (Sec. 606(ww), Tax Law). The deduction will apply to all wages and salaries in the first five years of tax benefits. In the remaining five years, for single individuals, heads of households, and married couples, the deduction will apply to the first $200,000, $250,000, and $300,000 of wages, respectively. The total number of new employees eligible for the deduction will be capped at 10,000 per year. (See ¶203)

Sales and use tax provisions: A business will be eligible for a credit or refund of sales and use taxes imposed on the retail sale of tangible personal property or services and similar taxes. The credit or refund shall be allowed for 120 consecutive months beginning with the month during which the business locates in the tax-free NY area. (See ¶2112)

¶114

Property tax provisions: Private universities and colleges will maintain tax-exempt status on property that is currently tax exempt and that they subsequently lease to businesses participating in the START-UP NY program. Only the portion of the property that is used for purposes of the START-UP NY program will be exempt. (See ¶ 2504)

Transfer tax provisions: Conveyances of real property located in tax-free NY areas to businesses located in those areas that are participating in the START-UP NY program are exempt from state and local real estate transfer tax or real property transfer tax. In addition, any lease of property to an eligible business also is exempt from any state or local real estate transfer tax or real property transfer tax. This lease provision applies to taxable years beginning on or after January 1, 2014. (See ¶ 2712)

Telecommunications tax provisions: A taxpayer that is a business or owner of a business that is located in a tax-free NY area is allowed a credit equal to the excise tax on telecommunication services (¶ 2708) and passed through to the business to the extent not otherwise deducted in computing New York adjusted gross income.

Penalties for fraud: In the case of a business that acts fraudulently in connection with the START-UP NY program, the business will be immediately terminated from the program; subject to applicable criminal penalties, including the felony crime of offering a false instrument for filing in the first degree; and required to pay back all tax benefits that the company and its employees have received (clawback provisions). (See ¶ 2508)

Additional information: See Reg. Secs. 220.1—220.20, New York Department of Economic Development, effective October 23, 2013; *TSB-M-13(7)C, (6)I, (11)M, (1)MCTMT, (7)S,* New York Department of Taxation and Finance, October 22, 2013, CCH NEW YORK TAX REPORTS, ¶ 407-949.

• *Credit for taxes withheld*

New York allows as a credit against tax the amount of taxes withheld from wages.

¶115 Minimum Income Tax—Disallowance of Credits

Law: Secs. 622, 636, Tax Law (CCH NEW YORK TAX REPORTS, ¶ 16-037).

New York personal income tax credits, except for the real property tax circuit breaker credit (¶ 122), the earned income credit and child and dependent care credit (¶ 121 and 126), and the credit for tax withheld (¶ 114), are not allowed against the minimum income tax. (Sec. 622(d), Tax Law; Sec. 636(d), Tax Law)

¶116 Credits Against Tax—Household Credit

Law: Sec. 606, Tax Law (CCH NEW YORK TAX REPORTS, ¶ 16-910).

A household credit is allowed to taxpayers with household gross incomes not exceeding $28,000 for single individuals and $32,000 for married individuals, heads of households, or surviving spouses. (Sec. 606(b), Tax Law) For residents, the credit may not exceed the total of the state income tax on taxable income and the supplemental tax relating to the tax table benefit recapture, reduced by the credit for child and dependent care (¶ 121), the credit for income taxes paid to other states (¶ 117), and the credit for trust beneficiaries receiving accumulation distributions (¶ 118). For nonresidents and part-year residents, the credit may not exceed the total of the state personal income tax on taxable income and the supplemental tax relating to the tax table benefit recapture, determined as if residents.

• *Amount of credit*

Residents: The amount of the credit for an individual who is not married nor the head of a household nor a surviving spouse is determined as follows (Sec. 606(b), Tax Law):

¶115

Household gross income	Amount of credit
Not over $5,000	$75
Over $5,000 but not over $6,000	$60
Over $6,000 but not over $7,000	$50
Over $7,000 but not over $20,000	$45
Over $20,000 but not over $25,000	$40
Over $25,000 but not over $28,000	$20

The amount of the credit for a husband and wife, head of a household, or surviving spouse is determined as follows:

Household gross income	Amount of credit
Not over $5,000	$90 plus an amount equal to $15 multiplied by a number that is one less than the number of exemptions for which the taxpayer (or taxpayers) is entitled to a deduction under IRC Secs. 151(b) and 151(c)
Over $5,000 but not over $6,000	$75 plus such an amount
Over $6,000 but not over $7,000	$65 plus such an amount
Over $7,000 but not over $20,000	$60 plus such an amount
Over $20,000 but not over $22,000	$60 plus an amount equal to $10 multiplied by a number that is one less than the number of exemptions for which the taxpayer (or taxpayers) is entitled to a deduction under IRC Secs. 151(b) and 151(c)
Over $22,000 but not over $25,000	$50 plus such an amount
Over $25,000 but not over $28,000	$40 plus an amount equal to $5 multiplied by a number that is one less than the number of exemptions for which the taxpayer (or taxpayers) is entitled to a deduction under IRC Secs. 151(b) and 151(c)
Over $28,000 but not over $32,000	$20 plus such an amount

When a resident husband and wife are required to file separate New York State personal income tax returns, the household credit is divided equally between both spouses; the unused portion of either spouse's credit may not be claimed by the other spouse. (Reg. Sec. 106.2)

¶117 Credits Against Tax—Taxes Paid to Other States or to a Province of Canada by Residents

Law: Sec. 620, Tax Law (CCH NEW YORK TAX REPORTS, ¶16-825).

Comparable Federal: Secs. 901—905 (U.S. MASTER TAX GUIDE, ¶1311).

Forms: IT-112-R, New York State Resident Credit.

A credit is allowed to residents for income taxes paid to other states or their political subdivisions or to the District of Columbia or a province of Canada on income that is also subject to New York taxation. (Sec. 620, Tax Law)

The credit is subject to the following two limitations:

— The credit may not exceed the percentage of the tax otherwise due, determined by dividing the portion of the taxpayer's New York income subject to taxation by the other jurisdiction by the total amount of the taxpayer's New York income.

CCH Example

Mr. Black is a resident of New York State. His gross income from salary, interest and dividends was $40,000, of which $10,000 was salary paid him for services rendered in Massachusetts. The Massachusetts tax on the $10,000 after allowable deductions and personal exemptions was $225, while his New York tax, before allowance of a tax credit, was $2,100.

The maximum allowable credit is computed as follows:

$$\frac{\$10,000 \ (\text{Mass. gross income})}{\$40,000 \ (\text{N.Y. gross income})} \times \$2,100 \ (\text{New York tax due before credit}) = \$525.$$

Since the actual Massachusetts tax of $225 is less than the maximum credit, the smaller amount is the allowable credit. The net tax due New York is $1,875 ($2,100 *minus* $225).

— The credit may not reduce the tax below the amount of tax that would have been due if the income subject to taxation by the other jurisdiction were excluded from the taxpayer's New York income.

Practitioner Comment: Limitations on Credit

Sourcing: The credit for taxes paid to other states or provinces is limited to items of income sourced to those locations. Items of income that have no source—interest, dividends, stock sales, etc.—are ineligible for a credit. Consequently, a domiciliary of one state who is a statutory resident of New York can be taxed twice on the same income. According to New York's courts, this result violates neither the United States' nor New York's Constitution (*Tamagni*, 91 NY2d 530, *cert. denied* 525 US 931 (1998); CCH NEW YORK TAX REPORTS, ¶ 403-055). Some commentators have suggested that this position is no longer valid in light of the U.S. Supreme Court ruling in *Comptroller of the Treasury of Maryland v. Wynne*, 135 S. Ct. 1787 (2015).

Year in which credit may be claimed: The credit for taxes paid to other states or provinces is available only for the year the tax is imposed by the other jurisdiction, not the year the amount is actually paid. A New York resident was assessed additional tax by Massachusetts for the tax years 1978-1986. While he paid the liability in 1994, he was unable to claim the New York credit in 1994. According to New York's Tax Department, the credit was available only for the 1978-1986 tax years. The taxpayer could not, presumably, apply the credit to those years since the statute of limitations precluded an amendment of the relevant returns (*Matter of Kazis*, NYS TAT 5/16/02; CCH NEW YORK TAX REPORTS, ¶ 404-183).

Mark S. Klein, Esq., Hodgson Russ LLP

• *Out-of-state lottery winnings*

A New York resident who won money in the Pennsylvania state lottery and paid income tax to that state on the amount, was also liable for New York state tax. Since the income was derived from a lottery ticket, which is intangible personal property, no credit was allowed for income taxes paid to the jurisdiction where it was obtained (*Siwula*, Decision of the State Tax Commission, August 17, 1979; CCH NEW YORK TAX REPORTS, ¶ 98-110).

• *Taxpayers claiming foreign tax credit*

In the case of a taxpayer who elects to claim the foreign tax credit for federal income tax purposes, the credit for income tax imposed by a province of Canada is allowed for the portion of the provincial tax not claimed for federal purposes for the taxable year or a preceding taxable year. (Sec. 620(b), Tax Law) To the extent that the provincial tax is claimed for federal purposes for a succeeding taxable year, the amount of the credit must be added back in the succeeding taxable year.

For credit against the separate tax on lump-sum distributions for income taxes imposed by other states or a province of Canada upon the ordinary income portion of a lump-sum distribution (see ¶ 107).

Practitioner Comment: New Audit Initiative Targets Credits

A new audit initiative carefully examines the amount of credit taken by New York residents for taxes paid to other states. A common scenario involves a New York resident who works in New Jersey and pays tax to New Jersey on 100% of wages. The New York auditors review the travel and entertainment expense reports from the New Jersey employer to see if the taxpayer really spent 100% of his time in the New Jersey office. If the taxpayer spent 20% of his time traveling outside of New Jersey for business, New York will disallow 20% of the credit for the taxes paid to New Jersey. Even though the taxpayer paid New Jersey, New York takes the position that New Jersey was overpaid, and New York will only provide a credit for taxes that were legally required by New Jersey, not what the taxpayer chose to gratuitously pay.

Mark S. Klein, Esq., Hodgson Russ LLP

¶117

¶118 Credits Against Tax—Trust Beneficiary Receiving Accumulation Distribution

Law: Secs. 621, 635, Tax Law (CCH New York Tax Reports, ¶ 16-951).

Comparable Federal: Sec. 667 (U.S. Master Tax Guide ¶ 567).

A resident trust beneficiary receiving an accumulation distribution is entitled to credit against tax the proportionate part of any tax paid by the trust in any taxable year that would not have been payable if the trust income had been distributed. (Sec. 621, Tax Law) The credit cannot reduce the tax otherwise payable to less than the amount that would have been payable if the beneficiary excluded part of the distribution from New York adjusted gross income. A nonresident beneficiary of a trust whose New York source income includes all or part of an accumulation distribution by such trust will be allowed a credit computed in the same manner as the credit to a resident trust beneficiary. (Sec. 635, Tax Law)

¶119 Credits Against Tax—Investment Tax Credit

Law: Sec. 606, Tax Law (CCH New York Tax Reports, ¶ 16-830).

Forms: IT-212, Investment Credit.

A credit is allowed with respect to tangible personal property and other tangible property, including buildings and structural components of buildings, that is (1) principally used by the taxpayer in the production of goods (other than electricity) by manufacturing, processing, assembling, refining, mining, extracting, farming, agriculture, horticulture, floriculture, viticulture or commercial fishing, (2) industrial waste treatment facilities or air pollution control facilities, used in the taxpayer's trade or business, (3) research and development property, (4) principally used by the taxpayer in the financial services and banking industries (credit available until October 1, 2015; see ¶ 924), (5) principally used in the taxpayer's trade or business of providing investment advisory services for a regulated investment company or lending, loan arrangement or loan origination services to customers in connection with the purchase or sale of securities, or (6) principally used as a film production facility by a qualified film production company. (Sec. 606(a)(2)(A), Tax Law)

Practitioner Comment: Scope of ITC

The investment tax credit for the production of goods is extremely broad and does not require that the taxpayer sell the goods that it produces. For example, a ski resort can qualify for an investment tax credit for snow making equipment even though it doesn't sell snow (*Plattekill Mountain Ski Center*, TSB-H-85(28)C). Similarly, medical diagnostic imaging devices such as X-ray, CAT-scan, ultrasound or MRI equipment all qualify for the credit (*Mitnick*, TSB-D-91(2)I; CCH New York Tax Reports, ¶ 253-434, and *Albany Equipment Management Associates*, TSB-A-88(10)I; CCH New York Tax Reports, ¶ 252-358).

Mark S. Klein, Esq., Hodgson Russ LLP

In order to qualify for the credit, the property must (1) be depreciable pursuant to IRC Sec. 167, (2) have a useful life of four years or more, (3) be acquired by purchase as defined in IRC Sec. 179(d), and (4) have a situs in New York.

Investment credit base: The investment credit base is the cost or other basis, for federal income tax purposes, of tangible personal property and other tangible personal property less the amount of the nonqualified nonrecourse financing with respect to the property to the extent such financing would be excludible from the credit base pursuant to former IRC Sec. 46(c)(8). (Sec. 606(a)(1), Tax Law)

Amount of the credit: The amount of the credit is determined by computing a percentage of the investment credit base. (Sec. 606(a)(1), Tax Law) The percentage to be used is that percentage appearing in Column 2 that is opposite the appropriate period in Column 1 in which the tangible personal property was acquired, constructed, reconstructed or erected:

Column 1	Column 2
1987 and thereafter	4% (7% for research and development property)
July 1, 1982, through December 31, 1986	6%
June 1, 1981, through June 30, 1982	5%
1979 through May 31, 1981	4%
1978	3%
1974 through 1977	2%
1969 through 1973	1%

In the case of an acquisition, construction, reconstruction or erection that was commenced in any one period and continued or completed in any subsequent period, the credit will be the sum of the portions of the investment credit base attributable to each such period.

Carryover: Any amount of credit allowed for a taxable year beginning after 1986, and not deductible in such year may be carried over to the 10 taxable years next following such taxable year. In lieu of carrying over the excess, a taxpayer who qualifies as an owner of a new business may, at his or her option, receive the excess as a refund. (Sec. 606(a)(5), Tax Law)

For tax years 2010, 2011, and 2012, taxpayers with more than $2 million in aggregated business tax credits were required to defer the amounts above $2 million until 2013. The total amount of credits deferred were paid back to taxpayers over tax years 2013, 2014, and 2015. (Secs. 33, 34, Tax Law; *TSB-M-10(11)I,* New York Department of Taxation and Finance, September 13, 2010, CCH New York Tax Reports, ¶406-976)

Leased property: No credit is allowed on account of otherwise qualified property that is leased by the taxpayer to another. (Sec. 606(a)(4), Tax Law)

Recapture: If the property ceases to be in qualified use (because of its disposition or otherwise) during the taxable year for which the credit is to be taken, the credit will be modified by a ratio that relates the months of qualified use to the months of useful life. (Sec. 606(a)(7), Tax Law) In instances where the property ceases to be in qualified use or is disposed of prior to the end of its useful life, the difference between the credit taken and the credit allowed for actual use must be added back in the year of disposition. However, this adjustment is not required if the property has a useful life of more than 12 years and has been in qualified use for more than 12 years.

Recapture of the investment tax credit will only be required where property on which the investment tax credit was claimed remains in qualified use for less than the number of months shown in the chart below:

IRC Section	Description of Property	Months of Qualified Use
168	3 yr. property	36
168	property other than 3 yr. property	60
168	buildings and structural components	144
167	all	144

The amount required to be added back is augmented by an amount equal to the product of that amount and the interest rate in effect on the last day of the taxable year.

Nonqualified nonrecourse financing addback: Nonqualified nonrecourse debt reduces the basis of property on which the credit is calculated. Consequently, increases in already existing nonqualified nonrecourse debt, as defined under federal law (26 U.S.C. § 46(c)(8)), with respect to a property eligible for credit, require an addback in the year of the increase in debt. The addback is an amount equal to the decrease in the credit that would result from reducing the basis of the property by the increased nonrecourse debt.

¶119

Retail enterprise: The credit is available to a retail enterprise that invests in a qualified rehabilitated building as defined in former IRC Sec. 48(a)(1)(E) (Sec. 606(a)(11), Tax Law). The retail enterprise must be registered as a vendor under the sales and use tax law, be primarily engaged in the retail sale of tangible personal property, and be eligible for a credit under IRC Sec. 38 (general business credit).

Employment incentive: Taxpayers that are allowed the investment tax credit, except those allowed the optional credit for research and development property, are also eligible for the employment incentive credit (¶120).

Financial services industry: The financial services investment tax credits are available until October 1, 2015, for qualified property that is principally used in the ordinary course of a taxpayer's business (Sec. 210(12)(b), Tax Law; see also *TSB-M-09(3)C*, January 16, 2009, CCH New York Tax Reports, ¶406-296):

— as a broker or dealer in connection with the purchase or sale of stocks, bonds, other securities, or commodities or in providing lending, loan arrangement, or loan origination services to its customers in connection with the purchase or sale of securities;

— as a provider of investment advisory services for a regulated investment company (as defined in Internal Revenue Code (IRC) section 851); or

— for Article 9-A taxpayers, as an exchange registered as a national securities exchange within the meaning of sections 3(A)(1) and 6(A) of the Securities Exchange Act of 1934, as a board of trade as defined in section 1410(a)(1) of the Not-for-Profit Corporation Law, or as an entity that is wholly owned by and that provides automation or technical services to one or more such national securities exchanges or boards of trade.

For additional details, see ¶924.

¶120 Credits Against Tax—Employment Incentive

Law: Sec. 606, Tax Law (CCH New York Tax Reports, ¶16-830).

Forms: IT-212-ATT, Claim for Historic Barn Rehabilitation Credit and Employment Incentive Credit.

Taxpayers that are allowed the investment tax credit (¶119), except those allowed the optional credit for research and development property, are also eligible for the employment incentive credit. (Sec. 606(a-1), Tax Law) The employment incentive credit is allowed for each of the two taxable years following the taxable year for which the investment tax credit is allowed if the average number of employees during the taxable year the employment incentive credit is claimed is at least 101% of the average number of employees during the employment base year, which is defined as the tax year immediately preceding the tax year for which the investment tax credit is allowed. In the case of a new business, the employment base year is the taxable year for which the investment tax credit is allowed. If the credit exceeds tax liability for a taxable year, the excess may be carried over to the next 10 taxable years. Alternatively, a taxpayer who qualifies as an owner of a new business may receive the excess credit as a refund.

The amount of the credit is determined as follows:

— If the average number of employees during the taxable year is at least 101% but less than 102% of the average number of employees in employment base years, the employment incentive credit will be 1.5% of the applicable investment credit base;

— If the average number of employees during the taxable year is at least 102% but less than 103% of the average number of employees in employment base years, the employment incentive credit will be 2% of the applicable investment credit base; and

— If the average number of employees is 103% or more of that in base years, the credit will be 2.5% of the investment credit base.

For tax years 2010, 2011, and 2012, taxpayers with more than $2 million in aggregated business tax credits were required to defer the amounts above $2 million until 2013. The total amount of credits deferred were paid back to taxpayers over tax years 2013, 2014, and 2015. (Secs. 33, 34, Tax Law; *TSB-M-10(11)I*, New York Department of Taxation and Finance, September 13, 2010, CCH NEW YORK TAX REPORTS, ¶406-976)

¶121 Credits Against Tax—Child and Dependent Care Expenses

Law: Sec. 606, Tax Law (CCH NEW YORK TAX REPORTS, ¶16-911).

Comparable Federal: Sec. 21 (U.S. MASTER TAX GUIDE, ¶1301).

Forms: IT-216, Claim for Child and Dependent Care Credit.

A credit is allowed against New York personal income tax for certain household and dependent care services necessary for gainful employment. (Sec. 606(c), Tax Law) The credit is a percentage of the credit allowed under IRC Sec. 21 for the same taxable year (regardless of whether the federal credit is claimed).

Credit amount: The percentage of the federal credit allowed ranges from 20%, for taxpayers whose New York adjusted gross income (AGI) is $65,000 and above, to 110%, for taxpayers whose AGI is $25,000 and below, calculated as follows:

— *Income less than $40,000:* For a person whose New York adjusted gross income is less than $40,000, the applicable percentage is 100%, plus 10% multiplied by a fraction. The numerator of the fraction is the lesser of (1) $15,000 or (2) $40,000 less the New York adjusted gross income (but not less than zero), and the denominator is $15,000. The result of this calculation is that, for a taxpayer whose adjusted gross income is $25,000 or less, the New York credit is 110% of the federal credit. This phases down to 100% of the federal credit as income rises to $40,000.

Income $40,000 and above: If adjusted gross income exceeds $40,000, the applicable percentage is 20% of the federal credit, plus 80% of that credit multiplied by a fraction. The numerator is the lesser of (1) $15,000 or (2) $65,000 less the New York adjusted gross income (but not less than zero), and the denominator is $15,000. The result of this calculation is that, for a taxpayer whose adjusted gross income is between $40,000 and $50,000, the New York credit is 100% of the federal credit, but this decreases to 20% of the federal credit as income increases to $65,000 or more.

CCH Example: Calculation of Child Care Credit

A taxpayer has employment-related child and dependent care expenses for the taxable year that qualify for a federal credit of $480 under IRC Sec. 21. Her New York adjusted gross income for the year is $60,000. Her New York credit is the sum of 20% of the federal credit ($96) plus 80% of that credit times a fraction. The numerator of the fraction is $5,000 (the lesser of $15,000 or $65,000 minus $60,000) (her New York adjusted gross income), and the denominator is $15,000. That fraction (reduced to $1/3$) times 80% of the federal credit ($384) equals $128 (rounded). Her New York credit is ($96 + $128), or $224.

Residents: For resident individuals, the credit is applied against all taxes under the New York personal income tax, after the application of allowable credits. If the credit exceeds the taxpayer's personal income tax liability, the amount of the excess may be refunded as an overpayment of tax, without interest. (Sec. 606(a)-(d), Tax Law)

Nonresidents: For nonresident individuals, the credit is applied only against New York State taxes imposed under Sec. 601(a)-(d), Tax Law, after the application of the household credit (¶116).

Part-year residents: For part-year residents individuals, the credit is applied against New York State taxes imposed under Sec. 601(a)-(d), Tax Law, after the application of the household credit (¶116). Any excess credit remaining after such application may be allowed against the minimum income tax (see Chapter 5) and the separate tax on the ordinary income portion of lump-sum distributions (¶107).

Any excess credit remaining after application as noted above is multiplied by a fraction, the numerator of which is the taxpayer's federal adjusted gross income for the period of residence (computed as if the taxable year for federal income tax purposes were limited to the period of residence) and the denominator of which is the taxpayer's federal adjusted gross income for the taxable year. The amount so determined will be refunded to the taxpayer.

Husband and wife: In the case of a husband and wife who file a joint federal return, but who are required to determine their New York taxes separately, the credit may only be applied against the tax imposed on the spouse with the lower taxable income, computed without regard to the credit. A husband and wife who are not required to file a federal return may claim the credit only if they file a joint New York return.

NYC child care credit: A local child care tax credit is available against New York City personal income tax, applicable to taxable years beginning on or after January 1, 2007. The tax credit is designed to assist low-income families with the cost of child care for children under the age of four. See ¶3009.

¶122 Credits Against Tax—Real Property Taxes Paid

Law: Sec. 606, Tax Law (CCH NEW YORK TAX REPORTS, ¶16-827).

Forms: IT-214, Claim for Real Property Tax Credit for Homeowners and Renters.

Beginning with assessment rolls used to levy school district taxes for the 2016-2017 school year, the School Tax Relief (STAR) exemption program (discussed at ¶2504) is closed to new applicants, and a new refundable personal income tax credit is established in its place (see ¶162). Four other personal income tax credits are available to individuals based upon real property taxes paid, as discussed below.

• *Real property circuit breaker credit*

A real property tax circuit breaker credit is available to qualified resident individual taxpayers with household gross incomes of $18,000 or less (Sec. 606(e), Tax Law).

Credit amount: The credit is the amount of "excess real property taxes" over a percentage of household gross income ranging from 3.5% for taxpayers with household gross incomes of $3,000 or less to 6.5% for taxpayers with household gross incomes of more than $14,000 but less than $18,000. The credit is available to property owners and tenants who meet certain conditions. Excluded are individuals whose residences are wholly exempt from taxation, owners of real property valued in excess of $85,000, persons claimed as a dependent by another taxpayer, and tenants paying adjusted rents exceeding $450 per month.

The maximum circuit breaker credit ranges from $75 ($375 for persons age 65 or older) for taxpayers with household gross incomes of $1,000 or less down to $41 ($86 for persons age 65 or older) for taxpayers with household gross incomes of more than $17,000 but less than $18,000. (Sec. 606(e)(3), Tax Law)

Planning considerations: Residents of a proprietary adult home were denied credits because they collectively constituted a household with an income exceeding the statutory limit (*Crociata et al. v. State Tax Commission* (1986, Sup Ct, Albany Cty), aff'd (1988) 134 AD2d 112, 523 NYS2d 923; CCH NEW YORK TAX REPORTS, ¶251-857).

The real property tax circuit breaker credit is reduced by any other personal income tax credits to which the taxpayer is entitled.

• *Enhanced real property tax circuit breaker credit*

A refundable enhanced real property tax circuit breaker credit is available for tax years 2014 through 2019. Homeowners and renters who reside in New York City and have a household gross income of less than $200,000 annually are eligible for the credit (Sec. 606(e-1), Tax Law). The credit applies to excess real property tax above a certain percentage of household gross income and is a maximum of $500.

Qualifying property taxes include all real property taxes, special ad valorem levies and special assessments, exclusive of penalties and interest, levied on the residence of a qualified taxpayer and paid during the taxable year. This threshold varies from 4 to 6% of income and credit rates range from 1.5 to 4.5% of excess real property tax. (Sec. 606(e-1), Tax Law)

Credit amount: Taxpayers with a household income of less than $100,000 have a burden threshold of 4% and a credit percentage of 4.5%. Taxpayers with a household income of $100,000 - $150,000 have a burden threshold of 5% and a credit percentage of 3.0%. Taxpayers with a household income of $150,000 - $200,000 have a burden threshold of 6% and a credit percentage of 1.5%. (Sec. 606(E-1), Tax Law)

Filing: Eligible circuit breaker recipients must claim the credit on their personal income tax return (or stand-alone form for claimants not required to file a tax return). (Sec. 606(e-1), Tax Law)

Planning considerations: If the credit amount exceeds the amount of tax due, the excess will be treated as an overpayment to be credited or refunded without interest. Only one credit per household and per qualified taxpayer is allowed per taxable year. If two or more members of a household qualify for the credit, the credit must be equally divided. (Sec. 606(e-1), Tax Law)

• *Real property tax freeze credit*

In order to qualify for the tax freeze credit, a homeowner must:

— be eligible for the STAR property tax exemption (discussed at ¶2504); and

— live in an eligible taxing jurisdiction that both: (i) limits any increase in its tax levy to a property tax cap set by State law ("cap-compliant"); and (ii) develops and implements a Government Efficiency Plan determined to be compliant by the New York State Division of Budget.

(Sec. 606(bbb), Tax Law; *Publication 1030,* New York Department of Taxation and Finance, July 14, 2014, CCH NEW YORK TAX REPORTS, ¶408-134)

The credit is applicable against school district and municipal taxes levied outside of New York City. Credits against school tax increases will be provided for school years 2014-15 and 2015-16. Credits against all other municipal taxes will be provided in 2015 and 2016. The credits will be sent as an advance payment, with the initial 2014-15 school tax payment occurring in the fall of 2014. (Sec. 606(bbb), Tax Law)

Credit amount: Eligible taxpayers residing in an eligible taxing jurisdiction will receive a credit equal to the greater of:

(1) the change in their real property taxes from the prior year, or

(2) the product of their previous year's taxes and the lessor of 2% or the inflation factor used in the real property tax cap determination.

¶122

Planning considerations: Tax bill increases due to a physical improvement, exemption loss, or disproportionate tax bill increase due to a general reassessment of all properties are not included in the credit.

STAR eligibility requires that (1) the combined gross income of all owners residing on the parcel does not exceed $500,000; and (2) the property serves as the primary residence for the homeowner.

There is no requirement for the homeowner to calculate or apply for the freeze credit.

New York City homeowners are not eligible for the credit because New York City is not subject to the property tax cap. However, New York City homeowners and renters are eligible for the circuit breaker tax credit.

• *Real property tax credit for qualified manufacturers*

Effective for tax years beginning on or after January 1, 2014, a credit is available for qualified New York manufacturers (Sec. 606(xx), Tax Law). A "manufacturer" is defined as a taxpayer principally engaged in the production of goods by manufacturing, processing, assembling, refining, mining, extracting, farming, agriculture, horticulture, floriculture, viticulture or commercial fishing. But, the generation and distribution of electricity, the distribution of natural gas, and the production of steam associated with the generation of electricity are not qualifying activities. (Sec. 210-B (43), Tax Law; see *TSB-M-15(3.1)I,* New York Department of Taxation and Finance, July 24, 2015, CCH NEW YORK TAX REPORTS, ¶408-488)

A qualified manufacturer must satisfy the existing receipts and property tests (Sec. 210-B(43)(B)(2), Tax Law):

(1) at least 50% of receipts must be from manufacturing; and

(2) either all or at least $1 million of manufacturing property is in New York.

A manufacturer that fails the receipts test may still qualify for the credit if it employs at least 2,500 people in manufacturing in New York and has $100 million in manufacturing property in New York (Sec. 606(xx), Tax Law).

Credit amount: The credit is equal to 20% of the real property taxes paid during the taxable year for real property owned by qualified manufacturers in New York and principally used for manufacturing. The credit is also allowed for property taxes paid on real property leased from an unrelated third party if the taxes are paid pursuant to explicit requirements in a written lease and remitted directly to the taxing authority. (Sec. 606(xx), Tax Law)

Planning considerations: The credit cannot be claimed if the real property taxes that are the basis for the credit are included in the calculation of another credit already claimed. Also, for personal income taxpayers the credit is limited to real property taxes not deducted from the taxpayer's New York adjusted gross income (Sec. 606(xx)(2)(B)(1), Tax Law).

If the property taxes that were the basis of the credit are later reduced, the taxpayer must add back the excess of (1) the amount of credit originally allowed for a taxable year over (2) the amount of credit determined on the reduced property taxes. This addback must be made in the same taxable year that the final order reducing the taxes is issued (Sec. 606(xx), Tax Law). The credit cannot reduce a taxpayers tax liability to less than $25.

Leased property: The term "real property tax" includes taxes paid by the taxpayer upon real property principally used by the taxpayer in manufacturing if the taxpayer leases the real property from an unrelated third party if the following conditions are satisfied:

(I) the tax must be paid by the taxpayer as lessee pursuant to explicit requirements in a written lease, and

(II) the taxpayer as lessee has paid such taxes directly to the taxing authority and has received a written receipt for payment of taxes from the taxing authority.

In the case of a taxpayer that, during the taxable year, is principally engaged in the production of goods by farming, agriculture, horticulture, floriculture, viticulture, or commercial fishing, the taxpayer is eligible if the taxpayer satisfies the above conditions and the taxpayer leases the real property from either a related or unrelated party. (Sec. 606(xx)(2)(B)(1)(ii), Tax Law; *TSB-M-15(3.1)I*, New York Department of Taxation and Finance, July 24, 2015, CCH NEW YORK TAX REPORTS, ¶ 408-488)

¶123 Credits Against Tax—Shareholders of S Corporations

Law: Sec. 606, Tax Law (CCH NEW YORK TAX REPORTS, ¶ 16-952).

Shareholders of federal S corporations, where the election to be treated as a New York S corporation is in effect, may claim a credit against the personal income tax equal to their *pro rata* share of the S corporation's credit base. (Sec. 606(i), Tax Law) The base includes the investment tax credit (¶ 119), empire zone investment tax, wage tax and capital tax credits (¶ 124), agricultural property tax credit (¶ 130) and the credit for employment of persons with disabilities (¶ 125). If the corporation qualifies as a new business pursuant to Sec. 210(12)(j), Tax Law, the shareholder will be treated as an owner of the business, unless he or she has previously received a refund.

Practitioner Comment: Additional Mortgage Recording Tax Credit

Although shareholders of S corporations are entitled to a *pro rata* share of most of the entity's credits, New York's Department of Taxation and Finance has taken the position that shareholders are not entitled to a portion of the S corporation's special additional mortgage recording tax credit. See 2015 Instructions to CT-34-SH-I, Page 2.

Mark S. Klein, Esq., Hodgson Russ LLP

¶124 Credits Against Tax—Empire Zones

Law: Secs. 15, 606, 210.19, Tax Law (CCH NEW YORK TAX REPORTS, ¶ 16-845—16-865).

Forms: IT-601, Claim for EZ Wage Tax Credit; IT-601.1, Claim for ZEA Wage Tax Credit; IT-602, Claim for EZ Capital Tax Credit; IT-603, Claim for EZ Investment Tax Credit and EZ Employment Incentive Credit; IT-604, Claim for QEZE Credit for Real Property Taxes and QEZE Tax Reduction Credit; IT-605, Claim for EZ Investment Tax Credit and EZ Employment Incentive Credit for the Financial Services Industry; DTF-621, Claim for QETC Employment Credit; DTF-622, Claim for QETC Capital Tax Credit.

Before the program's sunset date of June 30, 2010, there were six credits available to taxpayers that relocate to or stimulate private business enterprise within designated empire zones (EZs). Transitional provisions are explained in *TSB-M-10(6)C, (12)I, (19)S*, New York Department of Taxation and Finance, December 8, 2010, CCH NEW YORK TAX REPORTS, ¶ 407-074.

Empire zones: New York has designated more than 100 empire zones. The New York State Empire Zone Development agency website (**http://www.esd.ny.gov/BusinessPrograms/Data/EmpireZones/Zone_Coordinators.pdf**) has contact information for each empire zone.

Empire Zone reform: The sunset date for the empire zone program was June 30, 2010. Also, zones are to be designated as "investment zones" (for economically disadvantaged areas) or "development zones"(for county areas). The Excelsior jobs program, discussed at ¶ 135, replaced the expired Empire Zones program to provide job creation and investment incentives to firms in targeted industries.

The 2009-2010 budget legislation implements reform measures to the Empire Zone program and the Empire Zone income tax credits by decertifying businesses that have received more benefit from the program than they have provided and by increasing the cost-benefit ratio test for entry into the program from 15 to 1 to 20 to 1 (10 to 1 for manufacturers). The legislation also moved up the program's sunset date from June 30, 2011, to June 30, 2010. Applicable to taxable years beginning on and after January 1, 2008, carryover credits are not allowed for taxpayers that are decertified for failure to meet the 20:1 cost benefit analysis. For details, see *TSB-M-09(5)C*, CCH NEW YORK TAX REPORTS, ¶ 406-367.

Deferred credits: For tax years 2010, 2011, and 2012, taxpayers with more than $2 million in aggregated business tax credits were required to defer the amounts above $2 million until 2013. The total amount of credits deferred were paid back to taxpayers over tax years 2013, 2014, and 2015. (Secs. 33, 34, Tax Law; TSB-M-10(11)I, New York Department of Taxation and Finance, September 13, 2010, CCH NEW YORK TAX REPORTS, ¶ 406-976)

- *Empire zone investment tax credit*

Taxpayers are allowed a credit equal to 8% of the cost or other basis for federal income tax purposes of tangible personal property and other tangible property, including buildings and structural components of buildings, located within a designated empire zone. (Sec. 606(j), Tax Law) The acquisition, construction, reconstruction or erection of the property must begin on or after the date of the designation and prior to the termination of the designation. Where the acquisition, construction, reconstruction or erection continues or is completed after the period that the zone is certified, the credit is limited to 8% of the portion of the cost or other basis for federal income tax purposes that is attributable to the period of the zone's designation as an empire zone, and is determined by multiplying the cost or basis by the percentage that the expenditures paid or incurred during the certified period bears to the total of all acquisition, construction or erection expenditures. The credit must be claimed.

Eligibility requirements: To be eligible for the credit, the property must (1) be depreciable pursuant to IRC Sec. 167, (2) have a useful life of four years or more, (3) be acquired by purchase (as defined in IRC Sec. 179(d)), (4) have a situs in a designated empire zone, and (5) be principally used by the taxpayer in the production of goods (other than electricity) by manufacturing, processing, assembling, refining, mining, extracting, farming, agriculture, horticulture, floriculture, viticulture, or commercial fishing, or be principally used by the taxpayer in the financial services and banking industries (placed in service on or after October 1, 1998, and before October 1, 2008). (Sec. 606(j)(2), Tax Law)

The credit includes qualified property that is used as industrial waste treatment facilities or air pollution control facilities in a taxpayer's trade or business, or as research and development property.

The credit generally is not available for property that is leased to another person or corporation.

Recapture of credit: When property on which an empire zone investment tax credit has been claimed is disposed of or ceases to be in qualified use prior to the end of its useful life, a portion of the credit must be recaptured. The amount of the recapture is dependent upon the federal class-life of the property and the number of continuous years during which the property remained in qualified use. An exception applies to credits allowed to partners with respect to certain manufacturing property (Sec. 606(j)(6)(H), Tax Law).

Decertification of business enterprise: The decertification of a business enterprise in an empire zone will, as of the effective date of the decertification, constitute the disposal or cessation of the qualified use of any property on which the credit was taken.

¶124

If decertification is based upon a finding that the business enterprise (1) made material misrepresentations of fact on its application for certification, (2) failed to construct, expand, rehabilitate, or operate facilities substantially in accordance with the representations contained in the application, or (3) substantially violated laws for the protection of workers, the credit will be recaptured for all taxable years with interest at the underpayment rate in effect on the last day of the taxable year.

The credit will not be reduced below any investment tax credit to which the taxpayer is entitled.

Carryover of unused credit: With one exception, empire zone investment tax credits not used in one taxable year may be carried forward until exhausted. (Sec. 606(j)(4), Tax Law) Decertified business enterprises may not carry the credit beyond the seventh taxable year following the year in which the credit was allowed. In lieu of carrying unused credits over to subsequent years, a taxpayer that qualifies as the owner of a new business may receive 50% of the excess as a refund.

For tax years 2010, 2011, and 2012, taxpayers with more than $2 million in aggregated business tax credits were required to defer the amounts above $2 million until 2013. The total amount of credits deferred were paid back to taxpayers over tax years 2013, 2014, and 2015. (Secs. 33, 34, Tax Law; TSB-M-10(11)I, New York Department of Taxation and Finance, September 13, 2010, CCH NEW YORK TAX REPORTS, ¶406-976)

• *Empire zone employment incentive credit*

The empire zone employment incentive credit is allowed for three years following the taxable year for which the empire zone investment tax credit is allowed. (Sec. 606(j-1), Tax Law) The empire zone employment incentive credit is equal to 30% of the empire zone investment tax credit. The empire zone employment incentive credit is only available if the average number of employees employed in the empire zone during the taxable year the credit is allowed is at least 101% of the average number of employees for the tax year immediately preceding the year for which the empire zone investment tax credit is allowed. If the credit exceeds tax liability for a taxable year, the excess may be carried over to the following year or years. A taxpayer who qualifies as an owner of a new business may receive 50% of the excess credit as a refund.

For tax years 2010, 2011, and 2012, taxpayers with more than $2 million in aggregated business tax credits were required to defer the amounts above $2 million until 2013. The total amount of credits deferred were paid back to taxpayers over tax years 2013, 2014, and 2015. (Secs. 33, 34, Tax Law; TSB-M-10(11)I, New York Department of Taxation and Finance, September 13, 2010, CCH NEW YORK TAX REPORTS, ¶406-976)

• *Empire zone and ZEA wage tax credits*

Taxpayers are allowed a credit for wages paid to full-time employees in newly created jobs in empire zones and, before June 13, 2004, zone equivalent areas (ZEAs). (Sec. 606(k), Tax Law) The credit is larger for employers who hire targeted employees. A "targeted employee" is a New York resident who receives empire zone wages and who qualifies as any of the following:

— an eligible individual for the federal work opportunity tax credit (IRC Sec. 51);

— eligible for benefits under the provisions of the federal Workforce Investment Act (P.L. 105-220, as amended) as a dislocated worker or low-income individual;

— a recipient of public assistance benefits;

¶124

— an individual whose income is below the U.S. Department of Commerce poverty rate;

— a member of a family whose family income is below the federal poverty rate; or

— (for tax years beginning after 2004) is an honorably discharged member of any branch of the U.S. armed forces.

Credit amount: The amount of the credit is equal to the sum of the following (Sec. 606(k)(4), Tax Law):

—$3,000 multiplied by the average number of the taxpayer's full-time targeted employees (excluding general executive officers) who received empire zone wages for more than one-half of the taxable year and, with respect to more than one-half of the period of employment by the taxpayer during the taxable year, received an hourly wage that was at least 135% of the state minimum wage; and

—$1,500 multiplied by the average number of full-time employees (excluding general executive officers and targeted full-time employees) who received empire zone wages for more than one-half of the taxable year.

For a taxpayer certified in an investment zone, the dollar amount of the credit per employee is increased by $500 for each qualifying employee who received wages in excess of $40,000.

Duration of credits: The empire zone wage tax credits may be claimed for up to five years. The ZEA wage tax credits expired June 13, 2004; for tax years after that date, only carryover credits may be claimed. No empire zone credits may be claimed more than five years after designation of the empire zone.

Carryovers: Credits not used during one year may be carried forward to the following year or years and deducted from the tax for such years. In lieu of carrying a credit forward, a taxpayer that qualifies as a new business may elect, on its report for the taxable year with respect to which the credit is allowed, to treat 50% of the amount of the carryover as an overpayment of tax to be credited or refunded. (Sec. 606(k)(5), Tax Law)

For tax years 2010, 2011, and 2012, taxpayers with more than $2 million in aggregated business tax credits were required to defer the amounts above $2 million until 2013. The total amount of credits deferred were paid back to taxpayers over tax years 2013, 2014, and 2015. (Secs. 33, 34, Tax Law; TSB-M-10(11)I, New York Department of Taxation and Finance, September 13, 2010, CCH New York Tax Reports, ¶ 406-976)

• *Empire zone capital tax credit*

Taxpayers are allowed a credit equal to 25% of the sum of the following investments and contributions made during the tax year: (1) for taxable years beginning before 2005, qualified investments made in, or contributions in the form of donations made to one or more empire zone capital corporations; (2) qualified investments in certified zone businesses that, during the 12-month period immediately preceding the month in which such investment is made, employed full-time within New York an average of 250 or fewer individuals, excluding general executive officers, computed pursuant to the provisions of Sec. 606(k)(2)(c), Tax Law, except for investments made by or on behalf of an owner of the business, including, but not limited to, a stockholder, partner or sole proprietor, or any related person as defined in IRC Sec. 465(b)(3); and (3) contributions of money to community development projects. (Sec. 606(l), Tax Law)

The total amount of the empire zone capital tax credit allowable to a taxpayer for all years, taken in the aggregate, may not exceed $300,000 ($150,000 in the case of a husband or wife required to file a separate return) and may not exceed $100,000

($50,000 in the case of a husband or wife required to file a separate return) with respect to the investments and contributions described in each of the listed categories. In addition, the amount of any credit and carryovers may not exceed 50% of the taxpayer's tax liability (computed without regard to credits).

For tax years 2010, 2011, and 2012, taxpayers with more than $2 million in aggregated business tax credits were required to defer the amounts above $2 million until 2013. The total amount of credits deferred were paid back to taxpayers over tax years 2013, 2014, and 2015. (Secs. 33, 34, Tax Law; TSB-M-10(11)I, New York Department of Taxation and Finance, September 13, 2010, CCH NEW YORK TAX REPORTS, ¶406-976)

• *QEZE credit for real property tax*

A refundable credit is allowed for real property taxes paid by a taxpayer that is a sole proprietor of a qualified empire zone enterprise (QEZE) or a member of a partnership that is a QEZE on property owned by the QEZE and located within an empire zone for which the QEZE is certified. (Sec. 606(bb), Tax Law)

To claim the credit, a tenant is required to pay the real property taxes directly to the taxing authority. Property tax payments to a lender's escrow account were disqualified because they were deemed to be payments made through an intermediary and not direct payments to the taxing authority. (*Balbo*, New York Division of Tax Appeals, Tax Appeals Tribunal, DTA Nos. 825765 and 826269, August 18, 2016, CCH NEW YORK TAX REPORTS, ¶408-839).

CCH Advisory: Real Property Taxes Did Not Include Special Assessments

The New York Tax Appeals Tribunal affirmed the determination of an administrative law judge (ALJ) in a personal income tax case concerning a qualified Empire Zone enterprise (QEZE) real property tax credit claim that included certain special assessments. The ALJ held that it was proper for the Division of Taxation to disallow a portion of the claim that was based on payment of a road benefit tax. Although the tax was levied for an apparent municipal purpose, it was unquestionably a special assessment. Such assessments are not eligible real property taxes for purposes of the credit because special assessments are excluded from the term "tax" under the Real Property Tax Law definitions. The taxpayers had argued that a broad interpretation of the taxes eligible for inclusion in the credit was supported by the legislative history of the Empire Zones program, but that position was rejected. (*Ginsberg*, New York Division of Tax Appeals, Tax Appeals Tribunal, DTA Nos. 822853, 822855, 822856, 822857, 822858, 822859, and 822860, November 3, 2011, CCH NEW YORK TAX REPORTS, ¶407-409) See also, to the same effect, (*Burdick*, New York Division of Tax Appeals, Administrative Law Judge Unit, DTA No. 823485, October 27, 2011, CCH NEW YORK TAX REPORTS, ¶407-398).

A QEZE is a business enterprise that is certified under Article 18-B of the General Municipal Law and that annually meets the employment test.

Employment test: For a business entity first certified before April 1, 2005, the employment test is met for a taxable year if (1) the business enterprise's employment number in empire zones for the taxable year equals or exceeds its employment number in the zones for the base period, and (2) the business enterprise's employment number in New York State outside of the zones for the taxable year equals or exceeds its employment number in New York outside of the zones for the base period.

For entities first certified between August 1, 2002, and March 31, 2005, if the base period is zero years and the enterprise has an employment number in an empire zone of greater than zero with respect to a taxable year, then the employment test will be met only if the enterprise qualifies as a new business. For entities first certified before August 1, 2002, if the entity had a base period of zero years or zero employment in the base period, then the employment test will be met only if the enterprise qualifies as a new business.

¶124

For a business enterprise first certified on or after April 1, 2005, the employment test will be met with respect to a taxable year if the business enterprise's employment number in the state and the empire zones for that taxable year exceeds its employment number in the state and the empire zones, respectively, for the base period. If the base period is zero years or the base period employment is zero and the enterprise has an employment number in the zone of greater than zero with respect to a taxable year, then the employment test will be met only if the enterprise qualifies as a new business.

Test year: The employment test year is the taxable year that ended immediately before the test date. The test date is July 1, 2000, or a later date on which the QEZE is certified.

If a business enterprise does not have a taxable year that ends on or before the test date, the test year is the last calendar or fiscal year ending on or before its test date (whether or not the enterprise in fact had a taxable year during that period).

Credit amount: For businesses certified on or after April 1, 2005, the credit is equal to the product of 25% of the total wages, health benefits, and retirement benefits (up to $40,000) paid to or on behalf of net new employees during the taxable year. The credit is limited to $10,000 per employee. Certain adjustments (as well as a maximum credit limitation) may apply. (Sec. 15(b)(2)(A), Tax Law)

For tax years 2010, 2011, and 2012, taxpayers with more than $2 million in aggregated business tax credits were required to defer the amounts above $2 million until 2013. The total amount of credits deferred were paid back to taxpayers over tax years 2013, 2014, and 2015. (Secs. 33, 34, Tax Law; TSB-M-10(11)I, New York Department of Taxation and Finance, September 13, 2010, CCH NEW YORK TAX REPORTS, ¶406-976)

Formula for calculation of credit (prior years): For businesses certified before April 1, 2005, the QEZE property tax credit is the product of (the benefit period factor) × (the employment increase factor) × (the eligible real property taxes paid during the taxable year).

The benefit period factor is as follows:

— for the first 10 taxable years, 1.0;
— for the 11th taxable year, .8;
— for the 12th taxable year, .6;
— for the 13th taxable year, .4;
— for the 14th taxable year, .2; and
— for the 15th taxable year, 0.

The employment increase factor is the amount, not to exceed 1.0, that is the greater of:

— the excess of the QEZE's employment number in the empire zones in which the QEZE is certified for that year over the QEZE's test year employment number in such zones, divided by the test year employment number in those zones (*Note:* If the taxpayer's employment number in the zones for the taxable year exceeds the employment number in the zones for the test year, and the test year employment number is zero, then the employment increase factor will be 1.0); or

— the excess of the QEZE's employment number in the zones in which the QEZE is certified for that year over the QEZE's test year employment number in such zones, divided by 100.

The maximum credit that may be taken is the greater of the employment increase limitation or the capital investment limitation. (Sec. 15(f), Tax Law) The employment increase limitation is equal to the product of $10,000 and the excess of the QEZE's employment number in the empire zones for the taxable year over that employment number for the QEZE's test year. The capital investment limitation is the product of (a) 10% of the greater of the cost or other basis for federal income tax purposes of the real property owned by the QEZE and located in empire zones on the later of January 1, 2001 or the effective date of the QEZE's certification or the cost or other basis of such property on the last day of the taxable year, and (b) the percentage of the real property physically occupied and used by the QEZE or by a related person to the QEZE.

Refund: If the QEZE credit for real property taxes exceeds the taxpayer's tax for the taxable year, the excess may be refunded, without interest.

For federal income tax purposes, the Internal Revenue Service has determined that all or a portion of the QEZE credit for real property taxes that is refunded, or credited as an overpayment to estimated tax, may be a recovery of property tax previously deducted and is therefore considered income to the taxpayer.

For New York state corporate franchise tax and personal income tax purposes, any refund of the QEZE credit for real property taxes is considered a refund of franchise tax or income tax. Accordingly, under existing state law, the amount of the refund of the QEZE credit for real property taxes included in the taxpayer's federal taxable income or federal adjusted gross income is not taxable to New York state. Therefore, New York state taxpayers are allowed a subtraction for that refund amount in computing their New York taxable income. A memorandum describes how to report the subtraction on New York state corporate franchise tax returns and personal income tax returns, as well as the necessary amended return requirements. (*TSB-M-10(9)C, (15)I,* New York Department of Taxation and Finance, December 31, 2010, CCH NEW YORK TAX REPORTS, ¶ 407-084)

Recapture: A portion of the credit will be recaptured if the real property taxes that were the basis for the allowance of the credit are subsequently reduced as a result of a final order. (Sec. 15(g), Tax Law)

Resources: Additional details and examples are included in TSB-M-06(2)I, CCH NEW YORK TAX REPORTS, ¶ 300-499.

• *QEZE tax reduction credit*

A tax reduction credit is allowed to a taxpayer that is a sole proprietor of a qualified empire zone enterprise (QEZE) or a member of a partnership that is a QEZE that is certified pursuant to Article 18-B of the General Municipal Law, and that annually meets the employment test (see above). (Sec. 16, Tax Law)

Formula for calculation of credit: The QEZE tax reduction credit is the product of (the benefit period factor) × (the employment increase factor) × (the zone allocation factor) × (the tax factor).

The benefit period factor is as follows:

— for the first 10 taxable years, 1.0;

— for the 11th taxable year, .8;

— for the 12th taxable year, .6;

— for the 13th taxable year, .4;

— for the 14th taxable year, .2; and

— for the 15th taxable year, 0.

The employment increase factor is the amount, not to exceed 1.0, that is the greater of:

— the excess of the QEZE's employment number in the empire zones in which the QEZE is certified for that year over the QEZE's test year employment number in such zones, divided by the test year employment number in those zones (Note: If the taxpayer's employment number in the zones for the taxable year exceeds the employment number in the zones for the test year, and the test year employment number is zero, then the employment increase factor will be 1.0); or

    — the excess of the QEZE's employment number in the zones in which the QEZE is certified for that year over the QEZE's test year employment number in such zones, divided by 100.

The zone allocation factor is a percentage representing the taxpayer's presence in the empire zone based on property and payroll.

The tax factor is the larger of the tax amounts for the taxable year as computed under Sec. 601(a)-(d), Tax Law.

For the computation of the tax factor for sole proprietors, partners, and S corporation shareholders of a QEZE, see *TSB-M-02(8)I*, CCH NEW YORK TAX REPORTS, ¶ 300-376.

For tax years 2010, 2011, and 2012, taxpayers with more than $2 million in aggregated business tax credits were required to defer the amounts above $2 million until 2013. The total amount of credits deferred were paid back to taxpayers over tax years 2013, 2014, and 2015. (Secs. 33, 34, Tax Law; TSB-M-10(11)I, New York Department of Taxation and Finance, September 13, 2010, CCH NEW YORK TAX REPORTS, ¶ 406-976)

Resources: Additional details and examples are included in *TSB-M-06(2)I*, CCH NEW YORK TAX REPORTS, ¶ 300-499.

¶125 Credits Against Tax—Employment of Qualified Disabled Persons

Law: Secs. 606, 210-B(48), Tax Law (CCH NEW YORK TAX REPORTS, ¶ 16-875).

Forms: IT-251, Credit for Employment of Persons with Disabilities.

A credit is allowed for employing qualified disabled persons equal to 35% of the first $6,000 in wages for the employee's first year of employment. (Sec. 606(o), Tax Law) To be qualified, individuals must be certified by the Education Department as handicapped, and must have completed or be enrolled in an individualized rehabilitation plan and who has worked. The employment period must be full-time for at least 180 days or 400 hours.

An additional credit for hiring workers with developmental disabilities is discussed below.

When an employee's wages also constitute qualified first-year wages for purposes of the federal work opportunity tax credit for vocational rehabilitation referrals under IRC Sec. 51, the amount of the credit is 35% of the first $6,000 in wages for the qualified employee's second year. This has the effect of requiring that the employee be employed for two years. The credit cannot reduce the business's tax to less than the statutory minimum, but to the extent any excess credit remains, it may be carried over to the following year.

For tax years 2010, 2011, and 2012, taxpayers with more than $2 million in aggregated business tax credits were required to defer the amounts above $2 million until 2013. The total amount of credits deferred were paid back to taxpayers over tax years 2013, 2014, and 2015. (Secs. 33, 34, Tax Law; TSB-M-10(11)I, New York Department of Taxation and Finance, September 13, 2010, CCH NEW YORK TAX REPORTS, ¶ 406-976)

• *Credit for hiring persons with developmental disabilities*

The Workers with Disabilities Tax Credit Program, which is administered by the Department of Labor, provides an additional tax incentive to employers for employing individuals with developmental disabilities. The credit is available for qualified wages paid after January 1, 2015 and expires on January 1, 2020. (Sec. 210-B(48), Tax Law)

Credit amount: The nonrefundable credit is equal to 15% of the qualified wages for qualified full-time employees and 10% of the qualified wages for qualified part-time employees. The annual credit allocation is $6 million. (Sec. 210-B(48), Tax Law)

Planning considerations: Full-time employment is defined as working at least 30 hours per week, and part-time employment at least 8 hours per week, each for at least 6 months (Sec. 210-B(48), Tax Law).

In order to be eligible for the program, taxpayers must apply to the Department of Labor Commissioner by November 30 of the prior year to become a qualified employer, and will be issued a preliminary certificate of eligibility. At the end of the tax year, the employer must obtain a final certificate of eligibility from the department that states the maximum amount of credit allowed and provides verification for the credit claims. An employer is not allowed to concurrently claim this credit and any other credit for the employment of persons with disabilities for the same employee. (Sec 25-B, Labor Law).

Any unused credit may be carried forward for up to 3 years.

¶126 Credits Against Tax—Earned Income Credit

Law: Sec. 606(d), Tax Law (CCH NEW YORK TAX REPORTS, ¶16-820).

Comparable Federal: Sec. 32 (U.S. MASTER TAX GUIDE ¶1375).

Forms: IT-215, Claim for Earned Income Credit.

An earned income credit (EIC) is allowed against New York personal income tax, equal to 30% of the federal EIC (Sec. 606(d), Tax Law). New York conforms to the federal EIC eligibility rules; see *Important Notice N-16-2*, New York Department of Taxation and Finance, February 2016, (CCH NEW YORK TAX REPORTS, ¶408-641).

The EIC allowed to any taxpayer must be reduced by the taxpayer's household credit (¶116). Therefore, a taxpayer will not receive the benefit of both the EIC and the household credit.

Residents: For resident taxpayers, the EIC is applied against all taxes imposed under the New York State personal income tax, after the application of all other personal income tax credits. (Sec. 606(d), Tax Law) If the available credit exceeds the taxpayer's personal income tax liability (as so reduced), the amount of the excess may be refunded as an overpayment of tax, without interest.

Nonresidents: For nonresidents, the EIC is applied only against the New York taxes imposed under Sec. 601(a)-(d), Tax Law, after the application of the household credit (¶116) and the child care credit (¶121). (Sec. 606(d), Tax Law) The taxes imposed under Sec. 601(a)-(d) consist of the regular tax and the tax benefit recapture, computed as if the individual were a resident.

If the EIC is:

— less than the above amount, the remaining tax (the base tax) is multiplied by the income percentage to arrive at the New York State tax before other credits and taxes;

— more than the above amount, the excess credit cannot be used to reduce any other personal income taxes. The excess cannot be refunded.

The base tax is equal to the taxes computed under Sec. 601(a)-(d), Tax Law, as if the individual were a resident, reduced, respectively, by the household credit (¶116), the child care credit (¶121), and the earned income credit. The income percentage is the percentage computed by dividing the individual's New York source income for the entire year by the individual's New York adjusted gross income for the entire year.

Part-year residents: (a) For part-year residents, the EIC is first applied against the New York taxes computed under Sec. 601(a)-(d), Tax Law, after the application of the household credit and the child care credit. If the earned income credit is:

— less than the above amount, the remaining tax (the base tax) is multiplied by the income percentage to arrive at the New York tax before other credits and taxes,

— more than the above amount, proceed to paragraph (b).

(b) Any excess credit from paragraph (a) is applied against the New York separate tax on a lump-sum distribution (¶107) and the New York minimum income tax (¶502).

(c) Any excess remaining from paragraph (b) is multiplied by a fraction whose numerator is the taxpayer's federal adjusted gross income for the resident period, and whose denominator is the taxpayer's federal adjusted gross income for the entire tax year. The amount determined from this step will be refunded to the taxpayer, without interest.

Husband and wife: In the case of a husband and wife who file a joint federal return but are required to determine their New York taxes separately, the EIC may be applied against the tax of either spouse or divided between them as they may elect.

Noncustodial parents: For taxable years beginning after 2005 and before 2017, an enhanced EIC is available to any resident taxpayer, 18 or older, who meets all of the following requirements (Sec. 606(d-1), Tax Law):

— the taxpayer is the parent of a minor child or children with whom the taxpayer does not reside;

— the taxpayer has an order that has been in effect for at least one-half of the taxable year requiring him or her to make child support payments that are payable through a support collection unit; and

— the taxpayer has paid an amount in child support in the taxable year at least equal to the amount of current child support due during the taxable year for every order requiring him or her to make child support payments.

The credit is equal to the greater of the following: (1) 20% of the amount of the earned income tax credit that would have been allowed to the taxpayer under IRC Sec. 32 (absent the application of IRC Sec. 32(b)(2)(B)) if the child or children satisfied the requirements for a qualifying child under IRC Sec. 32(c)(3), provided that the credit must be calculated as if the taxpayer had only one child; or (2) the product of 2.5 multiplied by the amount of the earned income tax credit that would have been allowed to the taxpayer under IRC Sec. 32 if the taxpayer satisfied the eligibility requirements under IRC Sec. 32(c)(1)(A)(ii).

CCH Caution: Recordkeeping

The Division of Taxation properly disallowed a New York taxpayer's earned income credit after he failed to sustain his burden of proof in establishing receipt of earned income on his personal income tax return. The taxpayer, a self-employed, licensed taxi driver, kept no records or receipts of his income for the year at issue. He admitted to estimating his income. A failure to accurately prove earned income justified the denial of his claim for the earned income credit (*Sanchez*, New York Division of Tax Appeals, Small Claims, DTA No. 820220, September 15, 2005, CCH NEW YORK TAX REPORTS, ¶405-201).

¶127 Credits Against Tax—Film Production Credit

Law: Secs. 24, 31, 606(gg), Tax Law (CCH NEW YORK TAX REPORTS, ¶16-891).

For tax years beginning before 2020, a credit is available to qualified film production companies, or sole proprietors of qualified film production companies, for a portion of the qualified production costs of a qualified film. (Sec. 24, Tax Law; Sec. 606(gg), Tax Law) The credit is allowed for the taxable year in which the production of the qualified film is completed.

• *Definitions*

"Qualified production costs" means production costs only to the extent such costs are attributable to the use of tangible property or the performance of services within New York directly and predominately in the production (including pre-production and post-production) of a qualified film. (Sec. 24(b)(1), Tax Law)

"Production costs" means costs for tangible property used and services performed directly and predominately in the production (including pre-production and post-production) of a qualified film. Production costs generally include technical and crew production costs, such as expenditures for film production facilities, props, makeup, wardrobe, film processing, camera, sound recording, set construction, lighting, shooting, editing, and meals. (Sec. 24(b)(2), Tax Law)

Production costs do not include:

— costs for a story, script, or scenario to be used for a qualified film; and

— wages or salaries or other compensation for writers, directors, including music directors, producers, and performers (other than background actors with no scripted lines).

A "qualified film" is a feature-length film, television film, relocated television production, television pilot and/or each episode of a television series, regardless of the medium (Sec. 24(b)(3), Tax Law). A qualified film must have a minimum budget of $500,000 (Sec. 31(a)(5), Tax Law).

A qualified film does not include:

— a documentary film, news or current affairs program, interview or talk program, "how-to" (*i.e.*, instructional) film or program, film or program consisting primarily of stock footage, sporting event or sporting program, game show, award ceremony, film or program intended primarily for industrial, corporate or institutional end-users, fundraising film or program, daytime drama (*i.e.*, daytime soap opera), commercials, music videos or "reality programs"; or

— a production for which records are required to be maintained with respect to any performer in such production (reporting of books, films, etc. with respect to sexually explicit conduct).

A "qualified film production facility" is a film production facility in New York that contains at least one sound stage having a minimum of 7,000 square feet of contiguous production space. (Sec. 24(b)(5), Tax Law)

A "qualified film production company" is a corporation, partnership, limited partnership, or other entity or individual principally engaged in the production of a qualified film and in control of the qualified film during production. (Sec. 24(b)(6), Tax Law) Members of a partnership that is a qualified film production company may claim the credit.

• *Credit amount*

The amount of the credit is the product (or, in the case of a partnership, the partner's pro rata share of the product) of 30% (10%, for taxable years before 2008), and the qualified production costs paid or incurred in the production of a qualified film; provided that the qualified production costs (excluding post production costs) attributable to the use of tangible property or the performance of services at a qualified film production facility in the production of the qualified film equal or exceed 75% of the production costs (excluding post production costs) paid or incurred that are attributable to the use of tangible property or the performance of services at any film production facility within and without New York in the production of the qualified film. (Sec. 24(a)(2), Tax Law)

¶127

If the qualified production costs (excluding post production costs) attributable to the use of tangible property or the performance of services at a qualified film production facility in the production of the qualified film is less than $3 million, then the portion of the qualified productions costs attributable to the use of tangible property or the performance of services in the production of the qualified film outside of a qualified film production facility is allowed only if the shooting days spent in New York outside of a film production facility in the production of the qualified film equal or exceed 75% of the total shooting days spent within and without New York outside of a film production facility in the production of the qualified film. (Sec. 24(a)(2), Tax Law)

If the amount of the credit is between $1 million and $5 million, the credit is paid out in two equal installments over a two year period beginning in the taxable year in which the production of the qualified film is completed. If the credit is greater than $5 million, it is paid out in three equal installments in consecutive years beginning with the taxable year in which the production of the qualified film is completed.

Effective July 24, 2012, the qualified film and television post-production credit increased from 10% to 30% in the New York metropolitan commuter region, including New York City and Albany, Dutchess, Nassau, Orange, Putnam, Rockland, Schenectady, Suffolk and Westchester Counties (Sec. 31(a)(2), Tax Law). An additional 5% (for a total of 35%) in tax credits is available for post-production expenditures in locations elsewhere in the state (Sec. 31(c), Tax Law).

Upstate credit enhancement: In 2015 through 2019, film and post production projects are eligible for an additional credit equal to 10% of the wages or salaries of individuals employed by a qualified film or independent film production company for services performed in specified counties (Sec. 24(a)(5), Tax Law).

Maximum credit: The maximum amount of the credits allowed in any calendar year is $60 million.

• *Planning considerations*

If the amount of the credit allowable for any taxable year exceeds the taxpayer's tax for that year, the excess is treated as an overpayment of tax to be credited or refunded, with no interest (Sec. 606(gg), Tax Law).

An additional $420 million allocation is added annually over tax years 2010 through 2019, with $7 million of the annual allocation available for a separate post-production tax credit. Starting in 2015, the allocation dedicated to the post production credit increases from $7 million to $25 million annually.

New York City allows the credit against its personal income tax on residents, except that the percentage of qualified production costs used to calculate the credit is 5%. See ¶3009.

¶128 Credits Against Tax—Historic Barn Renovation

Law: Sec. 606(a)(12), Tax Law (CCH New York Tax Reports, ¶16-895).

Comparable Federal: Sec. 47 (U.S. Master Tax Guide ¶1347).

Forms: IT-212-ATT, Claim for Historic Barn Rehabilitation Credit and Employment Incentive Credit.

A credit is allowed in the amount of 25% of qualified rehabilitation expenditures paid or incurred in connection with the renovation of a qualified historic barn located within New York. (Sec. 606(a)(12), Tax Law) The term "barn" means a building originally designed and used for storing farm equipment or agricultural products, or for housing livestock.

Qualified rehabilitation expenses: To be eligible for the credit, expenditures must be qualified as the basis for the federal rehabilitation credit described in IRC Sec. 47. In general, under the federal provisions, a taxpayer may claim a credit equal to a specified percentage of its expenditures incurred to substantially rehabilitate a qualifying structure. The expenses must be properly chargeable to a capital account for property for which depreciation is allowable (*i.e.,* property used in a trade or business). The building that is being rehabilitated must have been placed in service prior to the commencement of the rehabilitation work, and it either must be a certified historic structure or have been first placed in service prior to 1936. A building will be considered to be substantially rehabilitated if the expenditures incurred during the 24-month period selected by the taxpayer and ending with or within the taxable year exceed the greater of the adjusted basis of the building or $5,000. Under certain circumstances, the rehabilitation work may extend over a number of taxable years ((TSB-M 97(1)I), CCH NEW YORK TAX REPORTS, ¶ 300-235).

A taxpayer may not claim both the regular investment tax credit on manufacturing property (¶ 924) and the investment tax credit for rehabilitation of historic barns on the same property. In addition, no credit will be allowed for any rehabilitation that (1) converts a qualified barn to a residential purpose, (2) immediately prior to the rehabilitation was used for residential purposes, or (3) materially alters the historic appearance of the barn.

CCH Advisory: Possible Property Tax Benefit

In addition to the income tax credit, the increase in assessed valuation of a rehabilitated historic barn may be exempt for property tax purposes. Local property tax authorities should be consulted (¶ 2504).

For tax years 2010, 2011, and 2012, taxpayers with more than $2 million in aggregated business tax credits were required to defer the amounts above $2 million until 2013. The total amount of credits deferred were paid back to taxpayers over tax years 2013, 2014, and 2015. (Secs. 33, 34, Tax Law; TSB-M-10(11)I, New York Department of Taxation and Finance, September 13, 2010, CCH NEW YORK TAX REPORTS, ¶ 406-976)

¶ 129 Credits Against Tax—Solar Energy System Equipment

Law: Sec. 606(g-1), Tax Law (CCH NEW YORK TAX REPORTS, ¶ 16-995).

Forms: IT-255, Solar Electric Generating Equipment Credit.

A solar energy credit is available against personal income tax in the tax year of installation for all residents who install devices that generate solar electric energy (Sec. 606(g-1), Tax Law). The credit includes equipment that uses solar radiation to provide heating, cooling, and/or hot water. Qualified expenditures include all material, labor, and architectural charges, but do not include interest or finance charges.

Effective August 17, 2012, the term "qualified solar energy system equipment expenditures" now includes the following:

    — the purchase of solar energy system equipment that is installed in connection with residential property that is (1) located in New York and (2) used by the taxpayer as his or her principal residence at the time the solar energy system equipment is placed in service;

    — the lease of solar energy system equipment under a written agreement that spans at least 10 years where such equipment owned by a person other than the taxpayer is installed in connection with residential property that is (1) located in New York and (2) used by the taxpayer as his or her principal residence at the time the solar energy system equipment is placed in service; or

— the purchase of power under a written agreement that spans at least 10 years where under the power purchased is generated by solar energy system equipment owned by a person other than the taxpayer that is installed in connection with residential property that is (1) located in New York and (2) used by the taxpayer as his or her principal residence at the time the solar energy system equipment is placed in service.

Credit amount: The credit is equal to 25% of qualified expenditures for solar electric generating equipment installed in the taxpayer's primary residence, provided that it is located in New York, with a maximum credit of $5,000.

Planning considerations: There is an expenditure cap for the credit equal to $6 multiplied by the number of watts included in the rated capacity of the equipment.

If equipment is installed in a principal residence shared by two or more taxpayers, the credit is prorated according to the percentage of expenditures contributed by each taxpayer.

When a condominium association or cooperative housing corporation buys a solar energy system, a taxpayer who is a member of the condominium management association or who is a tenant-stockholder in the cooperative housing corporation may claim a proportionate share of the total expense as the expenditure for the purposes of the credit attributable to his or her principal residence. Additionally, the solar energy system equipment requirement for condominium associations or cooperative housing corporation is set at 50 kilowatts.

Credit in excess of tax liability may be carried over for up to five years.

Caution: For tax years 2010, 2011, and 2012, taxpayers with more than $2 million in aggregated business tax credits were required to defer the amounts above $2 million until 2013. The total amount of credits deferred were paid back to taxpayers over tax years 2013, 2014, and 2015. (Secs. 33, 34, Tax Law; TSB-M-10(11)I, New York Department of Taxation and Finance, September 13, 2010, CCH NEW YORK TAX REPORTS, ¶ 406-976)

¶130 Credits Against Tax—Farmers' School Tax Credit

Law: Secs. 606(n), 606(n-1), Tax Law (CCH NEW YORK TAX REPORTS, ¶ 16-995).

Forms: IT-217, Claim for Farmers' School Tax Credit.

A credit for allowable school district property taxes is available if at least $2/3$ of the taxpayer's federal gross income in excess of $30,000 is from farming. In addition to traditional agricultural income, "federal gross income from farming" for purposes of the credit includes income from the production of maple syrup or cider, from a commercial horse boarding operation, from the sale of wine from a licensed farm winery, or from a managed Christmas tree operation. For tax years beginning after 2010, for otherwise-eligible farmers, payments from the New York farmland protection program will be included as federal gross income from farming. (Sec. 606(n)(2), Tax Law)

CCH Advisory: Income Averaging Allowed

For tax years beginning after 2003, a taxpayer may use the average of federal gross income from farming for the tax year and the income from farming for the two immediately preceding tax years for purposes of determining the taxpayer's eligibility to receive the agricultural property tax credit (Sec. 210.22, Tax Law; TSB-M-03(8)I, December 16, 2003, CCH NEW YORK TAX REPORTS, ¶ 300-410).

"Qualified agricultural property" means land located in New York that is used in agricultural production, plus land improvements, structures, and buildings (excluding buildings used for the taxpayer's residential purpose) that are located on the land

and that are used or occupied to carry out production. The term also includes land set aside or retired under a federal supply management or soil conservation program or land that is subject to a conservation easement. (Sec. 210(22)(d), Tax Law).

For tax years beginning after 1998, the credit was broadened to allow it to farmers who pay school district property taxes under a contract to buy agricultural land in the future. This allows a farmer who is the actual property taxpayer, but not yet the taxpayer of record, to claim the credit.

Unless the parties have agreed to an unequal division, qualified agricultural property owned by a taxpayer and related parties will be divided and alloted equally between them, and the taxpayer's base acreage will be limited to his or her alloted share.

Credit amount: The credit equals the total school property taxes paid on up to 350 acres of qualified agricultural property in New York, plus 50% of the school taxes paid on acreage in excess of 350 acres. Adjustments in the amount of the credit will be made if the taxpayer's New York adjusted gross income exceeds $200,000. (Sec. 606(n), Tax Law)

Limitation: If a taxpayer's New York adjusted gross income exceeds $200,000, allowable school property taxes are reduced by the percentage that (1) the lesser of $100,000 or the taxpayer's New York adjusted gross income over $200,000 (2) bears to $100,000. However, farmers may reduce their adjusted gross income by the amount of principal payments made on farm debts during the taxable year, thereby increasing the amount that may be earned before the credit is phased out. (Sec. 606(n), Tax Law)

Refund of excess credit: Unlike the agricultural property tax credit against Art. 9-A corporation franchise taxes (¶ 934), excess credit may not be carried forward and used in subsequent tax years. Instead, the taxpayer may claim a refund in the amount of any excess credit as an overpayment of tax (¶ 4004). No interest will be paid on any such refund.

Conversion of property to nonqualified use: No credit will be allowed for any taxable year in which qualified agricultural property is converted by a taxpayer to a nonqualified use. If property is converted to a nonqualified use within two years following the taxable year for which the credit was first claimed, credits allowed for the prior years must be recaptured and added back to the conversion year. If the property converted to a nonqualified use includes land, and the conversion is of only a portion of such land, the credit allowed with respect to converted property must be determined by multiplying the entire credit for the taxable years prior to the conversion year by a fraction, the numerator of which is the acreage converted and the denominator of which is the entire acreage of the land owned by the taxpayer immediately prior to the conversion. No recapture will be required if the conversion is involuntary within the meaning of IRC Sec. 1033. (Sec. 606(n), Tax Law)

The shareholders of an eligible C corporation may elect to take into account their pro rata shares of the corporation's income and principal payments on farm indebtedness. (Sec. 606(n)(9), Tax Law)

¶ 132 Credits Against Tax—Emerging Technology

Law: Secs. 606(q), 606(r), 606(nn), Tax Law; Sec. 3102-e, Public Authorities Law (CCH NEW YORK TAX REPORTS, ¶ 16-890).

Forms: DTF-621, Claim for QETC Employment Credit; Form DTF-622, Claim for QETC Capital Tax Credit.

The credits for employment and capital investment relating to qualified emerging technology companies are available to sole proprietors, partnerships, and limited liability companies under the personal income tax law. See ¶ 936 for additional discussion of the credits.

A "qualified emerging technology company" is a company located in New York that has total annual product sales of $10 million or less and that either (1) has its primary products or services that are classified as emerging technologies under the Public Authorities Law, or (2) has research and development activities in New York and a ratio of research and development funds to net sales that equals or exceeds the average ratio for companies surveyed by the National Science Foundation. It also includes re-manufacturing technologies, defined as processes whereby eligible commodities are restored to their original performance standards and diverted from the solid waste stream. (Sec. 3102-e, Public Authorities Law)

• *Credit for QETC facilities, operations, and training*

Eligible taxpayers may qualify for a refundable credit with three components relating to certain research and development (R&D) property, research expenses, and high-technology training expenditures. An eligible taxpayer (1) may have no more than 100 employees, at least 75% of which are employed in New York State, (2) must have a ratio of research and development funds to net sales at least equal to 6% during the taxable year, and (3) may have gross revenues of no more than $20 million for the taxable year prior to the year the credit is claimed. (Sec. 606(nn)(2), Tax Law)

Credit amount: The credit is the sum of the following amounts: (1) 18% of expenditures for R&D property used for testing, inspection, or quality control; (2) 9% of "qualified research expenses"; and (3) up to $4,000 per employee of "qualified high-technology training expenditures". (Sec. 606(nn)(3)-(5), Tax Law)

Planning considerations: An eligible taxpayer may generally claim the credits for four consecutive years, but one additional year is allowed for a taxpayer that is located in an academic incubator facility and relocates within New York to a nonacademic incubator site. The value of the credits may not exceed $250,000 per eligible taxpayer per year. (Sec. 606(nn)(6), Tax Law)

Applicable to taxable years beginning on or after January 1, 2010, if a taxpayer is a partner in a partnership or a shareholder of a New York S corporation, then the $2.5 million annual cap is applied at the entity level, so that the aggregate credit allowed to all of the partners or shareholders of each such entity in a taxable year will not exceed the cap amount (Sec. 28, Tax Law).

For tax years 2010, 2011, and 2012, taxpayers with more than $2 million in aggregated business tax credits were required to defer the amounts above $2 million until 2013. The total amount of credits deferred were paid back to taxpayers over tax years 2013, 2014, and 2015. (Secs. 33, 34, Tax Law; TSB-M-10(11)I, New York Department of Taxation and Finance, September 13, 2010, CCH NEW YORK TAX REPORTS, ¶ 406-976)

¶133 Credits Against Tax—Purchase of Automatic Defibrillator

Law: Sec. 606(s), Tax Law (CCH NEW YORK TAX REPORTS, ¶ 16-954).

Forms: IT-250, Claim for Credit for Purchase of an Automated External Defibrillator.

A credit against corporate franchise (income), personal income, and insurance franchise (income) taxes is available for the purchase of automated external defibrillators. (Sec. 606(s), Tax Law) The credit is equal to the cost of each defibrillator or $500, whichever is less. However, the credit may not reduce the tax below the minimum amount due.

For tax years 2010, 2011, and 2012, taxpayers with more than $2 million in aggregated business tax credits were required to defer the amounts above $2 million until 2013. The total amount of credits deferred were paid back to taxpayers over tax years 2013, 2014, and 2015. (Secs. 33, 34, Tax Law; TSB-M-10(11)I, New York Department of Taxation and Finance, September 13, 2010, CCH NEW YORK TAX REPORTS, ¶ 406-976)

¶134 Credits Against Tax—Credit for Disabled-Accessible Vehicles

Law: Sec. 606(tt), Tax Law (CCH New York Tax Reports, ¶16-953).

A company providing taxicab or livery service may claim a corporate franchise tax credit for (1) the incremental cost associated with upgrading a vehicle so that it is accessible by individuals with disabilities or (2) purchasing a new accessible vehicle (Sec. 606(tt), Tax Law; *TSB-M-12(1)I*, February 8, 2012, CCH New York Tax Reports, ¶407-471). To qualify for the credit, a vehicle must comply with federal regulations promulgated pursuant to the Americans with Disabilities Act applicable to vans under 22 feet in length, by the federal Department of Transportation, in Code of Federal Regulations, title 49, parts 37 and 38, and by the federal Architecture and Transportation Barriers Compliance Board, in Code of Federal Regulations, title 36, section 1192.23, and the Federal Motor Vehicle Safety Standards, Code of Federal Regulations, title 49, part 57.

Credit amount: The amount of the credit may not exceed $10,000 per vehicle (Sec. 606(tt), Tax Law).

Caution: For tax years 2010, 2011, and 2012, taxpayers with more than $2 million in aggregated tax credits for companies who provide transportation to individuals with disabilities are required to defer the amounts above $2 million until 2013. The total amount of credits deferred were paid back to taxpayers over tax years 2013, 2014, and 2015. (Sec 33.1 Tax Law; Sec 34.1 Tax Law)

Planning considerations: If the credit amount exceeds the taxpayer's tax for the taxable year, the excess may be carried forward and used in subsequent years (Sec. 606(tt), Tax Law).

The credit is applicable to tax years beginning on or after January 1, 2011, and is set to expire December 31, 2022.

¶135 Credits Against Tax—Excelsior Jobs Program

Law: Sec. 350 *et seq.,* Economic Development Law; Secs. 31, 187-q, and 606(qq), Tax Law; Reg. Secs. 190.1—196.6 (CCH New York Tax Reports, ¶16-876).

Forms: IT-607.

The Excelsior Jobs Program, administered by Empire State Development (ESD), provides job creation and investment incentives to firms in targeted industries, including biotechnology, pharmaceuticals, clean technology, green technology, financial services, agriculture and agricultural cooperatives, and manufacturing.

The 2015-16 budget law (Ch. 59 (A.B. 3009), Laws 2015) expands eligibility under the Excelsior Jobs Program to include certain business entities operating in music production or as an entertainment company. "Entertainment company" is defined to include entities principally engaged in the production or post-production of motion pictures, instructional videos, televised commercial advertisements, animated films or cartoons, music videos, television programs, or programs primarily intended for radio broadcast. Certain types of companies are specifically excluded (*e.g.,* those principally engaged in the live performance of events) (Sec. 352(7), Econ. Dev. Law). "Music production" means the process of creating sound recordings of at least eight minutes, recorded in professional sound studios, and intended for commercial release; the term does not include live concert recordings, recordings that are primarily spoken word or wildlife or nature sounds, or recordings produced for instructional use or advertising or promotional purposes. (Sec. 352(11), Econ. Dev. Law)

There are specific job requirements for each industry. The program includes the following corporate franchise, bank franchise, insurance franchise, and personal income tax credits (Part MM, Ch. 59 (A.B. 9709), Laws 2010):

— a jobs tax credit in the amount of 6.85% of gross wages for each net new job, effective March 31, 2011 (previously, up to $5,000 per job);

— an investment tax credit, equal to 2% of qualified investments;

— a 50% research and development credit, based on the federal credit, up to 3% of R&D expenditures (10%, with no cap, prior to March 31, 2011); and

— a real property tax credit.

Credits were first available for tax years beginning in 2011.

Under 2011-2012 budget legislation (Ch. 61 (S.B. 2811), Laws 2011, effective March 31, 2011), the tax benefit period of the jobs program is extended from five years to 10 years. The legislation made several other changes, as noted. See also *TSB-M-11(6)I*, New York Department of Taxation and Finance, June 8, 2011, CCH NEW YORK TAX REPORTS, ¶407-279.

Beginning in 2015, the definition of "net new jobs" is expanded to include jobs obtained by an entertainment company in New York (1) as a result of the termination of a licensing agreement with another entertainment company, (2) that are at risk of leaving the state as a direct result of the termination, (3) that are either full-time wage-paying jobs or equivalent to full-time wage-paying jobs requiring at least 35 hours per week, and (4) that are filled for more than six months. (Sec. 352(12)(b), Econ. Dev. Law)

The maximum aggregate credit components are reduced from $200 million to $183 million for 2016 through 2021, from $150 million to $133 million for 2022, from $100 million to $83 million for 2023, and from $50 million to $36 million for 2024 (Sec. 359. Econ. Dev. Law). The 2016-17 budget package provides that 100% of the unawarded amounts remaining at the end of 2024 can be allocated in subsequent years (Sec. 354(5). Econ. Dev. Law). However, no tax credits are allowed for taxable years beginning on or after January 1, 2027.

• *Credit amounts*

Jobs tax credit: The value of the jobs credit is determined on the basis of marginal wages plus benefits, as follows:

— $50,000 or less: 5%;

— $50,001 to $75,000: 4%

— Over $75,000: 1.33%, to a maximum of $5,000 per job.

Taxpayers generally must create at least 25 new jobs, but the threshold is reduced to ten jobs for businesses accepted into the START-UP NY program (see ¶114). In addition, a taxpayer that creates at least 75% of the estimated jobs will be allowed a proportionally reduced credit (Sec. 354(5), Econ. Dev. Law).

A business entity operating predominately in music production must create at least five net new jobs, and a business entity operating predominantly as an entertainment company must create or obtain at least 100 net new jobs (Sec. 353(3), Econ. Dev. Law).

Investment tax credit: The EJP-ITC is equal to 2% of the cost of qualified investments which are, generally, depreciable property located in New York with a useful life of four or more years. The property must be placed in service on or after the date the ESD issues the taxpayer a certificate of qualification.

Research and development credit: The EJP-R&D credit is equal to 10% of the amount of the taxpayer's federal R&D credit for qualified expenditures attributable to New York. Qualified expenditures are as set forth in IRC Sec. 41. A participant in the Excelsior Jobs Program may claim both the Excelsior investment tax credit component and the investment tax credit for research and development property, based on expenditures on the same property.

Real property tax credit: The EJP-RPTC credit equals 50% of the property taxes assessed and paid in the year immediately prior to the taxpayer's application to the ESD and declines by 5% each year for ten years. Effective March 31, 2011, property improvements that increase the value of real property are factored into the amount of the RPTC component. This credit is also refundable. It is available for projects in areas that are either (1) formerly designated as Investment Zones under the Empire Zones program, or (2) "regionally significant," as defined in Sec. 352(16), Econ. Dev. Law.

Effective March 31, 2011, the real property tax credit (RPTC) component schedule was amended to phase down from 50% to 5% over 10 years (5% each year) instead of five years (10% each year), reflecting the lengthening of the benefit period. Also, costs and expenses included in the basis of the Excelsior R&D credit component are allowed to be used for the qualified emerging technology company facilities, operations, and training credit.

CCH Advisory: Investment Credits

A participant in the Excelsior Jobs Program may claim both the Excelsior investment tax credit component and the investment tax credit for research and development property, based on expenditures on the same property (TSB-M-11(6)C, New York Department of Taxation and Finance, June 8, 2011, CCH NEW YORK TAX REPORTS, ¶407-280).

• *Planning considerations*

Taxpayers must apply to ESD, which can issue up to $50 million in new credit certificates annually against a total annual program cost of $250 million.

All four of the credits are refundable. (Part MM, Ch. 59 (A.B. 9709), Laws 2010)

¶136 Credits Against Tax—Long-Term Care Insurance

Law: Secs. 606(i-1), (aa), Tax Law (CCH NEW YORK TAX REPORTS, ¶16-920).

Form: CT-249, Claim for Long-Term Care Insurance Credit.

A credit is allowed for long-term care insurance premiums paid for a policy or for continuing coverage under a policy during the taxable year. (Sec. 606(i-1), Tax Law; Sec. 606(aa), Tax Law)

• *Credit amount*

The credit is equal to 20% of the premium payments during the taxable year (Sec. 606(aa), Tax Law).

• *Planning considerations*

Limitations and carryovers: For nonresidents and part-year residents, computation of the credit is limited to the percentage of the taxpayer's income derived from New York sources, applicable to taxable years beginning on or after January 1, 2005. (Sec. 606(aa)(2), Tax Law)

In order to qualify for the credit, the taxpayer's premium payment generally must be for a long-term care insurance policy approved by the Superintendent of Insurance. However, certain group contracts delivered or issued for delivery outside New York will be deemed to qualify for purposes of the credit without the need to seek the Superintendent's approval.

The credit may not reduce the tax below zero. However, any amount remaining may be carried forward indefinitely.

Practitioner Comment: Double Dipping Allowed

Both residents and nonresidents may be able to claim a New York State credit for long-term care premiums (using Form IT-249) even though the taxpayers may have already claimed an itemized deduction for the same premiums on their federal and state income tax returns.

Mark S. Klein, Esq., Hodgson Russ LLP

¶137 Credits Against Tax—Urban Youth Jobs Tax Credit (formerly, Youth Works Program)

Law: Sec. 606(tt), Tax Law (CCH NEW YORK TAX REPORTS, ¶16-925).

The New York Youth Works Tax Credit Program provides tax incentives to qualified businesses employing at-risk youths in full-time and part-time positions in 2012 through 2018. The program is administered by the Department of Labor. (Sec. 606(tt), Tax Law; TSB-M-12(3)I, CCH NEW YORK TAX REPORTS, ¶407-472) For further details, see the corporate franchise tax discussion at ¶953.

¶138 Credits Against Tax—Low-Income Housing

Law: Secs. 18, 606(x), Tax Law; Secs. 21(5), 22, Public Housing Law (CCH NEW YORK TAX REPORTS, ¶16-905).

Comparable Federal: Sec. 42 (U.S. MASTER TAX GUIDE ¶1334).

Forms: DTF-624, Low-Income Housing Credit; DTF-625, Low-Income Housing Credit Allocation Certification; DTF-625-ATT, Low-Income Housing Annual Statement.

A credit is allowed for the construction or rehabilitation of qualified low-income housing. (Sec. 18, Tax Law; Sec. 606(x), Tax Law)

Qualified housing: Generally, the credit is allowed for the construction of rent-restricted housing in New York that qualifies for the federal low-income housing credit. (Sec. 18, Tax Law)

CCH Advisory: Difference from Federal Credit

The federal credit (IRC Sec. 42) requires that a project be rent-restricted, and that either (1) at least 20% of the residential units of a project must be occupied by tenants whose income is 50% or less of area median gross income, or (2) at least 40% of the units must be occupied by tenants whose income is 60% of the area median. However, the New York credit may be claimed if the project either meets the federal requirements or if it is rent-restricted and at least 40% of the residential units are occupied by tenants whose income is 90% or less of area median gross income.

The credit may be passed on to successor owners of low-income buildings that already receive the credit.

• *Credit amount*

The amount of the credit is the applicable percentage of the qualified basis of each eligible low-income building. Eligible low-income housing buildings cannot receive in the aggregate more than a specified amount in credit. The cap amount is $64 million in 2016-17, and is being increased over a five-year period to $104 million. (Sec. 22, Public Housing Law) The Commissioner may set a limit on the amount of credit each low-income building may receive.

The credit amount allocated to a project will be allowed each year for 10 years. (Sec. 18, Tax Law; Sec. 606(x), Tax Law)

For tax years 2010, 2011, and 2012, taxpayers with more than $2 million in aggregated business tax credits were required to defer the amounts above $2 million until 2013. The total amount of credits deferred were paid back to taxpayers over tax years 2013, 2014, and 2015. (Secs. 33, 34, Tax Law; TSB-M-10(11)I, New York Department of Taxation and Finance, September 13, 2010, CCH NEW YORK TAX REPORTS, ¶406-976)

• *Planning considerations*

Limitations and carryovers: Limitations are generally the same as for claiming the federal credit.

The credit and any carryovers may not reduce the tax below zero. However, any amount remaining may be carried forward indefinitely.

Recapture: The project must continue to qualify as low-income housing for a 15-year period in order to avoid partial recapture of the credit. (Sec. 21(2), Public Housing Law)

¶139 Credits Against Tax—Green Buildings

Law: Secs. 19, 606(y), Tax Law (CCH NEW YORK TAX REPORTS, ¶16-889a).

Comparable Federal: Sec. 48 (U.S. MASTER TAX GUIDE ¶1351).

Forms: DTF-630, Claim for Green Building Credit.

A green building tax credit is available to enhance the supply of environmentally sound buildings in New York. (Sec. 19(a)(1), Tax Law) The credit includes six components, which are based on the capitalized costs (excluding land costs) of constructing green buildings, rehabilitating buildings to become green buildings, and purchasing and installing fuel cells, photovoltaic modules, and environmentally sensitive non-ozone depleting refrigerants.

The credit may be claimed over a five-year period by owners or tenants of eligible buildings, or by successor owners or tenants. In the year of a sale or termination of tenancy, the credit amount is allocated between the former and successor owners or tenants based upon the number of days during the year that the building was used by each.

Eligible buildings: A building or project must contain at least 20,000 square feet of interior space and must not require a federal or state construction permit because it is located on wetlands. (Sec. 19(b)(6), Tax Law) In addition, the building must be:

— classified b2, b3, b4, c1, c2, c5, or c6 for purposes of the New York State Uniform Fire Prevention and Building Code; or

— a residential multi-family building with at least 12 dwelling units; or

— one or more residential multi-family buildings with at least two dwelling units that are part of a single or phased construction project; or

— any combination of buildings described above.

Certifications: A taxpayer claiming the credit must obtain from the New York State Department of Environmental Conservation (DEC) an initial credit component certification, as well as an eligibility certification for each year in which the credit is claimed.

• *Credit amount*

The maximum amount of the credit for each component is specified in the initial credit component certification. The maximum amounts that may be claimed in each of the five years are as follows:

— *Green whole-building credit component:* 1.4% of allowable costs (1.6%, if the building is located in an economic development area), but not to exceed aggre gate costs of $150 per square foot for the base building and $75 per square foot for tenant space (Sec. 19(a)(2), Tax Law);

— *Green base building credit component:* 1% of allowable costs (1.2%, if the building is located in an economic development area), but not to exceed aggregate costs of $150 per square foot (Sec. 19(a)(3), Tax Law);

— *Green tenant space credit component:* 1% of allowable costs (1.2%, if the building is located in an economic development area), but not to exceed aggregate costs of $75 per square foot (Sec. 19(a)(4), Tax Law);

— *Fuel cell credit component:* 6% of allowable costs, but not to exceed aggregate costs of $1,000 per kilowatt (Sec. 19(a)(5), Tax Law);

— *Photovoltaic module credit component:* 20% of the incremental costs of a building-integrated module or 5% of the cost of a nonintegrated module, but not to exceed aggregate costs of $3 per watt (Sec. 19(a)(6), Tax Law);

— *Green refrigerant component:* 2% of the cost of air conditioning equipment using a non-ozone depleting refrigerant. (Sec. 19(a)(7), Tax Law)

• *Planning considerations*

The green building credit provisions are applicable to property that is placed in service, or that has received a final certificate of occupancy, in taxable years beginning after 2000. (Sec. 19(a), Tax Law)

Limitations and carryovers: Credit component certifications are limited to $25 million, and aggregate dollar limitations apply to each year through 2014.

The credit and any carryovers may not reduce the tax below zero. However, any amount remaining may be carried forward indefinitely. (Sec. 606(y)(2), Tax Law)

For tax years 2010, 2011, and 2012, taxpayers with more than $2 million in aggregated business tax credits were required to defer the amounts above $2 million until 2013. The total amount of credits deferred were paid back to taxpayers over tax years 2013, 2014, and 2015. (Secs. 33, 34, Tax Law; TSB-M-10(11)I, New York Department of Taxation and Finance, September 13, 2010, CCH NEW YORK TAX REPORTS, ¶ 406-976)

¶140 Credits Against Tax—College Tuition

Law: Sec. 606(t), Tax Law (CCH NEW YORK TAX REPORTS, ¶ 16-915).

Forms: IT-272, Claim for College Tuition Credit For New York State Residents.

A refundable credit for college tuition expenses is available for full-year resident taxpayers. (Sec. 606(t), Tax Law) Alternatively, for taxpayers who choose not to use this credit, a personal income tax itemized deduction can be used in its place (¶ 303).

• *Eligible expenses*

Expenses that qualify for the credit include tuition required for the enrollment or attendance of the taxpayer, the taxpayer's spouse, or a New York tax dependent of the taxpayer at an institution of higher education. Tuition paid by scholarships or financial aid is not eligible, and tuition for postgraduate study is also excluded.

Tuition for attendance at a business, trade, technical, or other occupational school is eligible if the institution is nationally accredited or recognized and approved by the Regents of the University of the State of New York, and if the institution provides a course of study leading to the granting of a post-secondary degree, certificate, or diploma. (Sec. 606(t), Tax Law)

Practitioner Comment: Double Dipping Allowed

A New York State college credit or deduction can be claimed for undergraduate tuition expenses for eligible students enrolled at an institution of higher learning. Qualified taxpayers are eligible for the credit or deduction even if the identical tuition expenses were deducted in computing the taxpayer's federal adjusted gross income (which, in turn, reduced New York AGI). (See *Publication 10-W* Q&A #13, CCH NEW YORK TAX REPORTS, ¶ 19-561)

Mark S. Klein, Esq., Hodgson Russ LLP

• *Credit amount*

The maximum amount of qualified college tuition expenses allowed in computing the credit or deduction is $10,000 per student, as follows (Sec. 606(t)(4), Tax Law):

— For expenses of $5,000 or more, the amount of credit is 4% of the allowable expenses; and

— For expenses of less than $5,000, the credit equals the lesser of $200 or the amount spent.

• *Planning considerations*

Refunds: If the amount of the credit exceeds the taxpayer's tax liability, the excess is refundable, without interest. (Sec. 606(t)(5), Tax Law)

Practitioner Comment: Coordinate Payments

Taxpayers wishing to maximize their use of New York's college incentive programs need to carefully coordinate their payments to institutions of higher learning. For example, parents of a college student should pay the student's undergraduate tuition expenses directly so that the payment qualifies for the college tuition credit/deduction. This credit is not available for payments of ancillary expenses or graduate school. Tax deductible payments for other college expenses (room, board, books, supplies, etc.), graduate school or for the education of nondependents are available using New York's family tuition account (see ¶203).

Mark S. Klein, Esq., Hodgson Russ LLP

¶141 Credits Against Tax—Fuel Cell Electric Generating Equipment (Expired)

Law: Sec. 606(g-2), Tax Law (CCH NEW YORK TAX REPORTS, ¶16-889b).

For taxable years beginning before 2009, a credit was allowed for a portion of the cost of qualified fuel cell electric generating equipment for use by the taxpayer in New York. (Sec. 606(g-2), Tax Law)

• *Credit amount*

The credit was equal to 20% of qualified expenditures, but could not exceed $1,500 per generating unit for any tax year. (Sec. 606(g-2), Tax Law)

• *Planning considerations*

Limitations and carryovers: Credits exceeding the tax due for a given year could be carried over for five tax years. (Sec. 606(g-2), Tax Law)

Multiple taxpayers: If multiple taxpayers could claim the credit, the credit was prorated according to the amount each taxpayer contributed to the expenditures.

¶142 Credits Against Tax—Historic Property and Historic Home Rehabilitation

Law: Sec. 606[oo], Tax Law (CCH NEW YORK TAX REPORTS, ¶16-896).

A refundable credit against the personal income tax is available for the rehabilitation of historic properties (Sec. 606[oo], Tax Law), and an historic home-ownership rehabilitation credit is also available (Sec. 606[pp], Tax Law).

• *Credit amounts*

Credit for rehabilitation of historic properties: The credit is equal to 100% (30%, for taxable years beginning before 2010 and after 2019) of the federal credit allowed for the same taxable year under IRC Sec. 47(c)(2) with respect to a certified historic structure that is located in a census tract that is at or below 100% of the median family income (Sec. 606[oo], Tax Law). The credit amount may not exceed $5 million.

Credit for historic home rehabilitation: The credit amount equals 20% of the qualified rehabilitation expenditures made by the taxpayer with respect to a qualified historic home (Sec. 606[pp](1), Tax Law). The credit may not exceed $50,000 ($25,000, for taxable years beginning before 2010) for a particular home, nor may it exceed that amount for more than one residence in a taxable year (Sec. 606[pp](2), Tax Law).

• *Planning Considerations*

State and local agency approval of expenditures is required for the historic home rehabilitation credit (Sec. 606[pp](1), Tax Law).

The credit for rehabilitation of historic properties is refundable for qualified rehabilitations placed in service on or after January 1, 2015; otherwise, unused credits may be carried over to following years without limitation.

The personal income tax credit for rehabilitation of an historic home is refundable if the credit exceeds the taxpayer's tax for the taxable year and the taxpayer's New York adjusted gross income is $60,000 or less; otherwise, any excess credit may be carried forward until exhausted (Sec. 606[pp](2)(b), Tax Law). For additional information, see *TSB-M-10(8)C, (14)I,* New York Department of Taxation and Finance, December 15, 2010, CCH NEW YORK TAX REPORTS, ¶ 407-076.

Recapture: If the federal credit is recaptured under IRC Sec. 47, New York will recapture an amount equal to 100% of the federal recapture amount (Sec. 606[oo](2), Tax Law). Recapture is required with respect to the historic home rehabilitation credit if the home is disposed of or if the taxpayer ceases to use the home as a residence within two years of purchase or final certification. (Sec. 606[pp](11), Tax Law)

The historic home rehabilitation credit may be allowed in the taxable year in which the final certification step of the certified rehabilitation is completed.

Caution: For tax years 2010, 2011, and 2012, taxpayers with more than $2 million in aggregated business tax credits are required to defer the amounts above $2 million until 2013. The total amount of credits deferred were paid back to taxpayers over tax years 2013, 2014, and 2015. (Secs. 33, 34, Tax Law; TSB-M-10(11)I, New York Department of Taxation and Finance, September 13, 2010, CCH NEW YORK TAX REPORTS, ¶ 406-976)

¶143 Credits Against Tax—Brownfield Cleanup Program Credits

Law: Secs. 21, 22, and 23, Tax Law; Sec. 606(dd), (ee), (ff), Tax Law (CCH NEW YORK TAX REPORTS, ¶ 16-915).

Three brownfield credits may be claimed by taxpayers that own or develop a qualified site for which a certificate of completion has been issued to the taxpayer by the Commissioner of Environmental Conservation. Any excess credit amounts will be credited or refunded. (Secs. 606(dd), (ee), (ff), Tax Law; TSB-M-08(13)C and TSB-M-08(8)I, December 23, 2008, CCH NEW YORK TAX REPORTS, ¶ 406-260)

For tax years 2010, 2011, and 2012, taxpayers with more than $2 million in aggregated business tax credits were required to defer the amounts above $2 million until 2013. The total amount of credits deferred were paid back to taxpayers over tax years 2013, 2014, and 2015. (Secs. 33, 34, Tax Law; TSB-M-10(11)I, New York Department of Taxation and Finance, September 13, 2010, CCH NEW YORK TAX REPORTS, ¶ 406-976)

The following changes became effective July 1, 2015:

— the definition of a "brownfield site" includes any real property where a contaminant is present at levels greater than the soil clean-up objectives or other health-based or environmental standards, criteria or guidance;

— amounts paid to related parties are excluded when calculating the tangible property credit component, but related-party service fees may be included in the calculation;

— the number of days to execute an environmental easement is changed from "within 60" to "within 180" days of commencement of the remedial design for owners of inactive hazardous waste disposal sites; and

— taxpayers wishing to claim tax credits under the program for any sites accepted on or before December 31, 2022, must have received the required certificate of completion on or before March 31, 2026.

• *Brownfield redevelopment credit*

The amount of the brownfield redevelopment tax credit equals the sum of the following three components: (1) site preparation; (2) tangible property; and (3) on-site groundwater remediation. (Sec. 21, Tax Law) The site preparation component equals the applicable percentage of the site preparation costs paid or incurred by the taxpayer with respect to a qualified site. The tangible property credit component equals the applicable percentage of the cost or other basis for federal income tax purposes of tangible personal property and other tangible property, including buildings and structural components of buildings, that constitute qualified tangible property. However, taxpayers must exclude the acquisition cost of any item of property with respect to which a credit was allowable to another taxpayer when determining the cost or other basis of such property. The on-site groundwater remediation component equals the applicable percentage of the on-site groundwater remediation costs paid or incurred by the taxpayer with respect to the qualified site.

In general, the applicable percentage is 10% for personal income tax and 12% for the other tax types. However, the applicable percentage is increased by 8% if at least 50% of the qualified site is located in an environmental zone and increased by 2% if the soil has been remediated to soil category 1. Qualified sites can only be deemed located in an environmental zone if they are the subject of a brownfield site cleanup agreement entered into before September 1, 2010 (Sec. 21(c), Tax Law).

The credit must be recaptured if the certificate of completion is revoked or the qualified property is disposed of or ceases to be in qualified use.

CCH Advisory: Allocation of Credit

A personal income tax advisory opinion discusses the allocation of a brownfield redevelopment tax credit among partners of a limited partnership when the costs incurred by the partnership are over multiple tax years and ownership interest in the partnership changes. A partner's distributive share of a credit is determined in accordance with the partner's interest in the partnership. The tangible property credit component of the brownfield credit is allowed for the tax year in which the qualified tangible property is placed in service on a qualified site after a certificate of completion has been issued. (TSB-A-06(8)I, November 30, 2006, CCH NEW YORK TAX REPORTS, ¶405-563)

Practitioner Comment: New York Respects Special Allocations of Brownfields Remediation Credit

New York's Department of Taxation and Finance has held that it will respect a special allocation of the tangible personal property component of the Brownfields redevelopment tax credit that is based on the special allocation of the depreciation deductions between the members of a limited liability company. Critical to this determination were the following facts: (1) the LLC was classified as a partnership; (2) all of the members of the LLC were individuals or trusts already subject to New York State personal income tax or corporations subject to the New York State corporation franchise tax; and (3) the special allocation had substantial economic effect under the federal rules. (TSB-A-09(4)I, 5/13/09, CCH NEW YORK TAX REPORTS, ¶406-401)

Mark S. Klein, Hodgson Russ LLP

¶143

• *Credit for remediated brownfields*

The remediated brownfield credit for real property taxes equals 25% of the product of the benefit period factor, the employment number factor, and the eligible real property taxes paid or incurred by the developer of the qualified site during the taxable year. (Sec. 22, Tax Law)

The employment number factor is determined by the average number of full-time employees at the qualified site. If the average number of employees is at least 25 but less than 50, the factor is 0.25; at least 50 but less than 75 employees, the factor is 0.5; at least 75 but less than 100 employees, the factor is 0.75; and at least 100 employees, the factor is 1. The credit is limited to the product of $10,000 and the developer's average number of full- time employees.

The credit must be recaptured if a developer's eligible real property taxes that are the basis for the credit are subsequently reduced. The recapture amount equals the amount of the credit originally allowed for a taxable year over the amount of credit determined based on the reduced eligible real property taxes.

• *Environmental remediation insurance credit*

The amount of the environmental remediation insurance credit equals the lesser of $30,000 or 50% of the environmental remediation insurance premiums paid on or after the date of the brownfield site agreement executed by the taxpayer and the Department of Environmental Conservation. (Sec. 23, Tax Law) If the remediation certificate issued to the taxpayer is revoked by a determination, the credit amount is added back in the taxable year in which the determination is final and no longer subject to judicial review.

¶144 Credits Against Tax—Security Training

Law: Secs. 26, 606(ii), Tax Law (CCH NEW YORK TAX REPORTS, ¶16-955).

Qualified building owners may claim a refundable security training tax credit. (Sec. 606(ii), Tax Law)

• *Qualifications*

Qualified security officers must have completed a qualified security training program. (Sec. 26, Tax Law) "Qualified building owner" means a building owner whose building entrances, exits, and common areas are protected by security personnel licensed under Article 7-A of the General Business Law, whether or not such personnel are employed directly by the building owner or indirectly through a contractor.

• *Credit amount*

The credit amount equals the sum of the number of qualified security officers providing protection to buildings owned by the taxpayer, multiplied by $3,000. (Sec. 26, Tax Law) Any credit amount not deductible in a taxable year will be treated as an overpayment of tax to be credited or refunded without interest.

• *Planning considerations*

The New York Office of Homeland Security may issue credit certifications for taxpayers meeting the applicable standards and demonstrating that they have provided (or will provide within the year) the appropriate training to all employees for whom the credit will be claimed. (Sec. 26, Tax Law)

The maximum aggregate amount of tax credits allowed in any calendar year will be $5 million. Any excess credit amounts will be credited or refunded. (Sec. 606(ii), Tax Law)

For tax years 2010, 2011, and 2012, taxpayers with more than $2 million in aggregated business tax credits were required to defer the amounts above $2 million until 2013. The total amount of credits deferred were paid back to taxpayers over tax years 2013, 2014, and 2015. (Secs. 33, 34, Tax Law; TSB-M-10(11)I, New York Department of Taxation and Finance, September 13, 2010, CCH NEW YORK TAX REPORTS, ¶ 406-976)

¶145 Credits Against Tax—Special Additional Mortgage Recording Tax

Law: Secs. 606(f)(3), Tax Law (CCH NEW YORK TAX REPORTS, ¶ 16-829).

A credit may be claimed in the amount of the special additional mortgage recording tax paid by the taxpayer or, in the case of a taxpayer who is a partner, the partner's pro rata share of the amount of the special additional mortgage recording tax paid by the partnership. (Sec. 606(f)(3), Tax Law)

• *Planning considerations*

The credit is not allowed with respect to mortgages recorded on property located in Erie County or in the Metropolitan Commuter Transportation District that is principally improved by one or more structures containing, in the aggregate, not more than six residential dwelling units, each dwelling unit having its own separate cooking facilities. (Sec. 606(f)(3), Tax Law)

Carryovers: The special additional mortgage recording tax credit not used in one taxable year may be carried forward to subsequent years until exhausted. Alternatively, the taxpayer may elect to treat the unused credit amount as an overpayment to be credited or refunded. (Sec. 606(f)(3)(b), Tax Law)

For tax years 2010, 2011, and 2012, taxpayers with more than $2 million in aggregated business tax credits were required to defer the amounts above $2 million until 2013. The total amount of credits deferred were paid back to taxpayers over tax years 2013, 2014, and 2015. (Secs. 33, 34, Tax Law; TSB-M-10(11)I, New York Department of Taxation and Finance, September 13, 2010, CCH NEW YORK TAX REPORTS, ¶ 406-976)

¶146 Credits Against Tax—Nursing Home Assessment Credit

Law: Secs. 606(hh), Tax Law (CCH NEW YORK TAX REPORTS, ¶ 16-921).

Forms: IT-258, Claim for Nursing Home Assessment Credit.

A credit is allowed with respect to a residential health care facility assessment (see ¶ 2715) that is imposed on the health care facility and passed through to the taxpayer. The credit is equal to the amount that is directly related to the assessment, separately stated and accounted for on the billing statement of a resident of a residential health care facility, and paid directly by the individual taxpayer. (Sec. 606(hh)(1), Tax Law)

• *Planning considerations*

If the credit amount exceeds the taxpayer's tax for the taxable year, the excess is credited or refunded to the taxpayer. (Sec. 606(hh)(2), Tax Law)

If an individual other than the resident of the home is actually paying the portion, then that individual, rather than the resident, is entitled to claim the credit. If two or more individuals are directly paying the total nursing home bill, the total portion of the assessment paid must be divided among them according to the percentage of the total nursing home expenses paid by each individual.

If a resident assigns his or her long-term insurance benefits to a nursing home, the resident is treated as having paid that amount towards the total nursing home bill. The credit cannot be claimed for any portion of the assessment paid directly to the nursing home by a health insurance policy, with public funds (e.g., Medicaid or Medicare), or by a trust or other entity.

¶145

If a nursing home does not separately state the portion of the assessment passed through to a resident on the resident's billing statements, the nursing home should provide a summary statement indicating the total portion of the assessment paid by or on behalf of the resident during the year. (*TSB-M-06(1)I*, Technical Services Bureau, Taxpayer Services Division, New York Department of Taxation and Finance, January 25, 2006, CCH NEW YORK TAX REPORTS, ¶ 300-498)

¶147 Credits Against Tax—Production of Commercials

Law: Sec. 28, Tax Law; Reg. Secs. 180.1—180.8 (CCH NEW YORK TAX REPORTS, ¶ 16-892).

A credit is available for qualified commercial production companies that incur qualified production costs to produce a qualified commercial in New York (Sec. 28, Tax Law). A "qualified commercial" is an advertisement that is recorded on film, audiotape, videotape, or digital medium in New York for multi-market distribution by way of radio, television networks, cable, satellite, or motion picture theaters.

"Production costs" are any costs for tangible property used and services performed directly and predominantly in the production (including pre-production and post-production) of a qualified commercial (Sec. 28(b)(2), Tax Law). Excluded are:

— costs for a story, script or scenario to be used for a qualified commercial; and

— wages or salaries or other compensation for writers, directors, including music directors, producers and performers (other than background actors with no scripted lines who are employed by a qualified company and musicians).

Production costs generally include technical and crew production costs, such as expenditures for commercial production facilities and/or location costs, film, audiotape, videotape or digital medium, props, makeup, wardrobe, commercial processing, camera, sound recording, scoring, set construction, lighting, shooting, editing, and meals.

• *Credit amount*

The amount of credit that may be claimed by a production company is a percentage of its qualified production costs, depending upon the total qualified production costs expended and, in some cases, the principal place of business of the production company. Each year, the first $1 million of the credit is available pro rata to all qualified production companies, and amounts to 20% of the excess of New York production costs over those of the average of the three previous years for which the credit was applied, up to $300,000 per taxpayer. Another $3 million of credit is available to production companies that film or record qualified commercials within the Metropolitan Commuter Transportation District, and amounts to 5% of the qualified production costs of at least $500,000 expended in New York during the taxable year. Another $1 million of credit is available to production companies that film or record qualified commercials outside the Metropolitan Commuter Transportation District, and amounts to 5% of the qualified production costs of at least $100,000 expended in New York during the taxable year. (Sec. 28(a)(2), Tax Law)

• *Planning considerations*

At least 75% of the qualified production costs must have been incurred in New York (Sec. 28(a)(1), Tax Law).

A production company's total qualified production costs must be greater in the aggregate during the current calendar year than the average of the three previous years for which the credit was applied. Until a qualified production company has established a three-year history, however, the credit will be based on either the previous year or the average of the two previous years, whichever is greater. (Sec. 28(a)(2)(i), Tax Law)

The credit provisions apply to taxable years beginning after 2006 and are set to expire on December 31, 2018.

For tax years 2010, 2011, and 2012, taxpayers with more than $2 million in aggregated business tax credits were required to defer the amounts above $2 million until 2013. The total amount of credits deferred were paid back to taxpayers over tax years 2013, 2014, and 2015. (Secs. 33, 34, Tax Law; TSB-M-10(11)I, New York Department of Taxation and Finance, September 13, 2010, CCH NEW YORK TAX REPORTS, ¶ 406-976)

¶148 Credits Against Tax—Alternative Fuel Vehicle Refueling and Electric Vehicle Recharging Property Credit

Law: Secs. 187-b, 210(24), Tax Law (CCH NEW YORK TAX REPORTS, ¶ 16-885).

A personal income tax credit is available for investment in alternative fuel refueling and electric vehicle recharging property. For details, see the corporate franchise tax discussion at ¶ 935.

¶149 Credits Against Tax—Alcoholic Beverage Production

Law: Sec. 37, Tax Law; Sec. 606(i), Tax Law (CCH NEW YORK TAX REPORTS, ¶ 16-956).

For taxable years beginning on or after January 1, 2016, the beer production credit is renamed the alcoholic beverage production credit and expanded to include cider, wine, and liquor (Sec. 37, Tax Law).

Corporate franchise and personal income tax credits are available for New York's craft breweries and, beginning in 2016, producers of cider, wine, and liquor. The law also exempts small breweries from paying the annual beer label registration fee, creates a farm brewery license to promote the use of local ingredients, and exempts farm breweries, wineries, and distilleries from certain tax filing requirements. To qualify for the credit, an eligible beer producer must produce no more than 60 million gallons of beer in New York in the taxable year (Sec. 37(a), Tax Law).

Credit amount: For tax years beginning on or after January 1, 2012, the credit is 14 cents per gallon for the first 500,000 gallons and 4.5 cents for additional gallons up to 15 million additional gallons for beer, cider, or wine and up to 300,000 additional gallons for liquor produced in New York in the same tax year. (Sec. 37(b), Tax Law). For additional guidance, see *TSB-M-12(8)C*, August 21, 2012, CCH NEW YORK TAX REPORTS, ¶ 407-626, *TSB-M-16(5)C,(3)I*, August 1, 2016, CCH NEW YORK TAX REPORTS, ¶ 408-824, and *TSB-M-16(6)C, (4)I. (5)M, (7)S*, August 1, 2016, CCH NEW YORK TAX REPORTS, ¶ 408-823.

Special rules exist for partners and S corporation shareholders. If a taxpayer is a partner in a partnership or a shareholder of a New York S corporation, the maximum credit amount will be applied at the entity level of the partnership or New York S corporation. Accordingly, the aggregate credit amount allowed to all partners or shareholders of a partnership or New York S corporation cannot exceed $745,000 for a tax year. (*TSB-M-12(8)C*, (7)I, August 21, 2012, CCH NEW YORK TAX REPORTS, ¶ 407-626)

Planning considerations: Personal income taxpayers must file Form IT-636, Alcoholic Beverage Production Credit, with their tax returns.

There is no limitation on the credit for personal income taxpayers, and the credit may reduce the tax to zero. If the credit allowed exceeds the tax, the excess may be treated as an overpayment of tax to be credited or refunded. However, no interest will be paid on the refund.

The beer production credit is not subject to the temporary deferral of certain tax credits under sections 33 and 34 of the Tax Law.

¶150 Credits Against Tax—Clean Heating Fuel

Law: Sec. 606(mm), Tax Law (CCH New York Tax Reports, ¶16-888).

A credit is allowed for bioheat that is used for space heating or hot water production for residential purposes within New York and that is purchased on or after July 1, 2006, and before January 1, 2020. "Bioheat" is a combination of biodiesel and conventional heating oil (Sec. 606(mm), Tax Law).

Beginning January 1, 2017, the credit does not apply to bioheat that is less than 6% biodiesel per gallon of bioheat.

Credit amount: The credit amount equals 1¢ per gallon for each percent of biodiesel included in the bioheat, not to exceed 20¢ per gallon, purchased by the taxpayer (Sec. 606(mm), Tax Law).

For additional information, see TSB-M-08(1)I, May 29, 2008, CCH New York Tax Reports, ¶406-068.

For tax years 2010, 2011, and 2012, taxpayers with more than $2 million in aggregated business tax credits were required to defer the amounts above $2 million until 2013. The total amount of credits deferred were paid back to taxpayers over tax years 2013, 2014, and 2015. (Secs. 33, 34, Tax Law; TSB-M-10(11)I, New York Department of Taxation and Finance, September 13, 2010, CCH New York Tax Reports, ¶406-976)

¶151 Credits Against Tax—Volunteer Firefighters and Ambulance Workers

Law: Sec. 606(e-1), Tax Law (CCH New York Tax Reports, ¶16-900).

A $200 personal income tax credit is available to qualifying volunteer firefighters and ambulance workers. In the case of a husband and wife who file a joint return and who both individually qualify, the credit amount is $400 (Sec. 606(e-1), Tax Law). To qualify for the credit, a person must have actively served as a volunteer firefighter or ambulance worker for the entire taxable year.

CCH Caution: Property Tax Exemption

A volunteer firefighter or ambulance worker who claims a property tax exemption for a portion of his or her primary residence based on such volunteer service (see ¶2504) may not also claim this credit (Sec. 606(e-1), Tax Law).

¶152 Credits Against Tax—Conservation Easement Property Taxes

Law: Sec. 606(kk), Tax Law (CCH New York Tax Reports, ¶16-900).

A credit is available in the amount of 25% of the school district, county, and city real property taxes paid on land that is under a conservation easement. The credit amount claimed by a taxpayer may not exceed $5,000 in any given year. (Sec. 606(kk), Tax Law)

For tax years 2010, 2011, and 2012, taxpayers with more than $2 million in aggregated business tax credits were required to defer the amounts above $2 million until 2013. The total amount of credits deferred were paid back to taxpayers over tax years 2013, 2014, and 2015. (Secs. 33, 34, Tax Law; TSB-M-10(11)I, New York Department of Taxation and Finance, September 13, 2010, CCH New York Tax Reports, ¶406-976)

¶153 Credits Against Tax—Child Credit

Law: Sec. 606(c-1), Tax Law (CCH New York Tax Reports, ¶16-912).

A refundable credit based on the federal child tax credit is provided to resident taxpayers with children from ages 4 through 16 (Sec. 606(c-1), Tax Law).

Credit amount: The credit is generally equal to the greater of $100 times the number of qualifying children or 33% of the child tax credit allowed under IRC Sec. 24 for the same taxable year for each qualifying child. However, in the case of a taxpayer whose federal adjusted gross income exceeds the applicable threshold amount set forth by IRC Sec. 24(b)(2), the credit will only be equal to 33% of the child tax credit allowed under IRC Sec. 24 for each qualifying child (Sec. 606(c-1)(1), Tax Law).

Planning considerations: In the case of a husband and wife who file a joint federal return but are required to determine their New York taxes separately, the credit may be applied against the tax imposed on either, or divided between them as they may elect (Sec. 606(c-1)(3), Tax Law).

¶154 Credits Against Tax—Biofuel Production

Law: Secs. 28, 606(jj), Tax Law (CCH New York Tax Reports, ¶16-887).

A biofuel production credit is available for taxable years beginning after 2005 and before 2020. "Biofuel" means a fuel that includes biodiesel and ethanol in accordance with standards approved by the New York state energy and research development authority (Sec. 28, Tax Law).

Credit amount: The credit equals 15¢ for each gallon of biofuel produced at a biofuel plant, after the production of the first 40,000 gallons per year presented to market. The credit is capped at $2.5 million per taxpayer per taxable year for up to four consecutive taxable years per biofuel plant. (Sec. 28, Tax Law; Sec. 606(jj), Tax Law)

For tax years 2010, 2011, and 2012, taxpayers with more than $2 million in aggregated business tax credits were required to defer the amounts above $2 million until 2013. The total amount of credits deferred were paid back to taxpayers over tax years 2013, 2014, and 2015. (Secs. 33, 34, Tax Law; TSB-M-10(11)I, New York Department of Taxation and Finance, September 13, 2010, CCH New York Tax Reports, ¶406-976)

Planning considerations: A taxpayer wishing to claim a credit under this section must annually certify the amount of biofuel produced at the eligible biofuel plant during a taxable year, and that the biofuel produced meets all existing standards for biofuel (Sec. 28(c), Tax Law).

Applicable to taxable years beginning on or after January 1, 2010, if a taxpayer is a partner in a partnership or a shareholder of a New York S corporation, then the $2.5 million annual cap is applied at the entity level, so that the aggregate credit allowed to all of the partners or shareholders of each such entity in a taxable year will not exceed the cap amount (Sec. 28, Tax Law).

¶155 Credits Against Tax—Economic Transformation and Facility Redevelopment Program

Law: Sec. 400 *et seq.*, Economic Development Law; Sec. 35, Tax Law (CCH New York Tax Reports, ¶16-876a).

The Economic Transformation and Facility Redevelopment Program provides a fully refundable credit available to personal income taxpayers, agricultural cooperatives, general business corporations, banks, and insurance companies and consisting of four components (Sec. 35, Tax Law):

— Jobs tax credit component: 6.85% of the gross wages of each net new job created;

— Investment tax credit (ITC) component: 10% of the cost of investments at a closed facility, with a facility-based cap of $8 million; 6% of the cost of investments elsewhere in an ETA, with a cap of $4 million per entity (if the participant is a partnership, a limited liability company, or an S corporation, the $4 million limitation is applied at the entity level);

— Job training credit component: 50% of training expenses for employees displaced by a facility closure, up to $4,000 per employee per year (the employees for whom the expenditures are made must be employed in a full-time, full-year position primarily located at the site in the economic transformation area during the training, and for 180 days after its completion); and

— Real property tax credit component (RPTC): 50% of real property taxes for projects located entirely within the grounds of a closed facility, declining by 10% a year; 25% of real property taxes for projects elsewhere in an ETA, declining by 5% a year.

To be eligible for the economic transformation and facility redevelopment program tax credit, the taxpayer must meet all the following requirements (Sec. 35, Tax Law):

— The taxpayer must be a participant or the owner of a participant in the economic transformation and facility development program. The commissioner of economic development must have issued a certificate of to the taxpayer or to an entity in which the taxpayer is an owner. A copy of the certificate is required to be attached to the taxpayer's report or return.

— The taxpayer or the entity in which the taxpayer is an owner must be a qualified new business.

— The taxpayer or the entity in which the taxpayer is an owner must create and maintain at least five net new jobs in the economic transformation area.

Planning considerations: The benefit period for the tax credits is five consecutive taxable years, beginning with the first taxable year in which the five net new jobs are created. However, in no event may that benefit period start later than two years after the certificate of eligibility is issued. If, in any year of the benefit period, the taxpayer fails to maintain the required level of five net new jobs (measured quarterly), the taxpayer will not be allowed a credit for that year. Such failure to be allowed a credit will not extend the taxpayer's benefit period. (Sec. 35, Tax Law)

If the participant at the end of its benefit period has not created sufficient net new jobs and made sufficient qualified investments to achieve a benefit-cost ratio of at least 10 to one, the taxpayer will be required to add back as tax in the last year of its benefit period the portion of the economic transformation and facility redevelopment tax credits claimed in the years of its benefit period necessary to achieve a cost benefit ratio of 10 to one. (Sec. 35, Tax Law)

The program is scheduled to expire on December 31, 2021.

The program is administered by Empire State Development (ESD). Application materials are available at **http://esd.ny.gov/index.html**.

¶156 Credits Against Tax—Empire State Jobs Retention Program

Law: Sec. 606(tt), Tax Law; Sec. 36, Tax Law (CCH NEW YORK TAX REPORTS, ¶16-876b).

The Empire State Jobs Retention Program has been established to create financial incentives to retain strategic businesses and jobs that are at risk of leaving the state due to the impact on business operations of an event (such as a natural disaster) leading to an emergency declaration by the governor. The program offers qualifying businesses a tax credit based on a percentage of the gross wages paid for retained jobs that otherwise would have been impacted by the event. (Sec. 36, Tax Law; Sec. 606(tt), Tax Law; TSB-M-12(3)I, CCH New York Tax Reports, ¶ 407-472)

For further details, see the corporate franchise tax discussion at ¶ 954.

¶157 Credits Against Tax—Minimum Wage Reimbursement Credit

Law: Secs. 38, 606(aaa), Tax Law (CCH New York Tax Reports, ¶ 16-876d).

A personal income tax credit is available for employers that hire employees at the minimum wage rate (Sec. 606(aaa), Tax Law). An eligible employer is defined as a corporation (including a New York S corporation), a sole proprietorship, a limited liability company or a partnership (Sec. 38(b), Tax Law).

For further details, see the corporate franchise tax discussion at ¶ 956.

¶158 Credits Against Tax—Hire a Veteran Credit

Law: Sec. 606(a-2), Tax Law (CCH New York Tax Reports, ¶ 16-876c).

A personal income tax credit is available for employers that hire qualified veterans (Sec. 606(a-2), Tax Law). For further details, see the corporate franchise tax discussion at ¶ 957.

¶159 Credits Against Tax—Family Tax Relief Credit

Law: Sec. 606(vv), Tax Law (CCH New York Tax Reports, ¶ 16-912a).

Applicable to tax years 2014 through 2016, a family tax relief credit is allowed for eligible taxpayers (Sec. 606(vv), Tax Law). To be eligible for the credit, the taxpayer (or taxpayers filing joint returns) on the personal income tax return filed for the taxable year two years prior, must have:

— been a New York resident;

— claimed at least one dependent child who was under the age of 17 on the last day of the taxable year;

— had New York adjusted gross income of at least $40,000 but no greater than $300,000; and

— had a tax liability of greater than or equal to zero.

Credit amount: The credit is equal to $350 for each year that the taxpayer meets the eligibility requirements above (Sec. 606(vv)(4), Tax Law).

Planning considerations: If the amount of the family tax relief credit allowed exceeds the taxpayer's tax for the taxable year, the excess will be treated as an overpayment of tax to be credited or refunded accordingly.

Advance payment of the credit by the Department of Taxation and Finance (former Sec. 606(VV)(4), Tax Law) is no longer available after 2014.

¶160 Credits Against Tax—Musical and Theatrical Production Credit

Law: Sec. 24-a, Tax Law; Reg. Sec. 240.1 *et seq.* (CCH New York Tax Reports, ¶ 12-136).

Effective for tax years beginning on or after January 1, 2015 and expiring on January 1, 2019, a credit is available against the New York corporate franchise tax and personal income tax for 25% of the qualified production expenditures and transportation costs incurred by eligible production companies to produce a live, dramatic stage presentation in a qualified production facility on a tour that consists of eight or more shows in three or more localities (Sec. 24-a, Tax Law; Reg. Sec. 240.1 *et seq.*). For further details, see the corporate franchise tax discussion at ¶ 959.

¶157

¶161 Credits Against Tax—Employee Training Incentive Credit

Law: Sec. 606(ddd), Tax Law; Sec. 441, Economic Development Law (CCH NEW YORK TAX REPORTS, ¶16-880).

For taxable years beginning on or after January 1, 2015, a refundable tax credit is available for eligible training costs incurred on or after April 13, 2015, by employers that procure eligible training for their employees (Sec. 606(ddd), Tax Law). The credit equals 50% of a taxpayer's eligible training costs, up to a credit of $10,000 per employee completing eligible training, and 50% of the stipend paid to an intern, up to a credit of $3,000 per intern completing eligible training. For further details, see the corporate franchise tax discussion at ¶960.

¶162 Credits Against Tax—Property Tax Relief Credit

Law: Sec. 606(n-1), Tax Law; Sec. 425(16), Real Property Tax Law (CCH NEW YORK TAX REPORTS, ¶16-829a).

A property tax relief credit against the personal income tax is available for tax years 2016 through 2019. The credit may be claimed by resident homeowners who have income not exceeding $275,000 and who live in school districts that comply with the property tax cap. (Sec. 606(n-1), Tax Law)

To be eligible for the credit, a taxpayer must:

— own and primarily reside in real property receiving the STAR exemption authorized by Sec. 425, Real Property Tax Law, or the school tax relief (STAR) credit authorized by Sec. 606(eee), Tax Law;

— be a resident of New York State; and

— have qualified gross income no greater than $275,000.

However, a credit will not be allowed if the taxpayer's property is located:

— in an independent school district that has adopted a budget in excess of the applicable tax levy limit,

— in a city with a dependent school district that has adopted a budget in excess of the applicable tax levy limit, or

— in New York City (but see below).

Transitional provisions: Beginning with the 2016-2017 school district assessment rolls, the STAR exemption is closed to new applicants and a new refundable personal income tax credit is available instead. Current recipients of STAR exemptions are permitted to keep the exemptions as long as they continue to own their homes, but upon transfer of the property to a new owner, the new owner would only be eligible for the income tax credit program. Current STAR exemption recipients have the option of giving up their STAR exemptions in favor of the personal income tax credit, though it is not required.

If the owners of a parcel that is receiving the STAR exemption want to claim the personal income tax credit in lieu of such exemption, they all must renounce that exemption in the manner provided by Sec. 496, Real Property Tax Law, and must pay any required taxes, interest and penalties, on or before December 31 of the taxable year for which they want to claim the credit. Any such renunciation is irrevocable. (Sec. 425(16), Real Property Tax Law)

Each year the credit is allowed, the commissioner will identify taxpayers who meet the income eligibility requirements for the property tax relief credit using information from personal income tax returns on file for the two years prior (2014, 2015, 2016, and 2017, respectively). The Tax Department will compute the property tax relief credit amount and mail checks to eligible taxpayers.

Credit amount: For tax year 2016, if an eligible taxpayer resides within the metropolitan commuter transportation district (MCTD) and outside New York City, the amount of the credit is $130. If an eligible taxpayer resides outside the MCTD, the amount of the credit is $185. (Sec. 606(n-1)(3)(A), Tax Law)

For tax years 2017, 2018, and 2019, if an eligible taxpayer owns and primarily resides in real property receiving the basic STAR exemption or the basic STAR credit, the amount of the property tax relief credit equals the STAR tax savings multiplied by a percentage as shown in the tables below (Sec. 606(n-1)(3)(b), Tax Law; *TSB-M-16(1)I*, June 3, 2016, CCH New York Tax Reports, ¶ 408-753):

- *Tax Year 2017*

Qualified gross income in 2017

If gross income is:	The percentage is:
Not over $75,000	28%
Over $75,000 but not over $150,000	20.5%
Over $150,000 but not over $200,000	13%
Over $200,000 but not over $275,000	5.5%
Over $275,000	no credit

- *Tax Year 2018*

Qualified gross income in 2018

If gross income is:	The percentage is:
Not over $75,000	60%
Over $75,000 but not over $150,000	42.5%
Over $150,000 but not over $200,000	25%
Over $200,000 but not over $275,000	7.5%
Over $275,000	no credit

- *Tax Year 2019*

Qualified gross income in 2019

If gross income is:	The percentage is:
Not over $75,000	85%
Over $75,000 but not over $150,000	60%
Over $150,000 but not over $200,000	35%
Over $200,000 but not over $275,000	10%
Over $275,000	no credit

- *Tax Years 2017-2019*

If an eligible taxpayer owns and primarily resides in real property receiving the *enhanced* STAR exemption or the *enhanced* STAR credit, the amount of the property tax relief credit equals the STAR tax savings multiplied by a percentage as shown in the table below (Sec. 606(n-1)(3)(c), Tax Law):

Tax Year	Percentage
2017	12%
2018	26%
2019	34%

Only one credit per residence is allowed per tax year. In addition, the amount of the credit may not exceed the school district taxes due for the residence for that tax year.

A full credit is allowed to owners of cooperative apartments and a minimum credit amount is provided in the case of mobile homes (*i.e.*, no less than the credit that would be allowed for property with a $20,000 assessed value). (Sec. 606(e-1)(1)(D), Tax Law; Sec. 606(ggg)(6)(B), Tax Law)

Registration: Homeowners who register by July 1 will receive a STAR check in September, which will be worth the same amount as the exemption. Those who register after July 1 will receive a check later. Homeowners may register for STAR on the Tax Department's website at **https://www.tax.ny.gov/pit/property/star/register-for-star-credit.htm**. Telephone registration is also available at (518) 457-2036 from 8:30 a.m. to 4:30 p.m.

Planning considerations: A taxpayer is not eligible for this credit if the school district taxes levied upon the residence during the tax year remain unpaid 60 days after the last date they could have been paid without interest. In the case of a school district where the taxes are paid in installments, a taxpayer is not eligible for the credit if the taxes remain unpaid 60 days after the date the last installment could have been paid without interest. Accordingly, if a taxpayer receives the property tax relief credit for a tax year, and the taxes that were levied in that same year remain unpaid on the 60th day after the last date they could have been paid without interest, the amount of property tax relief credit received by the taxpayer must be added back as tax on the taxpayer's personal income tax return for the tax year in which the sixtieth day occurs. (Sec. 606(n-1), Tax Law)

In the case of a taxpayer whose federal itemized deductions include an amount for real estate taxes paid, the New York itemized deduction otherwise allowable must be reduced by the amount of the property tax relief credit (Sec. 606(eee)(12), Tax Law).

New York City: For taxable years beginning after 2015, a school tax reduction credit against state personal income tax is available to New York City residents (Sec. 606(ggg), Tax Law). A credit may not be claimed by a taxpayer with federal adjusted gross income (with certain exclusions) of more than $250,000.

For married individuals filing jointly and surviving spouses, the credit is equal to $125. For an unmarried individual, a head of a household or a married individual filing a separate return, the credit is $62.50. (Sec. 606(ggg)(2), Tax Law)

¶163 Credits Against Tax—Farm Workforce Retention Credit

Law: Secs. 42, 210-B(1), Tax Law; Sec. 606(i)(1)(B), Tax Law (CCH New York Tax Reports, ¶16-876e).

For taxable years beginning on or after 2016 and before 2022, a taxpayer that is a farm employer or an owner of a farm employer may claim a new farm workforce retention credit available against the corporate franchise and personal income taxes (Sec. 42, Tax Law; Sec. 606(eee), Tax Law; *TSB-M-16(7)C, (5)I,* New York Department of Taxation and Finance, September 23, 2016, CCH New York Tax Reports, ¶408-856).

A "farm employer" is a New York S corporation, a sole proprietorship, a limited liability company or a partnership that is also an eligible farmer (Sec. 42(b), Tax Law).

An "eligible farmer" is a taxpayer whose federal gross income from farming (including payments from New York's farmland protection program) for the taxable year is at least $2/3$ of the taxpayer's "excess federal gross income," which is the amount of federal gross income from all sources that exceeds $30,000 for the taxable year (Sec. 42(c), Tax Law).

An "eligible farm employee" is an individual who is employed for at least 500 hours per taxable year by a farm employer in New York (Sec. 42(d), Tax Law).

Credit amount: The credit amount is determined by multiplying the total number of eligible farm employees by a dollar amount for each taxable year, as follows (Sec. 42(e), Tax Law):

> 2017—$250;
> 2018—$300;
> 2019—$500;
> 2020—$400;
> 2021—$600;

Planning considerations: The amount of this credit generally may not reduce the taxpayers tax below the amount of the fixed dollar minimum tax (Sec. 210-B(1), Tax Law; Sec. 606(i)(1)(B), Tax Law).

If a farm employee is unable to work due to a documented illness or disability, the hours the individual worked may be combined with the hours worked by a replacement for the worker when determining whether or not the 500 hour threshold has been met for a taxable year (Sec. 42(d), Tax Law).

PERSONAL INCOME TAX

CHAPTER 2
GROSS INCOME

¶201 "Gross Income" Defined

Comparable Federal: Sec. 61 (U.S. MASTER TAX GUIDE, ¶61, 1401).

There is no definition of "gross income" for New York personal income tax purposes. Since federal adjusted gross income is adopted as a starting point by New York with certain modifications (see ¶202 and 203), the items of federal gross income are generally also adopted.

¶202 New York Adjusted Gross Income—Residents

Law: Sec. 612, Tax Law (CCH NEW YORK TAX REPORTS, ¶15-105, 15-505, 16-335).

Comparable Federal: Sec. 62 (U.S. MASTER TAX GUIDE, ¶61, 1401).

New York adjusted gross income of a resident individual is the resident's federal adjusted gross income for the taxable year with certain modifications. (Sec. 612(a), Tax Law) The modifications are discussed at ¶203 and following.

By the adoption of federal adjusted gross income as the starting point for the determination of New York taxable income (¶203), New York in effect adopts the federal treatment of items of income.

Net operating losses: Taxpayers are required to use the same carryback period for New York State income tax purposes as used for federal purposes.

For any carryback or carryforward year where the amount of NOL deduction allowed for New York purposes is limited, the difference between the NOL deduction allowed on the federal income tax return and the NOL deduction allowed for New York state income tax purposes must be accounted for. Beginning with New York state income tax returns for tax years 2013 and after, the difference must be accounted for by using a New York addition modification to federal adjusted gross income (individuals) or federal taxable income (estates and trusts). For additional information, see *Publication 145, Net Operating Losses (NOLs) for New York State Resident Individuals, Estates, and Trusts,* CCH NEW YORK TAX REPORTS, ¶19-625.

• *Victims of terrorism*

Under the New York September 11th Victims and Families Relief Act (S.B. 7356, Laws 2002), no New York state or local taxation, including personal income and estate taxes, may be imposed on any payment from the federal September 11th Victim Compensation Fund.

IRC Sec. 139, as added by the federal Victims of Terrorism Relief Act of 2001 (P.L. 107-134), exempts from federal taxation any federal, state, or local government payments made in connection with a qualified disaster, including those resulting from terrorist attacks or military action. Consequently, no modification of federal adjusted gross income is necessary for New York personal income tax purposes with respect to payments from the federal September 11th fund.

• *Husband and wife*

If a husband and wife file a joint federal income tax return but are required to determine their New York income separately, they must compute their New York adjusted gross incomes as if their federal adjusted gross incomes had been computed separately. (Sec. 612(f), Tax Law)

Practitioner Comment: Installment Sales

A taxpayer who terminates his or her New York residence is placed on the accrual method of accounting on the day of departure. If the taxpayer is entitled to installment sales proceeds, the outstanding balance of the proceeds is treated as income at the time the taxpayer moves out of New York. The taxpayer must pay tax on this amount or, in the alternative, post a bond or other security with the Department of Taxation and Finance to insure that tax is paid as the installment sale proceeds are received. Conversely, taxpayers who move into New York are able to deduct from their income amounts received after the move as a result of installment sales occurring prior to the change in residence. (Reg. Secs. 154.10, 154.11)

Mark S. Klein, Esq., Hodgson Russ LLP

Shareholders of S corporations are discussed at ¶205.

¶203 New York Adjusted Gross Income—Residents— Modifications to Federal Adjusted Gross Income

Law: Secs. 612, 617-a, Tax Law; Reg. Sec. 112.2 (CCH NEW YORK TAX REPORTS, ¶15-510, 16-005 *et seq.*, 16-205 *et seq.*).

The starting point for the determination of New York adjusted gross income for resident individuals is federal adjusted gross income for the taxable year (¶202). This amount is subject to the following modifications (additions and/or subtractions):

Add

—Interest on obligations of other states and their political subdivisions. (This interest, exempt from federal income tax, is taxable in New York.) (Sec. 612(b)(1), Tax Law)

—Any interest or dividends on obligations or securities of federal authorities, commissions or instrumentalities that are exempt from federal income taxes, but not from state income taxes (generally, federal obligation interest is not exempt from federal tax). (Sec. 612(b)(2), Tax Law)

—Income taxes imposed by New York or any other taxing jurisdiction, to the extent deductible in determining federal adjusted gross income and not credited against federal income tax. (Sec. 612(b)(3), Tax Law)

¶203

—Interest, deducted in arriving at federal adjusted gross income, on loans incurred to buy or carry securities the interest from which is exempt for New York State income tax purposes. (Sec. 612(b)(4), Tax Law)

—Expenses paid or incurred for the production of income that is exempt in New York but taxable for federal purposes, or for the management, conservation or maintenance of property producing such income, and amortizable premiums on bonds, the income from which is exempt from New York but not federal tax (for example, federal bonds), are added to the extent deducted in determining federal adjusted gross income. (Sec. 612(b)(5), Tax Law) For treatment of Build America bonds, see TSB-M-10(4)I, March 12, 2010, CCH New York Tax Reports, ¶ 406-721.

—Amounts deducted on the federal return as an allowance for percentage depletion (¶ 207).

—When gain from the sale or disposition of property is included in federal gross income, the amount of reduction in the basis of the property attributable to the credit for solar and wind energy systems (which was allowed for taxable years ending before December 31, 1986) must be added to federal adjusted gross income in determining New York adjusted gross income. If the gain affected the determination of a net capital gain for federal income tax purposes for tax years beginning before 1987, only 40% of the amount of the reduction in basis attributable to the credit is added. (Sec. 612(b)(29), Tax Law)

—The amount of member or employee contributions to a retirement system or pension fund picked up or paid by a public employer pursuant to the state Retirement and Social Security Law or under the Administrative Code of the City of New York, for contributions made after June 1989. This provision will remain in effect as long as such contributions are not included in federal adjusted gross income under the Internal Revenue Code until distributed or made available to the member. (Sec. 612(b)(26), Tax Law)

—Amounts deducted or deferred from an employee's salary under a flexible benefits program established pursuant to Sec. 23 of the General Municipal Law or Sec. 1210-a of the Public Authorities Law. (Sec. 612(b)(31), Tax Law)

—For fractional plan members of the New York City Employee Retirement System (NYCERS) and New York City Board of Education Retirement System (BERS), the amount by which an employee's salary is reduced for health insurance and welfare benefits pursuant to Sec. 12-126.1(b), 12-126.2(b), NYC Adm. Code. (Sec. 612(b)(32), Tax Law).

—Real property taxes paid on qualified agricultural property and deducted in determining federal adjusted gross income, to the extent of the amount of any agricultural property tax credit allowed under Sec. 606(i) or (n), Tax Law. (Sec. 612(b)(3), Tax Law)

—Adjustments relating to safe harbor leases and ACRS/MACRS deductions. (Sec. 612(b)(23)-(25), Tax Law)

—Deferred gain from investments in emerging technologies (¶ 210).

—An addition modification is required for environmental remediation insurance premiums that were deducted in determining federal taxable income. (Sec. 612(b)(37), Tax Law)

—For taxable years beginning after 2002, and applicable to property placed in service on or after June 1, 2003, the New York personal income tax is decoupled from federal accelerated depreciation provisions under IRC Sec. 168(k), except with respect to qualified Resurgence Zone property and qualified New York Liberty Zone property (Sec. 612(b)(8), (c)(16), (k), (l), and (m), Tax Law; TSB-M-04(1)I, CCH New York Tax Reports, ¶ 300-420).

—An addition modification is required for the amount deducted by a taxpayer (except an eligible farmer) under IRC Sec. 179 for a sport utility vehicle with a vehicle weight over 6,000 pounds (Sec. 612(b)(36), Tax Law; TSB-M-04(1)I, CCH NEW YORK TAX REPORTS, ¶ 300-420).

—For any carryback or carryforward year where the amount of NOL deduction allowed for New York purposes is limited, the difference between the NOL deduction allowed on the federal income tax return and the NOL deduction allowed for New York state income tax purposes must be accounted for. Beginning with New York state income tax returns for tax years 2013 and after, the difference must be accounted for by using a New York addition modification to federal adjusted gross income (individuals) or federal taxable income (estates and trusts). For additional information, see *Publication 145, Net Operating Losses (NOLs) for New York State Resident Individuals, Estates, and Trusts*, CCH NEW YORK TAX REPORTS, ¶ 19-625.

—*Royalties:* For taxable years beginning after 2002, certain royalty payments made by the taxpayer to a related member during the taxable year must be added back, to the extent deductible in calculating the taxpayer's federal adjusted gross income. (Sec. 612(r), Tax Law) For additional information, see ¶ 1002 and 1003.

—An addition modification is required for the IRC Sec. 199 deduction for qualified production activities income (Sec. 612(b)(38), Tax Law).

—New York provides for various additions to be made by S Corporation shareholders in determining New York adjusted gross income (¶ 205).

Subtract

—Interest on obligations of the United States and its possessions. (Sec. 612(c)(1), Tax Law) Such interest income includes the amount received as dividends from a regulated investment company so long as at least 50% of the total assets of the company consists of obligations of the United States and its possessions. Such interest income includes dividends received from a regulated investment company that has been designated as interest income in a written notice to shareholders not later than 60 days following the close of its taxable year.

—Interest or dividends on obligations or securities of any federal authority, commission or instrumentality that are taxable for federal purposes, but exempt for state purposes. International Bank bonds have been held not to be federal obligations. (Sec. 612(c)(2), Tax Law)

—Pensions of officers and employees of New York, its subdivisions or agencies (including interest on amounts withdrawn), to the extent included for federal purposes, as well as pensions received as beneficiaries of deceased employees. Federal pensions received by officers and employees of the United States, any territory, possession, or political subdivision, the District of Columbia, and any agency or instrumentality of any of the foregoing, to the extent that such pension is includible in federal gross income. (Sec. 612(c)(3)(i), Tax Law)

—Pensions and annuities (not excluded under the provision immediately above) received by an individual 59½ years of age or older from an employee retirement plan, an individual retirement account or annuity or a self-employed retirement plan. (Sec. 612(c)(3-a), Tax Law) The amount of pension and annuity income and disability income (described immediately below) excluded may not exceed $20,000. Such pension and annuity income does not include lump-sum distributions subject to the separate tax on the ordinary income portion of lump-sum distributions.

¶203

Practitioner Comment: Distribution from Non-Qualified Pension Plan can Qualify for $20,000 Annual Exclusion

An administrative law judge reversed Tax Department policy that denied the $20,000 exemption to distributions from a non-qualified pension plan if the plan proceeds were reported on a W-2 or were subject to federal income tax withholding. The court held that a payment that meets the criteria of Sec. 612(c)(3-a), Tax Law, is all that is necessary to qualify for the exemption. The employer's reporting method is irrelevant. According to the judge, "because a payment may be reported as wages for FICA purposes does not preclude treating such payment as a [qualified] pension or annuity payment . . . ." (*Bourns,* New York Division of Tax Appeals, Administrative Law Judge Unit, DTA Nos. 821366 and 821404, 2/21/08, CCH NEW YORK TAX REPORTS, ¶405-990; see also *TSB-A-10(1)I,* April 10, 2010, CCH NEW YORK TAX REPORTS, ¶406-702).

Mark S. Klein, Esq., Hodgson Russ LLP.

Practitioner Comment: Beneficiaries

New York's regulations extend the $20,000 pension and annuity exclusion to beneficiaries who receive payments qualifying as a pension or annuity created by a decedent who reached 59$\frac{1}{2}$ years of age, regardless of the age of the beneficiary. Special rules apply if the deceased has more than one beneficiary. (Reg. Sec. 112.3(c)(2)(iv)(a))

Mark S. Klein, Esq., Hodgson Russ LLP

CCH Advisory: IRAs and Roth IRAs

New York conforms to the federal income tax treatment of Roth IRAs in all respects (TSB-M-98(7)I, Department of Taxation and Finance, December 24, 1998; CCH NEW YORK TAX REPORTS, ¶300-277). Although contributions to a Roth IRA are not tax deductible, there is no tax on account earnings as they accrue or when they are distributed to an account holder during retirement. If distributions are subject to federal income tax for failing to meet distribution qualifications, they are also subject to New York personal income tax.

New York's pension and annuity exclusion for individuals 59$\frac{1}{2}$ years or older may be applied to Roth IRAs. A taxpayer who converts from a traditional IRA to a Roth IRA may exclude up to $20,000 of the conversion from taxation. If the individual converted an IRA in 1998 and spread the tax over four years, the individual may claim a $20,000 exclusion in each of those years.

Roth distributions and conversions for a nonresident filing a New York income tax return are not treated as New York source income in accordance with federal rules preventing states from taxing the pension income of nonresidents (P.L. 104-95, 104th Cong., 1st Sess.; 4 USC § 114(a)). Part-year residents must treat distribution and conversion income as New York source income if the income is received or recognized while they are New York residents. If a four-year conversion period is elected while the taxpayer is a New York resident, the entire amount of the converted income must be included in New York source income. If a change in residence does not occur in the first year of the conversion, only $\frac{1}{4}$ of the conversion income must be reported as New York source income for the first year. If a change in residence occurs in the second year, the remaining $\frac{3}{4}$ of the conversion income must be reported as New York source income in the second year. An individual who posts a bond or security is allowed to continue including $\frac{1}{4}$ of the conversion income in each of the four conversion years.

A taxpayer who receives a distribution or elects a conversion after terminating New York residency does not have to treat any income as New York source income.

—Disability income included in federal gross income to the extent the disability income would have been excluded under federal provisions in effect prior to 1984. The amount of disability income and pension and annuity income (described above) excluded may not exceed $20,000. (Sec. 612(c)(3-b), Tax Law)

—Social security benefits to the extent includible in federal gross income. (Sec. 612(c)(3-c), Tax Law)

—Gain on sale or other disposition of property to the extent that the New York tax basis on December 31, 1959 (or on the last day of a 1959-1960 fiscal year) is higher than the federal basis. (Sec. 612(c)(4), Tax Law)

—Any amount of annuity, other income or gain properly reported and taxed under the former personal income tax law (Article 16). (Sec. 612(c)(5), Tax Law)

—Interest or dividend income on obligations or securities exempt for New York purposes by the statute authorizing the issue, but taxable for federal income tax purposes. (Sec. 612(c)(6), Tax Law)

—Refund or credit of income tax included in federal gross income. (Sec. 612(c)(7), Tax Law)

—Interest on loans to buy securities taxable in New York but exempt for federal purposes (for example, bonds of other states), connected with a trade or business, and not deducted in determining federal adjusted gross income. (Sec. 612(c)(9), Tax Law)

—Expenses paid or incurred for the production of income that is taxable in New York but exempt for federal purposes, or for the management, conservation or maintenance of property producing such income, and amortizable bond premiums on bonds taxable in New York but exempt for federal purposes, to the extent that such expenses or premiums are attributable to the taxpayer's trade or business. (Sec. 612(c)(10), Tax Law)

—Amounts required to be deducted as a New York depletion allowance (¶207).

—The portion of wages and salaries not allowed as a business expense deduction for federal purposes because the federal work incentive program (WIN) credit or work opportunity credit was taken.

—A percentage of gains from new business investments (¶208).

—Subtractions relating to accelerated depreciation (property placed in service in taxable years beginning before 1994) (¶209).

—Accelerated payments or payments of death benefits or special surrender values under life insurance policies pursuant to Sec. 1113(a), Insurance Law, upon diagnosis of a terminal illness (that is, a life expectancy of 12 months or less) or of a medical condition requiring extraordinary medical care or treatment. Such payments are subtracted only to the extent that they are included in gross income for federal tax purposes. (Sec. 612(c)(30), Tax Law)

—To the extent included in gross income for federal gross income, viatical settlement proceeds. (Sec. 612(c)(30), Tax Law) "Viatical settlements" are agreements between a viatical settlement company and the owner of a life insurance policy insuring the life of a person who has a catastrophic or life-threatening illness or condition where, in exchange for the owner's assignment, transfer, sale, devise, or bequest of the death benefit or ownership of the policy, the company agrees to pay compensation or value less than the expected death benefit of the policy.

—To the extent included in federal gross income, contributions to the Executive Mansion Trust Fund (Sec. 54.15, Arts and Cultural Affairs Law).

—Contributions of up to $5,000 ($10,000 for married couples filing a joint return) to a Family Tuition Account to the extent such contributions are not eligible for a federal deduction or credit. Nonqualified withdrawals are included in income in the year of receipt to the extent they are attributable to contributions that the taxpayer deducted for New York State personal income tax purposes (*TSB-M-00-5*, December 15, 2000; CCH NEW YORK TAX REPORTS, ¶300-333). (Sec. 612(c)(32), (33), Tax Law)

¶203

CCH Advisory: College Savings

The New York State College Choice Tuition Savings Program (Sec. 695 *et seq.*, Education Law) conforms to the federal college savings program provisions in IRC Sec. 529. The definition of "account owner" includes a person who enters into a tuition savings agreement as a fiduciary or agent on behalf of a trust, estate, partnership, association, company or corporation. A maximum account balance will be periodically adjusted by the state to reflect higher education costs.

The personal income tax exclusion for college savings account contributions is available only to the account owner (Sec. 612(c)(32), Tax Law).

See ¶140 for information on the alternative credit for payments for college tuition.

—Amounts previously taxed that the taxpayer is later required to repay under claim of right may be subtracted in the year of repayment. (Sec. 662, Tax Law)

—Distributions and qualified settlements made to a taxpayer because of his or her status as a victim of Nazi persecution or as a qualified spouse or descendant of such a victim, to the extent such distributions are included in federal adjusted gross income. A subtraction modification is also allowed for items of income attributable to assets that were stolen from, hidden from, or otherwise lost to a victim of Nazi persecution immediately prior to, during, and immediately after World War II. (Sec. 612(c)(35), (36), Tax Law)

—Gain realized from investments in emerging technologies (¶210).

—Certain royalty payments made to a related member (anti-PIC or expense disallowance provisions). (Sec. 612(r), Tax Law) For additional information, see ¶1002 and ¶1003.

—Various subtractions to be made by S Corporation shareholders in determining New York adjusted gross income (¶205).

—Any recapture amount included in federal adjusted gross income that is attributable to a post-2002 federal deduction under IRC Sec. 179 for a sport utility vehicle with a vehicle weight over 6,000 pounds. (Sec. 612(c)(37), Tax Law; *TSB-M-04(1)I*, CCH NEW YORK TAX REPORTS, ¶300-420)

—Income received by a member of the New York state organized militia as compensation for performing active duty service of the state or federal government within New York. (Sec. 612(c)(8-b), Tax Law)

—Organ donors may subtract up to $10,000 from federal adjusted gross income for unreimbursed travel expenses, lodging expenses, and lost wages incurred by the taxpayer with respect to his or her organ donation. The taxpayer must claim the modification in the taxable year in which the human organ transplantation occurs. The modification may be claimed by a taxpayer only once, and it is not available to nonresidents or part-year residents. (Sec. 612(c)(38), Tax Law)

—Employees working at businesses accepted into the START-UP NY program (see ¶114) may claim a personal income tax deduction equal to the wages earned from the business in the tax-free area. The deduction will apply to all wages and salaries in the first five years of tax benefits. In the remaining five years, for single individuals, heads of households, and married couples, the deduction will apply to the first $200,000, $250,000, and $300,000 of wages, respectively. The total number of new employees eligible for the deduction will be capped at 10,000 per year. (Sec. 612(c)(40), Tax Law)

—for taxable years beginning on and after January 1, 2014, any distributions from length of service defined contribution or benefit plans to volunteer firefighters and ambulance workers over the age of 59 1/2. (Sec. 612(c)(41), Tax Law)

¶203

QEZE credit for property taxes: For federal income tax purposes, the Internal Revenue Service has determined that all or a portion of the QEZE credit for real property taxes that is refunded, or credited as an overpayment to estimated tax, may be a recovery of property tax previously deducted and is therefore considered income to the taxpayer.

For New York state corporate franchise tax and personal income tax purposes, any refund of the QEZE credit for real property taxes is considered a refund of franchise tax or income tax. Accordingly, under existing state law, the amount of the refund of the QEZE credit for real property taxes included in the taxpayer's federal taxable income or federal adjusted gross income is not taxable to New York state. Therefore, New York state taxpayers are allowed a subtraction for that refund amount in computing their New York taxable income. A memorandum describes how to report the subtraction on New York state corporate franchise tax returns and personal income tax returns, as well as the necessary amended return requirements. (*TSB-M-10(9)C, (15)I*, New York Department of Taxation and Finance, December 31, 2010, CCH New York Tax Reports, ¶ 407-084)

Small business subtraction: For taxable years beginning after 2013, a small business having business income and/or farm income may claim a subtraction equal to 3% of the net items of income, gain, loss, and deduction attributable to the business or farm entering into federal adjusted gross income, but not less than zero. The subtraction amount increases to 3.75% for taxable years beginning after 2014 and to 5% for taxable years beginning after 2015. The term "small business" means a sole proprietor or a farm business that employs one or more persons during the taxable year and that has net business income or net farm income of less than $250,000. (Sec. 612(c)(39), Tax Law)

A taxpayer who has items of income, gain, loss, or deduction from more than one small business or farm business for the tax year must apply the income limitation to each business separately. A net loss from one business cannot be used to offset the net income from another business for purposes of meeting the net income limitation. A memorandum discusses the employment requirement and explains how the subtraction modification amount is computed. In addition, illustrative examples are provided (*TSB-M-14(3)C, (5)I*, July 21, 2014, CCH New York Tax Reports, ¶ 408-149).

Add or Subtract

For beneficiaries of an estate or trust, a fiduciary adjustment (¶ 703) is added or subtracted.

Property acquired from a decedent: In the case of a sale or other disposition of property acquired from a decedent, an amount to reflect the gain or loss where a federal estate tax return was not required to be filed and the alternate valuation method was adopted for New York. In such case the federal basis (value at date of death) may differ from New York (value on alternate valuation date). (Sec. 612(r), Tax Law)

Partners: For members of partnerships, the additions or subtractions noted above are made to their distributive share of the partnership items (¶ 707). The result is New York adjusted gross income.

Practitioner Comment: Rules for Public Employee Pensions

As a result of federal law, Section 457 government plan distributions are not considered "wages" for income tax purposes. Nevertheless, distributions from New York State's Deferred Compensation Plan (for public employees of New York State and its political subdivisions) are treated as income from qualified pension and annuity plans under Section 612(c)(3-a) of the Tax Law. Distribution of funds in these plans will not be subject to tax if they are rolled over into either IRAs or other qualified plans. Furthermore, taxpayers who have reached 59¹/₂ years of age who receive distributions from the IRA or other qualified plan are eligible for the $20,000 annual exclusion (*Gorewitz*, TSB-A-02(2)I).

Mark S. Klein, Esq., Hodgson Russ LLP

¶204 New York Adjusted Gross Income—Modifications—Reduction of Gain for Higher New York Basis

Law: Sec. 612, Tax Law (CCH New York Tax Reports, ¶ 15-545, 16-215).

If the New York basis for property as of December 31, 1959, for calendar-year taxpayers (or as of the last day of the 1959-1960 fiscal year for fiscal-year taxpayers) is higher than the federal basis, the portion of any gain on the sale of the property, up to the excess of New York basis over federal basis, is subtracted from federal adjusted gross income in computing New York adjusted gross income. (Sec. 612(c)(4), Tax Law)

¶205 New York Adjusted Gross Income—Shareholders of S Corporations

Law: Sec. 612, Tax Law (CCH New York Tax Reports, ¶ 16-113, 16-317).

Comparable Federal: Secs. 1361—1377 (U.S. Master Tax Guide ¶ 309—333).

Additions: In determining New York adjusted gross income, a shareholder of a New York S corporation must make the following additions to federal adjusted gross income:

— An amount equal to the shareholder's *pro rata* share of the corporation's reductions for taxes described in IRC Secs. 1366(f)(2) (relating to built-in gains) and 1366(f)(3) (relating to excess net passive income). (Sec. 612(b)(18), Tax Law)

— S corporation distributions to the extent not included in federal gross income for the taxable year because of the application of IRC Secs. 1368, 1371(e), or 1379(c), which represent income not previously subject to New York State personal income tax because New York S corporation status had not been elected. (Sec. 612(b)(19), Tax Law)

— When gain or loss is recognized for federal income tax purposes upon the disposition of stock or indebtedness of a federal S corporation, the amount of the increase in the basis of such stock or indebtedness pursuant to IRC Sec. 1376(a) (relating to passive investment income), as such section was in effect for taxable years beginning before 1983, and IRC Sec. 1367(a)(1)(A) and (B), for each taxable year of the corporation beginning after 1980, for which the election to be treated as a New York S corporation was not in effect. (Sec. 612(b)(20), Tax Law)

— A shareholder of a federal S corporation that is a New York C corporation must add to federal adjusted gross income any item of loss or deduction of the corporation included in federal gross income pursuant to IRC Sec. 1366. (Sec. 612(b)(21), Tax Law)

Subtractions: When gain or loss is recognized for federal income tax purposes upon the disposition of stock or indebtedness of a federal S corporation, a shareholder of a New York S corporation may subtract from federal adjusted gross income the amount of the reduction in the basis of such stock or indebtedness pursuant to IRC Sec. 1376(b) (relating to passive investment income), as such section was in effect for taxable years beginning before 1983, and IRC Sec. 1367(a)(2)(B) and (C), for each taxable year of the corporation beginning after 1980, for which the election to be treated as a New York S corporation was not in effect. (Sec. 612(b)(21), Tax Law)

A shareholder of a federal S corporation that is a New York C corporation may deduct from federal adjusted gross income any item of income of the corporation that was included in federal gross income pursuant to IRC Sec. 1366. (Sec. 612(b)(22), Tax Law). For taxable years beginning after 2006, New York corporations that are federal S corporations also must be New York S corporations; see ¶853.

Practitioner Comment: Special Rules for Shareholders of Ineligible Corporations

Foreign S corporations that are not subject to New York State's tax jurisdiction are unable to make a New York S election. In this situation, New York's Tax Department treats the corporation's shareholders as if New York S status was affirmatively elected. New York resident shareholders are taxed on their distributive share of the corporation's income, while nonresident shareholders are exempt from tax. New York State tax auditors, when faced with this issue, carefully scrutinize the corporation's nexus with New York State. If nexus is found, the corporation is treated as a federal S corporation that failed to make a New York S election, causing it and its shareholders to be taxed as though it were a New York C corporation (Publication 35—*New York Tax Treatment of S Corporations and Their Shareholders*, Department of Taxation and Finance (3/2000)).

Mark S. Klein, Esq., Hodgson Russ LLP

¶206 New York Adjusted Gross Income—Nonresidents

Law: Secs. 631, 638, Tax Law (CCH NEW YORK TAX REPORTS, ¶16-505 *et seq.*).

Forms: Form IT-203, Nonresident and Part-Year Resident Income Tax Return.

The New York adjusted gross income of a nonresident individual or part-year resident is determined by applying the New York modifications to the taxpayer's federal adjusted gross income. See ¶403 for discussion of apportionment of salaries and wages of nonresidents.

New York taxable income: Nonresidents and part-year residents are liable for tax on New York source income, including income received by nonresidents related to a business, trade, profession, or occupation previously carried on in New York, whether or not as an employee, including income from termination agreements and covenants not to compete. (Sec. 631(a), Tax Law; Sec. 631(b)(1)(f), Tax Law; *TSB-M-10(9)I*, August 31, 2010, CCH NEW YORK TAX REPORTS, ¶406-958; *TB-IT-615*, New York Department of Taxation and Finance, December 15, 2011, CCH NEW YORK TAX REPORTS, ¶407-441; *TB-IT-620*, New York Department of Taxation and Finance, December 15, 2011, CCH NEW YORK TAX REPORTS, ¶407-440)

Computation of tax liability: Nonresident individuals are required to compute their tax liability in the following manner:

— The amount of tax is initially computed as if the taxpayer were a resident for the entire year;

— The tax is reduced by any applicable household credit (¶116), and the child and dependent care credit (¶121), which are also computed as if the taxpayer were a resident for the entire year. The figure resulting after the application of these credits is known as the "base tax";

— The base tax is multiplied by a percentage, which is determined by dividing the taxpayer's New York source income for the entire year by the taxpayer's New York adjusted gross income for the entire year; and

— The resulting amount is further reduced by any other applicable New York credits.

Married taxpayers filing a joint return, in the case of one spouse having no income from New York sources, are required to enter in the Federal Amount column of Form IT-203 the combined amount of each item of income that the taxpayers included in their joint federal return. The taxpayers' federal adjusted gross income is entered on Line 18 of Form IT-203. The New York modifications (¶ 203) are applied to the taxpayers' federal adjusted gross incomes to yield their New York adjusted gross income on Line 30. Their New York adjusted gross income is reduced by the taxpayers' itemized or standard deduction and dependent exemptions to yield New York taxable income (Line 35) to which the tax tables are applied. The child and dependent care and household credits are subtracted from the tax to yield the base tax (Line 42) to which the income percentage (Line 43) reflecting New York source income is applied to finally yield the allocated New York tax on Line 44. The allocated tax is then reduced to reflect any other available credits or increased to reflect other taxes due to New York State.

Practitioner Comment: Worldwide Income Can Be Used to Determine a Nonresident's Tax Rates

Since nonresidents of New York must compute their initial tax liability as if the taxpayers were residents for the entire year, all income earned in the calendar year before a taxpayer moves to New York (and all income earned after a taxpayer leaves New York) is included in the initial computation. As a result of this methodology, the rate of tax applied to the taxpayer is based on income earned both within and outside of New York State. According to New York's courts, this computational method is valid, even though it creates a larger tax liability for the nonresident. (*Nathan vs. Commissioner of Taxation and Finance*, 883 NYS2d 367 (3d Dep't. 2009); CCH NEW YORK TAX REPORTS, ¶ 406-463)

Mark S. Klein, Hodgson Russ LLP

• *New York source income*

Nonresidents and part-year residents are liable for tax on taxable income derived from sources within New York. (Sec. 631(a), Tax Law)

The New York source income of a nonresident individual is the sum of the net amount of items of income, gain, loss and deduction entering into federal adjusted gross income, derived from or connected with New York sources including an individual's (1) distributive share of partnership income, gain, loss and deduction, (2) pro rata share of S corporation income, loss, and deduction, increased by reductions for taxes described in IRC Sec. 1366(f), and (3) share of estate or trust income, gain, loss, and deduction. Also included in New York source income are modifications applicable to these items, including any modifications attributable to the nonresident as a partner or shareholder of a New York S corporation. (Sec. 638(a), Tax Law)

The New York source income of a part-year resident individual is the sum of the following: (1) federal adjusted gross income for the period of residence, computed as if the individual's taxable year for federal income tax purposes were limited to the period of residence; (2) New York source income for the period of nonresidence determined in accordance with Sec. 631, Tax Law, as if the individual's taxable year for federal income tax purposes were limited to the period of nonresidence; and (3) certain special accruals. (Sec. 639, Tax Law)

Practitioner Comment: Like-Kind Exchanges Can Escape NY Tax

Since New York's computation of income begins with federal AGI, there is no provision to capture the untaxed gain of a like-kind exchange (under IRC Sec. 1031) of New York property. In view of the fact that New York has no jurisdiction to tax a nonresident on the sale of non-New York property, nonresidents who exchange New York property for replacement property located out of state will escape New York tax on all of the gain when the out-of-state property is ultimately sold. Of course, the converse of this rule also applies. If a nonresident exchanges non-New York real estate for property within New York, the ultimate sale of the parcel will result in a New York tax on the entire gain.

Mark S. Klein, Esq., Hodgson Russ LLP

Income and deductions from New York sources: Items of income, gain, loss and deduction derived from or connected with New York sources are those attributable to (Sec. 631(b)(1), Tax Law):

(1) the ownership of any interest in real or tangible personal property in New York;

(2) a business, trade, profession, or occupation carried on in New York;

(3) the ownership of shares issued by an electing shareholder of an S corporation;

(4) winnings of more than $5,000 from a wager placed in a lottery conducted by the New York Division of the Lottery; or

(5) gains from the sale, conveyance, or other disposition of shares of stock in a cooperative housing corporation in connection with the grant or transfer of a proprietary leasehold by the owner, and subject to the provisions of Tax Law Article 31 (*i.e.,* the New York real estate transfer tax), whether such shares are held by a partnership, trust, or otherwise.

Income from intangibles, such as annuities, interest, dividends, and gains from the sale of intangibles, is considered to be from New York sources only to the extent that the property is (Sec. 631(b)(2), Tax Law):

(1) used in a business, trade, profession, or occupation in New York; or

(2) winnings, from a wager placed in a lottery conducted by the Division of the Lottery if the proceeds exceed $5,000.

Similarly, for nonresidents, deductions with respect to capital losses and net operating losses are limited to those based on items of income, gain, loss, and deduction derived from or connected with New York sources.

CCH Advisory: Former Residents' Lottery Winnings

A resident who wins more than $5,000 in the New York State lottery and receives guaranteed annual payments of the winnings must, upon becoming a nonresident, accrue to the period of residence the value of the future lottery payments (Sec. 639, Tax Law). Alternatively, the taxpayer may authorize withholding of New York State (Sec. 639(d), Tax Law) and, if applicable, New York City (Sec. 11-1771(b)(3)(B), NYC Adm. Code) income taxes from the payments.

There is apparently no settled law concerning the proper method of determining the present value of the future payments (*Blanco*, Division of Tax Appeals, Administrative Law Judge Unit, April 8, 1999; CCH NEW YORK TAX REPORTS, ¶ 403-347; affirmed by *TAT*, April 6, 2000, CCH NEW YORK TAX REPORTS, ¶ 403-637, and by Supreme Court, Appellate Division, Third Judicial Department, No. 87650, April 19, 2001, CCH NEW YORK TAX REPORTS, ¶ 403-909).

Income derived by a nonresident athlete, entertainer or performing artist from closed-circuit and cable television transmissions of an event (other than events occurring on a regularly scheduled basis) taking place in New York as a result of the rendition of services by such nonresident constitutes income derived from New York sources only to the extent that the transmissions were received or exhibited in New York. (Sec. 631(b)(3), Tax Law)

¶206

Severance pay: Termination or severance pay is not included in the definition of "total compensation for services rendered as a member of a professional athletic team" and thus is not New York source income (*TSB-A-09(11)I*, September 22, 2009, CCH New York Tax Reports, ¶ 406-553).

Alimony: The U.S. Supreme Court held unconstitutional Sec. 631(b)(6), Tax Law, which denied nonresidents the right to deduct alimony payments authorized by IRC Sec. 215 (*Lunding*, US SCt, Dkt. 96-1462, January 21, 1998; CCH New York Tax Reports, ¶ 402-918).

Broker trading for own account: A nonresident, other than a dealer, is not considered to be in a business, trade, profession, or occupation carried on in New York solely because of the purchase and sale of property or the purchase, sale, or writing of stock option contracts, or both, for his or her own account. See discussion at ¶ 402.

Military pay: Pay for service in the armed forces received by an individual not domiciled in New York is not income from New York sources. See discussion at ¶ 403.

Victims of terrorism: Under the New York September 11th Victims and Families Relief Act (S.B. 7356, Laws 2002), no New York state or local taxation, including personal income and estate taxes, may be imposed on any payment from the federal September 11th Victim Compensation Fund.

IRC Sec. 139, as added by the federal Victims of Terrorism Relief Act of 2001 (P.L. 107-134), exempts from federal taxation any federal, state, or local government payments made in connection with a qualified disaster, including those resulting from terrorist attacks or military action. Consequently, no modification of federal adjusted gross income is necessary for New York personal income tax purposes with respect to payments from the federal September 11th fund.

Apportionment: For apportionment and allocation of income of a nonresident partly from New York sources, see Chapter 4.

Stockholders in S corporations: Nonresidents who are shareholders of electing New York S corporations include their pro rata share of the S corporation's items of income, loss and deduction to the extent the items are derived or connected with New York sources. In determining the amount derived or connected with New York sources, the corporation's business allocation percentage is used. (For full discussion, see *TSB-M-84(8)C*, CCH New York Tax Reports, ¶ 9-940).

For additional information on the New York-source income of nonresident S corporation shareholders, see ¶ 857.

Regarding nonresidents' sales of co-op shares, see *TSB-M-04(5)I*, CCH New York Tax Reports, ¶ 300-438; see also "*Income and deductions from New York sources*" above.

Members of New York Insurance Exchange: In the case of a nonresident individual or partner of a partnership doing an insurance business as a member of the New York Insurance Exchange, any item of income, gain, loss, or deduction from such business is not considered to be derived from New York sources. (Sec. 631(b)(5), Tax Law)

REMICs: Nonresident holders of interests in Real Estate Mortgage Investment Conduits, in determining New York source income, will include only the income received from REMICs when such interests are employed in a trade, business, profession, or occupation carried on in New York State.

Holders of interests in REMICs (regular or residual) are required to report their holdings as business capital and any income earned as business income (*TSB-M-87(22)C*, CCH New York Tax Reports, ¶ 10-000).

• *Retirement income of former residents*

Federal law curtails states' rights to subject retirement income of former residents to state income taxation (P.L. 104-95, 104th Cong, 1st Sess.; 4 USC 114(a)). The statute protects from source taxation all pension income or other retirement distributions received from IRC Sec. 401(a) trusts exempt from taxation under IRC Sec. 501(a), simplified IRC Sec. 408(k) plans, IRC Sec. 403(a) annuity plans, IRC Sec. 403(b) annuity contracts, IRC Sec. 7701(a)(37) individual retirement plans, IRC Sec. 457 deferred compensation plans, IRC Sec. 414(d) government plans and IRC Sec. 501(c)(18) trusts. Also included are prohibitions on out-of-state taxation of distributions from three non-qualified plans. First, plans described in IRC Sec. 3121(v)(2)(C) are protected if payments are made at least annually and spread over the actual life expectancy of the beneficiaries. Second, the same plans are protected if payments are spread over at least a ten-year period. Third, in instances where plans are trusts under IRC Sec. 401(a), but exceed limitations set forth in IRC Secs. 401(a)(17) and 415, the pensions are exempted from out-of-state taxation.

Practitioner Comment: Retirement Income

Even if a pension or other retirement benefit fails to qualify for exemption under the federal law, New York also exempts all payments to nonresidents that qualify as an "annuity". A qualifying annuity payment must be pursuant to a written agreement and be paid out at a uniform rate in money only (not securities or other property), at regular intervals, at least annually, and for not less than half of the recipient's life expectancy. (Reg. Sec. 132.4(d))

Mark S. Klein, Esq., Hodgson Russ LLP

Retired partners: The prohibition applies to the retirement income of a nonresident retired partner, as well as a nonresident retired employee, and the application of a predetermined formula cap or a cost-of-living adjustment in a nonqualified deferred compensation plan does not make the retirement income of such nonresidents subject to state taxation. See *TSB-M-07(2)I*, January 24, 2007, CCH New York Tax Reports, ¶405-601. See also ¶403, ¶855.

Exercise of stock options: Income from the exercise of stock options granted to an employee in connection with his employment could not be allocated to and taxed by New York as personal income, if in the period that the income was realized, the employee was a nonresident with no working days in New York (*Hopkins*, New York Division of Tax Appeals, Administrative Law Judge Unit, DTA No. 821812, January 8, 2009, CCH New York Tax Reports, ¶406-291).

• Sale of entity interest

Applicable to sales or exchanges of entity interests occurring on or after May 7, 2009, gains from the sale of interests in certain partnerships and other entities are included in nonresidents' New York source income, to the extent attributable to ownership of New York real property. Specifically, the term "real property located in this state" includes an interest in a partnership, LLC, S corporation, or non-publicly traded C corporation with 100 or fewer shareholders that owns real property located in New York and that has a fair market value that equals or exceeds 50% of all of the entity's assets on the date of the sale or exchange of the taxpayer's interest in the entity (Sec. 631(b)(1)(A)(1), Tax Law; *TSB-M-09(5)I*, May 5, 2009, CCH New York Tax Reports, ¶406-381).

Only those assets that the entity owned for at least two years before the date of the sale or exchange are to be used in determining the fair market value of all of the entity's assets on that date. The gain or loss derived from New York sources from the taxpayer's sale or exchange of an interest in such an entity is the total gain or loss for federal income tax purposes from that sale or exchange, multiplied by a fraction. The numerator of the fraction is the fair market value of the real property located in New York on the date of the sale or exchange, and the denominator is the fair market value of all of the entity's assets on that date.

¶206

¶207 Modifications for Disallowance of Federal Percentage Depletion

Law: Sec. 612(b)(10), (i), Tax Law (CCH NEW YORK TAX REPORTS, ¶ 16-037, 16-243).

Comparable Federal: Secs. 611, 613, 613A (U.S. MASTER TAX GUIDE ¶ 1289).

Amounts deducted on the federal return as an allowance for percentage depletion must be added to federal adjusted gross income in determining New York adjusted gross income. (Sec. 612(b)(10), Tax Law) However, with respect to the property as to which such addition to federal adjusted gross income is required, an allowance for depletion may be subtracted from federal adjusted gross income in the amount that would be deductible under IRC Sec. 611 if the deduction for an allowance for depletion had not been used. (Sec. 612(i), Tax Law)

¶208 Modifications Relating to New Business Investments

Law: Sec. 612(o), Tax Law (CCH NEW YORK TAX REPORTS, ¶ 16-070, 16-270).

"New business investment" refers to investments issued before 1988. (Sec. 612(o)(1)(A), Tax Law)

A taxpayer may subtract from federal adjusted gross income a portion of an amount constituting a new business investment gain. (Sec. 612(o), Tax Law) The amount of the subtraction is as follows: 25% of the gain if the new business investment was held at least four years but less than five years; 50% if the investment was held at least five years but less than six years; and 100% if the investment was held at least six years. If the modification is less than 100%, a further 10% subtraction is permitted when the new business investment gain is reinvested in a new business investment under prescribed conditions.

¶209 Modifications Relating to Depreciation Deductions

Law: Sec. 612, Tax Law (CCH NEW YORK TAX REPORTS, ¶ 15-010, 16-040, 16-245).

Comparable Federal: Secs. 168, 179 (U.S. MASTER TAX GUIDE ¶ 1201—1284).

There is no ACRS modification for property placed in service in 1994 or later.

For property placed in service in taxable years beginning before 1994, the amount allowable under the federal accelerated cost recovery system pursuant to IRC Sec. 168 must be added to federal adjusted gross income. (Sec. 612(b)(25), Tax Law) However, this requirement does not apply to property subject to IRC Sec. 280-F (relating to luxury automobiles) or to property placed in service in New York in taxable years beginning after 1984.

For property placed in service in taxable years beginning before 1994, a deduction from federal adjusted gross income is allowed equal to the depreciation allowable under IRC Sec. 167 as that section would have applied to property placed in service on December 31, 1980. However, this deduction does not apply with respect to luxury automobiles or to property placed in service in New York after 1984.

• *Other depreciation modifications*

Federal bonus depreciation: For taxable years beginning after 2002, and applicable to property placed in service on or after June 1, 2003, the New York personal income tax is decoupled from federal accelerated depreciation provisions, except with respect to qualified Resurgence Zone property and qualified New York Liberty Zone property. Decoupling includes the special depreciation provisions in the federal Economic Stimulus Act of 2008. See ¶ 203.

Federal SUV expensing: For taxable years beginning after 2002, an addition modification is required for the amount deducted by a taxpayer (except an eligible farmer) under IRC Sec. 179 for a sport utility vehicle with a vehicle weight over 6,000 pounds. A subtraction modification is enacted for any recapture amount included in federal adjusted gross income attributable to such deduction (Sec. 612(b)(36), (c)(37), Tax Law; *TSB-M-04(1)I*, CCH New York Tax Reports, ¶ 300-420). No further modifications are required with respect to the federal Economic Stimulus Act of 2008.

¶210 Modifications Relating to Gain from Investments in Emerging Technologies

Law: Sec. 612(u), (v), Tax Law (CCH New York Tax Reports, ¶ 15-710, 16-070, 16-270).

Gain from the sale of any emerging technology investment acquired on or after March 12, 1998, and held for more than 36 months will be recognized only to the extent that the gain realized exceeds the cost of any qualified emerging technology investment purchased by the taxpayer within 365 days from the date of the sale. Consequently, such deferred gain may, at the taxpayer's election, be subtracted from the taxpayer's federal adjusted gross income in the year of the sale. (Sec. 612(u), (v), Tax Law)

The amount deferred will be added to the taxpayer's federal adjusted gross income when the reinvestment is sold.

PERSONAL INCOME TAX

CHAPTER 3
DEDUCTIONS

¶301 In General

Resident individuals take the New York standard deduction (¶306) unless (1) they have itemized deductions for federal income tax purposes, and (2) they elect to itemize deductions for New York (¶302). The same rule applies for nonresidents (¶305).

Husband and wife: Deductions may be itemized only if both elect to do so—see ¶302.

CAUTION: New York no longer allows the federal deduction for state and local sales taxes in the computation of an individual's New York itemized deduction (*TSB-M-10(8)I,* August 20, 2010, CCH NEW YORK TAX REPORTS, ¶406-943).

• *Deductions for Ponzi scheme losses*

Federal IRS Revenue Ruling 2009-9 describes the tax rules that apply for federal income tax purposes to losses from "Ponzi-type" fraudulent investment arrangements. The IRS also issued Revenue Procedure 2009-20, providing an optional safe harbor procedure for computing and reporting losses for which the discovery year is a taxable year beginning after 2007.

The Department of Taxation and Finance recognizes the federal safe harbor for purposes of computing New York itemized deductions for personal income tax purposes. Accordingly, if the federal theft loss deduction is computed based upon the safe harbor, that amount is to be used in computing the New York itemized deduction. For New York State purposes, itemized deductions are subject to certain limitations. (TSB-M-09(7)I, May 29, 2009, CCH NEW YORK TAX REPORTS, ¶406-406; see also Publication 145, *Net Operating Losses (NOLs) for New York State Resident Individuals, Estates, and Trusts,* CCH NEW YORK TAX REPORTS, ¶19-625)

¶302 New York Itemized Deductions—Residents

Law: Sec. 615, Tax Law; Reg. Secs. 115.1—115.3 (CCH NEW YORK TAX REPORTS, ¶15-545).

Resident individuals who have itemized deductions on their federal income tax returns may elect to itemize deductions for New York or take the standard deduction. (Sec. 615(a), Tax Law)

The New York itemized deduction of a resident individual is equal to the total amount of that individual's deductions from federal adjusted gross income, other than federal deductions for personal exemptions, as provided for federal purposes for the taxable year, with certain modifications described at ¶303. In addition, however, the otherwise allowable New York itemized deductions are reduced for taxpayers with income above specified levels, as described at ¶304.

Husband and wife: When both husband and wife are required to file New York returns and have taken itemized deductions on their federal return or returns, they may take New York itemized deductions only if both elect to itemize. The total of the New York itemized deductions of a husband and wife whose federal taxable income is determined on a joint return, but whose New York incomes are required to be determined separately, will be divided between them as if their federal taxable incomes had been separately determined. (Sec. 615(b), Tax Law)

College tuition deductions: A personal income deduction is available for college tuition expenses, up to $10,000 annually for each student (¶303). An alternative credit is available (¶140).

For New York standard deduction, see ¶306.

¶303 New York Itemized Deductions—Residents—Modifications

Law: Sec. 615, Tax Law; Reg. Sec. 115.2 (CCH NEW YORK TAX REPORTS, ¶15-545).

New York itemized deductions for a resident individual are the same as the federal itemized deductions, with the following modifications:

Subtract

—Amount of federal deduction for New York, New York City, and other income taxes, and, except for tax years beginning in 2009 only, the amount of any federal deduction for state and local general sales and use taxes. (Sec. 615(c)(1), Tax Law)

—Interest on loans incurred to buy or carry securities the income from which is exempt for New York but taxable for federal purposes (for example, interest on loans to buy federal bonds). (Sec. 615(c)(2), Tax Law)

—Expenses paid or incurred for the production or collection of income that is exempt for New York but taxable for federal purposes, or for the management, conservation, or maintenance of property held for such income, and amortizable bond premiums on bonds exempt for New York but taxable for federal purposes. (Sec. 615(c)(3), Tax Law)

—Premiums paid for long-term care insurance to the extent they are deductible in determining federal taxable income. (Sec. 615(c)(4), Tax Law)

—Real property taxes imposed on renters on or after the April 1 occurring more than six months after an Internal Revenue Service ruling to the effect that renters may deduct the taxes for federal income tax purposes. Since the Internal Revenue Service has not ruled on this issue, this section has never gone into effect. (Sec. 615(c)(5), Tax Law)

—In the case of a shareholder of a federal S corporation, (1) when the election to be treated as a New York S corporation has not been made, S corporation items of deduction included in federal itemized deductions, and (2) in the case of a New York S termination year, the portion of such items assigned to the period beginning on the day the election ceases to be effective. (Sec. 615(c)(6), Tax Law)

—*Innovation Hot Spots:* Individuals who are sole proprietors of a qualified entity, or are partners/members/shareholders of a partnership, limited liability company, or New York S corporation, respectively, that is a qualified entity are allowed a deduction for the amount of income or gain attributable to operations at the Hot Spot (Sec. 38(1)(c), Tax Law; see also ¶114). This benefit is also available under the New York City personal income tax on residents (¶3010).

¶303

Add

—Interest on loans incurred to buy or carry securities the interest from which is taxable for New York but exempt for federal purposes (for example, interest on loans to buy bonds of other states). (Sec. 615(d)(2), Tax Law)

—Expenses paid or incurred for the production or collection of income that is taxable for New York but exempt for federal purposes, or for the management, conservation or maintenance of property held for such income, and amortizable bond premiums on bonds taxable for New York but exempt for federal purposes. (Sec. 615(d)(3), Tax Law)

—100% of allowable college tuition expenses, up to $10,000 annually (Sec. 615(d)(4), Tax Law). No deduction is allowed if the taxpayer claims the alternative credit for tuition expenses, as discussed at ¶140.

¶304 Reduction in New York Itemized Deductions

Law: Sec. 615, Tax Law (CCH NEW YORK TAX REPORTS, ¶15-545).

Higher-income New York taxpayers are allowed only a percentage of their total federal itemized deductions. The percentage varies according to the taxpayer's New York adjusted gross income (AGI) and filing status, as summarized below (Sec. 615(f), Tax Law):

— The first percentage is equal to 25% of a ratio, whose determination depends on a taxpayer's filing status. For unmarried individuals and married individuals filing separate returns, the ratio's numerator is the lesser of either $50,000 or the excess of New York AGI over $100,000, and the denominator is $50,000. For married individuals filing jointly, and for surviving spouses, the numerator is the lesser of $50,000 or the excess of New York AGI over $200,000, and the denominator is $50,000. For a head of household, the numerator is the lesser of $50,000 or the excess of New York AGI over $150,000, and the denominator is $50,000;

— The second percentage is equal to 25% of a ratio, the numerator of which is the lesser of $50,000 or the excess of the taxpayer's New York AGIe over $475,000, and the denominator of which is $50,000.

Reduction of deduction for charitable contributions: For tax years 2009 and after 2015, the amount of charitable contributions allowed as a New York itemized deduction is reduced to 50% of the individual's federal itemized deduction for charitable contributions by taxpayers with New York AGI above $1 million. For individuals with federal AGI over $10 million in tax years 2010 through 2017, the charitable deduction is reduced to 25% of the federal deduction (Sec. 615(g), Tax Law).

Practitioner Comment: Special Problem for Gambling Losses

The interplay of the federal and New York itemized deduction rules can lead to some very harsh results for high-income taxpayers with substantial gambling winnings and losses. For example, a taxpayer with income of over $500,000 a year who loses $100,000 a year through gambling activities (stemming from $200,000 of winnings and $300,000 of losses) will be taxed as if the gambling activities generated $100,000 of gain! Under

New York's tax rules, the taxpayer's gambling losses ($300,000) are limited to gambling winnings ($200,000). The resulting losses ($200,000) are an itemized deduction subject to the 50% reduction for high-income taxpayers. This reduces the taxpayer's losses to $100,000. This is the amount that is used to offset the $200,000 of gambling winnings, resulting in a gain of $100,000. (See *e.g., Karlsberg,* TAT, 3/1/10, CCH NEW YORK TAX REPORTS, ¶406-716, and *Lippman* (NYS ALJ 8/20/09), CCH NEW YORK TAX REPORTS, ¶406-506).

Mark S. Klein, Esq., Hodgson Russ LLP

¶305 New York Deductions—Nonresidents

Law: Sec. 631, Tax Law (CCH NEW YORK TAX REPORTS, ¶15-545).

Nonresidents are allowed the same itemized deductions as resident individuals. In addition, nonresident taxpayers who do not itemize are allowed the same standard deduction as resident individuals. (Sec. 631, Tax Law)

See the discussion concerning alimony paid by nonresidents at ¶206.

For New York deductions available to resident and nonresident individuals, see ¶301—¶303 and ¶306.

¶306 New York Standard Deduction

Law: Secs. 614, 634, Tax Law (CCH NEW YORK TAX REPORTS, ¶15-540).

The inflation-adjusted New York standard deduction amounts for 2016 are as follows:

Unmarried individuals: The New York standard deduction of an unmarried resident individual who is not the head of a household, nor a surviving spouse, nor an individual whose federal exemption amount is zero, is $7,950 ($7,900 for 2015). (Sec. 614(a), Tax Law)

Husband and wife filing jointly and surviving spouse(" marriage penalty"): Husbands and wives whose New York taxable incomes are determined jointly and surviving spouses are entitled to a New York standard deduction of $15,950 ($15,850 for 2015). (Sec. 614(b), Tax Law)

Heads of households: The New York standard deduction of a person who is the head of a household is $11,150 ($11,100 for 2015). (Sec. 614(c), Tax Law)

Married individuals filing separately: For married individuals filing separately, the New York standard deduction is $7,950 ($7,900 for 2015). (Sec. 614(d), Tax Law)

Dependents: For a resident whose federal exemption amount is zero (a dependent individual), the New York standard deduction is $3,100 (also $3,100 for 2015). (Sec. 614(e), Tax Law)

Nonresidents: Nonresidents are allowed the same standard deduction as resident individuals.

Indexing: For tax years through 2017, the New York standard deduction will continue to be indexed by the cost-of-living adjustment. For tax years 2018 and after, the standard deduction will be fixed at the amount allowable for tax year 2017.

PERSONAL INCOME TAX

CHAPTER 4
ALLOCATION AND APPORTIONMENT

¶401 In General

A nonresident is taxable on income from New York sources only (¶ 207).

The following paragraphs deal with the apportionment of business income (¶ 402) and the allocation of salary and wages earned partly inside and partly outside New York by a nonresident (¶ 403). There is no allocation or apportionment of the income of a resident.

¶402 Apportionment of Business Income

Law: Sec. 631, Tax Law; Reg. Secs. 132.15, 132.16, 132.21, 137.6 (CCH NEW YORK TAX REPORTS, ¶ 16-505 *et seq.*).

If a nonresident individual, or a partnership of which a nonresident individual is a member, carries on a business, trade, profession or occupation both within and without New York, the items of income, gain, loss and deduction attributable to the business, trade, profession or occupation must be apportioned and allocated to New York on a fair and equitable basis in accordance with approved methods of accounting (Reg. Sec. 132.15).

However, if the books and records of the business do not disclose, to the satisfaction of the Commissioner, the proportion of the net amount of the items of income, gain, loss and deduction attributable to the activities of the business carried on in New York, the proportion will be determined by multiplying:

(1) the net amount of the items of income, gain, loss and deduction of the business by

(2) the average of the property, payroll, and gross income percentages.

• *Apportionment formula*

The three-factor formula is the formula generally used in the administration of state taxes, being the average ratio (of the amount within New York to the total everywhere) of the following items (Reg. Sec. 132.15):

— real and tangible personal property connected with the business (average of opening and closing balances);

— payrolls;

— gross sales or charges for services performed. The sales or charges allocated to New York include all sales negotiated or consummated and charges for services performed by an employee, agent, or independent contractor chiefly situated at, or otherwise connected with, offices or agencies located in New York.

¶403 Salaries and Wages of Nonresidents

Law: Reg. Secs. 132.4, 132.17, 132.18, 132.19, 132.20, 132.22 (CCH NEW YORK TAX REPORTS, ¶ 15-175, 16-545, 16-570).

New York income from earnings of all nonresident employees, including corporate officers (but excluding salespersons whose compensation depends on the volume of business transacted), includes that portion of the total compensation for services which the total number of working days employed within New York bears to the total number of working days everywhere (Rule Sec. 132.18).

Nonworking days, such as Saturdays, Sundays, holidays, days of absence because of illness or personal injury, vacations, or leave with or without pay, are excluded. The items of gain, loss, and deduction of the employee attributable to that individual's employment, derived from or connected with New York sources, are similarly determined.

Practitioner Comment: Necessity or Convenience?

A major area of contention during audits is New York's rule that any allowance claimed for days worked outside New York must be based on performance of services that, of necessity, as distinguished from convenience, obligates the employee to out-of-state duties in the service of the employer. This rule has been applied to employees who were specifically requested by their employer to work at home (*Phillips*, NYS TAT (4/15/99), *aff'd*, 700 NYS2d 566 (3rd Dept. 1999), CCH New York Tax Reports, ¶403-546). It was also applied to a taxpayer who lived in Tennessee (*Huckaby*, NY Court of Appeals, No. 8, March 29, 2005; CCH New York Tax Reports, ¶405-078). However, wages will not be allocated to New York under the convenience test if the taxpayer performs *no* services in New York (*Friedman*, NYS ALJ (6/27/02)).

In 2006, New York's tax department slightly revised its position concerning the application of the convenience rule and provided a variety of tests that can be used to determine if a taxpayer's home office is a *bona fide* office of the employer. (*TSB-M-06(5)I*, CCH New York Tax Reports, ¶300-512)

Note: As a result of New York's initiative, federal legislation was introduced to prohibit one state's taxation of a telecommuter from another state. SeeS. 2813, The Multistate Worker Tax Fairness Act of 2016.

Mark S. Klein, Esq., Hodgson Russ LLP

• Pensions and other retirement benefits

Federal legislation enacted in 1996 (P.L. 104-95, 104th Cong, 1st Sess.; 4 USC 114(a)) sharply curtails the rights of states to reach across their borders to subject retirement income of former residents to state income taxation. The legislation prohibits source taxation of pension income or other retirement distributions received from IRC Sec. 401(a) trusts exempt from taxation under IRC Sec. 501(a), simplified IRC Sec. 408(k) employee pension plans, IRC Sec. 403(a) annuity plans, IRC Sec. 403(b) annuity contracts, IRC Sec. 7701(a)(37) individual retirement plans, eligible IRC Sec. 457 deferred compensation plans, eligible IRC Sec. 457 deferred compensation plans, IRC Sec. 414(d) government plans, and IRC Sec. 501(c)(18) employee pension trusts created before June 25, 1959. In addition, the legislation prohibits source taxation of distributions from IRC Sec. 3121(v)(2)(C) nonqualified deferred compensation plans if payments are made at least annually and spread over the actuarial life expectancy of the beneficiaries or spread over at least a 10-year period. If the plan is a trust under IRC Sec. 401(a) but exceeds the limits of IRC Sec. 401(a)(17) or IRC Sec. 415, the payouts cannot be subject to out-of-state tax. All of these provisions apply to amounts received after 1995.

In addition, federal P.L. 109-264 (H.R. 4019) (2006), provides that the prohibition applies to the retirement income of a nonresident retired partner, as well as a nonresident retired employee, and that the application of a predetermined formula cap or a cost-of-living adjustment in a nonqualified deferred compensation plan does not make the retirement income of such nonresidents subject to state taxation. These changes apply to amounts received after December 31, 1995. See *TSB-M-07(2)I*, January 24, 2007, CCH New York Tax Reports, ¶405-601.

¶403

• *Specific wages and professions*

Members of professional athletic teams: Nonresident members of professional athletic teams must allocate their wages to New York based on the number of games played within and outside the state. Income is apportioned on the basis of the number of duty days spent in one state compared to duty days spent in all states. (Rule Sec. 132.22) "Duty days" include:

(1) all days during the taxable year from the beginning of the team's official preseason training through the last game in which the team competes or is scheduled to compete;

(2) days that do not fall within the designated period on which a member of a professional team renders a service for a team (*e.g.*, participation in instructional leagues, the "Pro Bowl," or promotional caravans); and

(3) days during the off-season when a team member undertakes training and rehabilitative activities, but only if conducted at the team's facilities.

A "member of a professional athletic team" includes active players, players on the team's disabled list, and any other player who is required to travel, travels with and performs services on behalf of the team on a regular basis (*e.g.*, coaches, managers, trainers, etc.).

Salespersons: In the case of a salesperson whose compensation depends directly on the volume of business, New York income is the proportion of the compensation received which the volume of business transacted by that individual in New York bears to the total volume of business transacted everywhere. (Rule Sec. 132.17)

Ships' crews: All compensation received by a nonresident employee for services on a vessel operating exclusively in New York is New York source income. In addition, all items of income, gain, loss, and deduction attributable to such employment are New York source income. However, income items attributable to employment on a vessel operating between New York and foreign ports, or ports of other states, are not New York source income. (Rule Sec. 132.19)

Practitioner Comment: Nonresidents Who Perform Duties on Vessels

As a result of federal legislation (Section 11108 of Title 46 of the United States Code), New York cannot tax any compensation paid to nonresidents who are (1) engaged on a vessel to perform assigned duties in more than one state as a licensed pilot, or (2) engaged to perform regularly assigned duties as a master, officer, or crewman on a vessel operating on the navigable waters of more than one state. (TSB-M-02(4)I)

Mark S. Klein, Esq., Hodgson Russ LLP

Interstate rail and motor carriers: Compensation paid by a motor private carrier or a rail or motor carrier providing transportation subject to the jurisdiction of the Surface Transportation Board (formerly the Interstate Commerce Commission) pursuant to Subchapter I or II, Chapter 105, Title 49, U.S.C., to an employee who performs regularly assigned duties in two or more states is regarded as income derived from the individual's state of residence. Accordingly, when a nonresident receives compensation as an employee of an interstate rail carrier, an interstate motor carrier or an interstate motor private carrier for performing regularly assigned duties in two or more states, the compensation does not constitute income derived from New York sources, even though the services may have been performed in New York. (Rule Sec. 132.11(b))

Military pay: Compensation paid by the United States for active service in the United States Armed Forces performed by an individual not domiciled in New York does not constitute income derived from New York sources. Accordingly, where a nondomiciliary is paid compensation by the United States for active service in the armed forces, the compensation received by the individual does not constitute income derived from New York sources, even though the service is performed in whole or in part within New York. However, any other income that a nonresident member of the armed forces receives from New York sources may be subject to tax. This includes any income or gain from property located in New York from a business, trade or profession carried on within the state. (Rule Sec. 132.11(a))

Interstate air carriers: Compensation paid to a nonresident employee of an interstate air carrier for regularly assigned duties performed in New York State and one or more other states is taxable as income from New York sources if the employee earned more than 50% of the compensation in New York. An employee is considered to have earned more than 50% of the compensation in New York if the employee's scheduled flight time in New York is more than 50% of the total scheduled flight time in the calendar year. (Rule Sec. 132.11(c))

• *Stock options, stock appreciation rights*

Regulations provide for a grant-to-vest allocation period for statutory stock options, nonstatutory stock options without a readily ascertainable fair market value at the time of grant, and stock appreciation right (Reg. Secs. 132.24, 132.25, and 154.6).

PERSONAL INCOME TAX

CHAPTER 5

MINIMUM INCOME TAX ON TAX PREFERENCES (Repealed)

¶501 In General

For taxable years beginning before 2014, a minimum income tax was imposed on the New York minimum taxable income of every individual, estate, or trust, in addition to any other tax imposed under Article 22 of the Tax Law.

The minimum income tax (also called an "add-on tax" or alternative minimum tax) was imposed on the New York minimum taxable income of every individual, estate or trust (former Sec. 602, Tax Law). Minimum taxable income was determined with reference to items of tax preference (see below).

¶502 Imposition and Rate of Minimum Income Tax (repealed)

Law: Former Secs. 602, 622, 636, Tax Law (CCH NEW YORK TAX REPORTS, ¶ 15-405 *et seq.*).

Comparable Federal: Secs. 55—59 (U.S. MASTER TAX GUIDE ¶ 1401—1440).

Forms: IT-220, Minimum Income Tax.

Prior to repeal (see ¶ 501), the tax was imposed on the New York minimum taxable income of every individual, estate, or trust at the rate of 6%. (former Sec. 602, Tax Law)

Minimum taxable income was determined with reference to items of tax preference. For purposes of the minimum income tax, the term "items of tax preference" means the federal items of tax preference, as defined in IRC Sec. 57, of a resident individual, estate, or trust, for the taxable year, with certain modifications and an adjustment provision. (former Sec. 622(a), Tax Law) See also ¶ 504.

¶503 Basis of Tax—Minimum Taxable Income (repealed)

Law: Former Secs. 602, 622, Tax Law (CCH NEW YORK TAX REPORTS, ¶ 15-415).

Comparable Federal: Secs. 55—59 (U.S. MASTER TAX GUIDE ¶ 1401—1440).

Prior to repeal (see ¶ 501), the tax was imposed on the New York minimum taxable income of individuals, estates, and trusts.

• *Resident individuals, estates, or trusts*

Prior to repeal (see ¶ 501), the New York minimum taxable income of a resident individual, estate or trust was the sum of the items of tax preference (defined at ¶ 504) reduced (but not below zero) by the aggregate of the following (former Sec. 622(a), Tax Law; former Sec. 636(a), Tax Law):

(1) Specific deduction (¶ 505);

(2) The tax on New York taxable income for the taxable year, reduced by the sum of allowable credits (except the credit for tax withheld); and

(3) To the extent that the sum of the items of tax preference exceeds the sum of (1) and (2) above, the amount of any net operating loss of the taxpayer, as determined for federal income tax purposes, that remains as a net operating loss carryover to a succeeding taxable year. The amount of any net operating loss used to reduce the sum of the items of tax preference must be treated as an item of tax preference in the next succeeding taxable years, in order of time, in which such net operating loss carryover reduces federal taxable income.

• *Nonresident or part-year resident individuals, estates, or trusts*

For a nonresident taxpayer, the term "items of tax preference" (¶502) means the items of tax preference derived from or connected with New York sources, including special accrual provisions applicable to a nonresident or part-year resident individual, estate, or trust, for the taxable year. The New York minimum taxable income of a nonresident or part-year resident individual, estate, or trust is the sum of the items of tax preference, reduced (but not below zero) by the aggregate of the following (former Sec. 622(a), Tax Law, former Sec. 636(a), Tax Law):

(1) The applicable specific deduction (¶505);

(2) The tax on New York taxable income for the taxable year, reduced by the sum of allowable credits (except the credit for tax withheld); and

(3) To the extent that the sum of the items of tax preference exceeds the sum of (1) and (2) above, the amount of any net operating loss of the taxpayer that remains as a net operating loss carryover to a succeeding taxable year. In such case, however, the amount of such net operating loss used to reduce the sum of the items of tax preference will be treated as an item of tax preference in the next succeeding taxable years, in order of time, in which such net operating loss carryover reduces federal taxable income.

¶504 Items of Tax Preference (repealed)

Law: Former Sec. 622, Tax Law (CCH New York Tax Reports, ¶15-420, 15-430).

Comparable Federal: Secs. 55—59 (U.S. Master Tax Guide ¶1401—1440).

For purposes of the repealed minimum tax (¶503), the term "items of tax preference" means the federal items of tax preference, as defined in IRC Sec. 57, of a resident individual, estate or trust, for the taxable year with certain modifications, and adjusted as indicated below.

New York modifications: The New York computation required modifications to the federal items of tax preference, as follows (former Sec. 622(b), Tax Law):

— The federal items of tax preference for depletion are excluded from the computation of items of tax preference for New York;

— Except with respect to recovery property subject to the provisions of IRC Sec. 280-F (luxury automobiles) and recovery property placed in service in New York in taxable years beginning after 1984, the federal item of tax preference with respect to the accelerated cost recovery deduction will be excluded from the computation of items of tax preference;

— In the case of a shareholder of a federal S corporation, when the New York S corporation election has not been made, the federal items of tax preference of the corporation are excluded from the computation of items of tax preference; and

— The federal item of tax preference with respect to tax-exempt interest will be excluded from the computation of items of tax preference.

Adjustment: The items of tax preference will be adjusted when the tax treatment giving rise to such items will not result in the reduction of tax for any taxable year. (former Sec. 622(e), Tax Law)

¶505 Specific Deduction (repealed)

Law: Former Secs. 622, 636, Tax Law (CCH NEW YORK TAX REPORTS, ¶15-425).

Prior to repeal (see ¶501), the Tax Law provided a specific deduction in determining New York minimum taxable income, as follows:

Resident individuals: The specific deduction was $5,000 for resident individuals and married persons filing joint returns and $2,500 for married individuals filing separate returns. (former Sec. 622(c)(1), Tax Law)

Nonresidents or part-year residents: The specific deduction from minimum taxable income for nonresident or part-year resident individuals was an amount that bears the same ratio to $5,000, or $2,500, in the case of a married individual filing a separate return, as the taxpayer's items of tax preference bear to the taxpayer's total items of tax preference computed as if the taxpayer were a resident for the taxable year. (former Sec. 636(c)(1), Tax Law)

The deduction could not exceed $5,000 ($2,500 in the case of a married individual filing a separate return).

Resident estates and trusts: The deduction was an amount, not over $5,000, that bears the same ratio to $5,000 as the items of tax preference of the estate or trust computed as described in ¶504 bear to the sum of the items of tax preference of the estate or trust computed under the laws of the United States for the taxable year, with the modifications described in ¶504, but without regard to any apportionment of the items of tax preference between such estate or trust and the beneficiaries of the estate or trust under the laws of the United States. (former Sec. 622(c)(2), Tax Law)

Nonresident or part-year resident estates and trusts: The deduction was an amount, not over $5,000, that bears the same proportion to $5,000 as its items of tax preference (derived from or connected with New York sources) bear to the sum of the items of tax preference computed as if it were a resident estate or trust for the taxable year (¶504), but without regard to any apportionment of the items of tax preference between the estate or trust and its beneficiaries. (former Sec. 636(c)(2), Tax Law)

PERSONAL INCOME TAX

CHAPTER 6
RETURNS, ESTIMATES, PAYMENT OF TAX, WITHHOLDING

¶601 Returns—Time and Place of Filing

Law: Secs. 651, 659, Tax Law; Reg. Secs. 158.12, 2600-1.1 *et seq.* (CCH NEW YORK TAX REPORTS, ¶ 17-150 *et seq.*, 89-102).

Comparable Federal: Secs. 6072, 6081, 6091 (U.S. MASTER TAX GUIDE, ¶ 3, 118—122, 1501, 2525—2545).

Forms: See ¶ 602.

Calendar-year returns of annual income are due for individuals, partnerships, estates, and trusts on or before April 15. Fiscal-year taxpayers must file returns on or before the 15th day of the fourth month following the close of the fiscal year. These due dates are the same as for federal returns. (Sec. 651(a), Tax Law)

Partnerships having a resident partner or having any income derived from New York sources are required to file a partnership return. (Sec. 658(c), Tax Law) The return must be filed on or before the 15th day of the third (before 2016, fourth) month of the taxable year, except that the due date for the return of a partnership consisting entirely of resident aliens is the date prescribed for the filing of its federal partnership return for the taxable year.

Due dates for nonresident alien individuals are the same as for federal returns.

MCTDMT: Beginning with tax year 2015, self-employed individuals (including partners) paying MCTDMT must do so on their personal income tax returns. MCTMT due dates are now the same as the personal income tax due dates. (**http://www.tax.ny.gov/bus/mctmt/mctmt_changes_self_employed.htm**).

• *Return preparers*

If a tax return preparer prepared authorized tax documents for more than 10 different taxpayers during any calendar year beginning on or after January 1, 2012, and if in any succeeding calendar year he or she prepares one or more authorized tax documents using tax software, then for that succeeding calendar year and each subsequent calendar year, all authorized tax documents prepared by that preparer must be filed electronically. Any return or report including one or more tax documents that cannot be filed electronically will not be deemed to be an authorized tax document for purposes of the electronic filing requirements under Sec. 29, Tax Law. (*Important Notice N-12-4*, New York Department of Taxation and Finance, April 2012, CCH NEW YORK TAX REPORTS, ¶ 407-529; see also ¶ 3704)

The E-file mandate applies to individuals and tax return preparers through December 31, 2019 (*TSB-M-16(4)C, (2)I, (5)S*, New York Department of Taxation and Finance, July 22, 2016, CCH NEW YORK TAX REPORTS,¶ 408-810)

Preparers subject to the e-file mandate must continue to e-file all of their clients' authorized tax returns in all future years regardless of the number of returns prepared. (Publication 58, *Information for Income Tax Return Preparers*, January 2015, CCH NEW YORK TAX REPORTS, ¶ 19-614)

Registration: A "tax return preparer" is an individual who prepares a substantial portion of any return for compensation. Tax preparers must register if they are paid to prepare at least one New York State return in a calendar year as a tax return preparer or help to issue or administer a refund anticipation loan or refund anticipation check.

"Commercial tax return preparers" must pay a $100 registration fee if they (1) are paid to prepare 10 or more New York State tax returns in the previous calendar year and will be paid to prepare at least one tax return in the current calendar year; or (2) will be paid to prepare 10 or more tax returns in the current calendar year.

No fee is required for a tax return preparer who does not meet the definition of a commercial tax return preparer. Additionally, there is no fee for an individual who only meets the definition of a facilitator.

Tax preparers, commercial tax return preparers, and facilitators may register on the department's website (**http://www.tax.ny.gov/tp/reg/tpreg.htm**) or by contacting the Call Center at (518) 457-1929. For details, see Publication 58, *Information for Income Tax Return Preparers*, January 2015, CCH NEW YORK TAX REPORTS,¶ 19-614.

Qualifications: Commercial tax return preparers who prepare New York returns must meet certain minimum qualifications. As part of the requirements, commercial tax return preparers must do the following:

— meet applicable IRS requirements;

— complete continuing education requirements; and

— pass a New York state tax competency exam.

Continuing education: Commercial preparers with less than three years of experience must complete 16 hours of continuing education coursework and four hours of coursework each calendar year thereafter. Commercial preparers with three or more years of experience must complete four hours of continuing education coursework each calendar year starting in 2015. (Reg. Sec. 2600-2.2)

Certain tax return preparers (*i.e.,* attorneys, certified public accountants, public accountants, and enrolled agents) are generally not subject to the requirements under the regulations; however, the regulations provide that the department may coordinate with other taxing authorities and professional licensing or other regulatory bodies to make disciplinary referrals with respect to such individuals. (Reg. Sec. 2600-1.1 *et seq.*)

The department also amended an existing personal income tax regulation to eliminate a provision that had allowed a person to be an income tax return preparer without regard to educational qualifications and professional status requirements. (Reg. Sec. 158.12)

• *Report of federal changes—Amended returns*

If the amount of a taxpayer's federal taxable income, federal items of tax preference, total taxable amount, ordinary income portion of a lump-sum distribution or includible gain of a trust for transfers in trust, or credit for employment-related expenses or the amount of any federal foreign tax credit affecting the calculation of the credit for Canadian provincial taxes is changed by the Internal Revenue Service or

¶601

other competent authority, or as the result of a renegotiation of a contract or subcontract with the United States, or if a taxpayer's claim for a credit or refund of federal income tax is disallowed, the taxpayer, employer or payor must report the change or correction within 90 days after the final determination or change or correction. The allowance of a tentative carryback adjustment based on a net operating loss carryback is treated as a final determination. (Sec. 659, Tax Law)

Any taxpayer filing an amended federal income tax return and any employer or payor filing an amended federal return of income tax withheld must also file an amended New York return within 90 days.

Practitioner Comment: Failure to Report Federal Changes

Failure to report a federal change of income results in an indefinite extension of the statute of limitations on assessment. In *Merkowitz*, ALJ 2/16/06, CCH NEW YORK TAX REPORTS, ¶ 405-311, an ALJ upheld a 2000 assessment against taxpayers who failed to report a federal change made to their 1975-1979 income tax returns.

Mark S. Klein, Esq., Hodgson Russ LLP

¶602 Filing Requirements; Forms

Law: Secs. 651, 658, Tax Law (CCH NEW YORK TAX REPORTS, ¶ 17-150 *et seq.*, 89-102).

Comparable Federal: Secs. 6012, 6014, 6017 (U.S. MASTER TAX GUIDE, ¶ 109—124).

Residents: An income tax return must be filed for every resident individual (Sec. 651(a)(1), Tax Law):

— required to file a federal income tax return for the taxable year;

— having federal adjusted gross income for the taxable year, increased by the amounts required to be added to federal adjusted gross income in determining New York adjusted gross income, in excess of $4,000, or in excess of his or her New York standard deduction, if lower;

— subject to the minimum income tax; or

— having received during the taxable year a lump sum distribution any portion of which is subject to the separate tax on the ordinary income portion of a lump sum distribution.

Nonresidents: A return must be filed by every nonresident or part-year resident individual (Sec. 651(a)(3), Tax Law):

— having New York source income for the taxable year, and having federal adjusted gross income for the taxable year, increased by the amounts required to be added to federal adjusted gross income, in excess of his or her standard deduction;

— subject to the minimum income tax; or

— having received during the taxable year a lump sum distribution any portion of which is subject to the separate tax on the ordinary income portion of a lump sum distribution.

Estates or trusts: Returns must be filed by every *resident* estate or trust (Sec. 651(a)(2), Tax Law):

— required to file a federal income tax return for the taxable year;

— having any New York taxable income for the taxable year;

— subject to the minimum income tax; or

— having received during the taxable year a lump sum distribution any portion of which is subject to the separate tax on the ordinary income portion of a lump sum distribution.

A *nonresident* estate or trust or part-year resident trust must file a return if it (Sec. 651(a)(4), Tax Law):

— has New York source income for the taxable year;

— is subject to the minimum income tax; or

— has received during the taxable year a lump sum distribution any portion of which is subject to the tax on the ordinary income portion of a lump sum distribution.

Partnerships: Every partnership having a resident partner or having any income derived from New York sources must file a New York return. (Sec. 658(c)(1), Tax Law) For combined return for 50 or more qualified nonresident partners, see ¶ 708.

S corporations: Every federal S corporation for which an election to be treated as a New York S corporation is in effect must file a New York return. (Sec. 658(c)(2), Tax Law)

Withholding: See ¶ 608— ¶ 610.

Information at source: See ¶ 810.

CCH Advisory: Child's Income

A child's investment income over $1,300 is often reported on the parent's federal return. In that case, the child's income is also reported on the parent's New York return. However, it may be advantageous to file a separate New York return for the child because, in that way, there will be no New York tax on the first $3,000 of the child's investment income (¶ 306).

• *Forms*

Forms are prescribed by the Commissioner and may be obtained from the district offices of the New York State Income Tax Bureau or from the Taxpayer Assistance Bureau, W.A. Harriman Campus, Albany, New York 12227.

Forms may be obtained by calling toll-free 1-800-462-8100.

Forms also may be downloaded from the Department's website at **http:/ www.tax.ny.gov/forms**

Forms in current use include the following:

No.	Description
IT-201	Resident Income Tax Return
IT-201-X	Amended Resident Income Tax Return
IT-203	Nonresident and Part-Year Resident Income Tax Return
IT-204	Partnership Income
IT-205	Fiduciary Income Tax Return
IT-211	Special Depreciation Schedule
IT-220	Minimum Income Tax
IT-2105	Estimated Income Tax Payment Voucher for Individuals
IT-2105.1	Reconciliation of Estimated Income Tax Account
IT-2105.9	Underpayment of Estimated Income Tax By Individuals and Fiduciaries

¶603 Returns—Husband and Wife

Law: Secs. 171, 651, Tax Law (CCH NEW YORK TAX REPORTS, ¶ 17-150 *et seq.*, 89-102).

Comparable Federal: Sec. 6013 (U.S. MASTER TAX GUIDE, ¶ 109).

Forms: See ¶ 602.

Whether a husband and wife may file a joint New York return is determined by how they filed their federal returns. (Sec. 651(b)(1), Tax Law, Sec. 651(b)(2), Tax Law) If no federal returns are filed, a husband and wife may elect to file either joint or separate New York returns. (Sec. 651(b)(3), Tax Law)

Same-sex married persons: See the discussion at ¶ 104.

• *Separate federal returns*

If a husband and wife file separate federal returns, they must file separate New York returns. (Sec. 651(b)(1), Tax Law) The Commissioner is also allowed to require separate income tax returns if one spouse demonstrates to the satisfaction of the Commissioner that:

> (1) the address or whereabouts of the other spouse is unknown;

> (2) reasonable efforts have been made to locate the missing spouse; and

> (3) good cause existed for the failure to file a joint New York income tax return.

Separate returns may also be allowed in cases in which:

> (1) the other spouse has refused to sign a joint New York tax return;

> (2) reasonable efforts have been made to have the spouse sign the return;

> (3) objective evidence of alienation of the spouse exists;, and

> (4) good cause existed for the failure to file a joint return.

• *Joint federal returns*

If a husband and wife file a joint federal return, they must file a joint New York return, except if either husband or wife is a resident and the other is a nonresident. (Sec. 651(b)(2), Tax Law) If either husband or wife is a resident and the other is a nonresident, they must file separate New York returns unless the husband and wife determine their federal taxable income jointly and both elect to determine their joint New York taxable income as if both were residents.

Practitioner Comment: Special Rule for New York City Residents

Married couples eligible to file a joint New York State tax return must separately compute their New York City tax liability if only one spouse was a New York City resident. According to the Department of Taxation and Finance, the couple must "compute on a separate sheet of paper the NYC resident tax on the New York State taxable income of the city resident as if you had filed separate federal returns reduced by the NYC household credit (if applicable)". See 2015 Instructions for IT-201, line 51.

Mark S. Klein, Esq., Hodgson Russ LLP

In *Brady v. State of New York* (1993, NY CtApp); CCH NEW YORK TAX REPORTS, ¶ 400-680, the New York Court of Appeals ruled that a nonresident married couple filing a joint federal return must use the combined income of both spouses to determine the base tax subject to the New York source income percentage allocation, but did not address a ruling of the lower court that held that a nonresident spouse with no New York source income could not be required to file a joint state return. As a result, the Department of Taxation and Finance has advised that, where a joint federal return is filed and one spouse is a nonresident with no New York source income, a joint state return must be filed that includes the income of both spouses reported on the federal return. However, the spouse without New York source income cannot be required to sign the return and cannot be held liable for tax, penalties or interest that may be due (*Important Notice N-92-31*, Department of Taxation and Finance; CCH NEW YORK TAX REPORTS, ¶ 400-934).

CCH Advisory: Spousal Liability

New York has adopted federal provisions regarding relief from joint and several liability (see IRC Sec. 6015). For information on innocent spouse relief, see *Publication 89, Innocent Spouse Relief (And Separation of Liability And Equitable Relief)*, Department of Taxation and Finance, **http://www.tax.ny.gov/pdf/publications/income/pub89.pdf**.

¶604 Group Returns for Nonresident Athletes

Law: Sec. 651, Tax Law; Reg. Sec. 151.18 (CCH New York Tax Reports, ¶17-150 *et seq.*, 18-801a, 89-102).

Forms: IT-203-TM, Group Return for Nonresident Athletic Team Members.

Professional athletic teams may request permission to file group income tax returns on behalf of their qualified nonresident athletes who elect to participate in the group return in lieu of each athlete filing a personal income tax return. (Reg. Sec. 151.18) A team electing the group return must apply in writing for permission; the filing of a group return does not constitute a request. The application requires individual powers of attorney from each electing member. Electing members must be nonresidents for the entire year and have no other New York source income other than that derived from the professional sport.

A similar option is offered to nonresident partners and to members of limited liability companies and limited liability partnerships (¶708).

For information on allocation of wages to New York by nonresident members of professional athletic teams, see ¶403.

¶605 Extension of Time

Law: Secs. 657, 696 Tax Law; Reg. Sec. 157.2, (CCH New York Tax Reports, ¶15-175, 17-150 *et seq.*, 89-102).

Comparable Federal: Sec. 6081 (U.S. Master Tax Guide, ¶120).

Forms: IT-370, Application for Automatic Extension of Time to File for Individuals.

The Commissioner may grant a reasonable extension of time for filing any return, declaration, statement or other required document or for payment of tax or estimated tax (or any installment). The extension may not exceed six months for an individual, unless the taxpayer is abroad or in the military service. (Sec. 657, Tax Law). The extension may not exceed five months for a partnership or fiduciary return (except for electing large partnerships allowed a six-month federal extension) (Reg. Sec. 157.2(a)).

Automatic extension: An individual who is required to file a New York personal income tax return for any taxable year will be allowed an automatic six-month extension of time to file such return if an application is prepared on Form IT-370, *Application for Automatic Extension of Time to File for Individuals.*

Death of spouse: New York grants an automatic 90-day extension for paying personal income taxes or filing a personal income tax return when a taxpayer's spouse dies within 30 days prior to the April 15 deadline. No penalties or interest will be assessed or imposed upon a taxpayer during the extension. (Sec. 657(c), Tax Law)

An extension of time to file a New York State personal income tax return automatically extends the time to file New York City resident personal income tax and nonresident earnings tax returns.

• *Military personnel*

Extensions of time are provided for members of the Armed Forces and support personnel serving in an area designated as a combat zone or in a qualified hazardous duty area (*Important Notice N-02-5*, Department of Taxation and Finance, February, 2002; CCH NEW YORK TAX REPORTS, ¶320-086). Extension provisions also include personnel serving outside the United States in a contingency operation. See ¶111 for a list of designated combat zones and qualified hazardous duty areas. Service members directly supporting operations in Afghanistan or Iraq from other locations, who are receiving imminent danger pay or hostile fire pay, are deemed to be serving in the combat zone.

Extensions apply to the following (Sec. 696, Tax Law):

— filing a return of income tax (except withholding tax);

— payment of income tax (except withholding) or any liability to the state in respect thereof;

— filing a petition or application;

— allowance of credit or refund of income tax;

— filing claim for credit or refund;

— assessment of income tax;

— giving or making notice or demand for payment of tax or liability to the state with respect thereto;

— collection of any liability in respect of income tax;

— bringing of suit by or on behalf of the state in respect of any income tax liability; or

— any other act required or permitted by Article 22 or specified in regulations prescribed under Sec. 696, Tax Law.

Additionally, the above-described period is disregarded in determining the amount of any credit or refund (including interest).

Armed forces members are entitled to an exemption from New York personal income tax for military pay received while serving in a combat zone to the same extent that military pay is exempt from federal income tax. See ¶111.

CCH Advisory: Military Collection Deferral

Regular members of the Armed Forces, Reserve Forces, and National Guard who have been called to active duty and owe back New York personal income taxes may qualify for a deferral of the collection of the back income taxes owed under the New York State Soldiers' and Sailors' Civil Relief Act if they can show that their ability to pay the taxes is impaired because of their military service. The deferral only applies to income taxes that became due before or during the military service, and extends the payment deadline to six months after active military service ends. No interest or penalty will accrue during the deferral period. To take advantage of the deferral, a taxpayer must show both an inability to pay the tax and that this inability resulted from military service. A taxpayer must have received a notice of tax due, or be on an installment agreement with the state before applying for the deferral (*Important Notice N-02-3*, New York Department of Taxation and Finance, February 2002, CCH NEW YORK TAX REPORTS, ¶320-084).

¶605

Effective November 4, 2016, and applicable to any assessed taxes for which there is an outstanding tax liability, the extension provision does not apply to the collection of personal income tax liabilities with respect to any period of continuous hospitalization described in Sec. 696(a), Tax Law, and the next 180 days thereafter (Sec. 696(i), Tax Law)

Death of military member: In the case of the death of a member of the armed services while in active service in a combat zone as described above, or as a result of injuries sustained while so serving, the personal income tax will not apply for the tax year in which the date of death falls, or for a prior tax year ending on or after the first day served in the combat zone. No returns will be required on behalf of the individual or the individual's estate for such year, and the unpaid tax for that year, if any, will not be assessed for that year. Also, any assessment will be abated and any collected tax refunded.

Additional information may be found in Publication 361, *New York State Income Tax Information for Military Personnel and Veterans.*

¶606 Estimated Tax

Law: Secs. 663, 685, Tax Law; Reg. Secs. 163.1—163.5, 185.3 (CCH NEW YORK TAX REPORTS, ¶17-150 *et seq.,* 89-104, 89-206).

Comparable Federal: Sec. 6654 (U.S. MASTER TAX GUIDE, ¶2679, 2875).

Forms: IT-2105, Estimated Income Tax Voucher; IT-2658, Reports of Estimated Tax for Corporate Partners and Nonresident Individual Partners and Shareholders; IT-2663, Application for Certification for Recording of Deed and Nonresident Estimated Income Tax Payment Voucher.

New York residents and part-year residents with New York source income are required to make annual payments of estimated tax when they expect to owe, after withholding and credits, at least $300 of New York, New York City, or Yonkers tax for the current tax year, and their withholding and credits are expected to be less than the smaller of (1) 90% of the tax shown for the current tax year, or (2) 100% of the tax shown on the prior year's return (provided a return was filed and the taxable year consisted of 12 months). (Sec. 685(d), Tax Law)

In order to avoid the penalty for underpayment of estimated tax, the total amount of estimated tax and withholding tax paid must be:

— at least 90% (66 2/3% for farmers and fishermen) of the amount of income tax due as shown on the previous year's return (or 90% of the tax due if no return was filed); or

— 100% of the tax shown on the previous year's return (110% of that amount if the taxpayer is not a farmer or a fisherman and the New York adjusted gross income shown on that return is more than $150,000 or, if married filing separately for the current year, more than $75,000).

CCH Advisory: Nonresident's Sales of Real Property

Upon the sale of real property within New York by a nonresident taxpayer, the taxpayer must estimate the personal income tax liability on the gain, if any, from the sale or transfer. The estimation is to be done using an estimated tax rate equal to the highest rate of tax for the taxable year. Certain exceptions are set forth in the statute, *e.g.,* if the property being sold is a principal residence of the seller, within the meaning of IRC Sec. 121. For details, see *TSB-M-03(4)I,* CCH NEW YORK TAX REPORTS, ¶300-398 and *TSB-M-03(4.1)I,* CCH NEW YORK TAX REPORTS, ¶300-407. See also *TSB-M-04(5)I,* CCH NEW YORK TAX REPORTS, ¶300-438, regarding requirements with respect to sales of cooperative housing shares.

Due dates for payment: The dates upon which installments of estimated tax become due are dependent upon when the requirements to make estimated tax payments are first met. For calendar year taxpayers whose requirements are met before April 1, estimated tax installments are due in four equal installments on April 15, June 15, September 15, and January 15 of the following tax year. When the requirements to make estimated tax payments are first met after March 31 and before June 1, 50% of the required annual payment is due on June 15, 25% is due on September 15, and 25% is due on the following January 15. When the requirements are met after May 31 and before September 1, 75% of the required annual payment is due on September 15, and 25% is due on the following January 15. When the requirements are met after August 31, 100% of the required annual payment is due on the following January 15. (Reg. Sec. 185.3)

Corresponding dates apply to fiscal year taxpayers. Any installment may be paid prior to its due date.

The "required annual payment" of estimated tax is the lesser of 90% of the tax shown on the return for the taxable year, or 100% of the tax shown on the return for the previous taxable year (provided a return was filed and the taxable year consisted of 12 months).

Penalty threshold: There is no addition to tax if the tax due shown on the return, after credit for withholding and estimated tax payments, is less than $300. Previously, the threshold was $100.

Farmers and fishermen: Qualified farmers and fishermen may elect to make one payment of estimated tax, equal to $66^2/3\%$ of their total tax liability, on January 15 of the following tax year. Estimated tax payments will not be required if the New York return is filed, and total amount due is paid, on or before March 1.

An individual will be regarded as a farmer or fisherman if federal gross income from farming or fishing (including oyster farming) for the year is at least two-thirds of the total federal gross income from all sources for the taxable year or federal gross income from farming or fishing (including oyster farming) shown on the person's return for the preceding taxable year is at least two-thirds of the total federal gross income from all sources shown on the return.

- *Nonresident withholding by pass-through entities*

Partnerships (other than publicly traded partnerships), limited liability companies (LLCs), and S corporations having income from New York sources are required to make estimated tax payments on behalf of partners, members, or shareholders that are nonresident individuals or C corporations, with respect to their distributive or pro rata shares of such income. For details, see ¶858 and ¶3602.

- *Underpayment of tax*

Penalties are imposed on the underpayment of estimated tax. The amount of the penalty is determined by applying the applicable annual interest rate (¶607) to the amount of the underpayment for the period of the underpayment. The period will run from the due date for the required installment to the earlier of the 15th day of the fourth month following the close of the taxable year or, with respect to any portion of the underpayment, the date on which the portion is paid. The amount of the underpayment is the excess of the required installment over the amount, if any, of the installment paid on or before the due date for the installment. (Sec. 685(c)(1), (2), Tax Law)

Taxpayers who file returns for the prior taxable year on or before January 31 and pay the full amount owed are not subject to any additions to tax with respect to any underpayment of the fourth required payment for the taxable year.

Required installment: For individuals required to pay four installments of estimated tax, each installment must equal 25% of the required annual payment. The required annual payment is the lesser of (1) 90% of the tax shown on the return for the taxable year (if no return is filed, 90% of the tax for such year), or (2) subject to the limitations noted below, 100% of the tax shown on the return for the preceding taxable year (provided a return was filed and the year consisted of 12 months). (Sec. 685(c)(4), Tax Law)

Annualized income exception: When an individual establishes that an annualized income installment is less than the required installment determined pursuant to the preceding paragraph, the required installment will be reduced to an amount equal to the annualized income installment. Subsequent required installments will be increased until the amount of the reduction has been recaptured. (Sec. 685(c)(4), Tax Law)

The "annualized income installment" is the excess, if any, of the amount of the applicable percentage of the tax for the taxable year computed by placing on an annualized basis the taxable income and minimum taxable income for months in the taxable year ending before the due date for the installment, over the aggregate amount of any prior required installments for the taxable year. The applicable percentage of the tax is $22^1/2\%$ in the case of the first installment, 45% in the case of the second installment, $67^1/2\%$ in the case of the third installment, and 90% in the case of the fourth installment, and is computed without regard to any increase in the rates applicable to the taxable year unless such increase was enacted at least 30 days before the due date of the installment.

Additions to tax—Exemptions: No addition to tax will be imposed on a New York resident or nonresident who had New York adjusted gross income who did not have any tax liability for the preceding taxable year (consisting of 12 months), or if the tax shown on the return for the current taxable year, reduced by allowable credits, is less than $300.

No addition to tax will be imposed on any installment due after the death of a taxpayer.

Waiver of tax: The Commissioner of Taxation and Finance may waive any addition to tax upon a determination that, due to casualty, disaster, or other unusual circumstances, such addition would be against equity and good conscience. The Commissioner also may waive any addition to tax with respect to an underpayment when an individual attained age 62 or became disabled during the current or prior taxable year, and the failure to make the required payment was due to reasonable cause and was not willful. (Sec. 685(d)(4), Tax Law)

¶607 Payment of Tax

Law: Secs. 652, 657, 697, Tax Law (CCH New York Tax Reports, ¶ 17-150 *et seq.*, 89-102, 89-108).

Comparable Federal: Sec. 6151 (U.S. Master Tax Guide, ¶ 2525—2545).

Any tax due on a return must be paid by the date fixed for filing, without regard to any extension of time for filing. (Sec. 652, Tax Law)

For time and place of filing returns and estimated tax, see ¶601 and ¶606, respectively. For information on payment methods, installment payments, electronic filing, electronic funds transfers, and mailing requirements, see ¶3602.

Individuals whose income is limited to wages, salaries, tips, and like remuneration for services performed as an employee, interest, dividends, and unemployment compensation may elect to have the Commissioner compute the tax due. In such cases, any tax determined to be due must be paid by the later of (1) 10 days from the date of the issuance of the notice and demand, or (2) the date on which the return is due (without regard to any extensions of time).

E-file requirements: Any tax liability or other amount due shown on or required to be paid with authorized tax documents that are required to be filed electronically must be paid electronically as well. For additional information, see ¶3602 and Publication 84, *New York State Handbook for E-filers of Personal Income Tax Returns.*

Currency: For personal and corporation income tax purposes, New York tax law conforms to the federal treatment of convertible virtual currency as detailed in *IRS Notice 2014-21.* The notice provides that convertible virtual currency is treated as property for U.S. federal tax purposes. General tax principles that apply to property transactions apply to transactions using convertible virtual currency. (*TSB-M-14(5)C, TSB-M-14(7)I,* and *TSB-M-14(17)S,* December 5, 2014, CCH NEW YORK TAX REPORTS, ¶408-293)

• *Extension of time*

The Commissioner may grant a reasonable extension of time for payment of tax. (Sec. 657(a), Tax Law) If an extension of time is granted, the Commissioner may require the taxpayer to furnish a bond or other security in an amount not exceeding twice the amount for which the extension is granted.

Credit card payments: The Department of Taxation and Finance accepts credit card payments for personal income tax liabilities and balances due on extension payments. The credit cards accepted are American Express, MasterCard, and Discover/ Novus.

Interest: The Commissioner determines interest rates on underpayments and overpayments of taxes on the basis of federal short-term rates established for Internal Revenue Code purposes by the United States Secretary of the Treasury. For rates, see ¶807.

¶608 Withholding—General

Law: Secs. 171-h, 671, 673, 674, Tax Law; Reg. Secs. 171.1, 171.4, 171.5, 171.6 (CCH NEW YORK TAX REPORTS, ¶16-605 *et seq.*).

Comparable Federal: Secs. 3401, 3402 (U.S. MASTER TAX GUIDE, ¶2601—2663).

Forms: See ¶609.

New York provides for the withholding of the New York personal income tax from wages of all resident employees for services performed either within or outside New York and from wages of nonresidents for services performed within the state. (Reg. Secs. 171.1, 171.6)

In general, the New York withholding provisions parallel the federal. The New York law specifically adopts the federal terms (such as "wages," "employer," "employee," "payroll period," "withholding exemptions"). There is, however no New York withholding on compensation paid to a seaman who is a member of the crew on a vessel engaged in foreign, coastwise, intercoastal, interstate, or noncontiguous trade.

No withholding is required for employees under 18 years of age, employees under 25 years of age who are full-time students, and employees over 65 years of age; provided that the employees had no income tax liability in the prior year and can reasonably anticipate none in the current year.

The Commissioner is authorized to issue regulations permitting withholding of tax from nonwage remuneration and also from other payments.

Same-sex married persons: See the discussion at ¶104.

Household employers: For personal income withholding, sales and use tax, and unemployment compensation purposes, the Department of Taxation and Finance has issued a tax bulletin that summarizes New York State reporting and filing requirements and certain federal requirements for household employers. (*Tax Bulletin TB-MU-350*, CCH NEW YORK TAX REPORTS, ¶ 19-578)

Supplemental unemployment compensation benefits, annuity payments, lottery winnings, and supplemental wages: For purposes of withholding, the following payments are treated as if they were payments of wages by an employer to an employee for a payroll period (Sec. 671(b), Tax Law):

— Any supplemental unemployment compensation benefit paid to an individual to the extent includible in the individual's New York adjusted gross income or New York source income;

— Any payment of an annuity to an individual to the extent includible in such individual's New York adjusted gross income or New York source income if, at the time the payment is made, a request that such annuity be subject to withholding is in effect;

— Any amount that is deducted or deferred from an employee's salary under a flexible benefits program established pursuant to Sec. 23 of the General Municipal Law or Sec. 1210-a of the Public Authorities Law;

— Any payment of winnings from a wager placed in a lottery conducted by the Division of the Lottery, if the proceeds exceed $5,000 and are payable pursuant to a prize claim made by an individual who was a state resident at the time of the selection of the prize winning lottery ticket;

— Any member or employee contributions to a retirement system or pension fund picked up by an employer pursuant to the state Retirement and Social Security Law, Education Law, or the Administrative Code of the City of New York; and

— Any amount by which an employee's salary is reduced for health insurance and welfare benefit fund surcharges pursuant to Sec. 12-126.2, NYC Adm. Code.

Reporting newly hired employees: Employers, as defined in IRC Sec. 3401(d), are required to report specified information to the Department of Taxation and Finance regarding their newly hired employees who will be employed in the state. (Sec. 171-h, Tax Law) Employers must report the information within 20 calendar days from the hiring date, which is considered to be the first day on which compensated services are performed by the employee (*i.e.*, the first day when any services are performed for which the employee will be paid wages or other compensation, or the first day when an employee working for commissions is eligible to earn commissions). Employers who file by magnetic media must report the information using submissions made 12 to 16 days apart.

Employers who have employees working in more than one state and file by magnetic media need only designate one of the states to report any newly hired employees. (Sec. 171-h, Tax Law)

Withholding exemptions: The number of New York withholding exemptions that an employee receiving taxable wages may claim may not exceed the number of New York exemptions to which the employee is entitled, whether the employee is a resident or nonresident, and such additional New York withholding exemptions as may be prescribed by regulations or instructions of the Commissioner of Taxation and Finance, taking into account the applicable standard deduction and such other factors as he or she finds appropriate. The amount of each New York withholding exemption is the amount of New York exemption to which the employee is entitled, whether the individual is a resident or a nonresident. (Sec. 671(c), Tax Law)

¶608

Practitioner Comment: Exemptions in Excess of Fourteen

If an employee claims a withholding exemption in excess of fourteen, a copy of the IT-2104 must be sent to the Department of Taxation and Finance. See Reg. 171.4(d)(4)(i) and instructions to the 2016 Form IT-2104. This can trigger an audit of the employer or the taxpayer submitting the form.

Mark S. Klein, Esq., Hodgson Russ LLP

Resident employees of employer required to withhold other state or local income taxes: An employer required to deduct and withhold income taxes of other states or their political subdivisions or of the District of Columbia from wages paid to a New York resident shall deduct and withhold from those wages the amount of New York income tax determined according to the withholding tables or other method (¶610) *less* the amount required to be deducted and withheld for the other jurisdiction. (Reg. Sec. 171.5)

Withholding from unemployment benefits: Individuals filing for unemployment benefits may elect to have state personal income tax deducted and withheld from the payments. Previously, the authorization for withholding was limited to federal income tax. (Sec. 596, Labor Law)

Practitioner Comment: Duty to Withhold

Even businesses located outside of New York State are obligated to withhold New York income tax on the wages paid to their employees who happen to be New York residents. They must also withhold tax on a portion of the compensation paid to a nonresident of New York who occasionally visits the State on business. Auditors appear to have increased their activity in this area and pursue border businesses that meet the sales tax nexus requirements (¶2002; Sec. 671, Tax Law). These audits can raise additional issues since corporate officers are frequently held personally liable for the uncollected taxes if they are considered a "person required to collect . . . tax" under Sec. 685(g) of the Tax Law (*Gruenhagen*, NYS TAT (11/15/90), CCH NEW YORK TAX REPORTS, ¶253-408). Additionally, there is no statute of limitations for an assessment against a person required to collect tax who fails to do so.

Mark S. Klein, Esq., Hodgson Russ LLP

Pensions of former residents: Federal law curtails states' rights to subject retirement income of former residents to state income taxation (P.L. 104-95, 104th Cong, 1st Sess.; 4 USC 114(a)). The statute protects from source taxation all pension income or other retirement distributions received from IRC Sec. 401(a) trusts exempt from taxation under IRC Sec. 501(a), simplified IRC Sec. 408(k) plans, IRC Sec. 403(a) annuity plans, IRC Sec. 403(b) annuity contracts, IRC Sec. 7701(a)(37) individual retirement plans, IRC Sec. 457 deferred compensation plans, IRC Sec. 414(d) government plans and IRC Sec. 501(c)(18) trusts. Also included are prohibitions on out-of-state taxation of distributions from three non-qualified plans. First, plans described in IRC Sec. 3121(v)(2)(C) are protected if payments are made at least annually and spread over the actual life expectancy of the beneficiaries. Second, the same plans are protected if payments are spread over at least a ten-year period. Third, in instances where plans are trusts under IRC Sec. 401(a), but exceed limitations set forth in IRC Secs. 401(a)(17) and 415, the pensions are exempted from out-of-state taxation.

The law was amended in 2006 to clarify the treatment of nonresident retired partners; see *TSB-M-07(2)I*, January 24, 2007, CCH NEW YORK TAX REPORTS, ¶405-601, for the Department of Taxation and Finance's discussion of the 2006 amendment. See also *TSB-A-11(10)I*, New York Commissioner of Taxation and Finance, November 17, 2011, CCH NEW YORK TAX REPORTS, ¶407-422.

• *Wage reporting requirements*

The New York Department of Taxation and Finance requires all employers to complete the state W-2 box according to the guidelines below for any employee who has federal wages subject to New York state personal income tax withholding (*TSB-M-02(3)I*, May 1, 2002, CCH NEW YORK TAX REPORTS, ¶ 300-359). Except for New York state and local government employers, these guidelines are also applicable to the amount required to be reported on New York State Form NYS-45, *Quarterly Combined Withholding, Wage Reporting and Unemployment Insurance Return.*

Full-year New York residents: The amount of wages that must be reported in the state W-2 box is the same as the amount of federal wages required to be reported in box 1, Wages, tips, other compensation (federal box 1).

Full-year New York nonresident employees who perform all of their services in New York: The amount of wages that must be reported in the state W-2 box is the same as the amount of federal wages required to be reported in federal box 1.

Full-year New York nonresident employees who do not perform any services in New York: If an employee does not perform any services in New York for the entire tax year, the employer is not required to report any New York state wages in the state W-2 box.

Full-year New York nonresident employees who perform only a portion of their services in New York: If at any time during the tax year a nonresident employee performs services in New York, the amount of wages that must be reported in the state W-2 box is the same amount of federal wages required to be reported in federal box 1. That amount is federal wages before any allocation that the employee may have claimed.

Part-year New York residents: For a part-year New York resident, the amount of wages that must be reported in the state W-2 box is the same amount as the federal wages required to be reported in federal box 1. The amount is federal wages before any allocation that the employee may have claimed.

Reporting of wages on Form NYS-45: Employers must report on Form NYS-45, column (d), part (C), the same amount of federal wages paid to every individual employed at any time during the year as required to be reported in the state W-2 box. For governmental employers, the amount reported in Form NYS-45 must also include any taxable IRC Sec. 414(h) contributions and any IRC Sec. 125 amounts from a New York City flexible benefits program.

Withholding requirements for nonresidents: An employer must deduct the New York income tax on all wages paid to a nonresident employee for services performed in New York. Wages paid to a nonresident employee for services rendered entirely outside New York are not subject to withholding.

Practitioner Comment: Withholding Tax "Safe Harbor"

In 2012, New York State's Department of Taxation and Finance issued guidance exempting employers from withholding New York taxes on nonresident employees who are assigned to a primary work location outside of New York and who work in New York on 14 or fewer days in a calendar year. This 14-day safe harbor rule does not apply to deferred compensation or to payments made to nonresident athletes and entertainers performing services in New York. (*TSB-M-12(5)I*, Taxpayer Guidance Division, New York Department of Taxation and Finance, July 5, 2012, CCH NEW YORK TAX REPORTS, ¶ 407-589)

Mark S. Klein, Esq., Hodgson Russ, LLP

¶608

If a nonresident employee performs services partly within and partly outside New York, the employee should file Form IT-2104.1, Certificate of Nonresidence and Allocation of Withholding Tax, showing the employee's estimate of the percentage of services to be performed in New York State and to be subject to withholding. This percentage is determined as discussed at ¶ 403.

The employer is required to withhold the proper amount of tax. An employer is required to withhold tax from all wages paid to a nonresident employee who works partly within and partly without New York unless the employee files Form IT-2104.1 or unless the employer keeps adequate current records to determine the amount of wages from New York sources.

Practitioner Comment: Liability for Withholding

Although an officer or other person required to collect withholding taxes can become personally liable for an employer's failure to withhold, that liability is not limited to the tax that was not collected; it extends to any interest or penalties that may have been imposed against the employer, as well. (TSB-M-09(12)C, October 20, 2009, CCH NEW YORK TAX REPORTS, ¶ 406-574)

Mark S. Klein, Esq., Hodgson Russ, LLP

¶609 Withholding—Returns and Payment

Law: Secs. 9, 672, 674, 685, Tax Law; Reg. Secs. 174.1, 2396.4 (CCH NEW YORK TAX REPORTS, ¶ 16-665, 89-102, 89-108, 89-206).

Comparable Federal: Secs. 3402, 3403, 3501, 6011 (U.S. MASTER TAX GUIDE, ¶ 2650, 2658).

Forms: The following are the principal forms in current use in connection with withholding tax:

Form Number	Form Title	Federal Counterpart
WT-1-MN	Return of Tax Withheld	
NYS-45	Quarterly Combined Withholding, Wage Reporting and Unemployment Insurance Return	
IT-2102	Wage and Tax Statement	Form W-2
IT-2104	Employee's Withholding Allowance Certificate	Form W-4
IT-2104.1	Certificate of Nonresidence and Allocation of Withholding Tax	

• *Payment of withholding tax*

If an employer, after having made a payroll, has been required to deduct and withhold (but has not paid over) a cumulative amount of $700 or more of tax during a calendar quarter and was required to remit a cumulative aggregate amount of $15,000 or more of withholding tax during the calendar year preceding the previous year, the employer must remit the tax on or before the third business day following the date of making the payroll. Employers required to deduct and withhold a cumulative amount of $700 or more of tax during a calendar quarter who remit a cumulative aggregate amount of less than $15,000 of withholding tax during the calendar year preceding the previous calendar year must remit the tax on or before the fifth business day following the date of payment. Employers who are qualified educational organizations or health care providers must remit the tax on or before the fifth business day following the date of payment. (Sec. 674(a)(1), Tax Law)

Employers who have withheld, but have not paid over, a cumulative aggregate amount of less than $700 at the close of a calendar quarter must pay over the tax quarterly. Employers required to provide wage reporting information for employees must file a quarterly combined return detailing the preceding calendar quarter's withholding tax transactions, wage reporting information, and other information required by the Commissioner. (Sec. 674(a)(2), Tax Law)

The return covering the last calendar quarter of each year must also include withholding reconciliation information for the calendar year, and is to be filed no later than the last day of the month following the last day of each calendar quarter. The return covering the last calendar quarter of each year must be filed no later than January 31 of the succeeding year.

Combined returns: Employers liable for withholding and unemployment insurance contributions, or for payments in lieu of such contributions, must file quarterly combined withholding, wage reporting, and unemployment insurance returns. The returns must be filed no later than the last day of the month following the last day of each calendar quarter. The wage reporting information covering the last calendar quarter of the preceding year and the withholding reconciliation information required for that year must be filed by January 31. When filing a combined quarterly return, the employer must pay, in a single remittance, the unemployment insurance contributions and aggregate withholding taxes required to be paid over with the return. Any overpayment of unemployment insurance contributions or aggregate withholding taxes made by an employer with the quarterly combined return may be credited only against the employer's liability for such contributions or taxes, respectively. (Sec. 674(a)(4), Tax Law)

• *Electronic fund transfers (EFT)*

A taxpayer required to deduct and withhold an aggregate of $35,000 or more of withholding taxes for either of the semiannual periods ending June 30 or December 31 must make each required fund payment by electronic fund transfer (Sec. 9(b), Tax Law). For additional information on EFT requirements, see ¶3602.

• *Penalties*

Employers required to file quarterly combined returns who fail to comply with wage reporting requirements are subject to a maximum penalty of $10,000. For failure to include on the return the required or correct information relating to individual employees, a penalty of $1 will be imposed for each employee about whom information is required. The penalty is increased to $5 and $25 dollars, respectively, for the second and third failures. Employers who file returns more than 30 days after notification of failure to comply are subject to a penalty equal to the sum of $50 multiplied by the number of employees actually shown on its late filed return. (Sec. 685(v), Tax Law)

Employers who fail to file a quarterly combined return, or who file a return beyond the required due date, are subject to a penalty equal to the greater of $1,000 or the sum of $50 multiplied by the number of employees shown on the last quarterly reporting return filed by the employer. Employers who fail to include required quarterly information are subject to a penalty equal to 5% of the quarterly tax liability required to be shown by the employer for the quarter covered by the return. (Sec. 685(v), Tax Law)

Employers who fail to include all of the annual withholding information relating to individual employees on a quarterly return covering the last calendar quarter of a year are subject to a penalty equal to $50 multiplied by the number of employees for whom the information is inaccurate or incomplete. (Sec. 685(v), Tax Law)

Practitioner Comment: Liability for Penalty

An employer's obligation to withhold tax from its employees is separate and distinct from the employee's obligation to pay his or her own taxes on time. Accordingly, even if New York receives all of the tax to which it is entitled from an individual employee, it can impose a penalty (and interest) against an employer for not withholding the correct amount at the correct time (*Harrison*, NYS ALJ (2/1/96), *aff'd*, NYS TAT (2/20/97); CCH New York Tax Reports, ¶402-656 and *Republic New York Corporation*, NYS TAT (10/16/97); CCH New York Tax Reports, ¶402-836).

Mark S. Klein, Esq., Hodgson Russ, LLP

For additional withholding penalties, see ¶809.

¶609

¶610 Withholding—Tables and Methods

Law: Reg. Sec. 171.4 (CCH NEW YORK TAX REPORTS, ¶ 16-620).

Comparable Federal: Sec. 3402 (U.S. MASTER TAX GUIDE, ¶ 2614, 2616).

New York law parallels federal law in providing for withholding of tax by wage bracket tables or other methods.

• *Current withholding tables*

Withholding tables are reproduced in CCH NEW YORK TAX REPORTS, at ¶ 16-620.

New York City withholding tables and methods are available in CCH NEW YORK CITY TAX REPORTS, at ¶ 516-610.

Withholding tables and methods for New York State, New York City, and Yonkers are provided in Publication NYS-50-T, *Employer's Guide to Unemployment Insurance, Wage Reporting, and Withholding Tax*, which is available from the Department of Taxation and Finance at **https://www.tax.ny.gov/pdf/publications/withholding/nys50_t_nys.pdf**.

PERSONAL INCOME TAX

CHAPTER 7

ESTATES AND TRUSTS, PARTNERSHIPS

¶701 Estates and Trusts—General

The New York personal income tax is imposed on the income of estates and trusts as well as on the income of individuals. In general, the information on the federal return is the starting point for the determination of the New York taxable income of estates and trusts, just as for individuals.

For resident estates and trusts (defined at ¶102), the starting point is federal taxable income subject to certain modifications, including a "fiduciary adjustment" (¶703) that allocates modifications between the estate or trust and the resident beneficiaries.

For nonresident estates and trusts (defined at ¶102), the starting point is items of income, gain, loss, and deduction from New York sources included in federal distributable net income (¶704) plus items of income, gain, loss, and deduction from New York sources that are recognized for federal income tax purposes but excluded from federal distributable net income.

If the income of a trust is taxable to the grantor for federal income tax purposes because of certain provisions relating to retained control, power of revocation, or other reason, the federal treatment will be followed by New York.

Practitioner Comment: Executors of New York Estates Can Use the Federal Alternate Valuation Rules Even When No Federal Estate Tax Return is Required

New York's estate tax filing threshold and applicable exclusion are significantly less than their federal counterparts. As a result, some estates are required to file New York estate tax returns even though they have no federal tax obligations.

Under federal law, an executor can elect an alternate valuation method under certain circumstances, but only if that election decreases federal estate taxes. See IRC Sec. 2032. Even though there is no provision in New York law that allows the use of an alternate valuation to reduce New York estate taxes, New York has agreed to adopt the federal rule and will allow the use of an alternate valuation method for purposes of computing the gross estate on a New York estate tax return. (NYT-G-09(1)M)

Mark S. Klein, Hodgson Russ LLP

¶702 Resident Estates and Trusts—New York Taxable Income

Law: Secs. 612, 618, Tax Law (CCH New York Tax Reports, ¶ 15-205, 15-215).

The New York taxable income of a resident estate or trust is its federal taxable income modified as follows (Sec. 618, Tax Law):

— With respect to gains from the sale or other disposition of property, excluded from federal distributable net income, subtractions from federal taxable income are made for the following: (Sec. 618(2), Tax Law):

(1) the portion of any gain, from the sale or other disposition of property having a higher adjusted basis for New York income tax purposes than for federal income tax purposes on December 31, 1959 (or on the last day of 1959-60 fiscal year), that does not exceed such difference in basis; and

(2) the amount of any gain from the sale or other disposition of property that had been previously reported under Article 16 by the estate or trust or by a decedent as a result of whose death the estate or trust acquired the right to the gain.

— The share of the estate or trust in the "fiduciary adjustment" is also added to or subtracted from its federal taxable income (¶703). (Sec. 618(3), Tax Law)

— The amounts specified in the following Tax Law provisions must be added to federal taxable income:

(1) Sec. 612(b)(10), amounts deducted on the federal return as an allowance for percentage depletion;

(2) Sec. 612(b)(17), amounts required to be added in the case of a sale or other disposition of property acquired from a decedent where no federal estate tax return was required;

(3) Sec. 612(b)(18)—(b)(20), certain amounts required to be added by shareholders of a federal S corporation when an election to be treated as a New York S corporation has not been made or when such election terminates on a day other than the first day of a taxable year of a corporation;

(4) Sec. 612(b)(21), amounts required to be added because of adjustments to the basis of stock in S corporations for taxable years in which the election to be treated as an S corporation shareholder was not made;

(5) Sec. 612(b)(22), new business investment deferral;

(6) Sec. 612(b)(23)—(b)(25), and (b)(27), accelerated depreciation;

(7) Sec. 612(b)(26), employer-paid contributions to retirement system or pension fund; and

(8) Sec. 612(b)(29), basis reduction relating to former credit for solar and wind energy systems.

— *Net operating losses:* For any carryback or carryforward year where the amount of NOL deduction allowed for New York purposes is limited, the difference between the NOL deduction allowed on the federal income tax return and the NOL deduction allowed for New York state income tax purposes must be accounted for. Beginning with New York state income tax returns for tax years 2013 and after, the difference must be accounted for by using a New York addition modification to federal adjusted gross income (individuals) or federal taxable income (estates and trusts). For additional information, see Publication 145, *Net Operating Losses (NOLs) for New York State Resident Individuals, Estates, and Trusts,* available at **https://www.tax.ny.gov/pdf/publications/income/pub145.pdf**

— The amounts specified in the following Tax Law provisions may be subtracted from federal taxable income:

(1) Sec. 612(c)(13), the New York depletion allowance;

(2) Sec. 612(c)(15), that portion of wages and salaries paid or incurred for the taxable year for which a deduction is not allowed pursuant to IRC Sec. 280C;

(3) Sec. 612(c)(19), amounts that may be subtracted in the case of a sale or other disposition of property acquired from a decedent when no federal estate tax return was required;

(4) Sec. 612(c)(20) and (c)(23), a percentage of gains from new business investments;

(5) Sec. 612(c)(21), amounts that may be subtracted because of adjustments to the basis of stock in federal S corporations for taxable years for which the election to be treated as a New York S corporation shareholder was not made;

(6) Sec. 612(c)(22), amounts that may be subtracted by shareholders when an election to be treated as an S corporation shareholder has not been made or when such election terminates on a day other than the first day of a taxable year of a corporation; and

(7) Sec. 612(c)(24)—(c)(26) and (c)(28), accelerated depreciation modifications.

Applicable to income accumulated by a trust in a tax year starting on or after January 1, 2014, the 2014-2015 New York budget legislation amended the Tax Law and the New York City Administrative Code to impose tax on:

(1) residents who are grantors of exempt resident trusts that qualify as non-grantor incomplete gift trusts (so-called "ING trusts") on the income from such trusts. The fact that the transfer of property to the trust was an incomplete gift means that the New York grantor has retained some degree of control over the property, thereby creating nexus for New York to tax the grantor on the income from that property (Sec. 612(b)(41); *TSB-M-14(3)I*, May 16, 2014, CCH NEW YORK TAX REPORTS, ¶ 408-096); and

(2) residents who are beneficiaries of all other exempt resident trusts or nonresident trusts on the distributions of accumulated income that they receive from such trusts (Sec. 612(b)(40); *TSB-M-14(3)I*, May 16, 2014, CCH NEW YORK TAX REPORTS, ¶ 408-096).

¶703 Resident Estates and Trusts—New York Fiduciary Adjustment

Law: Sec. 619, Tax Law; Reg. Sec. 119.1 (CCH NEW YORK TAX REPORTS, ¶ 15-205).

A resident estate or trust may realize items of income or gain or incur items of loss or deduction that, if received or incurred by an individual taxpayer, would give rise to one or more modifications. (Reg. Sec. 119.1) In the case of a resident estate or trust, all such modifications are combined in the New York fiduciary adjustment, which must be allocated among the estate or trust and its beneficiaries. The net amount of modifications comprising the fiduciary adjustment does not include any modification with respect to any amount that, pursuant to the terms of the governing instrument, is paid or permanently set aside for a charitable purpose during the taxable year and any modification with respect to gains from the sale or other disposition of property, to the extent excluded from federal distributable net income. (Sec. 618(b), Tax Law)

Shares of the fiduciary adjustment: The respective shares of an estate or trust and its beneficiaries in the New York fiduciary adjustment are in proportion to their respective shares of federal distributable net income of the estate or trust. (Sec. 618(c), Tax Law) If the estate or trust has no federal distributable net income for the taxable year, the share of each beneficiary in the New York fiduciary adjustment is in proportion to his or her share of the estate or trust income for the year, under local law or the governing instrument, that is required to be distributed currently and any other amounts of such income distributed in such year. Any balance of the New York fiduciary adjustment is allocated to the estate or trust.

Alternate attribution of modifications: The Commissioner may, by regulation, establish such other method or methods of determining to whom the items comprising the fiduciary adjustment will be attributed, as may be appropriate and equitable. (Sec. 618(c), Tax Law) Such method may be used by the fiduciary in his or her discretion whenever the allocation of the fiduciary adjustment set forth in the statute would result in an inequity that is substantial both in amount and in relation to the amount of the fiduciary adjustment.

¶704 Nonresident Estates and Trusts—New York Taxable Income

Law: Secs. 601(e), 633, 638, Tax Law (CCH NEW YORK TAX REPORTS, ¶15-205, 15-215, 16-505).

Nonresident estates and trusts and part-year resident estates and trusts compute their tax in the following manner (Sec. 601(e), Tax Law):

— A tax is first computed as if the estate or trust were a resident of New York State for the entire taxable year. This figure is known as the "base tax."

— The base tax is then multiplied by a percentage that is determined by dividing the estate's or trust's New York *source* income for the entire year by the estate's or trust's New York adjusted gross income for the entire year.

— The resulting amount is then reduced by any New York State credits to which the estate or trust may be entitled and/or increased by any other New York State taxes for which it may be liable. This resulting figure is the New York State personal income tax for the year.

• *New York source income*

The New York source income of a nonresident estate or trust is determined as follows (Sec. 633(a), Tax Law):

— (1) The estate's or trust's share of income, gain, loss and deductions from New York sources included in federal distributable net income is determined (Sec. 633(a)(1), Tax Law); and

— (2) The amount derived from or connected with New York sources of any income, gain, loss and deduction which would be included in the determination of federal adjusted gross income if the estate or trust were an individual and which is recognized for federal income tax purposes but excluded from the definition of federal distributable net income of the estate or trust is added or subtracted, as the case may be. (Sec. 633(a)(2), Tax Law)

Deductions with respect to capital losses, passive activity losses and net operating losses are based solely on income, gains, losses and deductions derived from or connected with New York sources, but otherwise determined in the same manner as the corresponding federal deductions. (Sec. 633(b), Tax Law)

For part-year resident trusts, New York source income is the sum of (Sec. 638(b), Tax Law):

(1) the New York adjusted gross income for the period of residence, determined as if the trust were an individual whose taxable year for federal purposes was limited to the period of residence; and

(2) the New York source income for the period of nonresidence, as determined in accordance with Sec. 633, Tax Law, as if the taxable year for federal purposes were limited to the period of nonresidence.

¶705 Nonresident Estates, Trusts, and Beneficiaries— Determination of Shares in Income, Gain, Loss, and Deductions

Law: Sec. 634, Tax Law (CCH NEW YORK TAX REPORTS, ¶ 15-215, 15-235).

The share of a nonresident estate or trust, and the share of a nonresident beneficiary of any estate or trust, in estate or trust income, gain, loss, and deduction from New York sources is determined as follows (Sec. 634(a), Tax Law):

A determination is made of those items of gain, loss, and deduction that are derived from or connected with New York sources, that enter into the definition of federal distributable net income of the estate or trust for the taxable year, and that would be included in the determination of federal adjusted gross income if the estate or trust were an individual.

• *Allocation among estate or trust and beneficiaries*

The amounts determined above are allocated among the estate or trust and its beneficiaries in proportion to their respective shares of federal distributable net income. (Sec. 634(a)(2), Tax Law) The amount so allocated has the same character for New York personal income tax purposes as for federal income tax purposes. When an item entering into the computation of such amounts is not characterized for federal income tax purposes, it will have the same character as if realized directly from the source from which realized by the estate or trust, or incurred in the same manner as incurred by the estate or trust.

• *Alternate methods of determining shares*

If the estate or trust has no federal distributable net income for the taxable year, each beneficiary's share will be in proportion to the beneficiary's share of the estate or trust income for such year, under local law or the governing instrument, that is required to be distributed currently, and any other amounts of such income distributed in such year. (Sec. 634(b)(1), Tax Law) Any balance will be allocated to the estate or trust.

The Commissioner may, by regulation, establish such other method or methods of determining the respective shares of the beneficiaries and of the estate or trust in its income derived from New York sources as may be appropriate and equitable. (Sec. 634(b)(2), Tax Law) Such method may be used, in the discretion of the fiduciary, whenever the allocation of such respective shares under the statutory method would result in an equity that is substantial in amount.

¶706 Partners and Partnerships—General

Law: Sec. 601, Tax Law (CCH NEW YORK TAX REPORTS, ¶ 15-185).

Comparable Federal: Secs. 701—761, 7701 (U.S. MASTER TAX GUIDE ¶ 63, 401—481).

In general, the treatment of partnership income is the same for federal and New York personal income tax purposes. The partnership is not subject to the personal income tax; however, the partners are subject to tax in their individual capacities. For additional information, see ¶ 855.

Practitioner Comment: Partnership Business Allocation Rules Differ Significantly From Those Used by Corporations

Partnerships and LLCs taxed as partnerships continue to allocate their income based on the percentage of their property, payroll, and receipts in New York. On the other hand, after 2015, corporations (including S corporations) allocate income solely on the receipts factor, using customer-based sourcing. These distinctions must be taken into account when selecting the best form of doing business, since the tax impact on nonresident partners/members/shareholders can be quite significant.

Mark S. Klein, Esq., Hodgson Russ LLP

• *Limited liability companies*

Members of limited liability companies and limited liability investment companies that are treated as partnerships for federal tax purposes are treated a partners for New York personal income tax purposes, and are subject to tax in their individual capacities. See discussion at ¶113 and ¶856.

¶707 Resident Partners and Shareholders of S Corporations

Law: Secs. 617, 617-a, Tax Law; Reg. Sec. 154.6 (CCH NEW YORK TAX REPORTS, ¶15-185).

In determining the New York adjusted gross income and the New York taxable income of a resident partner or a resident shareholder of an S corporation, any modification that relates to an item of partnership or S corporation income, gain, loss, or deduction is made in accordance with the partner's distributive share or the shareholder's pro rata share, for federal income tax purposes, of the item to which the modification relates. (Sec. 617(a), Tax Law) If a partner's distributive share or a shareholder's pro rata share of any such item is not required to be taken into account separately for federal income tax purposes, the partner's or shareholder's share of the item will be determined in accordance with his or her share, for federal income tax purposes, of partnership or S corporation taxable income or loss generally.

Character of items: Each item of partnership and S corporation income, gain, loss, or deduction has the same character for a partner or shareholder for New York personal income tax purposes as for federal income tax purposes. (Sec. 617(b), Tax Law) If an item is not characterized for federal income tax purposes, it will have the same character for a partner or shareholder as if realized directly from the source from which realized by the partnership or S corporation or incurred in the same manner as incurred by the partnership or S corporation.

New York tax avoidance or evasion: If a partner's distributive share of an item of partnership income, gain, loss, or deduction is determined for federal income tax purposes by special provision in the partnership agreement with respect to the item, and the principal purpose of the provision is the avoidance or evasion of New York income tax, the partner's distributive share of the item, and any required modification, will be determined as if the partnership agreement made no special provision with respect to the item. (Sec. 617(c), Tax Law)

For additional information on taxation of partners and shareholders, see ¶856.

¶708 Nonresident Partners and Electing Shareholders of S Corporations

Law: Sec. 632, Tax Law; Reg. Secs. 137.6, 151.17 (CCH NEW YORK TAX REPORTS, ¶15-185).

In determining the New York source income of a nonresident partner of any partnership, there is included only the portion derived from or connected with New York sources of the partner's distributive share of items of partnership income, gain, loss, and deduction entering into the partner's federal adjusted gross income. Similarly, in determining the New York source income of an electing nonresident shareholder of an S corporation there is included only the portion of the shareholder's *pro rata* share of items of S corporation income, loss, and deduction entering into the shareholder's federal adjusted gross income, increased by reductions for taxes described in IRC Sec. 1366(f)(2) and (3). (Sec. 832(a), Tax Law)

In determining the New York sources of a nonresident partner's income, no effect is given to a provision in the partnership agreement that (Sec. 832(b), Tax Law):

    (1) characterizes payments to the partner as being for services or for the use of capital;

    (2) allocates to the partner, as income or gain from sources outside New York, a greater proportion of the partner's distributive share of partnership income or gain from sources outside New York to partnership income or gain from all sources, except as specifically authorized by the Commissione; or

¶707

(3) allocates to the partner a greater proportion of a partnership item of loss or deduction connected with New York sources than the partner's proportionate share, for federal income tax purposes, of partnership loss or deduction generally, except as authorized by the Commissioner.

CCH Advisory: Source Income of Nonresident Shareholders

In making the determination with respect to a shareholder's *pro rata* share of items of S corporation income, loss, and deduction entering into his or her federal adjusted gross income, only the portion derived from or connected with New York sources is included. The determination of the source of S corporation items is made at the corporation level using the allocation methods that apply under Tax Law Article 9-A (corporate franchise tax) or Article 32 (bank franchise tax). The New York source income of a nonresident individual also includes any New York addition and subtraction modifications under Tax Law Sec. 612(b) and (c) relating to income derived from or connected with New York sources. The New York source of a Sec. 612 modification follows the source of the pass-through item to which it relates. For example, if 35% of the S corporation's business income is derived from New York sources, 35% of the Sec. 612(b)(25) addition modification for federal ACRS depreciation would also be derived from New York sources. Accordingly, a New York S corporation subject to the corporate franchise tax is required to compute its business allocation percentage and its investment allocation percentage using the applicable method under Article 9-A. The S corporation must then report these percentages to its nonresident shareholders along with each shareholder's *pro rata* share of the items of income, gain, loss, and deduction included in federal adjusted gross income, as well as the items that relate to Sec. 612(b) and (c). (*TSB-A-08(1)I*, January 4, 2008, CCH NEW YORK TAX REPORTS, ¶405-957)

The Commissioner may, on application, authorize the use of such other methods of determining a nonresident partner's portion of partnership items derived from or connected with New York sources, and the modifications related thereto, as may be appropriate and equitable, on such terms and conditions as may be required. (Sec. 832(c), Tax Law)

For method of determining items of income, gain, loss, or deduction from New York sources, see ¶206. For additional information on taxation of nonresident and part-year resident partners and shareholders, see ¶856.

Practitioner Comment: Part-Year Residents

A part-year resident partner of a partnership (or shareholder of an S corporation) may prorate his or her distribution of a New York partnership's (or S corporation's) income between the taxpayer's resident and nonresident period (*Greig*, NYS TAT (9/16/99), CCH NEW YORK TAX REPORTS, ¶403-452 and TSB-M-00(1)I, CCH NEW YORK TAX REPORTS, ¶300-314).

Mark S. Klein, Esq., Hodgson Russ LLP

• *Tiered partnerships*

When a nonresident partner is a member in a partnership ("upper-tier partnership") that is a member in another partnership ("lower-tier partnership"), the source and character of the nonresident partner's distributive share of each partnership item of the upper-tier partnership that is attributable to the lower-tier partnership will retain the source and character determined at the level of the lower-tier partnership. The source and character are not changed by reason of the fact that the partnership item flows through the upper-tier partnership to the nonresident partner. (Reg. Sec. 137.6)

• *Group tax return for nonresident partners, LLC and LLP members*

A partnership that is required to file a New York partnership return may be granted approval to file a group New York nonresident personal income tax return on behalf of 35 or more qualified partners who elect to have the partnership file on their behalf. A similar option is available to nonresident partners of limited liability partnerships (LLPs) and limited liability companies (LLCs). (Reg. Sec. 151.17)

Nonresident groups cannot include any estates or trusts in their New York state nonresident group returns (*Important Notice N-09-5*, New York Department of Taxation and Finance, March 2009, CCH NEW YORK TAX REPORTS, ¶406-353).

• *Tax avoidance or evasion*

The Commissioner of Taxation and Finance is authorized to disregard a personal service corporation or S corporation if it is determined that the entity was formed or used to avoid or evade the New York personal income tax (Sec. 632-A, Tax Law).

Practitioner Comment: New Audit Initiative

Auditors from the New York State Department of Taxation and Finance have begun aggressively challenging nonresident S corps, PCs and PAs that are partners in a partnership doing business in New York State. The use of these entities can frequently reduce the New York source income that is taxable to the nonresident shareholder or member. Even if these entities were established for a valid business purpose, the Tax Department's efforts to disregard them seem to be based on the tax costs to New York State.

Mark S. Klein, Esq., Hodgson Russ LLP

PERSONAL INCOME TAX

CHAPTER 8
ADMINISTRATION, DEFICIENCIES, TAXPAYER REMEDIES

¶801 Administration of Tax—General

Law: Sec. 697, Tax Law (CCH NEW YORK TAX REPORTS, ¶89-060).

The New York personal income tax law is administered by the Department of Taxation and Finance, W.A. Harriman Campus, Albany, NY 12227-0125. For additional information, see ¶3601.

¶802 Deficiencies—Procedure

Law: Secs. 681, 684, Tax Law (CCH NEW YORK TAX REPORTS, ¶89-164).

Similar to corporation franchise (income) tax provisions. Discussion at ¶1502 and ¶3702 applies.

¶803 Jeopardy Assessments

Law: Sec. 694, Tax Law (CCH NEW YORK TAX REPORTS, ¶89-168).

Comparable Federal: Sec. 6861 (U.S. MASTER TAX GUIDE, ¶2715).

Similar to corporation franchise (income) tax provisions. Discussion at ¶1503 and ¶3702 applies.

¶804 Bankruptcy and Receivership

Law: Sec. 658, Tax Law (CCH NEW YORK TAX REPORTS, ¶89-170).

Comparable Federal: Secs. 6036, 6871—6873 (U.S. MASTER TAX GUIDE, ¶505, 506).

The New York personal income tax law provides that all receivers, trustees in bankruptcy, assignees for the benefit of creditors and other like fiduciaries must give notice of their qualification to the Commissioner.

¶805 Transferee Liability

Law: Sec. 693, Tax Law (CCH NEW YORK TAX REPORTS, ¶89-166).

Comparable Federal: Secs. 6901—6904 (U.S. MASTER TAX GUIDE, ¶2743).

Similar to corporation franchise (income) tax provisions. Discussion at ¶1505 applies.

¶806 Statute of Limitations on Assessments

Law: Sec. 683, Tax Law (CCH New York Tax Reports, ¶89-164).

Comparable Federal: Secs. 1311—1314, 6501—6504 (U.S. Master Tax Guide, ¶2726).

Similar to corporation franchise (income) tax provisions. Discussion at ¶1506 applies.

If a taxpayer omits over 25% of items of tax preference, or the total taxable amount or ordinary income portion of a lump-sum distribution from the return, the limitation period is six years after the return was filed.

If a trust omits an amount of includible gain that is in excess of 25% of the amount of includible gain, the tax may be assessed within six years after the return was filed.

Practitioner Comment: Application of Six-Year Statute of Limitations

Although a nonresident may pay only a small fraction of what they would owe to New York as a resident, the filing of a nonresident tax return should still entitle the taxpayer to a three-year statute of limitations, even if the tax liability, after audit, is many times greater than what was disclosed on the original return. The six-year statute of limitations applicable to a 25% omission is generally limited to undisclosed income, not improperly allocated amounts. Since 100% of the taxpayer's federal income was disclosed on the nonresident tax return (IT-203), the six-year statute of limitations should not be implicated. See also *United States v. Home Concrete & Supply, LLC,* 132 U.S. 1836 (2012).

Mark S. Klein, Esq., Hodgson Russ LLP

¶807 Interest on Underpayments or Overpayments

Law: Secs. 684, 688, Tax Law (CCH New York Tax Reports, ¶89-204).

Comparable Federal: Sec. 6601, 6611 (U.S. Master Tax Guide, ¶2765, 2838—2845).

The interest rate on an underpayment of personal income tax is set quarterly based on the federal short-term rate determined by the United States Secretary of the Treasury for Internal Revenue Code purposes, rounded to the nearest full percentage or increased to the next full percentage (in the case of $1/2$% multiple), plus 4%. The rate may not be less than 6%. Interest is compounded daily.

For the most current interest rate available at the time of publication, see ¶3704. Interest rates per annum, compounded daily and established quarterly, have been set in the recent past as follows:

Period	Overpayments	Underpayments
4/1/16—12/31/16	3%	7.5%
10/1/11—03/31/16	2%	7.5%
4/1/11—9/30/11	3%	7.5%
1/1/11—3/31/11	2%	7.5%
4/7/09—12/31/10	3%	7.5%
4/1/09—4/6/09	3%	6%
1/1/09—3/31/09	4%	8%
10/1/08—12/31/08	5%	7%
7/1/08—9/30/08	4%	6%
4/1/08—6/30/08	5%	7%
1/1/08—3/31/08	6%	8%
7/1/06—12/30/07	7%	9%
10/1/05—6/30/06	6%	8%
4/1/05—9/30/05	5%	7%
10/1/04—3/31/05	4%	6%
7/1/04—9/30/04	3%	6%
4/1/04—6/30/04	4%	6%
10/1/03—3/31/04	3%	6%
7/1/03—9/30/03	6%	6%
4/1/01—6/30/01	7%	7%
1/1/01—3/31/01	8%	8%

The interest rate applicable to underpayments of withheld taxes is the rate applicable for corporation franchise taxes (¶1507, ¶3704). Interest can be avoided if additions and penalties are paid within 21 days after a notice and demand for payment is made, 10 business days if the amount for which the notice and demand is made is $100,000 or more.

Interest on overpayments of tax is paid (1) from the date of the overpayment to the due date of an amount against which a credit is taken or (2) from the date of the overpayment to a date (to be determined by the Commissioner) preceding the date of a refund check by not more than 30 days, whether or not the refund check is accepted by the taxpayer. Interest is not paid on overpayments if the overpayment is credited or refunded within 45 days after the last date for filing the return or amended return, or within 45 days after the return was filed, whichever is later; within 45 days after a claim for credit or refund was filed on which the overpayment was claimed; or within six months after the filing of a demand that a portion of the overpayment and interest not be credited against past-due support or the amount of default in repayment of certain loans on debts owed to state agencies.

When an amended personal income tax return or a claim for refund or credit is filed to obtain a refund of overpaid New York personal income tax, the payment of interest on the refund is not limited to the time period after the filing of the return or claim. Interest on a refund may be paid for the time period preceding the filing of an amended return or claim. However, no interest will be paid on the period between the filing of the amended return or claim and the refund, if the refund is provided within 45 days after the filing of the return or claim.

¶808 Refund or Credit of Overpayment

Law: Secs. 686, 687, 3013, Tax Law (CCH NEW YORK TAX REPORTS, ¶89-224).

Forms: IT-113-X, Claim for Credit or Refund of Personal Income Tax.

A claim for credit or refund of an overpayment must be filed within three years from the time the return was filed or two years from the time the tax was paid, whichever period expires later. (Sec. 687(a), Tax Law) If no return was filed, the claim must be filed within two years from the time the tax was paid. The amount of the credit or refund may not exceed the portion of the tax paid within the applicable two- or three-year period preceding the filing of the claim.

CCH Advisory: Untimely Claim

A taxpayer's mental illness was not a recognizable reason to extend or ignore the statute of limitations for her claim for a refund of her New York personal income taxes. The taxpayer acknowledged that her claim was beyond the allotted time period, but argued that her severe depression prevented her from timely filing her refund claim. Her argument was rejected. (*Gunderson,* New York Division of Tax Appeals, Small Claims, DTA No. 821517, February 7, 2008, CCH NEW YORK TAX REPORTS, ¶405-977)

Notice of federal change or correction: A claim for credit or refund of any overpayment of tax attributable to a federal change or correction must be filed within two years from the time that the notice of change or correction or amended return was required to be filed with the Commissioner. (Sec. 687(c), Tax Law) If a required report of federal changes, corrections, or disallowances is not filed within the 90-day period, no interest will be payable on any claim for credit or refund of the overpayment attributable to the federal change or correction.

Overpayment attributable to net operating loss carryback: A claim for credit or refund of the portion of any overpayment attributable to the application of a net operating loss carryback must be filed within three years from the time the return was due for the taxable year of the loss. (Sec. 687(d), Tax Law)

CCH Advisory: Interest on Refund Due to NOL Carryback

The New York Department of Taxation and Finance has issued a personal income tax advisory opinion concerning the interest due on a refund caused by a net operating loss (NOL) carryback when the return for the loss year was filed before the extended due date and the refund was not paid to the taxpayer within 45 days of the refund claim. The opinion concludes that interest should be allowed from the due date of the loss year return, without regard to extensions of time to file. (*TSB-A-10(10)I*, New York Commissioner of Taxation and Finance, October 28, 2010, CCH NEW YORK TAX REPORTS, ¶ 407-051)

Application of refund against debts owed state agencies or student loans: The Commissioner of Taxation and Finance may credit an overpayment of income tax and interest on the overpayment against past-due support, past-due legally enforceable debts owed to state agencies, overpayments of public assistance benefits that the taxpayer is required to repay to the Department of Social Services, or against a default in repayment of a guaranteed student, state university, or city university loan. (Sec. 686(a), Tax Law) A refund will be made only upon the filing of a return and upon a certificate of the Commissioner approved by the Comptroller. The Comptroller, as a condition precedent to the approval of a certificate, may examine the facts disclosed by the return of the person who made the overpayment and other available information and data. If an overpayment of tax is claimed as a credit against estimated tax for the succeeding taxable year, the amount of the overpayment is considered as a payment of the income tax for the succeeding taxable year, and no claim for credit or refund of the overpayment will be allowed for the taxable year for which the overpayment arises. (Sec. 686(e), Tax Law)

Right to receive refund by check: The Taxpayer Refund Choice Act allows taxpayers to receive their personal income tax refunds by paper check. The bill also allows taxpayers to opt out of any prepaid debit card or direct deposit program for payment of tax refunds and requires the Department of Taxation and Finance to provide taxpayers with a clear written statement setting forth these taxpayer rights. The bill is repealed after five years. (Sec. 3013, Tax Law)

¶809 Penalties

Law: Secs. 685, 1801, 1802, 1804, 1806, 1810, Tax Law (CCH NEW YORK TAX REPORTS, ¶ 89-202).

Comparable Federal: Secs. 6651, 6653, 7201—7207 (U.S. MASTER TAX GUIDE, ¶ 2801—2898).

Similar to corporation franchise (income) tax provisions. Discussion at ¶ 1508 and ¶ 3704 applies.

Partnerships and S corporations that willfully fail to file timely reports or returns, or neglect to file complete reports or returns, are subject to a penalty for each month, or fraction of each month, that the failure continues (not to exceed five months). The penalty is equal to $50 multiplied by the number of partners or shareholders who, during any part of the taxable year, were subject to tax. (Sec. 685(h)(2), Tax Law)

Small partnerships: Although federal and New York filing requirements and penalty provisions are substantially similar, New York law, unlike IRC Sec. 6231(a)(1)(B), does not contain special exceptions for small partnerships of 10 or fewer partners. Although small partnerships must file timely and complete returns, the New York Department of Taxation and Finance has indicated that small partnerships that failed to file timely or complete returns for prior years because of reliance on a federal ruling may be entitled to a one-time waiver of penalties (*TSB-M-90(6)(I)*, Department of Taxation and Finance, CCH NEW YORK TAX REPORTS, ¶ 19-099).

Withholding taxes: In case of nonwillful failure to make a return and pay over withheld taxes by the due date, a penalty of 5% of the tax per month of delinquency is imposed, not exceeding 25% in the aggregate, and interest is included. If the failure to collect, account for, and pay over the tax is willful, the law provides a penalty of 100% of the tax. In the case of fraudulent intent, a penalty of up to $1,000 is imposed. Criminal penalties are also provided. (Sec. 685(f), Tax Law)

Innocent spouse relief: See Publication 89, *Innocent Spouse Relief (And Separation of Liability And Equitable Relief)*, Department of Taxation and Finance, **http://www.tax.ny.gov/pdf/publications/income/pub89.pdf**.

For additional withholding penalties, see ¶609.

Failure to deposit taxes as required by the personal income tax law or by regulation: 5% of amount not deposited as required.

Estimated tax: See ¶606.

¶810 Information at Source

Law: Secs. 658, 1703, Tax Law; Reg. Sec. 158.10 (CCH NEW YORK TAX REPORTS, ¶89-102).

Comparable Federal: Secs. 6039, 6041—6052 (U.S. MASTER TAX GUIDE, ¶406, 2565).

The Department of Taxation and Finance retains authority to require information returns at any time with respect to amounts it deems necessary to enforce tax law provisions. (Sec. 658, Tax Law)

The law requires the filing of information returns by payment settlement entities, third-party settlement organizations, electronic payment facilitators, and other third parties acting on behalf of payment settlement entities (Sec. 1703, Tax Law).

¶811 Taxpayer Remedies

Law: Secs. 171(3-a), (18-d), 651(b)(5), 2008, 2012, 2016, Tax Law (CCH NEW YORK TAX REPORTS, ¶89-222 *et seq.*).

Similar to corporation franchise (income) tax provisions. Discussion at ¶1510 applies. See also ¶3801.

A timely filed income tax return claiming a credit or refund for overpayment of tax for the immediate preceding year constituted an informal claim for a credit or refund (*Miles*, Division of Tax Appeals, Tax Appeals Tribunal, CCH NEW YORK TAX REPORTS, ¶253-314).

Spousal liability: Federal provisions apply (¶603).

PART II.5

PASS-THROUGH ENTITIES

Chapter 8.5
INCOME TAX TREATMENT OF PASS-THROUGH ENTITIES

¶850 Introduction

This chapter covers the various types of pass-through entities (also known as "flow-through entities"), the treatment of the pass-through entity at the entity level, the tax treatment of pass-through entity owners, reporting requirements, unified reporting options for nonresidents, and penalties.

¶851 Limited Liability Companies

Law: Secs. 2(5), 601(f), 658, Tax Law; Secs. 101—1403, Limited Liability Company Law; Secs. 102-a, 507, Banking Law (CCH NEW YORK TAX REPORTS, ¶ 10-240, 10-265, 10-340, 15-185).

Comparable Federal: Treas. Reg. Secs. 301.7701-1 through 301.7701-3 (U.S. MASTER TAX GUIDE, ¶ 402B).

New York generally adopts the federal income tax treatment of a limited liability company (LLC) as set out in the federal "check-the-box" regulations (Treas. Reg. Secs. 301.7701-1 through 301.7701-3). An LLC may elect classification as either a corporation, partnership, or "disregarded entity", unless the entity meets certain specifications requiring classification as a corporation. Classification of an LLC for New York corporate franchise (income) tax purposes is dependent upon the LLC's federal income tax classification as either a corporation, partnership, or disregarded entity. LLCs classified as partnerships for federal purposes are not subject to New York income tax (Sec. 601(f), Tax Law).

LLC organizational provisions are found in the Limited Liability Company Law (Sec. 201 et seq.) An LLC, unlike a partnership, can be formed in New York with a single member (Sec. 203, Limited Liability Company Law), although a one-person LLC will not be viewed as a partnership by the Internal Revenue Service (IRS). See also ¶ 921.

Foreign limited liability companies. —Foreign LLCs may apply for authority to do business in New York, subject to provisions analogous to those found in the New York Partnership Law (Sec. 801, Limited Liability Company Law). A foreign LLC authorized to do business in New York will have the same powers to conduct business in New York as it has in its home state, but can not have greater powers than those of a domestic LLC. A foreign LLC may not engage in any profession in New York, although this rule does not apply to foreign registered limited liability partnerships (Sec. 805, Limited Liability Company Law).

Professional service limited liability companies. —New York authorizes the establishment of professional service LLCs and imposes additional requirements on such entities (Sec. 1205, Limited Liability Company Law). These requirements parallel those contained in the Business Corporation Law for professional service corporations.

Foreign professional limited liability companies. —New York authorizes foreign professional service LLCs to register in New York (Sec. 1301, Limited Liability Company Law). These professional service LLCs may only provide services through individuals authorized to render such services in New York (Sec. 1302, Limited Liability Company Law).

Limited liability investment companies. —New York permits certain investment companies to organize themselves as limited liability investment companies (LLICs) (Sec. 507, Banking Law). The option is open only to Article 12 investment companies that serve as holding companies for foreign banking operations. For New York tax purposes, LLICs will be regarded as limited liability companies (Sec. 2(5), Tax Law). For additional information, see ¶1611.

Limited liability trust companies. —New York permits certain trust companies that do not receive deposits from the general public to be formed and operated as limited liability trust companies (LLTCs) (Sec. 102-a, Banking Law). The option is open only to Art. 12 investment companies that serve as holding companies for foreign banking operations.

• *Annual filing fees*

Limited liability company (LLC), limited liability partnership (LLP), and partnership filing fees are based on New York source gross income. The fees for LLCs and LLPs range from $25 (if New York source gross income is $100,000 or less) to $4,500 (if New York source gross income exceeds $25 million). LLCs that are disregarded entities for federal income tax purposes must pay a filing fee of $25. Provisions authorizing New York City to impose such filing fees are amended to make similar changes.

Fees for partnerships rage from $500 (if New York source gross income is $1 million) to $4,500 (if New York source gross income exceeds $25 million). Partnerships (other than LLPs under Article 8-B of the Partnership Law and foreign LLPs) with less than $1 million in New York source gross income are exempt from the filing fee.

The full amount of the filing fee due must be paid within 30 days after the last day of the taxable year. (Sec. 658(c)(3), Tax Law; *TSB-M-09(8)I*, July 8, 2009, CCH NEW YORK TAX REPORTS, ¶406-442)

For additional information on filing fees, see ¶859.

• *Federal income tax provisions*

The federal check-the-box regulations (Treas. Reg. Secs. 301.7701-1 through 301.7701-3) set forth a step-by-step analysis for determining the appropriate federal income tax classification of an entity. After determining whether a separate tax entity exists, the analyst must then distinguish between the various business entities available. Some of these entities may make use of the federal elective regime to choose their classification for income tax purposes. Occasionally, the initial tax classification will require a revaluation due to a change in the numerical membership of the entity. These analytical concepts are exin more detail below.

¶851

Determine whether a separate entity exists: Determining an organization's federal income tax classification is a two-step process. The first step in the analysis is to determine whether there is an "entity" that is separate and apart from its owners for federal tax purposes (Treas. Reg. Sec. 301.7701-1(a)(1)). Generally, a joint venture or other contractual arrangement where the participants carry on a trade, business, financial operation, or other venture for profit is a separate entity. The mere co-ownership of property, or a joint undertaking simply to share expenses, however, does not create a separate entity for federal income tax purposes (Treas. Reg. Sec. 301.7701-1(a)(2)). Note that a joint undertaking that is not an entity under local law may very well be a separate entity for federal tax purposes, and that an entity recognized under local law may not constitute a separate entity for federal tax purposes (Treas. Reg. Sec. 301.7701-1(a)(3)). Specific IRC sections may provide special classification treatment for certain organizations (Treas. Reg. Sec. 301.7701-1(b)).

Once an organization is recognized as a separate entity for federal income tax purposes, the second step is to determine whether that entity is either a "trust" or a "business entity." A trust is distinguishable from a business entity in that the trust lacks associates and an objective to carry on a business for profit (Treas. Reg. Sec. 301.7701-4). The definition of a business entity, however, is more complex.

Distinguish between certain business entities: A business entity is any entity recognized for federal income tax purposes that is not more properly classified as a trust or subject to special treatment under the IRC. Such a business entity with two or more members can be classified as either a "corporation" or as a "partnership" (See Treas. Reg. Sec. 301.7701-2(c)(1)). A business entity with only one owner can be classified as a corporation, or it can be disregarded as an entity separate from its owner. If a one-owner entity is disregarded for federal tax purposes, then the entity's activities are treated as if it were a sole proprietorship, if the owner is an individual, or as a branch or a division, if the single owner is a bank or a corporation (Treas. Reg. Secs. 301.7701-2(a) and (c)(2)).

Use of the elective regime: Any business entity that is not required to be treated as a corporation for federal income tax purposes may elect its classification under Treas. Reg. Sec. 301.7701-3. An eligible entity with at least two members can elect to be classified as either a partnership or as a corporation. An eligible entity with only a single owner can elect to be classified as a corporation or it can be disregarded as an entity separate from its owner (Treas. Reg. Sec. 301.7701-3(a)). In order to provide most eligible entities with the tax classification that they would likely choose without requiring them to actually file an election form (federal Form 8832, Entity Classification Election (see below)), the entity classification regulations provide certain default classification rules that attempt to match the taxpayers' expectations (thus reducing the number of elections that need be filed). These entity default classifications are effective until the entity affirmatively elects to change its classification.

Under the pass-through default rule for a "domestic" entity, a newly formed eligible entity will be classified as a partnership if it has at least two members, or it will be disregarded as an entity separate from its owner if it has a single owner (Treas. Reg. Sec. 301.7701-3(b)(1)). An entity is a domestic entity if it is created or organized in the United States, under the laws of the United States, or under that of any state or the District of Columbia.

The default rules for a foreign entity are generally based on whether the members of the foreign entity possess limited liability. A member does not have limited liability if the member, by virtue of being a member, has personal liability for all or any portion of the debts of the entity. Generally, only the statute or law of a particular country providing for limited or unlimited liability is relevant. However, where the underlying statute allows the entity to specify in its organizational documents whether the members will have limited liability, the organizational documents may be relevant (Treas. Reg. Sec. 301.7701-3(b)(2)(ii)).

Thus, a foreign eligible entity will be classified as a corporate entity if all of the members have limited liability. A foreign eligible entity will be classified as a partnership if it has two or more members and at least one member does not have limited liability. The entity will be disregarded as an entity separate from its owner if it has a single owner and that owner does not have limited liability (Treas. Reg. Sec. 301.7701-3(b)(2)(i)). For both domestic and foreign entities, the default classification for an entity in existence prior to 1997 is the classification that the entity claimed immediately prior to that date, unless the entity elects otherwise. However, if an eligible entity with a single owner claimed to be a partnership, the entity is now disregarded as an entity separate from its owner (Treas. Reg. Sec. 301.7701-3(b)(3)).

Making a classification election: If the default rules do not provide the desired tax classification, then an eligible entity may elect to be classified differently. The election is as simple as checking a box on Form 8832, Entity Classification Election.

Although the election is generally effective on the date filed, a taxpayer can specify another date, provided that date is not more than 75 days prior to the date on which the election is filed and not more than 12 months after the date on which the election is filed (Treas. Reg. Sec. 301.7701-3(c)(1)(iii)).

A copy of Form 8832 must also be attached to the entity's federal tax or information return for the year in which the election is to be effective. If the entity is not required to file a return for that year, then a copy of Form 8832 must be attached to any direct or indirect owner's federal income tax return or information return for the owner's tax year in which the election is effective. Although the failure of the entity or an owner to attach a copy of Form 8832 to the applicable return will not void an otherwise valid election, such a failure may give rise to penalties against the non-filing party. Other applicable penalties may also apply to parties that file federal tax or information returns inconsistent with their entity's election.

To ensure that the taxpayers who recognize the tax consequences of a conversion election approve of that election, the election must be signed by every owner on the date of the deemed conversion transaction (Treas. Reg. Sec. 301.7701-3(c)(2)(iii)).

The ability of an entity to make multiple classification elections is limited by prohibiting an eligible entity from changing its classification more than once during any 60-month period. However, the IRS may waive this 60-month limitation when there has been a more than 50% change in the ownership of the entity (Treas. Reg. Sec. 301.7701-3(c)(1)(iv)).

Reclassification due to numerical membership changes: An entity's default classification may change as a result of a change in the number of its members. Specifically, an eligible entity classified as a partnership will become a disregarded entity when the entity's membership is reduced to one member, and a disregarded entity will be classified as a partnership when the entity has more than one member (Treas. Reg. Sec. 301.7701-3(f)(2)).

¶852 Partnerships

Law: Secs. 208, 601(f), Tax Law (CCH New York Tax Reports, ¶10-220—10-235, 15-185).

Comparable Federal: Secs. 701-761, 7704 (U.S. Master Tax Guide, ¶401-481).

New York generally follows IRC Sec. 701—IRC Sec. 761, the federal income tax provisions addressing partners and their partnerships, because the starting point for New York entire net income is federal taxable income before the net operating loss and special deductions (see ¶202). (Sec. 208(1), Tax Law) Since New York follows the federal income tax treatment of a partnership and its partners, income and losses, including net operating losses (NOLs) of the partnership flow to its partners (Sec. 601(f), Tax Law).

Aside from limited liability partnerships (LLPs) classified as associations for federal income tax purposes, partnerships are not subject to the general corporate franchise (income) tax under Article 9-A. However, a corporate partner of a partnership is subject to the Article 9-A corporate franchise (income) tax.

Electing large partnerships.—New York has no provisions comparable to IRC Sec. 771—IRC Sec. 777, the federal income tax provisions that authorize the election of electing large partnership (ELP) status.

Practitioner Comment: No Special Forms for Electing Large Partnerships

An electing large partnership under federal law must still file a "regular" partnership return using the IT-204. According to the Tax Department, "New York does not conform to the electing large partnership provisions". (See Instructions to 2015 IT-204, Page 2)

Mark S. Klein, Esq., Hodgson Russ LLP

Publicly traded partnerships.—New York follows IRC Sec. 7704, under which a publicly traded partnership (PTP) is taxed as a corporation unless at least 90% of its gross income consists of qualifying passive income, without significant modification. After analyzing the applicable New York provisions relative to the PTP, an overview of the relevant federal income tax provisions is provided.

• *Interaction of federal and state provisions*

The term "partnership" has the same meaning as set forth in IRC Sec. 761(a) whether or not the election provided in that IRC section has been made (Reg. Sec. 1-2.6). In addition, the term "partnership" does not include a corporation as defined in Reg. Sec. 1-2.5(b).

A partnership may be either a general partnership or a limited partnership. In a general partnership, all partners share in the partnership's income and liabilities and all partners have, as a matter of law, a right to participate in the partnership management. However, the general partners can agree to turn management of the partnership over to one or more managing partners.

• *Federal income tax provisions*

For federal income tax purposes, a "partnership" is defined as "a syndicate, group, pool, joint venture, or other unincorporated organization through or by means of which any business, financial operation, or venture is carried on and which is not a corporation, trust, or estate." (IRC Sec. 761(a)) Under the "check-the-box" regulations discussed at ¶851, the determination of whether an entity is taxable as a partnership or as an association taxable as a corporation is simplified. Understandably, for federal tax purposes, a "partner" is simply a member of the partnership (IRC Sec. 761(b)).

A general partnership is not a separate taxable entity. Although the general partnership must file Form 1065, a federal information tax return, it does not pay any federal income tax. Rather, the general partnership serves as a conduit to the underlying partners. Any income, loss, deduction, or credit attributable to the general partnership's business activities is first computed at the entity level and is then passed through to the partners according to their "distributive share." A partner's distributive share is generally determined by the partnership agreement, which defines the partners' business relationship to one another and to the general partnership. (See IRC Sec. 761(c)). These pass-through shares must then be included and reported on the partners' own federal income tax returns.

Since the general partnership format directly passes the relevant tax items through to the partners without an entity-level tax, the double taxation of income that burdens the C corporation is avoided. Additionally, any tax loss attributable to the general partnership's business that is passed through to the partners may be used, subject to the IRC Sec. 465 at-risk rules and the IRC Sec. 469 passive activity limitation rules, to offset any of the partners' own taxable income from other sources, which is often beneficial.

¶852

While a general partnership's income is generally computed like that of an individual, there are certain exceptions. As stated above, a number of items must be separately stated. (IRC Sec. 703(a)(1)) Furthermore, several deductions are not permitted in computing partnership income since these deductions will be made instead at the partner level. The impermissible deductions are as follows (IRC Sec. 703(a)(2)):

—the deduction for those personal exemptions provided by IRC Sec. 151;

—the deduction for taxes provided by IRC Sec. 164(a);

—the IRC Sec. 170 charitable contribution deduction;

—the IRC Sec. 172 net operating loss deduction;

—the additional itemized deductions for individuals provided by IRC Sec. 211 and following; and

—the IRC Sec. 611 deduction for oil and gas well depletion.

Through the partnership agreement, a general partnership has great flexibility in allocating tax items to its partners. In determining a partner's distributive share of income, gain, loss, deduction, or credit, the partnership agreement generally controls. (IRC Sec. 704(a)) However, if the partnership agreement does not provide for the partners' distributive shares, or if the partnership chooses to allocate such income items in a manner disproportionate to the partners' interests in the partnership, or if the allocation to the partners under the agreement does not have "substantial economic effect," then each partner's distributive share is determined in accordance with that partner's interest in the partnership, taking into account all of the relevant facts and circumstances (IRC Sec. 704(b)). In order for an allocation to have such substantial economic effect, the allocation must be consistent with the underlying economic arrangement of the partners and must be substantial. In business terms, this means that the economic benefit or burden that corresponds to the allocation must flow to the partner receiving such economic benefit or burden.

When a partner contributes property to a general partnership, the income, gain, loss, or deduction with respect to that property generally must be shared among the partners so as to take into account the variation between the partnership's basis in the property and the property's fair market value at the time that it was contributed. If property that is contributed by a partner is distributed by the partnership (other than to the contributing partner) within seven years of being contributed, then the contributing partner is treated as recognizing gain or loss from the sale of the property in an amount equal to the gain or loss that would have been allocated to the partner if the property had been sold at fair market value at the time of the distribution. (IRC Sec. 704(c)) This federal tax rule prevents parties from using a partnership to disguise what is actually an outright sale of the allegedly contributed property. Note that a special allocation rule applies with respect to contributed property that retains a "built-in loss" (IRC Sec. 704(c)(1)(C)(i)).

Termination of partnership: An existing general partnership continues until it is terminated. (IRC Sec. 708(a)) For these purposes, a partnership terminates if no part of any business, financial operation, or venture of the partnership is carried on by the partners or if there is a sale or exchange of 50% or more of the total interest in partnership capital and profits within a 12-month period. (IRC Sec. 708(b)(1)) If two or more partnerships are merged or consolidated, then the partnership deemed to continue is the one whose members own an interest of more than 50% of the capital and profits of the resulting partnership. If a partnership is divided into two or more partnerships, then the resulting partnerships are considered to be a continuation of the original partnership, except for a resulting partnership the members of which owned 50% or less of the prior partnership (IRC Sec. 708(b)(2)).

• *Limited partnerships and limited liability partnerships*

New York generally follows IRC Sec. 701—IRC Sec. 761, the federal income tax provisions addressing partners and their limited partnerships, because the starting point for computing New York entire net income is federal taxable income (Sec. 208(1), Tax Law). Since New York follows the federal income tax treatment of limited partnerships (LPs) and limited liability partnerships (LLPs) and their limited partners, income and losses, including net operating losses (NOLs) of the LP and LLP flow to their partners. (Sec. 601(f), Tax Law)

¶853 S Corporations

Law: Secs. 208(1-B), 208, 210(1)(g), 658, Tax Law (CCH New York Tax Reports, ¶ 10-215, 15-185).

Comparable Federal: Secs. 1361-1379 (U.S. Master Tax Guide, ¶ 305-349).

New York generally follows the federal income tax treatment of an S corporation and its shareholders as set out in IRC Sec. 1361—IRC Sec. 1379. However, there are some differences for New York corporate franchise tax purposes, as discussed below. See also ¶ 914.

Certain New York corporations that are federal S corporations also must be New York S corporations (see "Mandatory election," below).

• *Interaction of federal and state provisions*

New York S corporations are subject to a corporate-level tax (Sec. 210(1)(g), Tax Law). For tax years beginning after 2002, the law with respect to New York S corporations was amended to eliminate the tax on the entire net income base and to impose only the fixed dollar minimum tax (see ¶ 905).

New York S corporation treatment is afforded only to general business corporations (Article 9-A corporations), and Article 32 banking corporations. It is not afforded to special corporations that are taxable under Articles 9 or 33 of the Tax Law.

New York City: S corporation status is not recognized for purposes of the New York City general corporation tax. Therefore, a federal S corporation that makes the S election for New York State purposes would still be a C corporation for New York City general corporation tax. (*Publication 35*, CCH New York Tax Reports, ¶ 13-040)

S corporation election.—In general, New York S corporation treatment is elective, not automatic. Shareholders must make a separate New York S election to be taxed as a New York S corporation. If this separate election is not made, the corporation is treated as a C corporation for New York tax purposes (Publication 35, CCH New York Tax Reports, ¶ 13-040).

A corporation may elect to be a New York S corporation only if it meets all of the following qualifications (*TSB-M-98(4)C*, CCH New York Tax Reports, ¶ 300-251):

—the corporation is already a federal S corporation, or the corporation is making a federal S election at the same time it is making its New York S election;

—the corporation is an eligible corporation; and

—all the corporation's shareholders agree to make the New York S election.

The election will be effective for the entire year for which it is made and for all succeeding years until the election is terminated. The election must be made at any time during the preceding tax year, or on or before the 15th day of the third month of the tax year to which the election will apply. For taxable years of two and one-half months or less, an election made not later than two months and 15 days after the first day of the taxable year will be treated as timely filed for that year.

Mandatory election: For taxable years beginning after 2006, if an entity is an eligible S corporation for federal tax purposes and has not made the election to be a

New York S corporation, it will be deemed a New York S corporation if the corporation's investment income for the current taxable year is more than 50% of its federal gross income for the year. This does not apply to S corporations that are subject to the bank franchise tax. (Sec. 660(i), Tax Law)

Late and invalid S elections.—If an election is made by an eligible S corporation for any taxable year after the election filing deadline for that taxable year, or if no election is made at all, and it is determined by the Commissioner that there was a reasonable cause for the failure to make a timely election, the Commissioner may treat that election as timely filed for that taxable year. (*TSB-M-03(5)C*, CCH NEW YORK TAX REPORTS, ¶ 300-405; *Publication 35*, CCH NEW YORK TAX REPORTS, ¶ 13-040)

Practitioner Comment: Professional Advice Can Be Reasonable Cause

Reliance on the advice of a professional can provide a reasonable basis for the late filing of a New York State S election. In one case, a taxpayer mistakenly believed his corporate attorney, who advised him that a federal S election was effective for New York State tax purposes. Since the taxpayer relied "in good faith" on the attorney's advice and it was "reasonable" for the taxpayer to rely on the erroneous advice he was given (the lawyer was supposedly a corporate law specialist), reasonable cause existed for the late filing (by over 10 years) of the New York S election. (*Michael and Blanche Dohan*, ALJ, DTA No. 819599, 1/6/05, CCH NEW YORK TAX REPORTS, ¶ 405-006)

Mark S. Klein, Hodgson Russ LLP

When an S election is retroactively validated for federal purposes, pursuant to IRC Sec. 1362(f), then the Commissioner may retroactively validate the New York election. The validation will apply for any taxable years occurring within the period validated by the Internal Revenue Service. As above, any retroactive validations require both the shareholders and the corporation to recognize the tax consequences of the election for the retroactive period.

Authority to disregard: For taxable years beginning after 2006, the Commissioner of Taxation and Finance is authorized to disregard personal service corporations or S corporations formed or availed of primarily to avoid or evade New York income tax (Sec. 632-a, Tax Law).

Estimated taxes.—Under certain circumstances, New York S corporations that have income derived from New York sources are required to make estimated tax payments on behalf of nonresident shareholders. (Sec. 658(c)(4), Tax Law) Such nonresident withholding is discussed further at ¶ 3602. See also *Important Notice N-03-30*, CCH NEW YORK TAX REPORTS, ¶ 320-134.

Net operating loss (NOL).—A New York S corporation is allowed a net operating loss deduction (NOLD) that is based upon the deduction allowed under IRC Sec. 172. However, the following rules apply (*Instructions*, Form CT-3-S, New York S Corporation Franchise Tax Return):

—A deduction is not allowed for an NOL sustained during any tax year:

(i) beginning before January 1, 1990; or

(ii) in which the corporation was not subject to corporate franchise (income) tax under Art. 9-A of the Tax Law; or

(iii) in which the corporation was a New York C corporation.

—IRC Sec. 172 federal losses must be adjusted in accordance with Art. 9-A, Secs. 208(9)(a), 208(9)(b), and 208(9)(g) of the Tax Law.

—The New York State NOLD is limited to the amount required under IRC Sec. 172 to reduce FTI to zero.

¶853

—An NOL can be carried back or forward. Both a New York C year and a New York S year are counted as a tax year for determining the number of tax years for which an NOL may be carried back or carried forward.

—For NOLs sustained in tax years beginning after August 5, 1997, the NOL may be carried back two years (with an exception for certain disaster losses), but may be carried forward for 20 years.

—For NOLs sustained in tax years beginning on or before August 5, 1997, the NOL could be carried back three years and carried forward 15 years.

—For taxpayers eligible for the five-year carryback of NOLs arising in tax years ending in 2001 and 2002 for federal tax purposes, a five-year carryback was allowed for purposes of computing the New York State NOLD under Art. 9-A.

—A New York S year is treated as a tax year for purposes of determining the number of tax years to which the NOL may be carried back or forward. (Sec. 208(9)(f)(4), Tax Law)

—The New York State NOL carryback is computed as if the corporation elected under IRC Sec. 172 to relinquish the carryback provisions, except for the first $10,000 for each loss year, which may be carried back to preceding years.

—Any portion of the New York $10,000 NOL carryback that was not carried back to preceding years may be carried forward.

—The New York NOLD for any particular year is limited to the federal NOLD for that year. (For purposes of this limitation, a corporation that has elected to carryback up to $10,000 of its NOL for New York State purposes should compute its federal NOLD as if it only carried back the same $10,000)

—An S corporation may elect to relinquish the carryback period. The election must be filed on or before the due date (or extended due date) of the return for the loss year. Any corporation that does not make an election on time must carry back the first $10,000 of the NOL before the loss can be carried forward.

Terminating a New York S election.—An election to be a New York S corporation will terminate (1) on the day the election to be a federal S corporation terminates under IRC Sec. 1362(d), or (2) on the day a person becomes a new shareholder of the corporation and that person affirmatively refuses to consent to the New York S election. (*Publication 35,* CCH NEW YORK TAX REPORTS, ¶ 13-040)

Revoking a New York S election.—An election to be a New York S corporation may be revoked only if shareholders who collectively own more than 50% of the outstanding shares of stock of the corporation consent to the revocation. The revoking shareholders must hold their stock on the day that the revocation is filed. A revocation is effective (*Publication 35,* CCH NEW YORK TAX REPORTS, ¶ 13-040):

—on the first day of the corporation's tax year, if the revocation is made on or before the 15th day of the third month of the tax year;

—on the first day of the following tax year of the corporation if the revocation is made after the 15th day of the third month of the tax year; or

—on the date specified, if the revocation specifies a date on or after the date of revocation.

Re-electing to be a New York S corporation.—A termination or revocation of the New York S election does not bar a corporation that continues to be a federal S corporation from making another New York S election for a succeeding tax year. There is no five year disqualification period, as applies for federal tax purposes. However, the corporation must meet the qualifications to make the New York S election. (Publication 35, CCH NEW YORK TAX REPORTS, ¶ 13-040)

Metropolitan Transportation Business Tax Surcharge.—A New York S corporation is not subject to the Metropolitan Transportation Business Tax surcharge under Article 9-A. (*Publication 35,* CCH NEW YORK TAX REPORTS, ¶ 13-040)

Qualified subchapter S subsidiaries.—In most instances, New York will follow the federal qualified subchapter S subsidiaries (QSSS or QSub) treatment in the Article 9-A taxes. QSubs are not subject to the corporate net income tax, provided certain conditions are met. (Sec. 208(1-B), Tax Law) If the QSub is exempt, the assets, liabilities, income, deductions, property, payroll, receipts, capital, credits, and all other tax attributes and elements of economic activity of the QSub are considered to be those of the parent corporation. The parent company may be either a C corporation or an S corporation. For additional information, see ¶ 914.

• *Federal income tax provisions*

A corporation that is taxed on its taxable income pursuant to the provisions of Subchapter C of the IRC is called a "C corporation." For such a corporation, corporate earnings and profits is the amount that remains after the deduction of its expenses and taxes. A dividend is a corporation's distribution of these earnings and profits to a shareholder. In most cases, this dividend is taxable to the recipient shareholder. Thus, a portion of a C corporation's net income is taxed twice—once when it is earned by the corporation and again when the distributed dividend is included on the shareholder's own tax return.

To avoid this so-called double taxation, an eligible corporation can elect to be taxed under Subchapter S of the IRC and thus become an "S corporation." Only a corporation that meets certain statutory requirements relative to the place of incorporation and the number and types of shareholders and classes of stock can elect to be treated as an S corporation. Once qualified, an S corporation normally does not pay any federal income tax itself. Instead, the S corporation generally passes through all of its income, gain, loss, deductions, and credits to a shareholder, and these items are then included *pro rata* on the shareholder's own tax return. For this reason, an S corporation is called a "pass-through entity." While most tax items are aggregated at the entity level and passed through to the shareholders, some items are reported separately by the S corporation since the deductibility of these items involves matters that vary with each shareholder's own situation and may warrant separate computations. If the special tax rules for an S corporation do not cover a specific issue, then the usual C corporation rules govern (IRC Sec. 1371(a)).

For federal income tax purposes, an S corporation must file an annual return on Form 1120S, U.S. Income Tax Return for an S corporation, which is due on or before the 15th day of the third month following the close of the corporate tax year, which generally must be a calendar year (IRC Sec. 1378).

Eligible corporations and shareholders.—Only a corporation that meets certain statutory criteria is eligible to elect S corporation status. Once a qualified corporation makes this election, the entity must continue to meet these standards or the S corporation status, and all of its tax benefits, will be lost.

To be eligible, an interested corporation must meet all of the following conditions (IRC Sec. 1361(b)):

—it must be a U.S. domestic corporation;

—it may not have more than 100 shareholders;

—each shareholder must be either an individual, estate, or a specified type of trust;

—each shareholder must be a U.S. citizen or resident alien;

—it may have only one class of stock; and

—it must not be an "ineligible" corporation.

For purposes of computing the number of corporate shareholders, a number of special rules are applicable. For example, a husband and wife (and their estates) are treated as one shareholder. Furthermore, all members of a family may be treated as one shareholder for purposes of the rules limiting the number of permissible shareholders in an S corporation. The term "members of a family" includes the common ancestor and all lineal descendants of the common ancestor (not more than six generations removed), plus spouses (or former spouses) of these individuals. (IRC Sec. 1361(c)(1))

As indicated above, other than an individual, various specialized entities are also eligible to be an S corporation shareholder, including (IRC Secs. 1361(c)(2), (c)(3), (c)(6), (d), and (e)):

—a trust that is treated as completely owned by a U.S. citizen or resident (grantor trust);

—a trust that qualified under the item above before the deemed owner's death, and that continues to exist for no more than two years beginning on the day of death;

—a trust to which stock is transferred according to a will, but only for a two-year period;

—a trust created primarily to exercise the voting power of the stock transferred to it;

—an estate of a decedent or of an individual in bankruptcy;

—a qualified tax-exempt retirement trust or charitable organization;

—a qualified Subchapter S trust (QSST); or

—an electing small business trust (ESBT).

However, a foreign trust may not be an S corporation shareholder. Finally, an IRA or Roth IRA may be a shareholder in a bank that is an S corporation to the extent of bank stock held by the IRA on October 22, 2004 (that is, the IRA account owner, an individual, is effectively treated as the shareholder) (IRC Secs. 1361(c)(2)(A) and (B)).

QSubs: Of special note in regard to the many eligibility requirements, an S corporation is permitted to own a "qualified Subchapter S subsidiary" (QSSS or QSub). (IRC Sec. 1361(b)(3)) A QSub includes any domestic corporation that would be eligible to be an S corporation itself if the stock of the entity were owned by the shareholders of the parent. The parent must own 100% of the subsidiary's stock, and must elect to treat this entity as a QSub. Once an election is made, all of the QSub's assets, liabilities, income, deductions, and credits are treated as those of the parent S corporation. If a QSub ceases to qualify as such, either because the subsidiary fails to qualify or the parent revokes the election, then another QSub election for that subsidiary may not be made for five years without IRS consent.

Electing S corporation status.—With the unanimous signed consent of all its shareholders, an existing qualified corporation must elect S corporation status on or before the 15th day of the third month of its tax year in order for the election to be effective beginning with that year. (IRC Secs. 1362(a)(2) and (b)(1)) This S corporation election is made on federal Form 2553, Election by Small Business Corporation, with the requisite shareholder consents attached. Each shareholder's consent is binding and may not be withdrawn after the corporation makes a valid election.

Termination of an S corporation election: A valid S corporation election remains effective until it is expressly revoked by shareholders holding more than half of the outstanding shares (including nonvoting stock) (IRC Sec. 1362(d)(1)), or automatically terminates because the corporation ceases to qualify as an S corporation (IRC Sec. 1362(d)(2)) or the corporation receives "excessive passive investment income" (IRC Sec. 1362(d)(3)). The IRS may disregard an inadvertent termination if steps are taken to correct the condition that rendered the corporation ineligible to be an S corporation and the corporation and its shareholders agree to make the requisite IRS adjustments. This waiver relief includes terminations connected with QSubs. (IRC Sec. 1362(f)) Otherwise, S corporation status, once terminated, generally cannot be reelected for five tax years.

Computation of income.—An S corporation must compute its taxable income so that the tax items can be passed through to its shareholders. In computing and reporting its taxable income, an S corporation must break down its income and deductions into two general categories: (1) nonseparately computed income and deductions; and (2) separately stated income and deductions (IRC Sec. 1363(b)). The nonseparately computed items are essentially the corporation's gross income from its trade or business operations and its trade or business deductions. The net ordinary income or loss is passed through as a lump-sum figure to the shareholders. The separately stated items are any income (including tax-exempt income), loss, or deduction that may have to be separately reported by the individual shareholders. These items are reported directly by each shareholder and are excluded from the computation of the nonseparately computed items. The more common types of income items to be stated separately include rents, royalties, interest, dividends, and capital gains or losses realized by the corporation. The more common types of deductions to be stated separately include charitable contributions, certain foreign taxes, mineral exploration costs, and expenses for the production of income.

Some special deduction rules are applicable to an S corporation. Generally, an S corporation cannot claim deductions for foreign taxes, net operating loss (NOL) carrybacks or carryovers, charitable contributions, excess itemized deductions allowed individuals, capital loss carrybacks and carryovers, or the oil and gas wells depletion deduction.

An S corporation is not entitled to deduct an NOL because such a loss is deductible by the corporation's shareholders. Also, since expenses incurred by an S corporation in the production or collection of income from property held for investment purposes are treated as itemized deductions by the corporation's shareholders, these expenses are not deductible by the corporation but are reported separately by the shareholders. The costs of providing fringe benefits to shareholder-employees who on any day of the tax year own more than 2% of the outstanding shares are not deductible in computing the corporation's taxable income from business operations. (IRC Sec. 1372)

Tax on excess passive investment income: An S corporation with Subchapter C earnings and profits and passive investment income totaling more than 25% of its gross receipts is taxed on its "excess net passive income," as statutorily defined, at the highest corporate rate. (IRC Sec. 1375(a))

Built-in gains tax: A corporate-level tax is imposed on any gain realized by a corporation that arose prior to the S corporation election (i.e., the "built-in" gain) (IRC Sec. 1374). The tax is equal to the highest applicable corporate tax rate times the S corporation's net recognized built-in gain, as statutorily defined. The gain is recognized by the S corporation through sale, distribution, or collection within any tax year during the 10-year recognition period beginning the first day that the S corporation election is effective. This corporate-level tax does not apply to a corporation that has been an S corporation for all of its tax years. (IRC Sec. 1374(c)(1)) The built-in gain rule is intended to prevent a corporation from electing S status in an effort to avoid taxation on gain relating to property that it owns. If the corporation waits 10 years, then it can avoid taxation on this built-in gain.

All gains realized from the disposition of an asset during the recognition period are presumed to be recognized built-in gains except to the extent that the S corporation can establish that the gain is from an asset that was acquired after the beginning of the recognition period or from appreciation realized after the start of the recognition period.

¶853

LIFO recapture tax: A C corporation that elects S corporation status and that used the last-in, first-out (LIFO) method to maintain its inventory assets during the last tax year before the S corporation election became effective must include in its gross income a LIFO recapture amount when it finally converts to S corporation status (IRC Sec. 1363(d)(1)). The LIFO recapture amount is the amount, if any, by which the amount of the inventory assets using the first-in, first-out (FIFO) method exceeds the inventory amount of such assets under the LIFO method (IRC Sec. 1363(d)(3)). This provision is designed to give LIFO method taxpayers treatment similar to their FIFO counterparts by requiring the LIFO taxpayer to recapture the benefits derived from using the LIFO method and, thereby, eliminating the potential disparity between these two methods of accounting.

¶854 RICs, REITs, REMICs, and FASITs

Law: Secs. 5, 8, 209, 1515, Tax Law; Reg. Secs. 3-11.1(a), 3-12.1(a), 3-12.1(c) (CCH NEW YORK TAX REPORTS, ¶ 10-355-10-370).

Comparable Federal: Secs. 851-860, 860A-860L, 1361-1379 (U.S. MASTER TAX GUIDE, ¶ 2301-2369).

This paragraph discusses the tax treatment of certain investment pass-through entities and their shareholders, including:

— Regulated investment companies (RICs);

— Real estate investment trusts (REITs);

— Real estate mortgage investment conduits (REMICs); and

— Financial asset securitization trusts (FASITs).

Investment partnerships are discussed above at ¶852. Limited liability investment companies are discussed at ¶851.

• *Regulated investment companies (RICs)*

A regulated investment company (RIC) (commonly known as a "mutual fund") is a corporation that acts as an investment agent for its shareholders, typically investing in government and corporate securities. On behalf of its shareholders, the RIC makes and manages various investments, earning dividends and interest on these investments, passing them on as dividends to the shareholders, and ideally retaining nothing after accounting for expenses.

As a type of pass-through entity, a RIC may entirely avoid taxation at the entity level if all of its income is annually distributed to its shareholders as dividends. Even if less than all of its income is distributed, but a minimum distribution threshold is satisfied (i.e., 90%), only the undistributed investment company income and net undistributed capital gains will be subject to tax. However, if this 90%-threshold is not met, then all of the RIC's income is subject to tax. (IRC Sec. 852(a)(1))

New York generally follows IRC Sec. 851—IRC Sec. 855 and IRC Sec. 860, the federal income tax provisions addressing RICs, subjecting them to corporate franchise (income) tax to the same extent as under federal law.

Interaction of federal and state provisions. —A corporation that is a RIC is subject to New York corporate franchise (income) tax provisions under Article 9-A, rather than the banking franchise (income) tax imposed under Article 32. (Sec. 209(7), Tax Law; Reg. Sec. 3-12.1(a))

Computation of income.—For purposes of the Article 9-A corporate franchise (income) tax, a RIC is subject to tax measured by the entire net income base, the minimum taxable income base, or the fixed dollar minimum, whichever is greater. (Sec. 209(7), Tax Law; Reg. Sec. 3-12.1(a))

The entire net income base of a RIC is federal "investment company taxable income", as defined in IRC Sec. 852(b)(2) and as modified by IRC Sec. 855, plus the amount taxable under IRC Sec. 852(b)(3), subject to the New York modifications that apply to corporations, except the 50% dividend exclusion and the net operating loss deduction, which are not allowed. (Reg. Sec. 3-12.1(b))

Combined reports: A "captive" RIC that is owned or controlled by one or more corporations subject to corporation franchise (income) tax must be included in a combined report with such corporations (Sec. 1515(f)(4)(v), Tax Law). There are exceptions for RICs owning subsidiary RICs, as well as for RICs owned by banks.

Apportionment factors.—New York has adopted special rules not found in the Uniform Division of Income for Tax Purposes Act or the Multistate Tax Commission regulations for the apportionment of income for management services rendered to RICs. (See ¶1303)

Dividends.—If a RIC pays dividends after the close of a taxable year and such dividends were declared before the date its report must be filed (including extensions), it may treat the dividends as having been paid during the taxable year. (Reg. Sec. 3-12.1(c))

New York City.—RICs are subject to the NYC general corporation tax (see ¶2803).

• *Real estate investment trusts (REITs)*

In many ways, a real estate investment trust (REIT) resembles a regulated investment company (RIC), except that a REIT is utilized for passive real estate, rather than for stock, investments. A REIT calculates its income as if it were a regular C corporation, except that certain adjustments apply, the most important of which is the deduction for dividends paid. As with a RIC, if a REIT distributes 90% or more of its ordinary income as dividends, and meets certain requirements as to ownership, management, purpose, and asset diversification, then the REIT is entitled to a deduction for all dividends paid that may be used to offset its income. If applicable, then, similar to other pass-through entities, there is only one level of federal income tax, and that is at the shareholder level. If an entity qualifies as a REIT, income that is distributed to its investors is taxed directly to them without first being taxed at the REIT level. Any retained earnings, of course, are taxed at the regular corporate rates (i.e., the highest corporate tax rate under IRC Sec. 11). A REIT is also subject to tax at the highest corporate rate on its net income from foreclosure property. Furthermore, a 4% excise tax is imposed on any undistributed income. (IRC Sec. 857)

New York generally follows IRC Sec. 856—IRC Sec. 860, the federal income tax provisions addressing REITs, and subjects them to the corporate franchise (income) tax (Article 9-A) rather than the bank franchise (income) tax (Article 32).

Interaction of federal and state provisions.—A corporation, trust, or association that is a REIT as defined in IRC Sec. 856(a), and that meets the requirements of IRC Sec. 856(c), will be treated as a REIT subject to New York corporate franchise (income) tax under Article 9-A of the Tax Law, rather than the bank franchise (income) tax under Article 32. (Sec. 209(5), Tax Law; Reg. Sec. 3-11.1(a))

Computation of income.—A REIT is subject to the New York corporation franchise (income) tax measured by the entire net income base, the minimum taxable income base, or the fixed dollar minimum, whichever is greater. (Sec. 209(5), Tax Law; Reg. Sec. 3-11.1(a))

The entire net income base of a REIT is federal "real estate investment trust taxable income", as defined in IRC Sec. 857(b)(2) and as modified by IRC Sec. 858, plus the amount of taxable income under IRC Sec. 857(b)(3). This amount is subject to the New York modifications that apply to corporations (i.e. additions and subtractions), except for the 50% dividend exclusion, which is not allowed. In addition, the income must be modified as required for optional depreciation. (Sec. 209(5), Tax Law; Reg. Sec. 3-11.1(b))

Combined reports: A "captive" REIT that is owned or controlled by one or more corporations subject to corporation franchise (income) tax must be included in a combined report with such corporations (Sec. 1515(f)(4)(v), Tax Law). There are exceptions for REITs owning subsidiary REITs, as well as for REITs owned by banks.

New York City.—REITs are subject to the NYC general corporation tax (see ¶ 2803).

• Real estate mortgage investment conduits (REMICs)

A real estate mortgage investment conduit (REMIC) is an entity that holds a fixed pool of mortgages and issues multiple classes of interests in itself to investors (IRC Sec. 860D). Under federal income tax law, a REMIC is generally not taxed on its income, but rather its income is taxable to the holders of its interests. In general, it is treated as a partnership, with its interests allocated to, and taken into account by, the holders of the interests in the REMIC. (IRC Sec. 860A—IRC Sec. 860C)

REMICs are exempt from New York income tax. A REMIC is not treated as a corporation, partnership or trust for purposes of the tax law, and the assets of a REMIC are not included in the calculation of any franchise tax liability under the tax law. However, the exemption does not extend to holders of regular or residual interests in a REMIC or to income from such interests. (Sec. 8, Tax Law)

Interaction of federal and state provisions.—A REMIC can assume any form of business entity (corporation, partnership, etc.). A REMIC can be created by a corporation as a segregated pool of assets, in which case such assets would not be included in the capital or asset base in the franchise tax computation of that corporation (*TSB-M-87(22)C*, CCH NEW YORK TAX REPORTS, ¶ 10-000). REMIC interest holders (regular or residual), as defined in IRC Sec. 860G, are not exempt from income tax on their interests. Rather, these interest holders are required to report their holdings as business capital and any income earned as business income.

If any entity ceases to be a REMIC at any time during the taxable year, such entity shall not be treated as a REMIC for such taxable year or any succeeding taxable year.

New York City.—REMICs are NOT subject to the NYC general corporation tax (see ¶ 2804).

• Financial asset securitization investment trusts (FASITs)

A financial asset securitization investment trust (FASIT) is used to secure debt obligations, such as credit card receivables, home equity loans, and auto loans.

New York has no provisions comparable to former IRC Secs. 860H—IRC Sec. 860L, the federal income tax provisions addressing Financial Asset Securitization Investment Trusts (FASITs). The general New York franchise tax laws and regulations are applicable.

The American Jobs Creation Act of 2004 (P.L. 108-357) repealed IRC Secs. 860H through 860L, which permitted the establishment of FASITs for federal income tax purposes. However, the repeal does not apply to any FASIT in existence on October 22, 2004, to the extent that any regular interests already issued by the FASIT remain outstanding in accordance with their original terms (AJCA Sec. 835(c)(2)).

¶855 Tax Treatment of Pass-Through Entities

Law: Secs. 210(3)(a), (8), 632-A, Tax Law; Reg. Secs. 3-8.8, 3-13.3, 4-6.1, 4-6.5, 17-1.1 (CCH NEW YORK TAX REPORTS, ¶ 11-515, 15-185, 16-113, 16-317, 16-565).

Comparable Federal: Secs. 701-761, 1361-1379 (U.S. MASTER TAX GUIDE, ¶ 305-349, 401-481).

As discussed in previous paragraphs, New York generally adopts the federal treatment of most pass-through entities (also known as "flow-through entities"). Federal law treats pass-through entities as separate entities, but requires that the entities' income, gain, losses, deductions and credits be passed-through to the entity's owners, generally in proportion to their ownership interests. An advisory opinion discusses the application of federal P.L. 86-272 to S corporations and their shareholders and to limited liability companies (LLCs) and their members (*TSB-A-08(7)C* and *TSB-A-08(4)I*, New York Commissioner of Taxation and Finance, December 15, 2008, CCH NEW YORK TAX REPORTS, ¶ 406-270).

• *Allocation and apportionment*

All flow-through entities use the three-factor formula of allocation (Reg. Sec. 4-6.5), except for S corporations, which use a single sales factor (Sec. 210(3)(a)(10), Tax Law).

For partnerships (including LLCs treated as partnerships and LLPs), allocation takes place at the entity level. A taxpayer that is a corporate partner must allocate its part of the partnership's property, receipts, and payroll within and outside New York (Reg. Sec. 4-6.5). See below for additional information.

Tax reform: A memorandum discusses how the state's corporate tax reform legislation affects the apportionment factor computation for a New York S corporation, as well as the determination of New York source income for nonresident and part-year resident shareholders of New York S corporations. For tax years beginning on or after January 1, 2015, the business apportionment factor reflects a corporation's New York market-based receipts. See *TSB-M-15(7)C, (6)I*, December 1, 2015, CCH NEW YORK TAX REPORTS, ¶ 408-575.

Practitioner Comment: Special Rule for Real Estate

Although partnerships are required to use a three-factor allocation methodology, income and deductions connected with the rental of real property, and gain or loss from the sale or exchange of real property are not subject to allocation, but are considered derived entirely from the situs of the real estate. Reg. § 132.16. This rule is not limited to gains derived from the sales of rental properties, but applies equally to sales of operating businesses, like hotels. See Ronald and Maxine Linde, (NYS TAT May 24, 2012).

Mark S. Klein, Esq., Hodgson Russ LLP

Tiered partnerships.—In the case of tiered partnerships, the factors flow-through (are included in the factors for) the various tiers. Where a partner is a member in a partnership (an "upper tier partnership") that is a partner in another partnership (a "lower tier partnership"), the source and character of each member's distributive share of each partnership item of income, capital, gain, loss or deduction of the upper tier partnership that is attributable to the lower tier partnership will retain the source and character determined at the level of the lower tier partnership. The source and character are not changed by reason of the fact that the item flows through the upper tier partnership to the member. (Reg. Sec. 3-13.3)

Discretionary allocation by Commissioner.—The Commissioner is authorized to adjust the business allocation percentage or the investment allocation percentage when the percentage does not properly reflect the activity, business, income, or capital of a taxpayer within New York. (Sec. 210(8), Tax Law; Reg. Sec. 4-6.1) The Commissioner may adjust the business allocation percentage by any of the following methods:

—Excluding one or more of the property, receipts or payroll factors;

—Including one or more other factors, such as expenses, purchases or contract values (less subcontract values);

—Excluding one or more assets in computing the allocation percentage provided that the income therefrom is also excluded in determining entire net income or minimum taxable income; or

—Applying any other method calculated to effect a fair and proper allocation.

The New York Department of Taxation and Finance has issued a personal income tax advisory opinion addressing the determination of New York source income for guaranteed payments received by a nonresident partner. The guaranteed payments constituted a distributive share of partnership income. Provided that the partnership records allocated items of income, gain, loss, and deduction to New York on a fair and equitable basis, in accordance with approved methods of accounting, the partner was required to include in his New York source income the amount of guaranteed payments reported by the partnership as New York source income. (*TSB-A-06(9)I*, November 30, 2006, CCH NEW YORK TAX REPORTS, ¶ 405-564)

Allocation of net operating loss.—Before deducting any net operating loss (NOL), a taxpayer with both business income and investment income in a taxable year to which a net operating loss is carried must apportion the loss between business and investment income. (Reg. Sec. 3-8.85) The amount of loss to be subtracted from business income and investment income is computed by multiplying the net operating loss deduction by a ratio. The ratio is a fraction, the numerator of which is investment income and the denominator of which is entire net income, both before deduction of the NOL.

• *Accounting periods and methods*

Except to the extent required by differences between New York and federal tax law, pass-through entities must use the same accounting periods and methods used on their federal returns (Reg. Sec. 17-1.1).

• *Corporate partners*

The New York Department of Taxation and Finance has issued comprehensive guidance on the computation of tax for corporations that are partners in partnerships or that are members of limited liability companies (LLCs) treated as partnerships, applicable to taxable years beginning on or after January 1, 2007 (*TSB-M-07(2)C* and *TSB-M-07(1)I*, January 17, 2007, CCH NEW YORK TAX REPORTS, ¶ 405-595).

Except for certain foreign corporate limited partners, a taxpayer that is a partner in a partnership must compute its tax with respect to its interest in the partnership under either the aggregate or entity method. The regulations discuss each method and set forth the determination of the applicable methodology (Reg. Sec. 4-6.5). Under the aggregate method, a corporate partner takes into account its distributive share of receipts, income, gain, loss, or deduction and its proportionate part of assets, liabilities, and transactions from the partnership. Under the entity method, a corporate partner is treated as owning an interest in a partnership entity, and the interest is considered an intangible asset that constitutes business capital. The regulations make it clear that the aggregate method, which was required under the previous regulations, is the preferred method.

Tax reform: Information regarding economic nexus has been revised to explain how the deriving receipts test is applied to limited corporate partners and corporate members of Limited Liability Companies (LLCs) treated as partnerships, in addition to general corporate partners; see **https://www.tax.ny.gov/bus/ct/ corp_tax_reform_faqs.htm**.

• *Tax avoidance or evasion*

The Commissioner of Taxation and Finance is authorized to disregard a personal service corporation or S corporation if it is determined that the entity was formed or used to avoid or evade the New York personal income tax (Sec. 632-A, Tax Law).

Practitioner Comment: Statute of Limitations Measured by Partner's Return, Not the Flow Through Entity

The tax liability of limited liability companies and partnerships can be asserted against the entities or their members/partners. Regardless of how the tax is assessed, the statute of limitations for any assessment is calculated using the returns of the member/partner. The filing date of the LLC or partnership is irrelevant. See *Wilmorite, Inc. v. Tax Appeals Tribunal*, Appellate Division, 3rd Div., July 30, 2015, CCH NEW YORK TAX REPORTS, ¶408-495.

Mark S. Klein, Esq., Hodgson Russ LLP

¶856 Treatment of Owners' Income

Law: Sec. 617, Tax Law (CCH NEW YORK TAX REPORTS, ¶15-185, 16-113, 16-317).

Comparable Federal: Secs. 701-761, 1366, 1367 (U.S. MASTER TAX GUIDE, ¶309-322, 401-488).

• *Resident partners and S corporation shareholders*

In determining the New York adjusted gross income and the New York taxable income of a resident partner or resident shareholder, any modification that relates to an item of partnership income, gain, loss or deduction will be made in accordance with the partner's distributive share, for federal income tax purposes, of the item to which the modification relates (Sec. 617(a), Tax Law). If a partner's distributive share of any such item is not required to be taken into account separately for federal income tax purposes, the partner's or shareholder's share of the item will be determined in accordance with the partner's share, for federal income tax purposes, of partnership or S corporation taxable income or loss generally.

For additional information, see ¶707. Allocation of partnership income is discussed at ¶855. For a personal income tax credit available to shareholders of S corporations, see ¶123.

Modifications to federal adjusted gross income by an S corporation shareholder for purposes of determining New York adjusted gross income are discussed at ¶205.

An advisory opinion discusses the application of federal P.L. 86-272 to S corporations and their shareholders and to limited liability companies (LLCs) and their members (*TSB-A-08(7)C* and *TSB-A-08(4)I*, New York Commissioner of Taxation and Finance, December 15, 2008, CCH NEW YORK TAX REPORTS, ¶406-270).

CCH Advisory: Metropolitan Commuter Transportation Mobility Tax

The New York Department of Taxation and Finance has issued an advisory opinion discussing the application of the metropolitan commuter transportation mobility tax (MCTMT) to the partners in a New York partnership that sells antique merchandise at various shows throughout the country.

Individuals (including partners in partnerships) who have net earnings from self-employment allocated to the Metropolitan Commuter Transportation District (MCTD) are subject to the MCTMT. However, if the total net earnings from self-employment allocated to the MCTD are $10,000 or less for the tax year, no MCTMT is due. In this case, the partnership maintains inventory in its partners' home, located in the MCTD. Further, the direction and control of the partnership's business activities take place in the MCTD, and the books and records of the business are located in the MCTD. Therefore, the partnership is carrying on business activity in the MCTD.

If an individual has net earnings from self-employment from activity both within and outside the MCTD, those net earnings must be allocated for purposes of determining whether or not the $10,000 annual threshold has been met and computing the amount of MCTMT due. Allocation is done using the same rules that apply for purposes of the allocation of business income earned within and outside the state under the personal income tax rules. (*TSB-A-10(2)MCTMT*, New York Commissioner of Taxation and Finance, October 28, 2010, CCH NEW YORK TAX REPORTS, ¶ 407-052)

- *Shareholder basis adjustments*

The computation and determination of a shareholder's basis in S corporation stock is important for a number of reasons. This basis, which should be adjusted at least annually:

—caps the loss amount that the shareholder may claim from the corporation;

—determines whether corporate operating or liquidating distributions are taxable; and

—helps measures the gain or loss on the sale of the S corporation stock.

A shareholder's S corporation stock basis is first increased by the shareholder's portion of the following (IRC Sec. 1367(a)(1)):

—all corporate income items (including tax-exempt income) that are separately computed and passed through to the shareholder, except for income from an S corporation's discharge of indebtedness that is excluded from corporate income (see IRC Sec. 108(a));

—nonseparately computed corporate income; and

—the excess of the corporation's depletion deductions over the basis of the property subject to depletion.

However, no increase in basis may be made for any pass-through item of corporate gross income unless that increase is, in fact, reported on the shareholder's tax return. (IRC Sec. 1367(b)(1)) Unlike with a partnership, a shareholder's proportionate share of the S corporation's debt to the shareholders is not included in the basis determination.

Stock basis is then decreased (but not below zero) in the following order by the shareholder's portion of (IRC Sec. 1367(a)(2)):

—nontaxable corporate return-of-capital distributions;

—a corporate expense not deductible in computing the entity's taxable income and not properly chargeable to the capital account;

—the depletion deduction for any oil or gas wells held by the S corporation to the extent that this deduction does not exceed the shareholder's proportionate share of the adjusted basis of the property;

—all corporate loss and deduction items that are separately stated and passed through; and

—the nonseparately computed loss of the corporation.

Note that a shareholder may make a binding election to permanently alter these ordering rules and to reduce his or her stock basis by losses and deductions before nondeductible expenditures.

In the case of amounts other than corporate nontaxable return-of-capital distributions that would reduce the shareholder's stock basis to less than zero, the excess is applied to reduce (but not below zero) the shareholder's basis in any indebtedness of the S corporation to the shareholder. Any net increase in basis in a subsequent year is applied first to restore the basis of indebtedness before it may be applied to increase the basis of stock. (IRC Sec. 1367(b)(2))

- *Distributions*

An S corporation distribution generally constitutes a nontaxable return of a shareholder's stock basis. However, in certain cases, part of a distribution may be taxable as a dividend, as a long-term or short-term capital gain, or as both.

A shareholder who receives a distribution from an S corporation must wait until the end of the corporation's tax year to determine whether, and to what extent, the distribution is taxable to the shareholder. A crucial factor in this determination is whether the S corporation has earnings and profits from years when it was a C corporation because an S corporation distribution is treated differently depending upon whether the corporation has such accumulated earnings and profits.

For federal income tax purposes, an S corporation does not accumulate earnings and profits from year to year because all of its current earnings and profits are taxed to the shareholders annually. (IRC Sec. 1371(c)) However, an S corporation can have accumulated earnings and profits attributable to tax years for which an election was not in effect or a corporate acquisition that results in a carryover of earnings and profits.

   • *Limited liability company members*

An LLC that elects to be taxed as a partnership is a pass-through entity in which profits and losses are passed through to members. For additional information, see ¶ 113. Allocation of partnership income is discussed at ¶ 855.

¶857 Nonresident Owners

   Law: Sec. 632, Tax Law (CCH New York Tax Reports, ¶ 15-105).

Partners: In determining the New York source income of a nonresident partner of any partnership, there is included only the portion derived from or connected with New York sources of the partner's distributive share of items of partnership income, gain, loss or deduction entering into the partner's federal adjusted gross income (Sec. 632(a)(1), Tax Law).

In determining the New York sources of a nonresident partner's income, no effect will be given to a provision in the partnership agreement that:

   —characterizes payments to the partner as being for services or for the use of capital;

   —allocates to the partner, as income or gain from sources outside New York, a greater proportion of the partner's distributive share of partnership income or gain from sources outside New York to partnership income or gain from all sources, except as specifically authorized by the Commissioner; or

   —allocates to the partner a greater proportion of a partnership item of loss or deduction connected with New York sources than the partner's proportionate share, for federal income tax purposes, of partnership loss or deduction generally, except as authorized by the Commissioner (Sec. 632(b), Tax Law).

S corporation shareholders: In determining the New York source income of an electing nonresident shareholder of an S corporation, there is included only the portion of the shareholder's *pro rata* share of items of S corporation income, loss, and deduction entering into the shareholder's federal adjusted gross income, increased by reductions for taxes on built-in gains or excessive net passive income (see IRC Sec. 1366(f)(2) and (3)). (Sec. 632(a)(2), Tax Law)

Amendments enacted as part of the 2010-2011 budget package that concern the IRC Sec. 453(h)(1)(A) treatment of installment payments and IRC Sec. 338(h)(10) treatment of subsidiary sales are discussed in *TSB-M-10(10)I,* August 31, 2010, CCH New York Tax Reports, ¶ 406-959.

For tax years beginning on or after January 1, 2015, the business apportionment factor reflects a corporation's New York market-based receipts. To calculate amounts derived from New York sources, nonresident shareholders apply the S corporation's business apportionment factor to all New York S corporation items of income, gain, loss, and deduction (and any related Sec. 612, Tax Law, modifications) that are included in New York adjusted gross income. For part-year resident shareholders, the allocation applies only to the New York S corporation items received during the nonresident period (and any related Sec. 612 modifications). See *TSB-M-15(7)C, (6)I*, December 1, 2015, CCH NEW YORK TAX REPORTS, ¶408-575.

For additional information, see ¶707 and ¶708. Allocation of partnership income is discussed at ¶855.

CCH Advisory: Gain Was Not NY Source Income

In a New York personal income tax case involving a deemed asset sale under IRC Sec. 338(h)(10), the Tax Appeals Tribunal affirmed an administrative law judge's determination that the gain received by nonresidents from the sale of their S corporation stock was not New York source income. The federal election was designed to provide very specific and limited federal tax consequences, but it did not affect the substance of the transaction, which was a stock sale. A plain reading of Sec. 208(9), Tax Law, regarding the calculation of entire net income for S corporations, makes it clear that S corporations must compute their income for New York tax purposes as if the Sec. 338(h)(10) election had not been made. Accordingly, the fictitious deemed asset sale and the deemed distribution in complete liquidation did not apply to the transaction in this case for New York purposes. Therefore, the gain from the deemed asset sale could not be included in the entire net income of the S corporation in determining its New York franchise tax under Article 9-A, and the gain also could not be passed through, *pro rata*, as New York source income to the S corporation's shareholders. (*Baum*, New York Division of Tax Appeals, Tax Appeals Tribunal, DTA Nos. 820837 and 820838, February 12, 2009, CCH NEW YORK TAX REPORTS, ¶406-321)

• Part-year residents

The amount of an individual's distributive or *pro rata* share of items of partnership income, gain, loss, and deduction to be included in New York source income is computed using the following formula (*TSB-M-00(1)I*, CCH NEW YORK TAX REPORTS, ¶300-314):

Step 1: Multiply the individual's distributive or *pro rata* share of income, gain, loss, and deduction for federal income tax purposes for the tax year by a fraction, the numerator of which is the number of days in the individual's tax year that the individual was a resident of New York State and the denominator of which is the total number of days in the individual's tax year.

Step 2: Multiply the individual's federal distributive or *pro rata* share of income, gain, loss, and deduction for federal income tax purposes for the tax year by a fraction, the numerator of which is the number of days in the individual's tax year that the individual was a nonresident of New York State and the denominator of which is the total number of days in the individual's tax year. This result is then multiplied by the partnership's New York allocation percentage for the year.

Step 3: Add the amounts computed in Step 1 and Step 2. This is the amount includable in New York source income. The same steps are used to determine the amount of the distributive or *pro rata* share of New York addition and subtraction modifications from the partnership to be included in New York source income. In addition, if an individual is a partner of more than one partnership, these steps must be repeated for each partnership.

CCH Advisory: Partners' Retirement Income

In 2006, an administrative law judge ruled that payments made to a nonresident under a partnership agreement constituted retirement income from a plan described in IRC Sec. 3121(v)(2)(C) and were part of a series of substantially equal periodic payments made for a period of not less than 10 years. Accordingly, under 4 U.S.C. 114, New York was precluded from imposing tax on the payments (*McDermott,* DTA No. 820099, February 2, 2006, CCH NEW YORK TAX REPORTS, ¶ 405-304). Subsequently, the New York Department of Taxation and Finance issued a memorandum regarding payments made in recognition of prior services to a retiring or retired nonresident or part-year resident partner under a nonqualified retirement plan maintained by a partnership. It was the Department's position that such payments were not covered by 4 U.S.C. Sec. 114, which provides that only the state of which a person is a resident or domiciliary may tax the person on his or her retirement income. According to the Department, payments received by a nonresident or part-year resident retiring or retired partner under such plans, where the payments did not constitute an annuity under Reg. Sec. 132.4(d), had to be taken into account in computing the partner's New York personal income tax liability. (*TSB-M-06(3)I,* CCH NEW YORK TAX REPORTS, ¶ 300-508)

However, federal legislation enacted in 2006 (P.L. 109-264 (H.R. 4019)) provides that the prohibition applies to the retirement income of a nonresident retired partner, as well as a nonresident retired employee, and that the application of a predetermined formula cap or a cost-of-living adjustment in a nonqualified deferred compensation plan does not make the retirement income of such nonresidents subject to state taxation. These changes apply to amounts received after December 31, 1995. See *TSB-M-07(2)I,* January 24, 2007, CCH NEW YORK TAX REPORTS, ¶ 405-601. See also ¶ 206, ¶ 403.

¶858 Withholding; Estimated Tax

Law: Sec. 658(c), Tax Law; Reg. Secs. 151.17, 151.19 (CCH NEW YORK TAX REPORTS, ¶ 16-640, 89-102, 89-104).

Comparable Federal: Secs. 701-761, 1366, 1367 (U.S. MASTER TAX GUIDE, ¶ 2447).

Forms: Form IT-2658, Report of Estimated Tax for Nonresident Individual Partners and Shareholders; Form CT-2658, Report of Estimated Tax for Corporate Partners; Form TR-99, Application for Permission to File a Group Return; Form IT-203-S, Group Return for Nonresident Shareholders of New York S Corporations.

Partnerships, limited liability companies (LLCs), and S corporations are not required to withhold income from their partners, members, or shareholders.

• *Estimated tax*

Partnerships, S corporations, and LLCs that have income from New York sources are required to pay estimated taxes on behalf of nonresident individual or C corporation partners, members, or shareholders on their distributive or *pro rata* shares of such income. (Sec. 658(c)(4), Tax Law; *TSB-M-04(1)I,* CCH NEW YORK TAX REPORTS, ¶ 300-420)

These provisions do not apply with respect to a partner, member, or shareholder if the estimated tax required to be paid by the entity for that partner, member, or shareholder does not exceed $300 for the taxable year or if the partner, member, or shareholder has elected to be included in an authorized group return (see below). In addition, the Commissioner may issue a waiver with respect to partners, members, or shareholders who are not subject to New York income tax (or who establish that they are filing New York income tax returns and paying estimated taxes when due) and in other circumstances when it is determined that withholding is not necessary to ensure collection of income tax on New York source income allocable to the nonresident or C corporation. (Sec. 658(c)(4), Tax Law; *TSB-M-04(1)I,* CCH NEW YORK TAX REPORTS, ¶ 300-420)

Further, estimated tax payments are not required for partners, members, or shareholders that are resident S corporations. (Instructions, Form IT-2658, Report of Estimated Tax for Nonresident Individual Partners and Shareholders)

For purposes of these provisions, the term "estimated tax" refers to a partner's, member's, or shareholder's distributive or *pro rata* share of the entity income derived from New York sources, multiplied by the highest rate of tax prescribed by Tax Law Sec. 601 for the taxable year of any partner, member, or shareholder who is an individual taxpayer and reduced by the distributive or *pro rata* share of certain credits derived from the entity. (Sec. 658(c)(4)(A), Tax Law)

Statements: Within 30 days after the estimated tax is paid, an entity is required to furnish a written statement to its partners, members, and shareholders showing the estimated taxes paid on their behalf. The entity is also required to provide certain information to the Commissioner, including information necessary to identify the estimated tax paid by the entity for each partner, member, or shareholder. (Sec. 658(c)(4)(E), Tax Law)

The statement must show that the payment is to be treated as a payment of estimated tax when the partners or shareholders file their New York returns; the statement cannot be a federal form W-2 or any other form or document that would indicate that the payment is income tax withheld—see *Important Notice N-04-11*, CCH New York Tax Reports, ¶ 320-144. See also Instructions to CT 2658.

Practitioner Comment: Estimated Tax Statements

Although flow-through entities are required to issue statements identifying the estimated taxes paid on behalf of nonresident partners, members and shareholders, there is no "official" form for this purpose. Many practitioners have reflected these payments in one of the state and local tax boxes on the federal withholding tax form (W-2). New York's Department of Taxation and Finance has announced that this practice is unacceptable. Instead, a separate, self-created withholding tax statement is required. *See* Instructions to CT-2658.

Mark S. Klein, Esq., Hodgson Russ LLP

Due dates: Estimated payments are due on April 15, June 15, September 15, and January 15 of the next year. S corporations may pay the entire amount due with the first payment (April 15), or pay in four equal installments. The payments must be made by these dates whether the entity keeps its books on a calendar-year basis or a fiscal-year basis. (*TSB-M-04(1)I*, CCH New York Tax Reports, ¶ 300-420; *Instructions*, Form IT-2658, Report of Estimated Tax for Nonresident Individual Partners and Shareholders; *Instructions*, Form CT-2658, Report of Estimated Tax for Corporate Partners)

A booklet, CT-2658/IT-2658-P, contains copies of the forms and instructions needed to make the estimated payments. See also *Important Notice N-03-25* regarding the use of computer-generated forms to report the estimated tax payments.

Waivers: The Commissioner may issue waivers for partners, members or shareholders who are not subject to New York income tax or establish that they are filing New York income tax returns and paying estimated taxes when due. Also, the Commissioner may issue a waiver in other circumstances in which he or she determines that withholding is not necessary to ensure collection of income tax on New York source income allocable to the nonresident or C corporation.

Penalties: See ¶ 3704.

- *Group returns*

Partnerships and LLCs: "Qualified electing nonresident partners" are allowed to make an election to file on a group basis (Reg. Sec. 151.17(c)). To be classified as a "qualified electing nonresident partner," the partner or member of an LLC must:

(1) be a nonresident of New York for the entire taxable year;

(2) have not maintained a permanent place of abode in New York State at any time during the taxable year;

(3) the partner or the partner's spouse must: (a) have no New York source income other than the partner's distributive share of partnership income (as determined under Regs. 137.1—137.6) allocated to New York State; (b) not be subject to the minimum income tax; (c) not be subject to the separate tax on the ordinary income portion of a lump sum distribution; and

(4) must waive the right to claim the New York standard or itemized deduction, personal exemptions, any capital loss carryover or net operating loss carryback or carryover, and any credits against New York State personal income tax (Reg. Sec. 151.17(c)).

S corporations: A New York S corporation is permitted to file a New York group nonresident personal income tax return on behalf of its qualified nonresident shareholders who elect to have the S corporation file on their behalf (Reg. Sec. 151.19). Form TR-99, Application for Permission to File a Group Return, should be used by a New York S Corporation to request permission to file a group nonresident return on behalf of its shareholders.

MCTDMT: Partnerships, LLCs, and LLPs may request approval to file returns for the Metropolitan Commuter Transportation District mobility tax on a group basis (*TSB-M-09(2)MCTMT*, August 5, 2009, CCH NEW YORK TAX REPORTS, ¶ 406-476).

¶859 Returns

Law: Sec. 209 (5), (7), Sec. 658(c), Tax Law; Reg. Sec. 158.9 (CCH NEW YORK TAX REPORTS, ¶ 17-155, 89-102).

Forms: Form CT-3-S, New York S Corporation Franchise Tax Return; Form CT-4-S, New York S Corporation Franchise Tax Return Short Form; Form IT-204, Partnership Return; Form IT-370-PF, Application for Automatic Extension of Time to File for Partnerships and Fiduciaries; Form IT-372-PF, Application for Additional Extension of Time to File for Partnerships and Fiduciaries; Form IT-204-LL, Limited Liability Company/Limited Liability Partnership Filing Fee Payment Form.

The following discussion details the return requirements for various types of pass-through entities (Sec. 658(c), Tax Law).

• *S corporations*

Every federal S corporation for which an election to be treated as a New York S corporation is in effect must file a New York return if the corporation does business, employs capital, owns or leases property, or maintains an office in the state (Sec. 658(c)(2), Tax Law). New York S corporations must file Form CT-3-S, New York S Corporation Franchise Tax Return, or Form CT-4-S, New York S Corporation Franchise Tax Return Short Form.

Attachments: Taxpayers must attach a copy of their *pro forma* federal Form 1120 and a copy of the actual federal Form 1120S that was filed.

Taxpayers must also attach Form CT-34-SH, New York S Corporation Shareholders' Information Schedule. In addition, CT-3-S filers must also attach Form CT-3-S-ATT, Schedules A, B, C, D, and E, to report the business allocation percentage, computation and allocation of capital, computation of subsidiary and investment income, and the issuer's allocation percentage.

Due date: Returns must be filed within two-and-a-half months after the end of the reporting period (i.e., if reporting for the calendar year, the return is due by March 15). (Sec. 658(c)(2), Tax Law)

Extensions: If the deadline cannot be met, taxpayers should file Form CT-5.4, Request for Six-Month Extension to File New York S Corporation Franchise Tax Return, and pay estimated franchise tax on or before the original due date of the return. Additional extensions will not be granted beyond six months. (Reg. Sec. 6-4.4; Form CT-5.4, Request for Six-Month Extension to File New York S Corporation Franchise Tax Return)

Composite returns: See "Group returns" at ¶ 858.

¶859

Termination year: In the termination year of an S corporation (the year the corporation allows its S corporation election to lapse and become a C corporation), a return is filed for both the S short year and the C short year, which are treated as separate taxable years. The due date for the S short year is the same as that for the C short year.

- *Partnerships*

Every partnership having a resident partner or having any income derived from New York sources must file a New York return (Sec. 658(c)(1), Tax Law). Partnerships must file Form IT-204, Partnership Return, all supporting attachments, and Form IT-204-ATT, Partners' Identifying Information - Attachment to Form IT-204. There are no specific forms used to report income/loss and apportionment for partners.

For tax years after 2015, calendar year taxpayers' returns are due on the March (previously, April) 15 following the end of the calendar year (Sec. 658(c)(1), Tax Law). Fiscal year returns are due the 15th day of the third (previously, fourth) month after the end of the tax year (Sec. 658(c)(3)(A), Tax Law).

Filing fee: Every partnership having any income derived from New York sources is subject to an annual filing fee calculated as follows (Sec. 658(c)(3), Tax Law; *TSB-M-09(8)I,* July 8, 2009, CCH NEW YORK TAX REPORTS, ¶ 406-442):

— $500 if New York source gross income is exactly $1 million;

— $1,500 if New York source gross income is more than $1 million but not over $5 million;

— $3,000 if New York source gross income is more than $5 million but not over $25 million; and

— $4,500 if New York source gross income is more than $25 million.

Partnerships (other than LLPs under Article 8-B of the Partnership Law and foreign LLPs) with less than $1 million in New York source gross income are exempt from the filing fee. For taxable years beginning before 2009, the filing fee requirement applied only to LLPs.

The full amount of the filing fee due must be paid within 60 days after the last day of the taxable year. (Sec. 658(c)(3), Tax Law; *TSB-M-09(8)I,* July 8, 2009, CCH NEW YORK TAX REPORTS, ¶ 406-442)

Attachments required: IRS Forms 1065 or 1065-B and Schedules K-1, New York Form IT-204-ATT, and all supporting attachments to Form IT-204 must be attached. (Instructions, 2004 Form IT-204, Partnership Return)

If the partnership conducts business entirely outside of New York and a return is being filed because the partnership has a New York resident partner, federal Schedules K-1 need not be attached for nonresident partners and Schedule A need not be completed. Instead, complete Schedule B and include the totals for all partners and include on Form IT-204-ATT a list of the resident partners. The partnership must also attach a statement to the return indicating:

—that the partnership has no income derived from New York sources;

—that all other partners in the partnership are nonresidents of New York;

—the number of nonresident partners; and

—that copies of federal Schedules K-1 will be submitted if deemed necessary at any time during the course of an audit.

If the partnership conducts business entirely within or within and outside of New York, all resident and nonresident partners need to be included on Form IT-204-ATT.

Extensions: New York Form IT-370-PF, Application for Automatic Extension of Time to File for Partnerships and Fiduciaries, must be filed by the due date of the return in order to receive an automatic three-month extension. IRS Form 8736 may be filed in lieu of New York Form IT-370-PF; however, IRS Forms 2758 and 4868 are not acceptable substitutes (Reg. Sec. 157.2(b)(2); Instructions, Form IT-204, Partnership Return). Partnerships may file Form IT-372-PF, Application for Additional Extension of Time to File for Partnerships and Fiduciaries, for an additional three-month extension. Form IT-372-PF must be filed on or before the extended due date of the original return. Except in cases of undue hardship, the New York Department of Taxation and Finance will not accept Form IT-372-PF if Form IT-370-PF is not filed first.

Composite returns: See "Group returns" at ¶858.

Information returns: When a partnership has elected to be excluded from the partnership provisions of IRC Sec. 761 and state and federal partnership returns are not required, but where federal information returns (IRS Form 1099) are required to be filed, similar information returns may be required to be furnished to New York. (Reg. Sec. 158.9)

• *Limited liability companies*

New York conforms with the federal classification of LLCs and, thus, an LLC that is treated as a partnership for federal income tax purposes will be treated as an LLC for New York corporate income tax purposes.

LLCs must file Form IT-204, Partnership Return, all supporting attachments, and Form IT-204-ATT, Partners' Identifying Information—Attachment to Form IT-204. There are no specific forms used to report income/loss and apportionment for members. Domestic or foreign LLCs that are required to file a New York partnership return are also required to file Form IT-204-LL, Limited Liability Company/Limited Liability Partnership Filing Fee Payment Form, within 30 days of the last day of the tax year. (Form IT-204-LL may not be attached to Form IT-204) For additional information, see *Important Notice N-08-16*, New York Department of Taxation and Finance, December 2008, CCH NEW YORK TAX REPORTS, ¶406-248.

For tax years after 2015, calendar year taxpayers' returns are due on the March 15 (previously, April 15) following the end of the calendar year. Fiscal year returns are due the 15th day of the third (previously, fourth) month after the end of the tax year. (Sec. 658(c)(3)(A), Tax Law)

Attachments required: IRS Forms 1065 or 1065-B and Schedules K-1, New York Form IT-204-ATT, and all supporting attachments to Form IT-204 must be attached. (*Instructions*, Form IT-204, Partnership Return)

If the LLC conducts business entirely outside of New York and a return is being filed because the LLC has a New York resident member, federal Schedules K-1 need not be attached for nonresident members and Schedule A need not be completed. Instead, complete Schedule B and include the totals for all members and include on Form IT-204-ATT a list of the resident members. The LLC must also attach a statement to the return indicating:

—that the LLC has no income derived from New York sources;

—that all other members in the LLC are nonresidents of New York;

—the number of nonresident members; and

—that copies of federal Schedules K-1 will be submitted if deemed necessary at any time during the course of an audit.

¶859

If the LLC conducts business entirely within or within and outside of New York, all resident and nonresident members need to be included on Form IT-204-ATT.

Extensions: See "Partnerships," above.

Composite returns: See "Group returns," at ¶858.

Information returns: When an LLC has elected to be excluded from the partnership provisions of IRC Sec. 761 and state and federal partnership returns are not required, but where federal information returns (IRS Form 1099) are required to be filed, similar information returns may be required to be furnished to New York. (Reg. Sec. 158.9)

- *Tax return preparers*

Information on rules that apply to preparers of New York personal income tax returns (including partnership and fiduciary returns), the requirements of the Tax Preparer Registration Program, and the electronic filing mandate are included in Publication 58, *Information for Income Tax Return Preparers*, January 2015, CCH NEW YORK TAX REPORTS, ¶19-614.

- *Limited liability partnerships*

New York conforms with the federal classification of LLPs and, thus, an LLP that is treated as a partnership for federal income tax purposes will be treated as an LLP for New York corporate income tax purposes. For reporting details, see "Partnerships," above.

- *RICs and REITs*

A "captive" RIC or REIT that is owned or controlled by one or more corporations subject to corporation franchise (income) tax must be included in a combined report with such corporations (Sec. 209(5), (7), Tax Law). There are exceptions for REITs owning subsidiary REITs and RICs owning subsidiary RICs, as well as for REITs and RICs owned by banks. See also ¶854.

¶860 Penalties

Penalties are discussed at ¶809 and ¶3704.

PART III

CORPORATION FRANCHISE (INCOME) TAX

CHAPTER 9
IMPOSITION OF TAX, RATES, EXEMPTIONS, CREDITS

¶940   Excelsior Jobs Program
¶941   Low-Income Housing Credit
¶942   Green Building Credit
¶943   Brownfield Cleanup Program Credits
¶944   Film Production Credit
¶945   Credit for Fuel Cell Electric Generating Equipment (Expired)
¶946   Credit for Security Training
¶947   Credit for Disabled-Accessible Vehicles
¶948   Credit for Historic Property Rehabilitation
¶949   Credit for Production of Commercials
¶950   Credit for Clean Heating Fuel
¶951   Credit for Conservation Easement Property Taxes
¶952   Credit for Biofuel Production
¶953   Urban Youth Jobs Tax Credit (formerly, Youth Works Credit)
¶954   Empire State Jobs Retention Program
¶955   Credit for Craft Breweries
¶956   Minimum Wage Reimbursement Credit
¶957   Hire a Veteran Credit
¶958   Real Property Tax Credit for Qualified Manufacturers
¶959   Musical and Theatrical Production Credit
¶960   Employee Training Incentive Credit
¶961   Farm Workforce Retention Credit

¶901 Overview of Corporation Franchise (Income) Tax

• *In General*

A New York corporation franchise tax was first imposed in 1880. The present codification, Article 9-A of the Tax Law, entitled "Franchise Tax on Business Corporations," was enacted in 1944. However, the law has been extensively amended since that time.

The franchise tax is imposed at rates listed at ¶905 on domestic corporations for the privilege of exercising the corporate franchise and on foreign corporations for the privilege of doing business, employing capital, owning or leasing property, or maintaining an office in New York during the fiscal or calendar year.

The tax is primarily based on entire net income allocated to New York. Any of three alternative bases—allocated capital, minimum income, or a fixed dollar minimum—must be used if a greater tax results. In addition to the tax on entire net income or on the alternative bases, there is a tax on allocated subsidiary capital (repealed for taxable years beginning after 2014).

"Entire net income" is principally federal taxable income with certain inclusions, exclusions, and adjustments. By adopting federal taxable income as a starting point, New York adopts generally the federal treatment of items of income, gain, loss, and deduction, with specific exceptions.

The various bases of tax and the modifications of federal taxable income are discussed at Chapters 10, 11, and 12. Allocation of income and capital in the case of corporations doing business within and without New York is treated at Chapter 13.

Returns, payments, and estimated taxes are discussed at Chapter 14, while taxpayer remedies, penalties, interest, and administration are the subjects of Chapter 15. Additional information on administrative topics, including recordkeeping, refunds, audits, and contact information for taxing agencies is found in Part IX, "Administration and Procedure," Chapters 36 through 40.

¶901

• *S corporations*

A corporate level tax is imposed on S corporations. Although administrative provisions relating to collection, payment, and reporting generally follow the provisions applicable to corporations that have not elected S status (that is, C corporations), differences do exist (see ¶853 and ¶914).

• *Federal legislation*

Expensing of assets: New York conforms to federal changes extending the enhanced IRC Sec. 179 deduction, except that an addition modification is required for the amount deducted by a taxpayer (except an eligible farmer) under IRC Sec. 179 for a sport utility vehicle with a vehicle weight over 6,000 pounds. (Sec. 208(9)(b)(16), Tax Law) (see ¶1002)

Bonus depreciation: For taxable years beginning after 2002, and applicable to property placed in service on or after June 1, 2003, the New York corporate franchise (income) tax, bank franchise (income) tax, insurance franchise (income) tax, and personal income tax are decoupled from federal accelerated depreciation provisions under IRC Sec. 168(k), except with respect to qualified Resurgence Zone property and qualified New York Liberty Zone property.

The federal Emergency Economic Stabilization Act of 2008 (EESA) (P.L. 110-343) includes special depreciation provisions for qualified refuse and recycling property (IRC Sec. 168(m)) and qualified disaster property (IRC Sec. 168(n)). New York has not decoupled from these provisions.

• *Recent New York legislation*

Corporate tax reform: The 2014-2015 budget law makes numerous changes to the corporate tax provisions, applicable to taxable years beginning on or after January 1, 2015, as follows.

— The Article 32 bank franchise tax is repealed, and banks are merged into the Article 9-A corporate franchise tax. The legislation also repeals the organization and license taxes and maintenance fees under Secs. 180 and 181, Tax Law; (¶926, ¶2714, ¶4001, ¶4002)

— Under Article 9-A, subtraction modification provisions are added for (1) qualified residential loan portfolios and (2) community banks and small thrifts; (¶1003)

— An economic nexus provision is added to impose tax on businesses having receipts within New York of $1 million or more in a taxable year. In addition, the legislation amends the nexus provisions to remove the exception for the use of fulfillment services; (¶902)

— The legislation eliminates the minimum taxable income base, as well as the separate tax on subsidiary capital. In addition, the capital base tax is phased out over six years, beginning in 2016; (¶905; ¶1201 *et seq.*)

— "Business income" is redefined to mean entire net income minus investment income and other exempt income. In no event will the sum of investment income and other exempt income exceed entire net income. If the taxpayer makes the fixed percentage method election under Sec. 210-A(5)(a)(1), Tax Law, then all income from qualified financial instruments will constitute business income; (¶1301)

— A new provision is created to define "other exempt income" as the sum of exempt CFC income and exempt unitary corporation dividends; (¶1301)

— The existing entire net income exclusions for income from subsidiary capital and 50% of dividends from non-subsidiaries are removed (¶1003);

— With respect to an alien corporation (not treated as a domestic corporation under any provision of the IRC), the definition of "entire net income" is

¶901

modified to refer to income that is effectively connected with the conduct of a trade or business within the U.S., as determined under IRC Sec. 882; (¶1001)

— The legislation revises the definitions of "business capital," "investment capital," and "investment income."; (¶1301)

— The MTA surcharge under Sec. 209-B, Tax Law, is made permanent, and the rate is increased from 17% to 25.6% for taxable years beginning after 2014 and before 2016. For subsequent years, the rate is 28%, as adjusted by the commissioner; (¶905)

— The legislation creates new Sec. 210-A, Tax Law, generally providing for the market-based sourcing of receipts, based on customer location; (¶1303)

— The legislation also adds Sec. 210-C, Tax Law, to generally require combined reporting if the taxpayer is engaged in a unitary business and a 50% common ownership test is met; (¶1404)

— With respect to net operating losses (NOLs), the legislation provides for (1) a prior NOL conversion subtraction and (2) a deduction for NOLs generated in taxable years beginning after 2014. (¶1008)

Corporate tax reform technical changes: The 2015-2016 budget law makes several technical changes to the corporate tax reform provisions, retroactive to tax years beginning after 2014, as follows (Ch. 59 (A.B. 3009), Laws 2015):

The amount of investment income that may be deducted is capped at 8% of the taxpayer's entire net income in cases where the taxpayer's investment income is determined without regard to the interest deductions allowed and makes numerous other technical changes to the corporate tax reform statute. (¶1001)

The law clarifies that net operating losses (NOLs) are required to be carried back to the earliest of the three years. Additionally, taxpayers are entitled to make an irrevocable election to relinquish the entire carryback period. (¶1001)

The law adds apportionment rules for marked-to-market gains (¶1301) as well as for receipts from the operation of vessels (¶1303).

¶902 Corporations Subject to Tax

Law: Sec. 209, Tax Law; Reg. Sec. 1-3.3 (CCH New York Tax Reports, ¶10-075, 10-210).

Comparable Federal: 11, 12, 501 (U.S. Master Tax Guide, ¶201).

All domestic corporations, and all foreign corporations doing business, or employing capital, or owning or leasing property, or maintaining an office in New York, are subject to the corporation franchise tax, unless specifically exempted or subject to other New York franchise taxes. (Sec. 209, Tax Law)

Exempt corporations are discussed at ¶903.

CCH Advisory: Banks Now Subject to Corporation Franchise Tax

Effective for taxable years beginning on or after January 1, 2015, the Article 32 bank franchise tax is repealed, and banks are merged into the Article 9-A corporate franchise tax (Ch. 59 (S.B. 6359), Laws 2014).

• *Domestic corporations*

A domestic corporation is subject to the tax by reason of its possession of the privilege to exercise its corporate franchise in New York. (Sec. 209, Tax Law) Consequently, the tax is imposed on a domestic corporation for every fiscal or calendar year, or other period of its existence, whether or not it does business, employs capital, owns or leases any property, maintains any office, or engages in any activity, within or without New York. For the same reason, a domestic corporation must pay the tax even though it carries on its business entirely outside New York.

• *Foreign corporations (nexus)*

A foreign corporation that does business, or employs capital, or owns or leases property, or maintains an office in New York or, for taxable years beginning after 2014, derives receipts of $1 million or more from activity in New York, is subject to the franchise tax irrespective of whether it has qualified to do business in New York (Sec. 209, Tax Law).

Corporate partners: Information regarding economic nexus has been revised to explain how the deriving receipts test is applied to limited corporate partners and corporate members of Limited Liability Companies (LLCs) treated as partnerships, in addition to general corporate partners; see **https://www.tax.ny.gov/bus/ct/ corp_tax_reform_faqs.htm**.

Practitioner Comment: Limited Partnership Interest

A corporation subject to New York State's franchise tax solely based on its ownership of an interest in a limited partnership doing business in New York can make an irrevocable election to compute its tax by taking into account only its distributive share of the income, capital, gain, loss or deduction of the limited partnership with New York activity. (20 NYCRR § 3-13.1)

Mark S. Klein, Esq., Hodgson Russ LLP

The following activities do not constitute doing business, employing capital, owning or leasing property, or maintaining an office in New York (Sec. 209(2), Tax Law; Reg. Sec. 1-3.3):

— the maintenance of cash balances with banks or trust companies in New York;

— the ownership of stock or securities kept in New York in a safe deposit box, safe, vault, or other receptacle rented for the purpose, or pledged as collateral security, or deposited with one or more banks or trust companies, or brokers who are members of a recognized security exchange, in safekeeping or custody accounts;

— the taking of any action by any such bank or trust company or broker, which is incidental to the rendering of safekeeping or custodian service to the corporation;

— the maintenance of a New York office by a corporation officer or director who is not an employee of the corporation if the corporation is not otherwise doing business or engaging in taxable activity in New York;

— the keeping of corporation books and records in New York by a non-employee if the corporation is not otherwise doing business or engaging in taxable activity in New York;

— for taxable years beginning before 2015, the use of fulfillment services of a person other than an affiliated person and the ownership of property stored on the premises of the person in conjunction with fulfillment services (defined as accepting orders or responding to consumer correspondence or inquiries electronically or via mail, telephone, fax, or the Internet; billing and collection activities; or shipping of orders from inventory);

CCH Advisory: Fulfillment Services

Temporarily storing inventory in the New York warehouse of a common carrier did not constitute doing business in New York by an out-of-state corporation and did not create nexus between the corporation and New York for purposes of imposing corporate franchise (income) tax. Sales of goods to the corporation's New York customer were fulfilled by using the common carrier for in-state delivery services, but a one-day supply of goods was temporarily stored at the common carrier's warehouse to ensure a stable flow of goods to the customer. Although the storage of inventory would subject the corporation to New York corporate franchise (income) tax under federal P.L. 86-272, a New York statute (Sec. 209(2), Tax Law) precluded the tax because the corporation was using the services of the common carrier to fulfill its customer orders (*Crowe, Chizek and Co., LLP* (Advisory Opinion), Commissioner of Taxation and Finance, TSB-A-98(25)C, December 2, 1998; CCH NEW YORK TAX REPORTS, ¶ 403-237).

On the other hand, a company that manufactured industrial blowers outside New York and shipped the blowers to a separate New York company that made certain customer-specific modifications to the blowers was subject to corporate franchise (income) tax because it was employing capital and owning personal property in New York on a regular basis. The out-of-state manufacturer was not entitled to an exemption for the use of fulfillment services, because the New York company's activities of adding motors and pulleys to the industrial blowers, pursuant to customers' specifications, before shipping the blowers to the out-of-state manufacturer's customers, exceeded the permissible scope of a fulfillment service (*Ernst & Young, LLP* (Advisory Opinion), New York Commissioner of Taxation and Finance, TSB-A-01(3)S and TSB-A-01(14)C, January 11, 2001; CCH NEW YORK TAX REPORTS, ¶ 403-864).

— advertising, processing orders, or maintaining a webpage on a New York server or through a New York Internet service provider (ISP) by a foreign company (TSB-M-97(1)C, Department of Taxation and Finance; CCH NEW YORK TAX REPORTS, ¶ 300-224);

— the trading of stocks, securities, or commodities by a foreign corporation for the corporation's own account, whether the trading is conducted by the corporation or its employees, or by a broker, commission agent, custodian, or other agent (this exemption is not available to dealers of stocks, securities, or commodities); or

— any combination of the foregoing activities.

Practitioner Comment: Participation in Trade Shows

New York allows out-of-state taxpayers the ability to participate in trade shows within New York State for up to fourteen days (or part days) during the corporation's federal tax year without becoming subject to New York's franchise tax. The taxpayer can send employees and staff to the trade show but can only display goods and promote its services. No sales can be made, and all orders must be sent out of state for acceptance or rejection. (Reg. 1-3.3(a)(7))

Mark S. Klein, Esq., Hodgson Russ LLP

Professional employer organization: A professional employer organization based in Ohio was not subject to New York corporate franchise tax, even though there were two workers for whom the organization was withholding New York income tax. The two workers were New York residents, but they were drivers for an Ohio trucking company and did not work in New York. The organization was not doing business, employing capital, owning or leasing property, or maintaining an office in New York. Accordingly, the New York corporate franchise tax was not applicable, regardless of whether the organization was considered to be the employer of the truck drivers (TSB-A-04(17)C, New York Commissioner of Taxation and Finance, December 13, 2004, CCH NEW YORK TAX REPORTS, ¶ 404-993).

Sales of consigned property: The taxpayer, a Virginia corporation, has a sales force of approximately 16 independent contractors located in New York that sell and deliver its products to its customers. The taxpayer consigns its inventory to the independent contractors, so they can deliver the product after the sales are made. After the independent contractors make the sales and deliver the products, they write up the sales slips which detail the products that were sold, the purchase prices, and the customers' information. Those receipts are then forwarded to the taxpayer. Upon receiving the sales slips, the taxpayer bills the customers from its corporate offices located outside of New York. The taxpayer retains title to the products until they are sold to the customers.

The taxpayer had nexus with New York because it owns the products that it consigns to its independent contractors until they are sold to the customer. These products are property owned by the taxpayer in New York. Because the taxpayer's independent contractors make sales and deliver its products in New York and the taxpayer retains title to the products stored in New York until the products are sold, the taxpayer's activities go beyond those allowed under Public Law 86-272 and the fulfillment services exemption. The actions of the independent contractors did not fall under the definition of fulfillment services, because the independent contractors did more than just accept or just ship orders in New York. The independent contractors located in New York made sales visits to customers and delivered the taxpayer's products to customers from their consigned inventories located within New York. Therefore, the taxpayer is subject to corporate franchise tax in New York. (*TSB-A-13(4)C*, New York Commissioner of Taxation and Finance, March 4, 2013, CCH NEW YORK TAX REPORTS, ¶ 407-791)

Practitioner Comment: A Foreign Corporation can be Subject to Tax Even if its Sole Activity is Trading Securities

According to New York's tax regulations, a foreign corporation will be subject to New York tax if it has no physical office (other than the statutory office of the state of incorporation) and the officers or agents of the corporation are located in New York while they "regularly and continuously" sell securities. 20 NYCRR § 1-3.2(f)(1).

Mark S. Klein, Esq., Hodgson Russ LLP

¶903 Exempt Corporations

Law: Secs. 3, 13, 209, 209.8, Tax Law; Sec. 77, Cooperative Corporations Law; Reg. Sec. 1-3.4 (CCH NEW YORK TAX REPORTS, ¶ 10-245).

Comparable Federal: Sec. 501 (U.S. MASTER TAX GUIDE, ¶ 601—698).

Corporations subject to other franchise taxes and certain other specified corporations are exempt from the corporation franchise tax.

• *Corporations subject to other franchise taxes*

The following are exempt from the Article 9-A corporation franchise tax (but are subject to other franchise taxes):

— Cooperative farmers', fruit growers' and other like agricultural corporations (subject to Sec. 185 of Article 9, Tax Law);

— Transportation and transmission corporations that remain subject to Secs. 183 and 184 of Article 9, Tax Law (*Note:* See ¶ 922 for special rules concerning the taxation of railroad and trucking companies);

— Insurance companies subject to Article 33, Tax Law (except overcapitalized captive insurance companies (see ¶ 2702));

— For taxable years beginning before January 1, 2015, banks, trust companies, savings and loan associations, and other financial corporations formerly subject to Article 32, Tax Law;

— Bank holding companies filing combined returns with affiliated corporations described immediately above (under Sec. 1462 of Article 32, Tax Law) and

— For-profit health maintenance organizations (beginning with taxable years after 2008).

• *Other exempt corporations*

In addition, the following corporations are exempt:

— Nonstock corporations that are organized and operated exclusively for nonprofit purposes (Reg. Sec. 1-3.4);

— Any domestic corporation exclusively engaged in the operation of vessels in foreign commerce (Sec. 3, Tax Law);

— Any trust company organized under a law of New York, all of the stock of which is owned by not less than 20 New York savings banks (Sec. 209(4), Tax Law);

— Limited-dividend housing companies (Sec. 93, Private Housing Finance Law);

— Limited-profit housing companies (Sec. 209(4), Tax Law);

— Housing development fund companies organized under Article 11, Private Housing Finance Law (Sec. 209(4), Tax Law);

— An organization organized exclusively for the purpose of holding title to property (under IRC Sec. 501(2) and (25)), and that turns over the net income so derived to an exempt organization (Sec. 209(9), Tax Law);

— Certain cooperative agricultural marketing, agricultural financing, or heating and cooling service companies (Sec. 77, Cooperative Corporations Law; Reg. Sec. 1-3.4(a)(7));

— Income from securities issued by the North Coast Power Authority (Sec. 1205-L, Public Authorities Law);

— Qualified settlement funds and grantor trusts established to resolve and satisfy claims relating to World War II, the Holocaust, victims or targets of Nazi persecution, or treatment of refugees fleeing Nazi persecution are exempt from all state and local taxes imposed on or measured by income (as well as from sales and use taxes and the NYC commercial rent tax) (Sec. 13, Tax Law);

— The ISO, a nonprofit corporation created to facilitate consumer access to competitively priced bulk electricity is exempt from New York corporate franchise (income) tax, utility (gross receipts) tax, and franchise tax on gross earnings from sales of electric energy (*New York Independent System Operator, Inc.*, Commissioner of Taxation and Finance, TSB-A-00(1)C, January 14, 2000; CCH NEW YORK TAX REPORTS, ¶403-573);

Domestic International Sales Corporations (DISCs): See ¶919.

Inactive corporations: A domestic corporation that is no longer doing business, employing capital, or owning or leasing property in New York is exempt from the fixed dollar minimum tax for tax years following its final tax year provided that the corporation (Sec. 209.8, Tax Law):

— does not have any outstanding Article 9-A franchise taxes for its final tax year or any prior tax year; and

— has filed a final Article 9-A franchise tax return (original or amended) covering the period through the date the corporation no longer does business, employs capital, or owns or leases property in New York.

For details, see *TSB-M-06(5)C*, CCH NEW YORK TAX REPORTS, ¶300-523. See also ¶906.

• *Federal comparison*

These exemptions do not parallel the federal corporation income tax exemptions. The New York exemption of nonprofit, nonstock corporations is, however, generally broad enough to encompass the federal exemption for charitable, religious, educational, and similar nonprofit organizations.

¶903

New York has adopted the federal concept of taxing unrelated business income of such organizations (¶2713).

¶904 Tax Bases—In General

Law: Sec. 210, Tax Law (CCH NEW YORK TAX REPORTS, ¶10-505).

Comparable Federal: Sec. 63 (U.S. MASTER TAX GUIDE, ¶124, 126).

The New York corporation franchise tax is primarily a tax measured by entire net income (the "business income base" for tax years after 2014) or the portion thereof allocated to New York *plus* a tax (repealed for taxable years beginning after 2014) on the value of subsidiary capital, if any, allocated to New York. (Sec. 210, Tax Law)

"Entire net income" is federal taxable income with certain exceptions and modifications. For discussion of entire net income as a basis of tax, see Chapter 10, beginning at ¶1001.

In lieu of entire net income, any of the following alternative bases must be used if a greater tax would result:

— Business and investment capital allocated to New York; see ¶1103; *or*

— Minimum income (for taxable years beginning before 2015; see ¶1105); *or*

— Fixed dollar minimum (¶905).

For discussion of the three alternative tax bases, see Chapter 11, beginning at ¶1101.

For taxable years beginning before 2015, the former tax on the value of allocated subsidiary capital (see Chapter 12, beginning at ¶1201) was added to the tax measured by entire net income or any of the alternative bases to determine tax liability.

¶905 Tax Rates

Law: Secs. 209-A, 209-B, 210, Tax Law; Reg. Secs. 9-1.1 and 9-1.2 (CCH NEW YORK TAX REPORTS, ¶10-380).

Comparable Federal: Sec. 11 (U.S. MASTER TAX GUIDE, ¶33).

The New York corporation franchise tax is the largest of the four amounts under A, *plus* the amount computed under B. (Sec. 210(1), Tax Law)

A

(1) *Business income base:* The rate is reduced from 7.1% to 6.5% for taxable years beginning on or after January 1, 2016 on the allocated entire net income (business income) base. See the special rules for manufacturers, QETCs, small business taxpayers, and S corporations, below (Sec. 210(1)(a), Tax Law) r; *or*

(2) *Business capital base:* The tax on the capital base is being phased out over six years, beginning in the 2015 taxable year. The rate on each dollar of allocated business capital for 2016 is 0.125%. The rates are reduced for qualified New York manufacturers, QETCs, and cooperative housing corporations; see "Phase-out of capital base tax rates" below. *or*

(3) *Alternative minimum tax:* The minimum taxable income base (alternative minimum tax) is eliminated for tax years beginning on or after January 1, 2015. For taxable years beginning on or after January 1, 2007, and before January 1, 2015, the rate was 1.5% of the taxpayer's minimum taxable income base (former Sec. 210(1)(c), Tax Law).;

or

(4) *Fixed dollar minimum tax:* For taxable years beginning after 2014, the income brackets above $25,000,000 were added, so the maximum tax before 2015 was $5,000.

The fixed dollar minimum varies according to the taxpayer's New York receipts, as follows (Sec. 210(1)(d), Tax Law):

New York receipts	Fixed dollar minimum
Not more than $100,000	$25
$100,001 to $250,000	$75
$250,001 to $500,000	$175
$500,001 to $1,000,000	$500
$1,000,001 to $5,000,000	$1,500
$5,000,001 to $25,000,000	$3,500
$25,000,001 to $50,000,000	$5,000
$50,000,001 to $100,000,000	$10,000
$100,000,001 to $250,000,000	$20,000
$250,000,001 to $500,000,000	$50,000
$500,000,001 to $1 billion	$100,000
Over $1 billion	$200,000

Innovation Hot Spots: A qualified entity that is located within an innovation hot spot is subject only to the fixed dollar minimum tax (Sec. 209(11), Tax Law; *TSB-M-13(6)C*, CCH New York Tax Reports, ¶ 407-897; *TSB-M-14(1)C*, CCH New York Tax Reports, ¶ 408-039).

• *Reduced rates for qualified manufacturers and QETCs*

The tax rate on the business income base for qualified New York manufacturers is reduced to zero in 2014 and thereafter. Previously, the corporate franchise tax rate on the entire net income (business income) base was reduced to 6.5% for taxable years beginning on or after January 31, 2007 and before January 1, 2014 (Sec. 210(1)(a)(vii), Tax Law; Sec. 210(1)(b)(iii), Tax Law; Sec. 210(1)(c)(iii), Tax Law; Sec. 210(1)(d)(6), Tax Law).

For tax year 2015, the capital base tax rate is reduced from 0.15% to 0.136% for qualified New York manufacturers.

Qualified emerging technology companies (QETCs): QETCs are no longer considered qualified New York manufacturers for purposes of the reduced rate on the income base. The tax rate on the business income base is 5.9% for 2014, 5.7% for 2015, 5.5% for 2016 and 2017, and 4.875% for 2018 and therafter (Sec. 210(1)(a)(vii), Tax Law).

Fixed dollar minimum tax: For tax year 2015, the fixed dollar minimum (FDM) tax for qualified New York manufacturers and QETCs that are not S corporations is as follows:

New York receipts	Fixed dollar minimum
Not more than $100,000	$22
$100,001 to $250,000	$66
$250,001 to $500,000	$153
$500,001 to $1,000,000	$439
$1,000,001 to $5,000,000	$1,316
$5,000,001 to $25,000,000	
Over $25,000,000	$4,385

For tax year 2016 and 2017, the fixed dollar minimum (FDM) tax for qualified New York manufacturers and QETCs that are not S corporations is as follows:

New York receipts	Fixed dollar minimum
Not more than $100,000	$21
$100,001 to $250,000	$63
$250,001 to $500,000	$148
$500,001 to $1,000,000	$423
$1,000,001 to $5,000,000	$1,269
$5,000,001 to $25,000,000	$2,961
Over $25,000,000	$4,230

For tax year 2018, the fixed dollar minimum (FDM) tax for qualified New York manufacturers and QETCs that are not S corporations is as follows:

New York receipts	Fixed dollar minimum
Not more than $100,000	$19
$100,001 to $250,000	$56
$250,001 to $500,000	$131
$500,001 to $1,000,000	$375
$1,000,001 to $5,000,000	$1,125
$5,000,001 to $25,000,000	$2,625
Over $25,000,000	$3,750

S corporations: For tax year 2015, the fixed dollar minimum (FDM) tax for qualified New York manufacturers and QETCs that are S corporations is as follows:

New York receipts	Fixed dollar minimum
Not more than $100,000	$22
$100,001 to $250,000	$44
$250,001 to $500,000	$153
$500,001 to $1,000,000	$263
$1,000,001 to $5,000,000	$877
$5,000,001 to $25,000,000	$2,631
Over $25,000,000	$3,947

For tax year 2016 and 2017, the fixed dollar minimum (FDM) tax for qualified New York manufacturers and QETCs that are S corporations is as follows:

New York receipts	Fixed dollar minimum
Not more than $100,000	$21
$100,001 to $250,000	$42
$250,001 to $500,000	$148
$500,001 to $1,000,000	$254
$1,000,001 to $5,000,000	$846
$5,000,001 to $25,000,000	$2,538
Over $25,000,000	$3,807

For tax year 2018, the fixed dollar minimum (FDM) tax for qualified New York manufacturers and QETCs that are S corporations is as follows:

New York receipts	Fixed dollar minimum
Not more than $100,000	$19
$100,001 to $250,000	$38
$250,001 to $500,000	$131
$500,001 to $1,000,000	$225
$1,000,001 to $5,000,000	$750
$5,000,001 to $25,000,000	$2,250
Over $25,000,000	$3,375

A "manufacturer" is a taxpayer principally engaged in the production of goods by manufacturing, processing, assembling, refining, mining, extracting, farming, agriculture, horticulture, floriculture, viticulture, or commercial fishing (Sec. 210(1)(a)(vi), Tax Law). The generation and distribution of electricity, the distribution of natural gas, and the production of steam associated with the generation of electricity are specifically excluded.

A "qualified New York manufacturer" is a manufacturer having property in New York that is described in Sec. 210(12)(b)(i)(A), Tax Law, provided that either the adjusted basis of such property for federal income tax purposes at the close of the taxable year is at least $1 million or all of the manufacturer's real and personal property is located in New York. In addition, certain taxpayers defined as qualified emerging technology companies under the Public Authorities Law may also qualify. (Sec. 210(1)(a)(vi), Tax Law)

Combined group: For purposes of computing the capital base in a combined report, the combined group will be considered a manufacturer only if the combined group, during the taxable year, is principally engaged in the specified activities or any combination thereof. A taxpayer or a combined group is principally engaged in such activities if, during the taxable year, more than 50% of the gross receipts of the taxpayer or combined group, respectively, are derived from the sale of goods produced by those activities. In computing a combined group's gross receipts, intercorporate receipts must be eliminated. (Sec. 210(1)(b)(2), Tax Law)

Eligible qualified New York manufacturers: Under the 2014 budget bill, a rate of 0% applies for purposes of the ENI (business) base beginning with tax year 2014. For taxable years beginning after 2011 and before 2014, the entire net income rate was reduced to 3.25%, the minimum taxable income rate was reduced to 0.75%, and the fixed dollar minimum (FDM) tax bases were reduced by half (Sec. 210, Tax Law). Beginning with the 2015 tax year, eligible qualified New York manufacturers are subject to the FDM schedule for qualified New York manufacturers.

The criteria for an eligible qualified manufacturer includes a property test and a receipts test, and factors such as regional unemployment, the economic impact that manufacturing has on the surrounding community, population decline within the region, and median income within the region (Sec. 210(1)(a)(vi), Tax Law; *TSB-M-13(1)C*, January 8, 2013, CCH New York Tax Reports, ¶407-755).

* *Small business taxpayers*

A "small business taxpayer" is a taxpayer that:

    (1) has an entire net income of not more than $390,000 for the taxable year,

    (2) falls within the Internal Revenue Code definition of a small business; and

    (3) is not part of an affiliated group.

In the case of a taxpayer with a short taxable year, entire net income is annualized to determine eligibility for the small business tax rates. If the taxpayer is eligible, tax is calculated on the annualized income on a pro rata basis. (Sec. 210(1)(f), Tax Law)

Business income base: A flat 6.5% rate applies to all small business taxpayers in tax years beginning on or after January 1, 2016. (Sec. 210(1)(a), Tax Law). Previously, for small business taxpayers with an entire net income/business income base of $290,000 or less, the corporate franchise tax was imposed at the rate of 6.5%. For taxpayers having an entire net income/business income base over $290,000, but not exceeding $390,000, the tax amount was $18,850, plus 7.1% of the amount over $290,000, plus 4.35% of the amount over $350,000 but not over $390,000.

Capital base: If the tax of a small business taxpayer is greater computed on the capital base than when it is computed on the entire net income base, solely by reason of the application of the special rate applicable to small business taxpayers, then the tax is imposed without reference to the taxpayer's capital base. In other words, the small business taxpayer must choose the capital base only when it exceeds the tax computed on the entire net income base at the generally applicable rate. Small business taxpayers are exempt from the capital base tax in their first two years.

For reduction of the fixed dollar minimum when the tax period is less than nine months, see ¶1107.

Computation of the entire net income/business income base and the alternative tax bases is covered in Chapters 10 and 11, respectively.

* *S corporations*

S corporations pay only the fixed dollar minimum tax (Sec. 210(1)(g), Tax Law; see also *TSB-M-03(5)C*).

For taxable years beginning on and after January 1, 2014, the fixed dollar minimum for S corporations that are not qualified New York manufacturers or QETCs is computed as follows (Sec. 210.1(d)(4), Tax Law):

New York receipts	Fixed dollar minimum
Not more than $100,000	$25
$100,001 to $250,000	$50
$250,001 to $500,000	$175
$500,001 to $1,000,000	$300
$1,000,001 to $5,000,000	$1,000
$5,000,001 to $25,000,000	$3,000
Over $25,000,000	$4,500

* *Reduced business income rates for qualified emerging technology companies (QETCs)*

The entire net income (business income) base tax rate for qualified emerging technology companies (QETCs) is reduced from 5.9% in 2014 to 5.7% (2015), 5.5% (2016 and 2017), 4.875% (2018 and thereafter). (Sec. 210(1)(a)(vi), Tax Law)

* *Phase-out of capital base tax rates*

The capital base tax is being phased out over six years beginning in 2016, as follows (Sec. 210(1)(b), Tax Law).

For qualified New York manufacturers and QETCs, the rates are: 0.132% (2015), 0.106% (2016), 0.085% (2017), 0.056% (2018), 0.038% (2019), 0.019% (2020), and 0% (2021 and thereafter).

For cooperative housing corporations, the rates are: 0.04% (through 2019), 0.025% (2020), and 0% (2021 and thereafter).

For other taxpayers, the rates are: 0.15% (2015), 0.125% (2016), 0.1% (2017), 0.075% (2018), 0.05% (2019), 0.025% (2020), and 0% (2021 and thereafter).

For tax years beginning on or after January 1, 2015, the tax is capped at $350,000 for qualified New York manufacturers and QETCs, and at $5 million for all other taxpayers.

• *Metropolitan Commuter Transportation District surcharge*

A surcharge is imposed on that portion of the corporation franchise tax attributable to business activity carried on within the Metropolitan Commuter Transportation District, which consists of the City of New York and the counties of Dutchess, Nassau, Orange, Putnam, Rockland, Suffolk, and Westchester. (Sec. 209-B, Tax Law) See ¶1319 for a discussion of the apportionment of tax within and without the District.

The tax rate is 28% for 2016 and subsequent years, unless adjusted by the commissioner (Reg. Secs. 9-1.1 and 9-1.2; *TSB-M-16(1)C*, New York Department of Taxation and Finance, April 26, 2016, CCH New York Tax Reports, ¶408-721). The surcharge rate was increased from 17% to 25.6% for taxable years beginning after 2014 and before 2016 (Sec. 209-B(1), Tax Law).

S corporations: New York S corporations are not subject to the MCTD business tax surcharge (Sec. 209-B(1), Tax Law).

• *MCTD mobility (payroll) tax*

The Metropolitan Commuter Transportation District Mobility Tax (MCTDMT) is imposed on certain employers and self-employed individuals engaging in business within the Metropolitan Commuter Transportation District (MCTD). Specifically, the tax applies to (Sec. 800, Tax Law; Sec. 801, Tax Law; TSB-M-09(1)MCTMT, June 1, 2009, CCH New York Tax Reports, ¶406-407):

(1) employers required to withhold New York state income tax from employee wages and whose payroll expense exceeds $312,500 ($2,500, prior to April 1, 2012) in any calendar quarter; and

(2) individuals with net earnings from self-employment allocated to the MCTD that exceed $10,000 for the tax year. (see ¶106)

Educational institutions, including libraries, the United Nations, federal agencies, public corporations, and federally chartered credit unions are not subject to the MCTDMT (Sec. 800, Tax Law; TSB-A-09(1)MCTMT, New York Commissioner of Taxation and Finance, October 28, 2009, CCH New York Tax Reports, ¶406-594).

Employers accepted into the START-UP NY program (see ¶923) are exempt from the MCTDMT (Sec. 803(b), Tax Law).

Rate of tax: For employers (including professional employer organizations), the MCTDMT is imposed at the following rates (Sec. 801, Tax Law; *TSB-M-12(2)MCTMT*, New York Department of Taxation and Finance, April 5, 2012, CCH New York Tax Reports, ¶407-528):

— 0.11% for employers with payroll expense no greater than $375,000 in any calendar quarter;

— 0.23% for employers with payroll expense no greater than $437,500 in any calendar quarter;

— 0.34% for employers with payroll expense exceeding $437,500 in any calendar quarter.

For quarters before the quarter beginning April 1, 2012, the tax rate was 0.34% of total payroll expense for employees employed within the MCTD.

An employer cannot deduct from an employee's wages or compensation any amount representing all or a portion of the tax imposed on the employer (Sec. 802, Tax Law).

Any exemption from tax specified in any other New York state law does not apply to the new tax. (Sec. 803, Tax Law)

Payment of tax: For employers, the tax must be paid quarterly, at the same time as the statewide wage reporting system report is required (see ¶608). Generally, employers subject to electronic funds transfer must pay the tax on payroll expense at the same time as the withholding tax remitted under the electronic payment reporting system and the electronic funds transfer system. (Sec. 804, Tax Law)

The Department of Taxation and Finance has a website dedicated to the tax at **http://www.tax.ny.gov/bus/mctmt/default.htm**. Also, *Publication 420* provides guidance with respect to computing, reporting, and paying the MCTDMT.

CCH Advisory: MCTDMT Upheld Against Constitutional Attack

A New York appellate court has reversed a lower court's ruling that the metropolitan commuter transportation mobility tax (MCTMT) was unconstitutionally passed by the Legislature without a home rule message. The lower court found that the tax was a special law that did not serve a substantial state interest (*Mangano v. Silver*, Supreme Court, 10th Judicial District (New York), No. 14444/10, August 22, 2012, CCH NEW YORK TAX REPORTS, ¶407-628).

However, the appellate court concluded that the law, which provides a funding source for the preservation, operation, and improvement of essential transit and transportation services in the Metropolitan Commuter Transportation District, does serve a substantial state concern. Therefore, the law was not unconstitutionally passed without a home rule message. (*Mangano v. Silver*, Appellate Division of the Supreme Court of New York, Second Department, Nos. 2012-09463 and 2012-09991, June 26, 2013, CCH NEW YORK TAX REPORTS, ¶407-866; motion for leave to appeal denied, New York Court of Appeals, January 14, 2014)

¶906 Domestic Corporations Ceasing to Possess Franchise

Law: Sec. 209, Tax Law (CCH NEW YORK TAX REPORTS, ¶10-210).

The New York corporation franchise tax is imposed for all or any part of each calendar or fiscal year during which the taxpayer possesses a franchise. Consequently, every domestic corporation is required to pay a tax measured by its entire net income (or other applicable basis) up to the date on which it ceases to possess a franchise. (Sec. 209, Tax Law)

A domestic corporation may cease to possess a franchise because of its dissolution, its merger into or consolidation with another corporation, or the surrender, revocation, or annulment of its charter. A dissolved corporation may, however, become subject to tax by continuing to conduct business other than the liquidation and winding up of its affairs. (Reg. Sec. 1-2.2)

Practitioner Comment: Dissolution by Proclamation

A corporation that fails to file tax returns or pay franchise taxes for two or more consecutive years may be dissolved by the Secretary of State upon referral by the Tax Department. Once dissolved, the corporation has no legal authority to transact business. If the corporation owns title to real estate, the property can not be sold until the corporation's authority is reinstated. This requires the payment of all outstanding tax, interest and penalties (TSB-M-86(5)C).

Mark S. Klein, Esq., Hodgson Russ LLP

¶907 Foreign Corporations Ceasing to Do Business in New York

Law: Secs. 209, 211, 213, Tax Law (CCH NEW YORK TAX REPORTS, ¶ 10-075, 10-210).

The consent of the Commissioner of Taxation and Finance must be obtained by every foreign corporation that seeks to surrender its authority to do business in New York. When an application for consent to dissolution is filed, the corporation will not be liable for any tax imposed for the following year or period, provided (1) its certificate of dissolution is filed in the office of the Secretary of State prior to the last day of the corporation's final period, and (2) it does not conduct business in that tax year or period.

A foreign corporation ceasing to do business or to engage in taxable activity in New York must pay a corporation franchise tax for the portion of the calendar or fiscal year prior to cessation. The entire net income or other basis of tax is determined in the same manner as for a domestic corporation ceasing to possess a franchise (¶ 906).

The foreign corporation is required to file a report on the date of cessation, or at such other time as the Commissioner may require, covering each year or period for which no report was filed.

¶908 Real Estate Corporations

Real estate corporations are subject to the corporation franchise tax imposed by Article 9-A of the Tax Law. Prior to 1962, such corporations were subject to a special franchise tax.

For treatment of real estate investment trusts, see ¶ 918.

¶909 Omnibus Corporations and Taxicab Corporations

Law: Secs. 183, 184, Tax Law (CCH NEW YORK TAX REPORTS, ¶ 10-210, 40-225).

Omnibus corporations and taxicab corporations are subject to the business corporation franchise tax during any period when the New York motor fuel tax rate is greater than 2¢ per gallon. The motor fuel tax rate currently exceeds 2¢ per gallon (see ¶ 2709).

¶910 Cooperative Housing Corporations

Law: Sec. 210(1)(b), Tax Law (CCH NEW YORK TAX REPORTS, ¶ 10-380).

Comparable Federal: Sec. 216(b) (U.S. MASTER TAX GUIDE, ¶ 699).

Cooperative housing corporations are subject to a special capital base tax rate (¶ 905).

New York adopts the federal definition of cooperative housing corporations (IRC Sec. 216(b)).

¶911 Regulated Investment Companies (RICs)

Law: Secs. 1.20, 209, 211, 1515, Tax Law (CCH NEW YORK TAX REPORTS, ¶ 10-355).

A regulated investment company (as defined for federal income tax purposes) is subject to the corporation franchise (income) tax measured by the entire net income base, the minimum taxable income base (repealed for taxable years beginning after 2014), or the fixed dollar minimum, whichever is greater. For tax rates, see ¶ 905.

"Entire net income" of a RIC is federal "investment company taxable income" with certain modifications. For additional information, see ¶854.

A RIC is permitted to deduct dividends paid to its shareholders in determining its federal taxable income (*Dreyfus Special Income Fund, Inc. v. State Tax Commission* (1988, NY Ct App) 72 NY2d 874, CCH NEW YORK TAX REPORTS, ¶252-102).

Captive RICs: A captive RIC is a regulated investment company that is not regularly traded on an established securities market and more than 50% of the voting stock is owned or controlled, directly or indirectly, by a single corporation that is not exempt from federal income tax and is not a RIC (Sec. 2.10, Tax Law). A captive RIC must be included in a combined return with the corporation that owns or controls more than 50% of its voting stock (Sec. 209(7), Tax Law; Sec. 211(4)(a)(6), Tax Law; Sec. 1515(f)(4)(ii), Tax Law).

¶912 Merger, Consolidation, or Reorganization

Law: Sec. 209, Tax Law; Reg. Sec. 3-2.6 (CCH NEW YORK TAX REPORTS, ¶1-440, 10-540).

Comparable Federal: Secs. 338, 354, 356, 361, 381, 382 (U.S. MASTER TAX GUIDE, ¶2205—2247).

Because the New York taxable income computation starting point is federal taxable income, New York generally follows the federal income tax treatment with respect to corporate distributions, reorganizations, and liquidations.

Domestic corporations ceasing to possess a franchise and foreign corporations ceasing to do business in New York as a result of a merger, consolidation, or reorganization must pay a franchise tax for the portion of the year prior to such merger, consolidation, or reorganization. See ¶906 for domestic corporations and ¶907 for foreign corporations.

Every domestic corporation desiring to dissolve or to consolidate with a foreign corporation must obtain the consent of the Commissioner prior to consolidation. The procedure is the same as for a domestic corporation that desires to dissolve (¶906).

¶913 Corporations Doing Business Within and Without the State

Law: Sec. 210, Tax Law (CCH NEW YORK TAX REPORTS, ¶6-005, 6-011).

Businesses that own or rent property, pay compensation, or derive business receipts from a jurisdiction other than New York may apportion their business income.

For full discussion of the allocation of income and capital, see Chapter 13, beginning at ¶1301.

¶914 S Corporations

Law: Secs. 208(1-B), 210, Tax Law (CCH NEW YORK TAX REPORTS, ¶10-215, 10-380).

Comparable Federal: Secs. 1371—1379 (U.S. MASTER TAX GUIDE, ¶301—345).

Corporations electing New York S corporation status pay only the fixed dollar minimum tax (Sec. 210(1)(g), Tax Law). See ¶905 for computation of the tax.

• *Qualified subchapter S subsidiaries*

A qualified subchapter S subsidiary (QSSS or QSub), as defined in IRC Sec. 1361(b)(3)(B), is not subject to the corporate net income tax, provided certain conditions are met. (Sec. 208(1-B), Tax Law) If the QSub is exempt, the assets, liabilities, income, deductions, property, payroll, receipts, capital, credits, and all other tax attributes and elements of economic activity of the QSub are considered to be those of the parent corporation. The parent company may be either a C corporation or an S corporation.

¶912

An exempt QSub is a nonexcluded New York QSub that is owned by a parent that is either a New York S corporation or a New York C corporation that is subject to corporation franchise (income) tax. If the QSub is not a taxpayer, a New York C corporation that owns the QSub must make an election to include the QSub's tax attributes in the calculation of its own net income or the C corporation company will be taxed as if the federal QSub election had not been made. Upon election by the parent, all assets, liabilities, income, deductions, property, payroll, receipts, capital, credits, and all other tax attributes and elements of economic activity of the QSub are considered to be those of the parent corporation. A non-New York S corporation that is not a corporation franchise (income) taxpayer and owns a QSub that, but for the QSub provisions would have been subject to corporation franchise (income) tax, may make an election to be taxed as a New York S corporation. For any taxable year that such an election is not in effect, the QSub will be taxed as a New York C corporation, and its entire net income must be determined as if the federal QSub election had not been made. (Sec. 208(1-B), Tax Law)

Termination of election: Special rules apply if a taxpayer's election of New York S corporation status is terminated on a day other than the first day of its taxable year—see ¶ 905 and 1107.

Credits: See ¶ 929.

Net operating loss deductions: See ¶ 1008.

Metropolitan Commuter Transportation District surcharge: New York S corporations are exempt (¶ 905).

¶915 Accounting Periods and Methods

Law: Sec. 208(9)(d), Tax Law; Reg. Secs. 2-1.1—2-2.2 (CCH NEW YORK TAX REPORTS, ¶ 10-520).

Comparable Federal: Secs. 441—483 (U.S. MASTER TAX GUIDE, ¶ 1501—1577).

By the adoption of federal taxable income as the starting point for determining "entire net income," the primary basis of the New York corporation franchise tax, New York also adopts the federal accounting periods and methods. (Reg. Sec. 2-2.1(a))

• *Accounting methods*

New York law expressly provides that the Commissioner may determine the year or period in which any item of income or deduction is to be included without regard to the method of accounting used by the taxpayer in order to properly reflect the entire net income of the taxpayer. (Sec. 208(9)(d), Tax Law; Reg. Sec. 2-2.1(a))

• *Accounting periods*

The accounting periods are generally the same for federal and New York purposes. By regulation, New York permits a 52-53 week accounting period when such period is used for federal returns. (Reg. Sec. 2-1.4)

Special provisions govern the situation where the New York return covers a different period than the federal return (¶ 916). This situation occurs when a foreign corporation begins (or ceases) to do business in New York during its federal taxable year, or when an election to be taxed as a New York S corporation is terminated on a day other than the first day of the taxable year.

¶916 When Period Covered Differs for New York and Federal Returns

Law: Sec. 208, Tax Law; Reg. Secs. 2-1.1—2-2.2, 4-6.4 (CCH NEW YORK TAX REPORTS, ¶ 10-510, 10-520).

The period covered by the taxpayer's New York corporation franchise tax return will be different from the period covered by its federal income tax return when a foreign corporation commences to do (or ceases to do) business in New York during its federal taxable year. In such case its entire net income is determined by multiplying its federal taxable income (as adjusted by additions (¶1002) and deductions (¶1003)) by the number of calendar months or major fractions thereof covered by its New York report and dividing the result by the number of calendar months or major fractions thereof covered by the federal report. (Sec. 208(h), Tax Law)

When this method does not properly reflect the taxpayer's income, the Commissioner is authorized to determine the taxpayer's entire net income solely on the basis of its income during the New York taxable period. (Sec. 208(h), Tax Law)

• *S corporations*

See ¶905 for calculation of the fixed dollar minimum for S corporations in a termination year.

¶917 Professional Service Corporations

Law: Sec. 210, Tax Law; Reg. Sec. 4-7.1 (CCH New York Tax Reports, ¶11-515).

Professional service corporations are taxed using an investment allocation percentage (¶1307) that is 100%. (Reg. Sec. 4-7.1)

¶918 Real Estate Investment Trusts (REITs)

Law: Sec. 2.9, 209, 1515, Tax Law; Reg. Sec. 4-11.1 (CCH New York Tax Reports, ¶10-360, 10-365, 10-510).

Comparable Federal: Secs. 857, 858, 860A—860G (U.S. Master Tax Guide, ¶1501—1577, 2343—2367).

A "real estate investment trust," as defined for federal purposes, is subject to the New York corporation franchise tax measured by the entire net income base, the minimum taxable income base (repealed for taxable years beginning after 2014), or the fixed dollar minimum, whichever is greater. For tax rates, see ¶905.

Entire net income is federal "real estate investment trust taxable income," with certain modifications.

Captive REITs: A captive REIT is a real estate investment trust that is not regularly traded on an established securities market and more than 50% of the voting stock is owned or controlled, directly or indirectly, by a single corporation that is not exempt from federal income tax and is not a RIC (Sec. 2.10, Tax Law). A captive RIC must be included in a combined return with the corporation that owns or controls more than 50% of its voting stock (Sec. 209(7), Tax Law; Sec. 211(4)(a)(6), Tax Law; Sec. 1515(f)(4)(ii), Tax Law).

• *REMICs*

An entity that is treated for federal income tax purposes as a real estate mortgage investment conduit (REMIC) is exempt from New York corporate income tax.

For additional information on REITs and REMICs, see ¶854.

¶919 Domestic International Sales Corporations (DISCs)

Law: Secs. 208, 209, 210, 211, Tax Law; Reg. Secs. 3-9.1—3-9.6 (CCH New York Tax Reports, ¶10-255).

Because of changes in federal law, domestic international sales corporations (DISCs) have generally been replaced by foreign sales corporations (FSCs). DISCs have not been entirely abolished, however. For the tax treatment of FSCs, see ¶920, and CCH New York Tax Reports, ¶10-255.

¶917

A corporation that elects to be treated as a domestic international sales corporation (DISC) for federal income tax purposes will be treated as a DISC for New York corporation franchise tax purposes.

Notice of election: Filing a copy of the federal election (Form 4876) with the Corporation Tax Bureau will provide identification of the corporation as a DISC for corporation franchise tax purposes.

Returns: Corporation franchise tax returns of DISCs are due on or before the 15th day of the ninth month following the close of its fiscal year (September 15 for calendar-year taxpayers).

Combined reports: A corporation that owns or controls directly or indirectly substantially all the capital stock of a nonexempt DISC may elect (or may be required by the Commissioner) to file a combined report. In such case intercorporate dividends are not eliminated.

Consolidated returns: New York does not follow the federal provisions (IRC Sec. 1501—IRC Sec. 1504) allowing affiliated corporations to file consolidated returns. However, New York allows the filing of a consolidated return for all corporate stockholders in a tax-exempt DISC who file the consolidated reports with the DISC on Form CT-3C.

- *Tax treatment of DISCs*

Exempt: A DISC that during the taxable year (1) received more than 5% of its gross sales from the sale of inventory or other property that it purchased from its stockholders, (2) received more than 5% of its gross rentals from the rental of property that it purchased or rented from its stockholders, or (3) received more than 5% of its total receipts, other than sales and rentals, from its stockholders, is exempt from the corporation franchise tax.

Nonexempt: A DISC that does not meet the above requirements is subject to the corporation franchise tax computed on the basis of business and investment capital (¶1102) or the fixed dollar minimum (¶1107), whichever is greater plus, for taxable years beginning before 2015, the former tax on subsidiary capital (¶1205).

- *DISC stockholders*

Income received by an individual stockholder in a DISC is treated at ¶202.

In the case of a corporate stockholder in a DISC, the following provisions apply:

— Investments in the stocks, bonds or other securities of a DISC or any indebtedness from a DISC are not treated as either subsidiary capital or investment capital;

— Amounts deemed distributed from a DISC or former DISC, which are taxable as dividends for federal purposes, are treated as business income for New York (unless includable in a taxpayer's entire net income for a prior taxable year);

— Any gain recognized for federal purposes on the disposition of stock in a DISC or former DISC and treated under federal law as a dividend is treated as business income for New York;

— Any actual distribution from a DISC or former DISC is treated as business income for New York (unless made out of "other earnings and profits" for federal purposes, in which case the actual distribution is treated as either subsidiary income or investment income for New York).

A stockholder in an exempt DISC must adjust each item of its receipts, expenses, assets, and liabilities by adding its attributable share of each such DISC's or former DISC's receipts, expenses, assets, and liabilities. Intercorporate transactions are eliminated, and the stockholder's entire net income is reduced by subtracting the amount of the deemed distribution of current income, if any, from each such DISC already included in federal taxable income (the starting point for the determination of entire net income (¶1001)).

These adjusted figures are also used in computing the business allocation percentage (¶1303).

¶920 Foreign Sales Corporations (FSCs)

   Law: (CCH NEW YORK TAX REPORTS, ¶10-255).

   Comparable Federal: Secs. 921—927 (repealed) (U.S. MASTER TAX GUIDE, ¶2470).

Foreign sales corporations are corporations organized under the laws of a foreign country or a U.S. possession and had to conform to certain arm's-length pricing standards mandated by the General Agreement on Tariffs and Trade (GATT).

CCH Advisory: FSC Legislation Repealed

Because the World Trade Organization ruled that the foreign sales corporation regime constituted an illegal export subsidy, the federal provisions governing the taxation of FSCs (IRC Secs. 921—927) were repealed by P.L. 106-519, generally effective for transactions occurring after September 30, 2000. In their place, a new exclusion from gross income was enacted for extraterritorial income that meets the requirements of "qualifying foreign trade income" (IRC Sec. 114).

The American Jobs Creation Act (AJCA) of 2004 (P.L. 108-357) repealed the FSC/ETI regime, replacing it with a 9% tax deduction for domestic production (manufacturing) activity (IRC Sec. 199). New York has decoupled from the domestic production activity deduction for taxable years beginning after 2007 (see ¶1002).

New York has no special provisions covering the taxation of FSCs.

¶921 Limited Liability Companies (LLCs)

   Law: Sec. 601(f), Tax Law (CCH NEW YORK TAX REPORTS, ¶10-240).

   Comparable Federal: 704, 721, 731(b) (U.S. MASTER TAX GUIDE, ¶402B).

New York authorizes the formation of domestic and foreign limited liability companies (LLCs). For New York corporate income tax purposes, LLCs are treated as partnerships, unless classified as corporations for federal income tax purposes. (Sec. 601(f), Tax Law) If the LLC is classified as an association taxable as a corporation, the New York entity-level corporate income tax applies. For further information on LLC classification, see ¶113 and ¶851.

Practitioner Comment: Single-Member LLCs

New York has ruled that a single-member limited liability company will be disregarded for personal and corporate income tax purposes. According to the Tax Department, if the LLC is not classified as a separate entity for federal purposes, the entity will "not be considered a separate entity for New York tax purposes, and the LLC itself would not be subject to New York tax." Accordingly, a single-member limited liability company established by a corporation is treated as a division of the corporation (*McDermott, Will and Emery*, TSB-A-96(19)C, CCH NEW YORK TAX REPORTS, ¶402-467A).

Mark S. Klein, Esq., Hodgson Russ LLP

¶922 Railroad and Trucking Companies

   Law: Secs. 183(1)(b), (10), 183-a(1), Tax Law (CCH NEW YORK TAX REPORTS, ¶10-210, 10-245, 80-020).

Businesses formed for or principally engaged in the conduct of a railroad, palace car, sleeping car or trucking business or formed for or principally engaged in the conduct of two or more of such businesses are excluded from Art. 9 franchise taxes on transportation and transmission companies (¶2708), *unless* those businesses elect to continue to be subject to Art. 9 tax instead of corporation franchise (income) tax (Art. 9-A or Art. 32). (Secs. 183(1)(b) and 183(10), Tax Law)

Companies coming into existence after 1997 must make their election by the due date of their first return. An election to remain subject to Art. 9 tax will continue in effect until revoked by the taxpayer. A revocation of the election, once made, is irrevocable.

¶923 Credits and Other Tax Incentives—In General

Law: Secs. 33, 34, 38, 39, 40, 208.9(a)(18), 209.11, 612(c)(39), 210(26), (47), (49), 1119(d)(1), Tax Law; Sec. 1(16-v), Urban Dev. Corp. Act; Sec. 353, Secs. 430, *et seq.*, Econ. Dev. Law; Sec. 11-1712(c)(35); NYC Admin. Code; (CCH New York Tax Reports, ¶12-001, 12-002, 12-085e).

Comparable Federal: Secs. 38, 39 (U.S. Master Tax Guide, ¶1301—1384).

New York offers a large number of credits and other tax incentives, as discussed in the paragraphs that follow.

• *Carryovers; recapture*

Most credits may not reduce a taxpayer's tax liability below the greater of the minimum taxable income (repealed for taxable years beginning after 2014) or the fixed dollar minimum. With some exceptions, credits not used in one year may be carried forward indefinitely. Recapture of credits may be required if property does not remain in qualified use.

• *Effect of certain criminal convictions on credits*

If a taxpayer stands convicted (or is a shareholder of an S corporation or a partner in a partnership that is convicted) of certain penal law offenses concerning corruption, bribery, and misconduct, then the taxpayer will not be eligible for any tax credit allowed under the corporate franchise tax or any business tax credit allowed under the personal income tax. The provision applies to acts committed on or after April 30, 2014. (Sec. 41, Tax Law)

• *Order for claiming credits*

Credits that cannot be carried over and that are not refundable are deducted first, followed by empire zone (EZ) wage tax credits (¶929), whether or not a portion of those credits is refundable. Credits that can be carried over, and carryovers of such credits, are deducted next. Those credits whose carryovers are of limited duration are deducted before those whose carryovers are not limited. Credits that are refundable (other than the EZ wage credit) are deducted last. (Sec. 210(26), Tax Law)

• *Refunds of credits*

The New York Department of Taxation and Finance has issued a corporate and personal income tax memorandum explaining how refunds of certain state business tax credits are treated.

At the federal level, the Internal Revenue Service (IRS) previously determined that the amount of the Qualified Empire Zone Enterprise (QEZE) credit for real property taxes that is refunded, or credited as an overpayment to estimated tax, is considered income to the taxpayer. The IRS also has determined that amounts of the Empire Zone (EZ) investment tax credit and the EZ wage tax credit that are refunded or credited as an overpayment to estimated tax are considered income to the taxpayer and must be included in the taxpayer's federal taxable income or federal adjusted gross income.

At the state level, under existing New York law, the amount of the refund of these credits included in a taxpayer's federal taxable income or federal adjusted gross income is not taxable. Therefore, New York taxpayers are allowed a subtraction modification for that refund amount.

For information on how to apply the subtraction modification for tax years 2015 and after, taxpayers should refer to Forms CT-225, CT-225-A, and IT-225. The memorandum discusses the amended return requirements for both corporate franchise and personal income taxes.

If the IRS determines that other New York business tax credits refunded, or credited as an overpayment to estimated tax, are considered income to the taxpayer, then the memorandum notes that those credits will also be allowed a subtraction modification on New York returns. (TSB-M-10(9.1)C, (15.1)I, New York Department of Taxation and Finance, April 7, 2016, CCH NEW YORK TAX REPORTS, ¶ 408-713)

• *Repealed and expired credits*

Fuel cell electric generating equipment: For taxable years beginning before 2009, a credit was allowed for the cost of qualified fuel cell electric generating equipment for use by the taxpayer in New York. (Sec. 210(37), Tax Law) Credits exceeding the tax due for a given year may be carried over to subsequent years.

Empire zone credits: The Empire Zone program expired on June 30, 2010. Transitional provisions are explained in *TSB-M-10(6)C, (12)I, (19)S*, New York Department of Taxation and Finance, December 8, 2010, CCH NEW YORK TAX REPORTS, ¶ 407-074. Continuing eligibility for Empire Zone benefits is discussed in *TSB-M-11(2)C, (3)I, (4)S*, New York Department of Taxation and Finance, April 5, 2011, CCH NEW YORK TAX REPORTS, ¶ 407-188.

• *Business tax credits deferred*

Caution: For tax years 2010, 2011, and 2012, taxpayers with more than $2 million in aggregated business tax credits were required to defer the amounts above $2 million until 2013. The total amount of credits deferred was paid back to taxpayers over tax years 2013, 2014, and 2015. (Sec. 33.1, Tax Law; Sec. 34.1, Tax Law; TSB-M-10(5)(C), September 13, 2010, CCH NEW YORK TAX REPORTS, ¶ 406-976).

Form CT-500, *Corporation Tax Deferral Credit*, provides taxpayers with detailed instructions and schedules regarding the temporary deferral of tax credits.

• *Business Incubator and Innovation Hot Spot incentives*

The New York State Business Incubator and Innovation Hot Spot Support Act (Part C, Ch. 59 (S.B. 2609), Laws 2013) was enacted to support the growth of companies in the early stages of development. The Act authorizes the Empire State Development Corporation (ESD) to designate five "New York State Innovation Hot Spots" in SFY 2013-14 and an additional five in SFY 2014-15.

ESD is authorized to issue an annual request for proposals for grants and assistance based on available appropriations and to designate qualified applicants as New York State incubators. In addition, in each of state fiscal years 2013 and 2014, ESD is authorized to designate five qualified New York State incubators as New York State Innovation Hot Spots. These New York State Innovation Hot Spots can certify certain clients as a qualified entities eligible for tax benefits under Sec. 38, Tax Law.

Entities designated as Innovation Hot Spots must demonstrate an affiliation with and the support of at least one college, university, or independent research institution, and offer programs consistent with regional economic development strategies. Qualified entities in Innovation Hot Spots are eligible for the tax benefits listed below for five taxable years, beginning with the year the entity becomes a tenant in or part of an Innovation Hot Spot:

    — A qualified entity that is located within the Innovation Hot Spot is subject only to the fixed dollar minimum tax under Article 9-A (¶ 905).

    — Qualified entities located within and without the hot spot and corporate partners of qualified entities are allowed a deduction for the amount of income or gain attributable to operations in the hot spot (¶ 1003).

¶923

— Individuals who are sole proprietors of a qualified entity, or are partners/members/shareholders of a partnership, limited liability company, or New York S corporation, respectively, that is a qualified entity are allowed a deduction for the amount of income or gain attributable to operations at the hot spot (this benefit is also available under the New York City personal income tax on residents) (¶303; ¶3010).

— Qualified entities are also eligible for a credit or refund of sales and use tax imposed on the retail sale of tangible personal property or services (¶2109).

Taxpayers claiming the above tax benefits are not eligible for any other New York State exemptions, deductions, credits, or refunds to the extent the exemption, deduction, credit, or refund is attributable to the business operations in the innovation hot spot.

(Secs. 38, 208(9)(a)(18), 209(11), 612(c)(39), and 1119(d)(1), Tax Law; Sec. 1(16-v), Urban Development Corporation Act; Sec. 11-1712(c)(35); NYC Admin. Code; *TSB-M-14(1)C, (1)I, (2)S,* March 7, 2014, CCH New York Tax Reports, ¶408-039)

• *START-UP NY Program*

The SUNY Tax-Free Areas to Revitalize and Transform Upstate (START-UP) New York program (Ch. 68 (A.B. 8113), Laws 2013; Sec. 39, Tax Law; Sec. 40, Tax Law; Sec. 210(47), Tax Law) provides several personal and corporate income tax, sales and use tax, property tax, and transfer tax incentives to promote business and job creation by transforming public higher education through designated tax-free communities in upstate New York and other strategically-designated locations.

For 10 years, through applicable credits and refunds, participating businesses will pay no corporate franchise or personal income taxes on business income and no sales and use taxes on tangible personal property and services related to the area (¶903).

Applicability: The tax benefits apply to taxable years beginning on or after January 1, 2014, to calendar quarters beginning on or after January 1, 2014, to sales tax quarters beginning on or after March 1, 2014, or to transactions occurring on or after January 1, 2014, whichever is applicable. (Sec. 23, Part A, Ch. 68 (A.B. 8113), Laws 2013)

Qualifications: Among other requirements for eligibility, a business must be a new start-up company, an out-of-state company relocating to New York, or an expansion of an existing New York company. The business must also create and maintain net new jobs. Businesses will not be eligible if they compete with existing businesses that are not within the tax-free area, and certain types of businesses are specifically excluded (*e.g.,* restaurants, real estate management companies, and retail, wholesale, or personal service businesses). (Sec. 433, Econ. Dev. Law)

Corporate income tax provisions: A tax-free NY area tax elimination credit is provided. The amount allowed is the product of two factors (Sec. 40(b), Tax Law):

(1) the tax-free area allocation factor, which is the percentage representing the business's economic presence in the tax-free NY area in which the business was approved to locate, and

(2) the tax factor, which is the largest of the amounts of tax determined for the taxable year under Sec. 210(1)(a)—(d), Tax Law, after the deduction of any other corporate income tax credits allowable.

The legislation also enhances the Excelsior Jobs Program by reducing the applicable job creation requirements (*e.g.,* a participant is required to create ten manufacturing jobs, rather than 25 (Sec. 353(4), Econ. Dev. Law)). In addition, a taxpayer that creates at least 75% of the estimated jobs will be allowed a proportionally reduced credit. See also ¶940.

In addition, an exemption from the metropolitan commuter transportation mobility tax (MCTMT) is created (¶905).

Applicable to taxable years beginning on and after January 1, 2014, a refundable credit is available for the excise tax on telecommunication services paid by a START-UP NY business (Sec. 210(49), Tax Law). The credit is equal to the 2.5% of the excise tax paid on purchased telecommunication services under Article 9, Section 186-e, Tax Law.

Personal income tax provisions: Employees working at such businesses will be authorized to claim a personal income tax deduction equal to the wages earned from the business in the tax-free area. The deduction will apply to all wages and salaries in the first five years of tax benefits. In the remaining five years, for single individuals, heads of households, and married couples, the deduction will apply to the first $200,000, $250,000, and $300,000 of wages, respectively. The total number of new employees eligible for the deduction will be capped at 10,000 per year. (See ¶203)

Sales and use tax provisions: A business will be eligible for a credit or refund of sales and use taxes imposed on the retail sale of tangible personal property or services and similar taxes. The credit or refund shall be allowed for 120 consecutive months beginning with the month during which the business locates in the tax-free NY area. (See ¶2112)

Property tax provisions: Private universities and colleges will maintain tax-exempt status on property that is currently tax exempt and that they subsequently lease to businesses participating in the START-UP NY program. Only the portion of the property that is used for purposes of the START-UP NY program will be exempt. (See ¶2504)

Transfer tax provisions: Conveyances of real property located in tax-free NY areas to businesses located in those areas that are participating in the START-UP NY program are exempt from state and local real estate transfer tax or real property transfer tax. In addition, any lease of property to an eligible business also is exempt from any state or local real estate transfer tax or real property transfer tax. This lease provision applies to taxable years beginning on or after January 1, 2014. (See ¶2712)

Penalties for fraud: In the case of a business that acts fraudulently in connection with the START-UP NY program, the business will be immediately terminated from the program; subject to applicable criminal penalties, including the felony crime of offering a false instrument for filing in the first degree; and required to pay back all tax benefits that the company and its employees have received (clawback provisions). (See ¶2508)

Additional information: See Reg. Secs. 220.1—220.20, New York Department of Economic Development, effective October 23, 2013; *TSB-M-13(7)C, (6)I, (11)M, (1)MCTMT, (7)S,* New York Department of Taxation and Finance, October 22, 2013, CCH NEW YORK TAX REPORTS, ¶407-949.

¶924 Investment Tax Credit

Law: Secs. 208, 210(12), Tax Law (CCH NEW YORK TAX REPORTS, ¶12-055).

Comparable Federal: Secs. 46—59 (U.S. MASTER TAX GUIDE, ¶1345).

Forms: Form CT-46, Claim for Investment Tax Credit.

A taxpayer may claim a credit against tax on account of qualified property acquired, constructed, reconstructed, or erected in New York after 1968. (Sec. 210(12)(a), Tax Law; Reg. Sec. 5-2.5) The credit must be claimed for the first taxable year in which the qualified property is placed in service.

For application of the credit to the financial services industry, see below.

Investment credit base: The investment credit base is the cost or other basis, for federal income tax purposes, of qualified property less the amount of the nonqualified nonrecourse financing with respect to the property to the extent such financing would be excludable from the credit base pursuant to IRC Sec. 46(c)(8).

Amount of the credit: For property acquired in taxable years beginning after 1990, the amount of the credit is 5% of the first $350 million of the investment credit base and 4% of the amount above $350 million. For research and development property, the credit is 9% of the investment credit base. (Sec. 210(12)(a), Tax Law)

For credit amounts applicable to property acquired in years before 1991, see CCH New York Tax Reports, ¶ 12-055.

Caution: For tax years 2010, 2011, and 2012, taxpayers with more than $2 million in aggregated business tax credits were required to defer the amounts above $2 million until 2013. The total amount of credits deferred was paid back to taxpayers over tax years 2013, 2014, and 2015 (Sec. 33.1, Tax Law; Sec. 34.1, Tax Law; TSB-M-10(5)(C),September 13, 2010, CCH New York Tax Reports, ¶ 406-976).

Qualified property: The credit is allowed with respect to qualified tangible personal property and other tangible property, including buildings and structural components of buildings, that is (1) principally used by the taxpayer in the production of goods (other than electricity) by manufacturing, processing, assembling, refining, mining, extracting, farming, agriculture, horticulture, floriculture, viticulture, or commercial fishing, (2) industrial waste treatment facilities or air pollution control facilities, used in the taxpayer's trade or business, (3) research and development property, (4) principally used by the taxpayer in the financial services and banking industries (credit available for insurance corporations until October 1, 2015), or (5) principally used as a film production facility by a qualified film production company. (Sec. 210(12)(b)(i), Tax Law)

Practitioner Comment: Off-Site Equipment

Equipment can qualify for the investment tax credit even if it is not located on the taxpayer's premises. The taxpayer must exercise dominion and control over the assets, however (*Xerox*, TSB-A-98(24)C, CCH New York Tax Reports, ¶ 403-236).

Mark S. Klein, Esq., Hodgson Russ LLP

In order to qualify for the credit, the property must (1) be depreciable pursuant to Sec. 167, (2) have a useful life of four years or more, (3) be acquired by purchase as defined in IRC Sec. 179(d) (except certain leases to regulated brokers, dealers, or exchanges), and (4) have a situs in New York.

Practitioner Comment: Leased Property

Property acquired by lease may be eligible for the New York investment tax credit. The determinative factor is whether the lessee is treated as the beneficial owner of the property for federal tax purposes. If so, the lease will be regarded as an acquisition by purchase, rather than a rental arrangement, and the lessee will be entitled to a federal depreciation deduction. In such instances, the lessee will also be entitled to the New York investment tax credit if the property otherwise satisfies the requirements of the credit (TSB-M-91(3)C, CCH New York Tax Reports, ¶ 300-006).

A "true" lease of otherwise qualifying property disqualifies both the lessor and the lessee from the credit, even if a single taxpayer owns or controls both the lessor and the lessee (*Gropper v. Tax Appeals Tribunal*, NYS2d (3d Dep't. 2004), CCH New York Tax Reports, ¶ 404-880). However, if a corporation leases the property from its own single-member limited liability company, the taxpayer will be entitled to the investment tax credit if the single-member limited liability company is a disregarded entity for federal income tax purposes (*Deutsche Bank Securities*, TSB-A-04(11)C, CCH New York Tax Reports, ¶ 404-861).

Mark S. Klein, Esq., Hodgson Russ LLP

Retail enterprise: The credit is available to a retail enterprise that invests in a qualified rehabilitated building, as defined by federal law. The retail enterprise must (1) be registered as a vendor under the sales and use tax law, (2) be primarily engaged in the retail sale of tangible personal property, and (3) be eligible for the federal general business credit (IRC Sec. 38).

Limitation and carryover: The credit may not reduce the tax due to less than the higher of the minimum taxable income base (repealed for taxable years beginning after 2014) or the fixed dollar minimum (¶905).

If the amount of credit exceeds the tax for a particular year, the excess may be carried over to following years, with a 15-year limitation for tax years commencing in 1987 or thereafter. For taxable years commencing prior to 1987, the final year for carryovers of the investment credit was 2001.

In lieu of carrying over the excess, a taxpayer that qualifies as an owner of a new business may, at its option, receive the excess as a refund. "New business" is defined by Sec. 210(12)(j), Tax Law. For a discussion of 2002 changes to the definition, see TSB-M-02(5)C, CCH New York Tax Reports, ¶300-373.

Mergers and acquisitions: Neither the merger of a New York corporation into another corporation nor a corporate spin-off that is a tax-free reorganization causes recapture of the merged corporation's investment tax credit.

An election under IRC Sec. 338 to treat a parent corporation's sale of its stock in its wholly owned subsidiary as the sale of the subsidiary's assets would be recognized under New York law as a sale of the assets, and therefore would require the subsidiary to recapture investment credits claimed for the assets against New York corporate income tax. The recaptured amount would be the portion of the credits that reflects the remaining useful life of the assets. An investment tax credit for the assets could be claimed by the new version of the subsidiary (*TSB-A-98(20)C*, Department of Taxation and Finance, November 3, 1998, CCH New York Tax Reports, ¶403-210).

Practitioner Comment: New Business

If properly structured, a corporate spin-off can result in a "new business" eligible for the refundable investment tax credit (*Delphi Automotive Systems Corp.*, TSB-A-99(27)C, CCH New York Tax Reports, ¶403-526).

Mark S. Klein, Esq., Hodgson Russ LLP

Recapture upon disposition of property: If the property ceases to be in qualified use (because of its disposition or otherwise) during the taxable year for which the credit is to be taken, then the credit is modified by a ratio that relates the months of qualified use to the months of useful life. In instances where the property ceases to be in qualified use or is disposed of prior to the end of its useful life, the difference between the credit taken and the credit allowed for actual use must be added back in the year of disposition. Special provisions apply to the disposition of recovery property to which IRC Sec. 168 (ACRS) relates. (Sec. 210(12)(g), Tax Law)

The amount required to be added back is augmented by an amount equal to the product of the addback and the underpayment interest rate in effect on the last day of the taxable year.

Nonqualified nonrecourse financing addback: Nonqualified nonrecourse debt reduces the basis of property on which the credit is calculated. Consequently, increases in already existing nonqualified nonrecourse debt, as defined under federal law (26 U.S.C. §46(c)(8)), with respect to a property eligible for credit, require an addback in the year of the increase in debt. The addback is an amount equal to the decrease in the credit that would result from reducing the basis of the property by the increased nonrecourse debt. (Sec. 210(12)(a), Tax Law)

Application for credit: A claim for investment tax credit is made on Form CT-46, Claim for Investment Tax Credit.

CCH Advisory: ITC Carryover After IRC Sec. 338(h)(10) Transaction

The New York Department of Taxation and Finance issued a corporate franchise tax advisory opinion examining whether a parent corporation succeeds to an investment tax credit (ITC) carryover of its wholly-owned subsidiary if the parent sells the subsidiary's stock to a third-party purchaser and makes a joint election with the purchaser under IRC Sec. 338(h)(10) to treat the stock sale as a deemed asset sale. The opinion concludes that the parent corporation may succeed to the ITC carryover of the subsidiary, provided that the parent meets its burden of proof to substantiate the amount of the credit. (*TSB-A-11(3)C*, New York Commissioner of Taxation and Finance, February 18, 2011, CCH NEW YORK TAX REPORTS, ¶ 407-144)

• *Financial services industry*

The financial services investment tax credits are available until October 1, 2015, for qualified property that is principally used in the ordinary course of a taxpayer's business (Sec. 210(12)(b), Tax Law; TSB-M-09(3)C, January 16, 2009, CCH NEW YORK TAX REPORTS, ¶ 406-296):

— as a broker or dealer in connection with the purchase or sale of stocks, bonds, other securities, or commodities or in providing lending, loan arrangement, or loan origination services to its customers in connection with the purchase or sale of securities;

— as a provider of investment advisory services for a regulated investment company (as defined in Internal Revenue Code (IRC) section 851); or

— for Article 9-A taxpayers, as an exchange registered as a national securities exchange within the meaning of sections 3(A)(1) and 6(A) of the Securities Exchange Act of 1934, as a board of trade as defined in section 1410(a)(1) of the Not-for-Profit Corporation Law, or as an entity that is wholly owned by and that provides automation or technical services to one or more such national securities exchanges or boards of trade.

For taxable years ending on or after January 1, 2008, a taxpayer will be allowed the credits if one of the following eligibility tests are met (Sec. 210(12)(b), Tax Law; TSB-M-09(3)C, January 16, 2009, CCH NEW YORK TAX REPORTS, ¶ 406-296):

— 80% or more of the employees performing the administrative and support functions resulting from or related to the qualifying uses of the property are located in New York; or

— the average number of employees that perform the administrative and support functions resulting from or related to the qualifying uses of the property and are located in New York during the taxable year the credit is claimed is equal to or greater than 95% of the average number of employees that perform these functions and are located in New York State during the 36 months immediately preceding the taxable year for which the credit is claimed; or

— the number of New York employees employed during the current taxable year must be equal to or greater than 90% of the New York State employees on December 31, 1998 (if the taxpayer was a calendar year filer taxable in New York State in 1998); or the last day of its first taxable year ending after December 31, 1998, if the taxpayer was not a calendar year filer in 1998, or was not subject to tax in New York State for 1998.

However, if the taxpayer first becomes subject to tax in New York State after the taxable year beginning in 1998, then the taxpayer is not required to satisfy any of these eligibility tests for its first taxable year.

Additionally, property purchased by a taxpayer affiliated with a registered investment advisor or property leased by a taxpayer to an affiliated registered investment advisor is also eligible for the credit(s) if the property is principally used by the affiliate in a qualifying activity. For purposes of determining if the property is principally used by the taxpayer in a qualifying activity, the taxpayer may aggregate its uses as (1) a broker or dealer and (2) a provider of investment advisory services. In addition, the taxpayer may aggregate its uses for either or both of those activities with its affiliated regulated broker, dealer, and registered investment advisor. (Sec. 210(12)(b), Tax Law; TSB-M-09(3)C, January 16, 2009, CCH NEW YORK TAX REPORTS, ¶406-296)

¶925 Employment Incentive Tax Credit

Law: Sec. 210, Tax Law (CCH NEW YORK TAX REPORTS, ¶12-070).

Forms: CT-46, Claim for Investment Tax Credit.

A taxpayer qualifying for the investment tax credit (¶924) (other than at the optional rate applicable to research and development property) with respect to property the acquisition, construction, reconstruction, or erection of which began on or after January 1, 1987, is allowed an employment incentive credit for each of the two years next succeeding the taxable year for which the investment credit is allowed with respect to such property. (Sec. 210(12-D)(a)(1), Tax Law) The credit is allowed only if the average number of employees during the taxable year (except general executive officers) is at least 101% of the average number of employees during the employment base year (the taxable year immediately preceding the taxable year for which the investment tax credit was allowed).

Computation of credit: When the investment tax credit is allowed for a taxable year beginning after 1990, the credit is (1) 1.5% of the investment credit base if the average number of employees during the taxable year is less than 102% of the average number of employees in the employment base year, (2) 2% of the investment credit base if the average number of employees during the taxable year is at least 102% and less than 103% of the average number of employees in the employment base year, and (3) 2.5% of the investment credit base if the average number of employees during the taxable year is at least 103%. The computation of the average number of employees is specified in the statute. A parent corporation filing a combined report with a subsidiary is not required to determine employment levels on a combined basis. (Sec. 210(12-D), Tax Law)

Caution: For tax years 2010, 2011, and 2012, taxpayers with more than $2 million in aggregated business tax credits were required to defer the amounts above $2 million until 2013. The total amount of credits deferred was paid back to taxpayers over tax years 2013, 2014, and 2015. (Secs. 33, 34, Tax Law; TSB-M-10(5)C, New York Department of Taxation and Finance, September 13, 2010, CCH NEW YORK TAX REPORTS, ¶406-976)

Limitations and carryovers: The credit may not reduce the tax to less than the higher of the minimum taxable income base (repealed for taxable years beginning after 2014) or the fixed dollar minimum. (Sec. 210(1)(c), (d), Tax Law) If the credit does reduce the tax to such amount, any remaining unused credit may be carried over to the next 15 taxable years.

¶926 Credit for Annual Maintenance Fee of Foreign Corporations (repealed)

Law: Former Sec. 181, Tax Law (CCH NEW YORK TAX REPORTS, ¶ 12-129).

Forms: CT-8, Claim for Credit of Corporation Tax Paid (obsolete)

For taxable years beginning before 2015, the former annual maintenance fee paid by foreign corporations (¶ 2714) was allowed as a credit against the corporation franchise (income) tax. (Former Sec. 181, Tax Law)

¶927 Credit for Special Additional Mortgage Recording Taxes

Law: Sec. 210(17), Tax Law (CCH NEW YORK TAX REPORTS, ¶ 10-215, 12-125).

Forms: CT-43 and IT-256, Claim for Special Additional Mortgage Recording Tax Credit.

Taxpayers are allowed a credit against tax for the amount of special additional mortgage recording tax paid on certain mortgages. (Sec. 210(17), Tax Law) The credit is not allowed for special additional mortgage recording taxes paid on residential mortgages recorded on or after May 1, 1987, if the real property is located in Erie County or any of the counties within the Metropolitan Commuter Transportation District.

The credit may not reduce the tax to less than the higher of the minimum taxable income base (repealed for taxable years beginning after 2014) or the fixed dollar minimum (¶ 905). Any unused credit may be carried forward. However, corporate taxpayers who, as mortgagee, paid special additional mortgage recording tax on residential mortgages in any tax year beginning on or after January 1, 2015, may elect to treat the unused portion of the credit attributable to those mortgages as an overpayment of tax to be credited or refunded, rather than as a carryforward (Sec. 210-B(9)(b), Tax Law; see *TSB-M-16(3)C*, New York Department of Taxation and Finance, June 7, 2016, CCH NEW YORK TAX REPORTS, ¶ 408-764).

Caution: For tax years 2010, 2011, and 2012, taxpayers with more than $2 million in aggregated business tax credits were required to defer the amounts above $2 million until 2013. The total amount of credits deferred was paid back to taxpayers over tax years 2013, 2014, and 2015. (Secs. 33, 34, Tax Law; TSB-M-10(5)C, New York Department of Taxation and Finance, September 13, 2010, CCH NEW YORK TAX REPORTS, ¶ 406-976)

S corporations: The special additional mortgage recording tax credit is allowed for New York S corporations (at the entity level). The credit may be carried over from a New York C year to a New York S year or vice versa. (Sec. 210(21), Tax Law)

Practitioner Comment: Special Additional Mortgage Recording Tax Credit Not Available to S Corporation Shareholders

The special additional mortgage recording tax credit is available to individuals, partners in a partnership, members of an LLC (taxed as a partnership), estates and trusts, and beneficiaries of estates and trusts. It is not, however, available to shareholders of S corporations. Instead, it is allowed only as a credit against the S corporation's own tax. Since the tax imposed on S corporations is relatively minimal, this eliminates the majority of the value of this credit to S corporation shareholders. See instructions to Form IT–256.

Mark S. Klein, Esq., Hodgson Russ LLP

¶928 Credits for Employing Disabled Persons

Law: Secs. 210(23), 210-B(48), Tax Law (CCH NEW YORK TAX REPORTS, ¶ 12-070a).

Forms: CT-41, Claim for Credit for Employment of Persons with Disabilities.

A credit is allowed for employing qualified disabled persons. To be a qualified employee, an individual must meet the requirements of being certified by the Education Department as disabled and have completed (or be enrolled in) a rehabilitation plan, in addition to working full time for a minimum 180 days or 400 hours. (Sec. 210(23), Tax Law)

An additional credit for hiring workers with developmental disabilities is discussed below.

Credit amount: The amount of the credit is 35% of the first $6,000 in wages for the qualified employee's first-year of employment. (Sec. 210(23)(c), Tax Law) When an employee's wages also constitute qualified first-year wages for purposes of the federal work opportunity tax credit for vocational rehabilitation referrals under IRC Sec. 51, the amount of the credit is 35% of the first $6,000 in wages for the qualified employee's second year. This has the effect of requiring that the employee be employed for two years.

Caution: For tax years 2010, 2011, and 2012, taxpayers with more than $2 million in aggregated business tax credits were required to defer the amounts above $2 million until 2013. The total amount of credits deferred was paid back to taxpayers over tax years 2013, 2014, and 2015. (Secs. 33, 34, Tax Law; TSB-M-10(5)C, New York Department of Taxation and Finance, September 13, 2010, CCH NEW YORK TAX REPORTS, ¶406-976)

Limitations and carryovers: The credit cannot reduce the business's tax to less than the statutory minimum, but to the extent any excess credit remains, it may be carried over for an unlimited number of years. The credit is not refundable.

• *Credit for hiring persons with developmental disabilities*

The Workers with Disabilities Tax Credit Program, which is administered by the Department of Labor, provides an additional tax incentive to employers for employing individuals with developmental disabilities. The credit is available for qualified wages paid after January 1, 2015 and expires on January 1, 2020. (Sec. 210-B(48), Tax Law)

Credit amount: The nonrefundable credit is equal to 15% of the qualified wages for qualified full-time employees and 10% of the qualified wages for qualified part-time employees. The annual credit allocation is $6 million. (Sec. 210-B(48), Tax Law)

Planning considerations: Full-time employment is defined as working at least 30 hours per week, and part-time employment at least 8 hours per week, each for at least 6 months (Sec. 210-B(48), Tax Law).

In order to be eligible for the program, taxpayers must apply to the Department of Labor Commissioner by November 30 of the prior year to become a qualified employer, and will be issued a preliminary certificate of eligibility. At the end of the tax year, the employer must obtain a final certificate of eligibility from the department that states the maximum amount of credit allowed and provides verification for the credit claims. An employer is not allowed to concurrently claim this credit and any other credit for the employment of persons with disabilities for the same employee. (Sec 25-B, Labor Law).

Any unused credit may be carried forward for up to 3 years.

¶929 Credits Relating to Empire Zones (expired)

Law: Secs. 14, 15, 16, 209(b)(2), 210(1), (12)(j), (19), (20), (27), (28), Tax Law; Reg. Secs. 5-8.1, 5-8.2, 5-8.4, 5-9.1—5-9.5, 5-10.1—5-10.9 (CCH NEW YORK TAX REPORTS, ¶12-060—12-062a).

Forms: CT-601, Claim for EZ Wage Tax Credit; CT-601.1, Claim for ZEA Wage Tax Credit; CT-602, Claim for EZ Capital Tax Credit; CT-603, Claim for EZ Investment Tax Credit and EZ Employment Incentive Credit; CT-604, Claim for QEZE Credit for Real Property Taxes and QEZE Tax Reduction Credit; CT-604-CP, Claim for QEZE Credit for Real Property Taxes and QEZE Tax Reduction Credit for Corporate Partners; CT-605, Claim for EZ Investment Tax Credit and EZ Employment Incentive Credit for the Financial Services Industry; DTF-621, Claim for QETC Employment Credit; DTF-622, Claim for QETC Capital Tax Credit.

The Empire Zone program expired on June 30, 2010. Transitional provisions are explained in *TSB-M-10(6)C, (12)I, (19)S*, New York Department of Taxation and Finance, December 8, 2010, CCH NEW YORK TAX REPORTS, ¶ 407-074. Continuing eligibility for Empire Zone benefits is discussed in *TSB-M-11(2)C, (3)I, (4)S*, New York Department of Taxation and Finance, April 5, 2011, CCH NEW YORK TAX REPORTS, ¶ 407-188.

Six separate credits were available to businesses that relocated to, or stimulated private business development and job creation within, designated empire zones. In addition, an alternative credit, the ZEA wage credit (see below) was available in eligible zones not designated as empire zones. Zone equivalent areas (ZEAs) are census tracts and block numbering areas that had a poverty rate of least 20% and an unemployment rate at least $1^1/_4$ times the statewide unemployment rates as of the 1990 census and are eligible to be designated as empire zones, but have not been so designated. The Excelsior jobs program, discussed at ¶ 940, replaces the expired Empire Zones program to provide job creation and investment incentives to firms in targeted industries.

Empire Zone reform: The 2009-2010 budget legislation implemented reform measures to the Empire Zone program and the Empire Zone income tax credits by decertifying businesses that have received more benefit from the program than they have provided and by increasing the cost-benefit ratio test for entry into the program from 15 to 1 to 20 to 1 (10 to 1 for manufacturers). The program's sunset date was advanced from June 30, 2011, to June 30, 2010. Applicable to taxable years beginning on and after January 1, 2008, carryover credits are not allowed for taxpayers that are decertified for failure to meet the 20:1 cost benefit analysis.

Deferral of credits: For tax years 2010, 2011, and 2012, taxpayers with more than $2 million in aggregated business tax credits were required to defer the amounts above $2 million until 2013. The total amount of credits deferred was paid back to taxpayers over tax years 2013, 2014, and 2015. (Secs. 33, 34, Tax Law; TSB-M-10(5)C, New York Department of Taxation and Finance, September 13, 2010, CCH NEW YORK TAX REPORTS, ¶ 406-976)

Eligibility: To be eligible for any of the credits, a business must be certified under Article 18-B of the General Municipal Law.

Practitioner Comment: S Corporations Must be Separately Certified

An empire zone business designation is limited to the qualified taxpayer. Even though single member LLCs are disregarded entities, a single member LLC's empire zone qualification does not flow through to its 100% owned S-corporation. Since S corporations are treated as separate taxpayers, each S corporation must be certified in its own right in order to earn the Empire Zone credits. Once the S corporation is qualified, the applicable credits would then be passed through to the S corporation's owners in proportion to their ownership interest. NYT-G-07(5)C.

Mark S. Klein, Esq., Hodgson Russ LLP

Empire zones: New York has designated more than 100 empire zones. Contact information for counties and municipalities with empire zones is found at ¶ 2112. Zones are designated as "investment zones" (for economically disadvantaged areas) or "development zones"(for county areas).

For information regarding 2005 changes to the empire zone and qualified empire zone enterprise (QEZE) programs, see TSB-M-06(1)C, CCH NEW YORK TAX REPORTS, ¶ 300-499.

• *Empire zone investment tax credit (expired)*

Businesses were allowed a credit equal to 10% of the cost or other basis for federal income tax purposes of tangible personal property and other tangible property, including buildings and structural components of buildings, located within a designated empire zone. (Sec. 210(12-B), Tax Law; Reg. Sec. 5-10.1) The acquisition, construction, reconstruction, or erection of the property had to begin on or after the date of the designation and prior to the termination of the designation. When the acquisition, construction, reconstruction, or erection continued or was completed after the period that the zone was certified, the credit was limited to 10% of the portion of the cost or other basis for federal income tax purposes that was attributable to the period of the zone's designation as an empire zone, and was determined by multiplying the cost or basis by the percentage that the expenditures paid or incurred during the certified period bears to the total of all acquisition, construction or erection expenditures.

Caution: For tax years 2010, 2011, and 2012, taxpayers with more than $2 million in aggregated business tax credits were required to defer the amounts above $2 million until 2013. The total amount of credits deferred was paid back to taxpayers over tax years 2013, 2014, and 2015. (Secs. 33, 34, Tax Law; TSB-M-10(5)C, New York Department of Taxation and Finance, September 13, 2010, CCH NEW YORK TAX REPORTS, ¶ 406-976)

For application of the credit to the financial services industry, see *TSB-M-09(3)C,* January 16, 2009, CCH NEW YORK TAX REPORTS, ¶ 406-296.

Qualifications: To be eligible for the credit, the property had to (1) be depreciable pursuant to IRC Sec. 167, (2) have a useful life of four years or more, (3) be acquired by purchase (as defined in IRC Sec. 179(d)), (4) have a situs in a designated empire zone, and (5) be principally used by the taxpayer in the production of goods (other than electricity) by manufacturing, processing, assembling, refining, mining, extracting, farming, agriculture, horticulture, floriculture, viticulture, or commercial fishing, or be principally used by the taxpayer in the financial services and banking industries (placed in service on or after October 1, 1998, and before October 1, 2015). Property leased by a taxpayer to any other person or corporation was generally ineligible for the credit.

Note: The period of eligibility to claim the Empire Zone (EZ) ITC for the financial services industry was only available until April 1, 2014, because the EZs are deemed to be expired as of that date. However, a financial services business that placed property in service between April 1, 2014, and October 1, 2015, may claim the regular ITC for the financial services industry instead (*TSB-M-11(6)C,* New York Department of Taxation and Finance, June 8, 2011).

The credit includes qualified property that is used as industrial waste treatment facilities or air pollution control facilities in a taxpayer's trade or business, or as research and development property.

Recapture: Provisions exist for the recapture of a portion of the credit if property is disposed of or ceases to be in qualified use prior to the end of its useful life or during the year in which a credit is to be taken, or if the enterprise is decertified. An exception applies to credits allowed to partners with respect to certain manufacturing property.

CCH Advisory: Corporate Reorganizations

Generally, no disposition of property occurs when property is transferred from a corporation as part of a transaction that does not result in the recognition of gain or loss under the Internal Revenue Code (Reg. Sec. 5-10.8(g)). Such transactions include statutory mergers, consolidations, and reorganizations, including bankruptcy reorganizations. However, the property must continue in qualified use, and the acquiring corporation must be certified.

¶929

Limitations and carryovers: The credit may not reduce the tax to less than the tax computed on the minimum taxable income base (repealed for taxable years beginning after 2014) or the fixed dollar minimum, whichever is greater.

The credit may not be claimed for property on which elective deductions for air or water pollution control facilities or research and development facilities are claimed, or for which the investment tax credit (¶924) is taken.

With one exception, empire zone investment tax credits not used in one taxable year may be carried forward until exhausted. Decertified business enterprises may not carry the credit beyond the seventh taxable year following the year in which the credit was allowed. In lieu of carrying unused credits over to subsequent years, a taxpayer that qualifies as the owner of a new business may receive 50% of the excess as a refund.

Forms: The credit is claimed on Form DTF-603.

• *Employment incentive tax credit (expired)*

Taxpayers that qualify for the empire zone investment tax credit were allowed an additional credit for each of the three years next succeeding the taxable year for which the investment tax credit was allowed. (Sec. 210(12-c), Tax Law; Reg. Sec. 5-11.1) The credit, equal to 30% of the investment tax credit, was allowed only if the average number of employees employed by the taxpayer in the economic empire zone in which the property is located during the taxable year is at least 101% of the average number of employees employed by the taxpayer in that zone or, where applicable, in the geographic area subsequently constituting such zone, during the taxable year immediately preceding the year for which the investment tax credit was allowed.

Recapture: The empire zone employment incentive tax credit is required to be recaptured if, as a result of a deemed disposal of property because of decertification, recapture of the empire zone investment tax credit is required.

Limitations and carryovers: The employment incentive wage tax credit may not reduce the tax to less than the fixed dollar minimum. Prior to 2001, the credit could not reduce the tax to less than the higher of the minimum taxable income base (repealed for taxable years beginning after 2014) or the fixed dollar minimum. Credit that is not deductible may be carried over to following years until exhausted. For taxable years commencing in or after 2006, in lieu of the carryover, a taxpayer that is deemed to be a new business under Tax Law Sec. 14(j)(5) may elect to treat 50% of the carryover amount as an overpayment to be credited or refunded without interest. Otherwise, however, a corporation may not claim a refund of the empire zone employment incentive credit.

Caution: For tax years 2010, 2011, and 2012, taxpayers with more than $2 million in aggregated business tax credits were required to defer the amounts above $2 million until 2013. The total amount of credits deferred was paid back to taxpayers over tax years 2013, 2014, and 2015. (Secs. 33, 34, Tax Law; TSB-M-10(5)C, New York Department of Taxation and Finance, September 13, 2010, CCH NEW YORK TAX REPORTS, ¶406-976)

Forms: The credit is claimed on Form DTF-603.

• *Empire zone and ZEA wage tax credits (expired)*

Taxpayers were allowed a credit for wages paid to full-time employees in newly created jobs in an empire zone or a zone equivalent area (ZEA). (Sec. 210(19), Tax Law; Reg. Sec. 5-9.1) (*Note:* The ZEA wage tax credit expired on June 13, 2004, but ZEA wage tax credit carryforwards may still be used.) The credit is larger for employers who hire targeted employees. A "targeted employee" is a New York resident who receives empire zone wages and who qualifies as any of the following:

— an eligible individual for the federal targeted jobs tax credit (IRC Sec. 51);

— eligible for benefits under the federal Workforce Investment Act (P.L. 105-220, as amended) as a dislocated worker or low-income individual;

¶929

— a recipient of public assistance benefits;

— an individual whose income is below the U.S. Department of Commerce poverty rate;

— a member of a family whose family income is below the federal poverty rate; or

— an honorably discharged member of any branch of the U.S. armed forces.

Caution: For tax years 2010, 2011, and 2012, taxpayers with more than $2 million in aggregated business tax credits were required to defer the amounts above $2 million until 2013. The total amount of credits deferred was paid back to taxpayers over tax years 2013, 2014, and 2015. (Secs. 33, 34, Tax Law; TSB-M-10(5)C, New York Department of Taxation and Finance, September 13, 2010, CCH NEW YORK TAX REPORTS, ¶ 406-976)

CCH Advisory: Liberty Zone Employees

New York Liberty Zone business employees may be considered targeted employees for purposes of the empire zone and zone equivalent area wage tax credits for taxable years ending on or after 2001, provided that other requirements for targeted status are satisfied (*TSB-M-02(2)C*, Technical Services Bureau, Taxpayer Services Division, New York Department of Taxation and Finance, August 2, 2002, CCH NEW YORK TAX REPORTS, ¶ 300-370).

Credit amount: The amount of the credit is equal to the sum of the following:

—$3,000 multiplied by the average number of the taxpayer's full-time targeted employees (excluding general executive officers) who received empire zone wages for more than one-half of the taxable year and, with respect to more than one-half of the period of employment by the taxpayer during the taxable year, received an hourly wage that was at least 135% of the state minimum wage; and

—$1,500 multiplied by the average number of full-time employees (excluding general executive officers and targeted full-time employees) who received empire zone wages for more than one-half of the taxable year.

For a taxpayer certified in an investment zone, the dollar amount of the credit per employee is increased by $500 for each qualifying employee who received wages in excess of $40,000.

Limitations and carryovers: The total zone wage tax credit (including any carryovers) may not, in the aggregate, exceed 50% of the business corporation franchise tax (computed prior to the subtraction of any credits). In addition, the credit, together with carryovers, may not reduce the tax due to less than the higher of the minimum taxable income base (repealed for taxable years beginning after 2014) or the fixed dollar minimum.

Credits not used in a taxable year may be carried forward to subsequent years until exhausted. In lieu of carrying unused credits over to subsequent years, a taxpayer that qualifies as the owner of a new business may receive 50% of the excess as a refund.

Duration of credits: The empire zone and former ZEA wage tax credits may be claimed for up to five years. No empire zone credits may be claimed more than five years after designation of the empire zone.

Any employee for whom the empire zone wage tax credit is claimed for the taxable year based on employment within a designated ZEA is not eligible for purposes of the employment incentive credit (¶ 925).

¶929

Forms: The credits are claimed on Form CT-601, Claim for EZ Wage Tax Credit, or Form CT-601.1, Claim for ZEA Wage Tax Credit, as appropriate.

• *Empire zone capital tax credit (expired)*

Taxpayers were allowed a credit equal to 25% of the sum of the following investments and contributions made during the tax year: (1) for taxable years beginning before 2005, qualified investments made in, or contributions in the form of donations made to, one or more empire zone capital corporations; (2) qualified investments in certified zone businesses that, during the 12-month period immediately preceding the month in which such investment was made, employed full-time within New York an average of 250 or fewer individuals, excluding general executive officers, computed pursuant to the provisions of Sec. 210(19)(3), Tax Law, except for investments made by or on behalf of an owner of the business, including, but not limited to, a stockholder, partner or sole proprietor, or any related person as defined in IRC Sec. 465(b)(3); and (3) contributions of money to community development projects. (Sec. 210(20)(a), Tax Law; Reg. Sec. 5-8.1)

Caution: For tax years 2010, 2011, and 2012, taxpayers with more than $2 million in aggregated business tax credits were required to defer the amounts above $2 million until 2013. The total amount of credits deferred was paid back to taxpayers over tax years 2013, 2014, and 2015. (Secs. 33, 34, Tax Law; TSB-M-10(5)C, New York Department of Taxation and Finance, September 13, 2010, CCH NEW YORK TAX REPORTS, ¶406-976)

Limitations and carryovers: The total amount of the empire zone capital tax credit allowable to a taxpayer for all years, taken in the aggregate, may not exceed $300,000 and may not exceed $100,000 with respect to the investments and contributions described in each of the listed categories. Unused credits may be carried forward until exhausted. In addition, the amount of any credit and carryovers may not exceed 50% of the taxpayer's tax liability (computed without regard to credits).

Recapture of credit: All or a portion of the capital credit must be recaptured if ownership interests arising from qualified investments that were the basis for the credit are sold, transferred, or otherwise disposed of, or contributions or investments that were the basis for the credit are recovered.

The amount of the credit to be added back is determined by multiplying the portion of the credit originally allowed that is attributable to the property disposed of or the payment or contribution recovered by:

—100%, if the disposition or recovery occurs within the taxable year with respect to which the credit is allowed or within 12 months from the end of that year;

—67%, if the disposition or recovery occurs more than 12, but not more than 24, months after the end of the taxable year with respect to which the credit is allowed; or

—33%, if the disposition or recovery occurs more than 24, but not more than 36, months after the end of the taxable year with respect to which the credit is allowed.

No recapture is required if disposition or recovery occurs more than 36 months after the end of the taxable year with respect to which the credit is allowed.

• *QEZE credit for real property tax*

A credit is allowed for real property taxes paid by a qualified empire zone enterprise (QEZE) on property owned by the QEZE and located within an empire zone for which the QEZE is certified. Taxes paid by the QEZE on leased property may qualify under certain circumstances. (Sec. 15(e), Tax Law; Sec. 210(27), Tax Law)

A QEZE is a business enterprise that is certified under Article 18-B of the General Municipal Law and that annually meets the employment test.

¶929

Employment test: For a business entity first certified before April 1, 2005, the employment test is met for a taxable year if (1) the business enterprise's employment number in empire zones for the taxable year equals or exceeds its employment number in the zones for the base period, and (2) the business enterprise's employment number in New York State outside of the zones for the taxable year equals or exceeds its employment number in New York outside of the zones for the base period.

For entities first certified between August 1, 2002, and March 31, 2005, if the base period is zero years and the enterprise has an employment number in an empire zone of greater than zero with respect to a taxable year, then the employment test will be met only if the enterprise qualifies as a new business. For entities first certified before August 1, 2002, if the entity had a base period of zero years or zero employment in the base period, then the employment test will be met only if the enterprise qualifies as a new business.

For a business enterprise first certified on or after April 1, 2005, the employment test will be met with respect to a taxable year if the business enterprise's employment number in the state and the empire zones for that taxable year exceeds its employment number in the state and the empire zones, respectively, for the base period. If the base period is zero years or the base period employment is zero and the enterprise has an employment number in the zone of greater than zero with respect to a taxable year, then the employment test will be met only if the enterprise qualifies as a new business.

Test year: The employment test year is the taxable year that ended immediately before the test date. The test date is July 1, 2000, or a later date (prior to July 1, 2010) on which the QEZE is certified.

If a business enterprise does not have a taxable year that ends on or before the test date, the test year is the last calendar or fiscal year ending on or before its test date (whether or not the enterprise in fact had a taxable year during that period).

Credit amount: For businesses certified on or after April 1, 2005, the credit is equal to the product of 25% of the total wages, health benefits, and retirement benefits (up to $40,000) paid to or on behalf of net new employees during the taxable year. The credit is limited to $10,000 per employee. Certain adjustments (as well as a maximum credit limitation) may apply. (Sec. 15(b)(2)(A), Tax Law)

Formula for calculation of credit (prior years): For businesses certified before April 1, 2005, the QEZE real property tax credit is the product of (the benefit period factor) × (the employment increase factor) × (the eligible real property taxes paid during the taxable year).

The benefit period factor is as follows:

— for the first 10 taxable years, 1.0;

— for the 11th taxable year, .8;

— for the 12th taxable year, .6;

— for the 13th taxable year, .4;

— for the 14th taxable year, .2; and

— for the 15th taxable year, 0.

The employment increase factor is the amount, not to exceed 1.0, that is the greater of:

(1) the excess of the taxpayer's employment number in the empire zones in which the taxpayer is certified for that year over the taxpayer's test year employment number in such zones, divided by the test year employment number in those zones (*Note:* If the taxpayer's employment number in the zones for the taxable year exceeds the employment number in the zones for the test year, and the test year employment number is zero, then the employment increase factor will be 1.0.); or

¶929

(2) the excess of the taxpayer's employment number in the zones in which the taxpayer is certified for that year over the taxpayer's test year employment number in such zones, divided by 100.

Limitations and carryovers: The QEZE credit for real property taxes may not reduce the tax of the QEZE below the tax payable on either the minimum taxable income (repealed for taxable years beginning after 2014) or the fixed dollar minimum. However, any amount remaining may be refunded, without interest.

For federal income tax purposes, the Internal Revenue Service has determined that all or a portion of the QEZE credit for real property taxes that is refunded, or credited as an overpayment to estimated tax, may be a recovery of property tax previously deducted and is therefore considered income to the taxpayer.

For New York state corporate franchise tax and personal income tax purposes, any refund of the QEZE credit for real property taxes is considered a refund of franchise tax or income tax. Accordingly, under existing state law, the amount of the refund of the QEZE credit for real property taxes included in the taxpayer's federal taxable income or federal adjusted gross income is not taxable to New York state. Therefore, New York state taxpayers are allowed a subtraction for that refund amount in computing their New York taxable income. A memorandum describes how to report the subtraction on New York state corporate franchise tax returns and personal income tax returns, as well as the necessary amended return requirements. (*TSB-M-10(9)C, (15)I*, New York Department of Taxation and Finance, December 31, 2010, CCH NEW YORK TAX REPORTS, ¶ 407-084)

Caution: For tax years 2010, 2011, and 2012, taxpayers with more than $2 million in aggregated business tax credits were required to defer the amounts above $2 million until 2013. The total amount of credits deferred was paid back to taxpayers over tax years 2013, 2014, and 2015. (Secs. 33, 34, Tax Law; TSB-M-10(5)C, New York Department of Taxation and Finance, September 13, 2010, CCH NEW YORK TAX REPORTS, ¶ 406-976)

Maximum credit limitation: The maximum credit that may be taken is the greater of the employment increase limitation or the capital investment limitation, not to exceed the amount of real property taxes paid during the taxable year. (Sec. 15(f)(2), Tax Law) The employment increase limitation is equal to the product of $10,000 and the excess of the QEZE's employment number in the empire zones for the taxable year over that employment number for the QEZE's test year. The capital investment limitation is the product of (a) 10% of the greater of the cost or other basis for federal income tax purposes of the real property owned by the QEZE and located in empire zones on the later of January 1, 2001 or the effective date of the QEZE's certification or the cost or other basis of such property on the last day of the taxable year, and (b) the percentage of the real property physically occupied and used by the QEZE or by a related person to the QEZE.

Recapture: A portion of the credit will be recaptured if the real property taxes that were the basis for the allowance of the credit are subsequently reduced as a result of a final order.

Forms: The credit is claimed on Form CT-604 or Form CT-604-CP (corporate partners).

Resources: Additional details and examples are included in TSB-M-06(1)C, CCH NEW YORK TAX REPORTS, ¶ 300-499.

• *QEZE tax reduction credit*

A tax reduction credit is allowed against corporate franchise (income) tax for a qualified enterprise zone enterprise (QEZE) that is certified pursuant to Article 18-B of the General Municipal Law and that annually meets the employment test (see above).

Formula for calculation of credit: The QEZE tax reduction credit is the product of (the benefit period factor) × (the employment increase factor) × (the zone allocation factor) × (the tax factor).

The benefit period factor is as follows:

— for the first 10 taxable years, 1.0;

— for the 11th taxable year, .8;

— for the 12th taxable year, .6;

— for the 13th taxable year, .4;

— for the 14th taxable year, .2; and

— for the 15th taxable year, 0.

The employment increase factor is the amount, not to exceed 1.0, that is the greater of:

— the excess of the QEZE's employment number for the taxable year in the empire zones where the QEZE is certified over the QEZE's test year employment number divided by the test year employment numbers in those zones (*Note:* If the taxpayer's employment number in the zones for the taxable year exceeds the employment number in the zones for the test year, and the test year employment number is zero, then the employment increase factor will be 1.0.); or

— the excess of the QEZE's employment number for the taxable year in the empire zones where the QEZE is certified over the QEZE's test year employment number divided by 100.

The zone allocation factor is a percentage representing the taxpayer's presence in the empire zone based on property and payroll.

The tax factor is the larger of the tax payable for the taxable year on either the entire net income base or the minimum taxable income (repealed for taxable years beginning after 2014). For the computation of the tax factor for corporate partners of a QEZE and combined filers, see TSB-M-03(4)C, CCH New York Tax Reports, ¶ 300-391.

Limitations and carryovers: The QEZE tax reduction credit may not reduce the tax of the QEZE below the tax payable on the fixed dollar minimum base (¶ 904), except in the case of a taxpayer whose zone allocation factor is 100%.

Caution: For tax years 2010, 2011, and 2012, taxpayers with more than $2 million in aggregated business tax credits were required to defer the amounts above $2 million until 2013. The total amount of credits deferred was paid back to taxpayers over tax years 2013, 2014, and 2015. (Secs. 33, 34, Tax Law; TSB-M-10(5)C, New York Department of Taxation and Finance, September 13, 2010, CCH New York Tax Reports, ¶ 406-976)

Forms: The credit is claimed on Form CT-604 or Form CT-604-CP (corporate partners).

Resources: Additional details and examples are included in TSB-M-06(1)C, CCH New York Tax Reports, ¶ 300-499.

¶930 Minimum Tax Credit (repealed)

Law: Sec. 210(13), Tax Law (CCH New York Tax Reports, ¶ 12-127).

For taxable years beginning before 2015, a minimum tax credit was provided for use against tax computed on the entire net income base. (Sec. 210(13), Tax Law) The credit is designed to prevent double-counting of income that might otherwise arise because of timing items of tax preference and adjustments.

¶930

Credit amount: The credit was allowed for the excess, if any of the adjusted minimum tax imposed for all prior taxable years beginning after 1989, over the amount of the minimum tax credit allowable for the prior taxable years that was actually deducted from the taxpayer's corporate income tax otherwise due for those years. (Sec. 210(13), Tax Law)

The adjusted minimum tax for any taxable year is the excess (if any) of the amount of the minimum tax for that year over the highest of the amounts computed under the entire net income base, the capital base, and the fixed dollar minimum for that year, reduced by the amount that would be the excess (if any) of the minimum tax for that year if the only adjustment and item of tax preference taken into account was that provided for in IRC Sec. 57(a)(1), relating to depletion, and if such minimum tax were computed without adding the New York net operating loss deduction otherwise allowed in the case of taxable years beginning after 1989, pursuant to Sec. 208(8-B)(a)(3), Tax Law, and without subtracting the alternative net operating loss deduction in the case of taxable years beginning after 1993, over the highest of the entire net income base, the capital base, and the fixed dollar minimum for that year.

¶931 Credits—S Corporations

Law: Sec. 210, Tax Law (CCH NEW YORK TAX REPORTS, ¶10-215).

Franchise tax payable by New York S corporations may not be reduced by credits or carryovers of credits, other than the credit for the special additional mortgage recording tax (¶927), which may be elected by New York S corporations paying corporate income tax for taxable years beginning in or after 1994. Furthermore, credits allowable in a year in which a taxpayer elects New York S corporation status may not be carried over to other years by the taxpayer. Rather, the credits flow through to the S corporation shareholders, provided there is a comparable credit under the personal income tax. Shareholders may carry forward unused credits, to the extent permitted under the personal income tax. The carryover of the credit allowed for the special additional mortgage recording tax is determined without regard to whether the credit is carried from a New York C year to a New York S year, or vice-versa. (Sec. 210(21), Tax Law)

¶932 Credit for Servicing SONYMA Mortgages

Law: Sec. 210(21-a), Tax Law (CCH NEW YORK TAX REPORTS, ¶12-126).

A mortgage banker registered under Article 12-D, Banking Law, that meets certain regulatory requirements established by the State of New York Mortgage Agency (SONYMA) and has entered into agreements to service mortgages acquired by SONYMA may claim an annual credit against its Article 9-A franchise tax. (Sec. 210(21-a), Tax Law)

Credit amount: The credit is equal to the following (Sec. 210(21-a), Tax Law):

— on mortgages secured by liens on one- to four-family residential structures, 2.93% of the total interest and principal collected by the banker during its taxable year (subject to limitations noted below); and

— on mortgages secured by liens on real property improved by a structure occupied as the residence of five or more families living independently of each other, an amount equal to the interest collected by the banker during its taxable year, multiplied by a fraction, the denominator of which is the interest rate payable on the mortgage (computed to five decimal places), and the numerator of which is (1) 0.00125 in the case of a mortgage acquired by the SONYMA for less than $1 million, or (2) 0.00100 in the case of a mortgage acquired by the SONYMA for $1 million or more.

The amount of the credit may not exceed the total amount of Article 9-A taxes due for the banker's taxable year. There is no provision for carryovers.

Caution: For tax years 2010, 2011, and 2012, taxpayers with more than $2 million in aggregated business tax credits were required to defer the amounts above $2 million until 2013. The total amount of credits deferred was paid back to taxpayers over tax years 2013, 2014, and 2015. (Secs. 33, 34, Tax Law; TSB-M-10(5)C, New York Department of Taxation and Finance, September 13, 2010, CCH NEW YORK TAX REPORTS, ¶ 406-976)

Mortgage limitations: In computing the credit for the servicing of mortgages on one- to four-family residential structures, no credit is allowed to a banker for the collection of curtailments or payments in discharge of a mortgage.

A "curtailment" is any amount paid by mortgagors (1) in excess of the monthly constant due during the month of collection and (2) in reduction of the unpaid principal balance of the mortgage. In the absence of clear evidence to the contrary, amounts paid in excess of the monthly constant due during the month of collection are deemed to be in reduction of the unpaid principal balance of the mortgage.

Forms: The credit is claimed on Form CT-3, General Business Corporation Franchise Tax Return, or Form CT-3-A, General Business Combined Corporation Franchise Tax Return.

¶933 Credit for the Rehabilitation of Historic Barns

Law: Sec. 210(12)(*l*), Tax Law (CCH NEW YORK TAX REPORTS, ¶ 12-090).

Comparable Federal: Sec. 47.

Forms: CT-46-ATT, Claim for Rehabilitation Expenses for Retail Enterprises and Historic Barns.

A credit is allowed in the amount of 25% of the qualified rehabilitation expenditures paid or incurred in connection with the renovation of a qualified historic barn located within New York State. (Sec. 210(12)(*l*), Tax Law) The term "barn" means a building originally designed and used for storing farm equipment or agricultural products, or for housing livestock.

Caution: For tax years 2010, 2011, and 2012, taxpayers with more than $2 million in aggregated business tax credits were required to defer the amounts above $2 million until 2013. The total amount of credits deferred was paid back to taxpayers over tax years 2013, 2014, and 2015. (Secs. 33, 34, Tax Law; TSB-M-10(5)C, New York Department of Taxation and Finance, September 13, 2010, CCH NEW YORK TAX REPORTS, ¶ 406-976)

Qualified rehabilitation expenses: To be eligible for the credit, expenditures must be qualified as the basis for the federal rehabilitation credit described in IRC Sec. 47. In general, under the federal provisions, a taxpayer may claim a credit equal to a specified percentage of its expenditures incurred to substantially rehabilitate a qualifying structure. (Sec. 210(12)(*l*), Tax Law)

Limitations and carryovers: The expenses must be properly chargeable to a capital account for property for which depreciation is allowable (*i.e.,* property used in a trade or business). The building that is being rehabilitated must have been placed in service prior to the commencement of the rehabilitation work, and it either must be a certified historic structure or have been first placed in service prior to 1936. A building will be considered to be substantially rehabilitated if the expenditures incurred during the 24-month period selected by the taxpayer and ending with or within the taxable year exceed the greater of the adjusted basis of the building or $5,000. Under certain circumstances, the rehabilitation work may extend over a number of taxable years.

A taxpayer may not claim both the regular investment tax credit on manufacturing property (¶ 924) and the investment tax credit for rehabilitation of historic barns on the same property. In addition, no credit will be allowed for any rehabilitation that (1) converts a qualified barn to a residential purpose, or (2) materially alters the historic appearance of the barn.

The credit cannot reduce the tax below the minimum tax or the alternative minimum tax, whichever is greater. Any excess credit may be carried forward for the next 15 taxable years.

Forms: The credit is claimed by filing Form CT-46-ATT with Form CT-3, the General Business Corporation Franchise Tax Return, or Form CT-3-A, the General Business Corporation Combined Franchise Tax Return.

¶934 Farmers' School Tax Credit

Law: Sec. 210(22), Tax Law (CCH NEW YORK TAX REPORTS, ¶12-128).

Forms: CT-47, Claim for Farmers' School Tax Credit.

A credit for allowable school district property taxes is allowed to taxpayers if at least two-thirds of their federal gross income in excess of $30,000 is from farming (Sec. 210(22), Tax Law). In addition to traditional agricultural income, "federal gross income from farming" for purposes of the credit includes income from the production of maple syrup or cider, from a commercial horse boarding operation, from the sale of wine from a licensed farm winery, or from a managed Christmas tree operation (Sec. 210(22)(i), Tax Law). For tax years beginning after 2010, for otherwise-eligible farmers, payments from the New York farmland protection program will be included as federal gross income from farming. (Sec. 210(22)(b), Tax Law)

CCH Advisory: Income Averaging Allowed

A taxpayer may use the average of federal gross income from farming for the tax year and the income from farming for the two immediately preceding tax years for purposes of determining the taxpayer's eligibility to receive the agricultural property tax credit (Sec. 210.22, Tax Law; TSB-M-03(7)C, December 16, 2003, CCH NEW YORK TAX REPORTS, ¶300-410).

Definition: "Qualified agricultural property" means land located in New York that is used in agricultural production, plus land improvements, structures, and buildings (excluding buildings used for the taxpayer's residential purpose) that are located on the land and that are used or occupied to carry out production. The term also includes land set aside or retired under a federal supply management or soil conservation program or land that is subject to a conservation easement. (Sec. 210(22)(d), Tax Law)

CCH Advisory: Contract to Purchase Agricultural Land

The credit may be claimed by taxpayers that are farmers and that pay school district property taxes under a contract to buy agricultural land in the future. This allows a farmer that is the actual property taxpayer but not yet the taxpayer of record for agricultural land to claim the credit.

Credit amount: The credit equals the total school property taxes paid on qualified agricultural property in New York up to 350 acres, plus 50% of the school taxes paid on acreage in excess of 350 acres. (Sec. 210(22), Tax Law)

Note: This credit is not subject to the deferral of business tax credits for tax years 2010, 2011, and 2012. (Secs. 33, 34, Tax Law; TSB-M-10(5)C, New York Department of Taxation and Finance, September 13, 2010, CCH NEW YORK TAX REPORTS, ¶406-976)

Limitations and carryovers: The credit phases out for taxpayers with New York entire net income in excess of $200,000.

No credit will be allowed in an amount that reduces the taxpayer's liability to less than the minimum taxable income base (repealed for taxable years beginning after 2014) or fixed dollar minimum. Excess credits may be carried forward to subsequent years or, at the election of the taxpayer, treated as an overpayment of tax to be credited or refunded.

The shareholders of an eligible C corporation may elect to take into account their pro rata shares of the corporation's income and principal payments on farm indebtedness (see ¶130). In such case, the farm income of the C corporation is zero (Sec. 210(22)(j), Tax Law).

Conversion of property to nonqualified use: No credit will be allowed for any taxable year in which qualified agricultural property is converted by a taxpayer to a nonqualified use. If property is converted to a nonqualified use within two years following the taxable year for which the credit was first claimed, credits allowed for the prior years must be recaptured and added back to the conversion year. If the property converted to a nonqualified use includes land, and the conversion is of only a portion of such land, the credit allowed with respect to converted property must be determined by multiplying the entire credit for the taxable years prior to the conversion year by a fraction, the numerator of which is the acreage converted and the denominator of which is the entire acreage of the land owned by the taxpayer immediately prior to the conversion. No recapture will be required if the conversion is involuntary within the meaning of IRC Sec. 1033.

Forms: The credit is claimed by filing Form CT-47 with Form CT-3, the General Business Corporation Franchise Tax Return, or Form CT-3-A, the General Business Corporation Combined Franchise Tax Return.

¶935 Alternative Fuel Vehicle Refueling and Electric Vehicle Recharging Property Credit

Law: Secs. 187-b, 210(24), Tax Law (CCH NEW YORK TAX REPORTS, ¶12-080).

Forms: CT-40, Claim for Alternative Fuels Credit.

A credit is available for investment in alternative fuel vehicle refueling property and/or electric vehicle recharging property for tax years beginning on or after January 1, 2013, but before January 1, 2018 (Sec. 210(24), Tax Law). For property placed in service in taxable years beginning before January 1, 2005, an alternative fuels credit was also available for expenditures on electric vehicles, qualified hybrid vehicles, and clean-fuel vehicles. (Former Sec. 210(24)(a), Tax Law). Although those credits have expired, unused credits previously earned may be carried forward until used (*TSB-M-06(3)C*, CCH NEW YORK TAX REPORTS, ¶300-510).

Caution: For tax years 2010, 2011, and 2012, taxpayers with more than $2 million in aggregated alternative fuels tax credits were required to defer the amounts above $2 million until 2013. The total amount of credits deferred was paid back to taxpayers over tax years 2013, 2014, and 2015 (Sec. 33.1, Tax Law; Sec. 34.1, Tax Law; *TSB-M-10(5)(C)*, September 13, 2010, CCH NEW YORK TAX REPORTS, ¶406-976).

To qualify, the alternative fuel vehicle refueling property or electric vehicle recharging property must have been placed in service in New York, and none of the cost may been paid by grants awarded before January 1, 2015, including grants from the New York state energy research and development authority or the New York power authority (Sec. 210(24)(b), Tax Law).

"Alternative fuel vehicle refueling property" means all of the equipment needed to dispense any fuel at least 85% of the volume of which consists of one or more of the following: natural gas, liquified natural gas, liquified petroleum, or hydrogen. (Sec. 210(24)(c), Tax Law).

¶935

"Electric vehicle recharging property" means all of the equipment needed to convey electric power from the electric grid or another power source to an onboard vehicle energy storage system (Sec. 210(24)(c), Tax Law).

Credit amount: The credit for each installation of alternative fuel vehicle refueling property and electric vehicle recharging property is the lesser of $5,000 or 50% of the cost of the property (less any grants) that is placed in service in New York State during a taxable year beginning on or after January 1, 2013, but before January 1, 2018 (Sec. 210(24)(b), Tax Law). Multiple examples demonstrating how to correctly calculate the credit are found in *TSB-M-13(5)C, (3)I,* CCH NEW YORK TAX REPORTS, ¶ 407-879.

Planning considerations: To qualify for the credit, the property must be used more than 50% in a trade or business carried on by the taxpayer in New York State. Accordingly, the credit would not be allowed for a recharging system installed at an individual's residence and used solely to charge his or her personal automobile. (Sec. 210(24)(c), Tax Law)

Alternative fuel vehicle refueling property and electric vehicle recharging property ceases to be qualified if:

— the property no longer qualifies as alternative fuel vehicle refueling property or electric vehicle recharging property;

— 50% or more of the use of the property in a tax year is other than in a trade or business in New York State; or

— the taxpayer receiving the credit sells or disposes of the property and knows or has reason to know that the property will no longer qualify as alternative fuel vehicle refueling property or electric vehicle recharging property, or that 50% or more of the use of the property in a tax year will be other than in a trade or business in New York State.

If alternative fuel vehicle refueling property or electric vehicle recharging property ceases to be qualified at any time before the end of its recovery period, a recapture amount must be added back in the year in which the cessation occurs. The recovery period is the depreciable life of the property.

For corporations taxable under Secs. 183 and 184, Tax Law, the credit is first applied against the tax imposed under Sec. 183. The credit may not reduce the tax under Sec 183 below the minimum tax. Any excess is then applied against the tax imposed by Sec. 184. For corporations taxable under Sec. 185, the credit cannot reduce the tax below the minimum tax.

For corporations taxable under Article 9-A, the credit cannot reduce the tax below the higher of the tax on the minimum taxable income base (repealed for taxable years beginning after 2014) or the fixed dollar minimum tax. For Article 22 taxpayers, the amount of credit may reduce the tax to zero. (*TSB-M-13(5)C, (3)I,* CCH NEW YORK TAX REPORTS, ¶ 407-879)

Forms: Article 9 and Article 9-A corporation taxpayers claim the credit by filing Form CT-637, Alternative Fuels and Electric Vehicle Recharging Property Credit, with their franchise tax return. New York S corporations claim this credit by filing Form CT-637, showing the total amount of credit. The New York S corporation must provide each shareholder with information about his or her share of the credit from the S corporation.

Personal income tax taxpayers claim this credit by filing Form IT-637, Alternative Fuels and Electric Vehicle Recharging Property Credit, with their personal income tax return. Partnerships claim this credit by filing Form IT-637, showing the total amount of the credit. Partnerships must provide each partner with information about the partner's share of the credit from the partnership.

¶935

¶936 Emerging Technology Credits

Law: Secs. 28, 210(12-E), (12-F), (12-G), Tax Law; Sec. 3102-e, Public Authorities Law (CCH NEW YORK TAX REPORTS, ¶ 12-085, 12-085a).

Forms: DTF-621, Claim for QETC Employment Credit; Form DTF-622, Claim for QETC Capital Tax Credit.

Three credits are available to qualified emerging technology companies under the New York State Emerging Industry Jobs Act.

Caution: For tax years 2010, 2011, and 2012, taxpayers with more than $2 million in aggregated business tax credits were required to defer the amounts above $2 million until 2013. The total amount of credits deferred was paid back to taxpayers over tax years 2013, 2014, and 2015 (Sec. 33.1, Tax Law; Sec. 34.1, Tax Law; *TSB-M-10(5)(C)*, September 13, 2010, CCH NEW YORK TAX REPORTS, ¶ 406-976).

• *Definition of "qualified emerging technology company"*

A "qualified emerging technology company" (QETC) is a company located in New York that has total annual product sales of $10 million or less and that either (1) has its primary products or services that are classified as emerging technologies under the Public Authorities Law, or (2) has research and development activities in New York and a ratio of research and development funds to net sales that equals or exceeds the average ratio for companies surveyed by the National Science Foundation. (Sec. 3102-e, Public Authorities Law)

The credits include "remanufacturing" technologies, which are processes by which eligible commodities are restored to their original performance standards and diverted from the solid waste stream.

CCH Advisory: Research and Development Activities

Research and development activities that may qualify a company for the emerging technology credits include both basic and applied research in the sciences and engineering, but exclude research and development in the social sciences.

The average ratio of research and development funds to net sales is 3.0 (*TSB-M-99(2)C*, Department of Taxation and Finance, March 15, 1999, CCH NEW YORK TAX REPORTS, ¶ 300-281).

• *Qualified emerging technology employment credit*

To qualify for the credit, a QETC must employ at least 101% of its "base year employment," defined as the average number of individuals employed full-time by the QETC in New York during the three taxable years immediately preceding the first taxable year in which the credit is claimed. (Sec. 210(12-E), Tax Law)

Amount of credit: The credit is $1,000 for each employee in excess of the base year employment, and it may be claimed for three consecutive years. For tax years beginning after 2004, if the credit reduces the tax to the minimum (*i.e.*, the greater of the minimum taxable income amount (repealed for taxable years beginning after 2014) or the fixed dollar minimum for the taxable year), the excess credit amount will be treated as an overpayment to be credited or refunded without interest. (Sec. 210(12-E)(d), Tax Law)

Caution: For tax years 2010, 2011, and 2012, taxpayers with more than $2 million in aggregated business tax credits were required to defer the amounts above $2 million until 2013. The total amount of credits deferred was paid back to taxpayers over tax years 2013, 2014, and 2015. (Secs. 33, 34, Tax Law; TSB-M-10(5)C, New York Department of Taxation and Finance, September 13, 2010, CCH NEW YORK TAX REPORTS, ¶ 406-976)

• *QETC capital credit*

The credit is allowed for qualified investments in a QETC. A "qualified invest-ment" is the contribution of property to a corporation, partnership, or other business entity in exchange for stock or another ownership interest. (Sec. 210(12-F), Tax Law)

Amount of credit: The credit may be either 10% or 20% of qualified investments, with the applicable percentage depending upon the period (four years or nine years) for which the taxpayer certifies to the Commission that the investments will not be sold, transferred, traded, or disposed of. (Sec. 210(12-F)(a), Tax Law) The credit may not reduce the tax liability below the greater of the fixed dollar minimum or the minimum taxable income amount (repealed for taxable years beginning after 2014), nor may it reduce the tax otherwise due by more than 50%. Although the excess credit may be carried forward for an unlimited number of years, the total amount of credit that a taxpayer may claim for all taxable years is limited to either $150,000 or $300,000, again depending upon the certified holding period.

Caution: For tax years 2010, 2011, and 2012, taxpayers with more than $2 million in aggregated business tax credits were required to defer the amounts above $2 million until 2013. The total amount of credits deferred was paid back to taxpayers over tax years 2013, 2014, and 2015. (Secs. 33, 34, Tax Law; *TSB-M-10(5)C*, New York Department of Taxation and Finance, September 13, 2010, CCH New York Tax Reports, ¶406-976)

Recapture: The credit is subject to full or partial recapture if the investment is not held for the entire certified holding period.

For four-year property disposed of within 12 months of the taxable year for which the credit is allowed, 100% of the portion of the credit attributable to the property disposed of must be recaptured. The recapture is 75% if the property is disposed of in the second year after the taxable year in which the credit is allowed, 50% if the property is disposed of in the third year, and 25% if the property is disposed of in the fourth year.

For nine-year property disposed of within 12 months of the taxable year for which the credit is allowed, 100% of the portion of the credit attributable to the property disposed of must be recaptured. The recapture is 80% if the property is disposed of in the second, third, or fourth year after the taxable year in which the credit is allowed, 60% if the property is disposed of in the fifth or sixth year, 40% if the property is disposed of in the seventh or eighth year, and 20% if the property is disposed of in the ninth year.

• *Credit for QETC facilities, operations, and training*

Eligible taxpayers may qualify for a refundable credit with three components relating to certain research and development (R&D) property, research expenses, and high-technology training expenditures. An eligible taxpayer (1) may have no more than 100 employees, at least 75% of which are employed in New York State, (2) must have a ratio of research and development funds to net sales at least equal to 6% during the taxable year, and (3) may have gross revenues of no more than $20 million for the taxable year prior to the year the credit is claimed. (Sec. 210(12-G)(a), Tax Law)

Credit amount: The credit is the sum of the following amounts: (1) 18% of expenditures for R&D property used for testing, inspection, or quality control; (2) 9% of "qualified research expenses"; and (3) up to $4,000 per employee of "qualified high-technology training expenditures". (Sec. 210(12-G)(b)-(d), Tax Law)

Caution: For tax years 2010, 2011, and 2012, taxpayers with more than $2 million in aggregated QETC facilities, operations, and training tax credits were required to defer the amounts above $2 million until 2013. The total amount of credits deferred was paid back to taxpayers over tax years 2013, 2014, and 2015 (Sec. 33.1, Tax Law; Sec. 34.1, Tax Law; *TSB-M-10(5)(C)*, September 13, 2010, CCH New York Tax Reports, ¶406-976).

Planning considerations: An eligible taxpayer may generally claim the credits for four consecutive years, but one additional year is allowed for a taxpayer that is located in an academic incubator facility and relocates within New York to a nonacademic incubator site. The value of the credits may not exceed $250,000 per eligible taxpayer per year. (Sec. 606(nn)(f), Tax Law)

If a taxpayer is a partner in a partnership or a shareholder of a New York S corporation, then the $250,000 annual cap is applied at the entity level, so that the aggregate credit allowed to all of the partners or shareholders of each such entity in a taxable year will not exceed the cap amount (Sec. 28, Tax Law).

¶937 Automated External Defibrillator Credit

Law: Sec. 210(25), Tax Law (CCH New York Tax Reports, ¶12-115).

Forms: CT-250, Claim for Purchase of an Automated External Defibrillator.

A credit may be taken for the purchase of automated external defibrillators, such as those used for first-aid treatment of heart attacks. (Sec. 210(25), Tax Law)

Credit amount: The credit is equal to the cost of each defibrillator purchased, but may not exceed $500 per unit.

The credit may not reduce the tax below the greater of the minimum taxable income base (repealed for taxable years beginning after 2014) or the fixed dollar minimum, and there is no provision for carryover.

Caution: For tax years 2010, 2011, and 2012, taxpayers with more than $2 million in aggregated business tax credits were required to defer the amounts above $2 million until 2013. The total amount of credits deferred was paid back to taxpayers over tax years 2013, 2014, and 2015 (Sec. 33.1, Tax Law; Sec. 34.1, Tax Law; *TSB-M-10(5)(C)*, September 13, 2010, CCH New York Tax Reports, ¶406-976).

Forms: The credit is claimed on Form CT-250.

¶938 Economic Transformation and Facility Redevelopment Program Credits

Law: Sec. 400 *et seq.*, Economic Development Law; Sec. 35, Tax Law; Reg. Secs. 200.1 *et seq.* (CCH New York Tax Reports, ¶12-070c).

The Economic Transformation and Facility Redevelopment Program provides a fully refundable credit available to personal income taxpayers, agricultural cooperatives, general business corporations, banks, and insurance companies and consisting of four components (Sec. 35, Tax Law):

— *Jobs tax credit component:* 6.85% of the gross wages of each net new job created;

— *Investment tax credit (ITC) component:* 10% of the cost of investments at a closed facility, with a facility-based cap of $8 million; 6% of the cost of investments elsewhere in an ETA, with a cap of $4 million per entity (if the participant is a partnership, a limited liability company, or an S corporation, the $4 million limitation is applied at the entity level);

— *Job training credit component:* 50% of training expenses for employees displaced by a facility closure, up to $4,000 per employee per year (the employees for whom the expenditures are made must be employed in a full-time, full-year position primarily located at the site in the economic transformation area during the training, and for 180 days after its completion); and

— *Real property tax credit component (RPTC):* 50% of real property taxes for projects located entirely within the grounds of a closed facility, declining by 10% a year; 25% of real property taxes for projects elsewhere in an ETA, declining by 5% a year.

To be eligible for the economic transformation and facility redevelopment program tax credit, the taxpayer must meet all the following requirements (Sec. 35, Tax Law):

— The taxpayer must be a participant or the owner of a participant in the economic transformation and facility development program. The commissioner of economic development must have issued a certificate of to the taxpayer or to an entity in which the taxpayer is an owner. A copy of the certificate is required to be attached to the taxpayer's report or return.

— The taxpayer or the entity in which the taxpayer is an owner must be a qualified new business.

— The taxpayer or the entity in which the taxpayer is an owner must create and maintain at least five net new jobs in the economic transformation area.

Planning considerations: The benefit period for the tax credits is five consecutive taxable years, beginning with the first taxable year in which the five net new jobs are created. However, in no event may that benefit period start later than two years after the certificate of eligibility is issued. If, in any year of the benefit period, the taxpayer fails to maintain the required level of five net new jobs (measured quarterly), the taxpayer will not be allowed a credit for that year. Such failure to be allowed a credit will not extend the taxpayer's benefit period. (Sec. 35, Tax Law)

If the participant at the end of its benefit period has not created sufficient net new jobs and made sufficient qualified investments to achieve a benefit-cost ratio of at least 10 to one, the taxpayer will be required to add back as tax in the last year of its benefit period the portion of the economic transformation and facility redevelopment tax credits claimed in the years of its benefit period necessary to achieve a cost benefit ratio of 10 to one. (Sec. 35, Tax Law)

The program is scheduled to expire on December 31, 2021.

The program is administered by Empire State Development (ESD). Application materials are available at **http://esd.ny.gov/index.html**.

¶939 Long-Term Care Insurance Credit

Law: Sec. 210(25-a), Tax Law (CCH NEW YORK TAX REPORTS, ¶ 12-115a).

Forms: CT-249, Claim for Long-Term Care Insurance Credit.

A credit is allowed for long-term care insurance premiums paid for a policy or for continuing coverage under a policy during the taxable year. (Sec. 210(25-a), Tax Law)

• *Credit amount*

The credit is equal to 20% of the premium payments during the taxable year (Sec. 210(25-a), Tax Law).

Note: This credit is not subject to the deferral of business tax credits for tax years 2010, 2011, and 2012. (Secs. 33, 34, Tax Law; TSB-M-10(5)C, New York Department of Taxation and Finance, September 13, 2010, CCH NEW YORK TAX REPORTS, ¶ 406-976; TSB-M-10(5)C, New York Department of Taxation and Finance, September 13, 2010, CCH NEW YORK TAX REPORTS, ¶ 406-976)

• *Planning considerations*

Limitations and carryovers: In order to qualify for the credit, the taxpayer's premium payment generally must be for a long-term care insurance policy approved by the Superintendent of Insurance. However, certain group contracts delivered or issued for delivery outside New York will be deemed to qualify for purposes of the credit without the need to seek the Superintendent's approval.

The credit may not reduce the tax below the tax payable on either the minimum taxable income (repealed for taxable years beginning after 2014) or the fixed dollar minimum. However, any amount remaining may be carried forward indefinitely.

¶940 Excelsior Jobs Program

Law: Sec. 350 *et seq.,* Economic Development Law; Secs. 31, 187-q, and 210(41), Tax Law; Reg Secs. 190.1—196.6 (CCH NEW YORK TAX REPORTS, ¶ 12-070b).

Forms: CT-607.

The Excelsior Jobs Program, administered by Empire State Development (ESD), provides job creation and investment incentives to firms in targeted industries, including biotechnology, pharmaceuticals, clean technology, green technology, financial services, agriculture and agricultural cooperatives, and manufacturing.

The 2015-16 budget law (Ch. 59 (A.B. 3009), Laws 2015) expands eligibility under the Excelsior Jobs Program to include certain business entities operating in music production or as an entertainment company. "Entertainment company" is defined to include entities principally engaged in the production or post-production of motion pictures, instructional videos, televised commercial advertisements, animated films or cartoons, music videos, television programs, or programs primarily intended for radio broadcast. Certain types of companies are specifically excluded (*e.g.,* those principally engaged in the live performance of events) (Sec. 352(7), Econ. Dev. Law). "Music production" means the process of creating sound recordings of at least eight minutes, recorded in professional sound studios, and intended for commercial release; the term does not include live concert recordings, recordings that are primarily spoken word or wildlife or nature sounds, or recordings produced for instructional use or advertising or promotional purposes. (Sec. 352(11), Econ. Dev. Law)

There are specific job requirements for each industry. The determination of whether a business is operating predominantly in a named industry will be made solely on the activity at the project location without regard to operations at other locations in New York. (Sec. 31, Tax Law; Sec. 210(41), Tax Law; Sec. 353, Economic Development Law; Sec. 354(5), Economic Development Law):

The program includes the following corporate franchise, bank franchise, insurance franchise, and personal income tax credits (Sec. 31, Tax Law; Sec. 355, Economic Development Law):

— a jobs tax credit in the amount of 6.85% of gross wages for each net new job, effective March 31, 2011 (previously, up to $5,000 per job);

— an investment tax credit, equal to 2% of qualified investments;

— a 50% research and development credit, based on the federal credit, up to 3% of R&D expenditures (10%, with no cap, prior to March 31, 2011); and

— a real property tax credit.

Under 2011-2012 budget legislation (Ch. 61 (S.B. 2811), Laws 2011, effective March 31, 2011), the tax benefit period of the jobs program is extended from five years to 10 years. The legislation made several other changes, as noted. See also *TSB-M-11(6)C,* New York Department of Taxation and Finance, June 8, 2011, CCH NEW YORK TAX REPORTS, ¶ 407-280.

Beginning in 2015, the definition of "net new jobs" is expanded to include jobs obtained by an entertainment company in New York (1) as a result of the termination of a licensing agreement with another entertainment company, (2) that are at risk of leaving the state as a direct result of the termination, (3) that are either full-time wage-paying jobs or equivalent to full-time wage-paying jobs requiring at least 35 hours per week, and (4) that are filled for more than six months. (Sec. 352(12)(b), Econ. Dev. Law)

The 2016-17 budget package provides that 100% of the unawarded amounts remaining at the end of 2024 may be allocated in subsequent years (Sec. 354(5). Econ. Dev. Law). However, no tax credits are allowed for taxable years beginning on or after January 1, 2027. In addition, the maximum aggregate credit components are reduced from $200 million to $183 million for 2016 through 2021, from $150 million to $133 million for 2022, from $100 million to $83 million for 2023, and from $50 million to $36 million for 2024 (Sec. 359. Econ. Dev. Law).

• *Credit amounts*

Jobs tax credit: The value of the jobs credit is 6.85% of gross wages for each net new job created in New York (Sec. 355(1), Tax Law). Taxpayers generally must create at least 25 new jobs, but the threshold is reduced to ten jobs for businesses accepted into the START-UP NY program (see ¶923). In addition, a taxpayer that creates at least 75% of the estimated jobs will be allowed a proportionally reduced credit (Sec. 354(5), Econ. Dev. Law).

A business entity operating predominately in music production must create at least five net new jobs, and a business entity operating predominantly as an entertainment company must create or obtain at least 100 net new jobs (Sec. 353(3), Econ. Dev. Law).

Investment tax credit: The EJP-ITC is equal to 2% of the cost of qualified investments which are, generally, depreciable property located in New York with a useful life of four or more years. The property must be placed in service on or after the date the ESD issues the taxpayer a certificate of qualification.

Research and development credit: The EJP-R&D credit is equal to 10% of the amount of the taxpayer's federal R&D credit for qualified expenditures attributable to New York. Qualified expenditures are as set forth in IRC Sec. 41. A participant in the Excelsior Jobs Program may claim both the Excelsior investment tax credit component and the investment tax credit for research and development property, based on expenditures on the same property (TSB-M-11(6)C, New York Department of Taxation and Finance, June 8, 2011, CCH New York Tax Reports, ¶407-280).

Real property tax credit: The EJP-RPTC credit equals 50% of the property taxes assessed and paid in the year immediately prior to the taxpayer's application to the ESD and declines by 5% each year for ten years. Property improvements that increase the value of real property are factored into the amount of the RPTC component. This credit is also. refundable. It is available for projects in areas that are either (1) formerly designated as Investment Zones under the Empire Zones program, or (2) "regionally significant", as defined in Sec. 352(16), Econ. Dev. Law.

Effective March 31, 2011, the real property tax credit (RPTC) component schedule was amended to phase down from 50% to 5% over 10 years (5% each year) instead of five years (10% each year), reflecting the lengthening of the benefit period. Also, costs and expenses included in the basis of the Excelsior R&D credit component are allowed to be used for the qualified emerging technology company facilities, operations, and training credit (see ¶940).

• *Planning considerations*

Taxpayers must apply to ESD, which can issue up to $50 million in new credit certificates annually against a total annual program cost of $250 million.

All four of the credits are refundable. (Part MM, Ch. 59 (A.B. 9709), Laws 2010)

A business that is certified to receive Empire Zone credits will only be required to give up its Empire Zone certification at the location where it will claim Excelsior benefits rather than at all its locations. A taxpayer that had Empire Zone credits and was subsequently accepted into the Excelsior Jobs Program was allowed to claim both benefits because the EZ benefits at issue were earned prior to the taxpayer's acceptance into the Excelsior Jobs Program, and therefore no possibility of double-dipping existed (*TSB-A-13(8)C*, August 30, 2013, CCH New York Tax Reports, ¶407-910).

¶940

¶941 Low-Income Housing Credit

Law: Secs. 18, 210(30), Tax Law; Secs. 21(5), 22, Public Housing Law (CCH NEW YORK TAX REPORTS, ¶ 12-105).

Comparable Federal: Sec. 42 (U.S. MASTER TAX GUIDE, ¶ 1334).

Forms: DTF-624, Low-Income Housing Credit; DTF-625, Low-Income Housing Credit Allocation Certification; DTF-625-ATT, Low-Income Housing Annual Statement.

A credit is allowed for the construction or rehabilitation of qualified low-income housing. (Sec. 18, Tax Law; Sec. 210(30), Tax Law)

Qualified housing: Generally, the credit is allowed for the construction of rent-restricted housing in New York that qualifies for the federal low-income housing credit.

CCH Advisory: Difference from Federal Credit

The federal credit (IRC Sec. 42) requires that a project be rent-restricted, and that either (1) at least 20% of the residential units of a project must be occupied by tenants whose income is 50% or less of area median gross income, or (2) at least 40% of the units must be occupied by tenants whose income is 60% of the area median. However, the New York credit may be claimed if the project either meets the federal requirements or if it is rent-restricted and at least 40% of the residential units are occupied by tenants whose income is 90% or less of area median gross income.

The credit may be passed on to successor owners of low-income buildings that already receive the credit.

• *Credit amount*

The amount of the credit is the applicable percentage of the qualified basis of each eligible low-income building. Eligible low-income housing buildings cannot receive in the aggregate more than a specified amount in credit. The cap amount is $64 million in 2016-17, and is being increased over a five-year period to $104 million. (Sec. 22, Public Housing Law) The Commissioner may set a limit on the amount of credit each low-income building may receive.

The credit amount allocated to a project will be allowed each year for 10 years.

• *Planning considerations*

Limitations are generally the same as for claiming the federal credit.

The credit and any carryovers may not reduce the tax below the tax payable on either the minimum taxable income (repealed for taxable years beginning after 2014) or the fixed dollar minimum. However, any amount remaining may be carried forward indefinitely.

Caution: For tax years 2010, 2011, and 2012, taxpayers with more than $2 million in aggregated business tax credits were required to defer the amounts above $2 million until 2013. The total amount of credits deferred was paid back to taxpayers over tax years 2013, 2014, and 2015 (Sec. 33.1, Tax Law; Sec. 34.1, Tax Law; *TSB-M-10(5)(C)*, September 13, 2010, CCH NEW YORK TAX REPORTS, ¶ 406-976).

Recapture: The project must continue to qualify as low-income housing for a 15-year period in order to avoid partial recapture of the credit. (Sec. 21(2), Public Housing Law; Sec. 18, Tax Law)

Forms: The credit is claimed on Form DTF-624.

¶942 Green Building Credit

Law: Secs. 19, 210(31), Tax Law (CCH NEW YORK TAX REPORTS, ¶ 12-080a).

Comparable Federal: Sec. 48 (U.S. MASTER TAX GUIDE, ¶ 1351).

Forms: DTF-630, Claim for Green Building Credit.

A green building tax credit is available to enhance the supply of environmentally sound buildings in New York. (Sec. 19. Tax Law; Sec. 210(31), Tax Law) The credit includes six components, which are based on the capitalized costs (excluding land costs) of constructing green buildings, rehabilitating buildings to become green buildings, and purchasing and installing fuel cells, photovoltaic modules, and environmentally sensitive non-ozone depleting refrigerants.

The credit may be claimed over a five-year period by owners or tenants of eligible buildings, or by successor owners or tenants. In the year of a sale or termination of tenancy, the credit amount is allocated between the former and successor owners or tenants based upon the number of days during the year that the building was used by each.

Eligible buildings: A building or project must contain at least 20,000 square feet of interior space and must not require a federal or state construction permit because it is located on wetlands. In addition, the building must be:

— classified b2, b3, b4, c1, c2, c5, or c6 for purposes of the New York State Uniform Fire Prevention and Building Code; or

— a residential multi-family building with at least 12 dwelling units; or

— one or more residential multi-family buildings with at least two dwelling units that are part of a single or phased construction project; or

— any combination of buildings described above.

Certifications: A taxpayer claiming the credit must obtain from the New York State Department of Environmental Conservation (DEC) an initial credit component certification, as well as an eligibility certification for each year in which the credit is claimed.

• *Credit amount*

The maximum amount of the credit for each component is specified in the initial credit component certification. The maximum amounts that may be claimed in each of the five years are as follows:

— *Green whole-building credit component:* 1.4% of allowable costs (1.6%, if the building is located in an economic development area), but not to exceed aggregate costs of $150 per square foot for the base building and $75 per square foot for tenant space (Sec. 19(a)(2), Tax Law);

— *Green base building credit component:* 1% of allowable costs (1.2%, if the building is located in an economic development area), but not to exceed aggregate costs of $150 per square foot (Sec. 19(a)(3), Tax Law);

— *Green tenant space credit component:* 1% of allowable costs (1.2%, if the building is located in an economic development area), but not to exceed aggregate costs of $75 per square foot (Sec. 19(a)(4), Tax Law);

— *Fuel cell credit component:* 6% of allowable costs, but not to exceed aggregate costs of $1,000 per kilowatt (Sec. 19(a)(5), Tax Law);

— *Photovoltaic module credit component:* 20% of the incremental costs of a building-integrated module or 5% of the cost of a nonintegrated module, but not to exceed aggregate costs of $3 per watt (Sec. 19(a)(6), Tax Law);

— *Green refrigerant component:* 2% of the cost of air conditioning equipment using a non-ozone depleting refrigerant (Sec. 19(a)(7), Tax Law).

¶942

Caution: For tax years 2010, 2011, and 2012, taxpayers with more than $2 million in aggregated business tax credits were required to defer the amounts above $2 million until 2013. The total amount of credits deferred was paid back to taxpayers over tax years 2013, 2014, and 2015 (Sec. 33.1, Tax Law; Sec. 34.1, Tax Law; *TSB-M-10(5)(C)*, September 13, 2010, CCH NEW YORK TAX REPORTS, ¶ 406-976).

• *Planning considerations*

Credit component certifications are limited to $25 million, and aggregate dollar limitations apply to each year through 2014.

The credit and any carryovers may not reduce the tax below the tax payable on either the minimum taxable income (repealed for taxable years beginning after 2014) or the fixed dollar minimum. However, any amount remaining may be carried forward indefinitely.

Forms: The credit is claimed on Form DTF-630.

¶943 Brownfield Cleanup Program Credits

Law: Secs. 21, 22, and 23, Tax Law; Sec. 210 (33), (34), (35), Tax Law (CCH NEW YORK TAX REPORTS, ¶ 12-080b).

Three brownfield credits may be taken against New York corporate franchise (income) tax (Art. 9-A), personal income tax (Art. 22), corporation and utility taxes (Art. 9), bank franchise (income) tax (Art. 32), and insurance franchise (income) tax (Art. 33). The credits are available to taxpayers that own or develop a qualified site pursuant to a brownfield cleanup agreement with the Department of Environmental Conservation (DEC) for which a certificate of completion has been issued to the taxpayer by the DEC. Any excess credit amounts will be refunded. (Secs. 21, 22, and 23, Tax Law; Sec. 210 (33), (34), (35), Tax Law; *TSB-M-08(13)C* and *TSB-M-08(8)I*, December 23, 2008, CCH NEW YORK TAX REPORTS, ¶ 406-260; see also, *Publication 300*, New York Department of Taxation and Finance, July 2014)

Caution: For tax years 2010, 2011, and 2012, taxpayers with more than $2 million in aggregated business tax credits were required to defer the amounts above $2 million until 2013. The total amount of credits deferred was paid back to taxpayers over tax years 2013, 2014, and 2015 (Sec. 33.1, Tax Law; Sec. 34.1, Tax Law; *TSB-M-10(5)(C)*, September 13, 2010, CCH NEW YORK TAX REPORTS, ¶ 406-976).

The following changes became effective July 1, 2015:

— the definition of a "brownfield site" includes any real property where a contaminant is present at levels greater than the soil clean-up objectives or other health-based or environmental standards, criteria or guidance;

— amounts paid to related parties are excluded when calculating the tangible property credit component, but related-party service fees may be included in the calculation;

— the number of days to execute an environmental easement is changed from "within 60" to "within 180" days of commencement of the remedial design for owners of inactive hazardous waste disposal sites; and

— taxpayers wishing to claim tax credits under the program for any sites accepted on or before December 31, 2022, must have received the required certificate of completion on or before March 31, 2026.

• *Brownfield redevelopment credit*

The amount of the brownfield redevelopment tax credit equals the sum of the following three components: (1) site preparation; (2) tangible property; and (3) on-site groundwater remediation (Secs. 21, 210(33), Tax Law). The site preparation component equals the applicable percentage of the site preparation costs paid or incurred by the taxpayer with respect to a qualified site. The tangible property credit component equals the applicable percentage of the cost or other basis for federal income tax purposes of tangible personal property and other tangible property, including buildings and structural components of buildings, that constitute qualified tangible property. However, taxpayers must exclude the acquisition cost of any item of property with respect to which a credit was allowable to another taxpayer when determining the cost or other basis of such property. The on-site groundwater remediation component equals the applicable percentage of the on-site groundwater remediation costs paid or incurred by the taxpayer with respect to the qualified site.

In general, the applicable percentage for the tangible property component is 12% for corporation franchise (income) tax. However, the applicable percentage is increased by 8% if at least 50% of the qualified site is located in an environmental zone and increased by 2% if the site has been remediated to Track 1, which allows use for any purpose. If the qualified site is located in a brownfield opportunity area (BOA), an additional 2% is allowed. Qualified sites can only be deemed located in an environmental zone if they are the subject of a brownfield site cleanup agreement entered into before September 1, 2010 (Sec. 21(c), Tax Law). The applicable percentages are different for the site preparation credit component and the on-site groundwater remediation credit component for qualified sites accepted into the Brownfield Cleanup Program after June 23, 2008; see *TSB-M-08(13)C*, December 23, 2008, CCH New York Tax Reports, ¶ 406-260.

The amount of any grant received from the federal, state or local government by the taxpayer and used to pay for any of the costs described above, which was not included in the federal gross income of the taxpayer, is subtracted in computing the credit components.

The credit must be recaptured if the certificate of completion is revoked or the qualified property is disposed of or ceases to be in qualified use.

Practitioner Comment: New York Respects Special Allocations of Brownfields Remediation Credit

New York's Department of Taxation and Finance has held that it will respect a special allocation of the tangible personal property component of the Brownfields redevelopment tax credit that is based on the special allocation of the depreciation deductions between the members of a limited liability company. Critical to this determination were the following facts: (1) the LLC was classified as a partnership; (2) all of the members of the LLC were individuals or trusts already subject to New York State personal income tax or corporations subject to the New York State corporation franchise tax; and (3) the special allocation had substantial economic effect under the federal rules (TSB-A-09(7)C, 5/1309, CCH New York Tax Reports, ¶ 406-401).

Mark S. Klein, Hodgson Russ LLP

• *Credit for remediated brownfields*

The remediated brownfield credit for real property taxes equals 25% of the product of the benefit period factor, the employment number factor and the eligible real property taxes paid or incurred by the developer of the qualified site during the taxable year. (Secs. 22, 210(34), Tax Law)

The benefit period factor is a numerical value corresponding with a benefit period of 10 consecutive taxable years commencing in the taxpayer's taxable year during which the certificate of completion is issued for the qualified site or the taxpayer's first taxable year commencing on or after April 1, 2005, whichever is later. The benefit period factor for the 10 years is 1.0.

The employment number factor is determined by the average number of full-time employees at the qualified site. If the average number of employees is at least 25 but less than 50, the factor is 0.25; at least 50 but less than 75 employees, the factor is 0.5; at least 75 but less than 100 employees, the factor is 0.75; and at least 100 employees, the factor is 1. The credit is limited to the product of $10,000 and the developer's average number of full-time employees.

For purposes of the credit, eligible real property taxes includes taxes imposed on real property which consists of a qualified site owned by the developer, provided such taxes become a lien on the real property in a period during which the real property is a qualified site.

The credit must be recaptured if a developer's eligible real property taxes that are the basis for the credit are subsequently reduced. The recapture amount equals the amount of the credit originally allowed for a taxable year over the amount of credit determined based on the reduced eligible real property taxes.

If the qualified site is located in an enterprise zone (¶929), and the taxpayer meets the eligibility requirements for both the remediated brownfield credit and the qualified empire zone enterprise (QEZE) credit for real property taxes (¶929), the taxpayer is not allowed to claim both credits. The taxpayer must elect which credit to claim.

— changing the definition of a "brownfield site" to include any real property where a contaminant is present at levels greater than the soil clean-up objectives or other health-based or environmental standards, criteria or guidance;

— excluding amounts paid to related parties when calculating the tangible property credit component, but clarifying that related-party service fees may be included in the calculation;

— amending the number of days to execute an environmental easement from within 60 to within 180 days of commencement of the remedial design for owners of inactive hazardous waste disposal sites; and

— clarifying that taxpayers wishing to claim tax credits under the Brownfield Clean-Up Program for any sites accepted on or before December 31, 2022, must have received the required certificate of completion on or before March 31, 2026.

• *Environmental remediation insurance credit*

The amount of the environmental remediation insurance credit equals the lesser of $30,000 or 50% of the environmental remediation insurance premiums paid on or after the date of the brownfield site agreement executed by the taxpayer and the Department of Environmental Conservation. (Secs. 23, 210(35), Tax Law) The credit is allowed for the tax year in which the certificate of completion is issued to the taxpayer. Also, the credit is allowed only once with respect to a particular certificate of completion. If the certificate of completion issued to the taxpayer is revoked by a determination, the credit amount is added back in the taxable year in which the determination is final and no longer subject to judicial review. Any excess credit amounts are credited or refunded.

¶944 Film Production Credit

Law: Secs. 24, 31, 210(36), Tax Law; Reg. Secs. 170.1 *et seq.* (CCH NEW YORK TAX REPORTS, ¶12-085b).

For tax years beginning after 2003 and before 2020, a credit is available to qualified film production companies for a portion of the qualified production costs of a qualified film. The credit is allowed for the taxable year in which the production of the qualified film is completed. (Sec. 24(a), Tax Law; Sec. 210(36), Tax Law)

• *Definitions*

"Qualified production costs" means production costs only to the extent such costs are attributable to the use of tangible property or the performance of services within New York directly and predominately in the production (including pre-production and post-production) of a qualified film. (Sec. 24(b)(1), Tax Law)

"Production costs" means costs for tangible property used and services performed directly and predominately in the production (including pre- and post-production) of a qualified film. Production costs generally include technical and crew production costs, such as expenditures for film production facilities, props, makeup, wardrobe, film processing, camera, sound recording, set construction, lighting, shooting, editing, and meals. (Sec. 24(b)(2), Tax Law)

Production costs do not include:

— costs for a story, script, or scenario to be used for a qualified film; and

— wages or salaries or other compensation for writers, directors, including music directors, producers, and performers (other than background actors with no scripted lines).

A "qualified film" is a feature-length film, television film, relocated television production, television pilot and/or each episode of a television series, regardless of the medium (Sec. 24(b)(3), Tax Law). A qualified film must have a minimum budget of $500,000 (Sec. 31(a)(5), Tax Law).

A qualified film does not include:

— a documentary film, news or current affairs program, interview or talk program, "how-to" (*i.e.*, instructional) film or program, film or program consisting primarily of stock footage, sporting event or sporting program, game show, award ceremony, film or program intended primarily for industrial, corporate or institutional end-users, fundraising film or program, daytime drama (*i.e.*, daytime soap opera), commercials, music videos or "reality programs"; or

— a production for which records are required to be maintained with respect to any performer in such production (reporting of books, films, etc. with respect to sexually explicit conduct).

A "qualified film production facility" is a film production facility in New York that contains at least one sound stage having a minimum of 7,000 square feet of contiguous production space.

A "qualified film production company" is a corporation, partnership, limited partnership, or other entity or individual principally engaged in the production of a qualified film and in control of the qualified film during production. Members of a partnership that is a qualified film production company may claim the credit.

• *Credit amount*

The amount of the credit is 30% of the qualified production costs paid or incurred in the production of a qualified film; provided that the qualified production costs (excluding post production costs) attributable to the use of tangible property or the performance of services at a qualified film production facility in the production of the qualified film equal or exceed 75% of the production costs (excluding post production costs) paid or incurred that are attributable to the use of tangible property or the performance of services at any film production facility within and without New York in the production of the qualified film. (Sec. 24(a)(2), Tax Law)

If the qualified production costs (excluding post production costs) attributable to the use of tangible property or the performance of services at a qualified film production facility in the production of the qualified film is less than $3 million, then the portion of the qualified productions costs attributable to the use of tangible property or the performance of services in the production of the qualified film outside of a qualified film production facility is allowed only if the shooting days spent in New York outside of a film production facility in the production of the qualified film equal or exceed 75% of the total shooting days spent within and without New York outside of a film production facility in the production of the qualified film. (Sec. 24(a)(2), Tax Law)

If the amount of the credit is between $1 million and $5 million, the credit is paid out in two equal installments over a two year period beginning in the taxable year in which the production of the qualified film is completed. If the credit is greater than $5 million, it is paid out in three equal installments in consecutive years beginning with the taxable year in which the production of the qualified film is completed.

Effective July 24, 2012, the qualified film and television post-production credit increased from 10% to 30% in the New York metropolitan commuter region, including New York City and Albany, Dutchess, Nassau, Orange, Putnam, Rockland, Schnectady, Suffolk and Westchester Counties (Sec. 31(a)(2), Tax Law). An additional 5% (for a total of 35%) in tax credits would be available for post-production expenditures in locations elsewhere in the state (Sec. 31(c), Tax Law).

Upstate credit enhancement: In 2015 through 2019, film and post production projects are eligible for an additional credit equal to 10% of the wages or salaries of individuals employed by a qualified film or independent film production company for services performed in specified counties (Sec. 24(a)(5), Tax Law).

Note: The film production credit was not subject to deferral of tax credits for tax years 2010, 2011, and 2012. (Secs. 33, 34, Tax Law; TSB-M-10(5)C, New York Department of Taxation and Finance, September 13, 2010, CCH New York Tax Reports, ¶ 406-976)

Maximum credit: The maximum amount of the credits allowed in any calendar year is $65 million in 2008, $75 million in 2009, $85 million in 2010, $90 million for both 2011 and 2012, and $110 million in 2013.

New York budget legislation in 2010 and 2013 provides $420 million annually over tax years 2010 through 2019, with $7 million of the annual allocation available for a separate post-production tax credit. Starting in 2015, the allocation dedicated to the post production credit increases from $7 million to $25 million annually.

• *Planning considerations*

If the amount of the credit allowable for any taxable year exceeds the taxpayer's tax for that year, the excess is treated as an overpayment of tax to be credited or refunded, with no interest. The balance of the credit not credited or refunded may be carried over to the immediately succeeding tax year and may be deducted from the taxpayer's tax for that year.

¶945 Credit for Fuel Cell Electric Generating Equipment (Expired)

Law: Sec. 210(37), Tax Law (CCH New York Tax Reports, ¶ 12-001).

For taxable years beginning before 2009, a credit was allowed for the cost of qualified fuel cell electric generating equipment for use by the taxpayer in New York (Sec. 210(37), Tax Law). The credit could not exceed $1,500 per generating unit for any tax year. Credits exceeding the tax due for a given year may be carried over to subsequent years.

¶946 Credit for Security Training

Law: Secs. 26, 210(37), Tax Law; Reg. Secs. 1000.1, 1000.2, and 1000.3 (CCH New York Tax Reports, ¶ 12-001).

Qualified building owners may claim a refundable security training tax credit. (Sec. 210(37), Tax Law)

• *Qualifications*

Qualified security officers must have completed a qualified security training program. (Sec. 26, Tax Law) "Qualified building owner" means a building owner whose building entrances, exits, and common areas are protected by security personnel licensed under Article 7-A of the General Business Law, whether or not such personnel are employed directly by the building owner or indirectly through a contractor.

• *Credit amount*

The credit amount equals the sum of the number of qualified security officers providing protection to buildings owned by the taxpayer, multiplied by $3,000. (Sec. 26, Tax Law) Any credit amount not deductible in a taxable year will be treated as an overpayment of tax to be credited or refunded without interest.

Caution: For tax years 2010, 2011, and 2012, taxpayers with more than $2 million in aggregated business tax credits were required to defer the amounts above $2 million until 2013. The total amount of credits deferred was paid back to taxpayers over tax years 2013, 2014, and 2015. (Secs. 33, 34, Tax Law; TSB-M-10(5)C, New York Department of Taxation and Finance, September 13, 2010, CCH NEW YORK TAX REPORTS, ¶ 406-976)

• *Planning considerations*

The New York Division of Homeland Security may issue credit certifications for taxpayers meeting the applicable standards and demonstrating that they have provided (or will provide within the year) the appropriate training to all employees for whom the credit will be claimed. (Sec. 26, Tax Law) Any credit amount not deductible in a taxable year will be treated as an overpayment of tax to be credited or refunded without interest. (Sec. 210(37), Tax Law)

The maximum aggregate amount of tax credits allowed in any calendar year will be $5 million.

Practitioner Comment: Security Guard Training Credit

In order to qualify for the security guard training credit, eligible building owners must obtain a certificate of tax credit from the New York State Division of Homeland Security. The certification process requires proof that each security guard received an hourly wage of at least $10.85 and that each guard satisfactorily completed the Division of Homeland Security 40-hour Certified Enhanced Security Guard Training Program. Information on training classes and applications for the credit can be found on New York's Division of Homeland Security and Emergency Services website at **www.dhses.ny.gov**. The credit is claimed on Form IT-631.

Mark S. Klein, Esq., Hodgson Russ LLP

¶947 Credit for Disabled-Accessible Vehicles

Law: Sec. 210-B(38), Tax Law (CCH NEW YORK TAX REPORTS, ¶ 12-133).

A company providing taxicab or livery service may claim a corporate franchise tax credit for (1) the incremental cost associated with upgrading a vehicle so that it is accessible by individuals with disabilities or (2) purchasing a new accessible vehicle (Sec. 210(44), Tax Law; *TSB-M-12(1)C*, February 8, 2012, CCH NEW YORK TAX REPORTS, ¶ 407-471). To qualify for the credit, a vehicle must comply with federal regulations promulgated pursuant to the Americans with Disabilities Act applicable to vans under 22 feet in length, by the federal Department of Transportation, in Code of Federal Regulations, title 49, parts 37 and 38, and by the federal Architecture and Transportation Barriers Compliance Board, in Code of Federal Regulations, title 36, section 1192.23, and the Federal Motor Vehicle Safety Standards, Code of Federal Regulations, title 49, part 57.

Credit amount: The amount of the credit may not exceed $10,000 per vehicle (Sec. 210(44), Tax Law).

Caution: For tax years 2010, 2011, and 2012, taxpayers with more than $2 million in aggregated tax credits for companies who provide transportation to individuals with disabilities were required to defer the amounts above $2 million until 2013. The total amount of credits deferred was paid back to taxpayers over tax years 2013, 2014, and 2015 (Sec. 33.1, Tax Law; Sec. 34.1, Tax Law)

Planning considerations: If the credit amount exceeds the taxpayer's tax for the taxable year, the excess may be carried forward and used in subsequent years (Sec. 210(44), Tax Law).

The credit is set to expire December 31, 2022.

¶948 Credit for Historic Property Rehabilitation

Law: Sec. 210(40), Tax Law (CCH NEW YORK TAX REPORTS, ¶ 12-090a).

A credit is available against the corporation franchise, personal income, bank franchise, and insurance premiums taxes for the rehabilitation of certain historic properties in the taxable year the property is placed in service. (Sec. 210 (40), Tax Law)

• *Credit amount*

Taxpayers may claim a credit equal to 100% (30%, for taxable years beginning before 2010 and after 2019) of the federal credit allowed for the same taxable year under IRC Sec. 47(c)(2) with respect to a certified historic structure located in New York. The credit amount may not exceed $5 million ($100,000 for taxable years beginning before 2010 and after 2019). (Sec. 210(40), Tax Law; TSB-M-10(2)C, (3)I, February 3, 2010, CCH NEW YORK TAX REPORTS, ¶ 406-686)

Caution: For tax years 2010, 2011, and 2012, taxpayers with more than $2 million in aggregated business tax credits were required to defer the amounts above $2 million until 2013. The total amount of credits deferred was paid back to taxpayers over tax years 2013, 2014, and 2015 (Sec. 33.1, Tax Law; Sec. 34.1, Tax Law; *TSB-M-10(5)(C)*, September 13, 2010, CCH NEW YORK TAX REPORTS, ¶ 406-976).

• *Planning considerations*

A rehabilitation project must be located within a Census tract that is at or below 100% of the median family income (Sec. 210(40), Tax Law).

The credit is refundable for qualified rehabilitations placed in service on or after January 1, 2015; otherwise, unused credit may be carried over to following years without limitation (Sec. 210(40), Tax Law).

For additional information, see *TSB-M-10(8)C*, New York Department of Taxation and Finance, December 15, 2010, CCH NEW YORK TAX REPORTS, ¶ 407-076.

¶949 Credit for Production of Commercials

Law: Secs. 28, 210 [38], Tax Law; Reg. Secs. 180.1—180.8 (CCH NEW YORK TAX REPORTS, ¶ 12-085d).

A credit is available for qualified commercial production companies that incur qualified production costs to produce a qualified commercial in New York (Sec. 28, Tax Law). A "qualified commercial" is an advertisement that is recorded on film, audiotape, videotape, or digital medium in New York for multi-market distribution by way of radio, television networks, cable, satellite, or motion picture theaters.

"Production costs" are any costs for tangible property used and services performed directly and predominantly in the production (including pre-production and post-production) of a qualified commercial (Sec. 28(b)(2), Tax Law). Excluded are:

    — costs for a story, script or scenario to be used for a qualified commercial; and

— wages or salaries or other compensation for writers, directors, including music directors, producers and performers (other than background actors with no scripted lines who are employed by a qualified company and musicians).

Production costs generally include technical and crew production costs, such as expenditures for commercial production facilities and/or location costs, film, audiotape, videotape or digital medium, props, makeup, wardrobe, commercial processing, camera, sound recording, scoring, set construction, lighting, shooting, editing, and meals. Qualified production costs also include instances where the commercial production consists in its entirety of techniques such as visual effects, graphic design, or animation (Sec. 28(b)(2), Tax Law).

• *Credit amount*

The amount of credit that may be claimed by a production company is a percentage of its qualified production costs, depending upon the total qualified production costs expended and, in some cases, the principal place of business of the production company. Each year, the first $1 million of the $7 million available annually for the credit is dispersed *pro rata* to all qualified production companies, and amounts to 20% of the excess of New York production costs over those of the average of the three previous years for which the credit was applied, up to $300,000 per taxpayer. Another $3 million of credit is available to production companies that film or record qualified commercials outside the Metropolitan Commuter Transportation District, and amounts to 5% of the qualified production costs of at least $100,000 expended in New York during the taxable year. (Sec. 28(a)(2), Tax Law)

Caution: For tax years 2010, 2011, and 2012, taxpayers with more than $2 million in aggregated business tax credits were required to defer the amounts above $2 million until 2013. The total amount of credits deferred was paid back to taxpayers over tax years 2013, 2014, and 2015 (Sec. 33.1, Tax Law; Sec. 34.1, Tax Law; *TSB-M-10(5)(C)*, September 13, 2010, CCH NEW YORK TAX REPORTS, ¶ 406-976).

• *Planning considerations*

At least 75% of the qualified production costs must have been incurred in New York. (Sec. 28(a)(1), Tax Law)

A production company's total qualified production costs must be greater in the aggregate during the current calendar year than the average of the three previous years for which the credit was applied. Until a qualified production company has established a three-year history, however, the credit will be based on either the previous year or the average of the two previous years, whichever is greater. (Sec. 28(a)(2)(i), Tax Law)

The credit provisions apply to taxable years beginning after 2006 and are set to expire on December 31, 2018.

¶950 Credit for Clean Heating Fuel

Law: Sec. 210(39), Tax Law (CCH NEW YORK TAX REPORTS, ¶ 12-080e).

A credit is allowed for bioheat that is used for space heating or hot water production for residential purposes within New York and that is purchased on or after July 1, 2006, and before July 1, 2007, and on or after January 1, 2008, and before January 1, 2020. "Bioheat" is a combination of biodiesel and conventional heating oil. The credit applies to taxable years through 2016. (Sec. 210(39), Tax Law)

Beginning January 1, 2017, the credit does not apply to bioheat that is less than 6% biodiesel per gallon of bioheat.

Credit amount: The credit amount equals $0.01 per percent of biodiesel per gallon of bioheat, not to exceed 20¢ per gallon, purchased by the taxpayer. (Sec. 210(39), Tax Law)

Caution: For tax years 2010, 2011, and 2012, taxpayers with more than $2 million in aggregated business tax credits were required to defer the amounts above $2 million until 2013. The total amount of credits deferred was paid back to taxpayers over tax years 2013, 2014, and 2015. (Secs. 33, 34, Tax Law; TSB-M-10(5)(C), New York Department of Taxation and Finance, September 13, 2010, CCH NEW YORK TAX REPORTS, ¶ 406-976)

For additional information, see TSB-M-06(6)I at CCH NEW YORK TAX REPORTS, ¶ 300-519.

¶951 Credit for Conservation Easement Property Taxes

Law: Sec. 210 [38], Tax Law (CCH NEW YORK TAX REPORTS, ¶ 12-132).

A credit is available in the amount of 25% of the school district, county, and city real property taxes paid on land that is under a conservation easement. The credit amount claimed by a taxpayer may not exceed $5,000 in any given year. (Sec. 210(38), Tax Law)

Caution: For tax years 2010, 2011, and 2012, taxpayers with more than $2 million in aggregated business tax credits were required to defer the amounts above $2 million until 2013. The total amount of credits deferred was paid back to taxpayers over tax years 2013, 2014, and 2015 (Sec. 33.1, Tax Law; Sec. 34.1, Tax Law; *TSB-M-10(5)(C)*, September 13, 2010, CCH NEW YORK TAX REPORTS, ¶ 406-976).

¶952 Credit for Biofuel Production

Law: Secs. 28, 33, 34, 210 [38], Tax Law (CCH NEW YORK TAX REPORTS, ¶ 12-080d).

A biofuel production credit is available for taxable years beginning before 2020. "Biofuel" means a fuel that includes biodiesel and ethanol in accordance with standards approved by the New York state energy and research development authority. (Sec. 28, Tax Law)

Credit amount: The credit equals 15¢ for each gallon of biofuel produced at a biofuel plant, after the production of the first 40,000 gallons per year presented to market. The credit is capped at $2.5 million per taxpayer per taxable year for up to four consecutive taxable years per biofuel plant. (Sec. 28, Tax Law; Sec. 210(38), Tax Law)

Caution: For tax years 2010, 2011, and 2012, taxpayers with more than $2 million in aggregated business tax credits were required to defer the amounts above $2 million until 2013. The total amount of credits deferred was paid back to taxpayers over tax years 2013, 2014, and 2015 (Sec. 33.1, Tax Law; Sec. 34.1, Tax Law; *TSB-M-10(5)(C)*, September 13, 2010, CCH NEW YORK TAX REPORTS, ¶ 406-976).

Planning considerations: A taxpayer wishing to claim a credit under this section must annually certify the amount of biofuel produced at the eligible biofuel plant during a taxable year, and that the biofuel produced meets all existing standards for biofuel. (Sec. 28(c), Tax Law)

If a taxpayer is a partner in a partnership or a shareholder of a New York S corporation, then the $2.5 million annual cap is applied at the entity level, so that the aggregate credit allowed to all of the partners or shareholders of each such entity in a taxable year would not exceed the cap amount (Sec. 28, Tax Law).

¶953 Urban Youth Jobs Tax Credit (formerly, Youth Works Credit)

Law: Sec. 210 [44], Tax Law; Sec. 25-a, Labor Law; Reg. Secs. 210.1—216.6 (CCH New York Tax Reports, ¶ 12-120).

The Urban Youth Jobs Tax Credit Program provides tax incentives to qualified businesses employing at-risk youths in full-time and part-time positions in 2012 through 2017. The program is administered by the Department of Labor. (Sec. 210(44), Tax Law; Reg. Secs. 210.1—216.6; *TSB-M-12(3)C,* February 13, 2012, CCH New York Tax Reports, ¶ 407-474; *TSB-M-13(10)C, (9)I,* December 30, 2013, CCH New York Tax Reports, ¶ 407-993)

A qualified employee is an unemployed low-income or at-risk individual between the ages of 16 and 24 who resides in a city of 55,000 or more or a town of 480,000 or more and who is filling a position for which no other employee has been terminated, or where the employer has not otherwise reduced its workforce by involuntary terminations with the intention of filling the vacancy by creating a new hire.

Credit amount: A qualified employer is entitled to a tax credit in the following amounts:

— $500 per month for up to six months for each qualified employee employed in a full-time job, or

— $250 per month for up to six months for each qualified employee employed in a part-time job of at least 20 hours per week; and

— $1,000 for each qualified employee who is employed for at least an additional six months in a full-time job, and

— $500 for each qualified employee employed for at least an additional six months in a part-time job of at least 20 hours per week.

An additional $1,000 tax credit is allowed for each youth retained in full-time status for one additional year and an additional $500 for each youth retained in part-time status for one additional year.

The first amount of the credit is allowable for the taxable year in which the wages are paid to the qualified employee. The second amount of the credit is allowable in the taxable year in which the additional period ends. In no case may the credit exceed the maximum amount of credit listed on the certificate of eligibility (Sec. 210(44), Tax Law).

Planning considerations: There are five distinct pools of tax incentives with authorized allocation amounts, as follows (Sec. 25-a(a), Labor Law):

(1) Program One ($25 million) covers tax incentives allocated for 2012 and 2013;

(2) Program Two ($10 million) covers tax incentives allocated in 2014 to be used in 2014 and 2015;

(3) Program Three ($20 million) covers tax incentives allocated in 2015 to be used in 2015 and 2016;

(4) Program Four ($50 million) covers tax incentives allocated in 2016 to be used in 2016 and 2017;

(5) Program Five ($50 million) covers tax incentives allocated in 2017 to be used in 2017 and 2018.

Application deadlines for the five programs are as follows (Sec. 25-1(b), Labor Law):

— Program One: November 30, 2012;

— Program Two: November 30, 2014;

— Program Three: November 30, 2015;

— Program Four: November 30, 2016;

— Program Five: November 30, 2017;

The credit may not reduce the tax due for a year to less than the fixed dollar minimum tax. Any unused amount of credit in the current tax year will be treated as an overpayment of tax that will be refunded or credited against next year's tax liability. Interest will not be paid on the overpayment. (Sec. 210(44), Tax Law)

¶954 Empire State Jobs Retention Program

Law: Secs. 36, 210 [44], Tax Law; Reg. Secs. 210.1—216.6 (CCH New York Tax Reports, ¶ 12-070d).

The Empire State Jobs Retention Program has been established to create financial incentives to retain strategic businesses and jobs that are at risk of leaving the state due to the impact on business operations of an event (such as a natural disaster) leading to an emergency declaration by the governor. The program offers qualifying businesses a tax credit based on a percentage of the gross wages paid for retained jobs that otherwise would have been impacted by the event. (Sec. 36, Tax Law; Sec. 210(44), Tax Law; *TSB-M-12(3)C*, February 13, 2012, CCH New York Tax Reports, ¶ 407-474)

To be a participant in the program, an eligible business must apply to and be certified by the Empire State Development Corporation. Applications must be made within 180 days of the declaration of an emergency by the governor in the county where the business is located.

To be eligible to participate in the program, a business entity must operate in New York State predominantly:

— as a financial services data center or a financial services back office operation;

— in manufacturing;

— in software development and new media;

— in scientific research and development;

— in agriculture;

— in the creation or expansion of back office operations in the state; or

— in a distribution center.

A business entity must also meet the following requirements:

— it must be located in a county in which an emergency has been declared by the governor on or after January 1, 2011;

— it must demonstrate substantial physical damage and economic harm resulting from the event leading to the emergency declaration by the governor; and

— it must have had at least 100 full-time equivalent jobs in the county in which an emergency has been declared by the governor on the day immediately preceding the day the event leading to the declaration occurred, and must retain or exceed that number of jobs in New York.

The business must agree to allow the Tax Department and the Department of Labor to share tax and certain other information with the Empire State Development Corporation. If admitted into the Empire State Jobs Retention Program, the business must also agree to be permanently disqualified for Empire Zone tax benefits at any location or locations that qualify for Empire State Jobs Retention Program benefits.

Certain businesses are not eligible for the program (*e.g.*, a business entity engaged predominantly in the retail or entertainment industry, or a business entity that is not in compliance with all worker protection and environmental laws and regulations).

¶954

Credit amount: The amount of the credit is equal to 6.85% of the gross wages paid for the impacted jobs. The participant will receive a certificate of tax credit from the Empire State Development Corporation each year. The certificate will specify the amount of the credit allowed for that year.

Planning considerations: The credit may not be claimed prior to the tax year that begins on or after January 1, 2012, and before January 1, 2013.

The credit may be claimed for up to 10 consecutive tax years. The benefit period begins in the first year the participant receives a certificate of tax credit from the Empire State Development Corporation, or the first taxable year listed on the preliminary schedule of benefits, whichever is later.

If the participant fails to satisfy the eligibility criteria in any one year, it will lose the ability to claim the credit for that year. The inability to claim the credit in any one year will not extend the original 10-year eligibility period.

If a certificate of eligibility or a certificate of tax credit issued by the Empire State Development Corporation is revoked, the amount of credit claimed by the taxpayer prior to the revocation must be added back to tax in the taxable year in which the revocation becomes final.

The credit cannot reduce the tax due to less than the fixed dollar minimum tax. Any excess credit will be treated as an overpayment of tax that will be refunded or credited against next year's tax liability. Interest will not be paid on the overpayment.

¶955 Alcoholic Beverage Production Credit

Law: Sec. 37, Tax Law; Sec. 210-B(39), Tax Law (CCH NEW YORK TAX REPORTS, ¶12-134).

For taxable years beginning on or after January 1, 2016, the beer production credit is renamed the alcoholic beverage production credit and expanded to include cider, wine, and liquor (Sec. 37, Tax Law).

Corporate franchise and personal income tax credits are available for New York's craft breweries and, beginning in 2016, producers of cider, wine, and liquor. The law also exempts small breweries from paying the annual beer label registration fee, creates a farm brewery license to promote the use of local ingredients, and exempts farm breweries, wineries, and distilleries from certain tax filing requirements. To qualify for the credit, an eligible beer producer must produce no more than 60 million gallons of beer in New York in the taxable year (Sec. 37(a), Tax Law).

Credit amount: For tax years beginning on or after January 1, 2012, the credit is 14 cents per gallon for the first 500,000 gallons and 4.5 cents for additional gallons up to 15 million additional gallons for beer, cider, or wine and up to 300,000 additional gallons for liquor produced in New York in the same tax year. (Sec. 37(b), Tax Law). For additional guidance, see *TSB-M-12(8)C,* August 21, 2012, CCH NEW YORK TAX REPORTS, ¶407-626, *TSB-M-16(5)C,(3)I,* August 1, 2016, CCH NEW YORK TAX REPORTS, ¶408-824, and *TSB-M-16(6)C, (4)I. (5)M, (7)S,* August 1, 2016, CCH NEW YORK TAX REPORTS, ¶408-823.

Planning considerations: Corporate franchise taxpayers must file Form CT-636, Alcoholic Beverage Production Credit.

For corporate franchise taxpayers, the credit cannot reduce the tax due to less than the applicable fixed dollar minimum tax. However, if the credit allowed for any tax year reduces the tax to the minimum amount, any excess credit may be treated as an overpayment of tax to be credited or refunded. However, no interest will be paid on the refund.

Special rules exist for partners and S corporation shareholders. If a taxpayer is a partner in a partnership or a shareholder of a New York S corporation, the maximum credit amount will be applied at the entity level of the partnership or New York S corporation. Accordingly, the aggregate credit amount allowed to all partners or shareholders of a partnership or New York S corporation cannot exceed $745,000 for a tax year. (*TSB-M-12(8)C, (7)I*, August 21, 2012, CCH New York Tax Reports, ¶407-626)

¶956 Minimum Wage Reimbursement Credit

Law: Secs. 38, 210(46), Tax Law (CCH New York Tax Reports, ¶12-070f).

A credit is available, for taxable years beginning on or after January 1, 2014, for employers that hire eligible employees at the minimum wage rate (Sec. 38, Tax Law; Sec. 210(46), Tax Law; *TSB-M-13(8)C, (7)I*, December 30, 2013, CCH New York Tax Reports, ¶407-990). An eligible employer is defined as a corporation (including a New York S corporation), a sole proprietorship, a limited liability company or a partnership (Sec. 38(b), Tax Law).

An eligible employee is defined as an individual who is (Sec. 38(b), Tax Law):

(1) employed by an eligible employer in New York state;

(2) paid at the New York minimum wage rate during the taxable year by the eligible employer;

(3) between the ages of 16 and 19 during the period in which he or she is paid at the minimum wage rate by the eligible employer, and

(4) a student during the period in which he or she is paid at the minimum wage rate by the taxpayer.

Credit amount: The amount of credit allowed is the total number of hours worked during the taxable year by eligible employees for which they were paid at the New York minimum wage rate multiplied by the following amounts (Sec. 38(c), Tax Law):

— For taxable years beginning on or after January 1, 2014 and before January 1, 2015, 75 cents;

— For taxable years beginning on or after January 1, 2015 and before January 1, 2016, $1.31; and

— For taxable years beginning on or after January 1, 2016 and before January 1, 2019, $1.35.

However, if the federal minimum wage is increased above 85% of the New York minimum wage, the dollar amounts above would be reduced to the difference between the New York minimum wage and the federal minimum wage, effective on the date that employers are required to pay the increased federal minimum wage (Sec. 38(c), Tax Law).

Planning considerations: Employers are prohibited from discharging an existing employee and hiring an eligible employee for the sole purpose of qualifying for this tax credit (Sec. 38(d), Tax Law).

The credit cannot reduce the tax due to less than the fixed dollar minimum tax. However, if the amount of credit allowed for any taxable year reduces the tax to such amount, any amount of credit not deductible in that taxable year will be credited or refunded (Sec. 210(46)(b), Tax Law).

¶957 Hire a Veteran Credit

Law: Sec. 210(23-a), Tax Law (CCH New York Tax Reports, ¶12-070e).

For taxable years beginning on or after January 1, 2015 and before January 1, 2019, a corporate franchise tax credit is available for employers that hire a qualified veteran who commences employment before January 1, 2018 (Sec. 210(23-a)(a), Tax Law; *TSB-M-13(9)C, (8)I*, December 30, 2013, CCH New York Tax Reports, ¶407-992). The veteran must be hired and employed for not less than one year and not less than 35 hours each week. The credit may be claimed in the year in which the qualified veteran completes one year of employment by the taxpayer. If the taxpayer claims the hire a veteran credit, the taxpayer may not use the hiring of a qualified veteran that is the basis for this credit in the basis of any other corporate franchise tax credit. (Sec. 210(23-a)(a), Tax Law)

A qualified veteran is an individual who (Sec. 210(23-a)(b), Tax Law):

(1) served on active duty in the U.S. army, navy, air force, marine corps, coast guard or the reserves thereof, or who served in active military service as a member of the army national guard, air national guard, New York guard or New York naval militia, and who was released from active duty by general or honorable discharge after September 11, 2001;

(2) commences employment by the qualified taxpayer on or after January 1, 2014, and before January 1, 2016; and

(3) certifies by signed affidavit, under penalty of perjury, that he or she has not been employed for 35 or more hours during any week in the 180 day period immediately prior to his or her employment by the taxpayer.

Credit amount: The amount of the credit is 10% of the total amount of wages paid to the qualified veteran during the veteran's first full year of employment (Sec. 210(23-a)(d), Tax Law). However, if the qualified veteran is a disabled veteran, the amount of the credit is 15% of the total amount of wages paid to the veteran during the veteran's first full year of employment.

The credit may not exceed $5,000 for any qualified veteran or $15,000 for any qualified veteran who is a disabled veteran in any taxable year (Sec. 210(23-a)(d), Tax Law).

Planning considerations: Employers are prohibited from discharging an existing employee and hiring a qualified veteran for the sole purpose of qualifying for this tax credit (Sec. 210(23-a)(c), Tax Law).

The credit cannot reduce the tax due to less than the fixed dollar minimum tax. However, if the amount of credit allowed for any taxable year reduces the tax to that amount, any amount of credit not deductible in that taxable year may be carried over to the following three years (Sec. 210(23-a)(e), Tax Law).

¶958 Real Property Tax Credit for Qualified Manufacturers

Law: Secs. 210(48), 210-B(43), Tax Law (CCH NEW YORK TAX REPORTS, ¶ 12-135).

Effective for tax years beginning on or after January 1, 2014, a credit is available for qualified New York manufacturers (Sec. 210(48), Tax Law). A "manufacturer" is defined as a taxpayer principally engaged in the production of goods by manufacturing, processing, assembling, refining, mining, extracting, farming, agriculture, horticulture, floriculture, viticulture or commercial fishing. But, the generation and distribution of electricity, the distribution of natural gas, and the production of steam associated with the generation of electricity are not qualifying activities. (Sec. 210(48), Tax Law; see *TSB-M-15(3.1)C*, New York Department of Taxation and Finance, July 24, 2015, CCH NEW YORK TAX REPORTS, ¶ 408-488)

A qualified manufacturer must satisfy the existing receipts and property tests:

(1) at least 50% of receipts must be from manufacturing; and

(2) either all or at least $1 million of manufacturing property is in New York.

A manufacturer that fails the receipts test may still qualify for the credit if it employs at least 2,500 people in manufacturing in New York and has $100 million in manufacturing property in New York (Sec. 210(48), Tax Law).

Credit amount: The credit is equal to 20% of the real property taxes paid during the taxable year for real property owned by qualified manufacturers in New York and principally used for manufacturing. The credit is also allowed for property taxes paid on real property leased from an unrelated third party if the taxes are paid pursuant to explicit requirements in a written lease and remitted directly to the taxing authority. (Sec. 210(48), Tax Law)

Planning considerations: The credit cannot be claimed if the real property taxes that are the basis for the credit are included in the calculation of another credit already claimed.

Taxpayers must add back the amount of real property taxes deducted at the federal level (Sec. 210(48), Tax Law). Additionally, when the property taxes that were the basis of the credit are later reduced, the taxpayer must add back the excess of (1) the amount of credit originally allowed for a taxable year over (2) the amount of credit determined on the reduced property taxes. This addback must be made in the same taxable year that the final order reducing the taxes is issued (Sec. 606(xx), Tax Law). The credit cannot reduce a taxpayers tax liability to less than $25.

Leased property: The term "real property tax" includes taxes paid by the taxpayer upon real property principally used by the taxpayer in manufacturing if the taxpayer leases the real property from an unrelated third party if the following conditions are satisfied:

(I) the tax must be paid by the taxpayer as lessee pursuant to explicit requirements in a written lease, and

(II) the taxpayer as lessee has paid such taxes directly to the taxing authority and has received a written receipt for payment of taxes from the taxing authority.

Effective April 13, 2016, for corporation franchise tax purposes, In the case of a taxpayer that, during the taxable year, is principally engaged in the production of goods by farming, agriculture, horticulture, floriculture, viticulture, or commercial fishing, the taxpayer is eligible for the credit if the taxpayer satisfies the above conditions and the leases the real property from either a related or unrelated party. (Sec. 210-B(43)(b)(2), Tax Law)

¶959 Musical and Theatrical Production Credit

Law: Sec. 24-a, Tax Law; Reg. Sec. 240.1 *et seq.* (CCH NEW YORK TAX REPORTS, ¶ 12-136).

Effective for tax years beginning on or after January 1, 2015 and expiring on January 1, 2019, a credit is available against the New York corporate franchise tax and personal income tax for eligible production companies (Sec. 24-a, Tax Law; Reg. Sec. 240.1 *et seq.*). To be eligible, a company must produce a live, dramatic stage presentation in a qualified production facility on a tour that consists of eight or more shows in three or more localities (Sec. 24-a(B), Tax Law).

The term "qualified musical and theatrical production company" is defined as a corporation, partnership, limited partnership, or other entity or individual which or who is principally engaged in the production of a qualified musical or theatrical production and performs in a qualified production facility (Sec. 24-a(B)(5), Tax Law). "Qualified musical and theatrical production" means a for-profit live, dramatic stage presentation in a qualified production facility, certified pursuant to rules and regulations promulgated by the department of economic development, as a qualified touring production (Sec. 24-a(B)(1), Tax Law). A "qualified production facility" is defined as a 1,000 or more seat theater located outside of New York City for which ticket receipts constitute 75% or more of the total receipts (Sec. 24-a(B)(4), Tax Law).

Credit amount: Eligible production companies may claim a refundable tax credit equal to 25% of "qualified production expenditures," which are costs for tangible property used and services performed in the course of production, with personal compensation expenses capped at $200,000 per week (Sec. 24-a(B)(3), Tax Law). The credit is also allowed for transportation expenditures, which includes costs for packaging, crating, and transporting production equipment, sets, costumes, and cast and crew (Sec. 24-a(B)(6), Tax Law).

Planning considerations: The total amount of credit is capped at $4 million per year and the credit is administered by Empire State Development (ESD) (Sec. 24-a(A)(2), Tax Law).

¶960 Employee Training Incentive Credit

Law: Sec. 210-B(50), Tax Law; Sec. 441, Economic Development Law (CCH NEW YORK TAX REPORTS, ¶12-075).

For taxable years beginning on or after January 1, 2015, a tax credit is available against corporation franchise and personal income tax for eligible training costs incurred on or after April 13, 2015, by employers that procure certain training for their employees (Sec. 210-B(50), Tax Law).

To participate in the program, a business entity must satisfy the following criteria (Sec. 442, Econ. Dev. Law):

(1) The business entity:

(a) must operate in the state predominantly in a strategic industry;

(b) must obtain the eligible training from an approved provider;

(c) must create at least 10 net new jobs or make a significant capital investment of at least $1 million in new business processes or equipment in connection with the eligible training; and

(d) must be in compliance with all worker protection and environmental laws and regulations; and

(e) may not owe past due state taxes or local property taxes; or

(2) The business entity, or an approved provider in contract with such business entity, must be approved by the commissioner to provide eligible training in the form of an internship program in advanced technology; and:

— the business entity must be located in New York;

— the internship program must not displace regular employees;

— the business entity must have less than 100 employees; and

— the participation of an individual in an internship program may not last more than 12 months.

"Eligible training" is (Sec. 441(3), Econ. Dev. Law):

(a) training provided by an approved provider that is:

(i) to upgrade, retrain or improve the productivity of employees;

(ii) provided to employees filling net new jobs, or to existing employees in connection with a significant capital investment by a participating business entity;

(iii) determined by the commissioner to satisfy a business need on the part of a participating business entity;

(iv) not designed to train or upgrade skills as required by a federal or state entity;

(v) not training the completion of which may result in the awarding of a license or certificate required by law in order to perform a job function; and

(vi) not culturally focused training; or

(b) an internship program in advanced technology approved by the commissioner and provided by an approved provider, on or after August 1 2015, to provide employment and experience opportunities for current students, recent graduates, and recent members of the armed forces.

Credit amount: The credit equals 50% of a taxpayer's eligible training costs, up to a credit of $10,000 per employee completing eligible training, and 50% of the stipend paid to an intern, up to a credit of $3,000 per intern completing eligible training.

Planning considerations: Each business entity participating in the program must maintain all relevant records for the duration of its program participation plus three years. (Sec. 445, Econ. Dev. Law)

The total amount of tax credits listed on certificates of tax credit issued by the commissioner for any taxable year may not exceed $5 million, and the portion allocated to internship programs in advanced technology may not be less than $250,000 nor more than $1 million. (Sec. 446, Econ. Dev. Law)

The credit is refundable (Sec. 210-B(50)(b), Tax Law).

¶961 Credits Against Tax—Farm Workforce Retention Credit

Law: Secs. 42, 210-B(51), Tax Law (CCH New York Tax Reports, ¶12-070g).

For taxable years beginning on or after 2016 and before 2022, a taxpayer that is a farm employer or an owner of a farm employer may claim a new farm workforce retention credit available against the corporate franchise and personal income taxes (Sec. 42, Tax Law; Sec. 210-B(1), Tax Law; *TSB-M-16(7)C, (5)I,* New York Department of Taxation and Finance, September 23, 2016, CCH New York Tax Reports, ¶408-856).

A "farm employer" is a New York S corporation, a sole proprietorship, a limited liability company or a partnership that is also an eligible farmer (Sec. 42(b), Tax Law).

An "eligible farmer" is a taxpayer whose federal gross income from farming (including payments from New York's farmland protection program) for the taxable year is at least 2/3 of the taxpayer's "excess federal gross income," which is the amount of federal gross income from all sources that exceeds $30,000 for the taxable year (Sec. 42(c), Tax Law).

An "eligible farm employee" is an individual who is employed for at least 500 hours per taxable year by a farm employer in New York (Sec. 42(d), Tax Law).

Credit amount: The credit amount is determined by multiplying the total number of eligible farm employees by a dollar amount for each taxable year, as follows (Sec. 42(e), Tax Law):

> 2017—$250;
>
> 2018—$300;
>
> 2019—$500;
>
> 2020—$400;
>
> 2021—$600;

Planning considerations: The amount of this credit generally may not reduce the taxpayers tax below the amount of the fixed dollar minimum tax (Sec. 210-B(1), Tax Law).

If a farm employee is unable to work due to a documented illness or disability, the hours the individual worked may be combined with the hours worked by a replacement for the worker when determining whether or not the 500 hour threshold has been met for a taxable year (Sec. 42(d), Tax Law).

CORPORATION FRANCHISE (INCOME) TAX

CHAPTER 10

BASIS OF TAX—ENTIRE NET INCOME

¶1001 In General

Law: Sec. 208, Tax Law (CCH NEW YORK TAX REPORTS, ¶10-510).

Comparable Federal: Secs. 61, 63 (U.S. MASTER TAX GUIDE, ¶62, 214, 2301—2323, 2326—2340).

The primary base for the computation of the New York corporation franchise tax is "entire net income," redefined as the "business income base" for tax years beginning after 2014. Entire net income is defined as total net income from all sources, which is the same as the entire taxable income (but not alternative minimum taxable income) (1) that the taxpayer is required to report to the U.S. Treasury Department, (2) that the taxpayer would have been required to report to the U.S. Treasury Department if it had not elected Subchapter S status for federal income tax purposes, or (3) that the taxpayer, in the case of a corporation that is exempt from federal income tax, but which is subject to New York income tax, would have been required to report to the U.S. Treasury Department but for the exemption. (Sec. 208(9), Tax Law)

Computation of the entire net income base begins with the amount from line 28 of federal Form 1120 (*i.e.,* federal taxable income before net operating loss and special deductions). New York provides for certain inclusions, exclusions, and other modifications.

By adopting federal taxable income as a starting point, the New York corporation franchise tax law generally adopts the federal income tax treatment of items of gross income and deductions. It should be noted, however, that New York entire net income includes income within or without the United States, thereby including income of alien corporations from foreign sources not subject to federal taxation; see (Sec. 208(9), Tax Law). With respect to an alien corporation (not treated as a domestic corporation under any provision of the IRC), the definition of "entire net income" is modified for taxable years beginning after 2014 to refer to income that is effectively connected with the conduct of a trade or business within the U.S., as determined under IRC Sec. 882 (Sec. 208(9)(iv), Tax Law).

Entire net income (the "business income base") consists of "business income" less "investment income"(reduced by related interest expenses) and other exempt income. In no event will the sum of investment income and other exempt income exceed entire net income (Sec. 208(6)(a)(i), Tax Law). If the amount of interest deductions exceeds investment income, the excess of such amount over investment income must be added back to entire net income (Sec. 208(6)(a)(ii), Tax Law). The amount of investment income that may be deducted is capped at 8% of the taxpayer's entire net income in cases where the taxpayer's investment income is determined without regard to the interest deductions allowed (Sec. 208(6)(a)(iii), Tax Law). If the taxpayer makes the election to use the fixed percentage method for qualified financial instruments under Sec. 210-A(5)(a)(1), Tax Law, then all income from qualified financial instruments will constitute business income.

Regulated investment companies: See ¶911.

Real estate investment trusts: See ¶918.

Domestic international sales corporations (DISCs): See ¶919.

For allocation of entire net income, see Chapter 13.

Federal Economic Stimulus Act of 2008 (ESA): New York has decoupled from the special depreciation allowance included in ESA, but not from the increased expensing provisions. For details, see *TSB-M 08(8)C,* June 9, 2008, CCH NEW YORK TAX REPORTS, ¶406-078.

¶1002 Inclusions in Entire Net Income (Additions to Federal Taxable Income)

Law: Sec. 208, Tax Law; Reg. Sec. 3-2.2, Reg. Sec. 3-6.3 (CCH NEW YORK TAX REPORTS, ¶10-600—10-701).

The starting point for the computation of New York entire net income is federal taxable income (before net operating loss and special deductions). (Reg. Sec. 3-2.2(b)) The following items are included in New York entire net income but not in federal taxable income and must be added:

— Interest on any federal, state, or local government bonds exempt for federal purposes, including those of New York State governmental bodies (less any interest or carrying charges on loans to purchase such bonds) (¶1005);

— Federal taxes on profits or income deducted for federal purposes. (Such taxes are not currently deductible for federal purposes.) Taxes paid to United States possessions and foreign countries, including "in lieu" taxes, are added;

— Taxes on or measured by profits or income, or that include profits or income as a measure, paid to any other state of the United States, or any political subdivision thereof, or to the District of Columbia (Sec. 208(9)(b)(3), Tax Law; Reg. Sec. 3-2.3);

— New York corporation franchise tax, the franchise tax on banking corporations (repealed for tax years after 2014), the franchise tax on transportation and transmission corporations, together with the additional franchise and temporary metropolitan transportation business surcharge taxes on these businesses (¶1007);

— The entire amount allowable as an exclusion or deduction for stock transfer taxes imposed in determining the entire taxable income that the taxpayer is required to report to the U.S. Treasury Department, but only to the extent that such taxes are incurred and paid in market-making transactions (Reg. Sec. 3-2.3(a)(10));

— In the discretion of the Commissioner, interest directly or indirectly attributable, or carrying charges directly or indirectly attributable, to subsidiary capital or to income, gains, or losses from subsidiary capital. (Sec. 208(9)(b)(6), Tax Law) New York has an addition modification for interest on indebtedness paid to a corporate stockholder owning more than 50% of the taxpayer's issued and outstanding voting stock. (Sec. 208(4), Tax Law; Reg. Sec. 3-6.3) If the taxpayer does not make this addition, the indebtedness will not constitute subsidiary capital in the hands of the corporate stockholder, and the stockholder will not be able to exclude the interest from its entire net income as income from subsidiary capital. Interest on indebtedness paid to a corporate stockholder is only required to be added back by the payor when the corporate stockholder payee has deducted the interest as income attributable to subsidiary capital on its New York State franchise tax return;

— Income from sources without the United States received by alien corporations and not included in federal taxable income (Sec. 208(9)(c), Tax Law; Reg. Sec. 3-2.3(a)(9));

— Amount of any specific federal exemption or credit against income (refers to the former $3,000 federal exemption available to certain corporations and the former deduction for Western Hemisphere trade corporations) (¶ 1004);

— A corporation having a safe harbor lease must add back (1) any amount claimed as a deduction in computing federal taxable income solely as a result of an election made under IRC Sec. 168(f)(8) as it was in effect on December 31, 1983 (Sec. 208(9)(b)(8), Tax Law; Reg. Sec. 3-2.3(a)(15)), and (2) any amount the taxpayer would have been required to include in the computation of its federal taxable income had it not made the election permitted under IRC Sec. 168(f)(8) as it was in effect on December 31, 1983 (Sec. 208(9)(b)(9), Tax Law; Reg. Sec. 3-2.3(a)(16));

— In the case of a taxpayer who is separately or as a partner of a partnership doing an insurance business as a member of the New York Insurance Exchange, the taxpayer's distributive or pro rata share of the allocated entire net income of such business (however, if the allocated entire net income is a loss, the loss is not subtracted) (Reg. Sec. 3-2.3(a)(14));

— In those instances when a credit for the special additional mortgage recording tax is allowed, the amount allowed as an exclusion or deduction for the special additional recording tax in computing the entire taxable income that the taxpayer is required to report to the IRS must be added back in determining entire net income (Reg. Sec. 3-2.3(a)(12));

— For property placed in service in New York State in taxable years beginning before 1994, the amount allowable under the federal accelerated cost recovery system pursuant to IRC Sec. 168 (other than property subject to the provisions of IRC Sec. 280-F, relating to luxury automobiles, or to property that was placed in service in New York in taxable years beginning after 1984). (Reg. Sec. 3-2.3(a)(17)) For property placed in service in New York State after 1993, the New York depreciation rules are generally the same as the federal depreciation rules, with certain exceptions (such as a partial decoupling from federal bonus depreciation, as noted below);

— Upon disposition of recovery property, the amount, if any, by which the New York depreciation deduction exceeds the federal deduction;

— Real property taxes paid on qualified agricultural property and deducted in determining a taxpayer's federal taxable income, to the extent of the taxpayer's allowed agricultural property tax credit (¶ 934);

— Deferred gain from investments in emerging technologies (¶ 1003);

— For taxable years beginning after 2002, and applicable to property placed in service on or after June 1, 2003, the New York corporation franchise (income) tax is decoupled from federal accelerated depreciation provisions under IRC Sec.

168(k), except with respect to qualified Resurgence Zone property and qualified New York Liberty Zone property (Sec. 208(9)(a)(17), (b)(17), (o), (p), and (q), Tax Law). Decoupling includes the special depreciation provisions in the federal Economic Stimulus Act of 2008;

— Applicable to taxable years beginning after 2002, an addition modification is required for the amount deducted by a taxpayer (except an eligible farmer) under IRC Sec. 179 for a sport utility vehicle with a vehicle weight over 6,000 pounds (Sec. 208(9)(b)(16), Tax Law);

— *Royalties:* Royalty payments, including certain interest payments, directly or indirectly paid, accrued, or incurred in connection with one or more direct or indirect transactions with one or more related members during the taxable year must be added back, to the extent deductible in calculating federal taxable income (Sec. 208(9)(o), Tax Law). The addback is not required if (Sec. 208(9)(o)(2)(B), Tax Law):

(1) the taxpayer's related member paid significant taxes on the royalty payment in other jurisdictions;

(2) the related member paid all or part of the royalty payment it received to a third party for a valid business purpose;

(3) the related member is organized under the laws of a foreign country that has a tax treaty with the United States; or

(4) the taxpayer and the Tax Department agree to alternative adjustments that more appropriately reflect the taxpayer's income.

CCH Advisory: Anti-PIC Provisions

For taxable years beginning after 2012, the former subtraction for royalty income is repealed (see ¶ 1003).

For purposes of this addback provision against passive investment companies (PICs), "royalty payments" are defined as payments, directly connected to the acquisition, use, maintenance or management, ownership, sale, exchange, or any other disposition of licenses, trademarks, copyrights, trade names, trade dress, service marks, mask works, trade secrets, patents and any other similar types of intangible assets as determined by the Commissioner. The definition also includes amounts allowable as interest deductions under IRC Sec. 163 to the extent these amounts are directly or indirectly for, related to or in connection with the acquisition, use, maintenance or management, ownership, sale, exchange or disposition of these intangible assets. (Sec. 208(9)(o)(1)(C), Tax Law)

A "valid business purpose" consists of one or more business purposes other than the avoidance or reduction of taxation that, alone or in combination, constitute the primary motivation for some business activity or transaction that changes in a meaningful way, apart from tax effects, the economic position of the taxpayer, including increasing the taxpayer's market share or the entry by the taxpayer into new business markets. (Sec. 208(9)(o)(1)(D), Tax Law)

"Related member or members" means a related person as defined in IRC Sec. 465(b)(3)(c), except that 50% is substituted for 10%. "Controlling interest" generally means control of at least 30% of the combined voting power or 30% of the capital, profits, or beneficial interests. (Sec. 208(9)(o), Tax Law)

— For taxable years beginning after 2007, an addition modification is required for the IRC Sec. 199 deduction for qualified production activities income (Sec. 208(9)(b)(19), Tax Law);

— An addition modification is required for environmental remediation insurance premiums that were deducted in determining federal taxable income, to the extent of the amount of the environmental remediation insurance credit (see ¶ 943). (Sec. 208(9)(b)(18), Tax Law)

QEZE credit for property taxes: For federal income tax purposes, the Internal Revenue Service has determined that all or a portion of the QEZE credit for real property taxes that is refunded, or credited as an overpayment to estimated tax, may be a recovery of property tax previously deducted and is therefore considered income to the taxpayer.

For New York state corporate franchise tax and personal income tax purposes, any refund of the QEZE credit for real property taxes is considered a refund of franchise tax or income tax. Accordingly, under existing state law, the amount of the refund of the QEZE credit for real property taxes included in the taxpayer's federal taxable income or federal adjusted gross income is not taxable to New York state. Therefore, New York state taxpayers are allowed a subtraction for that refund amount in computing their New York taxable income. A memorandum describes how to report the subtraction on New York state corporate franchise tax returns and personal income tax returns, as well as the necessary amended return requirements. (*TSB-M-10(9)C, (15)I*, New York Department of Taxation and Finance, December 31, 2010, CCH NEW YORK TAX REPORTS, ¶ 407-084)

¶1003 Exclusions from Entire Net Income (Deductions from Federal Taxable Income)

Law: Secs. 208, 211, Tax Law; Sec. 54.15, Arts and Cultural Affairs Law (CCH NEW YORK TAX REPORTS, ¶ 10-800—10-900).

In computing New York entire net income, the following items may be deducted from federal taxable income:

— Income and gains from subsidiary capital (other than war loss recoveries) (repealed for taxable years beginning after 2014) (¶ 1009);

— 50% of all dividends from corporations, other than from subsidiaries, that were included in computing federal taxable income (repealed for taxable years beginning after 2014) (Sec. 208(9)(a)(2), Tax Law). However, for taxable years after 2007, no deduction was allowed to any member of an affiliated group for dividends received from a captive RIC or REIT that is required to be included in the combined report (Sec. 211(4)(b)(1), Tax Law);

— Bona fide gifts (Sec. 208(9)(a)(3), Tax Law);

— Refund or credit of any New York corporation franchise tax or the banking corporation franchise tax imposed for a prior year when the tax had not been deducted in any earlier year. Also, any refund or credit of a tax imposed under Sec. 183 (concerning the franchise tax on transportation and transmission corporations and associations), Sec. 183-a (the temporary metropolitan business surcharge on transportation and transmission corporations and associations), Sec. 184 (the additional franchise tax on transportation and transmission corporations and associations), and Sec. 184-a (the additional temporary metropolitan transportation business surcharge on transportation and transmission corporations and associations), Tax Law (Sec. 208(9)(a)(5), Tax Law; Reg. Sec. 3-2.4(a)(4));

— Receipts from school districts and from nonprofit religious, charitable or educational organizations for the operation of school buses (Sec. 208(9)(a)(4), Tax Law);

— Net operating loss deduction (¶ 1008);

— Any amount treated as dividends under IRC Sec. 78 (foreign dividend gross up) and not otherwise deducted under (1) and (2) above (Sec. 208(9)(a)(6), Tax Law; Reg. Sec. 3-3.4(a)(6));

— The portion of wages disallowed under IRC Sec. 280C for federal purposes because the taxpayer claimed a federal credit;

— In the case of a taxpayer who is separately or as a partner of a partnership doing an insurance business as a member of the New York Insurance Exchange, any item of income, gain, loss, or deduction of such business that is the taxpayer's distributive or pro rata share for federal purposes or that the taxpayer is required to take into account separately for federal purposes (Reg. Sec. 3-2.4(a)(8));

— For corporations having a safe harbor lease, a subtraction is allowed for (1) any amount included in federal taxable income solely as a result of an election made under IRC Sec. 168(f)(8) as it was in effect on December 31, 1983, and (2) any amount the taxpayer could have excluded from federal taxable income had it not made the election provided for in IRC Sec. 168(f)(8) as it was in effect on December 31, 1983 (Sec. 208(9)(a)(9) and (a)(10), Tax Law; Reg. Sec. 3-2.4(a)(9) and (10));

— Upon disposition of recovery property, the amount, if any, by which the federal deduction exceeds the New York depreciation deduction (Sec. 208(9)(a)(11), Tax Law);

— Gain from the sale of any emerging technology investment acquired on or after March 12, 1998, and held for more than 36 months will be recognized only to the extent that the gain realized exceeds the cost of any qualified emerging technology investment purchased by the taxpayer within 365 days from the date of the sale. (Sec. 208(9)(l), Tax Law) Consequently, such deferred gain may, at the taxpayer's election, be subtracted from the taxpayer's federal adjusted gross income in the year of the sale. The amount deferred will be added to the taxpayer's federal adjusted gross income when the reinvestment is sold (¶1002);

— Any recapture amount included in federal adjusted gross income that is attributable to a post-2002 federal deduction under IRC Sec. 179 for a sport utility vehicle with a vehicle weight over 6,000 pounds. (Sec. 208(9)(a)(16), Tax Law)

— Income or gain included in federal taxable income of a taxpayer that is a partner in a qualified entity or is a qualified entity that is located both within and without a New York state Innovation Hot Spot (see ¶923). (Sec. 38(1)(b), Tax Law; Sec. 208(9)(a)(18), Tax Law)

Modifications applicable to thrifts and community banks: There are three possible modifications:

(1) The first modification, eligibility for which is based on the eligibility for the prior New York State bad debt modification for thrift institutions, is available to thrifts and qualified community banks holding a qualified residential loan portfolio (Sec. 208.9(r), Tax Law). Taxpayers must choose to utilize this modification or the second modification discussed below.

(2) The second modification is available to small thrifts and qualified community banks for holding a significant amount of New York small business loans and New York residential mortgages (Sec. 208.9(s), Tax Law.) Taxpayers must choose to utilize this modification or the first modification discussed above.

(3) The third modification is available to small thrifts and qualified community banks that maintained a REIT on April 1, 2014 (Sec. 208.9(t), Tax Law). Taxpayers using this modification are precluded from using the two other modifications discussed above.

Foreign air carriers: Qualified foreign air carriers that hold foreign air permits issued by the U.S. Department of Transportation may compute entire net income without including amounts directly or indirectly attributable to (1) any income derived from the international operation of an aircraft (as described in and subject to IRC Sec. 883), (2) income without the United States that is derived from the operation of aircraft, and (3) income without the United States that is of a type described in IRC Sec. 881(a), except that it is derived from sources without the United States. (Sec. 208(9)(c)(c-1), Tax Law)

Royalties: For taxable years before 2013, taxpayers could subtract royalty payments received during the tax year from a related member to the extent those payments were included in calculating the taxpayer's federal taxable income and the payments were required to be added to federal taxable income by the related member (former Sec. 208(9)(o)(3), Tax Law). This subtraction is now repealed, but there are four exceptions to the requirement to add back royalty payments made by a related member (see ¶1002).

QEZE credit for property taxes: For federal income tax purposes, the Internal Revenue Service has determined that all or a portion of the QEZE credit for real property taxes that is refunded, or credited as an overpayment to estimated tax, may be a recovery of property tax previously deducted and is therefore considered income to the taxpayer.

For New York state corporate franchise tax and personal income tax purposes, any refund of the QEZE credit for real property taxes is considered a refund of franchise tax or income tax. Accordingly, under existing state law, the amount of the refund of the QEZE credit for real property taxes included in the taxpayer's federal taxable income or federal adjusted gross income is not taxable to New York state. Therefore, New York state taxpayers are allowed a subtraction for that refund amount in computing their New York taxable income. A memorandum describes how to report the subtraction on New York state corporate franchise tax returns and personal income tax returns, as well as the necessary amended return requirements. (*TSB-M-10(9)C, (15)I,* New York Department of Taxation and Finance, December 31, 2010, CCH NEW YORK TAX REPORTS, ¶407-084)

¶1004 Federal Exemptions and Credits

Law: Sec. 208, Tax Law (CCH NEW YORK TAX REPORTS, ¶10-510).

The amount of any specific federal exemption or credit against income must be added to federal taxable income in determining New York entire net income (Sec. 208(9)(b)(1), Tax Law). However, because credits are applied against federal tax after federal taxable income is determined, no adjustment is necessary.

¶1005 Interest and Dividends

Law: Secs. 208, 210-C, Tax Law (CCH NEW YORK TAX REPORTS, ¶10-610, 10-630).

Comparable Federal: Secs. 103, 243 (U.S. MASTER TAX GUIDE, ¶237, 724, 731, 732).

Interest and dividends (other than on subsidiary capital) that are not included in federal taxable income must be added in determining New York entire net income. (Sec. 208(9)(b)(2), Tax Law; Reg. Sec. 3-2.3)

Interest from New York State and local government bonds and from bonds of other state and local governments is included even though exempt for federal purposes. The New York corporation franchise tax is measured by and not imposed upon entire net income; consequently, federal bond interest may be included.

The federal deduction for dividends received is not allowed for New York franchise tax purposes. Since the federal taxable income used to start the computation of entire net income for New York franchise tax purposes is taken before this dividend deduction, no adjustment is required on the franchise tax return to add back this deduction. However, 50% of all dividends from corporations other than from subsidiaries that were used in computing federal taxable income are allowed as a deduction for franchise tax purposes (¶1003).

For exclusion of interest and dividends from subsidiary capital, see ¶1009.

Corporate tax reform: For taxable years beginning after 2014, investment income and other exempt income are not taxable and the deductions for interest expenses attributable to such income are disallowed (Sec. 208(6)(a), Tax Law). If actual expense attribution exceeds income, the excess expenses are required to be added back to income.

In lieu of computing actual interest expenses disallowed, taxpayers generally can elect a "safe harbor" to reduce investment and other exempt income by 40% (Sec. 208(6)(ba), Tax Law; see *TSB-M-15(8)C, (7)I*, New York Department of Taxation and Finance, December 31, 2015, CCH NEW YORK TAX REPORTS, ¶ 408-609). If the election is made, it covers both other exempt income and investment income.

The computation of expense attribution for a combined group is done on a "one company" basis. If the taxpayer chooses the 40% election, it applies to both the investment income and other exempt income of all members of the combined group. (Sec. 210-C(4)(e), Tax Law)

Frequently asked questions about the tax reform legislation are available at **http://www.tax.ny.gov/bus/ct/corp_tax_reform_faqs.htm**.

¶1006 Interest Related to Corporate Acquisitions

Law: Sec. 208, Tax Law (CCH NEW YORK TAX REPORTS, ¶ 10-540, 10-595).

For taxable years before 1997, acquiring or surviving corporations were required to make an adjustment to federal taxable income to arrive at entire net income by adding back 5% of the amount of interest paid or accrued by a taxpayer during the taxable year to the extent it was deducted in computing entire net income. For details, see previous editions of this Guidebook or the above-cited discussion in CCH NEW YORK TAX REPORTS.

¶1007 Taxes

Law: Sec. 208, Tax Law; Reg. Sec. 3-2.3 (CCH NEW YORK TAX REPORTS, ¶ 10-615).

In computing entire net income for New York corporation franchise tax purposes, all federal taxes on or measured by income or profits, the New York corporation franchise tax, the franchise tax on banking corporations (now repealed), and the franchise tax on transportation and transmission corporations, together with the additional franchise and temporary metropolitan business surcharge taxes on those businesses, which were deducted in computing federal taxable income, must be added back. (Sec. 208(9)(b)(3), Tax Law; Sec. 208(9)(b)(4), Tax Law; Reg. Sec. 3-2.3) Taxes paid to United States possessions and foreign countries, including "in lieu" taxes, are added.

Taxes of other states: The amount of taxes on or measured by profits or income, or that include profits or income as a measure, paid to any other state of the United States, or to any political subdivision thereof, or to the District of Columbia, must be added to federal taxable income. (Sec. 208(9)(b)(3-a), Tax Law; Reg. Sec. 3-2.3)

¶1008 Net Operating Loss

Law: Sec. 208, Tax Law; Sec. 210, Tax Law; Reg. Secs. 3-8.1—3-8.9 (CCH NEW YORK TAX REPORTS, ¶ 10-805).

Comparable Federal: Sec. 172 (U.S. MASTER TAX GUIDE, ¶ 1173—1188).

The following rules apply to NOLs incurred in tax years beginning on or after January 1, 2015 (Sec. 210(1)(a)(ix), Tax Law):

— NOLs can be carried back to the earliest of 3 years, provided no NOL earned in 2015 or later can be carried back to a tax year before 2015. Taxpayers may make an irrevocable election to relinquish the entire carryback period;

— NOLs can be carried forward 20 years;

— A taxpayer's NOL deduction (NOLD) in any specific tax year would be the sum of apportioned business losses that were incurred in tax years beginning on or after January 1, 2015, less any portion of such losses that were deducted as a NOLD in a prior tax year;

— The NOLD is no longer limited by the federal NOLD source year or amount;

— The NOLD is a deduction against apportioned business income;

— Taxpayers only have to use a NOLD in an amount necessary to bring the tax on business income down to the higher of the tax measured by capital or the fixed dollar minimum tax, with excess NOL carried forward;

— NOLD is not allowed for a NOL sustained during any year in which the corporation generating the loss was not subject to tax in New York; and

— The current separate return limitation year (SRLY) rules used when corporations enter or leave a combined group are continued.

• *Prior net operating loss conversion subtraction*

Net operating losses (NOLs) that were incurred before the 2015 tax year are converted into a PNOLC subtraction to stabilize their value for financial accounting purposes (Sec. 210(1)(a)(viii), Tax Law).

Taxpayers must first compute the value of the unabsorbed NOL for the base year by applying the taxpayer's (or combined group's) 2014 business allocation percentage and tax rate to the 2014 pre-apportionment New York NOL carryforward. The resulting product is then divided by 6.51. This amount is referred to as the "PNOLC subtraction pool".

Taxpayers have a choice to (a) use 1/10 of the PNOLC subtraction pool in each year for the next 20 years or (b) use 1/2 of the PNOLC subtraction pool in 2015 and 2016, but taxpayers that choose to deduct 1/2 of the subtraction in 2015 and 2016 will lose any amount not used after 2016. Otherwise, any unused portion is carried forward and added to the amount allowed in subsequent years. Years in which the subtraction cannot be used are counted in determining the 20-year period. Qualifying small business taxpayers are not subject to the use limits.

Where two or more taxpayers and/or groups that existed in tax year 2014 constitute one group in 2015, each taxpayer and/or group must compute its PNOLC subtraction separately based on its 2014 information. In 2015, the group's total PNOLC subtraction is the sum of the subtractions of each of its constituent taxpayers and/or groups. If a taxpayer leaves the group after 2015, the taxpayer takes its proportionate amount of the subtraction with it. If a taxpayer enters the group after 2015, its proportionate amount of the subtraction is added to the group's remaining subtraction amount.

The PNOLC subtraction is a deduction against apportioned business income. (Sec. 210(1)(A)(viii), Tax Law)

• *Prior law*

A net operating loss deduction is allowed in computing entire net income for New York corporation franchise tax purposes. A 20-year carryover and two-year carryback are permitted, but the carryback is limited to the first $10,000 of loss in any taxable year. (Sec. 208(9)(f), Tax Law; Reg. Sec. 3-8.1; Reg. Sec. 3-8.2) The New York deduction, while presumably the same as the federal deduction under IRC Section 172, is, however, subject to the following three limitations:

— No deduction is allowed for a loss sustained during any taxable year beginning prior to January 1, 1961, or for a loss sustained during any year in which the corporation was not subject to the corporation franchise tax under Article 9-A;

Example: A corporation is incorporated in Pennsylvania in January 2014. During the taxable year 2015 it sustains a net operating loss of $10,000. In January 2016, the corporation begins to do business in New York. For the taxable year 2016 it has entire net income of $10,000. A New York net operating loss deduction is not allowed for any part of the 2015 loss, because the corporation was not subject to New York franchise tax in 2015;

— Any net operating loss that may be carried forward or carried back for federal tax purposes is subject to adjustment for the additions and subtractions required by New York (¶1002, 1003);

— The New York net operating loss deduction generally may not exceed the deduction allowable for federal income tax purposes.

Practitioner Comment: Cumulative Carryforward

For tax years prior to 2015, the New York net operating loss may not exceed the deduction allowed for federal income tax purposes. However, when the taxpayer's carryback is limited to $10,000 for New York purposes (see above), the remaining loss can be carried forward, even if the carryforward exceeds the federal net operating loss carryforward. (Sec. 208.9(f), Tax Law)

Mark S. Klein, Esq., Hodgson Russ LLP

• *Election to relinquish carryback*

The filing of an election to relinquish the carryback of a loss with the Internal Revenue Service is considered to be binding for New York corporation franchise tax purposes. A taxpayer who has made the election should submit a copy of the federal election with its franchise tax report for the year of the net operating loss.

• *S corporations*

Deductions may not be taken by S corporations for net operating losses sustained during any year in which they had not elected New York S corporation status, or for net operating losses sustained during taxable years beginning prior to 1990. Similarly, corporations not electing New York S corporation status may not deduct net operating losses sustained during years in which they did elect New York S corporation status. For additional information, see ¶853.

• *Combined reports*

In the case of a corporation that reports for New York franchise tax purposes on a combined basis with one or more related corporations, either for the year in which the net operating loss is sustained or for the year in which a deduction for such loss is taken, the deduction of the net operating loss is subject to the limitations that would apply for federal income tax purposes if a consolidated federal return for the same related corporations had been filed, regardless of whether in fact such consolidated federal return was filed. Any carryback or carryover from a year in which a combined New York report was filed is based upon the combined net operating loss of the group of corporations. Only a proportionate part of the combined loss may be carried by a member of the group to a separate report for a preceding or succeeding taxable year in which a separate report is filed.

¶1009 Income, Gain, or Loss from Subsidiary Capital

Law: Sec. 208(9), Tax Law; Reg. Sec. 3-2.4 (CCH NEW YORK TAX REPORTS, ¶10-635, 10-810, 10-815, 10-825).

For taxable years beginning on or after January 1, 2015, the exemptions for income from subsidiary capital and 50% of dividends from nonsubsidiaries are eliminated (Sec. 208(9)(b), Tax Law). The income is reclassified as investment income, other exempt income, or business income.

Prior law: For taxable years beginning before 2015, income (including dividends and interest), gains, and losses from subsidiary capital were not included in entire net income for New York corporation franchise tax purposes. (former Sec. 208(9)(a)(1), Tax Law; Reg. Sec. 3-2.4(a)(1)) Appropriate additions or subtractions had to be made to federal taxable income.

CCH Advisory: Interest Related to Subsidiary Capital

The purpose of the exclusion of interest attributable to subsidiary capital is to prevent a parent corporation from obtaining a double tax benefit by taking a deduction for interest payments on loans incurred for directly or indirectly financing investments in subsidiaries while at the same time the parent's income derived from such investments is tax free (*F.W. Woolworth Co.*, New York Supreme Court, Appellate Division, Third Department, January 22, 1987, 126 AD2d 976, 510 NYS2d 926, CCH NEW YORK TAX REPORTS, ¶ 251-579). See also, *Carpenter Technology Corporation,* New York Supreme Court, Appellate Division, 3rd Department, No. 90083, June 27, 2002, CCH NEW YORK TAX REPORTS, ¶ 404-225.

¶1010 Allocation of Entire Net Income

For allocation of entire net income, see Chapter 13.

¶1011 Combined Reports

Law: Sec. 210-C, Tax Law (CCH NEW YORK TAX REPORTS, ¶ 11-550).

In the case of combined reports, all intercompany dividends are eliminated in computing combined entire net income (except in the case of non-exempt DISCs (¶ 919)).

For discussion of when combined reports are required or permitted, see ¶ 1404.

CORPORATION FRANCHISE (INCOME) TAX

CHAPTER 11
BASIS OF TAX—THREE ALTERNATIVE BASES

¶1101 In General

For taxable years beginning before 2015, the New York corporation franchise tax was measured by one of three alternative bases if a greater tax would result than from a tax measured on entire net income (discussed in Chapter 10). The alternative bases are:

— business and investment capital allocated to New York (¶1102);

or

— minimum taxable income (eliminated for tax years beginning on or after January 1, 2015; see ¶1105);

or

— fixed dollar minimum (¶1107).

The base that will produce the greatest amount of tax is used.

For taxable years beginning before 2015, the tax on subsidiary capital (repealed for taxable years beginning after 2014; see Chapter 12) is added to the tax measured by entire net income or one of the three alternative bases.

• *Taxable years beginning after 2014*

The minimum taxable income base (alternative minimum tax) is eliminated for taxable years beginning on or after January 1, 2015, as is the additional tax on subsidiary capital (Sec. 210, Tax Law). Accordingly, the tax is generally the highest of the amounts under the entire net income (ENI/business income base, the capital base, or the fixed dollar minimum). However, the capital base tax is being phased out over six years, beginning in 2016 (see ¶905).

¶1102 Capital Basis

Law: Secs. 208, 210, Tax Law; Reg. Secs. 3-3.2, 3-3.46, 3-3.7 (CCH New York Tax Reports, ¶10-535).

NOTE: the capital base tax is being phased out over six years, beginning in 2016 (see ¶905).

The New York corporation franchise tax is based on the corporation's business and investment capital, or the portion thereof allocated to New York, if a higher tax will result than from the other alternative bases of tax (entire net income, minimum taxable income, fixed dollar minimum).

Small business taxpayer: If the tax of a small business taxpayer is greater computed on the capital base than when it is computed on the entire net income base, solely by reason of the application of the special rate applicable to small business taxpayers, then the tax is imposed without reference to the taxpayer's capital base. In other words, the small business taxpayer must choose the capital base only when it exceeds the tax computed on the entire net income base at the generally applicable rate.

For definition of "small business taxpayer," see ¶905. Allocation provisions are discussed at ¶1103.

• *"Business capital" defined*

"Business capital" means all assets (exclusive of stock issued by the taxpayer or assets constituting subsidiary capital or investment capital), *less* liabilities, to the extent such liabilities are not deducted in computing subsidiary capital or investment capital. "Business capital" includes loans to a subsidiary, if the subsidiary is allowed to take the interest as a deduction for purpose of a New York franchise tax. The term also includes investments in the securities of a DISC, or any indebtedness from a DISC. (Sec. 208(7) and (8-A), Tax Law; Reg. Sec. 3-3.3)

• *"Investment capital" defined*

For taxable years beginning after 2014, the term "investment capital" means investments in stocks that are held by the taxpayer for more than six consecutive months but are not held for sale to customers in the regular course of business or, if the taxpayer makes the fixed percentage method election provided for in Sec. 210-A(5)(a)(1), Tax Law, are not qualified financial instruments as described in Sec. 210-A(5), Tax Law. Stock in a corporation that is conducting a unitary business with the taxpayer, stock in a corporation that is included in a combined report with the taxpayer pursuant to the commonly owned group election in Sec. 210-C(3), Tax Law, and stock issued by the taxpayer shall not constitute investment capital. (Sec. 208(5)(a), Tax Law)

Any liabilities that are directly or indirectly attributable to investment capital are deducted from investment capital. If the amount of those liabilities exceeds the amount of investment capital, the amount of investment capital will be zero. (Sec. 208(5)(b), Tax Law)

For special treatment of investments in stocks, bonds or other securities of a DISC or any indebtedness from a DISC, see ¶919.

Prior law: For taxable years beginning before 2015, "investment capital" means investments in stocks, bonds and other securities issued by any corporation (other than the taxpayer or a subsidiary) or by any government (federal, state, local or foreign) or governmental instrumentality. (Sec. 208(5), Tax Law; Reg. Sec. 3-3.2) In the discretion of the Commissioner, liabilities attributable to investment capital may be deducted.

Repurchase agreements and demand notes used by a commodities broker as short-term investments were properly treated as investment capital for franchise tax purposes. Both instruments were similar to repurchase agreements and demand notes actively traded in the over-the-counter market and were designed to enable to taxpayer to receive the most favorable rate of return on short-term investments. Furthermore, the instruments were issued for the purpose of financing a corporate enterprise and provided a distribution of rights in or obligations of the corporate enterprise. Therefore, the repurchase agreements and demand notes were treated as "other securities" and properly classified as investment capital (*C. Czarnikow, Inc.,* Division of Tax Appeals, Tax Appeals Tribunal, CCH NEW YORK TAX REPORTS, ¶253-788).

¶1102

CCH Advisory: Financing Agreements—Business or Investment Capital?

The Tax Appeals Tribunal (TAT) reversed an Administrative Law Judge (ALJ) determination that found that certain equipment financing agreements between a corporation and various government entities qualified as investment capital, the income from which constituted investment income. The ALJ concluded that the agreements were "other securities" under Reg. Sec. 3-3.2(c) because the corporation's government customers did in fact provide debt obligations to the corporation through the terms of the lease/sale financing agreements.

However, the TAT rejected the ALJ's reading of the regulation because it would define a security as something that is not a security under New York decisional law. Under the applicable case law, the leases and installment sales did not constitute securities, because the agreements were not investments in common enterprises and the profits were not expected solely from the work of others. In addition, the instruments did not possess the attributes of investments, but rather those of contracts to rent or purchase equipment at a fixed rate or price.

The TAT also found that the corporation's relationship to the leases and installment sales was of assistance in determining whether the instruments constituted business income or investment income. The corporation was in the business of selling, servicing, and leasing office equipment, and the instruments were created in the corporation's ordinary course of business. The business nature of the transactions did not change because the sales involved extensions of retail credit to customers or because the purchasers were government entities. Focusing on the corporation's relationship to and the substance of the transactions, the TAT concluded that the revenue streams from the leases and installment sales were properly construed as business income. (*Xerox Corp.,* New York Tax Appeals Tribunal, DTA No. 822620, January 12, 2012; CCH NEW YORK TAX REPORTS, ¶ 407-458)

• *Cash*

For taxable years beginning before 2015, cash on hand and on deposit could, at the election of the taxpayer, be treated either as business capital or as investment capital. (Sec. 208(7), Tax Law; Reg. Sec. 3-3.2)

• *Determination of amount of investment and business capital*

The amount of investment capital and business capital is determined by taking the average value of the gross assets (less deductible liabilities), and, if the period covered by the report is other than a period of 12 calendar months, by multiplying the value by the number of calendar months or major parts thereof included in the period, and dividing the product by 12. (Sec. 210(2), Tax Law; Reg. Sec. 3-3.46; Reg. Sec. 3-3.7) Real property and marketable securities will be valued at fair market value.

The capital base is not applicable to the first two taxable years of a taxpayer that, for one or both such years, is a small business corporation and meets certain statutory criteria.

¶1103 Allocation of Business and Investment Capital

Law: Sec. 210, Tax Law (CCH NEW YORK TAX REPORTS, ¶ 11-515).

Business capital is allocated by a "business allocation percentage," and investment capital is allocated by an "investment allocation percentage."

For full discussion of the allocation of business capital and investment capital, see Chapter 13.

¶1104 Tax Rate on Business and Investment Capital

Law: Sec. 210, Tax Law (CCH NEW YORK TAX REPORTS, ¶ 10-380).

For taxable years beginning after 2014, the capital base tax rates are as follows:

For qualified New York manufacturers and QETCs, the tax rates are: 0.15% (2015), 0.106% (2016), 0.085% (2017), 0.056% (2018), 0.038% (2019), 0.019% (2020), and 0% (2021 and thereafter).

For cooperative housing corporations, the rates are: 0.04% (through 2019), 0.025% (2020), and 0% (2021 and thereafter). For other taxpayers, the rates are: 0.15% (2015), 0.125% (2016), 0.1% (2017), 0.075% (2018), 0.05% (2019), 0.025% (2020), and 0% (2021 and thereafter). For tax years beginning on or after January 1, 2015, the tax is capped at $350,000 for qualified New York manufacturers and QETCs, and at $5 million for all other taxpayers.

See also ¶ 905.

Prior law: For taxable years beginning before 2015, when the business and investment capital basis is used, the tax is imposed, for taxable years beginning after 2007, at the rate of 0.15%. (previously, 0.178% for each dollar of the corporation's business and investment capital allocated to New York.)(Sec. 210(1)(b), Tax Law)

In the case of cooperative housing corporations, the rate is 0.4 mill per dollar of allocated business and investment capital.

In no event may the amount of the tax on business and investment capital exceed $1 million ($350,000 for New York qualified manufacturers). (The $1 million maximum for non-manufacturers was increased to $10 million by the 2008 budget legislation; it reverted to $1 million for taxable years beginning after 2010.)

For additional tax on subsidiary capital, see Chapter 12.

Manufacturers: Beginning in 2014, the tax rate applicable to the capital base is reduced for qualified manufacturers (see ¶ 905). A percentage reduction of 9.2% applies to the rate that was in effect for tax years beginning on or after January 1, 2013, and before January 1, 2014. (Sec. 210(1)(b)(iii), Tax Law):

¶1105 Minimum Taxable Income Base

Law: Secs. 208(8-B), 210, Tax Law; Reg. Secs. 3-4.1, 3-4.2 (CCH NEW YORK TAX REPORTS, ¶ 10-530).

CAUTION: This base is eliminated for tax years beginning on or after January 1, 2015.

The minimum taxable income base is the portion of the taxpayer's minimum taxable income allocated within the state, subject to any modification for double depreciation on tangible business property or the accelerated one-year write-off on research and development facilities. (Sec. 210(1)(c), Tax Law; Reg. Sec. 3-4.1)

"Minimum taxable income" defined: The term "minimum taxable income" is defined as the entire net income of the taxpayer for the taxable year (1) increased by the amount of the items of tax preference set forth in IRC Sec. 57, (2) determined with reference to certain federal adjustments, (3) increased by the New York net operating loss deduction, and (4) reduced by the alternative net operating loss deduction (¶ 1008). (Sec. 208(8-B), Tax Law; Reg. Sec. 3-4.2) The federal items of tax preference will be modified by deducting tax-exempt interest and accelerated depreciation or amortization on certain property placed in service before January 1, 1987.

For allocation provisions, see ¶ 1303 and following.

¶1106 Tax Rate on Minimum Taxable Income

Law: Sec. 210, Tax Law (CCH NEW YORK TAX REPORTS, ¶10-380).

CAUTION: This base is eliminated for tax years beginning on or after January 1, 2015.

The tax on minimum taxable income was 1.5% for tax years beginning after 2006 and before 2015 (former Sec. 210(1)(c), Tax Law).

For the former additional tax on subsidiary capital, see Chapter 12.

¶1107 Fixed Dollar Minimum Basis

Law: Sec. 210, Tax Law (CCH NEW YORK TAX REPORTS, ¶10-380).

The fixed dollar minimum tax is based on New York receipts. Before 2008, the tax was based on gross payroll. Special rates apply to New YOrk manufacturers. For rates, see ¶905.

S corporations: In the case of a termination year (¶916), the total of the tax calculated for the S short year and the C short year may not be less than the fixed dollar minimum tax calculated as if the taxpayer were a New York C corporation for the entire year.

Homeowners' associations: The fixed dollar minimum tax does not apply to home-owners' associations that have no homeowners' association taxable income for federal income tax purposes.

¶1108 Combined Reports

Law: Sec. 210-C, Tax Law (CCH NEW YORK TAX REPORTS, ¶11-550).

For taxable years beginning in 2015, the tax on a combined report is the highest of (Sec. 210-C(1)(a), Tax Law):

— the combined business income base multiplied by the business income tax rate;

— the combined capital base multiplied by the capital tax rate; or

— the fixed dollar minimum that is attributable to the designated agent of the combined group.

For the applicable tax rates, see ¶905.

In addition, the tax on a combined report includes the fixed dollar minimum tax specified for each member of the combined group, other than the designated agent, that is a taxpayer (Sec. 210-C(1)(a), Tax Law).

The combined business income base is the amount of the combined business income of the combined group that is apportioned to the state, reduced by any net operating loss deduction for the combined group. The combined capital base is the amount of the combined capital of the combined group that is apportioned to the state. (Sec. 210-C(1)(b), Tax Law)

For additional information on combined reporting, see ¶1404.

CORPORATION FRANCHISE (INCOME) TAX

CHAPTER 12

BASIS OF TAX—SUBSIDIARY CAPITAL

¶1201 In General

Law: Secs. 208, 210, Tax Law; Reg. Sec. 3-6.2 (CCH NEW YORK TAX REPORTS, ¶ 10-635, 10-810, 10-815, 10-825, 10-535).

NOTE: The separate tax on subsidiary capital is repealed for taxable years beginning after 2014. See ¶ 905.

Income, gains, and losses from subsidiary capital were excluded in computing entire net income. A tax was imposed on the portion of a corporation's subsidiary capital, if any, allocated to New York. This tax on subsidiary capital was in addition to the tax measured by entire net income, other alternative bases, or the fixed dollar minimum tax. See ¶ 905 for rates.

The subsidiary capital base is reduced for certain subsidiaries that are themselves subject to New York franchise taxes. See ¶ 1203 for discussion.

¶1202 "Subsidiary" Defined

Law: Sec. 208, Tax Law; Reg. Sec. 3-6.3 (CCH NEW YORK TAX REPORTS, ¶ 10-535).

A "subsidiary" is defined to mean a corporation over 50% of the voting stock of which is owned by the taxpayer. (Sec. 208(3), Tax Law)

¶1203 Subsidiary Capital

Law: Secs. 208, 210, Tax Law; Reg. Sec. 3-6.3 (CCH NEW YORK TAX REPORTS, ¶ 10-535).

NOTE: The separate tax on subsidiary capital is repealed for taxable years beginning after 2014. See ¶ 905.

Subsidiary capital included the following: (1) investments in stock of subsidiaries; and (2) the amount of indebtedness owed to the taxpayer by its subsidiaries, exclusive of accounts receivable acquired in the ordinary course of trade or business for services rendered or for sales of property held primarily for sale to customers, on which no interest was claimed and deducted by the subsidiary for the purpose of any New York franchise tax imposed by Articles 9-A, 32, or 33 of the Tax Law. (Reg. Sec. 3-6.3) In the discretion of the Commissioner, liabilities attributable to subsidiary capital may be deducted.

Determination of amount of subsidiary capital: The amount of subsidiary capital was determined by taking the average value of the gross assets (less deductible liabilities), and, if the period covered by the report is other than a period of 12 calendar months, by multiplying the value by the number of calendar months or major parts thereof included in the period, and dividing the product by 12. (former Sec. 210(2), Tax Law)

Real property and marketable securities are valued at fair market value, and the value of personal property other than marketable securities is the value shown on the books and records of the taxpayer in accordance with generally accepted accounting principles.

¶1204 Allocation of Subsidiary Capital

Law: Sec. 210, Tax Law (CCH NEW YORK TAX REPORTS, ¶11-510, 11-515).

NOTE: The separate tax on subsidiary capital is repealed for taxable years beginning after 2014. See ¶905.

Taxpayers were entitled to allocate subsidiary capital within and without New York. For method of allocation, see ¶1316.

¶1205 Tax Rate on Subsidiary Capital

Law: Sec. 210, Tax Law (CCH NEW YORK TAX REPORTS, ¶10-380).

NOTE: The separate tax on subsidiary capital is repealed for taxable years beginning after 2014. See ¶905.

The former tax measured by subsidiary capital was at the rate of 0.9 mill for each dollar of subsidiary capital allocated to New York. (former Sec. 210(1)(e), Tax Law)

The tax on subsidiary capital, if any, was added to the tax measured by one of the four alternative bases (entire net income, business and investment capital, minimum taxable income, or fixed dollar minimum). The resulting total was the amount of the New York corporation franchise tax.

CORPORATION FRANCHISE (INCOME) TAX

CHAPTER 13
ALLOCATION OF INCOME AND CAPITAL

¶ 1301 In General

Law: Secs. 210 and 210-A, Tax Law (CCH New York Tax Reports, ¶ 11-505).

In general, for taxable years beginning before 2015, a "business allocation percentage" (¶ 1303) was used to allocate business income and business capital. An "investment allocation percentage" (¶ 1307) was ordinarily used to allocate investment income and investment capital. Subsidiary capital was allocated by a "subsidiary allocation percentage" (¶ 1316) determined by the amount of capital employed in New York by the taxpayer's subsidiaries.

• *Corporate Tax Reform*

Under corporate tax reforms enacted as part of the 2014 budget legislation (Ch. 59 (S.B. 6359), Laws 2014), business income is apportioned based on a single receipts factor using customer sourcing rules, applicable to taxable years beginning after 2014 (Sec. 210-A, Tax Law; *Corporate Tax Reform*, New York Department of Taxation and Finance, **http://www.tax.ny.gov/bus/ct/corp_tax_reform.htm**). For details of sourcing, see ¶ 1303.

For taxable years beginning after 2014, business income equals entire net income (ENI) minus investment income and other exempt income. Business income includes the following (Sec. 210-A, Tax Law):

— interest income and gains and losses from debt instruments or other obligations, unless the income cannot be included in apportionable business income under the U.S. Constitution;

— gains and losses from stock of a unitary corporation;

— dividends and gains and losses from stock held in a non-unitary corporation for 6 months or less; and

— cash.

All non-interest deductions are now attributable to business income; see *TSB-M-15(8)C, (7)I*, December 31, 2015, CCH NEW YORK TAX REPORTS, ¶ 408-609.

Qualified financial instruments: If the taxpayer makes the fixed percentage election under Sec. 210-A(5)(a)(1), Tax Law, then all income from qualified financial instruments (QFIs) will constitute business income. Special rules apply to apportionment of gains from marked-to-market financial instruments (Sec. 210-A(5)(a)(2), Tax Law). The definition of a qualified financial instrument (QFI) has been amended to clarify that stock that generates other exempt income and is not marked to market under IRC section 475 or 1256, is not a QFI with respect to such other exempt income even if other stocks are marked to market in the tax year (Sec. 210-A(5)(a), Tax Law; see *TSB-M-16(3)C*, New York Department of Taxation and Finance, June 7, 2016, CCH NEW YORK TAX REPORTS, ¶ 408-764).

Investment income includes only income from stocks of non-unitary corporations held for more than six consecutive months and income that cannot be included in apportionable business income under the U.S. Constitution (Sec. 208(6), Tax Law). Certain interest, operating loss, and hedging transactions are excluded.

The new "other exempt income" category of income is defined as the sum of exempt CFC income and exempt unitary dividends (Sec. 208(6-A), Tax Law). "Exempt CFC income" is income received from a controlled foreign corporation that is conducting a unitary business with the taxpayer but is not included in the combined group. This includes Subpart F income and IRC Sec. 956 dividends. "Exempt unitary dividends" are dividends from unitary corporations not in the combined group because they are:

(1) taxable under another tax article;

(2) alien corporations not deemed domestic with no ECI; or

(3) less than 50% directly or indirectly owned.

S corporations: The New York Department of Taxation and Finance has issued a memorandum discussing how the state's corporate tax reform legislation affects the apportionment factor computation for a New York S corporation, as well as the determination of New York source income for nonresident and part-year resident shareholders of New York S corporations. For tax years beginning on or after January 1, 2015, the business apportionment factor reflects a corporation's New York market-based receipts. See *TSB-M-15(7)C, (6)I*, December 1, 2015, CCH NEW YORK TAX REPORTS, ¶ 408-575.

¶1302 Allocation of Entire Net Income

Law: Secs. 210, Sec. 210-A, Tax Law; Reg. Secs. 3-13.1, 3-13.3 (CCH NEW YORK TAX REPORTS, ¶ 10-220, 10-225, 11-515).

Under corporate tax reforms applicable to taxable years beginning after 2014, ENI/business income is apportioned based on a single receipts factor using customer sourcing rules (Sec. 210-A, Tax Law; *Corporate Tax Reform*, New York Department of Taxation and Finance, **http://www.tax.ny.gov/bus/ct/corp_tax_reform.htm**).

Prior law: After the taxpayer's entire net income has been ascertained (Chapter 10) the portion allocated to New York and subject to the franchise tax is determined by (1) multiplying business income by a business allocation percentage, (2) multiplying investment income by an investment allocation percentage, and (3) adding the two products. (Sec. 210(3)(c), Tax Law)

If a net operating loss deduction (¶ 1308) is allowable in computing entire net income, it is apportioned between business income and investment income in accordance with the ratio of each to entire net income (before the deduction) before applying the allocation percentages.

The business allocation figure cannot be used if there is no business income or if business income shows a loss. Likewise, the investment allocation percentage does not apply if investment income is zero or a loss.

• *Foreign limited partners*

A foreign corporate limited partner that is subject to business franchise tax (¶902) may elect to compute its tax by taking into account only its distributive share of the income, capital, gain, loss, or deduction of each limited partnership that is doing business, employing capital, owning or leasing property, or maintaining an office in New York, regardless of whether such share is actually distributed. (Reg. Sec. 3-13.1) This election does not apply if the limited partnership and corporate group are engaged in a unitary business and there are substantial inter-entity transactions between the limited partnership and the corporate group, or if the foreign corporation files on a combined basis. The election must be made at the time the report is filed, and cannot be revoked by the filing of an amended report. The election is binding on the partnership interest for all future taxable years.

If a foreign limited partner makes an election regarding one or more, but not all, limited partnerships of which it is a partner that are doing business, employing capital, or owning or leasing an office in New York, its tax with respect to each partnership for which it has made such an election must be determined by reducing its entire net income and capital derived from its distributive share of income, capital, gain, loss, or deduction by the portion of the permissible deductions and liabilities that are attributable to the election partnership. In computing tax with respect to non-election partnerships, deductions and liabilities otherwise included in the computation of such tax must be reduced by the portion attributed to each election partnership. (Reg. Sec. 3-13.1)

• *Tiered partnerships*

When a corporation is a member in a partnership ("upper-tier partnership") that is a member in another partnership ("lower-tier partnership"), the source and character of the partner's distributive share of each partnership item of the upper-tier partnership that is attributable to the lower-tier partnership will retain the source and character determined at the level of the lower-tier partnership. The source and character are not changed by reason of the fact that the partnership item flows through the upper-tier partnership to the corporation. (Reg. Sec. 3-13.3)

¶1303 Business Allocation Percentage

Law: Secs. 209, 210, Tax Law; Reg. Secs. 4-4.1—4-4.6, Reg. Secs. 4-6.2, 4-6.3, 4-6.5 (CCH New York Tax Reports, ¶11-505—11-540).

The receipts factor constitutes 100% of the business allocation percentage for taxable years beginning on or after January 1, 2007. The property and payroll factors were each reduced from 25% of the percentage to 0% in 2007. (Sec. 210(3)(a)(10), Tax Law)

When the business allocation percentage does not properly reflect the activity, business, capital, or income of the taxpayer in New York, the Commissioner may adjust the percentage (¶1314).

• *Corporate Tax Reform*

Under corporate tax reforms enacted as part of the 2014 budget legislation, applicable to taxable years beginning after 2014, business income is apportioned based on a single receipts factor using customer sourcing rules (Sec. 210-A, Tax Law; *Corporate Tax Reform*, New York Department of Taxation and Finance, **http://www.tax.ny.gov/bus/ct/corp_tax_reform.htm**).

Receipts from sales of electricity are sourced to the delivery location.

Net gains (not less than zero) from the sales of real property are sourced to the location of the property.

Royalties from the use of patents, copyrights, trademarks, and similar intangibles are sourced to New York if the intangibles are used within the state.

Receipts from digital products are generally sourced to the customer's primary use location of the product.

New sourcing rules are created for apportioning income from financial instruments.

— Qualified financial instruments (QFIs) are defined as financial instruments that are marked to market under IRC Secs. 475 or 1256, excluding loans secured by real property.

— Taxpayers can use one of two sourcing methods for QFIs:

(1) customer-based sourcing for each income stream that does not constitute tax exempt income; or

(2) elect to treat all income from QFIs as taxable business income and apportion 8% of the net income (dividend income, interest income, and net gains), not less than zero, from QFIs to New York.

— The 8% QFI election must be made on an annual basis, is irrevocable, and applies to all the QFI income of all members of a combined group.

— Non-qualified financial instruments (non-QFIs) are all financial instruments that do not meet the definition of QFI and the related income is subject to customer-based sourcing.

In cases where sourcing rules for financial transactions rely on commercial domicile, taxpayers are required to use the following hierarchy:

— location of the treasury function;

— seat of management and control; and

— billing address of the customer.

Receipts constituting the primary spread of selling concession from underwritten securities are sourced to the customer's location.

Receipts from credit card authorization processing and clearing and settling processing are sourced to the location where the credit card processor's customer accesses the processor's network.

All other credit card processing receipts are sourced to New York using the average of 8% and the percentage of New York access points.

Receipts from services are generally sourced to New York if the customer receives the benefit of the service in the state.

The special apportionment rules for trucking, railroad, transportation of gas through pipes, and aviation are used as the basis for the new receipts rules for these industries.

Existing sourcing rules continue generally for the following:

— sales of tangible personal property;

— rentals of real and tangible personal property;

— broker/dealer activities, except as described above;

— interest, fees, penalties, service charges, merchant discounts, and credit card fees;

— services provided to a Regulated Investment Company (RIC); and

— advertising.

¶1303

(Sec. 210-A, Tax Law; *Corporate Tax Reform,* New York Department of Taxation and Finance, **http://www.tax.ny.gov/bus/ct/corp_tax_reform.htm**).

• *Apportionment factors for special industries*

New York has adopted special rules not found in the Uniform Division of Income for Tax Purposes Act (UDITPA) or the Multistate Tax Commission (MTC) regulations for the apportionment of income for the following industries and activities:

Newspaper and magazine advertising: In the case of taxpayers engaged in the business of publishing newspapers or periodicals, receipts arising from sales of advertising contained in the newspapers and periodicals are deemed to arise from services performed within New York to the extent that the publications are delivered to points within New York. (Sec. 210(3)(a)(2)(B), Tax Law; Reg. Sec. 4-4.3)

Online advertising: A Department of Taxation and Finance advisory opinion concludes that receipts from advertisers that have a cost-per-click (CPC) price structure arrangement should be allocated to New York when a New York subscriber clicks on the advertisement. The company's receipts from advertisers that have fee structures based on cost-per-thousand impressions (CPM) arrangements should be allocated to New York based on the ratio of New York subscribers to subscribers everywhere. (TSB-A-09(5)C, March 9, 2009, CCH NEW YORK TAX REPORTS, ¶ 406-352)

Practitioner Comment: Allocating Receipts to Internet Activity

Prior to 2015, receipts from activities occurring through the Internetwere sourced to New York based on the percentage of New York viewers who read or clicked on (for a CPC price structure) an advertisement. Based on the nature of the Internet, a taxpayer may have no idea of the location of the customers that view or click on their advertising. In that case, a "reasonable method" of allocation must be devised. (*SmarTax, LLC,* TSB-A-09(8)C, New York Commissioner of Taxation and Finance, June 16, 2009, CCH NEW YORK TAX REPORTS, ¶ 406-430). This is often based on New York population statistics.

Mark Klein, Esq., Hodgson Russ LLP

Management services rendered to RICs: Services provided to regulated investment companies (mutual funds) are allocated on the basis of the domicile of the shareholders of the mutual fund. The New York percentage of shareholders is determined by averaging monthly percentages reflecting the number of shares held by New York domiciliaries compared to the number of shares held by domiciliaries outside New York State. (Sec. 210(3)(a)(6), Tax Law; Reg. Sec. 4-4.3)

Airlines: An airline's entire net income allocated to New York is calculated by multiplying the airline's business income by an allocation percentage that is the average of the following three percentage calculations: (1) divide 60% of aircraft arrivals and departures in New York by total aircraft arrivals and departures everywhere; (2) divide 60% of revenue tons handled at New York airports by total revenue tons handled everywhere; and (3) divide 60% of originating revenue within New York by total originating revenue everywhere. (Sec. 210(3)(a)(7), Tax Law)

Foreign air carriers: In determining their business allocation percentages, qualified foreign air carriers must exclude property, receipts, salaries, wages, and other personal service compensation to the extent employed in, or attributable to, the generation of income excluded from entire net income (¶ 1003).

Air freight forwarders: In the case of taxpayers principally engaged in the activity of air freight forwarding acting as principal and like indirect air carriage, receipts arising from the activity from services performed within New York State are determined as follows: 100% of the receipts if both the pick up and delivery associated with the receipts are made in New York State and 50% of the receipts if either the pick up or delivery associated with the receipts is made in New York State. (Sec. 210(3)(a)(2)(B), Tax Law)

Railroad and trucking companies: Railroad and trucking companies that elect to be taxed under the Art. 9-A entire net income basis of taxation for taxable years beginning after 1997 (¶922) must use a single-factor allocation percentage to allocate income to New York. The percentage is determined by dividing the taxpayer's mileage within New York for the period covered by its report by its mileage within and without New York during the same period. (Sec. 210(3)(a)(8), Tax Law)

Vessels: The amount of receipts from the operation of vessels included in the numerator of the apportionment fraction is determined by multiplying the amount of such receipts by a fraction, the numerator of which is the aggregate number of working days of the vessels owned or leased by the taxpayer in territorial waters of the state during the period covered by the taxpayer's report and the denominator of which is the aggregate number of working days of all vessels owned or leased by the taxpayer during such period. Receipts from the operation of vessels are included in the denominator of the apportionment fraction. (Sec. 210-A(6-a), Tax Law)

Security and commodity brokers (including OTC derivatives dealers): The income allocation formula for registered securities and commodities brokers and dealers provides for the allocation of certain receipts to the domicile of the customer rather than the mailing address of the firms' offices of record. Specifically, these provisions apply to brokerage commissions, margin interest, account maintenance fees, management or advisory service fees, interest on certain loans and advances, and gross income, including accrued interest or dividends, from certain principal transactions (Secs. 210(3)(a)(2)(B), Tax Law, 210(3)(a)(9), Tax Law, *TSB-M-00(5)C*, Department of Taxation and Finance, December 27, 2000, CCH NEW YORK TAX REPORTS, ¶300-335).

A regulation explains the application of the special rules to receipts of registered securities brokers or dealers from repurchase agreements and securities lending agreements (Reg. Sec. 4-4.7(b)) The regulation also addresses corporate partners (Reg. Sec. 4-4.7(c)).

CCH Advisory: Allocation for ' and Dealers' Principal Transactions

Registered broker dealers may elect to source the gross income from principal transactions (*i.e.*, transactions by the broker or dealer for its own account and not as an agent for a customer) based on the location of the customer to the principal transaction. (See *TSB-M-02(5)C*, Department of Taxation and Finance, September 24, 2002, CCH NEW YORK TAX REPORTS, ¶300-373).

Commissions from over-the-counter transactions are included in the receipts factor only if the order originates from or through a taxpayer's New York office. Otherwise, no portion of the commission income is attributable to New York. OTC derivatives dealers are specifically included in the provisions discussed above allowing registered securities or commodities brokers or dealers to allocate certain kinds of receipts based on the location of their customers (Sec. 210(3)(a)(9)(B), Tax Law; TSB-M-02(5)C, Department of Taxation and Finance, September 24, 2002, CCH NEW YORK TAX REPORTS, ¶300-373).

Television and radio broadcasting companies: The broadcasting of radio and television programs and commercial messages by antenna under a license granted by the Federal Communications Commission (FCC) is deemed to be a service, and receipts from such programs are included in the receipts factor. If a lump sum is received for such a service, the sum is attributed to New York and to other states according to the number of listeners or viewers in each state. (Reg. Sec. 4-4.3)

¶1303

The licensing of television films, including syndication and cable television receipts, however, is treated differently. The receipts are allocated to New York State as follows (TSB-M-86(4)C, CCH NEW YORK TAX REPORTS, ¶ 9-958):

— When a producer of a film sells the rights to a film to a network or other taxpayer, the taxpayer's receipts are allocated to New York by the audience participation method as described above;

— When the producer of the film sells the rights to a film to a cable television network, the receipts from the sale are allocated to New York State by the ratio that New York subscribers bear to total subscribers everywhere;

— When a network or other taxpayer is acting as an agent of the producer of the film, its receipts are receipts for services. The taxpayer must allocate such commissions to New York to the extent the services were performed in New York on the basis of the audience participation method described above. Sellers of closed-circuit and cable TV transmission rights of an event (other than events occurring on a regularly scheduled basis) taking place within the state as a result of the rendition of services by employees of the corporation as athletes, entertainers, or performing artists, must include those receipts in the receipts factor to the extent that the receipts are attributable to transmissions received or exhibited within New York.

Cable TV; video-on-demand: The New York Department of Taxation and Finance has issued a guidance document explaining that a corporation's receipts from cable programming and video-on-demand services should be allocated based on the location of the subscribers. Accordingly, the numerator of the corporation's receipts factor should include the amount of cable programming and video-on-demand receipts paid by New York subscribers, and the denominator should include such receipts paid by all subscribers. The determination of whether a subscriber is a New York subscriber should be based on the location at which the cable programming is delivered. If information is not available to determine the delivery location, then the delivery location is presumed to be the subscriber's mailing address in the corporation's records. In addition, the corporation should base the allocation of advertising revenue on the ratio of its New York subscribers to the number of cable programming subscribers everywhere. (NYT-G-07(1)C, New York Commissioner of Taxation and Finance, January 17, 2007, CCH NEW YORK TAX REPORTS, ¶ 405-594)

Sellers of closed-circuit and cable TV transmission rights: Receipts from the sale of rights for closed-circuit and cable television transmission of an event (other than events occurring on a regularly scheduled basis) taking place within the state as a result of the rendition of services by employees of the corporation as athletes, entertainers, or performing artists, are included in the receipts factor for the corporation to the extent that such receipts are attributable to transmissions received or exhibited within the state. (Sec. 210(3)(a)(2)(C), Tax Law)

Office equipment: If a taxpayer's property ownership is limited to office equipment, the Commissioner may, on the Commissioner's own motion or by application of the taxpayer, eliminate the property factor, and may substitute a business expense factor. The business expense factor is the percentage that the taxpayer's business expenses, other than salaries and wages, incurred or expended within New York State bear to the total of such expenses. (Reg. Sec. 4-6.2)

Pipeline companies: Receipts arising from the transportation or transmission of gas through pipes are allocated to New York on the basis of the taxpayer's transportation units both inside and outside the state. A "transportation unit" is the transportation of one cubic foot of gas over a distance of one mile. (Sec. 210(3)(a)(2)(B), Tax Law)

Bus companies and companies using rolling equipment: The average fair market value of buses and other rolling equipment (such as construction equipment or trucks) that are located within and outside of New York is included in the property factor of the business allocation percentage by multiplying the value by the ratio of mileage or time operated within the state to the total mileage or time within and outside of New York. Mileage or time operated while a bus is engaged in school operations is disregarded in computing the ratio. (Reg. Sec. 4-3.1)

Receipts of the taxpayer from transportation by bus are included in the numerator of the receipts factor by multiplying such receipts by the time, mileage, or other approved ratio. Mileage or time operated in school operations is also disregarded for computation of the receipts ratio. (Reg. Sec. 4-4.5)

Government contractors: Government contracts are awarded on several bases, including cost sharing, time and materials, fixed price, and cost plus a fee. Reimbursed costs, as well as fees, commissions, incentive payments, and any other type of remuneration paid to the taxpayer for performance of a government contract, must be included in computation of the allocation factors, even if these costs are not reported as receipts for federal income tax purposes. (Reg. Sec. 4-6.3)

If reimbursed wages are not deducted by the taxpayer on its federal income tax return, such wages should be allocated to New York in the year in which the net fee for the contract is included in gross income for federal income tax purposes.

The terms of the contract are used to determine when ownership of property has passed. In the absence of such a contract provision, property is treated as belonging to the taxpayer until shipment is made to the government. Property owned by the government may not be included in the property factor.

Practitioner Comment: E-Commerce Income

Prior to 2015, the allocation of receipts from the electronic transmission of materials (copyrighted data and similar information) was based on the location of modems used by customers to download the material. Absent proof to the contrary, the location of the customer's modems was presumed to be the customer's mailing address (*Insurance Services Office Inc.*, TSB-A-00(15)C, CCH NEW YORK TAX REPORTS, ¶ 403-773).

Mark S. Klein, Esq., Hodgson Russ LLP

• *Corporate partners*

Under the 2014 corporate tax reform, the current approach to partnership items of receipts, income, gain, loss, and deduction that flow through a partnership to a corporate partner as well as gains or losses from the sale of a partnership interest itself (*i.e.*, the current regulations) is retained. (Sec. 209(1)(f), Tax Law; Sec. 210(3), Tax Law)

A taxpayer that is a corporate partner must allocate its part of the partnership's property, receipts, and payroll within and outside New York using the three-factor formula. (Reg. Sec. 4-6.5)

The New York Department of Taxation and Finance has issued comprehensive guidance on the computation of tax for corporations that are partners in partnerships or that are members of limited liability companies (LLCs) treated as partnerships, applicable to taxable years beginning on or after January 1, 2007 (*TSB-M-07(2)C and TSB-M-07(1)I*, January 17, 2007, CCH NEW YORK TAX REPORTS, ¶ 405-595). See also (¶ 855).

¶1304 Property Factor in Business Allocation Percentage

Law: Sec. 210, Tax Law; Reg. Secs. 4-3.1, 4-3.2 (CCH NEW YORK TAX REPORTS, ¶ 11-530).

When applicable, the property factor of the business allocation percentage is the following fraction (Sec. 210(3)(a)(1), Tax Law):

$$\frac{\text{Average Value of Real and Tangible Personal Property in New York}}{\text{Average Value of Real and Tangible Personal Property Everywhere}}$$

The property factor of the business allocation percentage is determined by ascertaining the percentage that the average value of the taxpayer's real and tangible personal property, whether owned or rented to it, within New York during the period covered by its report bears to the average value of all the taxpayer's real and tangible personal property during the period (Sec. 210(3)(a)(1), Tax Law). The term "value of all of the taxpayer's real and tangible personal property" means the adjusted bases of the properties for federal income tax purposes. Provided, however, that the taxpayer may make a one-time revocable election to use fair market value as the value of all of its real and tangible personal property, provided that the election is made on or before the due date for filing a report and provided that the election does not apply to any taxable year with respect to which the taxpayer is included on a combined report unless each of the taxpayers included on the report has made such an election, which remains in effect for the year.

The value of property rented to the taxpayer is determined by multiplying gross rents payable for the rental of the property during the taxable year by eight. (Reg. Sec. 4-3.2)

Intangible property: In a case involving amounts paid by a corporation's television stations under license agreements to broadcast television programs, an appellate court has annulled the Tax Appeals Tribunal's decision that the corporation could not treat the amounts as payments for the rental of tangible personal property. Consistent with prevailing technology, the vast majority of the programming was delivered by satellite during the years in question. The Department of Taxation and Finance informed the corporation that programming delivered on videotape was tangible personal property. However, the department purported to distinguish programming delivered via satellite transmission, contending that such programming was not tangible personal property that could be included in the property factor. While the petition was pending, the department announced a new policy that programming delivered on videotape or other hardcopy forms would no longer be considered tangible property for taxable years beginning on or after January 1, 2008. In the absence of the department's change in interpreting the statute, the corporation would have prevailed because its method of receiving programming was for all relevant tax purposes indistinguishable from a method permitted as part of the property factor. The tribunal's determination that the programming was not tangible property was effectively the result of retroactively applying a new interpretation of the statute to the corporation, and therefore the determination had to be annulled. (*Meredith Corp.,* Appellate Division of the Supreme Court of New York, Third Department, No. 512597, 102 A.D.3d 156, 956 N.Y.S.2d 585, November 21, 2012, CCH NEW YORK TAX REPORTS, ¶ 407-705)

¶1305 Receipts Factor in Business Allocation Percentage

Law: Sec. 210, Tax Law; Reg Sec. 4-4.2 (CCH NEW YORK TAX REPORTS, ¶ 11-525, 11-540).

The receipts factor of the business allocation percentage is the following fraction (Sec. 210(3)(a)(2), Tax Law):

$$\frac{\text{Receipts from Sales of Tangible Personal Property, Services, Rentals, Royalties and Other Business Receipts Attributable to New York}}{\text{Receipts from Sales, Etc. Everywhere}}$$

The receipts factor is computed by ascertaining the percentage that the receipts of the taxpayer arising from the following sources bears to receipts from all business transactions, within or without New York (Sec. 210(3)(a)(2), Tax Law):

— sales of its tangible personal property when shipments are made to points within New York or are otherwise received in the state;

CCH Advisory: Receipts from Sales of Goods

A destination rule for the allocation of receipts from the sale of merchandise is in effect by regulation (Reg. Sec. 4-4.2).

Under the regulations, when a customer picks up merchandise from a seller in New York, the sale is presumed to occur in New York but will be treated as a sale outside New York if the customer can show that the merchandise was taken out of state. Similarly, if possession of merchandise is transferred out of state, the sale is presumed to occur out of state and receipts from the sale must be allocated to income received outside New York. But if evidence shows that the merchandise was taken to New York, then receipts must be allocated to New York income. Before the regulations were amended, merchandise was treated as being sold in the state where a customer took possession of the merchandise, regardless of the merchandise's ultimate destination (TSB-M-00(3)C, Department of Taxation and Finance, August 15, 2000, CCH NEW YORK TAX REPORTS, ¶ 300-325).

— services performed within New York (see ¶ 1303 for apportionment factors applicable to certain industries);

— rentals from property situated within New York;

— royalties from the use of patents and copyrights within New York;

— receipts from the sales of rights for closed-circuit and cable television transmissions of an event (other than events occurring on a regularly scheduled basis) taking place within New York as a result of the rendition of services by employees of the corporation as athletes, entertainers or performing artists, but only to the extent that the receipts are attributable to such transmissions received or exhibited within New York; and

— all other business receipts earned within New York.

S corporations: In determining the business allocation percentage of S corporations, the receipts factor is counted only once. (Sec. 210(3)(a)(4), Tax Law)

¶1306 Payroll Factor in Business Allocation Percentage

Law: Sec. 210, Tax Law; Reg. Secs. 4-5.1—4-5.3 (CCH NEW YORK TAX REPORTS, ¶ 11-535).

When applicable, the payroll factor of the business allocation percentage is the following fraction (Sec. 210(3)(a)(3), Tax Law):

$$\frac{\text{Wages, Salaries, and Other Personal Service Compensation of Employees Within New York}}{\text{Wages, Salaries and Other Personal Service Compensation Everywhere}}$$

Wages, salaries, and other personal service compensation are computed on the cash or accrual basis in accordance with the method of accounting used in the computation of the entire net income during the taxable period. (Sec. 210(3)(a)(3), Tax Law)

Compensation paid to general executive officers of a corporation is not included in the computation of the payroll factor. In order to be considered a general executive officer, the officer must have company-wide authority or have responsibility for an entire division.

The regulations state that employees within New York include all employees regularly connected with or working out of an office or place of business of the taxpayer within New York, irrespective of where the services of such employees were performed. (Reg. Sec. 4-5.1) However, if the taxpayer establishes that a substantial part of the payroll paid to employees attached to a New York office is for services performed outside of New York so that the general rule will not be equitable, the Commissioner may permit computation of the payroll factor on the basis of services actually rendered within and without the state.

¶1307 Investment Allocation Percentage (obsolete)

Law: Sec. 210, Tax Law (CCH NEW YORK TAX REPORTS, ¶ 11-515).

Note: For taxable years beginning after 2014, investment income and other exempt income are not taxable and the deductions for interest expenses attributable to such income are disallowed. If actual expense attribution exceeds income, the excess expenses are required to be added back to income. (See ¶ 1005)

The investment allocation percentage was determined by (1) multiplying the amount of a company's investment capital (¶ 1102) invested in each stock, bond or other security (other than governmental securities) during the period covered by its report by the allocation percentage of the issuer or obligor, (2) adding together the products so obtained, and (3) dividing the result by the total of the company's investment capital invested during the period in stocks, bonds and other securities. (Sec. 210(3)(b), Tax Law)

Issuer's allocation percentage: For purposes of the calculation discussed above, the allocation percentage of the issuer or obligor is the percentage of the appropriate measure that was required to be allocated within New York State on the report, if any, required of the issuer or obligor under the Tax Law for the preceding year for the following issuers or obligors (Reg. Sec. 4-7.1):

    — For those subject to the franchise tax on transportation and transmission corporations and associations (Sec. 183, Tax Law), and for those subject to the franchise tax on farmers, fruit growers, and other co-operative agricultural corporations (Sec. 185, Tax Law), the appropriate measure is capital stock (¶ 2708, 2711);

    — For those subject to the tax on business corporations (Art. 9-A), the appropriate measure is entire net capital (¶ 904);

    — For those subject to the franchise tax on insurance companies, except for savings and insurance banks and domestic insurance companies (Art. 33), the appropriate measure is gross direct premiums (¶ 2702).

In the case of an issuer or obligor subject to the banking corporation tax (Art. 32) as a corporation or association organized under the laws of New York State, of any other state or country, or of the United States, the issuer's allocation percentage is the alternative entire net income allocation percentage determined under Sec. 1454(c), Tax Law, for the preceding taxable year. The issuer's allocation percentage of a banking corporation having alternative entire net income for the preceding year derived exclusively from business carried on within New York State is 100%. A corporation or association that is organized under the laws of a country other than the United States to do a banking business determines its issuer's allocation percentage by dividing (1) the loans (including a taxpayer's portion of a participation in a loan) and financing leases within New York State, and all other business receipts earned within New York with respect to the issuer or obligor from all sources within and without the United States, by (2) the gross income of the issuer or obligor from all sources within and without the United States, for the preceding year, whether or not included in alternative entire net income for the year (Sec. 210(3)(b), Tax Law; Reg. Sec. 4-7.1; *TSB-M-86(6)C*, CCH NEW YORK TAX REPORTS, ¶ 9-959).

    In the case of an issuer or obligor that is a corporation either (1) subject to Art. 3-A, (2) registered under the Federal Bank Holding Company Act of 1956, or (3) registered as a savings and loan holding company, the issuer's allocation percentage is determined by dividing the portion of the entire capital of the issuer or obligor allocable to New York State for the preceding year by the entire capital, wherever located, of the issuer or obligor for the preceding year.

If a report for the preceding year is not filed or, if filed, does not contain information that would permit the determination of the issuer's allocation percentage, then the issuer's allocation percentage to be used is, at the discretion of the Commissioner, either the issuer's allocation percentage derived from the most recently filed report of the issuer or obligor or a percentage calculated, by the Commissioner, reasonably to indicate the degree of economic presence in New York State of the issuer or obligor during the preceding year.

If a taxpayer's investment allocation percentage is zero, interest received on bank accounts will be multiplied by the taxpayer's business allocation percentage.

The Commissioner may adjust any investment allocation percentage that does not properly reflect the investment activity, business, income, or capital of the taxpayer within New York (¶1315).

Professional service corporations must use an investment allocation percentage of 100%. (Reg. Sec. 4-7.1)

Practitioner Comment: Bank Interest

For tax years prior to 2015, interest earned from bank accounts can be allocated using a taxpayer's investment allocation percentage as long as it has an investment allocation percentage greater than 0% (*e.g.*, not composed exclusively of U. S. government obligations). (Sec. 210.3(b)(3), Tax Law.) However, interest income from sources other than bank accounts (*e.g.*, short-term U.S. treasury notes and bills) can be allocated at 0% if the taxpayer's investment capital is limited to government obligations and companies with a zero issuer's allocation percentage (*Banigan*, TSB-A-02(10)C, CCH NEW YORK TAX REPORTS, ¶404-243).

Mark S. Klein, Esq., Hodgson Russ LLP

¶1308 Allocation—Net Operating Loss

Law: Sec. 208, Tax Law; Reg. Sec. 3-8.8 (CCH NEW YORK TAX REPORTS, ¶11-515).

Before 2015, when deducting any net operating loss (NOL), a taxpayer with both business income and investment income in a taxable year to which a net operating loss is carried must apportion the loss between business and investment income. The amount of loss to be subtracted from business income and investment income is computed by multiplying the net operating loss deduction by a ratio. The ratio is a fraction, the numerator of which is investment income and the denominator of which is entire net income, both before deduction of the NOL. (Reg. Sec. 3-8.8)

¶1309 Allocation—Deductions

Law: Sec. 208, Tax Law; Reg. Sec. 4-8.4 (CCH NEW YORK TAX REPORTS, ¶11-515).

Investment income is reduced by any deductions allowed in computing entire net income that are attributable to investment income or investment capital. In such case, the deductions are not taken into account for business income. (Reg. Sec. 4-8.4)

For deduction of current liabilities in computing investment capital and subsidiary capital, see ¶1102 and 1203.

¶1310 Allocation of Business Capital

Law: Sec. 210, Tax Law (CCH NEW YORK TAX REPORTS, ¶11-515).

The amount of the business capital allocable to New York is computed by multiplying total business capital (defined at ¶1102) by the business allocation percentage (¶1303).

¶1308

¶1311 Allocation of Investment Capital

Law: Sec. 210, Tax Law (CCH NEW YORK TAX REPORTS, ¶11-515).

For taxable years beginning before 2015, the amount of investment capital allocable to New York was determined by multiplying total investment capital (defined at ¶1102) by the investment allocation percentage (¶1307).

¶1313 Adjustments to Allocation Percentages

Law: Secs. 210, 211, Tax Law (CCH NEW YORK TAX REPORTS, ¶11-515).

The Commissioner is authorized to adjust the business allocation percentage (¶1314) or the former investment allocation percentage (¶1315) where the percentage does not properly reflect the activity, business, income, or capital of a taxpayer within New York. The Commissioner is also authorized to eliminate assets in computing any allocation percentage (provided the income therefrom is also excluded from entire net income or minimum taxable income).

The law directs the Commissioner to publish all rulings of general interest in connection with the adjustment of the allocation percentages.

¶1314 Adjustments to Business Allocation Percentage

Law: Sec. 210, Tax Law (CCH NEW YORK TAX REPORTS, ¶11-515).

The Commissioner may adjust a business allocation percentage that does not properly reflect the activity, business, income or capital of a taxpayer within New York. The adjustments include the following:

— excluding one or more of the property, receipts, or payroll factors;

— including one or more other factors, such as expenses, purchases, or contract values (less subcontract values);

— excluding one or more assets in computing the allocation percentage provided that the income therefrom is also excluded in determining entire net income or minimum taxable income; or

— applying any other similar or different method calculated to effect a fair and proper allocation.

Procedures for requesting a discretionary adjustment to the method of allocation for purposes of the corporate franchise tax and the banking franchise tax are explained in *TSB-M-11(3)C,* New York Department of Taxation and Finance, April 5, 2011, CCH NEW YORK TAX REPORTS, ¶407-187.

CCH Advisory: Nonunitary Business

An Illinois-based corporation was entitled to an adjustment of its business allocation percentage because the statutory formula did not accurately reflect the taxpayer's nonunitary business activity in New York. The corporation held a 90% interest in a New York metal trading business, but primarily received income from motion pictures it had produced outside New York before acquiring the New York business. Because the motion picture production and metals trading operations did not constitute a unitary business, the State Tax Commission's failure to adjust the corporation's business allocation percentage to allow separate accounting for the businesses constituted an abuse of discretion (*Petition of Movie Service Functions, Inc.,* Division of Tax Appeals, ALJ, May 5, 1988 (File No. 801472), CCH NEW YORK TAX REPORTS, ¶252-143).

¶1315 Adjustments to Investment Allocation Percentage

Law: Sec. 210, Tax Law (CCH NEW YORK TAX REPORTS, ¶11-515).

For taxable years beginning before 2015, the Commissioner may adjust any investment allocation percentage that does not properly reflect the investment activity, business, income, or capital of the taxpayer within New York by excluding one or more assets in computing the percentage. In such case, the income from the excluded asset or assets must be excluded in determining entire net income or minimum taxable income. (former Sec. 210(8), Tax Law; Reg. Sec. 4-6.1)

¶1316 Allocation of Subsidiary Capital

Law: Sec. 210, Tax Law; Reg. Sec. 4-10.1 (CCH NEW YORK TAX REPORTS, ¶11-515).

NOTE: The separate tax on subsidiary capital is repealed for taxable years beginning after 2014. See ¶905.

Prior law: Every taxpayer was entitled to allocate subsidiary capital (defined at ¶1203) within and without New York.

Subsidiary capital was allocated to New York as follows (Reg. Sec. 4-10.1):

— Multiply the investment in each subsidiary by the issuer's allocation percentage; and

— Add together the products obtained.

¶1317 Metropolitan Commuter Transportation District Surcharge

Law: Sec. 209-B, Tax Law (CCH NEW YORK TAX REPORTS, ¶10-380, 11-515).

Taxpayers determine the portion of their business activity carried on within the Metropolitan Commuter Transportation District by use of a three-factor formula. To make the apportionment, the taxpayer initially determines three percentages comparing its property, receipts, and compensation within the District to its property, sales, and compensation throughout the state as a whole. (Sec. 209-B, Tax Law)

Property factor: The first percentage is the ratio that the average value of the taxpayer's real and tangible personal property within the district during the taxable period bears to the average value of its property within the state. Both owned and rented property are factored into the computation, with value determined in the same manner as for general franchise tax purposes.

Receipts factor: The second percentage is the ratio that the taxpayer's receipts derived from the following sources bear to receipts from all transactions within the state, during the taxable period:

— sales of tangible personal property when shipment is made to points within the Metropolitan Commuter Transportation District;

— services performed within the district;

— rentals from property situated in the district and royalties from the use of patents or copyrights within the district, as well as receipts from the sales of rights for closed-circuit and cable television coverage of certain events taking place within the district as the result of the rendition of services by employees of the taxpayer as athletes, entertainers, or performing artists, to the extent the receipts are attributable to transmissions received or exhibited within the metropolitan commuter transportation district; and

— other business receipts earned within the district.

Compensation factor: The third percentage is the ratio of total wages, salaries, and other personal service compensation of employees within the district, other than executive offices, to the total wages, salaries, and other personal service compensation of all the taxpayer's employees within the state, except general executive officers, during the taxable period.

These percentages are then added together, and the result is divided by the number of percentages. The taxpayer's franchise tax is multiplied by the resultant percentage to determine the tax upon which the surcharge is imposed.

- *Aviation*

Taxpayers principally engaged in the conduct of aviation (other than air freight forwarders acting as principal, and like indirect air carriers) determine the portion of their business activity carried on within the Metropolitan Commuter Transportation District by multiplying the franchise tax by the average of the following three factors (Sec. 209-B(2-a)(a), Tax Law):

— the percentage determined by dividing the taxpayer's aircraft arrivals and departures within the Metropolitan Commuter Transportation District during the period covered on the taxpayer's report by the total aircraft arrivals and departures within New York State. The following are not included in computing the arrival and departure percentage: arrivals and departures solely for the maintenance or repair, refueling (when no debarkation or embarkation of traffic occurs); arrivals and departures of ferry and personnel training flights; or arrivals and departures in the event of emergency situations. Additionally, the Commissioner may provide an exemption for all non-revenue flights including flights involving the transportation of officers or employees receiving air transportation to perform maintenance or repair services or where the officers or employees are transported in conjunction with an emergency situation or the investigation of an air disaster (other than a scheduled flight);

— the percentage determined by dividing the revenue tons handled by the taxpayer at airports within the Metropolitan Commuter Transportation District during the period by the total revenue tons handled by it at airports within New York State during the period; and

— the percentage determined by dividing the taxpayer's originating revenue within the Metropolitan Commuter Transportation District for the period by its total originating revenue within the entire state for the period.

CAUTION: Although the allocation factors for an aviation business subject to the corporation franchise (income) tax are reduced to 60% of the above factors for tax years beginning after 2000 (see ¶1303), the reduction does not apply to the Metropolitan Transportation District surcharge. The numerators of the allocation factors must still contain 100% of each factor attributed to New York State (*TSB-M-99(4)(C)*, December 28, 1999, CCH NEW YORK TAX REPORTS, ¶300-304).

- *Air freight forwarders*

Taxpayers principally engaged as air freight forwarders acting as principal and like indirect air carriers compute their receipts from services performed within the Metropolitan Commuter Transportation District as follows: 100% of the receipts if both the pick up and delivery associated with the receipts are made in the Metropolitan Transportation District and 50% of the receipts if either the pick up or delivery associated with the receipts is made in the Metropolitan Commuter Transportation District. Air freight forwarders may file reports on a combined basis only if all of the taxpayers included on the combined report agree to have the air freight forwarder included. (Sec. 209-B(2-a)(b), Tax Law)

- *Railroad and trucking companies*

Railroad and trucking companies that elect to be taxed under the Art. 9-A entire net income basis of taxation (¶922) must allocate income to the Metropolitan Commuter Transportation District by multiplying their Art. 9-A tax liability by a fraction, the numerator of which is the taxpayer's mileage within the District for the period covered by its report, and the denominator of which is its mileage within New York during the same period. (Sec. 209-B(2-b), Tax Law)

¶1317

CORPORATION FRANCHISE (INCOME) TAX

CHAPTER 14
RETURNS, ESTIMATES, PAYMENT OF TAX

¶1401 Returns—Time and Place for Filing

Law: Secs. 211, 658, Tax Law; Reg. Sec. 6-3.1 (CCH NEW YORK TAX REPORTS, ¶89-102).

Comparable Federal: Sec. 6072 (U.S. MASTER TAX GUIDE, ¶3, 118—122, 2525—2545).

Forms: See ¶1402.

Beginning in 2016, C corporations subject to tax are required to file an annual corporation franchise tax return within 3 1/2 (previously, 2 1/2 months after the close of the fiscal year (April 15 for calendar-year corporations)). (Sec. 211(1), Tax Law; Reg. Sec. 6-4.1) A complete copy of the taxpayer's federal return must be attached to the New York return.

Corporations are required to report to the Commissioner specified information relating to payments made to shareholders owning more than 50% of the corporation's capital stock, when such payments are treated as payments of interest in the computation of entire net income or minimum taxable income (¶1509).

S corporations: Similar to provisions applicable to C corporations, discussed above. (Sec. 658(c)(2), Tax Law) If a New York S election terminates on a day other than the first day of the taxable year, the S short year and the C short year will be treated as separate taxable years and will require separate returns. The due date for the return for the S short year, however, will be the same as that of the C short year.

Domestic international sales corporations (DISCs): See ¶919.

Information returns—foreign corporations: A foreign corporation that is not a taxpayer but that has an officer or employee within New York, must file an information report (Sec. 211(1), Tax Law).

Information returns—credit and debit card payments: Annual reports must be filed with the Tax Department relating to credit and debit card payments to payees with New York State addresses or who are New York State taxpayers (referred to collectively as New York State payees). These New York requirements follow the provisions of IRC Sec. 6050W to require that annual reports must be filed by payment settlement entities, third-party settlement organizations, electronic payment facilitators, or other third parties acting on behalf of payment settlement entities. (Sec. 1703, Tax Law)

IRC Sec. 6050W requires a reporting entity to file annual information returns (Form 1099-K) with the Internal Revenue Service (IRS) reflecting the transactions of its payees. Under the New York Tax Law provisions, a reporting entity that is required to file the information returns under IRC Sec. 6050W is also required to file either a duplicate information return with the Tax Department or to file a duplicate of any information returns related to New York State payees. The duplicate information return required must be filed within 30 days of the filing of the information returns. See *TSB-M-12(2)C*, February 8, 2012, CCH New York Tax Reports, ¶ 407-470.

• *Administration*

Returns are filed with the Department of Taxation and Finance at the address stated on the return. The return must be signed by a responsible officer (that is, the president, vice-president, treasurer, assistant treasurer, chief accounting officer, or any other officer duly authorized to act on behalf of the corporation).

• *Amended federal return or federal changes:*

A taxpayer filing an amended federal return is required to file an amended New York return within 90 days thereafter. Also, if any change or correction is made in taxable income by federal authorities, or where income is changed by renegotiation of government contracts or subcontracts, the taxpayer, including an S corporation taxpayer, is required to report such change or correction within 90 days (120 days, if a combined return was filed) of the final determination. The allowance of a tentative carryback adjustment based upon a net operating loss carryback for federal purposes is treated as a final federal determination. (Sec. 211(3), Tax Law; Reg. Sec. 6-1.3)

The taxpayer is required to concede the accuracy of the federal determination or to state wherein it is erroneous. In case of failure to file a report of the federal changes, a deficiency assessment may be made at any time—see Sec. 1083, Tax Law.

¶1402 Returns—Forms in Current Use

Law: Sec. 211, Tax Law (CCH New York Tax Reports, ¶ 89-070).

The forms in current use include the following:

Form No.	Description
CT-3	General Business Corporation Franchise Tax Return [Long Form]
CT-3-A	Combined Franchise Tax Return
CT-3-C	Consolidated Franchise Tax Return
CT-3-S	S Corporation Franchise Tax Return
CT-4	General Business Corporation Franchise Tax Report [Short Form]
CT-5	Application for Six-Month Extension for Filing a Franchise or Business Tax Return
CT-40	Claim for Alternative Fuels Credit
CT-41	Claim for Credit for Employment of Persons with Disabilities
CT-43	Claim for Special Additional Mortgage Recording Tax Credit
CT-44	Claim for Investment Tax Credit for the Financial Services Industry
CT-46	Claim for Investment Tax Credit and Employment Incentive Credit
CT-46-ATT	Claim for Rehabilitation Expenses for Retail Enterprises and Historic Barns
CT-47	Claim for Farmers' School Tax Credit
CT-222	Underpayment of Estimated Tax by a Corporation
CT-238	Claim for Rehabilitation of Historic Properties Credit
CT-242	Claim for Clean Heating Fuel Credit
CT-242	Claim for Conservation Easement Tax Credit
CT-243	Claim for Biofuel Production Credit
CT-248	Claim for Empire State Film Production Credit
CT-249	Claim for Long-Term Care Insurance Credit
CT-250	Credit for Purchase of an Automatic External Defibrillator
CT-324	Schedule of Optional Depreciation on Qualified New York Property
CT-400	Estimated Tax for Corporations
CT-601	Claim for EZ Wage Tax Credit
CT-602	Claim for EZ Capital Tax Credit
CT-603	Claim for EZ Investment Tax Credit and EZ Employment Incentive Credit
CT-604	Claim for QEZE Credit for Real Property Taxes and QEZE Tax Reduction Credit
CT-604-CP	Claim for QEZE Credit for Real Property Taxes and QEZE Tax Reduction Credit for Corporate Partners
CT-605	Claim for EZ Investment Tax Credit and EZ Employment Incentive Credit for the Financial Services Industry
CT-2658	Report of Estimated Tax for Corporate Partners
DTF-621	Claim for QETC Employment Credit
DTF-622	Claim for QETC Capital Tax Credit
DTF-623	Claim for Industrial or Manufacturing Business (IMB) Credit
DTF-624	Claim for Low-Income Housing Credit
DTF-625	Low-Income Housing Credit Allocation Certification
DTF-625-ATT	Low-Income Housing Credit Annual Statement
DTF-630	Claim for Green Building Credit
DTF-632	Claim for Transportation Improvement Contribution Credit

CCH Advisory: Amended Returns

An amended return should be filed in order to claim a corporate tax refund or credit of tax in situations where a Form CT-8 or CT-9, (obsolete after 2008) would have been filed, or to notify the Tax Department of a change to their federal taxable income or federal alternative minimum taxable income where a Form CT-3360, Federal Changes to Corporate Taxable Income (obsolete after 2009) would have been filed. Taxpayers must file the amended return reflecting the federal change within 90 days (120 days, if filing a combined return) after the date of the final determination of the IRS. See *Important Notice N-09-2,* January 2009, CCH NEW YORK TAX REPORTS, ¶ 406-284; *Important Notice N-09-18,* October 2009, CCH NEW YORK TAX REPORTS, ¶ 406-562.

Two report forms are in general use: the simplified form, Form CT-4, and the long form, Form CT-3. Form CT-3 must be used by any corporation that has investment or subsidiary capital, a place of business outside New York State, or tax liability in excess of $1,000 or claims a net operating loss deduction, optional deduction for depreciation, adjustment for waste treatment or air pollution control facilities, credit for eligible business facilities, investment tax credit, etc.

The return forms furnished by the Commissioner have the name and address of the taxpayer imprinted thereon, together with certain file numbers and code numbers. The pre-stenciled forms should be used by the taxpayer; if not, the file and code number should be exactly duplicated. Reproduction of corporation tax forms is permitted provided that the reproduction is substantially identical to the official version.

Forms may be ordered from: New York State Tax Department, Taxpayer Assistance Bureau, W.A. Harriman Campus, Albany, NY 12227-0125. Taxpayers requesting forms may also call toll free 1-800-462-8100.

Forms also may be downloaded from the Department's website at **http://www.tax.ny.gov/forms**

¶1403 Extension of Time

Law: Secs. 209-A, 209-B, 211, 213, 213-a, 213-b, Tax Law; Reg. Sec. 6-4.4 (CCH NEW YORK TAX REPORTS, ¶ 89-102).

Comparable Federal: Sec. 6081 (U.S. MASTER TAX GUIDE, ¶ 2509).

Forms: CT-5, Application for Six-Month Extension for Filing a Franchise or Business Tax Report.

The Commissioner may grant a reasonable extension of time for filing reports when good cause exists. (Sec. 211(1), Tax Law) Application should be made prior to the due date.

In the case of the annual corporation franchise tax report, an automatic six-month extension will be granted on condition that Form CT-5 is filed and a "properly estimated" tax is paid on or before the due date of the return. (Reg. Sec. 6-4.4) A filing extension does not extend the due date for payment of tax. On or before the expiration of the automatic six-month extension of time for filing a report, the Commissioner may grant additional three-month extensions of time for filing reports when good cause exists. No more than two additional three-month extensions of time for filing a report for any taxable year may be granted. An application for each additional three-month extension must be made in writing before the expiration of the previous extension.

The amount of tax paid is deemed to be properly estimated if it is either not less than 90% of the actual tax liability or not less than the preceding taxable year's (12 month) tax.

If the estimated tax for the year is likely to be more than $1,000, a first installment payment (¶1405) must also be made.

The Commissioner may grant an extension of time of up to three months for the filing of a declaration of estimated tax and of up to six months for the payment of an installment of estimated tax. Interest applies for the period of extension for payment. For rate of interest, see ¶1507.

• *Metropolitan Commuter Transportation District business tax surcharge*

A six-month extension of time for the filing of the MCTD business tax surcharge report will be granted only if the taxpayer, at the time of filing the application for extension, pays either 90% of the surcharge or an amount equal to, or greater than, the surcharge amount shown on the taxpayer's report for the preceding taxable (12 month) year. The amount cannot be less than the product of the following amounts: (1) the surcharge rate; (2) the fixed dollar minimum; and (3) a percentage equal to the portion of the taxpayer's business activity carried on within the MCTD in the preceding year, unless the taxpayer was not subject to the surcharge, in which instance the percentage is considered to be 100%.

¶1404 Combined Reports

> *Law:* Sec. 210-C, Tax Law; Reg. Secs. 4-1.2, 4-4.7, 6-2.2—6-2.5, 6-3.2 (CCH New York Tax Reports, ¶11-550).
>
> *Comparable Federal:* Secs. 1501—1505 (U.S. Master Tax Guide, ¶295, 297).
>
> *Forms:* CT-3-A, Combined Franchise Tax Return.

Corporations engaged in a unitary business that comply with a 50% capital stock ownership requirement must file combined reports if filing on a separate basis would distort their activities, business, income, or capital in New York. (Sec. 210-C, Tax Law)

For taxable years beginning on or after January 1, 2015, the requirements to file a combined report are:

(1) the unitary business test and

(2) more than 50% stock ownership test based on voting power (one corporation directly or indirectly owns another, or corporations are controlled by a common interest or by related parties). The substantial intercorporate transactions test is eliminated.

The New York combined group must include all domestic corporations, alien corporations deemed domestic corporations under the IRC (contiguous, stapled, and inverted corporations), alien corporations with effectively connected income (ECI), captive REITs and RICs not combinable under Article 33, and combinable captive insurance companies. (Sec. 210-C, Tax Law)

The existing captive REIT/RIC combination requirement is incorporated without the special exclusion for affiliated groups whose members own assets under $8 billion. The combined reporting requirements for captive insurance companies is changed to require combination with captive insurance companies, where less than 50% of the captives' premiums are from arrangements that constitute insurance for federal income tax purposes. Cross-article combination remains prohibited.

In addition, the single receipts factor apportionment for all taxpayers (see ¶1301) allows aviation, railroad, and trucking companies to be included in the combined group.

Group election: Taxpayers can also make a commonly owned group election covering a seven-year period. The group must include all unitary and non-unitary corporations that could be taxed under Article 9-A and that meet the ownership test. The election must be made when the original return is timely filed and may not be revoked during the 7 year period. (Upon expiration, the election is automatically renewed for another seven years unless the group affirmatively declines; if the election is affirmatively declined, a new election cannot be made for 3 years).

Each corporation in the group is deemed to have agreed to treat the income from the non-unitary businesses as if it were from the group's unitary business, and any corporation conducting a non-unitary business that is acquired during that period that could be taxed under Article 9-A is included in the combined group for the remainder of the election period.

The combined group is generally treated as if it were a single entity. Each taxpayer member of the combined group is liable for the group's whole tax, not just its *pro rata* share of the combined group's tax. The combined group must designate one taxpayer member to be the agent for administrative purposes (*e.g.*, filings, assessments, payments, and waivers).

The combined group's tax is the sum of:

(1) the greater of the tax on combined business income, the tax on combined business capital, or the fixed dollar minimum tax of the agent and

(2) the fixed dollar minimum tax for every other taxpayer member of the group.

Generally, combined income is computed using the federal intercorporate deferral rules. Credits, prior net operating loss conversion subtractions, net operating loss deductions, and capital losses can be used by the group, not just the corporation that generated the item, and are applied in computing the combined tax. (Sec. 210-C, Tax Law; *Corporate Tax Reform*, New York Department of Taxation and Finance, **http://www.tax.ny.gov/bus/ct/corp_tax_reform.htm**)

Prior law—Related corporations: In determining whether to permit or require the filing of a combined report, the Commissioner of Taxation and Finance had to determine whether each member corporation in the group meets any of the following criteria (Sec. 211(4), Tax Law; Reg. Sec. 6-2.2; *TSB-M-13(3)C*, June 5, 2013, CCH NEW YORK TAX REPORTS, ¶ 407-853):

— the corporation owns or controls, either directly or indirectly, substantially all of the capital stock of another corporation;

— substantially all of the capital stock of the corporation is owned or controlled either directly or indirectly by another corporation; or

— substantially all of the capital stock of the corporation and one or more other corporations is owned or controlled, either directly or indirectly, by the same interests.

"Substantially all" means ownership or control of 80% or more of the voting power of the issued and outstanding stock. Ownership includes actual or beneficial ownership. (Reg. Sec. 6-2-2(a)(2)) To be considered the owner, the stockholder must have the right to vote and receive dividends.

"Control" refers to situations in which the taxpayer controls the stock of another corporation, the taxpayer's stock is controlled by another corporation, or the taxpayer and one or more other corporations are controlled, directly or indirectly, by the same interests.

Related corporations having substantial intercorporate transactions with one or more of the related corporations must file a combined report, regardless of the transfer price for such intercorporate transactions (Sec. 211(4)(a), Tax Law; *TSB-M-07(6)C*, June 25, 2007, CCH NEW YORK TAX REPORTS, ¶ 405-770). "Substantial intercorporate transactions" may include, but are not limited to the following activities (Reg. Sec. 6-2.3(b)):

— manufacturing, acquiring goods or property, or performing services for related corporations;

— selling goods acquired from related corporations;

— financing sales of related corporations;

— performing related customer services using common facilities and employees;

— incurring expenses that benefit, directly or indirectly, one or more related corporations; and

— transferring assets, including intangible assets, from one or more related corporations.

Practitioner Comment: Combination Rules Preempt P.L. 86-272

An out-of-state corporation that otherwise meets the tests for combination can be forced to file as part of a combined group of New York corporations even though the out-of-state business has no connection or nexus with New York. New York's Court of Appeals held that New York's combination rules supersede Public Law 86-272. Under the Court's rationale, the out-of-state corporation is not being taxed by New York. Instead, New York is simply using the out-of-state corporation's business attributes to "measure the combined group's taxable in state activities" (*Disney Enterprises, Inc. v. Tax Appeals Tribunal of the State of New York*, New York Court of Appeals, 859 NYS2d 87 (2008); CCH New York Tax Reports, ¶406-016).

Mark S. Klein, Esq., Hodgson Russ LLP

Prior law—Presumption of distortion: The activities, business, income or capital of a taxpayer will be presumed to be distorted when a taxpayer reports on a separate basis if there are substantial intercorporate transactions among the corporations. (Reg. Sec. 6-2.3)

In determining whether substantial intercorporate transactions exist, the Commissioner will consider transactions directly connected with the business conducted by the taxpayer. Service functions will not be considered if they are incidental to the business of the corporation providing the service.

The substantial intercorporate transaction requirement is met if at least 50% of a corporation's receipts or expenses are from intercorporate transactions. It is not necessary that there be substantial intercorporate transactions between any one corporation and every other member of the unitary group; each corporation must, however, have substantial intercorporate transactions with one other corporation within the group or with a combined or combinable group of corporations.

In *Petition of Standard Manufacturing Co., Inc.;* (CCH New York Tax Reports, ¶400-271), the Tax Appeals Tribunal rejected the argument by the Division of Taxation that substantial intercorporate transactions between a taxpayer and a non-taxpayer, coupled with the unitary business and stock ownership requirements, created an irrebuttable presumption that combined reporting was necessary to avoid distortion and properly reflect income. Instead, the Tribunal held that when the stock ownership, unitary business, and substantial intercorporate transactions tests are met, only a presumption of distortion arises, which a taxpayer may rebut by showing that reporting on a separate basis results in a proper reflection of tax liability. See, also, *Petition of Express, Inc., et al.*, Department of Tax Appeals, Administrative Law Judge Unit, September 15, 1995; CCH New York Tax Reports, ¶402-131.

Affiliated companies are not required to file on a combined basis merely because they are involved in a unitary business (*Petition of Silver King Broadcasting of New Jersey, Inc.;* CCH New York Tax Reports, ¶402-470). Instead, the Division must identify with particularity the activities or transactions that it claims gives rise to distortion and explain how distortion arises from those activities or transactions. The mere identification of possible areas of distortion is not sufficient to require the filing of a combined report.

¶1404

Practitioner Comment: New Audit Target: Decombination

After years of aggressively searching for distortion of income in order to force related companies to file on a combined basis, a new audit initiative seems to be targeting businesses that file on a combined basis in an effort to identify companies that should be filing separately. These "decombination" audits are focused on companies with significant activities outside of New York that necessarily dilute the New York business allocation percentage.

Mark S. Klein, Esq., Hodgson Russ LLP

A captive RIC or captive REIT that is owned or controlled by one or more corporations subject to corporation franchise (income) tax must be included in a combined report with such corporations (Secs. 209(5), (7), 211.4(a)(6)(ii), Tax Law).

• *Excluded corporations*

A corporation required or permitted to make a combined report does not include (Sec. 210-C(2)(c), Tax Law):

(1) corporations subject to franchise taxes under Article 9 (certain corporations) or Article 33 (insurance companies) of the Tax Law;

(2) non-captive RICs or REITs;

(3) New York S corporations; or

(4) an alien corporation not treated as a "domestic corporation" under the Internal Revenue Code.

A captive RIC or captive REIT that is owned or controlled by one or more corporations subject to corporation franchise (income) tax must be included in a combined report with such corporations (Secs. 209(5), (7), 211.4(a)(6)(ii), Tax Law).

Prior law: For taxable years beginning before 2015, corporations organized outside the United States could not be included in combined reports (Sec. 211(5), Tax Law; Reg 6-2.5(b)).

A railroad or trucking business that allocates income pursuant to the single-factor formula (¶1303) may not make any report on a combined basis with any corporation that does not so allocate.

Air freight forwarders may file reports on a combined basis only if all of the taxpayers included on the combined report agree to have the air freight forwarder included (former Sec. 211(4), Tax Law).

• *Authorization to file combined report (pre-2015)*

To file on a combined basis, a unitary group of corporations need only file a complete combined report. (Reg. Sec. 6-2.4)

For the first year of filing the combined report and for any year in which the composition of the combined group changes the following information must be filed along with the combined report: (1) the exact name, address, employer identification number, and state of incorporation for each corporation included in the combined report; (2) information showing that each group member meets the unitary business, capital stock ownership, and nondistortion requirements; and (3) the name, address, employer identification number, and the state of incorporation of corporations (except alien corporations) that meet the capital stock requirement, but that are not included in the combined report. The information requested in (2) and (3) may be met by providing a copy of federal Form 851, Affiliations Schedule, with the franchise tax return (Reg. Sec. 6-2.4(a)(2); *TSB-M-98(1)C*, CCH NEW YORK TAX REPORTS, ¶ 300-242).

Additionally, the following information must be provided for at least the first nine months of the taxable year: (1) the nature of business conducted by each corporation included in the combined report or that meets the capital stock requirement but is not included in the combined report; (2) the source and amount of gross receipts of each corporation and the portion derived from transactions with the other combined or combinable corporations; (3) the source and amount of total purchases, services, and other transactions of each corporation and the portion related to transactions with the other combined or combinable corporations; and (4) any other data that shows the degree of involvement of the corporations with each other. In addition, the following information may be required to be submitted at another time such as in conjunction with an audit: (1) a statement providing details of why a report excluding certain corporations meeting the capital stock requirement would equitably reflect the New York activities of the corporations included and excluded; and (2) information establishing that each of the corporations included in the combined group meets the unitary business requirement.

• *Calculation of tax (pre-2015)*

Intercompany eliminations: The tax is measured by combined entire net income, combined minimum taxable income, combined pre-1990 minimum taxable income, or combined capital of all corporations included in the report. (Sec. 211(4), Tax Law) The tax measured by combined capital may not exceed the $350,000 limitation provided by statute. In computing combined entire net income, combined minimum taxable income, or combined pre-1990 minimum taxable income, intercorporate dividends as well as receipts are eliminated. In computing combined business and investment capital, intercorporate stockholdings and intercorporate bills, notes, and accounts receivable and payable, and other intercorporate indebtedness are eliminated; and in computing combined subsidiary capital, intercorporate stockholdings are eliminated. However, intercorporate dividends from a DISC or a former DISC not exempt from tax under Sec. 208(9)(i), Tax Law, that are taxable as business income are not eliminated.

Attribution of income to New York: If a combined report is filed, New York attribution of income is made on the basis of combined accounts from which intercorporate items are eliminated. (Reg. Sec. 4-1.2)

Receipts factor on combined reports: The receipts factor on combined reports is computed as though the corporations included in the report were one corporation. (Reg. Sec. 4-4.7) All intercorporate business receipts are eliminated in computing the factor. "Intercorporate receipts" refers to amounts received by any corporation included in the combined report from another member included in the report.

• *Filing and payment of tax*

The corporation responsible for paying the combined tax must file the combined franchise tax report. In addition, each corporation in the combined group must submit such other reports and other information as the Commissioner of Taxation and Finance may require. (Reg. Sec. 6-3.2(a))

¶1405 Estimated Tax—Declarations and Payment

Law: Secs. 209-B, 213-a, 213-b, 1085, 1086, Tax Law; Reg. Secs. 7-2.1, 7-3.4 (CCH NEW YORK TAX REPORTS, ¶89-104).

Comparable Federal: Secs. 6154, 6611, 6655 (U.S. MASTER TAX GUIDE, ¶225—231).

Forms: CT-400MN, Estimated Tax for Corporations; CT-222, Underpayment of Estimated Tax by a Corporation; CT-2658, Report of Estimated Tax for Corporate Partners.

Certain corporations subject to the corporation franchise tax are required to file declarations and pay estimated tax (Sec. 213-a(a), Tax Law; Reg. Sec. 7-2.1). The first New York installment of estimated tax becomes due on the basis of the preceding year's tax liability even though no declaration may be required for the current year.

The below requirements generally apply to estimated payments of the corporate franchise, bank franchise, insurance franchise, and Article 9 corporation taxes.

CCH Advisory: Pass-through Entities

S corporations and certain other pass-through entities having income from New York sources are required to make estimated tax payments on behalf of partners, members, or shareholders that are nonresident individuals or C corporations, with respect to their distributive or pro rata shares of such income. For details, see ¶ 3602.

Metropolitan Commuter Transportation District surcharge: Corporations subject to the Metropolitan Commuter Transportation District surcharge (¶ 905) whose franchise tax liability can reasonably be expected to exceed $1,000 also must make declarations and pay estimated tax on the surcharge. (Sec. 209-B, Tax Law) The estimated franchise tax reporting requirements, discussed below, are generally applicable to the declarations and payment of the estimated surcharge.

- *First installment of estimated tax*

For purposes of the corporate franchise, bank franchise, insurance franchise, and Article 9 corporation tax, the first installment of tax for the account of the current year is due at the time of filing the corporation franchise tax return for the preceding taxable year (or at the time of filing an application for extension of time for filing such report) if the tax liability for the preceding year is in excess of $1,000 (Sec. 213-b(a), Tax Law). The first installment amount is 30% if the preceding year's tax exceeded $100,000 (this is increased to 40% for taxable years beginning on or after January 1, 2010). This first installment is required to be paid irrespective of the corporation's estimated tax liability for the current year. Any overpayment resulting from the first installment will be refunded with interest.

MCTD surcharge: Taxpayers subject to the Metropolitan Commuter Transportation District surcharge whose franchise tax can reasonably be expected to exceed $1,000 must also file declarations of estimated surcharge and make estimated surcharge payments (Sec. 213-a, Tax Law; Sec., 213-b, Tax Law; Sec. 1085(c), Tax Law). Declarations and payments must be made at the time that estimated franchise tax declarations and payments are required to be made.

- *Declaration of estimated tax—Other installments of estimated tax*

Corporations subject to the corporation franchise tax are required to file declarations of estimated tax if their estimated tax liability for the taxable year can reasonably be expected to exceed $1,000. Declarations are due on or before June 15 for calendar-year taxpayers. However, if the requirements (that is, expected tax liability exceeding $1,000) are first met after May 31 and before September 1, the declaration is due on or before September 15; if requirements are first met after August 31 and before December 1, the declaration is due on or before December 15. Instead of the declaration due on December 15, the taxpayer may elect to file a completed report, with payment of any unpaid balance of tax by February 15. (Sec. 213-b(b)(1), Tax Law; Reg. Sec. 7-3.4(a)(1))

Corresponding dates apply to fiscal-year taxpayers.

For calendar-year taxpayers filing declarations on or before June 15, the amount of estimated tax is paid in three equal installments (after deducting the amount of any first installment based on the preceding year's tax liability) on June 15, September 15, and December 15. If the declaration is required to be filed by September 15, any estimated tax due is paid in two equal installments on September 15, and December 15. If the declaration is filed December 15, any estimated tax due is paid with the declaration.

For fiscal-year taxpayers filing declarations by the 15th day of the sixth month, the amount of estimated tax is paid in three equal installments (after deducting the amount of any first installment based on the preceding year's tax liability) on the 15th day of the sixth, ninth and 12th month. If the declaration is required to be filed by the 15th day of the ninth month of the fiscal year, any estimated tax is paid in two equal installments on the 15th day of the ninth month and the 15th day of the 12th month of the fiscal year. If the declaration is required to be filed by the 15th day of the 12th month of the fiscal year, any unpaid estimated tax is due with the declaration.

- *Amended declarations*

Amended or revised declarations may be made in any case in which the taxpayer finds that its estimated tax differs from the estimated tax reflected in its most recent declaration of estimated tax. (Sec. 213-a(d), Tax Law; Reg. Sec. 7-2.4) However, an amended declaration may only be made on an installment date. No refunds will be issued as a result of the filing of an amended declaration.

The amended declaration should be made on Form CT-400 and marked "AMENDED".

A return filed on or before the 15th day of the second month of the succeeding taxable year (February 15 for calendar-year taxpayers) is considered as an amended declaration required to be filed on or before the 15th day of the 12th month of the taxable year.

- *Underpayment of estimated tax*

An interest penalty is added to the tax when it is determined that there has been an underpayment of all or any part of an installment of estimated tax. The interest penalty is added for the period of underpayment but not beyond the normal due date of the annual return. (For rate of interest, see ¶1507.) Penalties for underpayment of estimated tax are applicable to underpayments of the estimated Metropolitan Commuter Transportation District surcharge.

The first installment of estimated tax is considered underpaid to the extent that it is less than 40% of the previous year's tax liability (see above).

Other installments are underpaid if they total less than 91% of the current year's tax liability. Taxpayers are partly relieved from the penalty if installments equal at least 80% of the tax liability; in that case, the interest penalty is 75% of the penalty otherwise determined.

Corporations with entire net income over $1 million: Penalties are imposed if estimated tax payments are less than 100% of the current year's liability for corporations with $1 million of entire net income in any of the three immediately preceding taxable years.

- *Avoidance of penalties for underpayment*

Taxpayers who have underpaid estimated taxes may nevertheless avoid penalties if they qualify by paying estimated tax equal to the following:

— the tax shown on the return for the preceding year (if it was a period of 12 months) (Sec. 1085(d)(1), Tax Law);

— the tax equal to current tax rates applied to last year's facts and law (Sec. 1085(d)(2), Tax Law);

— the amount equal to 91% of the tax for the current year computed on an annualized basis (Sec. 1085(d)(3), Tax Law);

— the amount equal to 91% of the tax for the current year computed on a recurring seasonal income basis. (Sec. 1085(d)(4), Tax Law)

These exceptions parallel, but are not identical to, the federal provisions.

¶1405

• *Overpayments*

Any overpayment of tax shown due on the annual corporation tax return attributable to payment of the first installment (based on the preceding year's tax) will be refunded with interest from the date of payment to the due date of the annual return. (For rate of interest, see ¶ 1507.) The Commissioner of Taxation is authorized to credit any overpayment of tax against a taxpayer's past-due legally enforceable debt owed to state agencies.

• *Where to pay*

Declarations and payments of estimated tax are sent to the Department of Taxation and Finance at the address indicated on the form (CT-400 or the manual version, CT-400MN).

• *Nonresident withholding by pass-through entities*

Partnerships (other than publicly traded partnerships), limited liability companies (LLCs), and S corporations having income from New York sources are required to make estimated tax payments on behalf of partners, members, or shareholders that are nonresident individuals or C corporations, with respect to their distributive or pro rata shares of such income. For details, see ¶ 3602.

¶ 1406 Payment of Tax

Law: Secs. 211, 213, Tax Law (CCH New York Tax Reports, ¶ 89-102).

Comparable Federal: Secs. 6151, 6161 (U.S. Master Tax Guide, ¶ 5, 2529).

Taxpayers must pay the full amount of any tax shown due (less any installment payments of estimated tax) at the time the report is required to be filed. The balance of any tax is, therefore, due on or before March 15 for calendar-year taxpayers or two and one-half months after the close of the taxable year for fiscal-year taxpayers. (Sec. 211(1), Tax Law; Reg. Sec. 6-4.1)

Extensions of time for the payment of the corporation franchise tax may be granted by the Commissioner (¶ 1403). Ordinarily, interest will be charged.

For payment of estimated tax, see ¶ 1405.

Currency: For corporation tax and personal income tax purposes, New York tax law conforms to the federal treatment of convertible virtual currency as detailed in *IRS Notice 2014-21.* The notice provides that convertible virtual currency is treated as property for U.S. federal tax purposes. General tax principles that apply to property transactions apply to transactions using convertible virtual currency. (*TSB-M-14(5)C, TSB-M-14(7)I,* and *TSB-M-14(17)S,* New York Department of Taxation and Finance, December 5, 2014, CCH New York Tax Reports, ¶ 408-293)

CORPORATION FRANCHISE (INCOME) TAX

CHAPTER 15
ADMINISTRATION, DEFICIENCIES, PENALTIES, TAXPAYER REMEDIES

¶1501 Administration of Tax—In General

Law: Secs. 170, 1096, Tax Law (CCH New York Tax Reports, ¶89-060).

The corporation franchise tax imposed by Article 9-A, Tax Law, is administered by the Department of Taxation and Finance. (Sec. 170, Tax Law; Sec. 1096, Tax Law) For information on the organization of the Department, see ¶3601. For contact information, see Chapter 39.

Article 27 of the Tax Law provides for corporate tax procedure and administration with respect to the franchise taxes imposed.

¶1502 Deficiencies—Procedure

Law: Secs. 1081, 1082, 1084, Tax Law (CCH New York Tax Reports, ¶89-164).

The Commissioner, after examining the return and determining that additional tax is due, may proceed as outlined below. For information on audits, see ¶3701. Assessments are discussed at ¶3702.

• *Notice*

The Commissioner may mail a notice of deficiency to the taxpayer by certified or registered mail to its last known address. (Sec. 1081(a), Tax Law) After 90 days (150 days if the taxpayer's last known address is outside the United States) the notice is an assessment of the amount of tax, additions to tax, interest and penalties specified in the notice, except as to such amounts as to which the taxpayer has filed a petition for redetermination of the deficiency. (Sec. 1081(b), Tax Law)

If no return is filed, the Commissioner is authorized to estimate the taxpayer's New York tax liability from any information in its possession and to mail a notice of deficiency to the taxpayer.

If an underpayment of tax is due to a mathematical error, the Commissioner will send a notice to the taxpayer of the amount due. (Sec. 1081(d), Tax Law) This notice is not deemed to be a notice of deficiency. No interest will be due if the return was timely filed and payment of the tax due is made within three months after the due date (or extended due date) of the return. (Sec. 1084(c), Tax Law)

• *Federal change*

If no report of federal changes is made or no amended New York return is filed when a federal return is amended, the Commissioner may assess a deficiency based upon the increased or decreased federal taxable income. The deficiency, interest, additions to tax and penalties due will be deemed to be assessed on the date of the mailing of the notice of additional tax due unless a report of the federal changes or an amended return is filed within 30 days after the mailing of the notice, accompanied by a statement showing wherein the federal determination and the notice of additional tax due are erroneous. (Sec. 1081(e), Tax Law)

• *Combined reports*

The Commissioner may determine a deficiency of tax against any taxpayer that was included in a combined report or that might have been included in a combined report (Sec. 1081(g), Tax Law); see ¶1404

¶1503 Jeopardy Assessments

Law: Sec. 1094, Tax Law (CCH NEW YORK TAX REPORTS, ¶89-168).

Comparable Federal: Secs. 6851, 6861 (U.S. MASTER TAX GUIDE, ¶2715).

The New York franchise tax provisions relating to jeopardy assessments and early termination of the taxable year are similar to the federal. (Sec. 1094, Tax Law) Under both laws, the collection of any jeopardy assessment may be stayed by filing a bond.

For additional information, see ¶3702.

¶1504 Bankruptcy and Receivership

Law: Sec. 209, Tax Law (CCH NEW YORK TAX REPORTS, ¶89-170).

Comparable Federal: Sec. 6012 (U.S. MASTER TAX GUIDE, ¶505, 2750).

New York law specifically provides that receivers, referees, trustees in bankruptcy and assignees conducting the business of a corporation are subject to the franchise tax on business corporations imposed by Article 9-A of the Tax Law. (Sec. 209(3), Tax Law)

¶1505 Transferee Liability

Law: Sec. 1093, Tax Law (CCH NEW YORK TAX REPORTS, ¶89-166).

Comparable Federal: Secs. 6901—6904 (U.S. MASTER TAX GUIDE, ¶2743).

The law contains provisions permitting assessment and collection of tax from persons secondarily liable. The period of limitations is extended for assessments against transferees by one year for every transfer, not to exceed an aggregate of three years. (Sec. 1093, Tax Law)

¶1506 Statute of Limitations on Assessments

Law: Secs. 25, 1083, Tax Law (CCH NEW YORK TAX REPORTS, ¶89-164, 89-190).

Comparable Federal: Secs. 6501—6504 (U.S. MASTER TAX GUIDE, ¶2726).

The New York rules for determining the time within which an assessment may be made are as follows:

General rule: Three years after the date the return was filed. (Sec. 1083(a), Tax Law)

Waiver: The taxpayer may agree to an extension of the limitation period. (Sec. 1083(c)(2), Tax Law)

Omission of over 25% of gross income: When a taxpayer omits from the return gross income in excess of 25% of the gross income stated in the return, the limitation period is six years after the return was filed (or deemed to be filed). (Sec. 1083(d), Tax Law) Similarly, a tax may be assessed at any time within six years after the return was filed if a taxpayer omits from the sum of its items of tax preference and adjustments required in the computation of minimum taxable income an amount in excess of 25% of the sum stated in the return.

For New York purposes, "gross income" means gross income for federal income tax purposes as reportable on a business corporation return under Article 9-A of the Tax Law. (Sec. 1083(d)(1), Tax Law) An amount is not deemed to be omitted if sufficiently disclosed on the return or on a statement attached to the return. (Sec. 1083(d)(2), Tax Law)

False or no return: When no return or a fraudulent return was filed, there is no period of limitation on assessment. (Sec. 1083(c)(1), Tax Law)

Failure to report changes or amendment of federal returns: When the taxpayer fails to report any change of federal taxable income or federal tax or fails to file an amended return when required, there is no period of limitation on assessment. (Sec. 1083(c)(3), Tax Law)

Practitioner Comment: Federal Statute of Limitations

Although the New York State statute of limitations remains open whenever a taxpayer's federal income tax audit results in a change to federal taxable income, these rules do not affect the federal statute of limitations when a taxpayer is undergoing a New York State audit that results in a change to federal taxable income. As a result, practitioners often attempt to prolong a New York State audit that impacts federal taxable income in an effort to eliminate the potential of any federal income tax consequences.

Mark S. Klein, Esq., Hodgson Russ LLP

Amended return filed or federal change reported: When the taxpayer files an amended return or report of federal changes, assessment (if not deemed made upon the filing of the report or amended return) may be made within two years after the date on which the report or amended return was filed. (Sec. 1083(c)(3), Tax Law)

Practitioner Comment: Report of Federal Changes

New York no longer allows the filing of form CT-3360, Federal Changes to Corporate Taxable Income. Instead, taxpayers must file amended returns reflecting the federal changes within 90 days (120 days if filing on a combined basis) after the date of a final determination of the Commissioner of Internal Revenue Service (Important Notice N 09 18, October 2009, CCH NEW YORK TAX REPORTS, ¶ 406-562). See also ¶ 1402.

Mark S. Klein, Hodgson Russ LLP

Deficiency attributable to carryback: When the deficiency is attributable to a net operating loss carryback or a capital loss carryback, it may be assessed at any time that a deficiency for the taxable year of the loss may be assessed. (Sec. 1083(c)(4), Tax Law)

Dissolving corporations—Request for prompt assessment: When a written request for prompt assessment has been made by a dissolving corporation or its fiduciary after its return is filed, assessment shall be made within 18 months after the request or within three years after the due date of the return, whichever is earlier. (Sec. 1083(c)(6), Tax Law)

Practitioner Comment: No Tax Liability for Certain Dissolved Corporations

A corporation that is dissolved voluntarily or by proclamation may have no liability for any taxes, interest or penalties for periods after the dissolution if the corporation is inactive or is a mere record title holder of New York real property as a nominee for the benefit of others. According to the Tax Department, these activities do not constitute "conducting business in New York State as contemplated by section 209.3 of the Tax Law." (*William F. Holden*, TSB-A-09(4)C, 3/1509, CCH NEW YORK TAX REPORTS, ¶404-324)

Mark S. Klein, Esq., Hodgson Russ LLP

Eligible business facility: When a report reflecting the revocation or modification of a certificate of eligibility upon which a credit was taken against tax (¶923) is filed, an assessment relating to the credit may be made within three years after the filing of the report. (Sec. 1083(c)(9), Tax Law)

MTA surcharge: The filing of a corporate franchise return does not serve to begin the running of the statute of limitations for the metropolitan transportation business tax. When MTA surcharge returns have not been filed, the surcharge may be assessed at any time (*Kaiser Aerospace & Electronics Corp.;* CCH NEW YORK TAX REPORTS, ¶402-619).

Recovery of erroneous refund: When an erroneous refund has been made, assessment of a deficiency arising out of the refund may be made within two years from the making of the refund (five years if it appears that any part of the refund was induced by fraud or misrepresentation of a material fact). (Sec. 1083(c)(5), Tax Law)

Suspension of running of period of limitation: The running of the period of limitation for assessment is suspended during the period after the mailing of a notice of deficiency until the assessment is deemed made following expiration of the appeal period. (Sec. 1083(e), Tax Law)

• *Tax avoidance transactions*

If a taxpayer fails to file, disclose or provide any statement, return or other information for any taxable year with respect to a listed tax avoidance transaction (Sec. 25, Tax Law), the time for assessment of tax is one year after the earlier of the date on which the statement, return, or information is filed, or the date that a list of taxpayers is provided following a request by the commissioner relating to a transaction. (Sec. 1083(c)(11), Tax Law) Tax may be assessed at any time within six years after the return was filed if the deficiency is attributable to an abusive tax avoidance transaction.

¶1507 Interest on Underpayments and Overpayments

Law: Secs. 1084, 1086, 1088, 1096, Tax Law (CCH NEW YORK TAX REPORTS, ¶89-204).

Comparable Federal: Sec. 6601, 6611 (U.S. MASTER TAX GUIDE, ¶2765, 2838—2845).

The Commissioner of Taxation and Finance determines interest rates on underpayments and overpayments of taxes on the basis of federal short-term rates established for Internal Revenue Code purposes by the United States Secretary of the Treasury. The federal rates are rounded to the nearest full percentage (or increased to the next full percentage in the case of $1/2\%$ multiple). The overpayment rate is the sum of the federal short-term rate plus 2%. The underpayment rate is the sum of the federal short-term interest rate plus 7%. If no rates are established, the rates are deemed to be set at 7.5% per annum.

For the most current interest rate available at the time of publication, see ¶3704 or CCH NEW YORK TAX REPORTS, ¶89-204. Interest rates per annum, compounded daily and established quarterly, have been set in the recent past as follows:

Period	Overpayments	Underpayments
3/31/16—12/31/16	3%	8%
10/1//11—3/31/16	2%	7.5%
4/1/11—9/30/11	3%	8%
1/1/11—3/31/11	2%	7.5%
4/7/09—12/31/10	3%	8%
4/1/09—4/6/09	3%	6%
1/1/09—3/31/09	4%	7%
10/1/08—12/31/08	5%	8%
7/1/08—9/30/08	4%	7%
4/1/08—6/30/08	5%	8%
/1/08—3/31/07	6%	9%
7/1/07—12/30/07	7%	10%
10/1/06—6/30/06	6%	9%
4/1/05—9/30/05	5%	8%
10/1/04—3/31/05	4%	7%
7/1/04—9/30/04	3%	6%
4/1/04—6/30/04	4%	6%
10/1/03—3/31/04	3%	6%
4/1/03—9/30/03	6%	7%
1/1/03—3/31/03	6%	6%
7/1/01—12/31/02	6%	7%
4/1/01—6/30/01	7%	8%
4/1/00—3/31/01	8%	9%

Application of overpayment as credit against tax: In the absence of a request for a refund, an overpayment of tax will be credited against the estimated tax liability for the succeeding taxable year. If the Commissioner notifies the taxpayer that the overpayment has been credited against the succeeding year's liability within three months after the last date prescribed (or permitted by extension of time) for filing the return on which the overpayment is claimed, or three months after the return is filed, whichever is later, and the taxpayer, after such notice, makes a claim for a refund of all or part of the overpayment, no interest will be allowed prior to the date of the refund claim.

Satisfaction of underpayment by credits: When any portion of the tax is satisfied by credits for overpayment, no interest is imposed on the portion of the deficiency extinguished by the credit for the period subsequent to the date on which the overpayment was made.

Mathematical or clerical error: Interest on underpayments of tax will not be charged where the underpayment is solely due to a mathematical or clerical error and the return has been filed on time and the tax is paid within three months of the due date (or extended due date of the return).

Penalties and additions to tax: Interest will apply on assessments, additions to tax and penalties if not paid within 21 days after notice and demand for payment (10 days, if the amount is $100,000 or more).

¶1508 Penalties

Law: Secs. 39-a, 1085, 1805, Tax Law (CCH NEW YORK TAX REPORTS, ¶ 89-206, 89-208).

Comparable Federal: Secs. 6651, 6653, 7201, 7203 (U.S. MASTER TAX GUIDE, ¶ 2801—2898).

Penalties are provided as follows:

For failure to file a timely return, not due to reasonable cause: 5% of the tax due for each month (or fraction thereof) of delinquency, up to a maximum of 25%. (Sec. 1085(a)(1), Tax Law)

If the return is not filed within 60 days of the prescribed filing date, the penalty may not be less than $100 or the amount of tax due, whichever is less.

For failure to pay tax shown on return, not due to reasonable cause: $1/2$ of 1% of the tax due for each month (or fraction thereof) of delinquency, up to a maximum of 25%. (Sec. 1085(a)(2), Tax Law)

For failure to pay tax required to be shown on return within 21 days of notice and demand (10 days, if $100,000 or more), not due to reasonable cause: ¹/₂ of 1% of the tax stated in such notice and demand for each month (or fraction thereof) of delinquency, up to 25%. (Sec. 1085(a)(3), Tax Law)

If any part of a deficiency is due to negligence or intentional disregard of the law or rules and regulations without intent to defraud: 5% of the deficiency and 50% of the interest payable for underpayment of tax. (Sec. 1085(b), Tax Law)

If any part of a deficiency is due to fraud: 50% of the deficiency and 50% of the interest payable for underpayment of tax. (Sec. 1085(f), Tax Law)

For failure with fraudulent intent to pay any tax, to make any return or declaration of estimated tax, or to supply any information required by law: A penalty of not more than $1,000. This penalty may be waived, reduced or compromised by the Commissioner. (Sec. 1085(g), Tax Law)

For substantial understatement of liability: 10% of any underpayment of tax resulting from a substantial understatement of tax. There is a substantial understatement of tax for the year where the amount of the understatement exceeds the greater of 10% of the tax required to be shown on the return or $5,000. (Sec. 1085(k), Tax Law)

For fraud in the START-UP NY program: In the case of a business that acts fraudulently in connection with the START-UP NY program (see ¶923), the business will be immediately terminated from the program; subject to applicable criminal penalties, including the felony crime of offering a false instrument for filing in the first degree; and required to pay back all tax benefits that the company and its employees have received. (Sec. 38-a, Tax Law)

Criminal penalties: Failure to pay or file with intent to evade or filing false or fraudulent returns are crimes. For additional information, see ¶3704. Any person who intentionally understates the corporate tax due by more than $1,500 is guilty of a class E felony.

For penalties in connection with failure to file a declaration or an underpayment of estimated tax, see ¶1405.

¶1509 Information at Source

Law: Secs. 211, 1085, 1703, Tax Law; Reg. Sec. 6-3.1 (CCH NEW YORK TAX REPORTS, ¶89-102, 89-142).

Comparable Federal: Sec. 6041 (U.S. MASTER TAX GUIDE, ¶406, 2496B, 2565).

State tax law requires the reporting of several types of tax information. A foreign corporation that is not a taxpayer, but which has an employee, including any officer, in New York State must file an information report. (Sec. 211(1), Tax Law) An exempt DISC is also required to file an information report. In addition, corporations are required to report to the Commissioner specified information relating to payments made to shareholders owning, directly or indirectly, individually or in the aggregate, more than 50% of the issued capital stock of the taxpayer, where such payments are treated as payments of interest in the computation of entire net income or minimum taxable income reported on the corporation franchise tax returns. (For the contents of the report, see Reg. Sec. 6-3.1(c), "Form of Reports," CCH NEW YORK TAX REPORTS, ¶12-837.) Failure to file such a report results in a penalty of $500, unless it is shown that the failure is due to reasonable cause and not to willful neglect.

The law requires the filing of information returns by payment settlement entities, third-party settlement organizations, electronic payment facilitators, and other third parties acting on behalf of payment settlement entities (Sec. 1703, Tax Law).

¶1510 Taxpayer Remedies

Law: Secs. 170, 171, 2008, 2012, 2016, Tax Law; Reg. Secs. 3000.13, 5000.1 (CCH New York Tax Reports, ¶¶ 89-222—89-240).

Upon notice issued by the Commissioner of Taxation and Finance of a determination of tax due, of a tax deficiency, of a proposed assessment, of a denial of a refund or credit application, or of the cancellation, revocation, suspension or denial of an application for a license, permit or registration or any other notice that gives a person the right to a hearing under Ch. 60 of the Tax Law, the taxpayer may request an information hearing with the Bureau of Conciliation and Mediation Services, a division within the Tax Department, or may elect to settle the dispute by filing a petition for a hearing before an administrative law judge in the Division of Tax Appeals. (Sec. 170(3-a), Tax Law)

For information about the Taxpayers' Bill of Rights, see ¶3801.

Additional information about conciliation conferences, small claims hearings, administrative appeals, and judicial review is presented at ¶3802.

• *Conciliation conferences*

Conciliation conferences are conducted informally by a conciliation conferee to resolve taxpayer disputes in a quick and inexpensive manner without resorting to a formal hearing. A conciliation order is binding upon the Department of Taxation and Finance and the taxpayer unless the taxpayer requests a hearing before an administrative law judge within 90 days after the conciliation order is issued.

Practitioner Comment: Conciliation Conferences Are Usually Worthwhile

Although taxpayers are allowed to bypass the conciliation process, most practitioners advise against it. The Bureau of Conciliation and Mediation Services reports that conciliation conferees are able to resolve more than 75% of the disputes that come before them. Moreover, even though a conciliation order is binding on the Tax Department, a taxpayer that is dissatisfied with the results of a conciliation conference can still appeal to the Division of Tax Appeals.

Mark S. Klein, Esq., Hodgson Russ LLP

• *Tax appeal hearings*

Tax Appeal hearings are formal proceedings conducted by an administrative law judge (ALJ). The ALJ will hear evidence and issue a determination, generally within six months after the completion of the hearing. (Sec. 2010, Tax Law) Either the taxpayer or the Department may request a review of the hearing decision by the Tax Appeals Tribunal within 30 days of notification of the ALJ's determination. After reviewing the record of the hearing and any oral and written arguments, the Tribunal will affirm or reverse the determination. The Department may not seek judicial review of a Tax Tribunal decision. However, the taxpayer may seek judicial review in the Appellate Division of the State Supreme Court.

• *Small claims hearings*

The taxpayer may elect to have a hearing held in the Small Claims Unit of the Division of Tax Appeals when the amount in controversy does not exceed $20,000 (not including penalties and interest) a year. This is an informal hearing conducted by an impartial presiding officer whose determination is final and not subject to review by any other unit in the Division of Tax Appeals. At any time before the conclusion of a small claims hearing, a taxpayer may discontinue the proceeding and request transfer to a formal hearing before the administrative law judge by writing to the Secretary of the Tax Tribunal. (Reg. Sec. 3000.13)

• *Compromise of tax liability*

A civil tax liability may be compromised where there is doubt as to liability and/or doubt as to collectibility, or if collection in full would result in undue economic hardship to the tax debtor (Sec. 171(18-a), Tax Law). The Commissioner may accept an offer in compromise of civil tax liability at any time before the tax is no longer subject to administrative review. (Sec. 171(15), (17), Tax Law; Reg. Sec. 5000.1 *et seq.*) The Attorney General may compromise any such liability after reference to the Department of Law for prosecution or defense at any time prior to the time the tax or administrative action taken by the Department of Taxation and Finance is no longer subject to judicial review. (Sec. 171(18)(c), Tax Law) Upon acceptance of such an offer, the matter may not be reopened except upon a showing of fraud, malfeasance or misrepresentation of a material fact. (Sec. 171(18)(a), Tax Law)

The Commissioner may accept a lesser amount of taxes, penalties, and interest in order to increase the pool of applicants for a potential offer, including those offers based on undue economic hardship that collection in full would impose. An offer in compromise will not be accepted for any reason where acceptance of such an offer would not be in the best interests of the state or would undermine voluntary compliance with the Tax Law. Offers in compromise cannot be used as a tax planning device by businesses or individuals. (Sec. 171(15), Tax Law)

Practitioner Comment: Offers in Compromise

In 2014, the Offer in Compromise Unit was moved from the Office of the Taxpayer Rights Advocate back to the Civil Enforcement Division. While the offer in compromise acceptance rate historically averaged approximately 40%, in recent years the acceptance rate and number of applications received have steadily increased. Since 2015, the percentage of acceptances has increased to almost 80% of the total of applications submitted, including withdrawn applications. The number of applications the Department received during the 2015-2016 fiscal year increased by nearly 50% from the previous fiscal year, due in part to recent legislation that expanded the program to include individuals who would experience undue economic hardship if required to pay in full their outstanding tax liabilities.

Mark S. Klein, Esq., Hodgson Russ LLP

• *Judicial review*

Tax Appeals Tribunal decisions are not subject to judicial review unless, within four months after notice of the decision is served on all parties, the taxpayer applies for judicial review pursuant to Article 78, Civil Practice Laws and Rules. Appeals from Tribunal decisions go directly to the Supreme Court, Appellate Division, Third Department. (Sec. 1016, Tax Law)

PART IV

FRANCHISE TAXES ON BANKING CORPORATIONS

CHAPTER 16
IMPOSITION OF TAX, RATES, EXEMPTIONS, CREDITS

¶1601 Overview of Bank Franchise Tax

CAUTION.—Effective for taxable years beginning on or after January 1, 2015, the Article 32 bank franchise tax is repealed, and banks are merged into the Article 9-A corporate franchise tax (Ch. 59 (S.B. 6359), Laws 2014). The discussion below is applicable to taxable years beginning before 2015, except as otherwise indicated.

Since 1927 and until 2015, New York imposed franchise taxes on banks and financial institutions. Prior to 1973, Article 9-C of the Tax Law imposed a tax on national banks and production credit associations and Article 9-B of the Tax Law imposed a tax on other banks and financial institutions.

The present franchise tax on banking corporations is codified as Article 32 of the Tax Law. The tax is imposed for the privilege of doing business or exercising the corporate franchise for the taxable year.

When originally added, many provisions of Article 32 were scheduled to expire for taxable years beginning on or after January 1, 1990, except the alternative minimum tax measured by assets, and those provisions that apply to savings banks and savings and loan associations. Under legislation enacted in subsequent years, this "sunset date" was extended many times and was finally made permanent (Part J, Ch. 61 (S.B. 2811), Laws 2010).

The basic tax rate (¶1605) is imposed on entire net income with certain exclusions, discussed below. If a greater tax results, either a minimum tax or one of two alternative taxes applies.

¶1602 Corporations Subject to Franchise Tax

Law: Secs. 1451, 1452, 1462(f)(2)(iv), Tax Law (CCH New York Tax Reports, ¶14-017).

For taxable years beginning before 2015, the tax was imposed on national banks and production credit associations located in New York and on the following corporations organized under the laws of New York: banks, savings banks, savings and loan associations, trust companies, subsidiary trust companies and other financial corporations. The term corporation includes associations and joint stock companies. The tax is also imposed on foreign banking corporations and other foreign financial corporations doing a banking business and on federal savings banks and federal loan associations.

Special rules apply to bank holding companies filing combined reports with corporations subject to Article 32 (¶1802).

For taxable years beginning on or after January 1, 2015, the tax is not applicable to corporations other than savings banks and savings and loan associations. However, the provisions relating to the alternative minimum tax measured by taxable assets continued to apply to all taxpayers for taxable years beginning on or after January 1, 2011. Also beginning in 2011, if a corporation meets the conditions below, it will be subject to the bank franchise tax even if it had previously elected to be subject to the general corporation tax, or had been grandfathered under the Gramm-Leach-Bliley transitional provisions.

The 2007 budget legislation established conditions under which certain corporations that elected to be taxable under Article 9-A, or are required to be taxed under 9-A pursuant to the Gramm-Leach-Bliley transitional provisions, became taxable under the Article 32 bank franchise tax. However, only a corporation that meets the definition of a "banking corporation" in Sec. 1452(a), Tax Law, was allowed to remain an Article 32 taxpayer under the transitional provisions (*Summary of Tax Provisions in SFY 2012-13 Budget,* New York Department of Taxation and Finance, April 2012). The conditions include the following (Sec. 1452(n), Tax Law):

— ceasing to be a taxpayer under Article 9-A;

— becoming subject to the fixed dollar minimum tax for inactive corporations;

— having no wages or receipts allocable to New York or otherwise becoming inactive;

— being acquired by an unaffiliated corporation in a transaction under IRC Sec. 338(h)(3); or

— becoming engaged in a different line of business as a result of acquiring a certain amount of assets.

Credit card issuers: For taxable years beginning after 2007, there is nexus under the bank franchise tax with respect to certain banking corporations having credit card customers in New York. Specifically, the law provides that a banking corporation is doing business in New York in a corporate or organized capacity if (Sec. 1451(c)(1)):

(1) it has issued credit cards to 1,000 or more customers with New York mailing addresses;

(2) it has merchant customer contracts with merchants, and the total number of locations covered by those contracts equals 1,000 or more locations in New York to which the banking corporation remitted payments for credit card transactions during the taxable year;

¶1602

(3) it has receipts of $1 million or more in the taxable year from its customers who have been issued credit cards by the banking corporation and have a New York mailing address;

(4) it has receipts of $1 million or more arising from merchant customer contracts with merchants relating to locations in New York; or

(5) the sum of the number of customers described in (1) plus the number of locations covered by its contracts described in (2) equals 1,000 or more, or the amount of its receipts described in (3) and (4) equals $1 million or more.

The term "credit card" includes bank, credit, travel, and entertainment cards (Sec. 1451(c)(2)). Receipts from processing credit card transactions for merchants are deemed to include merchant discount fees received by the banking corporation.

• *Transitional provisions*

Under Part HH of Ch. 63 (A.B. 11006), Laws 2000, transitional provisions relating to the enactment and implementation of the federal Gramm-Leach-Bliley Act of 1999 allowed certain corporations that were taxed under the corporate franchise tax or the bank franchise tax in 1999 to maintain that taxable status in 2000. The legislation also permited certain corporations owned by financial holding companies or are financial subsidiaries of banks to elect to be taxed under either the corporate franchise tax or the bank franchise tax for the 2000 taxable year.

Legislation extending the sunset date from January 1, 2001, to January 1, 2003 (Ch. 383 (S.B. 5828), Laws 2001) enacted similar provisions, (1) allowing certain corporations that were taxed under the corporate franchise tax or the bank franchise tax in 2000 to maintain that taxable status in 2001 and 2002, and (2) permitting certain corporations that are owned by financial holding companies or that are financial subsidiaries of banks to elect to be taxed under either the corporate franchise tax or the bank franchise tax for the 2001 and 2002 taxable years. Also, banking corporations that elected under the earlier transition provisions to be taxed as Article 9-A corporations are allowed to revoke the election.

Similar amendments extended the transitional provisions through taxable years beginning before 2004 ((Ch. 62, (A.B. 2106), Laws 2003), before 2006 (Ch. 60 (S.B. 6060-B), Laws 2004), before 2008 (Ch. 62 (S.B. 6460), Laws 2006), before 2010 (Ch. 60 (S.B. 2110), Laws 2007), before 2011 (Ch. 24 (A.B. 10096), Laws 2010), and before 2013 (Ch. 61 (S.B. 2811), Laws 2011)).

Legislation has established conditions under which certain corporations that elected to be taxable under Article 9-A, or are required to be taxed under 9-A pursuant to the Gramm-Leach-Bliley transitional provisions, will become taxable under the Article 32 bank franchise tax, as set forth above (Sec. 1452(n), Tax Law).

For a corporation or banking corporation in existence before 2008 and subject to the Article 32 bank franchise tax for its last taxable year beginning before 2008, additional legislation (Ch. 636 (S.B. 8633), Laws 2008) removed a restriction providing that such tax treatment would no longer continue for taxable years beginning after 2007 and before 2011 if a transaction or series of transactions occurring on or after January 1, 2008, resulted in the corporation no longer meeting the requirements to be a banking corporation (Sec. 1452(m), Tax Law). A similar amendment was made for purposes of the New York City banking corporation tax (¶2903).

The legislation also repealed a provision under which a banking corporation in existence prior to 2010 and subject to the Article 32 bank franchise tax for its last taxable year beginning before 2011 could be taxable under Article 32 for taxable years beginning on or after January 1, 2011, only if the corporation, in that taxable year, met the requirements to be a banking corporation or satisfied applicable requirements for a corporation to elect to be taxable under Article 32.

¶1603 Exempt Corporations

Law: Sec. 1452, Tax Law (CCH NEW YORK TAX REPORTS, ¶ 14-019).

Corporations subject to the business corporation franchise tax under Article 9-A of the Tax Law (¶ 902) were not subject to Article 32 taxes.

Any trust company, all of the stock of which is owned by not fewer than20 New York savings banks, is expressly exempt from tax.

¶1604 Tax Base

Law: Sec. 1455, Tax Law (CCH NEW YORK TAX REPORTS, ¶ 14-036).

The franchise taxes are primarily measured by the entire net income of the taxpayer. The entire net income is subject to allocation and apportionment if the taxpayer is doing business within and without New York.

The computation of entire net income and allocation and apportionment are discussed in Chapter 17.

An alternative minimum tax is imposed if a larger tax would result. The alternative minimum tax is based on taxable assets allocated to New York, alternative entire net income allocated to New York or a flat fee minimum.

"Taxable assets" is defined as the average value of those assets that are properly reflected on a balance sheet. Amounts received from the Federal Deposit Insurance Corporation or from the Federal Savings and Loan Insurance Corporation are excluded.

For allocation of taxable assets, see ¶ 1704.

"Alternative entire net income" is defined as entire net income without the deductions for a percentage of income from subsidiary capital and for a percentage of interest received from New York State and federal obligations.

For allocation of alternative entire net income, see ¶ 1704.

¶1605 Tax Rates

Law: Secs. 1455, 1455-A, Tax Law (CCH NEW YORK TAX REPORTS, ¶ 14-031).

The rates of the taxes imposed were as follows:

Net income: 7.1% on net income allocated to New York.

Alternative minimum tax (used if a higher tax results): The alternative minimum tax was the largest of the following:

—$1/10$ of a mill on each dollar of taxable assets allocated to New York. However, in the case of a taxpayer whose net worth ratio is less than 5% but greater than or equal to 4%, and whose total assets are comprised of 33% or more of mortgages, the rate was $1/25$ of a mill upon each dollar of taxable assets. Taxpayers whose net worth ratio is less than 4% and whose total assets are comprised of 33% or more of mortgages were subject to tax at the rate of $1/50$ of a mill upon each dollar of taxable assets; or

—3% of alternative entire net income allocated to New York; *or*

—Flat fee minimum: $250.

Metropolitan Commuter Transportation District surcharge: Similar to corporation franchise (income) provisions (¶ 905).

¶1603

¶1606 Credits—In General

Law: Sec. 1456(b), (g), Tax Law (CCH New York Tax Reports, ¶14-086, 14-087, 14-105).

Comparable Federal: Secs. 38, 39 (U.S. Master Tax Guide, ¶1301—1384).

For taxable years beginning before 2015, New York offered banks a large number of credits, as discussed in the following paragraphs. For taxable years beginning after 2014, banks are subject to the corporation franchise (income) tax. Credits are discussed beginning at ¶923

- *Carryovers*

Most credits may not reduce a taxpayer's tax liability below the minimum tax (¶1605). With some exceptions, credits not used in one year may be carried forward indefinitely. Recapture of credits may be required if property does not remain in qualified use.

- *Order for claiming credits*

Credits that cannot be carried over and that are not refundable are deducted first, followed by empire zone (EZ) wage tax credits (¶929), whether or not a portion of those credits is refundable. Credits that can be carried over, and carryovers of such credits, are deducted next. Those credits whose carryovers are of limited duration are deducted before those whose carryovers are not limited. Credits that are refundable (other than the EZ wage credit) are deducted last.

- *Deferral of credits*

For tax years 2010, 2011, and 2012, taxpayers with more than $2 million in certain tax credits were required to defer the amounts above $2 million until 2013. The total amount of credits deferred were to be paid back to taxpayers over tax years 2013, 2014, and 2015. (Sec 33.1 Tax Law; Sec 34.1 Tax Law). Additional details are available under the discussion in Ch. 9 of corresponding corporate income (franchise) tax credits and in *TSB-M-10(5)C*, New York Department of Taxation and Finance, September 13, 2010, CCH New York Tax Reports, ¶406-976.

¶1607 Credit for Servicing SONYMA Mortgages

Law: Sec. 1456(a), Tax Law (CCH New York Tax Reports, ¶14-096).

Similar to corporation franchise (income) tax provisions. Discussion at ¶931 applies.

¶1608 Credit for Special Additional Mortgage Recording Taxes Paid

Law: Sec. 1456(c), Tax Law (CCH New York Tax Reports, ¶14-097).

Similar to corporation franchise (income) tax provisions. Discussion at ¶927 applies.

¶1609 Credits Relating to Economic Development Zones (Empire Zones)

Law: Sec. 1456(e), Tax Law (CCH New York Tax Reports, ¶14-089).

For bank franchise tax purposes, an empire zone credit for wages and an economic development zone capital corporation credit were allowed, as were credits designated for qualified empire zone enterprises (QEZEs). Similar to corporation franchise (income) tax provisions, the Empire Zone program was ended effective June 30, 2010. Discussion at ¶929 applies.

¶1610 International Banking Facilities

Law: Secs. 1450, 1453, Tax Law (CCH NEW YORK TAX REPORTS, ¶14-060).

An international banking facility is allowed a deduction from entire net income for adjusted eligible net income received from international banking. The deduction is phased in over a 10-year period to maintain tax revenues.

¶1611 Limited Liability Investment Companies

Law: Sec. 601, Tax Law (CCH NEW YORK TAX REPORTS, ¶10-240).

New York permits certain investment companies that are established and regulated under Article 12, Banking Law, to organize themselves as limited liability investment companies (LLICs). The option is open only to Article 12 investment companies that serve as holding companies for foreign banking operations.

For New York tax purposes, LLICs are regarded as limited liability companies. Accordingly, an LLIC that is treated as a partnership for federal tax purposes is treated as a partnership for New York State income tax purposes. Members of LLICs that are classified as partnerships for federal purposes are taxed as partners in a partnership, and are liable for personal income tax in their separate or individual capacities.

LLICs that are treated as partnerships for federal tax purposes are subject to the same annual filing fees that apply to limited liability companies (¶112).

¶1612 Investment Tax Credit

Law: Sec. 1456(i), Tax Law (CCH NEW YORK TAX REPORTS, ¶14-088).

Taxpayers may claim a credit against the bank franchise tax with respect to tangible personal property and other tangible property, including buildings, placed in service on or after October 1, 1998, and before October 1, 2015. (Sec. 1456(i), Tax Law; TSB-M-09(3)C, January 16, 2009, CCH NEW YORK TAX REPORTS, ¶406-296)

Eligibility requirements: The credit is allowed with respect to tangible personal property and other tangible property, including buildings, that (1) are depreciable pursuant to IRC Sec. 167, (2) have a useful life of four years or more, (3) are acquired by purchase as defined in IRC Sec. 179(d), (4) has a situs in New York State, and (5) are (a) principally used by the taxpayer in the ordinary course of business as a broker or dealer in connection with the purchase or sale of stocks, bonds, or other securities as defined in IRC Sec. 475(c)(2) or commodities as defined in IRC Sec 475(e), or (b) are principally used by the taxpayer in the ordinary course of the taxpayer's business of providing investment advisory services for a regulated investment company as defined in IRC Sec. 851.

A credit is not allowed for otherwise qualified property that is leased by the taxpayer to another unless the property is leased to an affiliated broker or dealer and used in a qualified manner.

Computation of credit: The amount of the credit for taxable years beginning after 1997 is 5% with respect to the first $350 million of the investment credit base and 4% with respect to the investment credit base in excess of $350 million.

The "investment credit base" is defined as the cost or other basis, for federal income tax purposes, of tangible personal property and other tangible property less the amount of any nonqualified nonrecourse financing with respect to the property to the extent such financing would be excludable from the credit base under federal law.

Credit limitations, carryovers, and recapture of the investment tax credit are the same as provided for the corporation franchise (income) tax, discussed at ¶924.

¶1610

CCH Advisory: Loan Originations Insufficient for Credit

It was proper for the Division of Taxation to disallow the investment tax credit claimed by a financial corporation with respect to its acquisition and improvement of a building. Loan originations, without sales of the resulting securities, could not be considered broker or dealer activities as required for purposes of the credit. The corporation argued, in the alternative, that its other activities of purchasing, selling, and terminating positions in securities satisfied the principal usage test in order to qualify for the credit. Based on a review of square footage calculations, however, this alternative argument was rejected. *Astoria Financial Corp.*, New York Division of Tax Appeals, Administrative Law Judge Unit, DTA No. 820197, August 10, 2006, CCH NEW YORK TAX REPORTS, ¶ 405-444.

Application of the credit to financial services organizations is discussed in detail at ¶ 924.

¶ 1613 Defibrillator Credit

Law: Sec. 1456(j), Tax Law (CCH NEW YORK TAX REPORTS, ¶ 14-094).

Forms: CT-250, Claim for Purchase of an Automated External Defibrillator.

A credit against bank franchise (income) tax is available for the purchase of automated external defibrillators. (Sec. 1456(j), Tax Law) Discussion at ¶ 937 applies.

¶ 1614 Long-Term Care Insurance Credit

Law: Sec. 1456(k), Tax Law (CCH NEW YORK TAX REPORTS, ¶ 14-095).

Forms: CT-249, Claim for Long-Term Care Insurance Credit.

A credit is allowed against bank franchise (income) tax for 20% of the premium paid for approved long-term care insurance during the taxable year. (Sec. 1456(k), Tax Law) Discussion at ¶ 939 applies.

¶ 1615 Excelsior Jobs Program

Law: Sec. 350 *et seq.*, Economic Development Law; Sec. 1456(u), Tax Law (CCH NEW YORK TAX REPORTS, ¶ 14-090a).

Forms: CT-607.

Legislation effective July 1, 2010, enacted the Excelsior Jobs Program, which includes the following corporate franchise, bank franchise, insurance franchise, and personal income tax credits:

— a jobs tax credit of up to $5,000 per job;

— an investment tax credit, equal to 2% of qualified investments;

— a 10% research and development credit, based on the federal credit; and

— a real property tax credit.

The Excelsior program replaced the expired Empire Zones program to provide job creation and investment incentives to firms in targeted industries. (Ch. 59 (A.B. 9709), Laws 2010)

For additional information about this credit, see ¶ 940.

¶ 1616 Low-Income Housing Credit

Law: Secs. 18, 1456(l), Tax Law; Secs. 21(5), 22, Public Housing Law (CCH NEW YORK TAX REPORTS, ¶ 14-093).

Comparable Federal: Sec. 42 (U.S. MASTER TAX GUIDE, ¶ 1334).

Forms: DTF-624, Low-Income Housing Credit; DTF-625, Low-Income Housing Credit Allocation Certification; DTF-625-ATT, Low-Income Housing Annual Statement.

A credit against bank franchise (income) tax is allowed for the construction or rehabilitation of qualified low-income housing. (Secs. 18, 1456(l), Tax Law; Secs. 21(5), 22, Public Housing Law) Discussion at ¶941 applies.

¶1617 Green Building Credit

Law: Secs. 19, 1456(m), Tax Law (CCH NEW YORK TAX REPORTS, ¶14-091).

Comparable Federal: Sec. 48. (U.S. MASTER TAX GUIDE, ¶1351).

Forms: DTF-630, Claim for Green Building Credit.

A green building tax credit is available against bank franchise (income) tax to enhance the supply of environmentally sound buildings in New York. (Sec. 1456(m), Tax Law) The credit includes six components, which are based on the capitalized costs (excluding land costs) of constructing green buildings, rehabilitating buildings to become green buildings, and purchasing and installing fuel cells, photovoltaic modules, and environmentally sensitive non-ozone depleting refrigerants. (Sec. 19, Tax Law) Discussion at ¶942 applies.

¶1618 Brownfield Credits

Law: Sec. 23, Tax Law; Secs. 1456 (q), (r), (s), Tax Law (CCH NEW YORK TAX REPORTS, ¶14-086).

Three refundable brownfield credits may be taken against bank franchise (income) tax. The credits are designated the brownfield redevelopment tax credit, credit for remediated brownfields, and environmental remediation insurance credit. The credits are available to taxpayers that own or develop a qualified site for which a certificate of completion has been issued to the taxpayer by the Commissioner of Environmental Conservation.

For details of the credits, see ¶943.

¶1619 Credit for Historic Property Rehabilitation

Law: Sec. 1456(u), Tax Law (CCH NEW YORK TAX REPORTS, ¶16-896).

A credit is available against the corporation franchise, personal income, bank franchise, and insurance premiums taxes for the rehabilitation of certain historic properties in the taxable year the property is placed in service. (Sec. 210 (40), Tax Law) The credit is equal to 100% of the federal credit allowed for the same taxable year under IRC Sec. 47(c)(2) with respect to a certified historic structure located in New York.

A rehabilitation project is a targeted area residence as defined in IRC Sec. 147(j) or located within a census tract that is at or below 100% of the median family income. Unused credit may be carried over to following years without limitation (Sec. 210(40), Tax Law). For additional information about this credit, see ¶948.

¶1620 Credit for Security Training

Law: Secs. 26, 1456(t), Tax Law (CCH NEW YORK TAX REPORTS, ¶16-395).

For qualified building owners, a refundable security training tax credit is allowed for taxable years beginning after 2004 (Sec. 1456(t), Tax Law). The credit amount equals the sum of the number of qualified security officers providing protection to buildings owned by the taxpayer, multiplied by $3,000 (Sec. 26, Tax Law). For details, see ¶946.

¶1621 Economic Transformation and Facility Redevelopment Program Credits

Law: Sec. 400 *et seq.*, Economic Development Law; Sec. 35, Tax Law; Reg. Secs. 200.1 *et seq.* (CCH NEW YORK TAX REPORTS, ¶14-090b).

The Economic Transformation and Facility Redevelopment Program provides a fully refundable credit available to personal income taxpayers, agricultural cooperatives, general business corporations, banks, and insurance companies and consisting of four components (Sec. 35, Tax Law):

— *Jobs tax credit component:* 6.85% of the gross wages of each net new job created;

— *Investment tax credit (ITC) component:* 10% of the cost of investments at a closed facility, with a facility-based cap of $8 million; 6% of the cost of investments elsewhere in an ETA, with a cap of $4 million per entity (if the participant is a partnership, a limited liability company, or an S corporation, the $4 million limitation is applied at the entity level);

— *Job training credit component:* 50% of training expenses for employees displaced by a facility closure, up to $4,000 per employee per year (the employees for whom the expenditures are made must be employed in a full-time, full-year position primarily located at the site in the economic transformation area during the training, and for 180 days after its completion); and

— *Real property tax credit component:* 50% of real property taxes for projects located entirely within the grounds of a closed facility, declining by 10% a year; 25% of real property taxes for projects elsewhere in an ETA, declining by 5% a year.

For details, see ¶938.

¶1622 Minimum Wage Reimbursement Credit

Law: Sec. 1456(z), Tax Law (CCH NEW YORK TAX REPORTS, ¶14-090e).

A credit is available for employers that hire qualified veterans (Sec. 1456(z), Tax Law). For further details, see the Art. 9-A corporate franchise tax discussion at ¶956.

¶1623 Hire a Veteran Credit

Law: Sec. 1456(e-1), Tax Law (CCH NEW YORK TAX REPORTS, ¶14-090d).

A credit is available for employers that hire qualified veterans, Tax Law. For further details, see the Art. 9-A corporate franchise tax discussion at ¶957.

FRANCHISE TAXES ON BANKING CORPORATIONS

CHAPTER 17
COMPUTATION OF INCOME

¶1701 In General

CAUTION.—Effective for taxable years beginning on or after January 1, 2015, the Article 32 bank franchise tax was repealed, and banks were merged into the Article 9-A corporate franchise tax (Ch. 59 (S.B. 6359), Laws 2014). The discussion below is applicable to taxable years beginning before 2015, except as otherwise indicated.

This chapter deals with the computation of the entire net income measure of the franchise tax imposed by Article 32 of the Tax Law. The tax is computed on an alternative basis if a higher tax will result (¶ 1604).

¶1702 Entire Net Income

Law: Sec. 1453, Tax Law (CCH NEW YORK TAX REPORTS, ¶ 14-037).

Comparable Federal: Secs. 61, 63 (U.S. MASTER TAX GUIDE, ¶ 62, 214, 2383—2389).

For taxable years beginning before 2015, "entire net income" of banks was defined as total net income from all sources, which is the same as entire taxable income (but not alternative minimum taxable income) (1) that the taxpayer is required to report to the U.S. Treasury Department, (2) that the taxpayer, in the case of a corporation that is exempt from federal income tax (other than the tax on unrelated business taxable income) but is subject to New York bank franchise taxes, would have been required to report to the IRS but for the exemption, or (3) that, in the case of a corporation organized under the laws of a country other than the United States, is effectively connected with the conduct of a trade or business within the United States. Certain modifications apply.

By adopting federal taxable income as a starting point, the New York franchise tax on banking corporations generally adopts the federal income tax treatment of items of gross income and deductions.

For modifications to federal taxable income, see ¶ 1703.

For allocation and apportionment, see ¶ 1704.

¶1703 Modifications to Federal Taxable Income

Law: Sec. 1453, Tax Law (CCH NEW YORK TAX REPORTS, ¶ 14-042—14-063).

The starting point for the computation of New York entire net income is federal taxable income for the taxable year. For taxable years beginning before 2015, this amount was subject to the following modifications (additions and/or subtractions):

Add

—Any part of any income from dividends or interest on any kind of stock, securities or indebtedness (other than dividends received from foreign corporations by a domestic corporation that elected to take a foreign tax credit) that was excluded for federal purposes. Special rules apply to corporations organized under the laws of certain foreign countries. (Sec. 1453(b)(1), Tax Law);

—Taxes imposed by the United States, its possessions or a foreign country on income or profits (Sec. 1453(b)(2), Tax Law);

—The New York franchise tax imposed on banking corporations, transportation and transmission corporations, water-works companies, gas companies, electric or steam heating, lighting and power companies, and business corporations;

—In those instances where a credit for the special additional mortgage recording tax is allowed, the amount allowed as an exclusion or deduction for the special additional recording tax in computing the entire taxable income that the taxpayer is required to report to the U.S. Treasury Department must be added back in determining entire net income. In addition, unless the credit for the special additional mortgage recording tax is reflected in the computation of the gain or loss so as to result in an increase in the gain or decrease in the loss for federal income tax purposes, from the sale or other disposition of the property with respect to which the special additional mortgage recording tax was paid, there must be added to federal entire taxable income the amount of the special additional mortgage recording tax that was paid and that is reflected in the computation of the basis of the property;

—Certain depreciation deductions. For property placed in service in New York State after 1993 and before 2003, the New York depreciation rules are the same as the federal depreciation rules, including the special "bonus" depreciation allowances for certain property under IRC Sec. 168(k) and for qualified Resurgence Zone and Liberty Zone property. However, for taxable years beginning after 2002, and applicable to property placed in service on or after June 1, 2003, the bank franchise (income) tax is decoupled from federal accelerated depreciation provisions under IRC Sec. 168(k), except with respect to qualified Resurgence Zone property and qualified Liberty Zone property (Sec. 1453(b)(13), Tax Law);

—Deferred gain from investments in emerging technologies (see below);

An addition modification is required for the IRC Sec. 199 deduction for qualified production activities income (Sec. 1453(b)(14), Tax Law);

—*Anti-PIC:* Certain royalty payments made by the taxpayer to a related member during the taxable year must be added back, to the extent deductible in calculating the taxpayer's federal taxable income. For additional information, see ¶1002;

Subtract

—Any credit or refund of a tax that was not allowed as a deduction or exclusion for New York purposes in a prior year;

—Interest on indebtedness incurred to buy or carry securities the income from which is taxable for New York but exempt for federal purposes;

—Expenses paid or incurred attributable to income that is taxable for New York but exempt for federal purposes;

—Amortizable bond premiums on bonds the interest on which is taxable for New York but exempt for federal purposes;

—The portion of wages and salaries not allowed as a business expense deduction for federal purposes because the federal targeted jobs tax credit was taken;

—Amounts received from the Federal Deposit Insurance Corporation or the Federal Savings and Loan Insurance Corporation;

—An amount equal to 17% of interest income from subsidiary capital;

—An amount equal to 60% of dividend income, gains, and losses from subsidiary capital (with certain phased-in reductions for disallowed investment proceeds (Sec. 1453(e)(11), Tax Law));

—An amount equal to 22.5% of the interest on New York State or federal obligations;

—Certain investment proceeds from RICs or REITs (Sec. 1453(u), Tax Law).

—An amount equal to 60% of the amount by which gains from subsidiary capital exceed losses from subsidiary capital, to the extent such gains and losses were taken into account in determining the financial institution's entire net income;

—The gain from the sale of any emerging technology investment acquired on or after March 12, 1998, and held for more than 36 months, but only to the extent that the gain realized exceeds the cost of any qualified emerging technology investment purchased by the taxpayer within 365 days from the date of the sale. The amount deferred will be added to federal taxable income when the reinvestment is sold;

—Net operating losses (NOLs) to the extent deductible under IRC Sec. 172, subject to certain adjustments. Using a taxpayer's federal NOL deduction as a starting point, the following New York adjustments must then be made: (1) the federal NOL deduction must be adjusted to reflect inclusions and exclusions required by other provisions of the bank income tax act; and (2) the deduction under IRC Sec. 172 must be determined as if the taxpayer had elected to relinquish the entire carryback period with respect to NOLs. NOLs incurred after 2000 may be deducted only in a taxable year in which the corporation is subject to the bank income tax.

Other Modifications

Differences between federal provisions and prior New York law: Because of differences in the computation of income or deductions under the federal provisions and under former Articles 9-B and 9-C of the Tax Law (applicable to bank taxes prior to January 1, 1973), additions to or subtractions from federal taxable income may be required in connection with bad debts, depreciation of property placed in service before January 1, 1973, charitable contributions, capital loss carryforward, income, or gain from installment sales, and other income or deductions previously reflected in New York returns.

Gain or loss: Adjustments are required in connection with gain or loss on the sale or exchange of property with a New York basis that differs from the federal basis.

Bad debts and reserves for loan losses: For taxable years beginning on or after January 1, 2010, the following additions to federal taxable income are no longer required:

— the bad debt amount allowed as a deduction pursuant to IRC Sec. 166; and

— 20% of the excess of the New York bad debt deduction allowed pursuant to Tax Law Sec. 1453(i) over the amount that would have been allowed if a bad debt reserve had been maintained for all tax years on the basis of actual experience.

The following subtractions from federal taxable income are no longer allowed:

— the recapture amount of the balance of the reserve for losses on loans pursuant to IRC Sec. 585(c) that is included in federal taxable income;

— the amount included in federal taxable income as a result of a recovery of a loan; and

— for banks subject to the provisions of IRC Sec. 585(c), and not subject to Tax Law Sec. 1453(h), the amount determined pursuant to Tax Law Sec. 1453(i).

In addition, the establishment and maintenance of a New York reserve for losses on loans is no longer necessary for banks subject to the provisions of Tax Law Sec. 1453(i)(1).

¶1704 Allocation and Apportionment

Law: Sec. 1454, Tax Law (CCH NEW YORK TAX REPORTS, ¶ 14-076—14-079).

Allocation percentage: If entire net income, alternative entire net income, and taxable assets are derived from business carried on within and without New York State, the taxpayer is required to allocate entire net income or taxable assets by a weighted three-factor (payroll, receipts, deposits) formula.

For a corporation owned by a bank or bank holding company that provides management, administrative, or distribution services to investment companies, a single sales factor allocation percentage was phased-in over a three-year period. (Sec. 1454(b)(1-a), Tax Law) Specifically, for affected taxpayers, the weight of the receipts factor was increased from 40% to 50% in 2006, and then to 70% in 2007. The single receipts factor became fully effective for tax years beginning after 2007.

Receipts factor: Receipts are allocated to the state in which the income producing activity occurred or is located.

The receipts factor is weighted as two.

Allocation rules for banks performing mutual fund management activities are conformed to the method allowed for general business corporations. Specifically, bank taxpayers may situs receipts from management, administrative, or distribution services to regulated investment companies based on the proportion of shares held by New York shareholders.

The allocation provisions pertaining to receipts from credit card transactions provide that service charges, fees, and interest, as well as fees and penalties in the nature of interest, are earned within New York if the card holder has a New York mailing address. (Sec. 1454(a)(2)(D), Tax Law) This applies to bank, credit, travel, and entertainment card receivables. See also TSB-M-08(7)C, June 9, 2008, CCH NEW YORK TAX REPORTS, ¶ 406-076.

Payroll factor: The payroll factor is the percentage that 80% of the total wages, salaries or other personal service compensation during the taxable year of employees within the state (other than general executive officers) bears to total wages, salaries, or other personal service compensation of all employees everywhere (except general executive officers).

Deposits factor: The deposits factor is the percentage that the average value of deposits maintained at branches within the state during the taxable year bears to the average value of deposits maintained at branches within and without the state during the taxable year.

The deposits factor is weighted as two.

In allocating "alternative entire net income," the payroll factor is recomputed to include total (instead of 80%) wages, salaries, or other personal service compensation of employees (other than general executive officers) within the state. Each factor is weighted as one.

International banking facilities: Special rules apply to international banking facilities. (Sec. 1453(f), Tax Law)

¶1704

FRANCHISE TAXES ON BANKING CORPORATIONS

CHAPTER 18

RETURNS, ESTIMATES, PAYMENT OF TAX

¶ 1801 Returns—Time and Place of Filing

Law: Secs. 1455-A, 1462, Tax Law (CCH NEW YORK TAX REPORTS, ¶ 14-121, 14-124).

Comparable Federal: Secs. 6072, 6081 (U.S. MASTER TAX GUIDE, ¶ 3, 118—122, 2509, 2525—2545).

Forms: CT-32, Banking Corporation Franchise Tax Return; CT-32-A, Banking Corporation Combined Franchise Tax Return; CT-32-M, Banking Corporation MTA Surcharge Return.

CAUTION.—Effective for taxable years beginning on or after January 1, 2015, the Article 32 bank franchise tax is repealed, and banks are merged into the Article 9-A corporate franchise tax (Ch. 59 (S.B. 6359), Laws 2014). The discussion below is applicable to taxable years beginning before 2015, except as otherwise indicated.

Calendar-year taxpayers are required to file annual returns on or before March 15 (for fiscal-year taxpayers returns are due by the 15th day of the third month following the close of the taxable year).

Extensions of time: An automatic six-month extension of time is granted when the application for extension is filed with the Commissioner on or before the due date and is accompanied by the amount properly estimated as the tax due.

With respect to returns for periods to which surcharge provisions apply, a six-month extension may not be granted unless an amount equal to the surcharge rate multiplied by the properly estimated tax is also paid. Other extensions of time may be granted.

Federal changes: A report of federal changes or corrections in taxable income must be filed within 90 days (120 days if making a combined return) after the final determination. If an amended federal return is filed, an amended New York return must be filed.

¶ 1802 Combined Returns

Law: Secs. 2.9, 2.10, 1462, Tax Law; Reg. Sec. 21-2.6 (CCH NEW YORK TAX REPORTS, ¶ 14-123).

Comparable Federal: Secs. 1501—1504 (U.S. MASTER TAX GUIDE, ¶ 295, 297).

Forms: CT-32-A, Banking Corporation Combined Franchise Tax Return; CT-32-A/B, Combined Group Detail Spreadsheet; CT-32-A/C, Report by a Banking Corporation Included in a Combined Franchise Tax Return.

A banking corporation or bank holding company, exercising its corporate franchise or doing business in New York, may be required or permitted to file a combined return.

80% ownership or control: Any banking corporation or bank holding company (1) that owns or controls, directly or indirectly, 80% or more of the voting stock of one or more banking corporations or bank holding companies, or (2) whose voting stock is 80% or more owned or controlled, directly or indirectly, by a banking corporation or bank holding company, is required to file a combined return. However, the taxpayer or the Commissioner may show that the combined return fails to properly reflect the tax liability of the corporation.

65% ownership or control: In the discretion of the Commissioner, any banking corporation or bank holding company (1) that owns or controls, directly or indirectly, 65% or more of the voting stock of one or more banking corporations or bank holding companies, or (2) whose voting stock is 65% or more owned or controlled, directly or indirectly, by a banking corporation or bank holding company, may be required or permitted to file a combined return.

Captive RICs and REITs: A captive RIC or captive REIT is a regulated investment company or real estate investment trust that is not regularly traded on an established securities market and more than 50% of the voting stock is owned or controlled, directly or indirectly, by a single corporation that is not exempt from federal income tax and is not a RIC (Secs. 2.9, 2.10, Tax Law). A captive RIC or captive REIT must be included in a combined return with the corporation that owns or controls more than 50% of its voting stock (Sec. 1462(f)(2)(v)(B), Tax Law).

Credit card banks: Banking corporations that are considered to be doing business in New York solely under new criteria regarding credit card transactions (see ¶ 1602), the law has been amended to include provisions addressing when such corporations should be included in a combined return with other banking corporations or bank holding companies (Sec. 1462(f)(2)(v), Tax Law). For details, see TSB-M-08(7)C, June 9, 2008, CCH NEW YORK TAX REPORTS, ¶ 406-076.

¶1803 Estimated Tax

Law: Secs. 1455-B, 1460, 1461, Tax Law (CCH NEW YORK TAX REPORTS, ¶ 14-122).

Comparable Federal: Secs. 6154, 6611, 6655 (U.S. MASTER TAX GUIDE, ¶ 225—231).

The estimated tax provisions for banking corporations are similar to the provisions applicable to corporations taxable under Article 9-A, the business corporation franchise (income) tax (¶ 1405).

Metropolitan Commuter Transportation District surcharge: Banking corporations subject to the Metropolitan Commuter Transportation District surcharge whose franchise tax liability can reasonably be expected to exceed $1,000 also must make declarations and pay estimated tax on the surcharge.

¶1804 Payment of Tax

Law: Sec. 1463, Tax Law (CCH NEW YORK TAX REPORTS, ¶ 14-121).

Comparable Federal: Secs. 6151, 6161, 6601 (U.S. MASTER TAX GUIDE, ¶ 5, 2529).

Payment of the full amount of any tax shown due on the return (less any installment payments of estimated tax) must accompany the return (¶ 1801).

The tax is due on or before the 15th day of the third month following the close of the taxable year (March 15 for calendar-year taxpayers). Remittances are made payable to New York State Corporation Tax.

FRANCHISE TAXES ON BANKING CORPORATIONS

CHAPTER 19

ADMINISTRATION, DEFICIENCIES, PENALTIES, TAXPAYER REMEDIES

¶1901 Administration of Bank Taxes

NOTE.—Effective for taxable years beginning on or after January 1, 2015, the Article 32 bank franchise tax is repealed, and banks are merged into the Article 9-A corporate franchise tax (Ch. 59 (S.B. 6359), Laws 2014).

Same as corporation franchise (income) tax (¶ 1501).

¶1902 Assessments—Deficiencies

Same as corporation franchise (income) tax (¶ 1502).

¶1903 Penalties and Interest

Same as corporation franchise (income) tax (¶ 1507, 1508).

¶1904 Taxpayer Remedies

Same as corporation franchise (income) tax (¶ 1511).

PART V

SALES AND USE TAXES

CHAPTER 20
IMPOSITION OF TAX, BASIS, RATE

¶2001 Overview of Sales and Use Tax

A statewide sales and use tax covering a broad range of taxables was enacted in 1965. The tax is imposed by Article 28 of the Tax Law, and applies to (1) sales of tangible personal property, (2) sales of enumerated services, (3) use of tangible personal property and enumerated services, (4) sales of gas, electricity, refrigeration and steam, and of telephone and telegraph services (except interstate and international telephone and telegraph services), (5) occupancies of hotel rooms, (6) food and beverages sold by restaurants, taverns and caterers, (7) admission charges to certain places of amusement and to roof gardens, cabarets and similar places, and (8) social or athletic club dues. Exemptions, either specific or by definition, are provided.

The sales tax on tangible personal property is general in nature. On the other hand, the tax on services is selective, in that taxable services are enumerated, all others being exempt. The use tax, in general, is complementary to the sales tax. It does not apply if the taxable property or service has already been or will be subject to the sales tax.

The current state tax rates are specified at ¶2022.

Cities, counties (except counties wholly within a city), and certain school districts also are authorized by Article 29 of the Tax Law to levy sales and use taxes for city, county, or school district purposes.

With certain exceptions, the sales and use tax base for both state and local levies is required to be uniform. The local jurisdictions have the option of adopting either the entire state tax package or, in the alternative, one or more of these taxes, excluding the tax on sales or use of tangible personal property and on services (¶2024).

Local taxes are discussed at ¶2024, and rates are listed at ¶11.

Entertainment and information services: An additional tax is imposed on taxable entertainment and information services that are furnished, provided, or delivered by means of interstate or intrastate telephony, telegraphy, or telephone or telegraph services (¶2022).

- *Streamlined Sales and Use Tax Agreement*

The stated purpose of the Streamlined Sales and Use Tax (SST) Agreement is to simplify and modernize sales and use tax administration in the member states in order to substantially reduce the burden of tax compliance. The Agreement was developed by representatives of state governments, with input from local governments and the private sector. It came into effect on October 1, 2005, with a Governing Board made up of member states. New York is not a member of the Agreement because, although it has enacted legislation authorizing it to enter into the Agreement (Sec. 1173, Tax Law), it has not yet enacted the changes to its laws necessary to comply with the Agreement's requirements. However, as an Advisor State to the Governing Board it will serve in an *ex officio* capacity on the Board, with nonvoting status, and may speak to any matter presented to the Board for its consideration.

DoTF Policy Analysis: The likelihood that conforming to the Streamlined Sales and Use Tax (SST) Agreement will generate vast amounts of new sales tax revenue for New York from taxing remote sales is low, according to a report issued by the New York Department of Taxation and Finance's Office of Tax Policy Analysis. The report found that "the vast majority of large retailers" with both a physical presence and Internet or catalog sales are already registered to collect in New York. Uncollected tax on remote sales in 2005 was estimated to equal less than 3% of fiscal year sales tax receipts. Achieving full conformity would require a "broad-based revision" of the state's tax law, including changes in the taxability of many basic items and the elimination of exemption thresholds and multiple rates. Counties and cities would be particularly affected. For instance, New York City's taxation of a variety of services might have to change. The number of conforming changes could result in unanticipated revenue swings, the report states. While praising the Agreement as "an important step towards reducing" tax collection burdens, the report goes on to say that recent proposals to amend the Agreement "appear to make sales tax collection more complex" for multistate businesses. (*Sales Tax Special Interest Report—Streamlining New York's Sales Tax,* New York Department of Taxation and Finance, October 2006)

¶2002 Imposition of Tax—Constitutional Limitations

(CCH New York Tax Reports, ¶60-075, ¶60-080).

Federal and state constitutional provisions restrict the ability of states to levy sales and use taxes. Of the federal provisions, the Commerce and Due Process Clauses are the most frequently invoked.

¶2002

• *Commerce Clause requirements*

The Commerce Clause reserves to Congress the power to regulate commerce among the states, with foreign nations, and with Indian tribes. Although this provision was once interpreted as setting a virtual bar on a state's ability to tax interstate commerce, the U.S. Supreme Court, in *Complete Auto Transit, Inc. v. Brady* (1977, US SCt) 430 US 274, 97 SCt 1076, held that state taxes may impact upon interstate commerce if the following requirements are met:

— the tax is applied to an activity with substantial connection (nexus) with the state;

— it is fairly apportioned;

— it does not discriminate against interstate commerce; and

— it is fairly related to the services provided by the taxing state.

When international commerce is involved, in addition to the criteria above, a tax may not do either of the following:

— create a risk of multiple taxation; or

— prevent the federal government from "speaking with one voice" when regulating commercial relations with foreign governments.

The *Complete Auto* test, with refinements, continues to be the standard for determining the validity of a state tax on interstate commercial activity under the Commerce Clause.

In *National Geographic Society v. California Board of Equalization* (1977, US SCt) 430 US 551, the U.S. Supreme Court required the Society to collect use tax with respect to interstate mail order sales from its District of Columbia home office, on the basis of the physical presence of two National Geographic magazine advertising sales offices in California, the taxing state. The Court made the following two significant rulings: (1) the required nexus with the taxing state need not necessarily be directly related to the activity being taxed, but could be simply whether the facts demonstrate some definite link, some minimum connection, between the taxing state and the person it seeks to tax; and (2) the required physical presence of the vendor in the taxing state must be more than the "slightest presence."

• *Due process requirements*

The Due Process Clause prevents states from depriving any person of life, liberty, or property without due process of law. Not defined by the Constitution, the nature of due process itself has consequently been determined by case law. The Supreme Court has held that due process requires "some definite link, some minimum connection, between a state and the person, property, or transaction it seeks to tax" (*Miller Brothers Co. v. Maryland* (1954, US SCt) 347 US 340). In essence, the tax must be reasonably related to the protection, opportunities, and benefits given by the state.

Connected with the notion that a tax must be reasonably related to the benefits provided by the taxing state is the requirement that the tax must be fairly apportioned. This fairness requirement is an element of both the Commerce and Due Process Clauses, and according to the Supreme Court has two components (*Container Corp. of America v. FTB* (1983, US SCt) 463 US 159, 103 SCt 2933). First, an apportionment formula must have "internal consistency"; that is, the formula must be such that, if applied by every jurisdiction, it would result in no impermissible interference with free trade. Second, the formula must have "external consistency"; that is, the factor or factors used in the apportionment formula must actually reflect a reasonable sense of how income is generated. In essence, the external consistency component requires an analysis of whether the income being taxed is in proportion to the activity being conducted within the taxing state.

¶2002

• *Nexus*

Nexus is a requirement for taxation of interstate transactions under both the Commerce and Due Process Clauses. Until *Quill Corp. v North Dakota* (1992, US SCt) 504 US 298, the constitutionally required nexus between the taxing state and the activity, entity or property subject to the tax was applied indistinguishably for purposes of both Due Process and Commerce Clause analysis. Generally, some physical presence of the vendor in the taxing state was noted as a factor justifying the imposition of the sales and use tax collection obligation.

In *National Bellas Hess, Inc. v Department of Revenue of Illinois* (1967, US SCt) 386 US 753, the Court for the first time explicitly made some physical presence of the vendor in the taxing state a requirement under both the Commerce and Due Process Clauses for charging the vendor with the duty of collecting a use tax on mail order purchases by residents of that state. Physical presence within the taxing state was required, irrespective of the degree to which the vendor may have availed itself of the benefits and protection of the taxing state in other ways, such as by "regularly and continuously engag[ing] in exploitation of the consumer market of [that state]" (Fortas, J., dissenting (quoting *Miller Bros. Co. v Maryland*)).

The Court gave the following three reasons for requiring the vendor's physical presence in the taxing state: (1) without some physical presence, there would be no fair basis for making interstate commerce bear a share of the cost of local government; (2) a contrary rule would require the Court "to repudiate totally the sharp distinction," relied upon by state taxing authorities, between mail order sellers with local outlets or solicitors and "those who do no more than communicate with customers in the state by mail or common carrier as part of a general interstate business"; and (3) permitting imposition of the duty of collection of the tax in that case would subject national mail order businesses to oppressive administrative and record-keeping burdens.

In *Quill Corp. v. North Dakota* (1992, US SCt) 504 US 298, the Court ruled that the Commerce Clause, but not the Due Process Clause, barred North Dakota from requiring an out-of-state mail order company to collect and pay use tax on goods sold to North Dakota customers when the company had no outlets, sales representatives, or other significant property in the state. In so ruling, the Court reaffirmed that portion of *National Bellas Hess* that established under the Commerce Clause a "bright-line" rule that permits a state to compel out-of-state mail-order sellers having a physical presence in the state to collect its use taxes, but not those who do no more than communicate with customers in the state by mail or common carrier as part of a general interstate business.

However, the Court overturned *Bellas Hess* and its prior decisions to the extent that they indicate that the Due Process Clause requires a seller's physical presence in a state before the seller can be obligated to collect the state's use tax.

In *Orvis Co., Inc. v. Tax Appeals Tribunal of the State of New York* and *Vermont Information Processing, Inc. v. Tax Appeals Tribunal of the State of New York,* the New York Court of Appeals considered whether sporadic visits by a mail-order company's sales personnel for the purpose of soliciting orders from retailers, and occasional visits by a computer software and hardware developer's personnel to install software, train employees, and correct difficult or persistent problems, were sufficient to establish the substantial nexus standards of *Quill*. In both cases, the Appellate Division, after reviewing the activities of the taxpayer (12 trips by Orvis personnel over a three-year period; 30 to 40 trips during a comparable period by Vermont Information Processing personnel) within New York, concluded that the activities were insufficient and, therefore, annulled the determinations assessing the tax.

On appeal, the Court of Appeals rejected the Appellate Division's conclusion that *Quill* required a "substantial physical presence" by an out-of-state vendor in New York as a prerequisite to imposing a duty upon the vendor to collect and remit

¶2002

compensating use tax on products that are sold to New York clientele. Instead, after considering *Quill* in the context of its position in the evolution of Supreme Court doctrine limiting the authority of a state to assess or impose a duty to collect taxes arising out of the economic activity of a foreign business engaged in interstate commerce, the court held that *Quill* cannot be read as equating a substantial physical presence of a vendor in a taxing state with the substantial nexus prong of the *Complete Auto* test.

The court noted that, while a physical presence of the vendor is required under contemporary Commerce Clause standards, it need not be substantial. Rather, it must be demonstrably more than a "slightest presence" and may be manifested by the presence in the taxing state of the vendor's property or the conduct of economic activities in the taxing state performed by the vendor's personnel or on its behalf.

Applying the "demonstrably more than a slightest presence" standard, the court concluded that there was substantial evidence to support the Tax Appeals Tribunal's initial determination that the activities of Orvis and of Vermont Information Processing in New York were sufficient to impose an obligation to collect compensating use taxes on their taxable retail sales to New York customers. Orvis' substantial wholesale business in New York was accomplished by its sales force's direct solicitation of retailers through visits to their stores in New York. Vermont Information Processing's employees visited New York on 41 occasions during the three-year audit period to resolve problems and give additional instructions in the use of its software.

CCH Advisory: Commissioned Referrals Created Nexus

A manufacturer's use of independent referral sources who were paid a commission to find suitable retailers for the manufacturer's products in New York created sufficient nexus with New York to require the manufacturer to register as a vendor for New York sales tax purposes. The activities of the referral sources in New York satisfied the requirements of the slightest-presence test set forth in *Orvis* (*Ohio Table Pad Co.*, NY Division of Tax Appeals, April 22, 1999, CCH NEW YORK TAX REPORTS, ¶403-355).

Related activity: A taxpayer's physical contacts with a state need not be related to the activity being taxed. In *National Geographic Society v. SBE* (1977, US SCt) 430 US 551, the U.S. Supreme Court held that the presence in California of advertising sales offices for the National Geographic magazine provided sufficient nexus so that California could require National Geographic to collect the use tax on mail-order sales made to California by another division of the Society. Although the two advertising sales offices had nothing to do with the mail-order division, the offices benefited from California services, and thus provided the connection with the state that allowed California to require the Society to collect the state's use tax. The Court applied similar reasoning in *D.H. Holmes Co. v. MacNamara* (1988, US SCt) 486 US 24, in which a company with retail outlets in the state was required to pay use tax on catalogs ordered from an out-of-state printer and sent by mail to company customers.

Practitioner Comment: Promotional Activities

An out-of-state business may send employees into New York without creating nexus for sales tax purposes as long as the employees' activities are limited to meetings with New York printers, mailers and other producers of promotional materials (TSB-M-96(10)S, CCH NEW YORK TAX REPORTS, ¶300-223).

Mark S. Klein, Esq., Hodgson Russ LLP

Although the physical contacts with the state need not be related to the activity being taxed, the Division of Tax Appeals has indicated that the contacts must have some relationship with the conduct of an economic activity in order to meet Commerce Clause nexus standards. In *Petition of NADA Services Corporation*, CCH NEW

York Tax Reports, ¶ 402-293, an Administrative Law Judge concluded that although the "quality and quantity" of a taxpayer's contacts with New York were sufficient to meet Due Process Clause nexus standards, they were insufficient to rise above a "slightest presence" and, therefore, did not satisfy Commerce Clause requirements.

¶2003 Transactions Subject to Sales Tax—In General

Law: Sec. 490, Tax Law; Sec. 1105, Tax Law; Sec. 1110, Tax Law; Reg. Secs. 526.6—526.8, 527.1 (CCH New York Tax Reports, ¶ 60-020, ¶ 60-310, ¶ 60-340, ¶ 60-445).

The sales tax is imposed on receipts from the following (Sec. 1105, Tax Law):

— the retail sale of tangible personal property, including the rental of such property (other than for resale) (¶ 2005);

— the sale of gas, electricity, refrigeration, and steam, and of telephone and telegraph services (except interstate and international telephone and telegraph services, and gas, gas service, electricity or electronic service purchased for use in providing gas or electric service consisting of operating a gas pipeline, or distribution line, or an electric or distribution line and ensuring the necessary working pressure in an underground gas storage facility) (¶ 2006);

— the sale of enumerated services (¶ 2007);

— the sale of food and beverages by restaurants, taverns, and caterers, including any cover charges (¶ 2008);

— occupancies of hotel rooms (¶ 2009);

— admission charges to certain places of amusement and to roof gardens, cabarets and similar places (¶ 2010); and

— social or athletic club dues and initiation fees (¶ 2011).

All receipts of tangible personal property and specified services, all rents for occupancy and all amusement charges are presumed taxable, unless the contrary is established. The burden of proving exemption from tax is imposed on the person required to collect tax or the purchaser of the goods or services. However, where a properly completed resale certificate, exempt use or exempt organization statement has been furnished to the vendor, the burden of proof as to non-taxability of a receipt, amusement charge or rent is shifted to the purchaser.

Transactions subject to use tax are discussed at ¶ 2013.

Nonmonetary transactions: A trade, barter, or exchange is usually a swap for something that is not intended for resale. Many times, trades and barters are between individuals not in the business of selling the items (for example, one person agrees with another to trade a boat for a dirt bike of similar value). But occasionally, businesses trade or barter (for example, a plumber repairs a broken water heater for a mechanic in exchange for repair work on an automobile)and sales tax is due on the transaction. The tax is calculated on the value of the items or services given in trade. In any trade, barter, or exchange, the purchase price or taxable receipt is considered to be the value of what you gave in trade. (*TB-ST-860*, June 16, 2011, CCH New York Tax Reports, ¶ 407-296)

Virtual currency: The use of convertible virtual currency such as bitcoin, by a customer to pay for goods or services delivered in New York is treated as a barter transaction. For sales tax purposes, convertible virtual currency is intangible property. Since the purchase or use of intangible property is not subject to sales tax, any convertible virtual currency received by a party to a barter transaction is not subject to sales tax. However, if the party that gives convertible virtual currency in trade receives in exchange goods or services that are subject to sales tax, that party owes sales tax based on the market value of the convertible virtual currency at the time of the transaction, converted to U.S. dollars. If the party that trades property or services in exchange for receiving convertible virtual currency gives the other party a sales slip, invoice, or receipt, the first party must separately state the sales tax due in U.S.

dollars on the sales slip, invoice, or receipt. For additional information, see *TSB-M-14(17)S*, December 5, 2014, CCH New York Tax Reports, ¶408-293.

Practitioner Comment: Place of Taxation

New York's sales tax is based on the destination of the taxable property or where the service is performed. The point of transfer to a purchaser, of either delivery or possession, controls both the incidence of the tax and the appropriate rate (Reg. Sec. 525.2(a)(3)). Consequently, a retailer that ships otherwise taxable goods outside of New York will have no obligation to collect New York sales tax (of course, depending on the retailer's connection with the state of delivery, it may have a sales tax collection obligation in that state). For information or services delivered electronically, the location of the customer's modem represents the point of delivery. Special rules apply when a customer is able to access on-line services from more than one location (*KPMG, LLP*, TSB-A-03(5)C, CCH New York Tax Reports, ¶404-547; see also *TB-ST-155*, New York Department of Taxation and Finance, August 6, 2015, CCH New York Tax Reports, ¶408-506).

Mark S. Klein, Esq., Hodgson Russ LLP

• *Drop shipments (third-party sales)*

A drop shipment is a shipment of tangible personal property from a seller directly to the purchaser's customer, at the direction of the purchaser. These sales are also known as third-party sales because they require that there be, at arm's length, three parties and two separate sales transactions. Generally, a primary seller (generally a retailer) accepts an order from a customer, places this order with a third party seller, usually a manufacturer or wholesale distributor, and directs the third party seller to ship the goods directly to the primary seller's customer or to the primary seller's unaffiliated fulfillment services provider. Drop shipments are examined as two transactions: (1) the sale from the third-party seller to the primary seller, and (2) the sale from the primary seller to the primary seller's customer. (*TB-ST-190*, August 5, 2014, CCH New York Tax Reports, ¶408-178)

When all the parties are located in the state, the retailer furnishes a resale certificate to the primary seller, rendering the first sale a nontaxable transaction. The retailer then collects sales tax on behalf of the state on the secondary sale to its customer. However, different considerations arise when one or more of the parties are not within the state. New York will exempt the sale of the primary (or initial) seller to an out-of-state retailer not doing business in New York provided that the retailer presents a resale certificate or other appropriate evidence that the sale is made for resale. If the out-of-state secondary seller does not have New York nexus and consequently cannot be held liable for tax on the sale to its New York customer, then the customer becomes liable for use tax. (Sec. 1110, Tax Law)

• *Electronic commerce*

"Electronic commerce" or "E-commerce" is the sale of tangible or intangible goods or services by electronic means. In most cases, this means sales transactions in which the seller and the buyer communicate over the Internet. The object of the sale frequently is a product in electronic form or a service that is also delivered over the Internet, but it may also be tangible personal property or an electronic product in tangible form, such as a prepaid phone card, delivered by conventional means. Activities that are related to a sale, such as advertising, shopping, ordering, and payment, are also considered to be electronic commerce when they occur over the Internet or a private network.

Sales and use tax may apply to a variety of transactions in an electronic commerce environment. This may include taxes on charges for tangible personal property or taxable services purchased via the Internet, or intangible personal property that may or may not be comparable to tangible personal property otherwise available.

Federal Internet Tax Freedom Act (ITFA): The federal Internet Tax Freedom Act (P.L. 105-277, 112 Stat 2681), as amended by P.L. 107-75, P.L. 108-435, and P.L 110-108, bars state and local governments from imposing multiple and discriminatory taxes on electronic commerce, including taxes on Internet access, except for those that were imposed and enforced prior to October 1, 1998. The ITFA was made permanent by Congress on February 24, 2016, as part of the "Trade Facilitation and Trade Enforcement Act of 2015 (H.R. 644, 114th Congress). See also ¶2006.

Tangible personal property: The New York sales and use tax is imposed on receipts from retail sales of tangible personal property and specified services. "Tangible personal property" subject to the tax is defined to include prewritten computer software whether sold as part of a package, as a separate component, or otherwise, and regardless of the medium by means of which such software is conveyed. A "sale" of prewritten computer software includes any transfer of title or possession, any exchange, barter, rental, lease, or license to use, including merely the right to reproduce, for consideration. Software designed and developed to the specifications of a specific purchaser is exempt (¶2005, ¶2102).

Situs: A software company's sale of the license to use its basic software package constitutes the sale of prewritten software subject to New York sales tax, regardless of where the software is stored. The situs of the sale for sale tax purposes is the location associated with the license to use (*i.e.*, the location of the customer's employees that use the software). If the locations where the customer's employees will use the software are both in and out of New York, the taxpayer is only required to collect tax based on the portion of the taxable receipts attributable to the employees' use of the software at locations in New York. The determination of the proper local tax rate and jurisdiction is also based on the locations associated with the licensees' use. (*TSB-A-09(41)S*, September 22, 2009, CCH NEW YORK TAX REPORTS, ¶406-546)

"Prewritten computer software" is defined as software not designed and developed by the author or other creator to the specifications of a specific purchaser. "Prewritten software" includes software designed and developed by the author to the specifications of a specific purchaser when it is sold to a person other than such purchaser. Prewritten software that is modified to the specifications of a specific purchaser remains prewritten software, but may qualify for an exemption from sales and use tax if it is used directly and predominately in the production of tangible personal property for sale, or directly and predominately in research and development. In addition, charges for custom modifications or enhancements that are reasonable and separately stated on an invoice or billing statement are not subject to tax. Charges for website design and development services are exempt (¶2102).

Taxable sales include any charges by the vendor to the purchaser for shipping or delivery regardless of whether such charges are separately stated in the written contract, if any, or on the bill and regardless of whether the shipping or delivery is provided by the vendor or a third party (¶2013, ¶2015).

Internet access: Receipts from the sale of Internet access service are exempt from New York sales and use tax. "Internet access service" is defined as providing connection to the Internet by means of accepted Internet protocols. The provision of communication or navigation software, an e-mail address, e-mail software, news headlines, space for a website and website services, or other such services in conjunction with the provision of the connection to the Internet, when such services are merely incidental to the provision of the connection, are considered to be part of the exempt Internet access service (¶2102). However, see ¶2006, concerning taxability of the sale of DSL services to an Internet service provider.

A fee charged for computer timesharing in itself is not subject to New York sales and use tax. There is no transfer of title or possession of the computer; therefore, the

¶2003

transaction is not the retail sale of tangible personal property. However, all or part of a timesharing transaction may be taxable according to the type of information or service provided (¶2005).

Charges by a system operator to persons in New York for membership or for "on-line" time, for the purpose of exchanging or conveying information or software programs, are subject to sales and use tax. For example, the system operator of a commercial on-line computer information service charges a fee to its customers for downloading prewritten software programs and for access to a computer bulletin board that has features on software support and technical advice. Charges for the software programs are taxable as the sale of tangible personal property. Charges for access to the software support and technical advice are subject to tax as information services. The manner of delivery to the customer of the software or information services does not affect the taxable status of the transactions (¶2007).

Charges for remote access to processed data that is personal and individual in nature and that cannot be substantially incorporated into reports furnished to other persons are not subject to New York sales and use tax. Fees charged for storing the data also are not taxable (¶2102).

An advisory opinion discusses the sales tax application to the provision of Internet access to customers at coffee bars, food service businesses, and other retail locations in New York City. Charges for basic service to access the Internet for a specified per-minute charge are exempt from sales tax. Receipts for premium service that include additional charges for the use of pre-written propriety software programs for word processing, calculation, and presentation are subject to tax. When the charge for basic service to access the Internet is aggregated with the charge for use of the pre-written software for a single lump sum charge, the entire charge will be subject to sales tax unless the Internet access provider can reasonably identify the charges for Internet access from its books and records kept in the regular course of business. (*TSB-A-08(47)S*, October 16, 2008, CCH New York Tax Reports, ¶406-195; see also *TSB-A-09(19)S*, May 21, 2009, CCH New York Tax Reports, ¶406-410)

Digitized products—software, publications, music, and videos: As discussed above, prewritten computer software is specifically deemed to be tangible personal property for sales and use tax purposes, regardless of the medium by which it is conveyed to the purchaser. Therefore, software that is otherwise taxable remains subject to sales tax even if conveyed to the purchaser electronically.

The hard copy version of a publication that provided news, analyses, political forecasts, and recommendations on financial investment matters met the requirements of a periodical and was therefore exempt from New York sales and use tax. However, the electronic version of the publication did not qualify for exemption. The publication was published four times a year in print form and 12 times a year electronically (four quarterly versions with free monthly updates). To be exempt, an electronic version of a publication may not include anything that is not in the hard copy edition or issue. Because subscribers to the electronic version received free monthly updates to the quarterly hardcopy version, the electronic version did not have the same content as the hard copy version and was subject to tax. (*TSB-A-07(6)S*, March 16, 2007, CCH New York Tax Reports, ¶405-680)

E-books: The current policy of the Department of Taxation and Finance, until further notice, is that the sale of a book delivered electronically (e-book) does not constitute the sale of an information service subject to state and local sales and use tax under Sec. 1105(c)(1), Tax Law. However, the e-book must meet all of the following conditions:

— the purchase of the product does not entitle the customer to additional goods and services and any revisions done to the e-book are for the limited purpose of correcting errors;

— the product is provided as a single download;

— the product is advertised or marketed as an e-book or a similar term;

— if the intended or customary use of the product requires that the product be updated or that a new or revised edition of the product be issued from time to time (*i.e.*, an almanac), the updates or the new or revised editions are not issued more frequently than annually; and

— the product is not designed to work with software other than the software necessary to make the e-book legible on a reading device (*e.g.*, Kindle, Nook, iPad, iPhone or personal computer).

The policy is limited to products that are not, or do not include, prewritten computer software or any other product that constitutes tangible personal property under Sec. 1101(b)(6), Tax Law. (*TSB-M-11(5)S*, New York Department of Taxation and Finance, April 7, 2011, CCH NEW YORK TAX REPORTS, ¶407-192; see also *TSB-A-14(1)S*, New York Commissioner of Taxation and Finance, January 23, 2014, CCH NEW YORK TAX REPORTS, ¶408-007)

Digital music and videos: A company's sales of alpha-numeric codes that provide the means by which an individual can access and download digital music were not subject to New York sales or compensating use tax because they are sales of an intangible, regardless of whether a physical medium such as a paper certificate or plastic card is used to transmit the code. The individual who uses the code to download digital music is purchasing the same digital music as individuals who directly purchase digital music for download by making payment at the time of purchase by credit card or through third-party financial institutions. Therefore, the sales of the code are sales of an intangible not subject to tax. In addition, the company's charges for the electronic transfer of digital music via the Internet to customers, downloaded for use on the customers' computers or similar devices, are not subject to tax regardless of whether customers make payment by credit card or by using the company's alpha-numeric code previously purchased and transferred to the customer on a physical medium, by E-mail, or otherwise. (*TSB-A-07(14)S*, May 17, 2007, CCH NEW YORK TAX REPORTS, ¶405-732)

Likewise, a company's sales of videos delivered electronically over the Internet to customers' computers are not subject to New York sales or compensating use tax. In the same way that audio content (music) and visual content (photographs) delivered electronically are not subject to tax, the receipts from sales of videos that are delivered to customers electronically over the Internet and downloaded for use on the customer's computer or other device are receipts from the sale of an intangible and are not subject to tax under Secs. 1105(a) or 1110(a)(A), Tax Law. Also, the use of the Internet to sell and electronically deliver a video for download to a customer's computer does not constitute the provision of a taxable information service or entertainment service within the meaning and intent of Secs. 1105(c)(1) or 1105(c)(9), Tax Law. (*TSB-A-07(11)S*, April 12, 2007, CCH NEW YORK TAX REPORTS, ¶405-705; *TSB-M 08(22)S*, May 2, 2008)

Practitioner Comment: Digitized Products

Other than software, New York's sales tax does not apply to products that are digitized and transferred to a purchaser electronically. Consequently, otherwise taxable items such as photographs, artwork, graphic designs, music, movies, books, and videos are exempt from tax when transferred by methods such as email, wire feed, satellite uplink, on-line, etc. (TSB-A-12(10)S, CCH NEW YORK TAX REPORTS, ¶407-561). Transfers of the same information by disc, tape or other magnetic media are subject to tax since the disc and tapes constitute tangible personal property (*Google, Inc.*, TSB-A-08(22)S, CCH NEW YORK TAX REPORTS, ¶406-055; *Apple Computer, Inc.*, TSB-A-07(11)S, and TSB-A-07(14)S, CCH NEW YORK TAX REPORTS, ¶405-705, ¶405-732). But see *American Multi-Cinema, Inc.* (ALJ 6/21/12, CCH NEW YORK TAX REPORTS, ¶407-580), where an ALJ extended the exemption to movies delivered by hard drive.

Mark S. Klein, Esq., Hodgson Russ LLP

"Tangible personal property" subject to New York sales and use tax includes newspapers and periodicals when the vendor ships or delivers the entire edition or issue of the newspaper or periodical by means of electronic media. However, sales of publications that qualify as newspapers or periodicals are exempt from New York sales and use tax, whether the publications are sold in print form, in CD-ROM format, or in Internet versions (¶2104).

Services: The New York sales and use tax is imposed on receipts from specified services, including the "furnishing of information" (¶2007).

Information services performed on computer software are exempt from sales and use tax, except that when the services are provided to a customer in conjunction with the sale of tangible personal property they are exempt only if the charge is reasonable and separately stated. For example, software maintenance agreements that provide for the sale of both taxable items (such as prewritten computer software) and exempt services are taxed on the total charge for the maintenance agreement, unless the charge for the nontaxable items is reasonable and is separately stated in the mainte-nance agreement and billed on the invoice or other document of sale given to the purchaser (¶2007).

Electronically delivered entertainment service is a taxable service (¶2007).

Amounts charged by a developer of Internet websites to its clients for domain registration, host site maintenance, website development, and creation of interactive games for websites are not taxable, because such services are not included among the list of enumerated services subject to tax (¶2102).

A taxpayer's electronic discovery litigation support services were not subject to the New York sales tax imposed on information services, because they were personal and individual in nature (*TSB-A-10(59)S*, New York Commissioner of Taxation and Finance, November 23, 2010, CCH New York Tax Reports, ¶407-078). However, another taxpayer's sale of a license to use its prewritten computer software for litigation support and e-discovery services by providing customers with the capabil-ity to capture, review, or manage data was subject to state and local sales tax (*TSB-A-10(60)S*, New York Commissioner of Taxation and Finance, November 24, 2010, CCH New York Tax Reports, ¶407-079).

Another advisory opinion discusses the taxability of advice services as informa-tion services (*TSB-A-10(61)S*, New York Commissioner of Taxation and Finance, December 17, 2010, CCH New York Tax Reports, ¶407-083).

Nexus: As with mail order sales, a transaction involving an electronic sale to a purchaser by a vendor that has no physical presence in the purchaser's state raises nexus issues. Sales and use tax nexus and other constitutional issues are discussed at ¶2002.

Medical marijuana (cannabis): Effective July 5, 2014, New York has established a medical marijuana program for New York State and imposes a 7% excise tax on the gross receipts from the sale of medical marijuana by a registered organization to a certified patient or designated caregiver. The tax is to be paid by the registered organization and may not be added as a separate charge or line item on any sales slip, invoice, receipt or other statement of price given to the retail customer. The law expires seven years from the date of enactment.

"Registered organization" means a registered organization under Title V-A, Secs. 3364 and 3365 of the Public Health Law. A "certified patient " is a patient who is a resident of New York State or is receiving care and treatment in New York State as determined by the Commissioner in regulation, and is certified under Title V-A, Sec. 3316 of the Public Health Law. (Sec. 490, Tax Law)

¶2003

Cloud computing: Cloud computing is a term used to describe the delivery of computing resources, including software applications, development tools, storage, and servers over the Internet. Rather than purchasing hardware or software, a consumer may purchase access to a cloud computing provider's hardware or software. Cloud computing offerings are generally divided into three categories: software as a service, infrastructure as a service, and platform as a service.

Software as a service.—Under the SaaS model, a consumer purchases access to a software application that is owned, operated, and maintained by a SaaS provider. The consumer accesses the application over the Internet. The software is located on a server that is owned or leased by the SaaS provider. The software is not transferred to the customer, and the customer does not have the right to download, copy, or modify the software. Sales tax authority on SaaS transactions is still evolving. Some states have taken the position that SaaS transactions are a sale of software, reasoning that using software by electronically accessing it is no different than downloading it. Other states have deemed it a service based on the fact that no software is transferred. In some states, the taxability may depend on the specific facts and whether the object of the transaction is the use of software or some other purpose.

New York has no specific authority on the taxability of SaaS. However, the Department of Taxation and Finance has issued various Advisory Opinions on software accessed remotely. See, for example, *TSB-A-13(22)S,* July 25, 2013, CCH New York Tax Reports, ¶407-895(sales of access to forms via software stored on the taxpayer's website are subject to sales tax when accessed by a customer located in New York because the taxpayer's product is prewritten computer software); *TSB-A-09(44)S,* September 24, 2009, CCH New York Tax Reports, ¶406-551 (discusses the sales and use tax treatment of various Internet advertising, set-up, support, and service fees relating to real estate listings, including application service provider (ASP) fees for website functionality that are considered receipts from the sale of prewritten computer software and are subject to tax); *TSB-A-09(25)S,* June 18, 2009, CCH New York Tax Reports, ¶406-432 (web based software applications developed by the taxpayer for use by homecare agencies to track patient care and employee time and attendance, and for billing purposes, are subject to sales tax); *TSB-A-09(15)S,* April 15, 2009, CCH New York Tax Reports, ¶406-377 (charges for online access to "loan origination and processing services," which, among other things, allowed customers to complete and print certain loan processing documents, constituted receipts from the sale of prewritten computer software); *TSB-A-08(62)S,* November 24, 2008, CCH New York Tax Reports, ¶406-277 (license to use software product that allowed a customer to upload an image to a website and manipulate the image to show various colors and views, constituted the sale of prewritten computer software).

Platform as a service.—Under the PaaS model, the provider sells access to a platform and software development tools that a consumer uses to create its own applications. A consumer deploys the applications it creates onto the provider's infrastructure. The consumer has control over its deployed applications but does not control the underlying infrastructure. New York has no specific authority on the taxability of PaaS, but see above for various Advisory Opinions on software accessed remotely.

Infrastructure as a service.—IaaS providers sell access to storage, networks, equipment, and other computing resources that the provider operates and maintains. A consumer purchases the ability to store data or deploy and run software using the provider's equipment. The consumer does not manage or control the cloud infrastructure but has control over its applications and data. New York has no specific authority on the taxability of IaaS, but see *TSB-A-15(2)S,* April 14, 2015, CCH New York Tax Reports, ¶408-397 (cloud computing product allows customers to access a specific array of a processor, memory, and storage upon which customers run their own software applications).

¶2004 Persons Subject to Tax

Law: Secs. 12, 1101, 1105, Tax Law (CCH NEW YORK TAX REPORTS, ¶ 60-020).

Persons who are subject to tax include vendors, lessors, promoters, purchasers of tangible personal property, services, food and beverages, recipients of room charges at hotels and motels, and admission charges to shows. Liability for the payment of tax falls primarily on those persons required to collect the tax. Liability may, however, be transferred to the purchaser in the event that the tax is not paid by the person required to collect it (¶ 2203).

Practitioner Comment: Vendor

Although not technically a "vendor" under law, any credit company or qualified intermediary that comes into possession of receipts that include sales taxes nonetheless becomes a person subject to tax and acquires liability for all collected amounts (*Ford Motor Credit, TSB-A-02(20)S,* CCH NEW YORK TAX REPORTS, ¶ 404-241).

Mark S. Klein, Esq., Hodgson Russ LLP

The term "vendor," for purposes of the sales tax, includes the following (Sec. 1101(b)(8), Tax Law):

— Persons who make sales of tangible personal property or services, the receipts from which are subject to sales tax;

— Persons who maintain places of business within New York and make sales to persons within the state of tangible personal property or services subject to use tax;

— Persons who solicit business by employees, independent contractors, agents or similar representatives and, by reason of such solicitation, make sales to persons within the state of tangible personal property or services subject to use tax;

The definition of "vendor" specifies that the in-state activities of an affiliate in providing accounting or legal services or advice, or in directing the activities of a seller, including but not limited to making decisions about strategic planning, marketing, inventory, staffing, distribution, or cash management, do not make the seller a vendor. For examples, see *TSB-A-15(3)S,* March 18, 2015, CCH NEW YORK TAX REPORTS, ¶ 408-404.

CCH Advisory: Internet Retailers—the "Amazon law"

There is a rebuttable presumption that any person making taxable sales of tangible personal property or services ("seller") is a vendor subject to New York sales and compensating use tax when the seller enters into an agreement with a New York resident to directly or indirectly refer customers to the seller, whether by a link on an Internet Web site or otherwise, for a commission or other consideration, and the agreement generates sales of over $10,000 in the prior four quarterly reporting periods. In such a situation, the seller is presumed to be soliciting business in New York through an independent contractor or other representative and will have to charge sales tax on all sales into the state. This presumption may be rebutted by proof that the resident did not engage in any solicitation activities in New York on behalf of the seller that would satisfy the nexus requirement of the U.S. Constitution during the previous four quarterly periods in question. (Sec. 1101(b)(8)(vi), Tax Law; see also *TSB-M 08(3)S, May 8, 2008,* CCH NEW YORK TAX REPORTS, ¶ 406-047)

Rebuttal: A memorandum provides additional guidance relating to rebuttal of the presumption that a seller described above is a vendor required to be registered for sales tax purposes and collect state and local sales taxes (*TSB-M-08(3.1)S,* June 30, 2008, CCH NEW YORK TAX REPORTS, ¶ 406-097).

Statute challenged in court: The constitutionality of the statute was challenged by major Internet retailers on Commerce Clause, Due Process, and Equal Protection grounds (*Amazon.com, LLC v. Dept. of Taxation and Finance,* New York Supreme Court, New York County, No. 08601247, filed August 25, 2008; *Overstock.com, Inc. v. New York Department of Taxation and Finance,* New York Supreme Court, New York County, No. 107581/08, filed May 30, 2008). The suits were dismissed (*Amazon.com LLC v. New York Department of Taxation and Finance,* New York Supreme Court, New York County, Index No. 601247/08, January 12, 2009, CCH NEW YORK TAX REPORTS, ¶406-287; *Overstock.com, Inc. v. New York Department of Taxation and Finance,* New York Supreme Court, New York County, Index No. 107581/08, January 12, 2009, CCH NEW YORK TAX REPORTS, ¶406-294).

In subsequent action, the New York Court of Appeals found that the statute is constitutional on its face in relation to the Commerce Clause and the Due Process Clause (*Overstock.com, LLC v. New York State Department of Taxation and Finance,* Court of Appeals of the State of New York, Nos. 33 and 34, March 28, 2013, CCH NEW YORK TAX REPORTS, ¶407-797). Petitions for *Certiori* were denied by the U.S. Supreme Court on December 2, 2013.

— Persons who regularly or systematically solicit business in New York through the distribution of catalogs, advertising fliers or similar means and, by reason of such solicitation, make sales of tangible personal property subject to use tax to persons within New York, when the solicitation satisfies federal nexus requirements;

— Persons who make sales of tangible personal property or services subject to tax, and who regularly or systematically deliver the property or services in New York by means other than the U.S. mail or common carrier;

— Persons who make sales of tangible personal property subject to tax, when (1) the person making the sale retains an ownership interest in the property, and (2) the person to whom the property is sold brings it into New York and becomes or is a resident or uses the property in carrying on any employment, trade, business or profession within the state;

— Persons who make sales of property or services subject to tax to persons within New York and are authorized by the Commissioner to collect the tax;

— The United States and any of its agencies or instrumentalities, the United Nations or similar international organizations of which the United States is a member, or the state of New York, its agencies, instrumentalities, public corporations or political subdivisions, when selling services of a kind ordinarily sold by private persons.

The term "vendor" also includes certain exempt organizations that make sales of tangible personal property through a shop or store operated by the organization, or which sell food and drink in New York State.

Agents: Any salesman, representative, peddler, or canvasser may be treated as the agent of the vendor, distributor, supervisor, or employer under whom he or she operates or from whom he or she obtains tangible personal property or for whom he or she solicits business. Such an agent may be held jointly responsible with the principal, distributor, supervisor, or employer for the collection and payment of tax (Sec. 1101(b)(8)(ii)(A), Tax Law).

CCH Advisory: Electronic Commerce

The term "vendor" does not include a person who has advertising stored on a server or other computer equipment located in New York or a person whose advertising is disseminated or displayed on the Internet by an individual or entity having nexus with New York. Taxable E-commerce transactions are discussed at ¶2003.

Fulfillment services: The definition of a "vendor" excludes any person who purchases fulfillment services carried on in New York from a nonaffiliated person and a person that owns tangible personal property located on the premises of a nonaffiliated fulfillment services provider performing services for that person (Sec. 1101(b)(8), Tax Law). The purchaser of the fulfillment services must not otherwise be a vendor. "Fulfillment services" are defined as accepting orders or responding to consumer correspondence or inquiries electronically or via mail, telephone, fax, or the Internet; billing and collection activities; or shipping orders from inventory (Sec. 1101(b)(18), Tax Law).

Affiliated persons.—Persons are affiliated persons with respect to each other if one has a direct or indirect ownership interest of more than 5% in the other or if an ownership interest of more than 5%, direct or indirect, is held in each such person by another or by a group of persons that are affiliated persons with respect to each other. Thus, a foreign corporation may engage a nonaffiliated New York fulfillment service company to fill orders for it with merchandise stored in New York and the foreign corporation will not be considered a vendor (Sec. 1101(b)(8), Tax Law).

Persons who, individually or through affiliates or agents, bill entertainment or information services provided by telephonic or telegraphic means by a vendor of entertainment or information services, are regarded as vendors of such services (Sec. 1101(b)(8)(ii)(B), Tax Law).

Affiliate nexus: The definition of "vendor" has been expanded to provide that the presence of an affiliate in New York makes the remote affiliate a vendor under either of two conditions, as follows (Sec. 1101(b)(8)(i)(I), Tax Law; *TSB-M-09(3)S,* May 6, 2009, CCH New York Tax Reports, ¶ 406-386):

(1) the in-state affiliate uses in New York a trademark, service mark, or trade name that is the same or similar to that of the remote affiliate; or

(2) the in-state affiliate engages in activities that help the remote affiliate develop or maintain a market for its goods or services in New York, to the extent that those activities are sufficient to give the state nexus over the remote affiliate under the nexus requirements of the U.S. Constitution.

For purposes of determining whether condition (2) is met, the Department will consider whether the direct or indirect ownership exceeds 50%, *i.e.,* if one owns, directly or indirectly, more than 50% of the other or if more than 50% of each entity is owned, directly or indirectly, by the same entity or by an affiliated group. Condition (2) will be considered to be satisfied if the percentage of direct or indirect ownership exceeds 50% and the New York affiliate engages in any activities that are more than *de minimis* and that promote the development or maintenance of a market for the remote affiliate's products or services in New York.

The following activities will result in vendor status under Condition (2) (*TSB-M-09(3)S,* May 6, 2009, CCH New York Tax Reports, ¶ 406-386):

— referring New York customers to the remote affiliate;

— accepting merchandise returns from catalog, telephone, or Internet customers of the remote affiliate;

— soliciting New York customers using names and addresses from the remote affiliate's mailing list (including an email list);

— distributing catalogs or discount coupons on behalf of the remote affiliate;

— distributing or displaying advertising on behalf of the remote affiliate;

— accepting catalog, telephone, or Internet orders on behalf of the remote affiliate;

— fulfilling sales ordered from the remote affiliate's Web site or catalog (including in-store pick up of items ordered from a catalog or Web site);

— handling distributions or warehousing in New York of products sold by the remote affiliate;

— performing repair services on behalf of a remote affiliate (e.g., warranty services).

¶2004

Legislation retroactive to July 1, 2009, provides that an in-state affiliate that only provides accounting or legal services or advice, or directs the activities of the seller (including but not limited to, making decisions about strategic planning, marketing, inventory, staffing, distribution or cash management on behalf of an out-of-state seller in New York State) will not make the out-of-state seller a vendor for sales tax purposes (*TSB-M-10(12)S*, August 19, 2010, CCH NEW YORK TAX REPORTS, ¶406-941).

A remote affiliate that makes taxable sales in New York and meets the expanded definition of a vendor must register for sales tax purposes and obtain a Certificate of Authority. Vendor registration requirements are discussed at ¶2201.

The sales tax liability of vendors is discussed at ¶2203.

¶2005   Retail Sales of Tangible Personal Property

> *Law:* Secs. 1101, 1102, 1105(a), 1111(q), Tax Law; Sec. 27-1913, Environmental Conservation Law; Reg. Secs. 526.6—526.8 (CCH NEW YORK TAX REPORTS, ¶60-020, ¶60-310, ¶60-560, ¶60-570, ¶60-600, ¶60-630, ¶60-650, ¶60-645, ¶60-730, ¶61-180, ¶65-174).

Retail sales of tangible personal property are taxable. (For exemptions, see Chapter 21.)

Practitioner Comment: Corporate Transactions

New York's sales tax rules are not always intuitive. For example, a federal "A" reorganization (the merger of two corporations) is not subject to sales tax (Reg. Sec. 526.6(d)(1)(i)), but a "C" reorganization (the transfer of assets for stock) is fully taxable. Reg. Sec. 526.6(d)(6)(iv). Similarly, transfers of assets to a corporation upon its organization in consideration for stock are not subject to tax while transfers of assets to an existing corporation in consideration for stock are taxable. However, even in the latter case, the tax can be eliminated by structuring the transaction as a contribution to capital, without the issuance of additional stock. Reg. Sec. 526.6(d)(5). Consequently, detailed and specialized research is always recommended.

Mark S. Klein, Esq., Hodgson Russ LLP

Definitions: A "retail purchase" and a "retail sale" is defined as a sale of tangible personal property to any person for any purpose *other than* (1) for resale in the same form or as a physical component part of other tangible personal property or (2) for use in performing certain taxable services (including information services, certain processing and printing services, installation, maintenance and repair, and repair services upon tangible personal property, real estate maintenance service or repair, interior decorating and designing services, and protective and detective services) when the property so sold becomes a physical component part of the property upon which the services are performed or is later actually transferred to the purchaser of the services in connection with the performance of the services. (Sec. 1101(b)(4), Tax Law; Reg. Sec. 526.6)

"Tangible personal property" is defined broadly as "corporeal personal property of any nature." Thus, the sales tax applies generally to all tangible personal property, unless specifically exempted. However, for purposes other than for the tax on sales of utility services, the term does not include gas, electricity, refrigeration, and steam. Prewritten computer software (sold as part of a package, as a separate component, or otherwise), regardless of the medium by which such software is conveyed to the purchaser, is specifically included in the definition of the term "tangible personal property." (Sec. 1101(b)(6), Tax Law; Reg. Sec. 526.8)

The rental, lease, or license to use or consume tangible personal property is subject to tax since such transactions are included in the definition of "sale." (Sec. 1101(b)(5), Tax Law; Reg. Sec. 526)

Practitioner Comment: Intangible Assets

A frequently used tax planning technique involves the placement of taxable assets into a new subsidiary, partnership or single-member limited liability company in consideration for the issuance of stock, a partnership interest or a membership interest. This transfer is not a retail sale under Tax Reg. 526.6(d)(2) and (5). Once the property is in the new entity, the stock, partnership interest or membership interest can be sold to a third party. If structured properly in conjunction with an adequate business purpose, sales of these "intangible assets" are not subject to sales tax. An administrative law judge ruled that there is nothing wrong with a taxpayer gaining an advantageous sales tax position as a by-product of the above structure. According to the judge, "it is the form chosen by the taxpayer which is controlling and the fact that a taxpayer could have chosen a different form which would have had different consequences does not convert" a nontaxable transaction into a taxable one (*TJX Companies*, NYS ALJ (11/9/95), CCH New York Tax Reports, ¶402-246, *aff'd*, NYS TAT (2/13/97), CCH New York Tax Reports, ¶402-638).

Mark S. Klein, Esq., Hodgson Russ LLP

Investment-related transfers: Certain transfers to and from corporations and partnerships are excluded from the definition of the term "retail sale," including (Sec. 1101(b)(4)(iii), Tax Law):

— transfers of tangible personal property to a corporation, solely in consideration for the issuance of its stock, pursuant to a merger or consolidation;

— distributions of property by a corporation to its stockholders as a liquidating dividend;

— distributions of property by a partnership to its partners in whole or partial liquidation;

— transfers of property to a corporation upon its organization in consideration for the issuance of its stock; and

— contributions of property to a partnership in consideration for a partnership interest.

Transfers of aircraft or vessels: These exclusions from the definition of "retail sale" do not apply to transfers, distributions, or contributions of aircraft and vessels between affiliated entities. (Sec. 1111(q), Tax Law)

The base on which sales tax would be computed on any sale of an aircraft or vessel by virtue of a transfer that qualifies as a retail sale covered under this provision is the price the seller paid to acquire the aircraft or vessel unless the seller has owned the property for six months or more at the time of transfer, in which case the sales tax due may be computed based on the current market value of the aircraft or vessel at the time of the transfer of the property. The current market value must not exceed the cost of the aircraft or vessel.

Contractors, subcontractors, repairmen: Any sale of tangible personal property to a contractor, subcontractor, or repairman for use or consumption in erecting structures or buildings, or building on, or otherwise adding to, altering, improving, maintaining, servicing, or repairing real property is deemed to be a retail sale regardless of whether the tangible property is to be resold as such before it is so used or consumed. The application of sales and use tax to contractors' repair, maintenance, and installation services to real property is discussed in *TB-ST-129*, New York Department of Taxation and Finance, March 17, 2016, CCH New York Tax Reports, ¶408-696.

The sale of a new mobile home to a contractor, subcontractor, or repairman who, in such capacity, installs the new mobile home is not a retail sale. (Sec. 1105(c)(8), Tax Law)

Exemptions are allowed for materials used in work performed for exempt organizations and for capital improvements (¶2102).

A taxpayer's charges to its customers for delivering construction equipment the taxpayer rents to them are subject to sales tax whether or not the delivery charges are separately stated on the receipt. See *TSB-A-12(21)S*, New York Commissioner of Taxation and Finance, August 28, 2012, CCH NEW YORK TAX REPORTS, ¶407-637.

Trucks, trailers or tractor-trailers: The purchase of a truck, trailer, or tractor-trailer combination for rental or lease to an authorized carrier is a retail sale (Sec. 1101(b)(4)(i), Tax Law).

Motor fuel: Retail sales of motor fuel and diesel motor fuel are subject to sales tax (Sec. 1101(a)(4)(ii), Tax Law; Sec. 1105(a), Tax Law; Reg. Sec. 561.1(f)). Similarly, the use of motor fuel is subject to the compensating use tax (Sec. 1110, Tax Law). Certain alternative motor fuels are exempt; see ¶2106.

For electronic funds transfer and certified check payments required to be made by taxpayers subject to sales and use taxes on motor fuel, see ¶2203.

For basis of tax on motor fuel and diesel fuel, see ¶2015.

Cigarettes: Cigarettes and tobacco products are taxable as sales of tangible personal property (Reg. Sec. 526.5(b)(1)(i)).

For basis of tax, see ¶2015. For refund provisions, see ¶2210.

Motor vehicle rentals: The amount of sales and use and 5% special passenger car rental tax (¶2014) is computed on the total amount of the rental or lease charge.

Wrapping and packaging materials and supplies: Sales of certain cartons, containers and wrapping and packaging materials and supplies are not considered "retail sales" (¶2102).

Typography: Composition (cold type), typography (hot type) and progressive proofs (prepress) used or consumed directly and predominantly in production are considered to be exempt equipment, exempt from the New York State and local sales and use taxes outside of New York City, provided such equipment is used directly and predominantly in the production of tangible personal property for sale (*TSB-M-79(7.1)S*, CCH NEW YORK TAX REPORTS, ¶66-077a).

Computer software: Prewritten computer software, whether sold as part of a package or as a separate component, is subject to tax regardless of the medium by which it is conveyed (Sec. 1101(b)(6), Tax Law). "Prewritten computer software" consists of computer software (including prewritten upgrades) that is not designed and developed by the author or other creator to the specifications of a specific purchaser, as well as software that is specially designed and developed for a specific purchaser but is sold to someone other than the purchaser. Software designed and developed to the specifications of a specific purchaser (*i.e.,* custom software), however, is exempt (Sec. 1101(b)(14), Tax Law). A taxable "sale" of prewritten computer software includes a transfer of title or possession, any exchange or barter, rental, lease, or license to use, and reproduction rights. See also ¶2003 and ¶2102.

Computer hardware: Generally, computer hardware is subject to sales tax as tangible personal property (Sec. 1101(b)(6), Tax Law). However, computer system hardware used or consumed directly and predominantly in designing and developing computer software (such as websites) for sale is exempt (Sec. 1115(a)(35), Tax Law). The exemption also extends to "associated parts," which encompass any component of, or attachment to, computer system hardware that is used in connection with and is necessary to the performance of the hardware's operation (*i.e.,* motherboards, CPUs, modems, and network wiring and cables). In addition, machinery, equipment, and other tangible personal property used to provide access to the Internet and to sell website services by operators of Internet data centers are exempt.

¶2005

For applicability of the compensating use tax, see ¶2013. For exemptions from tax, see ¶2102.

CCH Advisory: Computer Hardware and Software

An advisory opinion discusses various scenarios and transactions that can be described as sales of computer hardware and software, installation of computer hardware and software (provided by either the taxpayer or a customer), consulting services (including research, evaluation, design, and troubleshooting), customization of computer software, and data conversion. (*TSB-A-07(28)S*, November 14, 2007, CCH NEW YORK TAX REPORTS, ¶405-912)

• *Waste tire management fee*

Tire retailers, including car dealers, must collect a waste tire management fee of $2.50 on retail sales of new tires for use on nearly all self-propelled or towed vehicles that could be registered for any reason. The fee also applies to new tires sold with a new or used vehicle, including spare tires. The fee expires on December 31, 2019. (Sec. 27-1913, Environmental Conservation Law; *TSB-M-16(4)M*, July 27, 2016, CCH NEW YORK TAX REPORTS, ¶408-813.)

Exemptions: Sales to government agencies and other specified entities are exempt from the fee. New tires that are purchased solely for the purpose of resale are not subject to the fee at the time of purchase for resale.

Devices operated or driven by a person with a disability and vehicles that run only on rails or tracks are exempt. Prior to September 19, 2004, an exemption applied to new tires purchased for motorcycles, all terrain vehicles, and limited use vehicles, such as golf carts.

Returns and payments: The fee is administered by the Department of Taxation and Finance. Retailers must collect the $2.50 fee, file returns for each quarter on Form MT-170, Waste Tire Management Fee Return, and remit $2.25 for each tire sold. This allows each tire retailer to retain 25¢ for each tire sold to help defray administrative costs. The returns are due by the last day of the month following the close of each quarter. A tire retailer that has more than one location within the state must file a combined return for all locations.

¶2006 Sales of Gas, Electricity, Telecommunication, and Other Utilities

Law: Secs. 1105(b), 1105-c, 1110(a)(H), Tax Law; Reg. Sec. 527.2 (CCH NEW YORK TAX REPORTS, ¶60-020, ¶60-445, ¶60-750).

Sales, other than for resale, of gas, electricity, refrigeration, or steam; gas, electric, refrigeration, or steam service; telephony or telegraphy; and telephone or telegraph services are taxable. Interstate and international telephony and telegraphy, as well as such telephone and telegraph services, are exempt. Exemptions are provided for certain uses, including residential use and specified industrial uses (¶2102, ¶2105, ¶2106).

Use tax: Use tax is specifically imposed on the use of gas or electricity, eliminating a disparity in taxation favoring out-of-state sellers (Sec. 1110, Tax Law). An exemption is provided for gas, gas service, electricity or electric service used or consumed directly and exclusively to provide gas or electric service consisting of operating a gas pipeline or gas distribution line or an electric transmission or distribution line, and ensuring the necessary working pressure in an underground gas facility.

HVAC services: Additional rent paid by a commercial tenant for overtime heating, ventilation, and air conditioning (HVAC) services provided by a landlord incidental to the rental of office space are not subject to tax. Tax is authorized only on receipts from transactions that can be identified as independent sales of utility or utility services (*Debevoise & Plimpton*, New York Court of Appeals, February 20, 1993, 593 NYS2d 974, CCH NEW YORK TAX REPORTS, ¶ 400-946).

Service provision: The fee that a utility charges a customer for getting the gas or electricity to the customer is subject to state and local sales tax as a charge for electric or gas service (*TSB-M-00(4)S*, Department of Taxation and Finance, June 9, 2000, CCH NEW YORK TAX REPORTS, ¶ 300-319).

CCH Advisory: Vehicle Charging Stations

The unit charge and any fee a taxpayer charges its customers for the sale of electricity at an electric vehicle charging station are subject to New York sales tax. The taxpayer owns and operates electric vehicle charging stations in New York. The taxpayer charges its customers a per unit fee (based on kilowatt hours) for electricity transferred to its customers' electric vehicles. Sec. 1105(b)(1)(A), Tax Law, imposes sales tax on the receipts from every sale of electricity and electric service of whatever nature. Although this tax is generally known as the "consumer's utility tax," the intention of this statute is to tax the enumerated sales and services whether or not rendered by a company subject to regulation as a utility company. Accordingly, the taxpayer's charges for electricity for charging electric vehicles are subject to sales tax. (*TSB-A-13(18)S*, New York Commissioner of Taxation and Finance, July 15, 2013, CCH NEW YORK TAX REPORTS, ¶ 407-886)

Telecommunications and Internet access: The Internet Tax Freedom Act (ITFA) was made permanent by Congress on February 24, 2016, as part of the "Trade Facilitation and Trade Enforcement Act of 2015 (H.R. 644, 114th Congress). The IFTA Amendments Act of 2007 (P.L. 110-108 (H.R. 3678)), includes the following provisions.

— The moratorium on state and local taxes on Internet access and multiple or discriminatory taxes on electronic commerce that was originally enacted in October 1998 was extended until October 1, 2015; see ¶ 2003.

— The grandfather clause that permits Internet access taxes that were generally imposed and actually enforced prior to October 1, 1998, was also extended until October 1, 2015. However, the grandfather clause does not apply to any state that had, more than 24 months prior to the enactment of the 2007 legislation, repealed its tax on Internet access or issued a rule that it no longer applies such a tax.

— State and local governments that continue to impose tax on telecommunications service purchased, used, or sold by a provider of Internet access had until June 30, 2008, to end these disputed taxes. However, this provision only operates if a public ruling applying such a tax was issued prior to July 1, 2007, or such a tax is the subject of litigation that was begun prior to July 1, 2007. Some states dispute the assertion that taxes they impose on telecommunications service purchased by Internet service providers to connect their customers to the Internet (so-called "backbone" services) were prohibited by Congress in the 2004 renewal of the moratorium. This amendment and the revised definition of "Internet access" (discussed below) is intended to resolve this issue and end state and local taxation of Internet "backbone" service.

— A new definition of "Internet access" was enacted. It means a service that enables users to connect to the Internet to access content, information, or other services. The definition includes the purchase, use, or sale of telecommunications by an Internet service provider to provide the service or otherwise enable users to access content, information, or other services offered over the Internet. It also includes incidental services such as home pages, electronic mail, instant messaging, video clips, and personal electronic storage capacity, whether or not packaged with service to access the Internet. However, "Internet access" does not include voice, audio or video programming, or other products and services using Internet protocol for which there is a charge, regardless of whether the charge is bundled with charges for "Internet access." See *TSB-M 08(2)S*, May 2, 2008, CCH NEW YORK TAX REPORTS, ¶406-042, as revised by *TSB-M 08(2.1)S*, August 29, 2008, CCH NEW YORK TAX REPORTS, ¶80-420.

— The moratorium was amended to clarify that it does not apply to state general business taxes, such as gross receipts taxes, that are structured in such a way as to be a substitute for or supplement the state corporate income tax. Therefore, Internet access providers may still be taxed on their receipts attributable to providing access under tax regimes such as the Michigan business tax, Ohio commercial activity tax, Texas margin tax, and Washington business and occupation tax.

Internet telephony: The New York Department of Taxation and Finance has issued a guidance document explaining how the sales tax and the telecommunications excise tax apply to telecommunication services that use voice over Internet protocol (VoIP). Such services enable the user to make and receive telephone calls. Accordingly, VoIP services constitute telephony for purposes of the sales tax, and they also constitute telecommunication services for purposes of the excise tax. The use of the Internet or Internet routing protocols for transmission of all or part of a call does not change this result.

If intrastate telephone services are provided with interstate and/or international telephone services for a single charge, the entire charge is subject to sales tax, unless there is a reasonable, separately stated charge for the interstate and/or international services on the invoice given to the customer. If the services offered are entirely interstate and/or international, the charges for such services are excluded from sales tax. Interstate and international calling services billed on a call-by-call basis are not subject to sales tax, but the provider must maintain records to indicate the origination and termination of such calls. If nontaxable property or discrete services (other than Internet access) are bundled with taxable VoIP services and sold to the customer for a single charge, the entire charge is subject to sales tax, unless the charge for such property and/or discrete services is reasonable and separately stated on the invoice provided to the customer.

Under the telecommunications excise tax, revenues derived from equipment and other services (other than Internet access) provided with VoIP services are considered gross receipts subject to tax. If VoIP services are bundled with Internet access for a single charge, the entire charge is subject to both sales and excise taxes, unless the Internet access provider can reasonably identify the charges for Internet access from its books and records kept in the regular course of business. (*NYT-G-07(2)C* and *NYT-G-07(3)S*, June 20, 2007, CCH NEW YORK TAX REPORTS, ¶405-760)

A report from New York Department of Taxation and Finance discusses the scope and nature of the telecommunications industry in New York and summarizes all of the taxes, fees, and assessments (including sales and use, corporate franchise, utility, and property taxes) to which the industry is subject. The report includes a matrix that attempts to show what taxes apply to the various services provided by the industry. (*Report on the Taxation of the Telecommunications Industry*, New York Department of Taxation and Finance, October 2009)

Electronic messaging: The New York Supreme Court, Appellate Division, confirmed the Tax Appeals Tribunal's (TAT's) decision that a company's charges for electronic messaging services were subject to sales tax because they were considered taxable telegraph services. (*Easylink Services, International, Inc. v. New York Tax Appeals Tribunal*, Appellate Division of the Supreme Court of New York, Third Department, No. 512864, December 6, 2012, CCH NEW YORK TAX REPORTS, ¶407-723)

¶2007 Services

Law: Secs. 1101, 1105, 1110, Tax Law; Reg. Secs. 527.3—527.7, 528.21—528.24 (CCH New York Tax Reports, ¶60-020, ¶60-340—¶60-740, ¶60-365, ¶61-735).

Sales, except for resale, of specified services are taxable. Services not specifically taxed by law are not subject to tax. Wages, salaries, and other compensation paid by an employer to an employee for rendering services otherwise taxable are not subject to tax.

Service contracts and extended warranties: Sales of service contracts in New York are considered to be sales of taxable repair and maintenance services, whether sold at point of purchase or aftermarket products. Businesses located in New York that make sales of service contracts must be registered as New York sales tax vendors. See *TB-ST-836*, New York Department of Taxation and Finance, June 5, 2015, ¶408-428.

Practitioner Comment: Separate Entities

All corporations, partnerships and limited liability companies (including single-member limited liability companies) are treated as separate entities for sales and use tax purposes. Consequently, a taxpayer can lose the exemption for wages, salaries, and other compensation paid by an employer to an employee if the employees are performing taxable services for one company and are compensated by another entity. New York's courts will generally bind taxpayers to the disadvantages arising out of the form of business chosen by them (*Tops, Inc.*, NYS TAT (11/22/89), and *107 Delaware Avenue Associates*, 64 NY2d 935 (1985)).

Mark S. Klein, Esq., Hodgson Russ LLP

• *Credit reporting services*

Charges for credit information services are subject to tax, except those transmitted orally (Reg. Sec. 527.3(a)(4)). The following services related to credit reporting are also subject to tax: (1) any fee for a written report; (2) any fee for an oral report, if preliminary to the written report; and (3) an annual fee for subscribing to a service, if the fee entitles the subscriber to a certain number of free reports, or to reduced charges on reports, unless the subscriber receives only oral reports (Reg. Sec. 527.3(a)(4)). Since a credit report is included within the definition of a taxable information service, the rules applicable to information services also apply to credit reporting services (see below). (Sec. 1105(c)(1), Tax Law; Reg. Sec. 527.3(a)(3))

• *Information services*

The services of furnishing information by printed, mimeographed, or multigraphed matter or by any other method of duplication (including the services of collecting, compiling, or analyzing information and furnishing reports) are taxable. Taxable information services include credit reports, tax or stock market advisory and analysis reports, and product and marketing surveys. An information service also includes the collection, compilation or analysis of any kind of information and the furnishing of reports to other persons (Sec. 1105(c)(1), Tax Law; Sec. 1110(a), Tax Law; Reg. Sec. 527.3). The seller of the information service (i.e., the information service provider) is required to charge, collect, and remit the applicable tax (Sec. 1131(1), Tax Law; Reg. Sec. 525.2).

Exclusions apply for the furnishing of information that is done orally, is personal or individual in nature, for services of advertising agents or other agents or representatives, and information services used by newspapers and radio and television broadcasters in the collection and dissemination of news. (Reg. Sec. 527.3)

CCH Advisory: What Are Information Services?

In general, furnishing information created or generated from a common database, or information that is widely accessible, is a taxable information service. The sale of a report that uses or relies on statistical models or historical data is also generally considered to be a taxable information service, as is the service of gathering information from a variety of sources and recasting that information into a report. The resulting reports are not considered personal or individual in nature because they contain information that can be incorporated into reports furnished to other persons. A sale includes the sale of a single report and also includes an ongoing payment for access to information, such as a subscription.

Whether or not a service qualifies as an information service depends on its primary function. The fact that one element of a service is an information service does not mean that the service as a whole is taxable as an information service. The department will determine a service's primary function based on an examination of the nature of the service being sold and what is being paid for by the purchaser. How the buyer subsequently uses the information purchased is not relevant to this inquiry. If a customer's chief purpose in paying for a service is to receive information from that service, whether it is the price of a stock, the chain of ownership of real property, or contact information for a person meeting certain qualifications, the service as a whole qualifies as an information service. This result holds true even if the customer receives other benefits as part of the service. (*TSB-M-10(7)S*, July 19, 2010, CCH NEW YORK TAX REPORTS, ¶ 406-882)

Practitioner Comment: Allocation of Information Services

The receipts from information services delivered both in and out of New York State can be allocated between New York and non-New York sales. If the information is delivered by a tangible medium (such as paper or disc), tax is due on the percentage of the total number of copies that are delivered into New York. If an information service is transmitted electronically, the tax can be allocated according to the number of the customer's offices in and out of New York that have access to the electronic reports (*Comeau*, TSB-A-90(43)S, CCH NEW YORK TAX REPORTS, ¶ 253-363).

Mark S. Klein, Esq., Hodgson Russ LLP

Mailing lists: Information services related to mailing lists are exempt from tax if performed on or directly in connection with promotional materials that are mailed, shipped or otherwise distributed from a point within New York to customers or prospective customers located outside New York, for use outside New York (Sec. 1115(n)(2), Tax Law).

Laboratory reports: Furnishing reports of the results of scientific laboratory analysis constitute the furnishing of information services, but are exempt from tax if (1) they are personal or individual in nature, and (2) the information contained in the report is not substantially incorporated in reports furnished to persons other than the purchaser or the purchaser's designee. (*TSB-M-95(8)S*, Department of Taxation and Finance, CCH NEW YORK TAX REPORTS, ¶ 300-132)

Abstracts of title: A tax bulletin explains the department's recent change in its interpretation regarding the application of sales and use tax to the sales of abstracts of title and other public record searches that became effective September 1, 2010. Taxable sales include sales to a title insurance company, to a prospective purchaser of real property, or to an attorney representing a prospective customer. Search companies making sales to title companies and their agents, title companies, examining counsels, and their customers are affected by this change. This bulletin explains how the sales and use taxes apply to these changes. (*TB-ST-5*, New York Department of Taxation and Finance, September 23, 2010, CCH NEW YORK TAX REPORTS, ¶ 406-984)

¶2007

• *Installation and maintenance services*

Tax is imposed on the services of installing tangible personal property (excluding a mobile home) or maintaining, servicing, or repairing tangible personal property (including a mobile home) not held for sale in the regular course of business (Sec. 1105(c)(3), Tax Law; Reg. Sec. 527.5). The tax applies even if the service is performed by coin-operated equipment or any other means and whether or not tangible personal property is transferred.

The following installation and maintenance services are specifically *excluded* from tax:

— laundering, dry cleaning, tailoring, weaving, pressing, shoe repairing, and shoe shining (¶2102);

— services of individuals who are not in a regular trade or business of offering their services to the public, and who are engaged directly by a private homeowner or lessee in or about their residences (Sec. 1105(c)(3)(i), Tax Law; Reg. Sec. 527.5(b)(6));

— installation of property that becomes an addition or capital improvement to real property, property, or land (¶2102);

— maintenance and repair services to commercial aircraft, machinery, or equipment (¶2102);

— maintenance and repair services to commercial vessels primarily engaged in interstate or foreign commerce (¶2102);

— services rendered upon tangible personal property for use or consumption directly or predominantly in farming (¶2107);

— maintenance and repair services to fishing vessels (¶2102);

— maintenance and repair services to railroad rolling stock primarily engaged in carrying freight in intrastate, interstate, or foreign commerce (Sec. 1105(c)(3)(viii), Tax Law);

— installation, repair, and maintenance services performed on a barge that (1) is not self-propelled, (2) has a cargo capacity of at least 1,000 short tons, (3) is used exclusively by the owner, lessee, or operator of the barge to transport goods or other property in the conduct of such person's business, and (4) is primarily engaged in interstate, or foreign commerce (Sec. 1115(g), Tax Law);

— services rendered to tangible personal property used or consumed directly and predominantly in the production of gas or oil by manufacturing, processing, generating, assembling, refining, mining or extracting (Sec. 1105(c)(3)(ix), Tax Law); and

— installation of tangible personal property by a person furnishing taxable gas, electric, refrigeration, steam or telephone and telegraph services when the tangible personal property is: (1) installed at the premises of the purchaser of the utility service; (2) for use in connection with a utility service; and (3) purchased and owned by the person purchasing the utility service (Reg. Sec. 527.5(a)(4)).

• *Miscellaneous services*

Broadcasting: Machinery, equipment, or other tangible personal property (including parts, tools, and supplies) used by a broadcaster in the production and post-production of live or recorded programs for the purpose of broadcast over-the-air, cable television transmissions, or direct broadcast satellite transmissions are exempt. Further, certain services rendered to a broadcaster in connection with its broadcasting business are also exempt. Those include but are not limited to editing, dubbing, and mixing when performed in connection with the production, post-production, or transmission of live or recorded programs. While advertising space and services are exempt from tax, the cost of the materials connected with supplying those services is taxable. (Sec. 1115(a)(38), Tax Law)

See also ¶2102 and ¶2105.

Practitioner Comment: Sales Tax Rules for Broadcasters

As a result of legislative and administrative developments, the New York State Department of Taxation and Finance issued *Publication 825*, CCH NEW YORK TAX REPORTS, ¶65-946, summarizing the various sales tax exemptions and exclusions applicable to radio and television broadcasters. This document is available under the "Publications, Regulations and Laws" section of the Tax Department's website at **www.tax.ny.gov.**

Mark S. Klein, Esq., Hodgson Russ LLP

Interior decorating and design services: Receipts from providing interior decorating and designing services, whether or not provided in conjunction with the sale of tangible personal property, are subject to tax. Interior decorating and design services include, but are not limited to: the preparation of layout drawing of furniture, fixtures and other furnishings which are not permanently attached to a building or structure; selection, purchase and arrangement of surface coverings, draperies, furniture, furnishings and other decorations; or any similar service. Architects and engineers are also required to collect this tax when the services they provide fall within those generally regarded as interior decorating and design. However, services that consist of the practice of architecture or engineering, as defined in Secs. 7301 and 7201 of the Education Law, are not regarded as interior decorating and design services. (Sec. 1105(c)(7), Tax Law; *Important Notice No. N-90-16*, CCH NEW YORK TAX REPORTS, ¶252-918)

Practitioner Comment: Sales by or to Licensed Architects and Engineers

In 2010, New York's Tax Department issued guidance in an effort to reduce the confusion created when licensed architects and engineers buy or sell interior decorating or design services. Under New York's rules, sales of interior decorating and design services to a licensed architect or engineer are taxable, even if the results of the interior decorating and design work are incorporated into the architect's or engineer's signed and sealed documents. Similarly, interior decorating and design services sold directly to a building owner are also taxable, even if those services are incorporated into the signed and sealed documents of a licensed architect or engineer (TSB-M-10(5)S, April 26, 2010, CCH NEW YORK TAX REPORTS, ¶406-786).

Mark S. Klein, Hodgson Russ LLP

The point of delivery determines the sales tax rate that applies to a sale of interior decorating or design services. (*TB-ST-400*, New York Department of Taxation and Finance, June 2, 2011, CCH NEW YORK TAX REPORTS, ¶407-271)

Meteorological services: Receipts from the sale of meteorological services are exempt from tax, regardless of whether they are provided orally, in written format, or delivered via the mail, by telephone, telegraph, or otherwise (Sec. 1105(c)(1), Tax Law).

• *Motor vehicle parking, garaging, and storing services*

Receipts from providing parking, garaging, or storing services for motor vehicles are generally taxable. The tax does not apply where the garage is part of premises occupied solely as a private one- or two-family dwelling. (Sec. 1105(c)(6), Tax Law)

CCH Advisory: Parking for Motor Vehicle Dealers

A vendor engaged in the business of selling or renting motor vehicles cannot use an exempt use certificate when purchasing parking, garaging, or storage services from a person operating a garage, parking lot, or similar place of business, for vehicles that are held for rental or sale. Therefore, vendors of parking services are required to collect sales tax from vendors who sell or rent motor vehicles on charges made for parking, garaging, or storing motor vehicles. (*TSB-M-08(4)S*, July 2, 2008, CCH NEW YORK TAX REPORTS, ¶406-102; *TSB-M-08(4.1)S*, August 14, 2008, CCH NEW YORK TAX REPORTS, ¶60-665)

Municipally owned and operated parking facilities are exempt from state and local sales and use taxes.

Receipts from parking, garaging, and storing services for motor vehicles are not subject to tax if paid to a homeowners association by its members.

New York City also imposes a tax on parking, which tax is administered as part of the combined city and state sales and use tax (3311).

*Lease or rental of real property for parking:*Sec. 1105(c)(6), Tax Law, imposes sales tax on the service of providing parking, garaging, or storage of motor vehicles by persons operating a garage (other than a garage that is part of premises occupied solely as a private one- or two-family dwelling), parking lot, or other place of business engaged in providing parking, garaging, or storage of motor vehicles. When a person makes payments under a lease (or rental) agreement that includes parking, garaging, or storage of motor vehicles, and the agreement constitutes a lease of real property, the payments are not subject to sales tax. (*TSB-M-08(14)S*, December 17, 2008, CCH NEW YORK TAX REPORTS, ¶ 406-250)

- *Printing and processing services*

Tax applies to the services of producing, fabricating, processing, printing, or imprinting tangible personal property when performed for a person who directly or indirectly furnishes the tangible personal property (not purchased for resale) upon which the services are performed. When such services are combined with the sale of property by the person performing the services, the entire transaction is taxable as a retail sale. (Sec. 1105(c)(2), Tax Law; Reg. Sec. 527.4(e)(1))

When the material is mailed to persons both within and without New York, the tax is imposed only upon that portion being mailed to destinations in New York.

- *Real estate services*

Maintaining, servicing, or repairing real property, property, or land (as defined in the Real Property Tax Law), whether the services are performed inside or outside of a building, is taxable but not the services of adding to or improving real property by a capital improvement (Sec. 1105(c)(5), Tax Law). A capital improvement is an addition to real property that (1) substantially adds to the value of the real property, or appreciably prolongs its useful life, (2) becomes part of the real property or is permanently affixed to it so that removal would cause material damage to the property or article itself, and (3) is intended to become a permanent installation. Capital improvements are discussed further at ¶ 2102.

Practitioner Comment: Inspection Services

Inspection services mandated by federal, state or local ordinances, that are not related to or performed in connection with repairing, maintaining or servicing tangible or real property, are not subject to tax (*Elevator Service Companies, TSB-A-96(67)S*, CCH NEW YORK TAX REPORTS, ¶ 402-547 (elevator inspection services); *Smokowski, TSB-A-97(18)S*, CCH NEW YORK TAX REPORTS, ¶ 402-701 (medical and X-ray equipment inspections)).

Mark S. Klein, Esq., Hodgson Russ LLP

- *Sewage and water services*

A utility company's charges for sewage services were subject to New York sales and use taxbecause a sewage service represents the maintenance of real property and is taxable. However, charges for water services are exempt from sales tax. Water is exempt from sales and use tax when delivered through pipes or mains to the customer. Accordingly, a utility company's sales of water through pipes or mains was exempt. To obtain refunds, the utility company's customers must file a refund claim within three years of the date when the tax was payable by the company to the Department of Taxation and Finance. (*TSB-A-11(2)S*, New York Commissioner of Taxation and Finance, December 28, 2010, CCH NEW YORK TAX REPORTS, ¶ 407-101)

• *Security services*

Tax is imposed on the sale of protective and detective services (Sec. 1105(c)(8), Tax Law). Such services include, but are not limited to: the operation of alarm and protection systems or services of whatever nature (*i.e.*, fire, burglar, medical, contamination, mechanical breakdown or malfunction, or any similar alarm or protection system or service); detective agency services; private investigator services; armored car services; bonded courier services; watchman and patrol services; fingerprinting services; lie detection services; guard services; bodyguard services; and guard dog services (Sec. 1105(c)(8), Tax Law). However, the term protective and detective services does not include those services performed by a licensed port watchman (Sec. 1105(c)(8), Tax Law).

Reception services: Provision of reception services has been treated as taxable by the Division of Taxation as "protective and detective services" (*AlliedBarton Security Services, LLC*, New York Division of Tax Appeals, Administrative Law Judge Unit, DTA Nos. 825169, 825690, 825691, 825692, and 825693, December 18, 2014, CCH NEW YORK TAX REPORTS, ¶ 408-300).

• *Storage and moving services*

The storing of tangible personal property not held for sale in the regular course of business and the rental of safe deposit boxes or similar space are taxable services (Sec. 1105(c)(4), Tax Law; *TB-ST-340*, New York Department of Taxation and Finance, March 18, 2011, CCH NEW YORK TAX REPORTS, ¶ 407-172). However, the rental of self-service mini-storage units is not deemed to be a taxable storage service. The storage of automobiles is taxable under this provision.

Portable storage containers: All transportation charges relating to the rental of portable storage containers to and from a customer's storage location are subject to sales and use tax as part of the receipt for the rental of tangible personal property under Sec.1101(b)(3), Tax Law. The general transportation service of moving the container from one customer location to another customer location would not be taxable. The rental of the portable storage containers, the sale of moving supplies and equipment, storage fees, warehouse access fees, and cancellation fees are all taxable. Insurance charges, container cleaning fees, and the charge for container repair services are not subject to sales and use tax. (*TSB-A-08(64)S*, November 19, 2008, released January 2009, CCH NEW YORK TAX REPORTS, ¶ 406-281)

Moving services: The service of transporting household goods (moving service) is not subject to sales tax unless the charge is included as part of the bill for the sale of taxable property or services (*i.e.*, a charge for shipping as part of the sale of taxable tangible personal property). Moving services include moving household goods to and from any destination. It also includes moving items from a building to a truck, from a truck to a building, or moving items within a building, whether or not transportation is provided. Office moves are treated the same as household moves. (*TB-ST-341*, Department of Taxation and Finance, March 18, 2011, CCH NEW YORK TAX REPORTS, ¶ 407-173)

Practitioner Comment: Transportation of Items in Storage

Although "stand-alone" transportation charges are not subject to tax, delivery charges imposed by a property storage company to pick up, deliver or move property to a customer's designated location are all subject to tax. Under New York's rules, transportation charges are subject to tax if they are imposed by a vendor in connection with any taxable service (*SAM (Store and More), LLC*, TSB-A-08(64)S, November 19, 2008, CCH NEW YORK TAX REPORTS, ¶ 406-281).

Mark S. Klein, Hodgson Russ LLP

Storage in transit: The transportation of tangible personal property (for example, by a moving service) is generally exempt from New York state and local sales tax. However, the storage of tangible personal property in New York is generally subject to sales tax. The DOTF has long recognized that some incidental storage of tangible personal property, commonly referred to as "storage in transit," is often provided as part of an exempt transportation service. Storage in transit usually occurs when events delay the delivery of goods by the mover to the customer's destination and the stored property is the responsibility of the mover.

The department has reconsidered its prior policy and, beginning in 2015, it recognizes storage in transit as incidental to the provision of an exempt transportation service, and thus not taxable, if specified conditions are met. General storage services remain subject to sales tax.

"General storage" refers to storage services that are provided outside the context of a moving service. The purpose of general storage is to have property stored at a facility by the storage service provider for a period of time, not to have property stored temporarily in the process of being moved from one location to another. General storage services provided in New York remain subject to sales tax. All charges shown on an invoice for a general storage service, including separately identified charges for pickup and delivery, are part of the taxable receipt for the storage service, regardless of the duration of the storage. Storage services are considered to be delivered at the location where the storage service originates for the customer, i.e., the location where the service provider takes possession of the property to be stored. (*TSB-M-14(16)S*, New York Department of Taxation and Finance, November 17, 2014, CCH New York Tax Reports, ¶408-271)

- *Telecommunication services*

Telephonic and telegraphic entertainment and information services: Charges for entertainment and information services (other than cable television services) furnished, provided, or delivered by telephonic or telegraphic means are subject to tax if they would otherwise be taxable as an information service furnished by printed, mimeographed, or multigraphed matter or by duplicating written or printed matter in any other manner. Such services include entertainment and information services provided through 800- or 900-numbers, mass announcement services or interactive information network services (Sec. 1105(b), Tax Law; Reg. Sec. 527.2(d)(1)). Sales by a telecommunication provider of wallpaper, music and sounds are not subject to state and local sales taxes on mobile telecommunications service under Sec. 1105(b)(2), Tax Law. However, receipts from the sale of games are taxable under Sec. 1105(a), Tax Law (*TSB-A-08(8)C* and *TSB-A-08(63)S*, November 24, 2008, CCH New York Tax Reports, ¶406-278).

An additional tax is imposed at the rate of 5% on taxable entertainment and information services that are furnished, provided, or delivered by means of interstate or intrastate telephony, telegraphy, or telephone or telegraph services, and that are received by the customer exclusively in an aural manner (Sec. 1105(c)(9), Tax Law).

The New York Department of Taxation and Finance has advised that the additional 5% tax on information and entertainment services applies only to services that are provided exclusively aurally (*Release No. 34*, October 17, 1993, CCH New York Tax Reports, ¶401-246). Accordingly, information and entertainment services that involve a written component, such as those that are provided from computer to computer or computer to written format, are not subject to the additional tax. This interpretation excludes from the additional tax informational computer services, but applies the tax to services that are exclusively heard by the customer.

Telephonic and telegraphic services:"Telegraphy and telephony" are taxable. The term includes use or operation of any apparatus for transmission of sound, sound reproduction, or coded or other signals (Reg. Sec. 527.2(d)(2)). The tax applies to every charge for telephone and telegraph services, including the monthly message charge, intrastate toll charges, and charges for special services (*i.e.*, installation, change of location, conference connections, tie-lines, WATS lines, and the furnishing of equipment) (Reg. Sec. 527.2(d)(5)).

Prepaid mobile calling services: Sales tax applies to prepaid mobile calling services under the same rules that apply to prepaid telephone calling services (tax generally imposed based on retail location). "Prepaid mobile calling service" means the right to use a commercial mobile radio service, whether or not sold with other property or services, that must be paid for in advance and is sold for use over a specified period of time or in predetermined units or dollars that decline with use in a known amount, whether or not that right is represented by or includes the transfer to the purchaser of an item of tangible personal property (Sec. 1101(b)(22)(B), Tax Law).

Internet access services: Telecommunications services, including Internet access services purchased, used or sold by an Internet service provider to provide Internet access are generally exempt from sales and use taxes and from telecommunications excise tax (see TSB-M 08(2)S, May 2, 2008, CCH NEW YORK TAX REPORTS, ¶ 406-042, as revised by *TSB-M 08(2.1)S*, August 29, 2008, CCH NEW YORK TAX REPORTS, ¶ 80-420). For the definition of "Internet access" and additional discussion, see ¶ 2006.

Practitioner Comment: Taxation of VoIP Services

New York State's Department of Taxation and Finance confirmed that it will impose tax on charges for Voice over Internet Protocol (VoIP) services used to make intrastate calls. The use of the Internet or Internet routing protocols for transmission of all or part of those calls does not affect the result. More importantly, under New York's tax rules, all VoIP calls billed to New York users will be presumed taxable unless the provider can establish otherwise. (NYT G-07(2)C and (3)S). See also ¶ 2006.

Mark S. Klein, Esq., Hodgson Russ LLP

Prepaid (debit) telephone cards: Prepaid telephone calling services other than for resale are taxable (Sec. 1105(b), Tax Law; Sec. 1110, Tax Law). However, receipts from the actual delivery of telephone service under a prepaid telephone calling plan (*e.g.*, receipts represented by a debit to a prepaid account) are excluded from tax. In addition, a sale of telephone service is deemed to be an exempt sale for resale if purchased by a vendor that resells it as a component of a prepaid telephone calling service.

"Prepaid telephone calling service" means the right to exclusively purchase telecommunication services that enable the origination of intrastate, interstate, or international telephone calls using an access number (such as a toll-free network access number) and/or an authorization code, whether manually or electronically dialed, for which payment to a vendor must be made in advance, regardless of whether the right is represented by a transfer of tangible personal property to the purchaser. A credit card will not constitute a prepaid telephone calling service under any circumstances. (Sec. 1101(b)(22), Tax Law)

Interstate telecommunications: Except for certain entertainment or information services (see above), receipts from the sale of interstate and international telephony and telegraphy and telephone and telegraph service are excluded from tax (Sec. 1105(b), Tax Law). Those states that do tax interstate communications may only impose the tax if the communication originates or terminates within the state and is either charged to a service address in the state or billed or paid within the state (*Goldberg v. Sweet*, U.S. Supreme Court, No. 87-826 and 87-1101, 488 US 252 (1989)).

¶2007

Cellular telephones: Cellular telephone services are subject to tax. Cellular services are exempt only if they were purchased for resale or involved interstate or international service. (*TSB-A-89(38)S,* Department of Taxation and Finance, October 11, 1989, CCH NEW YORK TAX REPORTS, ¶ 252-817)

New York law conforms to the provisions of the federal Mobile Telecommunications Sourcing Act (P.L. 106-252). Wireless telecommunications services are sourced to the customer's "primary place of use," which is the residential or primary business address of the customer and which must be located in the service provider's licensed service area. The jurisdiction in which the primary place of use is located is the only jurisdiction that may tax the communications services, regardless of the customer's location when an actual call is placed or received. Conforming changes are also made for excise (telecommunications) tax purposes (3108) (Ch. 85 (A.B. 9762), Laws 2002; *TSB-M-02(4)C* and *TSB-M-02(6)S,* New York Department of Taxation and Finance, July 30, 2002, CCH NEW YORK TAX REPORTS, ¶ 300-367).

Telephone and telegraph services used for news: Telephony, telegraphy and telephone and telegraph service used by newspapers, radio broadcasters and television broadcasters in the collection or dissemination of news are tax-exempt where the charge for such services is a toll charge or a charge for mileage services (including the associated station terminal equipment) (Sec. 1115(b)(i), Tax Law).

Telephone answering services: Telephone answering services, other than answering services that are merely an incidental element of another service provided to a customer, are subject to tax. (Sec. 1105(b), Tax Law; Sec. 1110, Tax Law)

Practitioner Comment: Tax Location

The receipts from a telephone answering service are subject to tax based on the location of the telephones that are being answered (the location of the answering service's customer's business or the customer's personal residence). The location of the call answering service itself is irrelevant (*TSB-M-91(13)S,* CCH NEW YORK TAX REPORTS, ¶ 300-023).

Mark S. Klein, Esq., Hodgson Russ LLP

• *Transportation services*

Sales tax is imposed on specified transportation services provided in New York (Sec. 1105(c)(10), Tax Law; *TSB-M-09(2)S,* May 6, 2009, CCH NEW YORK TAX REPORTS, ¶ 406-382; *TSB-M-09(7)S,* May 22, 2009, CCH NEW YORK TAX REPORTS, ¶ 406-400). Transportation service includes the service of transporting, carrying or conveying a person or persons by livery service, whether to a single destination or to multiple destinations, and whether the compensation paid by or on behalf of the passenger is based on mileage, trip, time consumed or any other basis. A "livery service" means service provided by limousine, black car or other motor vehicle (*i.e.* community cars or vans), with a driver, but excludes a taxicab, bus, and any scheduled public service. A "limousine" means a vehicle with a seating capacity of up to 14 people, excluding the driver. "Black car" means a for-hire vehicle dispatched from a central facility.

Receipts from the sale of a taxable transportation service include any handling, carrying, baggage, booking service, administrative, mark-up, additional, or other charge, of any nature, made in conjunction with the transportation service. Transportation service also includes transporting, carrying, or conveying property of the person being transported. However, transportation service does not include interstate services; ambulance, ambulette, or emergency service transportation; or services provided in connection with funerals. (Sec. 1101(b)(34), Tax Law; *TSB-M-09(7)S,* May 22, 2009, CCH NEW YORK TAX REPORTS, ¶ 406-400)

Receipts from the sale of transportation service are subject to sales tax only if the service begins and ends in New York (intrastate service) even if it passes outside the state during a portion of the trip. Transportation services that begin or end outside the state (interstate service) are not subject to tax. If a round-trip service starts in New York and proceeds to a destination in another state, and then later the return leg of the round-trip service ends up back in New York, a single charge for that round-trip service would not be taxable, since the trip was interstate in nature. (Sec. 1101(b)(34), Tax Law, CCH NEW YORK TAX REPORTS, ¶406-400)

Livery vehicles (NYC): Transportation services provided by an affiliated livery vehicle that either begin or end in New York City are excluded from the sales tax imposed on transportation services. An "affiliated livery vehicle" means a for-hire motor vehicle with a seating capacity of up to six persons, including the driver, other than a black car or luxury limousine, that is authorized and licensed by the taxi and limousine commission of a city of one million or more to be dispatched by a base station located in such city and regulated by such tax and limousine commission; and the charges for service provided by an affiliated livery vehicle are on the basis of flat rate, time, mileage, or zones and not on a garage to garage basis. (Sec. 1101(b)(34), Tax Law; *TSB-M-13(2)S,* February 25, 2013, CCH NEW YORK TAX REPORTS, ¶407-780)

Hail vehicles: The 50-cent-per-taxicab-trip tax imposed by Article 29-A, Tax Law, must be added to the fare for each taxable Hail vehicle trip. The state high court upheld the constitutionality of the HAIL Act (Ch. 602, Laws 2011, and Ch. 9, Laws 2012) by reversing a lower court decision that had prevented the implementation of the HAIL Act, originally set to go into effect on June 1, 2012. Accordingly, the tax and record keeping requirements as described in *TSB-M-12(3)M,* Tax on Hail Vehicle Trips in the Metropolitan Commuter Transportation District, are in effect. The tax and recordkeeping requirements apply to trips provided by any Hail vehicles that are required to be licensed by and otherwise meet the requirements of the New York City Taxi and Limousine Commission (TLC). (*TSB-M-13(8)M, TSB-M-13(6)S,* July 12, 2013, CCH NEW YORK TAX REPORTS, ¶407-878)

• *Waste removal services*

Receipts from the sale of an integrated real property maintenance service of removing, transporting, processing, and disposing of hazardous waste from out-of-state real properties, including in-state treatment and disposal charges, notwithstanding that these latter portions of the integrated service physically occurred in New York, did not provide sufficient nexus to support imposition of New York sales tax (*CWM Chemical Services, Inc.,* CCH NEW YORK TAX REPORTS, ¶404-317). In that case, the sale transaction occurred outside of New York, the real property upon which the taxable service was being performed was located outside of New York, and delivery of the service was initially undertaken outside of New York. Since there was no nexus, there was no tax imposed and, as a consequence, no tax to be apportioned. Conversely, it was noted that New York could impose sales tax on the entire unapportioned receipts for providing such integrated services for real property located in New York, notwithstanding that a portion of such integrated service occurred outside New York.

Prior to *CWM Chemical Services* it was held that the removal of hazardous or industrial waste from a customer's New York property for transportation and processing outside New York was taxable as an integrated trash removal service. In *Petition of General Electric,* CCH NEW YORK TAX REPORTS, ¶400-311, the Tax Appeals Tribunal rejected the petitioner's contention that the disposal of waste material through the process of incineration, which took place wholly outside New York, was a separate service from the "removal" of the waste from the petitioner's New York facility and the "transportation" of the waste to Arkansas. In addition, to the extent that the removal, transportation and disposal were all part of an integrated service, and a portion of the service occurred within New York, sufficient nexus existed between the activity and New York to justify the imposition of tax.

However, the imposition of tax on the *entire* receipt for the waste removal service was not fairly apportioned under Commerce Clause standards and created the possibility of double taxation. The Tribunal concluded that the tax was not internally consistent since, if Arkansas had the same tax as New York, it would also view waste removal as an integrated service and since one aspect of that service, *i.e.*, the processing, occurred wholly in Arkansas, then Arkansas could tax the entire receipt for the integrated service, just as New York taxed the entire receipt for the integrated service because the pick-up and removal occurred in New York. Similarly, the tax failed the external consistency test because, as the Tribunal noted, there was a practical way to apportion the New York State tax as a part of the entire service so as to clearly tax only that portion of the revenues from the interstate activity that reasonably reflects the in-state component of the activity taxed.

Transfer stations or construction and demolition processing facility: Removal of waste material from a facility regulated as a transfer station or construction and demolition debris processing facility by the New York Department of Environmental Conservation is exempt from New York sales and use tax, provided that the waste material to be removed was not generated by the facility. (Sec. 1105(c)(5), Tax Law; *TSB-M-05(13)S,* Department of Taxation and Finance, CCH NEW YORK TAX REPORTS, ¶ 300-487)

• *Services in NYC*

New York City imposes a tax on selected services, as discussed at ¶ 3315.

¶2008 Restaurant Meals, Catered Meals, Meals for Off-Premises Consumption

Law: Sec. 1105(d), Tax Law (CCH NEW YORK TAX REPORTS, ¶ 60-390).

Sales of food and/or beverages (alcoholic or nonalcoholic) in or by restaurants, taverns, or other establishments in New York or by caterers are taxable, where (1) the sale is for consumption on the premises where sold; (2) the vendor, or another person whose services are arranged for by the vendor, after delivery of the food or drink for consumption off the premises of the vendor, serves or assists in serving, cooks, heats or provides other services with respect to such food or drink; or (3) the sale is for consumption off the premises of the vendor (Sec. 1105(d)(i), Tax Law).

Cover, minimum, entertainment, or other charges, unless subject to the tax on admission charges (¶ 2010), are included in the amount subject to the tax.

Tax does not apply to sales of food (other than sandwiches) or drink for off-premises consumption, which are (a) sold in an unheated state and (b) of a type commonly sold for off-premises consumption in the same form and condition in food stores not principally engaged in selling foods prepared and ready to be eaten (Sec. 1105(d)(i), Tax Law).

The following sales are taxable, within the above rules:

Restaurant: When the sale is for consumption on the premises where sold; or

Catering: When the vendor (or any person whose services are arranged for by the vendor), after the delivery of the food or drink for consumption off the premises of the vendor, serves or assists in serving, cooks, heats, or provides other services with respect to the food or drink; or

---

Practitioner Comment: Catering

The law imposes a sales tax on the receipts from every sale of food and drink by caterers, including "any cover, minimum, entertainment or other charges." Tax Law 1105(d)(i) (emphasis added). New York sales and use tax auditors have taken the position that this language justifies the imposition of sales tax on all charges imposed by a caterer, even those that would ordinarily be exempt from tax (*e.g.*, the hiring of a band or the rental of hotel room meeting space). See *TB ST 110* (2011).

Mark S. Klein, Esq., Hodgson Russ LLP

CCH Advisory: Cooking vs. Catering

A cooking service that did not involve sales of food or drink to the customer was not taxable as a catering service (*Holtzman*, TSB-A-01(12)S, April 17, 2001, CCH New York Tax Reports, ¶ 403-935).

Sales of food and drink to an airline for consumption in flight are exempt, as are certain meals sold to students (Sec. 1105(d)(ii), Tax Law).

Take-out: When the sale is for off-premises consumption, but excluding food (other than sandwiches) or drink sold in an unheated state that is of a type commonly sold in the same form and condition in food stores not chiefly selling foods prepared and ready to be eaten.

Vending machine sales: The sales tax on beer, wine, or other alcoholic beverages, or any other sale of drink and food by restaurants, taverns, or other establishments includes those instances in which the sale is made through a vending machine that is activated by use of coin, currency, credit card, or debit card. However, food and drink sold through vending machines is exempt from tax if it would be exempt when sold at retail. (Sec. 1105(d)(i), Tax Law)

Tax bulletins: The New York Department of Taxation and Finance has issued numerous bulletins (TB-ST) that discuss various topics related to food and beverages. Specifically, the bulletins address the following:

— beverages sold by food stores, beverage centers, and similar establishments (*TB-ST-65*);

— candy and confectionery (*TB-ST-103*);

— catering and catering services (*TB-ST-110*);

— sales made by convenience stores and bodegas (*TB-ST-135*);

— dietary foods and health supplements (*TB-ST-160*);

— food and beverages sold from vending machines (*TB-ST-280*);

— food and food products sold by food stores and similar establishments, including supermarkets, grocery stores, and convenience stores (*TB-ST-283*);

— listings of taxable and exempt foods and beverages sold by food stores and similar establishments (*TB-ST-525*);

— production equipment and utilities used by supermarkets, grocery stores, and delicatessens (*TB-ST-690*);

— purchases by restaurants, taverns, and similar establishments (*TB-ST-695*);

— sales of food and beverages (both alcoholic and nonalcoholic) by restaurants, taverns, and similar establishments (*TB-ST-806*); and

— sandwiches (*TB-ST-835*).

The Tax Bulletins can be found on the department's website at **http://www.tax.ny.gov/pubs_and_bulls/tg_bulletins/bulletins_by_number.htm**.

¶2009 Hotel Room Occupancy

Law: Secs. 1104, 1105(e), 1111(r), 1116(g), 1119(e), Tax Law; Reg. Sec. 527.9 (CCH New York Tax Reports, ¶ 60-480, ¶ 60-580).

The sales and use tax applies to hotel occupancies, including occupancy in an apartment hotel, motel, or a boarding house or club, whether or not meals are served (Sec. 1105(e), Tax Law). The rent for occupancy is taxable, except for occupancies for at least 90 consecutive days (180 for New York City local tax), or where the rent is $2 or less per day. The rent is taxable even if it is payable in a consideration other than money.

The following occupancies are exempt: (1) the rental of a hotel room or suite of rooms containing no sleeping facilities and used solely as a place for meetings or other assemblies; (2) nursing homes, rest homes, convalescent homes, maternity homes for expectant mothers, residences or homes for adults or retarded persons; (3) summer camps; (4) college dormitories; and (5) bungalows, where no maid, food, entertainment or other common hotel services are provided by the lessor and the rental is for at least one week (Reg. Sec. 527.9(e)). Rents received from room occupancies in a hotel operated by a religious, charitable, scientific, etc. organization, in furtherance of the activities of the non-profit organization, are also tax-exempt (Sec. 1116(c), Tax Law).

For information about how sales tax is calculated on the charges for occupancy, see *TB-ST-331*, New York Department of Taxation and Finance, May 9, 2012, CCH New York Tax Reports, ¶ 407-553.

CCH Advisory: Cottages Rented with No Services

Rent received for occupancy of a bungalow or similar living unit is not subject to the sales tax on hotel occupancy, regardless of the length of stay, so long as no housekeeping services, food services, or other common hotel services (including entertainment or planned activities) are provided by the lessor. (*TSB-M-12(4)S*, Taxpayer Guidance Division, New York Department of Taxation and Finance, March 16, 2012; CCH New York Tax Reports, ¶ 407-509)

Educational institutions that operate hotels containing 100 or more rooms must collect sales tax from customers who do not qualify for a sales tax exemption pursuant to Sec. 1116-a, Tax Law.

A publication provides hotel and motel owners, operators, or managers with information related to sales tax that is specific to the hotel and motel industry, and help them understand their sales tax responsibilities (*Publication 848*, February 2015, New York Department of Taxation and Finance, CCH New York Tax Reports, ¶ 65-960). Also, a sales and use tax bulletin discusses the taxable and nontaxable services that hotels and motels commonly offer. The taxable sales and services discussed include the following: safe deposit rentals; check room for coats, hats, luggage, etc.; television and in-room movies; fax service; copy services; telephone service; room service; rental of recreation equipment or other items; separately stated service charges; sporting and other event tickets; and transportation services. The nontaxable sales and services discussed include the following: Internet access; valet and laundry services; admission charges; theater and similar tickets; and gratuities and tips. (*TB-ST-333*, New York Department of Taxation and Finance, December 16, 2010, CCH New York Tax Reports, ¶ 407-081)

Practitioner Comment: Defined "Hotel Operators"

The imposition of New York's tax on hotel room occupancy is limited to businesses that operate hotels and provide hotel-type services. Long-term stay facilities that do not offer typical hotel amenities (e.g., daily maid services, toiletries, check-in desks, etc.) are not subject to tax. See TSB-A-15(11)S and *ExecuStay*, TSB-A-03(15)S.

Mark S. Klein, Esq., Hodgson Russ LLP

Military and veterans' organizations: Duly authorized representatives of posts or organizations comprised of past or present members of the U.S. Armed Forces, when acting on behalf of those organizations, are not subject to hotel room occupancy taxes and are not required to pay sales taxes on hotel room occupancies. The representative must display an exempt organization certificate, issued by the post or organization, certifying that the representative is acting on its behalf. (Sec. 1116(g), Tax Law)

Rewards programs: The reimbursement paid or credited to owners and operators of hotels from a rewards program to participate in a marketing program was not consideration for hotel occupancy, and therefore, was not subject to New York sales tax. (*Marriott International, Inc.*, New York Division of Tax Appeals, Administrative Law Judge Unit, DTA Nos. 821078, 821079, 821080, 821219, 821374, 821375, 821376, 821380, 821381, 821383, 821384, 821385, and 821753, November 26, 2008, CCH NEW YORK TAX REPORTS, ¶ 406-236)

Audio-visual equipment: A sales tax advisory opinion discusses whether hotel owners are purchasing audio visual services (AV services) from a third party that rents audio visual equipment and provides related services (AV provider) to the hotel's guests and customers. The taxpayers are the owners of two hotels that have each entered into a contract with a third party to rent audio visual equipment and provide related services at their respective hotel locations to the hotel's guests and customers. The AV provider enters into a separate agreement with the customer to rent audio visual equipment and related services for a specific event at the hotel. The hotel is not a party to these agreements. The agreement between the AV provider and the customer does permit billing for the AV services provided at an event to be made through the customer's master account at the hotel. However, in many cases the customer chooses to be billed directly by the AV provider. In those instances where the AV provider enters into a separate agreement between itself and the hotel guests or customers for providing AV services at a specific event, the hotels are not purchasing the AV services from the AV provider. However, due to the nature of the contracts at issue, they may be considered to be acting as co-vendor in any instance where they collect the payment from the customer and that payment includes taxable receipts. As such, the hotels are jointly and severally liable for any sales tax due on the sales of AV service contracts if they collect the receipts and then turn such receipts over to the AV provider, and the AV provider subsequently fails to remit the tax due on such sales. This means that the hotels will be liable for tax if the AV provider fails to remit it to the department. However, the hotels are not required to remit tax on the sales if the AV provider has reported and remitted the tax due. (*TSB-A-11(27)S*, New York Commissioner of Taxation and Finance, October 17, 2011, CCH NEW YORK TAX REPORTS, ¶ 407-413).

Practitioner Comment: "Free" Breakfasts Cannot be Purchased for Resale

According to a recent decision of the Tax Appeals Tribunal, breakfasts that were included in a hotel's room rate were considered part of the hotel's overhead for providing a hotel service. As a result, the hotel's purchase of these meals did not qualify for the resale exclusion. A separately stated charge to the customer for the breakfasts may have produced a different result. (*Washington Square Hotel* (TAT July 19, 2016)

Mark S. Klein, Esq., Hodgson Russ LLP

• *Room remarketers*

State and local sales taxes must be paid on the full amount charged to customers by businesses such as Web-based travel companies (room remarketers) for hotel occupancy in New York. Although the legislation applies to the hotel room occupancy tax imposed and administered by New York City, it does not apply to locally imposed and administered occupancy taxes (local bed taxes). The authority of the City of New York to enact the hotel room occupancy tax applicable to online travel companies has been upheld; see *Expedia, Inc. v. City of New York Department of Finance*, New York Court of Appeals, No. 180, November 21, 2013, CCH NEW YORK TAX REPORTS, ¶ 407-974.

A "room remarketer" is "a person who reserves, arranges for, conveys, or furnishes occupancy, whether directly or indirectly, to an occupant for rent in an amount determined by the room remarketer, directly or indirectly, whether pursuant to a written or other agreement" (Sec. 1101(C)(8), Tax Law). If a business meets the definition of a room remarketer, its ability or authority to reserve, arrange for, convey, or furnish occupancy, directly or indirectly, and to determine rent therefore, is referred to as the "rights of a room remarketer." A room remarketer is not a permanent resident with respect to a room that the remarketer has furnished to its customer. Businesses, such as travel agencies, that reserve rooms on behalf of their customers and do not have the right to determine the amount of rent that their customer pays for the room (i.e., the rent is fixed and determined by the hotel, and is not allowed to be marked-up by the business that reserves the room on behalf of its customer) are not room remarketers.

Effect of legislation on rent for occupancy paid and received by room remarketers: A room remarketer constitutes an operator of a hotel to the extent that the room remarketer has acquired the rights of a room remarketer with respect to a room or rooms in a hotel. In addition, rent subject to the sales tax on occupancy of a room or rooms in a hotel now includes any service or other charge or amount paid as a condition of occupancy to a room remarketer. Accordingly, the full amount charged by a room remarketer to its customer for the right to occupy a room in a hotel in New York constitutes rent for occupancy of a room in a hotel, and is subject to state and local sales tax (Sec. 1105(e)(2), Tax Law). Furthermore, since the law provides that in these circumstances, a room remarketer is an operator of a hotel, the room remarketer must collect the sales tax, and where applicable, the $1.50 hotel unit fee imposed on every occupancy of a unit in a hotel located in New York City (NYC $1.50 fee) from its customer, and remit the amount collected to the Tax Department. The full amount paid by a room remarketer to a hotel operator for the ability or authority to reserve rooms in a hotel, to convey the rights of occupancy of the rooms to their customers, and to determine the amount of rent the room remarketer charges its customers for occupancy of the rooms constitutes rent for hotel occupancy subject to sales tax and, where applicable the NYC $1.50 fee.

Occupancy included with property, services, amusement charges, etc.: Effective September 1, 2012, when occupancy is provided for a single consideration with property, services, amusement charges, or any other items, whether or not such other items are taxable, the rent portion of the consideration for such transaction must be computed as follows: (a) either the total consideration received by the room remarketer multiplied by a fraction, the numerator of which is the consideration payable for the occupancy by the room remarketer and the denominator of which is such consideration payable for the occupancy plus the consideration payable by the remarketer for the other items being sold, or (b) by any other method as may be authorized by the Commissioner of Taxation and Finance. (Sec. 1111(r), Tax Law; *TSB-M-12(8)S*, Taxpayer Guidance Division, New York Department of Taxation and Finance, July 26, 2012, CCH New York Tax Reports, ¶ 407-612)

If the room remarketer fails to separately state the tax on the rent so computed on a sales slip, invoice, receipt, or other statement given to the occupant or fails to maintain records of the prices of all components of a transaction, the entire consideration shall be treated as rent subject to tax. Room remarketers are also required to report such sales tax due on the return due for the filing period in which the occupancy ends. (Sec. 1111(r), Tax Law)

In order to qualify for a refund or credit against the amount of tax collected and required to be remitted, a room remarketer can provide the name, business address, telephone number, and the address of the hotel where the occupancy took place if the room remarketer requests the hotel operator's certificate of authority number and is not provided that number. (Sec. 1119(e), Tax Law)

¶2009

Purchases of hotel room occupancies by room remarketers: Applicable to rent paid for hotel occupancies on or after June 1, 2016, an exemption is provided for the purchase of hotel room occupancies by room remarketers when those purchases are made from hotels for later resale and an exemption certificate (Form ST-120.2, Room Remarketer's Exempt Purchase Certificate). is provided to the hotel operator by the room remarketer within 90 days of the date it purchases the occupancy from the hotel operator (Sec. 1115(kk), Tax Law; Sec. 11-2502(1), NYC Adm. Code; *TSB-M-16(2)S*, New York Department of Taxation and Finance, May 4, 2016, CCH NEW YORK TAX REPORTS, ¶ 408-734). Previously, there was no an exemption for room remarketers' purchases of hotel room occupancies they supplied to their customers. Instead, room remarketers had to seek a credit or refund for the tax they paid to the hotel operators, as discussed below.

Refund or credit for sales tax and NYC unit fee paid by room remarketer: A room remarketer is allowed a refund or credit against the sales tax and, where applicable, the NYC $1.50 fee that the remarketer paid to the operator of a hotel (Sec. 1119(e), Tax Law). However, in order to qualify for the refund or credit for any sales tax quarterly period, the room remarketer must, for that quarter: (1) be registered as a person required to collect sales tax under Sec. 1134, Tax Law, and must collect sales tax on rent for hotel occupancy and, where applicable, the NYC $1.50 fee, from its customers; and (2) furnish the Certificate of Authority number of the operator of the hotel to whom the room remarketer paid the tax, if required on the room remarketer's application for refund or credit, or if otherwise requested by the Tax Department.

An application for refund or credit must be filed by a room remarketer using Form AU-11, Application for Credit or Refund of Sales or Use Tax, within three years after the date the tax was payable to the Tax Department by the operator of the hotel to whom the tax was paid by the room remarketer. If an application for credit has been filed, the room remarketer may immediately take the credit on the return that is due coincident with the application for credit, or immediately after the room remarketer files the application for credit. However, the taking of the credit on the return is deemed to be part of the application for credit. Treatment of hotel occupancy when sold with nontaxable products or services: The law also clarifies that where occupancy of a room or rooms in a hotel is sold together with property, services, amusement charges, or any other items that are not subject to sales tax (other nontaxable sales) for one charge, the one charge is subject to sales tax as rent for hotel occupancy. However, the law further clarifies that if the hotel operator, including a room remarketer, gives a sales slip, invoice, receipt, or other statement to the occupant, which states the amount of rent for occupancy, separately from the nontaxable charges, only the separately stated rent for occupancy is subject to sales tax. This is so only if the separately stated rent for occupancy is reasonable in relation to the amount charged for the nontaxable sales.

Sales tax registration: Room remarketers are deemed to be operators of a hotel, and are required to register for sales tax purposes as persons required to collect sales tax under Sec. 1134(a), Tax Law, by applying for a Certificate of Authority. Accordingly, room remarketers who are reselling occupancy of rooms in hotels located in New York must register for sales tax purposes and must apply for a Certificate of Authority. Once registered for sales tax purposes, a room remarketer must collect sales tax and other required fees, file returns, remit the amounts collected and keep records. In addition, a room remarketer who rents hotel occupancy to certain individuals and organizations that claim exemption from sales tax must obtain a properly completed exemption document or other required documentation from the individual or organization to allow them to purchase the hotel occupancy exempt from sales tax. *(TSB-M-10(10)S*, August 13, 2010, CCH NEW YORK TAX REPORTS, ¶ 406-930; see also *Finance Memorandum 10-3*, New York City Department of Finance, September 1, 2010)

¶2009

¶2010 Admission Charges

> *Law:* Sec. 1105(f)(1), (f)(3), Tax Law, Sec. 1116, Tax Law, Sec. 1122, Tax Law; Reg. Sec. 527.10 (CCH New York Tax Reports, ¶ 60-230, ¶ 60-580).

Admission charges are taxable if the charge is in excess of 10¢ (Sec. 1105(f)(1), Tax Law). Taxable charges for entertainment or amusement include admissions to sporting events such as: baseball or football games; stock car racing; college athletic events; carnivals; rodeos; and exhibitions (circuses are no longer subject to sales tax). (Sec. 1101(d)(2), Tax Law; Reg. Sec. 527.10(b)(1)(iv)).

CCH Advisory: Taxes on adult entertainment upheld

The New York Supreme Court, Appellate Division, held that the "amusement tax" (Sec. 1105(f)(1), Tax Law) and the "cabaret tax" (Sec. 1105(f)(3, Tax Law) were constitutional on their face and as applied to the taxpayers. Specifically, the taxpayers, who operated an adult entertainment club, challenged the sales taxes imposed on their "Beaver Bucks" or "scrip," which was the club's in-house currency used by patrons to tip topless dancers, floor hosts, and to gain admission to private rooms to view entertainers and for lap dances. The taxpayers asserted that the tax laws infringed on their right to free speech under the United States and New York Constitutions by imposing a differential tax on protected expression based on content, thereby penalizing disfavored expression without furthering any important governmental interest. The taxpayers also claimed that the tax laws violated the Equal Protection Clauses of the United States and New York Constitutions by discriminating against protected expression based on its content, and allowing for different treatment of New York businesses engaging in constitutionally protected activities. Further, the taxpayers claimed that the tax laws were unconstitutionally vague, and deprived them of their right to procedural due process.

The court rejected all of the taxpayers' constitutional arguments, concluding that the tax laws were of general application. The amusement tax applies to sales at "any place where any facilities for entertainment, amusement, or sports are provided" and the cabaret tax applies to sales at "any roof garden, cabaret or other similar place which furnishes a public performance for profit." In addition, the tax laws do not enforce any differential treatment based on the content of ideas or viewpoints expressed in the entertainment provided at the club. By enacting the exemptions for certain types of entertainment (*i.e.*, live theatre, musical performances, and choreographed dancing), the legislature simply exercised its authority to pick and choose among the forms of expression it decides to subsidize through a tax exemption. Further, the tax laws at issue were not even directed specifically at the dancing at the club, but rather at the sale of the "beaver bucks," which were used for multiple purposes in the club. Moreover, there was no suspect classification at issue in this matter, because the exemptions were rationally related to the legitimate cultural purpose of promoting cultural and artistic performances in local communities and thus do not deprive any class of business of equal protection of the law. Nor were the exemptions unconstitutionally vague as the taxpayers contended. Nevertheless, even if they were, the consequences were not constitutionally severe, as the government was merely subsidizing the arts and the opportunity for businesses to obtain an official clarification of whether the exemptions apply to them is sufficient to allay any concerns about unpredictable enforcement. (*CMSG Restaurant Group, LLC, v. The State of New York*, Appellate Division of the Supreme Court of New York, First Department, No. 153539/14 1214, November 3, 2016, CCH New York Tax Reports, ¶ 408-896)

Exemptions: Tax is not imposed upon charges for admission to: race tracks, combative sports matches or exhibitions taxed under another provision of New York law, dramatic or musical arts performances, or live circus performances, or sporting facilities where the patron is to be a participant (such as bowling alleys and swimming pools). (Sec. 1105(f)(1), Tax Law; Reg. Sec. 527.10(d))

Admissions to roof gardens, cabarets, and other similar places in New York are exempt under certain conditions (see ¶ 2110).

A charge solely for admission to an amusement park (an admission-only ticket) is subject to state and local sales taxes. A charge solely for the use of amusement rides is not taxable (*TSB-M-03(5)S,* July 31, 2003, CCH NEW YORK TAX REPORTS, ¶ 300-397).

In addition, a permanent exemption from sales tax applies to 75% of the admission charges to a qualifying place of amusement when the charge includes a fee for the use of amusement rides within the park (Sec. 1122, Tax Law). The exemption also applies to the tax imposed in the Metropolitan Commuter Transportation District (MCTD).

Specifically, a place of amusement qualifies for the exemption if it meets the following requirements (Sec. 1122, Tax Law):

(1) it exists on a year-round basis (regardless of whether it is open year round) at a fixed location in the state;

(2) the admission charge allows patrons to ride at least 75% of the amusement rides;

(3) the combined geographic area of the amusement rides equal at least 50% of the entire geographic area of the place of amusement; and

(4) it provides each person that receives an admission ticket, a ticket or paper receipt stating the amount of the admission charge paid by such person and the sales tax due.

Admission charges to the following places or events are also tax-exempt: agricultural fairs; historical homes and gardens; and historic sites, houses and shrines and museums; provided that no part of the net earnings inures to the benefit of any stockholder. (Sec. 1116(d)(3), Tax Law)

Practitioner Comment: There is Nothing Entertaining About Shopping

While New York taxes admission charges to "any place of amusement," the tax applies only where there is something "amusing" or "entertaining" at the venue. New York's Tax Appeals Tribunal recognized that "shopping, browsing or scrutinizing a vendor's goods" are not forms of amusement or entertainment. As a result, admissions to an antique and collectibles show were not subject to tax as long as the event did not offer "live entertainment, interesting demonstrations . . . or a dance." (*Antique World Inc.* (TAT February 22, 1996)

Mark S. Klein, Esq., Hodgson Russ LLP

¶2011 Social or Athletic Club Dues

Law: Secs. 1101(d)(1), 1105(f)(2), Tax Law: Reg. Sec. 527.11 (CCH NEW YORK TAX REPORTS, ¶ 60-230).

The tax is payable on social or athletic club dues (including assessments) if the dues of a member with full privileges are more than $10 a year, exclusive of initiation fee. The tax also applies on the initiation fee alone, regardless of dues, if such fee is more than $10 (Sec. 1105(f)(2), Tax Law). Fraternal societies, orders, or associations operating under the lodge system, fraternal associations of students of a college or university, or rod and gun clubs (i.e. fishing and hunting clubs) are not taxable.

The sales tax on life membership in a social or athletic club is imposed on the amount paid as life membership dues. Life members, other than honorary members, who have been paying the tax annually, continue to make annual payments until the total tax paid is equal to the tax that would have been due if the tax had been paid at the time the life membership was purchased (Sec. 1105(f)(2), Tax Law). Life memberships for which no consideration is given are not subject to tax (Reg. Sec. 527.11(a)(4)).

Honorary members are exempt from tax (Sec. 1105(f)(2), Tax Law).

Health and fitness clubs: New York makes a distinction between health and fitness clubs and athletic clubs. New York state and local sales taxes are imposed on dues and membership fees paid to any athletic club in the state. An athletic club is any club or organization whose material purpose or activity is the practice, participation in, or promotion of any sports or athletics (*i.e.*, a Judo club or curling club). However, a facility that provides steam baths, saunas, rowing machines, or other exercise equipment, or that promotes exercising solely for health or weight reduction purposes, as contrasted to sports, is not considered to be an athletic club.

New York City imposes its local sales tax on every sale of services by weight control salons, health salons, gymnasiums, Turkish and sauna baths, and similar facilities, including any charge for the use of these facilities. This tax does not apply to any of these facilities located outside of New York City. Therefore, dues, membership and initiation fees, and any charges paid for the use of these facilities located in New York City are subject to the New York City local sales tax. However, if a facility also provides access to participant sporting activities and facilities, such as a swimming pool or racquetball courts, to its members, the facility is not considered to be a weight control salon, health salon, gymnasium, or other establishment for New York City sales tax purposes. (*TB-ST-329*, New York Department of Taxation and Finance, April 20, 2011, CCH New York Tax Reports, ¶ 407-214)

Practitioner Comment: Sports and Athletic Facility Fees

The tax on athletic club dues does not apply to sports and athletic facility fees, even if those fees are characterized as "dues" and the business, itself, is advertised as a "club." New York State does not impose sales tax on fees paid to participate in a sport or to exercise in a health club, where the facility is not owned or controlled by its members (where the members possess a proprietary interest in the organization, participate in the selection of management, etc.). If the "membership" fee is actually a charge to use sporting facilities, it is not taxable (NY Reg. Sec. 527.11(b)(5) and *The Paris Health Club Inc.*, TSB-A-08(12)S, CCH New York Tax Reports, ¶ 405-997).

Mark S. Klein, Esq., Hodgson Russ LLP

Homeowners' association dues: Dues paid by owners or residents to a homeowners association that operates social or athletic facilities (whether or not for the exclusive use by the owners or residents) are exempt from tax. Payments made by homeowners associations for purchases of maintenance and repairs (including maintenance and repairs to social or athletic facilities) remain subject to sales tax. (Sec. 1105(f)(2), Tax Law)

¶2013 Transactions Subject to Use Tax

Law: Sec. 1110, Tax Law; Reg. Secs. 526.5, 526.9, 526.14, 531.1—531.6 (CCH New York Tax Reports, ¶ 60-020).

A use tax is imposed, unless the property or service has already been subject to the sales tax, on the use of property or services within New York (Sec. 1110, Tax Law).

Use tax is imposed on the following (Sec. 1110, Tax Law):

— Use of any tangible personal property purchased at retail in New York;

— Use of any tangible personal property manufactured, processed, or assembled by the user, if items of the same kind are offered for sale by the user in the regular course of business. The tax is also imposed upon the use of any tangible personal property manufactured, processed, or assembled by the user, but not offered for sale by the user in the regular course of business, if the item is either used as such or incorporated into structures, buildings, or real property by contractors, subcontractors, or repairmen erecting structures or buildings or otherwise making improvements to real property or maintaining, servicing, or repairing real property. The mere storage, keeping, retention, or withdrawal from storage of such property, however, without actual use, is not a taxable use. See also ¶ 2016;

— Use of any taxable information services, interior decorating and designing services, and protective and detective services;

— Use of any tangible personal property, however acquired (but not for resale), upon which certain taxable services are performed, such as processing, printing, installation, maintenance, or repair services, or interior decorating and designing;

— Use of computer software written or otherwise created by the user who, in the regular course of business, offers software of a similar kind for sale as such or as a component part of other property. However, the mere storage, keeping, retention, or withdrawal from storage of such software by its author or creator is not considered to be a taxable use;

— Telephone answering service; and

— Use of any prepaid telephone calling service.

Practitioner Comment: Displayed Artwork

Although the purchase and temporary storage (as inventory) of tangible personal property for resale is generally not considered a taxable use, the storage, keeping, and retention of artwork by displaying it on walls is a taxable event (*P-H Fine Arts*, 89 NY2d 804 (1996)).

Mark S. Klein, Esq., Hodgson Russ LLP

Gas and electricity: Use tax is specifically imposed on the use of gas or electricity, eliminating a disparity in taxation favoring out-of-state sellers. The amount of tax is based on the consideration given or contracted to be given for gas or electricity or for the use of gas or electricity. "Consideration" includes any charges for tangible personal property transferred in conjunction with gas or electricity and charges by the gas or electricity vendor for the transportation, transmission, or distribution of gas or electricity. Use tax does not apply to self-produced gas or self-generated electricity if there is no consideration given or contracted to be given for the gas or electricity. (Sec. 1110, Tax Law)

Shipping and delivery charges: Charges for shipping or delivery are included in the use tax base for tax imposed on the following (Sec. 1110, Tax Law):

— the use of tangible personal property purchased at retail;

— the use of tangible personal property manufactured, processed, or assembled by the user, when items of the same kind are not offered for sale by the user in the regular course of business and the item is either used as such or incorporated into a structure, building, or real property by a contractor, subcontractor, or repairman in erecting structures, or building on or otherwise making improvements to, real property, or maintaining, servicing, or repairing real property;

— the use of information services, interior decorating and designing services, and protective and detective services; and

— the use of tangible personal property upon which processing or printing, installation, or maintenance, or interior decorating or designing services, are performed (however, an exemption is provided for a vendor's separately stated charges to ship or deliver promotional materials to a purchaser's customers or prospective customers by means of the U.S. postal service).

For use tax exemptions, see ¶2104.

¶2014 Passenger Car Rentals Tax

Law: Secs. 1160, 1166-A, Tax Law (CCH New York Tax Reports, ¶60-570).

Rentals of passenger cars that qualify as retail sales are subject to a special additional tax at the rate specified at ¶2022. A comparable use tax is imposed on

¶2014

passenger cars rented by persons for use in the state, subject to certain limitations. Certain leases of passenger cars for a term of one year or more (¶2021) are not subject to tax.

Basis of tax: Tax is imposed on receipts from taxable rentals of passenger cars (Sec. 1160(a), Tax Law). The use tax is computed on the basis of the consideration given or contracted to be given for the use of the passenger car, excluding any credit for tangible personal property accepted in part payment and intended for resale plus transportation costs.

Separate charges for supplemental insurance in conjunction with charges for the rental of automobiles are not subject to sales tax or the special tax on passenger car rentals, but separate charges for fuel are subject to both taxes (TSB-A-03(26)S, June 12, 2003).

MCTD tax: A special supplemental sales and use tax is imposed on passenger car rentals within the Metropolitan Commuter Transportation District (MCTD), effective June 1, 2009, at the rate specified at ¶2022 on the receipts from the rental of a passenger car that is rented or used within the MCTD (Sec. 1166-A, Tax Law). The MCTD tax is in addition to the applicable state and local sales and use taxes and the statewide special tax on the rental of passenger cars (statewide special tax). The MCTD tax uses the same rules as the statewide special tax and therefore is calculated, administered, and collected in the same manner as that tax, except that it is only imposed on rentals or uses within the MCTD. Accordingly, if a rental of a passenger car within the MCTD is subject to the statewide special tax, it is also subject to the special supplemental tax. The special supplemental tax is also subject to the transitional provisions under Sec. 1106, Tax Law.

Vendors who provide the rental of passenger cars within the MCTD are required to collect the special supplemental tax from their customers and pay the special supplemental tax in the same manner and at the same time in which they remit the statewide special tax. (TSB-M-09(6)S, May 21, 2009, CCH New York Tax Reports, ¶406-399)

¶2015 Basis of Sales Tax

Law: Secs. 282-a, 1101, 1105, 1111(d), (e), 1132, Tax Law; Reg. Secs. 526.5, 534.7 (CCH New York Tax Reports, ¶60-560, ¶60-730, ¶61-110—¶61-190).

The sales tax is imposed on the sales price and the charge for any service, whether received in money or other consideration (Sec. 1105, Tax Law; Sec. 1110, Tax Law). Credits (other than trade-in allowances), expenses, or early payment discounts are not deductible from the sales price.

• *Transportation charges*

Shipping and delivery charges on tangible personal property delivered or services rendered are included in the taxable base (Sec. 1101(b)(3), Tax Law; Reg. Sec. 526.5(g)(1); *TB-ST-838*, New York Department of Taxation and Finance, May 14, 2012, CCH New York Tax Reports, ¶407-557). However, an exemption is provided for a vendor's separately stated charges to ship or deliver promotional materials to a purchaser's customers or prospective customers by means of the U.S. postal service.

Practitioner Comment: Shipping and Delivery

Shipping and delivery charges are subject to tax when they are imposed by a vendor in connection with its sale of taxable products or services (Sec. 1101(b)(3), Tax Law). There is no sales or use tax on shipping and delivery charges if they are separately contracted and paid for by the purchaser.

Mark S. Klein, Esq., Hodgson Russ LLP

- *Trade-in allowances*

Trade-in allowances may be deducted from the sales price if the property traded in is tangible personal property and is intended for resale by the vendor (Reg. Sec. 526.5(f)).

- *Federal and local excise taxes*

Excise taxes imposed on manufacturers, importers, producers, distributors or distillers are included in the receipts on which the sales tax is computed, even though the excise tax may be separately stated to the purchaser. Examples of excise taxes included in the sales tax base are the statewide and New York City taxes on alcoholic beverages and cigarettes; federal manufacturers excise taxes on certain automobiles and tires; federal gallonage taxes on alcoholic beverages; federal cigarette tax; and statewide excise tax on consumers of cigarettes. However, excise taxes imposed on the consumer are generally excluded from the receipts on which sales tax is included. Among the excise taxes excluded from the sales tax base are federal retail excise taxes on diesel fuel and special motor fuel, federal taxes on communication services, the state tax on gasoline and diesel fuel and the New York City tax on leaded motor fuel. (Reg. Sec. 526.5(a); *TSB-M-83(11)S*, Department of Taxation and Finance, CCH New York Tax Reports, ¶ 66-179)

- *Cancelled sales, returned merchandise*

The vendor of tangible personal property or services, the recipient of an amusement charge and the operator of a hotel are permitted to exclude receipts, charges or rents from the sales or use tax return where a contract of sale is cancelled or the property returned within the same reporting period as the sale. Application for a refund or credit is allowed where the contract is cancelled, the property returned, or the receipt ascertained to be uncollectible subsequent to payment of the tax. Claims for refunds or credits must be made within three years from the date the tax was payable. In the case of allowance for defective merchandise, the tax is paid by the purchaser upon the net amount due after allowance for the returned merchandise. (Sec. 1132(e), Tax Law; Reg. Sec. 534.6(a)(1))

- *Bad debts*

When a receipt, amusement charge, or hotel rent is wholly or partly uncollectible, the vendor of the tangible personal property or services, the recipient of the amusement charges or the operator of the hotel may apply to the Department of Taxation and Finance for a refund or credit of the tax paid. The claim must be made within three years from the date on which the tax was payable. (Sec. 1132, Tax Law; Reg. Sec. 534.7)

No credit or refund may be sought until an account has been found to be uncollectible and has been actually charged off for federal income tax purposes. A schedule of the computation of the state and local taxes for which the refund or credit is sought must be attached to the return upon which the credit is taken or to the application for refund.

Practitioner Comment: Three-Year limitation on Bad Debt Claims

As noted above, no sales tax credit or refund is allowed until an account has been charged-off for federal income tax purposes. Although the federal government allows taxpayers up to seven years to make a bad-debt determination, New York's sales tax credits are limited to those identified and charged-off within the first three years. Subsequent bad debts cannot be deducted. As a result, the vendor ends up remitting sales taxes on invoices that were never paid. See *Richard L. Feigen & Company*, (ALJ 7/10/14); CCH New York Tax Reports, ¶ 408-135.

Mark S. Klein, Esq., Hodgson Russ LLP

A refund or credit is not available for transactions that are financed by a third party or for debts assigned to a third party, whether or not the third party has recourse to the vendor on the debt.

Private label credit card accounts: No credit or refund may be claimed under former Sec. 1132(e-1), Tax Law, on or after July 1, 2010, regardless of the date of the underlying sales tax transaction or the date the bad debt is written off. Bad debt credits and refunds are governed by Sec. 1132(e), Tax Law, and such claims must be made according to Reg. Sec. 534.7, governing those bad credits or refunds. (*TSB-M-10(11)S*, August 19, 2010, CCH New York Tax Reports, ¶406-940)

If a recovery is made on a bad debt account that was the subject of a bad debt credit or refund under Sec. 1132(e-1), Tax Law, prior to its repeal, the lender or the vendor who received the bad debt credit or refund with regard to that account must report the appropriate amount of sales tax on the amount collected on the first subsequent sales tax return filed by the lender or the vendor who claimed the credit or refund. (*TSB-M-10(11)S*, August 19, 2010, CCH New York Tax Reports, ¶406-940)

Interest: Credits or refunds of tax attributable to bad debts will be made without interest. (Reg. Sec. 534.7(f))

• *Installation charges*

Charges for the installation of tangible personal property are generally taxable. However, charges for the installation of personal property which, when completed, will constitute an addition or capital improvement to real property are tax-exempt. (Sec. 1105(c)(3), Tax Law). (See ¶2007)

• *Motor fuel and diesel fuel*

The prepaid tax on motor fuel and diesel fuel is based on the regional average retail sales price per gallon, subject to certain maximums. The tax is to be included in the price shown on any metered pump or other dispensing device from which the fuel is sold to purchasers for delivery directly to a vehicle propelled by other than muscular power. See ¶2022 for prepayment rates.

When determining the tax required to be collected on the retail sale of motor fuel or diesel fuel, the amount of tax required to be prepaid is excluded from the receipts on which the tax is computed.

The prepaid sales tax on diesel motor fuel will not apply to the sale of previously untaxed qualified biodiesel to a person registered as a distributor of diesel motor fuel other than (1) a retail sale to such person or (2) a sale to such person that involves a delivery at a filling station or into a repository that is equipped with a hose or other apparatus by which such qualified biodiesel can be dispensed into the fuel tank of a motor vehicle. (Sec. 282-a(3)(b), Tax Law)

There is no exemption from the prepaid sales tax for B20 fuel. The prepaid sales tax for B20 fuel must be computed at the full amount and may not be reduced by 20%; see ¶2106.

¶2015A Coupons, Vouchers, and Discounts

Law: Reg. Sec. 526.5 (CCH New York Tax Reports, ¶61 130).

In general, when a coupon is redeemable by a manufacturer or third party, the original price is subject to tax. However, if the coupon is issued by the retailer, it is a method of advertising and the reduced price is subject to tax. (For details, see *TSB-M-78(13)S*, Department of Taxation and Finance, CCH New York Tax Reports, ¶66-064; see also *TB-ST-860*, New York Department of Taxation and Finance, June 16, 2011, CCH New York Tax Reports, ¶407-296)

¶2015A

• *Coupons*

Coupon issued to purchaser by manufacturer.—When a manufacturer issues a coupon entitling a purchaser to a credit on the item purchased, the tax is due on the full amount of the receipt (Reg. Sec. 526.5(c)(1)). The receipt is composed of the amount paid and the amount of the coupon credit. The coupon credit reflects payment or reimbursement by another party to the vendor.

> *Example:* A manufacturer issues coupons entitling the holder to a credit allowance of 12¢ on the purchase of a 63¢ item from a retailer. The applicable tax, here 7% (or 5¢), is computed on the 63¢ purchase price of the item, yielding a purchase price (inclusive of tax) of 68¢. The 12¢ credit is then deducted, resulting in an amount due from the purchaser of 56¢.

Manufacturer's coupon issued by store to purchaser.—If a store issues a coupon entitling a purchaser to a credit on the item purchased for which it is reimbursed by a manufacturer or distributor, the tax is due on the full amount of the receipt. The receipt is composed of the amount paid and the amount of the coupon credit. The coupon must indicate, by "mfr" or some other code, that reimbursement is made. The reimbursement from the manufacturer or distributor to the store may be made in any form such as cash or a credit against purchases or in additional merchandise.

> *Example:* A store issues a coupon, labeled "mfr," entitling the holder to a credit allowance of 12¢ on the purchase of a 63¢ item from a retailer. The applicable tax, here 7% (or 5¢), is computed on the 63¢ purchase price of the item, yielding a purchase price (inclusive of tax) of 68¢. The 12¢ credit is then deducted, resulting in an amount due from the purchaser of 56¢.

Store-issued coupon entitling purchaser to discounted price with no reimbursement for store owner.—When a store issues a coupon entitling a purchaser to a discounted price on the item purchased, and the store receives no reimbursement, the tax is due from the purchaser on the discounted price only, which is the actual receipt.

> *Example:* A store issues coupons entitling the holder to a credit allowance of 12¢ on the purchase of a 63¢ product from a retailer. In such instance, the 12¢ store coupon is subtracted from the 63¢ purchase price, yielding an adjusted purchase price of 51¢. The applicable tax, here 7% (or 4¢) is computed on the adjusted 51¢ purchase price, resulting in an amount due from the purchaser of 55¢.

Store-issued coupon entitling store owner to reimbursement where such fact is not disclosed to purchaser.—If a store issues a coupon involving a manufacturer's reimbursement, but does not disclose that fact to the purchaser on the coupon or in the advertisement, the vendor may collect from the purchaser only the tax due on the reduced price, but will be required to pay the tax on the entire receipt—the amount of the price plus the reimbursement received from the manufacturer or distributor (Reg. Sec. 526.5(c)(2)).

CCH Advisory: Hotel Discounts

When a customer makes a taxable purchase using a discount coupon issued by the hotel, sales tax applies to the amount paid by the customer after the value of the coupon is deducted. Gift certificates for a stated dollar amount are exempt from tax when given away or sold to a customer, but sales tax applies when the certificate is redeemed, assuming a taxable purchase is made. For example, tax applies when such a gift certificate is redeemed by a person who purchased it from an exempt charitable organization, although no tax will apply if the certificate is redeemed by the exempt organization itself for food and drink to be consumed by the organization. If a gift certificate for a free stay or meal is given to a dissatisfied customer or donated to an exempt organization, no tax is due when the certificate is redeemed. However, when a customer redeems a certificate for a free meal, the hotel is liable for sales or use tax on its cost for the taxable food, drinks, and other items served to the customer.

¶2015A

Items offered by a hotel on a complimentary basis are subject to New York sales and use tax when purchased by the hotel because they do not qualify as items purchased for resale. However, if the hotel contracts with a customer to provide conference facilities and, as part of the agreement, furnishes food and beverages to attendees at no charge, the food and beverages purchased by the hotel are exempt as items purchased for resale. In cases in which the hotel offers a complimentary item in conjunction with a taxable sale, *e.g.,* a free bottle of wine with the purchase of a meal, the item qualifies as a purchase for resale if all costs associated with furnishing the item are recovered in the selling price paid by the customer (*First Colony Company,* Commissioner of Taxation and Finance, *TSB-A-99(13)S,* March 1, 1999; CCH NEW YORK TAX REPORTS, ¶ 403-339).

- *Vouchers*

A Department of Taxation and Finance memorandum provides guidance on the application of sales and use tax to purchases involving vouchers sold by Web-based companies that are then redeemed by the purchaser at a business that sells the property or service. Specifically, it provides that the sale of certain vouchers by Web-based companies on behalf of businesses is not subject to sales or use tax at the time that the voucher is sold. However, sales or use tax is due at the time the voucher is redeemed with a vendor if the voucher is redeemed for taxable products or services.

Under a typical business model involving these vouchers, an online company (deal site) solicits customers to purchase vouchers through its website. The deal site collects the purchase price of the voucher from the customer. The vouchers sold by the deal site can be redeemed by the customer for products or services from a local business. The vouchers are typically priced lower than the usual selling price of the product or service obtained when the voucher is redeemed (i.e., a customer may purchase a voucher from a deal site for $25 that can be redeemed for products or services that normally sell for $50). The customer who has purchased a voucher will present the voucher to the local business as payment for the advertised product or service. Typically, the deal site retains a portion (usually about 50%) of the price paid by the customer for the voucher and pays the remaining portion of the price paid for the voucher to the local business. The deal site that sold the voucher may describe the amount it retains as its charge to the business for advertising or as a commission. Alternatively, the deal site may indicate that it is the agent of the business in collecting the purchase price from the purchaser.

Sales tax treatment of the sale of the discount voucher.—Sales tax is not due on the sale of the voucher by the deal site. However, if the voucher is redeemed for taxable products or services, sales tax is due at the time the voucher is redeemed by the customer.

Sales tax treatment when the voucher is redeemed.—No sales tax is due if the voucher is redeemed for products or services not subject to sales tax. However, sales tax is due and must be collected from the customer when a voucher is redeemed for taxable products or taxable services. In this case, the amount subject to sales tax depends on whether the voucher is a specific product or service voucher or a stated-face-value voucher.

Specific product or service voucher: A specific product or service voucher is a voucher without a specific stated value that may be redeemed only for a specified product or service or combination of products and/or services. A voucher qualifies as a specific product or service voucher even if the normal or regular selling price of the product or service is stated on the voucher. When this type of voucher is redeemed for a taxable product or service, the amount subject to sales tax is the total price that the customer paid the deal site for the voucher. However, when this type of voucher can be redeemed more than once for a specifically identified taxable product or service (*e.g.,* a voucher that can be redeemed for two automobile oil change services), the amount subject to sales tax on each redemption is determined by dividing the total amount that the customer paid for the voucher by the number of times the voucher may be redeemed.

¶2015A

There may be cases where a specific product or service voucher can be redeemed for a combination of products and/or services. In these cases, the customer does not have the option of purchasing the products or services separately through the redemption of the voucher. Therefore, if the combination of products and/or services includes both taxable and nontaxable products and/or services, the transaction will be treated as the sale of taxable and exempt items sold as a single unit. In that situation, the sales tax due from the customer must be computed on the total price the purchaser paid to the deal site for the voucher.

Stated-face-value voucher: A stated-face-value voucher is a voucher with a specifically stated value, and, when redeemed, the value of the voucher is applied towards the price of the products or services purchased by the customer. A stated-face-value voucher is generally treated in the same manner as a gift card. That is, it is treated as cash up to the stated face value of the voucher. Therefore, when this type of voucher is redeemed for taxable products or services, sales tax is computed on the selling price of the items before the value of the voucher is applied against the purchase price.

If a stated-face-value voucher is redeemed for products and services with a value equal to or more than the face value of the voucher, any sales tax due must be collected from the customer at the time the sale occurs. However, if the voucher is redeemed for products and services valued at less than the face value of the voucher, the business can handle the collection and remittance of any sales tax due in one of two ways. A business may choose to collect the sales tax from the customer on the total value of the taxable products and services at the time of the sale. Alternatively, the business may allow the customer to use the remaining value of the voucher to pay the sales tax on the transaction. In this latter approach it is important that vendors realize that they must remit the full amount of the tax due on the transaction to the department even if the vendor did not collect any cash from the customer when it sold taxable products or services in exchange for the voucher. (*TSB-M-11(16)S*, Taxpayer Guidance Division, New York Department of Taxation and Finance, September 19, 2011, CCH NEW YORK TAX REPORTS, ¶ 407-362).

• *Discounts*

Early payment discounts.—Early payment discounts (discounts that are granted by a vendor for the purpose of encouraging prompt payment on an account) are not deductible from receipts (Reg. Sec. 526.5(d)(1)).

> **Example:** A vendor grants a purchaser a 2% discount for paying the price of a $100 camera within 10 days, and expects payment of the full price if paid within 30 days. The sales tax, in a 7% area, is $7 on the taxable receipt of $100, whichever method of payment the customer chooses.

Practitioner Comment: What's in a Name?

The New York State sales tax rules frequently elevate form over substance. Thus while "early" or "prompt payment" discounts do not reduce the amount of the "receipt" subject to sales tax (Reg. Sec. 526.5(d)(1)), an "up front" payment discount can be deductible (*Terminix*, TSB-A-00(25)S).

Mark S. Klein, Esq., Hodgson Russ LLP

Reduced-price discounts.—Discounts that represent a reduction in price (such as trade discounts, volume discounts or cash and carry discounts) are deductible in computing receipts (Reg. Sec. 526.5(d)(2)).

> **Example:** A vendor grants a purchaser a 10% cash-and-carry discount on a $50 item. The taxable receipt will be the discounted price of $45. The applicable tax, here 7% (or $3.15) is computed on the $45 discounted price, resulting in an amount due from the purchaser of $48.15.

• *Store loyalty discount cards*

Discount cards (sometimes called purchase cards or scan cards) are cards issued by a retailer to a customer, free of charge, that allow the customer to purchase certain items at a lower price by presenting the card at the time of purchase. Purchases made with a discount card are taxed on the purchase price after the price reduction has been made by the retailer. (Reg. Sec. 526.5(c); *TSB-M-11(10)S*, New York Department of Taxation and Finance, June 29, 2011, CCH NEW YORK TAX REPORTS, ¶407-301; see also *TB-ST-145*, New York Department of Taxation and Finance, September 29, 2011, CCH NEW YORK TAX REPORTS, ¶407-376)

CCH Advisory: Supermarket Discount Cards

Cash discounts on products received by supermarket shoppers through the use of supermarket discount cards were not subject to New York sales tax. The supermarket chain that supplied the cards was not reimbursed for its discounts by the suppliers of products selected by the supermarket for discounts. The use of an electronically encoded supermarket discount card to obtain a product discount is the same as the use of a paper coupon to obtain a discount. As with paper coupons, there is no sales tax on a cash discount unless a supermarket is reimbursed for the discount by the supplier of discounted products (*PricewaterhouseCoopers LLP* (Advisory Opinion), Commissioner of Taxation and Finance, *TSB-A-99(10)S*, March 1, 1999, CCH NEW YORK TAX REPORTS, ¶403-336).

¶2016 Basis of Tax—Manufacturer Using Own Product

Law: Secs. 1110, Tax Law; Reg. Secs. 526.9, 531.3 (CCH NEW YORK TAX REPORTS, ¶60-510).

Manufacturers, assemblers, or processors who use their own product in the regular course of their business in New York compute the tax on the cost of materials. The storage, keeping, or withdrawal from storage of tangible personal property by the person who manufactured, assembled, or processed the property is not a taxable use. (Sec. 1110, Tax Law)

When items of the same kind are not offered for sale by the user in the regular course of business and the item is either used as such or is incorporated into real property by a contractor, subcontractor, or repairman in erecting structures or buildings or otherwise making improvements to realty, the tax is computed based on the consideration given for the tangible personal property manufactured, processed, or assembled into the property subject to tax plus the cost of transportation. (Sec. 1110, Tax Law)

Fabricators are not subject to tax on the part of the price representing value added to the tangible personal property that they install as an addition or capital improvement to real property. In such case, the basis of tax is the normal purchase price prior to such fabrication that a manufacturer, producer or assembler would charge an unrelated contractor.

¶2017 Basis of Tax—Installment Sales

Law: Sec. 1132(d), Tax Law (CCH NEW YORK TAX REPORTS, ¶61-180).

The sales tax must be paid on the total sales price, and not on the amount of installments (Sec. 1132(d), Tax Law). The Commissioner is authorized to provide, by regulation, that tax on receipts from installment sales be paid on the amount of each installment and upon the date when the installment is due. However, no such regulation has been adopted.

For treatment of cancelled sales, returned merchandise, and bad debts, see ¶2015.

¶2016

¶2018 Basis of Tax—Use Tax on Property Used Out of State and Later Brought Into New York

Law: Sec. 1111(b), Tax Law; Reg. Secs. 525.2(b), 531.3, 531.4 (CCH NEW YORK TAX REPORTS, ¶ 60-450).

Purchases by New York residents outside the state for use outside the state, and who subsequently make in-state use of the property, are subject to compensating use tax on the purchase price (Sec. 1111(b), Tax Law; Reg. Sec. 525.2(b); Reg. Sec. 531.3; Reg. Sec. 531.4). However, residents who can affirmatively show that they used the property outside New York for more than six months prior to its first use in New York, pay use tax on the current market value of the property (not to exceed its cost) at the time of its first use in New York (Sec. 1111(b)(1), Tax Law).

If tangible personal property is brought into New York for use in the performance of a contract or subcontract for a period of less than six months, the taxpayer has an option to pay tax on the fair rental value of the property for the period of use in New York (Reg. Sec. 531.4(c)).

¶2019 Basis of Tax—Mobile and Modular Homes

Law: Secs. 1101(b), 1111(f), 1111(p), Tax Law; Reg. Sec. 544.3 (CCH NEW YORK TAX REPORTS, 60-540).

Sales and use taxes are generally imposed upon sales of new mobile homes. The tax is applied to 70% of the retail selling price (Sec. 1111(f), Tax Law). This rule, however, is applicable only to the selling price allocable to the new mobile home, including any tangible personal property permanently incorporated by the manufacturer, and is *not* applicable to furniture, fixtures, furnishings, appliances, attachments, or similar tangible personal property not permanently incorporated as component parts of the mobile home at the time of manufacture (Reg. Sec. 544.3(a)(2)(i)).

Sales of new mobile homes to contractors, subcontractors or repairers who, in that capacity, install them, are exempt (Sec. 1101(b)(4), Tax Law). Also exempt are sales of used mobile homes.

Factory-manufactured homes do not constitute mobile homes for New York sales and use tax purposes, and as a result the rules concerning taxation of mobile homes are inapplicable.

Items of tangible personal property included in a mobile home by a manufacturer or dealer that are not permanently incorporated as component parts, such as furniture, draperies, and freestanding appliances, must be taxed to the purchaser at 100% of their selling price (Reg. Sec. 544.3(a)(2)(ii)).

Used mobile home: Sales of used mobile homes are exempt (Sec. 1115(a)(23), Tax Law). However, items of tangible personal property included in the sale and which were not permanently incorporated as a component part of the mobile home at the time of manufacture are taxable (Reg. Sec. 544.3(a)(4)).

• *Modular homes*

A modular home that is permanently affixed to real property is not treated as tangible personal property. However, if the modular home is to be removed from the realty, then the home and its component parts would be tangible personal property, whether sold as a whole or as pieces. Modular home modules sold to a dealer that will be used to build a model home are taxed at 100% of the charge to the dealer, including any charges for shipping and handling. (Sec. 1101(b)(6), Tax Law; *TSB-M-09(19)S*, November 24, 2009, CCH NEW YORK TAX REPORTS, ¶ 406-602)

The sales tax imposed on receipts from the retail sales of a new modular home module is computed on the sum of (Sec. 1111(p)(1), Tax Law):

(1) 60% of the vendor's receipts from the sale of the module, excluding any charges for shipping or delivery; and

(2) 100% of any charges by the vendor to the purchaser for shipping or delivery of the modules.

The compensating use tax imposed on the use of a new modular home module by its purchaser is computed on the sum of (Sec. 1111(p)(2), Tax Law):

(1) 60% of the amount described in Sec. 1110(B), Tax Law, excluding any charges for shipping or delivery; and

(2) 100% of any charges for shipping or delivery.

When a manufacturer installs modules it manufactured, the compensating use tax imposed on the use of modular home modules by their manufacturer to be installed at a building site to construct a modular home that constitutes a capital improvement is computed on the sum of (Sec. 1111(p)(3), Tax Law):

(1) 60% of the consideration for which the manufacturer conveys those modules to the modular home buyer on an installed basis, excluding any consideration for shipping and delivery, and excluding the consideration for the installation of those modules at the building site as a modular home if such installation charge is reasonable and separately stated; and

(2) 100% of any charges for shipping or delivery.

¶2020 Basis of Tax—Racehorses

Law: Sec. 1111(g), Tax Law; Reg. Sec. 527.14 (CCH New York Tax Reports, ¶ 60-250).

Sales tax is imposed upon most retail sales of a racehorse in New York. Use tax is due upon the amount paid by a resident of New York State for a racehorse purchased out-of-state and subsequently brought into New York State for racing purposes (Sec. 1111(g), Tax Law; Reg. Sec. 527.14).

In addition, the sale of racehorses made through claiming races within New York is subject to sales tax, but only on such portions of the total purchase price that exceed the highest of any prior purchase prices paid for the same horse during the same calendar year within the state. When no previous purchases have been made in the state within a calendar year, the full purchase price is taxable (Sec. 1111(g), Tax Law).

Exemptions: Certain exemptions apply to sales and uses of racehorses (Sec. 1115(m), Tax Law). An exemption is also provided for the services of training and maintaining a racehorse to race in a race or race meeting held, maintained or conducted under the racing, pari-mutuel wagering and breeding law or a similar law of another state; when such services are rendered by a trainer to the owner of the horse. Certain property and services used predominantly in commercial horse boarding operations are exempt from sales and use tax (*TSB-M-00(8)S*, Department of Taxation and Finance, CCH New York Tax Reports, ¶ 300-326; *TSB-M-00(8.1)S*, Department of Taxation and Finance, CCH New York Tax Reports, ¶ 300-382; *TB-ST-253*, August 7, 2014, CCH New York Tax Reports, ¶ 408-181).

¶2021 Basis of Tax—Leases for Terms of One Year or More

Law: Secs. 1111(i), 1117, Tax Law; Reg. Sec. 527.15 (CCH New York Tax Reports, ¶ 60-460, ¶ 60-570, ¶ 60-740).

Receipts and consideration due or contracted to be given for leases, options, or contracts to renew leases for a term of one year or more, involving (1) motor vehicles with a gross weight of 10,000 pounds or less, (2) vessels, including any inboard or outboard motor and any trailer leased in conjunction with the vessel, and, prior to

September 1, 2015, (3) noncommercial aircraft having a seating capacity of less that 20 passengers and a maximum payload capacity of less than 6,000 pounds, are deemed to have been paid or given as of the date of first payment under the lease (Sec. 1111(i)(A), Tax Law). Tax must be collected as of the date of first payment under the lease, option, or similar provision, or combination of them, or as of the date of registration with the Commissioner of Motor Vehicles, whichever is earlier.

A lease for a term of one year or more includes any lease for a shorter period that includes an option to renew, or similar provision, when the cumulative period for which the lease may be in effect is one year or more (Sec. 1111(i)(B), Tax Law).

Receipts due and consideration given under any such lease or other provision for excess mileage charges are subject to tax as and when paid or due.

- *Fleet leases*

If the lessee of a motor vehicle certifies in writing that more than 50% of the use of the vehicle will be in the lessee's trade or business, and the lease includes an indeterminate number of options to renew (or other similar contractual provision) or at least 36 monthly options to renew beyond the initial term, all receipts due or consideration given or contracted to be given under the lease for (1) the first 32 months, or (2) the period of the initial term of the lease, whichever is greater, will be deemed to have been paid or given, and are subject to tax (Sec. 1117(a), Tax Law). Accelerated tax payment provisions do not apply to any payments due or contracted to be given upon the exercise of an option to renew (or similar provision) after the first 32 months of the initial term, if longer.

- *Leases involving property subsequently brought into New York*

In the case of leases, options or contracts to renew leases that were originally entered into outside New York by a lessee who was (1) a New York resident who leased the property for use outside New York but subsequently brought the property into New York for use within the state, or (2) not a New York resident but subsequently became a New York resident and brought the property into New York for use within the state, any remaining receipts due or consideration given will be taxed as if the lease, option or contract had been exercised initially within New York. (Sec. 1117(a), Tax Law; Reg. Sec. 527.15)

Practitioner Comment: Leased Vehicles

Once the sales tax is paid on the long-term lease of a motor vehicle, the transaction is deemed concluded under New York State's sales tax law. Accordingly, no refunds are available to taxpayers who prematurely terminate their lease (*Miehle*, NYS TAT (8/24/00), CCH New York Tax Reports, ¶403-748), purchase the vehicle outright (*Bethel*, ALJ 4/3/03, CCH New York Tax Reports, ¶404-497), move out of New York State (*Torquato*, NYS TAT (10/12/00), CCH New York Tax Reports, ¶403-768), or have their vehicles stolen (*Moerdler*, NYS TAT (4/26/01), CCH New York Tax Reports, ¶403-917).

Mark S. Klein, Esq., Hodgson Russ LLP

¶2022 Rate of Tax

Law: Secs. 1105, 1105-A, 1105-C, 1107, 1109, 1110, 1111, 1210, 1210-A, 1212, Tax Law (CCH New York Tax Reports, ¶60-096, ¶60-310, ¶61-710, ¶65-285).

The New York State sales and use taxes are imposed at the rate of 4% (Sec. 1105, Tax Law; Sec. 1110, Tax Law).

Medical marijuana: A 7% excise tax is imposed on sales of medical marijuana (cannabis); see ¶2003.

• *Metropolitan Commuter Transportation District*

An additional state sales and use tax of ³/₈ of 1% is imposed in the Metropolitan Commuter Transportation District, which consists of New York City and the counties of Dutchess, Nassau, Orange, Putnam, Rockland, Suffolk, and Westchester (Sec. 1109(a), Tax Law; *TSB-M-05(7)S*, Department of Taxation and Finance, CCH NEW YORK TAX REPORTS, ¶ 300-469).

• *Cities, counties, and school districts*

Cities and counties in New York (except counties wholly within a city), as well as certain school districts, are authorized, pursuant to Article 29 of the Tax Law, to impose local sales and use taxes (Sec. 1210, Tax Law; Sec. 1211(a), Tax Law). The local taxes are in addition to the 4% state rate and the additional Metropolitan Commuter Transit District tax, where applicable.

In general, localities may levy an additional local tax at a rate no greater than 3% (Sec. 1210, Tax Law; Sec. 1211(a), Tax Law). However, certain localities are authorized to impose the additional local tax at the rate of 0.50%, 1%, 1.50%, 2%, 2.50% or 3%, and are subject to rate ceilings and specific applicability periods.

The local tax rate must be uniform.

School districts coterminous with, partly within, or wholly within cities having a population of less than 125,000 may impose a tax on sales of utility services at a rate of up to 3% in addition to the state, city, and county taxes. Thus, in such cities, utility services may be subjected to a tax of up to 10%. Cities having a population of less than 125,000 are all cities in the state except Albany, Buffalo, New York City, Rochester, Syracuse, and Yonkers.

For additional information on local taxes, see ¶ 2024.

For a chart of local sales and use taxes, see ¶ 11.

Local rate changes: Local sales tax jurisdictions are generally allowed to increase or decrease their local sales and use tax (sales tax) rate effective on March 1, June 1, September 1, or December 1 of each year. A bulletin describes how sales tax is applied when the sales tax rate in a locality changes (*TB-ST-895*, March 10, 2014, CCH NEW YORK TAX REPORTS, ¶ 408-044).

• *Passenger car rental tax*

Certain passenger car rentals are subject to a special 6% tax (¶ 2014). For any rental contract entered into before June 1, 2009, that expires after that date, the charge subject to the special tax at the 6% rate is determined by a special formula (TSB-M-09(1)S, April 30, 2009, CCH NEW YORK TAX REPORTS, ¶ 406-376).

MCTD tax: A special supplemental sales and use tax is imposed on passenger car rentals within the Metropolitan Commuter Transportation District (MCTD), effective June 1, 2009, at the rate of 5% on the receipts from the rental of a passenger car that is rented or used within the MCTD. The MCTD tax is in addition to the applicable state and local sales and use taxes and the statewide special tax on the rental of passenger cars (statewide special tax). (Sec. 1166-A, Tax Law)

• *Rates on residential energy sources and services*

New York State sales and use tax does not apply to retail sales of the following energy sources when used for residential purposes: wood used for heating purposes, fuel oil, coal, propane (except when sold in containers of less than 100 pounds), natural gas, electricity, steam, and gas and electric steam services (Sec. 1105-A, Tax Law). The state sales tax, however, is applicable to sales of (1) diesel motor fuel involving delivery at a filling station or into a repository equipped with a hose or other apparatus to dispense the fuel into a fuel tank of a motor vehicle, and (2) enhanced (non-highway) diesel motor fuel, except if used exclusively for residential purposes and delivered into a storage tank not equipped with a hose or other

¶ 2022

apparatus by which such fuel can be dispensed into the fuel tank of a motor vehicle and which storage tank is attached to the heating unit burning the fuel (Sec. 1105-A, Tax Law).

All of the exemptions and provisions that apply to unenhanced diesel motor fuel are allowed for dyed ultra-low-sulfur kerosene for the purposes of the motor fuel, petroleum business, and sales taxes. However, the exemption is not allowed if the dyed ultra-low-sulfur kerosene is delivered to a filling station or into a storage tank equipped with a nozzle or similar apparatus capable of dispensing the fuel into the tank of a motor vehicle. (*TSB-M-11(2)M, TSB-M-11(2)S*, Office of Tax Policy Analysis, New York Department of Taxation and Finance, March 11, 2011, CCH NEW YORK TAX REPORTS, ¶ 407-157; See also *TSB-M-11(12)M, TSB-M-11(18)S*, New York Department of Taxation and Finance, October 6, 2011, CCH NEW YORK TAX REPORTS, ¶ 407-379; *TB-ST-775*, New York Department of Taxation and Finance, September 17, 2012, CCH NEW YORK TAX REPORTS, ¶ 407-645)

Cities and counties, except for counties wholly contained within a city, are authorized to adopt reduced rates on sales and uses of residential energy sources or to exempt such sales and uses.

For exemption of tangible personal property (including parts, tools and supplies) used or consumed in production from local sales and use taxes, see ¶ 2024.

• *Computer software*

The compensating use tax on computer software created by the user is imposed at the current rate based on the consideration given or contracted to be given for the tangible personal property that constitutes the blank medium (*e.g.*, disks or tapes) used in conjunction with the software, or for the use of the property. The mere storage, keeping, retention, or withdrawal from storage of computer software by its author or creator is not considered to be a taxable use (Sec. 1110(g), Tax Law).

Since prewritten software constitutes tangible personal property for New York sales and use tax purposes, other prewritten software (not created by the user) is subject to use tax at the current rate based on the consideration given or contracted to be given for the software or the use of the software, plus delivery costs. See ¶ 2102.

For additional information, see *TB-ST-128*, August 5, 2014, CCH NEW YORK TAX REPORTS, ¶ 408-177.

• *Entertainment*

An additional tax is imposed at the rate of 5% on taxable entertainment and information services that are furnished, provided, or delivered by means of interstate or intrastate telephony, telegraphy, or telephone or telegraph services, and that are received by the customer exclusively in an aural manner. See ¶ 2007.

• *Motor fuels*

The sales tax on certain motor fuels is capped at 8¢ per gallon outside the Metropolitan Commuter Transportation District (MCTD) and 8.75¢ per gallon within the MCTD. If the price of fuel is below $2 per gallon, the sales tax will be proportionally applied at the regular state rate of 4% per dollar (plus the regular MCTD rate, where applicable).

Local taxes: Local governments, including New York City, are authorized to compute their local sales tax on gasoline at a rate of cents per gallon equal to $2 or $3, multiplied by the percentage rate of such taxes within the locality (Sec. 1111(m-1)(3), (4), Tax Law). For additional information, see *Publication 718-F*, New York Department of Taxation and Finance, August 2013, CCH NEW YORK TAX REPORTS, ¶ 65-921.

The state and local cents-per-gallon method applies only to qualified fuels. Qualified fuel is motor fuel or diesel motor fuel that is (1) sold for use directly and exclusively in the engine of a motor vehicle or (2) sold by a retail gas station (other than water-white kerosene sold exclusively for heating purposes in containers of no more than 20 gallons) (Sec. 1111(m-1), Tax Law).

Retail and wholesale sellers are required to pass along the tax savings to consumers or face penalties of up to $5,000 for each day such violation occurs. (Sec. 1817(t), Tax Law)

The New York Department of Taxation and Finance has issued a publication discussing the local sales and use tax rates on qualified motor fuel, diesel motor fuel, and B20 biodiesel. The publication also lists the localities that have elected the cents-per-gallon method of computing local sales tax on qualified fuel, and the applicable local cents-per-gallon rate. It also lists those localities that continue to use the percentage rate method of computing sales tax on qualified fuel, and the applicable percentage rate. (*Publication 718-F,* New York Department of Taxation and Finance, August 2013, CCH NEW YORK TAX REPORTS, ¶ 65-921)

Quarterly rate adjustments: The Commissioner of Taxation and Finance is required to establish a quarterly average price for motor fuel and diesel fuel. Counties and cities that have adopted the cents-per-gallon method must multiply the average price by the local sales tax rate. If the result is less than the locality's effective cents-per-gallon rate, localities must drop their cents-per-gallon rate to the lower rate, rounded to the nearest cent. Adjustments to a cents-per-gallon rate due to a change in the average price are published by the Commissioner and take effect on the first day of the next succeeding sales tax quarter. Local sales and use tax rates on qualified motor fuel, diesel motor fuel, and B20 biodiesel are listed in *Publication 718-F,* New York Department of Taxation and Finance, CCH NEW YORK TAX REPORTS, ¶ 65-921. The publication also lists the localities that have elected the cents-per-gallon method of computing local sales tax on qualified fuel, and the applicable local cents-per-gallon rates, as well as those localities that continue to use the percentage rate method of computing sales tax on qualified fuel, and the applicable percentage rates.

Similar calculations take place quarterly with respect to the state and MCTD sales tax rates. For the local sales tax collection charts for motor fuel or diesel motor fuel sold at retail, see *Publication 873,* Local Sales Tax Collection Charts for Motor Fuel or Diesel Motor Fuel Sold at Retail, New York Department of Taxation and Finance, CCH NEW YORK TAX REPORTS, ¶ 65-967. The charts show the amount of the local sales tax component in any given pump price of a gallon of automotive fuel. They are to be used to verify the sales tax due.

- *Vending machine sales of food and drink*

Sales of food and beverages from vending machines are generally taxed in the same manner as sales of the same items in food stores. This means that generally: items that are taxable when sold in a food store are exempt when sold from a vending machine; and items that are exempt when sold in a food store are exempt when sold from a vending machine. (*TB-ST-280,* April 13, 2011, CCH NEW YORK TAX REPORTS, ¶ 407-200) However, there are two exceptions to this general rule:

(1) hot beverages sold from a vending machine are always exempt; and

(2) candy and confectionery, fruit drinks that contain less than 70% of natural fruit juice, and soft drinks, sodas, and beverages that are ordinarily dispensed at soda fountains (other than coffee, tea, and cocoa), sold through any vending machine activated by the use of a coin, currency, credit card, or debit card that are taxable when sold by food stores are exempt when they are sold from a vending machine for $1.50 or less (75¢, before June 1, 2014 *TSB-M-14(7)S,* May 21, 2014, CCH NEW YORK TAX REPORTS, ¶ 408-097).

- *Prepayment rates*

Sales taxes on motor fuel, diesel fuel, and packaged cigarettes must be prepaid.

Motor fuel and diesel fuel: The rate of the prepaid sales tax for distributors of motor fuels was increased and the applicable regions were changed, effective June 1, 2014. Region 1 consists of the localities included in the Metropolitan Commuter Transportation District (MCTD), excluding all localities included in the counties of Nassau and Suffolk, and the prepaid rate in this region is increased from 14.75 cents to 17.50 cents. Region 2 consists of the localities included in the counties of Nassau and Suffolk, and the prepaid rate in this region is increased from 14 cents to 21 cents. Region 3 consists of the area of the state outside the first two regions, and the prepaid rate in this region is 16 cents. (Sec. 1111(e)(2), Tax Law; *TSB-M-14(6)S*, May 15, 2014, CCH NEW YORK TAX REPORTS, ¶ 408-092; *Important Notice N-14-6*, May 15, 2014, CCH NEW YORK TAX REPORTS, ¶ 408-093; *Important Notice N-14-7*, May 15, 2014, CCH NEW YORK TAX REPORTS, ¶ 408-094)

Alternative fuels: The prepaid tax on diesel motor fuel does not apply to (Sec. 1102(a), Tax Law):

— the sale of nonhighway diesel or qualified biodiesel motor fuel to a registered distributor of diesel motor fuel (other than a sale to such person at a filling station or into a repository equipped with a hose or other apparatus by which such fuel can be dispensed into the fuel tank of a motor vehicle); or

— the sale to or delivery at a filling station or other retail vendor of water-white kerosene if the filling station or other retail vendor only sells kerosene exclusively for heating purposes in containers of no more than 20 gallons.

Note, however, that there is no exemption from the prepaid sales tax for B20 fuel; see ¶ 2106.

Cigarettes: The prepaid sales tax on cigarettes is computed by multiplying the base retail price by a tax rate of 8%, and rounding the result to the nearest whole cent per package. The base retail price is adjusted on September 1 each year in accordance with a legislated formula. (*TB-ST-685*, New York Department of Taxation and Finance, November 26, 2014, CCH NEW YORK TAX REPORTS, ¶ 408-286)

For the period September 1, 2016, through August 31, 2017, the prepaid sales tax rate on cigarettes is 83¢ on packages of 20 cigarettes; and $1.04 on packages of 25 cigarettes. The prepayments were determined using a base retail sales price of $10.403 per 20-pack of cigarettes and $2.598 for each additional five cigarettes above 20 (*Important Notice N-16-6*, July 2016, CCH NEW YORK TAX REPORTS, ¶ 408–803).

CCH Advisory: Determining Correct Rate

The New York Department of Taxation and Finance maintains an electronic service on its website to help businesses properly report local sales tax. The service allows businesses anywhere to determine the correct local taxing jurisdiction, the combined state and local sales tax rate, and the local jurisdiction reporting code for use in filing New York sales tax returns. The tool can be accessed from the Department website at **http://www8.tax.ny.gov/JRLA/jrlaStart**.

¶2023 Rounding

Law: Sec. 1132, Tax Law; Reg. Sec. 530.4 (CCH NEW YORK TAX REPORTS, ¶ 60-130, ¶ 65-288).

Generally, when the tax to be paid includes a fraction of one cent, the fraction need not be paid where it is less than one-half cent and a full cent must be paid where the fraction is one-half cent or more. However, if the sales tax computation results in a tax of five mills or less, no sales tax is due. (Sec. 1132, Tax Law; Reg. Sec. 530.4)

¶2024 City, County, and School District Taxes

Law: Secs. 1105-A, 1107(a), 1109, 1210, 1212, Tax Law (CCH NEW YORK TAX REPORTS, ¶ 61-735, ¶ 61-710, ¶ 65-286, ¶ 65-287).

Article 29 of the Tax Law provides that cities, counties (except counties wholly within a city), and certain school districts may adopt the entire state tax package consisting of a tax on (1) sales of tangible personal property, (2) sales of certain utility services, (3) sales of certain other services, (4) sales of food and beverages purchased from restaurants, taverns, or caterers, (5) hotel occupancies, (6) admissions and club dues, and (7) the use tax. In the alternative, the local jurisdictions may adopt one or more of these taxes (except that the sales and use taxes on tangible personal property and on services may only be adopted as part of the entire state tax package). These taxes are in addition to the statewide tax.

Residential energy: Residential energy sources and services are not subject to the 4% state sales and use tax (see ¶ 2106). Counties and cities that impose a local sales and use tax may choose to either tax or exempt the residential energy sources and services. A publication lists the jurisdictions that impose a local tax on residential sales of gas, propane (in containers of 100 pounds or more), electricity, and steam, and the applicable tax rate. It also lists the jurisdictions that impose a local tax on residential sales of coal, fuel oil, and wood (for heating), and the applicable tax rate. Localities or school districts not listed in the publication do not impose a local tax on residential energy sources and services. (*Publication 718-R*, New York Department of Taxation and Finance, August 2012, CCH NEW YORK TAX REPORTS, ¶ 65-922)

Motor fuels: For the local sales tax collection charts for motor fuel or diesel motor fuel sold at retail, see *Publication 873*, Local Sales Tax Collection Charts for Motor Fuel or Diesel Motor Fuel Sold at Retail, New York Department of Taxation and Finance, CCH NEW YORK TAX REPORTS, ¶ 65-967. The charts show the amount of the local sales tax component in any given pump price of a gallon of automotive fuel. They are to be used to verify the sales tax due. See also *Publication 718-F*, New York Department of Taxation and Finance, August 2013, CCH NEW YORK TAX REPORTS, ¶ 65-921.

Prepaid telephone calling services: If a county, city, or school district that imposes sales and use taxes on consumer utilities and telecommunications services as described in Tax Law Sec. 1105(b), the taxes do not apply to prepaid telephone calling services. Only general sales and use taxes apply to prepaid telephone calling services. See also ¶ 2007.

Upon either election, the provisions of the local tax must be uniform.

New York City, prior to November 1, 2000, had to omit the statewide exemption for fuel and utilities used or consumed in producing tangible personal property and utilities (¶ 2106). Cities (other than New York City), counties, and school districts that impose the entire state tax package must exclude from tax all sales of tangible personal property for use or consumption directly and predominantly in the production of tangible personal property, gas, electricity, refrigeration, and steam for sale (¶ 2105). Effective June 1, 2006, New York City is authorized to reduce or eliminate its local sales and use tax on residential energy sources, such as fuel oil, coal, wood, propane, natural gas, electricity, steam and gas, and gas, electric and steam services (Sec. 1105-A(f), Tax Law).

Technically, the New York City local tax is imposed as an additional state tax, and the revenues therefrom are paid to the Municipal Assistance Corporation for the City of New York, which was created to assist New York City meet its obligations. The Metropolitan Commuter Transportation District tax (¶ 2022) is also imposed in New York City.

New York City imposes tax on certain services (¶ 3315).

Cities and counties, except counties wholly within a city, are authorized to adopt reduced rates on retail sales and uses of residential heating and energy sources or to eliminate the tax on such sales and uses.

The state and local taxes are administered jointly by the Commissioner.

The local taxes imposed to date are listed at ¶ 11.

¶2024

SALES AND USE TAXES

CHAPTER 21
EXEMPTIONS AND CREDITS

¶2101 In General

The following paragraphs deal with the exemptions from the sales and use taxes.

The most frequent exemption is in connection with sales for resale (¶2103). Other important exemptions relate to grocery food (¶2102), machinery and equipment used in manufacturing, etc. (¶2105), fuel and utilities used in manufacturing (¶2106), and property used in production on farms (¶2107).

¶2102 Exempt Property and Services

Law: Secs. 1101, 1105, 1105-A, 1115, 1118, 1132(c), Tax Law (CCH New York Tax Reports, ¶61-735, 60-250, 60-260, 60-310, 60-390, 60-400, 60-520, 60-540, 60-560, 60-640, 60-285, 60-665, 60-720, 60-740, 60-750, 61-010, 61-020).

Specific exemptions from sales and use taxes include the following:

• *Advertising and promotion*

Advertising services are exempt (Sec. 1105(c)(1), Tax Law). The exemption, however, is limited to the consultation and creative development of an advertising campaign as well as charges for the placement of advertising with media, without the transfer of tangible personal property. An advertising agency's creation of tangible personal property (layouts, print media proofs, product packaging prototypes, brochures, videos and similar items) is subject to tax. Consequently, in order to maintain the exemption from tax, the charges for the consulting and creative aspect of the advertising campaign must be separately stated on the invoice to the customer.

A bulletin explains how sales and use taxes apply to sales and purchases made by businesses that provide advertising services (TB-ST-10, February 3, 2014, CCH New York Tax Reports, ¶408-023).

Internet advertising: Charges for running advertisements on the Internet are not subject to tax, provided the taxpayer does not sell tangible personal property in conjunction with the services. (Sec. 1105(c)(1), Tax Law; Reg. Sec. 527.3(b)(5); TSB-A-95(33)S, CCH New York Tax Reports, ¶402-145).

Practitioner Comment: Audio and Video Materials

An advertiser's delivery of audio or video materials on disks or tape to a New York location is treated as a taxable sale of tangible personal property. If, however, the video is transferred electronically (through the Internet or a satellite feed), no tax is due. See *Universal Music Group,* TSB-A-01(15)S, CCH NEW YORK TAX REPORTS, ¶ 403-938. Alternatively, many taxpayers send the original disk or tape (known as the "master") to an out-of-state location where duplicate copies are made and sent to the New York customers. Under New York's rules, sales tax is limited to the cost of creating the duplicates and is not based on the cost of producing the original recordings.

Mark S. Klein, Esq., Hodgson Russ LLP

Promotional materials: Tangible personal property that is purchased and given away without charge, for promotional or advertising purposes, is subject to tax (Reg. Sec. 526.6(c)(4)(i)). Likewise, tangible personal property that is purchased for promotional or advertising purposes and sold for a minimal charge which does not reflect its true cost, or which is not ordinarily sold by that person in the operation of that person's business, is a retail sale to the purchaser (Reg. Sec. 526.6(c)(4)(ii)).

Promotional materials mailed, shipped, or otherwise distributed by a printer-mailer from points within New York to a mailing address outside New York State, for use outside the state, are exempt from sales and use taxes (Sec. 1115(n), Tax Law). Clerical functions performed on promotional materials being mailed out of state are also exempt.

Printed promotional materials and promotional materials upon which services have been directly performed are exempt from tax when the purchaser mails or ships the materials, or causes the materials to be mailed or shipped without charge to its customers (or prospective customers) by means of a common carrier, U.S. postal service, or similar delivery service. Services that would otherwise be taxable under Sec. 1115(c)(2), Tax Law, performed on such materials are also exempt.

Mechanicals, layouts, artwork, photographs, color separations, and like property are exempt when purchased, manufactured, processed, or assembled by a person who furnishes them to a printer and the printer uses the items directly and predominantly in the production of promotional materials that are exempt or in performing services that are exempt and that are for sale by the printer to the person who furnished the items.

"Promotional materials" include any advertising literature, other related tangible personal property and envelopes used exclusively to deliver the materials, as well as paper and ink furnished to the printer. Such other related tangible personal property includes free gifts (but not free samples), complimentary maps or other items given to travel club members, applications, order forms and return envelopes with respect to such advertising literature, annual reports, prospectuses, promotional displays, and Cheshire labels. However, invoices, statements, and the like are excluded from the definition of "promotional materials." Additionally, the exemption for promotional materials distributed within New York State is limited to materials that are "printed in the traditional sense." Catalogs or other promotional materials distributed by videotape, diskette, CD, DVD or the like are not eligible for the exemption. See *TSB-A-03(1)S,* January 23, 2003, CCH NEW YORK TAX REPORTS, ¶ 404-446. For additional information, see *TSB-M-01(4)S,* February 8, 2001, CCH NEW YORK TAX REPORTS, ¶ 300-341 and *TSB-M-97(6)S,* August 20, 1997, CCH NEW YORK TAX REPORTS, ¶ 300-228.

Practitioner Comment: Limits on Promotional Exemption

The exemption for promotional materials is limited to items distributed to existing or potential customers. Materials mailed to members of an organization, labor union, or political party are ineligible for the exemption since the recipients are not being asked to purchase anything (NYT G 08(1)S. See also *TSB-A-99(15)S;* CCH NEW YORK TAX REPORTS, ¶ 403-341). Similarly, prescription drug sales kits mailed to New York physicians do not qualify for the exemption since the physicians are not existing or prospective customers (*Promex Medical, Inc.,* TSB-A-99(23)S, CCH NEW YORK TAX REPORTS, ¶ 403-371).

Mark S. Klein, Esq., Hodgson Russ LLP

Advertising supplements: Advertising supplements, when distributed as inserts in a newspaper, periodical or shopping paper, are exempt (Reg. Sec. 528.6(e)(1)).

Mailing lists: Charges for the portion of a mailing list used in conjunction with the distribution of exempt promotional materials are exempt to the extent that the promotional materials are shipped to addresses outside New York. These charges are exempt whether the list is considered an information service or tangible personal property (Sec. 1115(n), Tax Law).

Storing exempt promotional services: Charges for storing exempt promotional materials are exempt from tax when the vendor of the storing service is also either the vendor of the exempt promotional materials or the vendor who rendered exempt services on the materials, and the purchaser of the storing service is the purchaser of the exempt promotional materials (Sec. 1115(n)(6), Tax Law).

The exemption does not apply to tangible personal property that is (1) purchased by a person (other than under the circumstances noted above) or (2) furnished by the manufacturer, processor, or assembler to an exempt vendor to be included as free gifts with the exempt promotional materials to be mailed or shipped to New York customers or prospective New York customers.

- *Agriculture*

For exemption of tangible personal property used in farming, etc. or in research and development, see ¶ 2107 and ¶ 2108.

- *Aircraft*

Sales of commercial aircraft are generally exempt (Sec. 1115(a)(21), Tax Law). However, the definition of "commercial aircraft" provides that an aircraft does not qualify for the exemption if it is used primarily to transport a purchaser's personnel or those of an affiliated entity (Sec. 1101(b)(17), Tax Law). For taxability of fractional share ownership transactions, see *TSB-A-09(23)S,* June 5, 2009, CCH NEW YORK TAX REPORTS, ¶ 406-424.

General aviation aircraft: Effective September 1, 2015, a sales and use tax exemption is available for general aviation aircraft, and machinery or equipment to be installed on such aircraft (Sec. 1115(a)(21-a), Tax Law). "General aviation aircraft" means an aircraft that is used in civil aviation and that is not a commercial aircraft, military aircraft, unmanned aerial vehicle or drone. See *TSB-M-15(3)S,* July 24, 2015, CCH NEW YORK TAX REPORTS, ¶ 408-483.

Also effective September 1, 2015, leases of noncommercial aircraft having a seating capacity of less than 20 passengers and a maximum payload capacity of less than 6,000 pounds are no longer subject to accelerated sales or use tax provisions; see ¶ 2021.

Aircraft services: Sales and use tax exemptions are allowed for maintenance and certain other services performed on aircraft, as well as tangible personal property purchased and used in performing the services, when the property is a lubricant or becomes a physical component part of the aircraft. An exemption also is allowed for storage of an aircraft rendered in conjunction with the provision of services to the aircraft. (Sec. 1115(dd), Tax Law) In addition to exempting the sales of tangible personal property and lubricants, the sale of any service that keeps an aircraft in a condition of fitness, efficiency, readiness or safety or restoring it to such condition, is also exempt (*TSB-M-04(8)S,* Department of Taxation and Finance, CCH NEW YORK TAX REPORTS, ¶ 300-445).

Commercial aircraft: Commercial aircraft primarily engaged in intrastate, interstate, or foreign commerce, machinery or equipment to be installed on such aircraft, property used by or purchased for the use of such aircraft for maintenance and repairs, and flight simulators purchased by commercial airlines are exempt. Services rendered with respect to such aircraft, machinery or equipment to be installed on such aircraft, and property for maintenance and repairs of such aircraft are also exempt (Sec. 1105(c)(3)(v), Tax Law).

Aircraft fuel: Fuel sold to airlines for use in airplanes is exempt (Sec. 1115(a)(9), Tax Law). Sales of fuel for use in commercial and general aviation aircraft are exempt from local sales taxes and from the prepayment of sales tax on motor fuels, effective December 1, 2017. (¶2106; ¶2203)

• *Clothing and footwear*

Except as noted below, sales of clothing and footwear are subject to tax as retail sales of tangible personal property (Sec. 1105(a), Tax Law; Reg. Sec. 526.8(a)(2); *TSB-M-11(3)S*, New York Department of Taxation and Finance, March 14, 2011, CCH New York Tax Reports, ¶407-159; *Publication 718-C*, New York Department of Taxation and Finance, CCH New York Tax Reports, ¶65-908; see also *TB-ST-122*, March 10, 2014, CCH New York Tax Reports, ¶408-042 and *TB-ST-530*, March 10, 2014, CCH New York Tax Reports, ¶408-043).

Clothing and footwear: The state and MCTD exemption for sales of clothing and footwear costing less than $110, including items used or consumed to make or repair such clothing and that become a physical component part of such clothing, was temporarily suspended from October 1, 2010, through March 31, 2011. Beginning April 1, 2011, the exemption was reinstated for clothing and footwear costing less than $55 per item until March 31, 2012. The exemption reverted to $110 on April 1, 2012. Local governments are given the option to maintain their current exemptions or opt into the new exemption schedule. (*TSB-M-10(16)S*, September 7, 2010, CCH New York Tax Reports, ¶406-968)

The exemption generally applies to articles of clothing worn on the body, although it does not apply to jewelry, watches, precious stones, or sporting equipment. It also applies to most items that become a physical component part of exempt clothing or that are used to make or repair exempt clothing, such as most fabric, thread, yarn, buttons, snaps, hooks, zippers, and like items. If exempt clothing or footwear is sold with other taxable merchandise as a single unit, the full price is subject to sales or use tax, unless the price of the clothing or footwear is reasonable and separately stated.

Delivery, shipping, and handling charges: Reasonable, separately stated charges for delivery of eligible clothing and footwear are not taken into account in determining if the cost of an item is less than $110 (*TSB-M-06(6)S*, March 29, 2006, CCH New York Tax Reports, ¶300-506).

Coupons: Manufacturer's coupons do not reduce the selling price for purposes of determining whether an item is less than $110. However, store coupons (for which the store receives no reimbursement) do reduce the selling price for purposes of determining whether an items is less than $110.

Local exemptions: Any county or city in New York is authorized to enact the sales tax exemption for clothing and footwear costing less than $110 or to adopt the state's revised exemption schedule. For a complete listing of local exemptions, see *Publication 718-C*, New York Department of Taxation and Finance, CCH New York Tax Reports, ¶65-908.

¶2102

The New York City exemption for clothing and footwear is the same as the statewide exemption. For details and New York City rates, see ¶3301.

Special reporting requirements: Vendors who make sales of exempt clothing, footwear, and items used to make or repair exempt clothing must file Schedule H to report those sales. All sales of these items must be separately reported on Schedule H for the locality in which the sales were made. Sales of exempt clothing, footwear, and items used to make or repair exempt clothing must be reported, by locality, whether they are subject to local tax or are exempt from both state and local taxes (*TSB-M-06(6)S*, March 29, 2006, CCH NEW YORK TAX REPORTS, ¶300-506).

CCH Advisory: Yard Goods and Clothing Components

The exemption for clothing costing less than $110 also applies to each item of fabric, thread, yarn, buttons, and the like that become a part of exempt clothing (*TSB-M-00(1)S*, January 24, 2000, CCH NEW YORK TAX REPORTS, ¶300-312). When fabric is purchased by the yard, the exemption is based on the total cost of fabric purchased as a single item, not the cost per yard. Therefore, a single-item purchase of five yards of a $50 per yard fabric does not qualify for the exemption, because the total cost of the purchase exceeds $110 (*Hoffman (Advisory Opinion)*, TSB-A-01(10)S, April 12, 2001, CCH NEW YORK TAX REPORTS, ¶403-929).

• *Computers and software*

Computer software, generally taxable, is exempt if designed and developed to the specifications of a specific purchaser, and transferred, directly or indirectly, by the purchaser to a corporation that is a member of an affiliated group or to a partnership in which the purchaser and other members of the affiliated group have at least a 50% capital or profits interest, provided that the transfer is not in pursuance of a plan having tax avoidance or evasion as its principal purpose. The exemption does not apply to pre-written computer software that is available for sale to customers in the ordinary course of the seller's business. Prewritten software that is modified or enhanced to meet the specifications of individual purchasers is also taxable, except to the extent the charges for the modification are reasonable and separately stated on the customer's invoice (Sec. 1101(b)(14), Tax Law; see also *TB-ST-128*, August 5, 2014, CCH NEW YORK TAX REPORTS, ¶408-177).

Practitioner Comment: Occasional Sales

Two isolated sales of customized software did not necessarily result in a conclusion that the software was offered for sale in the regular course of the seller's business. As a result, the use of the software was not subject to tax (*ITG, Inc.*, TSB-A-01(6)S, CCH NEW YORK TAX REPORTS, ¶403-885).

Mark S. Klein, Esq., Hodgson Russ LLP

Computer hardware: Computer system hardware that is used or consumed directly and predominantly in designing and developing computer software for sale is exempt (Sec. 1115(a)(35), Tax Law), as is computer system hardware used in an Internet data center (see below). The exemption applies to purchases, leases, and rentals of such hardware. In addition, hardware used in providing the service, for sale, of designing and developing Internet websites is also exempt from sales and use tax (Sec. 1115(a)(35), Tax Law; *TB-ST-243*, August 7, 2014, CCH NEW YORK TAX REPORTS, ¶408-180).

Software services: Charges for services provided to a customer in connection with the sale of computer software are exempt, provided such charges are reasonable and are separately stated on an invoice or other statement of the price given to the purchaser (Sec. 1115(o), Tax Law). If the software maintenance charge involves a prewritten software upgrade, the charge is subject to tax.

The service of designing and developing web pages is exempt.

Internet access: Charges for internet access are not services enumerated in the New York Tax Law and, thus, are not subject to state and local sales tax. Communications/navigation software, e-mail privileges, news headlines, and certain webpage services furnished as part of a combined Internet access service are incidental to the provision of Internet access, and the charge is not subject to tax. See *TSB-M-97(1)C and TSB-M-97(1)S,* CCH NEW YORK TAX REPORTS, ¶ 300-224. For additional information, see ¶ 2006.

Practitioner Comment: Sales Tax on Bundled Services

Providers of computer and Internet access facilities need to be aware of New York's "cheeseboard" rule, which imposes tax on the total amount of a transaction composed of taxable and exempt items if the items are sold as a single unit. (20 NYCRR § 527.1(b)). As a result, the provider of an Internet café must separately identify the charges attributable to exempt items (Internet access) and taxable activities (e.g., access to Microsoft Office programs). Failure to separately state the cost of the components will cause the entire charge to be subject to tax *(Icor Systems,* TSB-A-08(47)S, October 16, 2008, CCH NEW YORK TAX REPORTS, ¶ 406-195).

Mark S. Klein, Hodgson Russ LLP

Internet data centers: An exemption applies for machinery, equipment, and other tangible personal property purchased by the operator of an Internet data center located in New York when such property is to be placed or installed in an Internet data center and is directly related to the provision of Internet webpage services for sale by the operator of the center (Sec. 1115(a)(37), Tax Law; Sec. 1115(y), Tax Law).

In addition, property purchased by contractors for incorporation into the real property of the Internet data center is also exempt. Further, repair and maintenance services rendered to the exempt property is exempt from sales and use tax whether such property retains its character as tangible personal property or becomes a capital improvement to the Internet data center.

Exempt tangible personal property includes computer system hardware, such as servers or routers; prewritten computer software, storage racks, and cages for computer equipment; property relating to building systems designed for an Internet data center, such as interior fiber optic and copper cables; property necessary to maintain the proper temperature environment, such as air filtration, air conditioning equipment, and vapor batteries; property related to fire control, power generators, protective batteries; property that, when installed, constitutes raised flooring; and property related to providing security to the center.

An Internet data center must be specifically designed and constructed to provide a high security environment for the location of services and similar equipment on which Internet webpages reside.

• *Contractors*

Capital improvements to property: The installation of property that becomes an addition or capital improvement to real property, property, or land (as defined in the Real Property Tax Law) when installed is exempt (Sec. 1115(a)(17)l, Tax Law; see also Sec. 1109(b)(9), Tax Law; *TB-ST-113,* August 7, 2014, CCH NEW YORK TAX REPORTS, ¶ 408-175). A contractor making capital improvements to realty should receive a "Certificate of Capital Improvement" from the owner of the property.

CCH Advisory: Capital Improvements

A corporation's installation of various kinds of signage, including monument signs, pylon signs, and illuminated electric letters or signs, generally does not result in a capital improvement exempt from New York sales tax under Sec. 1101(b)(9), Tax Law. However, monument signs may be exempt capital improvements if they are installed by imbedding them in a concrete foundation, rather than merely bolting them onto a base. In the case of sign installations by tenants, the terms of the lease may determine the capital improvement status of the installation. It is immaterial whether the sign installations are done in conjunction with new construction or remodeling of the real property. Charges, whether or not separately stated, for engineering sealed drawings, freight and delivery, crating, final electrical hookups, removals with sign installation to follow, land surveys in conjunction with signs, trenching and boring (including conduit), other materials (i.e. fascia panels, electrical components, ballasts, and lamps), and permits required to be obtained by a contractor are considered expenses incurred by the taxpayer in making its sale and installation of the signage. If such installation constitutes a capital improvement to real property, the entire charge is not subject to sales tax. If, however, the installation does not qualify as a capital improvement, the total charge to the customer, including the taxpayer's costs for these services and miscellaneous items, is subject to sales tax. (*TSB-A-08(26)S*, June 9, 2008, CCH NEW YORK TAX REPORTS, ¶ 406-091)

An exemption is also provided for tangible personal property sold by a contractor, subcontractor, or repairman to a nonexempt organization for which the contractor, subcontractor, or repairman is making a capital improvement to real property, provided that the property sold by the contractor, subcontractor, or repairman becomes a capital improvement to the real property (Sec. 1115(a)(17), Tax Law). In that event, the contractor, subcontractor or repairman is treated as the consumer of the tangible personal property and must pay tax on the initial purchase of the property. Sales of tangible personal property to a contractor, subcontractor, or repairman for use in erecting a structure or building of an exempt organization, adding to, altering, or improving real property of such an organization or maintaining, servicing, or repairing real property are exempt, provided that the property is to become an integral component part of the structure or real property.

Sale and installation of an emergency home generator as a backup system in the event of power failures qualifies as a capital improvement under Tax Law Sec. 1101(b)(9)(i). (*TSB-A-06(18)S*, New York Commissioner of Taxation and Finance, June 26, 2006, CCH NEW YORK TAX REPORTS, ¶ 405-418)

Temporary facilities (scaffolding services): When provided in connection with a capital improvement project, a scaffolding service is one of the services covered by the exclusion from sales tax described in Reg. Sec. 541.8(a). As a result, amounts charged by a subcontractor for scaffolding services qualify as charges for a "temporary facility" that are not subject to sales tax, provided that the underlying construction project qualifies as a capital improvement and is supported by the issuance of a valid Form ST-124, *Certificate of Capital Improvement*. Both lump sum and separately stated contracts are treated the same for sales tax purposes. The subcontractor is, however, liable for the payment of sales tax on its own purchases or rentals of materials acquired to provide the scaffolding service because these purchases and rentals do not qualify as purchases for resale. The subcontractor or repairman must charge sales tax to the prime contractor on the complete lump sum charged for the scaffolding service or, alternatively, on all of the separately stated charges including dismantling of the scaffolding system. Moreover, the purchase of the scaffolding service by the prime contractor does not qualify as a purchase for resale, because the prime contractor is using the service for its own purposes and will not be reselling it.

Scaffolding materials purchased by a person exclusively for the purpose of reselling or renting them to others (*i.e.*, without the lessor providing any accompanying services), the scaffolding materials may be purchased for resale without payment of sales tax. (*TSB-M-14(15)S*, New York Department of Taxation and Finance, October 23, 2014, CCH NEW YORK TAX REPORTS, ¶ 408-252)

Practitioner Comment: Construction Services

Services not normally considered capital improvements (*e.g.*, debris removal, painting, interior cleaning) can nonetheless qualify for the exemption if the end result of the service is a capital improvement to real property (NY Reg. Sec. 527.7(b)(4); *Imowitz Koenig LLP*, TSB-A-02(60)S, CCH NEW YORK TAX REPORTS, ¶404-414; and *Hilton Hotels Corp.*, TSB-A-02(9)S, CCH NEW YORK TAX REPORTS, ¶404-201).

Mark S. Klein, Esq., Hodgson Russ LLP

• *Energy*

Residential heating and energy sources: The New York State sales and use tax is not imposed on retail sales of specified energy sources when used for residential purposes (See ¶2022). Cities and counties, except for counties wholly contained within a city, may also exempt such sales and uses. For further discussion see ¶2106.

Natural gas from well on property: An exemption is provided for natural gas used for personal residence consumption by a landowner from, or provided in exchange for gas from, a natural gas well located on such land owner's property, when the gas has been set aside for the land owner's use by lease (Sec. 1115(a)(25), Tax Law).

Energy distributed to cooperative corporation tenants: Sales of electricity, steam, and refrigeration (utilities) and electric, steam, and refrigeration services that are metered and generated or produced by a cogeneration facility owned or operated by certain cooperative corporations are exempt from New York sales and compensating use taxes (Sec. 1115(b)(iii), Tax Law). In order to qualify, the cooperative corporation must have at least 1,500 apartments and the energy or energy services must be distributed to the tenants or occupants of such cooperative corporations (Sec. 1115(b)(iii), Tax Law).

Wood pellets: It is the Department's position that wood pellets and other compressed wood products designed to be used in a stove or fireplace used for residential heating purposes constitute wood for purposes of Sec. 1105-A, Tax Law. Accordingly, purchases of these products for residential heating purposes are exempt from sales tax (*TSB-M-07(3)S*, May 16, 2007, CCH NEW YORK TAX REPORTS, ¶405-728).

Commercial fuel cell electricity generating systems equipment and sales of generated energy: Effective June 1, 2016, an exemption is provided for commercial fuel cell electricity generating systems equipment and the service of installing and maintaining such systems. "Fuel cell electricity generating systems equipment" means an electric generating arrangement or combination of components installed upon non-residential premises that utilize solid oxide, molten carbonate, proton exchange membrane or phosphoric acid fuel cell, or linear generator. (Sec. 1115(kk)(1), Tax Law)

Also effective June 1, 2016, an exemption is provided for the sale of hydrogen gas or electricity by a person primarily engaged in the sale of fuel cell electricity generating system equipment and/or electricity generated by such equipment pursuant to written agreement under which the electricity is generated by commercial fuel cell electricity generating system equipment that is: (Sec. 1115(kk)(2), Tax Law)

(1) owned by a person other than the purchaser of such electricity;

(2) installed on the non-residential premises of the purchaser of such electricity;

(3) placed in service; and

(4) used to provide heating, cooling, hot water or electricity to such premises.

For additional information, see *Publication 718-FC*, New York Department of Taxation and Finance, May 2016, CCH NEW YORK TAX REPORTS, ¶408-752.

¶2102

• *Food and beverages*

Food, food products, beverages (including vegetable juices, iced tea mix and fruit juices containing at least 70% natural fruit juice), dietary foods, and health supplements sold for human consumption are exempt when sold by a retail food store (Sec. 1115(a)(1), Tax Law). The exemption does *not* apply to (1) candy and confectionery, (2) fruit drinks containing less than 70% of natural fruit juice, (3) soft drinks, sodas, and beverages (other than coffee, tea, and cocoa) of the kind ordinarily dispensed at soda fountains, (4) prepared or heated foods, and (5) beer, wine, or other alcoholic beverages. In addition, the exemption does *not* apply to food served by restaurants or caterers. (See ¶2008) However, food and drink sold to an airline for consumption in flight are exempt, as are certain meals sold to students (Sec. 1105(d)(ii), Tax Law).

Sales of unprepared food or drink for off-premises consumption that are sold in an unheated state and of a type commonly sold for off-premises consumption in the same form and condition in food stores not principally engaged in selling foods prepared and ready to be eaten are exempt (Sec. 1105(d)(i), Tax Law). This exemption applies to all food sold through a vending machine that is exempt when sold at a retail food store and all heated beverages sold through vending machines.

A comprehensive list of exempt food and beverages has been issued; see *TB-ST-525*, New York Department of Taxation and Finance, April 13, 2011, CCH New York Tax Reports, ¶407-202, also available at **http://www.tax.ny.gov/pubs_and_bulls/tg_bulletins/st/listings_of_taxable_and_exempt_food.htm**.

Practitioner Comment: Candy or Food?

New York's sales tax rules have been subject to significant ridicule for imposing tax on jumbo marshmallows (as candy) while exempting miniature marshmallows (as cooking ingredients). And while the Tax Department eliminated this distinction by exempting all marshmallows from tax. (Reg. Sec. 528.2(a)(4).) Many observers are still waiting for the Tax Department to address some of the law's other interesting distinctions (*e.g.,* Twix, the chocolate, caramel cookie, is exempt from tax if it is sold from a supermarket's cookie aisle, but taxable if it is purchased from the candy shelves) (*TSB-A-93(38)S,* CCH New York Tax Reports, ¶401-196).

Mark S. Klein, Esq., Hodgson Russ LLP

Food or drink sold by senior citizen independent housing community: Sales tax does not apply to receipts from sales of food or drink (other than beer, wine, or other alcoholic beverages) by a senior citizen independent housing community to residents or guests of residents for consumption on the premises of the community. A senior citizen is a person who is at least 55 years old. The food or drink must be served in the residents' rooms or in the community's dining facility that is not open to the public. The exemption does not apply to food or drink sold through vending machines (Sec. 1115(w), Tax Law).

Dietary supplements: A company's receipts from the sales of products that it markets and distributes as dietary supplements in the form of ready-to-drink beverages, liquid concentrates, powdered drink mixes, and chews were exempt from state and local sales and use taxes because the products were dietary foods and health supplements. As required by sales and use tax regulations, the labels of the taxpayer's products highlight their dietary properties (*i.e.,* their antioxidant effect) and that they are intended to increase the user's energy. The fact that they also supplement the ordinary diet or substitute for natural foods is evident from the products' ingredients and the supplement facts chart that illustrates how the products support nutritional needs by meeting or exceeding the daily requirements for many vitamins considered essential for good health. When sold for human consumption, as the taxpayer's products are, these products are exempt from state and local sales and use taxes. (*TSB-A-11(4)S,* New York Commissioner of Taxation and Finance, February 18, 2011, CCH New York Tax Reports, ¶407-143)

Food stamps: Receipts from the sale of certain otherwise taxable foods (such as candy, soft drinks, cold sandwiches, bottled water and ice) that are eligible to be purchased with coupons issued pursuant to the Federal Food Stamp Act of 1977 from retail food stores and other approved participants are exempt, when the food is purchased with such coupons (Sec. 1115(k), Tax Law).

Water: Water when delivered to the consumer through mains or pipes is exempt (Sec. 1115(a)(2), Tax Law). However, bottled water and water sold as ice are taxable (Reg. Sec. 528.11(c)(4)(i); Reg. Sec. 528.3(c)).

Wine: Wine or wine products furnished by the official agent of a farm winery, winery, wholesaler, or importer at a wine tasting to a customer or prospective customer who consumes the wine at the tasting is not subject to sales and use taxation (Sec. 1115(a)(33), Tax Law).

Effective June 1, 2015, the wine tasting exemption is extended to include other alcoholic beverages (*i.e.,* liquor, beer or cider) and items used to package such beverages (*i.e.,* bottles, corks, caps, and labels). Also, the bill makes technical corrections to clarify that the exemption applies to tastings held off the premises of an alcoholic beverage producer. Charges for admission to tour the facilities of an alcoholic beverage producer are not taxable. (Sec. 1118(13), Tax Law; *TSB-M-15(1)S,* July 24, 2015, CCH New York Tax Reports, ¶ 408-481; *TB-ST-15,* August 10, 2015, CCH New York Tax Reports, ¶ 408-507)

• *Manufacturing*

For exemption of machinery and equipment and of fuel and utilities used in manufacturing, processing, mining, farming, etc., see ¶ 2105 and ¶ 2106.

• *Medicines, medical equipment, and prosthetic aids*

Drugs and medicines intended for use in the cure, mitigation, treatment, or prevention of illnesses or diseases in human beings and products consumed by humans for the preservation of health (other than cosmetics or toiletry articles) are exempt (Sec. 1115(a)(3), Tax Law). There is no requirement that the drugs and medicines be on prescription. The exemption does not apply to cosmetics and toilet articles, even if containing medicinal ingredients. A number of items previously identified as subject to sales tax are reclassified as exempt medical equipment or as exempt prosthetic aids, effective for sales made or services rendered on or after July 1, 2014 (*TSB-M-14(8)S,* May 27, 2014, CCH New York Tax Reports, ¶ 408-101). *Publication 840,* CCH New York Tax Reports, ¶ 65-950 (issued before reclassification) contains a list of the tax status of a variety of over-the-counter products containing drugs and medicines.

Medical equipment (including component parts thereof) and supplies are exempt (unless purchased at retail for use in performing medical and similar services for compensation) (Sec. 1115(a)(3), Tax Law). Services performed on exempt equipment are also exempt (Sec. 1115(g), Tax Law).

A comprehensive list of exempt medical equipment and supplies, prosthetic devices and similar items can be found in *Publication 822,* CCH New York Tax Reports, ¶ 65-945; see also *TB-ST-193,* August 5, 2014, CCH New York Tax Reports, ¶ 408-179.

Practitioner Comment: Medical Equipment and Supplies

Physicians and other providers of medical services must pay sales tax on all of the equipment and supplies used or consumed in the practice of medicine (such as stethoscopes, bandages, etc.). This includes the purchase, lease or rental of medical equipment (Reg. Sec. 528.4(h); TSB-A-13(21)S, July 19, 2013; CCH New York Tax Reports, ¶ 407-889).

Mark S. Klein, Esq., Hodgson Russ LLP

Oxygen: Medical oxygen and nitrous oxide are exempt from sales and use tax. Oxygen provided in connection with furnishing oxygen therapy services is exempt from tax. In addition, medical equipment used to dispense oxygen (i.e. regulators, humidifies, ring stands, etc.) is exempt from tax (Reg. Sec. 528.4).

Insulin: Insulin packaged with disposable syringes is exempt (Reg. Sec. 528.4).

Blood and plasma: Blood and its derivatives are exempt from tax (Reg. Sec. 528.4).

Hearing aids, eyeglasses, and other physical aids: Prosthetic aids, hearing aids, eyeglasses, and artificial devices (including component parts) purchased to correct or alleviate physical incapacity in human beings are exempt (Sec. 1115(a)(4), Tax Law). Services performed on these items are also exempt.

Medical marijuana (cannabis): The sale of medical marijuana and sales of related products purchased to administer medical marijuana are exempt from sales tax. However, a registered organization must register as a vendor in order to issue and accept certain sales tax exemption certificates. (*TSB-M-16(1)M,* New York Department of Taxation and Finance, January 7, 2016, CCH NEW YORK TAX REPORTS, ¶ 408-610)

CCH Advisory: Telecommunications Devices

Receipts from sales of telecommunication devices, television decoders, telephone amplifiers, telephone answering machines, and assistive listening devices for persons with disabilities were exempt from sales and use tax because the items qualified as prosthetic aids or artificial devices for persons with physical, hearing, and sight impairments. Sales of clocks, hotel guest room kits containing devices required by the Americans with Disabilities Act, and signaling devices were also exempt because they were primarily and customarily used for conveying some form of notice or warning to persons with hearing or sight impairments. Accessories that were clearly identifiable as replacement parts for exempt prosthetic aids and devices were exempt, but supplies such as carrying cases and printer paper used in conjunction with prosthetic aids and devices were not exempt.

Repair services performed on exempt prosthetic aids and devices were also exempt. Expense items, such as gas, meals, and lodging, incurred by the taxpayer in the performance of repair services on exempt prosthetic aids and devices were exempt only if the taxpayer qualified as an exempt organization or made purchases as agent for an exempt organization (*TSB-A-99(11)S,* March 1, 1999, CCH NEW YORK TAX REPORTS, ¶ 403-337).

Dental prosthetics: Prosthetic dental devices (including their component parts, but not related supplies) that completely or partially replace missing teeth or the functions of permanently inoperative or permanently malfunctioning teeth are prosthetic devices exempt from sales and use tax. These prosthetic dental devices include implants, dentures, bridges, full and partial crowns (both temporary and permanent), onlays, and inlays. Prosthetic dental devices do not include any products that are not primarily and customarily used for such purposes and that are generally useful in the absence of illness, injury, or physical incapacity. This includes products that are cosmetic in nature, such as laminate veneers, decorative caps, and specialty or jewelry teeth. For additional information, see *TSB-M-06(5)S,* March 20, 2006, CCH NEW YORK TAX REPORTS, ¶ 300-505.

Veterinarians: Services by veterinarians constituting the practice of veterinary medicine, including hospitalization for which no separate boarding charge is made, are exempt (Sec. 1115(f), Tax Law; *TB-ST-930,* New York Department of Taxation and Finance, July 27, 2012, CCH NEW YORK TAX REPORTS, ¶ 407-617). Other nonmedical services to pets and other animals including, but not limited to, boarding, grooming, and clipping are taxable. Special rules apply to certain race horses (see below).

Sales by a veterinarian of articles of tangible personal property designed for use in some manner relating to domestic animals or poultry (for example, collars, flea spray, medicine) are exempt. However, all purchases of such tangible personal property by a veterinarian are taxable.

¶2102

Guide, hearing, and service dogs: The sale or use of any goods or services necessary for the acquisition, sustenance, or maintenance of a guide dog, a hearing dog, or a service dog are exempt from tax (Sec. 1115(s), Tax Law). The guide, hearing, or service dog must be used by a person with a disability, as defined in New York Executive Law Sec. 292(21), to compensate for an impairment to his or her sight, hearing, or movement. Those eligible to claim the exemption are persons with a disability who use a guide dog, hearing dog, or service dog to do work or perform tasks for the person with respect to the disability and for which the dog is trained and an individual whose dependent is a person with a disability. People who have been given express authority by an eligible person to make purchases on the eligible person's behalf may also claim the exemption.

• *Miscellaneous exemptions*

Bullion: Retail sales of precious metal bullion sold for investment are exempt, provided that all required provisions for retailer registration are met, and that the consideration for the bullion is dependent only upon the value of its metal content (Sec. 1115(a)(27), Tax Law). The exemption applies to bars, ingots, and coins of gold, silver, platinum, palladium, rhodium, ruthenium, or iridium.

Precious metal bullion is deemed to be sold for investment if it is sold for more than $1,000 and the purchaser, user, or agent holds the bullion in the same form and does not manufacture, process, assemble, or fabricate it for its own use. The consideration for the bullion depends only on the value of the metal content if the consideration does not exceed a specified percentage of the greater of the daily closing bullion cash price of the metal in the open market or the coin's face value at prevailing rates of exchange. The applicable percentages are 140% for silver coins, 120% for gold coins of $1/4$ ounces or less, and 115% for other coins. For bars and ingots, the consideration may not be in excess of 115% of the bullion cash price of the metal. The average of the bid and asked prices is used when there is no closing price for the metal (Sec. 1115(a)(27), Tax Law).

Donated property: Tangible personal property manufactured, processed, or assembled and donated by the manufacturer, processor, or assembler to an exempt organization is exempt, provided that the manufacturer, processor, or assembler offers the same kind of property for sale in the regular course of business and makes no other use of the donated property. No refund or credit is allowed for sales and use taxes properly paid (Sec. 1115(l), Tax Law).

Practitioner Comment: Special Rules for Donated Property

The sales tax exemption for tangible personal property donated to an exempt organization is limited to property donated by a manufacturer, processor or assembler. A retailer that takes property out of inventory and donates it to a charity is subject to use tax on the original cost of the donated inventory. Similarly, artwork acquired by a New York resident and immediately loaned to an exempt art gallery is nonetheless subject to tax on the full purchase price.

Mark S. Klein, Hodgson Russ LLP

Feminine hygiene products: Effective September 1, 2016, feminine hygiene products, including but not limited to, sanitary napkins, tampons and panty liners are exempt from New York state and local sales and use taxes. (Sec 1115(a)(3-a), Tax Law; *TSB-M-16(6)S*, New York Department of Taxation and Finance, August 1, 2016, CCH NEW YORK TAX REPORTS, ¶ 408-820)

Film production: An exemption applies to tangible personal property used or consumed directly and predominantly in the production, including editing, dubbing, and mixing, of a film for sale, regardless of the medium used to convey the film to a purchaser (Sec. 1105-B(a), Tax Law; *TB-ST-276*, New York Department of Taxation and Finance, July 26, 2012, CCH New York Tax Reports, ¶407-615). For purposes of the exemption, "film" means feature films, documentary films, shorts, television films, television commercials, and similar productions. Also exempt are the services of producing, fabricating, processing, printing, imprinting, installing, maintaining, servicing, or repairing such property, as well as fuel, gas, electricity, refrigeration, or steam and related service used or consumed directly and exclusively in the production of a film for sale.

Flags: Sales of the United States and New York State flags are exempt, as are military service flags, such as blue star and gold star banners, and prisoner of war flags. (Sec. 1115(a)(11), Tax Law; *TSB-M-12(13)S*, November 27, 2012, CCH New York Tax Reports, ¶407-711). However, sales of confederate flags, colonial flags, historic flags, flag patches, pins, or decals are subject to tax. In addition, when an exempt flag is sold as part of a package that includes items related to display of the flag (such as a pole and bracket, halyard, lanyard, or finial), or is sold attached to a rod, staff, or pole, the entire sale is exempt from tax.

Furnishing information individual in nature: The furnishing of information that is personal or individual in nature and that is not or may not be substantially incorporated in reports furnished to other persons is exempt. Noncustomized information is subject to tax regardless of the method of delivery (by mail, fax, on-line access, etc.) (Reg. Sec. 531.1(b)(3)).

Practitioner Comment: Online Access to Personalized Information May Be Recharacterized

Although access to personalized online data is exempt from tax, New York auditors have been aggressively scrutinizing online sales of data processing services to see if the services can be characterized as a taxable license to use remote-based software. See *National Football League, TSB-A 09(37)S*, August 25, 2009, CCH New York Tax Reports, ¶406-523, where an on-line payroll service was treated as a taxable license to use payroll software, and *TSB-A-09(2)S*, January 29, 2009, CCH New York Tax Reports, ¶406-313, where an online e-learning course was subject to tax because the customer's access was characterized as a license fee for software.

Mark S. Klein, Esq., Hodgson Russ LLP

Medical emergency response services: Receipts from sales of alarm call services designed specifically to respond to medical emergencies are exempt from sales and compensating use taxes (Sec. 1115(r), Tax Law).

Meteorological services: Meteorological services are exempt from New York's sales and use taxes (Sec. 1105(c)(1), Tax Law). Exempt meteorological services include providing reports of weather conditions, providing weather forecasts and providing records of past weather history. The exemption applies to all forms of delivery (*e.g.*, printed on paper, provided by fax or telephone, accessed on-line, etc.). For more information, see *TSB-M-95(11)S*, CCH New York Tax Reports, ¶300-168.

Military decorations and patriotic items: Purchases of military decorations (*e.g.*, ribbons, medals, mini-medals, and lapel pins) by a veteran or active member of the United States military are exempt. The purchaser must show proof of his or her status in the form of discharge papers or other official documentation of actual military service (Sec. 1115(a)(11-a), Tax Law).

Purchases of military service flags, prisoner of war flags, and blue star banners are also exempt from sales tax (Sec. 1115(a)(11-b), Tax Law).

Morticians, undertakers, and funeral directors: Tangible personal property sold by morticians, undertakers, and funeral directors is exempt. The sale of a grave site, cemetery lot or burial right constitutes the sale of an interest in real property, and is, therefore, tax-exempt (Reg. Sec. 528.8(d)). However, sales to such persons of property for use in conducting funerals are specifically excluded from the resale exemption and are taxable. A funeral director's lease of a vehicle for use during funerals is also subject to tax (Sec. 1115(a)(7), Tax Law; Reg. Sec. 528.8(a)).

College textbooks: College textbooks purchased by full or part-time college students are exempt from New York State sales and use taxes (Sec. 1115(a)(34), Tax Law). In order to qualify for the exemption, the students must be enrolled at an institution of higher education, and the textbooks must be required or recommended for the student's course, either by the instructor or the institution. The exemption applies whether the books are printed, on CD-ROM, or on floppy disc, and whether purchased from a bookseller, through the Internet, from a mail-order service, or by other available means (Sec. 1115(a)(34), Tax Law). For additional information, see *TSB-M-98(4)S*, June 5, 1998, CCH NEW YORK TAX REPORTS, ¶300-253.

Theatrical productions: A state sales tax exemption similar to an existing New York City sales tax exemption (¶3301) is provided for tangible personal property and services used to produce live public theatrical and musical performances in a theater or similar place of assembly with a seating capacity of 100 or more anchored chairs, with at least five performances per week for a period of at least two consecutive weeks, and with the content of each performance being the same (Reg. Sec. 527.10(d)(2)). See also ¶2110.

Veterans' home gift shops: Retail sales of tangible personal property by any gift shop located in a veteran's home are exempt (Sec. 1115(ff), Tax Law).

• *Newspapers and periodicals; electronic publications*

Sales of newspapers and periodicals are exempt (Sec. 1115(a)(5), Tax Law; Sec. 1118(5), Tax Law; Reg. Sec. 528.6). Also exempt are advertising supplements when distributed as inserts in a newspaper or periodical. In addition, the use of ink and paper in the publication of newspapers and periodicals are exempt from the use tax. Purchases of tangible personal property which become a physical component part of newspapers or periodicals are made for resale and, therefore, are not subject to tax. (¶2104). Publications distributed free of charge are not excluded from qualifying as "newspapers".

Shopping papers (pennysavers): Sales of shopping papers (so-called pennysavers) to the publisher for distribution to the public without consideration are exempt. Advertisements in a qualified pennysaver may not exceed 90% of the available space in the issue. The determination of whether advertisements exceed 90% of the printed area of a shopping paper is made by averaging all issues on an annual basis. Printing services performed in publishing pennysavers are exempt. An exemption is also provided for sales of paper, ink, and other tangible personal property that become a physical component of a shopping paper (Sec. 1115(a)(20), Tax Law; Sec. 1115(i)(A), Tax Law). In addition, materials (such as paper, ink and other tangible personal property) purchased for use in connection with the publication of a shopping paper, and which are to become a physical component part of the paper, are exempt from sales and compensating use taxes (Sec. 1115(a)(20)).

Electronic publications: An exemption is provided for electronically delivered newspapers and electronic periodicals (Sec. 1101(b)(6), Tax Law). To qualify for the exemption, the newspaper or periodical must be shipped or delivered by a vendor to a purchaser by means of telephony, telegraphy, or other electronic media, and the subscription or sales price must be separately stated, including any charge by the vendor for shipping or delivery to the purchaser. Also, for the exemption to apply, the entire publication must be delivered, but no additional material not available in the printed edition, other than advertising, may be included in the electronic delivery. Additionally, in order to qualify as an exempt newspaper or periodical, the publication must be available in hard copy. Newspapers and periodicals available exclusively on-line are not exempt from tax (*TSB-A-03(13)S*, CCH NEW YORK TAX REPORTS, ¶404-508).

An "electronic news service" is defined as a service that is delivered or accessed electronically and that meets specified criteria. The service's predominant purpose must be the presentation of news content, which it must prominently feature (Sec. 1101(b)(37)(i)(A), Tax Law). "News content" is defined as the articles, photographs, and video and audio material concerning general news or specialized news and does not include listings, advertisements, catalogs, compilations, databases, or the like, while "non-news content" is defined to mean any information other than news content.

Electronic news services that do not exceed a subscription price cap are exempt (Sec. 1115(gg)(1), Tax Law). The cap amount for the exemption is 300% of the annualized average daily newsstand price of the three newspapers with the largest total paid national daily circulation (Sec. 1101(b)(37)(ii)(F), Tax Law). From June 1, 2016, to May 31, 2017, the cap amount is $2,920, unchanged from the previous period (*Important Notice N-16-3*, New York Department of Taxation and Finance, March 2016, CCH NEW YORK TAX REPORTS, ¶408-684).

In line with the idea that delivery of news content is the key feature of an exempt electronic news service, the service's news content must include general news that is accessible without the use of a search function and is newly published or updated at least daily unless the service specifies some other interval; provided, however, that the news content must be newly updated or published within a 24-hour period that precedes or immediately follows a time when the non-news content is newly published or updated. If the service features a search function at no extra charge that allows access to content other than the service's past or present news content, the service will only qualify as an electronic news service if the provider can prove that the search function is only an incidental part of the service. To qualify as an electronic news service, the service must not in whole or in substantial part constitute a listing, catalog, database, or compilation. (Sec. 1101(b)(37)(ii)(G), Tax Law)

Electronic periodicals are also exempt (Sec. 1115(gg)(2), Tax Law). An "electronic periodical" is a publication that is delivered or accessed electronically and that meets specified criteria (Sec. 1101(b)(38), Tax Law). The predominant purpose must be the presentation of news content, which it must prominently feature (Sec. 1101(b)(38)(i)(A), Tax Law). An electronic periodical may not be published more frequently than weekly and cannot be updated between issues, although the incidental addition of news content between issues would not prevent a publication from being an electronic periodical (Sec. 1101(b)(38)(i)(B), Tax Law). Because of the lesser flexibility of the exemption for electronic periodicals, those publications need not meet any subscription price cap to qualify for exemption.

• *Packaging*

Cartons, containers, wrapping and packaging materials and supplies: Cartons, containers, wrapping and packaging materials and supplies, and components thereof, for use and consumption by a vendor in packaging or packing tangible personal property for sale and which are actually transferred by the vendor to the purchaser are exempt (Sec. 1115(19), Tax Law; Reg. Sec. 528.20(a)(1)). In order to qualify for the exemption, however, the purchaser cannot have any contractual or legal obligation to return the packaging materials. Further details are provided by regulation (CCH NEW YORK TAX REPORTS, ¶65-229). See also *TB-ST-107*, August 5, 2014, CCH NEW YORK TAX REPORTS, ¶408-174. For a decision concerning intracompany transactions, see TSB-A-08(60)S, October 15, 2008, CCH NEW YORK TAX REPORTS, ¶406-275.

Cups, plates, food wrappers, and other containers purchased by restaurant vendors and actually transferred to the purchaser of such food or drink are exempt as sales for resale (Reg. Sec. 528.20(d)(1)). This exemption is limited to the "critical elements" of a fast-food purchase and does not apply to a restaurant's purchases of incidental property such as napkins, stirrers, eating utensils or straws *Celestial Food of Massapequa Corp. v. NYS Tax Commissioner*, 63 NY2d 1020, CCH NEW YORK TAX REPORTS, ¶ 251-149.

Practitioner Comment: Returnable Packaging

A customer's agreement to return shipping pallets precluded the distributor's ability to take a sales tax exemption for the pallets as either packaging materials or as items purchased for resale. Instead, New York's Tax Appeals Tribunal held that the pallets were "used" by the distributor (*Genesee Brewing Company, Inc.*, TAT (5/9/02), CCH NEW YORK TAX REPORTS, ¶ 404-181). According to the Tribunal, any customer agreement to return the packaging materials precluded a determination that the property was "actually transferred" to the customer (*Upstate Farms Cooperative*, TAT (5/2/02), CCH NEW YORK TAX REPORTS, ¶ 404-166). Soft drink bottlers, however, can purchase bottles for resale. In *Nehi Bottling Co. v. Gallman*, 333 NYS2d 824 (3d Dep't. 1972), aff'd. 34 NY2d 808 (1974), CCH NEW YORK TAX REPORTS, ¶ 403-758, the Court held that "so long as there is no evidence of an agreement and the party is under no legal obligation to return them, he having the right to retain them if he chooses to leave the money deposited as a payment for the bottles, amounts in law to a sale . . . ."

Mark S. Klein, Esq., Hodgson Russ LLP

• *Racehorses*

Receipts from the sale of certain racehorses are exempt from tax. For the purpose of the exemption, a "racehorse" includes only thoroughbred, standardbred, and quarter horses.

A racehorse may be purchased exempt from state and local sales taxes if it meets both of the following tests (Sec. 1118(3), Tax Law):

> — it is registered with the Jockey Club, the United States Trotting Association, or the National Steeplechase and Hunt Association (a horse purchased during the first 24 months of its life may qualify if it is eligible to be registered); and

> — it is purchased with the *intent* that it will be entered in an event on which pari-mutuel wagering is authorized by law.

The exemption does not apply to the purchase of any horse that is considered to be at least four years old and has never raced in an event on which pari-mutuel wagering is authorized by law.

Racehorses purchased outside New York and brought into this state are not subject to the compensating use tax if the purchase otherwise qualified for exemption (Sec. 1118(3), Tax Law).

For additional information, see *TB-ST-757*, August 7, 2014, CCH NEW YORK TAX REPORTS, ¶ 408-186.

Racehorse training services: The services of training and maintaining a racehorse to race in a race or race meeting held, maintained, or conducted according to the racing, pari-mutuel wagering, and breeding law, are exempt when rendered by a trainer to the owner of the racehorse (Sec. 1115(m)(1), Tax Law). Tangible personal property actually transferred by a trainer to the racehorse owner in conjunction with the rendering of exempt training services is also exempt. However, the initial purchase of such property by the trainer does not qualify for the resale exemption.

- *Services*

Services on property delivered outside New York for use outside New York: The following services, otherwise taxable, performed on property delivered to the purchaser outside of New York for use outside the state are exempt:

— information services;

— services of production, fabrication, printing, etc., for a person who furnishes the property, not purchased for resale, on which the service is to be performed;

— installation of tangible personal property, or the maintenance, servicing, etc., of tangible personal property not held for sale in the regular course of business;

— interior design and decorating services; and

— protective and detective services.

Sales of property delivered outside New York for use outside the state are discussed at ¶2103.

Clothing services: Laundering, dry cleaning, tailoring (including separately stated, reasonable charges for alterations to all clothing), weaving, pressing, shoe repairing and shoe shining services are exempt. Reasonable and separately stated charges for alterations to new or used clothing are exempt (Sec. 1105(c)(3)(ii), Tax Law; Reg. Secs. 527.4 and 527.5; *TSB M-02(4),* Department of Taxation and Finance, July 18, 2002, CCH New York Tax Reports, ¶300-365).

Practitioner Comment: Laundering Exemption Limited to Cleaning of Fabric

New York's Tax Department has limited the application of the laundering exemption to the cleaning of fabric (carpeting, clothing, etc.). Consequently, the services of cleaning or shampooing automobile carpets, upholstery and other interior surfaces covered in cloth or fabric are exempt from tax, while the cleaning of an automobile's exterior is taxable. (*TB-ST-105,* September 2010, CCH New York Tax Reports, ¶406-985).

Mark S. Klein, Esq., Hodgson Russ LLP

- *Telecommunications*

Telephone, telegraph, and information services used for news: Telephony and telegraphy and telephone and telegraph services used by newspapers and radio and television broadcasters in the collection or dissemination of news are exempt if the charge is a toll charge or charge for mileage services (including the associated station terminal equipment). Also exempt are information services used by newspapers and radio and television broadcasters in the collection and dissemination of news.

Telecommunication machinery and equipment: See ¶2105.

Broadcasters: Certain services rendered to a broadcaster in connection with its broadcasting business are exempt from sales and use tax, including, but not limited to, editing, dubbing, and mixing when performed in connection with the production, post-production, or transmission of live or recorded programs. An exemption for machinery and equipment used by broadcasters is discussed at ¶2105. See also *Publication 825,* New York Department of Taxation and Finance, CCH New York Tax Reports, ¶65-946.

Coin-operated telephone charges of 25¢ or less: Telephone and telegraph services paid for by inserting coins in coin-operated telephones where the charge is 25¢ or less are exempt. See also "Vending machine sales," at ¶2103.

- *Vehicles and vessels*

Commercial vessels and supplies: Commercial vessels primarily engaged in interstate or foreign commerce, and property used by or purchased for the use of such vessels for fuel, provisions, supplies, maintenance, and repairs (other than articles for the original equipping of a new ship) are exempt. The services of installing, maintaining, servicing, or repairing such vessels are also exempt (Sec. 1115(a)(8), Tax Law; Sec. 1105(c)(3)(iv), Tax Law; Reg. Sec. 527.5(b)(5)(i)). Examples of exempt services include: painting, hull cleaning, carpentry, hold cleaning and ship sealing, as well as repair and maintenance of radar, navigational aids, onboard cargo handling equipment, marine cargo containers, canvas and office equipment (Reg. Sec. 528.9(d)(1)). Services which are not exempt include: stevedoring, cargo weighing, piloting and clerking and checking during cargo handling (Reg. Sec. 528.9(d)(2)).

Effective June 1, 2015, an exemption is provided for sales, leases or uses of vessels in excess of $230,000 (Sec. 1115(jj), Tax Law). In addition, a use tax exemption is provided for the use of a vessel within New York until (1) the boat is registered, or is first required to be registered, under New York's vehicle and traffic laws, or (2) the boat is used in New York for more than 90 days (Sec. 1118(13), Tax Law). See *TSB-M-15(2)S*, July 24, 2015, CCH NEW YORK TAX REPORTS, ¶408-482.

Fishing vessels: Fishing vessels used directly and predominantly in the harvesting of fish for sale, and property used by or purchased for the use of such vessels for fuel, provisions, supplies, maintenance, and repairs, are exempt from tax (Sec. 1115(a)(24), Tax Law). For purposes of the exemption, a vessel used predominantly for sport fishing purposes is not a fishing vessel. Services of installing, maintaining, servicing, or repairing fishing vessels are also exempt.

Mobile homes: Sales of new mobile homes are taxable under special rules (¶2019). Sales of used mobile homes are exempt. However, the tax is imposed on items of tangible personal property included in the sale that were not permanently incorporated as a component part of the mobile home.

Certain sales of mobile homes to contractors are exempt as sales for resale, see ¶2019.

Services of installing a mobile home are exempt. However, the maintenance, servicing, or repair of such homes is generally taxable.

Trucks, tractors, and tractor-trailers: The rental or lease of trucks, tractors, or tractor-trailer combinations leased with operator to an authorized carrier as augmenting equipment for use in the transportation for hire of tangible personal property is exempt. (Sec. 1115(a)(26), Tax Law; *TB-ST-890*, August 7, 2014, CCH NEW YORK TAX REPORTS, ¶408-187). An exemption is also provided for tractors, trailers, or semitrailers when used in combinations that have gross vehicle weights in excess of 26,000 pounds, and for property installed on such vehicles for their equipping, maintenance, and repair. Moreover, the tax does not apply to installation, maintenance, or repair services performed on exempt tractors, trailers, or semitrailers or on exempt property installed on such tractors, trailers, or semitrailers.

Omnibus carriers providing local transit service: Omnibus carriers providing local transit service in New York and operating pursuant to a certificate of public convenience and necessity issued by the New York Commissioner of Transportation or by the Interstate Commerce Commission or under a contract with New York City are entitled to a credit or refund with respect to certain sales and use taxes paid (Sec. 1119(b), Tax Law; *TB-ST-890*, August 7, 2014, CCH NEW YORK TAX REPORTS, ¶408-187). The credit or refund applies to sales and use taxes paid on any omnibus, or on parts, equipment, lubricants, fuel and maintenance, service, or repairs for any omnibus, proportionate to the extent the omnibus carrier is engaged in providing local transit service. The Tax Commission may also issue a direct payment permit to an omnibus carrier for the purchase or use of an omnibus.

Vessels providing local transit service: A refund or credit is allowed for tax paid on the sale to or use by a vessel operator of a vessel with a seating capacity of more than 20 passengers used for the transportation on water of passengers for hire (Sec.

¶2102

1119(b), Tax Law; Reg. Sec. 534.10). The provision also applies with respect to parts, equipment, lubricants, diesel motor fuel, maintenance, servicing, or repair purchased and used in the operation of any such vessel by the operator. In order to qualify, the vessel operator must provide local transit service in New York. The credit or refund amount is calculated based on the operator's vessel hours in local transit service compared to the total hours operated in New York. If the "local transit service percentage" is: (a) less that 10%, there is no credit or refund; (b) 10%, there is a credit or refund of 10%; (c) greater than 10% but less that 70%, the credit or refund is 10% plus the product of 1.5 times each whole percentage in excess of 10%; and (d) 70% or more, there is a 100% credit or refund.

¶2103 Exempt Transactions

Law: Secs. 1101, 1115, 1117, 1119, Tax Law; Reg. Sec. 528.14 (CCH NEW YORK TAX REPORTS, ¶60-430, ¶61-010).

In addition to specific items of tangible personal property or services that are exempt, the following transactions result in exemptions:

Sales for resale: Sales for resale are not subject to tax (Sec. 1105, Tax Law). These include:

(1) a sale for resale in the same form as purchased;

(2) a sale for resale as a physical component part of tangible personal property; or

(3) a sale of tangible personal property purchased for use in the performance of certain taxable services when the property so sold becomes a physical component part of the property upon which the services are performed or is later actually transferred to the purchaser of the service in conjunction with the performance of the taxable service.

This provides an exemption for manufacturers for purchases of property that becomes a part of the manufactured product. The resale exemption can also apply to the sale of a service that is resold in a taxable transaction (*e.g.*, a jeweler that sends a watch to a repair service can claim the resale exemption since the repair services are being resold to the owner of the watch by the jeweler) (Sec. 1101(b)(4)(i), Tax Law).

Practitioner Comment: Gratuitous Transfers

The sale for resale exclusion usually applies when a vendor acquires property and transfers it to a purchaser. The context of that transfer must be carefully scrutinized, however, to insure that the transfer is contractually required and is not gratuitous. If property is transferred as a gesture of goodwill, without a legal obligation, the transfer is not a resale. Instead, the seller is using the property to enhance its own reputation and must pay tax on the property. For example, an automobile dealer's purchase of vehicles for use as free loaners was a purchase for resale, since the dealer was contractually obligated to provide loaners to customers (*West-Herr Ford, Inc.*, New York Supreme Court, Appellate Division, Third Judicial Department, No. 95463, 791 N.Y.S.2d 193, March 3, 2005, CCH NEW YORK TAX REPORTS, ¶405-053).

Mark S. Klein, Esq., Hodgson Russ LLP

Sales of motor vehicles, vessels, or trailers to certain nonresidents: Such sales to nonresidents may be nontaxable even though the nonresident takes delivery of the vehicle in New York State (Sec. 1117(a), Tax Law). The specific requirements for this exemption to apply are that the nonresident:

(1) may not have any permanent place of abode in New York State;

(2) may not be engaged in carrying on in New York a trade, employment, business, or profession in which the motor vehicle, vessel, or trailer will be used;

(3) must furnish to the vendor prior to delivery the required affidavit or evidence supporting the claim for exemption; and

(4) (a) the vendor does not issue to the purchaser a temporary certificate of registration, and (b) the purchaser does not register the vehicle, vessel, or trailer in New York prior to registering it in another state or jurisdiction.

Sale of motor vehicle to spouse, parent, or child: Sale of a motor vehicle by one spouse to the other, by a parent to a child, or by a child to a parent is exempt unless the vendor is a dealer (Sec. 1115(a)(14), Tax Law).

Military service exemption: An exemption from New York sales and use tax is available for a motor vehicle purchased in another state by a person while in U.S. military service when the motor vehicle is registered in New York upon such person's return, so long as he or she can provide proof of payment of sales and use tax on such motor vehicle from another state. (Sec. 1115(a)(14-a), Tax Law; *TSB-M-14(11)S,* July 22, 2014, CCH NEW YORK TAX REPORTS, ¶ 408-160)

Out-of-state delivery: There is no specific statutory exemption for sales of tangible personal property delivered outside the state for use outside the state. However, such sales presumably are exempted under the Commerce Clause of the Federal Constitution.

Practitioner Comment: Export Sales

New York's Tax Department has established a procedure that will exempt from tax certain sales made to individuals about to depart the United States. Under this procedure, a retail vendor selling tangible personal property to a customer can deliver the property to a ship or plane's representative who must agree that the property will not be turned over to the purchaser until "after the conveyance leaves the territorial limits of the United States." Additionally, the property cannot be returned to the United States (*TSB-A-81(68)S,* CCH NEW YORK TAX REPORTS, ¶ 02037). (See also *TSB-H-87(220)S,* CCH NEW YORK TAX REPORTS, ¶ 60-450) Vendors must carefully follow the documentation requirements of this procedure or they can become liable for the sales tax (*Maximilian Furs Co., Inc.,* NYS TAT (8/9/90), CCH NEW YORK TAX REPORTS, ¶ 253-227).

Mark S. Klein, Esq., Hodgson Russ LLP

Occasional maintenance services: Maintenance services are exempt from tax when rendered by an individual who does not offer those services to the public in a regular trade or business (*e.g.,* individuals who occasionally perform "odd jobs") and who does not regularly perform such services in their own business or as an employee (Sec. 1105(c)(5)(i), Tax Law).

Waste removal: Removal of waste material from a facility regulated as a transfer station or construction and demolition debris processing facility by the New York Department of Environmental Conservation is exempt from New York sales and use tax, provided that the waste material to be removed was not generated by the facility. (Sec. 1105(c)(5)(iv), Tax Law; *TSB-M-05(13)S,* CCH NEW YORK TAX REPORTS, ¶ 300-487)

Professional services: Professional, fiduciary, management, meteorological, and consulting services on an individual basis are exempt. Advertising services are also exempt, but the tangible personal property used in performing such services is taxable.

Certain sales to related persons: Effective September 1, 2015, a sales and use tax exemption is provided for certain related persons' tangible personal property or service transactions related to requirements pursuant to the Dodd-Frank Wall Street Reform and Consumer Protection Act. The exemption sunsets on June 30, 2019. (Sec. 1115[jj], Tax Law)

Exempt uses: Refunds or credits of sales and use taxes paid are allowed for the following transactions (Sec. 1119, Tax Law):

— the sale or use of tangible personal property when the purchaser or user, in the performance of a contract, later incorporates it into real property outside New York;

— the sale or use of tangible personal property purchased in bulk, or any portion thereof, that is stored but not used within New York and later reshipped outside the state;

— the sale or use of tangible personal property by a contractor or subcontractor if used solely in the performance of a preexisting lump sum or unit price construction contract;

— the sale or use within New York of tangible personal property, not purchased for resale, when the use within the state is restricted to fabricating the property (including incorporating it into, or assembling it with, other tangible personal property), processing, printing, or imprinting it and the property is then shipped outside New York for out-of-state use;

— the sale to or use by a veterinarian of drugs or medicine used in rendering professional services to livestock or poultry that are used in the production for sale of tangible personal property by farming, as well as sales of drugs and medicines to a person entitled to the farmer's exemption (¶2107) for use on such livestock or poultry;

— the sale of tangible personal property purchased for use in constructing, expanding, or rehabilitating industrial or commercial real estate (except property used exclusively for retail sales) located in an empire zone to the extent that the property becomes an integral part of the real property;

— the sale or use of omnibuses, parts, equipment, lubricants, motor fuel, diesel fuel, maintenance, servicing, or repair by omnibus carriers providing local transit service (¶2102);

— the sale or use of tangible personal property by the purchaser in performing certain taxable services (that is, information services, processing and printing services, installation and maintenance services, real estate maintenance and services, interior decorating and designing services, and protective and detective services (¶2007)).

Oil and gas production: Receipts derived from installing, maintaining, servicing, or repairing tangible personal property with respect to property used or consumed directly and predominantly in the production for sale of gas or oil by manufacturing, processing, generating, assembling, refining, mining, or extracting are exempt (Sec. 1115(a)(12), Tax Law). Similarly, maintenance and repair services rendered directly with respect to real property or land used or consumed in such oil or gas production are exempt. In addition, there is an exemption for parts with a useful life of one year or less, tools, and supplies for use or consumption directly and predominantly in such production (Sec. 1105-B, Tax Law).

Sales at private residences: Sales of tangible personal property (other than boats, snowmobiles or motor vehicles) by persons at their residences are exempt if neither the person nor any member of the household conducts a trade or business in which similar items are sold and if the receipts from such sales cannot reasonably be expected to exceed $600 in a calendar year. For persons aged 16 years or older, only sales made on three or fewer days per calendar year qualify for the exemption. Where a person reasonably expects that receipts from such sales will not exceed $600 in a calendar year but such receipts do exceed that sum, the exemption applies, but only to the first $600 of receipts in the calendar year (Sec. 1115(18), Tax Law). In addition, if a person 16 years of age or older has engaged in such sales for three days in a calendar year, the exemption does not apply to subsequent sales in that calendar year. However, sales at a private residence conducted by an auctioneer, sheriff or other third party; sales held to liquidate an estate; and sales of boats, snowmobiles or motor vehicles (except sales of motor vehicles between certain closely related family members), are taxable (Sec. 1115(a)(18), Tax Law).

Practitioner Comment: Casual Sales

Other than the $600-per-year exemption for sales of tangible personal property sold by a person at their residence (above), New York, unlike many other states, has no other casual sales tax exemption from sales and use taxes. In fact, the sale of any business asset, other than in the ordinary course of business, triggers tax on the sale itself as well as the bulk sale notice requirements under Sec. 1141(c), Tax Law (see ¶2207).

Mark S. Klein, Esq., Hodgson Russ LLP

Sales by railroad in reorganization to profitable railroad: Sales of tangible personal property by a railroad in reorganization to a profitable railroad are exempt (Sec. 1115(h), Tax Law).

Solicitation of sales by catalogs and flyers in interstate commerce only: Persons who regularly or systematically solicit business in New York by the distribution of catalogs, advertising flyers, letters, or other means and who thereby make sales to persons in New York of tangible personal property subject to the state's use tax, as well as those who sell tangible personal property or services subject to the New York use tax and who regularly or systemically deliver the property or services in New York by means other than the U.S. mail or common carrier, however, are considered to be vendors for sales tax purposes, when the solicitation satisfies federal constitutional nexus requirements (Sec. 1101(b)(8)(i)(E), Tax Law).

The term "vendor" also includes persons who make sales of, but retain an ownership interest in, tangible personal property subject to the use tax, that is brought into the state by a buyer who is or becomes a resident or that is used in carrying on any employment, trade, business, or profession in New York (Sec. 1101(b)(8)(i)(F), Tax Law). Persons providing billing services on behalf of vendors of entertainment or information services provided by telephonic or telegraphic means are also regarded as vendors (Sec. 1101(b)(18), Tax Law).

Native Americans: Sales to an exempt Native American nation or tribe, as well as certain sales by an exempt Native American nation or tribe, are exempt (¶2109). Distributors may import motor fuel into New York State without payment and pass-through of the prepaid sales tax, nor collection and payment of the retail sales and use tax, when the fuel is sold and delivered to an exempt Native American nation or tribe, a qualified Native American consumer, or a registered dealer (¶2005). An exempt Native American nation or tribe, a qualified Native American consumer, or a registered dealer may make exempt purchases of motor fuel upon which the seller has not passed through the prepaid sales tax, nor collected and paid the retail sales and use tax, provided delivery is taken on a qualified reservation.

Although sales of motor fuel and tobacco products on Native American reservations for use by Native American consumers are exempt from tax, sales on Native American reservations to non-Native American consumers are taxable (Reg. Sec. 529.9).

The New York Department of Taxation and Finance has issued a cigarette and sales and use tax memorandum that discusses the two alternatives for Indian nations and tribes and their members to obtain tax-exempt cigarettes, refund claim provisions, tax agreements with the state, individual Indian exemption forms, and tax return forms and instructions *(TSB-M-11(14)M, TSB-M-11(7)S*, May 9, 2011, CCH New York Tax Reports, ¶407-243).

The right of New York to impose recordkeeping requirements and set quotas on the amount of untaxed cigarettes and motor fuel that wholesalers licensed by the

Bureau of Indian Affairs may sell was affirmed by the U.S. Supreme Court in *Department of Taxation and Finance v. Milhelm Attea & Brothers, Inc.*, 512 U.S. 61, 114 S. Ct. 2028, June 13, 1994, CCH NEW YORK TAX REPORTS, ¶ 401-528.

Vending machine sales: Several exemptions apply to sales of tangible personal property made by coin-operated vending machines. Services to tangible personal property provided through coin-operated vending machines are generally taxable, except as provided below.

Sales of tangible personal property at 10¢ or less: Tangible personal property sold through coin-operated vending machines at 10¢ or less is not subject to tax if the retailer is primarily (50% or more of total receipts) engaged in making such sales and maintains satisfactory records (Sec. 1105(d)(i)(3), Tax Law).

Bulk vending machine sales of tangible personal property at 50¢ or less: An exemption is also provided for tangible personal property sold through coin-operated bulk vending machines at 50¢ or less, again if the retailer is primarily engaged in making such sales and maintains satisfactory records. If the machine accepts debit or credit cards, only coin or currency transactions are exempt (Sec. 1115(a)(13-a), Tax Law). A "bulk vending machine" is a vending machine containing unsorted merchandise, such as gumballs or candy, that dispenses the merchandise in approximately equal portions at random and without selection by the customer. Food and drink sold through a coin-operated bulk vending machine are exempt under this provision only when the bulk vending machine is located on premises that have no facilities provided for customers for on-premises consumption (Reg. Sec. 528.14(b)(1)).

Vending machine sales of food and drink at 75¢ or less: Candy and confectionery, fruit drinks that contain less than 70% of natural fruit juice, soft drinks, sodas, and beverages that are ordinarily dispensed at soda fountains (other than coffee, tea, and cocoa), and beer, wine or other alcoholic beverages are exempt from sales and use tax when sold for 75¢ or less through any vending machine activated by the use of a coin, currency, credit card, or debit card (Sec. 1115(a)(1), Tax Law). Hot beverages sold through a vending machine are also exempt from tax regardless of price.

Sales through coin-operated equipment: Specific exemptions are provided for the following, if purchased through coin-operated equipment (where the coin-operated equipment also accepts debit or credit cards, only transactions using coin or currency are exempt):

Photocopying: Copies sold through coin-operated photocopying machines at 50¢ or less (Sec. 1115(a)(31), Tax Law);

Car washing: Receipts of a car wash from washing or waxing a motor vehicle or other tangible personal property, when the purchaser or user personally performs these services on their own vehicle or property exclusively by means of coin-operated automated equipment (neither the vendor nor any employee may assist the purchaser in performing the services) (Sec. 1115(t), Tax Law);

Car vacuuming: Receipts of any facility from self-service vacuuming of a motor vehicle or other tangible personal property exclusively by means of coin-operated automated equipment (Sec. 1115(t), Tax Law); and

Luggage carts: Temporary transportation devices used to transport for a limited period of time luggage or merchandise a short distance within a facility of embarkation or disembarkation (such as an airport) or a facility where the merchandise was purchased that is sold through coin-operated equipment (Sec. 1115(a)(13-b), Tax Law).

Food and drink sold through vending machines: Sales of beer, wine, or other alcoholic beverages, or any other sale of drink and food by restaurants, taverns, or other establishments, including those instances in which the sale is made through a vending machine that is activated by use of coin, currency, credit card, or debit card, are subject to sales tax (Sec. 1115(a)(13), Tax Law).

¶2104 Use Tax Exemptions

Law: Secs. 1110, 1118, Tax Law (CCH New York Tax Reports, ¶60-020, ¶60-510).

Use of the following categories of property is exempt from use tax (Sec. 1118, Tax Law):

(1) property used by the purchaser in New York prior to the effective date of the tax (August 1, 1965);

(2) property purchased by the user while a nonresident of New York, except that the use is taxable if the property is incorporated into real property in New York in the performance of a contract. Property used in any employment, trade, business, or profession carried on in New York does not qualify for this exemption;

(3) property or services the sale of which is expressly exempt from sales tax;

(4) property that is converted into or becomes a component part of a product produced for sale by the purchaser;

(5) paper used in newspapers and periodicals;

(6) property used exclusively in the temporary construction, repair, etc., of structures or exhibits at the New York World's Fair;

(7) spare aircraft parts (including engines), consumable technical supplies, maintenance and ground equipment brought into New York from a foreign country by a foreign airline for use exclusively on its aircraft;

(8) a thoroughbred, standardbred, or quarter horse purchased outside the state and brought into the state to enter a racing event or events on which pari-mutuel wagering is authorized; provided the horse is not entered in racing events in the state on more than five days in any calendar year (The exemption provisions relating to nonresidents described at (2) above continue to apply);

(9) a horse purchased outside the state and brought into New York State for racing, to the extent that the value of the horse exceeds $100,000;

(10) certain registered racehorses purchased outside the state that may or may not meet the requirements in (8) or (9) above (¶2102).

Nonresident exemption: The use tax exemption under (2) above for property purchased by a nonresident of New York does not apply to the use of an aircraft, vessel, or motor vehicle purchased by a business entity for use in New York State primarily to carry, for business or pleasure, individuals employed by or otherwise associated in specified ways either with (1) the purchaser, if any of the transported individuals were New York residents at the time of the property's purchase, or (2) an affiliated entity of the purchaser, if the affiliated entity was a New York resident when the property was purchased. For purposes of these provisions, persons are affiliated with respect to each other if one of the persons has an ownership interest of more than 5% (whether direct or indirect) in the other, or if an ownership interest of more than 5% (whether direct or indirect) is held in each of the persons by another person or by a group of other persons that are affiliated with respect to each other. (Sec. 1118(2), Tax Law)

Self-use by manufacturers: See ¶2016.

Sales or use tax paid to other states: Property or services on which a retail sales or use tax was due and paid, without any right to refund or credit, to another state or jurisdiction within another state are exempt, provided the other state or jurisdiction allows a corresponding exemption when a sales or use tax is paid to New York (Sec. 1118(7), Tax Law).

The New York use tax, however, does apply to the extent of the difference in rates if the New York tax is higher. If a New York local use tax also applies, the New York state and local use taxes will apply to the extent of the difference in rates if the aggregate (state and local) New York tax is higher.

¶2104

A reciprocal credit for sales or use tax paid to another state and/or locality in that state may be available if all the following conditions are met:

— the state and/or locality where the purchase was made allows a corresponding credit for sales or use tax paid to New York state and/or localities in New York;

— the purchaser was legally liable for the tax and paid the tax to the other state and/or locality;

— the tax paid to the other state and/or locality on the purchase is a sales or use tax;

— the purchaser has no right to a refund or credit of the tax paid to the other state and/or locality; and

— the purchaser has proof of payment, such as a receipt showing the amount or rate of tax paid to the other state and/or locality.

For additional information on the reciprocal credit, see *TB-ST-765*, New York Department of Taxation and Finance, October 9, 2013, CCH NEW YORK TAX REPORTS, ¶ 407-939.

¶2105 Machinery and Equipment

Law: Secs. 1105-B, 1115(a)(12), 1210, Tax Law; Reg. Sec. 528.13 (CCH NEW YORK TAX REPORTS, ¶ 60-510, ¶ 60-530, ¶ 60-620, ¶ 60-630, ¶ 60-640, ¶ 60-720, ¶ 60-740).

Machinery and equipment used or consumed directly and predominately in producing for sale tangible personal property, gas, electricity, refrigeration, or steam by manufacturing, processing, generating, assembling, refining, mining, or extracting are exempt (Sec. 1115(a)(12), Tax Law). Receipts from installing, maintaining, servicing, or repairing real or personal property for use in production of gas or oil for sale are exempt, as are sales of parts for use less than one year, tools, and supplies for such use or consumption (see ¶ 2103).

Parts, tools, and supplies used in connection with machinery or equipment used or consumed directly and predominately in producing for sale tangible personal property are exempt (Reg. Sec. 528.13).

Practitioner Comment: Forklifts and Racks

New York's exemption for equipment used directly and predominantly in production can extend to forklift trucks that load and unload raw materials, as well as racks used to store raw materials used in the production process (*TSB-A-02(17)S*, CCH NEW YORK TAX REPORTS, ¶ 404-238). The exemption can also apply to charges for repair services to production-based forklift trucks (*TSB-A-04(22)S*, CCH NEW YORK TAX REPORTS, ¶ 404-915).

Mark S. Klein, Esq., Hodgson Russ LLP

Oil and gas: All pipe, pipeline, drilling and service rigs, vehicles, and associated equipment used in the drilling, production, and operation of oil, gas, and solution mining activities to the point of sale to the first commercial purchaser are exempt. See ¶ 2103.

Gas or electricity: Gas or electricity used for gas or electric service is exempt. See ¶ 2106.

Internet data centers: An exemption applies for machinery, equipment, and other tangible personal property purchased by the operator of an Internet data center located in New York when such property is to be placed or installed in an Internet data center and is directly related to the provision of Internet website services for sale by the operator of the center (¶2102). An Internet data center consists of a data center specifically designed and constructed to provide a high security environment for the location of services and similar equipment on which Internet websites reside and provide uninterrupted Internet access to its customers' web pages in a secure environment and continuous Internet traffic management for its customers' web pages. In addition, property purchased by contractors for incorporation into the real property of the Internet data center is also exempt. Further, repair and maintenance services rendered to the exempt property is exempt from sales and use tax whether such property retains its character as tangible personal property or becomes a capital improvement to the Internet data center (Sec. 1115(a)(37), Tax Law; Sec. 1115(y), Tax Law; see also *TSB-A-12(30)S*, New York Commissioner of Taxation and Finance, December 3, 2012, CCH NEW YORK TAX REPORTS, ¶407-737).

Pollution control: Machinery and equipment used for disposing of industrial waste as part of a process for preventing water or air pollution is considered to be used directly and predominantly in production by manufacturing, processing, generating, assembling, refining, mining, or extracting and is, therefore, exempt from tax if (Sec. 1115(a)(12), Tax Law):

— purchased by a manufacturer and used predominantly to actually treat, bury, or store waste materials from a production process; and

— more than 50% of the waste treated, buried, or stored results from the production process.

An exemption is provided for machinery or equipment used in the control, prevention, or abatement of pollution or contaminants from manufacturing or industrial facilities.

Broadcasters: Machinery, equipment, or other tangible personal property (including parts, tools, and supplies) used by a broadcaster directly and predominantly in the production and post-production of live or recorded programs for the purpose of broadcast over-the-air, cable television transmissions, or direct broadcast satellite system transmissions are exempt (Sec. 1115(a)(38), Tax Law).

Purchases of parts and equipment by a satellite television provider that it supplied to its customers for a monthly fee so they could receive satellite television programming were subject to sales and use tax because they were not purchased for resale. The Appellate Division of the Supreme Court of New York held that the Tax Appeals Tribunal rationally determined that the taxpayer did not acquire the equipment for the purpose of rental to its customers. Rather, as the Tax Appeals Tribunal concluded, the taxpayer's primary purpose was to provide satellite television service and it used the equipment to supply that service to its customers. (*Echostar Satellite Corp. v. Tax Appeals Tribunal*, Appellate Division of the Supreme Court of New York, Third Department, No. 508200, December 9, 2010, CCH NEW YORK TAX REPORTS, ¶407-068)

Telecommunications: An exemption applies to telecommunications machinery and equipment used or consumed directly and predominantly in receiving, initiating, amplifying, processing, transmitting, retransmitting, switching, or monitoring telecommunications services for sale or Internet access services for sale (Sec. 1115(a)(12), Tax Law).

Also exempt are telephone central office equipment or station apparatus, and comparable telegraph equipment, used directly and predominantly in receiving at destination or initiating and switching telephone or telegraph communication.

New York City: The machinery and equipment exemption is applicable to the New York City local sales and use tax.

An exemption exists for machinery and equipment used directly and predominantly in loading, unloading, and handling cargo at marine terminal facilities located in New York City that handled more than 350,000 twenty foot equivalent units

(TEU's) in 2003. The exemption also applies to the $^3/_8$% sales and use taxes for the Metropolitan Commuter Transportation District (MCTD). However, the exemption does not apply to the 4% local sales and use taxes imposed by Sec. 1107 of the Tax Law within New York City (Sec. 1115(a)(41), Tax Law; *TSB-M-05(14)S*, CCH NEW YORK TAX REPORTS, ¶300-488).

Cities (other than New York City), counties, and school districts: Cities, other than New York City, counties and school districts imposing the entire state tax package (¶2024) must exclude from tax all sales of tangible personal property for use or consumption directly and predominantly in the production for sale of tangible personal property, gas, electricity, refrigeration or steam by manufacturing, processing, generating, assembling, refining, mining, extracting, farming, agriculture, horticulture or floriculture and all sales of certain telephone and telegraph equipment.

In claiming this exemption a manufacturer must furnish the vendor with an Exempt Use Certificate (Form ST-121).

¶2106 Fuel and Utilities

Law: Secs. 1101, 1102, 1105-A, 1107(b)(1), 1115(a)—(c), (j), (w), 1210(a)(1), Tax Law; Reg. Secs. 527.13, 528.3, 528.10, 528.11 (CCH NEW YORK TAX REPORTS, ¶60-530, ¶60-560, ¶60-750).

Fuel, utilities (gas, electricity, refrigeration, and steam) and utilities services used or consumed directly and exclusively in the production of tangible personal property, gas, electricity, refrigeration, or steam by manufacturing, processing, assembling, generating, refining, mining, extracting, farming, agriculture, horticulture, floriculture, or commercial horse boarding operations, are exempt (Sec. 1115(c), Tax Law; see also *TB-ST-587*, New York Department of Taxation and Finance, April 15, 2015, CCH NEW YORK TAX REPORTS, ¶408-383; *TB-ST-917*, New York Department of Taxation and Finance, April 15, 2015, CCH NEW YORK TAX REPORTS, ¶408-384).

The exemption is strictly limited to utilities used in production. Thus, fuel, gas, electricity, refrigeration and steam and like services are subject to tax when used or consumed in the heating, cooling or lighting of buildings or in the preparation of food and drink or in the storage of tangible personal property. Manufacturers claim the exemption by giving an exempt use certificate.

The exemption is applicable to sales and uses of non-highway diesel fuel and to certain amounts of such fuel in a 30-day period for use or consumption directly and exclusively in the production for sale of tangible personal property by farming, but only if consumed other than on the state highways. However, sales of diesel fuel that involve a delivery at a filling station or into a repository equipped with a hose or other apparatus by which the fuel can be dispensed into the fuel tank of a motor vehicle arc taxable (¶2005).

The taxation of diesel motor fuel depends on whether it is classified as highway diesel motor fuel or non- highway diesel motor fuel:

— Non-highway diesel motor fuel is any diesel motor fuel designated for use other than on a public highway (except for the use of the public highway by farmers to reach adjacent farmlands), and is dyed diesel motor fuel;

— Highway diesel motor fuel is any diesel motor fuel that is not non-highway diesel motor fuel.

Highway diesel motor fuel is subject to diesel motor fuel excise tax, petroleum business tax, and prepaid sales tax when it is first sold in New York State. When the fuel is designated for off-highway use and is dyed for federal tax purposes at the terminal, it is considered non-highway diesel motor fuel.

Non-highway diesel motor fuel is exempt from the diesel motor fuel excise tax and the prepaid sales tax, and either exempt or partially exempt from the petroleum business tax. These exemptions or partial exemptions apply as long as the fuel is not used on New York public highways (except by farmers to reach adjacent farmlands), or delivered to a filling station or into a tank equipped with a nozzle capable of fueling a motor vehicle (except for delivery at a farm site). For additional information, see (*TSB-M-11(6)M, TSB-M-11(11)S,* July 29, 2011, CCH NEW YORK TAX REPORTS, ¶ 407-325).

Water and sewer line protection programs: A sales and use tax exemption is available for water and sewer service line protection programs sold to residential property owners (Sec. 1115(ii), Tax Law; *TSB-M-14(14)S,* October 7, 2014, CCH NEW YORK TAX REPORTS, ¶ 408-244).

New York City: Under Article 29, Tax Law, the fuel and utilities exemption applies to the local sales and use tax imposed by New York City.

• *Energy consumed in research and development*

Gas, electricity, refrigeration, and steam, and gas, electric, refrigeration, and steam service, used or consumed directly and exclusively in research and development in the experimental or laboratory sense are exempt (Sec. 1115(b)(ii), Tax Law). "Research and development," for purposes of the exemption, does not include the ordinary testing or inspection of materials or products for quality control, efficiency surveys, advertising, promotions, or research in connection with literary, historical, or similar projects.

Refund or credit: The user may claim a refund or credit for the tax paid on the portion of energy use that qualifies for the exemption. The user must maintain adequate records and must submit an engineering survey or the formula used in arriving at the amount used in an exempt manner.

Other R&D-related exemptions: For information on other exemptions related to research and development activities, see ¶ 2108 and *TB-ST-773,* February 3, 2014, CCH NEW YORK TAX REPORTS, ¶ 408-025.

• *Residential and commercial energy sources and services*

Sales and use taxes are not imposed upon retail sales or uses of fuel oil, coal, propane (except when sold in containers of less than 100 pounds), natural gas, electricity, and steam, or upon gas, electric, and steam services, when used for residential purposes (Sec. 1105-A(a), Tax Law). The tax also does not apply to wood used for residential heating purposes.

When energy sources or services billed on a single meter are used for both residential and nonresidential purposes, and residential purposes constitute 75% or more of the usage, the entire amount billed is exempt. If the percentage of residential use is less than 75%, the amount billed is allocated. The percentage attributable to residential use is determined by dividing the total area of the space used for residential purposes, excluding common areas, by the total area of the premises (residential and nonresidential), excluding common areas, rounded to the nearest 10% (Sec. 1105-A(d), Tax Law).

CCH Advisory: Energy for Condominium Common Areas

Purchases of energy sources by a residential condominium association or a trailer park for common residential areas, such as parking lots, play areas, club houses, community buildings, swimming pools, hallways, and stairways, qualified as purchases for residential purposes and, therefore, were exempt from state sales and use tax and either exempt from local sales and use tax or subject to a reduced local tax rate.

The exemptions and reduced tax rate applied to purchases such as fuel oil, coal, propane, gas, electricity, and steam, or gas, electric, and steam services to heat, light, or operate the common areas. Purchases of energy sources and services to operate water pumps and sewer pumps for residences also qualified as purchases for residential purposes and therefore were exempt or subject to a reduced local tax rate (*TSB-A-00(31)S,* CCH NEW YORK TAX REPORTS, ¶ 403-766).

Local taxes: Localities may adopt reduced rates on retail sales and uses of certain residential energy sources or may exempt such sales and uses. New York City is authorized to reduce or eliminate its local sales and use tax on residential energy sources, such as fuel oil, coal, wood, propane, natural gas, electricity, steam and gas, and gas, electric and steam services (Sec. 1105-A(f), Tax Law). Taxes and rates in specific localities are listed in (*Publication 718-R*, New York Department of Taxation and Finance, CCH NEW YORK TAX REPORTS, ¶ 65-922, also at **https://www.tax.ny.gov/ pdf/publications/sales/pub718r.pdf**).

The New York Department of Taxation and Finance maintains an online service to help consumers and businesses determine whether the proper local sales tax is being charged on purchases of utility or telecommunication services. Sales and purchases covered by the new service include natural gas and electricity, telephone services, heating oil, propane, and firewood. By entering a street address and zip code, a vendor or customer can confirm the local sales tax jurisdiction, current jurisdiction code, and tax rate. The service is available at **http://www8.nystax.gov/ UTLR/utlrHome**.

Solar energy for homes: Receipts from the retail sale and installation of residential solar energy systems equipment are exempt from state sales and use taxes (Sec. 1115(ee), Tax Law). "Residential solar energy systems equipment" is defined as an arrangement or combination of components installed in a residence that utilizes solar radiation to produce energy designed to provide heating, cooling, hot water and/or electricity. Such arrangement or combination of components does not include equipment that is part of a non-solar energy system or that uses any sort of recreational facility or equipment as a storage medium. Therefore, "residential solar energy systems equipment" does not include such items as pipes, controls, insulation, or other equipment that are part of a conventional gas, oil, or electric heating or cooling system, and does not include equipment that uses any sort of recreational facility, such as a swimming pool or a hot tub, as a storage medium. All municipalities, including New York City, are authorized to grant the same exemption.

Solar energy for nonresidential buildings: The sale and the installation of commercial solar energy systems equipment are exempt from New York state sales and use tax (Sec. 1115(hh), Tax Law). Purchases are also exempt from local sales tax in jurisdictions that enact the exemption; see *Publication 718-CS*, New York Department of Taxation and Finance, CCH NEW YORK TAX REPORTS, ¶ 65-998, also at **https:// www.tax.ny.gov/pdf/publications/sales/pub718cs.pdf**. For purposes of the exemption, "commercial solar energy systems equipment" means an arrangement or combination of components installed upon nonresidential premises that utilize solar radiation to produce energy designed to provide heating, cooling, hot water and/or electricity. Such arrangement or component does not include equipment that is part of a non-solar energy system. Also, municipalities are authorized to provide for the same exemption (Sec. 1210(a)(1), Tax Law; *TSB-M-12(14)S*, December 4, 2012, CCH NEW YORK TAX REPORTS, ¶ 407-716).

Cogenerated energy for cooperative apartments: Sales of electricity, steam, and refrigeration and electric, steam, and refrigeration services that are metered and generated or produced by a cogeneration facility owned or operated by certain cooperative corporations are exempt from New York sales and compensating use taxes. In order to qualify, the cooperative corporation must have at least 1,500 apartments and the energy or energy services must be distributed to the tenants or occupants of such cooperative corporations (Sec. 1115(b)(iii), Tax Law).

Solar energy system equipment and electricity: Effective December 1, 2015, the exemptions for solar energy system equipment are expanded to include electricity generated by such equipment that is sold under a power purchase agreement (Sec. 1115(ee), Tax Law; *TSB-M-15(5)S,* November 4, 2015, CCH NEW YORK TAX REPORTS, ¶408-558). Specifically, the law expands the existing exemptions from state and local sales tax for residential and commercial solar equipment to include electricity purchased from a person primarily engaged in the sale of solar energy systems equipment and/or electricity generated by such equipment if the electricity is sold under a written agreement and generated by equipment that is:

(1) owned by a person other than the purchaser of the electricity;

(2) installed at the purchaser's residence or nonresidential premises; and

(3) used to provide heating, cooling, hot water or electricity.

Existing local option provisions are amended to include the expanded exemptions (Sec. 1210(a)(1), (4), Tax Law).

• *Gas or electricity used for gas or electric service*

An exemption from state and local sales and use taxes is provided for certain purchases of gas or electricity used to provide gas or electric service. Specifically, the exemption applies to gas or electricity—or gas or electric service—used or consumed directly and exclusively to provide gas or electric service consisting of operating a gas pipeline or distribution line or an electric transmission or distribution line and ensuring the necessary working pressure in an underground gas storage facility (Sec. 1115(w), Tax Law).

Additional details may be found in *TSB-M-00(4)S,* June 9, 2000, CCH NEW YORK TAX REPORTS, ¶300-319.

• *Natural gas used for personal residence consumption*

Natural gas used for personal residence consumption by a landowner from (or provided in exchange for gas from) a natural gas well located on the property is exempt, where the gas has been set aside for the property owner's use by lease (Sec. 1115(a)(25), Tax Law).

• *Water*

Water delivered to the consumer through mains or pipes is exempt (see ¶2102). The tax, however, is imposed upon water sold in bottles or by means other than through mains or pipes. Water sold as ice or in any other form is taxable.

• *Fuels*

CCH Advisory: Diesel Motor Fuel Reclassified

Beginning September 1, 2011, the manner in which diesel motor fuel is classified is redefined for purposes of the diesel motor fuel excise tax (Article 12-A), petroleum business tax (Article 13-A), and sales tax (Article 28). The terms "enhanced diesel motor fuel" and "unenhanced diesel motor fuel" are obsolete. Accordingly, it is no longer necessary to determine if fuel is labeled as diesel fuel, No. 1 diesel fuel, No. 2 diesel fuel, or similar designation, or if it is a blended product that it will be used as diesel fuel in a motor vehicle. Also, the fuel's sulfur content is irrelevant to determination of its taxability. Instead, based on the new definitions, the taxation of diesel motor fuel depends on whether it is classified as highway diesel motor fuel or non-highway diesel motor fuel. (*TSB-M-11(6)M, TSB-M-11(11)S,* New York Department of Taxation and Finance, July 29, 2011, CCH NEW YORK TAX REPORTS, ¶407-325)

"Highway diesel motor fuel" is any diesel motor fuel that is not non-highway diesel motor fuel (Sec. 282(16-a), Tax Law). "Non-highway diesel motor fuel" is any diesel motor fuel designated for use other than on a public highway (except for the use of the public highway by farmers to reach adjacent farmlands), and is dyed diesel motor fuel (Sec. 282(16), Tax Law).

Highway diesel motor fuel is subject to diesel motor fuel excise tax, petroleum business tax, and prepaid sales tax when it is first sold in New York State. When the fuel is designated for off-highway use and is dyed for federal tax purposes at the terminal, it is considered non-highway diesel motor fuel. Non-highway diesel motor fuel is exempt from the diesel motor fuel excise tax and the prepaid sales tax, and either exempt or partially exempt from the petroleum business tax. These exemptions or partial exemptions apply as long as the fuel is not used on New York public highways (except by farmers to reach adjacent farmlands), or delivered to a filling station or into a tank equipped with a nozzle capable of fueling a motor vehicle (except for delivery at a farm site). (Sec. 282-a, Tax Law)

The definition of "motor fuel" is amended to include E85 and fuel-grade ethanol, among other products (Sec. 282(2), Tax Law). The definition of E85 is amended to describe it as a fuel blend consisting of ethanol and motor fuel that meets the American Society for Testing and Materials (ASTM) International active standard D5798 for fuel ethanol (Sec. 282(22), Tax Law). Previously, the law defined E85 as consisting of 85% ethanol and the remainder of which is motor fuel. (Sec. 282(2), Tax Law)

As a result of these changes, the sales and use tax law, in addition to other Tax Law articles, is amended to change the references to "automotive fuel" to "petroleum product" to avoid confusion with the use of that term as defined in Article 12-A and 13-A and in order to avoid the unintended consequence of changing the sales tax base. Article 37, related to crimes and other offenses as well as seizures and forfeitures, is amended to conform to the definitional changes made to the diesel fuel tax structure and to add a seizure provision for diesel motor fuel that would parallel the seizure provisions that already exist for motor fuel. Conforming changes are made to sections of the Criminal Procedures Law that were necessitated by the definitional changes made in Article 28. Also, various provisions of the Tax Law and the New York City Administrative Code are repealed because they are either outdated or have expired. (¶2106)

Sales tax definition: "Petroleum products" are motor fuel or diesel motor fuel, not including kerosene or propane used for residential purposes (Sec. 1101, Tax Law). This term replaces the term "automotive fuel" for sales tax purposes only.

For additional information on the taxation of motor fuels, see ¶2709, Motor Fuels Tax, and ¶2716, Tax on Petroleum and Aviation Fuel Businesses. For information on sales of dyed water-white kerosene, undyed kerosene, and kerosene sold as highway diesel motor fuel, see *TSB-M-11(12)M, TSB-M-11(18)S,* New York Department of Taxation and Finance, October 6, 2011, CCH NEW YORK TAX REPORTS, ¶407-379.

Various fuels used for specific purposes are exempt from sales and use taxes.

Diesel fuel: Enhanced [highway] diesel fuel used exclusively for residential purposes is exempt, but only when delivered into a storage tank that is attached to the heating unit burning the fuel and that is not equipped with a hose or other apparatus for dispensing the fuel into the fuel tank of a motor vehicle (Sec. 105-A(a), Tax Law).

Fuel sold to airline for use in airplanes: Fuel sold to an airline for use in its airplanes is exempt (Sec. 1115(a)(9), Tax Law). The taxability of fueling services furnished to an airline for use in its airplanes is dependent upon when title to the fuel vests in the airline. The charge for defueling an airplane is a taxable service to the airline as a service to tangible personal property.

Sales and uses of kero-jet fuel are exempt, including prepayment of the sales tax on motor and diesel motor fuels (Sec. 1115(j), Tax Law).

Fuel used in commercial and general aviation aircraft: Effective December 1, 2017, sales of fuel for use in commercial and general aviation aircraft are exempt from local sales taxes (Sec. 1210(a)(1)(i), Tax Law) and from the prepayment of sales tax on motor fuels (Sec. 1102(a)(1), Tax Law).

Fuel used by commercial vessels engaged in interstate commerce: An exemption is provided for fuel used by commercial vessels primarily engaged in interstate or foreign commerce (Sec. 1115(a)(8), Tax Law).

Fuel used by commercial fishing vessels: Fuel used by commercial fishing vessels that are engaged directly and predominantly in the harvesting of fish for sale is exempt (Sec. 1115(a)(24), Tax Law). The exemption does not include any vessel used predominantly for sport fishing purposes.

Fuel for firefighting and ambulance use: Purchases of motor fuel and diesel motor fuel by fire companies, fire departments, or voluntary ambulance services for their own use and consumption in firefighting vehicles, apparatus, or equipment, or emergency rescue or first aid response vehicles, apparatus, or equipment, owned and operated by the department, company, or service, are exempt from tax (Sec. 1116(b)(5), Tax Law).

• *Alternative motor fuels*

A sales and use tax exemption applies until September 1, 2021, to the following types of alternative fuels that are used or consumed directly and exclusively in motor vehicle engines (Sec. 1115(a)(42), Tax Law; *TSB-M-14(12)S,* July 24, 2014, CCH NEW YORK TAX REPORTS, ¶ 408-162):

— E85 (a mix of 85% ethanol and 15% motor fuel);

— CNG (fuel composed primarily of methanol suitable for motor fuel use); and

— hydrogen (fuel composed primarily of molecular hydrogen suitable for motor vehicle use).

In addition, a partial exemption is available for B20 fuel so that the sales and use tax is imposed at 80% of the cents-per-gallon rate (Sec. 1111(n), Tax Law). Note, however, that there is no exemption from the prepaid sales tax for B20 fuel. The prepaid sales tax for B20 fuel must be computed at the full amount and may not be reduced by 20%; see *TSB-M-16(3)M, TSB-M-16(4)S,* New York Department of Taxation and Finance, July 22, 2016, **https://www.tax.ny.gov/pdf/memos/multitax/ m16_3m_4s.pdf.**"B20" is a mixture consisting by volume of 20% biodiesel and 80% diesel motor fuel. However, if a county or city does not make the cents-per-gallon election, sales and use tax will be imposed on 80% of the receipts from the retail sale or taxable use of B20. Further, New York City is authorized to exempt or impose reduced rates on retail sales and uses of certain residential energy sources and services.

The sales and use tax exemption for compressed natural gas (CNG) includes natural gas purchased and used to produce CNG for use exclusively and directly in the engine of a motor vehicle (Sec.1115(a)(42), Tax Law; *TSB-M-13(3)S,* May 17, 2013, CCH NEW YORK TAX REPORTS, ¶ 407-837).

The definition of compressed natural gas (CNG) includes liquefied natural gas (LNG); see *TSB-M-13(1)M, TSB-M-13(1)S,* January 8, 2013, CCH NEW YORK TAX REPORTS, ¶ 407-756.

Local taxes: Local governments, including New York City, are authorized to compute their local sales tax on gasoline at a rate of cents per gallon equal to $2 or $3, multiplied by the percentage rate of such taxes within the locality.

Effective December 1, 2017, sales of fuel for use in commercial and general aviation aircraft are exempt from local sales taxes (Sec. 1210(a)(1)(i), Tax Law; Sec. 1210(a)(4)(xiv), Tax Law).

Prepayments: Sales tax prepayments are not required for CNG, hydrogen, and E85 when delivered to a filling station and placed in the filling station's storage tank for such E85 to be dispensed directly into a motor vehicle for use in its operation. Also, effective December 1, 2017, sales of fuel for use in commercial and general aviation aircraft are exempt from the prepayment of sales tax on motor fuels. (Sec. 1102(a)(1), Tax Law)

The New York Department of Taxation and Finance has issued a publication discussing the local sales and use tax rates on qualified motor fuel, diesel motor fuel, and B20 biodiesel. The publication also lists the localities that have elected the cents-per-gallon method of computing local sales tax on qualified fuel, and the applicable local cents-per-gallon rate. It also lists those localities that continue to use the percentage rate method of computing sales tax on qualified fuel, and the applicable percentage rate (*Publication 718-F*, New York Department of Taxation and Finance, CCH NEW YORK TAX REPORTS, ¶ 65-921, also at **https://www.tax.ny.gov/pdf/publications/sales/pub718f.pdf**).

¶2107 Farmer's Exemptions

Law: Secs. 1105(c)(3)(vi), 1115(a)(6), (19-a), (c), Tax Law; Reg. Sec. 528.7 (CCH NEW YORK TAX REPORTS, ¶ 60-250).

Tangible personal property (whether or not incorporated in a building or structure) for use or consumption directly and predominantly in the production for sale of tangible personal property by farming, including stock, dairy, poultry, fruit, fur bearing animal, graping, and truck farming, is exempt (Sec. 1115(a)(6), Tax Law). The term "farming" includes ranching, operating nurseries, greenhouses, vineyard trellises, or other similar structures used primarily for the raising of agricultural, horticultural, vinicultural, viticultural, or floricultural commodities, and operating orchards. Farming also includes aquaculture, silviculture, and the raising, growing, and harvesting of woodland products, such as Christmas trees (*TSB-M-99(4)S*, CCH NEW YORK TAX REPORTS, ¶ 300-300).

Milk crates: Milk crates are exempt when purchased by a dairy farmer or licensed milk distributor used exclusively and directly for the packaging and delivery of milk and milk products to customers (Sec. 1115(a)(19-a), Tax Law).

Posts and wire: Posts and wire used to make and maintain a trellis for grapes are exempt.

Motor vehicles: The exemption applies to motor vehicles if more than 50% of the vehicle's use is on property farmed by the purchaser or user or in direct trips between properties farmed by the purchaser or user (Sec. 1115(a)(6), Tax Law).

Silos: Tangible personal property for use in erecting or altering a silo used in farming is exempt if the property becomes an integral component part of the silo. Materials used to construct the concrete foundations of silos are also exempt if those materials become an integral part of the foundation (Reg. Sec. 528.7(a)(1)(ii)).

Electric fencing: The purchase of electric fences used in farming and various other building materials is exempt (Sec. 1101(b)(21), Tax Law).

Personal protective equipment: Personal protective equipment purchased by a person engaged in farming for use or consumption in farm production is exempt from New York State and local sales and use taxes, including New York City sales and use tax, if it is used or consumed by the farmer or the farmer's employee while engaged directly or predominantly in farm production. "Personal protective equipment" is tangible personal property designed to protect against environmental, chemical, mechanical, or processing hazards encountered while engaged directly in farm production that may cause injury or impairment through absorption, inhalation, or physical contact. It does not include clothing or apparel. Examples of personal protective equipment include devices to protect the eyes, face, ears, and head, or safety shoes (Reg. Sec. 528.7(e)).

Fuels and utilities: Farmers are also exempt from tax on purchases of fuel and utilities used predominantly in farm production or commercial horse boarding operations (Sec. 1115(c), Tax Law). However, by regulation, the tax on fuel and utility services must be initially paid and refunds claimed periodically on any exempt portions (Reg. Sec. 528.7(f)(2)). For additional information, see *TB-ST-244*, New York Department of Taxation and Finance, April 15, 2015, CCH NEW YORK TAX REPORTS, ¶ 408-382.

Services: The services of installing, maintaining, servicing, and repairing tangible personal property used or consumed directly and predominantly in farm production are exempt. Services used predominantly in either farm production or commercial horse boarding operations, or in both, are exempt (Sec. 1105(c)(3)(vi), Tax Law; Reg. Sec. 528.7(a)(2); *TB-ST-244*, New York Department of Taxation and Finance, April 15, 2015, CCH NEW YORK TAX REPORTS, ¶408-382).

Claim form: Farmers claim the exemption by filing the Farmer's Exemption Certificate (Form ST-125).

¶2108 Research and Development Exemption

Law: Secs. 1115(a)(10), (b)(ii), Tax Law; Reg. Sec. 528.11 (CCH NEW YORK TAX REPORTS, ¶60-510).

Tangible personal property for use or consumption directly and predominantly in research and development in the experimental or laboratory sense is exempt (Sec. 1115(a)(10), Tax Law). The exemption does not extend to installation and repair services for property used or consumed directly and predominantly in research and development (Reg. Sec. 528.11(a)(2)). "Research and development" does not include the ordinary testing or inspection of materials for quality control. Efficiency surveys, management studies, consumer surveys, advertising, promotions, and research for literary or historical projects are not considered research and development for purposes of the exemption (Reg. Sec. 528.11).

"Research and development in the experimental or laboratory sense" means research which has any of the following as its ultimate goal: (1) basic research in a scientific or technical field of endeavor; (2) advancing the technology in a scientific or technical field of endeavor; (3) the development of new products; (4) the improvement of existing products; or (5) the development of new uses for existing products (Reg. Sec. 528.11(b)(1)).

Gas, electricity, refrigeration, and steam as well as gas, electric, refrigeration, and steam service, are exempt if used or consumed directly and exclusively for research and development in the experimental or laboratory sense (Sec. 1115(b)(ii), Tax Law).

Other R&D-related exemptions: For information on other exemptions related to R&D activities, see *TB-ST-773*, February 3, 2014, CCH NEW YORK TAX REPORTS, ¶408-025.

Practitioner Comment: Research and Development Exemption Can Apply to Computers and Software

The exemption for "property purchased for use or consumption directly or predominantly" in research and development can include a computer aided design/computer aided manufacturing system as long as the combined hardware and software is used over 50% of the time in the research and development process. (*Dresser-Rand*, TSB-A-97(5)S)

Mark S. Klein, Esq., Hodgson Russ LLP

¶2109 Exempt Organizations

Law: Secs. 1115(a)(15), (a)(16), 1116, Tax Law (CCH NEW YORK TAX REPORTS, ¶60-094, ¶60-420, ¶60-580, ¶65-254).

The sales and compensating use taxes do not apply to any sales or amusement charges by or to certain organizations, or to any use or occupancy by them. The exempt organizations are as follows (Sec. 1116(a), Tax Law):

(1) The state of New York, its agencies, instrumentalities, public corporations (including a public corporation created pursuant to agreement or compact with another state or Canada), or political subdivisions when such organizations are the

purchasers, users, or consumers. The exemption for sales by these organizations applies only to sales of services or property of a kind not ordinarily sold by private persons;

(2) The United States, its agencies and instrumentalities, insofar as such organizations are immune from taxation as purchasers, users or consumers, or where such organizations sell services or property not ordinarily sold by private persons;

National banks: Federal legislation (12 U.S.C. §548) permits the imposition of sales and use taxes on national banks.

Federal savings and loan associations: Sales to such organizations are considered to be taxable (12 U.S.C. §1464).

Credit unions: Purchases by federal and New York State chartered credit unions are exempt (12 U.S.C. §1768; Sec. 1116(a)(9), Tax Law; *TSB-M-06(4.1)S,* Taxpayer Guidance Division, New York Department of Taxation and Finance, July 12, 2012, CCH NEW YORK TAX REPORTS, ¶407-596).

(3) The United Nations, or any international organization of which the United States is a member, as well as diplomatic missions and diplomatic personnel, as a purchaser, user, or consumer, or as a seller of services or property not ordinarily sold by private persons;

(4) Nonprofit organizations organized and operated exclusively for religious, charitable, scientific, testing for public safety, literary, or educational purposes, or to foster national or international amateur sports competition, or for the prevention of cruelty to children or animals;

(5) Posts or organizations of past or present members of the United States armed forces or an auxiliary unit or society organized in New York and meeting certain membership requirements, no part of the net earnings of which inures to the benefit of any private shareholder or individual. Authorized representatives of such organizations, when acting on behalf of those organizations, are not subject to hotel room occupancy taxes and are not required to pay sales taxes on hotel room occupancies (¶2009);

(6) The following Native American nations or tribes residing in New York State: Cayuga, Oneida, Onondaga, Poospatuck, Saint Regis Mohawk, Seneca, Shinnecock, Tonawanda, and Tuscarora, when the nation or tribe is the purchaser, user, or consumer;

(7) Not-for-profit corporations operating as health maintenance organizations subject to the provisions of Article 44 of the Public Health Law;

(8) Rural electric cooperatives;

(9) Qualified settlement funds and grantor trusts established to resolve and satisfy claims relating to World War II, the Holocaust, victims or targets of Nazi persecution, or treatment of refugees fleeing Nazi persecution.

Retail sales of tangible personal property by any shop or store operated by an organization described in paragraph (4), (5), or (6) are taxable. Similarly, sales of food or drink in or by a restaurant, tavern, or other establishment operated by an organization described in paragraph (1), (4), (5), or (6) are taxable unless the purchaser is an exempt organization. Sales of tangible personal property by a rural electric cooperative are taxable unless the purchaser is an exempt organization. Motor vehicle parking, garaging, or storing services by an organization described in paragraph (4) or (5) operating a garage or parking lot are taxable. Motor fuel and diesel fuel subject to the prepaid tax or the sales and use tax are also taxable, except for purchases of motor fuel by a hospital for its own use and consumption or purchases of diesel fuel by an organization described in paragraph (4) for its own heating use and consumption (¶2005).

Practitioner Comment: Not all Federally Exempt Organizations are Exempt from Sales Taxes

Receipt of a federal income tax exemption under IRC Sec. 501(c) does not mean that the organization is necessarily exempt from New York State sales taxes. In order to qualify for the sales tax exemption, the organization must be both organized and "operated exclusively" for religious, charitable, scientific or educational purposes. If the actual operations of the organization include a significant social aspect (*e.g.*, sponsoring networking events), the entity will not qualify for the exemption. (Regulation 529.7(c)(1)(iii))

Mark S. Klein, Esq., Hodgson Russ LLP

Sales by nonprofit organizations: All nonprofit tax-exempt organizations are required to collect sales and compensating use tax on additional retail sales, including online and mail-order catalogue sales, and rentals or s of tangible personal property (Sec. 1116, Tax Law; Reg. Secs. 526.10, 529.7, 529.8, and 529.9). Specifically, the following exempt organization sales are subject to state and local sales and compensating use taxes:

— retail sales of tangible personal property by any shop or store operated by an exempt organization;

— services provided under Secs. 1105(b) and 1105(c)(5), Tax Law, whether or not sold from the exempt organization's shop or store;

— retail sales of tangible personal property and services under Secs. 1105(b) and 1105(c)(5), Tax Law, by that organization that are made with a degree of regularity, frequency, and continuity by remote means, such as by telephone, the Internet, or mail order; or

— retail sales of tangible personal property by lease or rental by the exempt organization as lessor, whether or not at a shop or store.

Services described in Sec. 1105(b), Tax Law, are commonly known as consumer utility services. Services described in Sec. 1105(c)(5), Tax Law, consist of maintaining, servicing, and repairing real property.

For additional information, see *TSB-M-08(5)S*, August 11, 2008, CCH New York Tax Reports, ¶60-580, and *TSB-M-08(15)S*, December 18, 2008, CCH New York Tax Reports, ¶406-257.

Occupancy in a hotel operated on the premises of a nonprofit organization in furtherance of the activities of the nonprofit organization is not subject to the tax on hotel occupancy.

Materials that are incorporated into construction work performed for an exempt organization are exempt from tax when purchased by the contractor (¶2102).

Veteran's home gift shops: Retail sales of tangible personal property by any gift shop located in a veteran's home are exempt from sales and compensating use taxes (Sec. 1115(ff), Tax Law).

Trash removal by municipal corporations: Trash removal, when the service is rendered by or on behalf of a municipal corporation (other than New York City), is exempt (Sec. 1116(e), Tax Law).

Innovation Hot Spots: A qualified entity that is a tenant in (or is part of) a New York State Innovation Hot Spot is eligible for a credit or refund for the 4% state sales and use tax and the 3/8% tax imposed in the Metropolitan Commuter Transportation District on the retail sale of tangible personal property and certain taxable services. The credit or refund is allowed for 60 months, beginning with the first full month

¶2109

after the qualified entity becomes a tenant or becomes part of an Innovation Hot Spot. (Secs. 38(1)(d), 1119(d)(1), Tax Law; see also *TSB-M-14(2)S*, March 7, 2014, CCH NEW YORK TAX REPORTS, ¶ 408-039)

- *Purchases by governmental entities*

For purposes of New York sales and use, motor fuel, diesel motor fuel, and petroleum business taxes, the Department of Taxation and Finance has issued *Publication 765, Sales and Fuel Excise Tax Information for Properly Appointed Agents of New York Governmental Entities*. The publication explains the scope of the exemption, the legal requirements that generally must be satisfied for an agency relationship to exist, and the new procedures that the Department has created in order for a properly appointed agent to make purchases exempt from sales and fuel excise taxes.

A New York governmental entity and its properly appointed agent must complete Form DTF-122, Certification of Agency Appointment by a New York Governmental Entity. When making a purchase of tangible personal property or services on behalf of a New York governmental entity, the agent must provide the vendor with a copy of a properly completed Form ST-122, Exempt Purchase Certificate for an Agent of a New York Governmental Entity. When making a purchase of motor fuel, diesel motor fuel, or residual petroleum product on behalf of a New York governmental entity, the agent must provide the vendor with a copy of a properly completed Form FT-122, Fuel Tax Exempt Purchase Certificate for an Agent of a New York Governmental Entity (*TSB-M-05(6)S* and *TSB-M-05(3)M*, June 8, 2005, CCH NEW YORK TAX REPORTS, ¶ 300-467).

CCH Advisory: State Contractors

As a result of concerns regarding the scope of the sales tax exemption applicable to contractors working for New York State and its instrumentalities, rules arre imposed and forms promulgated to govern all purchases made by agents on behalf of a New York State governmental entity (*TSB-M-05(6)S*, CCH NEW YORK TAX REPORTS, ¶ 300-467).

¶2110 Exempt Admission Charges

Law: Secs. 1105, 1116, 1123, Tax Law; Reg. Secs. 527.10, 527.11 (CCH NEW YORK TAX REPORTS, ¶ 60-230).

Admission charges are not taxable, subject to the restrictions noted below, if all of the proceeds inure exclusively to the benefit of the following organizations (Sec. 1116(d)(1), Tax Law):

— an exempt nonprofit organization, war veterans post or Native American nation or tribe (as described at (4), (5), or (6) under "Exempt Organizations" (¶ 2109));

— societies or organizations conducted for the sole purpose of maintaining symphony orchestras or operas and receiving substantial support from voluntary contributions;

— national guard organizations; and

— local police or fire departments, or voluntary fire or ambulance companies, or police or fire department retirement or disability funds.

Amusement park admissions: A permanent exemption from state and local sales tax exists for 75% of the admission charges to a qualifying place of amusement. The exemption also applies to the sales tax imposed by the state in the Metropolitan Commuter Transportation District (MCTD).

- *Restrictions on exempt admission charges*

Some admission charges are taxable, even when performances are for the benefit of the above organizations, as follows (Sec. 1116(d)(2), Tax Law):

— admissions to athletic games or exhibitions are taxable unless the proceeds inure exclusively to the benefit of elementary or secondary schools or, in the case of an athletic game between elementary or secondary schools, the entire gross proceeds inure to an exempt organization (as described at (4) under "Exempt Organizations" (¶ 2109)); and

— carnivals and rodeos are taxable if there are any paid professional performers unless the entire net profit inures exclusively to the benefit of a charitable or educational organization that has as its charitable or educational purpose the operation of a school and the operation of such a carnival or rodeo.

Admission charges to the following are nontaxable if no part of the net earnings inures to the benefit of any stockholders (Sec. 1116(d)(3), Tax Law):

— admissions to agricultural fairs when the proceeds are used exclusively for the improvement, operation, etc., of such fairs;

— admissions to historical homes and gardens; and

— admissions to historic sites, houses, shrines, and museums operated by organizations devoted to the preservation of such places.

For other exempt admissions, see ¶ 2010.

• *Nontaxable admission charges*

Tax is not imposed upon charges for admission to: race tracks, boxing, sparring or wrestling matches or exhibitions taxed under another provision of New York law, dramatic or musical arts performances, or live circus performances, motion picture theaters or sporting facilities where the patron is to be a participant (such as bowling alleys and swimming pools) (Sec. 1105(f)(1), Tax Law; *TB-ST-535*, August 7, 2014, CCH New York Tax Reports, ¶ 408-183).

Admission charges to an establishment where live dramatic or musical art performances are offered and food, refreshments or merchandise served or sold incidentally to such performance are exempt from tax (Reg. Sec. 527.10(d)(2)). For sales tax purposes, variety shows, magic shows, circuses, animal acts, ice shows, aquatic shows and similar performances are not considered "dramatic or musical arts performances."

Practitioner Comment: Admission to Adult Entertainment Facility Not Exempt from Tax

New York's highest court held that nude dancing and similar types of "adult entertainment" do not qualify for the sales tax exemption applicable to "live dramatic or musical arts performances." According to the Court, the exemption envisions performances that are "cultural and artistic" and does not extend to performances that attempt to recreate dances viewed on YouTube. (*677 New Loudon Corp. d/b/a Nite Moves v, TAT,* __NY3d__ (2012); CCH New York Tax Reports, ¶ 407-673; *certiorari denied,* October 15, 2013, U.S. Supreme Court, Dkt. 13-38). A recent decision of New York's Tax Appeals Tribunal further held that charges for private room dances, even if choreographed, were similarly taxable since the rooms for private performances do not constitute a "theatre, hall or place of assembly". (*677 New Loudon Corp.* (TAT 8-25-16)).

Mark S. Klein, Hodgson Russ LLP

Admission charges to a roof garden, cabaret, or other similar place to attend a dramatical or musical arts performance are exempt if the following conditions are satisfied (Sec. 1123, Tax Law):

— the admission charges are separately stated;

— separately stated charges for food, drink, service, and merchandise are not less on a day when the place offers performances than on days when it does not offer them, or if the place is open for business only when it offers performances, separately stated charges for food, drink, service, and merchandise are comparable to charges for comparable items at other similar places, restaurants, and taverns; and

— the place retains and makes available the menus and any other statements of its charges, showing all of its charges for food, drink, service, merchandise, and admission.

Admission charges to the following places or events are also tax-exempt, provided that no part of the net earnings inures to the benefit of any stockholder: agricultural fairs; historical homes and gardens; and historic sites, houses and shrines and museums (Sec. 1116(d)(3), Tax Law).

¶2111 Vendor Collection Credit

Law: Secs. 10, 1136, 1137(f), Tax Law (CCH New York Tax Reports, ¶61-270).

A business is eligible for the vendor collection credit if it files sales tax returns on a quarterly basis (Form ST-100) or on an annual basis (Form ST-101). The following businesses are not eligible for the vendor collection credit: businesses that file, or are required to file, their sales tax returns on a monthly basis (Form ST-809 and Form ST-810), and businesses enrolled in the PrompTax program for sales tax. (*TB-ST-925,* New York Department of Taxation and Finance, November 2, 2010, CCH New York Tax Reports, ¶407-034)

The vendor credit is equal to 5% of the state, local, and other taxes and fees (excluding penalties or interest) required to be reported on, and paid or paid over with such returns that are timely filed (i.e. state and local basis) (Sec. 1137(f), Tax Law). The maximum amount of the credit is $200 (Sec. 1137(f), Tax Law).

Limitation of credit: The vendor credit was eliminated, effective June 1, 2010, for certain large vendors who file or are required to file a monthly part-quarterly return pursuant to Sec. 1136(a)(2), Tax Law, or vendors who pay or are required to pay tax electronically pursuant to Sec. 10, Tax Law.

¶2112 Empire Zones and Other Localized Exemptions

Law: Secs. 1115, 1119, Tax Law; Sec. 874, General Municipal Law (CCH New York Tax Reports, ¶60-360).

For purchases made on or before June 30, 2010, a refund or credit of sales and use tax was allowed to a person who paid the tax on tangible personal property purchased for use in constructing, expanding, or rehabilitating industrial or commercial real property located in an area designated as an Empire Zone pursuant to Article 18-B of the General Municipal Law (Sec. 1115(z), Tax Law; *TSB-M-10(6)S,* June 30, 2010, CCH New York Tax Reports, ¶406-868).

A business enterprise or taxpayer that was certified before the program expired may continue to claim Empire Zone (EZ) tax benefits if it moves or expands after the expiration into a new property that is within the zone where the business or taxpayer was certified. If a business enterprise or taxpayer discontinues the business operations on which its EZ certification was predicated, the business enterprise or taxpayer would no longer be deemed to be certified as an EZ business for Tax Law purposes and would no longer be able to claim EZ tax benefits. (*TSB-M-11(2)C, (3)I, (4)S,* New York Department of Taxation and Finance, April 5, 2011, CCH New York Tax Reports, ¶407-188)

The refund or credit is only available to the extent that such property becomes an integral component part of the real property. The refund or credit does not apply for property used exclusively by one or more registered vendors primarily engaged in the retail sale of tangible personal property (Sec. 1115(z), Tax Law).

No refund or credit is allowed for local taxes paid unless the local law so provides. The refund or credit does not apply to the New York City sales and use taxes or to the sales and use taxes imposed for the benefit of the Metropolitan Commuter Transportation District.

• *Qualified empire zone enterprises (QEZEs)*

For purchases made on or before June 30, 2010, New York offered sales and use tax credits or refunds for Qualified Empire Zone Enterprises (QEZEs) under the

Empire Zone Program. The credits or refunds do not apply for local sales and use tax purposes unless the city, county, or school district imposing the tax elects to provide the QEZE credit or refund (Sec. 14, Tax Law; Sec. 1119(d), Tax Law; *TSB-M-09(12)S*, July 23, 2009, CCH NEW YORK TAX REPORTS, ¶406-460; *Important Notice N-09-14*, July 2009, CCH NEW YORK TAX REPORTS, ¶406-462). All sales to QEZEs are fully taxable as of September 1, 2009. Prior to that date, a sales and use tax exemption was available for items and services, including utility services, sold to a QEZE for use in designated areas.

A QEZE is a business enterprise that has been certified as eligible to receive benefits under Article 18-B of the General Municipal Law and that annually meets an employment test (described at ¶124).

For the credit or refund to apply, at least 50% of the tangible personal property or services must be directly used or consumed by the QEZE in the empire zone (100%, in the case of utility services) (*Important Notice N-01-7*, February 1, 2001, CCH NEW YORK TAX REPORTS, ¶320-068). Motor vehicles purchased or rented must be predominantly used by the QEZE in the empire zone in order to qualify for the exemption. The same standard applies to tangible personal property used in or on a motor vehicle, such as a battery, diesel motor fuel, an engine, engine components, motor fuel, a muffler, tires, and similar property.

Empire Zone reform: The Empire Zone program's sunset date is June 30, 2010.

The exemption also applies to property used by a contractor in improving or maintaining the real property of a QEZE or in erecting a structure for such an enterprise. The exemption does not apply for local sales and use tax purposes unless the city, county, or school district imposing the tax elects otherwise.

Forms: To make an exempt purchase, the QEZE had to give the vendor Form ST-121.6, Qualified Empire Zone Enterprise (QEZE) Exempt Purchase Certificate. A contractor who purchased property or services for use in a qualifying project for a QEZE had to provide the vendor with Form ST-120.1, Contractor Exempt Purchase Certificate. A properly completed exemption document accepted in good faith relieves the vendor from responsibility for collecting the sales tax.

For additional information, see *TSB-M-02(5)S*, New York Department of Taxation and Finance, CCH NEW YORK TAX REPORTS, ¶300-366, and *TSB-M-05(7)S*, CCH NEW YORK TAX REPORTS, ¶300-469.

- *Empire zones*

Additional information on Empire Zones is found at ¶12-060 in CCH NEW YORK TAX REPORTS.

- *Lower Manhattan exemptions*

In order to encourage businesses to locate or relocate in lower Manhattan, incentive measures have been enacted that include sales tax exemptions and a commercial rent tax exemption (Ch. 2 (S.B. 5930), Laws 2005).

Sales tax exemptions: Two sales and use tax exemptions exist for certain purchases of tangible personal property and services related to new commercial office space leases (as opposed to ground leases) of 10 years or more. The exemptions differ based on the location of the leased premises in two specific eligible areas. The first area (Eligible Area A) consists of a broad area of lower Manhattan below City Hall. The second area (Eligible Area B) consists of the World Trade Center site, the World

Financial Center, and the Battery Park City area. The exemptions provided for in Eligible Area B are broader in scope and longer in duration than those provided for in Eligible Area A. Accordingly, for leased commercial office space located within both eligible areas, the broader exemptions granted in Eligible Area A apply. The exemptions apply to the state and local sales and use taxes imposed in New York City, including the additional tax imposed by the state within the Metropolitan Commuter Transportation District (MCTD). The exemptions do not apply to sales and use taxes imposed by other counties or cities within New York. (Sec. 1115(ee), Tax Law; *TSB-M-05(12)S*, CCH NEW YORK TAX REPORTS, ¶300-479)

To qualify for the exemptions, the term of the lease for the commercial office space must be for a term of 10 years or more beginning on or after September 1, 2005, but not later than September 1, 2015 (Eligible Area A) or September 1, 2017 (Eligible Area B). The sales tax exemptions for Eligible Area A will expire on December 1, 2016. The sales tax exemptions for Eligible Area B will expire on December 1, 2018. (*TSB-M-09(14)S*, August 27, 2009, CCH NEW YORK TAX REPORTS, ¶406-510)

Commercial rent tax exemption: A five-year exemption is provided from the commercial rent tax for new and renewed leases with a term of at least five years for leases of property for retail sales that are located in the New York City Liberty Zone and the World Trade Center area and that begin July 1, 2005, through June 30, 2015 (Sec. 11-704(i)(2)(b), NYC Adm. Code). See also ¶3302.

• *Economic transformation areas*

The Economic Transformation and Facility Redevelopment Program provides incentives to attract new businesses and jobs in communities affected by the closing of certain correctional and youth facilities. Generally, an economic transformation area means an area limited to the site of a closed facility or an area within a certain radius of a closed facility. The designation of the size of an economic transformation area will vary depending on factors including, but not limited to, the closed facility's location and the population density, poverty rate, unemployment rate, and the loss of jobs at that facility and in the region. Special rules apply for areas within the Metropolitan Commuter Transportation District and the Port Authority District. (*TSB-M-11(9)S*, New York Department of Taxation and Finance, June 10, 2011, CCH NEW YORK TAX REPORTS, ¶407-285)

Incentive refunds of sales and use taxes. In addition to economic transformation and facility redevelopment income tax credits available, a participant may be eligible for a refund of New York state sales or use tax paid for certain purchases of tangible personal property. The tangible personal property must be used in construction, expansion, or rehabilitation of industrial or commercial real property and must become an integral part of the property that is located within an economic transformation area. To qualify, the tangible personal property must be purchased or contracted to be purchased after the participant receives its Certificate of Eligibility and be incorporated into real property before a certificate of occupancy is issued for the real property. (Sec. 1119(f), Tax Law; *TSB-M-11(9)S*, New York Department of Taxation and Finance, June 10, 2011, CCH NEW YORK TAX REPORTS, ¶407-285)

A refund is also available for sales tax paid on certain purchases of tangible personal property used by contractors. The tangible personal property must be used in erecting a structure or building after the participant has received its Certificate of Eligibility, or in adding, altering, or improving a participant's real property, property, or land. To qualify, the tangible personal property must become an integral part of the property improvements and the structure, building, real property, property, or land and must be located within an economic transformation area. The tangible personal property must be in the contractor's inventory on or after the day the participant receives its Certificate of Eligibility, or the contractor must purchase or be contracted to purchase the property after the participant receives its Certificate of Eligibility. The tangible personal property must be incorporated into the real property before a certificate of occupancy is issued. There is no refund available for tax paid on services that the contractor may provide in relation to the tangible personal property, including the services of installing the tangible personal property. The refunds described above are applicable only to the 4% state portion of the sales tax paid. They do not apply to any local sales tax imposed by a county or city and do not apply to the sales tax imposed in the Metropolitan Commuter Transportation District (MCTD). The participant or contractor may only apply for a refund once per sales tax quarter, and the amount cannot be claimed as a credit on a sales tax return. Refunds must be claimed within three years after the tax was payable to the department. The provisions are scheduled to expire on December 31, 2021. (Sec. 1119(f), Tax Law; *TSB-M-11(9)S*, New York Department of Taxation and Finance, June 10, 2011, CCH NEW YORK TAX REPORTS, ¶ 407-285)

• *Industrial development agencies*

Industrial Development Agencies (IDAs) promote and develop recreational, industrial, and commercial facilities for the benefit of the people of New York. Purchases of tangible personal property made in order to carry out its purposes are exempt from sales tax. The agency may extend to a designated agent or project operator its sales tax exemption. However, the agency must give the affected taxing jurisdiction 30-days notice as to whom the person will be by filing Form ST 60. The form must disclose the IDA's name address and phone number; the name, address, phone number, and employee identification number of the project operator or agent; the name and address of the project; a brief description of the goods or services intended to be exempted as well as an estimate of their value; the effective dates of the appointment; and the name, title, telephone number and dated signature of the officer or employee signing the form. Also, effective March 28. 2013, the IDA must indicate the project to which the benefits are being provided and supply any other information the department may require. (Sec. 874, General Municipal Law; *TSB-M-97(11)S*, December 27, 1997, CCH NEW YORK TAX REPORTS, ¶ 300-238)

Contractors and others (purchasers) appointed as agents for the IDA should obtain a letter from the IDA written on IDA letterhead, signed by a responsible officer of the IDA and containing a statement identifying the contract, the project, and the purchaser, and authorizing the purchaser to make purchases for the project as agent of the IDA. When making purchases as agent, the purchaser need only provide the supplier with a copy of this letter to establish the exemption. The supplier must identify the project on each bill and invoice for such purchases and indicate on the bill or invoice that the IDA or agent for the IDA was the purchaser. If an IDA amends, revokes, or cancels its appointment of an agent, or if an agent's appointment becomes invalid for any reason, the IDA must send a letter to the department within 30 calendar days indicating the change in appointment. Form ST-60 includes instructions with respect to this requirement. Failure to file Form ST 60 could result in the revocation of the IDA's authority to provide state and local sales and use tax exemption benefits. (*Important Notice N-13-3*, April 30, 2013, CCH NEW YORK TAX REPORTS, ¶ 407-816)

Practitioner Comment: IDA Exemption Can Apply to Vehicles

New York's courts have held that industrial development agencies can provide a sales tax exemption for the purchase of automobiles and trucks, where the industrial development agency specifically designated the taxpayer as its agent to purchase the vehicles. The fact that the vehicles may be temporarily used outside of the agency's jurisdiction is irrelevant. (*Elmer W. Davis v. Commissioner of Tax and Finance*, Appellate Division of the Supreme Court of New York, Third Department, No. 511256, 104 A.D.3d 50, 957 N.Y.S.2d 427, December 27, 2012; CCH NEW YORK TAX REPORTS, ¶ 407-750)

Mark S. Klein, Esq., Hodgson Russ LLP

• *START-UP NY program*

New York has enacted the SUNY Tax-Free Areas to Revitalize and Transform Upstate (START-UP) New York program, which provides personal and corporate income tax, sales and use tax, property tax, and transfer tax incentives to promote business and job creation by transforming public higher education through tax-free communities in upstate New York and other strategically-designated locations. An exemption from the Metropolitan Commuter Transportation Mobility Tax (MCTMT) is also created. In addition, the Excelsior Jobs Program is enhanced by reducing the applicable job creation requirements (*e.g.*, a participant is required to create 10 manufacturing jobs, rather than 25). Also, a taxpayer that creates at least 75% of the estimated jobs is allowed a proportionally reduced credit. Details are as follows (Ch. 68 (A.B. 8113), Laws 2013, effective June 24, 2013, unless otherwise noted; *TSB-M-13(7)C, (6)I, (11)M, (1)MCTMT, (7)S*, New York Department of Taxation and Finance, October 22, 2013; CCH NEW YORK TAX REPORTS, ¶ 407-909):

Applicability: The tax benefits apply to taxable years beginning on or after January 1, 2014, to calendar quarters beginning on or after January 1, 2014, to sales tax quarters beginning on or after March 1, 2014, or to transactions occurring on or after January 1, 2014, whichever is applicable.

Qualifications: Among other requirements for eligibility, a business must be a new start-up company, an out-of-state company relocating to New York, or an expansion of an existing New York company. The business must also create and maintain net new jobs. Businesses will not be eligible if they compete with existing businesses that are not within the tax-free area, and certain types of businesses are specifically excluded (*e.g.*, restaurants, real estate management companies, and retail, wholesale, or personal service businesses).

Sales and use tax provisions: A business will be eligible for a credit or refund of sales and use taxes imposed on the retail sale of tangible personal property or services and similar taxes. The credit or refund shall be allowed for 120 consecutive months beginning with the month during which such business locates in the tax-free NY area. (Sec. 39(f), Tax Law)

The Empire State Development agency website (**http://www.empire.state.ny.us/**) has information on the START-UP NY program.

SALES AND USE TAXES

CHAPTER 22
RETURNS, PAYMENT, ADMINISTRATION

¶2201 Registration

Law: Secs. 5-a, 1131, 1134, 1135, Tax Law; Reg. Sec. 533.1 (CCH NEW YORK TAX REPORTS, ¶60-020, ¶61-240, ¶65-530—¶65-555).

Forms: DTF-17, Application for Registration as a Sales Tax Vendor.

Every person required to collect sales and use taxes commencing business or opening a new place of business, every person purchasing or selling tangible personal property for resale commencing business or opening a new place of business, every person selling automotive fuel (including those that are not distributors), any of the foregoing who takes possession of or pays for business assets in a bulk sale, and any person required to register that has had its certificate of authority revoked, must register with the Commissioner (Sec. 1134(a)(1), Tax Law). Even though a business is located in another state, if it has customers in New York, it may be required to register as a vendor for New York sales tax purposes if the business has sufficient connection with New York State. Generally, the certificate of registration must be filed at least 20 days prior to commencing business or opening a new place of business or purchasing, selling, or taking of possession or payment, whichever comes first.

Practitioner Comment: Home-Based Sellers Can Be Considered Vendors

New York State has issued a bulletin reminding taxpayers that sales tax collection and registration is required for all businesses, even those that operate exclusively from the taxpayer's home. This includes taxpayers that sell items on a regular basis through online auctions or other Internet-based sites. (TB–ST–807).

Mark S. Klein, Hodgson Russ LLP

Upon registration, the Department of Taxation and Finance will issue a certificate of authority to collect the tax together with duplicate certificates for any additional places of business (Sec. 1134(a)(2), Tax Law) (See *Publication 750, A Guide to Sales Tax in New York State,* November 1, 2015, CCH NEW YORK TAX REPORTS, ¶65-975). There is no registration fee.

Vendors who regularly or systematically deliver tangible personal property or services in New York State by means other than the United States mail or common carrier are required to file a certificate of registration within 30 days after the day on which the cumulative total number of occasions that they came into the state to deliver such property or services, for the immediately preceding four quarterly periods ending on the last day of February, May, August, and November, exceeds 12 (Sec. 1101(b)(8)(i)(4), Tax Law).

For vendors who regularly or systematically solicit business in the state by distributing catalogs, advertising flyers or letters or other means of solicitation, where the solicitation satisfies federal nexus requirements, a certificate of registration must be filed within 30 days after the day on which the cumulative total of their gross receipts from sales of property delivered in the state, for the immediately preceding four quarterly periods ending on the last day of February, May, August, and November, exceeds $300,000 and the number of such sales exceeds 100 (Sec. 1101(b)(8)(i)(5), Tax Law).

Vendors who retain an ownership interest in property or services subject to tax must file a certificate of registration within 30 days after the property is brought into the state by a buyer who is or becomes a resident, or uses the property in any manner in carrying on any employment, trade, business, or profession within the state (Sec. 1101(b)(8)(i)(6), Tax Law).

Show promoters: Promoters of flea markets and similar shows are required, at least 10 days prior to the opening of a show, to file with the Commissioner a notice stating the location and date of such show (Sec. 1134(b)(1), Tax Law). Within five days after the receipt of the notice, the Commissioner will issue to the show promoter, without charge, a permit to operate the show (Sec. 1134(b)(2), Tax Law). If a permit is denied, the show promoter has a right to a hearing in the Division of Tax Appeals.

Show promoters must not permit any person to display for sale or to sell tangible personal property or services subject to tax at a show unless the person is registered and displays a certificate of authority. The permit must be prominently displayed at the main entrance to the show (Sec. 1134(b)(2), Tax Law). If a permit has not been received by the show promoter in time, and if a notice has been properly filed, the requirement to display the permit is considered to have been complied with, unless and until the show promoter receives the permit or receives a notice from the Commissioner denying the permit.

Promoters of entertainment events: Promoters of entertainment events must, at least 20 days prior to the event, file with the Commissioner a notice and application for an entertainment promoter certificate (Sec. 1134(c)(1), Tax Law).

Contractors: Contracts entered into by contractors and subcontractors (including their affiliates) with state agencies are generally not valid if they made sales deliveries by any means to locations within New York of tangible personal property or taxable services having a value in excess of $300,000 during the immediately preceding four sales tax quarters, and are not registered for New York sales and use tax purposes with the Commissioner of the Department of Taxation and Finance. Contractors must certify their compliance and the compliance of any affiliates and subcontractors before a contract valued at more than $100,000 with a state agency may take effect (Sec. 5-a (2)(b), Tax Law; *TB-ST-118,* New York Department of Taxation and Finance, June 12, 2013, CCH New York Tax Reports, ¶ 407-862).

¶2202 Returns

Law: Secs. 1133(b), 1136, 1137-A, 1142, 1145, Tax Law; Reg. Sec. 533.3 (CCH New York Tax Reports, ¶ 61-220, ¶ 62-530).

Forms: ST-100, New York State and Local Quarterly Sales and Use Tax Return; ST-130, Purchaser's Report of Sales and Use Tax.

¶2202

Every person who is required to register with the Commissioner of Taxation and Finance, or who voluntarily registers, is required to file returns (Sec. 1136(a), Tax Law). If at any time during the course of a year, a vendor's total tax due is in excess of $3,000, the vendor must file a quarterly or monthly return, rather than an annual return (Reg. Sec. 533.3(d)(6)). Payment of tax accompanies the return (Sec. 1137(e)(1), Tax Law; see also *TB-ST-275*, New York Department of Taxation and Finance, June 13, 2014, at **http://www.tax.ny.gov/pubs_and_bulls/tg_bulletins/st/filing_requirements _for_sales_and_use_tax_returns.htm**).

No tax due: Taxpayers who file periodic sales tax returns, but have no taxable sales to report, now may file online using the Department's "No Sales Tax Due" online return. Taxpayers may access this through the Department's Online Tax Center located at **https://www.tax.ny.gov/bus/st/stmp.htm**

Quarterly returns: Every person required to register with the Commissioner of Taxation and Finance whose taxable receipts, amusement charges and rents total less than $300,000, and any distributor whose sales of petroleum products total less than 100,000, in every quarter of the preceding four quarters, are required to file a quarterly return. If the Commissioner of Taxation and Finance deems it necessary to protect revenue, he or she may give notice to quarterly filers requiring such persons to file either short-form or long-form part quarterly returns, in addition to filing a quarterly return. (Sec. 1136(a)(1), Tax Law; TB-ST-275, New York Department of Taxation and Finance, June 16, 2011, CCH New York Tax Reports, ¶407-297).

Monthly returns: Every person whose taxable receipts, amusement charges and rents total $300,000 or more, and any distributor whose sales of automotive fuel total 100,000 gallons or more, in any quarter of the preceding four quarters, must, in addition to filing a quarterly return, file either a long-form or short-form part-quarterly return on a monthly basis (Sec. 1136(a)(2), Tax Law). Persons required to file monthly may elect to file either a long-form or short-form, part-quarterly return. A "long-form, part-quarterly return" reports the actual sales and use taxes for the preceding month. A person filing a "long-form, part-quarterly return" for each of the months contained in a quarter is also required to file a quarterly return for the quarter. A "short-form, part-quarterly return" may be used for the first two months of any quarter to report sales and use taxes for each month on the basis on one-third of the combined state and local sales and use taxes paid in the comparable quarter of the preceding year.

A person who is required to register and who is selling automotive fuel but is not a distributor of motor fuel must file an information return quarterly, or monthly if the Commissioner deems it necessary (Sec. 1136(a), Tax Law).

Filing of surety bond or other security: Any person who fails to collect, truthfully account for or pay over the sales tax, or file sales tax returns and whose financial condition is found to impair the ability to pay over tax may be required, upon notice from the commissioner, to collect such taxes and deposit them at least one time per week in a separate account in any banking institution in the state. Such notice may require either that the account be held in trust for and payable to the commissioner or that the person authorize the commissioner to debit the account. Any person who fails to comply with such notice is required to file a bond. The commissioner may revoke or suspend any person's sales tax certificate of authority if the person fails to obtain such a bond or fails to comply with such a notice issued by the commissioner. (Sec. 1137(e)(3), Tax Law)

Due dates: The returns and information returns required to be filed quarterly must be filed for quarterly periods ending on the last day of February, May, August, and November of each year. Each return and each information return must be filed within 20 days after the end of the quarterly period covered by the return. Monthly returns are due on or before the 20th day of the succeeding month (Sec. 1136(b), Tax

Law; *TB-ST-275*, New York Department of Taxation and Finance, June 13, 2014, at http://www.tax.ny.gov/pubs_and_bulls/tg_bulletins/st/filing_requirements_for_ sales_and_use_tax_returns.htm).

Practitioner Comment: Delinquent Taxpayers' Filing Requirements

New York's Tax Department has begun to impose additional filing requirements on taxpayers with a history of late filing or payment of sales taxes. Once notified by the Department, affected taxpayers may be required to deposit collected sales taxes into a separate bank account at a Tax Department-approved bank. The State may also require deposits be made on a weekly basis and that the taxpayer begin filing monthly sales tax returns instead of quarterly or less frequently. Failure to comply with these requirements could cause the business's certificate of authority to be suspended or revoked. (*TSB-M-11(9)S*. Department of Taxation and Finance, June 10, 2011, CCH NEW YORK TAX REPORTS, ¶ 407-285)

Mark S. Klein, Esq., Hodgson Russ LLP

Purchasers' returns: Persons not required to file periodic returns, who purchase or use taxable property or services without paying tax to the seller, must file returns within 20 days from the date of purchase.

Casual sales: Reports of casual sales must also be filed by persons not required to file periodic returns who make taxable sales of tangible personal property or services. Reports of casual sales must show the amount of sales of tangible personal property and services, food and drink, amusement charges, and rents and the amount of purchases subject to use tax, for each jurisdiction, as well as totals of all jurisdictions (Reg. Sec. 533.3(g)).

Sales for resale: Persons required to register only because they are purchasing or selling tangible property for resale, and who are not required to collect any tax or pay any tax directly to the Commissioner, must file an annual information return (Sec. 1136(a), Tax Law).

Sales to itinerant vendors: The Commissioner of Taxation and Finance is authorized to adopt regulations requiring persons registered or required to be registered under Sec. 1134, Tax Law, to file reports regarding sales for resale within the state of tangible personal property or services to itinerant vendors (Sec. 1136(h), Tax Law).

Show promoters and entertainment promoters: Every show and entertainment promoter must file a monthly report within 20 days after the end of the preceding month for all shows or all entertainment events, respectively, for which the person was a promoter during the preceding month. Such reports must list the date and place of each show or event and the name, address and certificate of authority number, by show or event, of every person permitted to display for sale or who made sales of tangible personal property or services subject to tax at the show or event (Sec. 1136(f), Tax Law).

Signature methods of tax return preparers: Tax return preparers are authorized to sign original tax returns, amended tax returns, claims for refund, and requests for extension of time to file manually or by means of a rubber stamp, mechanical device, or computer software program. These alternative methods of signing must include either a facsimile of the individual preparer's signature or the individual preparer's printed name.

Electronic filing: Some taxpayers must use Sales Tax Web File to file their quarterly sales and use tax returns. Taxpayers may electronically file their sales tax return early and schedule their payment through the due date. As a quarterly sales tax filer, a taxpayer must Web File if its business meets all three of the following conditions:

¶2202

— it does not use a tax preparer to prepare the required filings;

— it uses a computer to prepare, document or calculate the required filings or related schedules or is subject to the corporation tax e-file mandate; and

— it has broadband Internet access.

(*Release,* New York Department of Taxation and Finance, May 31, 2011)

To use Sales Tax Web File to electronically file quarterly or part-quarterly returns, taxpayers should visit the Department's Web site at **www.nystax.gov** and register on the Online Tax Center.

• *Information returns*

Annual information returns are required from persons required to register solely because they are purchasing or selling tangible personal property for resale and who are not required to collect or pay any tax directly to the Commissioner (Sec. 1136(a), Tax Law). The annual return covers the period from March 1 through the end of the following February.

In addition to all other returns, the following persons must file annual information returns:

— every insurer licensed to issue motor vehicle physical damage or motor vehicle property damage liability insurance for motor vehicles registered in New York if, during the period covered by the return, it has paid consideration or an amount under an insurance contract for the servicing or repair of a motor vehicle on behalf of an insured. For each person to whom the insurer paid the consideration, the return must report the total amount paid for that period, along with other required information (*TSB-M-09(8)S,* July 2, 2009, CCH NEW YORK TAX REPORTS, ¶ 406-438);

— every franchisor that has at least one franchisee that is required to be registered for sales and use tax purposes. For each franchisee, the return must include the gross sales of the franchisee in New York reported by the franchisee to the franchisor, the total amount of sales by the franchisor to the franchisee, and any income reported to the franchisor by each franchisee, along with additional information (*TSB-M-09(9)S,* July 7, 2009, CCH NEW YORK TAX REPORTS, ¶ 406-439); and

— every wholesaler, if it has made a sale of an alcoholic beverage, without collecting sales or use tax during the period covered by the return, except (i) a sale to a person that has furnished an exempt organization certificate to the wholesaler for that sale; or (ii) a sale to another wholesaler whose license under the alcoholic beverage control law does not allow it to make retail sales of the alcoholic beverage (*TSB-M-09(8)S,* July 7, 2009, CCH NEW YORK TAX REPORTS, ¶ 406-440).

For each vendor, operator, or recipient to whom the wholesaler has made a sale without collecting sales or compensating use tax, the return must include the total value of those sales made during the period covered by the return and the vendor's, operator's or recipient's state liquor authority license number, along with other information. (Sec. 1136(i)(2), Tax Law)

Exemption: Licensed farm wineries, farm distilleries, farm breweries producing less than 60,000 barrels annually, and non-farm wineries producing less than 150,000 finished gallons of wine are exempt from the sales tax annual information return filing requirements imposed by Sec. 1136(i)(1)(C), Tax Law. See also *TSB-M-15(6)S,* December 15, 2015, CCH NEW YORK TAX REPORTS, ¶ 408-594.

Due dates: Annual information returns are due on or before March 20th of each year, covering the period from March 1 of the previous year through February 28 or 29 of the current year. (Sec. 1136(i)(1), Tax Law)

¶2202

• *Penalties*

Any person failing to file a return or to pay over any tax due within the time required may be subject to civil penalties and interest. In addition, any person who willfully fails to make a required return or report (other than a return of compensating use tax) at the required time will be guilty of a misdemeanor (Sec. 1817(a), Tax Law; Sec. 1816, Tax Law). (See ¶ 3704)

Penalties are provided for failure to file returns or pay the tax on time—10% of the amount of tax due (if the failure is less than one month). If the failure is for more than one month, an additional 1% penalty is imposed for each additional month or fraction thereof during which the failure continues, not exceeding 30% in the aggregate. When a return is more than 60 days late, the penalty imposed will be at a minimum the lesser of $100 or the amount of tax required to be shown on the return. If a person required to register with the Commissioner fails to file a return, the penalty will be at least $50. In addition, interest is imposed (¶ 2211).

However, if the failure to file a return or pay the tax on time is due to fraud, a penalty of 50% of the amount of the tax due is added to the tax. In addition, interest is imposed (¶ 2211).

Recordkeeping: Every person required to collect tax must keep records of every sale or amusement charge or occupancy and of all amounts paid, charged or due and of the tax payable on forms required by the Commissioner of Taxation and Finance. (Sec. 1135(a)(1), Tax Law) (*Publication 900*, Important Information for Business Owners, CCH NEW YORK TAX REPORTS, ¶ 65-971) The burden of proving that any receipt, amusement charge or rent is not taxable is on the vendor or the customer. To satisfy its burden of proof, a vendor must maintain records sufficient to verify all transactions. (Reg. Sec. 533.2(a)(1)) In addition, any vendor who has elected to maintain any portion of their records in an electronic format will be required to provide those electronic records to the Department of Revenue upon request. The electronic records must be provided regardless of whether or not the vendor maintains and provides the records in a hard copy format. Failure to provide the records electronically will result in additional penalties. Additional penalties are imposed for every quarter in which a vendor fails to maintain adequate records in any format and for any vendor who fails to provide records in auditable form. (Sec. 1135(h), Tax Law; Sec. 1145, Tax Law)

¶ 2203 Payment of Tax

> *Law:* Secs. 10, 1101, 1102, 1111, 1131, 1132, 1133, 1137, 1142, Tax Law; Reg. Sec. 533.4 (CCH NEW YORK TAX REPORTS, ¶ 60-560, ¶ 61-210, ¶ 61-220, ¶ 61-230, ¶ 61-460, ¶ 89-325).

> *Forms:* FT-945/1045, Report of Sales Tax Prepayment on Motor Fuel/Diesel Motor Fuel.

Except in the case of distributors of motor fuel and cigarettes, who are required to prepay their sales taxes, payment of the tax accompanies the return (for return due dates, see ¶ 2202).

The collection of sales and use taxes is generally performed by persons required to collect the tax. "Persons required to collect the sales and use tax" include every vendor of tangible personal property or services, every recipient of amusement charges, every operator of a hotel, and any officer, director, or employee of a corporation or dissolved corporation, or any employee of a partnership or individual proprietorship under a duty to act for the entity (Sec. 1131(1), Tax Law).

Every person required to collect the sales and use tax is required to collect the tax from the customer when collecting the price, amusement charge, or rent to which it applies (Sec. 1132(a), Tax Law). Persons required to collect the tax are personally liable for the tax imposed, collected, or required to be collected (Sec. 1133(a), Tax Law).

Practitioner Comment: Timing of Sales Tax Remittance

The remittance of New York sales tax is based on the accrual method of accounting and is due at the time title or possession of property is transferred to a purchaser. The timing of the purchaser's payment is irrelevant. Even installment sales are not respected for sales tax collection purposes. In these situations, a seller has the obligation to remit the full amount of the sales tax upon the initial sale. If, for whatever reason, the seller does not receive the full purchase price, a proportional credit for the sales tax is available to the extent the remaining payment qualifies as a "bad debt" for federal income tax purposes (*TSB-A-03(8)S*, CCH NEW YORK TAX REPORTS, ¶404-475).

Mark S. Klein, Esq., Hodgson Russ LLP

Purchasers who do not pay the tax to the vendor or other persons required to collect the tax must pay the tax directly to the Commissioner (Sec. 1133(b), Tax Law).

Utilities, like other taxpayers, pay the amount of tax computed by applying the state tax rate (and any local rate, if applicable) to taxable sales and services. (See ¶2006 for taxable sales and services.) When the tax commission fixes an effective rate for any portion of their receipts, amusement charges or rents, utilities may elect to use the effective rate for computing the tax on such receipts, amusement charges or rents.

Sales of building materials: Material suppliers ("materialmen") primarily engaged in selling building materials to contractors, subcontractors, or repairmen can collect and remit sales tax due on the sales of materials at the time and to the extent the receipts or consideration from the sale are received (Sec. 1132(a), Tax Law).

If a material supplier receives a portion of the consideration, the tax due on that portion must be collected and remitted at the time received. Further, if a material supplier finances a sale with any person other than a contractor, subcontractor, or repairman, the material supplier will be deemed to have received payment and will be required to collect and remit tax on the next return due. For additional information on the pay-when-paid application procedure, recordkeeping, filing of returns, and payment of taxes, see (*TB-ST-555*, Department of Taxation and Finance, July 27, 2012 CCH NEW YORK TAX REPORTS, ¶407-616).

- *Collection of taxes on motor vehicles by registration agents*

Sales and compensating use taxes on motor vehicle sales may be collected by a registration agent who is not the seller of the motor vehicle. A registraton agent must be registered with the Commissioner of Taxation and Finance and certified by the Commissioner of Motor Vehicles as authorized to perform the function of registering motor vehicles or accepting applications for certificates of motor vehicle title (Sec. 1142(13), Tax Law).

Once authorized, registration agents are required to collect sales and use taxes for motor vehicles registered by the agent and to pay the collected taxes to the Commissioner. Registration agents are personally liable for the payment of the taxes collected, including penalties and interest. In addition, agents are required to keep records, and to make those records available to the Commissioner. Agents are also required to maintain the same level of confidentiality required of Department of Taxation and Finance employees. Further, agents are required to post a bond or other security. Finally, registration agents authorized to collect taxes are required to post a certificate issued by the Commissioner of Taxation and Finance (Sec. 1142(13), Tax Law).

- *Prepayment of tax by distributors of motor fuel and diesel fuel*

Distributors are required to prepay sales tax on each gallon of motor fuel (except as set forth at ¶2005) they import or manufacture within New York State for sale, use, distribution or storage. Distributors must also prepay sales tax on the sale or use of diesel fuel (except as set forth at ¶2005). The prepaid sales tax is passed through to each successive purchaser until the motor fuel or diesel fuel is sold at retail to the consumer. The vendor making the retail sale must collect sales tax computed on the actual selling price at the tax rate in effect in the locality where the motor fuel is delivered to the purchaser. The receipts on which the retail sales tax on motor fuel or diesel fuel is based does not include the amount of prepaid sales tax (Sec. 1102(a), Tax Law). See ¶2022 for prepayment rates.

Alternative fuels are generally exempt from sales tax (see ¶2106). Note, however, that there is no exemption from the prepaid sales tax for B20 fuel.

Fuel used in commercial and general aviation aircraft: Sales of fuel for use in commercial and general aviation aircraft are exempt from the prepayment of sales tax on motor fuels, effective December 1, 2017 (Sec. 1102(a)(1), Tax Law).

Prepayments: The prepayment of tax on motor fuel and diesel motor fuel was changed from a percentage rate of tax to a cents- per-gallon tax, effective June 1, 2006. Specifically, within the Metropolitan Commuter Transportation District (Region 1), the tax is determined by multiplying the average retail sales price per gallon by 14.75 cents. Outside the Metropolitan Commuter Transportation District (Region 2), the tax is determined by multiplying the average retail sales price per gallon by 14 cents (Sec. 1111(e)(2), Tax Law).

Credits: Credit for prepaid tax is claimed on Form FR, *Sales and Use Tax on Qualified Motor Fuel and Diesel Motor Fuel*. Despite the title, credit may be claimed for sales of both qualified and non-qualified fuel on this form (*Important Notice N-07-17*, September 13, 2007, CCH NEW YORK TAX REPORTS, ¶405-840). "Qualified fuel" is motor fuel or diesel that is (1) sold for direct and exclusive use in the engine of a motor vehicle, or (2) sold by a retail gas station (except kerosene for heating) (*TSB-M 06(8)S*, June 28, 2006, CCH NEW YORK TAX REPORTS, ¶300-517). Examples of nonqualified fuel sales are sales of heating oil for commercial purposes and sales of aviation gasoline or kero-jet fuel by a fixed-base operator.

• *Prepayment of tax for alternative fuels*

CNG and hydrogen fuels are exempt from the prepaid sales tax requirement. In addition, E85 fuel is exempt from the prepaid tax provided it is delivered to and placed in a storage tank of a filling station to be dispensed directly into a motor vehicle for use in its operation (Sec. 1102(a), Tax Law) (*TSB-M-06(10)S*, CCH NEW YORK TAX REPORTS, ¶405-333). The exemption does not apply to sales of B20; see ¶2106.

Effective August 1, 2013, sales of previously untaxed highway diesel motor fuel by a person registered as a distributor of diesel motor fuel to another person registered as a distributor of diesel motor fuel are exempt from the excise tax, petroleum business tax, and prepaid sales tax if the fuel is delivered by pipeline, railcar, barge, tanker or other vessel to a terminal of a licensed/registered operator, or sold within a diesel fuel terminal where it was delivered. (*TSB-M-13(7)M, TSB-M-13(5)S*, Taxpayer Guidance Division, New York Department of Taxation and Finance, July 11, 2013, CCH NEW YORK TAX REPORTS, ¶407-877)

See ¶2022 for prepayment rates.

• *Prepayment of tax by cigarette dealers*

Cigarette dealers are also required to prepay a portion of the sales tax on packages of cigarettes (Sec. 1103, Tax Law). See ¶2022 for prepayment rates.

• *Electronic fund transfers*

The Department of Taxation and Finance requires tax payments to be made by electronic fund transfers (EFT) or certified check by taxpayers whose sales and use taxes, prepaid sales and use taxes on motor fuel and diesel motor fuel, or petroleum

¶2203

business taxes exceed certain statutory thresholds. Under the terms of this program, the Department will make an initial eligibility determination within 45 days after June 1 of each year by examining the taxpayer's tax liability for the June 1 through May 31 period preceding the June 1 through May 31 period that precedes the initial determination (Sec. 10, Tax Law).

The threshold amounts for the applicable June 1 through May 31 period are as follows (Sec. 10(b)(1), Tax Law):

— more than $500,000 of state and local sales and use taxes (excluding the tax on paging devices);

— more than $5 million of prepaid state and local sales and use taxes on motor fuel and diesel motor fuel; or

— more than $5 million of the total of the tax on motor fuel and diesel motor fuel and the tax on petroleum businesses (excluding the tax on carriers).

A taxpayer will be required to participate in the program only with respect to taxes for which the applicable dollar thresholds noted above have been met. In determining whether the threshold has been met, every taxpayer who is identified by either its own federal employer identification number or its own separate New York State employer identification number is treated as a separate taxpayer (Sec. 10, Tax Law).

Taxpayers who do not meet the dollar thresholds noted above may apply for permission to participate in the Program on a voluntary basis.

Exemptions: A taxpayer liable for state and local sales and use taxes is exempt from EFT or certified check payment requirements provided that the taxpayer demonstrates to the satisfaction of the Commissioner that for the two most recent consecutive quarters, the taxpayer's state and local sales and compensating use taxes due are less than 50% of the state and local sales and use taxes properly payable by the taxpayer for the comparable two quarters of the preceding year, *and* that (1) the sum of the taxpayer's tax liability for the two most recent consecutive quarters together with (2) the product of the taxes properly payable by the taxpayer for the first two consecutive quarters of the preceding year, multiplied by the percentage by which the taxpayer's tax liability for the two most recent consecutive quarters falls below the tax liability for the two comparable quarters of the preceding year, is less than $250,000.

Taxpayers liable for prepaid state and local sales and use taxes are also exempt provided that the taxpayer demonstrates to the satisfaction of the Commissioner that, for the most recent six-month period, the prepaid state and local sales and use taxes on motor fuel and diesel motor fuel are less than 50% of the taxpayer's tax liability for the comparable six-month period of the preceding year and that (1) the sum of the taxpayer's liability for the most recent six-month period, together with (2) the product of the applicable taxes properly payable by the taxpayer for the six-month period immediately preceding the most recent six-month period, multiplied by the percentage by which the taxpayer's tax liability for the most recent six-month period falls below the tax liability for the comparable six-month period of the preceding year, is less than $2.5 million (Sec. 10, Tax Law).

A vendor that would otherwise be required to remit state and local sales and use taxes by EFT will be permitted to remit payment by EFT or certified check at the same time that it files its quarterly sales tax returns if (1) its sales and use tax liability for the "look-back period" was less than $4 million, and (2) within any two of the most recent four consecutive sales tax quarters, it was a materialman (as defined in Sec. 2, Lien Law), primarily engaged in furnishing building materials to contractors, subcontractors, or repairmen for the improvement of residential real property. The vendor must also be authorized by the Lien Law to file a mechanics lien upon the real property and improvements (Sec. 10, Tax Law).

¶2203

Amount of payment: Payments are required to be made in the following amounts (Sec. 10, Tax Law):

— *Taxpayers paying state and local sales and use taxes:* 75% of $1/3$ of the taxpayer's tax liability for the comparable quarter of the preceding year, or the taxpayer's total liability for such taxes during the period ending on the 22nd day of each month; and

— *Taxpayers paying prepaid state and local sales and use taxes on motor fuel and diesel motor fuel:* $3/4$ of the taxpayer's tax liability for the comparable month of the preceding year, or the taxpayer's total liability for such taxes during the period ending on the 22nd day of each month. See ¶2022 for prepayment rate.

EFT payment requirements: Taxpayers who are required to make payments by EFT or certified check because their state and local sales and use tax liability exceeds the above thresholds must file quarterly returns and make monthly remittances by EFT or certified check of either (1) 75% of $1/3$ of the taxpayer's total sales and use tax liability for the comparable quarter of the preceding year or (2) the taxpayer's total tax liability during the period ending on the 22nd day of the month and (a) for payments due in January, February, April, May, July, August, October, or November, the taxpayer's remaining tax liability for the immediately preceding calendar month, or (b) for payments due in March, June, September, or December, the taxpayer's remaining liability for the immediately preceding sales tax quarter (Sec. 10(c)(1)(A), Tax Law). For months for which a return is not required to be filed, payment by EFT or certified check constitutes the filing of a return.

• *Motor vehicles, trailers, snowmobiles, and motorboats*

Proof of payment of tax or exemption is required for registration of motor vehicles, trailers, snowmobiles, watercraft, or all-terrain vehicles, other than renewal by the same owner (Sec. 1132(f), Tax Law).

For penalties for failure to pay the tax when due, see ¶2202.

• *Liability for payment*

The Tax Law imposes personal responsibility for payment of sales tax on certain owners, officers, directors, employees, partners, or members (responsible persons) of a business that has an outstanding sales tax liability (Sec. 1133(a), Tax Law; Reg. Sec. 526.11). Being personally liable means that the personal assets, including a home, car, savings account, etc., could be taken by the Tax Department to satisfy the sales tax liability of their business. Personal responsibility can apply even if the owner has an employee or an accountant handle the businesses sales tax matters. In addition, an owner can be held personally responsible even though the business is a corporation or a limited liability company (LLC). The liability applies whether or not the tax imposed was collected (Reg. Sec. 532.3(a)(1)).

Relief from liability: The Department of Taxation and Finance announced a new policy, effective March 9, 2011 and subsequently revised, that provides some relief to the *per se* personal liability for certain limited partners and members (*TSB-M-11(17)S*, New York Department of Taxation and Finance, September 19, 2011, CCH NEW YORK TAX REPORTS, ¶407-363). Under the policy, the following limited partners and limited liability company (LLC) members who otherwise are responsible persons under Sec. 1131(1), Tax Law, may be eligible for relief:

— limited partners (of a limited partnership) may be approved for relief if they demonstrate that they were not under a duty to act in complying with the Tax Law on behalf of the partnership, and

¶2203

— LLC members who can document that their ownership interest and percentage distributive share of the profits and losses of the LLC are less than 50% may be approved for relief if they demonstrate that they were not under a duty to act on behalf of the company in complying with the Tax Law.

¶2204 Direct Payment Permits

Law: Sec. 1132(c), Tax Law; Reg. Sec. 532.5 (CCH New York Tax Reports, ¶61-250).

Forms: AU-298, Application for a Direct Payment Permit.

In cases in which it is not possible at the time of acquisition for a purchaser of tangible personal property or services to determine whether such property or services will be put to an exempt or taxable use, the purchaser may apply for a direct payment permit, which waives collection by the vendor and allows the purchaser to pay the tax directly to the Commissioner. Direct payment permit holders are required to notify vendors from whom they make purchases of their status by submitting a copy of the direct payment permit with the first purchase order (Sec. 1132(c)(2), Tax Law).

A direct payment permit may not be used (1) as a device to defer payment of the sales tax on purchases, (2) as a substitute for a resale certificate or other exemption certificate, or (3) as a device to transfer the permit holder's privileges to another person (Sec. 1132(c)(2), Tax Law).

Omnibus carriers providing local transit service in New York may also apply to the Commissioner for a direct payment permit, waiving collection by the vendor and authorizing them to pay the tax on the purchase of an omnibus directly (Sec. 1132(c)(2), Tax Law).

Practitioner Comment: Vendor's Acceptance

Unlike exemption and resale certificates, there is no time limit governing a vendor's acceptance of a direct pay permit. Instead, they can be obtained at any time (*Latz Landscaping*, TAT 10/26/06, CCH New York Tax Reports, ¶405-505).

Mark S. Klein, Esq., Hodgson Russ LLP

Revocation: A direct payment permit may be revoked for: (1) failure by the holder to timely file sales and use tax returns and timely pay any tax due; (2) any misuse of the privileges granted by the permit or failure to comply with any requirements with respect to the permit; or (3) a change in the business operation, so that it is possible to determine the use of purchases at the time made (Reg. Sec. 532.5(g)(1)).

¶2205 Exemption and Resale Certificates

Law: Sec. 1132(c), Tax Law; Reg. Secs. 532.4, 532.6 (CCH New York Tax Reports, ¶60-650, ¶61-020, ¶61-440).

Forms: See below.

Sales are taxable unless the vendor takes from the purchaser a proper resale certificate or exempt organization statement (Sec. 1132(c)(1), Tax Law). The resale certificate should be signed by and indicate the name, address, and registration certificate number of the purchaser, and declare that the property or service was purchased for resale. The resale certificate must be received within 90 days after the delivery of the property or the rendition of the service (Reg. Sec. 532.4(b)(2)(iii)). Receipts from the sale of property purchased under a resale certificate are not subject to tax at the time of purchase by the person who will resell the property. Instead, the receipts are taxable at the time of the retail sale (Reg. Sec. 526.6(c)(3)).

The acceptance by the vendor of a statement or other proof that the purchaser is an exempt organization or that the purchase is for an exempt use also relieves the vendor from liability for the tax, as does the acceptance of a validated direct payment permit from the purchaser (¶2204).

Practitioner Comment: Vendor's Acceptance

An out-of-state seller may accept a New York sales tax resale certificate, Form ST-120, from an out-of-state purchaser for merchandise that is shipped directly by the seller to the purchaser's customer in New York, *i.e.*, drop shipped into New York, if the out-of-state purchaser is neither registered nor required to be registered with the New York State tax department as a sales tax vendor and is registered with another state or located in a state that does not require registration. The purchaser should indicate on the resale certificate its registration number issued by the state in which it is registered to collect tax or indicate that it is located in a state that does not require registration. Upon acceptance of a properly completed resale certificate within 90 days of the sale, the seller is protected from liability for New York sales or use tax (*Kahn, Hoffman, Nonenmacher & Hochman, LLP* (Advisory Opinion), Commissioner of Taxation and Finance, TSB-A-00(20)S, 4/25/00, CCH NEW YORK TAX REPORTS, ¶ 403-683).

Mark S. Klein, Esq., Hodgson Russ LLP

A properly completed exemption certificate may be accepted in good faith if a taxpayer has no actual knowledge that the certificate is false or fraudulent.

Blanket resale certificates: A purchaser may provide the vendor with a blanket resale certificate to cover additional purchases of the same general type of property or service. Each vendor accepting a resale certificate must, for verification purposes, maintain a method of associating a sale made for resale with the resale certificate on file. A blanket certificate has no definitive expiration date. Instead, it is valid as long as it is properly completed and the purchaser information on the form remains accurate (Reg. Sec. 532.4(d)).

MTC Uniform Sales and Use Tax Certificate: New York does not currently allow vendors to accept the MTC Uniform Sales and Use Tax Certificate for resales.

Retention of resale certificate: The resale certificate must be retained for at least three years after the due date of the return to which it relates, or the date the return was filed, if later (Form ST-120).

Forms: Principal exemption certificates are the following: Exempt Organization Certification (Form ST-119.1); Resale Certificate (Form ST-120); Exempt Use Certificate (Form ST-121); and Farmer's Exemption Certificate (Form ST-125).

• *Electronic resale and exemption documents*

The New York Department of Taxation and Finance has authorized the use and acceptance of electronic versions of certain sales and use tax resale and exemption documents (e-certificates). The paper resale and exemption forms prescribed by the Department may still be used.

E-certificates are not available from the Department. At their discretion, purchasers and sellers may establish the means to electronically issue and receive e-certificates. The Department does not prescribe specific technologies or technical specifications for executing e-certificates nor does the Department require the use of particular types of hardware or software. However, an e-certificate must reproduce in its entirety the current paper resale or exemption form issued by the Department and must contain all of the language that is on the current paper form. Also, an e-certificate must contain prescribed e-certification and electronic signature language.

An e-certificate and all applicable instructions, must be available to both the purchaser and the seller. However, it is not necessary that the instructions be included when issuing an e-certificate to the seller in order for the e-certificate to be considered accepted in good faith or properly completed. If the paper resale or exemption form may be issued as a blanket certificate or as a single-purchase certificate, the corresponding e-certificate may also be issued as a blanket certificate or as a single-purchase certificate.

Signatures: To be relieved of liability for failure to collect tax, a seller must accept in good faith an e-certificate that is properly completed within 90 days after delivery of the property or the rendition of the service. A properly completed e-certificate includes the purchaser's (or authorized representative's) signature. In the case of an e-certificate, this requires an electronic signature that is in lieu of any written signature required on the paper counterpart. There is no requirement to affix a physical signature on the e-certificate. An electronic signature has the same validity and effect as a handwritten signature.

Recordkeeping: Sellers must keep e-certificates as part of the records required to be kept under the Tax Law and sales and use tax regulations. An e-certificate must comply with all of the requirements for retaining records, including the requirements that it be capable of being accurately reproduced so as to be perceptible by human sensory capabilities and be capable of being accessed by the Department if requested (TSB-M-07(1)S, March 1, 2007, CCH NEW YORK TAX REPORTS, ¶405-659).

¶2206 Records

Law: Secs. 341, 1135, 1145, Tax Law; Reg. Sec. 533.2 (CCH NEW YORK TAX REPORTS, ¶61-260, ¶61-420).

Persons required to collect tax must keep records of every sale or amusement charge or occupancy and of all amounts paid, charged or due, and of the tax payable on forms required by the Commissioner of Taxation and Finance (Sec. 1135(a)(1), Tax Law; *TB-ST-770*, June 2, 2011, CCH NEW YORK TAX REPORTS, ¶407-272). The burden of proving that any receipt, amusement charge or rent is not taxable is on the vendor or the customer. To satisfy its burden of proof, a vendor must maintain records sufficient to verify all transactions.

Records and returns are required to be preserved for three years from the due date of the return to which they relate or the date of filing, if later, unless the Commissioner consents to their destruction earlier or requires that they be kept longer (Sec. 1135(e), Tax Law).

Records on computer or microfilm: Records may be reproduced on any photographic, photostatic, microfilm, micro-card, miniature photographic or other process which actually reproduces the original record or may otherwise be retained as electronic records. Vendors wishing to retain general books of account on microfilm may do so provided they have met specific requirements (Sec. 1135(e), Tax Law).

Any vendor that has elected to maintain any portion of their records in an electronic format will be required to provide those electronic records to the Department upon request. The electronic records must be provided regardless of whether or not the vendor maintains and provides the records in a hard copy format. If a person fails to present or make available sales tax records for the Tax Department's review in a form that can be audited, the penalty is up to $1,000 for each quarter or part thereof for which the failure occurs. Failure to provide the records electronically will result in a penalty of up to $5,000 for each quarter or part thereof for which the failure occurs. (Sec. 1135(h), Tax Law; Sec. 1145, Tax Law).

Point-of-sale (POS) systems: When using POS systems, all sales and transactions are made through a computer system. The system should record every sale and track all transactions. Each POS transaction record must provide enough detail to independently determine the taxability of each sale and the amount of tax due and collected. Detailed information required for each sales transaction is listed in *TB-ST-770*, New York Department of Taxation and Finance, April 13, 2011, CCH NEW YORK TAX REPORTS, ¶407-195.

Practitioner Comment: Businesses Must Maintain Adequate Records

Businesses that fail to maintain adequate records (which can include copies of each sales slip, invoice, receipt or guest check) can be subjected to an estimated audit methodology that may or may not reflect the actual sales tax due. In the absence of adequate records, auditors have been allowed to perform a mark-up analysis of all purchases, use industry-specific sales or mark-up averages or simply record sales on a single day and extrapolate the result to a three-year audit period. The Tax Department's only obligation is to "adopt an audit method reasonably calculated to determine the amount of tax due . . . and exactness is not required." (*Beijing China Buffet, Inc.* (TAT 2/23/12), CCH NEW YORK TAX REPORTS, ¶407-495)

Mark S. Klein, Esq., Hodgson Russ LLP

¶2207 Bulk Sales

Law: Sec. 1141(c), Tax Law; Reg. Secs. 537.0—537.9 (CCH NEW YORK TAX REPORTS, ¶60-590, ¶61-210, ¶61-470).

Forms: AU-196.10, Notification of Sale, Transfer, or Assignment in Bulk.

In the case of a bulk sale, assignment, or transfer of all or any part of the business assets, other than in the ordinary course of business, by a person required to collect tax, the purchaser, transferee, or assignee must notify the Commissioner by registered mail of the proposed transfer at least 10 days before taking possession or making payment. Failure to notify the Commissioner renders the purchaser personally liable for payment of any taxes due the state from the seller up to an amount equal to the purchase price or fair market value of the assets sold.

If no notice is given or if, when given, the purchaser is notified that tax claims exist against the seller, any consideration due to be given to the seller is subject to a first priority lien for the taxes. The Commissioner will notify the purchaser of any taxes due within 90 days of receipt of the notice of sale. In the absence of such notification the purchaser is not obligated to withhold any payment from the seller (Sec. 1141(c), Tax Law; *TB-ST-70*, New York Department of Taxation and Finance, June 24, 2013, CCH NEW YORK TAX REPORTS, ¶407-864; see also *H & A Wine and Spirits, Inc.*, New York Division of Tax Appeals, Administrative Law Judge Unit, DTA No. 825984, September 10, 2015, CCH NEW YORK TAX REPORTS, ¶408-530).

Practitioner Comment: Acquiring Business Assets

A taxpayer's acquisition of the assets of an existing business (as opposed to the purchase of stock) can trigger the bulk sales notification requirements of Sec. 1141(c), Tax Law. Purchasers who insist on consummating a transaction before the end of the statute's 90-day notification period are advised to establish an escrow account or obtain some other type of financial protection in case the Tax Department asserts a preexisting liability of the seller.

Mark S. Klein, Esq., Hodgson Russ LLP

¶2208 Administration

Law: Secs. 1101(b)(8), 1142, Tax Law (CCH NEW YORK TAX REPORTS, ¶60-030, ¶61-620).

The state sales and use tax package and all local taxes based on the state tax are administered by the Department of Taxation and Finance, W.A. Harriman Campus, Albany, New York, 12227-0125. The functions performed include assessment, collection, determination, credit, or refund.

For additional information on the Department and its organizational structure, see ¶3601. For contact information, see Chapter 39.

The Commissioner is authorized to adopt rules and regulations for carrying out the purposes of the state and local sales and use tax, to extend the time period for filing a return or report for up to three months, to remit penalties but not interest computed at the rate of 6% per year when cause is shown, to publish lists of specific items of tangible personal property found to be exempt foods or drugs, and to set overpayment and underpayment rates of interest (Sec. 1142, Tax Law).

Practitioner Comment: Voluntary Disclosure Program

The New York State Department of Taxation and Finance aggressively pursues taxpayers who purchased valuables (*e.g.*, artwork, jewelry, antiques, etc.) outside of the State for ultimate use within New York. Purchases made within New York, where the vendor failed to collect sales taxes, are also being scrutinized. Since most individual taxpayers do not file sales and use tax returns, there is no statute of limitations on the State's ability to detect and pursue these taxes. Additionally, audits of affected taxpayers can result in assessments for the tax, penalties, interest at 14.5% and possible criminal referrals.

In an effort to encourage taxpayers to comply with the tax laws, New York has established a voluntary disclosure program. Under this policy, qualifying taxpayers who voluntarily disclose and pay their sales and use tax liabilities before they receive notice of a pending audit, can limit their exposure to the tax on purchases made during the last three years, eliminate all potential penalties, reduce the interest rate applicable to their liabilities and receive an assurance that the Tax Department will not pursue any criminal referral. Details regarding the voluntary disclosure program can be found at **www.tax.state.ny.us/e-services/vold/**.

Mark S. Klein, Esq., Hodgson Russ LLP

¶2209 Assessment of Tax

Law: Secs. 1138, 1139(b), 1147, 2006, 2016, Tax Law; Reg. Secs. 535.4, 535.5 (CCH New York Tax Reports, ¶61-410, ¶61-430, ¶61-520, ¶65-412—¶65-414).

The tax is self-assessing, in that it is based on receipts from sales and collected by the vendor. However, if no return is filed or if the return filed misstates the tax due, the Commissioner may compute the correct amount of tax due according to the best available information. Factors that may be used include stock on hand, purchases, rentals, number of employees, etc. (Sec. 1138(a)(1), Tax Law)

The service of a notice of determination will generally be sufficient to assess a sales tax deficiency unless the taxpayer, within 90 days from the date the notice is mailed applies to the Division of Tax Appeals for a hearing.

Practitioner Comment: Personal Liability for Tax

A business's failure to collect sales tax or remit use tax creates personal liability for officers, directors, employees or managers who are "under a duty to act" for the business under Sec. 1131(1), Tax Law. This liability extends to all members of a partnership, including limited partners, and all members of a limited liability company. According to the Tax Appeals Tribunal, all members of a limited liability company "are subject to *per se* liability for the taxes due from the limited liability company" (*Joseph P. Santo*, TAT (12/323/09), CCH New York Tax Reports, ¶406-645). As a result of concerns about the impact of this decision, New York's Department of Taxation and Finance is allowing special relief for LLC members who can demonstrate that they were not under a "duty to act" concerning the business's tax obligations. Additionally, the LLC member must have less than a 50% share of the profits and losses of the LLC. If they qualify, no penalty will be imposed on LLC members, and the liability of the eligible LLC member will be limited to an amount determined by multiplying the business's liability for sales taxes and interest by that person's percentage of ownership in the business, or the person's percentage share of profits and losses of the business, whichever is higher. This special relief does not apply to any general partners of a partnership nor to any partner of a limited liability partnership, See *TSB-M-11(17)S*, CCH NEW YORK TAX REPORTS, ¶ 407-363.

Mark S. Klein, Esq., Hodgson Russ LLP

Limitation period: The ordinary assessment limitation period is three years from the date of filing of a return. If no return has been filed as provided by law, or a false return with intent to evade the tax was filed, no assessment limitation period applies. The taxpayer may consent to an extension of the assessment period. The three-year limitations period for assessment is suspended until the time for filing a petition contesting the notice of assessment has expired or, if a petition is timely filed, until the decision of the Administrative Law Judge or Tax Appeals Tribunal becomes final (Sec. 1147(b), Tax Law). The period in which the Commissioner may make an assessment may be extended if the taxpayer, prior to the expiration of the limitation period, consents in writing to such an extension. Additional consents to extend the limitation period are permissible. (Sec. 1147(c), Tax Law)

Practitioner Comment: Statute of Limitations Not Extended for Substantial Understatement

Unlike the corporate and personal income tax laws (See ¶ 1506), there is no six-year statute of limitations for a substantial understatement of sales taxes.

Mark S. Klein, Hodgson Russ LLP

Jeopardy assessment: The Commissioner may make a jeopardy assessment if he or she believes the collection of the tax is in jeopardy (Sec. 1138(a), Tax Law). The collection of any jeopardy assessment may be stayed by the filing of a bond. For additional information, see ¶ 3702.

• *Audits*

Information on audits is presented at ¶ 3701.

¶2210 Refunds

Law: Secs. 1119, 1132, 1139, 1147(c), Tax Law; Reg. Secs. 534.1—534.9 (CCH NEW YORK TAX REPORTS, ¶ 61-120, 61-270, ¶ 61-620, ¶ 61-610).

Forms: AU-11, Application for Credit or Refund of Sales or Use Tax.

Application for refund or credit of tax erroneously, illegally, or unconstitutionally collected or paid may be filed within three years from the date on which the tax was payable (Sec. 1139(a), Tax Law). If a taxpayer has consented to extend the time for assessment, then the period within which the taxpayer may file for a refund does not expire prior to six months after the end of the period during which the assessment may be made. A refund application must be granted or denied within six months of its receipt by the Commissioner (Sec. 1139(b), Tax Law).

If the vendor makes the application, the vendor must be able to show that the tax has been repaid to the customer.

A taxpayer who fails to apply for a hearing but pays the outstanding tax deficiency, may request a refund within three years from the date that the return was filed, or two years from the date that the tax was paid (whichever is later) (Sec. 1139(c), Tax Law). If the refund request is denied, the taxpayer may petition the Division of Tax Appeals and obtain a hearing on the merits with respect to the tax liability.

¶2210

Practitioner Comment: Refund Authority

New York's Tax Commissioner has special discretionary authority under the personal income and franchise tax laws to refund taxes illegally or erroneously paid to the State, despite the expiration of the statute of limitations. See Secs. 697(d) and 1096(d), Tax Law. This special refund authority does not, however, apply to the sales tax law (*Kimberly Hotel*, TAT 5/4/06, CCH New York Tax Reports, ¶ 405-369).

Mark S. Klein, Esq., Hodgson Russ LLP

When a consumer returns a defective motor vehicle (a so-called lemon) and receives a refund of the purchase price, capitalized cost or portion thereof from the manufacturer because the manufacturer, its agents or dealers have been unable to correct a substantial defect or condition, the Commissioner will refund any sales tax paid by the consumer on the amount of the purchase price, capitalized cost, fees, and charges refunded (Sec. 1139(f), Tax Law).

Bulk sales: In the case of a bulk sale, when the tax was paid by the purchaser, transferee, or assignee, a claim for refund must be filed within two years after the giving of notice by the Commissioner (Sec. 1139(a), Tax Law).

Bad debts: See ¶ 2015.

Credit card sales of fuel: A third party, such as a credit card company or an oil company, is entitled to a refund or credit of New York petroleum business, motor fuel, or sales and use taxes paid on fuel when it is purchased by government entities using credit cards (Secs. 1138(a)(3)(e), and 1139(h), Tax Law). The refund claim is made by filing Form FT-505.1, Government Entity Credit Card Refund or Credit Election. Additional details are in TSB-M-08(12)S and TSB-M-08(9)M, November 5, 2008, CCH New York Tax Reports, ¶ 406-212.

Uncollectible credit card accounts: A retailer or lender may not claim a sales tax refund, deduction or credit when sales tax is paid up front on the entire amount of the sales price of a taxable item in an installment or credit sale on a private label credit card, and a portion of the purchase price is later charged off as uncollectible for federal income tax purposes (See ¶ 2015).

Interest: Interest is only allowed on refunds or credits granted for any tax, penalty, or interest which was erroneously, illegally, or unconstitutionally collected or paid. (Sec. 1139(d), Tax Law) There is no interest paid on refunds or credits due to an overpayment made with a short form part quarterly return. (Reg. Sec. 534.2) Interest does not attach to refunds and credits on tax payments attributable to canceled sales, returned or defective merchandise (Reg. Sec. 534.6) or bad debts (Reg. Sec. 534.7). In addition, there is no interest on refunds and credits for tax paid on the purchase of tangible personal property for certain specified uses (Reg. Sec. 534.2), on the purchase of certain services (Reg. Sec. 534.5), or on purchases of property or services by omnibus carriers engaged in local transit service (Reg. Sec. 534.4).

• *Incentive refunds*

For sales and use tax refunds available under the Economic Transformation and Facility Redevelopment Program, see ¶ 2112.

Practitioner Comment: Limitation on Sales Tax Refunds

While New York grants refunds of erroneously paid sales taxes, refunds are not available to a vendor for sales taxes that were erroneously collected. Collected taxes, even those collected in error, must be either remitted to New York State or returned to the customer. The refund belongs to the taxpayer who paid the tax, not to the taxpayer who collected it. See (*New Cingular Wireless PCS LLC*, ALJ, July 17, 2014, CCH New York Tax Reports, ¶ 408-163).

Mark S. Klein, Esq., Hodgson Russ LLP

¶2211 Interest on Underpayments or Overpayments

Law: Secs. 1139(d), 1142, Tax Law (CCH NEW YORK TAX REPORTS, ¶ 89-204).

The Commissioner of Taxation and Finance is authorized to set interest rates for overpayments and underpayment of tax (Secs. 1139(d), Tax Law; Sec. 1142, Tax Law). Rates are the same as those set for corporate franchise tax overpayments and underpayments (see ¶ 1507, ¶ 3704); however, if the interest rate on underpayments (based on the federal short-term plus 7%) drops below 14.5%, interest, compounded daily, will be computed at the rate of 14.5% per annum. If the failure to pay is due to reasonable cause and not willful neglect, the Commissioner may waive the interest in excess of the statutory rate.

Refunds: Interest does not accrue on sales and use tax refunds claimed on a late return or on an application for refund or credit before the date the return or the application is filed in processible form with the Tax Department. No interest will be paid on the refund if the refund is issued either within three months after the later of the return's due date or filing date or within three months after the filing date of an application for a sales tax refund or credit. (Tax Law section 1139(d))

For the most current interest rate available at the time of publication, see ¶ 3704. Interest rates per annum, compounded daily, have been established in the recent past as follows:

Period	Overpayments	Underpayments
4/1/16—12/31/16	3%	14.5%
1/1/15—3/31/16	2%	14.5%
10/1/11—12/31/14	2%	14.5%
4/1/11—9/30/11	3%	14.5%
1/1/11—3/31/11	2%	14.5%

¶2212 Advertising Absorption of Tax Illegal

Law: Secs. 1132, 1133(d), Tax Law (CCH NEW YORK TAX REPORTS, ¶ 61-210).

No person required to collect any New York State or local sales or use tax shall advertise or hold out to the public in any manner that the tax is not being collected. The amount of the tax must be separately stated.

PART VI

ESTATE, GIFT, and GENERATION-SKIPPING TRANSFER TAXES

CHAPTER 23
ESTATE TAX

¶ 2301 The Law

The Estate Tax Law (Article 26, Tax Law, Ch. 60, C.L.), is effective for estates of decedents dying on or after April 1, 1963. The tax is based on estate tax provisions of the federal Internal Revenue Code, with certain modifications for New York tax purposes. The tax applies to transfers of the New York taxable estate of resident and nonresident decedents. For a general overview applicable to the estates of individuals with dates of death on or after April 1, 2014, see **https://www.tax.ny.gov/pit/estate/etidx.htm**.

The Estate Tax is administered by the Department of Taxation and Finance, State Campus, Albany, New York 12227.

The respective Surrogate's Courts are given jurisdiction to determine all questions arising under Article 26 of the Tax Law.

CCH Comment: Same-sex spouses.

On June 26, 2013, the U.S. Supreme Court decision, in the matter of *United States v. Windsor*, held Section 3 of the Defense of Marriage Act to be unconstitutional. As a result of the decision, for New York State estate tax purposes, estates of individuals legally married to same-sex spouses are entitled to claim the same deductions and elections allowed for estates of individuals legally married to different-sex spouses, including the marital deduction, for all years open under the statute of limitations.

For New York estate tax purposes, equal treatment has been given to estates of individuals legally married to different-sex spouses and same-sex spouses since the enactment of the Marriage Equality Act, applicable to estates of individuals dying on or after July 24, 2011. This treatment now also applies to estates of individuals legally married to same-sex spouses who died prior to July 24, 2011, as a result of the high court's decision.

Accordingly, taxpayers affected by the Supreme Court decision may amend any previously filed estate tax return where the statute of limitations to apply for a refund remains open. Generally, a claim for credit or refund of an overpayment of estate tax must be filed by a taxpayer within the later of:

> — three years from the date the original return was filed (if the original return was filed before the due date, three years from the due date), or

> — two years from the date the tax was paid.

To amend an estate tax return, file Form ET-706, New York State Estate Tax Return, following the directions given in *TSB-M-11(8)M, Implementation of the Marriage Equality Act Related to the New York State Estate Tax*, New York Department of Taxation and Finance, July 29, 2011, CCH NEW YORK TAX REPORTS,¶407-329. (*TSB-M-13(9)M*, New York Department of Taxation and Finance, July 18, 2013, CCH NEW YORK TAX REPORTS,¶407-882)

Under the New York Constitution, moneys, credits, securities and other intangible personal property within the state which are not used by the owner in carrying on any business in the state are deemed to be located at the domicile of the owner for purposes of taxation. If held in trust, these intangibles are not deemed to be located in New York for purposes of taxation merely because the trustee is domiciled in New York. However, if no other state has jurisdiction to subject such property held in trust to a death tax, it may be deemed property having a taxable situs within New York for purposes of death taxation. Intangible personal property is not taxed ad valorem, and no excise tax is levied solely because of its ownership or possession, except that the income may be taken into consideration in computing any excise tax measured by income generally. Undistributed profits are not taxed. (Sec. 3, Art. 16, New York Constitution)

CCH Comment: Decoupling from Federal Law

Prior to April 1, 2014, the estate tax payable to New York State was limited to the maximum amount allowed on the federal estate tax return as a credit for state death taxes. (Sec. 952, Tax Law; TSB-M-97(8)M, CCH NEW YORK TAX REPORTS,¶300-241) As a result, the total amount of the New York State estate tax paid would be deductible from any federal estate tax that may be payable.

This kind of estate tax is sometimes referred to as a *pickup tax, sponge tax,* or *sop tax* because it picks up or absorbs the portion of the federal estate tax that would otherwise be paid to the federal government if the state tax was not imposed. (*Instructions for Form ET-706*, New York Estate Tax Return) However, the New York law is tied to the federal law as it existed, with all amendments made through July 22, 1998. (Sec. 951, Tax Law) The federal enactment of the Economic Growth and Tax Relief Reconciliation Act of 2001 (EGTRRA), (Pub L No 107-16, 107th Cong, 1st Sess (June 7, 2001)), phased out the federal credit for state death taxes over four years, then replaced it with a deduction and, ultimately by 2010, repealed the federal estate tax in its entirety.

Further, the federal legislation contained a sunset provision, so after 2010, the federal estate law reverted to its status prior to EGTRRA's enactment. New York did not adopt any of these changes. As a result of this new divergence from federal law, New York once again imposes a tax in excess of the amount for which federal credit is given.

Part X of Chapter 59 of the Laws of 2014 amended the estate tax to decouple the tax from Federal law. The unified threshold of $1 million is replaced with an applicable credit equal to the tax on a basic threshold amount (see ¶2302). The basic threshold will equal the Federal basic threshold amount with annual indexing for those dying on or after January 1, 2019.

¶2301

Gifts taxable under Section 2503 of the Internal Revenue Code that were not otherwise included in Federal Gross Estate and that were made during the three years ending on the date of death must be added to the New York Gross Estate. However, gifts made while the decedent was a nonresident of New York State and gifts made prior to April 1, 2014 or on or after January 1, 2019 are not included.

The Generation Skipping Tax was repealed as of April 1, 2014.

A constitutional provision prohibiting the giving away of state moneys has been held to prevent the retroactive application of changes in the Tax Law. (*In re Harbord's Estate*, New York Surrogate's Court, Westchester County, Apr. 30, 1951, CCH NEW YORK TAX REPORTS,¶01590; aff'd Appellate Division of the Supreme Court of New York, Second Department, Mar. 3, 1952, CCH NEW YORK TAX REPORTS,¶01213)

¶2302 Rates and Exemptions

For estates of decedents dying on or after April 1, 2014, an estate tax is imposed on the transfer of the New York estate by every deceased individual who, at his or her death, was a resident of New York State.

Basic exclusion amount: If the decedent's New York taxable estate is less than or equal to the basic exclusion amount ($2,062,500 from April 1, 2014, through March 31, 2015; $3,125,000 from April 1, 2015, through March 31, 2016; $4,187,500 from April 1, 2016, through March 31, 2017; $5,250,000 from April 1, 2017, through December 31, 2018; and $5 million plus an annual cost-of living adjustment beginning January 1, 2019), the estate will receive a credit equal to the amount of tax due.

Practitioner Comment: No Portability of Spousal Exclusion

New York's estate tax, unlike the federal law, does not provide for the portability of a deceased spouse's unused exemption. Consequently, practitioners should evaluate the efficacy of a credit shelter trust to help reduce a couple's New York State estate tax exposure.

Mark S. Klein, Esq., Hodgson Russ LLP

If the decedent's New York taxable estate exceeds the basic exclusion amount by an amount that is less than or equal to five percent of such amount, the credit will be the amount of tax that would be due if the amount on which the tax is to be computed were equal to the basic exclusion amount multiplied by one, minus a fraction, the numerator of which is the decedent's New York taxable estate minus the basic exclusion amount, and the denominator of which is five percent of the basis exclusion amount, but not exceeding the tax imposed. No credit will be allowed to the estate of any decedent whose New York taxable estate exceeds 105% of the basis exclusion amount. This is similar to the loss of the benefit of the $1 million unified threshold under prior law.

Practitioner Comment: Special Rules for Certain Artwork

Although New York's estate tax applies to nonresidents who owned tangible personal property located in New York at the time of their death, a special exception applies to nonresidents who allow works of art to be placed on exhibition or loan to a public gallery or museum located in New York State. See Tax Law § 960(d).

Mark S. Klein, Esq., Hodgson Russ LLP

Effective for decedents dying on and after April 1, 2014, the New York state estate tax rates are as follows:

New York Taxable Estate					
From	To	Tax =	+	%	Of Excess Over
$0	$500,000	$0		3.06	$0
500,000	1,000,000	15,300		5.0	500,000
1,000,000	1,500,000	40,300		5.5	1,000,000
1,500,000	2,100,000	67,800		6.5	1,500,000
2,100,000	2,600,000	106,800		8.0	2,100,000
2,600,000	3,100,000	146,800		8.8	2,600,000
3,100,000	3,600,000	190,800		9.6	3,100,000
3,600,000	4,100,000	238,800		10.4	3,600,000
4,100,000	5,100,000	290,800		11.2	4,100,000
5,100,000	6,100,000	402,800		12.0	5,100,000
6,100,000	7,100,000	522,800		12.8	6,100,000
7,100,000	8,100,000	650,800		13.6	7,100,000
8,100,000	9,100,000	786,800		14.4	8,100,000
9,100,000	10,100,000	930,800		15.2	9,100,000
10,100,000	. . . . . .	1,082,800		16.0	10,100,000

¶2303 Charitable Exemptions

Charitable, religious, etc., exemptions provided in the federal law are allowable under the New York law.

¶2304 Computation

See *TSB-M-14(6)M*, Taxpayer Guidance Division, New York Department of Taxation and Finance, August 25, 2014, CCH NEW YORK TAX REPORTS, ¶408-207, also available at **http://www.tax.ny.gov/pubs_and_bulls/memos/estate_memos.htm**.

¶2305 Additional Estate Tax

See ¶2302.

¶2306 Taxable Transfers

The final federal determinations of fact are adopted for New York estate tax purposes, unless they are shown to be clearly erroneous. This provision applies not only to the inclusion of property in the gross estate and the allowance of deductions, but also to the amounts and values which are to be included and allowed. The optional federal provision for valuing a decedent's estate 6 months after death is applicable to decedents' estates for the purpose of the New York estate tax.

Residents: Transfers are taxable when made by:

— will;

— laws of descent;

— grant or gift if (a) possession or enjoyment of the property can, through ownership of such interest, be obtained only by surviving the decedent, and (b) the decedent has retained a reversionary interest in the property and the value of such reversionary interest exceeds 5% of the value of the property;

— transfers under which the transferor has retained for his life or a period not ascertainable without reference to his death or for a period which does not in fact end before his death (a) the possession or enjoyment of, or the right to the income from, the property, or (b) the right, either alone or in conjunction with any other person, to designate the persons who shall possess the property or the income therefrom; the retention of voting rights in retained stock is considered a retention of the enjoyment of the stock; grant or gift, including grants in trust, where the decedent retained a power to alter, amend, revoke or terminate the interest or where any such power was relinquished in contemplation of death.

Special types of property interests are treated as follows:

— dower or curtesy interest or statutory substitute are taxable;

— homestead rights are taxable;

— family allowances are taxable;

— insurance receivable by the executor is includible in the estate, and insurance receivable by named beneficiaries is includible to the extent that such amount is required to be included in the gross estate under the provisions for the taxing of estates contained in the Federal Revenue Act applicable to the estate of the decedent;

— tenancies in common are taxable to the extent of decedent's fractional interest therein;

— joint tenancy, including tenancy by the entirety and jointly held bank accounts, except such part as shown to have originally belonged to the survivor, but any part of the jointly held property for which adequate consideration has been paid the deceased by the surviving joint tenant is not included in the gross estate; provided that as to property received by decedent and spouse by gift, devise or bequest to be held in tenancy by the entirety, one-half the value is taxable, and where the law does not specify the interest of the joint owners, then the value of decedent's interest is to be determined by dividing the value of property by the number of joint owners, except that only one-half of qualified joint interests of a husband and wife are taxable;

— tenancies by the entirety—see "joint tenancy" above;

— property passing under any general power of appointment exercised by will, or by deed executed in contemplation of or intended to take effect at or after death is subject to tax;

— annuities are taxed as under federal law.

Nonresidents: The same types of transfers are taxable in estates of nonresidents as in the estates of resident decedents, if the property transferred is taxable in New York. See "Computation" for method of computation.

¶2307 Settlement of Domiciliary Disputes

Where there is a dispute over the question of the decedent's domicile, the Commissioner of Taxation and Finance may compromise the tax with the officials of the other state or states claiming to be the state of domicile.

Practitioner Comment: Domicile Factors

While the tax law does not define domicile, New York's Department of Taxation and Finance has published guidelines that identify the five most important factors. They include a comparison of the individual's use and maintenance of a New York residence compared to the nature and use patterns of a non-New York residence, the taxpayer's active involvement in a New York business, the amount of time spent in New York compared to time spent in the taxpayer's new home state, the location of the items that are "near and dear" to the taxpayer, and the location of the taxpayer's immediate family. See 2014 Nonresident Audit Guidelines at **http://www.tax.ny.gov/pdf/2014/misc/nonresident_audit_guidelines_2014.pdf**.

Mark S. Klein, Esq., Hodgson Russ LLP

¶2308 Property Subject to Tax

Residents: All real property and tangible personal property within the state and all intangible personal property wherever situated is taxable if made the subject of a taxable transfer.

Nonresidents: Only real property within the state of New York and tangible personal property having an actual situs in the state is taxable. Intangibles of a nonresident are not taxable.

¶2309 Deductions

The following items are deductible, although the statute does not make specific mention of them:

— funeral expenses;

— administration expenses;

— the marital deduction; for deaths occurring on or after January 1, 2010, and expiring July 1, 2016, where a federal estate tax return is not required, a disposition to a surviving spouse who is not a U.S. citizen that would otherwise qualify for the federal marital deduction is treated as qualifying for such deduction for purposes of the New York estate tax without requiring that such disposition pass to the surviving spouse in a qualified domestic trust, as required for federal purposes;

— claims against the estate to the extent of property subject to claims;

— unpaid mortgages on, or indebtedness in respect of, property where the value of the decedent's interest therein, undiminished by such mortgage or indebtedness, is included in the value of the gross estate;

— debts to the extent that full and adequate consideration was received therefor;

— losses incurred during settlement of the estate arising from fires, storms, shipwreck, or other casualty, or from theft, when not covered by insurance;

— the amount of insurance proceeds or other reparations for assets stolen from or otherwise lost by the decedent as a victim of Nazi persecution during World War II or as the spouse or descendants-in-need of the victim;

Credits are allowed under federal law for state death taxes, gift taxes, taxes on prior transfers, and foreign death taxes.

No estate tax deductions are allowed for any administration expenses, nor for any claims against the estate for expenses of medical care of the decedent, nor for any losses arising from fires, storms or other casualties, nor from theft, unless it is shown that these expenses have not been and will not be claimed as deductions for purposes of determining the federal or New York taxable income of the decedent or his estate for a taxable year commencing with the year 1961.

A credit is allowed for estate taxes paid pursuant to Article 26 on property transferred to a decedent and includable in his estate, by a decedent who died 10 years before or 2 years after the decedent's death.

A credit equal to 5% of the first $15 million in value of qualified property owned by the decedent in a closely held business that has vested in one or more qualified heirs is allowed.

¶2310 Return and Assessment

Jurisdiction: The surrogate's court having jurisdiction of the probate of the estate, has jurisdiction of all questions arising under the act, "including specifically, but without limitation, jurisdiction to finally determine the amount of the tax." Petitions to fix the tax are made to the surrogate. If it appears that the petition to determine the tax is insufficient to permit such determination to be made, or if it appears that more than 18 months have passed since the date of the decedent's death and no proceeding to determine the tax has been instituted, the surrogate may direct that an appraiser be appointed.

Return: A return must be filed by the executor for any resident estate and, in the case of nonresident estates, a return must be filed if the New York gross estate includes real and tangible personal property having an actual situs in New York. Any returns, statements, or other documents, or copies thereof, as required, must be filed within 9 months after the date of the decedent's death with the Commissioner of Taxation and Finance and with the Surrogate's Court in the county where the petition was filed to commence either a proceeding for probate of a will or a proceeding for administration in intestacy. The Commissioner of Taxation and Finance may grant a reasonable extension of time for filing any return. Except in the case of executors who are out of the country, no such extension shall exceed 6 months. Penalties, including fines of up to $10,000 and possible imprisonment, may be imposed where a taxpayer, with intent to evade the tax, (a) fails to file a return or report, (b) files a fraudulent return, report, statement, or other document, or (c) fails to disclose property of the estate that is subject to the tax.

Final determination: A copy of the final determination of the federal estate tax must be filed with the Commissioner of Taxation and Finance.

Compromise of tax: A compromise of taxes may be made with the Commissioner of Taxation and Finance where a taxpayer has been discharged in bankruptcy or is insolvent. Compromises involving more than $10,000 must be approved by a justice of the Supreme Court.

Payments of estate tax for estates in all counties should be sent to the New York State Department of Taxation and Finance, Estate Tax Accounts, Rm. 302, Bldg. 8, W.A. Harriman Campus, Albany, New York 12227. However, payments that accompany Form TT-102, Resident Affidavit, should be sent to the Estate Tax Audit Division, W.A. Harriman Campus, Albany, N.Y. 12227. (TSB-M-85(3), Estate and Gift Tax)

¶2311 Payment and Refund

Time for payment: The tax due shall be paid on or before the date fixed for filing the return, 9 months after the decedent's date of death. The Commissioner of Taxation and Finance may grant an extension of up to 12 months for paying the tax. If the gross estate includes the value of a reversionary or remainder interest in property, the payment of that part of the tax attributable to such interest may, at the election of the executor, be postponed until 6 months after the termination of the precedent interest or interests in the property. If the Commissioner finds that payment of the tax within such 6 months would result in undue hardship to the estate, the amount of the payment so postponed may be made payable, with interest, within a period not in excess of 3 years from the expiration of such 6 months. If the Commissioner finds that payment of the tax on the due date would result in undue hardship to the estate, the time for payment may be extended for up to 4 years from the decedent's date of death, and such payment may be required to be made in annual installments. Interest at the prevailing rate is attached during any such extension for payment of the tax. The taxpayer may be required to furnish a bond in an amount not exceeding twice the amount due if any extension is granted for payment of any amount of tax.

Receipt for payment: If a return has been filed and the Commissioner of Taxation and Finance is satisfied that no tax is due or that the tax paid is the full amount due or is the compromise amount agreed to, the executor shall be issued a certificate if no tax is due or a final receipt for tax due, as the case may be. Any person interested in the estate is, upon request, entitled to a duplicate certificate or final receipt upon payment of $10 to the Commissioner. Any certificate or receipt so issued shall in no way act as a bar to liabilities for additional taxes which may be due and owing.

Liability for payment: The executor is personally liable for the payment of the estate tax. In addition the spouse, etc., is personally liable, if the tax is not paid when due, to the extent of the interest in property received from decedent's estate. In the absence of a direction in a will to the contrary, the federal, New York and foreign death taxes paid or payable by estate representative are apportioned among the beneficiaries.

Reciprocity: Reciprocity with other states as to the collection of inheritance and estate taxes in nonresident estates, imposed by the state of domicile, is provided for.

Refunds: Any claim for refund of an overpayment of the estate tax must be filed by the executor within 3 years from the time the return was filed or 2 years from the time the tax was paid, whichever is later, or, if no return was filed, within 2 years from the time the tax was paid. If an agreement to extend the period for paying the tax is made within the period prescribed for filing a refund claim, the period for filing a claim for refund shall not expire prior to 6 months after the expiration of the period within which payment may be made pursuant to the extension agreement. A refund claim for a tax overpayment attributable to a federal change or correction required to be reported must be filed by the taxpayer within 2 years from the time the notice of change or correction or an amended return was required to be filed with the Commissioner of Taxation and Finance.

¶2312 Notice and Waivers

Residents: Waivers are not required.

Nonresidents: Waivers are not required.

ESTATE, GIFT, and GENERATION-SKIPPING TRANSFER TAXES

CHAPTER 24

GIFT TAX

¶2401 Gift Tax (repealed)

The New York gift tax was imposed on transfers by gift beginning on or after January 6, 1972, through December 31, 1999, by resident or nonresident individuals. The tax was patterned after the federal gift tax and incorporated the provisions of the Internal Revenue Code applicable to the taxation of gifts. The rates of tax were graduated. The amount of tax payable was determined cumulatively from the effective date of the tax (January 6, 1972) over the lifetime of the donor, through the repeal of the tax, effective January 1, 2000.

For gifts and transfers made after 1982 and before 2000, New York had restructured its estate and gift tax system to provide for unified rates and credits similar to the federal provisions.

¶2402 Generation-Skipping Transfer Tax (repealed)

Effective April 1, 2014, the New York generation-skipping transfer tax was repealed. As a result, the New York State generation-skipping transfer tax no longer applies to any distributions or terminations made after March 31, 2014. Form ET-500, Generation-Skipping Transfer Tax Return for Distributions, and Form ET-501, Generation-Skipping Transfer Tax Return for Terminations, must be filed for any taxable distributions and terminations made from January 1, 2014, through March 31, 2014. To be taxable for New York State purposes, the distribution or termination must have occurred at the same time as, and as a result of, the death of an individual. These returns had to be filed on or after January 1, 2015, but not later than April 15, 2015. (*TSB-M-14(1)M*, New York Department of Taxation and Finance, May 27, 2014, CCH NEW YORK TAX REPORTS, ¶ 408-102)

For decedents dying prior to April 1, 2014, the New York generation-skipping transfer tax was imposed on generation-skipping transfers that include New York property, to the extent of a federal generation-skipping transfer tax credit (determined under amendments enacted on or before July 22, 1998) for state generation-skipping transfer taxes paid. The tax is patterned after the federal generation-skipping transfer tax and incorporates the provisions of the Internal Revenue Code applicable to the taxation of generation-skipping transfers.

The generation-skipping transfer tax is administered by the Department of Taxation and Finance, State Campus, Albany, N.Y. 12227.

For additional information on the former New York tax, see previous editions of this GUIDEBOOK or the CCH STATE INHERITANCE, ESTATE, AND GIFT TAX REPORTER. The federal generation-skipping transfer tax is explained in detail in CCH FEDERAL ESTATE AND GIFT TAX REPORTS at ¶ 12,001—13,340.

PART VII

PROPERTY TAXES

CHAPTER 25
PROPERTY TAXES

¶2501 Overview of Property Tax

Property taxes in New York are imposed on real property and special franchises (¶2503) only. Personal property, whether tangible or intangible, is exempt from *ad valorem* taxation for both state and local purposes. In practice, New York State derives its revenue from income, franchise, sales and use, estate, and other special taxes. Taxes on real property are presently levied by local governments, which assess and collect the taxes pursuant to the provisions of the Real Property Tax Law and in accordance with the various county codes and special charters. The proceeds of these collections are retained by the local governments.

The purpose of this chapter is to give a general picture of the nature and application of the property tax and the manner of its administration. It is not intended to provide detailed coverage. It covers, generally, the questions of what property is subject to tax, the basis and rate of tax, and the requirements for filing returns and making payments.

• *Administrative agencies*

In 2010, New York merged the state Office of Real Property Services (ORPS) and the state Board of Real Property Services (BRPS) into the Department of Taxation and Finance (DOTF). The commissioner of taxation and finance has assumed the duties of ORPS and BRPS. The Office of Real Property Tax Services (ORPTS) and a separate and independent state BRPS are created within the DOTF. (Secs. 200, 201, Real Property Tax Law)

¶2502 Imposition of Tax

Law: (CCH NEW YORK TAX REPORTS, ¶20-101, 21-850).

Property taxation is governed primarily by Chapter 50-a, Real Property Tax Law, the New York Constitution, and by unconsolidated county laws, special city and village charters and ordinances. The counties are the principal local taxing units, but much of the actual administration and collection of taxes is accomplished at the municipal level. Cities, towns, villages, and school and special districts also have independent powers of taxation for their own purposes.

The Office of Real Property Services within the Department of Taxation and Finance (DoTF) is charged with the supervision of the assessment process on real property and special franchises throughout the state. Tax jurisdictions may appeal county equalization rates set by the county equalization agency to the State Board of Real Property Services, a separate and independent agency within DoTF. These rates are used in the distribution of financial assistance and the apportionment of state aid to municipalities and school districts, the equalization of assessments of special franchises for local assessment purposes, and the computation of constitutional tax limits of municipalities and certain school districts.

¶2503 Property Subject to Tax

> *Law:* Secs. 102, 300, 304, 480, 480-a, 481, Real Property Tax Law (CCH New York Tax Reports, ¶20-103, 20-113, 20-143, 20-233).

All real property in the state is subject to tax unless specifically exempt (Sec. 300, Real Property Tax Law). See ¶2504 for a list of exemptions.

The term "real property" includes:

— land, including trees, mines, minerals, quarries and fossils;

— buildings and other structures, including bridges, wharves and piers and the value of the right to collect wharfage, cranage or dockage thereon;

— railroads and railroad structures, substructures and superstructures, tracks and so forth;

— telephone and telegraph lines, wires, poles, supports and enclosures for electrical conductors when owned by a telephone company, save for certain equipment owned by other than a telephone company;

— mains, pipes and tanks for conducting steam, heat, water, oil, electricity or any property, substance or product capable of transportation or conveyance therein or that is protected thereby;

— boilers, ventilating apparatus, elevators, plumbing, heating, lighting and power generating apparatus, shafting other than counter-shafting and equipment for the distribution of heat, light, power, gases and liquids;

— trailers and mobile homes (but not recreational vehicles); and

— special franchises.

Buildings and structures can be subject to the real property tax even if they are not permanently attached to the land. The determining factor is whether the structure is intended to remain a permanent structure on land. See *Opinion of Counsel,* SBEA 114 (1/27/93); *Metromedia v. Tax Commission,* 60 NY2d 85 (1983).

Cellular telephone towers and related equipment have been held to be taxable as fixtures; see *Matter of T-Mobile Northeast, LLC v DeBellis,* Appellate Division of the Supreme Court of New York, Second Department, No. 2014-01836, October 26, 2016, CCH New York Tax Reports,¶408-888.

All real property assessments are against the real property itself, which is liable for sale for any unpaid taxes or special *ad valorem* levies. (Sec. §304).

Special franchises: Property subject to tax includes the franchise, right, authority, or permission to construct, maintain, or operate in, under, above, or through any public street, highway, or public place, pipes, tanks, conduits, wires, and the like for conducting water, steam, light, power, gas, or other substances. These are known as "special franchises" and are taxed directly as property upon their value. (Sec. 102.17, Real Property Tax Law).

Specially assessed property: To encourage reforestation, special assessment is available for any tract of forest land that meets certain requirements. (Sec. §480.2(a), Real Property Tax Law).

Owners of certain lands used in agricultural production are entitled to an agricultural value assessment, provided the land meets the following requirements (Sec. 481, Real Property Tax Law; Sec. 301 *et seq,* Ag. and Markets Law):

— the land is located within an agricultural district; (Sec. 305, Agriculture and Markets Law) or

— the owner commits the land exclusively to agricultural uses for a period of eight years (the owner may withhold any portion of a parcel from agricultural commitment, in which case only the portion for which a commitment is filed is exempt). (Sec. 306, Agriculture and Markets Law)

If the land is eligible for agricultural assessment, the portion of the value of the land in excess of its agricultural assessment value is exempt (Sec. 305, Agriculture and Markets Law). The State Board of Equalization and Assessment determines agricultural assessment values, based on soil productivity and capability (Sec. 304-a, Agriculture and Markets Law).

¶2504 Property Exempt

Law: Secs. 301—306, 310, Ag. and Markets Law; Secs. 400—496, Real Property Tax Law; Sec. 1021-L, Public Authorities Law (CCH NEW YORK TAX REPORTS, ¶ 20-505).

Personal property, whether tangible or intangible, is expressly excluded from *ad valorem* taxation. Intangible property is excluded by the State Constitution and both tangible and intangible personal property are exempt under the Real Property Tax Law. In addition, the law provides for the following principal exemptions from property tax:

• *Agricultural property*

The definition of "land used in agricultural production" includes a six-year exemption for land of at least seven acres used as a single operation for the production for sale of orchard or vineyard crops, provided that the land is used solely for the purpose of planting a new orchard or vineyard. The definition also includes certain commercial equine operations (see below). The land must be owned or rented by a newly established farm operation in its first, second, third, or fourth year of agricultural production. (Sec. 301(4)(i), Ag. and Markets Law). The term "viable agricultural land" is defined as a qualifying farm operation as provided in Sec. 301, Ag. and Markets Law.

Buildings and other permanent structures: Structures and buildings essential to the operation of lands actively developed to agricultural or horticultural use, and actually used and occupied to carry out such operation, constructed after January 1, 1969, and prior to January 1, 2019, are exempt to the extent of any increase in value by reason of such construction or reconstruction for a period of ten years. The exemption includes housing for farm employees, indoor exercise arenas for training and exercising horses, and beekeeping operations (Sec. 483.2, Real Property Tax Law). "Agricultural and horticultural use" includes the activity of raising, breeding and boarding of livestock, including commercial horse boarding operations. Rollback taxes will be imposed in the event there is a conversion to nonagricultural or nonhorticultural uses during the period the exemption was granted. (Secs. 483.1, 483.7, Real Property Tax Law).

Structures permanently affixed to agricultural land for the purpose of preserving and storing forage in edible condition, farm feed grain storage bins, silos, commodity sheds, manure storage and handling facilities (including composters and anaerobic digesters), and bulk milk tanks and coolers used to hold milk awaiting shipment to market are exempt from taxation, special *ad valorem* levies and special assessments. The exemption will only be granted upon the application of the owner of the property upon which the structures are located. The application must be filed on or before the appropriate taxable status date (¶2506) with the assessor of the municipality having the power to assess real property. No renewal is necessary once an exemption has been granted (Secs. 483-a, 483-a.1, 483-a.2, Real Property Tax Law).

Orchards and vineyards: A limited property tax exemption is allowed for certain land used for crop expansion or replanting in connection with an orchard or vineyard. The exemption is allowed for a period not exceeding six years, beginning on the first eligible taxable status date following the replanting or expansion, provided the following conditions are met (Ag. and Markets Law Sec. 305.7):

— the land used for crop expansion or replanting is part of an existing orchard or vineyard that (1) is located on land used in agricultural production within an agricultural district, or (2) is part of an existing orchard or vineyard that is eligible for an agricultural assessment where the owner has filed an application for agricultural assessment;

— the land eligible for the exemption does not in any one year exceed 20% of the total acreage of the orchard or vineyard that is located on land used in agricultural production within an agricultural district, or 20% of the total acreage of the orchard or vineyard eligible for an agricultural assessment where the owner has filed an application for agricultural assessment (land located in a declared disaster area is not subject to the 20% limitation); and

— the land eligible for such real property tax exemption is maintained as land used in agricultural production as part of the orchard or vineyard for each year that the exemption is granted.

Equine operations: A farm operation includes a commercial equine operation, which means an agricultural enterprise consisting of at least seven acres and stabling at least 10 horses, regardless of ownership, that receives $10,000 or more in annual gross receipts from fees generated through the provision of commercial equine activities (Secs. 301(4), (11), (17), Ag. and Markets Law). Those activities include, but are not limited to: riding lessons; trail-riding activities; the training of horses; the production for sale of crops, livestock, and livestock products or both the provision of such commercial equine activities and such production. A commercial equine operation does not include operations whose primary on-site function is horse racing.

Quarantined lands: Farm lands seized by the state for the purpose of enforcing a quarantine and to fumigate lands infested with golden nematode, may, at the discretion of the assessing unit, be exempt from tax (not school levies, special *ad valorem* taxes, or special assessments) during the period the land is in the possession of the state and under such quarantine and treatment (Sec. 482, Real Property Tax Law).

Special rules apply for the assessment of land used in agricultural production. (Sec. 481, Real Property Tax Law; Sec. 300 *et seq*, Ag. and Markets Law).

Temporary greenhouses: Temporary greenhouses are exempt from taxation, special *ad valorem* levies and special assessments. The owner of the property must file an application on a form to be prescribed by the state board. (Sec. 483-c, Real Property Tax Law).

Farm labor camps: Farm or food processing labor camps or commissaries are exempt, as well as any other structures used to improve the health, living, and working conditions for farm laborers, provided that the structures are in compliance with applicable health, labor, and building code standards.

Agricultural societies: Property owned by agricultural societies, permanently used for a meeting hall or exhibition grounds, is exempt (Sec. 450, Real Property Tax Law).

Agricultural assessment: Any owner of land used in agricultural production within an agricultural district is eligible for an agricultural assessment (Sec. 305(1), Ag. and Markets Law). The applicant must furnish to the assessor such information as the commissioner of taxation and finance shall require.

The process to recertify agricultural assessments has been simplified. A landowner must certify that the landowner continues to meet the eligibility requirements for receiving an agricultural assessment for the same acreage that initially received the assessment by filing a form prescribed by the Tax Commissioner. The landowner must maintain records documenting the property's eligibility and is required to apply for agricultural assessment for any change in acreage, regardless of whether land is added or removed, after the initial grant of agricultural assessment. A new owner of the land who wishes to receive an agricultural assessment must make an initial application for the assessment. (Sec. 305(1), Ag. and Markets Law)

• *Business property*

A 10-year partial exemption is allowed for the cost of construction, alteration, installation or improvement of certain business property (Sec. 485-b, Real Property Tax Law). However, the exemption does not include fire district taxes. To qualify for the exemption, the property must be used primarily for the buying, selling, storing or developing of goods and services, the manufacture and assembly of goods, or the processing of raw materials. The expenditure must be for a commercial business or industrial activity and not for ordinary maintenance or repairs. Also, the cost of the work must exceed $10,000. The exemption is calculated as a percentage of the increase in assessed value of the property resulting from the improvement, construction, alteration or installation as computed in the initial year of the 10-year period following the filing of the initial application. The amount of the exemption decreases 5% per year as follows:

First year of exemption, 50%; second year, 45%; third year, 40%; fourth year, 35%; fifth year, 30%; sixth year, 25%; seventh year, 20%; eighth year, 15%; ninth year, 10%; tenth year, 5%; eleventh year and thereafter, 0% (Sec. 485-b.2, Real Property Tax Law). A county, city, town or village may, by local law, and a school district that levies school taxes may, by resolution, accelerate or reduce percentages of exemption. The exemption does not apply in New York City.

The exemption base and annual exemption may be recomputed in any year in which the level of assessment increases by 15% or more.

No business investment exemption will be granted concurrent with, or subsequent to, any other real property tax exemption granted to the same improvements. However, an exemption will be granted if, during the period of the previous exemption, payments in lieu of tax were made to local governments in an amount equal to or greater than the amount of tax due if an exemption was not granted. This exemption will be granted for a number of years equal to the 10-year exemption less the number of years the property would have previously been exempt (Sec. 485-b, Real Property Tax Law).

Industrial development property: Real property owned by or under the jurisdiction, supervision or control of an industrial development agency is entitled to the exemption set forth in the general municipal law. An application for exemption must be made by the agency on a form prescribed by the state board, which must be filed in the office of the assessor on or before the appropriate taxable status date for the year in which the exemption is first claimed. The application must include an extract of the terms of any agreement relating to the project. No subsequent application is required in later years, unless the terms of the agreement are modified or changed. Railroad real property owned by or under the jurisdiction, supervision or control of an industrial development agency which is leased by the agency to a railroad company is exempt as provided under the general municipal law, and from special *ad valorem* levies and special assessments to the extent that the assessed valuation of the property exceeds the railroad ceiling on the property as determined in accordance with the earnings ratio (Secs. 412-a, 412-b, Real Property Tax Law).

Banking development districts: A sliding exemption from New York real property taxes is available to banks that establish branches in banking development districts. The exemption is available for 10 years starting at 50% of a taxpayer's exemption base amount and decreasing by 5% per year to 5% of the base amount in the 10th year. The exemption base upon which the exemption applies is the increase in assessed value attributable to the alteration, construction, installation or improvement to the real property on which the bank is located. The exemption base may be readjusted if new

¶2504

improvements are made or the level of assessment increases by 15% or more. Grants are available to municipalities to study the need for a banking district (Sec. 485-f, Real Property Tax Law).

- *Capital improvements*

Municipalities (other than New York City) are authorized to adopt a resolution exempting certain capital improvements to residential buildings after a public hearing. Such buildings can be exempt from tax for a period of one year to the extent of 100% of the increase in assessed value attributable to the reconstruction, alteration or improvement, as well as for an additional period of seven years, the extent of such exemption decreasing by $12^1/2\%$ each year during the additional period. The exemption is limited to $80,000 of the increased market value of the property attributable to the reconstruction, alteration or improvement. Municipalities may, by local law, decrease the exemption limitation to an amount not less than $5,000. Any increase in market value that exceeds $80,000 or a lower amount specified in the local law is ineligible for exemption (Sec. 421-f, Real Property Tax Law).

- *Cemeteries*

Property used exclusively for cemetery purposes is exempt, provided the cemetery is not operated for profit. The term "cemetery purposes" means land and buildings, whether privately or publicly owned or operated, used for the disposal or burial of deceased human beings, by cremation or in a grave, mausoleum, vault, columbarium or other receptacle. It also includes land and buildings actually used and essential to the providing of cemetery purposes including, but not limited to, the on-site residence of a full-time caretaker and a storage facility for necessary tools and equipment (Sec. 446, Real Property Tax Law).

- *Churches and religious property*

Real property held in trust by a clergyman or minister for the benefit of the members of his or her church is exempt, provided that the property is used exclusively for religious, charitable, hospital, educational, or moral or mental improvement. (Secs. 436, 420-a, Real Property Tax Law).

CCH Advisory: For-profit Use Was Not Inconsistent with Religious Exemption

Real estate owned by a religious corporation was exempt from New York property tax because the primary or principal use of the property was for a tax-exempt purpose of its owner notwithstanding the operation of a for-profit summer camp on the property. The town argued that the religious corporation was no longer using the real property exclusively for carrying out thereupon one or more of its religious purposes and was not entitled to the exemption. The stated purpose of the summer camp was to generate funds for educational and religious purposes. However, the town failed to prove that the operation of a religious summer camp was inconsistent with the intended principal use of the land.

The court noted that the fact that the property is leased or licensed to other parties, or the fact that the owner derives some profit from the use of the property, does not defeat a tax exemption pursuant to Real Property Tax Law Sec. 420-a(1), so long as the primary or principal use of the property is for a tax-exempt purpose of its owner. A tax-exempt property will generally retain its tax-exempt status even where a nonexempt, for-profit independent contractor conducts commercial operations on the property, so long as those operations are in furtherance of the property's tax-exempt purposes. (*Congregation Rabbinical College of Tartikov, Inc. v. Town of Ramapo,* New York Supreme Court, Appellate Division, Second Judicial Department, No. 03267, April 20, 2010, CCH NEW YORK TAX REPORTS, ¶ 406-780)

Parsonages: Property owned by religious corporations and actually used by the officiating clergymen for residential purposes, is exempt. Property owned by a minister, priest, or rabbi of any denomination, engaged in the work assigned by the church or denomination of which he or she is a member, or who is unable to work due to impaired health or age, is exempt to the extent of $1,500 if he or she is a resident and inhabitant of New York. The same holds true for unremarried surviving spouses (Secs. 460, 462, Real Property Tax Law).

Interdenominational centers: Property owned by interdenominational centers, established to promote cooperation between various religious denominations, is exempt (Sec. 430, Real Property Tax Law).

• *Crime victims and good samaritans*

A property tax exemption is allowed for the assessed value of improvements to one-, two- and three-family residences that are made on behalf of a crime victim or good samaritan who is physically disabled as a result of a crime and who is either the property's resident owner, a member of the resident owner's household, or a resident of the property. To qualify, the improvement must facilitate and accommodate the disabled use and accessibility to the property.

A "victim" is someone who has personally suffered a physical injury as a direct result of a crime. A "good samaritan" is someone, other than a law enforcement officer, who (1) apprehends a person who committed a crime in the samaritan's presence or who committed a felony, (2) acts to prevent or attempts to prevent a crime, or (3) assists a law enforcement officer in making an arrest.

The owner of the property must make application for the exemption to the local assessor on forms prescribed by the state board. The application must be filed with a certified statement of physical disability or blindness and a police report or crime victim's board report substantiating that the physical disability was inflicted as a result of a crime (Sec. 459-b, Real Property Tax Law).

• *Dental societies*

In the absence of a local law providing otherwise, property situated in a city having a population of 175,000 or more, owned by a dental society of any judicial district, is eligible for a limited exemption, provided the property is used exclusively for the purposes of the dental society. The maximum exemption for property located in the first, second, tenth or eleventh judicial district may not exceed $100,000; in all other judicial districts, the maximum exemption may not exceed $50,000 (Sec. 474, Real Property Tax Law).

• *Disabled persons*

Real property owned by one or more disabled persons whose income is limited as a result of the is exempt from New York real property tax to the extent of 50% of the assessed value of the property. Disabled owners are eligible for the partial exemption if their income or combined income for the tax year immediately preceding the date of the application for exemption did not exceed $3,000 or, if a local law has been enacted, the owner's income was not less than $3,000 and not more than $26,000. The exemption applies only to property that is the legal residence of the owner and used exclusively for residential purposes. If any part of the property is not used for residential purposes, that portion will be subject to tax and the remainder will be entitled to the exemption (Sec. 459-c, Real Property Tax Law).

Improvements pursuant to Americans With Disabilities Act: Municipalities and villages may provide a limited 10-year exemption for real property altered, installed, or improved subsequent to the effective date of the Americans With Disabilities Act (P.L. 101-336) for purposes of removing architectural barriers for the disabled (Sec. 459-a, Real Property Tax Law).

Municipalities may elect to exempt the increase in value attributable to improvements used for the purpose of facilitating and accommodating the use and accessibility of property by the physically disabled resident owner of the property or the physically disabled member of the owner's household who resides on the property (Sec. 459, Real Property Tax Law).

Physically disabled persons: Local governments may provide for an exemption for improvements to residential property for use by persons who are physically disabled. To qualify as physically disabled, an individual must submit a certified statement from a licensed physician stating that he or she has a permanent physical impairment which substantially limits one or more of such individual's major life activities. Alternatively, a certificate of legal blindness from the State Commission for the Blind and Visually Handicapped or an award letter for a disability pension from the U.S. Department of Veterans Affairs may be submitted (Secs. 459, 459-a, 459-b, 459-c, Real Property Tax Law).

DRIE program: Disabled persons of limited income may be eligible for the DRIE program, similar to the SCRIE program discussed below under "Senior Citizens".

Optional exemption: One or more owners of real property who qualify for the property tax exemption for disabled persons and/or the exemption for senior citizens may choose the more beneficial exemption of the two (Secs. 455, 459-c, Real Property Tax Law).

• *Empire zones*

Local governments may provide for a limited exemption for property constructed, altered, installed, or improved in designated economic development zones. Ordinary maintenance and repairs are not included. For exemptions beginning within the first seven years following the creation of the zone, property will be entitled to an exemption equal to 100% of the increase in assessed value attributed to the construction, alteration, installment, or improvement. For exemptions beginning in the eighth, ninth, and 10th year, the exemption is 75%, 50%, and 25%. (Sec. 485-e, Real Property Tax Law)

The base amount of the exemption is equal to the increase in assessed value attributable to the construction, alteration, installation or improvement as determined in the initial year the application is made. The base amount remains constant for the authorized term of the exemption unless there is subsequent construction, alteration, installation or improvement during the term of the exemption, in which case the base amount is revised to include the associated increase in assessed value. If there is a change in level of assessment of 15% or more, the base amount is adjusted by the change in level of assessment and the exemption amount recomputed. (Sec. 485-e, Real Property Tax Law)

No business investment exemption will be granted concurrent with, or subsequent to, any other real property tax exemption granted to the same improvements. However, an exemption will be granted if, during the period of the previous exemption, payments in lieu of tax were made to local governments in an amount equal to or greater than the amount of tax due if an exemption was not granted. This exemption will be granted for a number of years equal to the 10-year exemption less the number of years the property would have previously been exempt (Sec. 485-e, Real Property Tax Law).

• *Energy and environmental conservation*

Solar or wind energy systems or farm waste energy systems constructed or existing prior to July 1, 1988, or constructed after January 1, 1991, and prior to January 1, 2025, are exempt from taxation for a period of 15 years to the extent of the increase in valuation by reason of the inclusion of the solar or wind energy system. Construction of a system is deemed to have begun when a contract or interconnection agreement with a utility is fully executed and the deposit, if required, is made. The owner or developer of a system must provide written notification to the appropriate local jurisdiction or jurisdictions upon execution of the contract or the interconnection agreement. Upon notification of the start of construction, a taxing jurisdiction must notify the developer or owner within 60 days if such jurisdiction's intention is to require an agreement for payment in lieu of taxes.

¶2504

"Solar or wind energy system" means an arrangement or combination of solar or wind energy equipment designed to provide heating, cooling, hot water or mechanical, chemical or electrical energy by the collection of solar or wind energy and its conversion, storage, protection and distribution. Pipes, controls, insulation and other equipment that are part of the normal heating, cooling or insulation system of a building are not included. However, certain materials are included to the extent they exceed the energy efficiency standards required by law (Sec. 487, Real Property Tax Law).

In addition, oil and gas rights, and other elements of economic units, are exempt from taxation if the gas produced is collected from a landfill or used to power farm waste energy systems or farm waste electric generating equipment, applicable to property on assessment rolls based on taxable status dates occurring before 2018.

Insulation or other energy conservation measures added to one-two-three-or four-family homes that qualify for financing under a home conservation plan, or a conservation-related state or federal tax credit or deduction, are exempt to the extent of any increase in value of such homes by virtue of such addition (Sec. 487-b, Real Property Tax Law).

Environmental conservation facilities: Industrial waste treatment facilities constructed or reconstructed after May 12, 1965, and air pollution control facilities constructed or reconstructed after September 1, 1974, to comply with environmental conservation laws, are exempt to the extent of any increase in value by reason of the construction or reconstruction. The term "industrial waste treatment facilities" includes facilities for the treatment, neutralization or stabilization of industrial waste from a point immediately preceding the point of such treatment, neutralization or stabilization to the point of disposal, including the necessary pumping and transmitting facilities, but excluding such facilities installed for the primary purpose of salvaging materials which are usable in the manufacturing process or are marketable.

The term "air pollution control facilities" includes facilities which remove, reduce, or render less noxious air contaminants emitted from air contamination sources from a point immediately preceding the point of such removal, reduction, or rendering to the point of discharge of air, meeting emission standards as established by the Department of Environmental Conservation. This includes flue gas desulfurization equipment and attendant sludge disposal facilities, fluidized bed boilers, precombustion coal cleaning facilities and certain other facilities. This does not include facilities installed for the primary purpose of salvaging materials that are usable in the manufacturing process or are marketable or those facilities that rely for their efficacy on dilution, dispersion or assimilation of air contaminants in the ambient air after emission (Secs. 477, 477-a, Real Property Tax Law).

Nuclear power plants: Local governments and school districts are authorized to exempt nuclear powered electric generating facilities from property taxes, special *ad valorem* levies, and special assessments. A qualifying facility is one that generates electricity using nuclear power for sale, directly or indirectly, to the public, including the land upon which the facility is located, equipment used to generate the electricity, and equipment leading from the facility to the interconnection with the electric transmission system. The owner must enter into an agreement to make payments in lieu of taxes. The exemption expires January 1, 2031. (Sec. 485, Real Property Tax Law).

- *Fallout shelters*

Property constructed, altered, or improved to include a fallout shelter complying with the provisions of the New York State Defense Emergency Act and the regulations of the state civil defense commission is exempt to the extent that the increase in the value of the property is attributable to the fallout shelter facility, subject to a maximum exemption of $100 multiplied by the number of occupants which the shelter is designed to accommodate (Sec. 479, Real Property Tax Law).

¶2504

• *First-time homebuyers*

Localities may enact a partial exemption for a period of up to five years for newly constructed primary residential property purchased by one or more persons, each of whom is a first-time home buyer and has not been married to a homeowner in the three years prior to applying for the exemption (Sec. 457, Real Property Tax Law). In the first year, 50% of the property's assessed valuation is exempt. Thereafter, the exemption amount is phased out by 10% each year. Property purchased on or after December 31, 2016, does not qualify for the exemption unless the purchase was made under a binding written contract entered into before December 31, 2016.

Qualifications for the exemption include a purchase price limitation and a household income limitation, both based on maximum price and income amounts set by the State of New York Mortgage Agency for the county in question under the Low Interest Rate Mortgage Program. A locality may increase the purchase price limit used for eligibility by up to 25%.

Reconstruction, alteration, and improvements exceeding $3,000 in value may also qualify for exemption if performed under the written contract for sale or a written contract entered into by the first-time home buyer within 90 days after the closing of the sale.

• *Forest land*

Privately owned tracts of certified forest land containing at least 50 contiguous acres (exclusive of any portion not devoted to the production of forest crops) are exempt to the extent of 80% of the assessed valuation or the amount by which the assessed valuation exceeds the product of the latest state equalization rate or special equalization rate multiplied by $40, whichever is less. The land must be exclusively devoted to and suitable for forest crop production, and must be stocked with forest trees sufficient to produce a merchantable forest crop within 30 years of the time of the original certification. The owner must certify that it is committed to continued forest crop production for an initial period of ten years and file an initial application with the assessor. There is another exemption for reforested lands of at least 15 acres that have been planted with an average of not less than 800 trees per acre, or that have been under-planted with an average of not less than 300 trees per acre, or upon which the majority of the mature timber has been removed leaving an immature stand of timber that will produce merchantable timber or pulpwood within 30 years (Secs. 480, 480-a, Real Property Tax Law).

• *Fraternal organizations*

The grand lodge of a fraternal organizations, used for its meetings or meetings of the general assembly of its members or subordinate bodies, or by other fraternal organizations for the same purpose, is exempt, provided the entire income produced by the property is used to support institutions for the care of indigent members and their families (Sec. 428, Real Property Tax Law).

• *Governmental property*

Property owned by the United States is exempt. Property owned by the United Nations, or any similar world wide organization of which the United States is a member, is exempt. Property owned by a foreign government which is a member of the United Nations or similar world-wide organization, used for maintaining offices, quarters or the residence of its representatives, is also exempt (Secs. 400, 402, 416, 418, 490, Real Property Tax Law).

Property owned by the State of New York or any department or agency thereof is exempt. Property owned by the New York State employees' retirement system or the New York State teachers' retirement system is exempt.

Property owned by a municipal corporation, located within its borders and held for public use is exempt. Property received in tax foreclosure is deemed "held for public use" for three years from the date of deed. Property owned by a municipal corporation, located outside its borders, used as a public park, aviation field or highway, for flood control or soil conservation purposes is exempt if the municipal governing board agrees in writing (see *In the Matter of Town of Rye v. Assessor of City of Rye*, Appellate Division of the Supreme Court of New York, Second Department, No. 2013-08072, July 27, 2016, CCH NEW YORK TAX REPORTS, ¶ 408-825). Property used as a sewage disposal plant or system owned by a municipal corporation, located outside its borders, may be wholly or partially exempt if the governing board agrees in writing. Municipalities with populations less than 100,000 or between 225,000 and 300,000 may wholly or partially exempt land owned by the municipality outside its borders used as a water plant, pumping station, water treatment plant, watershed or reservoir. County reforested lands are exempt. Aqueducts of the New York City water supply system are also exempt (Secs. 402, 490, 404, 406, Real Property Tax Law).

Property owned by a school district or board of cooperative educational services is exempt. Property located within a special district's boundaries and used exclusively for the purposes for which the special district was created, is exempt. Property not within the special district's boundaries, used as a water plant, pumping station, water treatment plant, reservoir, or sewer disposal plant or system, is exempt to the extent agreed upon by the governing board in writing (Secs. 490, 408, 410, 410-a, Real Property Tax Law).

Public authorities: Real property owned by public authorities under the public authorities law may be exempt (Sec. 412, Real Property Tax Law).

Corporation franchise tax and property tax exemptions have been enacted for the North County Power Authority. However, the authority will be liable for payments in lieu of taxes (1) to municipalities and school districts that are equal to taxes and assessments that would have been received by the jurisdiction and (2) for corporation franchise tax. Income derived from securities issued by the authority is exempt from tax, except for estate and gift taxes. The authority must register for state and local sales and use tax purposes before making sales of property or services. (Sec. 1021-L, Public Authorities Law)

Special districts and special water districts: Certain property owned by a special district not within district boundaries and used for a sewage disposal plant or water plant, pumping station, water treatment plant or reservoir may be wholly or partially exempted from taxation and exempt from special *ad valorem* levies and special assessments provided its governing board so agrees in writing. Property owned by special water districts in Oswego or Cayuga Counties not within district boundaries may be wholly exempt from taxation and exempt from special *ad valorem* levies and special assessments if used as a pumping station, water treatment plant, pipeline and/or reservoir under certain conditions (Secs. 410-a, 410-b, Real Property Tax Law).

- *"Green" improvements*

If adopted by local law, ordinance or resolution, a property tax exemption is authorized for the construction of improvements to real property initiated on or after January 1, 2013, that meet Leadership in Energy and Environmental Design (LEED) certification standards for green buildings, the green building initiative's green globes rating system, the national green building standards as approved by the American National Standards Institute, or substantially equivalent standards for certification using a similar program for green buildings as determined by a municipal corporation. The required certification may be determined by an accredited professional under any of the named standards. (Sec. 470, Real Property Tax Law)

The exemption amount ranges from 100% in the first year for certified/silver, gold, or platinum LEED exemption to 20% in the 10th year for platinum LEED exemption. The value of the construction must exceed $10,000 and is documented by a building permit, if required, or other appropriate documentation as required by the assessor. A municipal corporation may establish a maximum exemption amount in its local law, ordinance, or resolution. If approved by the assessor, the exemption becomes effective for the assessment roll that is prepared after the taxable status date. A municipal corporation may establish a maximum exemption amount in its local law, ordinance, or resolution. For purposes of the exemption, "construction of improvements" does not include ordinary maintenance and repairs. (Sec. 470, Real Property Tax Law)

• *Historic property*

Property (not exceeding six acres in any one locality) acquired by historical societies for the inclosure, preservation, and erection of monuments, and property owned by soldier monument corporations, is exempt (Secs. 442, 444, Real Property Tax Law).

If authorized by local law, real property that is altered or rehabilitated for historic preservation is eligible for an exemption from New York property tax and special *ad valorem* levies. The exemption is allowed to the extent of any increase in value attributable to such alteration or rehabilitation according to a 10-year schedule. For the first five years, 100% of the value of alterations is exempt. For the next four years, the percentage decreases in increments of 20% from 80% to 20% until it is zero in the 10th year. To be eligible for exemption, the property must be designated as a landmark or contribute to the character of an historic district and the alterations must be made for means of historic preservation and approved by the local preservation commission. Owners of historic real property must apply for the exemption on a form prescribed by the State Board of Real Property Services and file it with the assessor of the county, city, town, or village that assesses property for taxation on or before the appropriate taxable status date of such locale (Sec. 444-a, Real Property Tax Law).

Historic barns: Municipalities may provide for a partial exemption for the reconstruction or rehabilitation of historic barns. To qualify, the barn must have been at least partially completed prior to 1936, and must have originally been designed and used for storing farm equipment or agricultural products, or for housing livestock. An otherwise qualified historic barn may not receive the exemption if it is used for residential purposes, if the historic appearance of the barn was materially altered by the reconstruction or rehabilitation, or if the barn received the agricultural buildings exemption within the prior 10 years (Sec. 483-b, Real Property Tax Law).

When a county, city, town, village, or school district has authorized the exemption, the increase in assessed value that otherwise would result from the reconstruction or rehabilitation of a qualified historic barn will be totally exempt in the first year. The exemption is then reduced by 10% each year for the next nine years (Sec. 483-b, Real Property Tax Law).

• *Housing*

Cities with populations exceeding 325,000 are authorized through January 1, 2019, to enact legislation providing an exemption for up to 32 years for any increase in the assessed valuation of certain multiple dwellings resulting from improvements to eliminate substandard living conditions. Tax abatements may also be granted for such conversions and improvements. Local law may elect to exempt a portion of the value of improvements where part of the building is used for nonresidential purposes so that the exemption or abatement is allowed only on the portion used for residential purposes (Sec. 489, Real Property Tax Law). This is known as the "J-51" program in New York City (NYC Adm. Code Sec. 11-243). Rental units in buildings receiving these benefits must be registered with the State Division of Housing and Community Renewal (DHCR), and are generally subject to rent stabilization for at least as long as the J-51 benefits are in force (see *Roberts v. Tishman Speyer Properties, L.P.*, New York Court of Appeals, No. 131, October 22, 2009, CCH NEW YORK TAX REPORTS, ¶ 406-578).

¶2504

Cities with more than 325,000 inhabitants are authorized through 2019 to exempt increases in assessed valuation for certain improvements to multiple dwellings used for single-room occupancy. Such improvements may include installation or replacement of wiring and plumbing, elevators, walls, floors, ceilings, street connections, windows, boilers or burners, bathroom facilities, security devices and fuel conservation measures. Annual certification must be provided to the local housing agency. Qualifying real property may also be granted an annual tax abatement of $12^1/2\%$ of the improvement cost for a period not to exceed 20 years (Secs. 488-a, 489, Real Property Tax Law).

Limited profit housing companies: Property owned by a limited profit housing company, a limited dividend housing company, or a housing development fund company, is exempt from tax to the extent of the increase in value over the value at the time of acquisition by the housing company (Secs. 414, 467-c, Real Property Tax Law).

Low income housing: Certain low income housing in New York City is exempt from tax. The real property must be owned by a corporation, partnership or limited liability company formed for the purpose of providing housing accommodations for persons and families of low income. The owner must: participate in the federal low income housing tax credit program; enter into a regulatory agreement with the municipality, the state or the housing trust fund corporation; have received a loan from the municipality, the state or the housing trust fund corporation; and be organized as a nonprofit housing development fund company, a nonprofit housing corporation, a wholly-owned subsidiary of such a company, or a partnership or limited liability company controlled by such a company (Sec. 420-c, Real Property Tax Law).

CCH Advisory: Market Rent

A not-for-profit corporation's property tax exemption appeal was granted because all the properties at issue were used primarily to support the corporation's charitable activities. The corporation provided housing to people who were at high risk of becoming homeless. The fact that government subsidies raised the amount received for low-income housing to an equivalent of market rates did not defeat the exemption. In addition, a charitable organization that requires tenants to participate in programs that address their problems is eligible to obtain an exemption even though most of its tenants pay market rent. (*Association for Neighborhood Rehabilitation, Inc. v. Board of Assessors of City of Ogdensburg,* Appellate Division of the Supreme Court of New York, Third Department, No. 509888, February 24, 2011, CCH NEW YORK TAX REPORTS, ¶407-133)

Residential investment: A partial exemption is authorized for the construction of residential real property in cities having a population of at least 31,000 but not more than 32,000, and in cities of at least 34,000 but not more than 35,000.

Urban redevelopment action area projects: Local governments may grant exemptions by contract to redevelopment company projects for a maximum of 25 years and may grant a mutual redevelopment company a partial exemption for another 25 years. Upon expiration, the abatement may be granted for up to an additional 50-year period or until such time as the property ceases to provide affordable housing. (Sec. 125, Priv. Hous. Fin. Law).

Local governments may also provide exemptions for developments and improvements to multiple dwellings.

Co-ops and condos: There is a partial abatement available for cooperative apartments and condominiums in New York City, so long as the owner owns no more than three such units in any one property. Other localities may provide an exemption for certain cooperative or condominium homesteading and rental projects (Secs. 421-e, 467-a, Real Property Tax Law).

Infant home corporations: Property owned by an infant home corporations, actually dedicated and used by such corporation exclusively as a place of free maintenance, care, and recreation of children under six years of age, is exempt from tax (Sec. 440, Real Property Tax Law).

Multiple dwellings: There is a partial exemption from New York City real property taxes for newly constructed multiple dwellings with three or more residential units (Sec. 421-a, Real Property Tax Law). Construction must be commenced before June 15, 2015, and the affordable rental units must remain as rent-stabilized units for 35 years after completion of the construction (Sec. 421-a(2)(a)(iv)(A), Real Property Tax Law). The exemption extends for three years following completion of construction, except that a special provision extends the exemption period an additional 36 months for multiple dwellings constructed between January 1, 2007, and June 30, 2009. Towns, villages or cities other than New York City that have declared an emergency under the Emergency Tenant Protection Act may also elect to exempt new residential buildings (Sec. 421-c, Real Property Tax Law). The local legislature of any city, town or village outside of New York City may exempt certain new or rehabilitated multiple dwellings financed by notes, bonds or other obligations of the New York State Housing Finance Agency (Sec. 421-d, Real Property Tax Law).

Any city, town or village not eligible for the Sec. 421-a or Sec. 421-c exemptions may be allowed by local law to provide a property tax exemption for the construction or substantial rehabilitation of multiple dwellings where at least 20% of the units qualify as affordable units (Sec. 421-m, Real Property Tax Law). This provision is effective June 24, 2011, and remains in full force and effect at a minimum until and including June 15, 2019.

There is also a partial exemption for owners of newly constructed or substantially reconstructed 1 and 2 family dwellings in New York City that will be occupied as a residence for the first time. An eligible building must be either newly constructed or substantially reconstructed 1 or 2 family dwelling, the building must be owner-occupied, and it cannot have any commercial and/or professional space. The buildings must have been completed by July 1, 2011 (Sec. 421-b, Real Property Tax Law).

Certain multiple dwellings within an eligible area of New York City may be exempt from real property taxation for local purposes (other than assessments for local improvements) on the amount of the assessed value attributable exclusively to physical improvement, for a period of 12 consecutive years beginning with the tax year immediately following the issuance of a certificate of eligibility, and real property taxes are abated for a period of 14 years. The periods are extended to 13 and 15 years respectively if the building is a designated landmark. An eligible multiple dwelling is a Class A multiple dwelling (except for a hotel) created from conversion of a nonresidential building. The exemption/abatement is equal to the amount of the assessed value attributable to the physical improvement, and decreases by 20% in each of the last four years of the exemption period (Sec. 421-g, Real Property Tax Law).

Municipal housing authorities: Property owned by a municipal housing authority is eligible for limited exemptions. The local government may, however, enter into agreements for payments in lieu of taxes (Sec. 414, Real Property Tax Law).

Newly constructed homes: Local legislatures may provide an exemption for first-time homebuyers of newly constructed primary residential property from taxation levied by or on behalf of any county, city, town, village or school district for up to five years. 50% of the assessed valuation is exempt from tax in year one, 40% in year two, 30% in year three, 20% in year four, with 10% in the final year. The purchase price of the new home must fall within the purchase price limits set by the New York mortgage agency low interest rate mortgage program. Moreover, a first-time homebuyer must meet certain household income limits set by the New York mortgage agency low interest rate program (Sec. 457, Real Property Tax Law).

Nonprofit health maintenance corporation: Property owned by a non-profit health maintenance corporation subject to the provisions of the Public Health Law, used exclusively for corporate purposes, is exempt (Sec. 486-a, Real Property Tax Law).

For exemptions specific to New York City, see 3309.

• *Miscellaneous exemptions*

START-UP NY provisions: New York has enacted the SUNY Tax-Free Areas to Revitalize and Transform Upstate (START-UP) New York program, which, among other benefits, provides property and transfer tax exemptions to promote business and job creation by transforming public higher education through tax-free communities in upstate New York and other strategically-designated locations.

Private universities and colleges will maintain tax-exempt status on property that is currently tax exempt and that they subsequently lease to businesses participating in the START-UP NY program. Only the portion of the property that is used for purposes of the START-UP NY program will be exempt (Sec. 420-a Real Property Tax Law). For an overview of all tax-related aspects of the program, see *TSB-M-13(7)C, (6)I, (11)M, (1)MCTMT, (7)S*, New York Department of Taxation and Finance, October 22, 2013, CCH ¶407-949.

Madison Square Garden: Property within New York City used by both an N.H.L. hockey team and N.B.A. basketball team for home games, is exempt from property taxes to the extent that said taxes are by lease the obligation of the owners of the franchises, provided such owners enter into a 10-year agreement with the city to play home games at the facility (Sec. 429, Real Property Tax Law).

Off-street parking facilities: Local governments may provide for an exemption for certain off-street parking facilities, providing underground shelter complying with the provisions of the New York State Defense Emergency Act, for a period of up to 25 years after the taxable status date immediately following completion of construction, reconstruction, remodeling, or alteration. At least 75% of the building's total floor area must be used for parking, and the building must have a minimum parking capacity of 250 cars in New York City, 150 cars in Buffalo, Rochester, Syracuse, Utica, Albany and Yonkers, and 75 cars elsewhere (Sec. 478, Real Property Tax Law).

Volunteer firefighters: Property owned by an incorporated association of volunteer firefighters or voluntary ambulance companies is exempt from tax, subject to a limit of $20,000. Villages may provide for an additional $500 exemption for property owned by members of the village volunteer fire department or the village volunteer fire company.

A 10% exemption may be granted for the primary residences of certain volunteer firefighters and ambulance workers residing in certain counties. To be eligible for the exemption, an applicant must have been certified as an enrolled member of an incorporated volunteer fire company, fire department, or incorporated ambulance service for at least five years (Secs. 464, 466, 466-a, 466-b, 466-c, Real Property Tax Law).

Any municipality may provide an exemption from New York property tax for unremarried spouses of members of volunteer fire companies or volunteer ambulance services killed in the line of duty. The unremarried spouse must be certified by the authority having jurisdiction for the incorporated volunteer fire company, fire department or incorporated voluntary ambulance service, the deceased volunteer must have been an active member of the volunteer organization for at least five years, and the deceased volunteer must have been previously receiving the exemption (Sec. 466-f, Real Property Tax Law). A similar exemption is available to the unremarried spouse of a deceased volunteer who was an enrolled member for at least 20 years (Sec. 466-h, Real Property Tax Law).

Fire patrol and salvage corporations: Fire patrol and salvage corporation property used exclusively for housing or storing property is exempt, provided the property is used and the services are rendered indiscriminately and without charge for the public benefit (Sec. 468, Real Property Tax Law).

Pharmaceutical colleges: In the absence of a local law providing otherwise, property situated in a city having a population of 175,000 or more, owned by an incorporated pharmaceutical society which has established a college of pharmacy, is exempt from tax, provided no rent is derived and the property is used exclusively for the purposes of the college. (Sec. 472, Real Property Tax Law).

Property held by trustees: Property held in trust for hospital, public playground or library purposes, is exempt (Sec. 438, Real Property Tax Law).

Rehabilitation of vacant residential buildings: Construction of qualified new residential structures or total rehabilitation of qualified vacant residential structures determined to be unoccupied hazards initiated on or after January 1, 2013, in cities with a population of 130,000 to 160,000 may be exempt from city and school taxation (Sec. 485-o, Real Property Tax Law).

Retirement systems: Property owned by retirement systems is exempt (Sec. 488, Real Property Tax Law).

• *Music and performing arts*

Cities with populations in excess of 175,000 may exempt property owned by and used to operate a music academy, provided the academy, for the prior year, did not earn any net income upon the net cost of the academy and its furniture. Property within New York City, acquired by an organization that is organized and operated as an institute of arts and sciences and used to house an academy of music, is also exempt (Secs. 434, 424, Real Property Tax Law).

Performing arts: An "opera house" owned by any corporation organized to sustain, encourage and promote musical art and to educate the general public in music is exempt so long as the property is used for the production of opera and providing operatic and musical performances and other related educational activities. A portion may be leased for public performances, opera, ballet, concerts, lectures, meetings, graduation exercises or other educational or non-commercial uses for the purposes of income, if such income is necessary for and actually applied to the maintenance and support of the corporation.

A "performing arts" building is exempt when owned by any corporation organized to sustain, encourage and promote musical and performing art, including opera, concerts, ballet, drama and other forms of artistic expression, and to educate the general public in the musical and performing arts. The property must be used for the production of musical and performing art and other related educational activities either directly or indirectly by leasing or otherwise making the facilities available for the use of other non-profit corporations to educate the general public in, or to foster interest in, musical or performing art. A portion of the property may be leased or used for public performances, theatrical performances, opera, ballet, concerts, lectures, meetings, graduation exercises or other related educational or noncommercial uses for the purposes of income, if such income is necessary for and actually applied to the maintenance and support of the owner corporation or other nonprofit corporation.

Real property owned by a nonprofit corporation created by an act of the U.S. Congress organized and used exclusively for the purposes of stimulating public interest in the drama as an art, presenting theatrical productions, advancing interest in the drama by furthering the production of plays, furthering the study of the drama, and sponsoring, encouraging and developing the art and technique of the theatre through the operation of a school is exempt up to $1.5 million (Secs. 426, 427, 432, Real Property Tax Law).

- *Native American reservations*

Property located on a Native American reservation and owned by the tribe, nation, or band occupying the property is exempt (Sec. 454, Real Property Tax Law).

Parcels of historic reservation land reacquired by an Indian tribe on the open market were not exempt from New York property tax, according to the U.S. Supreme Court, because the passage of time, the tribe's delay in seeking relief, and developments in the area spanning several generations raised equitable principles that precluded the tribe from asserting sovereign dominion over the parcels *(City of Sherrill v. Oneida Indian Nation of N.Y.*, U.S. Supreme Court, Dkt. 03-855, reversing the U.S. Court of Appeals for the Second Circuit, March 29, 2005, CCH NEW YORK TAX REPORTS, ¶405-077).

CCH Advisory: Tribal Sovereign Immunity from Suit

New York property tax foreclosure actions against an Indian tribe for the nonpayment of property taxes were barred because the tribe was immune from suit under the doctrine of tribal sovereign immunity. The Oneida Indian Nation of New York (OIN) repurchased land, through open-market transactions, that had once been a part of the Oneida Nation's reservation and asserted that such land was exempt from property tax. The U.S. Supreme Court held that the land was subject to taxation in *City of Sherrill v. Oneida Indian Nation of New York*, 544 U.S. 197 (2005). However, the appellate court affirmed the decision of the district court that the foreclosure actions were barred by the OIN's sovereign immunity from suit. Tribal sovereign authority over reservation lands and tribal sovereign immunity from suit are distinct concepts. (*Oneida Indian Nation of New York v. Madison County*, U.S. Court of Appeals for the Second Circuit, Nos. 05-6408-cv, 06-5168-cv, and 06-5515-cv, April 27, 2010, CCH NEW YORK TAX REPORTS, ¶406-787; petition for certiorari granted October 12, 2010, *Madison County v. Oneida Indian Nation of New York*, U.S. Supreme Court, Dkt. 10-72)

The U.S. Supreme Court accepted the request of the New York counties to review this ruling, but prior to oral arguments, counsel for the Oneida Indian Nation informed the high court that the Nation had passed an ordinance waiving its sovereign immunity to enforcement of property taxation through foreclosure. The Court then remanded the case to the U.S. Court of Appeals for the Second Circuit to address whether to revisit its ruling on sovereign immunity in light of the decision by the Oneida Indian Nation to waive its immunity from foreclosure. Also, the high court directed the lower court to proceed, if necessary, to address other questions in the case. (*Madison County v. Oneida Indian Nation of New York*, U.S. Supreme Court, Dkt. 10-72, January 10, 2011, CCH NEW YORK TAX REPORTS, ¶407-091)

On remand, the U.S. Court of Appeals for the Second Circuit concluded that the Nation had abandoned its claims premised on tribal sovereign immunity from suit, as well as its claims based upon the federal Nonintercourse Act. In addition, the appellate court vacated the lower court's judgments to the extent that they rested upon a determination that the Nation was entitled to property tax exemptions under state law. The appellate court concluded that supplemental jurisdiction should not be exercised over the Nation's state law claims. Because no grounds remained in support of the lower court's award of permanent injunctive relief, the appellate court vacated both of the lower court's injunctions in their entirety. However, with respect to property taxes and related assessments accruing prior to March 29, 2005, the appellate court affirmed the lower court's ruling that the Nation was not liable for the payment of penalties or interest. (*Oneida Indian Nation of New York v. Madison County*, U.S. Court of Appeals for the Second Circuit, Nos. 05-6408-cv (L), 06-5168-cv (CON), and 06-5515-cv (CON), October 20, 2011, CCH NEW YORK TAX REPORTS, ¶407-390)

- *Nonprofit and limited profit organizations*

Property of nonprofit organizations organized or conducted exclusively for religious, charitable, hospital, educational, or moral or mental improvement of men, women, and children, or held in trust for the benefit of a religious denomination is exempt, provided no member, employee or officer is entitled to receive any pecuniary profit from the organization's operations. Also generally exempt is property of nonprofit organizations organized or conducted exclusively for bible, tract, benevolent, missionary, infirmary, public playground, scientific, literary, bar association, medical society, library, patriotic, or historical purposes, for the development of good sportsmanship for persons under 18 years of age, or the enforcement of laws relating to children or animals, used exclusively for carrying on such purposes. Any portion not exclusively used for such purposes shall be subject to tax. However, such property will be subject to tax by the municipal corporation in which the property is located, if the governing board, after a hearing, adopts an ordinance to that effect (Secs. 420-a, 420-b, Real Property Tax Law).

Nonprofit/limited profit medical, nursing, housing companies: Property owned by limited profit corporations used exclusively to provide housing and auxiliary facilities for faculty members, students, employees, nurses, interns, resident physicians, researchers and other personnel and their immediate families in attendance or employed at colleges, universities, educational institutions, child care institutions, hospitals and medical research institutions, or for handicapped or aged persons of low income, is exempt from tax (Sec. 422, Real Property Tax Law).

Property owned by nonprofit nursing home companies, used exclusively to provide facilities for nursing care to sick, invalid, infirm, disabled, or convalescent persons of low income, or to provide health-related services to persons of low income, is exempt (Sec. 422, Real Property Tax Law).

Property owned by nonprofit housing development fund companies, used exclusively to provide housing for handicapped or aged persons of low income, is exempt (Sec. 422, Real Property Tax Law).

Property owned by nonprofit companies organized under Article 75 of the mental hygiene law is exempt if used exclusively to provide care, treatment, training, education and residential accommodations for the mentally ill (Sec. 422, Real Property Tax Law).

Property owned by companies organized pursuant to the membership corporations law and Article 7-A of the private housing finance law are exempt where used exclusively to provide programs, services and other facilities for the aging (Sec. 422, Real Property Tax Law).

Limited profit nursing homes: Property owned by a limited profit nursing home company may be eligible for a limited exemption from tax (Sec. 414, Real Property Tax Law).

CCH Advisory: Leased Property

A not-for-profit organization that provided religious, charitable, and educational services was denied a property tax exemption because legal title to the property was not held in the corporation's name. Statutory exemption provisions allow the exemption for property owned, but not leased, by a corporation or association organized or conducted exclusively for religious, charitable, or educational purposes. Because the organization entered into a 99-year lease for the property, the corporation had not acquired legal title to the property and could not claim the exemption. (*Al-Ber, Inc. v. New York City Department of Finance*, Appellate Division of the Supreme Court of New York, Second Department, No. 2009-11875, January 25, 2011, CCH NEW YORK TAX REPORTS, ¶ 407-108)

• *Railroad property*

Property held and used by municipal railroad corporations is exempt (Sec. 456, Real Property Tax Law). Subsidized railroad real property is exempt. Bridges, viaducts, and similar structures constructed after 1958, as a result of the creation of a new highway, street, or roadway and carrying railroad facilities over such highway, street, or roadway are exempt. No assessment of any bridges, viaducts, and other similar structures lengthened or reconstructed after 1958, as the result of the widening, reconstruction, or relocation of an existing highway, street, or roadway, may be increased by reason of such relocation or reconstruction, except that the original portion of such bridges, viaducts, or other similar structure may be varied in accordance with the changes made generally in assessments on other local real property.

Railroad real property is exempt to the extent of any increase in value from certain additions, betterments, improvements or reconstructions made after the last taxable status date prior to April 21, 1959. Included are the installation of automatic grade crossing protective devices, the reconstruction or replacement of signals, railroad bridges, stations, freight houses, classification yards, repair shops or other such facilities; and the construction or reconstruction of any grade separation structure, such as bridges, viaducts, tunnels, retaining walls and embankments constructed for the purpose of eliminating or avoiding highway railroad crossings at grade.

Railroad property other than subsidized railroad real property is exempt from taxation to the extent that the assessed valuation exceeds the railroad ceiling. A railroad ceiling for the railroad real property (other than subsidized railroad real property) of each railroad is established annually by the state board.

Railroad passenger stations in cities with populations exceeding one million residents are exempt (Secs. 489-c, 489-cc, 489-d, 489-dd, 489-e, 489-ee, 476-a, Real Property Tax Law).

- *School tax relief (STAR) exemption*

Beginning with assessment rolls used to levy school district taxes for the 2016-2017 school year, the School Tax Relief (STAR) exemption program is closed to new applicants, and a new refundable personal income tax credit is established in its place (see ¶162). Current recipients of STAR exemptions are permitted to keep the exemptions as long as they continue to own their homes, but upon transfer of the property to a new owner, the new owner would only be eligible for the income tax credit program. Current STAR exemption recipients have the option of giving up their STAR exemptions in favor of the personal income tax credit, though it is not required. (Sec. 425(16), Real Property Tax Law)

If the owners of a parcel that is receiving the basic STAR exemption want to claim the personal income tax credit instead, they all must renounce that exemption in the manner provided by Sec. 496, Real Property Tax Law, and must pay any required taxes, interest and penalties, on or before December 31 of the taxable year for which they want to claim the credit. Any such renunciation is irrevocable. (Sec. 425(16), Real Property Tax Law)

The STAR property tax exemption is for the primary residences of homeowners (known as the basic exemption) and an enhanced exemption is available through 2019 for the primary residences of senior citizens (persons aged 65 and older). The basic exemption for homeowners is $30,000 and for senior citizens, $60,100 for the 2009-2010 school year. The base figure for the enhanced exemption is indexed for inflation after 2009. (Sec. 425, Real Property Tax Law). In certain specified counties, the exemption amounts are modified by a sales price differential factor determined by the state board of real property services. In order for property to qualify for the enhanced senior citizens exemption provided by the STAR program, the combined income of all the owners and owners' spouses residing on the property for the income tax year immediately preceding the date of application for the exemption may not exceed a specified, indexed amount. The combined income of all owners of a parcel may not exceed $500,000.

Effective January 1, 2016, the STAR exemption includes farm dwellings owned by a limited liability company (LLC) if the property serves as the primary residence of one or more of the owners. The same provisions continue to apply to farm dwellings owned by S corporations and partnerships. (Sec. 425(3)(d), Real Property Tax Law)

¶2504

The following additional qualifications and conditions apply:

Senior citizens' age: Age eligibility is based upon age as of December 31 of the tax year.

— Although property will generally qualify for the enhanced exemption only if all owners satisfy the age requirement, in the case of property owned by spouses or siblings, only one of the owners must be 65 years of age.

— In the case of property owned by a husband and wife, one of whom is at least 65 years of age, the exemption will not be rescinded solely because of the death of the older spouse, as long as the surviving spouse is at least 62 years of age.

— If an owner is absent from his or her residence while receiving health-related care as an inpatient of a residential health care facility, the enhanced exemption may still be granted, provided that during the owner's confinement the property is not occupied by anyone other than the owner's spouse or another co-owner.

Registration: Homeowners who purchased their primary residence after August 1, 2015, must register for STAR with New York State instead of applying with their assessor, while those who bought their home between May 1, 2014, and August 1, 2015, must register with the state if:

(1) they bought their home after the 2015 STAR application deadline, or

(2) they have never applied for the STAR benefit on their primary residence.

Such homeowners will receive a STAR check instead of an exemption on their school property tax bill. Property owners who bought their home before May 1, 2014, will continue to receive the STAR property tax exemption and do not need to take any action.

After initial eligibility is established, the commissioner will endeavor to confirm the continuing eligibility of STAR recipients through means other than re-registration, such as by reviewing relevant data appearing on personal income tax returns. The commissioner may direct the removal or denial of a STAR exemption under specified circumstances and is required to provide the property owners with notice and an opportunity to demonstrate eligibility before taking such action. The State Board of Real Property Services has the power to hear and determine reviews relating to determinations of STAR eligibility made by the Department of Taxation and Finance. (Sec. 425(14), Real Property Tax Law)

Effective April 1, 2014, if late registration for the STAR program is accepted after the Basic STAR exemption has already been removed from the subject property, the Commissioner is authorized to remit directly to the property owner the tax savings that the exemption would have yielded had it not been removed. The Commissioner may direct the assessor to restore the exemption on a prospective basis without a new application, unless there is reason to believe the property owner is no longer eligible. (Sec. 425(14)(a)(iii), Real Property Tax Law)

Suspension of STAR benefits: STAR property tax exemption benefits are suspended if past-due state tax liabilities exceed $4,500. The amount of the STAR benefits that are forfeited will be applied against the outstanding tax liability (Sec. 425(f), Real Property Tax Law). This provision is applicable to school years 2013-14, 2014-15 and 2015-16.

Senior citizens' income: Generally, an application for the enhanced exemption must be filed each year. However, seniors may elect to have their renewal application processed automatically, with annual income verification performed by the Department of Taxation and Finance. Seniors electing to participate in the program will not have to present tax returns to their local assessors, and each year they will receive a postcard indicating information on record, COLA changes, and a reminder to report any changes in their status. This notification process would also be applicable where senior citizens designate a third party to be notified when enhanced STAR renewal applications are due.

Failure to reapply for enhanced exemption: Although the enhanced exemption will be discontinued if a qualifying senior citizen fails to file an annual renewal application, the assessor must nevertheless grant the basic exemption that is generally available to other owners.

Applications for renewal of enhanced STAR senior citizen property tax exemptions may be filed after the taxable status date in certain cases. No later than the last day for paying taxes without incurring cost or penalty, owners may submit a written request to the assessor requesting a filing extension. Requests much contain an explanation of why the deadline was missed and be accompanied by a renewal application. The assessor may extend the deadline and grant the exemption if good cause existed for failure to timely file the renewal application and if the applicant is otherwise entitled to the exemption. (Sec. 425(6)(a-2), Real Property Tax Law)

Apartment co-ops and manufactured homes: With respect to residents of cooperative apartments and owners of trailers and mobile homes, who are allowed to apply for the STAR exemption even though the tax bill generally goes to the landowner or cooperative corporation, the law is clarified to ensure that the correct amounts are credited to the correct parties. Specifically, the assessor is now required to provide the landowner or cooperative apartment corporation with a statement setting forth the exemption attributable to each eligible tenant-stockholder, trailer, or mobile home. Cooperative apartment corporations must provide each eligible tenant-stockholder with a written statement detailing how the exemption is being credited.

Co-op apartment corporations may credit the exemption to tenant-stockholders. There are four options: (1) a full credit against the fees and charges of any single month within the current assessment cycle, with any balance to be credited in full for subsequent months until exhausted; (2) a proportional credit over six months during the current assessment cycle; (3) a proportional credit over 12 months during the current assessment cycle; or (4) a lump sump payment of the total savings to the tenant-stockholder. The exemption must be fully credited during the assessment cycle for which each tenant-stockholder is eligible for STAR. In addition, cooperative apartment corporations are required to inform eligible tenant-stockholders about the full value of their STAR benefits and how the amounts were calculated.

Special assessing units: The local legislative body of a county that is a special assessing unit may provide for the partial abatement of county taxes of senior citizens who qualify for and receive the enhanced STAR exemption (Sec. 425-a, Real Property Tax Law).

Effective November 21, 2015, all property tax assessing units are required to participate in the enhanced STAR exemption (Sec. 425(4)(b)(iv), Real Property Tax Law).

Local property tax rebates: When a property owner is entitled to the basic or enhanced STAR exemption, the owner or owners also may receive a local property tax rebate. (Sec. 1306-b, Real Property Tax Law)

Rebates are distributed to taxpayers by the Commissioner of Taxation and Finance.

Recoupment: The Department of Taxation and Finance may use data collected through the registration process to recoup improperly granted STAR exemptions on one or more of the three preceding assessment rolls, along with interest. The law establishes notice and grievance procedures associated with any such recoupment.

Neither assessors nor boards of assessment review have authority to consider objections to recoupment of an exemption; rather, such actions may be challenged only before the department. In order for the recoupment procedure to be considered timely, the required notice must be mailed no later than three years after the conclusion of the school year for which the exemption in question was granted. (Sec. 425(15), Real Property Tax Law)

Practitioner Comment: Nonresidents Ineligible for STAR Exemption

The STAR exemption from real property taxes is limited to the homeowner's primary residence. Taxpayers who establish a primary residence in a new state are required to notify the local New York assessor that the New York property no longer qualifies for the STAR exemption. New York's income tax auditors will frequently cite the failure to terminate the STAR exemption as evidence that the taxpayer still resides in the New York home (2014 New York State Nonresident Audit Guidelines ¶ V.C. 7).

Mark S. Klein, Hodgson Russ LLP

Grace period: Senior citizens who qualify for the school tax relief (STAR) exemption may be allowed a grace period of five business days to make payments of property taxes without penalty or interest if the governing body of a municipal corporation, other than a county, adopts this delayed payment provision (Sec. 925-b, Real Property Tax Law).

Renunciation: A property owner may voluntarily renounce his or her claim to a school tax relief (STAR) exemption. The owner must file an application form authorized by the tax commissioner, together with a $500 application fee, with the county director of real property tax services (or the commissioner of finance in New York City) no later than 10 years after the levy of taxes on the assessment roll. The assessed value of the property will be multiplied by the tax rate or rates that were applied to that assessment roll, and interest will be added to the product for each month or portion thereof since the levy of taxes on the assessment roll. The property owner must pay the total amount due to the county treasurer within 15 days of the mailing of the form. (Sec. 496, Real Property Tax Law)

Property tax freeze credit: A personal income tax credit (see ¶ 122) is available to homeowners who are eligible for the STAR exemption, and live in a taxing jurisdiction that (1) limits any increase in its tax levy to a property tax cap set by state law (see ¶ 2505), and (2) develops and implements a Government Efficiency Plan determined to be compliant by the New York State Division of Budget. Qualified homeowners will receive a freeze credit equal to the greater of the actual increase in their homeowner's tax bill or the previous year's tax bill multiplied by an inflation factor. In the first year of the program, homeowners will receive the credit if their local government or school district stays within the property tax cap. In the second year, homeowners will receive the credit for taxes from any taxing jurisdictions in which the homeowner resides that stay within the property tax cap and put forward a compliant plan to save 1% of their tax levies in each of the following three years. New York City homeowners are not eligible for the freeze credit because New York City is not subject to the property tax cap. (Sec. 606(bbb), Tax Law; *Publication 1030*, New York Department of Taxation and Finance, July 14, 2014, CCH New York Tax Reports, ¶ 408-134)

- *Senior citizens*

Local governments may provide for an exemption allowing persons 65 years of age or older to exclude up to 50% of the assessed value of property used for residential purposes, provided certain income limitations are met (Sec. 467, Real Property Tax Law). Proceeds from a reverse mortgage are not considered income for purposes of calculating eligibility.

If the property is owned by a husband and wife or by siblings, the exemption will be permitted if at least one spouse or sibling is 65 years of age. Divorced or separated property-owners may also qualify for relief, provided the property previously qualified for, and received, the senior citizen exemption when occupied by both spouses.

Title to cooperative apartments owned by a cooperative apartment corporation is deemed to be vested in the corporation's tenant-shareholders. Therefore, if an apartment owned by a cooperative apartment corporation and occupied by a tenant-shareholder is eligible for a tax exemption, the amount of the exemption must be credited against the assessed valuation of the property, and the resulting tax reduction must be credited by the corporation against the amount of the taxes otherwise chargeable to or payable by the tenant-shareholder.

Optional exemption: One or more owners of real property who qualify for the property tax exemption for disabled persons and/or the exemption for senior citizens may choose the more beneficial exemption of the two (Secs. 455, 459-c, Real Property Tax Law).

Senior citizen or disabled persons rent increase exemptions (SCRIE and DRIE): Local governments may also provide for limited tax abatements for rent-controlled and rent-regulated property occupied by senior citizens or disabled persons with limited incomes. The abatement amount is equal to the portion of any increase in the legal regulated rent that causes it to exceed $1/3$ of the combined income of all members of the household, or if the senior citizen or disabled person receives a monthly allowance for shelter pursuant to the social services law, the amount of any increase in maximum rent or legal regulated rent that is not covered by the maximum allowance for shelter that the senior citizen is entitled to receive. The amount of the abatement is deducted from the legal maximum rent or legal regulated rent for the dwelling unit of the senior citizen. (Sec. 467-b(3), Real Property Tax Law) No abatement is allowed if the combined income of all members of the household for the income tax year immediately preceding the date of application exceeds $4,000 or the income limit set by the local law, which may not exceed $50,000 ($29,000 prior to July 1, 2014). (Secs. 467-b; 467-c, Real Property Tax Law).

If the head of household dies or permanently leaves a household, the eligible surviving members of the household may apply to transfer the former head of household's property tax SCRIE or DRIE benefit. The option to transfer either benefit is available for six months after the head of household dies or permanently leaves the household or for 90 days after the date of notice from the supervising agency informing the household that the rent increase exemption benefit has expired, whichever is later. (Secs. 467-b(4-a); 467-c(4-a), Real Property Tax Law)

Individuals who are dropped from the Senior Citizen Rent Increase Exemption (SCRIE) and the Disability Rent Increase Exemption (DRIE) programs due to a nonrecurring item of income may reapply the next year and be accepted at the previously frozen rent amount (Sec. 467-b(2)(d)(1), Real Property Tax Law).

In New York City, anyone granted a rent increase exemption order that is in effect as of January 1, 2015, or that takes effect on or before July 1, 2015, may continue in the programs even if their rent does not meet the $1/3$ ratio of rent-to-income requirement. Going forward, new applicants are subject to the 1/3 ratio requirement. (Sec. 467-b(2)(c), Real Property Tax Law)

Both programs are scheduled to expire June 30, 2020.

Granny units: A county, city, town, village, or school district may exempt any increase in the assessed value of residential property resulting from the construction or reconstruction of the owner's principal residence for the purpose of providing living quarters for the owner's parent or grandparent who is age 62 or older (Sec. 469, Real Property Tax Law).

The exemption must not exceed the lesser of (1) the increase in assessed value resulting from the construction or reconstruction, (2) 20% of the total assessed value of the improved property, or (3) 20% of the median sale price of residential property in the county. If granted, the exemption is applicable only to construction or reconstruction that occurs after August 30, 2000, and only during taxable years in which at least one parent or grandparent maintains a primary place of residence in the living quarters.

Certain municipalities are empowered to exempt residential real property to the extent of any increase in assessed value resulting from the construction or reconstruction of the property for the purposes of providing living quarters for a senior citizen who is 65 years of age or older, or individuals considered disabled and receiving social security disability benefits (Sec. 467-d, Real Property Tax Law).

• *Veterans*

Local governments are authorized to exempt up to 15% of the assessed value of the primary residence owned by (or held in trust for the benefit of) a war veteran, the veteran's spouse, or the veteran's unremarried surviving spouse. If there is no unremarried surviving spouse, the exemption will apply if the property passes by devise or descent to the veteran's dependent father, mother, or children under 21 years of age, and is used by at least one as his or her primary residence. The maximum amount of the exemption may not exceed the lesser of $12,000, or the product of $12,000 multiplied by the latest state equalization rate (or, in the case of a special assessing unit, the latest class ratio). Veterans are not required to refile annually for the exemption. Seriously disabled veterans are also exempt from special district charges and assessments, and special *ad valorem* levies. (Sec. 458-a.2, Real Property Tax Law).

Effective January 2, 2016, municipalities are authorized to prorate a veteran's property tax exemption if the veteran moves within the same county, or in the case of NYC, within the same city (Sec. 458(9), Real Property Tax Law). Previously, proration was authorized for veterans relocating within the same city, town, or village.

Localities are authorized to further increase the maximum amount of a New York property tax exemption for veterans, applicable only to local laws adopted on or after January 2, 2016 (Sec. 458-a.2, Real Property Tax Law).

Additional exemption: Veterans who received a campaign ribbon, service medal, or expeditionary medal from the armed forces, the navy, or the marine corps, or a global war on terrorism expeditionary medal, as a result of service in a combat theatre or combat zone of operation may be entitled to an additional residential property exemption equal to 10% of the assessed value of the property, subject to a maximum of $8,000, or the product of $8,000 multiplied by the latest state equalization rate (or, in the case of a special assessing unit, the latest class ratio) (Sec. 458-a.2, Real Property Tax Law).

Qualifying veterans are those who served in the active military, naval or air service during a period of war (Sec. 458-a.1, Real Property Tax Law). The exemption is also available to reserve members of the U.S. armed forces who have served on federal active duty during a period of war, and who remain affiliated with their reserve component unit.

School tax exemption: After public hearings and adoption of a resolution, the governing body of a New York school district is authorized to grant eligible veterans exemption from their school taxes, effective December 18, 2013 (Sec. 458-a.2(d)).

Gold Star parents: Parents of a child who died in the line of duty ("Gold Star parents") may qualify for the additional exemption, at local option.

Gold Star parents are generally entitled to a 15% property tax exemption on their primary residence, and those whose son or daughter received a commendation are entitled to an additional 10% exemption (Sec. 458-a.7, Real Property Tax Law).

Cold War veterans: Municipalities are authorized to adopt a local law that allows a property tax exemption for residential real property owned by, or held in trust for, Cold War veterans. The exemption provisions are available to Cold War veterans who reside in cooperative apartments when they are tenant-stockholders of cooperative apartment corporations. Localities may grant the exemption in an amount equal to either 10% or 15% of the assessed value of the property for a period of 10 years. An additional exemption may apply if the veteran has a service-connected disability. If adopted, the exemption applies to county, city, town, and village property taxes. Effective August 19, 2016, school districts are authorized to provide, by resolution, an exemption from school taxes for eligible Cold War veterans. A Cold War veteran is a person who served on active duty in the U.S. Armed Forces during the period from September 2, 1945, to December 26, 1991 (Sec. 458-b, Real Property Tax Law).

Municipalities and counties may increase or decrease the maximum exemption amounts that are allowed to Cold War veterans. Also, the state board of equalization may establish a special equalization rate to recompute a Cold War veteran's exemption when there has been a material change in the level of assessment since the establishment of the latest state equalization rate. (Sec. 458-b, Real Property Tax Law)

Disabled veterans: Veterans who received a compensation rating from the United States as a result of a service-connected disability may be entitled to a residential property exemption equal to the assessed value of the property multiplied by 50% of the veteran's disability rating. The maximum amount of the exemption may not exceed the lesser of $40,000, or the product of $40,000 multiplied by the latest state equalization rate (or, in the case of a special assessing unit, the latest class ratio) (Sec. 458-a.2, Real Property Tax Law).

Effective July 1, 2015, real property purchased with eligible funds proceeds of a pension, bonus or insurance, or dividends or refunds on such insurance, or payments received as prisoner of war compensation from the United States government, for honorably discharged veterans of World War I, World War II, or the Korean conflict, who sustained permanent disability while on military duty, may also qualify for a $7,500 exemption (previously, $5,000) (Sec. 458(1), Real Property Tax Law).

"Recompute" exemption: A revised "recompute" veterans' exemption is permitted, upon adoption of a local law, when additional eligible funds upon which an original veterans' exemption was based are subsequently received by the veteran. The "recompute" exemption is in lieu of any other veterans' exemption and is equal to the sum of the original exemption and any additional funds received multiplied by the change in assessment level (Sec. 458.5(d), Real Property Tax Law).

The primary residence of a seriously disabled veteran, who has received pecuniary assistance from the United States and applied it towards the acquisition of a suitable housing unit, is exempt from tax, including special district charges, assessments and special *ad valorem* levies. The exemption includes housing for unremarried surviving spouses that continues to be used as the spouse's primary residence. The exemption may be transferred to any new housing unit that is to be used as the unremarried surviving spouse's primary residence.

Local governments may also provide for limited exemptions for property purchased by veterans with the proceeds from specified eligible funds. An unremarried surviving spouse of a veteran may transfer the exemption to any new housing unit that is to be used as his or her primary residence (Sec. 458.3, Real Property Tax Law).

An exemption is also allowed for eligible veterans who are tenant shareholders of a cooperative. The exemption is allowed for that proportion of the assessment of such real property owned by a cooperative apartment corporation determined by the relationship of such real property vested in such tenant-shareholder to such real property owned by such cooperative apartment corporation in which such tenant-shareholder resides. Any exemption that is granted will be credited by the appropriate taxing authority against the assessed valuation of such real property. The reduction in real property taxes realized thereby will be credited by the cooperative apartment corporation against the amount of such taxes otherwise payable by or chargeable to such tenant-shareholder (Sec. 458.8, Real Property Tax Law).

Veterans' organizations: Property owned, used and occupied by veterans' organizations is exempt (Sec. 452, Real Property Tax Law). Municipalities may exempt from local taxes any portion of the property rented to community, charitable, educational, or other organizations that may not be tax-exempt entities (Sec. 452(c), Real Property Tax Law).

¶2505 Basis and Rate of Tax

Law: Art. XVI, Sec. 2, N.Y. Const., Sec. 305, Real Property Tax Law (CCH NEW YORK TAX REPORTS, ¶ 20-080, 20-605).

Real property may not be assessed at more than full value and, except in New York City and Nassau County, must be assessed at a uniform percentage of value (Sec. 305, Real Property Tax Law).

In general, tax rates for a particular tax district (county, city, town, village, special or school district) are determined by dividing the amount of money to be raised by the assessed valuation of the real property of the district. It must be noted, however, that the amounts to be raised by taxes on real estate are subject to constitutional limitations.

• *Levy limitation (tax cap)*

Until June 15, 2020, annual property tax levy increases by local governments, school districts, and special districts are limited to 2% or the rate of inflation, whichever is less (Sec. 3-c, General Municipal Law; Sec. 2023-a, Education Law). The tax levy cannot exceed the cap unless 60% of voters (for school districts) or 60% of the total voting power of the governing body (for local governments) approve the increase. The cap does not apply to New York City.

The cap is subject to limited exceptions, such as judgments or court orders arising out of tort actions that exceed 5% of a locality's levy or growth in tax levies due to economic development. For additional information, see *Publication 1000,* New York Department of Taxation and Finance, September 2011.

¶2506 Assessment Procedure and Adjustment

Law: Secs. 301, 302, 305, 510, 511, 551, 551-a, 553, 600, 702—706, 1803-a, Real Property Tax Law (CCH NEW YORK TAX REPORTS, ¶ 20-605—20-650, 21-505—21-560).

Unlike most other states, New York does not have a statewide assessment ratio; assessment is a municipal responsibility, and assessment ratios vary from locality to locality.

The Real Property Tax Law requires all municipalities to have fair assessments every year (Secs. 301, 305, Real Property Tax Law; see also *Publication 1112,* New York Department of Taxation and Finance, January 2016, CCH NEW YORK TAX REPORTS, ¶ 408-640). However, the Legislature has not granted the state Office of Real Property Services (ORPS) any enforcement authority regarding fair assessment practices. Consequently, according to the ORPS, the extremes in property tax equity range from communities that have not reassessed in over fifty years to cities, towns and counties that are reassessing annually.

The taxable status of real property in cities and towns is generally determined and assessed according to its condition and ownership as of March 1 (the "taxable status date") and is valued as of the preceding July 1 (the "valuation date"). Dates may differ in some counties. Certain special assessing units that are cities are authorized to adjust their current base proportions for fiscal year 2014 by no more than 1% (Sec. 1803-a(1)(y), Real Property Tax Law).

The assessor establishes the assessment rolls of all property within the assessing unit's boundaries. The roll is then used for the levy and collection of county, municipal and school district taxes (Secs. 301, 302, Real Property Tax Law).

Property tax assessors are authorized to notify taxpayers of anticipated increases in assessments (preliminary assessments) before the tentative assessment roll is filed. If the tentative assessment is different from the preliminary assessment, the assessor is required to send another notice no sooner than 120 days preceding the date on which the tentative assessment roll is scheduled to be filed and no later than 10 days prior to the date for hearing complaints regarding assessments. The notice also must include information concerning upcoming board of assessment review meetings and the availability of publications at the assessor's office that contain procedures for contesting an assessment (Sec. 510, Real Property Tax Law).

A tentative assessment roll must be completed by May 1, and made available for public inspection until the fourth Tuesday in May. After this date, complaints relating to the tentative roll may be heard. After all complaints have been heard and the assessment roll has been corrected, it is verified. The final assessment roll must be filed by July 1 (Secs. 506, 516, Real Property Tax Law).

Superstorm Sandy damage: Taxing jurisdictions could provide relief to property owners for damage to the improvements on property caused by Superstorm Sandy (*i.e.*, the storms, rains, winds, or floods during the period beginning October 29, 2012, and ending November 3, 2012). The legislation applies to all improved properties; it is not limited to residential property. The legislation effectively provided relief if an assessment roll had a taxable status date prior to October 28, 2012, for taxes levied on that roll that were payable without interest on or after October 28, 2012. (Secs. 1 through 8, Ch. 424 (A.B. 8075), Laws 2013)

The relief program could be adopted by an eligible county and any city, town, village, school district, or special district that is wholly or partly contained within an eligible county. The deadline for taxing jurisdictions to opt into the program was December 6, 2013.

The provisions of the legislation were available only to taxpayers in eligible municipalities that opted to offer the relief. "Eligible county" means a county, other than a county wholly contained within a city, included in FEMA-4085-DR, the notice of the presidential declaration of a major disaster for the state of New York. Specifically, the eligible counties are Greene, Nassau, Orange, Putnam, Rockland, Suffolk, Sullivan, Ulster, and Westchester.

An eligible municipality that opted in had the further option of offering relief to those whose buildings and other property improvements lost less than 50% of their value. If the municipality opted into the legislation without opting to offer relief at levels below 50%, the relief was available only to those whose buildings and other property improvements lost 50% or more of their value.

Adoption of the program by a county did not apply to other local governments within the county; each municipality, school district, or special district that wished to offer the option to its property owners had to separately adopt a resolution.

To receive relief, the property owner in a participating municipality had to submit a written request to the assessor (using Form RP-5849-APP), along with supporting documentation. A municipal official could authorize relief of up to $7,500 without requiring an action of the tax levying body. The deadline for a property owner to apply for assessment relief was January 21, 2014. (*Summary of Legislation, Superstorm Sandy Assessment Relief Act,* New York Department of Taxation and Finance, October 2013, CCH NEW YORK TAX REPORTS, ¶ 407-969) Sandy Assessment Relief.

Stipulated reductions of tentative assessments: Taxpayers and assessors may stipulate to an assessed value (Sec. 525, Real Property Tax Law).

CCH Advisory: Assessment Agreement Invalid

An agreement between a taxpayer and a town supervisor that provided a specified formula to value the taxpayer's property for New York property tax assessment purposes was deemed invalid by an appellate court. The taxpayer argued that the assessments should be established by applying the formula set out in the agreement. However, the court concluded that the agreement prevented the assessor from performing the statutory duties of valuing the property and determining the most appropriate assessment method. The court also noted that there is no statutory authority to permit the predetermination of an assessment by an agreement, even if the assessor participates in forming the agreement. (*PNL Stillwater, LLC v. Board of Assessors of Town of Stillwater*, Appellate Division of the Supreme Court of New York, Third Department, No. 513707, April 26, 2012, CCH NEW YORK TAX REPORTS, ¶ 407-544)

Appeal from erroneous or illegal assessment: Appeals from erroneous or illegal assessments are commenced by filing a complaint with the assessor prior to the time fixed for review by the board of assessment review (usually the fourth Tuesday in May). The board of assessment review must give the property owner ten days' notice of the scheduling of a hearing to consider the complaint and determine the assessment of the property. (Secs. 510-512, Real Property Tax Law).

Small claims assessment review: A simplified review procedure of excessive or unequal assessments is available for assessments on one-, two- or three-family owner-occupied residential property, and on property that is unimproved and is not of sufficient size, as determined by the assessing unit or special assessing unit, to contain one-, two-, or three-family dwellings (Sec. 730, Real Property Tax Law). The equalized value of this property, however, must not exceed $450,000 and the total assessment reduction requested must not exceed 25% of the assessed property value. Homes owned by limited partnerships or trusts can qualify for small claims assessment review.

A petition for small claim review must be filed within 30 days after the completion and filing of the final assessment roll containing the assessment, and may only be filed if the property owner has first filed an administrative complaint (Sec. 730, Real Property Tax Law).

Judicial review: After an assessment roll is finalized (including correction and revision of assessments and determinations by a county board of assessment review), the actions of the tax assessors and review boards are subject to judicial review. The proceeding must be brought at a Special Term of the Supreme Court in the judicial district in which the assessment was made, within 30 days after the final completion and filing of the assessment roll.

Practitioner Comment: Failure To File

Failure to timely file a petition for review is a complete defense to the petition, and the petition will be dismissed. Grounds for reviewing an assessment include excessive, unequal or unlawful valuation or misclassification of the property.

Mark S. Klein, Esq., Hodgson Russ LLP

If the court determines that the assessment is illegal, the assessment will be ordered to be stricken from the assessment roll; if the assessment is held to be erroneous or unequal, the roll will be adjusted. If taxes have already been paid, a refund, with interest, may be ordered. When a final order is entered directing the refund of taxes collected under an excessive, unequal, or unlawful assessment, or as a result of a misclassification of property, interest will be computed from the date the tax was paid. The annual rate of interest on such refunds is the lesser of 9% or the quarterly rate set by the Commissioner of Taxation and Finance (Secs. 702, 704, 706, Real Property Tax Law).

¶2506

• *Special franchises*

Special franchises, except railroads, are assessed by the state Office of Real Property Services (ORPS). If the special franchise owner of the assessing unit objects to the assessment, a written complaint specifying the objection must be filed with the state Board of Real Property Services at least 10 days prior to the date specified for the hearing. (Secs. 600, 610, 202, Real Property Tax Law).

Following the hearing, the Board determines the final assessment of each special franchise, and files a certificate of final assessment with the assessing unit. Written notice of the final assessment must also be provided to the special franchise owner (Secs. 612, 614, 616, 618, Real Property Tax Law).

Special franchise assessments may be reviewed as assessments of real property. The proceeding for review must be filed within 60 days after the notice of final assessment.

• *Railroad franchises*

Railroad franchises are assessed locally rather than by the ORPS (Sec. 600, Real Property Tax Law).

¶2507 Returns and Payment

Law: Secs. 924, 925, 972, 1120, 1166, Real Property Tax Law (CCH NEW YORK TAX REPORTS, ¶21-010, 21-101).

There are no statutory requirements for returns in connection with property taxes, except in the case of special franchises and certain railroad reports. Special franchises require an initial report soon after acquisition, and annual reports thereafter (Secs. 600, 602, Real Property Tax Law).

Assessment is made against the real property, which may be sold for unpaid taxes or special assessments. However, owners of property, or of an interest in property, are personally liable for property taxes if they are residents of the city or town in which the property or interest is assessed and if their names are correctly entered on the tax roll (Sec. 926, Real Property Tax Law).

• *Payment to tax collector*

Taxes are payable to the collecting officer of the assessing unit by January 31, or within 30 days of the date of receipt of the tax roll and warrant, whichever is later. Taxes may be paid at the times and places indicated in the notice of receipt of the tax roll and warrant, as well as during usual business hours during the period of collection. Payment may also be sent by mail or designated delivery service to the appropriate collecting officer. Taxes are timely paid if received in an envelope bearing a U.S. postmark, including any date recorded or marked by a designated delivery service as provided in IRC Sec. 7502, dated no later than the due date of the tax payment. If the postmark is illegible or does not appear, payment will be deemed to have been made on the date of delivery. If the last day for payment falls on a Saturday, Sunday, or public holiday, an extension of time for payment is automatically in effect until the first business day following that date.

Payment under protest: Voluntary payment of assessed taxes without protest may preclude a subsequent recovery, even if the taxes were subsequently declared to be illegal; see *City of Rochester v. Angelo Chiarella, et al.* N.Y. Court of Appeals, March 29, 1983, 461 N.Y.S. 2d 244, 448 N.E. 2d 98, 55 N.Y. 2d 316, CCH NEW YORK TAX REPORTS, ¶250-715.

Senior citizens: Senior citizens who qualify for the school tax relief (STAR) exemption (see ¶2504) may be allowed a grace period of five business days to make payments of property taxes without penalty or interest if the governing body of a municipal corporation, other than a county, adopts this delayed payment provision (Sec. 925-b, Real Property Tax Law).

- *Enforcement provisions*

Tax districts seeking to foreclose tax liens must file proceedings *in rem* (Sec. 1120, Real Property Tax Law).

Effective January 1, 2016, oil, gas, and mineral rights are to be sold along with any property sold pursuant to a property tax foreclosure sale (Sec. 1166(1), Real Property Tax Law).

- *Payment of taxes by credit card*

Local governments may accept payments of municipal "fines, civil penalties, rent, rates, taxes, fees, charges, revenue, financial obligations or other amounts, including penalties, special assessments and interest" by credit card. Local governments that elect to accept payments by credit card must enter into an agreement with one or more financing agencies or credit card issuers for that purpose, and may require any person who makes payments by credit card to pay a "service fee" to the local government as a condition for using the credit card.

If a municipal charge is paid by credit card, the underlying legal obligation will remain intact, and any receipt will be deemed conditional, until the local government receives "final and unconditional payment of the full amount due" from the financing agency or credit card issuer. For example, a tax lien would not be canceled immediately upon the acceptance of a credit card payment, but would remain in effect until the payment became final and unconditional (Sec. 5, Gen. Mun. Law).

- *Installment payments*

County legislative bodies may adopt by local law a provision for the payment of property taxes in a number of equal installments unless the taxes are paid through a real property escrow account (Sec. 972, Real Property Tax Law). The local law sets the number of installments and the due dates of each installment. The due date of the first installment must be no later than the last day of the month in which the taxes would otherwise be payable without interest and the last installment can be no later than the last day of the fiscal year for which it was levied. In the case of a school district, the last installment can be no later than August 31 following the conclusion of the fiscal year. Each installment, other than the first, is subject to interstate rates that may be set lower than the state rate (¶2508). If an installment is not paid on or before the due date, additional interest is added. The installment program applies to all types of property unless the local law establishing the program limits it to one or more of the following types of property:

> — property that has been assessed as a one, two or three family residence;

> — property that is exempt from taxation because it is owned by someone 65 years of age or older;

> — property containing improvements that are exempt from taxation because the resident owner or member of the resident owner's family is disabled; or

> — property that is owned by, or used as, the principal residence of a person who receives supplemental security income.

- *Installment payments of school district taxes*

A school district may, by resolution, provide that New York real property tax in excess of $50 levied by the county board of supervisors may be paid in three installments. The first installment must be at least 50% of the total tax due or such other amount as may be prescribed by resolution and must be paid no later than the last day of the one-month collection period prescribed by law. The second payment must be at least 50% of the remaining tax due, or such other amount as may be prescribed by resolution, plus interest at the rate set by law and paid by a specific

¶2507

date (under the 1998 program, that date is August 15). The third and final payment must comprise the remaining tax due, plus interest, and must be paid by the date specified in the resolution for the expiration of the warrant, which is not later than the following November 15.

The installment program applies to all property within the school district unless it is explicitly limited to specific classes of property (Sec. 1326-a, Real Property Tax Law).

Delinquent taxes: A tax district may enact local law allowing for the installment payment of eligible delinquent taxes. A property owner is not eligible where there is a delinquent tax lien on the same property for which the application is made or on another property owned by the same person (unless the delinquent tax lien is made part of the agreement); the applicant owned property which was foreclosed upon within the last three years; or the owner defaulted on an installment payment agreement within three years of application (Sec. 1184, Real Property Tax Law).

¶2508 Administration, Penalties, Refunds

Law: Secs. 104, 201, 202, 316—320, 496, 500—506, 523—527, 556, 924, 924-a, Real Property Tax Law; Sec. 39-a, Tax Law (CCH NEW YORK TAX REPORTS, ¶21-405, 21-550, 21-855).

Taxes are considered late and must be paid with interest after the later of January 31 or 31 days after receipt of the tax roll and warrant by the collecting officer (Sec. 924, Real Property Tax Law).

The main remedy available to a taxpayer in connection with property taxes is an administrative or judicial proceeding to review the assessment on the grounds that the assessment is excessive, unequal, or unlawful, or that the real property is misclassified. However, voluntary payment may extinguish the right to refund. Generally, refund applications must be filed within three years of the date of annexation of the tax warrant (Secs. 524, 556, 726, Real Property Tax Law).

Interest rate on late payment of taxes and delinquencies: The interest rate on late payment of taxes and delinquencies is set by the Commissioner of Taxation and Finance pursuant to Sec. 697(j), Tax Law. The annual rate may not be less than 12% (Sec. 924-a, Real Property Tax Law).

Disaster relief: Deadlines for the collection of New York local property taxes without penalty or interest may be extended for up to 20 days by the Governor, as a result of a state disaster emergency, upon the request of the chief executive officer of the municipal or district corporation within the affected area (Sec. 925-a, Real Property Tax Law).

Refunds: If the tax was attributable to a clerical error or an unlawful entry and application is made within three years of the annexation of the warrant for the tax, tax levying bodies may refund to a taxpayer any amount of tax paid, or may provide a credit against an outstanding tax (Sec. 556, Real Property Tax Law). Tax levying bodies may also issue a refund or credit with respect to tax attributable to an error in essential fact other than the omission of the value of an improvement present on real property prior to the taxable status date. The application must be made within three years from the annexation of the tax warrant.

Effective October 21, 2014, an assessor that failed to use the separate assessment method for low-income housing under Sec. 581-a, Real Property Tax Law, may make a correction through the correction of errors law (Sec. 550(2)(j), Real Property Tax Law).

Penalties: See ¶3704

CCH Advisory: Penalties for Fraud in the START-UP NY Program

If the commissioner of economic development finally determines that any business participating in the START-UP NY program has acted fraudulently in connection with its participation in that program, the business will be:

— immediately terminated from the program;

— subject to applicable criminal penalties, including but not limited to the felony crime of offering a false instrument for filing in the first degree; and

— required to add back to tax the total value of the tax benefits that the business has received and that the employees of the business have received.

The amount required to be added back must be reported on the business's corporate franchise report if the business is taxed as a corporation or on the corporate franchise tax reports or personal income tax returns of the owners of the business if the business is taxed as a sole proprietorship, partnership or New York S corporation. (Sec. 39-a, Tax Law)

• *Electronic tax administration*

The tax commissioner is authorized to establish standards for Electronic Real Property Tax administration (E-RPT), including electronic communication means to furnish tax notices and other documents (Sec. 104, Real Property Tax Law). The measure permits the electronic filing, issuance, or payment of:

— exemption applications;

— petitions for administrative and judicial reviews of assessments;

— applications for corrections;

— statements of taxes;

— the payment of taxes;

— receipts for tax payments; and

— taxpayer notices.

In addition, real property taxes may be paid via the Internet under the terms and conditions of the General Municipal Law.

Municipalities may provide by local law for electronic property tax administration in accordance with the standards of the tax commissioner. Taxpayers will not be required to accept notices, statements of taxes, receipts for the payment of taxes, or other documents electronically unless they have so elected. (Sec. 104(3), Real Property Tax Law)

¶2509 New York City

The provisions of the Real Property Tax Law apply generally to New York City. However, certain assessment and collection provisions are superseded by the New York City Charter and Administrative Code (¶3309).

PART VIII

MISCELLANEOUS TAXES

CHAPTER 26
UNEMPLOYMENT INSURANCE TAX
(Including Disability Benefits)

¶2601 Unemployment Insurance—Overview

The Unemployment Insurance Law, summarized below, is imposed by Article 18, Labor Law, enacted by Ch. 705, Laws 1944, and as amended. The law is administered by the Industrial Commissioner through the Unemployment Insurance Division, Building #12, State Campus, Albany, New York 12240; One Main Street, Brooklyn, New York 11201.

Complete details are contained in CCH UNEMPLOYMENT INSURANCE REPORTS.

¶2602 Unemployment Insurance—Coverage

Unemployment insurance coverage is discussed at this paragraph.

Employer.—An employer becomes liable for contributions under the law as of the first day of any calendar quarter in which it has paid remuneration of $300 of more. An employer of persons in personal or domestic service in a private home becomes liable for contributions if it has paid them cash remuneration of $500 or more in a calendar quarter, liability commencing as of the first day of such quarter. A successor by operation of law to an employer subject to the Law becomes subject on the day of succession. An employer not covered by the Law may voluntarily elect coverage. The term "employer" also includes the State of New York and any municipal corporation or governmental subdivision.

Nonprofit organizations become subject to the law if they pay remuneration of $1,000 or more in a calendar quarter, or if they employ four or more persons on each of 20 days during the current or preceding calendar year, each day being in a different calendar week.

Any Indian tribe, subdivision, subsidiary or business enterprise wholly owned by such Indian tribe is subject to the Act.

Practitioner Comment: New York Statutory Employees

Liability for the unemployment insurance is generally limited to employer-employee relationships under the common law of "master-servant". In addition, New York's unemployment insurance statutorily imposes tax on employers of: (1) agents or commissioned drivers who deliver meat, vegetables, bakery products, and beverages (except milk); (2) most full-time salespeople; (3) professional musicians, models, and other performers; and (4) many persons performing services for construction contractors. See IA 318.14 and IA 318.29.

Mark S. Klein, Esq., Hodgson Russ LLP

Employment.—Service under any contract of employment for hire, express or implied, written or oral, with exceptions listed below.

Services by certain agent-drivers or commission-drivers and traveling or city salesmen are covered.

Services by an employee in the construction industry are covered unless the presumption of employment can be overcome.

Services by a professional musician or other person engaged in the performing arts for a television or radio station or network, film production, theater, hotel, restaurant, night club or similar establishment unless, by written contract, such person is stipulated to be an employee of another covered employer.

Whenever any helper, assistant or employee or an employer engages any other person to aid in his work, the employer is also the employer of the other person, whether such person is paid by the helper, assistant or employee or by the employer, provided the employment has been with the knowledge, actual, constructive or implied, of the employer.

The services of a person performed at a place of religious worship as a caretaker or for the performance of duties of a religious nature, or both, are employment if the employer makes application to this effect and the application is approved in writing.

Practitioner Comment: Unemployment Insurance Coverage Limited to New York Activities

New York's unemployment insurance coverage is limited to employment that is localized in New York State. This requires that the claimant's services were either performed entirely in New York or if performed in more than one state, that the activities outside of New York were incidental, temporary or transitory. It is irrelevant that New York may impose its income tax on the out-of-state wages under the so-called "convenience rule" (See ¶ 403). As a result, someone working from their Florida home for a New York employer could owe New York income tax on their wages but would not be covered by New York unemployment insurance (TSB-M-06(5)I and *Maxine Allen v. Commission of Labor*, 100 NYS2d 282 (2003)).

Mark S. Klein, Hodgson Russ LLP

Exemptions.—Baby sitters—not applicable to services performed for nonprofit organizations or governmental entities.

Golf caddies—not applicable to services performed for nonprofit organizations or governmental entities.

Licensed real estate broker or sales associate if substantially all of the remuneration is directly related to sales or other output rather than to number of hours worked; and his services are performed pursuant to a written contract providing that

¶2602

the broker or associate is an independent contractor, will be paid by commissions, and will be permitted certain freedoms with respect to the performance of his services.

Railroad employees covered by Railroad Unemployment Insurance Act.

Relatives, *i.e.*, service for employer by his spouse or minor child.

Service for an educational institution by a student in regular attendance, or by a spouse of that student if spouse's employment is under a program of assistance to the student.

Services performed by a minor in casual labor consisting of yard work and household chores in and about a residence or the premises of a nonprofit organization, not involving the use of power-driven machinery. Service by any child under age 14 is exempt. Not applicable to services performed for nonprofit organizations or governmental entities.

Services performed for a nonprofit organization by a person participating in a youth service program designed to foster a commitment to community service and occupational and educational development, but only if the person performs services in the community or attends school and receives a stipend designed to cover expenses and is eligible for an award or scholarship upon leaving the program.

Students attending elementary or secondary schools during the day who perform part-time work during school year or regular vacation periods. This exclusion is not applicable to nonprofit organizations and governmental entities.

Service by student under 22 enrolled at nonprofit or public educational institution in a full-time work study program. This exemption does not apply to program established for an employer or group of employers.

Agricultural employers.—Agricultural labor is covered if performed for an employer who employed 10 or more workers in such labor in 20 weeks in the current or preceding calendar year or paid cash remuneration of $20,000 or more for such labor in any quarter of the current or preceding calendar year. When agricultural labor is supplied by a crew leader, the employing unit for which the services are performed is the employer of the crew members unless the crew leader is registered under the Farm Labor Contractor Registration Act of 1963 or substantially all of the crew members operate or maintain mechanized equipment that is provided by the crew leader. In either of these instances, the crew leader is the employer.

Government and nonprofit employers: Nonprofit services.—Coverage is mandatory for services performed for nonprofit organizations which have paid cash remuneration of $1,000 or more in any calendar quarter, or have employed four or more persons on each of 20 days during the current or preceding calendar year, each day being in a different calendar week.

Services for a nonprofit organization do not include the following:

Religious duties of a minister or member of a religious order, a lay member of a church engaged in religious functions, and a caretaker of a church, unless an election for coverage has been made.

Patients performing services in a sheltered workshop or other rehabilitation facility.

Nonprofit organizations may pay regular contributions or may use the reimbursement method, i.e., employers' payments equal the amount of benefits paid to claimants and charged to their account.

Government and nonprofit employers: Nonprofit services.—Coverage is mandatory for services performed for nonprofit organizations which have paid cash remuneration of $1,000 or more in any calendar quarter, or have employed four or more persons on each of 20 days during the current or preceding calendar year, each day being in a different calendar week.

¶2602

Services for a nonprofit organization do not include the following:

Religious duties of a minister or member of a religious order, a lay member of a church engaged in religious functions, and a caretaker of a church, unless an election for coverage has been made.

Patients performing services in a sheltered workshop or other rehabilitation facility.

Nonprofit organizations may pay regular contributions or may use the reimbursement method, i.e., employers' payments equal the amount of benefits paid to claimants and charged to their account.

Wages.—An employer's taxes are computed on the basis of the amount of taxable wages it has paid. Wages include every form of compensation for employment paid by the employer to an employee, whether paid directly or indirectly, including salaries, commissions, bonuses, and the reasonable money value of board, rent, housing, lodging, or similar advantages. Gratuities received in the course of employment from a person other than the employer are also wages.

The most important limitation on the term "wages" is the taxable wage base: remuneration of more than $8,500 paid in a calendar year to an individual by an employer with respect to employment is not "wages". Wages paid for services in another state and wages paid by the employer's predecessor are included in the limitation. Among the various exclusions from wages are the following:

— standby pay to employees 65 years or older;

— payments under plans established on account of retirement, sickness, or accident disability;

— payments for sickness or accident disability made over six months after the employee's separation from work;

— certain trust or annuity plan payments; and

— payment of an employee's FICA tax without deduction from wages.

Payment for unused vacation at termination of employment is taxable only if legal right to the payment has accrued to the employee's benefit. If there is no legal right, it is termed a dismissal payment that is not taxable unless the employer is subject to the Federal Act.

¶2603 Unemployment Insurance—Tax Rates

Most employing units pay taxes or "contributions," as they are called, under the experience-rating provisions of the Law. Experience rating is a means of varying individual employer tax rates on the basis of individual history as to employment, wages, and unemployment. Under the tax and experience-rating provisions of the New York law, an employer may pay a tax or "contribution" rate of as much as 8.9% or as low as zero.

Newly liable employers (those who, together with the previous owners of the business, if any, have not been liable for taxes more than one full calendar year before January 1) are taxed at a set rate on wages paid during the calendar year. The new employer normal tax rate is calculated each year based on the size of fund index and is equal to the rate for an employer with a positive account percentage of less than 1%, except that the rate will not exceed 3.4%. This rate is in addition to the subsidiary tax and the Re-employment Service Fund tax.

Once an employer acquires enough experience to be "qualified," its rate can be either considerably higher or considerably lower. The determining factors are the employer's own "account percentage" and the state-wide "size-of-fund index". The employer's account percentage is determined as of the computation date (December 31 preceding the year for which rates are being determined) by subtracting benefits charges from the contributions credited to its account and dividing by its average taxable payroll for the five-year period beginning ending on the previous September 30. In the case of employers with fewer than 21 consecutive quarters of liability and a positive account percentage ending on the computation date, the account percentage is multiplied by a "benefit equalization factor" ranging from 1.00 to 3.00. The "size of fund index" is the lesser of the following two percentages: fund balance on the computation date divided by total taxable payrolls for all employers for the payroll year ending on the previous September 30, or such fund balance divided by the average of the totals of all taxable payrolls for the five consecutive one-year periods ending on the previous September 30.

A "qualified employer" is one whose account reflects its experience with respect to unemployment throughout not less than the four consecutive calendar quarters ending on December 31 preceding the year for which rates are being determined, who paid some remuneration in the one-year period ending on the previous September 30, and who filed all contribution reports that may have been prescribed during the three-year period ending on this September 30 by the following December 31.

The law provides tables of contribution rates from which, on the basis of the "size-of-fund index," a schedule of rates is determined to apply for a given calendar year. From this schedule the individual employer's rate is determined on the basis of its account percentage. To the rates in the schedule (and to other employers' rates as well) is added a subsidiary tax whenever the state fund balance in the general account falls below zero on the computation date. Subsidiary rates may range from zero to .925%, depending on the amount the fund is below certain limits.

An employer may make a voluntary contribution in order to improve its account balance and achieve a better rate. If such contributions are to achieve an improved rate for a given year they must be paid before April 1 of that year. In addition to the features mentioned in this brief survey of the tax provisions of the New York law, there are a number of other, special provisions.

Nonprofit organizations may directly reimburse the fund for benefits paid to former employees, rather than be subject to the regular experience-rating provisions of the law.

• *SUTA dumping*

If an employer transfers its organization, trade or business, or a portion thereof, to another employer and, at the time of the transfer, there is at least 10 percent common ownership, management or control of the two employers, then the unemployment experience attributable to the transferred organization, trade or business will be transferred to the employer to whom the organization, trade or business is so transferred. Note that the term "organization, trade or business" includes the employer's workforce.

If following a transfer of experience, the commissioner determines that a substantial purpose of the transfer was to obtain reduced liability for contributions, then the experience rating accounts of the employers involved will be combined into a single account and a single rate will be assigned to that account.

Whenever an individual is not an employer liable for contributions at the time he or she acquires the organization, trade or business of an employer, the unemployment experience of the acquired business will not be transferred to that individual if the commissioner finds that the individual acquired the business solely or primarily for the purpose of obtaining a lower rate of contributions. Instead, the individual will be assigned a rate as discussed below. In determining whether the organization,

¶2603

trade or business was acquired solely or primarily for the purpose of obtaining a lower rate of contributions, the commissioner will evaluate factors that include, but are not limited to the following: The cost of acquiring the organization, trade or business; whether the individual continued the business enterprise of the acquired business; how long such business enterprise was continued; or whether a substantial number of new employees were hired for performance of duties unrelated to the business activity conducted prior to acquisition.

¶2604 Unemployment Insurance—Returns and Reports

Each employer must file a Quarterly Combined Withholding Wage Reporting and Unemployment Insurance Return (Form NYS-45 and NYS-45-ATT) with the appropriate taxes due no later than the last day of the month following the last day of each calendar quarter. Filing via magnetic media is required for employers with 250 or more employees, magnetic media filing is encouraged for all other employers.

¶2605 Unemployment Insurance—Benefits and Eligibility

An individual's weekly benefit amount is determined as 1/26 of high-quarter wages, except that the benefit amount for an individual whose high-quarter wages are $3,575 or less is to be computed as 1/25 of high-quarter wages. The maximum weekly benefit amount is determined as one-half the state average weekly wage. Each unemployed worker's benefit rate is determined by the worker's average weekly wage. An "effective day" is a full day of total unemployment falling within a week in which the claimant received not more than the maximum weekly benefit amount in compensation and had four or more days of total unemployment. Only those days of total unemployment in excess of three days within such week, however, are deemed effective days, with the result that a claimant can accumulate no more than four effective days in one week. The maximum duration of benefits during an individual's benefit year is 104 effective days (effectively 26 weeks), but there is also a federal-state extended benefits program during periods of high unemployment that may increase benefit duration for a New York claimant by half (13 weeks).

To be eligible for benefits, an unemployed individual must file a "valid original claim." The individual will be deemed to have filed a "valid original claim" if

(a) the individual is able to work and available for work,

(b) the individual has been unemployed for 1 waiting-period week (4 effective days),

(c) the individual is not subject to any disqualification or suspension, and

(d) the individual's previously established benefit year, if any, has expired.

In addition to meeting conditions (a) through (d) above, an individual must have been paid remuneration during at least two calendar quarters of the base period, with at least one and one-half times the high-quarter earnings and at least $1,600 paid during the high quarter. In addition to filing a valid original claim, the claimant must register as totally unemployed and report for work or otherwise give notice of continuance of unemployment. An otherwise eligible claimant will not become ineligible for benefits because of regular attendance at an approved vocational training course.

Disqualification from benefits: A benefit claimant may meet the above eligibility requirements and still be disqualified from benefits for leaving work voluntarily without good cause, leaving work to marry, losing employment due to misconduct or a labor dispute, losing employment as the result of an act constituting a felony in connection with employment or making false statements or representations for the purpose of obtaining benefits. A person who refuses suitable work also loses the right to benefits. No benefits are payable to an individual for any week with respect to which the individual is entitled to unemployment benefits under another law, and the law contains special provisions concerning paid vacations or holidays and the receipt of pension or retirement payments.

¶2604

Special restrictions that generally prohibit the payment of benefits during school summer recesses or other similar periods apply in the case of claimants who have been employed in an instructional, research, or principal administrative capacity in an institution of education.

¶2606 Unemployment Insurance—Administration

The New York Unemployment Insurance Law is administered by the Commissioner of Labor.

Practitioner Comment: Collateral Impact of Unemployment Insurance Audit

Pursuant to a number of information-sharing agreements, the results of a New York State unemployment insurance audit are often shared with both the Internal Revenue Service and New York's income tax auditors. And while the unemployment insurance tax consequences of mischaracterizing employees as independent contractors are often financially insignificant, the federal and state income tax consequences, coupled with FICA taxes, can be quite considerable.

Mark S. Klein, Esq., Hodgson Russ LLP

¶2607 Disability Benefits—Coverage

An employer is subject to the law if it has in employment one or more employees on at least 30 days in any calendar year. Separate rules apply to an employer of personal or domestic employees. An employer may become subject by voluntarily electing coverage or by acquiring the trade or business of a covered employer. Public entities, municipal corporations, fire districts, and other political subdivisions may elect coverage.

An "employee" under the Act is any person engaged in employment in the service of an employer, except that the spouse or minor child of the employer, a minister, priest, rabbi or member of a religious order, sextons, Christian Science readers, and persons engaged in a professional or teaching capacity or as volunteers for a religious, charitable, or educational institution, recipients of charitable aid or of rehabilitative services from a religious or charitable institution, and certain domestic or personal workers and certain corporate officers are excluded from the term "employee".

"Employment" means employment in any trade, business or occupation carried on by an employer, exclusive of governmental agencies, railroad, seamen, farm laborers, casual workers, golf caddies, and part-time workers who are day students in elementary or secondary schools.

¶2608 Disability Benefits—Tax Rates

Both employers and employees are liable for contributions under the law. Employee contributions are deducted by the employer from the employee's wages, unless a plan or agreement between the employer and his employees provides otherwise. If there is no such plan and no deduction is made, the employer is allowed one month after the payment of wages to collect contributions through payroll deduction.

Employers are authorized to make deductions from employees' wages at the rate of of 1% of such wages, but not more than 60 cents a week for each employee. The cost of providing disability benefits in excess of the contributions collected from employees is borne by the employer. The amounts so contributed by the employer and his employees are to be used by the employer to provide for the payment of sickness disability benefits to his employees.

"Carriers," a term which includes the State Fund, insurance companies insuring the payment of disability benefits, and employers acting as self-insurers, are liable for the three assessments under the statute: annual and emergency assessments to replenish the Special Fund (a fund providing benefits for the disabled unemployed), and an annual assessment for expenses of administering the disability statute.

¶2609 Disability Benefits—Returns and Reports

Employers must keep records of information prescribed by the Board.

¶2610 Disability Benefits—Benefits and Eligibility

An employer may provide for payment of disability benefits in one or more of three ways:

(1) through the payment of premiums to the State Fund;

(2) through the payment of premiums to an approved insurance company;

(3) through the employer acting as a self-insurer.

If an employer has a "plan," it must provide benefits "at least as favorable" as those provided under the law.

"Disability" during employment means the inability of an employee, as a result of injury or sickness not arising out of and in the course of an employment, to perform the regular duties of the employment or the duties of any other employment which the employer may offer the individual at the regular wages and which the injury or sickness does not prevent the employee from performing. "Disability" during unemployment means the inability of an employee, as a result of injury or sickness not arising out of and in the course of an employment, to perform the duties of any employment for which the individual is reasonably qualified by training and experience.

Except in the case of a claimant who is disabled while unemployed and who would have been entitled to unemployment insurance were it not for the disability, or in the case where the employer's plan provides otherwise, there is a seven-day waiting period before benefits are payable. "Day of disability" means any day on which the employee was prevented from performing work because of disability and for which he or she has not received regular remuneration. The weekly benefits payable to a disabled worker is one-half of his or her "average weekly wage" for the last eight weeks preceding disability, but not more than $170 nor less than $20. Where the average weekly wage is less than $20, the weekly benefit amount is the average weekly wage. The duration of benefits is limited to 26 weeks during a period of 52 consecutive weeks, or during any one period of disability.

No benefits are payable:

(1) for any period of disability during which the employee is not under a physician's, podiatrist's, practising psychologist's, chiropractor's, nurse midwife's, or dentist's care,

(2) for any disability occasioned by the employee's willful intention to bring about injury to, or the sickness of, himself or another,

(3) for any day of disability during which the employee performed work for remuneration or profit,

(4) for any day of disability for which the employee is entitled to receive from the employer, or a fund to which the employer contributes, remuneration equal to or greater than the weekly benefit,

(5) for any period for which the employee is subject to suspension or disqualification of the accumulation of unemployment insurance benefit rights, or

(6) for any period for which the employee receives unemployment insurance benefits or workers' compensation for occupational disability with respect to the same disability.

¶2611 Disability Benefits—Administration

The New York Disability Benefits Law is administered by the Worker's Compensation Board, 100 Broadway-Menands, Albany, New York 12241 and 215 W. 125th St., New York, New York 10027.

MISCELLANEOUS TAXES

CHAPTER 27
OTHER STATE TAXES

¶2701 Scope of Chapter

This chapter outlines briefly the New York State taxes that have not already been covered in the *Guidebook*. The purpose is merely to indicate in general terms who is subject to the tax, who is exempt, the basis and rate of tax, report and payment requirements, and by whom the tax is administered.

The chapter does not discuss various occupational license, inspection, and miscellaneous fees that are imposed by the state under the New York Consolidated Law chapters that govern each industry. For additional information, see the Business Wizard application at **https://bw.licensecenter.ny.gov/BW/guestHomeAction.els**.

¶2702 Insurance Taxes

Law: Secs. 11, 21, 33.1, 34.1,1500-1520, Tax Law; Sec. 9108, Insurance Law (CCH NEW YORK TAX REPORTS, ¶ 88-001 *et seq.*).

Forms: CT-33, Insurance Corporation Franchise Tax Return; CT-33-C, Captive Insurance Company Franchise Tax Return; CT-33-D, Tax on Premiums Paid or Payable To an Unauthorized Insurer.

Domestic, foreign and alien insurance companies are subject to franchise taxes imposed under Article 33 of the Tax Law. The Article 33 taxes consist of (1) a franchise and (2) an additional franchise tax based on gross premiums less certain deductions. (Secs. 1501(a); 1502; 1510, Tax Law) For taxable years beginning on and after January 1, 2009, for-profit HMOs are subject to the insurance franchise tax instead of the corporation franchise tax (Art. 9-A, Tax Law) (TSB-M-09(7)C, May 22, 2009, CCH NEW YORK TAX REPORTS, ¶406-402). Nonprofit HMOs, which are required to obtain a certificate of authority under Article 44 of the Public Health Law, are not subject to Article 33 taxes.

Various insurance law provisions have been amended to comply with the federal Nonadmitted and Reinsurance Reform Act of 2010 under the Dodd-Frank Wall Street Reform and Consumer Protection Act (P.L. 111-203).

Guidance on taxation of unauthorized insurers is provided in *TSB-M-12(4)C*, Taxpayer Guidance Division, New York Department of Taxation and Finance, February 17, 2012, CCH NEW YORK TAX REPORTS, ¶407-483.

Additional temporary franchise tax: An additional temporary franchise tax is authorized on insurance companies (other than those whose premiums are received solely as consideration for accident and health insurance policies). Imposition of the tax is contingent upon the transfer of certain funds by the Medical Malpractice Insurance Association into the New York General Fund. These transfers are to be made pursuant to a schedule submitted to the Association by the Director of the Division of the Budget. If the funds are transferred in accordance with the terms of the schedule, the temporary tax is without force and effect. (Sec. 9111-b, Insurance Law)

• *Exemptions*

The following are exempt from the franchise taxes imposed by Article 33 of the Tax Law: federal, state and local governments and their instrumentalities; any charitable, religious, missionary, educational or philanthropic nonstock corporation exempted by the Insurance Law in effect immediately prior to January 1, 1940; any retirement system or pension fund that does exclusively an annuity business; any nonprofit medical expense indemnity or hospital service corporation; any incorporated or unincorporated fraternal benefit society or, in the event of the conversion of such society into a mutual life insurance company or the reinsurance of the business of such society by the Superintendent of Insurance pursuant to an order of liquidation, premiums payable under insurance benefit certificates issued by such society prior to the conversion or reinsurance; any domestic corporation for the insurance of domestic animals on the cooperative or assessment plan; town or county cooperative insurance corporations; nonprofit voluntary employees' beneficiary associations that are exempt for federal purposes; and nonprofit property/casualty insurance companies organized under Sec. 6703, Insurance Code. (1512(a), Tax Law)

Certain exemptions apply only to the additional franchise tax on premiums. Premiums from the following types of insurance are excluded or deducted in determining the amount of premiums subject to the additional franchise tax: annuity contracts, joint underwriting of group health insurance for persons 65 years of age or older, ocean marine insurance and reinsurance contracts from corporations or other insurers authorized to transact business in New York. (Sec. 1510(c), Tax Law)

Also exempt from the additional franchise tax on premiums are nonprofit corporations for the benefit of charitable institutions, etc. Writing insurance on property outside the state or on lives of nonresidents and life insurance companies, exempt from federal income tax, organized to establish nonprofit voluntary employees beneficiary associations, writing insurance on lives of nonresident risks. (Sec. 1512(b)(1), (2), Tax Law)

Except in the case of foreign and alien title insurance corporations, premiums (other than those for accident and health insurance) written, procured or received in New York for insurance on property or risks located or resident outside the United States are exempt from the additional franchise tax on premiums. (Sec. 1512(b)(3), Tax Law)

¶2702

Special provisions apply to the New York Insurance Exchange and its members (¶2703).

• *Basis and rate*

Franchise tax: The franchise tax is the greatest of the following (Sec. 1502, Tax Law):

(1) 7.1% of the taxpayer's allocated entire net income, or portion thereof allocated within New York State, for the taxable year; or

(2) 1.6 mills for each dollar of the taxpayer's total business and investment capital allocated within New York State for the taxable year; or

(3) 9% on 30% of the taxpayer's entire net income plus salaries and other compensation paid to the taxpayer's elected or appointed officers and to every stockholder owning in excess of 5% of its issued capital stock minus $15,000 and any net loss for the reported year, or the portion of the sum allocated within New York State; or

(4) $250;

plus 0.8 of a mill for each dollar of the taxpayer's subsidiary capital allocated within New York for the taxable year.

An additional franchise tax is imposed on life insurance companies at the rate of 0.7% of life premiums.

Premiums tax: A premiums tax is imposed on every domestic, foreign, and alien insurance corporation (including for-profit HMOs, but not life insurance companies) that (1) is authorized to transact business in New York under a certificate of authority from the Superintendent of Insurance, or (2) is a risk retention group. The tax is imposed on all gross direct premiums, less return premiums thereon, written on risks located or resident in New York. The tax is computed in the same manner set forth in Sec. 1510(a), Tax Law, (as it applied to taxable years beginning before January 1, 2003), except that the rate is 1.75% for accident and health insurance contracts and 2% for other non-life insurance premiums. The tax may not be less than $250. Life insurance companies are subject to a 1.5% premiums tax or the tax applicable under existing provisions, whichever is greater.

Practitioner Comment: Deductible Reimbursement Payments Are Not Premiums

New York's Department of Taxation and Finance has acquiesced to the Administrative Law Judge's determination in American Zürich Insurance Company (ALJ, 10/14/10) and agreed that, in most circumstances, "amounts received or accrued by an insurance company from its insured policyholder as deductible reimbursements were not premiums for purposes of the tax on premiums . . . ." This change of policy is effective for all open years. Timely refund claims will be honored. (*TSB–M–12(6)C,* July 9, 2012; CCH NEW YORK TAX REPORTS, ¶407-594)

Mark S. Klein, Esq., Hodgson Russ LLP

Depreciation: The New York insurance franchise tax is decoupled from federal accelerated depreciation provisions, except with respect to qualified Resurgence Zone property and qualified New York Liberty Zone property.

Production activities: An addition modification is required for the IRC Sec. 199 qualified production activities deduction, applicable to taxable years beginning after 2007.

Independently procured insurance: Contracts of commercial insurance directly placed with an insurer not authorized to do business within New York are subject to a premiums tax at the rate of 3.6%. Applicable to taxable insurance contracts having an effective date on or after July 21, 2011, insurance franchise tax provisions are amended to limit the imposition of the tax on independently procured insurance to persons whose home state is New York and to provide that if the taxable insurance contract covers risks located both within and outside the state and the taxpayer's home state is New York, then 100% of the premiums are allocable to New York. (Sec. 1551, Tax Law)

Annuity insurers: If more than 95% of an insurance corporation's premiums are received as consideration for annuity contracts, gross direct premiums subject to tax include all amounts received as consideration for annuity contracts and premiums for policies and insurance that exceed 95% of all premiums received (Sec. 1505(c), Tax Law).

Captive insurance companies: New York allows the formation of captive insurance companies and imposes a gross premiums tax (in lieu of the franchise tax, additional franchise tax and surcharge) on such companies. (Sec. 1502-b, Tax Law) Overcapital-ized captive insurance companies are excluded from the definition of an insurance corporation subject to tax under Article 33, insurance franchise tax, and are required to be included in a combined return with the closest controlling stockholder under either Article 9-A corporate franchise tax, or Article 32, bank franchise tax (TSB-M-09(9)C, August 31, 2009, CCH NEW YORK TAX REPORTS, ¶406-513).

Captive insurance companies must pay a tax on all gross direct premiums and assumed reinsurance premiums, less return premiums, written on risks located or resident in New York. The tax imposed on captive insurance companies is imposed on all gross direct premiums at a rate of 0.4% on all or any part of the first $20 million of premiums, 0.3% on all or part of the second $20 million of premiums, 0.2% on all or part of the third $20 million of premiums and 0.075% on each dollar of premiums thereafter. (Sec. 1502-b(a), Tax Law)

Further, the tax imposed on assumed reinsurance premiums is 0.0225% on all or any part of the first $20 million of premiums, 0.0150% on all or any part of the second $20 million of premiums, 0.0050% on all or any part of the third $20 million of premiums and 0.0025% on each dollar of premiums thereafter. (Sec. 1502-b(a), Tax Law)

The tax imposed is the greater of the sum of the tax imposed on gross direct premiums and assumed reinsurance premiums or $5,000.

Retaliatory taxes: New York has retaliatory provisions that subject foreign insur-ance companies to not less than the rates of tax that their home states impose on New York insurance companies. In computing retaliatory taxes paid to New York, foreign insurance companies may include metropolitan commuter transportation district surcharges (*United Services Automobile Association,* New York Court of Appeals, No. 94, April 30, 1996, CCH NEW YORK TAX REPORTS, ¶402-389).

Metropolitan Commuter Transportation District Surcharge: The Metropolitan Com-muter Transportation District surcharge on insurance corporations is similar to that imposed under the corporation franchise (income) provisions (¶905). The temporary surcharge (see above) is not included in the calculation. (Sec. 1505-a, Tax Law)

The amount of the surcharge is calculated as if the franchise tax rate were 9% and the maximum tax were 2.6%. (Sec. 1505-a(3), Tax Law)

- *Credits*

Order of credits: Tax credits under the insurance franchise (income) tax must be applied in the following order:

(1) Empire Zone (EZ) capital credit; (2) EZ and ZEA wage tax credits; (3) non-carryover credits that are not refundable; (4) carryover credits with limited

¶2702

carryover periods; (5) carryover credits with unlimited carryover periods; and (6) refundable credits. (Sec. 1511(t), Tax Law; TSB-M-02(5)C, CCH NEW YORK TAX REPORTS, ¶ 300-373).

Credits against tax: (Sec. 1511, Tax Law).

Special additional mortgage recording taxes paid: Similar to corporation franchise (income) tax provisions (¶ 927).

Retaliatory taxes: New York insurance companies may credit a percentage of retaliatory taxes paid to other states. The benefit of this credit is limited for insurers operating within the Metropolitan Commuter Transportation District (MCTD). Other states impose retaliatory taxes against these insurers that take into account all Article 33 taxes, including the MCTD surcharge.

Life insurance company assessments: A credit is available for a portion of the assessments paid to the Life Insurance Company Guaranty Corporation.

Excelsior jobs program: the Excelsior Jobs Program provides corporate franchise, bank franchise, insurance franchise, and personal income tax credits, as follows (Sec. 1511(y), Tax Law):

— a jobs tax credit of up to $5,000 per job;

— an investment tax credit, equal to 2% of qualified investments;

— a 10% research and development credit, based on the federal credit; and

— a real property tax credit.

The Excelsior program is discussed in greater detail under the franchise (income) tax (see ¶ 940).

Employing disabled persons: Similar to corporation franchise (income) tax provisions (¶ 928).

Investing in certified capital companies (CAPCOs): Insurance companies in New York are allowed a credit against insurance franchise taxes for investing in "certified capital companies".

CAPCO Program One: Under certified capital company program one, the aggregate amount of certified capital for which tax credits may be allowed could not exceed $50 million for calendar year 1999 and an additional $50 million for the calendar year 2000 or thereafter.

CAPCO Program Two: The aggregate amount of certified capital for which tax credits may be allowed could not exceed $30 million for the calendar year 2001.

CAPCO Program Three: The aggregate amount of certified capital for which tax credits may be allowed could not exceed $150 million for the calendar year 2002.

CAPCO Program Four: The aggregate amount of certified capital for which tax credits may be allowed could not exceed $60 million for calendar year 2006. Credits were allocated to and vested in certified investors at the time of investment. Credits allowed under CAPCO Program Four are allowed for tax years beginning in 2006.

CAPCO Program Five: The aggregate amount of certified capital for which tax credits may be allowed may not exceed $60 million for calendar year 2007 (the certified capital could be invested beginning in calendar year 2005). (Sec. 11(h), Tax Law; Sec. 1511(k), Tax Law) Credits were allocated to and vested in certified investors at the time of investment. Credits allowed under CAPCO Program Five are allowed for tax years beginning in 2007. (Sec. 11(h), Tax Law)

The maximum amount of certified capital invested in any one certified capital company is $10 million in any one year, unless the aggregate amount has not been reached 60 days prior to the end of the year. In that case, an insurance company can invest more than $10 million in one certified capital company. The amount of the credit against insurance franchise taxes is 100% of the investment in a certified capital company, with 10% of the credit allowed in the first year and each of the following nine taxable years. However, the credits for investing in certified capital companies may not reduce the insurance company's tax liability to less than the minimum tax due under Sec. 1502(a), Tax Law, but excess credit may be carried forward.

A taxpayer may transfer or sell CAPCO credits, in whole or in part, to affiliates subject to the insurance franchise (income) tax (Sec. 1511(k)(9), Tax Law; *TSB-M-06(2)C*, February 24, 2006, CCH NEW YORK TAX REPORTS, ¶ 300-503).

For tax years 2010, 2011, and 2012, taxpayers with more than $2 million in aggregated tax credits for certain investments in certified capital companies were required to defer the amounts above $2 million until 2013. The total amount of credits deferred were or will be paid back to taxpayers over tax years 2013, 2014, and 2015. (Sec 33.1 Tax Law; Sec 34.1 Tax Law)

Other premium taxes: Insurers are allowed a credit for the amount of taxes paid or accrued on premiums for any insurance against loss or damage by fire under the insurance law or various city charters.

Automated external defibrillator credit: A credit against insurance franchise (income) taxes is available for the purchase of automated external defibrillators. The credit is equal to the cost of each defibrillator or $500, whichever is less. However, the credit may not reduce the tax below the minimum amount due.

Long-term care insurance: A credit is allowed for 20% of the long-term care insurance premiums paid during the taxable year. The credit applies not only to premium payments for the purchase of a policy, but also to premium payments for continuing coverage under a qualifying long-term care insurance policy. See the discussion at ¶ 939.

Historic property rehabilitation: A credit is available for the rehabilitation of certain historic properties in the taxable year the property is placed in service. (Sec. 1511 (y), Tax Law) The credit is equal to 100% (30% after 2014) of the federal credit allowed for the same taxable year. For additional information about this credit, see ¶ 948.

Low-income housing: A credit is allowed for the construction or rehabilitation of qualified low-income housing. See the discussion at ¶ 941.

Green buildings: A credit is available to enhance the supply of environmentally sound buildings in New York. The credit includes six components, which are based on the capitalized costs (excluding land costs) of constructing green buildings, rehabilitating buildings to become green buildings, and purchasing and installing fuel cells, photovoltaic modules, and environmentally sensitive non-ozone depleting refrigerants. See the discussion at ¶ 942.

Brownfield credits: Three refundable brownfield credits are available. The credits are designated the brownfield redevelopment tax credit, credit for remediated brownfields, and environmental remediation insurance credit. The credits are available to taxpayers that own or develop a qualified site for which a certificate of completion has been issued to the taxpayer by the Commissioner of Environmental Conservation. Any excess credit will be refunded. For details of the credits, see ¶ 943.

Investment tax credit: A credit is allowed for a portion of the cost of tangible personal property placed in service on or after January 1, 2001, and before October 1, 2015, including buildings and structural components of buildings that are depreciable, have a useful life of four years or more, are acquired by purchase, have a situs in New York, and are principally used in the ordinary course of the taxpayer's trade or business as a securities or commodities broker providing investment advisory services for a regulated investment company or providing lending, loan arrangements, or loan origination services. The percentage to be used to compute the credit is 5% for the first $350 million of the investment credit base and 4% when the investment credit base exceeds $350 million. The credit generally may not reduce the tax below the minimum tax for any taxable year, but the excess may be carried over for up to 15 years; however, in the case of a new business, the excess may be refunded. See also the discussion of the investment tax credit against corporation franchise (income) tax at ¶924.

Insurance companies are entitled to relief from ITC recapture provisions with respect to property that was destroyed or ceased to be in qualified use as a direct result of the September 11, 2001 terrorist attacks. For details, see ¶924.

Application of the investment tax credit to financial services organizations is discussed at ¶924.

Estimated tax: Similar to corporation franchise (income) tax provisions (¶1405). The Metropolitan Commuter Transportation surcharge is also subject to estimated franchise tax reporting and payment requirements (Secs. 1513; 1514, Tax Law).

Retaliatory tax: Foreign insurance companies subject to the retaliatory tax are required to make estimated tax payments. The payment, due by December 15, must be equal to the lesser of 90% of the amount finally determined to be due for second preceding calendar year, or 80% of the amount finally determined to be due for the calendar year. (Sec. 1112(a)(2)(ii), Tax Law)

• *Returns and payment*

Returns are required to be filed with the Commissioner of Taxation and Finance on or before March 15 for calendar-year taxpayers (on or before the 15th day of the third month following the close of the taxable year for other taxpayers). Payment accompanies the return. Estimated tax payment requirements are generally the same as for the corporation franchise tax (see ¶1405).

A copy of the return is filed with the Superintendent of Insurance. (Sec. 1515, Tax Law)

Additional franchise tax: The additional franchise tax is paid in two installments. The first installment is due no later than 30 days after the Superintendent of Insurance determines the tax is to be paid, and must equal at least 90% of the tax ultimately determined to be due. The balance must be paid on the following March 25, accompanied by a return. (Sec. 9111-b(b), Tax Law)

Independently procured insurance contracts: Returns and payments of tax involving independently procured insurance contracts are due within 60 days of the end of the calendar quarter during which a taxable insurance contract took effect or was renewed. (Sec. 1554, Tax Law)

Combined reports: Insurance corporations must file on a combined basis with related corporations if there are substantial intercorporate transactions among the related corporations (Sec. 1515, Tax Law; TSB-M 08(2)C).

Administration: The Article 33 franchise taxes on insurance corporations are primarily administered by the Department of Taxation and Finance, W.A. Harriman State Campus, Albany, NY 12227.

• *Fire insurance fee*

Every insurance company authorized to do business in New York is required to collect a fire insurance fee from each holder of a fire insurance policy issued in New York on property or risks located in New York (excluding any policy insuring household furnishings and/or one or two family residential structures, schools, churches, and hospitals). (Sec. 9108, Insurance Law)

¶2702

The fee is imposed at the rate of $1^{1}/4$% on gross direct premiums; however, no fee is imposed on a policy covering inland marine, ocean marine, automobile, or aircraft physical damage. (Sec. 9108(b)(1), Insurance Law)

Fees are paid to the Superintendent of Insurance quarterly on April 15, July 15, October 15, and January 15 for the preceding calendar quarter. An annual statement is filed with the Superintendent of Insurance on or before February 15 covering the preceding calendar year. (Sec. 9108(b)(2), Insurance Law)

¶2703 Insurance Taxes—New York Insurance Exchange

Law: Sec. 1512, Tax Law; Secs. 6201, 6302, Insurance Law (CCH NEW YORK TAX REPORTS, ¶85-130, 85-180).

The New York Insurance Exchange provides a facility for the underwriting of reinsurance of all kinds of insurance, direct insurance of all kinds of risks located entirely outside the United States, and risks rejected by a committee of special risk insurers. (Sec. 6201, Insurance Law)

For purposes of the additional franchise tax based on premiums (¶2702), direct premiums written, procured, or received by a member or members of the New York Insurance Exchange are deemed to be written, procured, or received by the Exchange and taxable to the Exchange.

The franchise tax, the premiums tax, and the additional franchise tax do not apply to any corporation, association, joint stock company or association, person, society, aggregation or partnership doing an insurance business as a member of the New York Insurance Exchange (Sec. 1512(c), Tax Law). Corporations, associations, persons, societies, aggregations or partnerships must compute an allocated entire net income and transmit a return to the Commissioner of Taxation and Finance.

The New York Insurance Exchange itself is exempt from taxes, except that direct premiums written by exchange members on risks within New York are reportable by the Exchange, which must pay the tax. (Sec. 6302, Insurance Law)

¶2704 Motor Vehicle Registration

Law: Secs. 123, 125, 128, 143, 205, 250—253, 316, 370, 401, 415, 501—503, Vehicle and Traffic Law; Sec. 6110, Insurance Law (CCH NEW YORK TAX REPORTS, ¶37-101 *et seq.*).

Persons subject to tax: Registration taxes or fees are imposed upon the operation and ownership of commercial and non-commercial motor vehicles, including automobiles, omnibuses, trucks, tractors, trailers, semi-trailers and motorcycles.

Exemptions: Among the vehicles exempted from registration fees are ambulances, governmental vehicles, consular vehicles and disabled veterans' vehicles.

Basis and rate: The registration fees are based upon the weight of the vehicle to be registered, except in the case of passenger omnibuses where the fees are based upon seating capacity. Registrations and renewals expire on a date determined by the Commissioner. Provision is made for adjustment of fees on a monthly computation basis for registrations for more or less than a calendar year. There is a wide range of fees according to the classification of the motor vehicle to be registered.

Motor vehicle law enforcement fee: An annual motor vehicle enforcement fee of $1 is imposed on New York policy holders of insured motor vehicles. (Sec. 9110, Insurance Law) The fee is collected by insurance companies in addition to the premium charge.

MCTD fee: A supplemental fee of $25 per year is imposed on the registration and renewal of all registrants of motor vehicles who reside within the Metropolitan Commuter Transportation District.

Returns and payments: Other than accident reports, no returns are required to be filed. Fees are payable at the time the annual registration application is submitted.

Administration: The motor vehicle registration provisions are administered by the Department of Motor Vehicles.

¶2705 Highway Use Taxes

Law: Secs. 501—528, Tax Law (CCH NEW YORK TAX REPORTS, ¶40-009, 89-102).

Forms: MT-903-FUT, Fuel Use Tax Return; MT-903-MN, Highway Use Tax Return; IFTA-100-MN, IFTA Quarterly Fuel Use Tax Report.

CAUTION: Unapportioned HUT violates Commerce Clause

Summary judgment was granted in a challenge to the constitutionality of New York's highway use tax (HUT), which required the payment of fees by certain vehicles operating on public highways in the state. Under the challenged HUT provisions, each motor carrier was required to apply for a certificate of registration for each motor vehicle operated or to be operated on the public highways in New York, and each application for a certificate of registration was to be accompanied by a $15 fee. The use of decals as evidence of a valid certificate of registration was also required, the fee for which was $4 each.

The taxpayers contended that the because the fees were not apportioned based on miles traveled in New York, the fees imposed a higher per mile tax rate on out-of-state trucks, and thus constituted an undue burden on interstate commerce in violation of the Commerce Clause of the U.S. Constitution. The court agreed, citing evidence presented by the taxpayers that established that the cost per mile for the registration and decal taxes was greater for non-New York based businesses than it was for New York based businesses.

The state's contention that flat taxes were constitutionally permissible because they could not practically be apportioned was rejected, because, the court noted, there were several ways that registration and decal fees could be apportioned without imposing and undue administrative burden on the state. (*Owner Operator Independent Drivers Assoc. v. New York State Department of Taxation and Finance,* Supreme Court, 3rd Judicial District (New York), No. 5551-13, January 22, 2016, CCH NEW YORK TAX REPORTS, ¶408-769)

Three taxes are imposed upon the operation of trucks, tractors, trailers and semi-trailers over the highways of the state—the highway use tax (truck mileage tax), which is weight-oriented, the supplemental highway use tax, and the fuel use tax, which is related to the use of motor fuel within the state. All the provisions of the highway use tax apply to the additional highway use tax unless inconsistent. (Secs. 503, 503-a, 523, Tax Law)

Persons subject to tax: Highway use taxes are imposed on motor vehicles (that is, trucks, tractors and other self-propelled vehicles) meeting applicable weight and vehicle classification categories. The taxes are imposed upon the carrier, except that where the carrier is not the owner of the vehicular unit, each of the taxes is a joint and several liability upon both the carrier and owner. (Sec. 503.1, Tax Law)

Exemptions: Authorized vehicles that are used exclusively to transport household goods on New York public highways are exempt from highway use tax. However, a highway use tax assessment was properly sustained because in order to receive an exemption for transportation of household goods, the taxpayer needed to demonstrate that its shipments qualified as household goods under federal law rather than the more expansive definition provided by state law. The Appellate Division found that the federal definition of "household goods" was in conflict with the definition found in the state transportation law, and, therefore, the more restrictive federal law preempted the state law. Because the taxpayer, as a federally registered motor carrier engaged in the interstate transport of household goods, failed to demonstrate that its shipments qualified as household goods within the meaning of the federal law, the conclusion that the contested shipments were not exempt was affirmed. (*In the Matter of Atlas Van Lines, Inc. v. Tax Appeals Tribunal of the State of New York,* Appellate Division of the Supreme Court of New York, Third Department, No. 516631, October 23, 2014, CCH NEW YORK TAX REPORTS, ¶ 408-255)

The Commissioner of Transportation takes the position that the Interstate Commerce Commission Termination Act of 1995 (ICCTA) preempts the definition of "household goods" in New York State Transportation Law. However, items described by New York Transportation Law qualify for the definition of household goods provided by the ICCTA. Therefore, vehicles that are properly authorized and used exclusively to transport property that qualifies as "household goods" under New York Transportation Law Sec. 2.15(a) and the ICCTA are exempt from highway use tax under Sec. 504.5, Tax Law (TSB-A-09(1)M, January 15, 2009, CCH NEW YORK TAX REPORTS, ¶ 406-302).

A highway use tax exemption is allowed for any vehicle operated by a farmer or a related person or entity and used exclusively by the farmer or by the related person or entity to transport: the farmer's own agricultural commodities, products, pulpwood, or livestock (including packaged, processed, or manufactured products that were originally grown or raised on the farmer's own farms or orchards; farm products from farms contiguous to the farmer's own farms; or supplies and equipment for use or consumption on the farmer's own farms. For additional information, see *TSB-M-13(5)M,* May 17, 2013, CCH NEW YORK TAX REPORTS, ¶ 407-835).

Trip permits: Carriers whose trucks or tractors are only occasionally operated within New York may obtain highway use tax and fuel use tax trip permits, which remain in effect for a 72-hour period, upon payment of a $25 fee for each permit. (Sec. 502.1(d), Tax Law)

Highway Use Tax (Truck Mileage Tax)

There are two alternate bases and rate schedules: (1) the gross weight of vehicle, or (2) the unloaded weight of a truck or tractor. (Sec. 503.1, Tax Law)

New York Thruway: Miles traveled on the New York Thruway for which a fee, rental or charge has been paid are exempt from the supplemental highway use tax and the highway use tax.

• Gross weight method

The tax is based upon the gross weight of each vehicular unit and the number of miles it is operated on the public highways in New York. The applicable tax rate is based on the unloaded and gross weight of each tractor or other self-propelled device and each truck. The mileage traveled during any reporting period is divided into "laden miles" and "unladen miles." The tax is computed by multiplying the number of miles operated within New York by the appropriate tax rate as it appears in the following tables (Sec. 503.1(b), (c), Tax Law):

Gross Weight Method—Laden Miles

Gross Weight of Vehicle	Tax Rate (in mills)
1. 18,001 to 20,000 inclusive	6.0
2. 20,001 to 22,000 inclusive	7.0
3. 22,001 to 24,000 inclusive	8.0
4. 24,001 to 26,000 inclusive	9.0
5. 26,001 to 28,000 inclusive	9.5
6. 28,001 to 30,000 inclusive	10.0
7. 30,001 to 32,000 inclusive	10.5
8. 32,001 to 34,000 inclusive	11.0
9. 34,001 to 36,000 inclusive	11.5
10. 36,001 to 38,000 inclusive	12.0
11. 38,001 to 40,000 inclusive	12.5
12. 40,001 to 42,000 inclusive	13.0
13. 42,001 to 44,000 inclusive	14.0
14. 44,001 to 46,000 inclusive	15.0
15. 46,001 to 48,000 inclusive	16.0
16. 48,001 to 50,000 inclusive	17.0

Gross Weight of Vehicle	Tax Rate (in mills)
17. 50,001 to 52,000 inclusive	18.0
18. 52,001 to 54,000 inclusive	19.0
19. 54,001 to 56,000 inclusive	20.0
20. 56,001 to 58,000 inclusive	21.0
21. 58,001 to 60,000 inclusive	22.0
22. 60,001 to 62,000 inclusive	23.0
23. 62,001 to 64,000 inclusive	24.0
24. 64,001 to 66,000 inclusive	25.5
25. 66,001 to 68,000 inclusive	27.0
26. 68,001 to 70,000 inclusive	28.5
27. 70,001 to 72,000 inclusive	30.0
28. 72,001 to 74,000 inclusive	32.5
29. 74,001 to 76,000 inclusive	35.0
30. 76,001 and over	add 2 mills per ton and fraction thereof

Gross Weight Method—Unladen Miles

Tractors

Unloaded Weight	Tax Rate (in mills)
1. 7,001 to 8,500 inclusive	6.0
2. 8,501 to 10,000 inclusive	7.0
3. 10,001 to 12,000 inclusive	8.0
4. 12,001 to 14,000 inclusive	9.0
5. 14,001 to 16,000 inclusive	9.5
6. 16,001 to 18,000 inclusive	10.0
7. 18,001 and over	add five tenths of a mill per ton and fraction thereof

Trucks

Unloaded Weight	Tax Rate (in mills)
1. 18,001 to 20,000 inclusive	6.0
2. 20,001 to 22,000 inclusive	7.0
3. 22,001 to 24,000 inclusive	8.0
4. 24,001 to 26,000 inclusive	9.0
5. 26,001 to 28,000 inclusive	9.5
6. 28,001 to 30,000 inclusive	10.0
7. 30,001 and over	add five tenths of a mill per ton and fraction thereof

• *Unloaded weight of truck or tractor method*

An optional method of computing the tax is based on the unloaded weight of each self-propelled motor vehicle and the number of miles it is operated on the public highways of the state. The tax is computed by multiplying the number of miles operated within the state by the appropriate tax rate as it appears in the following table (Sec. 503.3, Tax Law):

Unloaded Weight	Tax Rate (in mills)
1. 8,001 to 9,000 inclusive	4
2. 9,001 to 10,000 inclusive	5
3. 10,001 to 11,000 inclusive	7
4. 11,001 to 12,000 inclusive	8
5. 12,001 to 13,000 inclusive	9
6. 13,001 to 14,000 inclusive	10
7. 14,001 to 15,000 inclusive	11
8. 15,001 to 17,500 inclusive	12
9. 17,501 to 20,000 inclusive	14
10. 20,001 to 22,500 inclusive	18
11. 22,501 to 25,000 inclusive	22
12. 25,001 and over	27

Unloaded Weight of Tractor	Tax Rate (in mills)
1. 4,001 to 5,500 inclusive	6
2. 5,501 to 7,000 inclusive	10
3. 7,001 to 8,500 inclusive	14
4. 8,501 to 10,000 inclusive	18
5. 10,001 to 12,000 inclusive	25
6. 12,001 and over	33

The election may be made only on the first return filed during the calendar year and applies to all vehicles included in the return (Sec. 503.3, Tax Law).

The gross weight and unloaded weight for miles traveled by a truck that is not drawing a trailer, semi-trailer, dolly or similar drawn device is determined without regard to any device drawn by the truck at other times or the weight of any load carried by the device. (Sec. 503.1(d), Tax Law)

Supplemental highway use tax: Carriers subject to the highway use tax are subject to a supplemental tax that is equal to 40% of the highway use tax, discussed above. Carriers that operate three or fewer vehicles used primarily to transport boltwood, logs, pulpwood or woodchips, or to transport raw, unprocessed milk in bulk, are exempt. (Sec. 503-b, Tax Law)

License requirements: Carriers must obtain a certificate of registration from the Tax Department for each truck, tractor, or other self-propelled vehicle, and any trailer, semi-trailer, or other attached device used to transport automotive fuel. Effective April 13, 2016, the $15 application fee and $4 decal or special decal fees for highway use tax registration decals are repealed and replaced with a single application fee of $1.50. A fee of $1.50 is also imposed for replacement due to loss, mutilation, or destruction of decals; however, no additional fee is charged for issuance of a corrected certificate of registration. A certificate of registration (or permit) does not have to be carried in the motor vehicle, but must be kept at the carrier's regular place of business. (Sec. 502, Tax Law; *Important Notice N-07-15*, New York Department of Taxation and Finance, July 1, 2007, CCH NEW YORK TAX REPORTS, ¶ 405-801)

For temporary trip permits, see discussion above.

• *Fuel Use Tax*

New York State is a participating member of the International Fuel Tax Agreement (IFTA). The IFTA simplifies the reporting of fuel taxes by allowing a motor carrier to report to its base jurisdiction all the fuel taxes that it owes to the various IFTA members' jurisdictions. (Secs. 523(a); 528(b), Tax Law; 20 NYCRR § 490.1(c))

A carrier's "base jurisdiction" is the IFTA member jurisdiction where (1) the carrier's qualified motor vehicles are based for vehicle registration purposes, (2) the operational control and operational records of those qualified motor vehicles are maintained or can be made available, and (3) some travel actually occurs by qualified motor vehicles in the carrier's fleet. (20 NYCRR § 490.2(a))

A qualified motor vehicle is any motor vehicle, other than a recreational vehicle, that meets any of the following criteria:

— it has two axles and a gross vehicle weight or registered gross vehicle weight of more than 26,000 pounds;

— it has three or more axles, regardless of weight; or

— it is used in combination and the gross vehicle weight of the combination is more than 26,000 pounds. (20 NYCRR § 490.2(h)(1))

Registration: Each vehicle registered to pay HUT also is required to affix a decal to the front bumper of the vehicle. This applies to all vehicles with a gross weight of more than 18,000 pounds, other than a truck transporting automotive fuel. The decal requirement also applies to vehicles that have an Automotive Fuel Carrier (AFC) certificate, which is any truck, trailer, semitrailer, or other "attached device" transporting automotive fuel on New York State highways and weighing more than 18,000 pounds.

• *Rate of tax*

New York's fuel use tax rate is determined by adding together (a) a fuel use component, equivalent to the applicable rate per gallon imposed by Article 12-A, Tax Law (tax imposed on gasoline and similar motor fuels), and (b) a sales tax component, equivalent to the rate per gallon applicable to receipts from the sale of a gallon of motor fuel or diesel motor fuel in effect under sales and compensating use taxes imposed by Secs. 1105 and 1110, Tax Law, plus the highest rate applicable to the receipts from the sale of a gallon of motor fuel or diesel motor fuel in effect in any locality in New York that imposes a local sales and compensating use tax on sales of motor fuel and diesel motor fuel. The total sales tax component may not exceed 7%.

The total equivalent rate per gallon is based on the average price per gallon (including all federal and state and any local taxes included in such price or imposed on the use or consumption of such fuels upon which the state and local sales tax is computed, but determined without the inclusion of any state or local sales tax on receipts from sales of such fuel) paid by the carrier during the reporting period for all motor fuel and diesel motor fuel purchased for use in its operations either within or without New York. The price for motor fuel and diesel motor fuel purchased by the carrier is deemed to be the prevailing price for motor fuel and diesel motor fuel, as established by the Commissioner each calendar quarter, applicable for the reporting period.

The tax is computed by multiplying the composite rate by the amount of motor fuel or diesel motor fuel used by the carrier in its operations within the state during each reporting period. The amount of miles traveled within the state is determined by dividing the number of miles traveled in the state subject to tax by the average miles per gallon for the type of fuel. Where the carrier's records are inadequate or incomplete, the qualified motor vehicles of a carrier required to file a return are presumed to have consumed, on the average, one gallon of diesel motor fuel for every four miles traveled, or one gallon of motor fuel for every three miles traveled. (Sec. 523(b), Tax Law)

For the fuel use tax rate for the current quarter, see CCH NEW YORK TAX REPORTS, ¶ 40-009.

Exemptions: The following vehicles are exempt from tax: road rollers, tractor cranes, truck cranes, power shovels, road building machines, snow plows, road sweepers, sand spreaders, well drillers, vehicular units engaged exclusively in the transportation of U.S. mail under contract, government and certain farm vehicles (see *TSB-M-13(5)M*, May 17, 2013, CCH NEW YORK TAX REPORTS, ¶ 407-835), vehicles owned and operated by a volunteer fire department, and certain vehicular units used exclusively in the transportation of household goods. Also, taxes do not apply to motor fuel and diesel motor fuel used by an omnibus carrier in the operation of the omnibus in local transit service in New York, pursuant to a certificate of public convenience and necessity issued by the Commissioner of Transportation or by the Interstate Commerce Commission, or pursuant to a contract, franchise or consent between the carrier and New York City (or a New York City agency). (Sec. 525, Tax Law; 20 NYCRR § 471.2)

Credits: Carriers subject to tax are allowed a credit against New York fuel use tax in an amount equal to the sum of the fuel tax and sales tax components. The fuel tax component is determined by multiplying the number of gallons of motor fuel or diesel motor fuel purchased by the carrier within the state during the return period, for use in its own operations either within or without the state, by the applicable rate per gallon imposed on such fuel by Article 12-A, Tax Law (gasoline and similar motor fuels tax). No credit is allowed unless Article 12-A taxes have been paid on the purchases of fuel by the carrier. (Sec. 524(a), Tax Law)

The sales tax component is determined by multiplying the number of gallons of motor fuel or diesel motor fuel purchased by the carrier within the state during the return period, for use in its own operations either within or without the state, by the applicable equivalent rate per gallon of the sales tax component of the tax rate. No credit is allowed unless applicable sales and use taxes on the purchases of fuel have been paid by the carrier. (Sec. 524(a), Tax Law)

Refund or carryover of unused credit: Motor carriers may claim a refund of New York fuel use tax credit for 49 months following the end of the reporting period in which the credit was derived. A carrier with a New York State International Fuel Tax

Agreement (IFTA) license may also claim a refund for outstanding fuel use tax credit for 49 months following the reporting period in which the credit was derived. IFTA carriers have the option, however, of having their credit applied toward fuel taxes that will come due during any of the eight reporting quarters that follow the quarter in which the credit was derived. NY Tax Law § 524.

IFTA reports contain a carrier's total credit balance, including the amount of unused credit. A refund of the credit must be requested directly on the IFTA report. If the unused credit is not on the report, carriers must request a refund by letter within 49 months after the reporting period in which the credit was derived. Unclaimed credit is forfeited after 49 months.

Carriers with IFTA licenses from states other than New York may claim a refund of New York fuel use tax credit that accrued in a reporting period prior to the carrier's participation in IFTA. The refund is available for 49 months following the end of the reporting period in which the credit was derived.

A carrier is entitled to a credit against prior fuel use taxes that it would have been entitled to carry forward, but for the termination of the tax. Credits or refunds may also be permitted for erroneous payments, or where the carrier establishes that the average price paid per gallon during a reporting period is less than the actual price paid. (Sec. 524(b), Tax Law)

• *Returns and payment*

Monthly highway use tax returns are required only where the carrier's total highway use tax liability for the preceding calendar year exceeded $4,000. Quarterly returns may be filed on or before the last day of the calendar month following the end of the calendar quarter, provided the carrier was not subject to highway use tax during the prior calendar year, or its highway use tax liability for the preceding year did not exceed $4,000. The Commissioner of Taxation and Finance may permit the filing of annual returns (due not later than January 31 of the succeeding year) provided the carrier was subject to highway use tax during the entire preceding calendar year and its highway use tax liability did not exceed $250. (Sec. 505, Tax Law)

Taxpayers may use the highway use tax (HUT) Web File system to file returns. Taxpayers will receive an electronic confirmation number with the date and time of filing the return, and can schedule an electronic payment for a date no later than the return's due date. Taxpayers are required to create an Online Services business account and can grant access to the account to a New York state tax preparer. The online account may be used to file monthly, quarterly, and annual highway use tax returns; no activity returns; final returns; and amended returns that were previously filed via the Internet. Additional information can be found on the department's website (**http://www.tax.ny.gov**).

Fuel use tax returns are due quarterly (Sec. 526, Tax Law).

Both taxes are payable at the time the returns are filed. (Secs. 506; 526(b), Tax Law)

License requirements: Carriers must obtain a certificate of registration from the Tax Department for each truck, tractor, or other self-propelled vehicle, and any trailer, semi-trailer, or other attached device used to transport automotive fuel. (Sec. 502, Tax Law).

The validity of certificates of registration and permits may be checked by police officers and law enforcement agencies by calling the Tax Department on a phone line reserved for their use only. (*Important Notice N-07-15*, New York Department of Taxation and Finance, July 1, 2007, CCH NEW YORK TAX REPORTS, ¶405-801; See also *TSB-M-07(3)M*, June 11, 2007, CCH NEW YORK TAX REPORTS, ¶405-749, and *Publication*

536, International Fuel Tax Agreement (IFTA) A Guide for New York State Carriers, New York Department of Taxation and Finance, May 1, 2014, CCH NEW YORK TAX REPORTS, ¶41-514)

Administration: The taxes are administered by the Department of Taxation and Finance, W.A. Harriman State Campus, Albany, NY 12227.

¶2706 Alcoholic Beverage Taxes

> *Law:* Secs. 424—438, Tax Law; (Secs. 17, 79-c, 107-a(4)(g), Alcoholic Beverage Control Law; Reg. Sec. 60.1).

> *Forms:* MT-40, Return of Tax on Wines, Liquors, Alcohol, and Distilled or Rectified Spirits; MT-50, Beer Tax Return (and Similar Fermented Malt Beverages).

Excise taxes on the sale and use of alcoholic beverages are imposed upon distributors and noncommercial importers of liquors, beer, and wine. Persons who receive alcoholic beverages from a distributor upon whom the state is not empowered to impose a tax against the distributor, and who then sell or use the beverage in a manner that would otherwise be taxable, are liable for the excise tax. (Secs. 424.1; 425, Tax Law)

Presumption of taxability: Until the contrary is established by substantial evidence, it is assumed that all alcoholic beverages found or possessed in New York are subject to tax. (Sec. 425-a, Tax Law)

- *Tax Rates*

Taxes are imposed at the following rates:

Type of Beverage	Rate per Gallon
Beer	$0.14
Still wines	0.30
Artificially carbonated sparking wines	0.30
Natural sparkling wines	0.30
Cider containing more than 3.2% alcohol by volume	0.0379
	Rate per Liter
Liquors (containing not more than 2% alcohol by volume)	$0.01
Liquors (containing not more than 24% alcohol by volume)	0.67
Liquors (containing more than 24% alcohol by volume, including wine over 24%)	1.70

Licensing fees: A broad range of annual license fees and permit fees applies to manufacturers, wholesalers and retailers.

Exemptions: The following sales of alcoholic beverages are exempt from tax:

— The sale of wine in sealed containers to religious organizations for sacramental purposes;

— The sale of beer to or by a voluntary unincorporated organization of the armed forces of the United States operating a place for the sale of goods pursuant to regulations of an executive agency of the United States;

— The sale of beer to certain foreign consular officers assigned to foreign consulates within New York, provided that American consular officers of equal rank who exercise their official functions at American consulates in such foreign country are granted reciprocal exemptions;

— One quart of alcoholic beverages (or one gallon if purchased in American Samoa, Guam, or the Virgin Islands) per month, purchased outside New York as an incident to a journey from which the purchaser is returning, and which is not intended for resale or commercial use. (Secs. 424.1(f); 424.4; 424.5, Tax Law)

Farm and craft brewers: The annual fee for a farm brewery license is $320. To be eligible, a farm brewery can manufacture only New York State-labeled beer in quantities not to exceed 60,000 barrels annually.

An alcoholic beverage tax exemption from the annual $150 beer label registration fee is provided for beer produced in small batches totaling 1,500 barrels of beer or less annually by both in-state and out-of-state brewers (Sec. 107-a(4)(g), Alcoholic Beverage Control Law; *TSB-M-13(6)M,* June 10, 2013, CCH NEW YORK TAX REPORTS, ¶407-855). These provisions are deemed to have been in full force and effect as of March 28, 2012.

• *Administration*

Statewide administration of the Alcoholic Beverage Control Law is vested in the State Liquor Authority (SLA) (Sec. 10, NY ABC Law). The SLA has many functions, powers and duties assigned to it. Licenses and permits may be issued or refused, limited in number, and revoked, cancelled or suspended by the SLA. The Authority is authorized to fix the rules and standards of manufacture and fermentation in order to insure the use of proper ingredients and methods in the manufacture of alcoholic beverages to be sold and consumed in New York. (Sec. 17, NY ABC Law).

A "one-stop shop" website is available for alcoholic beverage producers to get assistance regarding regulations, licensing, state incentives, and any other questions or issues facing the industry (**http://esd.ny.gov/NYSBeverageBiz.html**).

• *Direct Shipments to Customers*

An out-of-state direct shipper's license authorizes the holder to ship wine directly to adult New York residents as long as the state where the licensee is located allows New York individuals and licensees reciprocal shipping privileges. (Sec. 79-c, NY ABC Law)

¶2707 Cigarette and Tobacco Products Tax

> *Law:* Secs. 470—489, Tax Law; Reg. Sec. 71.2 (CCH NEW YORK TAX REPORTS, ¶55-001 *et seq.*).
>
> *Forms:* CG-5, Nonresident Agent Cigarette Tax Report; CG-6, Resident Agent Cigarette Tax Report; CG-11, Cigarette Tax Floor Tax Return; CG-15, Cigarette Use Tax Return.

A stamp tax is imposed on all cigarettes possessed for sale within New York, and is assessed only once on the same package of cigarettes. A comparable use tax is imposed on all cigarettes used in the state, subject to certain limitations. (Secs. 471, 471-a, Tax Law). Little cigars are classified as cigarettes.

Practitioner Comment: Cigars or Little Cigars

A cigar is any roll of tobacco wrapped in leaf tobacco or in any substance containing tobacco. In order to qualify as a "little cigar", the cigar must be:

(1) made of tobacco and provided in rolled form for smoking, and

(2) wrapped in some sort of tobacco, but not natural leaf tobacco.

Additionally, the product must either weigh four pounds or less per one hundred cigars or have a cigarette-type filter. Since the tax on cigars is 75% of the wholesale price, this distinction can make a significant difference. TB-TP-530 (2014)

Mark S. Klein, Esq., Hodgson Russ LLP

New York City imposes an additional tax (¶3303).

Tobacco products: Tobacco products used in New York, or possessed in New York by any person for sale or use, are subject to tax (Secs. 471; 471-a, Tax Law).

Exemptions: The following exemptions apply to the taxes imposed on cigarettes and tobacco products:

Cigarettes: Sales in interstate commerce, out-of-state sales, sales to the United States, sales to New York State, sales to qualified Native Americans on qualified Native American reservations (¶2103), or sales to or by voluntary unincorporated organizations of the Armed Forces, governmental entities, the United Nations, diplomatic missions and diplomatic personnel are not subject to the cigarette tax (Sec.

471(1), Tax Law; 20 NYCRR §74.1(c)). The use tax will not be imposed (1) if the cigarette tax has already been paid, (2) on the use of cigarettes that are exempt from the cigarette tax, or (3) on the use of 400 or fewer cigarettes, brought into the state by, or in the possession of, any person. (If more than 400 cigarettes are brought into the state by or are in the possession of any person, the first 400 cigarettes are also taxable.) (Sec. 471-a, Tax Law). Out-of-state mail sales, however, are subject to tax (*The Angelica Co., Inc.* (1966, NY SCt, NY Cty) 52 Misc2d 844, 276 NYS2d 766; CCH NEW YORK TAX REPORTS, ¶ 98-699).

In *Milhelm Attea & Brothers, Inc.,* CCH NEW YORK TAX REPORTS, ¶ 401-528, the U.S. Supreme Court ruled that federal statutes governing trade with Native Americans did not preempt New York State regulations that imposed recordkeeping requirements and set quotas on the amount of untaxed cigarettes that wholesale distributors licensed by the Bureau of Indian affairs could sell to tribal retailers.

Cigarette manufacturers are prohibited from selling unstamped cigarettes to stamping agents who have not provided them with certification that the cigarettes will not be resold in violation of Article 20 of the Tax Law (Tax on Cigarettes and Tobacco Products). An agent that violates Article 20 is subject to revocation or cancellation of its license. The Commissioner of Taxation and Finance is required to prescribe a form for the certification process and instructions on how to use the form. (A.B. 11258, Laws 2008)

CCH Advisory: Reservation Sales

Qualified Indians may purchase tax-exempt cigarettes for their own use on their own reservations. However, the exemption does not extend to purchases made by Indians off their reservations or on other reservations. Non-Indians may not purchase tax-exempt cigarettes. (Sec. 471-e, Tax Law)

Effective September 1, 2010, all cigarettes sold to Indian nations or tribes and reservation cigarette sellers must bear tax stamps. However, a dual system is implemented to collect taxes on all cigarettes sold on an Indian reservation to non-Indians and non-members of an Indian nation or tribe. The governing body of an Indian nation or tribe may elect to participate in the Indian tax exemption coupon system or an alternate prior approval system. Under both the coupon system and the prior approval system, the Department of Taxation and Finance will determine the quantity of tax-exempt cigarettes for each Indian nation or tribe annually in June, based on the probable demand of the qualified Indians on the Indian nation's or tribe's reservation plus an additional amount needed for official nation or tribal use. The department will then provide coupons or prior approvals to agents and wholesale dealers for tax-exempt sales to each nation in the amount that is determined. Both the coupon system and the prior approval system are in place for tax-free sales taking place on or after September 1, 2010 (Regs. 74.6 and 74.7).

The annual amount of stamped tax-exempt packs of cigarettes for each of the Indian nations or tribes for the 12-month period beginning September 1, 2016, and ending August 31, 2017, has been determined; see *Important Notice N-16-5,* New York Department of Taxation and Finance, July 2016, CCH NEW YORK TAX REPORTS, ¶ 408-798.

Tobacco products: A tobacco products tax is imposed on all non-cigarette tobacco products. The same exemptions apply (Sec. 471-b, Tax Law). The tobacco products use tax will not be imposed (1) if the tobacco products tax has already been paid, (2) on the use of tobacco products that are exempt from the tobacco products tax, or (3) on the use of 250 cigars or less, or five pounds of less or tobacco, brought into the state on, or in the possession of, any person. (Sec. 471-c, Tax Law)

- *Basis and rate of tax*

The cigarette tax rate is $4.35 per pack in New York State. See ¶ 3303 for rates in New York City. The tax rate for snuff is $2.00 per ounce. (Emergency Regs. 74.6 and

74.7, and *Release*, New York Department of Taxation and Finance, June 22, 2010; *Important Notice N-10-4*, New York Department of Taxation and Finance, June 2010, CCH NEW YORK TAX REPORTS, ¶ 406-862).

For packages containing more than 20 cigarettes, the rate of tax on the cigarettes in the package in excess of 20 is $1.0875 per five cigarettes or fraction thereof. The tobacco products tax (excluding snuff) is imposed at a rate of 75% of the wholesale price on all tobacco products (non-cigarette) possessed in New York by any person for sale or use. The taxes are imposed only once on the same cigarettes or tobacco products and it is presumed that all cigarettes and tobacco products in the state are subject to tax, unless it is established otherwise. The burden of proof that they are not taxable is on the person in possession of the cigarettes or tobacco products. (Secs. 471, 471-a, 471-b, 471-c, Tax Law)

Little cigars are subject to cigarette tax at the rate of $4.35 per pack of 20 (TSB-M-10(10)M, August 6, 2010, CCH NEW YORK TAX REPORTS, ¶ 406-925; *TB-TP-530*, New York Department of Taxation and Finance, August 28, 2014, CCH NEW YORK TAX REPORTS, ¶ 408-225).

A commission is allowed for the expenses incurred in affixing stamps.

• *Returns and payment*

The tax is paid by agents authorized to purchase and affix adhesive or metered stamps. Agents are required to file monthly reports on the 15th of each month showing the number of unstamped cigarettes on hand at the beginning and end of the preceding month, and cigarette stamps handled during the preceding month. Additional records are required of agents, dealers, vending machine owners, and cigarette transporters. All records must be kept for a period of three years, and are subject to inspection by the Commissioner of Taxation. Users are required to file returns, together with a remittance of the tax, within 24 hours after accrual of liability for the payment of the tax. (Sec. 473, Tax Law)

Distributors of tobacco products are required to file returns on or before the 20th day of each month, showing the quantity and wholesale price of all tobacco products that they imported or caused to be imported into New York, or that they manufactured in New York, during the preceding calendar month. The tax is due upon the filing of the return. A dealer is liable for the tax on all tobacco products in his possession at any time, upon which tax has not been paid or assumed by a distributor appointed by the Commissioner of Taxation and Finance. Users are required to file returns, together with a remittance of the tax, within 24 hours after accrual of liability for the payment of the tax. Persons who possess or transport more than 250 cigars or more than five pounds of tobacco upon the public highways, roads, or streets of New York, as well as dealers or distributors who so possess or transport more than 50 cigars or more than one pound of tobacco, are required to have in their possession invoices or delivery tickets for the tobacco products. Distributors and wholesale dealers of tobacco products are required to retain duplicative invoices. (Secs. 473-a; 474, Tax Law)

Wholesale dealers must electronically file quarterly informational returns with the Department of Taxation and Finance that detail their purchases, sales, and prices of tobacco products. An e-mail address and a password are needed to set up an account. The returns are due by the 20th day of March, June, September, and December for the quarterly periods ending on the last day of February, May, August, and November of each years (Reg. Secs. 75.2 and 90.1). Taxpayers with questions may contact the Taxpayer Contact Center at (518) 457-5735 for additional information (*Important Notice N-12-2*, New York Department of Taxation and Finance, February 2012, CCH NEW YORK TAX REPORTS, ¶ 407-489).

¶2707

Jenkins Act: The New York Department of Taxation and Finance has issued a cigarette and tobacco products tax memorandum that describes the new and expanded reporting requirements concerning reporting to the department under the Jenkins Act, as amended by the Prevent All Cigarette Trafficking Act (PACT), effective June 29, 2010. Reports are due by the 10th day of each calendar month. (TSB-M-10(7)M, Office of Tax Policy Analysis, New York Department of Taxation and Finance, August 3, 2010, CCH NEW YORK TAX REPORTS, ¶406-917)

Administration: The tax is administered by the Department of Taxation and Finance, W.A. Harriman State Campus, Albany, NY 12227.

• *Penalties*

A penalty is imposed at the rate of 10% of the tax due for the first month or fraction of a month, and 1% for each subsequent month or fraction of a month in which the tax remains unpaid, up to a maximum penalty of 30%. The total penalty and interest may not exceed 30% in the aggregate. (Sec. 481, Tax Law)

If a return is not filed within 60 days of the due date, the penalty may not be less than the lesser of the tax due or $100. In no event may this penalty be less than the penalty computed pursuant to the preceding paragraph. (Sec. 481.1(a)(i)(C), Tax Law)

Possession of unstamped cigarettes or untaxed tobacco products: Persons who possess or have under their control unstamped or unlawfully stamped packages of cigarettes may be subject to a penalty of not more than $600 for each 200 cigarettes in excess of 1,000 cigarettes. (Sec. 481(1)(b)(i), Tax Law)

The Department may impose a penalty of up to $200 for each 10 unaffixed false, altered, or counterfeit cigarette tax stamps, imprints, or impressions, or fraction thereof, in the possession or under the control of any person. In lieu of this penalty, other lesser monetary penalties may be imposed at the discretion of the Department (Sec. 481(1)(b)(ii)(A)(i), Tax Law; TSB-M-08(7)M, October 3, 2008, CCH NEW YORK TAX REPORTS, ¶406-179).

Tobacco products tax: Regarding tobacco products upon which the tobacco products sales or use tax has not been paid, the Commissioner may impose an additional penalty of not more than $75 for each 50 cigars or one pound of tobacco (or fraction thereof) in excess of 250 cigars or five pounds of tobacco in the possession or control of any person. An additional penalty of not more than $150 may be imposed for each 50 cigars or pound of tobacco (or fraction thereof) in excess of 500 cigars or ten pounds of tobacco in the possession or under the control of any person. Such additional penalties, however, may not exceed $7,500 in the aggregate. A separate penalty applies if a person knowingly possesses or has control of such cigars or tobacco. NY Tax Law § 481.1(b)(i), (ii).

In addition, a dealer or distributor that possesses or has control of cigars or tobacco upon which tobacco products tax has not been paid or assumed may be subject to a penalty of (1) not more than $75 for each 50 cigars or one pound of tobacco in excess of 50 cigars or one pound of tobacco and (2) not more than $150 for each 50 cigars or one pound of tobacco in excess of 250 cigars or five pounds of tobacco. The penalty may not exceed $15,000. NY Tax Law § 481.1(b)(i).

Increased penalties apply for knowing possession. (Sec. 481.1(b)(ii), Tax Law)

"Roll-your-own"(RYO) cigarette tobacco: A civil penalty of up to $5,000 per violation is imposed on distributors and tobacco product manufacturers who violate statutory provisions concerning certain certification requirements and prohibitions on the sale of uncertified "Roll-your-own"(RYO) tobacco. (Sec. 481(1)(d), Tax Law; TSB-M-08(8)M, October 28, 2008, CCH NEW YORK TAX REPORTS, ¶406-202)

Licenses: Agents, wholesale dealers, chain stores, and vending machine operators and distributors must obtain licenses to do business within New York. (Sec. 480, Tax Law)

The penalties imposed for violation of the cigarette and tobacco products tax registration provisions by retail dealers are a minimum of $1,000 but not exceeding $25,000 for a first violation, and a minimum of $10,000 but not exceeding $35,000 for a second or subsequent violation within three years following a prior finding of violation. The penalties imposed for violation of the registration provisions by vending machine owners or operators are a minimum of $750 but not exceeding $1,000 for a first violation, and a minimum of $1,000 but not exceeding $6,000 for a second or subsequent violation within three years following a prior finding of violation. (Sec. 480-a.3, Tax Law; *TSB-M-09(7)M,* July 31, 2009, CCH NEW YORK TAX REPORTS, ¶ 406-470)

¶2708 Public Utilities Taxes

Law: Sec. 189, Econ. Dev. Law; Secs. 183, 184, 186, 186-a, 186-e, Tax Law; Sec. 18-a, Public Service Law (CCH NEW YORK TAX REPORTS, ¶ 80-001 *et seq.*).

Forms: CT-183, Transportation and Transmission Corporation Franchise tax Return on Capital Stock; CT-183-M, Transportation and Transmission Corporation MTA Surcharge Return; CT-184, Transportation and Transmission Corporation Franchise Tax Return on Gross Earnings; CT-184-M, Transportation and Transmission Corporation MTA Surcharge Return; CT-186-A, Utility Services Tax Return—Gross Operating Income; CT-186-A/M, Utility Services MTA Surcharge Return; CT-186-E, Telecommunications Tax Return and Utility Services Tax Return.

Utilities doing business within New York are subject to (1) franchise taxes imposed on some transportation and transmission companies under Article 9, Secs. 183 and 184, Tax Law; (2) a tax on the furnishing of utility services under Sec. 186-a, Tax Law; and (3) a tax on telecommunication services providers imposed under Sec. 186-e, Tax Law. Utilities conducting business activities within the Metropolitan Commuter Transportation District are subject to a surcharge.

A temporary state energy and utility service conservation assessment is imposed on the gross operating receipts of public utility companies, including municipalities, corporations (including the Long Island power authority), and regulated public utility companies to encourage the conservation of energy and other resources provided through utility entities (Sec. 18-a(6)(a), Public Service Law). The assessment rates through 2017 are as follows (Sec. 18-a(6)(b), Public Service Law):

— Beginning April 1, 2013, through March 31, 2015: 2%;

— April 1, 2015, through March 31, 2016: 1.75%;

— April 1, 2016, through March 31, 2017: 1.5%; and

— 2017: 0.5% of the 2016 assessment.

The above rates are reduced for the Long Island Power Authority (Sec. 18-a(6)(b), Public Service Law).

Water and energy companies: A franchise tax on water, gas, electric, or steam heating, lighting, and power companies under Sec. 186, Tax Law, was repealed, effective for taxable years ending after January 1, 2000. These companies are now subject to the corporation franchise (income) tax under Article 9-A, Tax Law. Certain taxpayers with total-output contracts in effect on January 1, 2000, remain subject to the Sec. 186 tax until the expiration of the contracts.

Corporations principally engaged in transportation, transmission, or distribution of gas, electricity, or steam (TTD companies), formerly taxable under Article 9, Secs. 183 and 184, Tax Law, are also subject to Article 9-A.

Enhanced emergency telephone system surcharge: Municipalities are authorized to impose a telephone system surcharge to pay for the cost of providing enhanced emergency telephone systems. The surcharge may not exceed 35¢ ($1 in New York City) per access line per month on the customers of every service supplier, and may not be imposed on more than 75 access lines per customer per location. Lifeline customers, public safety agencies and municipalities that have enacted the surcharge are exempt from the surcharge. Telephone service suppliers must collect the surcharge from their customers, and remit the fees to the applicable county on a monthly basis. The surcharge will not be considered in the determination of gross income or gross operating income of the utility for purposes of the additional tax on utility services, discussed below. (Sec. 186-a.10, Tax Law)

Public safety communications surcharge: A state surcharge is imposed on each device used to access wireless communications service at the rate of $1.20 per month (Sec. 186-f, Tax Law; TSB-M-09(8)C, August 27, 2009, CCH New York Tax Reports, ¶406-511). In addition, certain counties and New York City (¶3307) are authorized to impose a surcharge of up to 30¢ per wireless device per month.

Cable television systems: Municipalities are authorized to impose a fee, tax or charge on cable television companies, subject to the condition that, when added to the state fee, the total tax does not exceed 1% of the company's annual gross receipts.

Administration: Utility taxes are administered by the Department of Taxation and Finance, W.A. Harriman State Campus, Albany, NY 12227.

• *Transportation and transmission companies*

Some transportation and transmission companies are subject to the franchise tax on capital stock (Sec. 183, Tax Law) and an additional tax on intrastate gross earnings. (Sec. 184, Tax Law)

Telephone businesses: The gross earnings tax on telecommunication services providers is limited to entities formed for or principally engaged in the conduct of a "local" telephone business (Sec. 184, Tax Law). A "local" telephone business means the provision or furnishing of telecommunication services for hire wherein the services furnished by the provider consist of carrier access service or the service originates and terminates within the same local access and transport area (LATA).

Exemptions: The following transportation and transmission companies are exempt from tax:

— corporations engaged exclusively in the operation of vessels in foreign or interstate commerce;

— ferry companies operating between boroughs of New York City under a lease granted by the city;

— corporations, joint-stock companies, and associations engaged in the conduct of aviation (including air freight forwarders acting as principal and like indirect air carriers);

— corporations principally engaged in providing telecommunication services between aircraft and dispatcher, aircraft and air traffic control or ground station and ground station (or any combination of the foregoing), when (1) at least 90% of the corporation's voting stock is owned, directly or indirectly, by air carriers, and (2) the corporation's principal function is to fulfill the requirements of the Federal Aviation Administration or the International Civil Aviation Organization (or successors thereto) relating to communication systems between aircraft and dispatchers, aircraft and air traffic control or ground station and ground station (or any combination thereof) for air safety and navigation purposes;

¶2708

— corporations, joint-stock companies or associations formed for or principally engaged in the transportation, transmission, or distribution of gas, electricity, or steam (TDD corporations);

— banking corporations subject to Article 32 franchise taxes (¶1601 and following); and

— omnibus and taxicab corporations, provided the state motor fuel tax remains greater than 2¢ per gallon (see ¶2709 for current rate). Out-of-state taxicab or omnibus corporations that conduct fewer than 12 trips into New York per calendar year are subject to an annual tax equal to $15 per trip. (To qualify for the per-trip tax, the corporation must neither own nor lease property, nor maintain an office, in New York. Secs. 183.1, 183-a.1, 184.1, 184-a.1, Tax Law)

CCH Advisory: Mobile Telecommunications

According to a new policy announced by the New York Department of Taxation and Finance, mobile telecommunication service providers are not taxable under Sec. 184, Tax Law, which imposes an additional franchise tax on certain transportation and transmission corporations. With regard to telecommunication services, the tax is limited to corporations that are formed for or principally engaged in a telegraph or local telephone business. Mobile telecommunication service providers' services are not limited to intra-LATA or carrier access service; therefore, such providers are not engaged in the conduct of a local telephone business. A mobile telecommunication service provider may be entitled to a refund if it previously paid the Sec. 184 tax and the statute of limitations for the tax year is open.

A now-superseded advisory opinion (*TSB-A-00(18)C*, Nov. 20, 2000, CCH New York Tax Reports, ¶403-838) concluded that wireless communications service providers engaged in intra-LATA and inter-LATA communications services were conducting a local telephone business. However, because the industry as a whole has changed, that conclusion no longer represents the department's view. (*TSB-M-15(6)C*, New York Department of Taxation and Finance, July 24, 2015, CCH New York Tax Reports, ¶408-485)

Trucking and railroad corporations: Businesses formed for or principally engaged in the conduct of a railroad, palace car, sleeping car or trucking business or formed for or principally engaged in the conduct of two or more of such businesses are subject to Article 9-A business corporation franchise taxes (or, in instances where the trucking or railroad corporation is a subsidiary of a banking corporation, Article 32 bank franchise taxes), *unless* those businesses elected to continue to be subject to Article 9 taxes. An election to remain subject to Article 9 tax continues in effect until revoked by the taxpayer. A revocation of the election, once made, is irrevocable. (Secs. 183.10, 183-a.1, 184.1, 184-a.1, Tax Law)

Cable TV systems: Taxpayers providing cable services were subject to the New York utility tax imposed on transmission companies under Tax Law Article 9, Secs. 183 and 184, rather than the corporate franchise (income) tax imposed on general business corporations under Tax Law Article 9-A (*NewChannels Corp. et al.*, New York Supreme Court, Appellate Division, Third Department, No. 86041, January 11, 2001; CCH New York Tax Reports, ¶403-834).

Basis and rate: The Sec. 183 tax on issued capital stock and Sec. 184 tax on gross earnings are determined as follows:

Capital stock tax: The franchise tax on capital stock is imposed at the greater of (a) 1.5 mills per dollar of the net value (not less than $5 per share) of issued capital stock allocated to New York, or (b) if dividends of 6% or more are paid, 0.375 of one mill for each 1% of dividends paid, to be computed upon the par value of the capital stock, or (c) $75. Special rules apply to stock without par value and to corporations having vessels engaged in foreign commerce. For tax years beginning after 2001, an exclusion from (b) applies to telephone companies that are subject to the gross earnings tax and that have no more than one million access lines in New York. (Sec. 183.3, Tax Law)

Gross earnings tax: The additional tax on intrastate gross earnings is imposed at the rate of 0.375% on gross earnings from all sources within New York. Unlike the Sec. 183 tax, there is no minimum tax. (Sec. 184.1, Tax Law)

Subject to certain limitations, railroads whose property is leased to other railroads will be taxed at the rate of $4^1/2$% on dividends paid during the calendar year that exceed 4% of the amount of capital stock. (Sec. 184.3, Tax Law)

The gross earnings tax on telecommunication providers is limited to entities formed for or principally involved in the conduct of a local telephone business; these companies must exclude from earnings 30% of separately charged inter-LATA, interstate or international telecommunication service derived from sales for ultimate consumption of telecommunication service to its customers. (Sec. 184.1, Tax Law)

Metropolitan Commuter Transportation District surcharge: Similar to corporation franchise (income) provisions (¶ 905).

For purposes of calculating the surcharge, the tax imposed under Sec. 184 is deemed to be imposed at a rate of 0.75% except that for eligible corporations, joint stock companies or associations that elect to be subject to the provisions of Sec. 183, the Sec. 184 tax is deemed to have been imposed at a rate of 0.6%.

Credits: The following credits are allowed:

Foreign corporation annual maintenance fees: Foreign transportation and transmission companies were allowed a credit against Secs. 183 and 184 taxes for the amount of former annual maintenance fees paid for the calendar year (¶ 2714).

Special additional mortgage recording tax credit: Similar to corporation franchise (income) provisions (¶ 927). (Sec. 187, Tax Law)

Credit for employing disabled persons: Similar to corporation franchise (income) tax provisions (¶ 928). However, in applying the credit to the transportation and transmission companies taxes, it must first be applied to the Sec. 183 franchise tax and then any excess may be applied against the Sec. 184 additional franchise tax. (Sec. 187-a, Tax Law)

Alternative fuels tax credit: Generally, this credit is similar to corporation franchise (income) tax provisions (¶ 935). (Sec. 187-b, Tax Law)

Long-term care insurance: A credit is allowed for 20% of the long-term care insurance premiums paid during the taxable year. See the discussion at ¶ 939. (Sec. 190, Tax Law)

Green buildings: A credit is available to enhance the supply of environmentally sound buildings in New York. The credit includes six components, which are based on the capitalized costs (excluding land costs) of constructing green buildings, rehabilitating buildings to become green buildings, and purchasing and installing fuel cells, photovoltaic modules, and environmentally sensitive non-ozone depleting refrigerants. See the discussion at ¶ 942. (Sec. 187-d, Tax Law)

Brownfield credits: Three refundable brownfield credits are available. The credits are designated the brownfield redevelopment tax credit, credit for remediated brownfields, and environmental remediation insurance credit. The credits are available to taxpayers that own or develop a qualified site for which a certificate of completion has been issued to the taxpayer by the Commissioner of Environmental Conservation. For details of the credits, see ¶ 943.

Credit for security training: For qualified building owners, a security training tax credit is allowed. (Secs. 26, 187-n, Tax Law) The credit amount equals the sum of the number of qualified security officers providing protection to buildings owned by the

¶2708

taxpayer, multiplied by $3,000. Any credit amount not deductible in a taxable year will be treated as an overpayment of tax to be credited or refunded without interest.

Returns and payment of tax: Transportation and transmission companies must file written reports with the Commissioner of Taxation and Finance on or before March 15 of each year, stating the company's condition at the close of the preceding year. Payment of tax accompanies the filing of the return.

Estimated tax: Transportation and transmission companies subject to the additional tax on gross earnings (Sec. 184, Tax Law) must file declarations of estimated tax if their estimated tax for the current year can reasonably be expected to exceed $1,000. See discussion at ¶1405.

• *Water, gas, steam, and electric companies*

Corporations, joint stock companies, associations, and publicly traded partnerships taxable as corporations that are formed for, or principally engaged in, the business of supplying electricity or water, steam, or gas (when delivered through mains or pipes) were subject to an annual franchise tax (Sec. 186 tax) that was repealed for taxable years ending after January 1, 2000. The Metropolitan Commuter Transportation District Surcharge imposed by Sec. 186-b, Tax Law, was also repealed. Taxpayers subject to the repealed tax are now generally subject to the corporation franchise (income) tax (Article 9-A, Tax Law, beginning at Chapter 9). For transitional provisions, see CCH NEW YORK TAX REPORTS, ¶80-101. In some unusual cases, a corporation that is a subsidiary of a banking corporation will be subject to the Article 32 franchise tax on banking corporations, rather than Article 9-A.

Certain independent power producers subject to Sec. 186, but not Sec. 186-a, have the option of remaining subject to Sec. 186 until existing output contracts are scheduled to expire.

• *Tax on furnishing of utility services*

Utilities doing business within New York that are subject to the jurisdiction of the Department of Public Service ("first class utilities"), and utilities *not* subject to the jurisdiction of the Department of Public Service that sell gas, electricity, steam, water, or refrigeration, delivered through mains, pipes, or wires, or furnish gas, electric, steam, water, or refrigerator service, by means of mains, pipes, or wires ("second class utilities"), are subject to an additional annual franchise tax. (Sec. 186-a tax)

Exclusion: An exclusion from gross income applies to receipts from the transportation, transmission, or distribution of gas or electricity (*i.e.,* noncommodity charges) to nonresidential customers. (Sec. 186-a.2(c)(1), Tax Law).

Practitioner Comment: Special Exceptions to Gross Receipts Tax

Section 186-a.2(c) of the Tax Law imposes a gross receipts tax on a utility's receipts from services as well as from the "profits from any transaction . . . within New York State whatsoever." However, when applying this language to sales of real property, other than inventory, profit is measured by reducing the selling price of the realty by its original cost, without any deduction attributable to depreciation. Expenses of the sale are also deductible. Additionally, if the utility is divesting itself of substantial assets, its "profit" can be computed on an aggregate basis, not on the sale of each individual asset (*Niagara Mohawk Power Corp.,* TSB-A-99(9)C, CCH NEW YORK TAX REPORTS, ¶403-314).

Mark S. Klein, Esq., Hodgson Russ LLP

Exemptions: The following utilities are exempt from tax:

— first class utilities with gross income for the calendar year of $500 or less; (Sec. 186-a.1, Tax Law)

— second class utilities with gross operating income for the calendar year of $500 or less; (Sec. § 186-a.1, Tax Law)

¶2708

— sleeping and parlor railroad car companies and railroads (other than street surface, rapid transit, subway and elevated railroads); (Sec. 186-a.2(a), Tax Law)

— omnibus carriers operating on New York public highways and omni-buses having a seating capacity of more than seven persons; (Sec. 186-a.2(a), Tax Law)

— the State of New York, its municipalities, political and civil subdivisions of the state or municipality, and public districts (provided that, with respect to gas, electricity, and gas or electric service—including the sale of the transporta-tion, transmission, or distribution of gas or electricity—such municipalities, subdivisions, and public districts will fall under this exclusion if they own and operate facilities that are used to generate or distribute electricity or to distribute gas, and they distribute and sell such gas or electricity solely at retail and solely within their respective jurisdiction; in addition, with respect to the sale of electricity or the transportation, transmission, or distribution of electricity, a municipality will fall under the exclusion if it sells electricity at retail and all such electricity (excluding temporary substitution power during outages or periods of reduced output) has been generated solely by, and purchased solely from, the state or a public authority of the state); (Sec. 186-a.2(b), Tax Law)

— corporations and associations that are organized and operated exclu-sively for religious, charitable or educational purposes, no part of the net cearnings of which inures to the benefit of any private shareholder or individual, and that are described under Sec. 1116(a)(4), Tax Law, where such organization resells such gas or electricity, or gas or electric service, as landlord to its tenants in buildings owned by the organization; NY Tax Law § 186-a.2(b)

— corporations organized and operated exclusively for the purpose of leas-ing from a city a water-works system designed to supply water at cost to users for discharge, either before or after industrial use, into a river within the city in order to improve the flow and condition of the river and thereby to provide a means to relieve the river from pollution; (Sec. 186-a.2(b), Tax Law) and

— limited dividend housing corporations organized under the State Hous-ing Law.

Cooperative utility corporations: Certain cooperative utility corporations that are organized without capital stock and qualify for federal tax exemption pursuant to IRC Sec. 501(c)(12) may, in lieu of Sec. 186-a tax, pay an annual $10 fee to the Commissioner of Taxation and Finance.

Basis and rate: Tax is imposed at the rate of 2.5% on the gross income of telecommunication service providers subject to the supervision of the Department of Public Service. (Sec. 186-e, Tax Law)

Additionally, an excise tax is imposed on the sale of mobile telecommunications services at the rate of 2.9% of gross receipts from any mobile telecommunications service provided by a home service provider where the mobile telecommunications customer's place of primary use is within New York State. (Sec. 186-e(2)(a)(2), Tax Law)

For other utilities subject to the supervision of the Department of Public Service, the gross income tax base for such utilities is broken into two parts, and the 2.5% rate is reduced, as follows: (1) on the portion of gross income derived from the transporta-tion, transmission, or distribution of gas or electricity by conduits, mains, pipes, wires, lines, or similar means, the rate was reduced to 2% on January 1, 2005; (2) on other gross income (*i.e.,* charges for the commodity of gas or electricity), the rate was reduced to 0% beginning January 1, 2005. (Sec. 186-a.1, Tax Law)

For other utilities not subject to the supervision of the Department of Public Service, the tax, which was imposed on gross operating income, was phased out beginning January 1, 2005. (Sec. 186-a.1, Tax Law)

For all of the above, no tax is imposed if gross income or gross operating income for the year is $500 or less.

Financial resource asset corporations: Electric corporations that, on or before July 16, 1989, were permitted by the Public Service Commission to establish financial resource assets for rate-making purposes are allowed a deduction against gross income. The deduction is equal to the amount by which the portion of gross income received in any year after 1991 exceeds the portion of gross income received in the 12-month period immediately preceding the month in which the financial resource asset is established. To be eligible for the deduction, electric corporations must, at the time of filing the franchise tax return, file a certificate from the Department of Public Service verifying that the calculation of the tax adjustment complies with these provisions. This adjustment is not applicable in calculating any other provision of law. The Metropolitan Commuter Transportation District Surcharge and temporary tax surcharge must be calculated and paid as if this adjustment were not allowed. (Sec. 186-a.2-a, Tax Law)

Metropolitan Commuter Transportation District surcharge: For all or parts of taxable years ending before December 31, 2018, the surcharge is imposed at the rate of 17% of the taxpayer's Sec. 186-a tax liability, after the deduction of credits otherwise allowable, except any utility credit provided by Article 13-A, Tax Law.

For telecommunications providers taxable under Sec. 186-a(1)(a), Tax Law, the surcharge is calculated as if the tax imposed under Sec. 186-a were imposed at a rate of 3.5%. The tax is applied only to that portion of the taxpayer's Sec. 186-a tax liability that is attributable to the taxpayer's gross income or gross operating income attributable to the taxpayer's business activity carried on within the MCTD.

On and after May 1, 2015, an additional surcharge on the gross receipts from mobile telecommunication services relating to the MCTD is imposed at the rate of 0.721% on utilities doing business in the MCTD (Sec. 186-c, Tax Law).

Credits: The following credits are allowed:

Foreign corporation annual maintenance fees: Foreign transportation and transmission companies were allowed a credit against Sec. 186-a, Tax Law, tax for the amount of the former annual maintenance fees paid for the calendar year (¶2714).

Special additional mortgage recording tax credit: Utilities are *not* allowed a credit against Sec. 186-a, Tax Law, tax for special additional mortgage recording taxes paid by the utility.

Transportation improvements: A refundable credit is provided to taxpayers who make a significant contribution to New York for the construction of certain transportation improvement projects and who also increase employment by more than 1,000 jobs in New York. See the discussion at ¶940.

Returns and payment of tax: Written reports must be filed with the Commissioner of Taxation and Finance on or before March 15 of each year, stating the company's condition at the close of the preceding year. Payment of tax accompanies the filing of the return.

Estimated tax: Utilities must file declarations of estimated tax if their estimated tax for the current year can reasonably be expected to exceed $1,000. See discussion at ¶1405.

¶2708

• *Telecommunication services providers*

Telecommunication services providers are subject to an annual excise tax on gross receipts from sales of telecommunication services (Sec. 186-e, Tax Law).

The term "telecommunication services" means telephony or telegraphy, or telephone or telegraph service. The term includes any transmission of voice, image, data, information, and paging through the use of wire, cable, fiber-optic, laser, microwave, radio wave, satellite, or similar media or any combination thereof. The term also includes services that are ancillary to the provision of telephone service, plus any equipment and services provided therewith.

Wallpaper, games, music, and sounds sold by a mobile telecommunications provider are not subject to the tax on the furnishing of utilities under Sec. 186-a, Tax Law, and the telecommunications excise tax under Sec. 186-e, Tax Law (TSB-A-08(8)C and TSB-A-08(63)S, November 24, 2008, CCH NEW YORK TAX REPORTS, ¶ 406-278).

The term does not include:

— separately stated charges for any service that alters the substantive content of the message received by the recipient from that sent; or

— cable television services. (Sec. 186-e.1(g), Tax Law)

Kiosk sales: Because a kiosk seller is not the provider of any of the telecommunication services available at the kiosks, it is not liable for the telecommunications excise tax. (*TSB-A-16(2)C, (15)S*, New York Commissioner of Taxation and Finance, April 25, 2016, CCH NEW YORK TAX REPORTS, ¶ 408-763)

CCH Advisory: Voice over Internet; Internet Access

The New York Department of Taxation and Finance has issued a guidance document explaining the telecommunications excise tax treatment of services using voice over Internet protocol (VoIP) and wireless VoIP. Gross receipts from VoIP or wireless VoIP telecommunication services are subject to the tax if the calls are intrastate or the calls originate or terminate in New York and are charged to a service address in New York. In addition, VoIP and wireless VoIP services may be subject to the tax as a mobile telecommunications service, if they fall within the applicable definition. The tax would apply if such service was provided by a home service provider and the customer's place of primary use was in New York (NYT-G-07(3)C, New York Commissioner of Taxation and Finance, June 21, 2007, CCH NEW YORK TAX REPORTS, ¶ 405-769).

Contrary to statements in TSB-M-08(4)C and TSB-M-08(2)S, May 2, 2008, CCH NEW YORK TAX REPORTS, ¶ 406-042, it is now the Department's view that the appropriate interpretation of the Internet Tax Freedom Act amendments of 2005 is that the telecommunications excise tax imposed by Tax Law Sec. 186-e on the telecommunications purchased, used, or sold by ISPs to provide Internet access was preempted by federal law on and after November 1, 2005. The Department believes this interpretation is more consistent with the intent of Congress. Accordingly, those telecommunications services were no longer subject to the excise tax effective November 1, 2005 (*TSB-M-08(4.1)C* and *TSB-M-08(2.1)S*, August 29, 2008; see also *TSB-A-09(15)C*, September 1, 2009, CCH NEW YORK TAX REPORTS, ¶ 406-530).

Sourcing: New York law conforms to the provisions of the federal Mobile Telecommunications Sourcing Act (P.L. 106-252). Wireless telecommunications services are sourced to the customer's "primary place of use," which is the residential or primary business address of the customer and which must be located in the service provider's licensed service area. The jurisdiction in which the primary place of use is located is the only jurisdiction that may tax the communications services, regardless of the customer's location when an actual call is placed or received (See *TSB-M-02(4)C* and *TSB-M-02(6)S*, New York Department of Taxation and Finance, July 30, 2002, CCH NEW YORK TAX REPORTS, ¶ 300-367).

Exclusions: The following sales of telecommunication services are excluded from tax:

— sales of telecommunication services to a telecommunication services provider when the services are purchased by the provider for resale as telecommunication services to its purchasers (*TSB-M-09(2)C*, January 12, 2009, CCH New York Tax Reports, ¶ 406-285); and

— sales of telecommunication services to air carriers solely for the purpose of air safety and navigation are excluded from the tax, provided (a) the service is provided by an organization, at least 90% of which (or, if a corporation, 90% of the voting stock of which) is owned, directly or indirectly, by air carriers, and (b) the organization's principal function is to fulfill the requirements of the Federal Aviation Administration or the International Civil Aviation Organization (or successors thereto), relating to the existence of a communication system between aircraft and dispatcher, aircraft and air traffic control or ground station and ground station (or any combination of the foregoing) for the purposes of air safety and navigation.

In addition, the tax does not apply to sales of telecommunication services under circumstances that would preclude the application of the tax by reason of the U.S. Constitution or other federal law. (Sec. 186-e.2(b), (c), Tax Law)

Internet access: Internet access is not considered a telecommunication service and, consequently, is not subject to the telecommunication excise tax. Additionally, the act of providing an Internet access service is not considered the carrying on of a telephone, local telephone, telegraph or transmission business for purposes of the other taxes imposed on public utilities. (Sec. 179, Tax Law)

The term "Internet access" refers to a connection to the Internet, usually by means of a temporary or dedicated telephone line. It includes items such as communications software, navigation software, an e-mail address, e-mail software, website space, and similar website services. (Secs. 179, 1115(v) Tax Law). In order to qualify for this exemption, the Internet access must "entail routing Internet traffic by means of accepted Internet protocols" which are discussed in *TSB-M-97(1.1)C*, issued November 15, 1999. Although access charges for the Internet qualify for the exemption, telephone calls to an Internet service provider to initiate access to the Internet are not exempt. (Sec. 179, Tax Law)

Basis and rate: The tax is imposed at the rate of 2.5% of gross receipts from (Sec. 186-e.2, Tax Law):

— any intrastate telecommunication services;

— any interstate and international telecommunication services (other than interstate and international private telecommunication services and mobile telecommunications taxable as noted below) that originate or terminate in New York and are charged to a New York State service address (regardless of where the amounts charged for the services are billed or ultimately paid);

— interstate and international private telecommunication services. The gross receipts of an interstate or international private telecommunication services provider, if not separately ascertainable for each use of the service, are subject to apportionment; and

The rate on the sale of mobile telecommunication services by a home service provider is 2.9% of gross receipts received on or after May 1, 2015, for mobile telecommunications services provided on or after that date to a customer whose place of primary use is within New York. Sales of telecommunication services other than sales of mobile telecommunication services continue to be taxed at the 2.5% rate. Similarly, the MTA surcharge rate imposed on the sale of mobile telecommunication services within the Metropolitan Commuter Transportation District (MCTD) is 0.721% (previously, 0.595%). (*TSB-M-15(5)C*, New York Department of Taxation and Finance, July 24, 2015, CCH New York Tax Reports, ¶ 408-484).

¶2708

Wireless communications service surcharge: A state surcharge is imposed on wireless communications service at the rate of $1.20 per month. In addition, certain counties are authorized to impose a charge of up to 30¢ per month on each wireless communications device. New York City has enacted the surcharge at the rate of 30¢ per month.

Metropolitan Commuter Transportation District surcharge: Similar to corporation franchise (income) provisions (¶ 905).

Credits: The following credits are allowed (Sec. 186-e.4, Tax Law):

Resold telecommunication services: A credit, equal to the amount of tax imposed on telecommunication services, is allowed to purchasers that are providers of telecommunication services when (1) the provider is not an interexchange or local carrier, and (2) the telecommunication services purchased are later resold by the purchaser as telecommunication services. To accomplish this result, the credit is determined by computing the tax on the resold service so that the tax is imposed on the difference between the amount of the charge made by the provider to the purchaser and the amount of the charge made by the purchaser for the resold service.

Like taxes paid to other jurisdictions: A credit is allowed to interstate or international telecommunication services for like taxes imposed by other states, countries or jurisdictions on sales of telecommunication services. The amount of the credit is be the amount of tax lawfully due and paid to the other state. The total credit may not exceed the tax due to New York.

Special additional mortgage recording taxes: A telecommunication services provider is *not* allowed a credit against Sec. 186-e tax for special additional mortgage recording taxes paid by the provider.

Foreign corporation annual maintenance fees: Foreign telecommunication services providers were allowed a credit against Sec. 186-e tax for the amount of the former annual maintenance fees paid for the calendar year (¶ 2714).

Returns and payment of tax: Written reports must be filed with the Commissioner of Taxation and Finance on or before March 15 of each year, stating the company's condition at the close of the preceding year. Payment of tax accompanies the filing of the return. (Sec. 186-e.6, Tax Law)

Estimated tax: Telecommunication services providers must file declarations of estimated tax is their estimated tax for the current year can reasonably be expected to exceed $1,000. See discussion at ¶ 1405.

¶2709 Motor Fuels Tax

Law: Secs. 282—289-f, 301-c, Tax Law (CCH NEW YORK TAX REPORTS, ¶ 40-001 *et seq.*).

Forms: FT-945/1045, Report of Sales Tax Prepayment On Motor Fuel/Diesel Motor Fuel; PT-100, Petroleum Business Tax Return; PT-101, Tax on Motor Fuels (Includes Aviation Gasoline); PT-102, Tax on Diesel Motor Fuels; PT-103, Tax on Residual Petroleum Product Businesses; PT-104, Tax on Kero-Jet Fuel; PT-106, Retailers of Heating Oil Only.

A tax is imposed upon motor fuel imported into the state for use, distribution, storage, or sale in the state, or manufactured in the state. A separate tax is imposed on the first sale or use of diesel motor fuel. "Motor fuel" means gasoline, benzol, reformulated blend stock for oxygenate blending, conventional blend stock for oxygenate blending, E85, fuel grade ethanol that meets the ASTM International active standards specifications D4806 or D4814 or other product that is suitable for use in operation of a motor vehicle engine, but if kerosene or crude oil is compounded or mixed with any other product or products, and the resulting compound or mixture is suitable for use in the operation of any such motor vehicle engine (Sec. 282(2), Tax Law). "Diesel motor fuel" means No. 1 Diesel fuel, No. 2 Diesel fuel, biodiesel, kerosene, fuel oil or other middle distillate and also motor fuel suitable for use in the operation of an engine of the diesel type (Sec. 282(14), Tax Law). Any product specifically designated as "No. 4 Diesel fuel" that is not suitable as a fuel used in the operation of a motor vehicle engine is explicitly excluded from the definition of "diesel motor fuel." (Secs. 284.1, 282-a, 282-b, 282-c, 282(14), Tax Law)

For highway use and fuel use taxes imposed on carriers, see ¶2705.

Motor fuel distributors: Distributors or motor fuel are required to register with the Department and file motor fuel tax returns (Sec. 283, Tax Law).

Motor fuel wholesalers: Effective December 1, 2016, wholesalers of motor fuel are required to register with the Department and file motor fuel tax returns (Sec. 283-d, Tax Law). "Wholesaler of motor fuel" is defined as a person, firm, association or corporation who (Sec. 282(27), Tax Law):

(1) is not a distributor of motor fuel;

(2) makes a sale of motor fuel in New York other than a retail sale not in bulk; and

(3) makes any purchases of motor fuel for resale within specified regions.

Unregistered wholesalers are prohibited from making sales of motor fuel in New York other than a retail sale not in bulk (Sec. 283-d, Tax Law).

CCH Advisory: Diesel Motor Fuel Reclassified

Beginning September 1, 2011, the manner in which diesel motor fuel is classified was redefined for purposes of the diesel motor fuel excise tax (Article 12-A), petroleum business tax (Article 13-A), and sales tax (Article 28). The terms "enhanced diesel motor fuel" and "unenhanced diesel motor fuel" are obsolete. Accordingly, it is no longer necessary to determine if fuel is labeled as diesel fuel, No. 1 diesel fuel, No. 2 diesel fuel, or similar designation, or if it is a blended product that it will be used as diesel fuel in a motor vehicle. Also, the fuel's sulfur content is irrelevant to determination of its taxability. Instead, based on the new definitions, the taxation of diesel motor fuel depends on whether it is classified as highway diesel motor fuel or non- highway diesel motor fuel. (*TSB-M-11(6)M, TSB-M-11(11)S,* New York Department of Taxation and Finance, July 29, 2011, CCH New York Tax Reports, ¶407-325)

"Highway diesel motor fuel" is any diesel motor fuel that is not non-highway diesel motor fuel (Sec. 282(16-a), Tax Law). "Non-highway diesel motor fuel" is any diesel motor fuel designated for use other than on a public highway (except for the use of the public highway by farmers to reach adjacent farmlands), and is dyed diesel motor fuel (Sec. 282(16), Tax Law).

Highway diesel motor fuel is subject to diesel motor fuel excise tax, petroleum business tax, and prepaid sales tax when it is first sold in New York State. When the fuel is designated for off-highway use and is dyed for federal tax purposes at the terminal, it is considered non-highway diesel motor fuel. Non-highway diesel motor fuel is exempt from the diesel motor fuel excise tax and the prepaid sales tax, and either exempt or partially exempt from the petroleum business tax. These exemptions or partial exemptions apply as long as the fuel is not used on New York public highways (except by farmers to reach adjacent farmlands), or delivered to a filling station or into a tank equipped with a nozzle capable of fueling a motor vehicle (except for delivery at a farm site). (Sec. 282-a, Tax Law)

Petroleum business tax definitions: "Commercial gallonage" is gallonage that (Sec. 300(k), Tax Law):

is non-highway diesel motor fuel or residual petroleum product;

is included in the full measure of the non-highway diesel motor fuel component or the residual petroleum product component of the petroleum business tax;

does not (and will not) qualify (A) for the utility credit or reimbursement, (B) as manufacturing gallonage, (C) for the not-for-profit organization exemption, or (D) for the heating exemption or reimbursement; and

will not be used (has not been used) in the fuel tank connecting with the engine of a vessel.

"Manufacturing gallonage" is non-highway diesel motor fuel or residual petroleum product used and consumed directly and exclusively in the production of tangible personal property for sale by manufacturing, processing, or assembly, but only if (Sec. 300(m), Tax Law):

all the fuel or product is delivered on the manufacturing site, or

the purchaser causes the fuel or product to be delivered to its manufacturing site.

Manufacturing gallonage may not be consumed on the public highways of New York, or delivered to a filling station or into a tank equipped with a nozzle capable of fueling a motor vehicle.

"Railroad diesel" is non-highway diesel motor fuel for use and consumption directly and exclusively for operating a locomotive or self-propelled vehicle run only on rails or tracks, but only if either (Sec. 300(l), Tax Law):

all the fuel is delivered into a storage facility which is not equipped with a nozzle capable of fueling a motor vehicle, and the facility is used only to fuel locomotives or self-propelled vehicles, or

all the fuel is delivered directly into fuel tanks of locomotives or self-propelled vehicles.

Sales tax definition: "Petroleum products" are motor fuel or diesel motor fuel, not including kerosene or propane used for residential purposes. This term replaces the term "automotive fuel" for sales tax purposes only.

Highway use tax and fuel use tax definition: "Automotive fuel" is both diesel motor fuel and motor fuel. This term has not changed and still applies for purposes of the highway use tax and fuel use tax/International Fuel Tax Agreement (IFTA).

Tax rates: The current tax rates remain in effect. See *Publication 908, Fuel Tax Rates,*(¶2716) for the current rate structure using the new terminology. The annual petroleum business tax rates will continue to be indexed and adjusted effective January 1 for monthly filers and March 1 for quarterly filers.

• *Exemptions*

The following are exempt from tax:

Alternative fuels: Sales of E85 fuel are exempt from motor fuel tax and petroleum business tax provided the E85 is delivered to and placed in a storage tank of a filling station to be dispensed directly into a motor vehicle for use in the operation of the motor vehicle (Secs. 289-c(1-a)(d), 301-b(6), Tax Law). The retailer may exclude the tax from the selling price. When E85 is not delivered to and placed in a storage tank of a filling station to be dispensed directly into a motor vehicle, the seller must include the applicable taxes and provide the purchaser with a properly completed Form FT-935, Certification of Taxes Paid on Motor Fuel, or an invoice showing that the taxes have been included. Certification is not required for a sale at retail.

In addition, sales of B20 fuel, or diesel motor fuel mixed with 20% biodiesel, are partially exempt from motor fuel tax and petroleum business tax (Secs. 289-c(1-a)(d), 301-b(7), Tax Law). The exemption is equal to 20% of the applicable taxes. Note, however, that there is no exemption from the prepaid sales tax for B20 fuel. The prepaid sales tax for B20 fuel must be computed at the full amount and may not be reduced by 20%; see *TSB-M-16(3)M, TSB-M-16(4)S*, New York Department of Taxation and Finance, July 22, 2016, **https://www.tax.ny.gov/pdf/memos/multitax/ m16_3m_4s.pdf.**

Sales of CNG or hydrogen for operation of a motor vehicle are also exempt from motor fuel tax and petroleum business tax (Secs. 289-c.1-a. (d), 301-b(8), Tax Law). This information should be reported on Form PT-101, Tax on Motor Fuels.

The above exemptions are repealed after August 31, 2021. Sales and use tax exemptions for alternative fuels are discussed at ¶2106. For additional details on alternative fuel exemptions, see *TSB-M-0(2)M,* New York Department of Taxation and Finance, August 11, 2006, CCH NEW YORK TAX REPORTS, ¶300-522, and *TSB-M-11(5)M, TSB-M-11(8)S,* New York Department of Taxation and Finance, June 10, 2011, CCH NEW YORK TAX REPORTS, ¶407-284.

Kerosene and crude oil: Kerosene and crude oil are not subject to motor fuel tax except when compounded into a mixture suitable for use as a motor fuel. However, kerosene is included within the definition of "diesel motor fuel" and, therefore, it is subject to diesel motor fuel tax (Sec. 282.2, Tax Law).

All of the exemptions and provisions that apply to unenhanced [non-highway] diesel motor fuel are allowed for dyed ultra-low-sulfur kerosene for the purposes of the motor fuel, petroleum business, and sales taxes. However, the exemption is not allowed if the dyed ultra-low-sulfur kerosene is delivered to a filling station or into a storage tank equipped with a nozzle or similar apparatus capable of dispensing the fuel into the tank of a motor vehicle. (*TSB-M-11(2)M, TSB-M-11(2)S,* New York Department of Taxation and Finance, March 11, 2011, CCH NEW YORK TAX REPORTS, ¶407-157)

Dyed or undyed ultra-low-sulfur kerosene is subject to tax as enhanced [highway] diesel motor fuel if certain conditions are met. Diesel motor fuel, other than kerosene, meeting the 15-parts-per-million (maximum) sulfur standard is considered enhanced [highway] diesel motor fuel regardless of its designation, and, therefore, all of the provisions related to enhanced diesel motor fuel apply. (*TSB-M-11(2)M, TSB-M-11(2)S,* New York Department of Taxation and Finance, March 11, 2011, CCH NEW YORK TAX REPORTS, ¶407-157)

Fuel not used in motor vehicles: Motor fuel or diesel motor fuel used to propel vehicles that do not fall within the definition of "motor vehicles" are exempt from tax. This includes the following: boats (other than pleasure boats); road building machinery; power shovels; tractor cranes; tractors used exclusively for agricultural purposes; and vehicles operated on rails or tracks, or used in any other manner except in the operation of motor vehicles upon or over the highways of the state. (Sec. 282(3), Tax Law; 20 NYCRR § 415.1(b); § 415.3(a))

CCH Advisory: Fuel Used in Fishing Boats

Some owners of pleasure boats have acquired commercial fishing licenses in an attempt to escape motor fuel, petroleum business, and/or sales and use taxes on fuel. However, the fact that a boat is licensed for commercial fishing does not necessarily entitle it to purchase tax-exempt fuel. The exemption applies only if the boat is used "directly and predominately (more than 50%) in the harvesting of fish for sale." The Department of Taxation and Finance will make an individual determination of fact in such cases (*Montauk Marine Basin* (Advisory Opinion), TSB-A-95(3)M, October 30, 1995; CCH NEW YORK TAX REPORTS, ¶402-362).

Fuels in tanks of vehicles entering the state: Motor fuel and diesel motor fuel brought into the state in the fuel tank of a motor vehicle and used solely for the vehicle's own propulsion are exempt from tax. (Sec. 282.1, Tax Law)

Interdistributor sales: Effective August 1, 2013, tax does not apply when highway diesel motor fuel is either (1) being delivered by pipeline, railcar, barge, tanker, or other vessel to a terminal, the operator of which is registered under Sec. 283-b, Tax Law, or (2) within a terminal where it has been so delivered (Sec. 282(a)(3)(b), Tax

¶2709

Law; *TSB-M-13(7)M, TSB-M-13(5)S,* July 11, 2013, CCH NEW YORK TAX REPORTS, ¶407-877). The exemption does not apply to any highway diesel motor fuel if it is removed from a terminal, other than by pipeline, barge, tanker, or vessel.

Sales to federal, state, and local government: Sales to the federal government and to the state of New York or its municipalities are exempt from tax.

Sales of fuel for immediate export: Sales of motor fuel for export to dealers or distributors licensed in another state are not taxable provided the vendor complies with regulations of the Commissioner relating to such sales. (Sec. 289-c, Tax Law)

Sales to the United Nations: The United Nations, as a retail purchaser of motor fuel, is exempt from motor fuels tax, provided that the fuel is acquired by the United Nations for its official use.

Diplomatic missions and diplomatic personnel: In certain instances, purchases of motor fuel by diplomatic missions and diplomatic personnel are exempt from motor fuels tax.

Qualified hospitals: Certain hospitals that hold current operating certificates from the New York Department of Health or the New York Department of Mental Hygiene and qualify as tax-exempt organizations may (1) import or cause motor fuel to be imported into New York State, (2) produce, refine, manufacture or compound motor fuel in New York State, or (3) purchase motor fuel in New York State, for their own use or consumption without payment of, or in the case of a purchase of such fuel, without having had passed through to them, motor fuel tax. In order to qualify as an exempt organization for sales and use tax purposes, the hospital must generally be organized and operated exclusively for religious, charitable, scientific, testing for public safety, literary or educational purposes, or to foster national or international amateur sports competition or for the prevention of cruelty to children. In addition, no part of a qualified hospital's net earnings may be used to benefit any private shareholder or individual.

Fuel sold for immediate export: Motor fuel upon which the seller has not passed through the motor fuel tax is exempt when it is acquired in the state by a duly registered or licensed distributor of, or dealer in, motor fuel in another state or province of a foreign country for immediate export to an identified facility in that state or province for the purpose of selling such motor fuel.

Sales to volunteer fire departments, Voluntary Ambulance Services and Volunteer Rescue Squads: Motor fuel and diesel motor fuel tax paid by a volunteer fire department or company, volunteer rescue squad supported by public funds, or volunteer ambulance service is refundable. (Sec. 301-c(p), Tax Law; *TSB-M-13(3)M,* May 17, 2013, CCH NEW YORK TAX REPORTS, ¶407-836)

Sales between registered distributors: Sales of motor fuel to a registered or licensed distributor or dealer of motor fuel in another state or in a province of a foreign country are exempt from tax provided that the fuel is exported immediately to an identified location in that state or province for purposes of selling it.

Aviation gasoline sold to "retail sellers of aviation gasoline": A registered motor fuel distributor who sells aviation gasoline to a fixed base operator registered as a "retail seller of aviation gasoline" may exclude motor fuel tax or taxes from the selling price of aviation gasoline (a) delivered to the fixed base operator's premises and (b) placed in a storage facility used exclusively for the purpose of fueling airplanes. Any person registered as both a motor fuel distributor and as a "retail seller of aviation gasoline" may exclude motor fuel taxes from the selling price on retail sales of aviation gasoline.

Special provisions—Diesel motor fuel: The following are exempt from the excise tax on diesel motor fuel (Sec. 282-a, Tax Law):

— sale or use of untaxed diesel fuel to or by certain exempt organizations when used by the organization for its own use or consumption;

— consumer sale or use of certain previously untaxed diesel fuel that is not enhanced and that is used exclusively for heating purposes or for use or consumption directly and exclusively in the production of tangible personal property, gas, electricity, refrigeration or steam for sale, but only if such fuel is consumed other than on the highways of New York;

— sale of previously untaxed unenhanced [non-highway] diesel fuel to a registered distributor of diesel motor fuel, other than retail sales to registered distributors of diesel motor fuel or sales that involve a delivery at a filling station or into a repository equipped to dispense fuel into the tank of a motor vehicle. Diesel fuel designated as 500 ppm sulfur NRLM (non-road, locomotive, marine) diesel fuel or similar designations (*e.g.*, 500 ppm dyed low sulfur nonroad diesel fuel) is unenhanced [non-highway] diesel motor fuel for petroleum business, motor fuel, and sales tax purposes. Special provisions apply, as long as such fuel is not delivered to a filling station or into a storage tank or other repository equipped with a nozzle or similar apparatus capable of dispensing the fuel into the tank of a motor vehicle (TSB-M-07(2)M, TSB-M-07(4)S, May 31, 2007, CCH NEW YORK TAX REPORTS, ¶405-742);

— sale or use of enhanced [highway] diesel fuel to or by a consumer exclusively for certain heating purposes only if delivered into a storage tank not equipped with a hose or other apparatus by which the fuel can be dispensed into the fuel tank of a motor vehicle and if the storage tank is attached to a heating unit burning such fuel subject to certification requirements pertaining to gallonage;

— sale or use consisting of no more than 4,500 gallons of diesel motor fuel in a 30-day period to or by a consumer for use or consumption directly and exclusively in the production for sale of tangible personal property by farming if all of the fuel is delivered on the farm site and is consumed other than on the highways of New York (except for use of the highway to adjacent farmlands);

— sale to the consumer consisting of not more than 20 gallons of water-white kerosene to be used and consumed exclusively for heating purposes;

— sale to or delivery at a filling station or other retail vendor of water-white kerosene if the retail vendor or filling station sells only water-white kerosene for heating purposes in containers of not more than 20 gallons; and

— sale of aviation gasoline to an airline for use in its airplanes or use of aviation gasoline by an airline in its airplanes. NY Tax Law § 282-a.3;

— sale of dyed enhanced [non-highway] diesel motor fuel by a distributor to another distributor that is primarily engaged in the retail heating oil business and that holds a direct pay permit.

CCH Advisory: Reservation Sales

Qualified Indians may purchase tax-exempt motor fuel for their own use on their own reservations. However, the exemption does not extend to purchases made by Indians off their reservations or on other reservations. Non-Indians may not purchase tax-exempt motor fuels. (Sec. 284-e, Tax Law)

• *Basis and rate of tax*

Effective September 1, 2011, the taxation of automotive fuels and petroleum products was amended to update the tax structure. The then-current tax rates were codified into statute as a starting point for indexing these rates, which are adjusted every year as of January 1 and published in the State Register (see *Publication 908* (¶2716)).

¶2709

The basic rates of tax are 8¢ per gallon of motor fuel, 10.2¢ per gallon of highway diesel motor fuel, and 9.3¢ per gallon of non-highway diesel motor fuel. The motor fuel tax is computed on the basis of the number of gallons of motor fuel imported into the state for use, distribution, storage or sale in the state or manufactured in the state by a registered distributor. The diesel motor fuel tax is computed based on the number of gallons sold in New York. (Secs. 284-284-c; 282-282-c, Tax Law)

Petroleum testing fee: A petroleum testing fee equal to $1/2$ of 1 mill (0.5) is imposed on each gallon of motor fuel imported, manufactured or sold in New York by a distributor. (Sec. 284-d, Tax Law)

• *Credits and refunds*

Refunds of motor fuel taxes are authorized as noted below. In lieu of a refund, a distributor may claim a credit on its monthly return.

Fuel used for tax-exempt purposes: Any person who buys motor fuel or diesel motor fuel on which tax has been paid, but uses the fuel for any purpose other than the operation of a motor vehicle on state highways or in pleasure or recreational motorboats, is entitled to a refund. A refund will not be granted, however, for tax paid on motor fuel or diesel motor fuel taken out of New York in the fuel tank of a motor vehicle for consumption outside the state. (Sec. 289-c, Tax Law)

Buses and taxis: The aggregate tax in excess of 4¢ per gallon paid on motor fuel or 6¢ per gallon paid on diesel motor fuel will be refunded to omnibus carriers and taxicab licensees upon application if such fuel is consumed by the operation of an omnibus or taxicab within the state. (Sec. 289-c.3, Tax Law)

A full refund of motor fuel or diesel motor fuel tax is allowed to any carrier operating an omnibus in local transit service pursuant to a certificate of convenience and necessity issued by the Commissioner of Transportation or the Interstate Commerce Commission or under a contract with New York City. (Sec. 289-c.3(d), Tax Law)

Nonpublic school operators: A nonpublic school operator is entitled to a refund of tax paid on motor fuel or diesel motor fuel if the fuel was consumed by the operator exclusively in education-related activities. (Sec. 289-c.3(e), Tax Law)

Voluntary ambulance services: Volunteer ambulance services, fire companies, fire departments, and rescue squads are entitled to a refund of tax paid on motor fuel and diesel motor fuel if the fuel was consumed in their owned and operated vehicles. (Sec. 301-c(p), Tax Law) A purchasing entity is eligible if it has paid the entire amount of tax and possesses documentary proof evidencing the absorption of the tax. (*TSB-M-13(3)M,* May 17, 2013, CCH NEW YORK TAX REPORTS, ¶ 407-836)

CCH Advisory: Government Credit Card Sales

Credit card companies and motor fuel or motor diesel fuel distributors that finance the purchase of such fuel by governmental entities using credit cards are allowed a credit or refund of New York motor fuel, petroleum business, and sales and use taxes on such purchases. According to the sponsor's memorandum, this provision is intended to conform to federal tax legislation that creates a system for credit card issuers and fuel distributors to receive refunds of the federal excise tax on fuel purchases by governmental entities using credit cards. Applicants must file Form FT-505.1, Government Entity Credit Card Refund or Credit Election. (Sec. 289-c(3)(h), Tax Law; TSB-M-08(12)S and TSB-M-08(9)M, November 5, 2008, CCH NEW YORK TAX REPORTS, ¶ 406-212)

• *Reports and payment*

Generally, reports are filed on a monthly basis with payment of the taxes accompanying the returns. The reports and payment are due not later than the 20th day of the month following the month for which the report is being made. (Sec. 287, Tax Law)

Direct payment permits: A registered distributor of diesel motor fuel may obtain a direct payment permit allowing the distributor to make tax-free purchases of dyed [non-highway] diesel motor fuel that is certified to be used solely as residential or commercial heating oil. (Sec. 283-d, Tax Law; TSB-M-06(5)M, TSB-M-06(13)S, November 10, 2006, CCH NEW YORK TAX REPORTS, ¶ 405-526) The holder of a direct pay permit must make payments of any motor fuel tax liability for such purchases directly to the Commissioner.

Electronic fund transfer payments: Taxpayers who are liable, on or after June 1 of any year, for more than $5 million of motor fuel taxes during the preceding one year period are required to make payment of tax by electronic funds transfer or certified check. (Sec. 10(b)(1)(C), Tax Law) For additional information, see ¶ 3602.

Payment by electronic funds transfer or certified check is due on or before the third business day following the 22nd day of each month. (Sec. 10(c), Tax Law)

Amount of payment: Taxpayers subject to electronic fund transfer and certified check requirements must pay $3/4$ of the total liability for motor fuel taxes payable by the taxpayer for the comparable month of the preceding year, *or* the taxpayer's total liability for such taxes during the period ending on the 22nd day of each month. (Sec. 10(c), Tax Law)

Refunds: The statute of limitations for applying for refunds, credits, or reimbursements of taxes on motor fue or diesel motor fuel and petroleum businesses is three years (Sec. 289-c, Tax Law).

Administration: The motor fuel tax and the tax on diesel motor fuel are administered by the Department of Taxation and Finance, W.A. Harriman State Campus, Albany, NY 12227.

¶2710 Mortgage Recording Taxes

Law: Secs. 250—267, Tax Law (CCH NEW YORK TAX REPORTS, ¶ 37-052).

Forms: MT-15, Mortgage Recording Tax Return.

Mortgage recording taxes are excise taxes imposed on the recording of mortgages on real property situated in New York. There are various taxes that may be imposed, including the following:

— the basic tax (imposed by Sec. 253(1), Tax Law);

— the additional tax (imposed by Sec. 253(2), Tax Law);

— the special additional tax (imposed by Sec. 253(1-a), Tax Law);

— the New York City tax (authorized by Sec. 253-a, Tax Law, and imposed by Sec. 11-2601, N.Y.C. Adm. Code) (¶ 3312);

— the city of Yonkers tax (authorized by Sec. 253-d, Tax Law, and imposed by Sec. 92-123, City of Yonkers Code);

— county taxes (see the county chart at ¶ 30); and

— the regional tax imposed in the Metropolitan Commuter Transportation District.

Unless expressly exempt from tax (see below), every mortgage involving real property situated, in whole or in part, in New York is subject to the basic tax and the special additional tax. Mortgages are also subject to the additional tax unless the imposition of that tax has been suspended by a local law, ordinance or resolution.

Mortgages involving real property located in whole or in part in New York City, city of Yonkers, or certain counties are subject to the respective local taxes.

• *Mortgages subject to tax*

The following mortgages on real property situated in New York and recorded on or after July 1, 1906, are subject to the recording tax: mortgages and deeds of trust imposing a lien on or affecting title to realty; executory contracts for sale of realty under which the purchaser has or is entitled to possession; contracts or agreements increasing mortgage indebtedness. (Sec. 250.2, Tax Law)

Exemptions: Every mortgage on real property situated in New York is subject to tax unless specifically exempted by statute or by operation of federal or state constitutional provision. Primary exemptions include the following:

— mortgages involving state or federal agencies (to the extent that such entities are exempt from taxation);

— mortgages on real property situated within New York that are transferred, assigned, or made to an agricultural credit association, or federal home loan bank;

— mortgages made pursuant to confirmed bankruptcy plans under Sec. 1129, Ch. XI, Bankruptcy Code;

— reverse mortgages recorded on or after December 2, 1993, that conform to the provisions of Sec. 280 or 280-a, Real Property Law;

— declarations or liens for common charges;

— mortgages executed by limited dividend housing companies created pursuant to Article 4, Private Housing Finance Law;

— mortgages of community senior citizen centers and service companies created pursuant to Article 7-A, Private Housing Finance Law;

— mortgages to secure the repayment of loans made pursuant to Article 8-B, Private Housing Finance Law;

— certain mortgages of redevelopment companies created pursuant to Article 5, Private Housing Finance Law;

— mortgages of a trust created pursuant to Article 20, Arts and Cultural Affairs Law;

— mortgages of community mental health services companies or mental retardation services companies created pursuant to Article 75, Mental Hygiene Law;

— mortgages given to or by Sec. 1411(f), Not-For-Profit Corporation Law, corporations;

— mortgages securing obligations issued under Section 6-a of the Banking Law (relating to obligations of certain persons 65 years of age or older that were incurred to satisfy real property indebtedness);

— mortgages executed by a fund formed for the purpose of insuring deposits and/or depositors created pursuant to Article 6-B, Banking Law;

— mortgages executed, given or made by a railroad redevelopment corporation during the first nine years of its existence;

— mortgages executed by voluntary nonprofit hospital corporations, voluntary fire companies, and voluntary ambulance services *(TSB-M-07(4)R, August 22, 2007, CCH NEW YORK TAX REPORTS, ¶405-831)*;

— mortgages of a nonprofit sponsor of a housing project under Article XI, Private Housing Finance Law; and

— mortgages of a limited profit housing company created pursuant to Article 2, Private Finance Housing Law.

Substitution of mortgagee: In *11814 Homes Corp.*, Tax Appeals Tribunal (4/4/96), New York's Tax Appeals Tribunal held that the mere substitution of one mortgagee for another, which did not secure a repayment of any additional indebtedness, did not create a new mortgage subject to tax.

Supplemental mortgages: Supplemental mortgages recorded for purposes other than creating or securing a new or additional indebtedness or obligation that may be secured by a recorded primary mortgage are exempt, provided a sworn statement claiming the exemption is filed with the recording officer at the time the supplemental mortgage is recorded. (Sec. 255, Tax Law; see also *Metropolitan and Fresh Pond Associates, LLC,* New York Division of Tax Appeals, Administrative Law Judge Unit, DTA No. 825001, June 19, 2014, ¶408-126)

Mortgage following a deed-in-lieu of foreclosure: A tax bulletin explains that mortgages assigned, modified, or otherwise transacted after the mortgaged property has been transferred by a deed in lieu of foreclosure are treated as new mortgages. Mortgage recording tax must be paid on the full amount of the debt secured when the new mortgage is recorded. (*TB-MR-575*, New York Department of Taxation and Finance, January 6, 2014, CCH NEW YORK TAX REPORTS, ¶407-996)

Credit line mortgages: The basis of tax on credit line mortgages is the maximum amount of the indebtedness secured. An additional amount of tax will be imposed whenever the total amount of monies advanced or re-advanced exceeds the maximum principal amount that was originally used to compute the tax. (20 NYCRR §647.3). However, as long as the correct amount of mortgage tax was paid at inception, a credit line mortgage secured by a 1 to 6 family owner/occupied dwelling, or on other real estate where the credit line secures a maximum debt of under $3,000,000, no additional taxes will be imposed on the making of advances and re-advances under the line of credit, regardless of the cumulative total of the liabilities. This policy only applies when the advances and re-advances are made to the original borrower of the credit line mortgage. See 20 NYCRR §647.4. See also *TB-MR-570*, New York Department of Taxation and Finance, January 6, 2014, CCH NEW YORK TAX REPORTS, ¶407-995.

Reverse mortgages: Reverse mortgages are exempt from all mortgage recording taxes and fees, provided the lender provides documentation in a format sufficient to enable a recording officer to determine that the transaction qualifies as a reverse mortgage. If documentation is not provided, mortgage recording tax will be determined on the basis of the maximum principal amount that the authorized lender is obligated to lend to the borrower. The maximum amount is determined without regard to contingencies relating to the addition of unpaid interest to principal, or relating to any percentage of the future appreciation of the property securing the loan as consideration to the making of the loan. If the proceeds are increased after the recording of the mortgage, the new obligation serves as the measure of the tax unless an exemption applies. (Sec. 252-a.2, Tax Law)

Lease as mortgage substitute: A transaction is not a transfer of real property subject to New York real estate transfer tax when title is conveyed at the termination of a lease in satisfaction of a debt and the lease functions in lieu of a conventional mortgage (properly recorded) Such transactions are entered into solely to effect and secure the financing of another party's acquisition of the real property. (*TSB-A-08(2)R*, New York Commissioner of Taxation and Finance, April 28, 2008, NEW YORK TAX REPORTS, ¶406-058)

Unrecorded negative pledge agreements: The Department of Taxation and Finance has held that unrecorded negative pledge agreements are not mortgages for mortgage recording tax purposes. (*TSB-M-95(1)R*; CCH NEW YORK TAX REPORTS, ¶300-139)

¶2710

Exemptions: The following mortgages are exempt from *special additional mortgage recording taxes:*

IRC Sec. 501(a) nonprofit organization: Nonprofit corporations exempt from federal income taxation under IRC Sec. 501(a) are exempt from the special additional mortgage recording tax. However, the other party to the mortgage may be liable for payment of the tax.

Residential natural persons: A mortgagee of real property who is a natural person is exempt from the payment of special additional recording taxes where the mortgaged premises consist of real property improved by a structure containing six residential units or less, each with their separate cooking facilities. (Sec. 253.1-a, Tax Law)

Credit unions: An exemption from the special additional mortgage recording tax is available for residential mortgages made by state-chartered credit unions. (Sec. 486-a, Banking Law; *TSB-M-08(5)R*, October 27, 2008, CCH NEW YORK TAX REPORTS, ¶406-193; TSB-M-10(1)R, March 30, 2010, CCH NEW YORK TAX REPORTS, ¶406-762)

Mortgages issued by federal credit unions were subject to the New York mortgage recording tax because the language used in the Federal Credit Union Act (FCUA) did not explicitly specify immunity from the tax for mortgages and loans (*Hudson Valley Federal Credit Union v. New York State Department of Taxation and Finance,* New York Court of Appeals, No. 154, October 18, 2012, CH NEW YORK TAX REPORTS, ¶407-671; *TSB-M-12(1)R,* December 6, 2012, CCH NEW YORK TAX REPORTS, ¶407-722).

• *Basis and rates of tax*

Mortgage recording taxes are computed on the amount of the principal debt or obligation that is or may be secured by the mortgage. The first $10,000 of mortgage indebtedness on one- and two-family residences is exempt from the additional tax (see below). Special rules exist for determining the basis of pre-1906 mortgages, supplemental mortgages, executory contracts, trust mortgages, credit line mortgages, mortgages for an indefinite amount, and mortgages securing property located in two or more tax districts or within and without New York. (Sec. 253.2, Tax Law)

Tax rates: The basic tax is imposed at the rate of 50¢ for each $100 (or major fraction thereof) of principal debt or obligation that is secured by the mortgage. If the principal debt or mortgage is less than $100, a tax of 50¢ is imposed. (Sec. 253.1, Tax Law)

The additional mortgage recording tax is generally imposed at the rate of 25¢ per $100 (or major fraction thereof) on the principal indebtedness secured. However, the additional tax imposed in the Metropolitan Commuter Transportation District is 30¢ for each $100 of principal debt secured by a mortgage (Sec. 253(2), Tax Law). The MCTD consists of the City of New York and Counties of Dutchess, Nassau, Orange, Putnam, Rockland, Suffolk and Westchester. Where a mortgage subject to the additional tax secures real property that is principally improved (or is to be principally improved) by a one- or two-family residence or dwelling, the first $10,000 of principal debt or obligation is deducted from the total principal debt or obligation secured by the mortgage, and the additional tax is computed on the remaining amount. (Sec. 253.2, Tax Law; *TB-MR-5,* New York Department of Taxation and Finance, July 5, 2012, CCH NEW YORK TAX REPORTS, ¶407-592)

The special additional tax is imposed at the rate of 25¢ for each $100 and each remaining major fraction thereof of principal debt or obligation that is, or under any contingency may, be secured at the date of execution of the mortgage or at any time thereafter. (Sec. 253.1-a, Tax Law)

Yonkers rates: The city of Yonkers mortgage recording tax is imposed at the rate of 50¢ for each $100 and each remaining major fraction thereof of principal debt or obligation that is, or under any contingency may be, secured at the date of the execution of the mortgage or at any time thereafter, on property located in whole or in part in the City of Yonkers. The tax is imposed on mortgages recorded beginning September 1, 1993, and ending on or before August 31, 2017. A tax of 50¢ is imposed if the principal debt or obligation secured by the mortgage is less than $100. The total mortgage recording tax rate for the City of Yonkers is $1.80 for each $100 secured by a mortgage. (Sec. 253-d, Tax Law)

For a chart listing mortgage recording taxes by county, see ¶30.

Credit: A special credit is allowed in the case of the first conveyance of each unit in a condominium subject to a purchase money mortgage where the tax has been paid on a construction contract mortgage or blanket mortgage on the condominium.

For construction mortgages, the credit is allowed where the proceeds were applied to the construction of a condominium unit and where the first condominium unit of the condominium plan is sold within two years after the construction mortgage is recorded. In addition, the credit is allowed for blanket mortgages, provided that the proceeds of the blanket mortgage were applied exclusively to (1) payment of a construction mortgage, (2) capital expenditures or expenses for the development or operation of the condominium, or (3) the purchase of land or buildings for the condominium, provided that the purchase was made no more than two years prior to the recording of the declaration of condominium, and where the first condominium unit of the condominium plan is sold within two years after the blanket mortgage is recorded. (Sec. 339ee, Tax Law) 20 NYCRR § 651.1; § 651.2.

• *Returns and payment*

The tax is payable to the recording officer of the county where the realty or part thereof is situated. The tax is due when the mortgage is recorded. NY Tax Law § 257.

Mortgages of real property that are subject to the tax and on which no tax has been paid cannot be released, discharged of record or received in evidence nor can such mortgage be extended. (Sec. 258, Tax Law)

Administration: The mortgage recording tax is administered by the Department of Taxation and Finance, W.A. Harriman State Campus, Albany, NY 12227.

¶2711 Tax on Cooperative Agricultural Corporations

Law: Sec. 185, Tax Law (CCH NEW YORK TAX REPORTS, ¶11-515 *et seq.*).

Forms: CT-185, Cooperative Agricultural Corporation Franchise Tax Return.

An annual franchise tax is imposed on domestic and foreign cooperative agricultural corporations based on the amount of the corporation's capital stock within New York during the preceding year. (Sec. 185.1, Tax Law)

• *Basis and rate of tax*

The tax is imposed at the rate of (1) one mill per dollar of net value of issued capital stock allocated to New York (the net value being deemed to be not less than $5 per share, or not less than the average price for which the stock sold during the year or not less than the difference between the corporation's assets and liabilities), (2) if dividends of 6% or more are paid, $1/4$ of one mill for each percent of dividend paid applies to such stock, the dividend rate being computed on the face value of par value stock apportioned to New York or on the amount paid-in on no par stock apportioned to New York, or (3) $10, whichever is the greatest. (Sec. 185.2, Tax Law)

• *Credits*

Credit for special additional mortgage recording tax paid: The credit allowed is similar to that allowed under the corporate franchise (income) provisions (see ¶927).

¶2711

Green buildings credit: A green buildings tax credit has been enacted in order to enhance the supply of environmentally sound buildings in New York. The credit is based on the costs of constructing green buildings, rehabilitating buildings to become green buildings, and purchasing fuel cells, photovoltaic modules, and environmentally sensitive non-ozone depleting refrigerants. The credit amount is spread over five years and may be carried forward. For additional information, see ¶942.

QEZE credit for real property taxes: The Qualified Empire Zone Enterprise (QEZE) credit for real property taxes could be claimed against the franchise tax on cooperative agricultural corporations. See ¶929 for additional information on the credit. If the amount of the credit exceeds a taxpayer's tax liability for the year, the excess is treated as an overpayment of tax to be credited or refunded.

The following credits were also available to agricultural cooperatives: empire zone investment tax credit, empire zone employment incentive credit, and empire zone wage tax credit.

• *Reports and payment*

Reports and payment of tax are due on or before March 15 to the Department of Taxation and Finance, W.A. Harriman State Campus, Albany, NY 12227.

¶2712 Real Estate Transfer Tax

Law: Secs. 1401*et seq.*, Tax Law; Reg. Sec. 575.7 (CCH NEW YORK TAX REPORTS, ¶37-051).

Forms: Form TP-584, Combined Real Estate Transfer Tax Return, Credit Line Mortgage Certificate, and Certification of Exemption from the Payment of Estimated Tax.

The real estate transfer tax is imposed on each conveyance when the consideration is in excess of $500. The grantor is liable for the payment of the base tax, unless the grantor fails to pay the tax or is exempt, in which case the grantee becomes liable. The grantee is also liable for payment of the additional tax imposed on residential real property conveyances. (Secs. 1402(a), 1402-a(a), 1404, Tax Law)

For purposes of the tax, the term "conveyance" means the transfer or transfers of any interest in real property by any method, including but not limited to, the sale, exchange, assignment, surrender, option, taking by eminent domain, transfer, or acquisition of a controlling interest in any entity with an interest in real property. A taxable conveyance also includes the creation of certain leases or subleases. (Sec. 1401(e), Tax Law)

A transfer or acquisition of a "controlling interest" in a corporation occurs "when a person, or group of persons acting in concert, transfers or acquires a total of 50% or more of the voting stock" in the corporation. In the case of a partnership, association, trust or other entity with an interest in real property, the tax is triggered when a total of 50% or more of the capital, profit or beneficial interest in the entity is transferred or acquired by a person or group of persons acting in concert. See 20 NYCRR § 575.6.

"Consideration" is the price paid in dollars or otherwise and includes the discharge of an obligation. It also includes payments for an option or contract to purchase real property (including the value of rental or other payments attributable to the exercise of an option to renew), and the amount of any mortgage, lien, or other encumbrance, whether or not the underlying indebtedness is assumed, provided, however, that with respect to conveyances or transfers of one-, two- or three-family houses and individual residential condominium units or interests therein, and conveyances or transfers in which the consideration or value of the interest conveyed is less than $500,000, the consideration or value of the interest conveyed shall exclude the value of any lien or encumbrance remaining thereon at the time of sale. (Sec. 1401(d), Tax Law)

With respect to conveyances of shares of stock allocated to an individual residential unit in a cooperative housing corporation in connection with the transfer of proprietary leasehold interests (other than the original conveyance by the corporation or sponsor), consideration will not include the value of any liens on stock certificates or other evidences of an ownership interest in and a proprietary lease from a corporation or partnership formed for the purpose of cooperative ownership of a residential interest remaining thereon at the time of conveyance. (Sec. 1401(d)(v), Tax Law)

When real property is transferred by a referee or sheriff pursuant to a court order in a foreclosure proceeding ordering the sale of the property, the referee or sheriff effectuating such transfer will not be liable for any interest or penalties under the real property transfer tax laws or Article 37 of the Tax Law, relating to seizures and forclosures. (Sec. 1422 *et seq.*, Tax Law)

Practitioner Comment: Filing Requirements

New York's real property transfer tax is collected by the clerk of the county where the property is located, before the deed will be accepted for filing. This ensures that tax is collected on all direct transfers of property. When a taxpayer transfers or acquires an interest in an entity that owns real property, there is no need to file a deed since the entity remains in title to the property. In that event, the parties must file form TP 584 with the Department of Taxation and Finance in Albany within 15 days of the transfer to remit the tax that is due on the transaction.

Mark S. Klein, Hodgson Russ LLP

The transfer tax is imposed on original and subsequent conveyances of shares of stock in a cooperative housing corporation in connection with the transfer of proprietary leasehold interests. NY Tax Law § 1405-B.

CCH Advisory: Estimated Tax on Gain

No deed in New York may be recorded unless each nonresident transferor has received a certification from the Commissioner of Taxation and Finance regarding payment of the estimated personal income tax or has signed a certification on Form TP-584 that the requirement to pay estimated tax does not apply. For information on estimated tax, see ¶ 606.

Leases: Three possible transactions involving leases qualify as taxable conveyances of real property for transfer tax purposes:

     — *Grant of lease or sublease without option to purchase*—The creation of a lease or sublease not coupled with an option to purchase is a taxable conveyance of an interest in real property only where (Sec. 1401(e), Tax Law):

         (1) the sum of the term of the lease or sublease and any options for renewal exceeds 49 years;

         (2) substantial capital improvements are or may be made by or for the benefit of the lessee or sublessee; and

         (3) the lease or sublease is for substantially all of the premises constituting the real property.

     — *Lease coupled with option to purchase*—An option to purchase real property coupled with the right of use or occupancy of the property is, for transfer tax purposes, the conveyance of a taxable interest in real property. (Reg. Sec. 575.7) Accordingly, the creation of a lease coupled with the granting of an option to purchase, regardless of the term of the lease, is a conveyance subject to the transfer tax.

     — *Assignments or surrender of lease*—The transfer of a leasehold interest by assignment or surrender, regardless of the term, is a conveyance subject to tax.

• *Basis and rate of tax*

Tax is imposed when the consideration is over $500 at the rate of $2 for each $500 (or fraction thereof) paid as consideration for the transfer.

Transfers to REITs: Transfers of interests in real property to qualified real estate investment trusts (REITs) (or to a partnership or corporation in which the REIT owns a controlling interest immediately following such conveyance), in connection with the initial formation of the REIT, are subject to real estate transfer tax at the rate of $1 for each $500 (or fractional part thereof) of consideration. The reduced rate is effective through September 1, 2017. (Sec. 1402, Tax Law; *TSB-M-11(3)R*, September 1, 2011, CCH NEW YORK TAX REPORTS, ¶407-356)

Additional tax: Conveyances of residential real property for which the consideration is $1 million or more are subject to an additional tax. The tax is imposed at the rate of 1% of the consideration attributable to the residential property. See "Mansion tax," discussed below.

Erie County: The additional tax imposed on conveyances of interests in real property located in whole or in part in Erie County is imposed at the rate of $2.50 for each $500 (or fractional part thereof), of the consideration or value. (Sec. 1425, Tax Law)

Exemptions: The following governmental entities are exempt from paying the real estate transfer tax: New York, its agencies, instrumentalities, subdivisions or public corporations; the United Nations; the United States, its agencies and instrumentalities. The exemption afforded these bodies does not relieve their grantees from liability for the tax. (Sec. 1405(a), Tax Law)

The following conveyances are not taxed:

— conveyances to any of the exempt governmental agencies noted above;

— conveyances used to secure a debt or other obligation;

— corrective conveyances (conveyances without additional consideration);

— conveyances without consideration and that do not relate to a sale (such as a gift);

— conveyances given in connection with a tax sale;

— conveyances that consist of a deed of partition;

— conveyances given pursuant to the federal bankruptcy act;

— conveyances to effectuate a mere change of identity or form of ownership or organization where there is no change in beneficial ownership (other than conveyances to a cooperative housing corporation of the real property comprising the cooperative dwellings);

— conveyances consisting of the execution of a contract to sell without the use or occupancy of the property or the granting of an option to purchase without the use or occupancy of the property;

— conveyances of an option or contract to purchase with the use or occupancy of the property, where the consideration is less than $200,000 and the property was used solely by the grantor as his personal residence and consists of a one-, two-, or three-family house, an individual residential cooperative unit, or the sale of stock in a cooperative housing corporation in connection with the transfer of a proprietary leasehold covering an individual residential cooperative unit;

— conveyances pursuant to devise, bequest or inheritance. (Secs. 1401(e), 1405(b), Tax Law)

START-UP exemption provisions: Conveyances of real property located in tax-free NY areas to businesses located in those areas that are participating in the START-UP NY program are exempt from state and local real estate transfer tax or real property transfer tax (Sec.1405(b)(11), Tax Law).

In addition, any lease of property to an eligible business also is exempt from any state or local real estate transfer tax or real property transfer tax (Sec. 39(g), Tax Law). This lease provision applies to taxable years beginning on or after January 1, 2014.

Cooperative housing corporation transfers: Transfer tax is imposed on the original conveyance of shares of stock in a cooperative housing corporation in connection with the transfer of a proprietary leasehold by the corporation or sponsor and the subsequent conveyance of stock in a cooperative housing corporation in connection with the transfer of a proprietary leasehold by the owner. When property has been converted into cooperative ownership, a credit is available. The amount of the credit is determined by multiplying the amount of the tax paid on the conveyance to the cooperative housing corporation by a percentage representing the extent to which the conveyance effectuated a mere change of identity or form of ownership, and then multiplying the resulting product by a fraction, the numerator of which is the number of shares conveyed in the transaction and the denominator of which is the total number of shares of the cooperative housing corporation. The credit may not be applied to reduce the tax to zero, and may not be applied to a tax paid more than 24 months prior to the date on which the first in a series of stock conveyances occurs. (Sec. 1405-B, Tax Law)

Credit: A grantor is allowed a credit against the tax due on a conveyance of realty to the extent tax was paid by the grantor on a prior creation of a leasehold or the granting of an option or contract to purchase all or a portion of the same real property. The credit is computed by multiplying the tax paid on the creation of the leasehold or the granting of the option or contract by a fraction, the numerator of which is the value of the consideration used in computing the tax paid that is not yet due to the grantor on the date of the subsequent conveyance, and the denominator of which is the total value of consideration used to compute the tax paid. (Sec. 1405-A, Tax Law)

Practitioner Comment: Duty to Inquire

Failure to pay the real estate transfer tax based on a reasonable interpretation of the law may not be sufficient to avoid the imposition of penalties, if that interpretation is ultimately rejected. There is an affirmative obligation placed on a taxpayer to request an advisory opinion or other guidance to determine the position of the Department of Taxation and Finance. Taxpayers that fail to inquire about the Department's position do so at their peril. According to a decision of New York's courts, the imposition of penalties "does not require an intent to deprive the government of its money but only something more than accidental non-payment [citations omitted]. Advancement of a reasonable legal theory in good faith or reliance on professional advice, in the absence of inquiry to ascertain the position of the Department of Taxation and Finance, does not constitute reasonable cause." (*CBS Corp. v. Tax Appeals Tribunal of the State of New York*, 867 NYS2d 270 (3d Dep't. 2008), CCH New York Tax Reports, ¶406-226; Mtn. App. den. 12 NY 3rd 703 (2009))

Mark S. Klein, Hodgson Russ LLP

• *Mansion tax*

An additional tax is imposed on conveyances of residential real property for which the consideration is $1 million or more (Sec. 1402-a(a), Tax Law; see also *Publication 577*, February 1, 2010, CCH New York Tax Reports, ¶39-515).

The so-called "mansion tax" was applied to a transaction involving a construction and purchase contract, despite the purchaser's assertion that the conveyance at issue was one of vacant land containing no residential real property. What was conveyed was an interest in residential real property, consisting of the lots and the contract for the purchase of a home to be built. An examination of the substance of the transaction supported a finding that the steps of the transaction should not be viewed separately. If the builder had obtained financing as originally planned, then the property would have been transferred when the home was completed and the conveyance would have been subject to the additional tax as a transfer of residential real estate in excess of $1 million. The severing of the transaction into the steps necessary to secure financing should not be afforded a different tax treatment. *Kelly*, New York Division of Tax Appeals, Administrative Law Judge Unit, DTA No. 819863, December 8, 2005, CCH NEW YORK TAX REPORTS, ¶405-259.

Multiple units: The transfer of two residential units with a combined value of $1.525 million was subject to the real estate transfer mansion tax, even though the taxpayers had purchased the units under two individual contracts for less than $1 million each, because the two units had already been consolidated by the previous owner, allowing the units to be combined into a single apartment. The units were fully accessible to each other, had a single kitchen, and functioned as a single-family residence. (*Sacks v. Tax Appeals Tribunal*, Appellate Division of the Supreme Court of New York, Third Department, No. 512527, October 25, 2012, CCH NEW YORK TAX REPORTS, ¶407-679)

Hotel condominiums: Hotel suite condominium units primarily used for commercial purposes do not qualify as residential units and, therefore, are not subject to the New York real estate transfer mansion tax. The units at issue are sold to individuals who will be entitled to occupy the units for a limited duration of time each year, but the units must be made available for rental as transient hotel accommodations pursuant to the New York City Department of Buildings requirements and zoning restrictions. The certificate of occupancy conforms to this requirement and states that the building has zero dwelling units. Further, the units are treated as hotel units for sales and hotel occupancy tax purposes. The application of the mansion tax is not dependent on the form of the underlying transactions but on the economic reality that characterizes the entire conveyance. The zoning approval and restrictive declaration from the New York City Department of Buildings imposes restrictions on the use of the property to ensure that it will qualify as a transient hotel that will be primarily used for commercial purposes. Therefore, the units are not subject to the mansion tax. (*TSB-A-13(4)R*, New York Commissioner of Taxation and Finance, August 30, 2013, CCH NEW YORK TAX REPORTS, ¶407-905)

• *Returns and payment*

The grantor and grantee are required to file a joint return for each conveyance, regardless of whether a tax is due. A joint return is not required to be filed for conveyance of an easement or license to a public utility where the consideration for the grant of the easement or license is $2 or less and is clearly stated as actual consideration in the instrument of conveyance. The return is filed with the recording officer before the instrument effecting the conveyance is recorded. If the return is filed with the Commissioner of Taxation and Finance at the time the tax is paid, a receipt must be filed with the recording officer before the instrument may be recorded. (Sec. 1409, Tax Law)

Collection of tax: The tax is required to be paid to the Commissioner of Taxation and Finance, or an appointed agent, not later than 15 days following the date of delivery of the instrument effecting the transfer.

¶2712

¶2713 Tax on Unrelated Business Income of Exempt Organizations

Law: Secs. 290—296, Tax Law (CCH NEW YORK TAX REPORTS, ¶ 32-205 *et seq.*).

Forms: CT-13, Unrelated Business Income Tax Return.

A tax (UBIT) is imposed on the unrelated business income of exempt organizations and trusts (as described in IRC Sec. 511(a)(2) and (b)(2)). The UBIT is imposed by Article 13 of the Tax Law and is similar to the federal tax on the unrelated business income of such organizations. (Sec. 290(a), Tax Law)

Exempt: Any corporation subject to tax under Article 9-A of the Tax Law (the New York corporate franchise (income) tax) is exempt.

An organization whose sole unrelated trade or business carried on in New York consists of activities constituting an unrelated trade or business solely by virtue of IRC Sec. 501(m)(2)(A) (relating to commercial-type insurance) is also exempt from the tax.

Practitioner Comment: ERISA Does Not Preempt the UBIT

New York State can impose a tax on the unrelated business income (UBIT) of a trust that holds and administers the assets of a retirement plan governed by the federal Employment Retirement Income Security Act of 1974 (ERISA). While the Tax Appeals Tribunal held that ERISA preempts state taxation of these plans (*McKinsey Master Retirement Plan Trust*, TAT (5/8/03, CCH NEW YORK TAX REPORTS, ¶ 404-540)), New York's Tax Department has stated that a subsequent decision of the United States Court of Appeals supersedes the Tribunal's opinion. As a result, an employee trust carrying on an unrelated trade or business in New York must file form CT-13 (Unrelated Business Tax Return) and pay the UBIT.

Mark S. Klein, Hodgson Russ LLP

Any income from the conduct of licensed games of chance or from rental of premises for the conduct of such games is exempt. Games of chance do not include bingo or lotto. (Sec. 290(c), Tax Law)

A not-for-profit political action committee was held not subject to the UBIT. For purposes of the opinion, the political action committee was assumed to be a qualifying political organization as described in IRC Sec. 527. (*TSB-A-05(15)C*, New York Commissioner of Taxation and Finance, October 24, 2005, CCH NEW YORK TAX REPORTS, ¶ 405-236)

• *Basis and rate of tax*

The tax is imposed on unrelated business income, which is defined as the federal unrelated business income of the taxpayer for the taxable year with the following modifications (Sec. 292(a), Tax Law):

(1) *New York tax on unrelated business income:* The amount of any New York tax on unrelated business income is added to the federal figure;

(2) *Refund or credit of New York unrelated business income tax:* The amount of any refund or credit for overpayment of New York unrelated business income tax is subtracted from federal unrelated business income;

(3) *Net operating loss deduction:* The net operating loss deduction is the same as the federal deduction, except that (a) the modification described in (1) and (2) must be made, (b) any net operating loss sustained during taxable years beginning before January 1, 1970, or in any taxable year in which the taxpayer was not subject to the New York unrelated business income tax, must be excluded, and (c) the deduction must not exceed the allowable federal deduction;

(4) *Production activities:* An addition modification is required for the IRC Sec. 199 qualified production activities deduction, applicable to taxable years beginning after 2007.

¶2713

Practitioner Comment: UBTI Does Not Apply to PACs

Although the New York tax on unrelated business taxable income applies to exempt organizations, the New York State Department of Taxation and Finance has ruled that it does not apply to not-for-profit political action committees formed under IRC Sec. 527 (*The Public Works Pac, Inc., TSB-A-05(15)C*, CCH NEW YORK TAX REPORTS, ¶ 405-236).

Mark S. Klein, Esq., Hodgson Russ LLP

If the taxpayer has a regular place of business outside New York, the unrelated business income is allocated by a three-factor (property, receipts, payroll) formula. (Sec. 293(Sec. 292(a)), Tax Law)

Tax rate: Tax is imposed at the rate of 9%.

The minimum tax is $250. (Sec. 290, Tax Law)

CCH Advisory: Minimum Tax

An exempt organization under IRC Sec. 501(c)(7) is subject to the minimum New York unrelated business income tax of $250 where it has income from investment activity but its federal unrelated business taxable income is zero for the year at issue. The minimum tax is imposed on an organization carrying on an unrelated trade or business in New York regardless of the amount of its unrelated business taxable income under Sec. 292 of the Tax Law. For purposes of Sec. 292, unrelated business income is the organization's federal unrelated business taxable income with the modifications contained in Sec. 292. Since the taxpayer's unrelated business taxable income for the year at issue is zero, and the modifications contained in Sec. 292 of the Tax Law do not appear to apply, the taxpayer does not have unrelated business taxable income for purposes of Sec. 292. Accordingly, the minimum tax imposed under Sec. 290(a) of the Tax Law applies (*The Polish American Citizens Club of Rochester, New York, Inc. (Advisory Opinion)*, TSB-A-04(14)C, July 22, 2004, CCH NEW YORK TAX REPORTS, ¶ 404-883).

• *Returns and payment*

Returns are due on or before the 15th day of the fifth month following the close of the taxable year (May 15 for calendar-year taxpayers). Payment accompanies the return. (Sec. 294(a), Tax Law)

Extension of time: An automatic six-month extension for the filing of the annual return will be allowed, provided the taxpayer, prior to the date on which the return is due, files an application for extension and pays the amount properly estimated as its tax. The amount paid shall be deemed properly estimated if it is either not less than 90% of the tax as finally determined or not less than the tax shown on the taxpayer's return for the preceding taxable year not less than 12 months. (Sec. 294(b), Tax Law)

Administration: The unrelated business income tax on exempt organizations is administered by the Department of Taxation and Finance, W.A. Harriman State Campus, Albany, NY 12227.

¶2714 Annual Maintenance Fee of Foreign Corporations (repealed)

Law: Former Sec. 181, Tax Law (CCH NEW YORK TAX REPORTS, ¶ 35-001).

Forms: CT-240, Foreign Corporation License Fee Return; CT-245, Maintenance Fee and Activities Return For a Foreign Corporation Disclaiming Tax Liability.

For taxable years beginning before 2015, every foreign corporation authorized to do business in New York (except banking corporations, fire, marine, casualty and life insurance companies, cooperative fraternal insurance companies and building and loan associations) had to pay an annual maintenance fee of $300. (former Sec. 181.2(a), Tax Law)

The fee was reduced by 25% if the tax period is more than six months but not more than nine months, and by 50% if the tax period is six months or less. (former Sec. 181.2(a), Tax Law)

The annual maintenance fee was payable within two and one-half months after the close of the corporation's calendar or fiscal year. (former Sec. 181.2(b), Tax Law)

The fee was allowed as a credit against corporate franchise (income) taxes. The fee could not, however, be credited against the former organization tax for domestic corporations or the former license tax on foreign corporations.

¶2715 Taxes on Health Facilities

Law: Sec. 2807-d, Public Health Law (CCH NEW YORK TAX REPORTS, ¶ 35-001 *et seq.*).

Hospitals are subject to a health facility tax on their gross receipts for patient services (Sec. 2807-d, Public Health Law). "Hospital" is broadly defined and includes general hospitals, public health centers, dental centers, rehabilitation centers, residential health care facility and diagnostic and treatment centers (Sec. 2801(1), Public Health Law). The health facility tax is based on the gross receipts received from all patient care services and other operating income, less personal needs allowances and refunds, on a cash basis (Sec. 2807-d(1)(a), Public Health Law).

Certain voluntary nonprofit and private proprietary general hospitals and any facility dedicated solely to the care of police, firefighters, and emergency service personnel are exempt from the health facility tax (Sec. 2807-d(1)(b), Public Health Law).

Rates of tax: An assessment is imposed at the rate of 0.35% on gross receipts received by general hospitals for periods on or after April 1, 2009 (Sec. 2807-d(2)(a)(v), Public Health Law).

The assessment was 6% of each residential health care facility's gross receipts received from all patient care services and other operating income on a cash basis for the period April 1, 2009, through March 31, 2011, for hospital or health-related services, including adult day services (Sec. 2807-d(2)(b), Public Health Law).

If the assessment is passed through to a resident of the facility, a personal income tax credit may be claimed by the resident (see ¶ 146).

¶2716 Tax on Petroleum and Aviation Fuel Businesses

Law: Sec. 301, Tax Law (CCH NEW YORK TAX REPORTS, ¶ 40-005, 40-007).

Forms: PT-100, Petroleum Business Tax Return; PT-101, Tax on Motor Fuels (Includes Aviation Gasoline); PT-102, Tax on Diesel Motor Fuels; PT-103, Tax on Residual Petroleum Product Businesses; PT-104, Tax on Kero-Jet Fuel; PT-106, Retailers of Heating Oil Only.

Article 13-A of the Tax Law imposes a privilege tax on petroleum and aviation fuel businesses operating in New York. The tax is determined on the basis of the volume of fuel imported or produced in New York.

Article 13-A also imposes a petroleum business carrier tax, which is a complement to and is collected with the fuel use tax (¶ 2705).

CCH Advisory: Diesel Motor Fuel Reclassified

Beginning September 1, 2011, the manner in which diesel motor fuel is classified is redefined for purposes of the diesel motor fuel excise tax (Article 12-A), petroleum business tax (Article 13-A), and sales tax (Article 28). The terms "enhanced diesel motor fuel" and "unenhanced diesel motor fuel" are obsolete. Accordingly, it is no longer necessary to determine if fuel is labeled as diesel fuel, No. 1 diesel fuel, No. 2 diesel fuel, or similar designation, or if it is a blended product that it will be used as diesel fuel in a motor vehicle. Also, the fuel's sulfur content is irrelevant to determination of its taxability. Instead, based on the new definitions, the taxation of diesel motor fuel depends on whether it is classified as highway diesel motor fuel or non- highway diesel motor fuel. (*TSB-M-11(6)M, TSB-M-11(11)S,* New York Department of Taxation and Finance, July 29, 2011, CCH NEW YORK TAX REPORTS, ¶407-325)

"Highway diesel motor fuel" is any diesel motor fuel that is not non-highway diesel motor fuel (Sec. 282(16-a), Tax Law). "Non-highway diesel motor fuel" is any diesel motor fuel designated for use other than on a public highway (except for the use of the public highway by farmers to reach adjacent farmlands), and is dyed diesel motor fuel (Sec. 282(16), Tax Law).

Highway diesel motor fuel is subject to diesel motor fuel excise tax, petroleum business tax, and prepaid sales tax when it is first sold in New York State. When the fuel is designated for off-highway use and is dyed for federal tax purposes at the terminal, it is considered non-highway diesel motor fuel. Non-highway diesel motor fuel is exempt from the diesel motor fuel excise tax and the prepaid sales tax, and either exempt or partially exempt from the petroleum business tax. These exemptions or partial exemptions apply as long as the fuel is not used on New York public highways (except by farmers to reach adjacent farmlands), or delivered to a filling station or into a tank equipped with a nozzle capable of fueling a motor vehicle (except for delivery at a farm site). (Sec. 282-a, Tax Law)

Petroleum business tax definitions: "Commercial gallonage" is gallonage that (Sec. 300(k), Tax Law):

> is non-highway diesel motor fuel or residual petroleum product;

> is included in the full measure of the non-highway diesel motor fuel component or the residual petroleum product component of the petroleum business tax;

> does not (and will not) qualify (A) for the utility credit or reimbursement, (B) as manufacturing gallonage, (C) for the not-for-profit organization exemption, or (D) for the heating exemption or reimbursement; and

> will not be used (has not been used) in the fuel tank connecting with the engine of a vessel.

"Manufacturing gallonage" is non-highway diesel motor fuel or residual petroleum product used and consumed directly and exclusively in the production of tangible personal property for sale by manufacturing, processing, or assembly, but only if (Sec. 300(m), Tax Law):

> all the fuel or product is delivered on the manufacturing site, or

> the purchaser causes the fuel or product to be delivered to its manufacturing site.

Manufacturing gallonage may not be consumed on the public highways of New York, or delivered to a filling station or into a tank equipped with a nozzle capable of fueling a motor vehicle.

"Railroad diesel" is non-highway diesel motor fuel for use and consumption directly and exclusively for operating a locomotive or self-propelled vehicle run only on rails or tracks, but only if either (Sec. 300(l), Tax Law):

> all the fuel is delivered into a storage facility which is not equipped with a nozzle capable of fueling a motor vehicle, and the facility is used only to fuel locomotives or self-propelled vehicles, or

> all the fuel is delivered directly into fuel tanks of locomotives or self-propelled vehicles.

Sales tax definition: "Petroleum products" are motor fuel or diesel motor fuel, not including kerosene or propane used for residential purposes. This term replaces the term "automotive fuel" for sales tax purposes only.

Highway use tax and fuel use tax definition: "Automotive fuel" is both diesel motor fuel and motor fuel. This term has not changed and still applies for purposes of the highway use tax and fuel use tax/International Fuel Tax Agreement (IFTA).

Tax rates: The current tax rates remain in effect. See *Publication 908, Fuel Tax Rates,*(below) for the current rate structure using the new terminology. The annual petroleum business tax rates will continue to be indexed and adjusted effective January 1 for monthly filers and March 1 for quarterly filers.

• *Petroleum businesses*

Imposition of tax: Petroleum businesses doing business, employing capital, owning or leasing property, or maintaining an office in New York are subject to a monthly tax on the volume of fuel imported, caused to be imported, or produced in New York. NY Tax Law § 301-a.

Supplemental tax: A supplemental tax is imposed on petroleum businesses. (Sec. 301-j., Tax Law)

"Petroleum business" defined: The term "petroleum business" means every corporation and unincorporated business (1) importing motor fuel, diesel motor fuel, or residual petroleum product or causing motor fuel, diesel motor fuel or residual petroleum product to be imported into the state for use, distribution, storage or sale in New York, or (2) producing, refining, manufacturing, or compounding motor fuel or petroleum product in New York. (Sec. 300(b)(1), Tax Law)

Corporations and unincorporated businesses selling or using diesel motor fuel or residual petroleum product in New York, other than making non-bulk retail sales or self-use of diesel motor fuel or residual petroleum product that has been the subject of a retail sale to the corporation or business, are regarded as petroleum businesses. (Sec. 300(b)(2), (3), Tax Law)

A corporation or unincorporated business involved in the enhancement of diesel motor fuel within New York, or which is registered by the Division of Taxation and Finance as a "distributor of kero-jet fuel only" is also regarded as a petroleum business. (Sec. 300(b)(2), Tax Law)

If nontaxable motor fuel is received by any person within New York, and the fuel later becomes subject to tax, the person possessing the fuel at the time it becomes subject to tax will be regarded as a petroleum business and will be liable to pay tax. (Sec. 301-a(j), Tax Law)

"Doing business" defined: A petroleum business will not be deemed to be doing business by virtue of all or any combination of the following: maintaining bank account balances in New York; owning shares or securities kept in safe deposit boxes within New York, pledged as collateral security, or deposited in safekeeping or custodial service by bank or trust companies; actions by banks, trust companies or brokers that are incidental to the rendering of custodial or safekeeping service to the petroleum business; maintenance of offices in New York by officers or directors who are not employees of the petroleum business; or the keeping of books or records in New York, if the books or records are not kept by employees and the petroleum business is not otherwise engaged in business within the state. (Sec. § 301-a(i), Tax Law)

Exemptions: The following sales and organizations are exempt: (1) sales to New York or the federal government; (2) sales to individuals; (3) sales for export; (4) sales for residential heating; (5) fuel used for farm production; (6) fuel used for manufacturing electricity; (7) fuel in tanks, including fuel in tanks of commercial fishing vessels; (8) sales to nonprofit organizations; (9) sales between commercial distributors; (10) commercial gallonage; (11) railroad diesel; and (12) diesel motor fuel or residual petroleum products used by passenger commuter ferries in the provision of mass transit of passengers. There is also a partial nonresidential heating exemption. (Secs. 301-b, 300(b)(1), 300(k), (l), Tax Law)

¶2716

Fuel used in manufacturing: Unenhanced [non-highway] diesel motor fuel or residual petroleum product sold and used directly and exclusively for manufacturing purposes is fully exempt from the petroleum tax (Sec. 301-a(g), Tax Law; TSB-M-97(10)M).

Nonresidential heating: A partial exemption is allowed for unenhanced diesel motor fuel or residual petroleum product sold by a registered petroleum business to a consumer exclusively for nonresidential heating purposes. The partial exemption is also available for enhanced diesel motor fuel sold for such purposes, but only if the fuel is delivered into a storage tank that is attached to a heating unit and not equipped to dispense such fuel into the tank of a motor vehicle. (Sec. 301-b(d), Tax Law; TSB-M-01(3)M; TSB-M-01(5)M)

Fuel used in farming: An exemption is allowed for sale or use consisting of no more than 4,500 gallons of diesel motor fuel in a 30-day period to or by a consumer for use or consumption directly and exclusively in the production for sale of tangible personal property by farming if all of the fuel is delivered on the farm site and is consumed other than on the highways of New York (except for use of the highway to adjacent farmlands). (Sec. 301-c(f), Tax Law; *TSB-M-15(2)M*, New York Department of Taxation and Finance, July 24, 2015, CCH NEW YORK TAX REPORTS, ¶ 408-486)

Fuel used in mining: Purchasers are eligible for a complete reimbursement of petroleum business tax paid on residual petroleum product and diesel motor fuel purchased for use in the production of tangible personal property for sale by mining or extracting. The fuel or product must be delivered at the mining or extracting site, and no portion of it may be consumed on the highways.

Products: Sales of the following products are exempt from tax: unblended kerosene sold or used for purposes other than the operation of motor vehicles; kero-jet fuel sold to consumers for use exclusively as jet aircraft fuel or to registered distributors of kero-jet fuel for non-bulk retail sales directly into fuel tanks for the operation of airplanes; aviation gasoline meeting the specifications set forth in American Standard Testing Material Specifications D910 or Military Specifications MIL-G-5572, imported, produced, refined, manufactured, or compounded within New York; residual petroleum product sold for use exclusively as bunker fuel in vessels; and crude oil and liquefied petroleum gases. (Sec. 301-b(a), Tax Law)

Alternative motor fuels: From September 1, 2006, until September 1, 2021, a petroleum business tax exemption is available for sales of E85 (85% ethanol), CNG (methane), or hydrogen fuel when delivered for storage in tanks and sold as motor vehicle fuel. In addition, a partial tax exemption equal to 20% of the amount of tax due is allowed for B20 (20% biodiesel) fuel. For details, see ¶ 2709.

• *Basis and rate of tax*

The monthly tax on petroleum businesses is determined on the basis of the sum of the following fuel and petroleum product components:

Motor fuel component: The motor fuel component is determined by multiplying the motor fuel and highway diesel motor fuel rate by the number of gallons of motor fuel imported or caused to be imported into New York by the petroleum business for use, distribution, storage, or sale in New York, or produced, refined, manufactured, or compounded in New York by the petroleum business during the month covered by the return.

Highway diesel motor fuel component: The highway diesel motor fuel component is determined by multiplying the motor fuel and highway diesel motor fuel rate by (1) the number of gallons of highway diesel fuel sold or used by the petroleum business in New York during the month covered by the return, and (2) with respect to any gallonage that has not previously been included in the measure of the tax imposed by

Article 13-A, the number of gallons of diesel motor fuel delivered to a filling station or into a motor vehicle's fuel tank for use in the operation of the motor vehicle, whichever occurs first.

Nonautomotive-type-highway diesel motor fuel/residual petroleum product component: The non-highway diesel motor fuel and residual petroleum product components are determined, respectively, by multiplying the nonhighway diesel motor fuel rate or residual petroleum product rate by the number of gallons of non-highway diesel fuel or residual petroleum product sold or used by the petroleum business in New York during the month covered by the return. (Sec. 301-a(a)-(d), Tax Law)

Fuel/petroleum product rates: Effective January 1 through December 31, 2016, aggregate fuel and petroleum product tax rates are as follows (*Publication 908*, Fuel Tax Rates, New York State Department of Taxation and Finance, January 1, 2016, **http://www.tax.ny.gov/pdf/publications/multi/pub908.pdf**):

	Cents per gallon (including tax and supplemental tax)
Motor fuel	17.0
Liquefied petroleum gases (LPG)	none
Compressed natural gas (CNG)	none
E85 (sales at a filling station)	none
Aviation gasoline	17.0
Retail sellers of aviation gasoline	6.8
Kero-jet fuel	6.8
Highway diesel motor fuel	15.25
Highway B20	12.20
Non-highway diesel motor fuel	
Exempt organizations	none
Farm use	none
Manufacturing	none
Commercial gallonage	9.3
B20 (commercial gallonage)	7.4
Nonresidential heating	5.0
B20 (nonresidential heating)	4.0
Railroad diesel	8.9
B20 (railroad diesel)	7.1
Electric corporation (without direct pay permit)	16.1
Electric corporation (with direct pay permit)	none
Commercial vessels (sales to)	1618
Dyed kerosene	none
Residual petroleum product	
Exempt organizations	none
Farm use	none
Manufacturing	none
Commercial gallonage	7.1
Nonresidential heating	3.8
Electric corporation (without direct pay permit)	13.9
Electric corporation (with direct pay permit)	none
Bunker fuel for vessels	none
Electric utility credit/reimbursement	
Nonhighway diesel	6.23
Residual petroleum product	6.20
Commercial gallonage reimbursement	6.8
Aviation gasoline credit/refund/reimbursement	10.2

Non-highway diesel motor fuel or residual petroleum product sold and used for manufacturing purposes are exempt from the petroleum business tax. Diesel fuel designated as 500 ppm sulfur NRLM (non-road, locomotive, marine) diesel fuel or similar designations (*e.g.*, 500 ppm dyed low sulfur nonroad diesel fuel) is *non-highway* diesel motor fuel for petroleum business, motor fuel, and sales tax purposes. Special provisions apply, as long as such fuel is not delivered to a filling station or into a storage tank or other repository equipped with a nozzle or similar apparatus capable of dispensing the fuel into the tank of a motor vehicle. (*TSB-M-07(2)M, TSB-M-07(4)S*, May 31, 2007, CCH NEW YORK TAX REPORTS, ¶405-742)

The Department of Taxation and Finance provides a schedule that lists the tax-per-trip method for tugboat and towboat operators (*Publication 908-CV*, January 2016, available at **http://www.tax.ny.gov/pdf/publications/multi/pub908cv.pdf**).

¶2716

CCH Advisory: Production of Industrial Gasses

The purchase of non-highway diesel motor fuel that is used to produce industrial gases is exempt from New York petroleum business, motor fuel, and sales and use taxes if such gases are not used for the purpose of heating, cooking, or lighting. The industrial gases produced constitute tangible personal property that is eligible for exemption from petroleum business, motor fuel, and sales and use taxes, and the taxpayer may claim the exemptions by providing its distributor with Form FT-1012, Manufacturing Certification for Diesel Motor Fuel and Residual Petroleum Product, on which it checks off box Part I. (TSB-A-09(4)M, TSB-A-09(63)S, New York Commissioner of Taxation and Finance, December 30, 2009, CCH NEW YORK TAX REPORTS, ¶406-611)

Credits against tax: Electric corporations subject to the supervision of the Department of Public Services that purchase or import residual petroleum products and non-highway diesel motor fuel to fuel generators for the production or manufacture of electricity, as well as residual petroleum product and non-highway diesel motor fuel purchased in New York through the use of direct pay permits, are entitled to a credit against, or reimbursement of, the tax on petroleum businesses. (Sec. 301-d(a), Tax Law)

The amount of the credit is listed in the above rate chart.

The credit rates are adjusted in the same manner applicable to fuel and petroleum product rates. (Sec. 301-d(b), Tax Law); N.Y. Dep't of Tax. and Fin. Pub. 908.

The credit must be first applied against the liability for the petroleum business tax for the period during which the liability arose. Excess credit, if any, may then be applied against liability for subsequent periods. (Sec. 301-d(b), Tax Law); N.Y. Dep't of Tax. and Fin. Pub. 908.

Commercial gallonage: A credit or reimbursement of tax is allowed against the non-highway diesel motor fuel component and the residual petroleum product component of the petroleum business tax with respect to commercial gallonage. "Commercial gallonage" is gallonage included in the full measure of the petroleum business tax component that does not qualify for either the utility credit or reimbursement allowed to electric corporations or the exemption from supplemental tax allowed to certain manufacturers. The amount of the credit or reimbursement is determined by multiplying eligible commercial gallonage by the basic credit or reimbursement per gallon. The basic credit or reimbursement per gallon is 50% of the sum of (1) the then current rate of the supplemental tax, and (2) the product of the current supplemental tax rate and the then current surcharge rate. The credit or reimbursement must first be applied against tax liability for the same period during which the credit or reimbursement arose. Excess credit or reimbursement may then be carried forward to subsequent periods. (Secs. 301-c(i); 300(k), Tax Law)

The amount of the commercial gallonage credit/reimbursement is listed in the above chart.

Minimum tax: There is no minimum tax.

• *Returns and payment*

Returns and payment of tax are due on or before the 20th day following the close of the taxable month. (Sec. 308(a), Tax Law)

Quarterly returns: The Commissioner of Taxation and Finance may permit quarterly, rather than monthly, returns by diesel motor fuel distributors that only make sales of diesel motor fuel for residential heating purposes and businesses registered as "distributors of kero-jet fuel only." (Sec. 308(a) Tax Law)

Electronic funds transfer payment: Taxpayers liable for more than $5 million of petroleum business taxes during the preceding one-year period are required to make

¶2716

payment of tax by electronic funds transfer or certified check. The amount of payment by such method is $3/4$ of the total liability for petroleum business taxes payable by the taxpayer for the comparable month of the preceding year, *or* the taxpayer's total liability for such taxes during the period ending on the 22nd day of each month. (Secs. 308(b); 10(b)(1), (2), Sec. 308(a)) For additional information on EFT payments, see ¶3602.

Reimbursement of tax: Purchasers of diesel motor fuel in New York who subsequently sell such fuel to consumers exclusively for residential heating purposes are eligible for a reimbursement of tax, subject to certain limitations. Purchasers of diesel motor fuel or motor fuel in New York who subsequently sell such fuel to the state of New York or the United States are eligible for reimbursement, provided that (1) the fuel is for the government organization's own use and consumption, (2) the tax has been paid on the fuel and the entire amount has been absorbed by the purchaser, and (3) the purchaser possesses documentary proof satisfactory to the Commissioner of Taxation and Finance evidencing the absorption by it of the entire amount of the tax. (Sec. 301-c(a), (b), Tax Law)

CCH Advisory: Government Credit Card Sales

Credit card companies and motor fuel or motor diesel fuel distributors that finance the purchase of such fuel by governmental entities using credit cards are allowed a credit or refund of New York motor fuel, petroleum business, and sales and use taxes on such purchases. According to the sponsor's memorandum, this provision is intended to conform to federal tax legislation that creates a system for credit card issuers and fuel distributors to receive refunds of the federal excise tax on fuel purchases by governmental entities using credit cards. Applicants must file Form FT-505.1, Government Entity Credit Card Refund or Credit Election. (Sec. 289-c(3)(h), Tax Law; TSB-M-08(12)S and TSB-M-08(9)M, November 5, 2008, CCH NEW YORK TAX REPORTS, ¶406-212)

Refunds for uncollectible debts: Petroleum businesses may apply for refunds of petroleum business taxes (including the supplemental tax) with respect to taxes paid for sales on accounts determined to be uncollectible. The refund will be permitted if (1) the gallons have been included in reports filed by the petroleum business and the tax paid, (2) the gallonage was sold in bulk by the petroleum business to a purchaser for the purchaser's own use and consumption, and (3) the sale gave rise to a debt that (a) is worthless and (b) is deducted as a worthless debt for federal income tax purposes for the taxable year covering the month in which the state refund claim is filed. (Sec. 301-l, Tax Law)

• *Carriers*

Imposition of tax: A monthly tax is imposed on motor fuel and diesel motor fuel imported into New York by carriers in the fuel tanks of vehicular units. (Sec. 301-h, Tax Law)

Basis and rate: The tax is measured by the number of gallons of motor fuel and diesel motor fuel imported into New York in the fuel tanks of vehicular units that have not previously been included in the measure of the tax on petroleum businesses and are consumed in New York in the operation of the vehicular unit, multiplied by the sum of the motor fuel and automotive-type diesel motor fuel rates applicable to petroleum businesses and the supplemental petroleum business tax rate. (Sec. 301-h(a), Tax Law)

Credit: A credit is allowed equal to the tax absorbed by the carrier with respect to any excess of gallonage purchased in New York during the reporting period, over the gallonage consumed in the state during such period. The credit may be claimed against the tax for which the carrier would otherwise be liable for the eight succeeding calendar quarters commencing with the end of the reporting period for which the excess was derived.

¶2716

In lieu of a credit, a claim for a refund may be filed. The claim must be filed within two years from the end of the reporting period for which the excess was derived and may not be filed more than quarterly. (Sec. 301-h(a), Tax Law)

• *Aviation fuel businesses*

Imposition of tax: A monthly tax is imposed on aviation fuel businesses for the privilege of engaging in business, doing business, employing capital, owning or leasing property or maintaining an office in New York. (Sec. 301-e(a), Tax Law)

An "aviation fuel business" is a corporation or unincorporated business that (1) imports or causes aviation gasoline or kero-jet fuel to be imported (including importing in aviation fuel tanks) into New York for use, distribution, storage or sale in the state, (2) produces, refines, manufactures, or compounds aviation gasoline or kero-jet fuel in the state, (3) sells or uses kero-jet fuel in New York (other than a retail sale not in bulk or self-use of kero-jet fuel that was sold to the corporation or unincorporated business at retail), or (4) is registered as a distributor of kero-jet fuel only. (Secs. 301-e(e); 300(b), Tax Law)

"Kero-jet fuel and aviation gasoline consumed in this state" is presumed to mean all such fuel consumed during takeoffs from points in New York.

Exemption: An exemption applies to an aviation fuel business servicing four or more cities in New York with nonstop flights between such cities.

Basis and rate: The tax on aviation fuel businesses is equal to the sum of the aviation gasoline component and the kero-jet fuel component. A supplemental tax is imposed on the aviation gasoline component of the tax. The components of the tax are determined as follows:

Aviation gasoline component: The aviation gasoline component is determined by multiplying the aviation gasoline rate by the number of gallons of aviation gasoline imported or caused to be imported into New York for use, distribution, storage, or sale in the state, or produced, refined, manufactured, or compounded in New York by the aviation fuel business.

Kero-jet fuel component: The kero-jet fuel component is determined by multiplying the kero-jet fuel rate by (1) the number of gallons of kero-jet fuel imported or caused to be imported into New York by an aviation fuel business and consumed in New York by such business in the operation of its aircraft, and (2) kero-jet fuel, which has not been previously included in the measure of the tax that is sold in New York by an aviation fuel business to persons other than those registered as aviation fuel businesses or consumed in New York by the aviation fuel business in the operation of its aircraft. (Sec. 301-e(a), (b), (c), Tax Law)

Kero-jet fuel included within the kero-jet fuel component in the calculation of the aviation fuel business tax is excluded in the calculation of the aviation fuel business surcharge.

Fuel/gasoline rates: See the above chart.

Credit: A motor fuel distributor is entitled to a partial credit or refund of tax paid on aviation gasoline sold to a fixed-base operator registered as a retail seller of aviation gasoline under Article 12-A, Tax Law. To be eligible for the credit or refund, the tax must have been paid by the distributor and not passed on to the retail seller. (Sec. 301-e(b)(2), Tax Law)

A retail seller of aviation gasoline will be entitled to a partial credit or refund of aviation gasoline delivered and stored at its fixed base operations premises, as of the time that the fuel is delivered and placed in the storage facility. (Sec. 301-e(b)(2), Tax Law)

An airline that is registered as a motor fuel distributor and imports aviation fuel into New York for use in its airplanes, where delivery and storage takes place as described in Sec. 289-c(1-a)(b)(i), Tax Law, is also allowed a partial credit or refund of tax on fuel imported and used in the operation of its airplanes. (Sec. 301-e(b)(2), Tax Law)

An aviation fuel business taxed as such by reason of importation in the fuel tank of airplanes is allowed a partial credit or refund for aviation gasoline consumed in New York. (Sec. 301-e(b)(2), Tax Law)

A partial credit or refund of the supplemental tax is also allowed with respect to aviation gasoline that qualifies for the partial credit or refund of the tax on aviation fuel. (Sec. 301-j(b), Tax Law)

Credit amount: See the chart above for the per gallon rate.

Reimbursement—Airlines: An aviation fuel business is entitled to reimbursement of the tax on aviation fuel purchased in New York and consumed exclusively in the operation of the business' aircraft outside New York where the entire amount of the tax has been absorbed by the aviation fuel business. Airlines are also entitled to a credit for aviation fuel that is imported into New York but consumed outside the state. (Sec. 301-e(d), Tax Law)

Refunds for uncollectible debts: Aviation fuel businesses may apply for refunds of petroleum business taxes (including the aviation business fuel supplemental tax) with respect to taxes paid for sales on accounts determined to be uncollectible. The refund will be permitted if (1) the gallons have been included in reports filed by the aviation fuel business and the tax paid, (2) the gallonage was sold in bulk by the aviation fuel business to a purchaser for the purchaser's own use and consumption, and (3) the sale gave rise to a debt that (a) is worthless and (b) is deducted as a worthless debt for federal income tax purposes for the taxable year covering the month in which the state refund claim is filed. (Sec. 301-1(a), Tax Law)

¶2717 Nonrefillable Beverage Containers Tax (Repealed)

The tax on beverage containers was repealed, effective October 1, 1998. The tax was imposed on sales of nonrefillable beverage containers containing not more than one gallon or 3.8 liters of carbonated soft drink, mineral water, or soda water at a rate of 1¢ per container.

¶2718 Environmental Protection and Spill Compensation Fund

Law: Secs. 172, 174, 179, 181, Navigation Law (CCH NEW YORK TAX REPORTS, ¶ 37-151).

The Environmental Protection and Spill Compensation Fund was established in 1978 to ensure the prompt cleanup and removal of petroleum discharges. The fund is subsidized by license fees levied against major facilities in New York.

License requirements: All persons operating, or causing to be operated, a major facility within New York are required to be licensed by the Commissioner of the Department of Environmental Conservation. Licenses are issued for a period not exceeding five years. (Sec. 174.1, .2, Navigation Law)

"Major facility" defined: The term "major facility" includes refineries, storage or transfer terminals, pipelines, deep water ports, drilling platforms, and any appurtenances attached to any of the foregoing that are used, or are capable of being used, to refine, produce, store, handle, transfer, process or transport petroleum. Vessels will be considered major facilities only when petroleum is transferred between them. Facilities with total combined above-ground or buried storage capacity of less than 400,000 gallons, however, are not regarded as major facilities. (Sec. 172.11, Navigation Law)

License fees: License fees are imposed on the first transfer point of barrels of petroleum at the rate of 1¢ per barrel. The fee is collected until the balance in the Environmental Protection and Spill Compensation Fund equals or exceeds $25 million. In subsequent fiscal years, no license fee will be imposed unless the current balance in the Fund falls below $20 million, or pending claims against the fund exceed 50% of the balance. If major discharges or spills result in claims against the fund that exceed its existing balance, the license fee will be reimposed at the rate of 8¢ per barrel transferred until the balance equals pending claims. The fund administrator may set the rate at less than 8¢ per barrel if a determination is made that the revenue generated by the lesser rate will be sufficient to pay outstanding claims within one year of the imposition of the license fee. (Sec. 174.4(a), Navigation Law)

Surcharge: In addition to the license fee, a $4^1/4$¢ surcharge is imposed on the transfer of each barrel of petroleum. The surcharge must be paid regardless of whether the license fee continues to be imposed. (Sec. 174.4(b), Navigation Law)

Reports: Each licensee must file a report with the Commissioner by the 20th day of the month following the close of the license period. The report must certify the number of barrels of petroleum transferred to the licensee's major facility during the prior month. Petroleum coming into the state will be regarded as "transferred" to the first major facility to receive it in New York. Reports must be filed even if no petroleum was transferred during the month. Payment of the license fee and surcharge must accompany the report. (Sec. 174.5, Navigation Law)

Administration: The Environmental Protection and Spill Compensation Fund is administered by the New York State Department of Environmental Conservation, Regulatory Fee—Oil Spill Revenue Bureau, 50 Wolf Road, Room 628, Albany, NY 12233-5024.

¶2719 Tax on Generation of Hazardous Waste

Law: Sec. 27-0923, Environmental Conservation Law (CCH New York Tax Reports, ¶37-151).

Forms: TP-550-MN, Return of Special Assessments on Generation, Treatment or Disposal of Hazardous Waste in New York State.

Article 27 of the Environmental Conservation Law imposes special assessments on persons involved in the production or treatment of hazardous waste.

Every person engaged within New York in the generation of hazardous waste is subject to a special assessment. (Sec. 27-0923.1, Env. Conserv. Law)

"Hazardous waste" defined: The term "hazardous waste" means any waste (or combination of wastes) that, because of its quantity, concentration, or physical, chemical or infectious characteristics may (1) cause, or significantly contribute to an increase in, mortality or an increase in serious irreversible, or incapacitating reversible illness, or (2) pose a substantial present or potential hazard to human health or the environment when improperly treated, stored, transported, disposed, or otherwise managed. (Sec. 27-0923.3, Env. Conserv. Law)

CCH Advisory: Disposal Tax Stricken

The New York Court of Appeals upheld a lower court's determination that the hazardous waste disposal tax was unconstitutional because it was facially discriminatory against interstate commerce in violation of the Commerce Clause of the U.S. Constitution. The tax on generation of hazardous waste remains in effect. (*CWM Chemical Services v. Roth,* New York Court of Appeals, No. 3, March 23, 2006, CCH New York Tax Reports, ¶405-337) (¶2719)

Information on refunds of disposal taxes paid is found in *TSB-M-06(1)M,* New York Department of Taxation and Finance, April 13, 2006, CCH New York Tax Reports, ¶300-511.

• *Basis and rate of tax*

The special assessments are imposed on the tonnage of hazardous waste produced. The assessments are prorated in the event of fractional tons. (Sec. 27-0923.3(b), Env. Conserv. Law)

The special assessment on generators of hazardous waste is determined as follows:

$27 per ton of hazardous waste that is disposed of in a landfill on the site where the waste was generated, or that is designated for removal or removed from the site of generation for disposal in a landfill, or that is removed from the site of generation for storage before disposal in a landfill;

$9 per ton of hazardous waste that is designated for removal or removed from the site of generation for incineration or for storage prior to incineration;

$2 per ton of hazardous waste that is incinerated on the site where the waste was generated; and

$16 per ton of hazardous waste that is designated for removal or removed from the site of generation for treatment or disposal, exclusive of disposal in a landfill or by incineration, or for storage before such treatment or disposal. (Sec. 27-0923.1, Env. Conserv. Law)

The actual method utilized to dispose of or treat hazardous waste governs the determination of the applicable rate per ton. If an assessment is reported and paid on the basis of a rate that is greater than the rate applicable to the actual method used to dispose of or treat the waste, the difference between the amount reported and paid and the amount due using the rate applicable to the method utilized is regarded as an overpayment and must be credited or refunded. (Sec. 27-0923.3(e), Env. Conserv. Law)

Exemptions: No special assessment is imposed on the resource recovery of any hazardous waste. "Resource recovery" does not include the removal of water from a hazardous waste. (Sec. 27-0923.3(a), Env. Conserv. Law)

No special assessment is imposed on the generation of universal wastes. (Sec. 27-0923.1(f), Env. Conserv. Law)

• *Reports and payment*

Separate reports for each site must be filed with the Department of Taxation and Finance on a quarterly basis on or before the 20th day of the month following the end of the calendar quarter. Payment of the assessment generally accompanies the report. No quarterly return or payment is required for a site when there is no activity subject to assessment during the quarter, or the total assessments attributable to the site for the quarter do not exceed $27. (Sec. 27-0923.4(e), Env. Conserv. Law)

A penalty of 25% is imposed, in addition to an estimate of tax due, for failure or refusal to file a return or furnish information to the Department of Taxation and Finance. Interest on deficiencies is fixed by statute at 15% per annum. (Sec. 27-0923.7(b), Env. Conserv. Law)

Administration: The special assessment is administered by the Department of Taxation and Finance, W.A. Harriman State Campus, Albany, NY 12227. The provisions of Article 27, Tax Law, generally apply (Chapter 7).

¶2719

¶2720 MCTD Tax on Taxicab Rides

Law: Secs. 1281—1285, Tax Law (CCH NEW YORK TAX REPORTS, ¶ 35-051, 80-040).

A 50-cent surcharge is imposed on taxicab rides that originate in New York City and terminate anywhere within the territorial boundaries of the New York City Metropolitan Commuter Transportation District (MCTD). Taxicab owners are required to pass along the surcharge to passengers by adjusting the fares, and taximeters must be adjusted to include the tax. (Sec. 1281, Tax Law) Liability for the tax is the taxicab owner's responsibility. If the owner has a designated agent, both the owner and the agent must share the liability.

Returns and payment: Persons liable for the surcharge must file returns with the Department of Taxation and Finance within 20 days after the end of each quarterly period ending on the last day of March, June, September, and December. Payment of the tax is due with returns filed with the Department or to designated financial institutions. Returns and reports must be retained for three years. (Sec. 1284, Tax Law; Sec. 1285, Tax Law; *TSB-M-13(8)M, TSB-M-13(6)S,* July 12, 2013, CCH NEW YORK TAX REPORTS, ¶ 407-878)

¶2721 Waterfront Commission Payroll Tax (Joint New York— New Jersey Compact)

Law: Secs. 9858, 9860, 9861, 9901, Unconsolidated Laws (CCH NEW YORK TAX REPORTS, ¶ 35-101).

A joint compact between New York and New Jersey created the Waterfront Commission of New York Harbor and provided for the imposition of an assessment on each employer of longshoremen, pier superintendents, hiring agents and port watchmen within the Port of New York District. The proceeds of the tax are used to defray the expenses of the Commission.

• *Basis and rate of assessment*

The assessment is determined by the Waterfront Commission on the basis of its estimate of the percentage of employer gross payroll payments that will be sufficient to finance the Commission's budget for the year (after taking into account funds available from reserves, federal grants and other funds on hand). The rate may not exceed 2% of gross payroll payments.

• *Returns and payment*

Returns and payments are due on or before the 15th day of January, April, July and October covering the preceding calendar quarter. The Commission may grant a reasonable extension of time whenever good cause exists.

Administration: The assessment is administered by the Waterfront Commission of New York Harbor, 42 Broadway, New York, NY 10004.

¶2722 Stock Transfer Tax

Law: Secs. 270—281-a, Tax Law (CCH NEW YORK TAX REPORTS, ¶ 37-053).

Forms: MT-650, Stock Transfer Tax Return.

A tax is imposed on the sale or transfer of shares of stock, certificates of stock, certificates of rights to stock, certificates of interest in property or accumulations, certificates of interest in business conducted by trustees, and certificates of deposit within the state of New York. (Sec. 270.1, Tax Law)

The original issuance of stock is not subject to tax. However, transfers of treasury stock are taxable. 20 NYCRR § 440.1(g)

The effects of the stock transfer tax were phased out through a series of rebates. However, the tax is maintained in order to meet certain funding requirements of the Municipal Assistance Corporation. (Sec. 280-a, Tax Law)

Exemptions: Certain transfers are exempt from tax only if accompanied by a proper exemption certificate. In some cases the exemption is strictly limited to a transfer from or to the name of a particular person. These exempt transfers are, in general, the following (Sec. 270.5, Tax Law):

— odd lot sales on an Exchange within the state of New York;

— transfers of collateral security, and the return thereof;

— transfers of security pursuant to some statutory provision, and the return thereof;

— transfers between a fiduciary and its nominee, or between nominees of the same fiduciary;

— transfers between the owner and his or her custodian, or between a custodian and its nominee, or between nominees of the same custodian;

— loans of stock, or the return thereof;

— transfers between broker and customer, for sale or to complete a purchase;

— transfers between a corporation and a nominee thereof registered with the Tax Commission as provided by regulation, or between two registered nominees of the same corporation;

— certain transfers or deliveries upon the instructions of a broker for the purpose of holding the shares or certificates subject to the instructions of a clearing corporation affiliated with a New York securities exchange, and certain transfers upon the instructions of the clearing corporation; and

— certain transfers or deliveries upon the instructions of a depositor in a system for the central handling of securities.

Other exemptions are set forth in Secs. 270, 270-b, and 270-c, Tax Law.

No tax applies to either party in the case of a sale or transfer in which the vendor or transferor is a governmental entity or international organization that is not subject to the tax. (Sec. 270.3, Tax Law)

By federal law, when the sole event in New York is the delivery or transfer to or by a "registered clearing agency" or a "registered transfer agent," as those terms are defined under the Securities Exchange Act of 1934, there is no stock transfer tax due and owing on and after December 1, 1975. However, where a sale, agreement to sell, memorandum of sale or any other delivery or transfer takes place in New York, the stock transfer tax due and owing thereon must be paid (*Opinion of Counsel*, Department of Taxation and Finance, December 1, 1975).

• *Basis and rate of tax*

The tax rate and basis are as follows:

Selling Price Per Share	Rate (per share)
Less than $5	$1^1/4$¢
$5 or more but less than $10	$2^1/2$¢
$10 or more but less than $20	$3^3/4$¢
$20 or more	5¢
Transactions Other Than Sales	**Rate (per share)**
Per share	$2^1/2$¢

When any single sale relates to shares of the same class that are issued by the same issuer, the tax shall not exceed $350. Certain multiple sales of the same issue, executed on the same day, are considered a single sale. (Secs. 270.2, 270-e, Tax Law)

Rebates: The effects of the stock transfer tax were phased out through a series of rebates.

A 100% rebate is currently allowed. However, a rebate is not allowed where the Department of Taxation and Finance has determined the amount of tax due because of the failure of the taxpayer to pay the required tax. (Sec. 280-a, Tax Law)

- *Returns and payment*

The tax is ordinarily collected by the sale of tax stamps through authorized agents, affixed and cancelled on the stock certificate or the memorandum of sale, or in the case of transactions shown only on the books of the corporation, on the books of the corporation. Alternate methods are available to members of a securities exchange in New York registered with the Securities and Exchange Commission, and certain others. Returns are not required unless the alternate collection methods are employed. (Secs. 270.4; 281-a, Tax Law)

Administration: The tax is administered by the Department of Taxation and Finance, W.A. Harriman State Campus, Albany, NY 12227. A branch office is maintained at 80 Centre Street, New York City.

¶2723 Taxes on Gaming and Wagering Contests

> *Law:* Secs. 451 *et seq.,,* 1105(f)(1), Tax Law; Secs. 227, 236, 532, Racing, Pari-mutuel Wagering and Breeding Law; Sec. 1400 *et seq.,* Racing, Pari-mutuel Wagering and Breeding Law (CCH NEW YORK TAX REPORTS, ¶ 35-301).

> *Forms:* Form MT-160, Authorized Combative Sports Tax Return; Form AU-212, New York State Pari-Mutuel Betting Tax Return.

New York imposes privilege taxes on certain gaming and wagering activities. Taxation of combative sports, thoroughbred horse racing (pari-mutuel taxes), and interactive fantasy sports are discussed below.

- *Authorized combative sports*

Every person holding any professional or amateur boxing, sparring or wrestling match or exhibition in New York is subject to a tax at a rate of 3% of gross receipts from ticket sales and/or broadcasting rights, except that in no event may the tax exceed $50,000 for any match or exhibition (Sec. 452, Tax Law).

On and after September 1, 2016, a gross receipts tax is imposed on authorized combative sports (*i.e.,* kick boxing, single discipline martial arts, or mixed martial arts events) held in New York at a rate of 8.5% of gross receipts from ticket sales, with no maximum tax, plus 3% ($50,000 maximum) of the sum of:

(i) gross receipts from broadcasting rights, and

(ii) gross receipts from digital streaming over the internet.

Except for the 8.5% tax, the tax imposed may not exceed $50,000 for any match or exhibition (Sec. 452, Tax Law; *TSB-M-16(6)M, 8(S),* New York Department of Taxation and Finance, August 18, 2016, CCH NEW YORK TAX REPORTS, ¶ 408-829).

Exemptions: The following are exempt from the tax on authorized combative sports (Sec. 455, Tax Law):

— matches or exhibitions conducted under the supervision or the control of the New York State National Guard or naval militia where all of the contestants are members of the active militia;

— matches or exhibitions where the contestants are all amateurs, sponsored by or under the supervision of any university, college, school or other institution of learning, recognized by the regents of the state of New York; and

— matches or exhibitions where the contestants are all amateurs sponsored by or under the supervision of the U.S. Amateur Boxing Federation or its local affiliates, or the American Olympic Association.

Admissions to combative sports events are exempt from sales tax (Sec. 1105(f)(1), Tax Law).

Returns and payments: Returns and payments of the gross receipts tax from broadcasting rights must be made on or before the last day of the month in which such gross receipts from broadcasting rights are received by the individual corporation, association or club holding such match or exhibition. If the taxpayer receives receipts subject to tax during the last five days of a month, the required return and payment of tax is not due until the fifth day of the succeeding month. Returns and payments of the gross receipts tax from ticket sales must be made within 10 business days after the holding of the match or exhibition. (Sec. 453, Tax Law)

• *Thoroughbred racing (pari-mutuel sports)*

Corporations and associations conducting pari-mutuel betting pay a percentage of the total pool to the Department of Taxation and Finance. For racing corporation or association pools, rates are as follows (Sec. 236, Racing, Pari-Mutuel Wagering and Breeding Law):

— 1.5% of regular and multiple bets,

— 6.75% of exotic bets, and

— 7.75% of super exotic bets, as well as 55% of the breaks.

An additional of 1% applies to all on-track bets where a racing association or corporation failed to expend at least of 1% of such bets during the prior calendar year on capital improvement enhancements.

For nonprofit racing corporations or associations, the tax on the total pool of regular and multiple bets is 20% of the breaks as well as 5% of regular bets and 4% of multiple bets. Exotic bets are subject to a tax of 7.5% plus 20% of the breaks. Super exotic bets are subject to a tax of 7.5% plus 50% of the breaks.

Nonprofit associations or corporations must pay 50% of the compensation received from wagers made on races simulcast outside New York to the State Thoroughbred Racing Capital Investment Fund (Sec. 238, Racing, Pari-Mutuel Wagering and Breeding Law).

There is a 4% tax on admissions (Sec. 227, Racing, Pari-Mutuel Wagering and Breeding Law).

New York City imposes a 5% surcharge on the portion of pari-mutuel wagering pools distributable to persons having placed bets at off-track betting facilities within the City. (Sec. 532, Racing, Pari-Mutuel Wagering and Breeding Law) Every other regional off-track betting corporation and off-track betting operator imposes a similar surcharge.

• *Interactive fantasy sports*

A privilege taxis imposed on interactive fantasy sports contests in New York, effective August 3, 2016 (Sec. 1400 *et seq*, Racing, Pari-mutuel Wagering and Breeding Law). Operators of interactive fantasy sports contests must register with the N.Y. State Gaming Commission (Sec. 1401(8), Racing, Pari-mutuel Wagering and Breeding Law).

"Interactive fantasy sports contest" or "contest" means a game of skill wherein one or more contestants compete against each other by using their knowledge and understanding of athletic events and athletes to select and manage rosters of simulated players whose performance directly corresponds with the actual performance of human competitors on sports teams and in sports events (Sec. 1401(8), Racing, Pari-mutuel Wagering and Breeding Law).

"Interactive fantasy sports gross revenue" is defined as the amount equal to the total of all entry fees not attributable to New York state prohibited sports events that

¶2723

a registrant collects from all players, less the total of all sums not attributable to New York state prohibited sports events paid out as winnings to all players, multiplied by the resident percentage for New York state; provided, however, that the total of all sums paid out as winnings to players may not include the cash equivalent value of any merchandise or thing of value awarded as a prize (Sec. 1401(9), Racing, Pari-mutuel Wagering and Breeding Law).

Tax rates: Registrants are required to pay a tax equivalent to 15% of their interactive fantasy sports gross revenue generated within New York; in addition, registrants must pay a tax equal to 0.5%, but not to exceed $50,000 annually (Sec. 1407, Racing, Pari-mutuel Wagering and Breeding Law).

Planning considerations: The gaming commission may perform audits of the books and records of an interactive fantasy sports operator with a permit or registrant, at such times and intervals as it deems appropriate, for the purpose of determining the sufficiency of tax payments (Sec. 1410, Racing, Pari-mutuel Wagering and Breeding Law).

PART IX

LOCAL TAXES

CHAPTER 28
NEW YORK CITY GENERAL CORPORATION TAX

¶2801 Scope of Chapter

This chapter discusses the principal provisions of the New York City general corporation tax, enacted as Subchapter 2 of the City Business Tax. Its purpose is to give a general description of the tax, its application and the manner of its administration. The administration provisions outlined (¶2815) are enacted as Subchapter 5, Corporate Tax Procedure and Administration, of the City Business Tax, which is also applicable to the tax on financial corporations (Chapter 29).

¶2802 History and Imposition of Tax

The New York City general corporation tax (Subchapter 2 of the City Business Tax) was enacted in 1966.

The tax is patterned after the New York State corporation franchise (income) tax imposed by Article 9-A of the Tax Law.

Domestic (New York State) and foreign corporations are taxed for the privilege of doing business in New York City. The privilege year is the fiscal or calendar year on which the tax is based.

• *NYC corporate tax reform*

The New York City corporate income tax system is significantly revised and updated, generally applicable to taxable years beginning on or after January 1, 2015.

However, S corporations remain subject to the existing New York City general corporation tax or banking corporation tax. (Ch. 60 (S.B. 4610), Laws 2015)

For affected corporations (*i.e.,* corporations and banks that are not S corporations), the new provisions make numerous changes, similar to those enacted last year for New York State' corporation franchise (income) tax, including the following (Sec. 11-651 *et seq.,* N.Y.C. Adm. Code):

— merging the banking and general corporation taxes; (¶2803)

— in place of the general 8.85% tax rate, allowing a reduced rate for certain small businesses and qualified manufacturing corporations; (¶2805)

— applying a 9% tax rate to certain financial corporations having more than $100 billion in assets; (¶2805)

— adopting combined reporting for unitary corporations that meet a more-than-50% stock ownership test; (¶2813)

— replacing the entire net income tax base with a business income tax base; (¶2805, ¶2807)

— adopting the phase-in of a single receipts factor, as previously contained in the general corporation tax; (¶2811)

— applying customer-based sourcing rules; (¶2811)

— eliminating the separate treatment of subsidiary capital and income; (¶2811)

— modifying the definitions of "investment capital" and "investment income" and exempting both from tax; (¶2805)

— for pre-2015 net operating losses (NOLs), providing for a prior NOL conversion subtraction; (¶2808)

— allowing a three-year carryback for NOLs incurred in tax years beginning after 2014; (¶2808)

— repealing the alternative minimum tax base for income plus compensation; (¶2805)

— eliminating the tax on assets for banks (¶2805), (¶2903); and

— increasing the maximum capital base tax to $10 million, but allowing a $10,000 reduction for all capital base tax calculations. (¶2805)

¶2803 Corporations Subject to Tax

Law: Secs. 11-602—11-610, 11-651, 11-654, NYC Adm. Code (CCH NEW YORK CITY TAX REPORTS, ¶505-200—505-215).

Under corporate tax reform legislation enacted in 2015, the New York City corporate income tax system was significantly revised, generally applicable to taxable years beginning on or after January 1, 2015 (Subchapter 3-A, Corporate Tax of 2015; Sec. 11-651, N.Y.C. Adm. Code, *et. seq.*).

S corporations and qualified subchapter S subsidiaries remain subject to the existing, pre-reform general corporation tax provisions (Sec. 11-602.1, N.Y.C. Adm. Code).

Beginning in 2015, the taxation of financial corporations (banks, bank holding companies, savings and loan companies, securities and commodities brokers, etc.) other than S corporations and their subsidiaries, is merged with that of general corporations (Sec. 11-654(e)(1)(i), N.Y.C. Adm. Code; see ¶2903).

• *Pre-reform provisions*

All domestic corporations, and all foreign corporations doing business, employing capital, owning or leasing property, or maintaining an office in New York City, are subject to the New York City general corporation tax, unless specifically exempted or subject to certain other New York City taxes.

¶2803

The term "corporation" includes associations that are classified as corporations pursuant to IRC Sec. 7701(a)(3) (including limited liability companies that are so classified) and publicly traded partnerships that are treated as corporations for federal tax purposes pursuant to IRC Sec. 7704. However, an unincorporated organization that would be treated as a corporation under the this definition, but was subject to New York City unincorporated business tax (Chapter 36) for taxable years beginning in 1995, may make a one-time election to continue to be subject to the unincorporated business tax for taxable years beginning in 1996 and thereafter.

Exempt corporations are treated at ¶ 2804.

The law specifically states that the following activities do not constitute doing business, employing capital, owning or leasing property, or maintaining an office in New York City:

— the maintenance of cash balances with banks or trust companies in New York City;

— the ownership of stock or securities kept in New York City in a safe deposit box, safe, vault or other receptacle rented for the purpose, or pledged as collateral security, or deposited in safekeeping or custodian accounts with one or more banks or trust companies, or brokers who are members of a recognized security exchange;

— the taking of any action, by any such bank or trust company or broker, that is incidental to the rendering of safekeeping or custodian service to the corporation;

— the maintenance of a New York City office by corporation officers or directors who are not employees of the corporation if the corporation is not otherwise doing business or engaging in taxable activity in New York City;

— the keeping of corporation books and records in New York City by a non-employee if the corporation is not otherwise doing business or engaging in taxable activity in New York City;

— any combination of the foregoing activities.

Federal restrictions: A foreign corporation will not be subject to the general corporation tax if it conducts only minimum activities within New York City. To be exempt, the activities of the foreign corporation must be limited to the following activities:

— the solicitation of orders by employees or representatives within the state for sales of tangible personal property, where the orders are sent outside New York State for approval or rejection and, if approved, are filled by shipment or delivery from a point outside New York; and

— the solicitation of orders for sales of tangible personal property by employees or representatives within the state in the name of or for the benefit of a prospective customer of the foreign corporation, provided the customer's orders are sent outside New York for approval or rejection and, if approved, are filled by shipment or delivery from a point outside New York.

CCH Advisory: Participation in Trade Shows

Foreign corporations that do not otherwise conduct business may participate in New York tradeshows for up to 14 days during the corporation's federal taxable year without becoming subject to New York City's general corporation tax (NYC Reg. 11-04(c)(1)(vi)). New York State has adopted a similar regulation (Reg. 1-3.3(a)(7)).

Period when subject to tax: A corporation incorporated or beginning to do business, employ capital, own or lease property, or maintain an office in New York City immediately becomes subject to the tax. Its first privilege year and base period is its first calendar or fiscal year (that is, the period beginning on the date of incorporation or of commencing to do business or engage in other taxable activity in New York City and ending on the last day of the accounting year).

Corporations ceasing to do business or engage in other taxable activity in New York City pay a tax for the privilege of doing business for the portion of the calendar or fiscal year prior to the cessation of doing business. A dissolved corporation continuing to do business remains subject to tax.

Other organizations: The general corporation tax also applies to certain organizations having the characteristics of a corporation, such as joint-stock companies or associations, and to various business and investment trusts.

S corporations: Small business corporations electing to be taxed as S corporations for federal income tax purposes are subject to the pre-reform provisions of the New York City general corporation tax.

Domestic international sales corporations (DISCs): DISCs and their shareholders are subject to taxation in the same manner as other corporations.

Professional service corporations: New York City has not adopted any specific provisions relating to professional service corporations.

Real estate investment trusts (REITs): REITs are subject to the New York City general corporation tax computed either on allocated entire net income or the flat fee minimum (¶2805). Entire net income is computed in the same manner as for New York State (¶918) except that a net operating loss is not allowed.

Regulated investment companies (RICs): RICs are subject to the New York City general corporation tax computed either on allocated entire net income or the flat-fee minimum (¶2805). Entire net income is computed in the same manner as for New York State (¶911).

¶2804 Exempt Corporations

Law: Secs. 11-122, 11-603, NYC Adm. Code; Rule Sec. 11-04 (CCH NEW YORK CITY TAX REPORTS, ¶505-220).

Insurance companies subject to the New York City insurance corporation tax are exempt from the New York City general corporation tax; see ¶3308.

Practitioner Comment: HMOs are Exempt Insurers

Income earned by health maintenance organizations (HMOs) is generated from the payment of premiums by clients for medical insurance coverage. The HMOs provide their members with protection against the economic loss that would be caused by an unexpected injury or illness. This is the essence of an insurance business. Consequently, HMOs are exempt from the general corporation tax. (*Aetna, Inc.,* NYC TAT (7/22/14), CCH NEW YORK CITY TAX REPORTS, ¶600-779)

Mark S. Klein, Esq., Hodgson Russ LLP

Other exempt corporations include the following:

— Utility companies (subject to the New York City utilities excise tax (¶3307)). Most utility companies subject to tax under New York City's utility tax are exempt from the general corporation tax, but vendors and resellers of utility services that are not closely supervised by the Department of Public Service are subject to both taxes. In computing the corporation tax, however, the vendors reduce business income allocated to the city by a percentage derived by dividing gross operating income subject to the utility tax by total gross operating income. The city may require other apportionment methods if necessary.

¶2804

In the case of a taxpayer that is a partner in a partnership subject to the New York City utility tax as a utility, entire net income does not include the taxpayer's distributive or *pro rata* share for federal income tax purposes of any item of income, gain, loss, or deduction of the partnership, or any item of income, gain, loss, or deduction of the partnership that the taxpayer is required to take into account separately for federal income tax purposes.

— Bank holding companies that file consolidated returns with affiliated corporations subject to the New York City financial corporation tax;

— A trust company organized under New York State law, all the stock of which is owned by at least 20 New York savings banks;

— Limited-profit housing companies organized under Article 2 of the Private Housing Finance Law;

— Housing development fund companies organized pursuant to Article 11 of the Private Housing Finance Law;

— Nonstock corporations organized and operated exclusively for nonprofit purposes and not engaged in substantial commercial activities;

— New York corporations exclusively engaged in operating vessels in foreign commerce;

— New York corporations principally engaged in the conduct of a ferry business that operates between any of the boroughs of New York City under a lease granted by the city, and city owned corporations principally engaged in an aviation, steamboat, ferry, or navigation business;

— Organizations that are organized exclusively for the purpose of holding title to property (under IRC Sec. 501(2) and (25)), and that turn over the net income so derived to an exempt organization; and

— Foreign corporations not taxable under P.L. 86-272 because their activities in New York State are limited to the solicitation of orders (¶902).

CCH Caution: Unprotected Activities

A corporation may become subject to the New York City general corporation tax if it engages in activities anywhere in New York State that remove it from the protection of P.L. 86-272 (Rule Sec. 11-04). See ¶902 for a listing of protected activities.

Exclusion of REMICs: An entity that is treated for federal income tax purposes as a Real Estate Mortgage Investment Conduit (REMIC) is not subject to the general business corporation tax. A REMIC is not treated as a corporation, partnership or trust for purposes of the general corporation tax, and the assets of a REMIC are not included in the calculation of any tax liability under the general corporation tax. The exemption does not apply to holders of regular or residual interests, as defined in IRC Sec. 860G, or on income from such interests.

¶2805 Basis and Rate of Tax

Law: Sec. 11-604, NYC Adm. Code; NYC Rule Secs. 11-34, 11-35, 11-36 (CCH NEW YORK CITY TAX REPORTS, ¶505-251, 505-401).

For taxable years beginning after 2014 and before 2018, corporations subject to the New York City general corporation tax must determine their tax under three (previously, four) alternative methods and pay whichever of the three produces the greatest liability.

For taxable years beginning after 2014 and before 2018, the alternatives are as follows (Sec. 11-604, NYC Adm. Code):

(1) a tax at the rate of 8.85% on allocated business income (9% for certain financial corporations having more than $100 billion in assets); or

(2) a tax at the rate of 0.15 on each dollar of allocated business capital (0.04 per dollar in the case of cooperative housing corporations), not to exceed $10 million (a $10,000 reduction applies to all capital tax calculations); or

(3) a fixed dollar minimum tax of that varies according to the taxpayer's New York City receipts, as follows (Sec. 11-604(1)(E), NYC Adm. Code):

The rate for qualified manufacturing corporations ranges from 4.425% to 8.85%, depending on the amount of business income.

The rate for small businesses ranges from 6.5% to 8.85%, depending on the amount of business income.

The portion of total business capital directly attributable to stock in a subsidiary that is taxable as a utility within the meaning of the New York City Utility Tax or would have been taxable as an insurance corporation under the former New York City Insurance Corporation Tax is taxed at the rate of 0.75%.

S corporations and qualified subchapter S subsidiaries remain subject to the existing, pre-reform general corporation tax provisions. (Sec. 11-602.1, NYC Adm. Code)

New York receipts	Fixed dollar minimum
Not more than $100,000	$25
$100,001 to $250,000	$75
$250,001 to $500,000	$175
$500,001 to $1,000,000	$500
$1,000,001 to $5,000,000	$1,500
$5,000,001 to $25,000,000	$3,500
$25,000,001 to $50,000,000	$5,000
$50,000,001 to $100,000,000	$10,000
$100,000,001 to $250,000,000	$20,000
$250,000,001 to $500,000,000	$50,000
$500,000,001 to $1 billion	$100,000
Over $1 billion	$200,000

For taxable years beginning after 2014, the alternative minimum tax base for income plus compensation is repealed. This was a tax at the rate of 8.85% of an amount that is 30% (subject to reduction; see below) of the taxpayer's entire net income plus salaries and other compensation paid to 5%-plus stockholders and less the sum of $40,000 (prorated for fractional years)

• *Entire net income (business income) base*

"Entire net income" is business income allocated to New York City, which is presumably the same as entire net taxable income that the corporation is required to report to the U.S. Treasury Department, with certain inclusions, exclusions and other modifications that are similar to those allowed for New York State corporation franchise (income) tax purposes (Sec. 11-652(c)(8), N.Y.C. Adm. Code).

The modifications required for New York City purposes are discussed below (¶ 2807). In the case of S corporations, the starting point for computing entire net income is the federal taxable income that would have been reported if an election under subchapter S of Chapter 1 of the Internal Revenue Code had not been made. A similar provision applies to qualified subchapter S subsidiaries.

New York City entire net income includes income within and without the United States, thereby including income of alien corporations from foreign sources not subject to federal taxation.

Entire net income consists of "business income". The term "business income" means entire net income minus investment income and other exempt income. In no event shall the sum of investment income and other exempt income exceed entire net income (Sec. 11-652(c)(7), N.Y.C. Adm. Code).

For allocation of entire net income, see ¶ 2811.

¶ 2805

• *Business capital base*

"Business capital" means all assets, other than investment capital and stock issued by the taxpayer, less liabilities not deducted from investment capital; provided, however, business capital shall include only those assets the income, loss or expense of which are properly reflected (or would have been properly reflected if not fully depreciated or expensed or depreciated or expensed to a nominal amount) in the computation of entire net income for the taxable year (Sec. 11-652(c)(6), N.Y.C. Adm. Code).

"Investment capital" generally means long-term investments in stocks, bonds and other securities, corporate and governmental, not held for sale to customers in the regular course of business, exclusive of stock in companies included with the taxpayer in a combined report and stock issued by the taxpayer (Sec. 11-652(c)(4), N.Y.C. Adm. Code).

The amount of business and investment capital is determined by taking the average value of the gross assets (less, liabilities deductible therefrom that are directly and indirectly attributable to investment capital, and for business capital, liabilities not deducted from subsidiary or investment capital), and, if the period covered by the report is other than a period of 12 calendar months, by multiplying the value by the number of calendar months or major parts thereof included in the period, and dividing the product by 12. For purposes of the determination, real property and marketable securities are valued at fair market value, and the value of personal property other than marketable securities is the value shown on the books and records of the taxpayer in accordance with generally accepted accounting principles.

Corporate tax reform: For tax years beginning after 2014, the maximum capital base tax is increased to $10 million, but a $10,000 reduction is allowed for all capital base tax calculations (Sec. 11-654.3(e)(ii)(D), N.Y.C. Adm. Code); (Sec. 11-654.3(e)(ii)(E), N.Y.C. Adm. Code).

• *Income plus compensation base (repealed for tax years after 2014)*

This base did not apply to regulated investment companies, real estate investment trusts, and certain small businesses.

Certain small businesses: Both the alternative income plus compensation tax base and the capital tax base under the General Corporation Tax were eliminated for corporations that (1) have less than $250,000 in gross income, (2) allocate 100% to the City, and (3) have no investment or subsidiary capital or income. Additionally, any such corporation that is not a New York State S corporation could elect to pay its tax based on its New York State entire net income (modified by adding back New York City corporate tax) rather than separately calculating New York City entire net income. (Sec. 11-604, N.Y.C. Adm. Code)

Computation of base: The tax base was determined as follows:

(1) add, to the taxpayer's entire net income (or net loss), 100% of all salaries and other compensation paid to every stockholder (including a stockholder who is also a corporate officer) owning in excess of 5% of the taxpayer's issued capital stock, but only to the extent that a deduction was allowed for such salaries and compensation in computing entire net income or net loss;

(2) deduct from such total: $40,000 (or a proportionate part thereof in the case of a return for less than a year); and

(3) multiply the balance by 15% (for taxable years beginning on or after January 1, 2010).

• *Subsidiary capital*

"Subsidiary capital" is defined as investments in the stock of subsidiaries and any indebtedness from subsidiaries, exclusive of accounts receivable acquired in the ordinary course of trade or business for services rendered or for sales of property held primarily for sale to customers, whether or not evidenced by written instrument, on which interest is not claimed and deducted by the subsidiary for tax purposes.

The amount of subsidiary capital is determined by taking the average value of the gross assets (less, liabilities that are directly or indirectly attributable to subsidiary capital), and, if the period covered by the report is other than a period of 12 calendar months, by multiplying the value by the number of calendar months or major parts thereof included in the period, and dividing the product by 12. For purposes of the determination, real property and marketable securities are valued at fair market value, and the value of personal property other than marketable securities is the value shown on the books and records of the taxpayer in accordance with generally accepted accounting principles.

¶2806 Credits Against Tax

Law: Sec. 1201-a, Tax Law; Secs. 11-604, 11-654, 22-622, NYC Adm. Code (CCH NEW YORK CITY TAX REPORTS, ¶507-001—507-035).

The New York City general corporation tax provides for the following tax credits:

• *Relocation and employment assistance program (REAP) credit*

A credit is allowed to businesses that have conducted substantial business operations outside of New York City or south of 96th Street in Manhattan for 24 months prior to relocation, and that relocate all or part of the business operations to eligible premises in other parts of the city, and enter into a contract to purchase or lease eligible premises or a parcel on which eligible premises will be constructed, on or after May 27, 1987, or owned such property prior to that date and have not applied for the property tax exemption for industrial or commercial properties. Eligible premises are nonresidential premises that are wholly contained in real property that is certified as eligible to receive benefits pursuant to the exemption for industrial and commercial properties. (Sec. 11-604(17); Sec. 22-621, NYC. Adm. Code)

The mayor is authorized to reduce REAP benefits in certain cases when an eligible business moves more than 100 jobs out of Lower Manhattan. Since July 1, 2003, REAP benefits may be made available to eligible businesses relocating to Lower Manhattan. The credit amount is $3,000 multiplied by the number of eligible aggregate employment shares maintained by the taxpayer during the taxable year with respect to eligible premises to which the taxpayer has relocated.

Eligible premises include nonresidential premises for which a minimum expenditure exceeding $25 per square foot has been made for improvements. If the premises are leased, the lease must have a term that does not expire until three years after the date of relocation or the lease commencement date, whichever is later.

The credit is allowed for the first taxable year during which the eligible aggregate employment shares are maintained with respect to the premises and for any of the 12 succeeding taxable years during which the shares are maintained with respect to the premises. Generally, initial certification had to be obtained before July 1, 2008.

Credit amount: The amount of the credit is determined by multiplying $1,000 by the number of eligible aggregate employment shares maintained by the taxpayer with respect to particular eligible premises during the taxable year. However, no credit is available for the relocation of any retail activity or hotel services.

An expanded credit of $3,000 per eligible employment share applies to businesses that relocated to districts zoned as revitalization areas.

¶2806

The amount of the credit available during the 12th year is determined by multiplying the number of eligible aggregate employment shares maintained with respect to the premises in the 12th year by the lesser of one and a fraction, the numerator of which is the number of days in the taxable year of relocation less the number of days the eligible business maintained employment shares in the eligible premises in the taxable year of relocation, and the denominator of which is the number of days in the 12th year during which the shares are maintained with respect to the premises.

An "employment share" is the sum of the number of full-time work weeks worked by each employee divided by the number of weeks in the taxable year, and the number of part-time work weeks worked by the employees divided by an amount equal to twice the number of weeks in the taxable year. The taxpayer's eligible aggregate employment shares are generally the amount by which the taxpayer's aggregate employment shares for a taxable year exceeds the taxpayer's aggregate employment shares for the taxable year preceding the year of relocation.

Multiple relocations: If an eligible business has obtained certifications for more than one relocation, the portion of the total amount of eligible aggregate employment shares to be multiplied by the applicable dollar amount for each certification of a relocation is the number of total attributed eligible aggregate employment shares determined with respect to such relocation.

Additional or replacement premises: Certain businesses are allowed to continue receiving REAP benefits after moving to designated additional or replacement premises.

Planning considerations: The REAP credit must be taken *before* all other credits against the general corporation tax, except the credit for unincorporated business tax paid. In addition, the amount of the credit allowed for any one year is limited to the tax imposed for that year. Excess credits may be carried forward, in order, to the five immediately succeeding taxable years and, to the extent not previously utilized, may be credited against the taxpayer's tax for those years.

Unless certain requirements are met, no certification of eligibility will be issued on or after July 1, 2017 (Sec. 22-622(b), NYC. Adm. Code).

• *Real estate tax escalation credit*

A corporation that has relocated to leased premises in New York City from a location outside New York State and has created at least 100 industrial or commercial employment opportunities in the City is allowed a credit against general corporation tax for the amount of any additional lease payments actually paid to the landlord that are based solely and directly upon increased real estate taxes on the relocation premises. The credit may be claimed only if the taxpayer's eligibility to receive the credit has been approved and certified by the Industrial and Commercial Incentive Board. The credit can be claimed annually for the term of the lease or for a 10-year period, whichever is shorter. (Sec. 11-604(13), NYC. Adm. Code)

"Employment opportunity" means the creation of a full-time position (not less than 30 hours per week of gainful employment) for an industrial employee (one engaged in the manufacturing or assembling of tangible goods or the processing of raw materials) or commercial employee (one engaged in the buying, seller or otherwise providing of goods and services other than on a retail basis directly to the ultimate user or consumer) and the actual hiring of the employee for that position (Sec. 11-604(13)(a)(2), NYC. Adm. Code).

• *Employment opportunity relocation costs credit*

A credit is allowed for relocation expenses ("employment opportunity relocation costs") incurred by a taxpayer in relocating in New York City from outside the state where the taxpayer creates a minimum of 10 industrial or commercial employment opportunities. The maximum credit is $300 for each commercial employment opportunity and $500 for each industrial employment opportunity relocated. However, no credit is allowed for industrial employment opportunities relocated to premises that are within an industrial business zone and for which a binding contract to purchase or lease was first entered into by the taxpayer on or after July 1, 2005 (Sec. 11-604(14)(a)(1), N.Y.C. Adm. Code).

The relocation costs credit may be taken by the taxpayer in whole or in part in the year in which the employment opportunities are relocated by the taxpayer, or in either of the following two years.

"Employment opportunity relocation costs" include: costs incurred in moving furniture, files, papers and office equipment into New York City from a location outside the state; costs in moving and installing machinery and equipment into New York City from a location outside the state; costs of installing telephones and other communication equipment required as a result of the relocation; costs incurred in the purchase of office furniture and fixtures required as a result of the relocation; and the cost of renovating the premises to be occupied as a result of the relocation (subject to the limitation that the renovation costs cannot exceed 75¢ per square foot of the total area utilized by the taxpayer in the occupied premises).

For definition of "employment opportunity", see discussion under "Real estate tax escalation credit", above.

• *Credit for partners in entities subject to UBT*

A credit is allowed against New York City general corporation tax for corporations that are partners in unincorporated businesses subject to New York City Unincorporated Business Tax (UBT) based on either entire net income or entire net income plus salaries and other compensation (Sec. 11-604(18), NYC. Adm. Code). The credit must be claimed before any other credits allowed against corporation tax.

Determination of credit: The credit is equal to the *lesser* of the following:

— the sum of (a) the UBT reported and paid by the unincorporated business for its taxable year ending within or with the taxable year of the corporation, and (b) the amount of any credit or credits allowed to the unincorporated business by Sec. 11-503(j), NYC Adm. Code (credit for income from partnerships subject to unincorporated business tax), for its taxable year ending within or with the taxable year of the corporation, multiplied by a fraction, the numerator of which is the net total of the corporation's distributive share of income, gain, loss and deductions of, and guaranteed payments from, the unincorporated business for the taxable year, and the denominator of which is the sum, for the taxable year, of the net total distributive shares of income, gain, loss and deductions of, and guaranteed payments to, all partners in the unincorporated business for whom or which the net total (as separately determined for each partner) is greater than zero. If the corporation is liable for general corporation tax based on entire net income plus certain salaries and other compensation, the amount so determined must be multiplied by $2655/4000$; or

— if, before the application of any credits, the corporation is liable for (a) the tax based on entire net income, the excess of the tax so computed, without the allowance of any credits, over the tax so computed, determined as if the corporation had no distributive share or guaranteed payments with respect to the unincorporated business, multiplied by $400/885$, or (b) the tax based on entire net income plus certain salaries and other compensation, the excess of the tax computed, without allowance of credits, over the tax so computed, determined as if the corporation had no such distributive share or guaranteed payments with respect to the unincorporated business. The amount so determined may not be less than zero.

¶2806

For additional information, see *Update on Audit Issues,* New York City Department of Finance, June 2008, CCH New York Tax Reports, ¶ 600-661.

Credit limitations: The sum of the credits allowed to a corporation for a taxable year with respect to all unincorporated businesses in which the corporation is a partner may not exceed (1) in the case of a corporation that, before the application of any credits, is liable for general corporation tax computed on entire net income, the tax so computed, without any allowance of any credits, multiplied by $400/885$, and (2) in the case of a corporation that, before the application of any credits, is liable for general corporation tax computed on entire net income plus certain salaries and other compensation, the tax so computed without allowance of any credits.

Corporations filing combined reports: Corporations that file combined reports must compute the credit as if the combined group were the partner in each unincorporated business from which any of the members of the group had a distributive share or guaranteed payments. However, if more than one member of the combined group is a partner in the same unincorporated business, for purposes of the calculation required above, the numerator of the fraction must be the sum of the net total distributive shares of income, gain, loss and deductions of, and guaranteed payments from, the unincorporated business of all of the partners of the unincorporated business within the combined group for which the net total (as separately determined for each partner) is greater than zero, and the denominator must be the sum of the net total distributive shares of income, gain, loss and deductions of, and guaranteed payments from, the unincorporated business of all partners in the unincorporated business for whom or which such net total (as separately determined for each partner) is greater than zero.

- *Sales and compensating use tax credit*

A credit is allowed against general corporation tax equal to the amount of sales and compensating use taxes paid with respect to the purchase or use of the services of installing, repairing, maintaining or servicing machinery, equipment, parts, tools, or supplies used directly and predominantly in the production of tangible personal property, gas, electricity, refrigeration, or steam for sale, or certain telephone central office equipment or station apparatus or comparable telegraph equipment. Interest paid in connection with such taxes is also allowed as a credit.

- *Credit for sales and use taxes paid on production machinery*

A credit is allowed for sales and use taxes paid with respect to the purchase or use by a taxpayer of machinery or equipment for use or consumption directly and predominantly in the production of tangible personal property, gas, electricity, refrigeration, or steam for sale. (Sec. 11-604(12), NYC Adm. Code) Parts having a useful life of one year or less, and supplies used in connection with the production equipment, are not eligible for the credit.

- *Film production credit*

New York City allows the empire state film production credit against general corporation tax through 2019 (Sec. 11-604(20), NYC Adm. Code). The credit is substantially identical to the state credit, except that the percentage of qualified production costs used to calculate the credit is 5%, instead of 10%. Up to $30 million in tax credits will be available each calendar year. For a discussion of the state credit, see ¶ 944.

- *Industrial business zone relocation credit*

Credits against the New York City general corporation tax and unincorporated business tax are available to eligible taxpayers that are engaged in industrial and manufacturing activities and that relocate to an industrial business zone (Sec.

¶2806

11-604(17-b), NYC Adm. Code). The credit amount equals $1,000 per full-time employee, not to exceed the lesser of actual relocation costs or $100,000.

The Industrial Business Zone Boundary Commission is authorized to designate industrial business zones (Sec. 22-625, NYC Adm. Code).

• *Biotechnology credit*

A refundable credit against the New York City general corporation tax and unincorporated business tax is available for biotechnology businesses. In order to claim the credit, a biotechnology firm must be a qualified emerging technology company (QETC) and must meet the following requirements (Sec. 11-604(21), NYC Adm. Code):

— have 100 or fewer full-time employees, with at least 75% of those employees employed in New York City;

— have a ratio of research and development funds to net sales of at least 6%; and

— have gross revenues not exceeding $20 million for the immediately preceding year.

Credit amount: For biotechnology firms that have increased their employment in the city by at least 5%, are newly formed, or are newly located to the city, the credit is provided as follows, up to $250,000:

— 18% for the acquisition of research and development property and related costs and fees;

— 9% for qualified research expenses; and

— 100% of certain training expenses, up to $4,000 per employee.

Planning considerations: Existing biotechnology firms that have not increased their employment by at least 5% are eligible for the credit, but at half the rate, up to $125,000. The total credits for a given year are capped at $3 million. If credits in a given year exceed the cap, the credit will be allocated on a prorated basis by the New York City Department of Finance. The credit is applicable for taxable years beginning on or after January 1, 2010, and before January 1, 2019. (Sec. 11-604(21), NYC Adm. Code)

• *Beer production credit*

A beer production credit is available against the New York City general corporation, and business corporation taxes, applicable to taxable years beginning on or after January 1, 2017. (Sec. 11-604(22), NYC Adm. Code; Sec. 11-654(22), NYC Adm. Code)

Credit amount: The credit is equal to 12 cents per gallon for the first 500,000 gallons produced in New York City and 3.86 cents per gallon for the next 15 million gallons produced in New York City in the taxable year.

Planning considerations: To be eligible for the credit, a taxpayer must be registered as a distributor under Tax Law Article 18 and must produce 60 million or fewer gallons of beer in the state during the taxable year.

Unused credit is refundable as an overpayment of tax; however, no interest will be paid.

¶2807 Computation of Entire Net Income

Law: Secs. 11-601—11-604, 11-652, NYC Adm. Code (CCH NEW YORK CITY TAX REPORTS, ¶505-401, 505-405).

The term "entire net income" means total net income from all sources, which shall be presumably the same as the entire taxable income the taxpayer is required to report for federal income tax purposes (Sec. 11-652(8), NYC Adm. Code).

CCH Caution: Computation Unconstitutional

In *Castle Oil Corp. v. City of New York* (CCH NEW YORK CITY TAX REPORTS, ¶600-213), the New York Supreme Court, Appellate Division, held that the requirement that New York City general corporation tax be computed without the exclusion, deduction or credit of the Article 13-a petroleum business tax was unconstitutional. The New York Court of Appeals affirmed on December 20, 1996, holding that since the enabling act required the City law to follow the state statute, the City exceeded its authority after the state law was amended to permit such deductions. Therefore, the City requirement was invalid as of September 1, 1990, the effective date of the state law amendment (*Castle Oil Corp. v. City of New York* 89 N.Y. 2d 334, 675 N.E. 2d 840, 653 N.Y.S. 2d 86, December 20, 1996; CCH NEW YORK CITY TAX REPORTS, ¶600-267).

—The New York City general corporation or banking corporation taxes;

—Taxes on or measured by profits or income or that include profits or income as a measure paid or accrued to any other state, or political subdivision thereof, or to the District of Columbia, including "in lieu" taxes;

—The amount allowed as an exclusion or deduction for stock transfer taxes imposed in determining entire taxable income reported for federal income tax purposes, but only to the extent that such taxes are incurred and paid in market-making transactions;

—The amount allowed as an exclusion or deduction for sales and use taxes in determining entire taxable income reported for federal income tax purposes, but only the portion that is not in excess of the credit for sales and use taxes paid on machinery or equipment used in production;

—The amount allowed as an exclusion or deduction in determining entire taxable income reported for federal income tax purposes, but only the portion of the exclusion or deduction that is not in excess of the amounts allowed for the real estate tax escalation credit;

—The amount allowed as an exclusion or deduction in determining entire taxable income reported for federal income tax purposes, but only the portion of the exclusion or deduction that is not in excess of the amount of the credit allowed for industrial or commercial employment opportunity relocation costs;

—The amount allowed as an exclusion or deduction in determining entire taxable income that is reported for federal income tax purposes, but only the portion of the exclusion or deduction that is not in excess of the amount of the credits allowed for sales and use taxes paid for purchases or uses by a nonresidential energy user of electricity or electric service purchased at retail from the Power Authority of the state of New York or the Port Authority of New York and New Jersey, including purchases or uses by a nonresidential fuel user of fuel or fuel service;

—Any part of any income from dividends or interest on any kind of stock, securities, or indebtedness;

—In the discretion of the Commissioner of Finance, any amount of interest directly or indirectly and any other amount directly or indirectly attributable as a carrying charge or otherwise to subsidiary capital or to income, gains or losses from subsidiary capital;

—For taxable years beginning after December 31, 1981, any amount claimed as a deduction in computing federal taxable income solely as a result of the safe harbor election made under IRC Sec. 168(f)(8), or any amount that would have been included in federal taxable income had the taxpayer not made the safe harbor lease election, as it was in effect for agreements entered into prior to January 1, 1984;

—For property placed in service in taxable years beginning prior to 1994, the amount allowable under the federal accelerated cost recovery system pursuant to IRC Sec. 168. However, this requirement does not apply to property subject to the provisions of IRC Sec. 280-F (relating to luxury automobiles) or to property that was placed in service in New York in taxable years beginning after 1984. For tax years beginning after 1993, the New York City depreciation rules are the same as the federal depreciation rules (*Caution:* See the discussion under "Depreciation," below);

—Upon disposition of recovery property, the amount, if any, by which the New York City depreciation deduction exceeds the federal deduction;

—The income from sources without the United States received by alien corporations and not included in federal taxable income;

—Members of New York Insurance Exchange—similar to corporation franchise (income) tax provisions discussed at ¶ 1002;

—Entire net income includes 100% of dividends on shares of stock with respect to which a dividend deduction is disallowed by IRC Sec. 246(c);

For taxable years beginning after 2007, an addition modification is required for the IRC Sec. 199 deduction for qualified production activities income (Sec. 11-602(8)(b)(18), N.Y.C. Adm. Code);

—*Royalties:* For taxable years beginning after 2002, certain royalty payments made by the taxpayer to a related member during the taxable year must be added back, to the extent deductible in calculating the taxpayer's federal taxable income. For additional information, see ¶ 1002.

Exclusions from Entire Net Income
(Deductions from Federal Taxable Income)

The computation of New York City entire net income requires the following items to be deducted from federal taxable income:

—Interest, dividends and gains from subsidiary capital (other than war loss recoveries) to the extent they were included in computing federal taxable income;

—Fifty percent of all dividends from corporations, other than subsidiaries, that were included in computing federal taxable income;

—Bona fide gifts;

—Refund or credit of any New York City general corporation tax, New York City banking corporation tax or New York State taxes imposed by Tax Law Articles 9 (corporation tax), 9-A (business corporation tax) or 32 (banking corporation tax) imposed for a prior year where the taxes had not been deducted in any earlier year;

—Receipts from school districts and from nonprofit religious, charitable or educational organizations for the operation of school buses, less any deductions allowed in computing federal taxable income attributable to such receipts;

—By regulation, foreign income, war-profits and excess profits taxes imposed by foreign countries or U.S. possessions that were utilized as a foreign tax credit instead of a deduction for federal income tax purposes are to be deducted from federal taxable income;

—Net operating loss deduction (¶ 2808);

—The portion of wages and salaries not allowed as a business expense deduction for federal purposes because the federal jobs tax credit was taken;

—Members of New York Insurance Exchange—similar to corporation franchise (income) tax provisions discussed at ¶ 1003;

¶ 2807

—For property placed in service in taxable years beginning before 1994, a deduction is allowed equal to the amount with respect to property that is subject to the provisions of IRC Sec. 168 allowable as the depreciation deduction under IRC Sec. 167 as that section would have applied to property placed in service on December 31, 1984. However, this deduction does not apply with respect to property subject to the provisions of IRC Sec. 280-F (relating to luxury automobiles) or to property that was placed in service in New York after 1984. For tax years beginning after 1993, the New York City depreciation rules are the same as the federal depreciation rules (*Caution:* See discussion under "Depreciation," below);

—Upon disposition of recovery property, the amount, if any, by which the federal deduction exceeds the New York City depreciation deduction;

—For taxable years beginning after 1981, any amount included in federal taxable income solely as a result of a safe harbor lease election made under IRC Sec. 168(f)(8), or any amount that would have been excluded in federal taxable income had the taxpayer not made the safe harbor lease election, as it was in effect for agreements entered into prior to January 1, 1984.

See ¶2809 for elective deduction for industrial waste treatment facilities and air pollution control facilities.

See ¶2810 for adjustment of gain where the fair market value on January 1, 1966, is higher than the federal basis.

See ¶2812 for special elective deduction, allowed against allocated entire net income, for certain business property or research and development facilities.

Partners in utilities: In the case of a taxpayer that is a partner in a partnership subject to the New York City utility tax as a utility, entire net income does not include the taxpayer's distributive or pro rata share for federal income tax purposes of any item of income, gain, loss, or deduction of the partnership, or any item of income, gain, loss, or deduction of the partnership that the taxpayer is required to take into account separately for federal income tax purposes.

CCH Advisory: Management Fees

In a New York City unincorporated business tax case regarding a management fee paid by a taxpayer to its corporate general partner, an appellate court has affirmed the Tax Appeals Tribunal's determination that the portion of the fee representing compensation for services rendered to the taxpayer by the corporate general partner's employees, who were also the taxpayer's partners, was not deductible by the taxpayer. The tribunal's conclusion that the claimed amount was not deductible was supported by substantial evidence and had a rational basis in the law. (*Tocqueville Asset Management L.P. v. New York City Tax Appeals Tribunal.*, Appellate Division of the Supreme Court of New York, First Department, No. 1663 39/15, July 5, 2016, CCH NEW YORK CITY TAX REPORTS, ¶600-809)

• *Depreciation*

A taxpayer subject to New York City general corporation tax that takes accelerated depreciation deductions under IRC Sec. 168(k) in calculating its federal taxable income must add that amount back to its entire net income base if the deduction is for property placed in service outside of New York. Under Sec. 11-602(j), NYC Adm. Code, the taxpayer can take a deduction for that property under IRC Sec. 167. For property placed in service *within* New York, however, a taxpayer may take *either* the IRC Sec. 167 deduction or the IRC Sec. 168 ACRS deduction.

In *R.J. Reynolds v. City of New York Department of Finance* (1997), (CCH NEW YORK TAX REPORTS, ¶600-314), the New York Supreme Court, Appellate Division, held that, by overtly differentiating between property placed in service within and without New York, based solely on the situs of the corporate taxpayer's activities, the City violated federal Commerce Clause principles. In addition, by only allowing taxpayers to take advantage of the accelerated depreciation scheme for property placed in service in New York, the City code provisions created a direct commercial advantage to local businesses, thereby discriminating against taxpayers whose property was located outside New York.

CCH Advisory: "Bonus" Depreciation

The accelerated depreciation deductions allowed by IRC Sec. 168(k) must be added back to federal taxable income for New York City business tax purposes. However, the federal accelerated depreciation is allowed for businesses located in the Resurgence Zone or the Liberty Zone (Ch. 93 (A.B. 11817), Laws 2002; NYC Local Law 17 (Introductory Number 220-A), Laws 2002; Finance Memorandum 02-3, New York City Department of Finance, September 26, 2002, CCH NEW YORK CITY TAX REPORTS, ¶ 600-458).

Sport utility vehicles: For purposes of the general corporation tax, banking corporation tax, and unincorporated business tax, in the case of a taxpayer that is not an eligible farmer, no deduction may be taken for the amounts allowable as a deduction under IRC Sec. 167, IRC Sec. 168, and IRC Sec. 179 with respect to a sport utility vehicle that is not a passenger automobile as defined in IRC Sec. 280F(d)(5). Instead, the deduction must be computed *as if* the sport utility vehicle *were* a passenger automobile as defined in IRC Sec. 280F(d)(5).

IRC Sec. 179 limits the amount that a federal taxpayer may deduct for an SUV, in lieu of depreciation, to $25,000 rather than the $100,000 amount that would otherwise apply. Passenger vehicle deduction limitations under IRC Sec. 280F do not apply to many SUVs because of their weight. However, under the New York City provisions, the IRC Sec. 280F limitations apply to all SUVs, regardless of weight. Accordingly, the applicable New York City deduction is based on the IRC Sec. 280F limitations that would apply if the SUV were a passenger automobile. The New York City limitations apply to depreciation deductions and IRC Sec. 179 deductions taken in tax years beginning on and after January 1, 2004, regardless of when the SUV was placed in service. The department has provided schedules setting forth the New York City limits for tax years beginning in 2004 through 2014 (*Finance Memorandum 14-1*, New York City Department of Finance, February 11, 2015, CCH NEW YORK TAX REPORTS, ¶ 600-794).

Upon the disposition of property to which Sec. 11-602(8)(o) applies, the amount of any gain or loss includible in entire net income must be adjusted to reflect the above inclusions and exclusions from entire net income attributable to such property.

Repurchase agreements: For purposes of the general corporation tax (GCT) and the unincorporated business tax (UBT), the New York City Department of Finance has issued a statement of audit procedure that provides guidance regarding the correct corporate income tax treatment of certain repurchase and reverse repurchase agreements and securities lending and borrowing transactions by financial services firms regularly engaged in such activities (*Statement of Audit Procedure PP-2008-12*, New York City Department of Finance, March 31, 2008, CCH NEW YORK TAX REPORTS, ¶ 600-632).

¶2808 Entire Net Income—Deduction of Net Operating Loss

Law: Secs. 11-602, 11-603, 11-654.1, NYC Adm. Code; Rule Secs. 11-27, 11-28 (CCH NEW YORK CITY TAX REPORTS, ¶ 505-437).

Corporate tax reform: In computing the business income subject to tax, taxpayers are allowed both a prior net operating loss conversion subtraction and a net operating loss deduction. The prior net operating loss conversion subtraction is applied against business income before the net operating loss deduction. (Sec. 11-654.1, NYC Adm. Code)

¶2808

The prior net operating loss conversion subtraction is calculated as specified in Sec. 11-654.1(1)(b), NYC Adm. Code.

A net operating loss is the amount of a business loss incurred in a particular tax year multiplied by the business allocation percentage for that year. The net operating loss deduction is the amount of net operating loss or losses from one or more taxable years that are carried forward or carried back to a particular taxable year. (Sec. 11-654.1(3), NYC Adm. Code) The net operating loss deduction does not include any net operating loss incurred during any taxable year beginning prior to January 1, 2015, or during any taxable year in which the taxpayer was not subject to the tax (Sec. 11-654.1(3)(b), NYC Adm. Code).

A net operating loss may be carried forward for up to 20 years, or carried back for up to three taxable years preceding the taxable year of the loss, but no loss may be carried back to a taxable year beginning before January 1, 2015. The loss must be carried to the earliest of the three taxable years preceding the taxable year of the loss. (Sec. 11-654.1(3)(d), NYC Adm. Code)

The carryback period may be irrevocably waived on the taxpayer's original timely filed return (determined with regard to extensions) for the taxable year of the net operating loss for which the election is to be in effect (Sec. 11-654.1(3)(g), NYC Adm. Code).

Prior law: For tax years before 2015, a net operating loss deduction was allowed in computing entire net income for the New York City general corporation tax (Sec. 11-602(8)(f), NYC Adm. Code). A carryover and carryback were permitted in the same manner as for federal purposes, although carrybacks were limited to the first $10,000 of loss in any taxable year ending after June 30, 1989.

The net operating loss allowable was apportioned between investment income and business income in the proportion that each bears to entire net income before such deduction.

Except as provided under tax reform, a New York City net operating loss that was carried back or forward as a deduction in some other year would, nevertheless, be used in computing the alternative net income-plus-compensation basis of tax for the year in which the loss was sustained.

Election to relinquish carryback: Similar to New York State corporation franchise (income) tax (¶1008). With respect to net operating losses sustained during taxable years ending after June 30, 1989, except for the first $10,000 of each of the losses, the net operating loss deduction allowed under IRC Sec. 172 must be determined as if the taxpayer had elected to relinquish the entire carryback period.

¶2809 Entire Net Income—Elective Deductions for Industrial Waste Treatment Facilities and for Air Pollution Control Facilities

Law: Sec. 11-602, NYC Adm. Code (CCH NEW YORK CITY TAX REPORTS, ¶505-440).

The taxpayer may elect to take deductions for expenditures paid or incurred during the taxable year for the construction, reconstruction, erection or improvement of industrial waste treatment facilities and air pollution control facilities (Sec. 11-602, NYC Adm. Code). These deductions may not be taken if double depreciation or one-year write-off allowances (¶2812) are taken on the same property.

This deduction is the same as that allowed in the New York State corporation franchise tax law, except that (1) the New York City deduction only applies to depreciable tangible property having a situs in New York City and used in the taxpayer's trade or business, the construction, reconstruction, erection or improvement of which is initiated, in the case of industrial waste treatment facilities, on or after January 1, 1966, and only for expenditures paid or incurred prior to January 1, 1972, and, in the case of air pollution control facilities, initiated on or after January 1, 1966, and (2) the required report of a change of use of the facility or of the failure to obtain a permanent certificate of compliance is made to the Department of Finance.

¶2810 Entire Net Income—Reduction of Gain when Fair Market Value on January 1, 1966, Is Higher than Federal Basis

Law: Sec. 11-602, NYC Adm. Code (CCH New York City Tax Reports, ¶505-444).

With respect to gain on the sale or other disposition of property (other than stock in trade and accounts and notes receivable acquired in the ordinary course of trade or business) acquired prior to January 1, 1966, a deduction from entire net income is allowed if the fair market value of the property on January 1, 1966, was higher than federal adjusted basis on that date. (Sec. 11-602, NYC Adm. Code)

Computation: The allowable deduction from entire net income is the difference between (1) the amount of the taxpayer's federal taxable income, and (2) the amount of the taxpayer's federal taxable income computed by using the special New York City basis for the property, plus or minus adjustments to basis, if smaller than (1).

For the purpose of computing the modification, the basis of the property may be taken to be the lower of the following:

— Its fair market value on January 1, 1966, plus or minus all adjustments to basis for federal income tax purposes for periods on and after January 1, 1966; or

— The amount realized from its sale or other disposition.

Limitation on total modification: The total modification for gain on such property may not exceed the taxpayer's net gain from the sale or other disposition of all such property.

The effect is that, for New York City purposes, gain on a sale or other disposition of property acquired before January 1, 1966, is computed by using January 1, 1966, value adjusted to date, or the amount realized on the sale (instead of federal adjusted basis) if this produces a smaller amount of gain than use of federal adjusted basis.

¶2811 Allocation of Income and Capital

Law: Sec. 11-605, NYC Adm. Code; Rule Sec. 11-63 (CCH New York City Tax Reports, ¶506-501—506-580).

The New York City general corporation tax provides for separate allocation of business income and capital. (Sec. 11-605, NYC Adm. Code; Rule Sec. 11-63).

In general, a "business allocation percentage" is used to allocate business income and business capital. For tax years beginning before 2015, an "investment allocation percentage" was ordinarily used to allocate investment income and investment capital. Subsidiary capital is allocated by a "subsidiary allocation percentage" determined by the amount of capital employed in New York City by the taxpayer's subsidiaries.

• *Business allocation percentage*

Beginning in 2009, a single sales factor is being phased in over 10 years (Sec. 11-604(3)(a)(10), N.Y.C. Adm. Code; *Finance Memorandum 09-2,* CCH New York City Tax Reports, ¶600-687). Specifically, the receipts factor is increased, and the payroll and property factors decreased, as indicated for the taxable years below:

— for 2009, 40% receipts —30% payroll —30% property;

— for 2010, 46% —27% —27%;

¶2810

— for 2011, 53% —23.5% —23.5%;

— for 2012, 60% —20% —20%;

— for 2013, 67% —16.5% —16.5%;

— for 2014, 73% —13.5% —13.5%;

— for 2015, 80% —10% —10%;

— for 2016, 87% —6.5% —6.5%;

— for 2017, 93% —3.5% —3.5%; and

— after 2017, 100% receipts.

If any of the percentages cannot be determined because the taxpayer has either no property, no payroll, or no business receipts/gross income within or outside the city, then for taxable years beginning in 2009 and thereafter, but before 2018, the computation must be made by taking the sum of the products determined for the factors that are present and dividing that sum by the sum of the weight factors that apply to each of the present factors in the calculation. This amount is then rounded to four decimal places. An allocation factor is not missing merely because its numerator is zero, but it is missing if both the numerator and denominator are zero. The rules contain examples illustrating the application of these provisions. (Rule Sec. 11-63)

Prior to 2009, the business allocation percentage was determined using the three factors of property, receipts and payroll, equally weighted. (Sec. 11-604(3), N.Y.C. Adm. Code)

The three factors that comprise the business allocation percentage are:

— *Property percentage:* the average value, at the beginning and end of the taxable year, of real property (including real property rented to the business) and tangible personal property connected with the business and located in New York City, divided by the values for all such property located both within and outside New York City;

— *Payroll percentage:* wages and other compensation paid to employees in connection with business in New York City divided by the total compensation paid to all employees wherever employed; and

— *Gross income percentage:* gross sales or service charges within New York City divided by all such sales and charges wherever made.

Manufacturing corporations: For taxable years beginning before January 1, 2011, a corporation that derives more than 50% of its gross receipts from the manufacture and sale of tangible personal property may elect to "double-weight" the receipts factor of its business allocation formula (that is, to add together its property, payroll and receipts percentages plus an additional percentage equal to the receipts percentage and divide the total by four). In the case of an affiliated group filing a combined report, an election is permitted under this provision only if the corporations included in the report would qualify as a manufacturing corporation if they were treated as a single corporation. (Sec. 11-604(3)(a)(8), N.Y.C. Adm. Code; Rule Sec. 11-63(c))

Practitioner Comment: Election to Double Weight

The election to double weight receipts is irrevocable and must be made on the taxpayer's original, timely filed (including extensions) return. A separate election must be made for each taxable year (NYC Reg. Sec. 11-63(c)(4)(iv)).

Mark S. Klein, Esq., Hodgson Russ LLP

Receipts from sales of tangible personal property are allocable to New York City if shipments are made to points within the City.

CCH Advisory: Dock Sales

Taxpayers having receipts from dock sales for tax periods beginning after 1999 may request permission to allocate those receipts in a manner consistent with New York State Reg. Sec. 4-4.2, which includes a "destination" rule with respect to dock sales (¶ 1305).

Under the state regulation, receipts from sales of tangible personal property are allocated to New York state under the following circumstances: (1) when shipment is made to a point within the state; (2) when possession of the property is transferred to the purchaser or the purchaser's designee within the state, unless the destination of the property is a point outside New York; or (3) when possession of the property is transferred to the purchaser or designee outside the state but the destination of the property is within the state. The regulation establishes a presumption that the destination of property is where the possession is transferred, unless the taxpayer provides sufficient evidence to establish the destination.

Prior to filing a return, a New York City taxpayer having dock sales will be allowed to request advance permission to allocate the receipts according to the state's destination rule. The request should contain a statement setting forth the reasons why the taxpayer believes the use of the dock sales rule is necessary to properly reflect the taxpayer's income within and outside the city, a detailed explanation of how the business allocation percentage would be calculated using the dock sales method, and a comparison of the receipts or gross income factor calculated using the dock sales rule and using the point of shipment rule. Taxpayers who receive permission to use the dock sales rule must attach a copy of the Department's response when filing the return (*Statement of Audit Procedure: Receipts from Dock Sales*, New York City Department of Finance, Audit Division, December 28, 2000; CCH NEW YORK CITY TAX REPORTS, ¶ 600-414).

Newspapers and broadcasters: For newspapers and periodicals, a subscriber is located in the City if the mailing address for the subscription is within the City. For program services, a subscriber is located in the City if the billing address for the subscription is within the City.

Valuation of property: In determining the property factor of the general corporation tax's business allocation formula, tangible property is valued at its federal adjusted basis, whether the property is owned or rented. Since a lessee does not have a federal adjusted basis for rented property, a clarifying amendment enacted in 1996 provides that the value of rented property is to be determined by multiplying the annual gross rent by eight.

Formula adjustment by Commissioner: Sections 11-604(8) and 11-604(9) of the Code authorize The Commissioner of Finance may adjust the business allocation percentage if he or she determines that use of the corporation's three-factor BAP does not properly reflect the corporation's activity, business, income or capital within the City. (Secs. 11-604(8) and (9), NYC Admin. Code; NYC Rule 11-67) The adjustment may include the exclusion of one or more factors in the calculation of BAP. The Taxpayer has the burden of demonstrating that the applicable three-factor formula results in a distortion of taxable income and causes the taxation of extraterritorial values. (*Finance Letter Ruling 074870-006*, New York City Department of Finance, March 6, 2008, CCH NEW YORK TAX REPORTS, ¶ 600-627)

Apportionment factors for special industries: New York City has adopted special rules for the apportionment of income for the following particular industries or activities: registered brokers and dealers of securities and commodities, aviation corporations, operators of vessels, certain vendors of utility services, publishing and broadcasting businesses, management services rendered to investment companies, and air freight forwarders acting as principal. (Sec. 11-603(4), N.Y.C. Adm. Code)

Consent to use alternative method: If a taxpayer believes that using the statutory method of allocation does not lead to a result that fairly and equitably reflects New

York City income, the taxpayer may obtain the department's consent to use a different allocation method by submitting a written request, separate and apart from the tax return, describing the alternative method. This is a change from the procedure that was in place in past years, in which an alternative method could be requested by checking a box on the return and submitting information with the return.

The request, which is applicable only to a single tax year, may be made before or after the filing of the return. Unless consent to use an alternative method is granted prior to the filing of the return, the statutory method for allocation must be used on the return. The written request must fully explain the proposed alternative allocation method. The explanation must provide full information regarding the nature and scope of the business activities carried on within and outside New York City and provide complete details of how the proposed method would allocate income on a more equitable basis than the statutory method. The taxpayer must submit calculations of the tax due under both the statutory method and the proposed alternative method. If the department consents to the use of the proposed alternative method of allocation and it results in a lower tax liability than the formula basis upon which the tax paid was calculated, the taxpayer may be entitled to claim a refund of the excess amount paid. (*Alternative Allocation Method Notice*, New York City Department of Finance, February 2, 2012)

- *Sourcing of receipts*

Receipts from various sales are included in the numerator of the receipts fraction as provided in Sec. 11-654.2(2), N.Y.C. Adm. Code:

Tangible personal property: Receipts from sales of tangible personal property where shipments are made to points within the city or the destination of the property is a point within the city;

Electricity: Receipts from sales of electricity delivered to points within the city. Receipts from sales of tangible personal property and electricity that are traded as commodities also are included;

Real property: Net gains (not less than zero) from the sales of real property located within New York City;

Rentals: Receipts from rentals of real and tangible personal property located within the city;

Royalties: Receipts of royalties from the use of patents, copyrights, trademarks, and similar intangible personal property within New York City are included. A patent, copyright, trademark, or similar intangible personal property is used within the city to the extent that the activities thereunder are carried on within the city.

Practitioner Comment: No Separate Office Required

A corporation is entitled to allocate part of its business income and capital outside of New York City as long as it is carrying on business both within and outside the City. A regular place of business outside of the City is no longer required. See 2014 Form NYC-3-L, Instructions to Schedule H.

Mark S. Klein, Esq., Hodgson Russ LLP

- *Investment allocation percentage*

The investment allocation percentage is computed for New York City purposes in basically the same manner as the New York State investment allocation percentage (¶ 1307). Alternative entire net income, contained in the numerator of the percentage, is the basis of the issuer's allocation percentage for a bank or trust company organized under the laws of the United States, New York State, or other state. Gross income is the basis of the issuer's allocation percentage for a bank or trust company organized under the laws of a country other than the United States.

If a taxpayer's investment allocation is zero, interest on bank accounts is multiplied by the business allocation percentage.

The New York Court of Appeals has ruled that excluding obligations of the United States from the denominator of the investment allocation percentage, while including obligations of states other than New York, violates the federal statute barring discriminatory treatment of federal obligations (*In the Matter of Forbes, Inc.* (1987, NY Ct App), CCH NEW YORK CITY TAX REPORTS, ¶251-300). The City Administrative Code has been amended to eliminate from the denominator the exclusion for obligations of the United States and its instrumentalities and obligations of New York State, its political subdivisions and instrumentalities.

- *Allocation of entire net income*

The portion of the entire net income/business income to be allocated within New York City is determined by multiplying business income by the determined business allocation percentage.

Prior law (except for S corporations): The portion of the entire net income to be allocated within New York City is determined by the following:

(1) Multiplying business income by the determined business allocation percentage;

(2) Multiplying investment income by the determined investment allocation percentage; and

(3) Adding the products obtained in (1) and (2).

If a net operating loss deduction (¶2808) is allowable in computing entire net income, it is apportioned between business income and investment income in accordance with the ratio of each to entire net income (before the deduction). The allocation percentages are applied after business income and investment income are so reduced.

CCH Advisory: Taxation of Gain Was Disproportionate

A taxpayer was not required to include its share of income from the sale of California real property owned by a limited partnership in which it had a 30% interest in its allocated New York City income subject to the general corporation tax, because that would result in a tax that is out of all appropriate proportion to the taxpayer's activities in New York City. (*Imperial Rental Investments, Inc.*, New York City Tax Appeals Tribunal, TAT(H)06-20(GC), April 1, 2009, CCH NEW YORK CITY TAX REPORTS, ¶600-682)

- *Subsidiary capital*

Determination of the portion of the subsidiary capital to be allocated to New York City is found through the method used for finding the portion of subsidiary capital to be allocated for New York State purposes (¶1316), but based on information required to be furnished to New York City on a New York City business tax report for the preceding year, without regard to any minimum. Alternative entire net income is the basis of the issuer's allocation percentage for a bank or trust company organized under the laws of the United States, New York State, or other state. Gross income is the basis of the issuer's allocation percentage for a bank or trust company organized under the laws of a country other than the United States.

The special elective deductions for new tangible business property and new research and development facilities (¶2812) are deducted from allocated entire net income.

¶2811

¶2812 Allocated Entire Net Income—Elective Deductions for Double Depreciation on New Tangible Business Property and Accelerated One-Year Write-Off on New Research and Development Facilities

Law: Sec. 11-604, NYC Adm. Code (CCH NEW YORK CITY TAX REPORTS, ¶505-450).

The taxpayer may elect to take double the federal depreciation allowance in connection with certain newly constructed, reconstructed, erected or acquired tangible business property having a situs in New York City (Sec. 11-604, NYC Adm. Code). In the case of research and development facilities, an election may be made to deduct the expenditures in one year. These special depreciation allowances are deducted from the portion of entire net income allocated to New York City.

Only one deduction (double depreciation or one-year depreciation write-off) is allowed in connection with any one item of property.

¶2813 Returns and Payment

Law: Secs. 11-605, 11-606, 11-653, 11-674, NYC Adm. Code; Rule Secs. 11-88, 11-89 (CCH NEW YORK CITY TAX REPORTS, ¶507-505, 507-518, 507-524, 507-530).

Forms: See below.

The New York City general corporation tax provisions relating to returns and payment parallel the state law.

Time and place of filing: Beginning in 2017, corporations subject to tax are required to file an annual general corporation tax return within three and one-half months after the close of the fiscal year (April 15 for calendar year taxpayers). Previously, the due date was March 15 for calendar-year taxpayers) (Sec. 11-653, NYC Adm. Code). Payment of the tax, or any balance of tax that remains to be paid after estimated tax payment, is due at the time the return is required to be filed.

Returns and remittances are mailed to the Department of Finance at the address designated on the form.

CCH Advisory: Electronic Filing

The New York City Department of Finance has a program for electronic filing; see **http://www1.nyc.gov/site/finance/taxes/tax-btef-faq.page**. Also, the Department is participating in the Fed/State 1120 Corporation Tax e-file program, under the IRS Modernized e-File (MeF) architecture. This program allows corporations to electronically file both their federal and New York City corporate returns together.

Foreign corporations claiming not to be subject to tax: Every foreign corporation claiming not to be subject to tax, but having an officer, agent or representative within New York City must file an information report (Form NYC-245).

Corporations ceasing to do business in New York City: Reports are due on the date of cessation, or at such other time as required by the Commissioner of Finance, covering each year or period for which no report was previously filed.

Federal or New York State changes: If any change or correction is made in taxable income, alternative minimum taxable income or other basis of tax by federal or New York State authorities, or if income is changed by renegotiation of government contracts or subcontracts, the taxpayer is required to report such change or correction within 90 days of the final determination (120 days in the case of a combined report) or as required by the Commissioner of Finance. The allowance of a tentative carryback adjustment based upon a net operating loss carryback or net capital loss carryback under IRC Sec. 6411 is treated as a final determination. The taxpayer is required to concede the accuracy of the determination or to state wherein it is erroneous. In case of failure to file a report of the federal or New York State changes, a deficiency assessment may be made at any time. A taxpayer filing an amended federal return is required to file an amended New York City return within 90 days thereafter.

The same requirement applies if there is a change or correction in taxable income of a shareholder of an S corporation that elected not to be taxed as a corporation for federal income tax purposes. This also applies to shareholders of qualified subchapter S subsidiaries.

• *Extension of time*

The Commissioner of Finance may grant a reasonable extension of time for filing reports when good cause exists.

In the case of the annual general corporation tax report, an automatic six-month extension will be granted if an application for such extension is filed within the prescribed time for the filing of the report and on the prescribed form and a properly estimated tax is paid with the application for automatic extension. The amount of tax paid is deemed to be properly estimated if it is either not less than 90% of the actual tax liability or not less than the tax for the preceding taxable year (12 months). Interest will be imposed on any balance of tax due. (For interest rate, see ¶2815)

If the tax for the period covered by the report is estimated to exceed $1,000, the installment payment for the account of the following year is also required with the application.

In the case of applications for automatic extensions of time for the filing of combined reports, one application may be used for all members of the combined group. The application must list all members of the group. The minimum tax for each member of the group, except the parent corporation, must accompany the application. The parent corporation, filing on behalf of the group, is responsible for payment of the combined tax at that time.

• *Combined reports*

For taxable years beginning on or after January 1, 2009, the filing of a combined return is mandatory if there are substantial intercorporate transactions among related corporations, regardless of the transfer prices charged in those transactions. A captive RIC or a captive REIT must be included in a combined return with a related New York City taxpayer where a greater-than-50% ownership test is met. (Sec. 11-605(4), N.Y.C. Adm. Code; *Finance Memorandum 09-2*, CCH NEW YORK CITY TAX REPORTS, ¶600-687) Generally, under prior law, every corporation subject to the New York City general corporation tax was considered a separate entity and had to file its own report on an individual basis.

In a combined report, the tax is measured by the combined entire net income or combined capital of all the corporations included in the report. In computing combined entire net income, intercorporate dividends are eliminated; in computing combined business and investment capital, intercorporate stockholdings, intercorporate bills, notes and accounts receivable and payable and other intercorporate indebtedness are eliminated; and in computing combined subsidiary capital, intercorporate stockholdings are eliminated.

If all of the corporations filing a combined return for New York State franchise tax purposes are doing business in New York City, they must file combined returns for New York City general corporation tax purposes. Where some of the corporations filing the combined return are not doing business in New York City, separate New York City returns are required unless permission to file jointly is granted.

NYC tax reform: For tax years after 2014, combined reporting is required for unitary corporations that meet a more-than-50% stock ownership test (Sec. 11-654.3(2), N.Y.C. Adm. Code).

¶2813

A taxpayer will not be permitted to make a report on a combined basis covering any other corporation where either the taxpayer or the other corporation, but not both, allocates in accordance with the special allocation provisions applicable to aviation corporations or corporations principally engaged in the operation of vessels.

Corporations that elect the application of IRC Sec. 936 (Puerto Rico and U.S. possession tax credit), with respect to a particular federal taxable year, are not permitted to make a report on a combined basis with respect to the same taxable year (or a portion of it) for New York City corporate income tax purposes.

Practitioner Comment: Election on Audit

A taxpayer who failed to make a timely election to file on a combined basis can raise the issue for the first time upon audit, and force the Tax Department to evaluate the propriety of the combined filing. If it otherwise qualifies, the taxpayer must be allowed to file the combined return, in spite of the late election (*Matter of Direct Pro and Direct Worldwide*, NYC TAT(H) 97-6(GC); NYC TAT(H) 97-7(GC) (2/23/99), CCH NEW YORK TAX REPORTS, ¶600-357).

Mark S. Klein, Esq., Hodgson Russ LLP

Inconsistent tax years: When a related corporation does not have the same year as the parent, the related corporation's activities for its taxable year that ends during the parent's taxable year are used for purposes of reporting and filing as part of a combined report. Accordingly, each corporation with a different tax year need not conform to the parent corporation's tax year in order to comply with the combined filing requirements, but a combined return, including all of the corporations, is still required. (*Finance Letter Ruling 11-4917*, New York City Department of Finance, July 28, 2011, released November 21, 2011, CCH NEW YORK CITY TAX REPORTS, ¶600-736)

- *Information returns*

The Commissioner of Finance may prescribe regulations and instructions requiring information returns relating to payments made to shareholders owning, directly or indirectly, individually or in the aggregate, more than 50% of the issued capital stock of the taxpayer, where such payments are treated as payments of interest in the computation of entire net income reported on such reports. A penalty equal to $500 is imposed for failure to file information returns unless the failure is shown to be due to reasonable cause and not willful neglect.

Forms in Current Use

The following forms are in current use:

No.	Description
NYC-3A	Combined General Corporation Tax Return
NYC-3L	General Corporation Tax Return [Long Form]
NYC-4S	General Corporation Tax Return [Short Form]
NYC-6	Application for Automatic Extension
NYC-8	General Corporation Tax Amended Return and/or Claim for Refund
NYC-245	Activities Report of Corporations
NYC-399	Schedule of NYC Depreciation Adjustments
NYC-400	Declaration of Estimated Tax by General Corporations

¶2814 Declarations and Payments of Estimated Tax

Law: Secs. 11-607, 11-608, 11-676, NYC Adm. Code (CCH NEW YORK CITY TAX REPORTS, ¶507-511).

Forms: NYC-400, Declaration of Estimated Tax by Corporations.

Declarations and payment of estimated New York City general corporation tax are mailed to the Department of Finance at the address designated on the form.

First installment: An installment of estimated tax for the account of the current year is due at the time of filing the New York City general corporation tax return for the preceding taxable year (or at the time of filing an application for extension of time for filing such return) if the tax liability for the preceding year is in excess of $1,000. This first installment, in the amount of 25% of the preceding year's tax, is required to be paid irrespective of the corporation's estimated tax liability for the current year and even though no declaration will be required for the current year. Any overpayment resulting from the first installment will be refunded with interest from the date of payment to the 15th day of the third month following the close of the taxable year, except that no interest is payable if the amount is less than one dollar or if the interest becomes payable solely because of a carryback of a net operating loss from a later taxable year. (See ¶2815 for the applicable rate of interest.)

• *Declarations*

Corporations subject to the general corporation tax are required to file declarations of estimated tax if their estimated tax liability for the taxable year can reasonably be expected to exceed $1,000. Declarations are due on or before the 15th day of the sixth month of the taxable year (June 15 for calendar-year taxpayers). However, if the requirements (that is, expected tax liability exceeding $1,000) are met after the last day of the fifth month and before the first day of the ninth month, the declaration is due by the 15th day of the ninth month (September 15 for calendar-year taxpayers). If the requirements are met after the last day of the eighth month and before the first day of the 12th month, the declaration is due by the 15th day of the 12th month (December 15 for calendar-year taxpayers).

Corporations required to file a declaration of estimated tax make installment payments of the estimated tax due after taking credit for the amount of any first installment based on the preceding year's tax liability and for the amount of any overpayment shown on the last year's report credited against this year's estimated tax. For declarations filed on or before the 15th day of the sixth month, the amount of estimated tax is paid in three equal installments—at the time of filing the declaration, on the 15th day of the ninth month, and on the 15th day of the 12th month. If the declaration is filed between the 15th day of the sixth month and before the 15th day of the ninth month, any estimated tax payments are due in two installments—at the time of filing the declaration and on the 15th day of the 12th month. If the declaration is filed after the 15th day of the ninth month (and was not required to be filed prior to that date), the estimated tax must be paid at the time of filing.

If a declaration is filed after the prescribed time, or after the expiration of any extension of time, all installments of tax payable at or before such time are due at the time of filing, and the remaining installments are due at the times and in the amounts they would have been payable if the declaration had been filed when due.

Amended declarations: Amended declarations should be filed if necessary to correct tax estimates and related payments.

Return in lieu of declaration: A return filed on or before the 15th day of the second month of the succeeding taxable year (February 15 for calendar-year taxpayers) is considered as a declaration or amended declaration otherwise required to be filed on or before the 15th day of the last month of the preceding taxable year.

Failure to file declaration or underpayment of estimated tax: An interest penalty is added to the tax when it is determined there has been an underpayment of all or any part of an installment of estimated tax. The penalty is added for the period of underpayment but not beyond the normal due date of the annual return. (For interest rate, see ¶2815.)

Penalties may be avoided under the same rules as apply for state corporation franchise (income) tax purposes (¶1405).

¶2814

¶2815 Administration, Deficiencies, Refunds

Law: Secs. 11-671—11-690, NYC Adm. Code (CCH NEW YORK CITY TAX REPORTS, ¶508-005, 508-010, 508-024—508-045, 508-250).

Subchapter 5 of the City Business Tax, "Corporate Tax Procedure and Administration," provides assessment, collection, refund, review, and administration provisions applicable generally to the New York City taxes on corporations: the general corporation tax, the financial corporation tax (Chapter 29) and the insurance corporation tax (¶3308). The provisions of Subchapter 5 are substantially the same as Article 27 of the Tax Law (also entitled "Corporate Tax Procedure and Administration"), except that the Commissioner of Finance is charged with the administration of New York City taxes while the New York State Commissioner of Taxation and Finance administers the New York State taxes. The state provisions are covered at Chapter 15 of this Guidebook.

Administration of tax: The Commissioner of Finance administers the New York City general corporation tax. Among the powers of the Commissioner is the power to inspect books and records.

• *Deficiency assessment*

The first step in a deficiency assessment, except in the case of a mathematical error, is usually the sending of a 90-day notice of deficiency by the Commissioner of Finance. The deficiency may be determined by an examination of the return or, if no return was filed, from any information in the Commissioner's possession. The deficiency assessment is deemed to be made after 90 days (150 days if the notice is addressed to a taxpayer whose last known address is outside the United States) except with respect to any tax or amount as to which the taxpayer files a petition for redetermination with the Commissioner of Finance. Where the taxpayer has not reported a change in federal or New York State taxable income, a notice of additional tax due is given. This becomes final within 30 days from the date of mailing unless the taxpayer files the required report or amended return showing wherein the federal or state determination is erroneous.

No assessment of a deficiency may ordinarily be made later than three years from the due date or filing date of the return, whichever is later. However, if more than 25% of gross income is omitted on the return, assessment may be made within six years. If no return is filed or a false or fraudulent return is filed, there is no time limit. In the case of a report or amended return required due to a federal or New York State change, assessment of a deficiency may be made within two years. If such a report or amended return is required, but is not filed, there is no time limit.

When the taxpayer fails to report a change of federal or state taxable income or tax, or fails to file an amended return, there is no period of limitation on assessment. When the taxpayer has reported federal or state changes, assessment may be made within two years of the report or amended return. The limitation period is also two years following a report showing a change in sales or use tax liability that affects a credit claimed against the general corporation tax.

Carrybacks: Deficiencies attributable to a net operating loss carryback or capital loss carryback may be assessed at any time that a deficiency for the taxable year of the loss may be assessed.

Jeopardy assessment: The Commissioner of Finance is authorized to make a jeopardy assessment of the deficiency (together with all interest, penalties and additions to tax) if the Commissioner believes that the assessment or collection of the deficiency will be jeopardized by delay.

• *Refunds*

A claim for credit or refund may ordinarily be made within three years from the date of filing the return or two years from the payment of tax, whichever is later. If no return was filed, the refund claim may be made within two years from the payment of the tax. Special limitation periods apply to refund based on net operating loss carryback, in the case of federal or New York State changes and other circumstances.

A petition for refund may be filed with the Commissioner of Finance if the taxpayer has previously filed a timely claim for refund and, either six months have elapsed since the filing of the claim, or a notice of disallowance has been sent by the Commissioner of Finance. If a notice of disallowance has been sent, the petition may be filed within two years from such notice. If a waiver of the notice has been filed, the petition may be filed within two years from the date of waiver.

Extension of limitation period by agreement: The assessment limitation period may be extended by a timely agreement. The limitation period applicable to a claim for credit or refund does not expire prior to six months after the expiration of the period in which an assessment may be made under such an agreement or an extension thereof.

• *Judicial review*

Determinations of the Commissioner of Finance are reviewable under Article 78 of the Civil Practice Law and Rules.

• *Interest on underpayments and overpayments*

The Commissioner of Finance determines interest rates on underpayments and overpayments of New York City business taxes (general corporation (income) tax, banking corporation (income) tax, unincorporated business income tax, and the tax on foreign and alien insurers) on the basis of federal short-term rates established by the United States Secretary of the Treasury for Internal Revenue Code purposes, rounded to the nearest full percentage (or increased to the next full percentage in the case of $1/2\%$ multiple). The overpayment rate is the sum of the federal short-term rate plus 2%. The underpayment rate is the sum of the federal short-term interest rate plus 7%. If no rates are established, the rates will be deemed to be set at 7.5% per annum. There is no minimum interest rate on overpayments of the general corporation tax or the tax on banking corporations.

Interest rates per annum, compounded daily, have been established in recent periods as follows:

Period	Overpayments	Underpayments
04/1/16—12/31/16	3%	8%
10/1/11—03/31/16	2%	7.5%
3/1/11—9/30/11	3%	8%
1/1/11—3/31/11	2%	7.5%
7/11/09—12/31/10	3%	8%
4/1/09—7/10/09	3%	6%
1/1/09—3/31/09	4%	7%
10/1/08—12/31/08	5%	8%
7/1/08—9/30/08	4%	7%
4/1/08—6/30/08	5%	8%
1/1/08—3/31/08	6%	9%
7/1/06—12/31/07	7%	10%
10/1/05—6/30/06	6%	9%
4/1/05—9/30/05	5%	8%
10/1/04—3/31/05	4%	7%
7/1/04—9/30/04	3%	6%
4/1/04—6/30/04	4%	7%
10/1/03—3/31/04	3%	6%
7/1/03—9/30/03	4%	7%
1/1/02—6/30/03	6%	6%

Mathematical error: Interest on underpayments of tax will not be charged where the underpayment is solely due to a mathematical error and the tax is paid within three months of the due date (or extended due date) of the return.

¶2815

Penalties and additions to tax: Interest will apply on additions to tax and penalties if not paid within 10 days after notice and demand for payment.

Carrybacks: Interest is not recomputed when the application of a net operating loss carryback or capital loss carryback reduces the tax for a previous year.

Satisfaction by credits: Where any portion of the tax is satisfied by credits for overpayment, no interest is imposed on the portion of the deficiency extinguished by the credit for the period subsequent to the date on which the overpayment was made.

LOCAL TAXES

CHAPTER 29

NEW YORK CITY TAX ON BANKING CORPORATIONS

¶2901 Scope of Chapter

This chapter discusses the New York City tax on banking corporations. It is designed to give a general description of the tax, the banks subject to tax, the basis and rate of tax and to outline return and payment requirements.

¶2902 History and Imposition of Tax

The New York City tax on banking corporations, enacted in 1972, is Part 4 of the City Business Tax. When originally added, many provisions were scheduled to expire for taxable years after 1989, except the alternative minimum tax measured by assets and provisions that apply to savings banks and savings and loan associations. Subsequent legislation has extended this "sunset date." Beginning January 1, 2010, the banking corporation tax is applicable only to savings and loan associations. However, the alternative minimum tax measured by taxable assets continues to apply to all taxpayers.

The tax, imposed on banks and other financial corporations "for the privilege of doing business in New York City" is a franchise, rather than income, tax. Therefore, it is not subject to a federal statute that exempts obligations of the United States government from state taxation (*Bankers Trust New York Corporation et al. v. Department of Finance* (1991, NY SCt, AppDiv) 171 AD2d 550, 567 NYS2d 438, *aff'd* (1992, NY Ct App) 583 NYS2d 821, 79 NYS2d 457, CCH NEW YORK CITY TAX REPORTS, ¶ 600-063).

The city tax is patterned after the New York State taxes on banks and financial corporations imposed by Article 32 of the Tax Law (see Part IV of this Guidebook). New York City has been given authority to amend the local law to maintain conformity with the state taxes.

¶2903 Banks and Other Financial Corporations Subject to Tax

Law: Secs. 11-639, 11-640, NYC Adm. Code (CCH NEW YORK TAX REPORTS, ¶ 510-201, 510-225).

For tax years beginning on or after January 1, 2015, the banking corporation tax (BCT) applies only if a corporation is an S corporation or a qualified subchapter S subsidiary under the IRC. Other corporations that were previously subject to tax under the BCT are now subject to tax under Subchapter 3-A of Chapter 6 of Title 11 of the New York City Administrative Code. Accordingly, such corporations will file Subchapter 3-A tax returns instead of BCT returns.

Prior law: For tax years beginning before 2015, and for S corporations no longer subject to the general corporation tax, a tax, for the privilege of doing business in New York City, is imposed on banks, savings and loan associations, trust companies and other financial institutions organized under the laws of New York State and on national banks, production credit associations and federal savings and loan associations located within New York City. Also taxed are foreign banking corporations and other foreign financial corporations doing a banking business in New York City.

Beginning in 2011, credit card companies with customers having a mailing address in New York City are subject to the banking corporation tax regardless of whether the credit card company has any physical location within New York City (Sec. 11-640(c), N.Y.C. Adm. Code).

The tax is imposed on entire net income (or on the alternative base if applicable).

Sunset date: As discussed above (¶2902), many taxpayers previously subject to the NYC bank tax became subject to the NYC tax on general corporations for taxable years beginning on or after January 1, 2011. Also beginning in 2011, if a corporation meets certain conditions, it is subject to the bank tax even if it had previously elected to be subject to the general corporation tax, or had been grandfathered as subject to GCT, under the Gramm-Leach-Bliley transitional provisions (Sec. 11-640(m), N.Y.C. Adm. Code). Transition provisions similar to those applicable under the state bank franchise tax apply (¶1602).

Exempt corporations: Corporations subject to the New York City general corporation tax, and any trust company all of the stock of which is owned by not fewer than 20 New York State savings banks, are expressly exempt from tax. Corporations subject to tax under Article 33, Tax Law (New York State tax on insurance corporations) are exempt from tax. The exemption does not apply to savings and insurance banks conducting life insurance business.

International banking facilities: Similar to state provisions (¶1610).

Gramm-Leach-Bliley Act transitional provisions: Similar to state provisions (¶1602).

For a corporation or banking corporation in existence before 2010 and subject to the Article 32 bank franchise tax for its last taxable year beginning before 2010, additional legislation (Ch. 24 (A.B. 10096), Laws 2010) removed a restriction providing that Article 32 tax treatment would no longer continue for taxable years beginning after 2010 and before 2011 if a transaction or series of transactions occurring on or after January 1, 2010, resulted in the corporation no longer meeting the requirements to be a banking corporation (Sec. 1452(m), Tax Law).

¶2904 Basis of Tax

Law: Sec. 11-641, NYC Adm. Code (CCH NEW YORK CITY TAX REPORTS, ¶510-401, 510-410).

The taxes are primarily measured by the entire net income of the taxpayer. The entire net income is apportioned where the taxpayer is doing business within and without New York City.

For computation of entire net income and allocation and apportionment, see ¶2907.

Before 2015, an alternative minimum tax was imposed if a larger tax would result. The alternative minimum tax is based on taxable assets allocated to New York City, alternative entire income allocated to New York City or a flat fee minimum.

The New York City provisions parallel the state tax (¶1604).

¶2905 Rate of Tax

Law: Sec. 1455-B, Tax Law, Sec. 11-643.5, NYC Adm. Code (CCH NEW YORK TAX REPORTS, ¶510-250).

The following tax rates apply:

Net income: 9% on net income allocated to New York City.

Alternative minimum tax (repealed): The alternative minimum tax is the largest of the following:

$^1/_{10}$ of a mill on each dollar of taxable assets allocated to New York City; or

3% of alternative entire net income allocated to New York City; or

Flat fee minimum: $125.

A special alternative minimum tax applies to banks organized under the laws of foreign countries (Sec. 11-643.5(b), N.Y.C. Adm. Code).

For tax years beginning after 2010, one of the alternative taxes under the Bank Tax's alternative minimum tax is based on taxable assets allocated to the city even if the bank is organized under the laws of a country other than the United States. Under this amendment, most banks are subject to a tax of $^1/_{10}$ of a mill, or one $^1/_{100}$ of a cent, for every dollar of taxable assets allocated to New York City, as banks organized in the United States are. However, certain banks with a net worth ratio of under 5% are taxed on their allocated assets at a lower rate, and a bank is not subject to the allocated asset tax for any part of a period in which that bank had outstanding net worth certificates issued under a certain provision of the Federal National Housing Act. (Sec. 11-643.5(b), N.Y.C. Adm. Code)

¶2906 Credits Against Tax

Law: Secs. 11-643.5, 11-643.7, NYC Adm. Code (CCH NEW YORK CITY TAX REPORTS, ¶510-820, 510-825).

The New York City banking corporation tax provides for the following credits against tax:

Relocation and employment assistance credit: A credit is allowed to businesses that have conducted substantial business operations at certain business locations in Manhattan for 24 months prior to relocation, and that relocate all or part of the business operations and enter into a contract to purchase or lease eligible premises (or a parcel on which eligible premises will be constructed). See the discussion at ¶2806.

Credit for distributions from partnerships subject to unincorporated business tax: A credit is allowed for banking corporations that are partners in unincorporated businesses subject to unincorporated business tax. To be eligible, the corporation must be liable for the basic banking corporation tax or the alternative minimum tax on alternative net income. The credit must be deducted before any other credits, and may not be used to change the basis on which a banking corporation's tax is computed. For additional details, see discussion at ¶2806.

¶2907 Computation of Entire Net Income—Allocation

Law: Secs. 11-641, 11-642, NYC Adm. Code; Rule Sec. 3-04 (CCH NEW YORKCITY TAX REPORTS, ¶510-401, 510-601).

"Entire net income" is the total net income from all sources that:

— the taxpayer is required to report to the U.S. Treasury Department;

— the taxpayer, in the case of a corporation that is exempt from federal income tax (other than the tax on unrelated business taxable income), but that is subject to the New York City banking corporation tax, would have been required to report to the U.S. Treasury Department, but for the exemption;

— in the case of a corporation organized under the laws of a country other than the United States, is effectively connected with the conduct of a trade or business within the United States determined under IRC Sec. 882, subject to certain modifications and adjustments;

— in the case of an S corporation or qualified S corporation subsidiary (QSSS), the taxpayer would have had to report for federal income tax purposes if no S or QSSS election had been made.

Entire net income is the same as entire taxable income (but not alternative minimum taxable income).

Deductions: The following are allowed as deductions in determining entire net income, to the extent not deductible in determining federal taxable income (Sec. 11-641(e), N.Y.C. Adm. Code):

(1) interest on indebtedness incurred or continued to purchase or carry obligations or securities, the income from which is subject to New York City banking corporation tax but exempt from federal income tax;

(2) ordinary and necessary expenses paid or incurred during the taxable year attributable to income which is subject to New York City banking corporation tax but exempt from federal income tax; and

(3) the amortizable bond premium for the taxable year on any bond, the interest on which is subject to New York City banking corporation tax but exempt from federal income tax.

A deduction is allowed for the portion of wages and salaries paid or incurred for the taxable year and not allowed as a business expense deduction under IRC Sec. 280C because federal employment credits and federal incentive program (WIN) credit were claimed. (Sec. 11-641(e), N.Y.C. Adm. Code)

Deductions are allowed for money and property received from the Federal Deposit Insurance Corporation pursuant to Sec. 13 of the Federal Deposit Insurance Act, and money and property received from the Federal Savings and Loan Insurance Corporation pursuant to Sec. 406 of the Federal National Housing Act. (Sec. 11-641(e), N.Y.C. Adm. Code)

A deduction is also allowed for 17% of interest income from subsidiary capital and 60% of dividend income, gains and losses from subsidiary capital. Also deductible is 22 1/2% of interest income on obligations of New York State, or of any political subdivision of New York State, or on obligations of the United States, other than obligations held for resale in connection with regular trading activities. (Sec. 11-641(e), N.Y.C. Adm. Code)

Bad debts: The bad debt deduction allowed under the City's banking corporation tax is the same as the bank's federal income tax deduction for bad debts. Before 2010, a special calculation applied in figuring the City deduction.

Depreciation: Taxpayers generally may deduct the amount allowed as a deduction under IRC Sec. 168 to the extent not excluded in the computation of entire net income (Sec. 11-641(e)(7), N.Y.C. Adm. Code).

CCH Advisory: "Bonus" Depreciation

The accelerated depreciation deductions allowed by IRC Sec. 168(k) must be added back to federal taxable income for New York City business tax purposes. However, the federal accelerated depreciation is allowed for businesses located in the Resurgence Zone or the Liberty Zone. (Ch. 93 (A.B. 11817), Laws 2002; NYC Local Law 17

(Introductory Number 220-A), Laws 2002; Finance Memorandum 02-3, New York City Department of Finance, September 26, 2002, CCH NEW YORKCITY TAX REPORTS, ¶ 600-458)

For treatment of sport-utility vehicles (SUVs), see below.

Franchise taxes not deductible: Entire net income is computed without deduction of the New York State franchise taxes imposed under Tax Law Articles 9 (corporation tax), 9-A (business corporation tax), 13-A (tax on petroleum business) and 32 (banking corporation tax) and the New York City general corporation and banking corporation taxes. Entire net income does not include any refund or credit of tax for which an exclusion or deduction was allowed in determining entire income for New York City general corporation tax purposes for any prior year.

Allocation: If entire net income, alternative entire net income and taxable assets are derived from business carried on within and without New York City, the taxpayer is required to allocate.

The New York City provisions are similar to the state tax, based on factors of payroll, receipts, and deposits (¶ 1704). However, beginning in 2009, banking corporations that substantially provide management administrative or distributive services to investment companies are phasing in a single sales factor to replace the current three-factor allocation formula. The new allocation formula is phased in as follows (Sec. 11-642(b)(1-a), N.Y.C. Adm. Code):

— for 2009, 46% receipts —18% payroll —36% deposits;

— for 2010, 52% —16% —32%;

— for 2011, 58% —14% —285%;

— for 2012, 64% —12% —24%;

— for 2013, 70% —10% —20%;

— for 2014, 76% —8% —16%;

— for 2015, 82% —6% —12%;

— for 2016, 88% —4% —8%;

— for 2017, 94% —2% —4%; and

— after 2017, 100% receipts.

If any of the percentages cannot be determined because the taxpayer has either no payroll, no receipts, or no deposits, then for taxable years beginning in 2009 and thereafter, but before 2018, the computation must be made by taking the sum of the products determined for the facto2s that are present and dividing that sum by the sum of the weight factors that apply to each of the present factors in the calculation. This amount is then rounded to four decimal places. An allocation factor is not missing merely because its numerator is zero, but it is missing if both the numerator and denominator are zero. The rules contain examples illustrating the application of these provisions. (Rule Sec. 3-04)

Royalties: Certain royalty payments made by the taxpayer to a related member during the taxable year must be added back, to the extent deductible in calculating the taxpayer's federal taxable income. For additional information, see ¶ 1002.

Sport utility vehicles: IRC Sec. 179 limits the amount that a federal taxpayer may deduct for an SUV, in lieu of depreciation, to $25,000 rather than the $100,000 amount that would otherwise apply. Passenger vehicle deduction limitations under IRC Sec. 280F do not apply to many SUVs because of their weight. However, under the New York City provisions, the IRC Sec. 280F limitations apply to all SUVs, regardless of weight. Accordingly, the applicable New York City deduction is based on the IRC Sec. 280F limitations that would apply if the SUV were a passenger automobile. The New York City limitations apply to depreciation deductions and IRC Sec. 179

deductions taken in tax years beginning on and after January 1, 2004, regardless of when the SUV was placed in service. The department has provided schedules setting forth the New York City limits for tax years beginning in 2004 through 2012 (*Finance Memorandum 14-1*, New York City Department of Finance, February 11, 2015, CCH NEW YORK TAX REPORTS, ¶ 600-794).

Upon the disposition of property, the amount of any gain or loss includible in entire net income must be adjusted to reflect the above inclusions and exclusions from entire net income attributable to such property.

Net operating losses: For losses incurred in tax years after 2008, banks are permitted to have a net operating loss (NOL) deduction. However, the deduction will only be allowed for NOLs carried forward to future tax years. No NOLs may be carried back to past years. (Sec. 11-641(k-1), N.Y.C. Adm. Code)

¶2908 Returns, Estimates, Payment

Law: Sec. 11-646, NYC Adm. Code (CCH NEW YORK TAX REPORTS, ¶ 511-001, 511-410).

Forms: NYC-1, Tax Return for Banking Corporations; NYC-1A, Combined Tax Return for Banking Corporations; NYC-400B, Declaration of Estimated Tax by Banking Corporations; NYC-6B, Banking Corporation Tax Application for Automatic Extension; NYC-6.1B, Banking Corporation Tax Application for Additional Extension; NYC-8, Claim for Credit or Refund of Corporation Tax.

All banks subject to the tax on banking corporations are required to file annual returns with the Commissioner of Finance and pay the tax, less estimated tax previously paid, on or before the 15th day of the third month following the close of the taxable year (March 15 for calendar-year taxpayers).

Extensions of time: An automatic six-month extension of time is granted where the application for extension is filed with the Commissioner of Finance on or before the due date and is accompanied by the amount properly estimated as the tax due. Further extensions of time not exceeding three months in the aggregate may be granted. Interest at the rate set by the Commissioner of Finance (¶ 2815) applies from the original due date with respect to any underestimation of tax (properly estimated tax is not less than 90% of the tax as finally determined or not less than the tax for the preceding taxable year (12 months)).

CCH Advisory: Electronic Filing

The New York City Department of Finance operates a program for electronic filing; see **http://www1.nyc.gov/site/finance/taxes/tax-btef-faq.page.**

Federal or New York State changes: Report of federal or New York State changes or corrections in taxable income, alternative minimum taxable income or other basis of tax must be filed within 90 days (120 days for a taxpayer making a combined return) after the final determination or as required by the Commissioner of Finance. If an amended federal or state return is filed, an amended New York City return must be filed within 90 days (120 days for a taxpayer making a combined return). The requirement for reporting federal and New York State changes has been extended to shareholders of S corporations and qualified subchapter S subsidiaries.

Combined returns: Combined returns are permitted or required by the Commissioner of Finance.

The New York City provisions are similar to the state tax (¶ 1802).

• *Declarations and payment of estimated tax*

The estimated tax provisions for banking corporations are generally similar to the provisions relating to corporations subject to the New York City general corporation tax (¶ 2814). Declarations and payments are made to the address designated on the form.

¶2908

¶2909 Administration, Deficiencies, Refunds

Law: Sec. 11-130, NYC Adm. Code (CCH New York City Tax Reports, ¶511-300).

The New York City tax on banking corporations is administered by the Commissioner of Finance.

The corporate tax procedure and administration provisions of the City Business Tax apply to banking corporations, as well as to corporations subject to the New York City general corporation tax. For outline, see ¶2815.

Data match requirement: Any bank doing business in the state of New York must implement a data match system to facilitate the identification and seizure of nonexempt financial assets of tax debtors identified by the Commissioner of Finance (Sec. 11-130(b)(2), NYC Adm Code).

Interest on underpayments and overpayments: The interest rates are the same as those for the general corporation tax (see ¶2815).

LOCAL TAXES

CHAPTER 30
NEW YORK CITY PERSONAL INCOME TAX ON RESIDENTS

¶3001 Scope of Chapter

This chapter discusses the principal features of the New York City personal income tax on residents. Persons subject to tax, basis of tax, and rate of tax are covered.

¶3002 History and Imposition of Tax

The New York City personal income tax on residents was first imposed in 1966.

The tax is imposed on the city taxable income of resident individuals, estates and trusts. The New York City Tax Reduction Act of 1987 enacted rates of tax that decrease each year. The rates vary by filing status.

The tax is imposed by Ch. 17 of Title 11 of the New York City Administrative Code.

In general, New York City adopts the New York State personal income tax provisions, except as to rates and as otherwise provided in Article 30.

Unlike the state law, the city personal income tax law relates only to residents. (Nonresidents were subject to a separate earnings tax until its repeal—see Chapter 35.)

¶3003 Persons Subject to Tax

Law: Sec. 1127, NYC Charter; Sec. 11-1705, NYC Adm. Code (CCH NEW YORK TAX REPORTS, ¶515-205—515-215).

The New York City personal income tax is imposed on the city taxable income of every resident individual, estate, and trust.

Practitioner Comment: New York City Does Not Tax New York City Source Income

Unlike New York State, New York City does not tax nonresidents on income derived from sources within New York City. Instead, New York City's personal income tax applies only to residents of New York City: those individuals domiciled in New York City or those taxpayers who are considered statutory residents (see below). As a result, a resident of Florida who sells New York City real estate will be taxed by New York State on any gain but will not owe any tax to New York City. Similarly, New York City residents who establish residence in another state may owe New York State tax on subsequently received deferred compensation, but no tax will be owed to New York City.

Mark S. Klein, Esq., Hodgson Russ LLP

Resident individual: A "city resident individual" is defined as an individual who (1) is domiciled in New York City, unless he or she maintains no permanent place of abode in the city, maintains a permanent place of abode elsewhere, and spends in the aggregate not more than 30 days of the taxable year in the city, or (2) is not domiciled in New York City but maintains a permanent place of abode in the city and spends in the aggregate more than 183 days of the taxable year in the city, unless such individual is in the armed forces of the United States.

Presence within New York City for any part of a calendar day is deemed to be a day spent within the city.

The term "city resident individual" does not include certain persons residing in foreign countries. (See ¶ 102 for similar state provisions.)

A "city nonresident individual" is an individual who is not a resident under the definition above.

CCH Advisory: Former Residents' Lottery Winnings

A resident who wins more than $5,000 in the New York State lottery and receives guaranteed annual payments of the winnings must, upon becoming a nonresident, accrue to the period of residence the value of the future lottery payments (Sec. 11-1754(c), NYC Adm. Code). Alternatively, the taxpayer may authorize withholding of New York City income taxes from the payments (Sec. 11-1771(b)(3)(B), NYC Adm. Code).

There is apparently no settled law concerning the proper method of determining the present value of the future payments (*Blanco*, Division of Tax Appeals, Administrative Law Judge Unit, April 8, 1999, CCH NEW YORK TAX REPORTS, ¶ 403-347).

• *Resident estate or trust*

A "city resident estate or trust" is defined as (1) the estate of a decedent who at his or her death was domiciled in New York City, (2) a trust, or a portion of a trust, consisting of property transferred by will of a decedent who at his or her death was domiciled in New York City, or (3) a trust, or portion of a trust, consisting of the property of (a) a person domiciled in New York City at the time such property was transferred to the trust, if such trust or portion of a trust was then irrevocable, or if it was then revocable and has not subsequently become irrevocable, or (b) a person domiciled in New York City at the time such trust, or portion of a trust, became irrevocable, if it was revocable when such property was transferred to the trust but has subsequently become irrevocable. A trust is deemed revocable if subject to a power to revest title in the person whose property constitutes such trust or portion of a trust. A trust becomes irrevocable when the possibility that such power may be exercised has been terminated.

¶3003

A "nonresident estate or trust" is an estate or trust that is not a resident estate or trust under the definition above.

A trust that, by reason of its purposes or activities, is exempt from federal income tax is exempt from New York City personal income tax, regardless of whether it is subject to federal income tax on unrelated business taxable income.

A resident trust is not taxable if (1) all the trustees are domiciled outside New York City, (2) the entire corpus of the trust, including real and tangible property, is located outside New York City, and (3) all income and gains of the trust are from or connected with sources outside the city and are determined as if the trust were a nonresident trust. Intangible property is considered to be located in New York City if at least one of the trustees is domiciled in the city. A banking corporation located outside New York City continues to be a nonresident corporate trustee even if it later becomes an office or branch of a corporate trustee domiciled in the city (Sec. 11-1705(b)(3), N.Y.C. Adm. Code).

• *City employees*

Nonresident employees of the City of New York are required, as a condition of employment, to pay to the city an amount equal to the personal income tax liability the employee would have had if he or she were a city resident. However, according to the city charter, the payment is not a tax.

The payment is computed and filed on Form NYC-1127.

CCH Advisory: Scope of Tax on City Employees

Charter Sec. 1127 applied not only to salaries that employees received from the city, but to all income wherever or however derived. Sec. 1127 requires nonresident municipal employees to agree to pay to the city the difference between what they would pay in city personal income tax if they were city residents and what they actually pay in city earnings tax and city personal income tax. The purpose of Sec. 1127, to equalize the city taxes paid by resident and nonresident city employees, could only be realized by applying Sec. 1127 to all income (*Fleming v. Giuliani*, New York Supreme Court, Appellate Division, First Judicial Department, No. 1536, August 21, 2003, CCH NEW YORK TAX REPORTS, ¶ 404-628).

¶3004 Tax Rates—In General

Law: (CCH NEW YORK TAX REPORTS, ¶ 515-300).

There are two New York City personal income taxes imposed on New York City residents, estates, and trusts (1) the base tax imposed by Sec. 11-1701, NYC Adm. Code, and (2) the additional tax surcharge imposed by Sec. 11-1704.1, NYC Adm. Code.

See ¶ 23 for the blended rate schedule, which combines the base tax and the surcharge.

Minimum income tax: In addition to other taxes, a tax is imposed on the city minimum taxable income of every city resident, estate, or trust.

¶3005 Tax Rates—Base Tax

Law: Sec. 11-1701, NYC Adm. Code (CCH NEW YORK TAX REPORTS, ¶ 515-320).

The New York City base tax is imposed on City taxable income at a graduated rate determined on the basis of income and filing status.

The applicability of New York City personal income rates set forth under Tax Law Sec. 1304(b) and Administrative Code Sec. 11-1701(b) was delayed until taxable years beginning after 2014. Accordingly, when the temporary rates enacted in 2003 under Tax Law Sec. 1304-D expired after 2005, the set of rates contained in Tax Law Sec. 1304(a) and Administrative Code Sec. 11-1701(a) apply through taxable years beginning before 2018. In addition, for taxable years beginning after 2008, the rates imposed under Administrative Code Sec. 11-1701(b) are conformed to the rates authorized by Tax Law Sec. 1304(b) (Ch. 636 (S.B. 5617), Laws 2005).

For taxable years beginning after 2009, the top base tax rate was increased from 3.2% to 3.4% for taxpayers having city taxable income over $500,000. See *TSB-M-10(7)I*, August 17, 2010; CCH NEW YORK TAX REPORTS, ¶ 406-935.

For taxable years beginning after 2014, the New York City STAR personal income tax rate reduction benefit is eliminated for taxpayers having income above $500,000 (Sec. 1304, Tax Law; Sec. 11-1701, NYC Adm. Code; *TSB-M-15(4)I*, May 8, 2015, CCH NEW YORK CITY TAX REPORTS, ¶ 600-789).

See ¶ 23 for the blended rate schedule, which combines the base tax and the additional tax surcharge.

Married filing joint returns and surviving spouses

For taxable years beginning after 2009

If the New York City taxable income is:	The tax is:
Not over $21,600	2.55% of the NYC taxable income
Over $21,600 but not over $45,000	$551 plus 3.1% of excess over $21,600
Over $45,000 but not over $90,000	$1,276 plus 3.15% of excess over $45,000
Over $90,000, but not over $500,000	$2,694 plus 3.2% of excess over $90,000
Over $500,000	$15,814* plus 3.4% of excess over $500,000

* increased to $16,803 for tax years beginning after 2014.

Heads of households

For taxable years beginning after 2009

If the New York City taxable income is:	The tax is:
Not over $14,400	2.55% of the NYC taxable income
Over $14,400 but not over $30,000	$367 plus 3.1% of excess over $14,400
Over $30,000 but not over $60,000	$851 plus 3.15% of excess over $30,000
Over $60,000, but not over $500,000	$1,796 plus 3.2% of excess over $60,000
Over $500,000	$15,876* plus 3.4% of excess over $500,000

* increased to $16,869 for tax years beginning after 2014.

Single, married filing separately, and resident estates and trusts

For taxable years beginning after 2009

If the New York City taxable income is:	The tax is:
Not over $12,000	2.55% of the NYC taxable income
Over $12,000 but not over $25,000	$306 plus 3.1% of excess over $12,000
Over $25,000 but not over $50,000	$709 plus 3.15% of excess over $25,000
Over $50,000 but not over $500,000	$1,497 plus 3.2% of excess over $50,000
Over $500,000	$15,897* plus 3.4% of excess over $500,000

* increased to $16,891 for tax years beginning after 2014.

¶3006 Tax Rates—Temporary Surcharge

Law: Sec. 11-1704, NYC Adm. Code (CCH NEW YORK TAX REPORTS, ¶ 515-310).

A temporary surcharge was imposed on the City taxable income of city residents, estates, and trusts for taxable years beginning after 1989 and before 1999.

¶3007 Tax Rates—Additional Tax Surcharge

Law: Sec. 11-1704.1, NYC Adm. Code (CCH NEW YORK TAX REPORTS, ¶ 515-315).

An additional surcharge is imposed on the City taxable income of resident individuals, estates, and trusts for taxable years beginning after 1990 and before 2018. The surcharge is calculated at the rate of 14% of the City personal income tax.

Administration: The additional tax surcharge is administered, collected, and distributed by the Commissioner of Taxation and Finance in the same manner as other City income taxes.

See ¶23 for the blended rate schedule, which combines the base tax and the surcharge.

¶3008 Tax Rates—Minimum Income Tax

Law: Sec. 11-1702, NYC Adm. Code (CCH New York Tax Reports, ¶515-305).

For tax years beginning before 2014, in addition to other taxes, a tax was imposed for each taxable year on the city minimum taxable income of every city resident individual, estate or trust at the rate of 2.85% of such city minimum taxable income (Sec. 11-1702, N.Y.C. Adm. Code; *TSB-M-06(4)I*, CCH New York Tax Reports, ¶300-509). The minimum income tax was eliminated by the 2013-2014 budget legislation.

¶3009 Credits

Law: Sec. 1310, Tax Law; Secs. 11-1706, 11-1721, NYC Adm. Code (CCH New York Tax Reports, ¶516-405).

The following credits are available against the New York City personal income tax:

• *Credit for trust beneficiary receiving accumulation distribution*

A resident beneficiary of a trust receiving an accumulation distribution may credit against the tax the proportionate part of any amount of New York City personal income tax paid by the trust in any preceding taxable year that would not have been payable if the trust income had been distributed. The credit cannot reduce the tax otherwise due to less than the amount that would have been payable if the beneficiary excluded his or her part of the distribution from New York City adjusted gross income.

This credit corresponds to the credit allowed for state personal income tax purposes (see ¶118).

• *Earned income credit*

A New York City personal income tax credit is available in the amount of 5% of the earned income credit allowed under IRC Sec. 32 (Sec. 11-1706(d), N.Y.C. Adm. Code).

If a taxpayer changes his or her status during the taxable year from City resident to City nonresident, or from City nonresident to City resident, the credit is limited to the amount determined by multiplying the amount of the credit by a fraction. The numerator is the taxpayer's City adjusted gross income for the period of residence, and the denominator is such taxpayer's City adjusted gross income determined as if he or she had been a City resident for the entire taxable year.

In the case of a husband and wife who file a joint return, but who are required to determine their City personal income taxes separately, the credit may be applied against the tax of either or divided between them as they may elect. In the case of a husband and wife who are not required to file a federal return, the credit is allowed only if the taxpayers file a joint City personal income tax return.

• *Household credit*

For an individual who is not married nor the head of a household nor a surviving spouse, a household credit will be allowed, to be determined according to the following table (Sec. 11-1706(b), N.Y.C. Adm. Code):

If household gross income is:	The credit is:
Not over $10,000	$15
Over $10,000 but not over $12,500	$10

For any husband and wife, head of household, or surviving spouse, a household credit will be allowed, to be determined by multiplying the number of exemptions for which the taxpayer is entitled to a deduction for the taxable year for federal income tax purposes by the credit factor for the taxable year as specified below:

If household gross income is:	The credit factor is:
Not over $15,000	$30
Over $15,000 but not over $17,500	$25
Over $17,500 but not over $20,000	$15
Over $20,000 but not over $22,500	$10

For a married person filing separately, a household credit will be allowed, to be determined by multiplying the number of exemptions for which the taxpayer is entitled to a deduction for the taxable year for federal income tax purposes by the credit factor for the taxable year as specified below:

If household gross income is:	The credit factor is:
Not over $15,000	$15
Over $15,000 but not over $17,500	$12.50
Over $17,500 but not over $20,000	$7.50
Over $20,000 but not over $22,500	$5

If a taxpayer changes status during the taxable year from resident to nonresident, or from nonresident to resident, the household credit will be prorated according to the number of months in the period of residence.

The amount of the credit may not exceed the amount of the tax, reduced by the credit for a trust beneficiary receiving an accumulation distribution.

• *NYC credit for child care expenses*

A local child care tax credit is available against New York City personal income tax. The credit is designed to assist low-income families with the cost of child care for children under the age of four.

Families with gross household incomes of up to $30,000 a year who pay child care expenses for children under age four qualify for the credit. The credit can be worth up to $1,000 and will be combined with the already existing state and federal child care tax credits. Families who qualify for the credit, but do not file taxes because they have no income, will receive a $1,000 refund check instead. (Sec. 11-1706(e), N.Y.C. Adm. Code)

• *Credit for unincorporated business income tax*

New York City provides for a credit against City personal income tax for a portion of the unincorporated business income tax (UBT) paid by a City resident. A New York City resident may be eligible for a credit of up to 100% of New York City unincorporated business income tax paid by an unincorporated business conducted by the resident and/or the proportionate share of the tax paid (after adding back the partnership credits under Sec. 11-503(j) and (m), Tax Law) by a partnership in which the city resident is a partner, as calculated under a formula. If the resident's City taxable income is $42,000 or less, the amount of the credit is 100% of the tax paid. If City taxable income is more than $42,000 but less than $142,000, the credit percentage is calculated as follows: subtract from 100% a percentage determined by subtracting $42,000 from City taxable income, dividing the result by $100,000, and multiplying by 77%. For income of $142,000 or more, the credit is 23%. (Sec. 11-1706(c), N.Y.C. Adm. Code)

• *College tuition credit or deduction*

A credit or deduction for certain college tuition expenses is available for City personal income tax purposes, up to $10,000 annually for each student (CCH NEW YORK TAX REPORTS, ¶ 516-405). This parallels the New York State credit, discussed at ¶ 140.

¶ 3009

• *State school tax reduction credit*

For taxable years beginning on or after January 1, 2016, the school tax relief credit for New York City taxpayers is converted from a city personal income tax credit into a state personal income tax credit (Sec. 606(eee), Tax Law); see ¶162.

• *Credit for general corporation tax payments by S corporations*

A personal income tax credit is allowed to city residents for certain general corporation tax payments made by New York S corporations. The credit is available for taxable years beginning on or after January 1, 2014, and before July 1, 2019. (Sec. 11-1706(f), N.Y.C. Adm. Code)

Credit amount: If city taxable income is $35,000 or less, the credit is 100% of the applicable *pro rata* amount of tax paid. If city taxable income is more than $35,000 but less than $100,000, the credit percentage is calculated as follows:

— subtract from 100% a percentage determined by subtracting $35,000 from city taxable income,

— divide the result by $65,000, and

— multiply by 100%.

If city taxable income is $100,000 or more, no credit is allowed. In addition, a formula is provided for calculating the credit for any taxable year that encompasses days occurring after June 30, 2015. (Sec. 11-1706(f), N.Y.C. Adm. Code)

• *Other credits*

The tax withheld from wages and the amount of estimated tax paid are allowed as credits against the New York City tax computed on the return.

Taxes paid to other jurisdictions: The New York City personal income tax law does not provide a credit for income taxes paid to other jurisdictions. The state tax law does. Thus, New York City residents working in New Jersey will not be allowed to credit the New Jersey commuter income tax against the New York City tax.

Separate tax on lump-sum distributions: Similar to state provisions (¶106).

¶3010 Computation of Income

Law: Secs. 11-1711—11-1716, 11-1722, NYC Adm. Code (CCH NEW YORK TAX REPORTS, ¶515-405).

The New York City taxable income of a resident individual is, for the most part, the same as his or her New York net income for state purposes. The New York net income of a resident individual is New York adjusted gross income (¶202) less the New York deduction (Chapter 3) and New York exemptions (¶104).

Sport utility vehicles (SUVs): For depreciation and expensing provisions applicable to SUVs, see ¶2807.

Business Incubator and Innovation Hot Spots program: Individuals who are sole proprietors of a qualified entity, or are partners/members/shareholders of a partnership, limited liability company, or New York S corporation, respectively, that is a qualified entity are allowed a deduction for the amount of income or gain attributable to operations at the Hot Spot. (Sec. 11-1712(c)(35); NYC Admin. Code)

¶3011 Estates, Trusts, and Decedents

Law: Sec. 11-1701, NYC Adm. Code (CCH NEW YORK TAX REPORTS, ¶515-301).

Resident estates and trusts: The New York City taxable income of a resident estate or trust is, for the most part, the same as its New York taxable income for state purposes (¶702).

Decedents: The treatment of income and deductions on a decedent's final return will be the same as for state purposes (¶110).

¶3012 Partners and Partnerships

Law: Sec. 11-1701, NYC Adm. Code (CCH New York Tax Reports, ¶515-205).

Partnerships having any income from New York City sources or having a resident partner are required to file a partnership return for New York City.

In general, the treatment of partnership income is the same for federal, New York State and New York City purposes. While the partnership is not subject to tax under the personal income tax law, the partners are taxed in their individual capacities. However, the partnership may be taxed under the New York City unincorporated business tax (Chapter 36).

The additions and subtractions relating to resident individuals, which relate to an item of partnership income, gain, loss, or deduction, are made to a partner's distributive share of such partnership item. Each item of partnership income, gain, loss, or deduction has the same character in the hands of a partner as such item has for federal income tax purposes. If an item is not characterized for federal income tax purposes, it has the same character in the hands of the partner as it had in the hands of the partnership. The partner's distributive share of an item not taken into account separately for federal income tax purposes is determined in accordance with his or her distributive share of partnership taxable income or loss generally.

Limited liability companies: See ¶113.

¶3013 Withholding of Tax

Law: Secs. 11-1771—11-1778, NYC Adm. Code (CCH New York Tax Reports, ¶516-605).

Forms: IT-2401.1, New York State, City of New York, and City of Yonkers Certificate of Nonresidence and Allocation of Withholding Tax.

The New York City personal income tax on residents is administered by the New York State Commissioner of Taxation and Finance. Following the recent enactment of a New York City personal income tax rate increase for high-income taxpayers, the Department of Taxation and Finance has issued a publication containing revised withholding computation rules. Effective for payrolls made on or after September 1, 2010, employers must use the rules and revised withholding methods included in the publication to compute the amount of New York City personal income tax to be withheld from employees. The publication also notes that the New York City supplemental withholding rate was increased from 4% to 4.75% effective September 1, 2010.

A new Form IT-2104, *Employee's Withholding Allowance Certificate*, is required. Additional information is available at **http://www.tax.state.ny.us/wt/rate.htm**. (Publication NYS-50-T.2, New York Department of Taxation and Finance, January 2011)

Requests for information or blank withholding forms should be sent directly to the Taxpayer Assistance Bureau, Albany, NY 12227.

Persons required to withhold: Employers who maintain an office or transact business in New York State and pay wages subject to the New York City personal income tax on residents are required to withhold the tax from such wages paid to a resident. Withholding does not apply to payments made for service in the armed forces of the United States, including Reserve and National Guard units. Also, by federal statute, withholding from wages of seamen is prohibited. Payments regarded as wages for purposes of federal withholding are wages for withholding of city personal income tax (¶3016).

Special rules apply to employees of interstate carriers.

¶3012

Practitioner Comment: NYC Withholding Rules

New York State employers are required to withhold New York City taxes on wages paid to all New York City residents. This requirement applies to employers doing business anywhere in New York State, regardless of whether the employer is doing business in New York City. See *NYS Withholding Tax Field Audit Guidelines,* Page 27 Example 2.

Mark S. Klein, Esq., Hodgson Russ LLP

Reporting of wages: The New York Department of Taxation and Finance requires all employers to complete the state W-2 box according to the following guidelines for any employee who has federal wages subject to New York City personal income tax withholding (TSB-M-02(3)I, Technical Services Bureau, Taxpayer Services Division, New York Department of Taxation and Finance, May 1, 2002, CCH NEW YORK TAX REPORTS, ¶ 300-359). Except for New York state and local government employers, these guidelines are also applicable to the amount required to be reported on New York State Form NYS-45, Quarterly Combined Withholding, Wage Reporting and Unemployment Insurance Return.

— For a full-year New York City resident employee, the amount of wages that must be reported in the Local wages, tips, etc. box on Form W-2 (local W-2 box) is the same amount as the federal wages required to be reported in federal box 1.

— For a part-year New York City resident, the employer must report in the local W-2 box only the amount of federal wages for the period the employee was a New York City resident.

— In the case of a full-year New York City nonresident, the employer is not required to report any wages in the local W-2 box.

Employer's liability: Employers required to withhold the tax are liable for such tax. The tax withheld is held in trust for the city. The employer is relieved from liability for any tax it did not withhold when the employee pays his or her total tax liability, but the employer remains liable for any interest or penalties applicable for such failure to withhold.

Withholding returns and payment: Employers are required to file combined withholding, wage reporting, and unemployment insurance returns. Combined New York State and City of New York returns and payment of withheld taxes are mailed to the Commissioner of Taxation and Finance. (For due dates, see ¶ 609)

¶ 3014 Returns, Estimates, Payment

Law: Secs. 11-1751—11-1754, NYC Adm. Code (CCH NEW YORK TAX REPORTS, ¶ 516-705).

The New York City personal income tax is administered by the New York State Commissioner of Taxation and Finance.

The New York City personal income tax on residents is reported on the appropriate New York State return (see Chapter 6). Returns and remittances are mailed to the Commissioner of Taxation and Finance.

The New York State provisions relating to due dates, extensions of time, reports of federal changes, and estimated taxes, etc., apply (¶ 601— ¶ 603, ¶ 605, ¶ 607).

Military personnel: The New York City Department of Finance has issued a memorandum discussing military relief provisions. With respect to income taxes, for example, whether a charge was incurred before or during military service, all collections will be deferred until six months after service ends. No interest will accrue during the deferral period. To comply with the federal Servicemembers Civil Relief Act and the New York State Soldiers' and Sailors' Civil Relief Act, the Department will allow all active duty military personnel to request relief by completing an affidavit that includes information about military service and the relief being requested (*Finance Memorandum 05-3*, New York City Department of Finance, June 17, 2005, CCH NEW YORK TAX REPORTS, ¶ 600-549).

Practitioner Comment: A Question of Residency

New York's nonresident income tax return (IT-203) requires a response to the following question: "Nonresidents: Did you or your spouse maintain living quarters in New York State?" New York's resident income tax return (IT-201) poses a similar question about living quarters in New York City. Auditors have begun aggressively targeting taxpayers that fail to or erroneously answer these questions. The New York State Department of Taxation and Finance has asserted civil penalties and, in some cases, initiated criminal proceedings against taxpayers who respond incorrectly.

Mark S. Klein, Esq., Hodgson Russ LLP

CCH Advisory: Penalty Threshhold

There will be no addition to tax if the tax due shown on the return, after credit for withholding and estimated tax payments, is less than $300.

¶3015 Administration, Deficiencies, Taxpayer Remedies

Law: Secs. 11-1781—11-1797, NYC Adm. Code (CCH NEW YORK TAX REPORTS, ¶ 516-805).

Administration of tax: The New York City personal income tax on residents is administered by the New York State Commissioner of Taxation and Finance.

The New York State provisions relating to assessment, deficiencies, civil penalties, interest, collection, and taxpayer remedies apply (Chapter 8).

¶3016 Withholding Tables and Methods

Law: (CCH NEW YORK TAX REPORTS, ¶ 516-610).

The New York State Department of Taxation and Finance periodically issues a revised set of withholding tables, setting forth the approved methods of determining the amount of the personal income tax on residents to be withheld.

In case of special situations, an employer may apply to the Commissioner of Taxation and Finance for permission to use another method.

Withholding tables are reproduced in CCH NEW YORK TAX REPORTS, ¶ 516-610.

Practitioner Comment: Supplemental Withholding Rates

Although the highest possible New York City personal income tax rate is 3.876%, the New York City resident withholding rate on supplemental wages (bonuses, commissions, overtime pay, sales awards, etc.) has been set at 4.25%. (*NYS-50-T-NYC*).

Mark S. Klein, Esq., Hodgson Russ LLP

LOCAL TAXES

CHAPTER 31

NEW YORK CITY EARNINGS TAX ON NONRESIDENTS

¶3101 Repeal of Tax

The New York City earnings tax on nonresidents (commuter tax) was repealed effective July 1, 1999. Legislation that became effective on that date enacted a partial repeal of the tax, so that the tax would be imposed only on nonresidents of New York City who commute to New York City from other states but not on those New York City nonresident commuters residing in New York State. As discussed below, this partial repeal was held to be unconstitutional, and a self-executing alternative provision thereby took effect, repealing the entire tax.

¶3102 History of Tax

Law: Sec. 1305, Tax Law; Sec. 25-m, General City Law (CCH NEW YORK TAX REPORTS, ¶518-030).

The New York City earnings tax on nonresidents was enacted in 1966 as one of a series of new taxes imposed by the City of New York as part of the reorganization of its tax structure. Under the enabling act the tax could only be imposed so long as the City imposes a personal income tax on residents, a tax now in effect.

The earnings tax on nonresidents, prior to repeal, was imposed on the wages earned, and net earnings from self-employment, within New York City, of every nonresident individual, estate, or trust.

• *Limitation of earnings tax held unconstitutional*

Under legislation effective July 1, 1999, a "nonresident individual" was defined as an individual who was not a resident of New York City or New York State. Previously, the term referred only to nonresidents of New York City. Consequently, the effect was to impose the tax on the New York City earnings of those who commute to the City from other states.

The amended tax was held to be unconstitutional even before it took effect (*Igoe et al.*, NY Supreme Court, New York County, June 25, 1999, CCH NEW YORK TAX REPORTS, ¶600-369). The Appellate Division upheld the decision, but refused to enjoin enforcement of the statute (*Igoe et al.*, NY SupCt, App Div, October 5, 1999, CCH NEW YORK TAX REPORTS, ¶600-379).

Affirming the lower court opinion, the New York Court of Appeals held that the partial repeal of the tax was a violation of the Privileges and Immunities and Commerce Clauses of the U.S. Constitution. The Court of Appeals further held that since the partial repeal was unconstitutional, the alternate provision in the statute repealing the entire commuter tax takes effect. Finally, the court held that a permanent injunction enjoining New York from enforcing the tax was inappropriate given that the refund process provides an adequate remedy at law (*The City of New York et al. v. The State of New York*, New York Court of Appeals, No. 1, No. 16, April 4, 2000, CCH NEW YORK TAX REPORTS, ¶600-395).

LOCAL TAXES

CHAPTER 32

NEW YORK CITY UNINCORPORATED BUSINESS TAX

¶3201 Scope of Chapter

This chapter deals with the New York City unincorporated business tax. The principal provisions relating to businesses subject to tax, basis and rates, returns, estimates, payment, and administration are outlined briefly.

¶3202 History and Imposition of Tax

The New York City unincorporated business tax is one of a series of taxes enacted by the City of New York in 1966 in a reorganization of its tax structure. The city tax is patterned after the former New York State unincorporated business tax imposed by Article 23 of the Tax Law.

¶3203 Businesses Subject to Tax

Law: Secs. 11-122, 11-501, 11-502, 11-506, 11-602, NYC Adm. Code (CCH NEW YORK CITY TAX REPORTS, ¶519-110).

The New York City unincorporated business tax (UBT) is imposed on any individual or unincorporated entity (including a partnership, fiduciary, or corporation in liquidation) engaged in any trade, business, profession, or occupation wholly or partly carried on within New York City. A partnership is any entity treated as a partnership for federal income tax purposes.

Self-employed professionals: The imposition of the New York City unincorporated business tax on self-employed professionals is constitutional (*Shapiro v. City of New York* (1973, NY Ct App) 32 NY2d 96, 343 NYS2d 323; appeal dismissed for want of a substantial federal question, U.S. Supreme Court, October 9, 1973, CCH NEW YORK TAX REPORTS, ¶198-216).

Practitioner Comment: Schedule C Audit Initiative

Since New York City's unincorporated business tax is imposed on all individuals who are self-employed, New York City tax auditors have begun matching New York City resident income tax returns that report income on a Schedule C with taxpayers filing unincorporated business tax returns. Although there may be situations where the New York City resident is involved in a trade or business exclusively outside of New York City, auditors are frequently dispatched to review the situation.

Mark S. Klein, Esq., Hodgson Russ LLP

Independent contractor or employee?: Independent contractors are subject to the UBT, but employees are not. The New York City Department of Finance has issued a statement of audit procedure (SAP) regarding the unincorporated business tax classification of real estate salespeople as employees or independent contractors. The SAP lists the mandatory safe harbor requirements for an individual to be classified as an employee rather than an independent contractor and notes that those meeting the requirements will not be subject to the tax with respect to their activities as real estate salespeople or associate brokers. An individual who does not meet the safe harbor requirements will be classified as an employee or independent contractor based upon an examination of the facts and circumstances of his or her particular situation. (Statement of Audit Procedure UBT-2009-1rev, New York City Department of Finance, February 12, 2009, CCH New York City Tax Reports, ¶ 600-681)

Utilities: For New York City purposes, any unincorporated business that is subject to the New York City tax on utilities (¶ 3307) is exempt from the city unincorporated business tax. However, an unincorporated business subject to the city tax on vendors of utility services (that is, a business not subject to the Department of Public Service that furnishes or sells gas, electricity, steam, water, refrigeration, telephony and/or telegraphy, or such services, or operates omnibuses) is taxable for New York City unincorporated business tax purposes on the percentage of its net income allocable to the city and not attributable to receipts taxed as a vendor of utility services.

¶3204 Exemptions

Law: Sec. 11-510, NYC Adm. Code (CCH New York City Tax Reports, ¶ 519-305).

The organizations and activities discussed below are exempt from the unincorporated business tax by reason of being specifically excluded from the statutory definition of "unincorporated business."

- *Employees, officers, and directors*

Services as an employee, or as an officer or director of a corporation, or as a fiduciary, do not subject an individual to unincorporated business tax, unless such services constitute part of a business regularly carried on by the individual.

Practitioner Comment: Director's Fees Should Be Reported as Other Income

Director's fees are exempt from the UBT unless the taxpayer is in the business of being a director. In order to preserve the exemption, director's fees should be reported on Line 21 of a board member's federal Form 1040 as "other income". Taxpayers who report director's fees on Schedule C – "profit or loss from business" (usually in order to claim expense deductions) provide auditors with strong evidence that the taxpayer is in the business of being a director.

Mark S. Klein, Esq., Hodgson Russ LLP

- *Purchases and sales for own account*

An individual or other unincorporated entity (other than a dealer) is not subject to unincorporated business tax solely by reason of (a) the purchase, holding and sale of property or the entry into, assumption, offset, assignment, or other termination of a position in property, or both, for its own account, (b) the acquisition, holding or disposition, other than in the ordinary course of a trade or business, of interests in an unincorporated entity that itself qualifies for the self-trading exemption, or (c) any combination of the activities noted above and any other activity not otherwise constituting the conduct of an unincorporated business.

For purposes of the New York City unincorporated business tax, the term "dealer" means an individual or unincorporated entity that (1) holds or disposes of property that is stock in trade of the taxpayer, inventory or is otherwise held for sale to customers in the ordinary course of the taxpayer's trade or business, or (2) regularly offers to enter into, assume, offset, assign or otherwise terminate positions in property with customers in the ordinary course of the taxpayer's trade or business. An individual or unincorporated entity will not be treated as a dealer based solely on its ownership of an interest in an entity that is a dealer, nor will an unincorporated entity be treated as a dealer based solely on the ownership by a dealer of an interest in that unincorporated entity.

Individuals or other unincorporated entities receiving $25,000 or less of gross receipts during a taxable year (determined without regard to any deductions) from an unincorporated business wholly or partly carried on within New York City will not be treated as not being engaged solely in exempt activities because of such receipts.

The "self trading" exemption encompasses investment activities routinely conducted in financial markets, such as dealings in notational principal contracts and derivative financial instruments. To protect against loss of the exemption when the unincorporated entity is also carrying on taxable business activities, a "primarily engaged" test has been established. Under this test, if an unincorporated entity is "primarily engaged" in activities qualifying for the self-trading exemption and/or the acquisition, holding or disposition of interests, as an investor, in unincorporated entities carrying on any unincorporated business in New York City, the entity's self-trading activities will not be subject to unincorporated business tax. Unincorporated entities that qualify for this partial exemption may exclude from their unincorporated business gross income any income and gains from activities qualifying for the self-trading exemption, including income with respect to securities loans, and other substantially similar income and gains from ordinary and routine trading and investment activity to the extent determined by the Commissioner of Finance.

An unincorporated entity will be considered to be "primarily engaged" in the designated activities if at least 90% of the gross value of its assets is represented by assets qualifying for the self-trading exemption, interests in unincorporated entities not carrying on any unincorporated business in the City, or investments in unincorporated entities carrying on any unincorporated business in the City held by the taxpayer as an investor. In determining whether a taxpayer meets the above test, the average gross value of the assets over the year will be taken into account under rules patterned after those applicable to the New York City General Corporation Tax. The Commissioner of Finance is, however, given discretion to use net values or to exclude assets if he or she deems it necessary to properly reflect the primary activities of the taxpayer. In addition, if a taxpayer holds securities purchased on margin or securities hedged by offsetting positions, the Commissioner may use net values in applying the 90% test.

• *Holding, leasing or managing real property*

An owner of real property, lessee or fiduciary is not subject to unincorporated business tax solely because he holds, leases or manages real property. If an owner of real property or lessee or fiduciary (except a dealer holding real property primarily for sale to customers in the ordinary course of his or her trade or business) who is holding, leasing or managing real property is also carrying on an unincorporated business in whole or in part in the city, such holding, leasing or managing of real property will not be deemed an unincorporated business if, and only to the extent that, such real property is held, leased or managed for the purpose of producing rental income from such real property or gain upon the sale or other disposition of the real property. The conduct by the owner, lessee or fiduciary, at the property, of a trade, business, profession or occupation will be deemed to be an incident to the holding, leasing or managing of the property and will not be deemed to be the conduct of an unincorporated business, provided the trade, business, profession or occupation is conducted solely for the benefit of tenants at the real property, as an incidental service to the tenants, and is not open or available to the general public.

¶3204

Income received by a property owner from building tenants who rent space in the building's public garage on a monthly or longer term basis is exempt from unincorporated business tax.

• *Sales representatives*

A person is not subject to unincorporated business tax *solely* because of selling goods, wares, merchandise or insurance for more than one person, firm or corporation unless he maintains an office, employs one or more assistants, or otherwise regularly carries on a business. In this connection, space utilized solely for the display of merchandise and/or for the maintenance and storage of business records is not considered an office and the employment of clerical and secretarial assistance is not considered the employment of assistants.

• *Tax exempt trusts*

Trusts or other unincorporated organizations that are exempt from federal income tax by reason of their purposes or activities is not deemed to be an unincorporated business (regardless of whether subject to federal or New York tax on unrelated business taxable income).

• *Businesses subject to general corporation tax*

Generally, a corporation or other entity subject to a corporation franchise tax is not subject to unincorporated business tax.

The definition of "corporation" for New York City general corporation tax purposes includes unincorporated associations that are classified as corporations pursuant to IRC Sec. 7701(a)(3) (including limited liability companies that are so classified) and publicly traded partnerships that are treated as corporations for federal tax purposes pursuant to IRC Sec. 7704. However, an unincorporated organization that would be treated as a corporation under this definition, but was subject to City unincorporated business tax for its 1995 taxable year (prior to a change in the definition), may make a one-time election to remain subject to the City unincorporated business tax for taxable years beginning in 1996 and thereafter. The election, once made, will remain in effect until revoked by the unincorporated organization.

¶3205 Basis of Tax

Law: Secs. 11-506, 11-507, 11-508, NYC Adm. Code; Rule Sec. 28-07 (CCH NEW YORK CITY TAX REPORTS, ¶519-200).

The tax is imposed on New York City unincorporated business taxable income.

The method of arriving at unincorporated business taxable income involves, at the outset, the determination of gross income through modifications to federal gross income and the determination of unincorporated business deductions through modifications to federal deductions for the business.

• *Additions to federal gross income*

The following additions are made to the federal gross income of an unincorporated business in connection with items attributable to the business (Sec. 11-506(bc), N.Y.C. Adm. Code):

—Interest on state and local bonds (other than New York);

—Interest or dividends on bonds of any federal authority, commission or instrumentality that is exempt from federal income tax but not from state or local income taxes;

—If the taxpayer exercised the election permitted for liberalized depreciation for research and development property and if the property was sold or otherwise disposed of during the taxable year, the amount of the depreciation must be added;

¶3205

—The entire amount allowable as an exclusion or deduction for stock transfer taxes in determining federal gross income but only to the extent that such taxes are incurred and paid in market-making transactions;

—The amount allowed as an exclusion or deduction for sales and use taxes imposed, but only that amount that is not in excess of the amount of credit permitted for sales and use taxes paid on certain machinery and equipment;

—The amount allowed as an exclusion or deduction for relocation rent expenses but only that amount that is not in excess of the credit permitted for such rental increases;

—The amount allowed as an exclusion or deduction in determining federal gross income for expenses involved in relocating industrial and commercial employment opportunities but only that amount that is not in excess of the credit permitted for such expenses;

—In the case of a taxpayer who is an eligible energy user, the amount allowed as an exclusion or deduction for energy charges in determining federal gross income, but only such portion of the exclusion or deduction that is not in excess of the sum of the special rebates in connection with the purchase or transport of electricity. A supplier of fuel services must add the entire amount allowed as a deduction;

—For taxable years beginning in 1982, except for qualified mass commuting vehicles, the amount that would properly be includible for federal income tax purposes had the taxpayer not made an election under IRC Sec. 168(f)(8) as it was in effect for safe harbor lease agreements entered into prior to January 1, 1984;

—Applicable to property placed in service in taxable years beginning before 1994, upon disposition of property (except for property subject to the provisions of IRC Sec. 168 placed in service in New York State for taxable years beginning after 1984 and property subject to IRC Sec. 280-F, concerning luxury automobiles), the amount, if any, by which the aggregate of the amounts allowable as a depreciation deduction under IRC Sec. 167 exceeds the aggregate of the amounts allowable as the accelerated cost recovery system deduction under IRC Sec. 168;

—The amount allowed as an exclusion or deduction for sales and use taxes in determining federal gross income, but only the amount that is not in excess of the amount of credits allowed with respect for sales and use taxes paid on electricity used in manufacturing, processing or assembling and purchases of certain energy sources by nonresidential users;

—In the event of a stock or asset acquisition during the taxable year or within the three immediately preceding taxable years, 5% of the acquisition-related interest is added, up to a limitation amount. The limitation amount is the product of the taxpayer acquisition-related interest and a fraction. The numerator of the fraction is (1) the taxpayer's total cost of any target corporation acquired in a corporate acquisition during the taxpayer's taxable year or in the three immediately preceding taxable years, or (2) in the case of an acquisition of all or substantially all of the assets of a corporation occurring on or after July 1, 1989, the value of the assets acquired during the taxpayer's taxable year or in the three immediately preceding taxable years. The denominator of the fraction is the taxpayer's average total debt for the taxable year;

—The amount allowed as an exclusion or deduction for sales and use taxes imposed by Sec. 1107, Tax Law (or for any interest imposed in connection therewith), in determining federal gross income, but only to the extent of the portion of the exclusion or deduction that is not in excess of the amount of the credit allowed pursuant to Sec. 11-503(k), NYC Adm. Code;

—The amount allowed as an exclusion or deduction in determining federal gross income of any loss, other than as a dealer, from the holding, sale, disposition, assumption, offset or termination of a position in property, or other substantially similar losses from ordinary and routine trading or investment activity to the extent determined by the Commissioner of Finance, realized in connection with activities described in Sec. 11-502(c)(2), NYC Adm. Code, if, and to the extent that, such activities are not deemed an unincorporated business carried on by the taxpayer pursuant to Sec. 11-502(c);

—In the case of a taxpayer that is an unincorporated entity described in Sec. 11-502(c)(4)(b), NYC Adm. Code, the amount allowed as an exclusion or deduction in determining federal gross income of any loss realized from the sale or other disposition of an interest in another unincorporated entity if, and to the extent that, such loss is attributable to activities of such other unincorporated entity not deemed an unincorporated business carried on by the taxpayer pursuant to Sec. 11-502(c);

—The amount allowed as an exclusion or deduction in determining federal gross income of any loss realized from the holding, leasing or managing of real property if, and to the extent that, such holding, leasing or managing of real property is not deemed an unincorporated business carried on by the taxpayer pursuant to Sec. 11-502(d), NYC Adm. Code; and

—The amount allowed as an exclusion or deduction in determining federal gross income of any loss realized from the provision by an owner, lessee or fiduciary holding, leasing or managing real property of the service of parking, garaging or storing of motor vehicles on a monthly or longer term basis to tenants at such real property if, and to the extent that, the provision of such services to such tenants is not deemed an unincorporated business carried on by the taxpayer pursuant to 11-502(d), NYC Adm. Code;

—*Royalties:* Certain royalty payments made by the taxpayer to a related member during the taxable year must be added back, to the extent deductible in calculating the taxpayer's federal taxable income. For additional information, see ¶ 1002.

CCH Advisory: "Bonus" Depreciation

The accelerated depreciation deductions allowed by IRC Sec. 168(k) must be added back to federal taxable income for New York City business tax purposes. However, the federal accelerated depreciation is allowed for businesses located in the Resurgence Zone or the Liberty Zone (Ch. 93 (A.B. 11817), Laws 2002; NYC Local Law 17 (Introductory Number 220-A), Laws 2002; Finance Memorandum 02-3, New York City Department of Finance, September 26, 2002, CCH New York City Tax Reports, ¶ 600-458).

Sport utility vehicles (SUVs): For depreciation and expensing provisions applicable to SUVs, see ¶ 2807.

• *Subtractions from federal gross income*

The following subtractions are made from the federal gross income of an unincorporated business in connection with items attributable to the business (Sec. 11-506(c), N.Y.C. Adm. Code):

—Interest on bonds of the United States and its possessions to the extent includible in federal gross income;

—Interest or dividends on bonds of any authority, commission or instrumentality of the United States that is includible in federal gross income, but which is exempt from state or local income taxes by federal statute;

—Interest or dividend income exempt by the New York State or New York City law authorizing the issuance of the obligations or securities on which paid, to the extent includible in federal gross income;

¶3205

—Any tax refund or credit for overpayment of income taxes levied by New York State, New York City or any other taxing jurisdiction or the petroleum business tax imposed by Article 13-A, Tax Law, to the extent includible in federal gross income;

—Gain on the sale or other disposition of property where the January 1, 1966, fair market value is higher than the federal basis;

—For taxable years beginning in 1982, except for qualified mass commuting vehicles, the amount properly includible in federal gross income solely as a result of a safe harbor lease election made under IRC Sec. 168(f)(8) as it was in effect for agreements entered into prior to January 1, 1984;

—Upon disposition of property (except for property subject to the provisions of IRC Sec. 168 placed in service in New York State for taxable years beginning after 1984 and property subject to IRC Sec. 280-F, concerning luxury automobiles), the amount, if any, by which the aggregate accelerated cost recovery systems deduction under IRC Sec. 168 exceeds the aggregate of the depreciation deduction under IRC Sec. 167;

—Fifty percent of dividends to the extent includible in federal gross income and not otherwise subtracted, other than (1) amounts described in Sec. 11-602(8)(b)(13) and (15), NYC Adm. Code (dividends related to sale of assets by target corporations), and (2) dividends from stock described in Sec. 11-602(3)(b) and (c), NYC Adm. Code. *Note:* The foregoing provisions of Sec. 11-602 were repealed for taxable years beginning after 1999. No subtraction is allowed for any portion of a stock dividend with respect to which a dividend deduction would have been disallowed by IRC Sec. 246(c) (relating to the dividends received deduction) if the unincorporated business were a corporation;

—The amount of any income or gain (to the extent includible in gross income for federal tax purposes) realized by an owner of real property, a lessee or a fiduciary from the holding, leasing or managing of real property to the extent that such holding, leasing or managing is not deemed to constitute an unincorporated business carried on by the taxpayer;

—The amount of any income or gain (to the extent includible in gross income for federal income tax purposes), including but not limited to, dividends, interest, payments with respect to securities loans, income from notional principal contracts, or income and gains, other than as a dealer, from the holding, sale, disposition, assumption, offset or termination of a position in, property, or other substantially similar income from ordinary and routine trading or investment activity to the extent determined by the Commissioner of Finance, realized in connection with activities described in Sec. 11-502(c)(2), NYC Adm. Code, if, and to the extent that, such activities are not deemed an unincorporated business carried on by the taxpayer pursuant to Sec. 11-502(c);

—In the case of a taxpayer that is an unincorporated entity described in Sec. 11-502(c)(4)(b), NYC Adm. Code, the amount of any income or gain (to the extent includible in gross income for federal income tax purposes) realized from the sale or other disposition of an interest in another unincorporated entity if, and to the extent that, such income or gain is attributable to activities of the other unincorporated entity not deemed an unincorporated business carried on by the taxpayer pursuant to Sec. 11-502(c); and

—The amount of any income or gain (to the extent includible in gross income for federal income tax purposes) realized from the provision by an owner, lessee or fiduciary holding, leasing or managing real property of the service of parking, garaging or storing of motor vehicles on a monthly or longer term basis to tenants at such real property if, and to the extent that, the provision of such services to such tenants is not deemed an unincorporated business pursuant to Sec. 11-502(d), NYC Adm. Code.

¶3205

• *Deductions*

The starting point for determination of New York City unincorporated business deductions is the items of loss or deduction directly connected with, or incurred in the conduct of, the business, or with any property employed in the business, to the extent those loss and deduction items are allowed for federal income tax purposes in the taxable year. Items of loss or deduction are subject to the following modifications (Sec. 11-507, N.Y.C. Adm. Code):

Charitable contributions: A deduction for charitable contributions is allowed to the same extent that the contributions would be deductible for federal income tax purposes if made by a corporation, but the deduction cannot exceed 5% of the amount by which unincorporated business gross income exceeds the sum of (a) unincorporated business deductions other than the charitable contributions deduction, and (b) the deductions for accelerated depreciation and research and development.

Net operating losses: The deduction is computed in the same way it would be computed for federal income tax purposes if the New York City unincorporated business were an individual, but based only upon New York City unincorporated business gross income and deductions. The federal net operating loss deduction used in computing the city deduction must be determined as if the unincorporated business had elected, pursuant to IRC Sec. 172, to relinquish the entire carryback period with respect to net operating losses, except for the first $10,000 of each loss sustained during taxable years ending after June 1989. A net operating loss may be carried forward in the same manner as for federal purposes. Partnerships are treated in a more restrictive fashion.

Payments to owner or partner: No deduction is allowed for amounts paid to a proprietor or partner for services or use of capital. For example, an individual was not entitled to deduct payments by his unincorporated business of one-half of his federal self-employment tax, the cost of his self-employed health insurance premiums, and contributions to a defined benefit plan, because these payments represented amounts paid or incurred to a proprietor for services or for the use of capital. Although the three deductions were allowable for federal income tax purposes, they were not proper deductions for unincorporated business tax purposes pursuant to Sec. 11-507(3), N.Y.C. Adm. Code (*Horowitz v. New York City Tax Appeals Tribunal*, 1, New York Supreme Court, Appellate Division, First Judicial Department, No. 8804 TAT(H)99-3(UB), June 5, 2007, CCH NEW YORK TAX REPORTS, ¶405-744; see also *Proskauer Rose, LLP v. Tax Appeals Tribunal of the City of New York*, New York Supreme Court, Appellate Division, First Judicial Department, No. 4786 103381/08, December 11, 2008, CCH NEW YORK TAX REPORTS, ¶600-672).

However, New York City allows a deduction for reasonable compensation for the personal services of a proprietor or of each partner actively engaged in the unincorporated business. This deduction, which is not subject to allocation, is limited to the lesser of (a) $10,000 for the owner or each active partner, or (b) 20% of the unincorporated business taxable income without the benefit of the deduction for the compensation for personal services or the unincorporated business exemptions.

Practitioner Comment: Payments to Retired Partners Not Deductible

Under New York City's unincorporated business tax, no deduction is allowed for payments made to a partner for services. (Sec. 11-507(3) of the Administrative Code of the City of New York). New York City's Department of Finance had taken the position that this disallowance included any payments made to a retired partner if the source of the payment was based on prior personal services. This position was also adopted by New York's Court of Appeals. According to the Court, if payments to retired partners were based on accounts receivable, they represented payment for personal services, and must be added back to the partnership's income. Presumably, if the retirement amounts had been computed using a non-service based criterion, they would have been deductible (*Buchbinder Tunick & Co. v. Tax Appeals Tribunal of the City of New York*, 100 NY2d 389(2003)). See also *Proskauer Rose LLP*, Tax Appeals Tribunal (1st Dep't. 2008).

Mark S. Klein, Esq., Hodgson Russ LLP

Income taxes: No deduction is allowed for income taxes imposed by New York City, New York State or any other taxing jurisdiction or the petroleum business tax imposed by Article 13-A, Tax Law.

Interest on loans to carry tax-exempt securities: No deduction is allowed for (a) interest on indebtedness incurred or continued to purchase or carry obligations or securities the income from which is exempt from the unincorporated business tax, (b) expenses paid or incurred for the production or collection of such income or the management, conservation or maintenance of property held for the production of such income, or (c) the amortizable bond premium on any bond the interest income from which is exempt from the unincorporated business tax.

However, a deduction is allowed for the following: (a) interest on indebtedness incurred or continued to purchase or carry obligations or securities the income from which is subject to New York City unincorporated business tax but exempt from federal tax; (b) ordinary and necessary expenses paid or incurred during the taxable year for the production or collection of such income or the management, conservation or maintenance of property held for the production of such income; and (c) the amortizable bond premium for the taxable year on any bond the interest on which is subject to the New York City unincorporated business tax but exempt from federal income tax.

Capital gains and losses: No deduction in respect of the excess of net long-term capital gain over net short-term capital loss is allowed in computing the unincorporated business tax since all capital gains connected with the unincorporated business are treated as ordinary income. Similarly, capital losses of the business are deductible as ordinary losses.

Federal accelerated cost recovery system: For taxable years beginning after 1981, except for property subject to IRC Sec. 280-F (concerning luxury automobiles) and property subject to the provisions of Sec. 168 that is placed in service in New York State for taxable years beginning after 1984, no deduction is allowed for the amount allowable as the accelerated cost recovery system deduction under IRC Sec. 168. Provided a safe harbor lease deduction has not been disallowed, a taxpayer is allowed with respect to property that is subject to IRC Sec. 168, the depreciation deduction allowable under IRC Sec. 167 as the section would have applied to property placed in service on December 31, 1980.

Depletion: Natural resource depletion cannot be deducted on a percentage basis, but is permitted in an amount allowable under IRC Sec. 611, which permits cost depletion.

Federal jobs tax credit adjustment: A deduction is allowed for the portion of wages and salaries paid or incurred for the taxable year and not allowed as a business expense deduction under IRC Sec. 280C, since the federal jobs tax credit was taken.

Elective deductions for tangible business property, research and development facilities, industrial waste treatment facilities, and air pollution control facilities: New York City allows elective deductions in connection with certain tangible business property, research and development facilities, industrial waste treatment facilities and air pollution control facilities. The city deductions for double depreciation on certain tangible business property and for one-year write-off of new research and development facilities are applicable only to depreciable property having a situs within New York City that is constructed, reconstructed, erected, or acquired for original use after

December 31, 1965. New York City has adopted provisions similar to the state franchise tax provisions relating to leased property and to property acquired after January 1, 1968, but has not adopted the state substitution of an investment tax credit for double depreciation.

Safe harbor leases: For taxable years beginning after 1981, except for qualified mass commuting vehicles, a deduction is allowed for any amount that the taxpayer could have excluded had it not made a safe harbor lease election under IRC Sec. 168(f)(8) for agreements entered into prior to January 1, 1984. If such an election was made, no deduction is allowed for the amount deductible for federal income tax purposes solely as a result of the election.

Sport utility vehicles: For taxable years beginning on or after January 1, 2004, in the case of a taxpayer that is not an eligible farmer, no deduction may be taken for the amount allowable as a deduction with respect to a sport utility vehicle that is not a passenger automobile as defined in IRC Sec. 280F(d)(5). Instead, the deduction must be computed as if the sport utility vehicle were a passenger automobile as defined in IRC Sec. 280F(d)(5). See also ¶2807.

• *Exemption*

Every unincorporated business is allowed an exemption of $5,000 without allocation. This exemption will be prorated for taxable years of less than 12 months. Proration is on the basis of $13.70 per day or, if the return is filed for a number of whole months, $416.67 per month.

• *Allocation*

An unincorporated entity that conducts business both within and without New York City may allocate to the city a fair and equitable portion of the excess of its unincorporated business gross income over its unincorporated business deductions.

Beginning in 2009, a single sales factor is being phased in over 10 years. (Sec. 11-508(i), N.Y.C. Adm. Code; *Finance Memorandum 09-2*, CCH NEW YORK CITY TAX REPORTS, ¶600-687) Specifically, the receipts factor is increased, and the payroll and property factors decreased, as indicated for the taxable years below:

— for 2009, 40% receipts —30% payroll —30% property;

— for 2010, 46% —27% —27%;

— for 2011, 53% —23.5% —23.5%;

— for 2012, 60% —20% —20%;

— for 2013, 67% —16.5% —16.5%;

— for 2014, 73% —13.5% —13.5%;

— for 2015, 80% —10% —10%;

— for 2016, 87% —6.5% —6.5%;

— for 2017, 93% —3.5% —3.5%; and

— after 2017, 100% receipts.

If any of the percentages cannot be determined because the taxpayer has either no property, no payroll, or no business receipts/gross income within or outside the city, then for taxable years beginning in 2009 and thereafter, but before 2018, the computation must be made by taking the sum of the products determined for the factors that are present and dividing that sum by the sum of the weight factors that apply to each of the present factors in the calculation. This amount is then rounded to four decimal places. An allocation factor is not missing merely because its numerator is zero, but it is missing if both the numerator and denominator are zero. The rules contain examples illustrating the application of these provisions. (Rule Sec. 28-07)

¶3205

For taxable years beginning after 2004 and before 2009, taxpayers were generally required to use the three-factor formula allocation method, unless that method did not fairly reflect the taxpayer's New York City income (Sec. 11-508, NYC Adm. Code). Certain taxpayers that were properly using the books and records method could elect to continue using that method for taxable years beginning before 2012.

For taxable years beginning after 2004, both real and personal property rented to the taxpayer are included in the property factor, valued at eight times the annual rent. (Sec. 11-508, NYC Adm. Code) Also, charges for services are allocable to New York City to the extent that the services are performed within the City.

Practitioner Comment: Where are Services Sourced?

Unlike New York City's business corporation tax, New York City's UBT sources the receipts from services to the principal office location of the employee performing the services. Beginning in 2015, New York City began sourcing receipts under its business corporation tax to the location where the services are delivered, regardless of the principal office location of the person performing the services. (20 NYCRR § 132.15(f)).

Mark S. Klein, Esq., Hodgson Russ LLP

Manufacturers: For taxable years before 2011, manufacturing firms (those deriving more than 50% of their gross receipts from the manufacture and sale of tangible personal property) were permitted, at their option, to "double weight" the receipts factor of their business allocation formula (Sec. 11-508(g), N.Y.C. Adm. Code; Rule Sec. 28-07(d)). Receipts from sales of tangible personal property are allocated to New York City only where the goods are shipped to points within the City.

Special rules apply to the allocation of business income by publishing and broadcasting companies, to the allocation of investment income by unincorporated businesses, and to receipts from management, administrative, or distribution services performed for regulated investment companies.

¶3206 Rate of Tax; Credits

Law: Sec. 11-503, NYC Adm. Code (CCH New York City Tax Reports, ¶519-120, 519-405—519-450).

The New York City tax on unincorporated business is imposed at the rate of 4% of unincorporated business taxable income allocated to New York City.

• *Fixed dollar credit*

A credit is allowed in an amount equal to the full amount of the tax if the taxpayer's unincorporated business tax liability is $3,400 or less. If the taxpayer's unincorporated business tax liability exceeds $3,400 but is less than $5,400, the credit is determined by multiplying the tax by a fraction, the numerator of which is $5,400 minus the amount of the tax and the denominator of which is $2,000. If the taxpayer's unincorporated business tax liability is $5,400 or more, no credit is allowed. (Sec. 11-503(b)(3-a), N.Y.C. Adm. Code)

• *Credit for partners*

Partners in an unincorporated business who are subject to unincorporated business tax and are required to include in unincorporated business taxable income their distributive share of income, gain, loss and deductions of, or guaranteed payments from, the unincorporated business, may claim a tax credit. The credit is equal to the lesser of the following:

— the sum of (a) the unincorporated business tax reported and paid by the unincorporated business for its taxable year ending within or with the taxable year of the partner, and (b) the amount of any credit or credits allowed to the unincorporated business (other than the fixed dollar credit) for its taxable year ending within or with the taxable year of the partner (to the extent that such credits do not reduce the unincorporated business's tax to an amount below zero), multiplied by a fraction, the numerator of which is the net total of the partner's distributive share of income, gain, loss and deductions of, and guaranteed payments from, the unincorporated business for the taxable year, and the denominator of which is the sum, for the taxable year, of the net total distributive shares of income, gain, loss and deductions of, and guaranteed payments to, all partners in the unincorporated business for whom or which such net total (as separately determined for each partner) is greater than zero; or

— the difference between the tax computed on the unincorporated business taxable income of the partner, without allowance of any credits, and the tax computed as if the partner had no such distributive share or guaranteed payments with respect to the unincorporated business. The amount so determined may not be less than zero.

The sum of the credits allowed to a partner for a taxable year with respect to all unincorporated business in which he or she is a partner may not exceed the tax imposed on the unincorporated business taxable income of the partner reduced by the fixed dollar credit. Also, the credit must be taken after the credit allowed by Sec. 11-503(b), NYC Adm. Code (unincorporated business tax fixed dollar credit), but before any other unincorporated business tax credits.

Excess credits may be carried forward and used in any of the succeeding seven taxable years. Where a partner is itself a partnership, no credit carryforward will be allowed unless one or more of its partners has a proportionate interest or interests, amounting to at least 80% of all interests in the unincorporated business gross income and unincorporated business deductions of the partnership that was allowed the credit for which the carryforward is claimed. The carryforward allowable on account of the credit may not exceed the percentage of the amount otherwise allowable, determined by dividing (1) the sum of the proportionate interests in the unincorporated business gross income and unincorporated business deductions of the partnership, for the year to which the credit is carried forward, attributable to such partners, by (2) the sum of such proportionate interests owned by all partners for the taxable year. The amount by which the carryforward otherwise allowable exceeds the amount allowable pursuant to the preceding sentence may not be carried forward to any other taxable year.

• *Credit for sales and use taxes paid on machinery*

Similar to New York City general corporation tax provisions (¶ 2806).

• *Relocation and employment assistance (REAP) credit*

Similar to New York City general corporation tax provisions (¶ 2806).

If an eligible taxpayer so elects, the credit may be taken against the utilities tax instead of the unincorporated business tax. No taxpayer that has previously received a certification of eligibility to take the credit against the unincorporated business tax will be permitted to make the election.

• *Film production credit*

New York City allows a film production credit against NYC unincorporated business tax through 2011 (Sec. 11-503(m), NYC Adm. Code). The credit is substantially identical to the state credit, except that the percentage of qualified production costs used to calculate the credit is 5%, instead of 10%. Up to $30 million in tax credits are available each calendar year.

For a complete discussion of the state film production credit, see ¶ 944.

¶ 3206

- *Industrial business zone relocation credit*

Credits against the New York City general corporation tax and unincorporated business tax are available to eligible taxpayers that are engaged in industrial and manufacturing activities and that relocate to an industrial business zone. (Sec. 11-503(n), NYC Adm. Code) The credit amount equals $1,000 per full-time employee, not to exceed the lesser of actual relocation costs or $100,000.

The Industrial Business Zone Boundary Commission is authorized to designate industrial business zones (Sec. 22-625, NYC Adm. Code).

- *Biotechnology credit*

Same as general corporation tax credit; see ¶2806.

- *Beer production credit*

A beer production credit is available against the New York City unincorporated business tax, applicable to taxable years beginning on or after January 1, 2017. (Sec. 11-503(22), NYC Adm. Code)

Credit amount: The credit is equal to 12 cents per gallon for the first 500,000 gallons produced in New York City and 3.86 cents per gallon for the next 15 million gallons produced in New York City in the taxable year.

Planning considerations: To be eligible for the credit, a taxpayer must be registered as a distributor under Tax Law Article 18 and must produce 60 million or fewer gallons of beer in the state during the taxable year.

Unused credit is refundable as an overpayment of tax; however, no interest will be paid.

¶3207 Returns, Estimates, Payment

Law: Secs. 11-511, 11-514, 11-517, 11-519, NYC Adm. Code (CCH New York City Tax Reports, ¶519-510, 519-530).

Forms: NYC-202, Unincorporated Business Tax Return for Individuals, Estates, and Trusts; NYC-204, Unincorporated Business Tax Return for Partnerships (Including Limited Liability Companies); NYC-5UB, Partnership Declaration of Estimated Unincorporated Business Tax; NYC-5UBTI, Declaration of Estimated Unincorporated Business Tax (for Individuals, Estates, and Trusts); NYC-62, Unincorporated Business Tax Application for Automatic Extension (for Individuals, Estates, and Trusts); NYC-64, Unincorporated Business Tax Application for Automatic Extension (for Partnerships); NYC-113, Unincorporated Business Tax Claim for Credit or Refund.

An unincorporated business is required to file a return if it has gross income (before any deduction for cost of goods sold or services performed) of more than $95,000 (Sec. 11-514(a)(4), NYC Adm. Code).

Payment of the tax, less estimated tax previously paid, is due at the time of filing of the return, by the 15th day of the fourth month following the close of the taxable year.

Partnership returns are due by the 15th day of the third month following the close of the taxable year.

CCH Advisory: Electronic Filing

The New York City Department of Finance has a program for electronic filing. Under the program, the Department will accept estimated tax payments and related forms, as well as applications for automatic extensions, for the New York City general corporation tax, banking corporation tax, and unincorporated business tax. See: **http:/ www1.nyc.gov/site/finance/taxes/business.page**.

Estimated tax: A declaration of estimated tax is generally required if a taxpayer's estimated tax can reasonably be expected to exceed $3,400 (Sec. 11-511(a)(4), NYC Adm. Code).

¶3208 Administration, Deficiencies, Taxpayer Remedies

Law: Secs. 11-524—11-537, NYC Adm. Code (CCH New York City Tax Reports, ¶519-620, 519-655).

The New York City unincorporated business tax is administered by the Commissioner of Finance.

The assessment, collection and administration provisions, including provisions relating to deficiencies and taxpayer remedies are the same as for the New York City personal income tax.

Receivers, trustees in bankruptcy, assignees for the benefit of creditors, and other like fiduciaries must give notice to the Commissioner of Finance of qualification as such, as may be required by regulation.

Practitioner Comment: Report of Federal and New York State Changes Mandatory

A taxpayer subject to the New York City unincorporated business tax must report the results of any federal or New York State tax audit that increases or decreases the taxpayer's taxable income (NYC Adm. Code Sec. 11-519). There is no statute of limitations for an assessment against the taxpayer that fails to give this notification (NYC Adm. Code Sec. 11-523(c)(1)).

Mark S. Klein, Esq., Hodgson Russ LLP

• *Interest on underpayments and overpayments*

The Commissioner of Finance determines interest rates on underpayments and overpayments of New York City unincorporated business tax on the basis of federal short-term rates established by the United States Secretary of the Treasury for Internal Revenue Code purposes, rounded to the nearest full percentage (or increased to the next full percentage in the case of $1/2\%$ multiple). The overpayment rate is the sum of the federal short-term rate plus 2%. The underpayment rate is the sum of the federal short-term interest rate plus 3% and may not be less than 6% per annum. If no rates are established, the rates will be deemed to be set at 6%.

Rates for the current and prior periods are listed at ¶2815.

LOCAL TAXES

CHAPTER 33
MISCELLANEOUS NEW YORK CITY TAXES

¶3301 Combined City and State Sales and Use Taxes

The New York City sales and use taxes are generally imposed at the rate of 4.5%. The revenues from these taxes are paid to the Municipal Assistance Corporation for the City of New York, which was created to assist New York City meet its obligations.

Combined tax rates: The combined state and local tax rate imposed in New York City is 8⁷/₈% (8.875%). This includes the 4% state tax, the ³/₈% Metropolitan Commuter Transportation District (MCTD) tax, and the 4.5% city tax.

The New York City sales and use tax generally conforms to the statewide tax. Also, New York City taxes certain services (¶3315).

Clothing and footwear: The New York City exemption for clothing and footwear is the same as the statewide exemption; see ¶2102; for historical and transitional information, see (*TSB-M-10(16)S*, September 7, 2010, CCH NEW YORK TAX REPORTS, ¶406-968)

Enhanced rate on certain services: NYC taxes are imposed at the rate of 4.5% on credit rating and credit reporting services and certain personal services, such as beauty, barbering, hair restoring, manicuring, pedicuring, and health salon services, through November 30, 2017. See ¶3315.

Motor fuels: Local governments, including New York City, are authorized to compute their local sales tax on gasoline at a rate of cents per gallon equal to $2 or $3, multiplied by the percentage rate of such taxes within the locality (Sec. 1111(m-1)(3), (4), Tax Law). For additional information, see (*Publication 718-F*, New York Department of Taxation and Finance, July 2009).

Alternative energy: New York City is authorized to reduce or eliminate its local sales and use tax on residential energy sources, such as fuel oil, coal, wood, propane, natural gas, electricity, steam and gas, and gas, electric and steam services. (Sec. 1105-A(f), Tax Law; Sec. 1210(o), Tax Law)

Machinery and equipment: Purchases of parts, tools, supplies, and services relating to tangible personal property used in manufacturing processes are exempt from New York City sales and use taxes to the same extent as they are exempt from state sales and use taxes.

Property used in live productions: Property used or consumed in the production of live dramatic or musical performances in a theater or other similar place of assembly in New York City is exempt from New York City sales and use taxes. The theater or other similar place of assembly must have a seating capacity of 100 or more rigidly anchored chairs; however, roof gardens, cabarets, or similar venues do not qualify. Certain services rendered with respect to exempt property are also exempt. These services include producing, fabricating, processing, printing, and imprinting performed on tangible personal property furnished by the customer and installing, maintaining, servicing, or repairing tangible personal property not held for sale in the regular course of business. The exemption, however, does not apply to tangible personal property that is permanently affixed to or becomes an integral part of a structure, building, or real property.

Commercial office space: Two sales and use tax exemptions exist for certain purchases of tangible personal property and services related to new commercial office space leases (as opposed to ground leases) of 10 years or more. The exemptions differ based on the location of the leased premises in two specific eligible areas. The first area (Eligible Area A) consists of a broad area of lower Manhattan below City Hall. The second area (Eligible Area B) consists of the World Trade Center site, the World Financial Center, and the Battery Park City area. (Sec. 1115(ee), Tax Law) (TSB-M-05(12)S, CCH NEW YORK TAX REPORTS, ¶ 300-479) See also ¶ 2112.

Online travel companies (remarketers): A hotel room remarketer, such as an online travel company, must collect state and local sales tax on the markup it charges the hotel guest. The room remarketer is liable for the sales tax based on the full room charge paid by 1 the hotel guest, but it can claim a refund or credit for the sales tax it pays to the hotel operator, provided it is registered as a sales tax vendor and collects the tax. (Sec. 11-2501, NYC Adm. Code; Sec. 11-2502, NYC Adm. Code; *Finance Memorandum 08-1REV*, New York City Department of Finance, August 23, 2011, CCH NYC TAX REPORTS, ¶ 600-728)

For additional information, see ¶ 2009 and ¶ 3310.

Practitioner Comment: Rental of Taxicab

Even though the lease of a taxicab was characterized as "shift payment" representing the use of the taxicab medallion, a portion of that fee also includes the rental of an automobile that was subject to sales tax both at the regular and additional (short-term automobile leasing) rate (*Best Taxi Management, Inc.*, NYS2d (3rd Dept., 2003), CCH NEW YORK TAX REPORTS, ¶ 404-100).

Mark S. Klein, Esq., Hodgson Russ LLP

The New York City parking tax (¶ 3311) is collected as part of the state tax package.

New York City imposes a tax on hotel occupancies in addition to the sales and use taxes (¶ 3310).

¶3302 Commercial Rent or Occupancy Tax

Law: Secs. 11-701 *et seq.*, NYC Adm. Code (CCH NEW YORK CITY TAX REPORTS, ¶ 532-001 *et seq.*).

Forms: CR-A, Commercial Rent Tax Annual Return; CR-Q, Commercial Rent Tax Quarterly Return.

Every tenant using premises in New York City for the purpose of any trade, business, profession, vocation, or commercial activity must pay a tax.

¶3302

The commercial rent or occupancy tax does not apply to premises located in the Borough of Manhattan north of the center line of 96th Street, or in the Boroughs of the Bronx, Brooklyn, Queens, or Staten Island.

- *Exemptions*

The following tenants are exempt from commercial rent or occupancy tax:

— the United States (to the extent that it is immune from taxation), New York State and its political subdivisions, the United Nations, or any world-wide organization of which the United States is a member;

— religious, charitable and educational nonprofit organizations and organizations for the prevention of cruelty to animals or children, when (a) no part of the organization's net earnings inure to the benefit of any private shareholder or officer, and (b) no substantial part of the organization's activities involve the carrying on of propaganda or otherwise attempting to influence legislation;

— tenants subject to commercial rent or occupancy tax aggregating $1 or less for the taxable year;

— tenants who use their premises for 14 days or less (whether or not consecutive) for a taxable year, who are not obligated to pay rent for a longer period;

— tenants (other than the operator of a hotel, apartment hotel or lodging house) who use premises for residential renting to others to the extent of 75% or more of the rentable floor space;

— tenants who use premises for certain dramatic or musical arts performances for less than four weeks, where the performances were not intended to continue for less than four weeks. Tenants who use premises for the production and performance of a theatrical work are exempt from the payment of commercial rent or occupancy tax with respect to rent paid for the premises for a period not exceeding 52 weeks. The exemption begins on the date that the production of the theatrical work commences. The term "theatrical work" means a performance (or repetition thereof) in a theater of a live dramatic performance (whether or not musical in part) that contains sustained plots or recognizable thematic material, including so-called legitimate theater plays or musicals, dramas, melodramas, comedies, compilations, farces, or reviews, provided that the performance is intended to be open to the public for at least two weeks. The term does not include performances of any kind in a roof garden, cabaret or similar place, circuses, ice skating shows, aqua shows, variety shows, magic shows, animal acts, concerts, industrial shows or similar performances, or radio or television performances, whether or not such performances are prerecorded for later broadcast (Rule Sec. 7-04);

— tenants whose annualized base rent does not exceed $249,999;

— tenants that are qualified settlement funds and grantor trusts established to resolve and satisfy claims relating to World War II, the Holocaust, victims or targets of Nazi persecution, or treatment of refugees fleeing Nazi persecution; and

— an exemption for new and renewed leases with a term of at least five years for leases of property for retail sales that are located in the New York City Liberty Zone and the World Trade Center area and that begin July 1, 2005, through June 30, 2013. (Sec. 11-704(i), NYC Adm. Code)

Presumption: There is a statutory presumption that all premises are taxable premises. The burden is on the person claiming the exemption to prove otherwise.

¶3302

Practitioner Comment: New Audit Initiative for Billboards

New York City has begun enforcing its commercial rent tax against billboard owners and advertisers, taking the position that the rental of billboard space represents the use of premises for commercial activity. Although there is no statute of limitations for businesses that never filed commercial rent tax returns, New York City's Department of Finance has agreed to limit its lookback to six years in an effort to encourage prospective compliance.

Mark S. Klein, Esq., Hodgson Russ LLP

• *Basis of tax*

Tax is computed on the tenant's "base rent." Base rent is, generally, the rent paid by a tenant to a landlord for a period, less the amounts received by or due to the tenant from a subtenant for the same period from any subtenant of any part of the premises. When base rent is for a period of less than one year, it must be annualized.

"Rent" defined: "Rent" is the consideration paid or required to be paid by a tenant for the use or occupancy of premises, valued in money, whether received in money or otherwise, including all credits, property or services of any kind, as well as any payments required to be made by a tenant on behalf of the landlord for real estate taxes, water and sewer charges, or any other expenses (including insurance) normally payable by the landlord who owns the premises. The term does not include expenses for improvement, repair, or maintenance of the tenant's premises.

The corporate operator of a Spanish language television network was not required to pay tax on improvements made to leased commercial office space in compliance with a lease provision requiring the expenditure as consideration for the rental. The statutory definition of "rent" excluded expenses for the improvement of the tenant's premises (*SIN, Inc. v. Department of Finance of the City of New York* (1988, NY Ct App) 528 NYS2d 524, CCH NEW YORK TAX REPORTS, ¶ 400-227).

If the rent paid by a tenant for occupancy of taxable premises is measured in whole or in part by the gross receipts from the tenant's sales at the premises, the rent, to the extent paid on the basis of such gross receipts, is deemed not to exceed 15% of such gross receipts.

If a tenant pays an undivided rent for premises used both for residential and commercial purposes, tax applies to the portion of the premises that is attributable to the part of the premises used for business purposes. There is a conclusive presumption that the rent attributable to business use is the amount that the tenant deducts as rent for the premises for federal income tax purposes.

Base rent—Deductions for rent received from subtenants: Rent received from a subtenant whose annualized base rent is less than $250,000, and rent received from a governmental entity, the U.N., or a nonprofit religious, charitable, or educational entity that is exempt from commercial rent or occupancy tax may be deducted by a prime tenant.

Base rent—Reductions resulting from tenant's own use of property: A tenant is entitled to deduct the following from base rent amounts paid by it for its own use of the premises:

— for railroad, air, or omnibus transportation purposes;

— as piers, in so far as they are used in interstate or foreign commerce;

— that are located in, above or under a public place and are defined by law as special franchise property;

¶3302

— that are advertising space or signs, vending machines, or newsstands in subway or elevated railroad premises operated by the New York City Transit Authority, when the rent is payable to the Transit Authority; or

— that is a parking space subject to the additional 8% parking tax imposed by Sec. 11-2049, NYC Adm. Code (¶3312).

Base rent—Special deduction: The base rent of taxable premises located in the Borough of Manhattan south of the center line of 96th Street may be reduced by 35%. This reduction must be made after all other commercial rent or occupancy rent exemptions and deductions have been taken.

Pre-1975 buildings in Lower Manhattan: A special base rent reduction is allowed for certain pre-1975 buildings in Lower Manhattan that are used for nonresidential or mixed-use purposes. For the exemption to be allowed, the premises must be leased for a minimum term of 10 years (if the tenant employs 50 or more employees in the taxable premises) or five years (if the tenant employs fewer than 50 employees) and the tenant must agree to make certain minimum expenditures on improvements to the premises. When the qualifications are met, the reduction would be available for a period of up to five years, as follows:

— in the first year of the benefit period, the special reduction would be equal to the base rent for the base year (thereby eliminating commercial rent or occupancy tax liability for the first year);

— for the first and second 12-month periods following the base year, the amount of the special reduction is equal to the lesser of the base rent for the base year or the rent paid for the applicable 12-month period;

— for the third 12-month period following the base year, the special reduction is equal to two-thirds of the lesser of the base rent for the base year or the rent paid for the 12-month period; and

— for the fourth 12-month period following the base year, the special reduction is equal to one-third of the lesser of the base rent for the base year or the rent paid for the 12-month period.

No reduction in base rent will be allowed for any period beginning after March 31, 2020 (Sec. 11-704(i)(2)(a), NYC Adm Code).

Base rent—Reductions for REAP: Certain participants in the Relocation and Employment Assistance Program (REAP) are entitled to limited 12-year base rent reductions for premises to which they relocate from outside the eligible area. The amount of the reduction is calculated based on the number of employees relocated. (Sec. 11-704(f), NYC Adm. Code)

CCH Advisory: Leasehold Improvements

A statement of audit procedure issued by the Department of Finance provides guidance to auditors in determining when tenant expenditures for leasehold improvements may be subject to New York City commercial rent tax. If a lease specifies a dollar amount for a work allowance that the landlord is obligated to provide, the tenant's payment of this obligation on behalf of the landlord in lieu of fixed rental payments is subject to tax. If a lease does not obligate the landlord to provide a specified work allowance, the tenant's leasehold improvement expenditures are not subject to tax. (*Statement of Audit Procedure CRT-2008-01*, New York City Department of Finance, April 7, 2008, CCH NEW YORK TAX REPORTS, ¶600-641)

• *Credits*

A credit is allowed to a tenant whose base rent is at least $250,000 but not more than $300,000. The credit is determined by multiplying 3.9% of the base rent by a fraction, the numerator of which is $300,000 minus the amount of base rent, and the denominator of which is $50,000.

• *Rate of tax*

Commercial rent or occupancy tax is imposed at a rate of 6% of base rent of $250,000 or over.

If the rent is for less than a year, the rate must be determined by assuming that the rent is on an equivalent basis for an entire year.

• *Returns and payment*

Returns and payment are due March 20, June 20, September 20, and December 20 for the preceding three-month period. The June 20 return is a final return for the preceding year ending May 31.

Landlords may be required to file information returns.

Returns are filed with and payment made to the Department of Finance.

¶3303 Cigarette Tax

Law: Secs. 11-1301 *et seq.*, NYC Adm. Code (CCH New York City Tax Reports, ¶555-002 *et seq.*).

Forms: CTX-AW, Application for a Wholesale Cigarette License or License to Operate Cigarette Vending Machines.

In addition to the state cigarette tax, the City of New York imposes a tax upon the possession in the City for sale, or the use of, cigarettes. All sales of cigarettes must bear valid tax stamps, effective January 18, 2014, and sales of loose cigarettes ("loosies") and loose little cigars are prohibited, effective March 19, 2014, all subject to penalties.

• *Exemptions*

The tax does not apply to (1) the use, other than for sale, of 400 cigarettes or fewer brought into the City on, or in the possession of, any person, (2) cigarettes sold to the United States or Armed Forces post exchanges, (3) cigarettes possessed by an agent or wholesale dealer for sale outside the City or State, and (4) cigarettes sold to the state of New York, to a public corporation or to an improvement district or other political subdivision of the state where it is the purchaser, user or consumer and does not purchase the cigarettes for resale. The use tax exemption applicable to 400 or fewer cigarettes brought into New York State or New York City on or in the possession of any person does not apply to mail order sales. These sales in any amount are taxable.

• *Basis and rate of tax*

The tax is imposed through 2017 at the basic rate of 75¢ for each 10 cigarettes or fraction thereof ($1.50 per package of 20). If a package contains more than 20 cigarettes, the rate of tax on the cigarettes in the package in excess of 20 is 38¢ for each five cigarettes or fraction thereof. The incidence of the tax is on the consumer. (Sec. 11-1302, N.Y.C. Adm. Code).

The combined state and city cigarette tax rate is $5.85 per pack of 20 cigarettes.

• *Returns and payment*

Wholesale dealers must secure licenses from the Commissioner of Finance. Agents file monthly returns with the Commissioner of Finance. The tax is collected by means of stamps or meter impressions.

* *Licensing*

Retail cigarette dealers must obtain a license from the Commissioner of Consumer Affairs at a biennial fee of $110 and wholesale dealers must obtain a license at a fee of $600 a year. For both retail and wholesale dealers, the fee for a duplicate license is $15.

* *Counterfeit stamp penalties*

A penalty is imposed of not more than $200 for each ten counterfeit stamps in excess of 100 counterfeit stamps.

¶3304 Real Property Transfer Tax

Law: Secs. 1240, Tax Law; Sec. 11-2101 *et seq.*, NYC Adm. Code (CCH NEW YORK CITY TAX REPORTS, ¶556-005 *et seq.*).

Forms: NYC-RPT, Real Property Transfer Tax Return.

The tax is imposed upon each deed of real property located in whole or in part in the City of New York where the consideration for the real property and any improvement thereon exceeds $25,000. The tax applies at the time of delivery to a grantee. (Sec. 11-2102, NYC Adm. Code)

In addition, New York City imposes its realty transfer tax on transfers of economic interests in real property where the consideration exceeds $25,000. "Economic interest in real property" is defined to include ownership of shares in a corporation that owns real property or an interest in a partnership, association, trust or other entity that owns real property.

The tax also applies to the original transfer of shares of stock in a cooperative housing corporation or cooperative plan sponsor in connection with the grant or transfer of a proprietary interest. Similar to state tax provisions (¶2712).

The transfer of an equitable title or interest in real property, such as a beneficial interest in a trust or a life estate, is a taxable conveyance and, therefore, is subject to New York City real property transfer tax. (*Update on Audit Issues: Real Property Transfer Tax --Transfer of Equitable Interest*, New York City Department of Finance, June 2008, CCH NEW YORK TAX REPORTS, ¶600-664)

Practitioner Comment: "Straw Man" Transfers

Although the New York City real property transfer tax applies to transfers of interests in real property within the City, the tax does not apply to any transfers from a "mere agent, dummy, straw man or conduit to his principal" or vice versa. New York City's Department of Finance issued a Statement of Audit Procedure governing audits of purported "dummy/straw man" transfers in connection with real estate syndications. The publication sets forth the criteria for exemption and imposes time limitations (one year) as well. (01-2-RPTT (626-02))

Mark S. Klein, Esq., Hodgson Russ LLP

Bulk transfers: The New York City Department of Finance has issued a real estate transfer tax memorandum to advise taxpayers and tax professionals of, and explaining the Department's current position and procedures with respect to, the determination of the tax rate with regard to bulk sales of cooperative apartments and residential condominium units. In order to determine whether a bulk sale has taken place, the department will look to the facts and circumstances of the specific case. The department recommends that purchasers request a letter ruling to obtain its position. (*Finance Memorandum 00-6REV*, New York City Department of Finance, September 8, 2011, CCH NEW YORK CITY TAX REPORTS, ¶600-727)

¶3304

CCH Advisory: Step Transactions

A decision by an administrative law judge (ALJ) which sustained a notice of determination asserting a New York City real property transfer tax was affirmed, because the events involved in the transfer of interest in the property were steps in a single transaction. The petitioner held a 45% tenant-in-common fee interest and a second entity held a 55% tenant-in-common fee interest. During one day, both parties formed a new entity (Owner LLC) and each contributed their respective interests in the property to the new owner entity. As consideration for the contributions, the petitioner received a 45% membership interest in Owner LLC and the second entity received a 55% membership interest in Owner LLC. The petitioner then sold its 45% membership interest in Owner LLC to the second entity, and claimed an exemption from the real estate transfer tax based on a mere change of identity or form of ownership or organization.

The "step transaction doctrine" is applied if either of two tests is satisfied:

(1) the end result test, where if it is evident that various steps are undertaken to achieve a specific ultimate result, they will be taxed as a single transaction; or

(2) the interdependence test, whereupon separate steps will be consolidated where it is clear that no single step would have been undertaken except as part of the whole transaction.

The ALJ correctly concluded that the step transaction doctrine applied to the transactions as a single transaction not exempt from the tax as a mere change of ownership or as a transfer of a non-controlling economic interest in the property. The Tax Appeals Tribunal noted that the actions on the day at issue were "wholly interrelated components of a single transaction whereby the petitioner conveyed its tenant-in-common interest in the property in exchange for cash and relief from liability under the mortgage loan." Further, all of the essential documents were executed the same day. (*In the Matter of GKK 2 Herald, LLC*, New York City Tax Appeals Tribunal, TAT(E)13-25(RP), July 15, 2016, CCH NEW YORK CITY TAX REPORTS, ¶ 600-810)

• *Exemptions*

The following transactions are exempt (Sec. 11-2106, NYC Adm. Code):

— conveyances where the consideration does not exceed $25,000;

— mortgages and releases of mortgages;

— leaseholds for a term of years or part of a year;

— transfers of burial plots;

— property devised under a will, or conveyed by an executor's deed in accordance with the terms of a will;

— conveyances by or to the United Nations or a similar organization of which the United States is a member;

— conveyances by or to religious, charitable or educational organizations, or organizations for the prevention of cruelty to animals or children, provided net earnings do not inure to the benefit of any private individual and such organization does not devote a substantial part of its activities for the purpose of propaganda or to influence legislation;

— conveyances to New York State, its agencies, instrumentalities, public corporations and political subdivisions;

— conveyances to the United States, its agencies and instrumentalities;

— deeds pursuant to contracts made prior to May 1, 1959;

— deeds from New York State or the federal government as a result of a sale at public auction pursuant to a contract made prior to May 1, 1959;

¶3304

— conveyances given solely as security for a debt, or for the purpose of returning such security;

— conveyances between an agent, dummy, straw man or conduit and a principal;

— deeds, instruments or transactions conveying or transferring real property or economic interests in real property that effect a mere change of identity or form of ownership or organization, to the extent that beneficial ownership remains the same (other than conveyances to a cooperative housing corporation of the land and building or buildings comprising the cooperative dwelling or dwellings); and

---

Practitioner Comment: Mere Change Exemption Subject to Step-Transaction Doctrine

Transfers made in connection with a "mere change of identity" must have "substance and independent significance" apart from the tax consequences. Although application of the New York City transfer tax is usually formulaic in nature, New York City's Tax Appeals Tribunal recently held that the form can be disregarded using the step-transaction doctrine if it appears that the only purpose for the structuring was to minimize transfer taxes. (*GKK 2 Herald LLC* (TAT(e) 13-25 (RP), July 15, 2016)).

Mark S. Klein, Esq., Hodgson Russ LLP

— certain transfers of interests in cooperative housing corporations stock and appurtenant proprietary leaseholds as a result of actions to enforce liens, security interests or other rights on or in the stock and proprietary leaseholds.

The state of New York, its agencies, instrumentalities, public corporations and political subdivisions are exempt from tax. The United States, its agencies and instrumentalities are also exempt. Such exemption does not, however, relieve a grantee from liability for the tax or from filing a return.

Foreclosure transfers: Effective September 23, 2014, the authorization for the city of New York to impose a tax upon the transfer of real property does not include the authorization to impose a civil or criminal penalty upon a referee or sheriff who conveyed property as a result of a court order in a foreclosure proceeding ordering the sale of the property. A new section is also added to the Administrative Code of the City of New York providing that when real property is transferred by a referee or sheriff pursuant to a court order in a foreclosure proceeding ordering the sale of the property, the referee or sheriff effectuating such transfer will not be liable for any interest or penalties authorized by the city's real property transfer tax or Chapter 40 of the Administrative Code. (Ch. 356 (A.B. 1582), Laws 2014) (¶3304)

• *Basis of tax*

The tax is measured by the consideration, being the price to be paid or required to be paid, including any mortgage, lien or other encumbrance on the property that existed before the delivery of the deed and remains after the delivery. (When the property is partly outside of the City, consideration is allocated.)

The amount subject to tax in the case of a grant of a leasehold interest is only the amount that is not considered rent.

The tax on transfers of economic interests applies to the transfer of a "controlling interest"—in the case of a corporation, 50% or more of the combined voting power or 50% or more of the total fair market value of all classes of stock; and in the case of a partnership, association, trust, or other entity, 50% or more of the capital, profits, or beneficial interest.

However, in the case of a corporation (other than a cooperative housing corporation), partnership, association, trust or other entity, the real property transfer tax applies to each transfer made on or after August 1, 1989, of shares of corporate stock, interest in the entity or beneficial interest in a trust, in connection with the grant or transfer of a proprietary leasehold.

The New York City Commissioner of Finance may not disregard a buyer and seller's good faith apportionment of the consideration received in connection with the transfer of real property and other assets. In *Petition of 761 Hotel Associates* (CCH NEW YORK TAX REPORTS, ¶ 600-238), a New York City Administrative Law Judge held that, because the allocation between real property and other assets was made in good faith, it must be accepted by the Commissioner for city real property transfer tax purposes even if another allocation would appear to be more appropriate.

CCH Advisory: Transfer to Spouse

A husband's transfer of his individual ownership of a property to joint ownership by him and his wife was not without consideration and one-half of the mortgage at the time of the transfer was subject to the New York City real property transfer tax. One-half of the mortgage was taxable consideration for the transfer because it was a lien on the property at the time of the transfer regardless of whether (1) the wife guaranteed the mortgage prior to the transfer or (2) any additional purchase price was paid for the property pursuant to the transfer. (*Song*, New York City Tax Appeals Tribunal, TAT(E)06-12(RP), September 29, 2008, CCH NEW YORK TAX REPORTS, ¶ 600-667)

• *Rate of tax*

The tax is imposed at the following rates (Sec. 11-2102, NYC Adm. Code):

With respect to conveyances in, or grants, assignments, or surrenders of a leasehold interest in one-, two-, or three-family houses or individual dwelling units in a dwelling occupied as the residence of four or more families living independently of each other:

1% of the consideration where the consideration is $500,000 or less;

1.425% of the consideration where the consideration is more than $500,000.

With respect to all other conveyances (or grants, assignments, or surrenders of leasehold interests):

1.425% of the consideration where the consideration is $500,000 or less;

2.625% of the consideration where the consideration is more than $500,000.

For purposes of any real property transfer tax which New York state has allowed cities with a population of one million or more to impose, the consideration for conveyances or transfers of individual residential property excludes the amount of any mortgage, lien, or encumbrance that existed before the delivery of the deed or transfer and remains after the date of delivery.

Real estate investment trusts—Rate reduction: Transfers of interests in real property after June 9, 1994, and before September 1, 2017, to qualified real estate investment trusts (REITs) or to a partnership or corporation in which a REIT owns a controlling interest immediately following such conveyance, where the conveyance is made in connection with the initial formation of the REIT, are subject to a real property transfer tax at a rate that is 50% of the general rate. Transfers of interests between July 13, 1996, and August 31, 2017, to qualified preexisting REITs (that is, transfers that do *not* occur in connection with the initial formation of the REIT), where the transferor receives and retains for at least two years an ownership interest in the REIT with a value that equals at least 50% of the value of the equity interest in the real estate transferred to the REIT, ware also eligible for the reduced tax rate. (Sec. 11-2102(e), NYC Adm. Code)

The tax is ordinarily payable by the grantor, but if the grantor does not pay or is exempt, the grantee must pay.

• *Returns and payment*

Returns signed by both grantor and grantee must be filed within 30 days of delivery of the deed. Any tax due accompanies the return. Ordinarily, returns are filed and any tax payment due is made at the time of recording the deed with the register. Returns are required (except by the United States or New York governmental bodies) even if no tax is due. (Sec. 11-2105, NYC Adm. Code)

Cooperative housing corporations must file an information return by July 15 of each year covering the preceding period of January 1 through June 30, and by January 15 of each year covering the preceding period of July 1 through December 31. The return must be filed by February 15, covering the reporting period beginning on January 6 of the preceding year and ending on January 5 of the year of filing.

Practitioner Comment: Identification of Hidden Buyers of New York City Real Property

Effective in 2015, every partnership or LLC that buys or sells real estate must list the name and Social Security number (or employer identification number) of every one of its general partners or members on New York City's transfer tax return (NYC – RPT). Most practitioners assume that this information will be shared with New York City resident income tax auditors.

Mark S. Klein, Esq., Hodgson Russ LLP

¶3305 Annual Vault Charge (Repealed)

The vault charge was repealed effective June 1, 1998.

¶3306 Motor Vehicle Taxes

> *Law:* Secs. 11-801 *et seq.*, 11-2204, NYC Adm. Code (CCH NEW YORK CITY TAX REPORTS, ¶ 550-002 *et seq.*).

New York City imposes (1) a tax on commercial motor vehicles, and (2) a motor vehicle use tax on passenger and suburban motor vehicles. (Sec. 11-802, NYC Adm. Code)

• *Tax on commercial motor vehicles*

The use of certain commercial vehicles upon the public highways and streets of New York City is subject to an excise tax. The tax is imposed on owners, including lessees and bailees having exclusive use of a vehicle for a period of 30 days or more, of (1) commercial motor vehicles used principally in the City or in connection with a business carried on within the City, and (2) motor vehicles for the transportation of passengers used regularly in the City. (Sec. 11-8902, NYC Adm. Code)

Exemptions: Exempt are: vehicles owned by the state or federal government, the United Nations, nonprofit religious, charitable or educational organizations, or by a foreign nation or its representative (for which no New York registration fee is payable); vehicles bearing dealer's license plates and used exclusively for demonstration or delivery; motor vehicles used principally for the transportation of children to and from schools and day camps operated by nonprofit agencies, or used exclusively for the transportation of persons in connection with funerals; and certain airport buses. Vehicles that do not travel on the New York City streets during the tax year, or that are in dead storage, are not taxed. (Sec. 11-803, NYC Adm. Code)

Basis and rate of tax: Commercial motor vehicles are taxed on the basis of the vehicles' maximum gross weight (that is, the motor vehicle's gross weight plus the weight of the maximum load to be carried by the vehicle), as follows (Sec. 11-802, NYC Adm. Code):

	Rate
10,000 lbs or less	$ 40
over 10,000 lbs and up to 12,500 lbs.	200
over 12,500 lbs and up to 15,000 lbs.	275
over 15,000 lbs.	300

Motor vehicles for passenger transportation are taxed at the following flat rates:

	Rate
Vehicles other than medallion taxicabs	$ 400
Medallion taxicabs	1,000

When the first taxable use occurs on or after December 1 and before March 1, the tax is imposed at 50% of the annual rate; if the first taxable use occurs on or after March 1, the rate is 25% of the annual rate. The payment of the tax covers the year from June 1 through May 31.

Returns and payment: Returns are required to be filed annually on or before June 20, or within two days after the acquisition of a motor vehicle subject to the tax. The tax is due and payable at that time; payment is evidenced by a stamp. (Sec. 11-807, NYC Adm. Code)

Medallion taxicabs: The tax imposed on medallion taxicabs is due and payable in two equal installments on or before the last day on which the return or supplemental return for the tax year is required to be filed and on or before the first day of December in the tax year. If a medallion taxicab is acquired after the first day of November in the tax year, the full amount of the tax imposed for the year is due and payable on or before the last day on which the medallion taxicab supplemental return is required to be filed.

Returns and payment are made to the Department of Finance. (Sec. 11-808, NYC Adm. Code)

• *Motor vehicle use tax*

The New York City motor vehicle use tax is imposed on the registration of passenger and suburban motor vehicles owned or leased by a resident of New York City (other than a resident who has not lived in the city more than 30 days in the year preceding the application for registration), by a nonresident who has lived in the city more than 183 days in the year preceding the application for registration and by persons, firms, copartnerships, trustees, associations, or corporations who conduct a business and who regularly keep, store, garage, or maintain a passenger or suburban vehicle in New York City. (Sec. 11-2202, NYC Adm. Code)

Exemptions: Exemptions include owners exempt from New York State registration fees (including municipalities, foreign consulates or diplomats, public authorities and certain disabled veterans), federal and state governments and their instrumentalities, United Nations, nonprofit religious, charitable, educational, etc., organizations, and nonresidents who are members of the armed forces of the United States (Sec. 11-2203, NYC Adm. Code). Any owner claiming an exemption must furnish a "City of New York Vehicle Use Exemption Certificate."

Basis and rate of tax: The tax is imposed at the rate of $15 on each vehicle at the time of registration. (Sec. 11-2202, NYC Adm. Code)

Administration and collection: The New York City motor vehicle use tax is administered by the Department of Finance, except that the tax is collected by the New York State Department of Motor Vehicles at the time of registration.

¶3306

¶3307 Public Utilities

Law: Secs. 11-1101 *et seq.*, 11-2323, 11-2343, NYC Adm. Code (CCH NEW YORK CITY TAX REPORTS, ¶ 580-002 *et seq.*).

Forms: NYC-UXP, Return of Excise Tax by Utilities; NYC-UXRB, Return of Excise Tax by Utilities (for Use by Railroads, Bus Companies, and Other Common Carriers Other Than Trucking Companies); NYC-UXS, Return of Excise Tax by Vendors of Utility Services [for Use by Persons (Other Than a Limited Fare Omnibus Company) Not Subject to the Supervision of the Department of Public Service Who Furnish or Sell Utility Services or Operate Omnibuses].

New York City imposes an excise tax on all utilities and vendors of utility services, including operators of omnibuses (Sec. 11-1102, NYC Adm. Code). If 80% or more of a taxpayer's gross receipts consist of charges for the provision of mobile telecommunications services to customers, the taxpayer is included under the definition of "utility" regardless of whether the taxpayer is supervised by the Department of Public Service.

• *Exemptions*

Sales for resale by vendors of utility services are excluded from the measure of tax.

Practitioner Comment: Internet Access

Although the New York City utility tax applies to receipts from the furnishing or selling of telecommunications services, New York City's Department of Finance has announced that it will not treat Internet access services as telecommunications services (*Department of Finance Memorandum 99-5 (10/26/99)*).

Mark S. Klein, Esq., Hodgson Russ LLP

• *Basis of tax*

The tax is based on gross income or gross operating income for the calendar month preceding each monthly return and is imposed for the privilege of exercising the franchise, holding property or doing business in New York City. Gross income and gross operating income include 84% of charges for the provision of mobile telecommunications services when the place of primary use is within the city. (Sec. 11-1102, NYC Adm. Code)

Partnerships: A taxpayer that is a partner in a partnership subject to the New York City tax imposed on utilities is not deemed to be carrying on the trade, business, profession, or occupation carried on by the partnership. (Sec. 11-1102(f), NYC Adm. Code)

If a partnership is subject to the utility tax as a utility or a vendor of utility services, no partner in the partnership is subject to the utility tax on the partner's distributive share of the partnership's gross income or gross operating income. If the partner is separately subject to the supervision of the Department of Public Service or is a utility or vendor of utility services based on activities exclusive of the partnership's activities, then that partner is subject to the utility tax only on its separate gross income or separate gross operating income.

• *Rate of tax*

The tax is imposed at the rate of 2.35% of the gross income of utilities, except that persons operating omnibuses with a carrying capacity of more than seven persons and subject to the supervision of the Department of Transportation, other than limited fare omnibuses, are taxed at the rate of 1.17% of gross income. Vendors of utility services are taxed at the rate of 2.35% of gross operating income, except that operators of omnibuses with a carrying capacity of more than seven persons and not subject to the supervision of the Department of Transportation are taxed at the rate of 1.17% of gross operating income. (Sec. 11-1102, NYC Adm. Code)

Limited fare omnibus companies are subject to tax at the rate of $1/10$th of 1% on gross income derived from commuter service and at the rate of 1.17% on gross income from all other sources.

The Department of Finance has held that revenues from sight-seeing tours and transportation services that used buses and drivers leased from unrelated bus companies were subject to New York City utility tax. The fact that the third-party lessor bus companies were also subject to utility tax as operators of omnibuses was not found to constitute an improper double taxation (*New York Tokyo Tours, Inc.,* Department of Finance, Bureau of Hearings, May 13, 1991. CCH NEW YORK TAX REPORTS, ¶ 600-003).

Persons operating or leasing sleeping and parlor railroad cars and certain railroads are taxable at the rate of 3.52% of gross income.

• *Credits*

A credit against tax for sales and use taxes paid on machinery and equipment used in production is allowed similar to the New York City general corporation tax (¶ 2806).

If an eligible taxpayer so elects, the credit for relocation and employment assistance (¶ 2806) may be taken against the utilities tax instead of the general corporation (income) tax, the banks income tax, or the unincorporated business tax. No taxpayer that has previously received a certification of eligibility to take the credit against any of those taxes will be permitted to make the election.

• *Enhanced emergency (911) telephone system surcharge*

A monthly 911 surcharge of $1 per telephone access line per month is imposed on the customers of every New York City telephone service supplier. The surcharge may not be imposed on more than 75 exchange access lines per customer per location. Telephone service suppliers must pay the surcharge on a monthly basis, and are entitled to retain an administrative fee equal to 2% of collections. (Sec. 11-2323, NYC Adm. Code)

The surcharge applies to Voice over Internet Protocol (VoIP) services (Sec. 11-2322, NYC Adm. Code). All eligible telecommunications service providers are required to include these 911 surcharges on New York City customer bills.

• *Wireless communications surcharge*

A monthly surcharge of 30¢ is imposed on each wireless communications device. (Sec. 11-2343, NYC Adm. Code)

• *Returns and payment*

Returns and payment are due on or before the 25th day of each month for the preceding calendar month. Returns are filed with and payment made to, the Department of Finance. (Sec. 11-1104, NYC Adm. Code)

¶3308 Insurance Companies

> *Law:* Secs. 11-901—11-909, NYC Adm. Code (CCH NEW YORK CITY TAX REPORTS, ¶ 585-005 *et seq.*).

> *Forms:* NYC-FP, Annual Report of Fire Premiums Tax Upon Foreign and Alien Insurers.

New York City imposes a fire department tax and a fire patrol assessment on certain insurance companies.

Fire Department Tax: A 2% tax on all fire insurance premiums, less return premiums, received during the preceding calendar year for insurance against loss in

New York City is imposed on foreign and alien fire insurance corporations, associations and individuals that insure property against loss or damage by fire. Mutual insurance companies taxed under Sec. 912, Insurance Law, and domestic insurance companies are exempt. Returns and payment are made annually to the Commissioner of Finance on or before March 1.

Fire patrol assessment: The fire patrol assessment is an apportioned assessment of the expenses of the Fire Patrol. (Sec. 14, Ch. 241, Laws 1930)

¶3309 Property Taxes

Law: Secs. 307-a, 458-a, 467-a(2), 467-c, 467-e, Real Property Tax Law; Sec. 1519, NYC Charter; Secs. 11-128, 11-209, 11-238, 11-241—11-267, NYC Adm. Code; Rule 50.01 *et seq.* (CCH NEW YORK CITY TAX REPORTS, ¶520-001 *et seq.*).

Provisions of the Real Property Tax Law (discussed in Chapter 25) are applicable to real property located within the City of New York, unless specifically superseded by special provisions of the New York City Charter or the New York City Administrative Code. Generally, the Real Property Tax Law determines whether property within the City is subject to tax; assessment and collection procedures, however, are governed by Charter and Code provisions.

Property subject to tax: Similar to state property tax provisions (¶2503). Special franchises are assessed by the State Board of Equalization and Review, and taxed at the rate applied to real property within New York City.

• *Exemptions*

Exemptions set forth in the Real Property Tax Law generally apply to property located within New York City (¶2504). In addition, the New York City Administrative Code and the New York City Charter provide for the following exemptions:

Buildings under construction: A building other than a commercial building in the course of construction, where the construction was commenced since the preceding January 5 and the building is not ready for occupancy on the following January 5, will not be assessed unless it is ready for occupancy, or is occupied in part, prior to April 15. For commercial buildings under construction, the exemption can extend for up to three years.

Housing—Single-family residences and duplexes: A 10-year full or partial decreasing exemption provided for newly constructed, reconstructed, or converted owner-occupied one- and two-family residences in New York City (Sec. 421-b(2), Real Property Tax Law). To qualify, projects must have been begun before July 1, 2006, and completed no later than July 1, 2011. The exemption includes certain owner occupied multiple dwellings containing no more than four units, provided that the dwellings were developed in a governmentally assisted project and were constructed, reconstructed, or converted on real property that was acquired by the federal government through the foreclosure of a federally-insured mortgage loan and conveyed to an owner approved by the local housing agency for the purpose of rehabilitation, in accordance with an agreement between the owner and the federal government.

Housing—New multiple dwellings (421-a program): New multiple dwellings in New York City may be eligible for either a 10-year, 15-year, 20-year, or 25-year partial exemption from tax, if they meet certain requirements (Sec. 421-a, Real Property Tax Law; Sec. 11-245, N.Y.C. Adm. Code). The 10-year exemption is mandatory under the Real Property Tax Law, while the 15- and 25-year exemptions are authorized by the Real Property Tax Law but subject to adoption by the New York City Department of Housing Preservation and Development. All three exemption provisions may be limited by the city government. The city government has adopted provisions relating to all three. The 20-year exemption applies under the Real Property Tax Law unless excluded by local law (Sec. 421-a(2)(a)(iv)(A), Real Property Tax Law).

Any dwelling that is occupied as the residence or home of three or more families living independently of each other is a multiple dwelling for purposes of these exemptions. Hotels are excluded. If specific conditions are met, a new multiple dwelling includes new residential construction and the concurrent conversion, alteration or improvement of a pre-existing building or structure (Sec. 421-a(1), Real Property Tax Law).

For all Sec. 421-a exemptions, construction must have commenced before June 15, 2015 (Sec. 421-a(2)(a)(iv)(A), Real Property Tax Law; Sec. 421-a(2)(c)(ii), Real Property Tax Law).

Practitioner Comment: New York Enforcing Requirements of 421-a Program

In 2015, New York began auditing building owners who took advantage of the State's 421-a exemption program to ensure that they were fulfilling the law's rent regulation requirements. According to New York Governor Cuomo "We will not tolerate landlords who break the law and deny their tenants rent-regulated leases, plain and simple". See New York Attorney General Press Release, August 26, 2015.

Mark S. Klein, Esq., Hodgson Russ LLP

Housing—Multiple dwellings (J-51 program): Increases in assessed valuation resulting from alterations and improvements to convert certain multiple dwellings or other buildings to Class A multiple dwellings, or to eliminate certain substandard conditions, may qualify for 14-year or 34-year exemptions from property tax (Sec. 11-243(b), NYC Adm. Code). Projects eligible for relief include the following:

— conversion of Class B multiple dwellings to Class A multiple dwellings;

— conversion of nonresidential buildings or structures located within New York, Bronx, Kings, Queens, or Richmond Counties to Class A multiple dwellings;

— alterations or improvements (visible from a public street) to the exterior of otherwise eligible designated historic landmark sites or structures, pursuant to a permit issued by the Landmarks Commission;

— alterations or improvements to otherwise eligible buildings or structures designed to conserve the use of fuel, electricity or other energy source; also, conversions to master electrical metering after July 16, 2001;

— alterations or improvements to existing dwellings to eliminate existing unhealthy or dangerous conditions or to replace inadequate or unhealthy sanitary conditions that represent fire or health hazards; and

— conversion of qualified lofts to Class A multiple dwelling units. Generally, the exemption will only apply if the gross cubic content of the building or structure is not increased as a result of the alteration or improvement. In addition, the conversion, alteration, or improvement must be completed within a specified period.

Eligible improvements to certain Class A and Class B multiple dwelling units that are commenced after July 1, 1980, and before June 30, 2015, and are completed within 36 months of commencement, may qualify for a 32-year tax exemption to the extent of any increase in the property's assessed valuation as a result of the improvement. (Sec. 11-244, N.Y.C. Adm. Code)

Increases in the assessed valuation attributable to the moderate rehabilitation of substantially occupied Class A multiple dwellings may qualify for exemption from property tax for a period of 34 years.

Qualified conversions, alterations and improvements may also qualify for tax abatements for up to 20 years. The amount of the abatement may not exceed $8^1/_3\%$ of the reasonable cost of the conversion, alteration or improvement.

¶3309

New construction of residential multiple dwellings may also qualify for partial real estate exemptions. Construction must be commenced before December 31, 2011.

To participate in the program, a redevelopment company must be organized and operated as a mutual redevelopment company and agree to continue ownership and operation of the rehabilitated building for 15 years or more (NYC Intro. No. 823, Laws 2008).

Manufacturing and industrial property (ICIP): New industrial or commercial construction projects may be entitled to full or partial exemption or to deferral of tax if certified as eligible by the New York City Department of Finance under the Industrial or Commercial Incentive Program (ICIP). Applications, as well as detailed information regarding eligible areas and deadlines, may be obtained by calling the Department of Finance ICIP Unit at (212) 669-2000 or by writing to the ICIP Unit at 1 Centre Street, Room 900, New York, NY 10007 (*New York City Tax Benefits Guide*, New York City Department of Finance, January 1998). The program is scheduled to expire on June 30, 2010.

Industrial and commercial property (ICAP): An abatement of taxes is available for the construction, alteration, or improvement of certain industrial or commercial properties in specified areas of New York City. Abatements are available for varying periods up to 25 years, for eligible industrial and commercial buildings that are built, modernized, rehabilitated, expanded, or otherwise physically improved. The amount of the abatement years depends on the amount of capital spent on construction work and the ultimate use of the property. Applicants are required make a minimum required expenditure (MRE) equal to at least 30% of the taxable assessed value of the project in the year of the issuance of the building permit or, if no permit is required, the start of construction. The MRE must be made no later than four years from the date of the issuance of the first building permit for the project, or, if no permit is required, the start of construction. An additional tax abatement benefit is also provided for industrial construction projects that meet a higher MRE of 40%. Abatement benefits granted may not exceed the real property taxes imposed on such property in any year, and no benefits will be granted for residential construction work. (Sec. 489-bbbbbb, Real Property Tax Law; NYC Intro No. 822, Laws 2008) The program is authorized until June 30, 2018 (Sec. 11-271, N.Y.C. Adm. Code). The reauthorizing legislation allows tax abatements for certain new peaking electric generating facilities in New York City.

Residential conversion projects: Property tax abatements and exemptions are authorized for commercial office buildings in Lower Manhattan that are converted to residential use. To be eligible, a building permit for the conversion had to have been issued between July 1, 1995, and June 30, 2006. Eligible buildings receive a tax exemption for 12 years (a percentage of the increase in value due to conversion) and a tax abatement for 14 years (a percentage of the tax that would have been due in the first year of the benefit period but for the abatement). Buildings designated as landmarks receive an additional year of benefits. (Sec. 421-g, Real Property Tax Law)

Nonprofit organizations: Nonprofit corporations and associations organized exclusively for religious, charitable, hospital, educational or cemetery purposes are exempt from taxation on property used for the stated purposes. Real property owned by a bar association, medical society, pharmaceutical society or dental society, however, is subject to tax.

Water-works property: Property owned by a water-works corporation subject to the provisions of the Public Service Law, used exclusively for the sale, furnishing and distribution of water for domestic, commercial and public purposes, is exempt.

Disabled persons: New York City provides a partial real property tax exemption of up to 50% of a property's assessed valuation for persons with disabilities whose incomes are limited due to such disabilities. The exemption applies to real property owned by one or more persons with disabilities and extends to property owned jointly or separately by a husband and wife or by siblings as long as one of them has a disability.

Only real property or the portion of real property used exclusively for residential purposes is entitled to the exemption. Further, the disabled person must use and occupy the real property as a legal residence unless the person is absent while occupying a residential health care facility.

The exemption is computed on the basis of the combined income of the owners of the property. The combined income amount may be reduced by the amount paid for a disabled person's stay in a residential health care facility.

The exemption is applied after all other applicable partial exemptions have been subtracted from the total amount assessed. However, the exemption may not be combined with the New York City real property tax exemption for persons 65 years of age or older.

Low-income housing: The New York City low-income housing property tax exemption, which was previously available to certain participants in the federal low-income housing tax credit program, is now applicable with respect to eligible real property that participates in, or has participated in, the tax credit program (Sec. 420-c, Real Property Tax Law). A regulatory agreement must require that units formerly assisted under the tax credit program be rented in accordance with the income requirements of the program. In addition, the exemption is no longer limited to owners receiving certain governmental loans.

"Eligible owner" is defined to mean one or more eligible entities holding legal and beneficial title to eligible real property or a legal and beneficial leasehold interest with a term of at least 30 years in eligible real property. "Eligible entity" means a corporation, partnership, or limited liability company at least 50% of the controlling interest of which is held by a charitable organization. The charitable organization must be (or must wholly owned and controlled by) an entity that is formed for purposes including the provision of housing accommodations for low-income persons and families and that has received written recognition of exemption under IRC Sec. 501(c)(3) or IRC Sec. 501(c)(4).

Senior citizens: Persons 65 years of age or older may exclude up to 50% of the assessed value of property used for residential purposes, provided certain income limitations are met (Sec. 11-245.3, NYC Adm. Code). The applicant for exemption must have owned the property for at least 12 consecutive months prior to the date of application. If the property is owned by a husband and wife, the exemption will be permitted if at least one spouse is 65 years of age. The exemption will not be rescinded upon the death of the older spouse, provided the surviving spouse is at least 62 years of age.

Senior Citizens Rent Increase Exemption (SCRIE): Under the Senior Citizens Rent Increase Exemption (SCRIE) program, certain low-income senior citizens living in rent-controlled, rent-regulated or publicly aided housing may receive a rent increase exemption order, and the owners of the property within which they live may benefit from a tax abatement. The annual maximum income eligibility level for the SCRIE program is $50,000. (Sec. 467-c, Real Property Tax Law; Sec. 26-405(m), NYC Adm. Code)

Anyone granted a rent increase exemption order that is in effect as of January 1, 2015, or that takes effect on or before July 1, 2015, may continue in the programs even if their rent does not meet the $1/3$ ratio of rent-to-income requirement. Going forward, new applicants are subject to the 1/3 ratio requirement. (Sec. 467-b(2)(c), Real Property Tax Law)

¶3309

Veterans: The property of war-time veterans, their spouses, or their unremarried surviving spouses or surviving dependents, is eligible for the alternative veterans' exemption if used as their primary residence or if the veteran or unremarried surviving spouse is absent from the property due to medical reasons or institutionalization (Sec. 458-a, Real Property Tax Law; Sec. 11-245.6, NYC Adm. Code). Property qualifying for the eligible funds or pro-rata veterans' exemptions prior to January 6, 1985, may continue to receive these exemptions.

A veteran's property tax exemption may be prorated if the veteran's primary residence moves within NYC (Sec. 458(9), Real Property Tax Law).

The City has increased the maximum alternative exemptions provided for under state law (¶2504) as authorized by Sec. 458-a of the Real Property Tax Law. Qualifying residential property of veterans is exempt to the extent of 15% of the assessed value of the property, not to exceed the lesser of $45,000 (up from $12,000 under state law), or the product of $45,000 multiplied by the latest class ratio. The residential property of veterans who served in a combat theatre or combat zone of operations, as documented by the award of a U.S. campaign ribbon or service medal, is granted an additional exemption of 10% of the assessed value of the property, not to exceed the lesser of $30,000 (up from $8,000 under state law), or the product of $30,000 multiplied by the latest class ratio. Finally, the residential property of war-time veterans who have received a compensation rating from the U.S. Veteran's Administration or from the U.S. Department of Defense due to a service-connected disability is exempt to the extent of the product of the assessed value of the property multiplied by 50% of the veteran's disability rating, not to exceed the lesser of $150,000 (up from $40,000 under state law), or the product of $150,000 multiplied by the latest class ratio.

Gold Star Parents: A partial exemption is available for Gold Star Parents (i.e., mothers and fathers of Americans killed while in military service for the United States during wartime). Gold Star Parents are generally entitled to a 15% property tax exemption. Further, Gold Star Parents having a son or daughter who received a commendation are eligible for an additional 10% exemption.

Cooperatives: New York City has adopted a local law providing that the portion of real property owned by a cooperative apartment corporation that is vested in a veteran tenant-shareholder qualifies for the veteran and alternative veteran exemptions. Secs. 458 and 458-a of the New York Real Property Tax Law authorizes such exemptions provided the municipality in which the real property is located adopts a local law providing for them. An exemption is allowed for that proportion of the assessment of such real property owned by a cooperative apartment corporation determined by the relationship of such real property vested in such tenant-stockholder to such real property owned by such cooperative apartment corporation in which such tenant-stockholder resides. The exemption also applies to the alternative exemption. Any exemption that is granted will be credited by the appropriate taxing authority against the assessed valuation of such real property. The reduction in real property taxes realized thereby will be credited by the cooperative apartment corporation against the amount of such taxes otherwise payable by or chargeable to such tenant-stockholder.

Proof of eligibility required: Applicants must submit proof of eligibility when applying for: the exemption for senior persons who are 65 years or older; the exemption for the disabled; the school tax relief (STAR) exemptions; the exemptions for veterans; and the exemption for clergy members (NYC L.L. 31, (Intro. No. 688), Laws 2012).

Athletic facilities: An exemption is provided for arenas located in New York City and used by both a professional major league hockey team and by a professional major league basketball team (currently, Madison Square Garden), to the extent that the taxes are the obligation of the owners of the franchises for the teams. The exemption applies only if the owners enter into a written agreement to play their home games within New York City for ten consecutive years. The property is taxable if either team ceases to play its home games in the arena.

Revocation of exemption: The Department of Finance has issued a memorandum describing its policy for revoking New York City property tax exemptions when a property owner is no longer eligible to receive an exemption. The document provides an overview of the exemption revocations, the exemption revocation policy, and information regarding the various exemptions at issue (*Finance Memorandum 05-5,* New York City Department of Finance, July 12, 2005, CCH NEW YORK CITY TAX REPORTS, ¶ 600-552).

• *Rebates and abatements*

Solar power: A property tax abatement is available for the construction of a solar electric generating system in connection with a class one, two, or four building in New York City. A "solar electric generating system" is a system that uses solar energy to generate electricity (Sec. 499-aaaa, Real Property Tax Law). Eligible solar electric generating system expenditures include reasonable expenditures for materials, labor costs properly allocable to on-site preparation, assembly and original installation, architectural and engineering services, and designs and plans directly related to the construction or installation of the solar electric generating system.

If the solar electric generating system was placed in service on or after August 5, 2008, and before January 1, 2011, the amount of the tax abatement was equal to the lesser of: (1) 8.75% of eligible solar electric generating system expenditures; (2) the amount of taxes payable in such tax year; or (3) $62,500. If the solar electric generating system was placed in service on or after January 1, 2011, and before January 1, 2013, the amount of the tax abatement is the lesser of: (1) 5% of such expenditures; (2) the amount of taxes payable in such tax year; or (3) $62,500.

If the solar electric generating system was placed in service on or after January 1, 2013, and before January 1, 2014, the amount of the tax abatement was the lesser of (1) 2.5% of eligible solar electric generating system expenditures, (2) the amount of taxes payable in such tax year, or (3) $62,500.

If the solar electric generating system is placed in service on or after January 1, 2014, and before January 1, 2017, for each year of the compliance period such tax abatement is the lesser of (1) 5% of eligible solar electric generating system expenditures, (2) the amount of taxes payable in such tax year, or (3) $62,500. (Sec. 499-bbbb, Real Property Tax Law).

The tax abatement begins on the July 1 following the approval of an application for tax abatement by a designated agency and may not be carried over to any subsequent tax year. Tax abatement applications must be filed no later than the March 15th before the first tax year, beginning July first, for which the tax abatement is sought. Tax abatements for eligible buildings held in the condominium form of ownership will be apportioned among all of the condominium tax lots within such buildings (Sec. 499-cccc, Real Property Tax Law).

Green roofs: A New York property tax abatement is available for the construction of a green roof on a class one, two, or four property in New York City, equal to $5.23 ($4.50, prior to July 1, 2014) per square foot of green roof space. A green roof is an addition to at least 50% of a roof's space on a eligible building that includes a growth medium and a vegetation layer of drought resistant and hardy plant species that covers at least 80% of the addition (Sec. 499-aaa, Real Property Tax Law). The amount of the tax abatement may not exceed the lesser of $200,000 or the tax liability for the eligible building in the tax year for which the tax abatement is taken (Sec. 499-bbb, Real Property Tax Law). The abatement begins on July 1 following the approval of an application for tax abatement by a designated agency and is available for one year. Tax abatement applications must be filed between January 1, 2009, and March 15, 2018 (Sec. 499-ccc, Real Property Tax Law).

Abatements for condominiums and cooperatives: A partial property tax abatement is allowed to certain homeowners of residential cooperative and condominium units in class-two multi-family residential properties (Sec. 467-a(2), Real Property Tax Law; Rule 50.01 *et seq.*). Tthe abatement may be granted to a cooperative or condominium dwelling unit held in trust solely for the benefit of a person or persons who would otherwise be eligible to receive a tax abatement if that person or persons legally owned the unit. The abatement is determined on the basis of the average assessment per residential unit.

In 2015 through 2018, if the average assessed value of residential units in the property is $50,000 or less, the abatement ranges from 25% to 28.1% of the net real property taxes due on the unit after allowance for other exemptions or abatements. If the average assessed value exceeds $50,000, but is equal to or less than $55,000, the abatement is 25.2%, and if the average assessed value exceeds $55,000 but is equal to or less than $60,000, the abatement is 22.5%. If the average assessed value exceeds $60,000, the abatement is 17.5%.

The Homeowner Tax Benefit Application is due onMarch 15, 2017, for benefits to begin July 1, 2017. The Coop Tax Benefit Change Form for 2016/2017 must be emailed or postmarked by February 1, 2017. The forms may be found on the department's website at **http://www1.nyc.gov/site/finance/benefits/property-bene-fit-forms/benefits-forms-property-owners-condo-coop.page**.

Commercial revitalization: Abatements are available through March 31, 2024 for nonresidential or mixed-use premises built before 1975 and located in designated abatement zones. Applicants are required to make certain minimum expenditures to improve the eligible premises (used for offices or retail stores), and the lease must have commenced between April 1, 1995, and March 31, 2018 (Sec. 499-a, Real Property Tax Law; Sec. 499-b, Real Property Tax Law; Sec. 499-c, Real Property Tax Law). Similar benefits are also available for eligible buildings in Title 4-A abatement zones (Sec. 499-aa, Real Property Tax Law; Sec. 499-bb, Real Property Tax Law; Sec. 499-cc, Real Property Tax Law).

Abatement for rent control or tenant protection buildings: Through June 15, 2019, a real property tax abatement is available for Class Two buildings located in New York City that are subject to either the emergency housing rent control law or the rent and rehabilitation law enacted pursuant to the emergency housing rent control law or to the Emergency Tenant Protection Act of 1974. The amount of the abatement will be determined by calculating 50% of the economic loss attributed to the building owner as a result of changes to the amortization period for such buildings, which will be measured by a specified fractional formula. An abatement will commence on July 1 following the approval of an application for tax abatement by the Department of Finance and may not be carried over to any subsequent tax year and may not reduce or be offset by any other tax benefit provided, approved or calculated by the city or the state. (Sec. 467-I, Real Property Tax Law)

CCH Advisory: Superstorm Sandy Relief

As authorized by New York State, New York City grants a partial abatement of taxes on real property that was seriously damaged during Hurricane Sandy and has since been rebuilt. The law provides relief to New York City residents affected by the storm whose property tax bill in City Fiscal Year 2015 is greater than the corresponding tax liability from City Fiscal Year 2013. The properties that are subject to the assessment limitations must satisfy the following conditions:

— the Department of Finance reduced the assessed value of the building on the property on the assessment roll completed in 2013 from the assessed value on the assessment roll completed in 2012 as a result of damage caused by Hurricane Sandy; and

— the Department of Finance increased or will increase the assessed value of the building on the property as a result of the repair or reconstruction of damage caused by Hurricane Sandy on any assessment roll completed from 2014 through 2020.

For properties that satisfy these conditions and that have not had repairs or reconstruction as of the assessment roll completed in 2015, the physical increase to their assessed value as a result of repairs or reconstruction that will be performed is limited to the amount of the physical decrease reflected on the assessment roll completed in 2013. Any increase in excess of the amount of the physical decrease reflected on the assessment roll completed in 2013 will be treated as an equalization (nonphysical) increase and subject to the limitations for equalization increases. The assessed values of the properties that satisfy the requisite conditions will not be higher than they would have been but for Hurricane Sandy. For class four and larger class two properties subject to transitional assessments, the limitation on physical increases will apply to the lower of the actual assessed value or the transitional assessed value.

For properties that satisfy these conditions and have already had repairs or reconstruction that constitutes a physical increase reflected on an assessment roll completed as of 2015, the assessed value as it appeared on the assessment roll completed in 2015 must be recalculated as if the law had been in effect. The Department of Finance is authorized to correct the 2015/2016 assessed value in accordance with the enacted law within 90 days of the effective date of a local law adopting these provisions. Subsequent physical increases reflected on an assessment roll completed from 2016 through 2020 will also be subject to the limitations. To the extent that the square footage used to determine the assessed value of the building on the property on a given assessment roll exceeds that reflected on the assessment roll completed in 2012, the law provides that the Department of Finance will recalculate the limitation on physical increases by multiplying it by the percentage of the excess square footage of the building. (Ch. 14 (A.B. 5620), Laws 2015; L.L. 67 (Intro. No. 1120), Laws 2013; NYC L.L. 20 (Intro. No. 360), Laws 2014; L.L. 34 (Intro. No. 727), Laws 2015)

New York City legislation allows property owners receiving the veterans tax exemption to receive a prorated exemption if they move from one property to another midway through the tax year, ensuring that veterans receive the maximum benefit possible. (L.L. 68 (Intro. No. 1064), Laws 2013, applicable to assessment rolls prepared on the basis of taxable status dates occurring on or after January 1, 2014)

• *Payment of tax*

The collection of New York City property taxes is the responsibility of the Department of Finance. Tax bills issued by the Commissioner must indicate the current taxes, plus arrears or special assessments related to the property. For real property with an assessed value of $250,000 or less, taxes are payable in four equal installments due July 1, October 1, January 1 and April 1; otherwise, property taxes are payable in two installments due July 1 and January 1. Property held in a cooperative form of ownership will not be deemed to have an assessed value of over $80,000 if the property's assessed value divided by the number of residential dwelling units is $80,000 or less per unit. For additional information on installment payments, see *Finance Letter Ruling 05-4*, New York City Department of Finance, June 23, 2005, CCH NEW YORK CITY TAX REPORTS, ¶ 600-550.

Discounts are allowed for early payments of tax. Real property with an assessed value of more than $80,000 is not allowed the discount for early installment payments unless the installment is paid no later than 30 days before the due date and the discount for such property is applied only until the due date.

Payment by EFT: The New York City Commissioner of Finance is specifically authorized to accept and require the payment of real property taxes by electronic funds transfer (EFT). The Commissioner requires the payment of real property taxes by EFT for properties with annual real property tax liability equal to or greater than $300,000. (Rule Sec. 44-01) For a complete discussion of EFT payment requirements, see ¶3602.

¶3310 Hotel Occupancy Tax

Law: Secs. 11-2501 *et seq.*, NYC Adm. Code; NYC Rule Sec. 12-01 (CCH NEW YORK CITY TAX REPORTS, ¶531-005 *et seq.*).

Forms: NYC-HTX, Hotel Room Occupancy Tax Return.

New York City imposes a tax on the occupancy of hotel rooms, including occupancy in an apartment hotel, motel, or a boarding house or club, whether or not meals are served. The hotel occupancy tax is based on the amount of money received from the occupant, including service fees. (Secs. 11-2501, 11-2502(a), N.Y.C. Adm. Code) This tax is in addition to the combined city and state sales tax on hotel occupancy (¶2009). New York City's hotel room occupancy tax has been amended to conform to the room remarketer provisions of the sales tax (see ¶3301).

"Occupancy" is the use or possession, or the right to the use or possession of any room or rooms in a hotel, or the right to the use or possession of the furnishings or to the services and accommodations accompanying the use and possession of the room or rooms. (Sec. 11-2501(4), N.Y.C. Adm. Code)

Subletting: Persons subletting hotel rooms are not defined as operators. Generally, if a person sublets a room after renting it from an operator, the taxable occupancy is the original occupancy. Under such circumstances, the original hotel operator is required to collect the tax from the original occupant. However, the original operator must collect the tax from the sublessee in cases where the original occupant or any sublessee of the room is directly or indirectly related to the original hotel operator, as follows (Rule Sec. 12-01):

— the original hotel operator owns directly or indirectly a 5% or greater interest in the occupant;

— the occupant owns directly or indirectly a 5% or greater interest in the original hotel operator;

— one or more persons own directly or indirectly 5% or greater interests in both the occupant and the original hotel operator; or

— the occupant is an officer, director, manager (including a manager of an LLC), trustee, fiduciary, or employee of the original hotel operator or is an individual who is a member of the family of an individual original hotel operator.

• *Exemptions*

No tax is imposed on permanent residents (that is, occupants of hotel rooms for at least 180 consecutive days). (Sec. 11-2502, N.Y.C. Adm. Code)

An occupant who, under the provisions of the rent stabilization program, requests a lease after August 31, 1990, is tentatively accorded the status of permanent resident, regardless of whether the occupant has satisfied the 180-consecutive-day requirement. The operator of the hotel will not be permitted to collect the additional tax from a permanent resident for any day, commencing with the date the lease is requested, which falls within a period of continuous occupancy. If the occupant ceases to occupy a room or rooms in the hotel prior to the completion of 180 continuous days of occupancy, however, the unpaid taxes will immediately become due, and must be collected from the occupant. (Sec. 11-2502, N.Y.C. Adm. Code)

Also exempt are the state of New York or its subdivisions, public corporations, the United States to the extent that it is immune from taxation, the United Nations or similar international organizations and religious, charitable or educational organizations.

Rents or occupancies in premises in which a religious, charitable or educational organization operates a hotel as part of its activities are not subject to tax. Persons displaced by the World Trade Center attack on September 11, 2001 are not subject to tax.

Room remarketers: Any occupancy conveyed or furnished by a hotel operator to a room remarketer for the purpose of reselling to an occupant after June 1, 2016, is exempt from the hotel tax. The hotel operator must provide the remarketer with a New York State Room Remarketer's Exempt Purchase Certificate in order to claim the exemption. The remarketer remains responsible for collecting and remitting the hotel tax on the sale to the occupant. (*Finance Memorandum 16-5,* New York City Department of Finance, May 24, 2016, CCH NEW YORK CITY TAX REPORTS, ¶ 600-807)

Practitioner Comment: Hotel Tax Initiative

The New York City Department of Finance has expanded the application of its hotel occupancy tax to short-term rentals of residential apartment units. It is irrelevant that the rentals of these same apartments are exempt from the combined New York City and State sales tax on hotel room occupancy (see ¶ 2009). Under State law, the rental of these units is considered the rental of real property. The City, on the other hand, considers them the rental of hotel rooms. Since the New York State and New York City statutory definitions of "hotel" are almost identical, practitioners expect that the City's new interpretation will be challenged.

Mark S. Klein, Esq., Hodgson Russ LLP

- *Basis and rate of tax*

The basic tax is imposed on the occupancy of each room in a hotel in New York City at the following rates (Sec. 11-2502(a), N.Y.C. Adm. Code):

Rent per day per room	Tax per day
$10 or more, but less than $20	$.50
$20 or more, but less than $30	1.00
$30 or more, but less than $40	1.50
$40 or more	2.00

If the rent is charged on a weekly, monthly or other term basis, the taxable rent per day is determined by dividing the rent for the term by the number of days in the term. Similar apportionment is made for rentals of a number of rooms, including suites of rooms.

Additional tax: In addition to the base rate, a tax is imposed for every occupancy of each room in a hotel in New York City at the rate of 5.875% of the rent or charge per day for each such room from December 20, 2013, through November 30, 2019. Beginning December 1, 2019, the rate is reduced to 5%. (Sec. 11-2502(a), N.Y.C. Adm. Code)

Room remarketers: A room remarketer is required to charge the occupant the amount of the tax that the remarketer owes to the department based on the "service fee" the occupant pays to the remarketer that is in excess of the amount that the remarketer pays to the hotel operator (termed "additional rent"). (Sec. 11-2501, N.Y.C. Adm. Code; Sec. 11-2502, N.Y.C. Adm. Code)

CCH Advisory: Service Fees May Not Be Included in Hotel Tax

In a case concerning a lawsuit brought by online travel companies (OTCs) against New York City, a New York appellate court reversed the lower court's order, which had found that the city could to impose tax on the entire amount paid by a consumer for a hotel room, including any service fees charged by travel intermediaries. The enabling legislation authorized the city to impose on a hotel occupant a tax at a rate of up to 6% of the rent or charge per day for each hotel room. Contrary to the lower court's finding, the plain language of the enabling legislation did not clearly and unambiguously provide the city with broad taxation powers with respect to imposing a hotel occupancy tax. Rather, it permitted the city to impose the tax on "hotel occupants." The plain meaning of this phrase did not encompass the service fees charged by the travel intermediaries. To extend the tax to cover these fees requires action by the New York Legislature, such as that taken in 2010. Accordingly, the appellate court declared that Local Law 43, Laws 2009, which contained the amendments in question, violated the New York Constitution. (*Expedia, Inc. v. City of New York Department of Finance*, Appellate Division, First Department, No. 6174 650761/09, November 29, 2011, CCH NEW YORK CITY TAX REPORTS, ¶ 600-738)

• *Returns and payment*

Quarterly returns are filed on March 20, June 20, September 20 and December 20 covering the preceding quarterly period. Payment accompanies the return. Returns and payment are made to the Commissioner of Finance.

Practitioner Comment: Hotel Taxes are Trust Funds

As is the case with sales and withholding taxes, the New York City hotel occupancy tax is considered a trust fund, so that hotel operators and "all officers of a corporate operator" are personally liable for the tax. This liability applies regardless of whether the tax was actually collected from the occupant of the hotel room. (NYC Adm. Code Sec. 11-2502(f)(3))

Mark S. Klein, Esq., Hodgson Russ LLP

¶3311 Parking Tax

Law: Secs. 11-2001 *et seq.*, NYC Adm. Code (CCH NEW YORK CITY TAX REPORTS, ¶ 560-030).

Forms: Application for Manhattan Resident Parking Tax Exemption.

The New York City parking tax is imposed on receipts from the service of providing parking, garaging or storing motor vehicles by persons operating a garage (other than a garage that is part of premises occupied solely as a private one-or two-family dwelling), parking lot or other place of business engaged in providing parking, garaging or storing for motor vehicles.

Practitioner Comment: Nonresidents Ineligible for the Exemption

Qualification for the New York City parking tax exemption is limited to residents of Manhattan. Income tax auditors frequently cross reference applications for the parking tax exemption with individuals who claim to be nonresidents of New York City. Since the rules are mutually exclusive, taxpayers who take both positions are put in a very awkward position.

Mark S. Klein, Esq., Hodgson Russ LLP

• *Basis and rate of tax*

The services of parking, garaging and storing motor vehicles within New York City are subject to the 4% state tax, the 6% New York City local tax, and the 0.375% Metropolitan Commuter Transportation District (MCTD) tax (for a combined state and local rate of 10.375%).

The borough of Manhattan has an additional 8% parking tax that applies unless the purchaser is a certified exempt resident (for a combined state and local rate of 18.375%).

• *Exemptions*

Manhattan residents who park, garage or store their motor vehicles on a monthly or longer-term basis are exempt from the 8% additional parking tax imposed in the Borough of Manhattan if they obtain exemption certificates from the New York City Department of Finance. Persons exempt from the additional Manhattan parking tax remain subject to the tax on New York City parking services (6% New York City tax, 4% New York State sales tax and $^3/_8$% Metropolitan Commuter Transportation District surcharge).

Receipts for parking, garaging, or storing motor vehicles paid to a homeowner's association by its members are not subject to the 6% New York City sales tax on parking or the 8% New York County (Manhattan) parking tax. The exemption includes parking charges paid by members of a homeowner's association to a person leasing a parking facility from the homeowner's association. To be exempt, the association's membership must be comprised exclusively of owners or residents of residential dwelling units and the association must own or operate the facility in which the services are provided or performed.

Organizations that are exempt from the New York State and New York City sales tax will remain exempt when they are the purchasers of parking services. However, if an exempt organization or governmental entity provides parking, garaging or storage services for motor vehicles, it must collect the tax for any charges made for such services.

Parking charges paid to municipally owned and operated parking facilities are exempt from state and local sales taxes other than the 8% Manhattan parking tax. Also, individual residents of Manhattan who lease their cars are entitled to an exemption from the 8% Manhattan parking tax to the same extent as is applicable to individuals who own their cars.

• *Returns, payment, administration*

The New York City parking tax is administered by the State Department of Taxation and Finance through the New York State Sales Tax Bureau. Returns and payment are made at the same time as the combined city and state sales and use tax returns and payment (¶2202, ¶2203) but special recordkeeping and enforcement provisions relating to parking garage operators in Manhattan are required.

For additional information on the parking tax, see *TB-ST-679*, New York Department of Taxation and Finance, June 20, 2014, CCH New York City Tax Reports, ¶600-775.

CCH Advisory: Manhattan Parking Operators

Special requirements are imposed on operators of parking facilities located in Manhattan who are required to collect New York state parking tax, New York City parking tax, and additional Manhattan parking tax. The Department discusses special recordkeeping requirements as well as how to claim a hardship exemption from the special requirements, special provisions concerning inspection of parking facilities, and special penalty provisions. Governmental entities and organizations that have received an exempt organization certificate for New York sales and use tax purposes are exempt from the special requirements (*Important Notice N-03-19*, New York Department of Taxation and Finance, July 2003, CCH New York Tax Reports, ¶320-126).

¶3312 Mortgage Recording Tax

Law: Secs. 11-260 *et seq.*, NYC Adm. Code (CCH New York City Tax Reports, ¶557-005 *et seq.*).

The New York City mortgage recording tax is imposed on the recording of a mortgage on real property situated within New York City. The city tax is similar to, and adopts by reference the administrative and collection provisions of, the state recording tax (¶2710).

Assignments of rent accruing from tenancies, subtenancies, leases or subleases within New York City are deemed to be mortgages for purposes of the tax. In certain instances, a principal indebtedness or obligation secured by a supplemental instrument or additional mortgage will also be subject to the mortgage recording tax.

Tax applies to a contract or agreement, whereby the proceeds of any indebtedness secured by a mortgage of real property in New York City are used to reduce all or any part of a mortgagee's equity interest in a wraparound or similar mortgage of the real property, regardless of whether the aggregate amount of indebtedness secured by mortgages of such real property is increased or added to. Also, tax generally applies to the recording of a spreading agreement or additional mortgage that imposes the lien thereof upon real property located in New York City and not originally covered by or described in a recorded primary mortgage. The Commissioner of Taxation and Finance is authorized to disregard transfers under certain circumstances, and there is a presumption that all transfers of one or both of such properties to related parties, within the 12-month period preceding the recording of the spreading agreement or additional mortgage, were undertaken for tax avoidance or evasion purposes. Such a presumption can only be rebutted with clear and convincing evidence to the contrary.

- *Basis and rate of tax*

The mortgage recording tax is imposed at the following rates:

$1 for each $100 or major fraction thereof with respect to real property securing a principal debt or obligation of less than $500,000;

$1.125 for each $100 or major fraction thereof with respect to one, two or three family houses, individual cooperative apartments and individual residential condominium units securing a principal debt or obligation of $500,000 or more;

$1.75 for each $100 or major fraction thereof with respect to all other real property.

When mortgages form part of the same or related transactions and have the same or related mortgagors, the mortgages may be aggregated to determine whether they are subject to a tax rate in excess of the minimum rate. If the Commissioner of Taxation and Finance finds that a mortgage transaction has been formulated for the purpose of avoiding or evading a rate of tax, rather than solely for an independent business or financial purpose, the Commissioner is authorized to treat all mortgages forming part of a transaction as a single mortgage for the purpose of determining the applicable rate of tax.

The lower residential rate, rather than the higher commercial rate, of New York City mortgage recording tax would be due upon the recording of a mortgage securing three separate but adjacent condominium units that were purchased with the intent to combine the units into a single residence. The transfer did not constitute a bulk sale subject to the higher rate because the petitioners demonstrated a clear intent, prior to closing, to combine the units into one primary residence. However, if the units are not merged, the petitioners will have underpaid and additional mortgage recording tax would be owed. (*TSB-A-14(1)R*, New York Commissioner of Taxation and Finance, July 2, 2014, CCH New York Tax Reports, ¶408-142)

- *Administration and collection*

The city tax is administered and collected by the Commissioner of Taxation and Finance in the same manner as the state tax. The tax is paid at the time of recording, together with the state tax. Taxes on supplemental instruments or additional mortgages are also administered and collected in the same manner as the state tax on supplemental mortgages.

¶3312

¶3313 Tax on Motor Fuels Containing Lead

Law: Secs 11-2033 *et seq.,* NYC Adm. Code (CCH New York City Tax Reports, ¶ 535-005 *et seq.*).

The tax is imposed on every distributor for each gallon of motor fuel containing one-half gram or more of tetra ethyl lead, tetra methyl lead or any other lead alkyls per gallon, sold within or for sale within the city by such distributor.

Basis and rate of tax: The tax is imposed at the rate of 1¢ per gallon.

Administration and collection: The tax is administered and collected by the Commissioner of Taxation and Finance in the same manner as the state gasoline tax (¶ 2709). However, refunds of this tax to certain omnibus carriers and taxicab licensees are not permitted.

¶3314 Alcoholic Beverage Taxes

Law: Secs. 11-2055 *et seq.,* 11-2401 *et seq.,* NYC Adm. Code (CCH New York City Tax Reports, ¶ 535-105 *et seq.*).

New York City imposes an excise tax on beer and liquor when sold or used within the city and also imposes a privilege tax on retail licensees within the city.

The excise tax is imposed on distributors and noncommercial importers.

The tax for the privilege of selling liquor, wine or beer at retail, for on or off premises consumption, within New York City is imposed on retail licensees of the State Liquor Authority.

• *Exemptions*

Exemptions from the excise tax include: sales of liquor to the United States, beers sold to or by a voluntary unincorporated organization of the U.S. armed forces or limited amounts of alcoholic beverages brought into the city by travelers.

Exempt from the tax on retail licensees are the United States, New York State and its political subdivisions, the United Nations and nonprofit religious, charitable and educational organizations.

• *Basis and rate of tax*

The excise tax is imposed at the following rates:

12¢ per gallon upon beer; and

26.4¢ per liter upon liquors.

The tax on retail licensees is imposed at the rate of 25% of the license fees payable under the state Alcoholic Beverage Control Law.

• *Returns, payment, administration*

The excise tax is administered by the New York State Commissioner of Taxation and Finance jointly with the state tax. (For due dates of returns and payment, see ¶ 2706.)

The tax on retail licensees is administered by the New York City Commissioner of Finance. Returns and payments are due on or before June 25 annually.

¶3315 Sales Tax on Selected Services

Law: Secs. 11-2001 *et seq.,* NYC Adm. Code (CCH New York City Tax Reports, ¶ 560-001 *et seq.*).

New York City sales tax is imposed on the sale of the following services:

— Retail sales (including rentals) of tangible personal property;

— Gas, electricity, refrigeration and steam, and telephone and telegraph services;

— Information services;

— Processing and printing services;

— Credit rating and credit reporting services, rendered in written or oral form or in any other manner. The tax on these services is scheduled to expire November 30, 2017;

— Protective and detective services (excluding such services performed by port watchmen). The tax applies to services provided by alarm or other protective systems, including protection against burglary, theft, fire, water damage, industrial malfunction or damage to property, or injury to persons. It also applies to all types of detective, armored car, guard, patrol and watchman services;

— Installation, repair and maintenance services performed upon tangible personal property;

— Storage and safe deposit rentals;

— Real estate maintenance, service, or repair;

— Parking, garaging or storing of motor vehicles (except receipts paid to a homeowner's association by its members for such services) (see 3311); and

— Maintaining, servicing or repairing real property, where such services consist of interior cleaning and maintenance services performed on a regular contractual basis for a term of 30 days or more, and including such services provided by a contractor to a landlord, managing agent or tenant or by a managing agent to a tenant whether under the terms of a lease or otherwise.

A New York City tax is also imposed on the receipts from beauty, barbering, hair restoring, manicuring, pedicuring, electrolysis, massage and similar services and on every sale of services by weight control salons, health salons, gymnasiums, turkish and sauna baths and similar establishments. However, services rendered by a physician, osteopath, dentist, nurse, physiotherapist, chiropractor, podiatrist, optometrist, ophthalmic dispenser or a person performing similar services licensed under title VIII of the Education Law and services performed on pets and other animals, are not taxable.

Practitioner Comment: Yoga is Not Considered Exercise

New York City sales tax is imposed on most personal fitness services, including facilities that offer pilates, aerobics, and similar exercise classes. Tax Bulletin ST–329. A facility that limits its services to yoga classes, however, is exempt from tax since, according to New York, "instruction in yoga is not an exercise activity...". (NYT–G–12(1)S)

Mark S. Klein, Esq., Hodgson Russ LLP

Interior decorating and design services: New York City's local sales and use tax does not apply to interior decorating and design services. When interior decorating and design services are sold in conjunction with other taxable services or property, the charge for the decorating and design services delivered in New York City must be separately stated on the bill given to the customer. If the charges are not separately stated, the entire charge (including the decorating and design charges) will be subject to tax at the combined state and local tax rate.

Interior decorating services that are performed in conjunction with the sale of tangible personal property by the decorator to the customer will be subject to tax if the tangible personal property associated with the decorating service is transferred or delivered to the customer, or the customer's designee, in New York State. In New York City, the portion of the bill that constitutes the sale of tangible personal property is subject to the combined state and local tax. However, if the interior decorating and design services are separately contracted for, and separately itemized on the bill or invoice given to the customer, the interior decorating and design services are subject only to the state and MCTD taxes.

¶3315

• *Exemptions*

Wages and other compensation received from an employer for performing any of the specified services do not constitute taxable receipts under these provisions.

Organizations exempt from the basic sales and use tax (¶2109) are exempt from the local New York City tax.

A refund or credit of any sales or use tax paid on tangible personal property used in a taxable service will be allowed against the taxes on services if the property has become a physical component of the property on which the service is performed, or has been transferred to the purchaser of the service in connection with its performance.

Beauty services, etc. performed on pets and other animals are not taxable.

• *Basis and rate of tax*

The New York City sales and use tax is generally imposed at the rate of 4.5%.

The separate New York City taxes on specified services, such as beauty, barbering, health salons, manicuring, pedicuring; protective and detective services; credit rating and reporting services; and repair and maintenance of real property are also imposed at the rate of 4.5%. The tax on such services can be imposed through November 30, 2017. (Sec. 11-2002(a), N.Y.C. Adm. Code; Sec. 11-2040(a), N.Y.C. Adm. Code)

All receipts from the sale of the services of transporting, transmitting, distributing, or delivering gas or electricity are subject to the 4.5% New York City local tax, even if purchased from someone other than the vendor of the gas or electricity. The commodities of gas and electricity themselves are already subject to New York City local tax. (*Important Notice N-09-12*, New York Department of Taxation and Finance, July 2009, CCH New York Tax Reports, ¶406-452)

• *Returns, payment, administration*

Returns and payment accompany the New York sales and use tax (¶2202, ¶2203).

The tax is administered by the New York State Commissioner of Taxation and Finance.

¶3316 Taxicab License Transfer Tax

Law: Secs. 11-1401 *et seq.*, NYC Adm. Code (CCH New York City Tax Reports, ¶536-005 *et seq.*).

Forms: NYC-TCLT Taxicab License Transfer Tax Return.

A tax is imposed on each transfer of a taxicab license or interest therein.

The transfer of the economic interest in a taxicab license resulting from the transfer of shares of stock of a corporation that holds the taxicab license, or resulting from the transfer of an interest in a partnership or association that holds the taxicab license, is treated as a transfer of the license and is subject to tax.

• *Exemptions*

Exemptions include the United States and New York State (including its political subdivisions) as purchaser, user, or consumer. Also exempt are the United Nations and nonprofit religious, charitable, and educational organizations.

The tax does not apply to the transfer of a taxicab license by a lease, license or other rental arrangement that does not exceed six months.

• *Basis and rate of tax*

The tax is imposed at the rate of 5% of the consideration given for the transfer.

When a taxicab or any other property is transferred in conjunction with the transfer of a license, the tax is computed on the total consideration less the fair market value of the taxicab or other property.

• *Returns and payment*

A joint return is filed by the transferee and the transferor at the time of payment of the tax. Payment is due at the time of approval of the transfer by the New York City Taxi and Limousine Commission, but not later than 30 days following the transfer. Payment is made to the New York City Taxi and Limousine Commission as agent of the Commissioner of Finance.

The tax is paid by the transferee. However, the transferor is liable for the tax if it is not paid by the transferee.

LOCAL TAXES

CHAPTER 34

YONKERS INCOME TAX SURCHARGE ON RESIDENTS

¶3401	Imposition of Tax, Basis, Rate
¶3402	Administration, Returns and Payment, Estimated Tax
¶3403	Withholding of Tax

¶3401 Imposition of Tax, Basis, Rate

Law: Secs. 1321—1344, Tax Law (CCH NEW YORK TAX REPORTS, ¶33-010, 33-015).

Imposition of tax: The City of Yonkers income tax surcharge is imposed on every city resident individual, estate, and trust. The tax is authorized for tax years beginning before 2018. (Sec. 1321, Tax Law)

Basis and rate of tax: Beginning in 2014, the surcharge is imposed at the rate of 16.75% (previously, 15% of the net state tax). The net state tax is the sum of all taxes imposed under Article 22 of the Tax Law (see Part II of the *Guidebook*) less applicable credits (other than the credit for taxes withheld).

For information on the 2014 rate increase, see *TSB-M-14(6)I*, New York Department of Taxation and Finance, August 20, 2014, CCH NEW YORK TAX REPORTS, ¶408-202.

¶3402 Administration, Returns and Payment, Estimated Tax

Law: Secs. 1321—1344, Tax Law (CCH NEW YORK TAX REPORTS, ¶33-005, 33-020).

Administration of tax: The tax is administered by the New York State Commissioner of Taxation and Finance.

Returns and payment: The City of Yonkers income tax surcharge is reported on the New York State personal income tax return and is paid together with the state tax.

¶3403 Withholding of Tax

Law: Sec. 1329, Tax Law (CCH NEW YORK TAX REPORTS, ¶33-025, 33-030).

Withholding of the City of Yonkers income tax surcharge is required.

Wage reporting requirements: The guidelines set forth for New York state (¶609) are also applicable to the amount of wages required to be reported in the local W-2 box for employees subject to Yonkers income tax withholding. In using the guidelines, employers should substitute *Yonkers* and *Local, wages, tips, etc.* box for New York state to determine the amount of Yonkers wages to be reported in the local W-2 box.

Withholding tables are reproduced at CCH NEW YORK TAX REPORTS, ¶33-030.

LOCAL TAXES

CHAPTER 35

YONKERS EARNINGS TAX ON NONRESIDENTS

¶ 3501	Imposition of Tax, Basis, Rate
¶ 3502	Administration, Returns and Payment, Estimated Tax
¶ 3503	Withholding of Tax

¶3501 Imposition of Tax, Basis, Rate

Law: Secs. 1340—1343, Tax Law (CCH NEW YORK TAX REPORTS, ¶ 33-105, 33-110).

Forms: Y-203, City of Yonkers Nonresident Earnings Tax Return.

Imposition of tax: The City of Yonkers earnings tax is imposed on wages earned and net earnings from self-employment within the City of Yonkers by every nonresident individual, estate and trust. The tax is authorized for tax years beginning before 2018. (Sec. 1340, Tax Law)

Basis and rate of tax: The tax is currently imposed at the rate of $1/2$ of 1% on the wages earned and net earnings from self-employment within the City of Yonkers.

Exclusion: In computing the amount of taxable wages and net earnings from self-employment the following exclusion is allowed:

Total of wages and net earnings	Exclusion allowable
Not over $10,000	$3,000
Over $10,000 but not over $20,000	2,000
Over $20,000 but not over $30,000	1,000
Over $30,000	None

¶3502 Administration, Returns and Payment, Estimated Tax

Law: Sec. 1342, Tax Law (CCH NEW YORK TAX REPORTS, ¶ 33-103, 33-115).

Administration of tax: The tax is administered by the New York State Commissioner of Taxation and Finance.

Returns and payment: The City of Yonkers earnings tax return is attached to the New York State personal income tax return and payment of any earnings tax due is paid at the time of filing.

¶3503 Withholding of Tax

Law: Sec. 1341, Tax Law (CCH NEW YORK TAX REPORTS, ¶ 33-120, 33-125).

Withholding of the City of Yonkers earnings tax is required.

Withholding tables and methods: Withholding tables are reproduced at CCH NEW YORK TAX REPORTS, ¶ 33-125.

PART X

ADMINISTRATION AND PROCEDURE

CHAPTER 36
ADMINISTRATION, RETURNS, RECORDS, AND REFUNDS

¶3601 Administrative Agencies

Law: Secs. 170, 171, 2000, 2002, Tax Law; Reg. Sec. 525.3 (CCH New York Tax Reports, ¶89-060, 89-064).

The New York Department of Taxation and Finance, headed by the Commissioner of Taxation and Finance, has jurisdiction over the administration of all state taxes. Contact information for the Department and for other taxing agencies is listed in Chapter 39.

• *Commissioner of Taxation and Finance*

The Commissioner of Taxation and Finance is the head of the Department of Taxation and Finance, and has the sole charge of the administration of the Department, except for the administration of the Division of Tax Appeals. The Commissioner makes all rules and regulations necessary to carry out New York's tax laws.

The Commissioner is authorized to assess and collect taxes due, and may issue refunds, abatements, and credits, and impose penalties where applicable. The Commissioner may also compromise civil liability, set rates of interest, and render advisory opinions and declaratory rulings.

• *Department of Taxation and Finance*

The Department of Taxation and Finance is divided into the following divisions:

Division of Taxation.—The Division of Taxation is headed by the Commissioner of Taxation and Finance and is divided into administrative bureaus as follows:

Corporation Tax Bureau: The Corporation Tax Bureau administers and collects the following taxes:

— corporate organization and qualification fees of foreign corporations;
— franchise tax—agricultural co-operative corporations;
— franchise tax—business corporations, domestic and foreign;
— franchise tax—financial corporations; national banking associations;
— franchise tax—gas, water, electric, or steam companies;
— franchise tax—insurance companies; insurance companies' premium tax (with Superintendent of Insurance);
— franchise tax—real estate corporations;
— franchise tax—transportation and transmission corporations;
— tax on importation of gas services; and
— utility services tax.

Income Tax Bureau: The Income Tax Bureau administers and collects the New York state and New York City personal income tax.

Sales Tax Bureau: The Sales Tax Bureau administers and collects the sales and use tax. The bureau registers vendors, collects all sales and use taxes, audits returns, conducts meetings with vendors, taxpayers and representatives of industry and consumer groups, and issues assessments, refunds, and credits. The bureau also advises all registered vendors of new enactments or rate changes by local taxing jurisdictions, and of amendments to statewide or local sales and use tax laws. The collection of delinquent sales and use taxes is undertaken by the Tax Compliance Division.

Miscellaneous Tax Bureau: The Miscellaneous Tax Bureau administers and collects the following taxes:

— alcoholic beverage tax (with State Liquor Authority);

— cigarette tax;

— estate tax;

— fuel tax on carriers;

— gift tax;

— hazardous waste assessments;

— highway use tax;

— motor carrier road tax;

— motor fuel tax;

— petroleum taxes; and

— racing taxes.

Office of Real Property Services.—The Office of Real Property Services and the local officers administer and collect the general property tax in New York.

Office of the State Treasurer.—The Office of the State Treasurer is responsible for the proper accounting of all state monies received and disbursed, for the investment of sole custody funds, and for the control of monies owed by the state. The Treasurer is the custodian of all state funds, and such public funds as Teachers Retirement, state insurance, and other miscellaneous funds. It is also responsible for the issuance and reconciliation of all checks, including unemployment benefit checks.

Division of Tax Appeals.—The Division of Tax Appeals administers disputes between the Department of Taxation and Finance and taxpayers. The Division of Tax Appeals is operated and administered by the Tax Appeals Tribunal, and is responsible for processing and reviewing petitions, providing hearings, rendering determinations and decisions, and all other matters relating to the administration of the administrative hearings process. The Division is separate from and independent of the authority of the Commissioner of Taxation and Finance.

Tax Appeals Tribunal.—The Tax Appeals Tribunal administers and operates the Division of Tax Appeals, a separate and independent division of the Department of Taxation and Finance. The Tax Appeals Tribunal consists of three Commissioners, who are appointed by the Governor, by and with the advice and consent of the Senate. Determinations in tax cases are issued by administrative law judges employed by the Division of Tax Appeals, who conduct any hearing or motion procedure authorized to be held within the Division of Tax Appeals. Appeals from these determinations may be made to the Tax Appeals Tribunal, which will issue a decision affirming, reversing, or modifying the administrative law judge's determination.

¶3601

- *Bureau of Conciliation and Mediation Services*

The Director of the Bureau of Conciliation and Mediation Services reports directly to the Commissioner of Taxation and Finance. This Bureau is responsible for providing conciliation conferences to taxpayers who have a right to a hearing under the Tax Law.

Operating units: The Bureau has two separate operating units, the Conciliation Conference Unit and the Control Unit. The former is responsible for scheduling and conducting conciliation conferences, resolving disputes, and issuing conciliation orders. The latter reviews all taxpayer responses to statutory notices, such as notices for taxes due.

- *Technical services*

The Technical Services Bureau develops regulations, interpretations and instructions concerning all tax laws administered by the Department. The Bureau issues regulations to be promulgated by the Commissioner, notices, newsletters, and bulletins. Upon enactment of legislation affecting the public, the Bureau produces instructions for use by taxpayers in complying with the new law.

Advisory opinions: Taxpayers who wish an interpretation of any tax administered by the Commissioner may request an advisory opinion (TSB-A) which is binding on the Commissioner for the particular taxpayer that requested it. The issuance of these opinions has been delegated to the Office of Counsel. The TSB-A process allows taxpayers to obtain information on matters not clearly covered in the Tax Law, regulations or publications. The Commissioner of Taxation and Finance must issue a TSB-A within 90 days of receipt of the petition. This 90-day period may be extended for good cause shown, up to 30 additional days (Sec. 171(24), Tax Law).

Practitioner Comment: Advisory Opinions Are No Longer Anonymous

New York's Department of Taxation and Finance has eliminated a taxpayer's ability to obtain an advisory opinion anonymously, or through a representative acting on behalf of unidentified persons or entities (TSB-M-08(10)C). This has had a chilling effect on taxpayers looking for guidance who fear that an adverse determination could trigger an audit.

Mark S. Klein, Esq., Hodgson Russ LLP

Technical Services Bureau Memoranda: In addition, Technical Services Bureau Memoranda (TSB-M) contain current information reflecting amendments to the Tax Law, Tax Commissioner policy decisions, departmental policy and procedural changes, regulation changes, opinions of Counsel, and general interpretation of law as the need arises. (Sec. 171(23), Tax Law).

Guidance letters: The New York Department of Taxation and Finance issues a document series called New York Tax Guidances (NYT-Gs) in order to improve voluntary compliance. The NYT-Gs are redacted versions of selected letters and memoranda written by the Department's Office of Counsel and selected Advisory Opinions where the petitions have been withdrawn. Based on the Department's interpretation of the Tax Law and regulations and on a particular set of facts, NYT-Gs are accurate on the date they are published and are limited to the facts set forth therein.

Tax Guidance Bulletins: The Taxpayer Guidance Division issues Tax Guidance Bulletins to help taxpayers quickly find guidance on a wide variety of tax subjects. Bulletins are available on the Department's Web site at **www.tax.state.ny.us**. The bulletins explain the general application of a provision of the Tax Law or the application of the Tax Law to a specific type of business or a particular type of transaction, but are not binding on the Department. Tax guidance bulletins are based on the statutes, regulations, court cases, and Tax Appeals Tribunal decisions in effect on the date they are issued.

¶3601

• *Additional state administrative agencies*

The following are tax administrative bodies in New York, in addition to the Department of Taxation and Finance. See Chapter 39 for contact information.

Secretary of State: The Secretary of State, through the Department of State, Division of Corporations and State Records, performs the filing functions of the State as to all domestic corporations, except banking, insurance, religious, and educational operations. The Secretary administers the provisions of Sec. 180 of the Tax Law, which imposes an organization tax upon domestic business corporations. Foreign corporations seeking to do business in New York (banking and insurance corporations excepted) must apply to the Secretary of State for authority to do business.

State Liquor Authority: The State Liquor Authority issues licenses for the sale of all alcoholic beverages.

Department of Motor Vehicles: The Department of Motor Vehicles, headed by the Commissioner of Motor Vehicles, issues motor vehicle registrations and drivers licenses, administers regulatory laws relating to motor vehicles and their drivers, including the Financial Security Law, and is responsible for the collection of fees imposed.

Department of Transportation: The Department of Transportation administers the oil spill cleanup and removal tax.

Department of Labor: The Unemployment Insurance Division of the Department of Labor administers and collects the unemployment insurance tax in New York.

Department of Insurance: The Superintendent of Insurance with the Corporation Tax Bureau administers and collects the taxes on all insurance firms.

Department of Environmental Conservation: The Department collects and administers the marine resource taxes.

Local taxing officers: The local taxing officers administer and collect the mortgage tax and, with the State Board of Real Property Services, the general property tax.

New York City: The revenue laws of New York City are administered by the Department of Finance. For contact information, see Chapter 39.

¶3602 Returns and Payments

> *Law:* Secs. 9, 10, 29, 171(19), 171-k, 658(c)(4), 3010, Tax Law; Sec. 5-b, Gen. Municipal Law; Reg. Secs. 2396.3, 2399.2; NYC Rule Secs. 12-07, 17-03 (CCH NEW YORK TAX REPORTS, ¶¶ 89-102—89-112, 89-188, 589-102—589-112).

Returns and due dates, including estimated tax requirements, are discussed specifically under each tax. Consult the Table of Contents or the Topical Index.

Return information for pass-through entities is discussed at ¶ 859. New York City taxes are discussed in Chapters 28 through 33.

• *Installment payments*

Taxpayers may be permitted to pay tax liabilities (including any interest, penalty or addition to tax) in installment payments, provided the Commissioner of Taxation and Finance (or the Commissioner of Finance in New York City) determines that installment payments will facilitate collection of the liability.

CCH Advisory: Installment Payment Agreements Online

Taxpayers who are unable to pay the full amount of their income tax liabilities may request permission to pay the tax (plus applicable interest and penalties) on an installment basis. This request can be made by mail with Form DTF-383 or electronically through the Tax Department's web site at **www.tax.ny.gov**.

Termination of agreement: An agreement for installment payments may be terminated if information provided by the taxpayer to the Commissioner prior to the date of the agreement is inaccurate or incomplete, or the Commissioner believes that collection of the liability to which the agreement relates is in jeopardy. The Commissioner may also alter, modify, or terminate an agreement if the financial condition of the taxpayer has significantly changed or if the taxpayer fails to pay any installment or other tax liability when due or fails to provide a financial condition update when requested.

- *Electronic filing*

Personal income tax returns: During 2012 through 2019, electronic filing is mandated for individuals who do not use a tax preparer, but instead prepare their own income tax returns using software. This mandate is due to sunset on December 31, 2019. (Sec. 29, Tax Law)

New York offers three different programs to file electronically: (1) Federal/State electronic filing program; (2) NYS Direct; and (3) Home PC On-line filing. Form IT-201-E, Declaration for Electronic Filing of Income Tax Return, must be completed and submitted with all required attachments for all electronically filed returns. If a taxpayer owes money, payment needs to be submitted with Form IT-201-V, Payment Voucher for Income Tax Returns Filed Electronically anytime on or before April 15. Employers can electronically file Form MTA-305, Employer's Quarterly Metropolitan Commuter Transportation Mobility Tax Return.

Corporation tax returns: Electronic filing is also mandated for corporations that do not use a tax preparer to prepare Article 9-A general business corporation and S corporation tax returns, use tax preparation software approved by the state, and have broadband Internet access. (Sec. 29, Tax Law)

Sales and use tax returns: New York state and local quarterly sales and use tax returns (ST-100) and New York state and local sales and use tax returns for a single jurisdiction (ST-102) may be filed online, through an approved E-service provider.

Mandatory electronic filing: If a tax return preparer prepares authorized tax documents for more than 10 different taxpayers during any calendar year beginning on or after January 1, 2012, and if in any succeeding calendar year he or she prepares one or more authorized tax documents using tax software, then for that succeeding calendar year and each subsequent calendar year, all authorized tax documents prepared by that preparer must be filed electronically (Sec. 29, Tax Law). A "tax document" is a return, report or any other document relating to a tax or other matter administered by the Commissioner.

For additional information on electronic filing, see *Publication 84, New York State Handbook for Electronic Filers of Personal Income Tax Returns.* See also *TB-IT-215,* June 11, 2013, CCH NEW YORK TAX REPORTS, ¶ 407-859; *TB-MU-210,* June 11, 2013, CCH NEW YORK TAX REPORTS, ¶ 407-860; and *TB-MU-220,* June 11, 2013, CCH NEW YORK TAX REPORTS, ¶ 407-861.

Signatures: Tax return preparers are authorized to use alternative methods (*i.e.,* rubber stamp, mechanical device, or computer software program) in signing original tax returns, amended tax returns, refund claims, and requests for extension of time to file. In addition to the personal income tax, the policy applies to tax returns, amended tax returns, refund claims, and requests for extension of time to file for all other taxes and fees administered by the New York Department of Taxation and Finance (TSB-M-05(1)C, TSB-M-05(1)I, TSB-M-05(1)S, and TSB-M-05(1)M, February 1, 2005, CCH NEW YORK TAX REPORTS, ¶ 300-453).

New York City property electronic filing: New York City tax returns may be filed electronically; see **https:/a836-btseservices.nyc.gov/production/eservices/_/.**

The New York City Department of Finance will accept property tax payments electronically (see **http://www1.nyc.gov/site/finance/taxes/property-bills-and-payments.page**, as well as estimated tax payments and applications for automatic extensions, for the New York City general corporation tax, banking corporation tax, and unincorporated business tax. Quarterly and annual commercial rent tax returns may be filed electronically, as well as returns for utility tax and hotel tax).

The program allows taxpayers, or their accounting or legal representatives, to file the forms electronically on or before the due date. Payments will then be debited from the taxpayers' accounts on the due date by Automated Clearing House (ACH) transfer. See also **http://www1.nyc.gov/site/finance/pay-now/pay.page**

• *Electronic funds transfer (EFT)*

Certain taxpayers are required to make tax payments by electronic funds transfer (EFT) or certified check. Also, the Department of Taxation and Finance will accept credit card payments for certain tax liabilities.

Voluntary participation: Any taxpayer that is not required to participate in the EFT Program may, at any time, submit a request to the Commissioner for permission to participate on a voluntary basis.

Personal income taxes: Each taxpayer (other than health care providers) that has a separate federal or state employer identification number and is required to deduct and withhold an aggregate of $35,000 or more of New York state personal income tax, New York City personal income tax, New York City income tax surcharge, or City of Yonkers income tax for a semiannual period ending in June or December must pay the tax by electronic funds transfer on or before the due date to a bank, banking house, or trust company designated by the Commissioner of Taxation and Finance. (Sec. 9(b), Tax Law)

Sales and use, motor fuel, and petroleum business taxes: Taxpayers whose sales and use taxes, prepaid sales and use taxes on motor fuel and diesel motor fuel, or petroleum business taxes exceed certain statutory thresholds must remit taxes by EFT or certified check. The Department will make an initial eligibility determination within 45 days after June 1 of each year by examining the taxpayer's tax liability for the June 1 through May 31 period preceding the June 1-May 31 period that precedes the initial determination.

The threshold amounts for the applicable June 1 through May 31 period are:

— more than $500,000 of state and local sales and use taxes (excluding the tax on paging devices);

— more than $5 million of prepaid state and local sales and use taxes on motor fuel and diesel motor fuel; or

— more than $5 million of the total of the tax on motor fuel and diesel motor fuel and the tax on petroleum businesses (excluding the tax on carriers).

A taxpayer is required to participate in the program only with respect to taxes for which the applicable dollar thresholds have been met. In determining whether the threshold has been met, every taxpayer who is identified by either its own federal employer identification number or its own separate New York state employer identification number is treated as a separate taxpayer. For exemptions from the EFT program, see ¶2203.

Taxpayers who do not meet the dollar thresholds noted above may apply for permission to participate in the program on a voluntary basis.

¶3602

Real property taxes: The New York City Commissioner of Finance is specifically authorized to accept and require the payment of real property taxes by electronic funds transfer (EFT). The Commissioner requires the payment of real property taxes by EFT for properties with annual real property tax liability equal to or greater than $300,000. (Rule Sec. 44-01)

• *Credit card payments*

The Department of Taxation and Finance accepts credit cards for payment of personal income tax liabilities (including New York City personal income taxes), quarterly estimated tax payments, and balances due on extension payments. New York utilizes the services of Official Payment Corporation and Link2Gov Corporation for the handling of these transactions. The State's credit card payment vendors will accept American Express, MasterCard, Visa, and Discover/Novus.

• *Internet payments*

Taxpayers can view and pay open New York tax assessments through the Individual Service Center or the Business Service Center (**http://www.tax.ny.gov**). After obtaining a password online, taxpayers may log in to the appropriate service center using their taxpayer identification number and password. The electronic Consolidated Statement of Tax Liabilities displays the current status of a taxpayer's open assessments, including balance due. Taxpayers with a balance due assessment can initiate an electronic funds withdrawal (ACH debit) or credit card payment.

Local governments: The governing board of any local government may provide for the acceptance of penalties, rents, rates, taxes, fees, charges, revenue, financial obligations or other amounts, including penalties, special assessments or interest via a municipal Internet website. However, submission via the Internet may not be the exclusive method allowed. Payments received via the Internet are considered received by the appropriate officer and paid by the taxpayer at the time the Internet transaction is completed and sent by the taxpayer. A local government authorizing Internet payments must provide a confirmation page to the taxpayer following the completion of the Internet transaction.

• *Rounding of fractional dollar amounts*

Amounts required to be included in returns, reports, or other statements may be entered at the nearest whole dollar amount. However, this does not apply to the items that must be taken into account in making the computations necessary to determine such amounts. Where the whole dollar reporting option is chosen, it must be used for all applicable amounts.

• *Mailing rules and legal holidays*

Generally, any tax return or document required to be filed with, or payment made to, the Department of Taxation and Finance or the New York City Department of Finance will be deemed filed as of the U.S. postmark date stamped on the envelope. Airborne Express, DHL, Federal Express, and UPS are private delivery companies whose "postmark dates" are treated as those of the U.S. mail. However, when delivery is made by courier, delivery messenger or similar service, the filing date will be the date the return or document is received. (Reg. Sec. 2399.2)

Payment by EFT: A payment made by electronic funds withdrawal is deemed to be made on the date the taxpayer specifies as the date for withdrawal, provided that: (1) the specified date is not beyond the last date prescribed for payment; (2) the funds are available for withdrawal; and (3) the document to which the funds apply is timely filed. If the document has not been timely filed, a payment made by electronic funds withdrawal by the last date prescribed for payment will be deemed timely if it can be associated with the proper tax liability, as evidenced by the taxpayer. (Reg. Sec. 2399.2)

¶3602

Payment by credit card: A payment by credit or debit card is deemed to be made on the date that the issuer of the card properly authorizes the transaction, provided that the payment is actually received by the Department in the ordinary course of business and is not returned due to correction of errors relating to the credit or debit card account. (Reg. Sec. 2399.2)

Weekends and legal holidays: When the deadline for filing a document or return falls on a Saturday, Sunday or a day that is a legal holiday in the State of New York, the filing of the return or document will be deemed timely if performed on the next succeeding day that is not a Saturday, Sunday or legal holiday. (Reg. Sec. 2399.3)

¶3603 Recordkeeping Requirements; Confidentiality

Law: Secs. 171-k, 341(f), 1135, 1142-A, 1146, 3038, Tax Law; Reg. Secs. 158.1—158.4, 158.8, 533.2, 2402.1, 2402.2; NYC Rule Secs. 4-17, 7-11, 12-14, 23-11, 28-19 (CCH New York Tax Reports, ¶ 89-142, 89-180, 89-184, 589-142, 589-180, 589-184).

Recordkeeping requirements vary by tax type, as discussed below. Under the record retention and electronic recordkeeping provisions of the New York Electronic Signatures and Records Act (Ch. 4, Laws 1999) and the federal Electronic Signatures in Global and National Commerce Act (P.L. 106-229), taxpayers are generally given the option of retaining required records in either hard-copy or electronic format.

The Department does not prescribe specific technologies or technical specifications for maintaining electronic records and does not require the use of particular types of hardware or software.

Corporate franchise (income) tax: There are no specific provisions in the corporate franchise (income) tax law dealing with recordkeeping requirements.

Personal income tax: Every person subject to New York personal income tax or liable for the collection of New York personal income tax, and any person required to file a New York return of information with respect to income, must keep such permanent books of account or records, including inventories, as are sufficient to establish the amount of gross income, deductions, credits, and other matters required to be shown by such person in any New York income tax return or New York information return.

Individuals deriving gross income from the business of farming, and individuals whose gross income includes salaries, wages or similar compensation for personal services rendered are required to keep such records as will enable the Commissioner to determine the correct amount of New York income subject to tax. No particular form is required for keeping the records, but systems of accounting must be used as will enable the Commissioner to ascertain whether liability for New York income tax is incurred or whether a New York information return is required to be filed and, if so, the correctness of the amounts required to be reported in any New York income tax return or New York information return.

The books, records and a copy of any New York income tax return, schedule, statement or other document required to be kept must be retained so long as the contents of the books, records or return may become material in the administration of the personal income tax law.

Paid preparers must retain a completed copy of the return for a period of three years after the due date of the return, including extensions. Records with respect to personal income tax withheld must be retained for a period of four years after the due date of the withheld tax for the return period to which the records relate, or the date the amount withheld was paid, whichever is later. Records with respect to information returns must be retained for a period of four years after the due date of the return.

Sales and use taxes: Every person required to collect sales and use tax must keep records of every sale or amusement charge or occupancy and of all amounts paid, charged or due and of the tax payable on forms required by the Commissioner. The burden of proving that any receipt, amusement charge or rent is not taxable is on the vendor or the customer. To satisfy its burden of proof, a vendor must maintain records sufficient to verify all transactions.

The records must include a true copy of each of the following, separately stating the tax charged: (1) sales slip, invoice, receipt, contract, statement or other memorandum of sale; (2) guest check, hotel guest check, receipt from admissions; and (3) cash register tape and any other original sales document. Where no written document is given to the customer, the seller must keep a daily record of all cash and credit sales in a day book or similar book. The sales record must provide sufficient detail to determine the taxable status of each sale and the amount of tax due and collected. Records must also be maintained substantiating points of delivery if delivery was made at a place other than the place of business. Exemption certificates must be dated and retained in order to prove exempt sales. Complete records must be kept to support deductions or claims for credit for bad debts, returned merchandise, and canceled sales. Documentation must be maintained to substantiate any exemption, exclusion, or exception claimed on the purchase of any tangible personal property or service.

Vendors who participate in the federal food stamp program: Retail food stores and other participants approved for participation in the federal food stamp program whose receipts may be subject to exemption are required to keep true and complete copies of applications, updates of applications, redemption certificates, returns and reports furnished to or by the U.S. government or New York State or their agencies in order to participate in the food stamp program or to redeem coupons issued under the federal food stamp act.

Entertainment promoters: Every entertainment promoter must keep a record of the date and place of each entertainment event and the name, address and certificate of authority number of every person permitted by the promoter to make taxable sales of tangible personal property at each event.

Automotive fuel vendors: Every person selling or holding large volumes of automotive fuel is required to keep records for the periods and in the manner prescribed by the Commissioner. The records must show: (1) the number of gallons of automotive fuel purchased, the price paid, the amount of tax prepaid and the applicable regional average retail sales price; and (2) the number of gallons sold, the price paid by the purchaser, the amount of prepaid tax, and the applicable regional average retail sales price or the amount of tax collected from retail sales.

Motor vehicle parking, garaging and storage services: Taxpayers who provide these services in New York City and who are required to pay state sales and use taxes, New York City temporary municipal assistance sales and use tax, and New York City sales and use tax on parking services in Manhattan were subject to special recordkeeping requirements.

Motor vehicle insurers: In addition to the recordkeeping requirements imposed for sales and use tax purposes, insurers licensed to issue physical or property damage liability insurance for motor vehicles registered in New York State, must keep such additional records as the Commissioner may prescribe and must retain all such records for a period of at least four years from the latest date of payment of any portion of the award.

Vendors accepting motor vehicle insurance damage award claimants' vouchers and stubs are required to retain the stubs and must submit the vouchers to the Commissioner with their current quarterly return, together with any schedule of vouchers received in lieu of tax, and must keep such other records in the form and for such period as required by the Commissioner. (Sec. 1135(a)(3), Tax Law)

¶3603

• *Preservation of records and returns*

Records and returns must be preserved for a period of three years from the due date of the return to which they relate, or the date of filing, if later, unless the Commissioner consents to their destruction earlier or requires that they be kept longer.

Records on computer or microfilm: Records may be reproduced on any photographic, photostat, microfilm, micro-card, miniature photographic, or other process that actually reproduces the original record or may otherwise be retained as electronic records. Vendors wishing to retain general books of account on microfilm may do so provided they have met specific requirements.

New York City: Recordkeeping requirements are generally similar to the state requirements.

• *Confidentiality*

It is unlawful for the Commissioner, an officer or employee of the Department of Taxation and Finance, or any other person to divulge in any manner information disclosed on a return or report, except in accordance with proper judicial order or as otherwise provided by law.

Any officer or employee of New York who willfully violates secrecy provisions must be dismissed from office and may not hold any public office for a period of five years. Such person may also be held civilly liable.

• *Intergovernmental tax collection agreements*

New York has entered into tax information exchange agreements with a number of states and Canadian provinces. The nature of the information subject to exchange includes, but is not limited to, the following:

— identifying data on taxpayers or potential taxpayers;

— copies of tax or information returns, including schedules and attachments;

— filing verification;

— nexus information and questionnaires;

— audit reports;

— collection and enforcement activities; and

— appeals and criminal tax matters with respect to any taxpayer or group of taxpayers.

FTA uniform agreement: New York State and New York City are both signatories to the Federation of Tax Administrators (FTA) uniform information exchange agreement, but both have exchange agreements that are independent of the FTA uniform agreement.

Tax avoidance transactions: The New York City Finance Commissioner and the Internal Revenue Service Area Director signed an agreement allowing New York City, New York state, and federal taxing authorities to share information about individuals and businesses that set up tax avoidance schemes, including offshore accounts.

The Abusive Tax Avoidance Transactions (ATAT) agreement was negotiated in a joint effort between individual states and the IRS' Small Business/Self- Employed Division. The agreement leaves procedures governing communication on more routine taxpayer compliance efforts unchanged, and maintains important separation of federal tax authority and protection of taxpayer privacy. Currently, 45 states and the District of Columbia have signed the memorandum.

The disclosure of returns and information between New York City, New York state, and IRS employees who deal with ATAT leads, cases, and audits, will be used

¶3603

to identify, examine, and bring ATAT participants into compliance with federal tax laws and regulations. In addition, the cooperation among the agencies will counter claims of those marketing tax schemes and scams (*Press Release*, NY Department of Taxation and Finance, December 16, 2003).

For information on tax shelter disclosure requirements, see ¶3703.

¶3604 Refunds

> *Law:* Secs. 683, 686—689, 697(d), 1083, 1086—1089, 1096(d), Tax Law; Reg. Sec. 36.1; Secs. 11-526, 11-677, 11-709, NYC Adm. Code (CCH New York Tax Reports, ¶89-224, 589-224).

A taxpayer who has paid an amount in excess of his or her tax liability for a given year (*i.e.*, an overpayment), may file a claim for refund or credit within the statutory period of limitations. An overpayment is a payment in excess of the amount that should have been assessed and collected as tax. Any tax assessed or collected after the applicable period of limitations has expired and any withholding taxes or estimated taxes paid in excess of actual tax imposed for the year are treated as overpayments.

Overpayment may be credited against estimated tax for the following tax year. To the extent so credited, a claim for refund is not allowed.

Corporate tax refunds: If an overpayment of corporate tax is claimed on a return or report, a refund is made only if application for the refund is made on the return or report. Otherwise, the overpayment is credited against the tax liability for the following year and against the estimated tax for the year, regardless of whether the taxpayer claims the overpayment as a credit in the declaration of estimated tax for the year. The Commissioner notifies the taxpayer that the overpayment has been so credited, and the taxpayer may, prior to the due date of the taxpayer's return for the year to which the overpayment has been credited, claim a refund of the overpayment.

CCH Advisory: Amended Returns

An amended return should be filed in order to claim a corporate tax refund or credit, or to notify the Tax Department of a change to their federal taxable income or federal alternative minimum taxable income. Taxpayers must file the amended return reflecting the federal change within 90 days (120 days, if filing a combined return) after the date of the final determination of the IRS. See *Important Notice N-09-2*, January 2009, CCH New York Tax Reports, ¶406-284; *Important Notice N-09-18*, October 2009, CCH New York Tax Reports, ¶406-562.

• *Disclosure of taxpayer's overpayment*

The Department of Taxation and Finance is required to disclose to a taxpayer all instances of tax overpayments made by the taxpayer and discovered by the Department during the course of an audit, assessment, collection, or enforcement proceeding. For tax overpayments disclosed under this provision, a taxpayer may apply for a refund or claim a credit within 120 days from the date on which the notice of disclosure is given to the taxpayer. A failure to apply within 120 days will result in the loss of the right to apply for a refund or credit. However, this limitation will not reduce the time within which a taxpayer may claim a credit or refund of a tax overpayment under any other applicable provision.

This provision may not be construed as requiring or permitting the payment of a refund or the granting of a credit with respect to any period that, because of a period of limitations, is not open for assessment or refund when the overpayment is discovered by the Department.

• *Special refund authority*

The Department of Taxation and Finance can refund personal income taxes and corporation taxes at any time, without regard to any period of limitations, where no questions of fact or law are involved and the tax was erroneously or illegally collected, or paid under a mistake of fact.

• *Redetermination of deficiency*

If a taxpayer has filed a petition for redetermination of a deficiency, the Commissioner of Taxation and Finance has jurisdiction to determine that the taxpayer has overpaid tax for the year in question and to allow a credit or refund without requiring a separate claim by the taxpayer. Similarly, if on judicial review of a decision of the Commissioner a court disallows the deficiency in whole or in part, the amount of disallowed deficiency, if previously paid, may be refunded or credited without a separate claim.

• *Interest on overpayments*

A taxpayer is entitled to interest on an overpayment of tax from the date of the overpayment until no more than 30 days before the date of the refund check, or if the overpayment is credited, to the due date of the amount against which the credit is taken. No interest is payable if the amount is less than $1.49.

If an overpayment is refunded within three months (45 days for overpayments of personal income tax) after the due date of the return (or date of actual filing if the return is filed after the due date), no interest is payable on the overpayment. Interest on a refund claimed by filing an amended return may be paid for the period preceding the filing of the amended return or claim, but no interest will be paid on the period between the filing of the amended return or claim and the refund, if the refund is provided within 45 days after the filing of the return or claim.

Generally, if a return is filed after the due date (including extensions), no interest is allowed for any day before the date the return is filed.

Overpayments credited against past-due support, against a past-due legally enforceable debt or against a defaulted guaranteed student, state university or city university loan cease to bear interest on the date that the Commissioner certifies the amount of the credit to the Comptroller.

For current rates, see ¶ 3704.

• *Refunds on loss carrybacks*

If an overpayment results from the carryback of a net operating loss (and/or capital loss for corporate taxpayers), the overpayment is considered to have occurred on the filing date of the loss year, without regard to extensions. If a refund or credit of the overpayment resulting from the carryback is made within three months of filing the claim (45 days for overpayments of personal income tax), no interest is payable. In the case of S corporations, where an overpayment results from a carryback of a net operating loss or net capital loss, interest on any resulting refund or credit ceases to accrue 12 months and 180 days after the last day of the tax year in which the loss arises unless a refund claim is filed within the 18-month period. The 18-month limitation does not apply to non-S corporations that do not use the federal quick refund procedures.

For interest rates, see ¶ 3704.

¶3604

- *Petition for refund*

A taxpayer may file a petition with the Commissioner for refund of an overpayment if six months have expired since a timely claim was filed, or the Commissioner has mailed to the taxpayer a notice of disallowance, in whole or in part, of the refund. If a notice of disallowance has been mailed, the petition for refund must be filed within two years of the mailing date unless the period has been extended by written agreement between the taxpayer and the Commissioner. The taxpayer may file a written waiver of the requirement that he be mailed a notice of disallowance of refund, in which case the two-year period for filing the petition runs from the date the waiver is filed.

In determining whether the taxpayer is entitled to a refund on petition, the Commissioner may determine all issues relating to whether an overpayment for the tax year has been made, and may offset overpayments against deficiencies for the same year that are time-barred.

Judicial review: The taxpayer is entitled to judicial review of a determination on a petition for refund. The application must be made within four months from the date that notice of the decision of the Tax Appeals Tribunal is mailed to the taxpayer. (For a discussion of judicial appeals, see ¶ 3801.)

- *Statute of limitations*

To be timely, a claim for refund or credit of an overpayment must generally be filed within three years of the date the return is filed or two years from the date the tax is paid, whichever is later. Where a claim is filed during the three-year period, it is limited to the tax paid during the three years plus any extension for filing the return. When a claim is made within the two-year period, the refund or credit is limited to the portion of the tax paid during the two years. If a taxpayer fails to file a return, recovery is limited to amounts paid within the two-year period before the claim is filed.

Practitioner Comment: Special Extension for Impaired Taxpayers

In 2014, New York enacted legislation similar to IRC Sec. 6511(h), which extends the statute of limitations on refunds for mentally or physically impaired taxpayers who are unable to manage their financial affairs. A similar provision was also enacted in New York City.

Mark S. Klein, Esq., Hodgson Russ LLP

Prepayments: For refund and credit purposes, advance remittances, such as withholding or estimated taxes, are considered paid on the due date. In determining the amount of an overpayment, the tax is the correct amount of tax as redetermined after audit.

Claims relating to federal tax changes: If an overpayment results from a change in the federal return required to be reported to the state, the claim for refund must be filed within two years from expiration of the 90-day period (120-day period for corporations filing a combined return) in which the report of change or amended return was due. If the claim is made outside the normal limitations period, the amount of the refund may not exceed the reduction in state tax attributable to the federal change. For corporate taxpayers, the refund must be computed without change of allocation of income or capital.

Loss carrybacks: A claim for refund when the overpayment results from the carryback of a net operating loss (and/or capital loss for corporate taxpayers) must be made within (1) three years from the due date of the return (including extensions) for the tax year when the loss occurred, (2) six months after expiration of an agreement to extend the time for assessment of a deficiency for the year of the loss, or (3) the period for filing a claim based on a federal change for the carryback year, whichever expires latest.

Mailed refund claim: A refund claim sent by mail is considered filed on the date of the postmark. The rule establishing the date of mailing as the date of filing applies, however, only if the document mailed is actually received. The risk of mishandling, either by the post office or the Department of Taxation and Finance, is on the taxpayer (*Matter of Filler*, Division of Tax Appeals, Tax Appeals Tribunal, August 24, 1989, CCH NEW YORK TAX REPORTS, ¶ 252-764).

Extension by agreement: A written agreement between the taxpayer and the Commissioner of Taxation and Finance to extend the period of limitations for assessment of tax also extends the period of limitations for a claim for refund or credit for the same period, plus an additional six months. If a claim is made within the additional six months, the amount of refund or credit may include not only the portion of the tax paid after the agreement but all of the tax that could have been refunded had a claim been filed on the date the extension agreement was executed.

Amount of overpayment: Even if the period of limitations on assessment and collection has run, the Commissioner may take into account any time-barred deficiency found to exist for the year in determining the extent to which a taxpayer has actually overpaid the tax. Moreover, rather than refund an overpayment, the Commissioner may credit it against any other tax liability of the taxpayer, or against any liability the taxpayer might have for past-due support or a past-due debt owed to a state agency.

• *Erroneous refunds*

A refund that is issued due to an error by the Department and that is not based upon claims made by the taxpayer is deemed an underpayment of tax on the date made. A deficiency created by an erroneous refund may be assessed within two years, or within five years if any part of the refund was induced by fraud or misrepresentation of a material fact.

ADMINISTRATION AND PROCEDURE

CHAPTER 37
AUDITS, ASSESSMENT, AND COLLECTION OF TAX

¶3701 Audits

Law: Secs. 171(3-a), 2008, Tax Law; Reg. Secs. 3000.2, 4000.2; Sec. 11-124, NYC Adm. Code (CCH NEW YORK TAX REPORTS, ¶89-132—89-148, 589-132—589-148).

The Department of Taxation and Finance conducts audits to verify that the correct amount of tax was paid.

The Audit Division of the Department of Taxation and Finance is responsible for all audit activities of the Department, including central office correspondence, desk audits and review of refund and credit claims, and field or office audits at the district offices. These audits are accomplished through the Central Office Audit Bureau and the District Office Audit Bureau. Uniform audit procedures are disseminated, monitored and evaluated by the Audit Evaluation Bureau. Objectivity in selecting cases for audit is assured through the use of sophisticated computerized techniques. Expertise needed to audit firms whose records are highly computerized is provided by the EDP Systems Audit Bureau.

New York City: The Audit Division of the New York City Department of Finance handles audits of all categories of city business taxpayers under the Department's jurisdiction.

Practitioner Comment: Above-the-Line Audits are Becoming More Common

Historically, New York State income tax audits were limited to New York-specific issues that would not ordinarily be reviewed by the Internal Revenue Service. Recently, however, many New York auditors have been scrupulously reviewing "above-the-line" issues. See e.g., *Anthony and Renata Conte*, ALJ, March 12, 2015, CCH NEW YORK TAX REPORTS, ¶408-360, involving the federal hobby loss rules, and *Erik and Kathryn Brandvold*, ALJ, March 19, 2015, CCH NEW YORK TAX REPORTS, ¶408-361, involving the federal passive activity loss rules.

Mark S. Klein, Esq., Hodgson Russ LLP

- *Audit procedures*

During an audit, the taxpayer will be required to provide the auditor with whatever records are necessary to verify the information provided on a tax return.

Field audits: Field audits usually take place at the taxpayer's business location and are initiated by a telephone call or letter from the auditor. Field audits are usually scheduled at least 15 days in advance to give the taxpayer time to assemble the required records. If a taxpayer needs more than 15 days to gather the necessary records, an extension of up to 30 days can be requested. For delays longer than 30 days, the request must be in writing and substantiate the need for extra time.

A field audit generally covers a three-year period, and can take anywhere from several days to a year or more to complete, depending on the complexity of the returns being audited and on the completeness and accuracy of the taxpayer's records. Most audits, however, take only three to four days to complete (*Publication 130-F, The New York State Tax Audit—Your Rights and Responsibilities*, available at **http://www.tax.ny.gov/pdf/publications/income/pub130f.pdf**).

Practitioner Comment: No Prohibition of Recurring Audits

Unlike the Internal Revenue Service, New York has no rule prohibiting recurring audits of the same issue. (*Trabold*, ALJ, 8/14/08)

Mark S. Klein, Hodgson Russ LLP

Desk audits: Desk audits are normally conducted by correspondence and by review of tax returns, refund requests, or other documents that the taxpayer has already submitted to the Department of Taxation and Finance. Sometimes, the audit includes information obtained from other sources, such as third-party information. It takes place solely within the Department and rarely involves any face-to-face contact between the technician and the taxpayer. The taxpayer is not routinely notified that a desk audit is taking place. In fact, the only way a taxpayer knows about a desk audit is if the Department finds it necessary to request additional information, or if it determines that the taxpayer either owes additional tax or is due a refund (*Publication 130-D, The New York State Tax Audit—Your Rights and Responsibilities*, available at **http://www.tax.ny.gov/pdf/publications/income/pub130d.pdf**).

CCH Advisory: Audit Methodology

In conducting an indirect sales and use tax audit of a retail convenience store, the Division of Taxation was permitted to use purchase records provided by a supplier and to apply a markup percentage because the retailer's records were inadequate and this methodology was rational. The retailer failed to produce cash register tapes, sales invoices, or any other original sales documentation to verify the amount of sales for the audit period (*SRS News, Inc.*, New York Division of Tax Appeals, Tax Appeals Tribunal, DTA No. 817006, September 12, 2002, CCH New York Tax Reports, ¶ 404-312).

Audit findings: When a field audit is completed, the taxpayer is notified of the findings. Following a desk audit, the taxpayer is notified of the findings if there are any additional taxes due.

The taxpayer receives a statement of any proposed audit changes explaining the reason for the additional taxes. The taxpayer is then given a reasonable period of time to respond to the audit findings. The auditor analyzes the taxpayer's response, and if appropriate, revises and resubmits the new findings. If, however, the audit results in a refund, the taxpayer automatically receives a refund check and a letter of explanation.

The taxpayer is asked to indicate agreement with the audit findings by signing the statement of proposed audit changes. A taxpayer who consents to a proposed audit adjustment cannot later contest the adjustment, although the taxpayer is entitled to apply for a refund or credit of the tax within the applicable time period (¶ 3604).

A taxpayer who does not agree with the findings should indicate the disagreement on the statement of proposed audit changes and return the form to the auditor. If the audit report is approved by Department of Taxation and Finance supervisory personnel, the taxpayer is sent a notice of determination or notice of deficiency for the taxes due, at which point the taxpayer may formally appeal the audit findings through either the Bureau of Conciliation and Mediation Services or the Division of Tax Appeals. For information on appeals, see ¶ 3802.

¶ 3701

CCH Advisory: Obtain Representation

If a significant controversy appears to be brewing, it is advisable for representation of the taxpayer to begin at the audit stage. The representative's function at this point is to facilitate the development of reasonable ground rules for the audit, *i.e.*, what will be examined, and to see to it that the taxpayer marshals the information necessary for the examination. At the same time, moreover, the representative may be in a position to do much to shape the course the audit will take.

• *Taxpayers' rights*

Many of the rights of a taxpayer are found in the Taxpayers' Bill of Rights (¶3801).

The audit examination must be conducted in accordance with professional auditing standards by an auditor who is familiar with generally accepted accounting procedures and auditing techniques. Specifically, the Department of Taxation and Finance must ensure that certain enumerated rights of the taxpayer are respected during an audit. These include:

— the right to know why certain information is being requested, how such information will be used, and the consequences of failing to submit the information;

— the right to confidentiality of information obtained from a tax return or during the course of an audit to any unauthorized person. However, the Department is permitted to share tax information with the IRS and other tax agencies pursuant to defined standards of secrecy and reciprocity;

— the right to have a representative of the taxpayer's choice at any point in the proceedings;

— the right to make an audio recording of any in-person interview, upon advance notice to the Department.

Power of attorney: A power of attorney generally is needed by the taxpayer's representative for all dealings with the Department of Taxation and Finance, proceedings before the Bureau of Conciliation and Mediation Services, and the Division of Tax Appeals.

The following types of self-representation, or representation by related persons, are permitted without a power of attorney:

— an individual represented by himself;

— a partnership by a general partner;

— a corporation by an officer;

— a minor (*i.e.*, an individual under 18 years of age), by a parent, guardian, spouse or return preparer; and

— an incapacitated person (*i.e.*, an individual who is mentally or physically incapable of filing a request or appearing on his own behalf), by anyone having a proper interest in doing so, for example, the committee of an incompetent.

In all other cases, the representative of the taxpayer needs a power of attorney. Appropriate representatives include an attorney, CPA, or PA licensed or enrolled in New York. A corporation may be represented by an employee.

Practitioner Comment: Residency Audits

Until recently, it was not uncommon for taxpayers to learn that they were under audit for a tax year that was about to expire under the statute of limitations. In addition to notification of the audit, the auditor's first correspondence to the taxpayer would

¶3701

contain a request that the taxpayer extend the statute of limitations to allow time for an adequate review of all applicable records. As a result of the issuance of the Audit Division's Residency Audit Guidelines, all personal income tax audits must now be commenced with at least 120 days remaining before the expiration of the statute of limitations for assessing additional taxes due. According to the Guidelines, "an audit is not to be commenced near the end of a statute of limitation period when an insufficient period of time remains to adequately address the issues of the audit. The first communication with the taxpayer should never be a request for voluminous documentation and a statement that the taxpayer will be assessed as a resident unless all the material is produced in an unreasonably short period of time or the taxpayer agrees to extend the statute. Such requests are unreasonable, and assessing additional taxes automatically unless the taxpayer agrees to extend the period is contrary to Audit Division policy and procedures" (*2014 Nonresident Audit Guidelines,* Page 85).

Mark S. Klein, Esq., Hodgson Russ LLP

• *Protest of audit*

A taxpayer who is dissatisfied with an assessment resulting from a tax audit may file a petition for a hearing with the Division of Tax Appeals, or request an informal hearing with the Bureau of Conciliation and Mediation Services.

New York City: An administrative appeal may be filed with the New York City Tax Appeals Tribunal, or a request for a conciliation conference may be filed with the Bureau of Conciliation.

• *Managed audits*

There are no official managed audits in New York. However, taxpayers may be allowed to enter into compliance agreements for sales and use tax. However, New York does not have statutory authority to enter into such agreements.

A Sales and Use Tax Compliance Agreement (SUTCA) is an agreement between a taxing agency and a taxpayer providing simplified procedures under which the taxpayer is to calculate and remit unpaid sales and use tax on its purchases. The agreement commonly provides that the tax to be paid on purchases covered by the agreement is determined applying an agreed-upon tax rate (determined through a review of the taxpayer's purchasing history) to the aggregate of the taxpayer's covered purchases, rather than being determined on a transaction-by-transaction basis (Sales and Use Tax Compliance Agreements, A Report of the Steering Committee, Federation of Tax Administrators, March 2000).

Sales and use tax compliance agreements (SUTCAs) are sometimes confused with managed audits because of the similar terminology that is used. While both SUTCAs and managed audits involve cooperation and written agreements between the taxing agency and the taxpayer, they are different. SUTCAs involve an up-front agreement specifying the manner in which tax is to be computed and remitted at the time of a purchase, the accuracy of which will be evaluated at a later point. Also, they govern the handling of tax obligations on a prospective basis (*Sales and Use Tax Compliance Agreements,* A Report of the Steering Committee, Federation of Tax Administrators, March 2000).

¶3702 Assessments

Law: Secs. 211, 288, 478, 681, 692, 694, 1081, 1092, 1094, 1138, 1147, Tax Law; Secs. 11-521, 11-672, 11-708, 11-810, 11-906, 11-1206, 11-1310, 11-1406, 11-2107, 11-2206, 11-2407, 11-2506, NYC Adm. Code (CCH NEW YORK TAX REPORTS, ¶89-164, 89-168, 589-164, 589-168).

When a taxpayer either fails to file a return or files a return showing a tax due that is less than the correct tax, the Department of Taxation and Finance may assess a tax deficiency. Except when collection of the tax is in jeopardy, deficiency assessments may not be summarily made. Certain procedural requirements must be satisfied in connection with assessing a deficiency in tax to afford the taxpayer an opportunity for review prior to assessment and collection.

Practitioner Comment: Proof of Mailing

The filing requirements for petitions and requests for conciliation conference are statutory and can not be extended. Failure to adhere to the mandated time limits will result in dismissal of the appeal and the loss of a taxpayer's prepayment adjudicative opportunities. Taxpayers must obtain a United States Postal Service postmark on the envelope containing the appropriate response (petition or request for conciliation conference), along with proof of mailing (using certified or registered mail) in order to avoid the risk of loss or delay of the mail. Absent a USPS postmark, late or misplaced mail will result in the dismissal of the taxpayer's protest. Certified mail, using a machine metered stamp date, is inadequate to prove mailing (*Hey's Enterprises, Inc.,* ALJ Order (6/6/02) CCH NEW YORK TAX REPORTS, ¶ 404-195).

Mark S. Klein, Esq., Hodgson Russ LLP

Generally, a deficiency must be assessed within three years of the due date of the return, or within six years if 25% or more of the taxpayer's income is omitted. However, if tax may be assessed at any time if: (1) no report is filed; (2) a false or fraudulent report is filed with the intent to evade tax; or (3) the taxpayer fails to file a report or an amended report.

New York City: The principles, procedures, and time limits discussed in this paragraph are generally applicable to assessments of New York City taxes by the Commissioner of Finance.

• *Notice of deficiency*

When the Department of Taxation and Finance determines that a deficiency exists, it must send a notice of deficiency to the taxpayer's last known address by certified or registered mail. This notice is sent to the fiduciary if the Department has received notice that a fiduciary relationship exists with respect to the taxpayer. (Sec. 681(a), Tax Law; Sec. 1081(a), Tax Law)

Income taxes: New York procedure parallels that of federal law, whereby after 90 days from the mailing of a notice of deficiency (150 days if the taxpayer's last known address is outside the United States), the notice becomes an assessment of the amount of tax specified in the notice, together with interest, additions, and penalties. Deficiencies may not be assessed unless a notice has been mailed to the taxpayer. (Sec. 1081, Tax Law)

Taxpayers are required to report any change in their federal return that has the effect of changing their New York tax liability (Sec. 211(3), Tax Law). If no report of federal change is made or no amended New York return is filed when a federal return is amended, the Commissioner may assess a deficiency based upon increased federal taxable income. The additional tax is deemed assessed 30 days after the notice is mailed (rather than the standard 90-day period described above) unless the taxpayer files the required report of change or amended return before the 30-day period has lapsed, together with a statement showing that the federal determination was erroneous.

Sales and use taxes: The sales and use tax is self-assessed, since the person required to collect the tax (such as a vendor) or the person required to pay the tax (such as a customer who has not paid the tax at the time of purchase) computes the tax and pays the tax at the time of filing returns. The Commissioner of Taxation and Finance, however, determines the tax if the return when filed is incorrect or insufficient, or if the return is not filed.

As with income taxes, a notice of the determination of the tax due will be mailed by registered or certified mail, to the person liable for the collection or payment of the tax. The determination becomes final unless the person against whom it is assessed, within 90 days, applies to the Division of Tax Appeals for a hearing, or unless the Commissioner redetermines the tax. If an application for a hearing has been filed on behalf of an entity and a determination of personal liability has been made on behalf of the person under a duty to act, only one application for hearing is required to be filed on behalf of the corporation, dissolved corporation, partnership, or individual proprietorship and on behalf of the personally liable individual.

Motor fuels tax: A determination of tax may be made within three years after an incorrect or insufficient return has been filed by a distributor. An assessment may be made at any time, however, for a distributor who has not registered, has failed to file a return, or has filed a wilfully false or fraudulent return with an intent to evade the tax. Such determinations of tax by the Commissioner are final unless a hearing is requested.

Cigarette and tobacco taxes: If any person files an incorrect or insufficient return, the Commissioner may determine the amount of tax due at any time within three years after the return was filed, whether or not it was filed on or after the due date. However, if no return is filed or the return is wilfully fraudulent, the determination may be made at any time. A determination is final unless the person against whom the tax is assessed applies, within 90 days after notice of the determination was given, to the Division of Tax Appeal for a hearing.

• *Jeopardy assessments*

If the Department of Taxation and Finance determines that the assessment or collection of a tax may be jeopardized by delay, it may assess and take steps to collect the tax without regard to the usual restrictions on deficiency assessments and collections. However, after the jeopardy assessment is made, the taxpayer is entitled to certain procedural rights, including prompt review of the propriety of the jeopardy assessment and seizure of property, restrictions on sale of property seized to collect the tax, and the right to petition the Department for redetermination of the deficiency. (Sec. 692, Tax Law; Sec. 694(a), Tax Law; Sec. 1092, Tax Law; Sec. 1094(a), Tax Law)

Termination of tax year: If the Department determines that collection of tax is in jeopardy before the return for the year is due, it may terminate the tax year of the taxpayer and assess tax for the short period. Early termination of the tax year is warranted only where collection of the tax might otherwise be defeated by, for example, the taxpayer's departure from the state, a plan to conceal himself or his assets, or a plan to dissipate property. This is a form of jeopardy assessment and is subject to the same post-assessment procedural restrictions applicable to other jeopardy assessments.

Time of jeopardy assessment: A jeopardy assessment may be made at any time before the Department's decision upon petition for redetermination of a tax deficiency becomes final, or the taxpayer has filed an application for judicial review of the decision, whichever is earlier. If no petition for redetermination of the deficiency has been filed or, if filed, the Department has not rendered a decision, a jeopardy assessment may be made for any amount determined to be due without regard to the amounts stated in the deficiency notice. If the jeopardy assessment is made after the Department's decision but before the decision becomes final, the jeopardy assessment can be made only in the amount of the deficiency determined in the decision.

Taxpayers' rights: If the jeopardy assessment is made before the mailing of a notice of deficiency, the notice must be mailed to the taxpayer within 60 days of the assessment. The taxpayer then has 90 days (150 days if the notice is sent outside the United States) to petition for a hearing to redetermine the deficiency.

¶3702

When a levy upon the taxpayer's property has been made under a jeopardy warrant before the Department of Taxation and Finance's decision on redetermination of the deficiency, the taxpayer is entitled to a prompt hearing to determine the probable validity of the pre-decision warrant remedy.

¶3703 Collection of Tax

Law: Secs. 171(18-a), 171-v, 174-b, 203, 211(3), 681—684, 692, 694, 1081—1084, 1092, 1094, Tax Law; Reg. Secs. 8-1.2, 2394.3, 2500.1—2500.7, 5000.1, 5000.5 (CCH New York Tax Reports, ¶ 89-162—89-192, 589-162—589-192).

If the tax, addition, penalty or interest remains unpaid for 21 calendar days after the notice and demand for payment is given (10 business days if the amount for which the notice and demand is given is equal to or exceeds $100,000), the Commissioner may, within six years after the assessment date, issue a warrant directing the sheriff or any officer or employee of the Department to levy upon and sell the real and personal property of the taxpayer for the payment of the amount assessed (Sec. 692(c), Tax Law; Sec. 1092(c), Tax Law). Also, effective March 28, 2013, through April 1, 2017, the Tax Commissioner is authorized to serve an income execution without filing a warrant. The taxpayer can obtain a stay of the warrant's execution by filing a bond or other security with the Department in the amount of the assessment (Sec. 694(h), Tax Law; Sec. 1094(h), Tax Law). The Commissioner is authorized to vacate warrants if the state's interests will not be jeopardized. The New York City Commissioner of Finance has similar authority.

A levy can also be made on bank accounts, and requires a bank to remove money from a taxpayer's account and send it to the Department of Taxation and Finance. A levy can also be made on money that any third party owes the taxpayer, such as a loan or rent owed to the taxpayer. If the taxpayer is a business, a levy can be made on the cash in the register.

A tax liability will not be enforceable and will be extinguished after 20 years from the first date a warrant could be filed by the commissioner (Sec. 174-b, Tax Law). The first date a warrant can be filed is the day after the last day specified for payment by the notice and demand issued for the tax liability where there is no right to a hearing with respect to such notice and demand. Where there is a right to a hearing with respect to a notice and demand for a tax liability, the first date a warrant may be filed means the day after opportunity for a hearing or review has been exhausted. The commissioner and the taxpayer can consent in writing to extend the time period during which tax warrants may be collected. (Sec. 174-b, Tax Law; *TSB-M-11(10)C, TSB-M-11(10)I, TSB-M-11(11)M, TSB-M-11(3)MCTMT, TSB-M-11(4)R, TSB-M-11(15)S,* September 9, 2011, CCH New York Tax Reports, ¶ 407-359)

Income executions: An income execution is a type of levy that may be used against a taxpayers' wages. Under an income execution procedure, the taxpayer will be asked to voluntarily submit a fixed amount of their wages, up to 10% of gross earnings, to the Department. If the taxpayer does not voluntarily pay the amount within 20 days of receiving the Department's notice and continue to pay this amount until the debt is fully paid, the taxpayer's employer will then be ordered to take up to 10% of the taxpayer's gross wages directly out of the taxpayer's paycheck and pay it to the Department on the taxpayer's behalf. The income execution remains in effect until the outstanding tax liability is paid in full.

Judicial proceedings: Judicial proceedings may be brought by the attorney general in the name of the state to recover unpaid taxes, additions to tax, and penalties or interest that have been assessed within six years prior to the date the action is commenced. The attorney general may also bring an action for forfeiture of the franchise of any corporation whose failure to file reports or pay taxes is intentional.

Collection agencies: The Taxpayer's Bill of Rights (¶3801) specifies that its provisions are applicable to all private contractors, including subcontractors and employees, that are under contract with the Department of Taxation and Finance for collection of outstanding tax liabilities.

Offsets: The State Department of Taxation and Finance is authorized to offset income tax refunds to collect warranted tax judgments against all New York City taxes, based on written agreements between the State and City Commissioners (Sec. 171-l, Tax Law). Also, overpayments of certain New York City taxes may be offset against outstanding debts owed the State. (Sec. 171-m, Tax Law)

CCH Advisory: Data Matching

To assist in the collection of debts, the Department is required to develop and operate a financial institution data match system for the purpose of identifying and seizing the nonexempt assets of tax debtors. In addition, each financial institution doing business in the state is required to operate a data match system and to provide certain information to the Department each calendar quarter for identified tax debtors maintaining an account at the institution.

Suspension of driver's licenses: Delinquent tax liabilities equal to or exceeding $10,000 may be enforced through the suspension of drivers' licenses (Sec. 171-v, Tax Law).

Practitioner Comment: Driver's License Suspension Program is a Success

The delinquent taxpayer driver's license suspension program has been a huge financial success. By the end of 2016, the program was responsible for suspending over 10,000 driver's licenses while generating over $400 million in revenue. As a result, there have been proposals to reduce the outstanding liability threshold to $5,000.

Mark S. Klein, Esq., Hodgson Russ LLP

• *Voluntary Disclosure and Compliance (VDC) Program*

An eligible taxpayer may avoid civil penalties and criminal prosecution by entering into a disclosure and compliance agreement with the Department and voluntarily disclosing past tax obligations. The Department may permit the taxpayer to enter into an installment payment plan if payment cannot be made immediately. The compliance agreement will include terms to require the taxpayer to comply with the Tax Law in the future. (Sec. 1700, Tax Law)

An "eligible taxpayer" is an individual, partnership, estate, trust, corporation, limited liability company, joint stock company, or any other company, trustee, receiver, assignee, referee, society, association, business or any other person subject to a tax administered by the Department. To be eligible, a taxpayer must meets the following criteria (Sec. 1700.2, Tax Law):

— the taxpayer is not currently under audit by the department;

— the taxpayer is voluntarily disclosing a tax liability that the department has not determined, calculated, researched or identified at the time of the disclosure;

— the taxpayer is not currently a party to any criminal investigation being conducted by an agency of the state or any political subdivision; and

— the taxpayer is not seeking to disclose participation in a tax avoidance transaction that is a federal or New York State reportable or listed transaction.

¶3703

Under the agreement, the commissioner may not use the taxpayer's disclosure as evidence in any proceeding brought against the taxpayer or reveal the contents of the disclosure to any law enforcement or other agency, with certain exceptions. The following penalties are waived (Sec. 1700.3, Tax Law):

    (1) failure to pay any tax;

    (2) failure to file a tax return or report;

    (3) failure to pay estimated tax; and

    (4) the additional rate of interest imposed under Sec. 1145, Tax Law.

The agreement maybe rescinded and civil penalties and/or criminal prosecution may be imposed for the intentional failure to pay the disclosed liability in accordance with the compliance agreement or the intentional violation of any term of the agreement.

NYC and NY State coordination: New York City has a VDC program that is very similar to the state program (Sec. 11-131, NYC Adm. Code). NYC's Department of Finance operates a unified program that allows a delinquent taxpayer to make one request to participate in both the state and city VDC programs without making separate requests to each jurisdiction. As part of the unified program, New York City will conform to state procedures, including those requiring taxpayers to identify themselves on their application. The taxpayer receives one agreement detailing the terms of both jurisdictions, and an authorized employee from each jurisdiction will sign the agreement. All requests to participate in the unified program must be made with the New York State Department of Taxation and Finance. (*Statement of Audit Procedure* PP-2009-1rev., New York City Department of Finance, August 5, 2009, CCH NEW YORK TAX REPORTS, ¶ 600-691)

Disclosure to tax authorities: The Department is permitted to disclose any return or report filed by a taxpayer under the VDC program to the IRS or the proper tax officer of any state or city, as otherwise permitted in the Tax Law. (*TSB-M-09(6)I, TSB-M-09(6)C, TSB-M-9(5)M, TSB-M-09(1)R, TSB-M-09(5)S,* Office of Tax Policy Analysis, New York Department of Taxation and Finance, May 13, 2009, CCH NEW YORK TAX REPORTS, ¶ 406-395.)

• *Compromise of tax liability*

The Commissioner of Taxation and Finance is authorized to compromise civil tax liability when there is doubt as to liability and/or doubt as to collectibility, or if collection in full would result in undue economic hardship to the tax debtor (Sec. 171(18-a), Tax Law). An offer in compromise is made only in response to an assessment. Therefore, it may only be made after the issuance of a statutory notice of assessment to the taxpayer, which is issued only after an audit is concluded.

The Commissioner may accept an offer in compromise of civil tax liability of $100,000 or less, exclusive of penalties and interest, at any time before the tax is no longer subject to administrative review. The Attorney General may compromise the liability after reference to the Department of Law for prosecution or defense at any time prior to the time the tax or administrative action taken by the Department of Taxation and Finance is no longer subject to judicial review. Upon acceptance of an offer in compromise, the matter may not be reopened except upon a showing of fraud, malfeasance, or misrepresentation of a material fact.

The Commissioner may accept a lesser amount of taxes, penalties, and interest in order to increase the pool of applicants for a potential offer, including those offers based on undue economic hardship that collection in full would impose. An offer in compromise will not be accepted for any reason where acceptance of such an offer would not be in the best interests of the state or would undermine voluntary compliance with the Tax Law. Offers in compromise cannot be used as a tax planning device by businesses or individuals. (Sec. 171(15), Tax Law)

Practitioner Comment: Offers in Compromise

In 2014, the Offer in Compromise Unit was moved from the Office of the Taxpayer Rights Advocate back to the Civil Enforcement Division. While the offer in compromise acceptance rate historically averaged approximately 40%, in recent years, the acceptance rate and number of applications received have steadily increased. Since 2015, the percentage of acceptances has increased to almost 80% of the total of applications submitted, including withdrawn applications. The number of applications the Department received during the 2015-2016 fiscal year increased by nearly 50% from the 2013-2014 fiscal year, due in part to recent legislation that expanded the program to include individuals who would experience undue economic hardship if required to pay in full their outstanding tax liabilities.

Mark S. Klein, Esq., Hodgson Russ LLP

• *Tax shelter disclosure*

Disclosure requirements are in effect with respect to reportable or listed transactions, including penalties for nondisclosure and underpayment, as well as an extended statute of limitations for assessments related to tax avoidance transactions. (Sec. 25, Tax Law; Reg. Secs. 2500.1—2500.7; *TSB-M-07(7)C* and *TSB-M-07(6)I*, June 28, 2007, CCH NEW YORK TAX REPORTS, ¶ 405-774). The provisions are set to expire July 1, 2019.

Under the regulations, a New York reportable transaction is a transaction that has the potential to be a tax avoidance transaction. The regulations describe three categories of such transactions, including New York listed transactions, New York confidential transactions, and New York transactions with contractual protection. Every taxpayer that has participated in a New York reportable transaction during its taxable year is required to disclose the participation with its tax return for that taxable year. On or before the date when disclosure would otherwise be required, a taxpayer may submit a request to the Department for a determination of whether a particular transaction is subject to the disclosure requirements. In addition, if a taxpayer is uncertain whether a transaction must be disclosed, the taxpayer may disclose the transaction with an indication that the disclosure is being filed on a protective basis (Reg. Secs. 2500.1—2500.7; *TSB-M-07(4)C* and *TSB-M-07(4)I*, March 8, 2007, CCH NEW YORK TAX REPORTS, ¶ 405-667).

• *Intergovernmental collection agreements*

There are a number of agreements among governmental agencies to provide for assistance in tax collection, both between the Internal Revenue Service and the states, and among the states themselves. See also ¶ 3603.

Abusive Tax Avoidance Transactions (ATAT) Memorandum: The Small Business/Self-Employed Division of the Internal Revenue Service has signed an ATAT Memorandum of Understanding with nearly all states, including New York. The Memorandum provides for information sharing on abusive tax avoidance transactions (*Memorandum of Understanding,* Internal Revenue Service, CCH NEW YORK TAX REPORTS, ¶ 89-184). The Memorandum authorizes the IRS and New York to:

— exchange tax returns and return information;

— share audit results from ATAT participant cases;

— exchange information on identified types of ATAT schemes; and

— share audit technique guides.

The IRS will provide states with a list of participants in a particular ATAT scheme on a semi-annual basis on July 31 and January 31. The IRS generally refers to an abusive tax shelter arrangement as the promise of tax benefits with no meaningful change in the taxpayer's control over or benefit from the taxpayer's income or assets.

¶3703

¶3704 Penalties and Interest

Law: Secs. 171(28), 211(2-a), 658(c)(4), 685, 697(j), 1085, 1145, 1801, 1803, 1805, 1808—1810, Tax Law; Reg. Sec. 158.12, 536.1, 2392, 2398.1, 2398.2, 2600-1 *et seq.* (CCH NEW YORK TAX REPORTS, ¶89-202—89-210, 589-204).

Below are the penalties and the interest rates generally applicable in New York.

• *Civil penalties*

Civil penalties are administered under specific provisions that specify procedures to be followed in cases of failure to file a return, failure to pay tax shown on return, deficiencies due to negligence or fraud, underpayment of estimated tax, and other situations warranting the imposition of penalties.

Failure to timely pay and/or file: When a taxpayer fails to file a return on the due date, including extensions to file, a penalty of 5% per month is imposed, up to a maximum aggregate amount of 25%. The penalty is imposed on the difference between the amount shown as due on the return, less withholding, estimated payments, partial payments and other credits to which the taxpayer is entitled. If no tax is owed, therefore, a taxpayer who files late does not incur this penalty.

The penalty for failure to file can be waived if the taxpayer can demonstrate that the failure to file was due to reasonable cause and not to wilful neglect.

The late filing penalty runs from the due date of the return (including extensions to file) to the date the return is actually received. It is not uncommon for a taxpayer to incur both failure to file and failure to pay delinquency penalties. If both penalties apply for a given month or part of a month, the penalty for failure to file is reduced by the penalty for failure to pay tax when due.

A minimum penalty applies when the return is more than 60 days late. The penalty is equal to the lesser of $100 or 100% of the tax due, *i.e.,* liability reduced by payments and credits. Thus, there is no minimum penalty if there is no tax liability, even where a return nonetheless must be filed. As in the case of the basic penalty (5% of tax per month, up to a maximum of 25%), this minimum penalty may not be imposed where the failure to file is shown to have been due to reasonable cause and not due to wilful neglect. Unlike the basic penalty, it is not reduced by the 5%-per-month failure to pay penalty.

A similar penalty is imposed for failure to pay a deficiency within 21 calendar days of notice and demand for payment (ten calendar days if the amount for which the notice and demand is made equals or exceeds $100,000). The amount to which the penalty rate is applied is the tax stated in the notice reduced by any partial payments. This penalty also may be waived if shown to be due to reasonable cause and not wilful neglect.

In the case of a disaster declared by the President or Governor, the Commissioner of Taxation and Finance may extend deadlines for payment of taxes for up to 90 days. In addition, regarding state disaster emergencies declared by the Governor, the deadlines for payment may be extended until the conclusion of the disaster (or up to 30 days thereafter).

Negligence: When any part of a deficiency is due to negligence or intentional disregard of the law, rules and regulations, but not to fraud, a two-part penalty applies. The first part of the penalty is equal to 5% of the deficiency. Once negligence or intentional disregard is found for any part of the deficiency, the 5% penalty is imposed on the entire underpayment. The second part of the penalty is equal to 50% of the interest otherwise due on the portion of the underpayment that is due to negligence or intentional disregard. The period for measuring the interest starts on the due date for payment of the tax (excluding extensions) and ends on the earlier of the date of assessment or payment.

In computing the amount of the deficiency on which the negligence penalty is imposed, the taxpayer's correct tax liability is reduced by any tax shown on a timely filed return (including extensions to file).

Negligence generally is defined as lack of due care, or failure to do what a reasonable and ordinarily prudent person would do under the circumstances.

Practitioner Comment: Penalties Often Imposed Automatically

While auditors historically evaluated a taxpayer's actions to determine if the imposition of negligence penalties was appropriate, a more recent trend involves auditors automatically imposing penalties and leaving it to the taxpayer to establish a basis for reasonable cause to abate them. This usually requires that the taxpayer provide a written statement explaining the basis for the reasonable cause.

Mark S. Klein, Esq., Hodgson Russ LLP

Mandatory electronic filing and payment: If a taxpayer does not utilize a tax return preparer to prepare an authorized tax document, but instead prepares that document itself using tax software, then all authorized tax documents prepared by the taxpayer using tax software must be filed electronically (Sec. 29(c), Tax Law).

For other than personal income tax, a taxpayer who is required to electronically pay any liability is assessed a penalty of $50 for each failure to electronically pay the liability (Sec. 29(e)(2), Tax Law). The penalty is imposed unless the taxpayer can show that the failure was due to reasonable cause and not wilful neglect.

The following additional penalties apply to a taxpayer who is required to e-file any authorized document but fails to e-file the authorized tax document:

— a penalty of $50 for each failure to e-file unless the taxpayer can show that the failure was due to reasonable cause and not wilful neglect, and

— a penalty under the applicable article for the failure to file a return or report, whether a paper return or report has been filed or not.

If a taxpayer who is required to e-file any authorized tax document fails to e-file the document, the taxpayer will not be eligible to receive interest on any overpayment until the document is filed electronically (Sec. 29(e)(4), Tax Law).

Fraud: If any part of a deficiency is due to fraud, a penalty of two times the deficiency is imposed. Once fraud is found, the penalty is imposed on the entire amount of the underpayment, not merely on the amount of the underpayment due to the fraud-tainted item.

If a fraud penalty is assessed, no negligence penalties or penalties for failure to timely file or pay tax may be imposed.

False or fraudulent document: A taxpayer that submits a false or fraudulent document to the Department of Taxation and Finance is subject to a penalty of $100 per document or $500 per tax return submitted. This penalty is in addition to any other penalties allowed under the tax law. (Sec. 685(cc), Tax Law)

A penalty of up to $5,000 is imposed on any person who, with the intent that tax be evaded, for a fee or other compensation, aids or assists in, or procures, counsels, or advises the preparation or presentation, of any return, report, declaration, statement or other document under the sales and use tax law that is fraudulent or false as to any material matter. This penalty applies if the person supplies any false or fraudulent information, whether or not the falsity or fraud is with knowledge or consent of the person authorized or required to present the return.

Substantial understatement of tax liability: A 10% penalty is imposed against taxpayers for substantial understatements of tax liability. A substantial understatement is an omission of tax on an annual return equal to at least 10% of the correct tax or $2,000 ($5,000 for corporations), whichever is greater. Since substantial understatements of tax can result from incorrect positions taken in good faith, taxpayers are excused for any portion of an understatement attributable to tax treatment of an item for which there was substantial authority, or where the facts affecting the taxpayer's treatment of the item are adequately disclosed in the return or in a statement attached to the return. The Commissioner may waive all or part of the penalty on the taxpayer's showing of good faith and reasonable cause for all or part of the understatement.

Fraudulent failure to perform required act: In addition to other penalties, the Commissioner of Taxation and Finance may impose a penalty of up to $1,000 against any person who, with fraudulent intent, fails to pay tax due or fails to make, sign, or certify any return, or supply information within the time required. This penalty may, in the discretion of the Commissioner, be waived, reduced, or compromised.

Underpayment of estimated tax: A taxpayer who underpays estimated tax is subject to a penalty based on the amount and duration of the underpayment.

For individuals, the amount of the penalty for underpayment of estimated taxes is computed by applying to the underpayment the interest rate in effect for the period as established by the Commissioner. The underpayment for penalty purposes is the difference between the actual payment and the required installment. The required installment is the lower of:

(1) 25% of the required annual payment, which in turn is the lesser of:

(a) 90% of the tax shown on the return (or if no return is filed, of the tax for such year); or

(b) 100% of the tax shown on the return filed for the preceding tax year, provided that the individual filed a return for that year and that it was a full tax year (12 months);

(2) an annualized income installment, which means in essence:

(a) annualizing the taxable income and minimum taxable income for the months ending before the due date for the installment, and computing the tax that would be due on such amounts;

(b) multiplying that tax by 22.5% for the first installment, 45% for the second installment, 67.5% for the third installment or 90% for the fourth installment; and

(c) subtracting from the product the aggregate of prior estimated tax payments.

Withheld tax generally is treated as a payment of estimated tax and is applied equally to the four installments. The taxpayer, however, may establish the actual dates and amounts of withholding, in which case these amounts are treated as payments of estimated tax on the actual withholding dates.

Penalty exceptions: Various exceptions apply to the imposition of the addition to tax, whereby no penalty is imposed:

— a *de minimis* rule prohibits imposition of a penalty where the tax (reduced by credits, including that for tax withheld) is less than $300;

— taxpayers who had no tax liability for the preceding year;

— installments due on or after the taxpayer's death;

— where the Department determines that "by reason of casualty, disaster or other unusual circumstances the imposition of such addition to tax would be against equity and good conscience"; or

— where the taxpayer retired after age 62 or became disabled, either in the tax year for which estimated tax payments were required or in the preceding tax year, and the Department determines that the underpayment was due to reasonable cause and not wilful neglect.

Corporations: Corporations are generally required to make estimated tax payments during the year equal to 91% of the current year's tax, although higher payments are required of large corporations. See ¶1405 for specific information on estimated tax requirements and penalties applicable to corporations and large corporations.

Withholding penalties: There are several penalties for noncompliance with withholding requirements. These penalties apply even if the tax required to be withheld is ultimately paid by an employee. For details, see ¶609 and ¶809.

Pass-through entities: Partnerships (except publicly traded partnerships), limited liability companies (LLCs), and S corporations failing to pay the estimated tax on behalf of nonresident partners, members, or shareholders (¶3602) are subject to a $50 penalty for each failure per partner, member, or shareholder, unless the failure is due to reasonable cause and not due to wilful neglect. An addition to tax is also applicable if there is an underpayment of estimated tax by the entity.

Failure to file information returns: New York tax law imposes penalties on the failure to file returns of information at source (*viz.*, Forms IT-2102 and IT-2102.1, similar to federal Forms W-2 and 1099), or annual information returns of partnerships and S corporations. The penalty applicable to returns of information at source is $50 per statement (up to an annual maximum of $10,000). The penalty applicable to partnership and S corporation information returns for each month of failure (up to five months) is equal to $50 multiplied by the number of partners or shareholders who were in the partnership or S corporation for any part of the tax year and were subject to tax for any part of that year.

Failure to supply identifying numbers: For failure to include one's identifying number in any return, statement or other document, a $5 penalty applies. For failure to furnish one's identifying number to another person or to include the identifying number of another person in a return, statement or other document, a $50 penalty applies. The maximum total amount of all such penalties during a calendar year is $10,000. The penalty for failure to supply one's own identifying number is not imposed unless the person fails to supply the number within 30 days after the Department of Taxation and Finance requests it. It is also not imposed if the failure is shown to be due to reasonable cause and not wilful neglect. Grounds that may establish reasonable cause include good faith reliance on an incorrect identifying number, waiting for the issuance of an identifying number, and failure to obtain an identifying number after repeated documentable attempts.

Frivolous tax returns: A penalty of up to $500 is imposed for filing a frivolous return. A return is frivolous when (1) it does not contain enough information on which to judge the substantial correctness of the self-assessment, or indicates on its face that the self-assessment is substantially incorrect; and (2) it takes a position that is frivolous or evinces an intent to delay or impede the administration of the tax. For additional information, see Publication 101, *Frivolous Positions Under the Personal Income Tax,* February 2010, available at **http://www.tax.ny.gov/pdf/publications/income/pub101.pdf.**

Aiding or assisting in fraudulent returns: A penalty of up to $1,000 ($10,000 for corporations) applies to persons who, for a fee or other compensation and with intent to evade tax, aid, assist in, procure, counsel or advise the preparation or presentation (in connection with an income tax or franchise tax matter) of any return, report, declaration, statement or other document that is fraudulent or false as to any material matter. Also proscribed is supplying false or fraudulent information. The penalty is imposed whether or not the falsity or fraud is with the knowledge or consent of the taxpayer.

¶3704

Failure to report interest payments: For failure by corporations to report payments of interest to shareholders owning more than 50% of the capital stock of the corporation, a penalty of $500 is imposed unless it is shown that the failure was due to reasonable cause and not due to wilful neglect.

Failure relating to issuer's allocation percentage: A $500 penalty applies against corporate taxpayers where a return does not contain the taxpayer's issuer's allocation percentage or the information necessary to compute the taxpayer's issuer's allocation percentage, unless it is shown that the failure is due to reasonable cause and not due to wilful neglect.

Failure relating to wage reports: An employer who fails to include required wage reporting information relating to individual employees on the return, or to include true and correct wage reporting information, and who fails to correct the failure for more than 30 days after notification of the failure is subject to the following penalty:

(1) up to $1 for each employee for the first failure for one reporting period in any eight consecutive reporting periods;

(2) up to $5 for each employee for the second failure for one reporting period in any eight consecutive reporting periods; and

(3) up to $25 for each employee for the third failure for any reporting period in any eight consecutive reporting periods, and for each such failure in any eight consecutive reporting periods that is subsequent to the third such failure.

An employer who fails to file a required quarterly combined withholding and wage reporting return in timely fashion is subject to a penalty of the greater of $1,000 or the product of $50 times the number of employees of the employer, up to $10,000 for any failure. The penalty is abated, however, if the employer files the return within 30 days after notification of the failure is sent by the Department of Taxation and Finance.

Bad check fee: A $50 fee is imposed for bad checks, bad money orders, or failed electronic funds withdrawals intended for payments of any taxes, fees, or assessments imposed by the Department of Taxation and Finance (Sec. 30, Tax Law).

• *Return preparers*

Tax return preparers and facilitators, except attorneys and CPAs licensed in New York and IRS-enrolled agents, are required to register electronically with the New York Department of Taxation and Finance and pay an annual fee of $100 (Sec. 32, Tax Law; *TSB-M-09(11)C, TSB-M-09(9)I, TSB-M-09(10)M, TSB-M-09(3)MCTMT, TSB-M-09(4)R, TSB-M-09(15)S,* October 1, 2009, CCH New York Tax Reports, ¶406-544 and *TSB-M-09(14)C, TSB-M-09(16)I, TSB-M-09(13)M, TSB-M-09(5)MCTMT, TSB-M-09(11)R,* and *TSB-M-09(21)S,* December 22, 2009, CCH New York Tax Reports, ¶406-629).

A "tax return preparer" is an individual who prepares a substantial portion of any tax return for compensation, and a "facilitator" is a person who individually or in conjunction or cooperation with another person: (1) solicits the execution of, processes, receives, or accepts an application or agreement for a refund anticipation loan or refund anticipation check; (2) serves or collects upon a refund anticipation loan or refund anticipation check; or (3) in any other manner facilitates the making of a refund anticipation loan or refund anticipation check.

Commercial tax return preparers who prepare New York returns must meet certain minimum qualifications. As part of the requirements, commercial tax return preparers must do the following (Reg. Sec. 2600-1.1 *et seq.*):

— meet applicable IRS requirements;

— complete 16 hours of course work, if new to the field of New York state tax preparation;

— pass a New York state tax competency exam; and

— annually participate in 4 hours of continuing professional education.

The education and testing requirements are to be phased in over time. The department may initially limit those requirements to tax return preparers who prepare personal income tax returns. The regulations also provide minimum standards of conduct for registered tax return preparers. Certain tax return preparers (*i.e.*, attorneys, certified public accountants, public accountants, and enrolled agents) are generally not subject to the requirements under the new regulations; however, the regulations provide that the department may coordinate with other taxing authorities and professional licensing or other regulatory bodies to make disciplinary referrals with respect to such individuals.

Upon completing the registration process, a tax return preparer or facilitator will receive a registration certificate. A tax return preparer or facilitator who does not register with the Department will not be allowed to represent clients before the Division of Taxation or the Division of Tax Appeals. Penalties are added for violations of these provisions. (Sec. 32, Tax Law)

Obligations of tax preparers: Generally, tax preparers are required to provide each of their customers with a receipt containing an address and phone number at which the preparer can be contacted throughout the year. If the actual person who prepared the return is an employee, partner, or shareholder of an entity that is a tax preparer, the general address and phone number of the entity should be on the receipt. In addition, as of January 1 of each year, tax preparers are generally required to obtain the current version of Publication 135, *Consumer Bill of Rights Regarding Tax Preparers*, from the Department's Web site (**www.tax.state.ny.us**) and reproduce it for their customers. Those tax preparers must give each customer a free copy of Publication 135 before any discussions take place with the customer. Certain tax preparers (*e.g.* licensed accountants and attorneys and, agents enrolled to practice before the Internal Revenue Service) are exempt from the requirement to provide a receipt with contact information and the requirement to give Publication 135 to potential customers.

All tax preparers are subject to certain refund anticipation loan (RAL) requirements. Specifically, tax preparers are prohibited from advertising RALs as refunds, and any advertisement by a tax preparer that mentions RALs must state conspicuously that RALs are, in fact, loans and that a fee or interest will be charged by the lending institution. In addition, before any RAL is entered into, the tax preparer facilitating the loan must provide a specific disclosure statement to the taxpayer in writing. (Reg. Secs. 2398.1, 2398.2, and 2398.3; *TSB-M-08(7)I*, New York Department of Taxation and Finance, November 20, 2008, CCH NEW YORK TAX REPORTS, ¶ 406-231; *TSB-M-09(13)I*, December 7, 2009, CCH NEW YORK TAX REPORTS, ¶ 406-617)

Penalties: Any individual who is a tax return preparer for any return or claim for refund and who is required to sign the return or refund claim is subject to a penalty of $50 for each failure to sign, with a maximum penalty of $25,000 for any calendar year.

For failure to furnish an identifying number on a return or refund claim, the person who is the tax return preparer of the return or claim is subject to a penalty of $50 per failure, up to $25,000 per year.

The penalty for failure to furnish a copy of the return or refund claim to the taxpayer is $50 per return or claim, up to $25,000 per year.

The penalty for failure to retain a copy of the return or refund claim or a list of taxpayers is $50 for each such failure, with a $25,000 maximum for any calendar year.

¶3704

Any tax preparer who violates any provision of the Consumers' Bill of Rights regarding tax preparers (Sec. 372, General Business Law), or any regulation promulgated as a result of that section, is liable for a civil penalty of not less than $250 but not more than $500 for the first violation and, for each succeeding violation, a civil penalty of not less than $500 but not more than $750.

New York City: The Commissioner of Finance is authorized to require tax preparers that prepare more than 100 tax returns in a single calendar year and again files more than 100 returns or other tax documents in a succeeding year using tax software, to file the returns electronically. Penalties will be imposed for the failure to electronically file or electronically pay, equal to $50 for each failure instance.

Tax preparers operating within New York City are not subject to the provisions of Article 24-C of the General Business Law for tax returns actually prepared within the city. Instead, Subchapter 8 of Chapter 4 of Title 20 of the Administrative Code of the City of New York provides rules that apply specifically to tax preparers operating in New York City. For more information on New York City's consumer bill of rights regarding tax preparers, visit the New York City Department of Consumer Affairs Web site (**http://www1.nyc.gov/site/dca/index.page**) or dial 311 (212-NEW-YORK from outside New York City).

Mandatory electronic filing and payment: Tax return preparers and software companies may not charge a separate filing fee for the electronic filing of authorized tax documents. Violations result in a civil penalty of $500 for a first violation and $1,000 for each succeeding violation.

If a tax return preparer prepared authorized tax documents for more than 10 different taxpayers during any calendar year beginning on or after January 1, 2012, and if in any succeeding calendar year he or she prepares one or more authorized tax documents using tax software, then for that succeeding calendar year and each subsequent calendar year, all authorized tax documents prepared by that preparer must be filed electronically. Any return or report including one or more tax documents that cannot be filed electronically will not be deemed to be an authorized tax document for purposes of the electronic filing requirements under Sec. 29, Tax Law.

If a tax return preparer is required to file authorized tax documents electronically but fails to file one or more of those documents electronically, then that preparer will be subject to a penalty of $50 for each failure to electronically file an authorized tax document, unless it is shown that the failure is due to reasonable cause and not due to wilful neglect. A taxpayer's election to electronically file a state or New York City tax return is not considered a reasonable cause for the failure to file, applicable to tax returns and other tax documents required to be filed electronically by tax return preparers on or after December 31, 2010.

If a return or transfer is rejected, a preparer is allowed a reasonable period of time to resubmit without penalty, applicable to electronic returns and payments made for tax years beginning after December 31, 2010.

If a taxpayer is required to electronically pay any tax liability or other amount due shown on, or required to be paid with, an authorized tax document required to be filed electronically, and that taxpayer fails to electronically pay one or more of those liabilities or other amounts due, then that taxpayer will be subject to a penalty of $50 for each failure to electronically pay (Sec. 29, Tax Law).

• *Criminal penalties*

Tax fraud acts: Article 37 of the Tax Law, which applies to all taxes administered by the Tax Department, includes a series of crimes entitled "Tax fraud acts". A tax fraud act means wilfully engaging in an act or acts or wilfully causing another to engage in an act or acts pursuant to which a person:

— fails to make, render, sign, certify, or file any return or report required by the Tax Law or by regulations promulgated thereunder within the time required;

— files or submits a return, report, statement or document with the state or any political subdivision of the state, or with any public office or public officer of the state or any political subdivision of the state, knowing that the return, report, statement or other document required under the Tax Law contains any materially false or fraudulent information or omits any material information;

— knowingly supplies or submits materially false or fraudulent information in connection with any return, audit, investigation, or proceeding or fails to supply information within the time required by or under the provisions of the Tax Law or any regulation promulgated thereunder;

— engages in any scheme to defraud the state or a political subdivision of the state or a government instrumentality within the state by false or fraudulent pretenses, representations or promises as to any material matter, in connection with any tax imposed under the Tax Law or any matter under the Tax Law;

— fails to remit any tax collected in the name of the state or on behalf of the state or any political subdivision of the state when the collection is required under the Tax Law;

— fails to collect any tax required to be collected under Articles 12-A, 18, 20, 22, or 28 or pursuant to the authority of Article 29 of the Tax Law;

— fails to pay any tax with intent to evade the tax; or

— issues an exemption certificate, interdistributor sales certificate, resale certificate, or any other document capable of evidencing a claim that taxes do not apply to a transaction, which he or she does not believe to be true and correct as to any material matter, which omits any material information, or which is false, fraudulent, or counterfeit.

A person wilfully engages in any of the above described tax fraud acts when a person engages in such an act with intent to defraud, intent to evade the payment of taxes or intent to avoid a requirement of the Tax Law, a lawful requirement of the Commissioner of Taxation and Finance or a known legal duty. Such acts are Class A misdemeanors.

Tax fraud acts committed with intent to evade tax are Class E, D, B, or C felonies, depending on the resulting amount of tax evasion.

• *Interest*

The interest rates on underpayments and overpayments of New York taxes are set quarterly based on the federal short-term rate established for Internal Revenue Code purposes by the U.S. Secretary of the Treasury, rounded to the nearest full percentage or increased to the next full percentage (in the case of $1/2\%$ multiple). Announcement of the rates are legally required, even if there are no changes from the previous quarter.

For corporate franchise (income) tax, the underpayment rate is the sum of the federal short-term interest rate plus 7% and the overpayment rate is the sum of the federal short-term interest rate plus 2%. If no rates are established, the rate will be deemed to be set at 7.5%.

For personal income tax, the interest rate is calculated as the federal short-term rate plus 5.5% for underpayments or plus 2% for overpayments. If no rate is set, it is deemed to be set at 7.5%.

Interest on any sales and use tax not paid is the greater of 14.5% per annum or the federal short-term interest rate plus 7%, imposed from the due date to the date paid whether or not any extension of time for payment was granted.

The minimum underpayment interest rate for all taxes is 7.5%

• *Recent interest rates*

The interest rates per annum, compounded daily, are specified below for refunds of tax and late payments and assessments of tax for the period April 1, 2016 through December 31, 2016. For earlier interest rates, see the specific taxes (consult the Table of Contents or Topical Index).

¶3704

Tax	Refunds	Late Payments and Assessments
Alcoholic Beverage	3%	8%
Boxing & Wrestling	3%	8%
Cigarette	NA	8%
Corporation	3%	8%
Diesel Motor Fuel	3%	8%
Estate	3%	7.5%
Fuel Use Tax	5%	5%
Generation-Skipping Transfer	3%	7.5%
Hazardous Waste	3%	15%
Highway Use	3%	8%
Income	3%	7.5%
MCTD mobility tax	3%	7.5%
Medical Marihuana	3%	8%
Mortgage Recording	3%	8%
Motor Fuel	3%	8%
Petroleum Business	3%	8%
Real Estate Transfer	3%	8%
Sales and Use	3%	14.5%
Tobacco Products	NA	8%
Waste Tire	3%	8%
Withholding	3%	8%

Practitioner Comment: Interest on Sales Tax Deficiencies Can Be Reduced

Although the statutory interest rate on sales and use tax underpayments is 14.5%, a taxpayer that is able to establish that the tax deficiency was due to reasonable cause and not wilful neglect can reduce the rate of interest to the federal short-term interest rate plus 5%. See Reg. 536.1(c).

Mark S. Klein, Esq., Hodgson Russ LLP

• *New York City*

New York City interest rates applicable to underpayments and overpayments of tax are set by the Commissioner of Finance on a quarterly basis. However, there are some differences from the state rates. For details, see ¶2815.

ADMINISTRATION AND PROCEDURE

CHAPTER 38
TAXPAYER REMEDIES

¶3801 Taxpayer Rights and Remedies

Law: Secs. 3000—3038, Tax Law (CCH NEW YORK TAX REPORTS, ¶89-222—¶89-240).

The New York Taxpayers' Bill of Rights requires the Department of Taxation and Finance to furnish taxpayers with nontechnical statements that explain taxpayers' rights with respect to audits, protests, the review of adverse decisions, refunds, complaints, and enforcement procedures.

The Taxpayers' Bill of Rights applies to all taxes and fees administered and collected by the Department of Taxation and Finance. It provides a variety of specific guarantees and remedies to individual and corporate taxpayers. These include:

— disclosure of rights of taxpayers and overpayments made by taxpayers;

— prompt and accurate answers to tax questions and requests for assistance;

— requirements of certain Department letters, notices and documents;

— procedures involving taxpayer interviews;

— the procedures for filing and processing refund claims and filing of taxpayer complaints;

— rights to protest an action taken by the Department, including administrative and judicial appeals;

— confidentiality of all tax information unless otherwise required by law;

— procedures regarding abatement of certain interest, penalties and additions to tax;

— giving more time to pay tax liabilities after receiving a notice of the liability before additional interest and certain penalties begin to accrue;

— procedures regarding disagreement with audit findings;

— procedures regarding assessments attributable to certain mathematical errors by the Department;

— the procedures the Department of Taxation and Finance may use in enforcing taxes;

— taxpayer agreements for payments of tax liability in installments;

— procedures for requesting cancellation, release or modification of liens;

— awarding of costs and certain fees;

— expanding innocent spouse relief;

— allowing levies to be released in certain hardship situations; and

— civil damages for failure to release a lien, for certain unauthorized collection actions, a wrongful levy, or unauthorized disclosure of returns and return information.

Practitioner Comment: Taxpayer Rights Advocate

In 2009, New York's Tax Department announced the creation of the office of Taxpayer Rights Advocate. The Taxpayer Rights Advocate reports directly to the Commissioner of Taxation and Finance and is charged with informing taxpayers of their rights and responsibilities with respect to audits, protests, collection activities, mediation services and enforcement procedures. The advocate is also responsible for identifying patterns in tax matters that may indicate systemic problems with the Department's procedures or policies. The advocate will also "assist the public with their tax problems when resolution has not been possible through normal Tax Department channels" (*Press Release*, 10/1/09).

Form DTF-911 should be used to request assistance from the Office of the Taxpayer Rights Advocate.

Mark S. Klein, Esq., Hodgson Russ LLP

¶3802 Appeals

Law: Secs. 170, 1007, 1090, 2000, 2002, 2010, 2012, 3000—3038, Tax Law; Secs. 512, 523-a, 524, 525, 550, 554, 702, Real Property Tax Law; Reg. Secs. 3000.13, 3000.15, 3000.17, 3000.20, 4000.5; Sec. 506, Civil Practice Law and Rules (CCH New York Tax Reports, ¶89-228—89-236, 589-234, 589-236).

The following is a general discussion of actions that may be taken by taxpayers who disagree with an assessment of tax or other action of the Department of Taxation and Finance, the New York City Department of Finance, or local assessors. For additional information, consult the discussion of the specific tax (consult the Table of Contents or Topical Index).

Practitioner Comment: New York's Freedom of Information Law (FOIL)

Once a taxpayer decides to appeal the results of an audit, she is well advised to request a full copy of the auditor's entire file under New York's Freedom of Information Law. The auditors' notes, emails, underlying investigative reports, narrative statement (also known as the DO-220.5) and field audit report (DO-1637.2) can provide valuable insight into the auditors' thought process and information that the auditors were able to unearth during the course of their investigation.

Mark S. Klein, Esq., Hodgson Russ LLP

• *Taxpayer conferences*

Conciliation conferences, conducted informally by a conciliation conferee, seek to resolve taxpayer disputes in a quick and inexpensive manner without resorting to a formal hearing.

The taxpayer's representative presents his or her side of the case, and an auditor presents the views of the Department of Taxation and Finance. The conciliation conferee then attempts to resolve any disagreements by narrowing the facts or legal issues in dispute. Relevant facts and legal arguments are tendered by each party in an informal manner through testimony, affidavits, briefs, letters, and other means.

As an incentive to taxpayers to employ this settlement process, the Commissioner of Taxation and Finance may delegate to the conferee the authority to waive or modify penalties, interest, or other additions to tax.

CCH Advisory: Conciliation Conferences

Conciliation conferences are strongly advised. Only in rare circumstances should they be bypassed, for example, where it is clear that nothing will be accomplished by a conference except the disclosure of information that the taxpayer's representative at this point chooses not to disclose. Conferences will usually result in a clearer definition of the issues, the elimination of agreed-upon matters, and a smoother formal hearing. Moreover, the Division of Tax Appeals has the authority to refer matters to the Bureau of Conciliation and Mediation Services for a conciliation conference where one has not been conducted, upon the request of a taxpayer and with the consent of the Office of General Counsel if the taxpayer intended to file a request rather than a petition for a formal hearing or if the conference would serve a useful purpose. (Sec. 3000.3(e), Tax Law)

Expedited matters: An expedited hearing process will apply in cases where a person receives any of the following specified notices that advises the person of:

— the proposed cancellation, revocation, or suspension of a license, permit, registration, or other credential issued by the Tax Department;

— the denial of an application for a license, permit, registration, or other credential issued under the authority of the Tax Law, except for an application to renew a sales tax Certificate of Authority;

— the imposition of a fraud penalty for aiding or assisting in the giving of fraudulent returns, reports, statements or other documents; or

— the imposition of a penalty equaling two times the amount of tax due for engaging in other fraudulent behavior under the Tax Law.

Any person who seeks review by the Bureau of Conciliation and Mediation Services of a specified notice must request a conciliation conference within 30 days of receipt of that notice. If a person seeks review by the Division of Tax Appeals of a conciliation order involving a specified notice, the hearing request must be made within 30 days after the conciliation order was issued.

Any person who receives a specified notice and seeks a hearing before the Division of Tax Appeals must file a petition with the Division of Tax Appeals within 30 days of the receipt of the notice unless the person has requested a conciliation conference as previously described. If the petition is not filed within the 30-day period, the actions described in the specified notice will be permanently and irrevocably fixed. The expedited hearing must be scheduled within 10 days of the receipt of the petition by the Division of Tax Appeals.

The determination of the administrative law judge must be rendered within 30 days of receipt of the petition by the Division of Tax Appeals. If an exception is taken to the determination of the administrative law judge, the decision of the Tax Appeals Tribunal in response to the exception must be issued within three months of receipt of the petition.

For additional information, see *(TSB-M-09(12)C, TSB-M-09(12)I, TSB-M-09(11)M, TSB-M-09(4)MCTMT, TSB-M-09(8)R, TSB-M-09(17)S,* October 20, 2009, CCH NEW YORK TAX REPORTS, ¶ 406-574)

Discontinuances: At any time prior to the issuance of the conciliation order the taxpayer may discontinue the conciliation conference by filing a request for a discontinuance with the Bureau of Conciliation and Mediation Services. The taxpayer will then have 90 days from the time the request for discontinuance is filed to petition for a hearing in the Division of Tax Appeals.

Outcome of conference: After the conclusion of a conference, the conciliation conferee will review the evidence, testimony and other materials submitted by the parties and attempt to work out a resolution of the matter in the form of a consent.

Execution of a consent within 15 days concludes the matter, and the taxpayer waives all rights to a hearing before the Division of Tax Appeals.

¶3802

If a taxpayer does not agree to a proposed consent or fails to execute it within 15 days, the conciliation conference is deemed to have been concluded without a resolution. An order to that effect will be rendered by the conferee within 30 days of the deemed conclusion date. The issuance date of a conciliation order is the date the order is mailed, not the date indicated on the face of the order or the date the order was signed by the conferee. For mailing rules and legal holidays, see ¶3602.

Force and effect: Absent a showing of fraud, malfeasance or misrepresentation of a material fact, conciliation orders are binding on the Division of Taxation. Conciliation orders are not, however, considered precedent, nor are they given any force or effect in any subsequent conciliation conference with regard to the taxpayer or any other taxpayer. In fact, a taxpayer cannot use a prior conciliation order in a subsequent conference even if it involves identical legal issues.

• *Small claims hearings*

A taxpayer may choose to initiate a small claims hearing, which is intended to afford a speedier resolution of tax controversies in a more informal atmosphere than hearings before administrative law judges. Small claims hearings are adversarial, but formal rules of evidence are relaxed to permit the officer to consider anything that the officer believes to be necessary or desirable for a just and equitable determination.

Jurisdiction: Small claims treatment is available for all taxes administered by the Commissioner of Taxation and Finance where the amount in controversy for any 12-month period does not exceed $20,000 ($40,000 in controversies involving sales and compensating use tax disputes), excluding penalties and interest. In New York City, the small claims limit is $10,000, excluding penalties and interest.

Procedure: The Small Claims Unit schedules hearings after a tax controversy is deemed at issue, that is, after the parties have served their pleadings (or the time for filing an answer has expired). The parties must then be given at least 30 days' notice of the initial hearing date, and 10 days' notice of the date of any subsequent hearing date (*i.e.,* after an adjournment or continuance). A hearing may be waived by the parties, in which case the determination will be made on the written submissions.

Discontinuance: At any time before the conclusion of a small claims hearing, a taxpayer may request that the small claims hearing be discontinued, and that the case be transferred to the docket of an administrative law judge by writing to the Secretary of the Tax Tribunal. The discontinuance is without prejudice on any subsequent proceedings before the administrative law judge.

Outcome of hearing: Determinations of presiding officers are final and must be rendered within three months after completion of the hearing or the submission of briefs, whichever is later. Determinations are not subject to review by any other unit in the Division of Tax Appeals or by any judicial body. On the motion of either party, the Tribunal may, however, order a rehearing upon proof or allegation of misconduct by the small claims presiding officer.

Determinations of presiding officers are not considered precedent, nor are they given any force or effect in other proceedings in the Division of Tax Appeals.

Practitioner Comment: Disposition Statistics

Although the resolution of a tax dispute is (or should be) based on the merits of the case, the Division of Tax Appeals has published statistics detailing the disposition of cases brought before it. During the 2014-2015 fiscal year (the most recent period for which statistics were available), administrative law judges sustained the Tax Department's deficiency notices 85.3% of the time. In small claims cases, the Tax Department's assessments were sustained 67% of the time. When a party appealed a decision of the administrative law judge to the Tax Appeals Tribunal, the ALJ was affirmed 85.2% of the time.

Mark S. Klein, Esq., Hodgson Russ LLP

• *Administrative appeals*

Taxpayers seeking administrative review of controversies with the Department of Taxation and Finance may request a formal hearing with the Division of Tax Appeals. The Division of Tax Appeals is intended to promote fairness, efficiency, and quality in the administrative review of tax matters. It is an autonomous unit of the Department of Taxation and Finance that is completely independent of the Commissioner of Taxation and Finance.

The original and two conformed copies of the petition (Form TA-10) are filed with the Supervising Administrative Law Judge, State of New York, Division of Tax Appeals, Riverfront Professional Tower, 500 Federal Street, Troy, NY 12180-2894.

Statute of limitations: Petitions for administrative review must be filed with the Division of Tax Appeals within the following statutory time limitations after mailing of notice by the Commissioner:

— appeal from a notice of deficiency involving personal income, franchise, petroleum business, and gift taxes, 90 days (150 days if addressed to a taxpayer whose last known address is outside the United States.);

— appeal from a notice of determination of sales and use, alcoholic beverage, tobacco, highway use, real property transfer, lubricating oil, real property transfer gains, mortgage recording, and motor fuels taxes, 90 days;

— appeal from a notice of determination of stock transfer or motor fuel taxes, 30 days; or

— petition for refund, two years.

Procedure: Once the pleadings have been filed, the petition is assigned to an administrative law judge (ALJ) and scheduled for a hearing. Parties must be given at least 30 days' notice of the first hearing date, and at least 10 days' notice of any adjourned or continued hearing date. The hearings are conducted formally, and the petitioner bears the burden of proof on most issues.

Outcome of hearing: The ALJ must render a determination within six months after completion of the hearing or the submission of briefs, whichever is later. The six-month period may be extended, for good cause shown, for an additional three months.

The determination of the ALJ is a final determination of any matters in controversy unless a party takes exception by requesting review by the Tax Appeals Tribunal within 30 days of the notice of the determination. Determinations of administrative law judges are not considered precedent, nor are they given any force or effect in other proceedings in the Division of Tax Appeals.

Practitioner Comment: Use of ALJ Determinations

Although determinations of ALJs are not technically precedential, both auditors and taxpayer representatives frequently cite ALJ determinations in the audit negotiation process to demonstrate how the tax laws are applied to similar sets of facts.

Mark S. Klein, Esq., Hodgson Russ LLP

Practitioner Comment: Access to Cases

Determinations issued by ALJs and all decisions of the Tax Appeals Tribunal are available online at **www.nysdta.org/whatsnew.htm**.

Mark S. Klein, Esq., Hodgson Russ LLP

New York City: Taxpayers seeking administrative review of disputes involving city-administered taxes may request a formal hearing with the New York City Tax Appeals Tribunal.

Review by Tax Appeals Tribunal: The Tribunal reviews the record and may, to the extent necessary or desirable, exercise all of the powers that it could have exercised if it had made the earlier determination. A decision affirming, reversing, modifying, or remanding the ALJ's determination must be issued within six months from the date that the exception was filed, the briefs were submitted, or oral argument was concluded, whichever is later.

The Department may not seek judicial review of a Tax Appeals Tribunal decision. A taxpayer may seek judicial review in the Appellate Division of the State Supreme Court.

Practitioner Comment: Single Opportunity to Present Evidence

A hearing before an administrative law judge of the Division of Tax Appeals is a taxpayer's first and only opportunity to present any evidence to a finder of fact. Absent extraordinary circumstances, no additional (or newly discovered) evidence can be submitted on behalf of the taxpayer at any later stage of the proceedings, including any appeals to the judicial courts.

Mark S. Klein, Esq., Hodgson Russ LLP

• *Appeal to state courts*

A decision of the Tax Appeals Tribunal may be appealed by the taxpayer to the Third Department of the Appellate Division of the State Supreme Court within four months after the decision is served on all parties. An adverse decision of the Third Department may, under certain circumstances, be appealed to the Court of Appeals, New York's highest court.

New York City: Appeals from the New York City Tax Appeals Tribunal are commenced in the Supreme Court, Appellate Division, First Department.

Declaratory judgment: Under certain circumstances, a taxpayer or an association of taxpayers can seek a declaratory judgment from the supreme court. The courts have sometimes permitted a taxpayer to maintain a declaratory judgment action against the taxing authority when the taxpayer claims that a taxing authority is unconstitutional on its face, a taxing statute is inapplicable to the taxpayer; or the taxing authority exceeded the scope of its jurisdiction.

• *Appeal to federal courts*

An assessment may be appealed to a federal court if a question involves the United States Constitution or federal law. Federal questions may arise from discrimination, diversity of citizenship, or interstate commerce.

Federal Tax Injunction Act: The Tax Injunction Act of 1937 (28 U.S.C. §1341) mandates that a federal district court "shall not enjoin, suspend or restrain the assessment, levy or collection of any tax under State law where a plain, speedy and efficient remedy may be had in the court of such State." Since enactment of the statute, only a sprinkling of state tax cases has been heard in federal courts. The principle statutorily set forth has evolved into the federal abstention doctrine as it has been amplified by case law, including two U.S. Supreme Court cases. In *Railroad Commission v. Pullman Co.* ((1941, US SCt) 312 US 496, 61 SCt 643), the Court called for abstention when interpretation of state statutes in state forums might in and of itself eliminate constitutional questions. A second case, *Younger v. Harris* ((1971, US SCt) 401 US 37, 91 SCt 746), held that abstention was proper in deference to a state's interest in ongoing proceedings in its own forums and deference to a state judiciary's power to consider constitutional claims.

¶3802

Criteria for exercising federal jurisdiction: The criteria for accepting jurisdiction were set forth by the Second Circuit (*In the Matter of Levy* (1978, USCA) 574 F2d 128). These criteria are as follows: (1) there are no unsettled questions of state law that affect federal claims; (2) present state proceedings would not be interrupted by exercise of federal jurisdiction; and (3) the most important questions of law presented by the suit are federal, not state, questions.

Administrative remedies: The requirements of 28 U.S.C. § 1341 do not prevent the state from requiring administrative actions prior to appeal to the state courts (*G.F. Alger Co. et al. v. Peck et al.* (1957, US SCt)).

Practitioner Comment: Taxpayers' Costs

Section 3030, Tax Law, allows certain taxpayers the ability to recover a variety of administrative and litigation costs, including attorney's fees, if they are a "prevailing party" in an action by or against the Tax Department where the Department cannot establish that its position was "substantially justified." Professional costs are capped at $75 an hour absent "special circumstances."

Mark S. Klein, Esq., Hodgson Russ LLP

• *Property tax appeals*

Taxpayers may file complaints of allegedly illegal or erroneous assessments with the local assessors at any time before the time fixed for review by the local board of assessment review. The board of assessment review of each municipality or village hears complaints beginning the fourth Tuesday in May, or as many days after that date that the board deems necessary. The board takes testimony and hears proofs, and may require the owner of the property, or any other person, to appear before the board and be examined, and to produce papers relating to the assessment.

Following the hearing, the board of assessment review determines the final assessed valuation or taxable assessed valuation. If the original assessment is determined to be unlawful, it may be ordered stricken from the roll, or entered on to the exemption portion of the roll if appropriate.

Hearing panel: The legislative body of a municipality or village may also establish an administrative hearing panel to hear assessment complaints. Complaints are made on forms provided by the Office of Real Property Services (ORPS). The findings of the panel do not fix the final assessment, but rather constitute recommendations to the board of assessment review. If a majority of the board disagree with the assessment determined by the panel, a hearing before the board is scheduled.

Correction of clerical errors: Taxpayers may apply to the county director of real property tax services for the correction of clerical errors, unlawful entries, or errors in essential fact. A tax levying body may enact a resolution delegating its authority to correct clerical errors, unlawful entries, or certain errors in essential fact on tax rolls to officials empowered to authorize payment of bills. The resolution may only be in effect during the calendar year of adoption and must provide that the designated official only has correction authority if the recommended correction is $2500 or less.

Judicial review: After the assessment roll is finalized, including correction and revision of assessments and determinations by a county board of assessment review, the actions of the tax assessors and review boards are subject to judicial review by a proceeding to review an assessment. The proceeding to review an assessment must be brought at a Special Term of the Supreme Court in the judicial district in which the assessment was made, within 30 days after the final completion and filing of the assessment roll.

The proceeding to review an assessment must be brought at a Special Term of the Supreme Court in the judicial district in which the assessment was made, within 30 days after the final completion and filing of the assessment roll.

ADMINISTRATION AND PROCEDURE

CHAPTER 39
NEW YORK RESOURCES

Department of Taxation and Finance—Taxpayer Assistance
W.A. Harriman Campus, Albany, NY 12227
Personal Income Tax Information Center 518-457-5181
TDD line for taxpayer assistance . . . . 518-485-5082, or
dial 711
Personal income tax refund information 518-457-5149
Corporation Tax Information Center 518-485-6027
Withholding Tax Information Center 518-485-6654
Metropolitan Commuter Transportation Mobility Tax 518-485-2392
Sales Tax Information Center 518-485-2889

Office of Real Property Tax Services 518-591-5232
Mortgage Recording and Real Estate Transfer Tax Information 518-457-8637
Miscellaneous Business Tax Information 518-457-5735
Estate Tax 518-457-5387
Tax Collections and Civil Enforcement Division 518-457-5434
Report Tax Evasion and Fraud 518-457-0578
Forms:
Forms and publications ordering 518-457-5431
Internet: **www.tax.ny.gov**

Empire State Development Corporation
633 Third Ave., 32nd Flr., New York, NY 10017-6706 212-803-3100
625 Broadway, Albany, NY 12245 518-252-5100
95 Perry Street, Suite 500, Buffalo, NY 14203 716-846-8200
Internet: **http://www.nylovesbiz.com** or **http://esd.ny.gov**
Email: esd@empire.state.ny.us

Department of Environmental Conservation
625 Broadway, Albany, NY 12233-0001 518-402-8044
Internet: **www.dec.ny.gov**
Email: dpaeweb@gw.dec.state.ny.us

Department of Labor—Unemployment Insurance
General information 888-469-7365
Internet: **www.labor.ny.gov**
Email: **labor.sm.ui.division@labor.ny.gov**

Department of Motor Vehicles 518-473-5595
Internet: **dmv.ny.gov**

Department of Transportation 518-457-6195
Internet: **www.dot.ny.gov**

Office of Real Property Tax Services
W.A. Harriman State Campus, Albany, NY 12227
General information 518-591-5232
Internet: **www.tax.ny.gov/bus/property**

Secretary of State—Corporations, State Records, and UCC Division
One Commerce Plaza, 99 Washington Ave., Suite 600., Albany, NY 12231 578-473-2492
Internet: **www.dos.ny.gov/corps**
Email: corporations@dos.ny.gov

New York City Department of Finance
Correspondence Unit, One Centre Street, 22nd Floor, New York, NY 10007
General information . . . . 311 or 212-NEW
YORK (639-9675)
TTY 212-639-9675

Payment and Adjudication Centers
Bronx: 3030 Third Ave., 2nd Flr., Bronx, NY 10455
Brooklyn: 210 Joralemon St., 1st Flr., Brooklyn, NY 10201
Manhattan: 66 John St., 2nd Flr., New York, NY 10038
Queens: 144-06 94th Ave., 2nd Flr., Jamaica, NY 11435
Staten Island: 350 St. Marks Place, Staten Island, NY 10301
Internet: **http:/www1.nyc.gov/site/finance**

PART XI

DOING BUSINESS IN NEW YORK

CHAPTER 40

FEES AND TAXES

¶ 4001	Domestic Business Entities
¶ 4002	Foreign Business Entities

¶4001 Domestic Business Entities

Law: Business Corporation Law; Sec. 102, *et seq.*; Limited Liability Company Law, Sec. 101, *et seq.*; Partnership Law, Article 8-A Revised Limited Partnership Act, Sec. 121-101, *et seq.* (CCH New York Tax Reports, ¶ 1-105).

New York has several business-related enactments addressing the formation, operation, combination, and dissolution, etc. of for-profit domestic corporations and other domestic business entities. These corporate, limited liability company (LLC), and assorted partnership enactments provide significant information regarding the internal operations of a corporation, LLC, partnership, or other business entity, such as ownership rights, voting rules, director/manager obligations, and bylaw/agreement contents, etc. These enactments also address the service fees that are applicable to the various interactions between the state and the above domestic business entities. Business law resources and the location of applicable fee information are specifically noted below.

Information statements: Each domestic and foreign corporation (and other business entities doing business in New York) must file biennial information statements with the Secretary of State stating the name and business address of its chief executive officer, the street address of its principal executive office, and the post office address to mail a copy of any process against it served upon the Secretary of State (Sec. 408, Bus. Corp. Law; Sec. 301, Limited Liability Company Law; Sec 121-1500, Partnership Law). However, beginning in 2016, the entity may provide this information on its tax returns filed with the Commissioner of Taxation and Finance for delivery to the Secretary of State, in which case the $9 filing fee will not be charged.

Corporate entities: New York's general corporation law provisions addressing domestic and foreign corporations are found within the New York Business Corporation Act. (Bus. Corp. Law, Sec. 102, *et seq.*)

All parties desiring to incorporate a for-profit domestic corporation in New York, that is, a corporation created under the laws of the state, must execute and file articles of incorporation with the Secretary of State. Among other items, such articles generally provide the name of the corporation, the number of shares that the corporation may issue, the address of the corporation's registered office in the state, and the name of its registered agent authorized to receive the service of process. The New York Secretary of State imposes and collects a service fee for this filing and for issuing a certificate of incorporation. The Secretary also charges other related fees for assorted corporate filing activities. Such fees are generally payable at the time that the requisite documents are filed. For additional, specific information on these fees and the amounts due, see **http://www.dos.ny.gov/corps/fees_corp.html**.

Other business entities: In addition to forming and operating as a domestic corporation, among other choices, a business taxpayer can choose to form and operate as either a domestic LLC or as one of the varied domestic partnership formats. The noncorporate business entity choices are briefly addressed below.

CCH Advisory: Online Filing System

Domestic business corporations and domestic limited liability companies can file their Certificates of Incorporation and Articles of Organization electronically. Electronic filing also eliminates the need to pay expedited processing fees. The online filing system is available Monday through Friday from 6:00 am to 7:30 pm through the Department of State's Division of Corporations website at **http://www.dos.ny.gov/corps/index.html**.

LLCs.—New York's general LLC law provisions addressing domestic LLCs are found within the New York Limited Liability Company Act. (Limited Liability Company Law, Sec. 101, *et seq.*)

All parties desiring to organize a for-profit domestic LLC in New York, that is, an LLC created under the laws of the state, must execute and file articles of organization with the Secretary of State. Among other items, such articles generally provide the name of the LLC, the address of the initial designated office, the name and address of the initial agent for service of process, and the name and address of each organizer. The New York Secretary of State imposes and collects a service fee for this filing and for issuing a certificate of organization. The Secretary also charges other related fees for assorted LLC filing activities. Such fees are generally payable at the time that the requisite documents are filed. For additional, specific information on these fees and the amounts due, see **http://www.dos.ny.gov/corps/fees_llc.html**.

Partnerships.—New York's general partnership law provisions addressing domestic partnerships are found within the New York Uniform Partnership Act. (Partnership Law, Article 8-A Revised Limited Partnership Act, Sec. 121-101, *et seq.*) The New York Secretary of State imposes and collects a service fee for certain filings and for the issuance of specified instruments. Such fees are generally payable at the time that the requisite documents are filed. For additional, specific information on these fees and the amounts due, see **http://www.dos.ny.gov/corps/fees_lp.html**.

• *Initial fees and taxes*

NOTE: The organization and license taxes and the annual maintenance fee under Secs. 180 and 181, Tax Law, were repealed by Ch. 59 (S.B. 6359), Laws 2014, applicable to taxable years beginning on or after January 1, 2015.

Organization tax: Prior to repeal, every stock corporation incorporated under any law of New York State and every corporation formed under the Business Corporation Law had to pay a tax of $1/20$ of 1% upon the amount of the par value of all par value shares that it is authorized to issue and a tax of 5¢ on each no par value share that it is authorized to issue. The minimum tax was $10. The tax was due and payable at the time of filing the certificate of incorporation with the Department of State.

Limited dividend housing corporations and railroad redevelopment corporations are exempt from this organization tax.

Changes in shares: Prior to repeal, the fees payable upon changes of shares of capital stock were as follows. The minimum is $10 in each case:

    — In a change from par value to no par value stock, the fee is 5¢ on each no par value share, less $1/20$ of 1% on par value so changed.

    — In a change from no par value into shares with par value, the fee is $1/20$ of 1% on par value shares, less 5¢ per share without par value so changed.

    — In a change from shares without par value into other shares without par value, the fee is 5¢ per share on shares without par value, less 5¢ on each share without par value so changed, and less 5¢ with respect to each share without par value not authorized previous to the change but resulting from the change and

¶4001

issued pursuant to terms upon which the change is made, if the change is effected more than five years from date of filing of the certificate of incorporation or certificate of amendment to effect the change.

— In a change from par value shares into both par value and no par value, the fee is $1/20$ of 1% on par value resulting from the change, plus 5¢ per share without par value resulting from the change, less $1/20$ of 1% on par value so changed.

— In a change from no par value shares into both par value and no par value, the fee is $1/20$ of 1% on par value resulting from the change, plus 5¢ per share on no par value shares resulting from the change, less 5¢ per share without par value so changed.

¶4002 Foreign Business Entities

Law: Business Corporation Law, Sec. 102 *et seq.*; former Tax Law, Sec. 180 *et seq.*; Limited Liability Company Law, Sec. 101, *et seq.*; Partnership Law, Article 8-A Revised Limited Partnership Act, Sec. 121-101, *et seq.* (CCH NEW YORK TAX REPORTS, ¶ 1-110).

New York has several business-related enactments addressing the qualification and operation of for-profit foreign corporations and other foreign business entities. These corporate, limited liability company (LLC), and assorted partnership enactments provide significant information regarding the internal operations of a corporation, LLC, partnership, or other business entity, such as ownership rights, voting rules, director/manager obligations, and bylaw/agreement contents, etc. These enactments also address the service fees that are applicable to the various interactions between the state and the above foreign business entities. Business law resources and the location of applicable fee information are specifically noted below.

Information statements: Each domestic and foreign corporation (and other business entities doing business in New York) must file biennial information statements with the Secretary of State stating the name and business address of its chief executive officer, the street address of its principal executive office, and the post office address to mail a copy of any process against it served upon the Secretary of State (Sec. 408, Bus. Corp. Law; Sec. 301, Limited Liability Company Law; Sec 121-1500, Partnership Law). However, beginning in 2016, the entity may provide this information on its tax returns filed with the Commissioner of Taxation and Finance for delivery to the Secretary of State, in which case the $9 filing fee will not be charged.

NOTE: The organization tax and license taxes and the annual maintenance fee under Secs. 180 and 181, Tax Law, were repealed by Ch. 59 (S.B. 6359), Laws 2014, applicable to taxable years beginning on or after January 1, 2015. Therefore, for those years, there is no longer a requirement to file Form CT-240.

Corporate entities: New York's general corporation law provisions addressing domestic and foreign corporations are found within the New York Business Corporation Act. (Bus. Corp. Law, Sec. 102 *et seq.*) Regarding the license fee imposed prior to 2015 under Tax Law Sec. 181, the Department of Taxation and Finance provides an overview at **http://www.tax.ny.gov/bus/ct/license_fee_art9.htm**.

In the same manner that the incorporation of a domestic corporation and its ability to do business in New York is a privilege to be conferred only by law and upon such conditions and payments as the state sees fit, the exercise of the corporate franchise in New York and the transaction of business in the state by a business entity created and incorporated elsewhere is a privilege upon which conditions may be imposed and for which fees may be charged. No foreign corporation may engage in any business in New York until all applicable fees have been paid and the entity has procured a certificate of authority from the New York Secretary of State to transact business in the state.

Upon the issuance of a certificate of authority by the Secretary of State, the foreign corporation possesses rights, privileges, duties, and restrictions comparable to those of a domestic corporation incorporated in the state.

A party desiring to qualify a foreign corporation in New York must apply for a certificate of authority from the Secretary of State. Among other items, such an application must generally provide the name of the corporation, the place of incorporation, the address of its principal office, the number of shares that the corporation may issue, the address of the foreign corporation's registered office in the state, and the name of its registered agent authorized to receive the service of process. A foreign corporation that transacts business in the state without a certificate of authority is liable to the state for the years or parts thereof during which it engaged in business without a certificate of authority. The charge will be an amount equal to all fees that would have been imposed upon the corporation had it applied for and received a certificate of authority and filed all of the required reports, plus all penalties for the failure to pay the fees. New York's Attorney General will bring proceedings to recover all amounts due to the state.

The New York Secretary of State imposes and collects a service fee for reviewing the application for, and issuing, a certificate of authority to a foreign corporation to "do business" (see below) in the state. The Secretary also charges other related fees for assorted corporate filing activities. Such fees are generally payable at the time that the requisite documents are filed. For additional, specific information on these fees and the amounts due, see **http://www.dos.ny.gov/corps/fees_corp.html**.

Other business entities: In addition to operating as a foreign corporation, among other choices, a business taxpayer can choose to operate as either a foreign LLC or as one of the varied foreign partnership formats. The noncorporate business entity choices are briefly addressed below.

LLCs.—New York's general LLC law provisions addressing foreign LLCs are found within the New York Limited Liability Company Act. (Limited Liability Company Law, Sec. 101, *et seq.*)

All parties desiring to qualify a for-profit foreign LLC in New York must present the LLC's articles of organization and apply for a certificate of authority from the Secretary of State. Among other items, the articles of organization generally provide the name of the LLC, the address of the initial designated office, the name and address of the initial agent for the service of process, and the name and address of each organizer.

The New York Secretary of State imposes and collects a service fee for reviewing the application for, and issuing, the certificate of authority. The Secretary also charges other related fees for assorted LLC filing activities. Such fees are generally payable at the time that the requisite documents are filed. For additional, specific information on these fees and the amounts due, see **http://www.dos.ny.gov/corps/fees_llc.html**.

Partnerships.—New York's general partnership law provisions addressing foreign partnerships are found within the New York Uniform Partnership Act. (Partnership Law, Article 8-A Revised Limited Partnership Act, Sec. 121-101, *et seq.*) The New York Secretary of State imposes and collects a service fee for certain filings and for the issuance of specified instruments. Such fees are generally payable at the time that the requisite documents are filed. For additional, specific information on these fees and the amounts due, see **http://www.dos.ny.gov/corps/fees_lp.html**.

• *Doing Business*

"Doing business," as far as a foreign business entity is concerned, refers to a link or connection that the entity establishes by its business operations or activities in a state. Whether a foreign business entity is doing business in a state is important in at least three areas of the law:

    (1) whether the entity has subjected itself to a state's laws on qualification to transact business in the state,

(2) whether the entity is subject to the state's taxing power, and

(3) whether the entity is amenable to suit in the state.

The concept of "doing business", however, is not similarly defined in these three areas. For additional, more specific information on this topic in the income taxation context, see ¶902 and in the sales and use tax context, see ¶2002 and ¶2004.

For miscellaneous fees that may also be applicable to foreign corporations, see ¶4001.

- *License tax*

Prior to repeal, applicable to taxable years beginning on or after January 1, 2015, every foreign corporation, except banking corporations, fire, marine, casualty and life insurance companies, cooperative fraternal insurance companies, and building and loan associations, doing business in New York, had to pay a license fee of $1/20$ of 1% on its issued par value capital stock employed within New York and 5¢ on each share of its capital stock without par value employed within the state for the privilege of exercising its corporate franchises or carrying on its business in such corporate or organized capacity in New York. The minimum first payment of the license tax was $10.

Every foreign corporation subject to tax under Article 9-A of the Tax Law was also subject to the license fee imposed for the privilege of exercising its corporate franchise, or of doing business, or employing capital, or of owning or leasing property in New York in a corporate or organized capacity, or of maintaining an office in the state.

REMICs: A real estate mortgage investment conduit (REMIC) was not required to pay the license fee (TSB-M-87(22)C, CCH NEW YORK TAX REPORTS, ¶10-000).

- *Annual maintenance fee*

Prior to repeal, applicable to taxable years beginning on or after January 1, 2015, every foreign corporation, except banking corporations, fire, marine, casualty and life insurance companies, cooperative fraternal insurance companies and building and loan associations authorized to do business in New York had to pay an annual maintenance fee of $300 for each year or portion of a year during which it was so authorized. However, the fee was reduced by 25% if the period for which the fee was imposed consisted of more than six months but not more than nine months and by 50% if the period for which the fee is imposed consisted of not more than six months.

The maintenance fee was allowed as a credit against the business corporation franchise tax (see ¶926).

REMICs: A real estate mortgage investment conduit (REMIC) was not required to pay the annual maintenance fee (TSB-M-87(22)C, CCH NEW YORK TAX REPORTS, ¶10-000).

PART XII

UNCLAIMED PROPERTY

CHAPTER 41
UNCLAIMED PROPERTY

¶4101 Unclaimed Property

State law requires banks, insurance companies, utilities, and other businesses to turn dormant savings accounts, unclaimed insurance and stock dividends, and other inactive holdings over to the state. If there has been no activity in the account for a set period of time, usually between two and five years, the money is considered unclaimed or abandoned. (*Frequently Asked Questions*, New York Office of Unclaimed Property)

For contact information, see **Administration** below.

Although not formally defined in the state law provisions, "escheat" is the vesting in the state of title or possession of property whose owner is unknown or, additionally in the case of real property, the ownership of which has been alienated by such specified criminal convictions as treason. (Sec. 201, Abandoned Property Law)

CCH Comment: Federal/state conflict

Escheat is an area of potential federal/state conflict. A federal statute may preempt state escheat provisions. For instance, it has been federal policy that the Employee Retirement Income Security Act of 1974 (ERISA) (particularly Sec. 514(a)) generally preempts state laws relating to employee benefit plans. Thus, funds of missing participants in a qualified employee benefit plan stay in the plan under the federal executive policy that state escheat laws are preempted by ERISA (Advisory Opinion 94-41A, Department of Labor, Pension and Welfare Benefit Administration, Dec. 7, 1994). However, some states have challenged the federal position on this and similar narrowly delineated situations. Thus, practitioners are advised that a specific situation where federal and state policy cross on the issue of escheat may, at this time, be an area of unsettled law.

In the case of federal tax refunds, IRC Sec. 6408 disallows refunds if the refund would escheat to a state.

New York has drawn a few provisions from the Uniform Property Acts of 1954 and 1981, but does not follow the Acts closely. Compliance with the procedures required to deal with abandoned property is briefly covered in the following paragraphs.

- *Presumption of abandonment*

A period of inactivity is required before abandonment is presumed. An absence of claims for a period of 10 years is the requirement for abandoned deposits held by federal courts. (Sec. 1201, Abandoned Property Law)

Seven years is the period for property held by the U.S. or any of its agencies. (Sec. 1216, Abandoned Property Law)

CCH Comment: 2011 budget bill

The 2011 budget bill reduced the dormancy period from five years to three years on condemnation awards, credit balances arising from loans, bank accounts (demand deposit, savings, time deposit, deposit and suspense), lost cash, money on deposit to secure funds, unredeemed gift certificates, and various other types of funds such as bail, certain trusts, escrow accounts, and child or spousal support which is held by the court because it has not been claimed. It also reduced the dormancy period from six years to three years on surplus from the sale of pledged property. *2011-12 New York State Executive Budget Revenue Article VII Legislation Memorandum - In Support*, April 4, 2011.

The dormancy period is three years for any amounts due on deposits or any amounts to which a shareholder of a savings and loan association or a credit union is entitled, held or owing by a banking organization. (Sec. 300(a), Abandoned Property Law)

The dormancy period also is three years for amounts held by banking organizations for the payment of interest on bonds and apportioned or transferred mortgages after the liquidation of the mortgage. (Sec. 300(b), Abandoned Property Law)

Five years is the dormancy period for money orders held and owing by an organization other than a banking organization. (Sec. 1309, Abandoned Property Law)

The requisite period is three years in the case of bank and savings and loan deposits, unknown owner court funds, or unclaimed condemnation awards. (Sec. 300(c), Abandoned Property Law; Sec. 600, Abandoned Property Law)

Three years of inactivity is required for uncashed checks Sec. 300(1)(c), Abandoned Property Law and before the contents of safe deposit boxes, stock dividends, stocks and bonds, wages held by security holders or brokers, or life insurance proceeds may be presumed abandoned. (Sec. 300(d), (e), (f), (g), Abandoned Property Law; Sec. 501, Abandoned Property Law; Sec. 511, Abandoned Property Law; Sec. 700, Abandoned Property Law)

The dormancy period is three years for lost property held by safe-deposit companies or banks. (Sec. 300(k), Abandoned Property Law)

Funds held for the benefit of minors are not subject to the escheat laws until the minor reaches the age of 18. (Sec. 600, Abandoned Property Law; Sec. 300(k)(3), Abandoned Property Law)

Utility deposits are considered abandoned two years after discontinuation of service. (Sec. 400, Abandoned Property Law)

(Sec. 1300, Abandoned Property Law)

The dormancy period is three years for services not rendered or goods not delivered and unclaimed money or securities held in escrow or otherwise by a corporation, individual, company, or business trust. (Sec. 1315, Abandoned Property Law)

Gift certificates and gift cards.—Sec. 1315, Abandoned Property Law, requires corporations to report outstanding checks issued for goods or services not delivered. This includes unclaimed accounts payable and account receivable credits, unrefunded charges, as well as gift cards. The law applies even if the instrument indicates an expiration date. The term "gift certificate" includes gift certificates designated for merchandise and/or services. Gift certificates are deemed reportable at face value even in instances in which an expiration date is indicated. The dormancy period under Sec. 1315 is five years. (Sec. 1315, Abandoned Property Law; Handbook for Reporters of Unclaimed Funds, *General Corporations*, Office of the State Comptroller)

¶4101

The term "gift certificate" includes written promises or electronic payment devices that:

— are usable at a single merchant or an affiliated group of merchants that share the same name, mark, or logo, or are usable at multiple, unaffiliated merchants or service providers;

— are issued in a specified amount;

— may or may not be increased in value or reloaded;

— are purchased and/or loaded on a prepaid basis for the future purchase or delivery of any goods or services; and

— are honored upon presentation.

The term does not include an electronic payment linked to a deposit account, or prepaid telephone calling cards regulated under the Public Service Law. Also, the term does not include healthcare flexible spending arrangements, nor does it include discount cards or discount programs. (Sec. 103, Unclaimed Property Law)

Insurance company demutualization.—Any amount, security, or other distribution payable or distributable to a resident as the result of a demutualization or similar reorganization of an insurance company is deemed abandoned if, for two successive years,

(1) all amounts, securities, or other distributions have remained unpaid to or unclaimed by the resident, and

(2) no written communication from the resident has been received by the holder.

(Sec. 501(2-a), Abandoned Property Law)

• *Business-to-business exemption*

New York does not have a business-to-business exemption. (Sec. 1315, Abandoned Property Law)

• *Report requirements*

Annual reports are due as follows:

General corporations, mutual funds, state, municipal, or other public stock/ bond issuers, brokers and dealers, title insurance companies: March 10, for property unclaimed as of December 31 of the preceding year. (Sec. 502, Abandoned Property Law; Sec. 512, Abandoned Property Law)

Banking institutions: For property as of June 30, preliminary report due August 1, negative report due August 10, publication notice due August 31, proof of publication due September 10, final report due November 10. (Sec. 303, Abandoned Property Law)

Insurance companies: For property as of January 1 (December 31 for superannuated policies), preliminary or negative report due April 1, publication notice due May 1, proof of publication due May 10, final report due September 10. (Sec. 703, Abandoned Property Law)

Utilities: For property as of July 1, preliminary or negative report due August 1, publication notice due August 31, proof of publication due September 10, final report due October 10. (Sec. 403, Abandoned Property Law

(NY Form AC2709, NY Handbook)

Court funds are accompanied by a report when delivered to the state comptroller by April 10 for property held as of January 1. (Sec. 602, Abandoned Property Law; Sec. 603, Abandoned Property Law)

Aggregate reporting.—Holders of unclaimed property may report in the aggregate, without specifying the name, address, or other identifying information of the owner, property amounting to $20 or less. (Sec. 1419, Abandoned Property Law)

Negative reporting.—New York does not require negative reporting. (*Handbook for Reporters of Unclaimed Funds*, New York State Comptroller)

• *Delivery of unclaimed property*

As noted above, most unclaimed property is delivered to the State Comptroller at the same time that the information report is filed. In addition, financial organizations are required to deliver by November 10 property abandoned as of June 30. (Sec. 303, Abandoned Property Law) Also, utilities deliver by October 10 property deemed abandoned as of July 1. (Sec. 403, Abandoned Property Law) Corporations deliver unclaimed condemnation awards by February 10 for abandoned property held as of the preceding July 1. (Sec. 1003, Abandoned Property Law)

• *Notice of abandoned property*

Financial organizations, utilities, insurance companies, and corporations holding abandoned condemnation awards are required to publish the names of the owners of unclaimed property within 30 days of the report to the State Comptroller. (Sec. 302, Abandoned Property Law; Sec. 402, Abandoned Property Law; Sec. 702, Abandoned Property Law; Sec. 1002, Abandoned Property Law)

County treasurers or, in the case of the City of New York, the Commissioner of Finance are similarly required to publish the names of persons believed to be the owners of abandoned court funds by February 1 of each year. (Sec. 601, Abandoned Property Law)

Due diligence.—At least 90 days prior to the applicable reporting date for the unclaimed property, the holder must send a written notice by first class mail to each person appearing to be the owner of property listed in an abandoned property report. However, these requirements do not apply if the holder does not have an address for the owner or can demonstrate that the only address that the holder has pertaining to the owner is not the owner's current address. (Sec. 1422, Abandoned Property Law)

With respect to property whose value exceeds $1,000, the holder is required to send a second written notice by certified mail, return receipt requested, at least 60 days prior to the applicable reporting date. Such notice is not required if the holder has received a claim from the owner of the property or the original mailing was returned as undeliverable. (Sec. 1422, Abandoned Property Law)

Penalties and interest.—Failure to make reports or to file any required affidavits will result in a penalty of $100 per day. The Comptroller may extend the time for making reports or filing affidavits, and may waive the payment of any penalty. Interest at 10% per annum of the value of the property will be imposed for failure to pay any sum or to deliver any property as required. Sec. 1412, Abandoned Property Law)

• *Claims for recovery*

Claims for recovery of sums escheated to the state are submitted to the State Comptroller, who has full authority to determine such claims. No time limit is specified in the law. A notice of the Comptroller's finding is sent to the claimant. (Sec. 1406, Abandoned Property Law)

• *Claimant remedies*

Claimants may apply to the State Comptroller within four months of notice for redetermination of a denied claim. If the Comptroller's decision remains unfavorable, the claim may be submitted within four months for review by the Supreme Court, Albany County. Ten days' notice to the Comptroller is required. (Sec. 1406, Abandoned Property Law)

- *Abandoned property location services*

Abandoned property location services are required to provide a written disclosure to consumers stating that abandoned funds held by the state may be obtained directly from the state comptroller's office without paying a fee. The disclosure would also have to include contact information for the comptroller. (Sec. 1416, Abandoned Property Law)

"Abandoned property location services" are any services provided for a fee that assists consumers in locating or retrieving unclaimed property held by the comptroller. However, the term does not apply to certain agreements between clients and their attorneys or accountants. (Sec. 1416, Abandoned Property Law)

- *Administration*

The unclaimed property laws are administered by the New York State Office of the State Comptroller, Office of Unclaimed Funds, 110 State Street, Albany, NY 12236.

Phone: 1-800-221-9311

Email: NYSOUF@osc.state.ny.us

Internet: http://www.osc.state.ny.us/index.htm

LAW AND REGULATION LOCATOR

The Law and Regulation Locator includes the sections of the New York Tax Law, the Charter of the City of New York, and the Administrative Code of the City of New York, as well as the New York State and City rules and regulations, that are discussed in the *Guidebook*.

Chapter 67
Disability Benefits Law

Regulations
New York Regulations

Rules
Rules of the City of New York

TOPICAL INDEX

»»→ References are to paragraph numbers.

ITE

NEW

NEW